AF814181

NATIONAL TESTING AGENCY (NTA)

UGC NET/JRF/SET

LAW

SOLVED PAPERS

2024-2012

Compiled by

Bhavtosh Agarwal

Bhavya Dubey, Jyoti Singh

arihant

SUCCESS AND NOTHING LESS

arihant
SUCCESS AND NOTHING LESS

ARIHANT PUBLICATIONS (INDIA) LIMITED

卐 **Administrative & Production Offices**

Regd. Office

'Ramchhaya' 4577/15, Agarwal Road, Darya Ganj, New Delhi -110002
Tele: 011- 47630600, 43518550

卐 **Head Office**

Kalindi, TP Nagar, Meerut (UP) - 250002
Tel: 0121-7156203, 7156204

卐 **Sales & Support Offices**

Agra, Ahmedabad, Bengaluru, Bareilly, Chennai, Delhi, Guwahati, Hyderabad, Jaipur, Jhansi, Kolkata, Lucknow, Nagpur & Pune.

卐 **PRICE** ₹525.00

卐 **PO No :** TXT-XX-XXXXXXX-X-XX

Published by Arihant Publications (India) Ltd.

For further information about the books published by Arihant, log on to www.arihantbooks.com or e mail at info@arihantbooks.com

PREFACE

NTA UGC NET examination is a highly prestigious and competitive examination conducted by NTA. The purpose of this exam is selection of candidates for Junior Research Fellowship and Assistant Professor.

Keeping in mind the importance of such exam, Arihant Publications presents **NTA UGC Solved Paper Series** – The only series that contains 100% detailed solution for each question.

This book **Law Previous Years' Solved Papers** contains all question papers from 2024-2012.

Salient Features of the Books

- 100% detailed & authentic explanations.
- All the facts and data have been provided with latest information.
- 5 Practice Sets also have been provided exactly based on the latest pattern of the examination for practice.

We have taken utmost care in preparing this book and put our best efforts to make it a perfect study resource for the aspirants, still we request all the respected teachers and the aspirants to provide us their valuable feedback or suggestions or reviews whatsoever you want to say about the book.

We assure you that we will try to incorporate all those points in the further edition of the book.

Author

About the UGC NET

NTA UGC NET

On behalf of UGC, National Testing Agency (NTA) conducts National Eligibility Test (NET) for determining the eligibility of Indian Nationals for the eligibility for Assistant Professorship or Junior Research Fellowship or both in Indian Universities and Colleges.

NTA will conduct NET in 84 subjects at 91 selected NET Examination cities spread across the country.

CONDITIONS OF ELIGIBILITY

- For General category 55% marks in Master degree, for SC / ST / OBC category 50% marks in Master degree.
- Candidates who have appeared OR will be appearing at the qualifying Master's degree (final year) examination and whose result is still awaited or candidates whose qualifying examination have been delayed may also apply for this test.
- The Ph.D degree holders whose master's level examination had been completed by 19th September 1991 (irrespective of date of declaration of result) shall be eligible for a relaxation of 5% in aggregate marks (i. e. from 55% to 50%) for appearing in NET.

AGE LIMIT & RELAXATION

- **Junior Research Fellowship:** Not more than 30 years. A relaxation up to 5 years is provided to the candidates belonging to OBC (Non creamy layer, as per the central list of OBC available on website).
- **Assistant Professor:** There is no upper age limit for applying for eligibility for Assistant Professor exemption (Eligibility for assistant professor).

EXAMINATION SCHEDULE

NATIONAL ELIGIBILITY TEST (NET)

Sec./Paper	Marks	Number of Questions
First I	100	50 Questions & all are Compulsory
Second II	200	100 Questions & all are Compulsory

CONTENTS

UGC-NET LAW SOLVED PAPER 2024 (August)

PAPER II

Directions *This paper contains* ***hundred (100)*** *objective type questions of* ***two (2)*** *marks each. All questions are compulsory.*

1. Match List-I with List-II

	List-I (Authors/Editors)		List-II (Titles of Books)
A.	J. Crowe and KW Scheuber	I.	The Handbook of International Humanitarian Law (ed), OUP
B.	Charlotte Lulf	II.	Persecution International Refugee Law and Refugees : A Feminist Approach
C.	Mathilde Crepin	III.	Conflict of Displacement and Legal Protection Understanding Asylum, Human Rights and Refugee Law
D.	Dieter Fleck and Michael Bothe	IV.	Principles of International Humanitarian Law

Codes

	A	B	C	D
1	I	II	IV	III
2	III	I	IV	II
3	II	I	III	IV
4	IV	III	II	I

Ans. (4)

Exp. The correct matching is A-IV, B-III, C-II, D-I.

J. Crowe and KW Scheuber is associated with 'Principles of International Humanitarian Law'. This book provides a clear and concise explanation of the central principles of international humanitarian law (or the law of armed conflict), while situating them in a broader philosophical, ethical and legal context.

Charlotte Lulf is known for her work on 'Conflict of Displacement and Legal Protection Understanding Asylum, Human Rights and Refugee Law.' The work analyses different models for interpreting the notion of persecution in international refugee law through a comparative lens. In particular, a feminist approach to refugee law is adopted to determine to what extent the notion of persecution can apply to gender related forms of violence and what are the challenges in doing so.

Mathilde Crepin has written about 'Persecution International Refugee Law and Refugees: A Feminist Approach.' This book looks into the ambit of the notion of persecution in international law and its relevance in the current geopolitical context, more specifically for refugee women.

Dieter Fleck and Michael Bothe are known as the editors of 'The Handbook of International Humanitarian Law (ed), OUP.' This highly influential book covers all aspects of international humanitarian law in international and non-international armed conflict situations and provides extensive explanatory commentary and case analysis by a team of distinguished and internationally renowned experts.

2. Arrange the following as per the procedure of Constitutional Amendment in United States of America.

I. Proposal by Congress or Convention of States
II. Governor of State submitting proposed Amendment to state's legislature for consideration
III. Ratification by state
IV. Governor intimating Congress about state decision
V. Getting ratification by two-third states

Choose the correct answer from the options given below.

1 I, II, III, IV, V 2 I, II, III, V, IV
3 II, III, IV, V, I 4 II, III, V, IV, I

Ans. (1)

Exp. The given options are incorrect.

Article V of the US Constitution provides for the process of amendment. It states that "The Congress, whenever two-thirds of both Houses shall deem it necessary, shall propose Amendments to this Constitution or on the Application of the Legislatures of two-thirds of the several states, shall call a Convention for proposing Amendments, which, in either case, shall be valid to all intents and purposes, as part of this Constitution, when ratified by the Legislatures of three-fourths of the several states, or by Conventions in three-fourths thereof, as the one or the other Mode of Ratification may be proposed by the Congress; provided that no Amendment which may be made prior to the year one thousand eight hundred and eight shall in any Manner affect the first and fourth Clauses in the Ninth Section of the first Article; and that no state, without its consent, shall be deprived of its equal Suffrage in the senate."

Thus, the correct order for the given question is as follows

1. Proposal by Congress or Convention of States
2. Getting ratification by two-third states.
3. Ratification by state
4. Governor of State submitting proposed Amendment to state's legislature for consideration and
5. Governor intimating Congress about state decision.

Thus, the correct order is I, V, III, II, IV.

3. Which of the following is not a source of International Law as per Article 38 of the Statute of International Court of Justice?

1 Judicial decisions (subject to Article 59 of Statute of ICJ)
2 Writing of most highly qualified publicists (subject to Article 59 of Statute of ICJ)
3 Community customary laws
4 General principles of law recognised by civilised nations

Ans. *(3)*

➲ *Exp.* Among the given options, community customary laws are not a source of International Law.

According to Article 38 of ICJ, the following are the sources of international law

International conventions, whether general or particular, establishing rules expressly recognised by the contesting states;

International custom, as evidence of a general practice accepted as law;

The general principles of law recognised by civilised nations; and

Judicial decisions and the teachings of the most highly qualified publicists of the various nations, as subsidiary means for the determination of rules of law (subject to Article 59).

4. Which of the following is not a feature of French administrative legal system?

1 Dual system of courts separating administrative and ordinary courts
2 Conseil d' Etat as the Supreme administrative court
3 Principle of Judicial Independence
4 Use of state decisis in administrative decisions

Ans. *(4)*

➲ *Exp.* State decisis (the doctrine that courts should follow precedents set by previous decisions) is not a feature of the French administrative legal system.

The French administrative legal system is known for the following features

Dual system of courts separating administrative and ordinary courts

Conseil d'État as the Supreme administrative court

Principle of Judicial Independence

5. Arrange the following in chronological order (section-wise) as stated in Motor Vehicles Act, 1988.

I. Procedure and power of claim tribunal
II. Award of claim tribunal
III. Claim tribunals
IV. Application for compensation

Choose the correct answer from the options given below.

1 I, II, III, IV 2 I, III, II, IV
3 III, IV, II, I 4 III, II, I, IV

Ans. *(3)*

➲ *Exp.* The correct chronological order as per the provisions of Motor Vehicles Act, is as follows

Section 165-Claim tribunals

Section 166- Application for compensation

Section 168-Award of claim tribunal

Section 169-Procedure and power of claim tribunal

6. Contributory negligence is a/an

1 obligation 2 crime
3 defence 4 right

Ans. *(3)*

➲ *Exp.* Contributory negligence is a defence under law. Contributory negligence in law, refers to a behaviour that contributes to one's own injury or loss and fails to meet the standard of prudence that one should observe for one's own good. Contributory negligence of the plaintiff is frequently pleaded in defense to a charge of negligence.

7. In which year, Limited Liability Partnership Rules of Third Amendment come up?

1 2023 2 2021 3 1930 4 2008

Ans. *(1)*

➲ *Exp.* The LLP (Third Amendment) Rules, 2023 were notified on 27th October, 2023. These rules mandate the Limited Liability Partnerships (LLPs) to maintain a register of partners, which is similar to the register of members maintained by the companies under the Companies Act, 2013. Additionally, as per the new rules, LLP is required to file a declaration regarding the beneficial interest in any contribution and to designate a partner to provide information to the registrar of companies. These amendments aim to streamline compliance requirements, promote transparency and ensure that the LLPs remain competitive in the global market by aligning with international standards.

8. Arrange the following cases in the chronologically order of their year of verdict.

I. Vineet Narain *v/s* Union of India
II. Kesavananda Bharati *v/s* State of Kerala
III. Minerva Mills Ltd. *v/s* Union of India
IV. DK Basu *v/s* State of West Bengal

Choose the correct answer from the options given below.

1 I, II, III, IV　　2 II, III, I, IV
3 IV, I, II, III　　4 II, III, IV, I

Ans. (4)

Exp. The correct chronological order is II, III, IV, I.

In the case of Kesavananda Bharati *v/s* State of Kerala, it was held by the Supreme Court that the Parliament has the right to change the provision of the Constitution, but it shall not change the basic structure of the Indian Constitution.

In the case of Minerva Mills Ltd. and Ors. *v/s* Union of India and Ors the Supreme Court of India had applied and evolved the basic structure doctrine of the Constitution of India. In the Minerva Mills Case, the Supreme Court provided key clarifications on the interpretation of the basic structure doctrine.

In DK Basu *v/s* State of West Bengal, the judgement by the bench of Justice AS Anand and Justice Kuldip Singh were composed of two parts: establishing procedural safeguards and elaborating a system of compensation for victims of police abuse. The judgement emphasised the global effort against torture.

In Vineet Narain *v/s* Union of India, commonly called the Jain Hawala Case-a three-judge bench of the Supreme Court had struck down the 1969 'Single Directive' of the Union Government, a consolidated set of instructions issued to the CBI by various ministers on the modalities of initiating and registering cases.

9. Match List-I with List-II.

	List-I (Descriptions)		List-II (Offences/Sections)
A.	Death caused by a child of 6 years	I.	Exception 4 to Section 300
B.	Death committed without premediation in a sudden fight	II.	Right of private defence
C.	Death of trespasser of the House who was escaping	III.	No offence
D.	Death is caused in safeguarding property from mischief by fire	IV.	Exception 2 to Section 300

Codes

	A	B	C	D		A	B	C	D
1	I	III	II	IV	2	III	II	IV	I
3	I	IV	III	II	4	III	I	IV	II

Ans. (4)

Exp. The correct matching is A-III, B-I, C-IV, D-II.

As per Section 82 of IPC, nothing is an offence it is done by a child below 7 years of age by virtue of 'doli incapax'

According to Exception 4 to Section 300 of IPC, culpable homicide is not murder if it is committed without premeditation in a sudden fight in the heat of passion upon a sudden quarrel and without the offender having taken undue advantage or acted in a cruel or unusual manner.

Further, according to Exception 2 to Section 300 of IPC, Culpable homicide is not murder if the offender, in the exercise in good faith of the right of private defence of person or property, exceeds the power given to him by law and causes the death of the person against whom he is exercising such right of defence without premeditation, and without any intention of doing more harm than is necessary for the purpose of such defence. Thus, death of a trespasser of the House who was escaping would fall in this ambit.

Further, if death is caused in safeguarding property from mischief by fire, it would fall in the ambit of private defence by virtue of section 103, IPC.

10. Which actions are covered under the offence of violation of privacy under Section 66-E of Information Technology Act, 2000?

1 Non-consensual capture, publication and transmission of intimate images
2 Knowingly transmission and publication of intimate images only
3 Non-consensual publication of intimate images only
4 Non-consensual and consensual capture, publication and transmission of intimate images

Ans. (1)

Exp. According to Section 66-E of Information Technology Act, whoever, intentionally or knowingly captures, publishes or transmits the image of a private area of any person without his or her consent, under circumstances violating the privacy of that person, shall be punished with imprisonment which may extend to three years or with fine not exceeding ₹ 2 lakh or with both.

11. Which of the following refers to "a clear and formal expression of recognition by a state through official communication or diplomatic statement"?

1 Implicit recognition
2 Collective recognition
3 Explicit recognition
4 Conditional recognition

Ans. (3)

Exp. Explicit recognition of a state refers to a clear and formal expression of recognition by a state, often through diplomatic statements, official communications or the exchange of ambassadors. This type of recognition leaves no ambiguity regarding the recognising state's position on the legitimacy of the new state or government.

12. After declaration of financial emergency, what is the maximum period of its operation without approval of Parliament?

1 One month　　2 Two months
3 Six months　　4 One year

Ans. (2)

Exp. As per Article 360 (2)(c), a proclamation issued under Article 360(1) shall cease to operate at the expiration of two months unless before the expiration of that period it has been approved by resolutions of both Houses of Parliament.

13. Which kind of intellectual property protection is available for trademark?

1 Statutory protection alone
2 Common law protection alone
3 Both statutory and common law protection
4 Protection under Trade and Merchandise Act, 1958

***Ans.* (3)**

Exp. Both statutory and common law protection is available for trademarks. The primary distinction between registered and unregistered trademarks is the level of protection available for registered and unregistered trademarks. The first is a statutory remedy, while the second is a common law remedy.

14. Match List-I with List-II.

List-I (Pre-requisites for Protections)	List-II (Kinds of IPR)
A. Distinctiveness	I. Copyright
B. Originality	II. Geographical Indication
C. Industrial application	III. Trademark
D. Quality and reputation of goods	IV. Patents

Codes

	A	B	C	D		A	B	C	D
1	I	II	IV	III	2	III	II	I	IV
3	III	I	IV	II	4	IV	III	I	II

***Ans.* (3)**

Exp. The correct matching is A-III, B-I, C-IV, D-II.

Distinctiveness is protected by trademark. A trademark may be eligible for registration or registrable, if it performs the essential trademark function and has distinctive character.

The concept of originality is protected by copyright. To be protected by copyright, works must be 'original' or be seen to have 'originality'. In the legal sense, a work being 'original' or having 'originality' refers to the notion of independent creation.

In certain jurisdictions' patent law, industrial applicability or industrial application is a patentability requirement according to which a patent can only be granted for an invention which is susceptible to industrial application, i.e. for an invention which can be made or used in some kind of industry.

A Geographical Indication (GI) is a sign used on products that have a specific geographical origin and possess qualities or a reputation that are due to that origin. In order to function as a GI, a sign must identify a product as originating in a given place.

15. Arrange the following legislations in the chronological order of their enactment.

I. Maintenance and Welfare of Parents and Senior Citizens Act
II. Rights of Persons with Disabilities Act
III. Protection of Women from DomesticViolence Act
IV. Forest Rights Act

Choose the correct answer from the options given below.

1 IV, I, III, II
2 III, IV, II, I
3 III, IV, I, II
4 II, III, IV, I

***Ans.* (3)**

Exp. The legislations according to their chronological order shall be III, IV, I, II.

Protection of Women from Domestic Violence Act, 2005 is an Act to provide for more effective protection of the rights of women guaranteed under the Constitution who are victims of violence of any kind occurring within the family and formatters connected therewith or incidental thereto.

The Forest Rights Act (FRA) of 2006 seeks to correct historical injustices by granting forest land and resource rights to forest-dwelling communities.

Maintenance and Welfare of Parents and Senior Citizens Act, 2007 is a legislation, initiated by the Ministry of Social Justice and Empowerment, Government of India to provide more effective provision for maintenance and welfare of parents and senior citizens.

The Rights of Persons with Disabilities Act, 2016 is a disability law passed by the Parliament of India to fulfill its obligations under the United Nations Convention on the Rights of Persons with Disabilities, ratified by India in 2007. The Act replaces the Persons with Disabilities Act, 1995.

16. Which of the following statements are correct in case of vicarious liability?

I. Relationship of Master Servant
II. No control of master over the manner of the doing work
III. Tort committed in course of employment
IV. Control of master on the manner of doing work

Choose the correct answer from the options given below.

1 I, II and III
2 II, III and IV
3 I, III and IV
4 I, II and IV

***Ans.* (3)**

Exp. Statements I, III and IV are correct. To constitute the tort of vicarious liability, the following essentials must be fulfilled

The wrongful act must have been committed by an employee or other agent,

The employee or other agent must have been acting within the scope of his or her employment or agency, and

The employer or other person must have had the ability to control the employee or agent.

17. According to Section 4 of Dissolution of Muslim Marriage Act, 1939, Apostasy from Islam of a Muslim wife

1 will dissolve her marriage ipso facto.
2 will not dissolve her marriage ipso facto.
3 dissolves her marriage and she loses her claim to dower.
4 dissolves her marriage and she does not lose her claim to dower.

Ans. (2)

➲ *Exp.* According to Section 4 of Dissolution of Muslim Marriages Act, 1939, the renunciation of Islam by a married Muslim woman or her conversion to faith other than Islam shall not by itself operate to dissolve her marriage.

18. Arrange the following reasonable restrictions provided for Freedom of Speech and Expression in Article 19(2) of the Constitution in their chronological order.

I. Contempt of court
II. Incitement to an offence
III. Public order
IV. Security of the state
V. Friendly relations with foreign states

Choose the correct answer from the options given below.

1 I, V, II, III, IV
2 IV, V, III, I, II
3 IV, I, II, III, V
4 IV, III, II, V, I

Ans. (2)

➲ *Exp.* The correct chronological order is IV, V, III, I and II. According to Article 19(2) of the Constitution, nothing in sub-clause (a) of clause (1) shall affect the operation of any existing law, or prevent the state from making any law, in so far as such law imposes reasonable restrictions on the exercise of the right conferred by the said sub-clause in the interests of the sovereignty and integrity of India, the security of the state, friendly relations with foreign states, public order, decency or morality or in relation to contempt of court, defamation or incitement to an offence.

19. Arrange the following conventions in the chronological order of their adoption.

I. Vienna Convention on the Protection of Ozone Layer
II. Stockholm Convention on Persistent Organic Pollutants
III. Convention on International Trade in Endangered Species of Wild Fauna and Flora (CITES)
IV. The Basel Convention on the Control of Transborder Movements of Hazardous Waste and their Disposal

Choose the correct answer from the options given below.

1 I, III, II, IV
2 III, I, IV, II
3 I, II, III, IV
4 IV, II, I, III

Ans. (2)

➲ *Exp.* The correct chronological order is III, I, IV, II.

CITES (1973) concerned about the overexploitation of many vulnerable species as a result of unregulated international trade, governments adopted the Convention on International Trade in Endangered Species of Wild Fauna and Flora (CITES) in 1973. The treaty entered into force in 1975 and now has 183 parties.

Vienna Convention on Protection of Ozone Layer (1985) is an important part of the international ozone regime, providing the forum for discussions on scientific research and observations of the ozone layer. It was adopted on 22nd March, 1985 and entered into force on 22nd September, 1988.

The Basel Convention on the Control of Transborder Movements of Hazardous Wastes and their Disposal (1989) was adopted on 22nd March, 1989 and entered into force on 5th May, 1992.

The Stockholm Convention (2004) is a global treaty that aims to protect human health and the environment from the effects of persistent organic pollutants (POPs). The convention entered into force on 17th May, 2004.

20. Nuisance is the interference with the person's right related to

1 possession
2 leave and license
3 use and enjoyment of land
4 ownership

Ans. (3)

➲ *Exp.* Nuisance is an unlawful interference with a person's use of enjoyment of land or some right over or in connection with it. If the interference is 'direct', the wrong is trespass; whereas, if the interference is 'consequential', it amounts to nuisance.

21. In which of the following judgement, the Supreme Court has held that the Exception 2 to Section 375 IPC is violative of the right of girl child below 18 years?

1 Navtej Singh Johar *v/s* Union of India
2 Prahlada *v/s* State of Haryana
3 Arnesh Kumar *v/s* State of Bihar
4 Independent Thought *v/s* Union of India

Ans. (4)

➲ *Exp.* In the case of Independent Thought *v/s* Union of India (2017), the Supreme Court of India held that Exception 2 to Section 375 of the Indian Penal Code (IPC), which allowed marital rape of a girl child aged between 15 to 18 years, was violative of the rights of a girl child below 18 years. The court therefore held Exception 2 to Section 375 to be against the provisions and objectives of POCSO and the social welfare aims of Article 15(3).

22. Which of the following is correct as per the Motor Vehicles Act, 1988?

I. Section 140 of the Motor Vehicles Act, 1988 deals with principle of no fault liability.
II. United Indian Insurance Ltd. *v/s* Karamchand (2011) deals with third parties.
III. Doctrine of pay and recover is covered under Section 149 of the Motor Vehicles Act, 1998.
IV. As per Section 173 of Motor Vehicles Act, 1988, an appeal to High Court from the award of Motor Accident Claim Tribunal to be preferred within 60 days from the date of the award.

Choose the correct answer from the options given below.

1 I, III and IV   2 I, II and III
3 II, III and IV   4 I, II and IV

***Ans.* (2)**

Exp. Statements I, II and III are correct.

Section 140 of the Motor Vehicles Act, 1988 provides for Liability to pay compensation in certain cases on the principle of no fault, thereby dealing with the principle of strict liability.

United Indian Insurance Ltd. *v/s* Karamchand (2011) deals with the insurance of motor vehicles against third-party risks.

As per Section 149(2) of the Motor Vehicles Act, the insurer can avoid liability only if it proves that the insured breached policy conditions, such as employing a disqualified or unlicensed driver, due to negligence or lack of reasonable care.

Statement IV is incorrect because as per Section 173(1), subject to the provisions of sub-section (2), any person aggrieved by an award of a claims tribunal may, within 90 days from the date of the award, prefer an appeal to the High Court.

23. Match List-I with List-II.

List-I (Cases)	List-II (Point of Laws)
A. NG Dastane *v/s* S. Dastane (1975) 2 SCC 326	I. Desertion as a ground of divorce
B. Court on its own motion (Lajja Devi) *v/s* State (2012) 193 DLT 61	II. Prohibition of Child Marriage Act, 2006 will prevail over personal law
C. Saroj Rani *v/s* Sudarshan Kumar AIR 1984 SC 1562	III. Section 23 (1) is not a bar to file a petition *v/s* 13 (1A) of Hindu Marriage Act
D. Bipin Chandra *v/s* Prabhawati AIR 1957 SC 176	IV. Cruelty as a ground of divorce

Codes

	A	B	C	D		A	B	C	D
1	IV	III	II	I	2	IV	II	III	I
3	III	IV	II	I	4	III	IV	I	II

***Ans.* (2)**

Exp. The correct matching is A-IV, B-II, C-III, D-I.

NG Dastane v/s S. Dastane (1975) Cruelty as a ground of divorce. This case is a landmark decision on cruelty in marriage and is one of the leading precedential authorities in matrimonial disputes related to the irretrievable breakdown of marriage.

Court on its own motion (Lajja Devi) *v/s* State (2012) Prohibition of Child Marriage Act, 2006 will prevail over personal law. It is one such case which not only deals with the issue of child marriage, but also brings forth certain other complexities which it entails especially when the marriage is against the wishes of the parents.

Saroj Rani v/s Sudarshan Kumar (1984) Section 23(1) is not a bar to file a petition v/s 13(1A) of Hindu Marriage Act. Saroj Rani was a landmark case that overruled the Andhra Pradesh High Court in T. Sareetha v/s Venkata Subbaiah (AIR 1983 AP 356) and affirmed the Delhi High Court judgement of Harvinder Kaur v/s Harmander Singh Choudhry (AIR 1984 Delhi 66). The Supreme Court upheld the constitutionality of the right to restitution of conjugal rights under Section 9 of the Hindu Marriage Act, 1955 (HMA), which was considered violative of the fundamental right to privacy in T. Sareetha.

Bipin Chandra v/s Prabhawati (1957) Desertion as a ground for divorce. In Bipin Chandra Shah v/s Prabhawati, AIR 1957 SC 176, the Supreme Court observed that the two essential conditions must be there before the spouse can be held guilty of desertion. They are; the factum of separation, and intention to bring cohabitation permanently to an end (animus deserendi).

24. Which of the following is not correct about Savigny?

1 Savigny was against natural law.
2 Volksgeist theory of savigny made it impossible for a comparative study of law.
3 Savigny did not recognise legislation as a potent source of law.
4 Savigny was in favour of codification of law.

***Ans.* (4)**

Exp. Statement (4) is incorrect because Savigny was not in favour of codification of law. He wanted German law to be developed on the pattern of Roman law. According to him, the codification of law may hamper its continuous growth, and when the legal system gets fully developed and established then the codification may take place. He has been known for the admiration of Roman law.

25. Which of the following kind of IPR is regarded as community property?

1 Industrial designs
2 Copyright
3 Patents
4 Geographical Indications

***Ans.* (4)**

Exp. Geographical Indications (GIs) are regarded as community property because they are associated with products originating from a specific region, and the rights to use them are shared by the producers from that region.

26. Identify the common law maxims concerning the double jeopardy.

I. Nemo bis punitur pro eodem delicto
II. Ex turpi causa non oritur actio
III. Nemo bis vexari debet pro eadem causa
IV. Novus actus interveniens
V. Nemo debet bis puniri pro uno delicto

Choose the correct answer from the options given below.

1 II, III and IV   2 I, III and V
3 II, IV and V   4 I, II, III and IV

Ans. (2)

➲ *Exp.* The correct answer is I, III and V.

Nemo bis punitur pro eodem delicto means that nobody can be punished, charged or convicted more than once for the same offense.

Nemo debet bis vexari pro una et eadem causa is a Latin legal maxim that translates to 'no one ought to be vexed twice for the same cause.'

Nemo bis punitur pro eodem delicto means that nobody can be punished, charged or convicted more than once for the same offense.

27. Match List-I with List-II.

List-I (Cyber Crimes)		List-II (Punishments)	
A.	Violation of bodily privacy	I.	Upto three years imprisonment and fine up to one lakh rupees
B.	Publishing or transmitting of material containing	II.	Extend upto life imprisonment
C.	Identity theft	III.	Upto five years imprisonment and fine upto ten lakh rupees
D.	Cyber terrorism	IV.	Upto three years imprisonment with fine not exceeding two lakh rupees

Codes

	A	B	C	D		A	B	C	D
1	I	IV	III	II	2	IV	III	I	II
3	III	IV	II	I	4	III	IV	I	II

Ans. (2)

➲ *Exp.* The correct matching is A-IV, B-III, C-I, D-II.

According to Section 66-E of IT Act (violation of bodily privacy), whoever, intentionally or knowingly captures, publishes or transmits the image of a private area of any person without his or her consent, under circumstances violating the privacy of that person, shall be punished with imprisonment which may extend to three years or with fine not exceeding two lakh rupees or with both.

According to Section 67 of IT Act (punishment for publishing or transmitting obscene material in electronic form), the punishment on first conviction shall be imprisonment of either description for a term which may extend to three years and with fine which may extend to five lakh rupees and in the event of second or subsequent conviction with imprisonment of either description for a term which may extend to five years and also with fine which may extend to ten lakh rupees.

According to Section 66-C of IT Act (punishment for identity theft), whoever, fraudulently or dishonestly make use of the electronic signature, password or any other unique identification feature of any other person, shall be punished with imprisonment of either description for a term which may extend to three years and shall also be liable to fine which may extend to rupees one lakh.

According to Section 66-F (2) of IT Act (punishment for cyber terrorism), whoever commits or conspires to commit cyber terrorism shall be punishable with imprisonment which may extend to imprisonment for life.

28. If a Muslim husband swears that he will not have sexual intercourse with wife for four months or more, it amounts to a form of divorce known as

1 I'la 2 Zihar 3 Tafweez 4 Mubarat

Ans. (1)

➲ *Exp.* The situation wherein a husband who is of sound mind and has attained the age of majority swears in the name of God that he will not have sexual intercourse with his wife and leaves her to observe iddat, he is said to make I'la.

If the husband resumes sexual intercourse within the iddat period being observed by wife, it will lead to cancellation of I'la. It is pertinent to note that I'la is not practised in India. Option (1) is thus the right answer here.

29. In which of the important circumstances, Parliament can legislate with respect to matters in the State List?

I. To make laws with respect to Goods and Services Tax imposed by such state
II. In matters of national interest
III. If a proclamation of emergency is in operation
IV. By consent of states
V. For giving effect to international agreements

Choose the correct answer from the options given below.

1 I, II, III 2 II, III, IV
3 I, III, IV, V 4 II, III, IV, V

Ans. (4)

➲ *Exp.* The correct answer is II, III, IV and V.

The Parliament has the power to legislate with respect to matters in the State List in the following cases

Article-249 allows Parliament to legislate with respect to a matter in the State List in the national interest.

Article-250 deals with the power of Parliament to legislate with respect to any matter in the State List if a proclamation of emergency is in operation.

Article-252 provides for the power of Parliament to legislate for two or more states by consent and adoption of such legislation by any other state.

Article-253 allows the Parliament to make legislation for giving effect to international agreements.

30. Which of the following is not part of 'International Bill of Rights'?

I. Magna Cart I, 1215
II. Universal Declaration of Human Rights, 1948
III. International Convenent on Civil and Political Rights, 1966
IV. Convention on Rights of the Child, 1989

Choose the correct answer from the options given below.

1 I and II 2 I and III
3 II and III 4 I and IV

Ans. (4)

Exp. Among the given options, I and IV are not a part of the International Bill of Rights. The 'International Bill of Rights' consists of the following

The Universal Declaration of Human Rights (UDHR), 1948

The International Convenent on Civil and Political Rights (ICCPR), 1966

The International Convenent on Economic, Social and Cultural Rights (ICESCR), 1966

31. Constitution of India confers original and exclusive jurisdiction on the Supreme Court in cases where there is a dispute

I. between two or more states.

II. dispute arising out any treaty entered into or executed before the commencement of the Constitution.

III. between Union Government and one or more states.

IV. between Union Government and any states on one side and one or more states on the other.

V. dispute arising out of substantial question of law of general importance.

Choose the correct answer from the options given below.

1 I, II and III 2 III, IV and V
3 II, III, IV and V 4 I, III and IV

Ans. (4)

Exp. According to Article 131 of the Constitution, subject to the provisions of this Constitution, the Supreme Court shall, to the exclusion of any other court, have original jurisdiction in any dispute

between the Government of India and one or more states;

between the Government of India and any state or states on one side and one or more other states on the other; or

between two or more states, if and in so far as the dispute involves any question (whether of law or fact) on which the existence or extent of a legal right depends

Provided that the said jurisdiction shall not extend to a dispute arising out of any treaty, agreement, covenant, engagement, named or other similar instrument which, having been entered into or executed before the commencement of this Constitution, continues in operation after such commencement or which provides that the said jurisdiction shall not extend to such a dispute.

32. Which of the following judicial decisions are related to Environmental Impact Assessment and Environmental Clearance?

I. Sterile Industries (India) Ltd. *v/s* Union of India

II. Balram Singh *v/s* UOI

III. Deepak Kumal *v/s* State of Haryana and Ors.

IV. Orissa Mining Corporation Ltd. *v/s* MOEF

Choose the correct answer from the options given below.

1 I, III and IV 2 I, II, IV
3 I, II and III 4 II, III and IV

Ans. (3)

Exp. Judicial decisions related to Environmental Impact Assessment and Environmental Clearance are I, II and III.

Sterlite Industries (India) Limited *v/s* Union of India (2013) The Court held that appellant is liable for a compensation amounting ₹ 100 crore for the creation of pollution in the environment. They directed the amount to be deposited to the Collector of Thoothukudi district.

Balram Singh *v/s* Union of India and Others (2023) relates to guidelines given by the honourable Supreme Court of India for eradication of the dehumanising practice of manual scavenging. The directions were comprehensive including every possible aspect required to eradicate manual scavenging from its roots.

Deepak Kumar *v/s* State of Haryana and Others (2012) In this case, the Court was of the considered view that it is highly necessary to have an effective framework of mining plan which will take care of all environmental issues and also evolve a long-term rational and sustainable use of natural resource base and also the bio-assessment protocol, which have to be given effect to, inculcating the spirit of Article 48A, Article 51A(g) read with Article 21 of the Constitution.

33. Arrange the following steps as per the law-making process of UK Parliament.

I. First and second reading

II. Royal asssent

III. Consideration of amendments

IV. Committee stage

V. Report stage

Choose the correct answer from the options given below.

1 I, V, IV, III, II 2 I, IV, III, V, II
3 I, IV, V, III, II 4 IV, I, V, III, II

Ans. (3)

Exp. A bill must go through the following as per the law-making process of the UK Parliament

First Reading The bill arrives in the Lords. This stage is a formality where the bill name is read in the chamber.

Second Reading The main debate on the purpose and key areas of the bill. At this stage, members discuss any concerns or specific areas where they think changes may be needed. There are usually no votes (divisions) at this stage.

Committee Stage Detailed line-by-line scrutiny of the text with amendments (suggested changes). Members start at the front of the bill and work through to the end. Votes may take place to decide whether to make the changes. Any member may take part and there is no time limit.

Report Stage A further opportunity to examine the bill and make changes. More amendments are debated and further votes take place to decide whether to make the changes.

Consideration of Amendments If the Lords has made changes to the draft law, it is sent to the commons to agree. The commons may accept the Lords change, make its own change in its place, or reject it. Any commons changes are sent back to the Lords. There may be several rounds of this process, known as 'ping pong'.

Royal Assent When both Houses have agreed the text, the bill is approved by the monarch and becomes a law or 'Act of Parliament'.

34. A person can be punished for an offence under Section 369 of IPC, for kidnapping or abducting child with intent to steal from the person. For the application of Section 369 of IPC, the child must be

1 under the age of 12 years
2 under the age of 15 years
3 under the age of 10 years
4 under the age of 14 years

Ans. (3)

Exp. As per Section 369 of IPC, whoever kidnaps or abducts any child under the age of 10 years with the intention of taking dishonestly any movable property from the person of such child, shall be punished with imprisonment of either description for a term which may extend to 7 years and shall also be liable to fine.

35. Which of the following are functions of Controller of Certifying Authorities under the Information Technology Act, 2000?

I. Exercising supervision over the activities of the Certifying Authorities
II. Certifying public keys of the Certifying Authorities
III. Laying down standards to be maintained by Certifying Authorities
IV. Summon and enforcing attendance of any subscriber and examining him on oath
V. Facilitation of the establishment of any electronic system by a certifying authority

Choose the correct answer from the options given below.

1 II, III, IV, V   2 I, II, III
3 I, II, III, IV   4 I, II, III, V

Ans. (4)

Exp. Among the given options, statements I, II, III and IV are the function of controller of certifying Authorities under the information Technology Act, 2000. Section 18 of the IT Act provides for the functions of Controller of Certifying Authorities. These functions are

Exercising supervision over the activities of the Certifying Authorities;

Certifying public keys of the Certifying Authorities;

Laying down the standards to be maintained by the Certifying Authorities;

Specifying the qualifications and experience which employees of the Certifying Authority should possess;

Specifying the conditions subject to which the Certifying Authorities shall conduct their business;

Specifying the contents of written, printed or visual materials and advertisements that may be distributed or used in respect of a 2 (electronic signature) Certificate and the public key. etc

36. Arrange the following general exceptions in the Indian Penal Code in the chronological order of their appearance in IPC.

I. Act done in good faith for the benefit of child by the consent of guardian
II. Act done in good faith for the benefit of person without consent
III. Communication made in good faith
IV. Act to which a person is compelled by threats

Choose the correct answer from the options given below.

1 I, II, III, IV   2 III, IV, II, I
3 I, II, IV, III   4 III, IV, I, II

Ans. (1)

Exp. The correct chronological order is I, II, III, IV, which as follows

Section 89: Act done in good faith for benefit of child or insane person or by consent of guardian.

Section 92: Act done in good faith for the benefit of a person without consent.

Section 93: Communication made in good faith.

Section 94: Act to which a person is compelled by threats.

37. Which one of the following offence is punishable in all the four stages of crime?

1 Rape   2 Murder
3 Dacoity   4 Kidnapping

Ans. (3)

Exp. Dacoity is the only offence which the legislature has made punishable, at four stages. When five or more persons assemble for the purpose of committing a dacoity, each of them is punishable under Section 399 of IPC.

38. Convention on biodiversity was signed at which International Conference/Summit?

1 Paris Climate Conference
2 Stockholm Conference
3 Rio Earth Summit
4 Hague Conference

Ans. (3)

Exp. The Convention on Biological Diversity was opened for signature at the Earth Summit in Rio de Janeiro on 5th June, 1992 and entered into force on 29th December, 1993. The United States is the only UN member state which has not ratified the convention. It has two supplementary agreements, the Cartagena Protocol and Nagoya Protocol.

39. Which of the following terms are defined under the Information Technology Act, 2000?

I. Computer network   II. Information
III. Data   IV. Secure System
V. Online

Choose the correct answer from the options given below.

1 I, IV and V   2 I, II, III and IV
3 I and IV   4 I, III, IV and V

Ans. (2)

➲ *Exp.* Computer Network, Information, Data and Secure System are defined under the IT Act, 2000. However, the term 'online' has not been defined in the Act.

40. According to Section 6 of the Environment (Protection) Act, 1986, which of the following authority has power to make rules to regulate environmental pollution?

1 National Green Tribunal
2 The Central Government
3 The State Government
4 The Pollution Control Board

Ans. (2)

➲ *Exp.* According to Section 6(1) of the Environmental (Protection) Act, the Central Government may, by notification in the Official Gazette, make rules in respect of all or any of the matters referred to in Section 3.

41. In which of the following case, it was held that the Preamble of the Constitution emphasises the need to secure to all its citizens Justice, Liberty, Equality and Fraternity?

1 Kesavananda Bharati *v/s* State of Kerala
2 KS Puttaswamy *v/s* UOI
3 National Legal Series Authority *v/s* Union of India
4 EP Royappa *v/s* State of Tamil Nadu

Ans. (1)

➲ *Exp.* In the landmark case of Kesavananda Bharati *v/s* State of Kerala, the Supreme Court of India held that the Preamble of the Constitution highlights the need to secure for all citizens Justice, Liberty, Equality and Fraternity. The case also established the 'basic structure doctrine,' asserting that certain fundamental aspects of the Constitution cannot be amended.

42. Which of the following Judgements are associated with the Legislative Supremacy of Parliament in UK?

I. Jackson *v/s* Attorney General (2005)
II. R *v/s* Secretary of State for Transport (Factor fame) (1991)
III. R *v/s* Secretary of State for the Home Department ex p. Leech (1994)
IV. O Reilly *v/s* Mackman (1983)
V. Ridge *v/s* Baldwin (1964)

Choose the correct answer from the options given below.

1 I, II, III and IV 2 I, II and III
3 I, II, IV and V 4 I, II, III and V

Ans. (2)

➲ *Exp.* Only the judgements given in options I, II and III dealt with the Legislative Supremacy of the Parliament in the UK.

Jackson *v/s* Attorney General (2005) The courts found for the Attorney General, determining that the Hunting Act, 2004 and Parliament Acts, 1911 and 1949 were lawful.

R (Factortame Ltd) *v/s* Secretary of State for Transport This was a judicial review case taken against the United Kingdom government by a company of Spanish fishermen who claimed that the United Kingdom had breached European Union Law (then Community Law) by requiring ships to have a majority of British owners if they were to be registered in the UK. The case produced a number of significant judgements on British constitutional law, and was the first time that courts held that they had power to restrain the application of an Act of Parliament pending trial and ultimately to disapply that Act when it was found to be contrary to EU law.

R *v/s* Secretary of State for the Home Department ex p. Leech (1994) The court held that Rule 33(3) is ultra vires Section 47(1) of the Prison Act, 1952 and violates Article 8 of the European Convention on Human Rights. Section 47(1) of the Prison Act, 1952 confers a power of rule making which may limit a prisoner's general civil rights in respect of the confidentiality of correspondence.

43. Which section of Biological Diversity Act, 2002 mandates approval of National Biodiversity Authority (NBA) before applying for any Intellectual Property Right in a foreign country?

1 Section 7 2 Section 19
3 Section 6 4 Section 8

Ans. (3)

➲ *Exp.* Section 6 of the Biological Diversity Act provides for application for Intellectual Property Rights not to be made without approval of National Biodiversity Authority. Section 6(1) states that any person or entity covered under sub-section (2) of Section 3 applying for an intellectual property right, by whatever name called, in or outside India, for any invention based on any research or information on a biological resource which is accessed from India, including those deposited in repositories outside India or traditional knowledge associated thereto, shall obtain prior approval of the National Biodiversity Authority before grant of such intellectual property rights.

44. Match List-I with List-II.

List-I (Jurists)	List-II (Theories)
A. Roscoe Pound	I. Life of the law has not been logic it has been experience.
B. Oliver Wendell Holmes	II. Law is uncertain and certainty of law is a legal myth.
C. Jhering	III. End of law should be to satisfy a maximum of wants with minimum of friction.
D. Jerome Frank	IV. Law is part of human conduct and in the idea of purpose.

Codes

	A	B	C	D
1	III	I	IV	II
2	II	I	IV	III
3	III	II	I	IV
4	II	III	IV	I

Ans. (1)

➲ *Exp.* The correct matching is A-III, B-I, C-IV, D-II.

According to **Roscoe Pound**, the end of law is to satisfy a maximum of wants with a minimum of friction or confrontation. Elaborating the functional aspect of law, Roscoe pound stated that the function of law is to reconcile the conflicting interest of individuals in the community and harmonise their inter-relations.

Justice **Oliver Wendell Holmes** Jr. famously maintained that "the life of the law has not been logic: it has been experience."

According to **Jhering**, law is an instrument which regulates human conduct/behaviour. Law means justice, morality, reason, order and righteous from the viewpoint of the society. Law means statutes, acts, rules, regulations, orders and ordinances from the point of view of the legislature.

Jerome Frank, a renowned American legal scholar and jurist, is credited with the statement that 'certainty of law is a legal myth.' Frank was a prominent figure in the field of legal realism, which challenged the notion that law is an objective and predictable system.

45. Match List-I with List-II.

List-I (Countries)		List-II (Procedure and Authority to Amend the Constitutions)
A.	United States of America	I. Sections 38-49
B.	India	II. Section 128 of the Constitution
C.	Australia	III. Article 368 of the Constitution
D.	Canada	IV. Article 5 of the Constitution

Codes

	A	B	C	D		A	B	C	D
1	IV	III	I	II	2	II	III	IV	I
3	IV	III	II	I	4	I	III	IV	II

Ans. (3)

➲ *Exp.* The correct matching is A-IV, B-III, C-II, D-I.

Article 5 of the **US Constitution** provides for the power to amend the Constitution.

The **Indian Parliament** has the power to amend the Constitution by virtue of Article 368.

The **Australian Constitution** provides for the power to amend the Constitution under Article 128.

Sections 38-49 of the **Canadian Constitution** provide for the power to amend the Constitution.

46. Independent director may be paid remuneration by way of

I. sitting fees

II. stock option

III. profit related commission approved by board members

IV. share in fixed asset of company

Choose the correct answer from the options given below.

1 I and III 2 II and IV
3 III and IV 4 I and II

Ans. (1)

➲ *Exp.* As per the provisions of Companies Act and SEBI (LODR) Regulations, independent directors receive remuneration in the form of sitting fees for attending the meetings of board or committee of the company and its subsidiaries where such director may be appointed.

Further, the remuneration payable to the independent directors in the form of commission may be paid within the monetary limits as may be approved by shareholders subject to the limit not exceeding 1% of the profits of the company computed as per applicable provisions of the Companies Act, 2013.

47. Which of the following cases are related to personal bias according to the principle of natural justice.

I. AK Kraipak *v/s* Union of India

II. Jacob Mathew *v/s* State of Punjab

III. Mohd Yunus Khan *v/s* State of Uttar Pradesh

IV. Gullapalli Nageswara Rao *v/s* State of Andhra Pradesh

V. Manak Lal *v/s* Prem Chand Singhvi

Choose the correct answer from the options given below.

1 I, II, III and IV 2 I, III and V
3 II, III and IV 4 II and IV

Ans. (2)

➲ *Exp.* Judgements given in options I, III and V deal with personal bias according to the principles of natural justice were

AK Kraipak *v/s* Union of India (1970) is one of the judgements where the Hon'ble Supreme Court held that fair adjudication is not only limited to judicial functions, but also in administrative matters. The case is considered an imperative dictum on the issue of personal bias.

The ruling in the Jacob Mathew *v/s* **State of Punjab,** 2005 offered protection to medical practitioners by establishing that only gross negligence, amounting to criminal negligence, could result in criminal charges.

Mohd Yunus Khan *v/s* State of Uttar Pradesh was held that the error of violating the principles of natural justice by the Disciplinary Authority has been of such a grave nature that under no circumstance can the past conduct of the appellant, even if not satisfactory, be taken into consideration.

Gullapalli Nageswara Rao *v/s* APSRTC (1959, SC) deals with bias relating to subject matter-scheme for nationalisation of motor transport notified by State Government was-quashed since the Secretary who initiated scheme and who heard objections was the same.

The case of Manak Lal *v/s* Dr. Prem Chand deals with the principles of natural justice and more importantly the rule against bias and how it is to be interpreted in India. It dives into the principles of natural justice and how they should be interpreted to ensure that there is utmost integrity and fairness in the administration of justice.

48. Inland instrument means

I. instrument drawn or made in India.
II. instrument made payable in India.
III. instrument drawn upon any person resident in India.
IV. instrument that is passed by Indian Parliament.

Choose the correct answer from the options given below.

1 I, II and III　　2 II, III and IV
3 I, III and IV　　4 II, I and IV

***Ans.* (1)**

➲ *Exp.* According to Section 11 of the Negotiable Instruments Act, a promissory note, bill of exchange or cheque drawn or made in India and made payable in, or drawn upon any person resident in, India shall be deemed to be an inland instrument.

49. Indicate the correct sequence of the following sources of Muslim Law.

I. The Quran　　II. The Ijma
III. The Hadis　　IV. The Qiyas

Choose the correct answer from the options given below.

1 I, II, III, IV　　2 I, III, II, IV
3 IV, III, II, I　　4 I, IV, III, II

***Ans.* (2)**

➲ *Exp.* The correct sequence for sources of Muslim Law is as follows

Quran
Sunna (traditions or hadis)
Ijma (consensus)
Qiyas (analogical deductions)

50. Which Amendment to the US Constitution is important in defining the powers reserved to the states?

1 Ist Amendment　　2 IXth Amendment
3 Xth Amendment　　4 Vth Amendment

***Ans.* (3)**

➲ *Exp.* The Xth Amendment grants all powers not given to the federal government, to the states. It states that "the powers not delegated to the United States by the Constitution, nor prohibited by it to the states, are reserved to the states respectively or to the people."

51. Which of the following led setting aside of practice of Triple Talaq as evident in the case of Shayara Bano *v/s* UOI (2017) SCC?

I. Muslim Personal Law (Shariat) Application Act, 1937 is not a Law regarding Triple Talaq and the practice is against the tenets of Holy Quran.
II. Section 2 of Shariat Application Act, 1937 is pre-constitutional legislation within the meaning of Article 13 (1) of Constitution and violative of Article 14.
III. Section 2 of Shariat Application Act, 1937 is pre constitutional legislation within meaning of Article 13 (1) of Constitution and violative of Article 15 of Constitution of India.
IV. Triple Talaq can be injuncted by Supreme Court to severe matrimonial relationship.

Choose the correct answer from the options given below.

1 I and II　　2 I and III
3 II and IV　　4 III and IV

***Ans.* (1)**

➲ *Exp.* Statements I and II are correct. In the landmark case of Shayara Bano *v/s* Union of India, the Supreme Court observed the following

The SC declared that the practice of Triple Talaq was unconstitutional with 3:2 majority. Justice Rohinton Nariaman, Justice UU Lalit and Justice Kurian Joseph gave the majority judgement.

As per majority, it was held that the Triple Talaq is not protected by the exception laid down in Article 25 of Constitution and the court found the said practice not an essential element of Islamic religion.

They stated that this practice was arbitrary and was against the basic practices of Shariat and basic tenets of Quran and thus it cannot be protected under the Fundamental Right.

Justice Kurian Joseph in his concurring opinion stated that "what is bad in Quran cannot be good in Shariat, and what is bad in theology is bad in law as well".

SC concluded that "this form of Talaq is manifestly arbitrary in the sense that the martial tie can be broken capriciously and whimsically by a Muslim man without any attempt at reconciliation to save it. This form of talaq must, therefore, be held to be violative of the Fundamental Right contained in Article 14 of the Constitution of India. The Muslim Personal (Shariat) Application Act, 1937, insofar as it seeks to recognise and enforce triple talaq is within the meaning of the expression 'laws in force' in Article 13(1) of Constitution and must be struck down as being void to extent that it recognises and enforces triple talaq."

52. As per Article 324 of the Constitution of India, any other Election Commissioner or a Regional Commissioner shall not be removed from office except on the recommendation of the

1 President
2 Chief Justice of India
3 Prime Minister
4 Chief Election Commissioner

***Ans.* (4)**

➲ *Exp.* As per the second provision to Article 324(5), any other Election Commissioner or a Regional Commissioner shall not be removed from office except on the recommendation of the Chief Election Commissioner.

53. Arrange the following international treaties/conventions in the chronological order of their adoption.

I. Budapest Treaty on international recognition of the deposit of micro-organism
II. Hague Agreement concerning the international registration of industrial design
III. WIPO Copyright Treaty
IV. Paris Convention for the protection of industrial property

Choose the correct answer from the options given below.

1 I, III, II, IV
2 IV, II, I, III
3 II, I, IV, III
4 IV, I, II, III

Ans. (2)

Exp. The correct chronological order is IV, II, I, III.

The Paris Convention, adopted in 1883, applies to industrial property in the widest sense, including patents, trademarks, industrial designs, utility models, service marks, trade names, geographical indications and the repression of unfair competition. This international agreement was the first major step taken to help creators ensure that their intellectual works were protected in other countries.

The Hague Agreement governs the international registration of industrial designs. First adopted in 1925, the Agreement effectively establishes an international system - the Hague System - that allows industrial designs to be protected in multiple countries or regions with minimal formalities.

Adopted in 1977, the Budapest Treaty concerns a specific topic in the international patent process: micro-organisms. All states party to the treaty are obliged to recognise micro-organisms deposited as a part of the patent procedure, irrespective of where the depository authority is located.

WIPO Copyright Treaty was adopted by the WIPO Diplomatic Conference on Certain Copyright and Neighbouring Rights Questions in Geneva, on 20th December, 1996.

54. Match List-I with List-II.

List-I (Commissions and Tribunals)	List-II (Initial Establishments)
A. National Commission for Backward Classes (NCBC)	I. 1992
B. National Commission for Women (NCW)	II. 2010
C. National Green Tribunal (NGT)	III. 2004
D. National Commission for Scheduled Castes (NCSC)	IV. 1993

Codes

	A	B	C	D		A	B	C	D
1	IV	I	II	III	2	I	II	III	IV
3	II	I	IV	III	4	II	III	I	IV

Ans. (1)

Exp. The correct matching is A-IV, B-I, C-II, D-III.

National Commission for Backward Classes (found in 1993) is an Indian constitutional body under the jurisdiction of the Ministry of Social Justice and Empowerment, Government of India established through the Constitution.

The National Commission for Women was set-up as statutory body in January 1992 under the National Commission for Women Act, 1990.

The National Green Tribunal established in 2010, as per the National Green Tribunal Act is a specialised judicial body equipped with expertise solely for the purpose of adjudicating environmental cases in the country.

The National Commission for Scheduled Castes (2004) is an Indian constitutional body under the jurisdiction of Ministry of Social Justice and Empowerment, Government of India established with a view to provide safeguards against the exploitation of Scheduled Castes and Anglo-Indian communities to promote and protect their social, educational, economic and cultural interests, special provisions were made in the Constitution.

55. What includes 'deliverable state', as per the definition of Section 2(3) of Sale of Goods Act 1930?

1 State of goods in which buyer is bound to take delivery
2 Identified goods
3 Ascertained goods
4 Goods out for delivery

Ans. (1)

Exp. As per Section 2(3) of Sale of Goods Act, goods are said to be in a 'deliverable state' when they are in such state that the buyer would under the contract be bound to take delivery of them.

56. Which of the following statement is incorrect?

1 A child in the mother's womb is a legal person.
2 A dead person has right to regulate his property according to his wishes when he is not living.
3 Animals are subjects of rights and duties just like human beings.
4 A partnership firm is not a legal person, therefore it cannot sue or be sued in its name.

Ans. (2)

Exp. Statement (2) is incorrect because a dead person is no more a legal entity. As soon as a person dies, he becomes incapable of enjoying rights or performing his duties. So, the legal personality of a person ends with their death. However, the law does take into account the wishes and desires of the deceased person, as shown in the will they might have left behind.

57. What does 'ratio decidendi' generally imply?

1 Reason for decision alone
2 Principles laid down in the case alone
3 Both (1) and (2)
4 Observations and opinions

Ans. (3)

Exp. The ratio decidendi is the reason for a court's decision and is part of the judgement delivered at the end of a case. Through analysis of the facts, the judge applies the appropriate rule or principle of law and makes a ruling on the verdict of a case.

58. Which of the following statement is incorrect regarding Asylum?

I. Article 14 of UDHR grants a right to asylum from persecution.
II. Asylum also includes transfer of person wanted by an arrest warrant to the prosecution country.
III. Granting of asylam per se excludes any possibility of extradition.
IV. Extradition and asylum are mutually exclusive.

Choose the correct answer from the options given below.

1 I, II and III
2 I and IV
3 II, III and IV
4 I, III and IV

Ans. (3)

Exp. Statements II, III and IV are incorrect regarding Asylum. Asylum is granted to protect individuals from persecution, while extradition involves surrendering a person wanted for criminal prosecution. Asylum typically prevents extradition.

Granting asylum usually protects an individual from extradition, there may be exceptions in cases where the person is accused of serious non-political crimes, such as terrorism or war crimes.

Though extradition and asylum are often treated separately, they are not mutually exclusive in all circumstances. Extradition may still occur if asylum is not granted or if there are exceptional circumstances.

59. Which of the following is not a condition for determining the capacity of male Hindu to adopt?

1 Consent of wife under certain circumstances
2 Majority
3 Soundness of mide
4 Must be necessarily married

Ans. (4)

Exp. According to Section 7 of Hindu Adoptions and Maintenance Act, any male Hindu who is sound mind and is not a minor has the capacity to take a son or a daughter in adoption:

provided that, if he has a wife living, he shall not adopt except with the consent of his wife unless the wife has completely and finally renounced the world or has ceased to be a Hindu or has been declared by a court of competent jurisdiction to be of unsound mind.

Explanation: If a person has more than one wife living at the time of adoption, the consent of all the wives is necessary unless the consent of any one of them is unnecessary for any of the reasons specified in the preceding proviso.

60. Who coined the English phrase 'International Law' for the first time?

1 Plato
2 Cisero
3 Aristotle
4 Jeremy Bentham

Ans. (4)

Exp. The term was coined by the English philosopher Jeremy Bentham.

International Law is the body of legal rules, norms and standards that apply between sovereign states and other entities that are legally recognised as international actors.

61. How many independent judges compose the International Court of Justice (ICJ)?

1 25
2 20
3 30
4 15

Ans. (4)

Exp. The International Court of Justice is composed of 15 judges elected to nine-years terms of office by the United Nations General Assembly and the Security Council. These organs vote simultaneously but separately.

62. According to Section 20 of the Green Tribunal Act, 2010, what are the principles that should be applied by the NGT while passing orders and decisions?

I. Principle of sustainable development
II. Precautionary principle
III. Polluter pays principle
IV. Principle of absolute liability

Choose the correct answer from the options given below.

1 I, II and IV
2 II, III and IV
3 I, II and III
4 I, III and IV

Ans. (3)

Exp. According to Section 20 of Green Tribunals Act, the Tribunal shall, while passing any order or decision or award, apply the principle of sustainable development, the precautionary principle and the polluter pays principle.

63. An independent director shall be eligible for reappointment on

1 passing ordinary resolution
2 passing special resolution
3 approval of board of director
4 approval of central government

Ans. (2)

Exp. According to Section 149(2) of Companies Act, subject to the provisions of Section 152, an independent director shall hold office for a term up to five consecutive years on the board of a company, but shall be eligible for reappointment on passing of a special resolution by the company and disclosure of such appointment in the Board's report.

64. Which of the following are offences against public tranquility as per Indian Penal Code, 1860?

I. Counterfeiting coin II. Unlawful assembly
III. Sedition IV. Rioting
V. Affray

Choose the correct answer from the options given below.

1 II, III and IV
2 I, II and IV
3 II, IV and V
4 I, III and V

Ans. (3)

Exp. Chapter VIII of IPC deals with offences against public tranquility. The following offences come under its ambit

Unlawful assembly (Section 141)
Rioting (Section 146)
Affray (Section 159)

65. The contents of an electronic record may be proved under which of the following sections of India Evidence Act, 1872?

1 Section 65-A
2 Section 65-B
3 Section 66
4 Sections 61 and 53

Ans. (2)

Exp. Section 65-A provides that the contents of electronic records may be proved in accordance with the provisions of Section 65-B. Thus, Section 65-A provides for a special procedure for proving of contents of electronic record. In furtherance thereof, Section 65-B provides for the procedure.

66. Under Section 24 of Indian Contract Act, 1872, if only a part of consideration or object is unlawful, the contract shall be

1 valid 2 voidable
3 void 4 illegal

Ans. (3)

Exp. According to Section 24 of the Contract Act, if any part of a single consideration for one or more objects, or any one or any part of any one of several considerations for a single object, is unlawful, the agreement is void.

67. Arrange the following legislations in the chronological order of their enactment.

I. Indian Divorce Act
II. Parsi Marriage and Divorce Act
III. Dissolution of Muslim Marriage Act
IV. Special Marriage Act

Choose the correct answer from the options given below.

1 II, I, IV, III
2 I, II, III, IV
3 III, II, IV, I
4 I, IV, II, III

Ans. (*)

Exp. The legislations in chronological order of their enactment are—Indian Divorce Act, 1869, Dissolution of Muslim Marriages Act, 1939, Parsi Marriage and Divorce Act, 1936, Special Marriage Act, 1954.

Note : This questions has been dropped by NTA-UGC.

68. Match List-I with List-II.

	List-I (Titles of Books)		List-II (Authors)
A.	Public International Law in Nutshell	I.	JL Taulbee and GV Glahn
B.	Law among Nations: An Introduction to Public International Law	II.	Martin Dixon
C.	Principles of Public International Law	III.	Thomas Buergenthal and Sean D. Murphy
D.	Text Book on International Law	IV.	Ian Brownlie

Codes

	A	B	C	D		A	B	C	D
1	IV	II	III	I	2	III	I	IV	II
3	II	I	III	IV	4	I	III	II	IV

Ans. (2)

Exp. The correct matching is A-III, B-I, C-IV, D-II

Public International Law in Nutshell is written by Thomas Buergenthal and Sean D. Murphy. This book provides an overview of contemporary international law and signposts for additional research, includes chapters on the law of the sea, international environmental law, the use of force and arms control.

Law among Nations: An Introduction to Public International Law is written by JL Taulbee and Gerhard von Glahn (late) who was a professor of Political Science at the University of Minnesota-Duluth.

Principles of Public International Law was written by Ian Brownlie. He was an English barrister and academic, specialising in international law. He was Chichele Professor of Public International Law from 1980-1999.

The Text book on International Law is written by Martin Dixon.

69. Match List-I with List-II.

	List-I (Rules)		List-II (Explanations)
A.	Rule of Foreseeability Test	I.	Two or more person combine to injure a third party by unlawful mean
B.	Rule of Proximity	II.	Re Polemis
C.	Tort of Conspiracy	III.	Negligence
D.	Test of Directness	IV.	Wagon Mound (No. 1) case

Codes

	A	B	C	D		A	B	C	D
1	IV	III	I	II	2	I	II	III	IV
3	III	IV	II	I	4	II	I	IV	III

Ans. (1)

➲ *Exp.* The correct matching is A-IV, B-III, C-I, D-II.

Overseas Tankship (UK) Ltd *v/s* Morts Dock and Engineering Co Ltd. commonly known as Wagon Mound (No. 1), is a landmark tort law case, which imposed a remoteness rule for causation in negligence. The Privy Council held that a party can be held liable only for loss that was reasonably foreseeable. Contributory negligence on the part of the dock owners was also relevant in the decision, and was essential to the outcome, although not central to this case's legal significance.

Proximity simply means that the parties must be 'sufficiently close', so that it is 'reasonably foreseeable' that one party's negligence would cause loss or damage to the other.

For a tort to become a conspiracy, there must be a common intention to harm the other person. If the real purpose of the combination is not to injure another, but to forward or defend the trade of those who enter into it, then no wrong is committed and no action will lie although damage to another ensues.

In Re Polemis and Furness, Withy and Co Ltd. is an English tort case on causation and remoteness in the law of negligence. The Court of Appeal held that a defendant can be deemed liable for all consequences flowing from his negligent conduct regardless of how unforeseeable such consequences are.

70. Arrange in chronological order of the following Fundamental Duties as appearing in the Constitution of India.

I. To safeguard public property and to abjure violence
II. To value and preserve the rich heritage of our composite culture
III. To develop the scientific temper
IV. To defend the country and render national service

Choose the correct answer from the options given below.

1 IV, I, II, III
2 I, III, IV, II
3 IV, III, II, I
4 IV, II, III, I

Ans. (4)

➲ *Exp.* The correct chronological order is IV, II, III, I.

According to Article 51A of the Constitution, it shall be the duty of every citizen of India

To abide by the Constitution and respect its ideals and institutions, the National Flag and the National Anthem;

To cherish and follow the noble ideals which inspired our national struggle for freedom;

To uphold and protect the sovereignty, unity and integrity of India;

To defend the country and render national service when called upon to do so;

To promote harmony and the spirit of common brotherhood amongst all the people of India transcending religious, linguistic and regional or sectional diversities; to renounce practices derogatory to the dignity of women;

To value and preserve the rich heritage of our composite culture;

To protect and improve the natural environment including forests, lakes, rivers and wild life, and to have compassion for living creatures;

To develop the scientific temper, humanism and the spirit of inquiry and reform;

To safeguard public property and to abjure violence;

To strive towards excellence in all spheres of individual and collective activity, so that the nation constantly rises to higher levels of endeavour and achievement;

who is a parent or guardian to provide opportunities for education to his child or, as the case may be, ward between the age of six and fourteen years.

71. Marriage of Hindu man with biological sister of his adopted sister is

1 void
2 valid
3 voidable
4 illegal

Ans. (2)

➲ *Exp.* The Hindu Marriage Act, does not consider the marriage between the biological sister of an adopted sister as void or prohibited.

Since, there is no legal provision that explicitly prohibits such a marriage, it is considered valid under the Hindu Marriage Act.

72. Which of the following is undefined in the International Convention on the "Protection of the Rights of all Migrant Workers and Members of their Family, 1990"?

1 Migrant worker
2 Unorganised worker
3 Seasonal worker
4 Frontier worker

Ans. (2)

➲ *Exp.* Other than unorganised workers, all other kinds of workers have been defined in the International Convention on the "Protection of the Rights of all Migrant Workers and Members of the Family, 1990".

73. Match List-I with List-II.

List-I (Concepts)	List-II (Section of Relevant Acts)
A. Unpaid seller	I. Section 16 of Sale of Goods Act, 1930
B. Caveat emptor and its exceptions	II. Section 45 of Sale of Goods Act, 1930
C. Minor admitted to benefits of partnership	III. Section 30 of Indian Partnership Act, 1932
D. Registration of partnership	IV. Section 69 of Partnership Act, 1932

Codes

	A	B	C	D
1	II	I	III	IV
2	I	II	IV	III
3	III	IV	II	I
4	IV	III	I	II

Ans. (1)

Exp. The correct matching is A-II, B-I, C-III, D-IV.

Unpaid sellers have been provided under **Section 45** of **Sale of Goods Act, 1930**. According to Section 45(1), the seller of goods is deemed to be an 'unpaid seller' within the meaning of this Act-when the whole of the price has not been paid or tendered; when a bill of exchange or other negotiable instrument has been received as conditional payment, and the condition on which it was received has not been fulfilled by reason of the dishonour of the instrument or otherwise.

Section 16 of Sale of Goods, 1930 Act provides for the rule of caveat emptor and its exceptions.

Section 30 of the Indian Partnership Act, 1932 provides for minors admitted to the benefits of partnership.

Section 69 of the Partnership Act, 1932 provides for registration of partnership.

74. Match List-I with List-II.

List-I (List in Constitutions)	List-II (Subjects)
A. Concurrent List	I. In civil matters
B. State List	II. Marriage and divorce
C. Union List	III. Public health and sanitation
D. Appellate Juristiction of Supreme Court	IV. Elections to the legislatures of state

Codes

	A	B	C	D		A	B	C	D
1	I	IV	II	III	2	IV	II	III	I
3	II	III	IV	I	4	III	IV	II	I

Ans. (3)

Exp. The correct matching is A-II, B-III, C-IV, D-I.

Concurrent List-Marriage and divorce
State List-Public health and sanitation
Union List-Elections to the legislatures of the state
Appellate Jurisdiction of Supreme Court-In civil matters

75. Muta marriage is

I. a temporary marriage.
II. recognised under Shia Law.
III. recognised under Sunni Law.
IV. a marriage for a fixed period: a day, month, year.
V. one in which dower need not be specified.

Choose the correct answer from the options given below.

1 I, II and IV   2 I, II and V
3 I, III and IV   4 I, III, IV and V

Ans. (1)

Exp. 'Muta' marriage is a marriage for temporary, but a fixed period after specifying dower. 'Muta' marriage recognised under Shia law. It is void under Sunni Law because the words used at the time of proposal and acceptance must denote an immediate and permanent union. The specified period may be a day, a month or a year or term of years.

76. Digital Signature Certificate issued by the Certifying Authority can be revoked

1 depending upon the type of certificate issued.
2 on the request of the subscriber.
3 under no circumstances.
4 on the basis of dispute between the partners of the firm.

Ans. (2)

Exp. Section 38(1) of the IT Act states that a Certifying Authority may revoke a Digital Signature Certificate issued by it:

where the subscriber or any other person authorised by him makes a request to that effect; or
upon the death of the subscriber; or
upon the dissolution of the firm or winding up of the company where the subscriber is a firm or a company.

77. Match List-I with List-II.

List-I (Judicial Decisions)	List-II (Fundamental Rights)
A. Sri Srinivasa Theatre *v/s* Government of Tamil Nadu	I. Article 20 (3) of the Constitution
B. KA Abbas *v/s* Union of India	II. Right to Environment
C. Selvi *v/s* State of Karnataka	III. Equality before Law
D. Rural Litigation and Entitlement Kendra *v/s* State of Uttar Pradesh	IV. Censorship

Codes

	A	B	C	D
1	I	II	III	IV
2	III	IV	I	II
3	II	I	IV	III
4	IV	II	I	III

Ans. (2)

Exp. The correct matching is A-III, B-IV, C-I, D-II.

Sri Srinivasa Theatre *v/s* Government of Tamil Nadu In this case, it was held that the expressions 'equality before law' and 'equal protection of law' do not carry the same meaning though there is a lot in common between them. The word 'law' in the first expression was more general in sense and in the second expression it was more specific.

KA Abbas *v/s* Union of India The court allowed the amendment holding the petitioner was right in contending that a person who invests capital in promoting or producing a film must have clear guidance in advance in the matter of censorship of films even if the law of pre-censorship is not violative of the Fundamental Right.

Selvi *v/s* State of Karnataka (Article 20(3) of the Constitution) This is a landmark case decided by the Supreme Court of India in 2010, which ruled that the use of narcoanalysis, brain mapping and polygraph tests on individuals without their consent is unconstitutional.

Rural Litigation and Entitlement Kendra *v/s* State of Uttar Pradesh This case highlights the conflict between industrial development and environmental conservation. Filed in the 1980s, this case brought attention to the detrimental effects of limestone quarrying in the Doon valley of Mussoorie and set significant precedents for environmental jurisprudence in India.

78. Match List-I with List-II.

List-I (IPR Treaties and Agreements)	List-II (Corresponding Subject Matters)
A. Strasbourg Agreement	I. Trademark
B. Nice Agreement	II. Audio-visual performance
C. Beijing Treaty	III. International patent classification
D. Singapore Treaty	IV. International classification of goods

Codes

	A	B	C	D		A	B	C	D
1	I	III	IV	II	2	III	II	I	IV
3	II	I	III	IV	4	III	IV	II	I

***Ans.* (4)**

Exp. The correct matching is A-III, B-IV, C-II, D-I.

Strasbourg Agreement is a hierarchical system which uses language-independent symbols to classify patents and utility models according to the area of technology to which they relate.

Nice Agreement establishes a international classification of goods and services for the purposes of registering trademarks and service marks.

Beijing Agreement was adopted on 24th June, 2012 and entered into force on 28th April, 2020. It deals with the intellectual property rights of performers in audio-visual performances.

Singapore Treaty is to create a modern and dynamic international framework for the harmonisation of administrative trademark registration procedures. Building on the Trademark Law Treaty of 1994 (TLT), the Singapore Treaty has a wider scope of application and addresses more recent developments in the field of communication technologies.

79. MK Ranjit Singh *v/s* UOI (2024) deals with which of the following issue?

1 Preservation of biodiversity and climate change
2 Immigrants and refugees
3 Offence against children
4 Cyber crimes

***Ans.* (1)**

Exp. MK Ranjit Singh *v/s* UOI (2024) deals with the preservation of biodiversity and climate change. The primary issue encircling the case was the protection of endangered species of birds and finding alternatives to the overhead power lines in the form of underground infrastructure.

80. In which year "WIPO Treaty on Intellectual Property, Genetic Resources and Associated Traditional Knowledge" has been adopted?

1 2023 2 2020
3 2024 4 2022

***Ans.* (3)**

Exp. The WIPO Treaty on Intellectual Property, Genetic Resources and Associated Traditional Knowledge (the Treaty) was adopted by the Member States of WIPO on 24th May, 2024, and it will come into force three months after there have been 15 ratifications and accessions. Key terms used in the treaty are defined in Article 2.

81. The maxim 'de minimis non curat lex' relates to

1 affray 2 annoyance
3 cheating 4 slight harm

***Ans.* (4)**

Exp. The maxim 'de minimis non curat lex' relates to slight harm. It is a common law principle whereby the court will not sit in judgement of extremely minor transgressions of the law. In general, the maxim refers that the courts will not intervene in disputes where the substance of the controversy is insignificant.

82. Which of the following statements are correct according to National Green Tribunal Act, 2010.

I. It repealed National Environment Tribunal Act, 1995.
II. It repealed National Environment Appellate Authorities Act, 1997.
III. The Act does mention about judicial pronouncements construing right to healthy environment as a part of right to life under Article 21 of the Constitution.
IV. The Act does not define environment.

Choose the correct answer from the options given below.

1 II, III and IV 2 I, II and IV
3 I, II and III 4 I, III and IV

***Ans.* (3)**

Exp. Statements I, II and III are correct. Statement IV is incorrect because the Act does define 'environment'.

83. Which of the following statements are correct as per International Court of Justice (ICJ)?

I. The judgement is final and without appeal.
II. No application for revision may be made at all.
III. The court shall deliver it's advisory opinion in open court.
IV. The members of ICJ are elected for 10 years.

Choose the correct answer from the options given below.

1 III and IV
2 II and IV
3 I and II
4 I and III

Ans. (4)

➲ *Exp.* Statements I and III are correct as an application for revision of a judgement may be made only when it is based upon the discovery of some fact of such a nature as to be a decisive factor, which fact was, when the judgement was given, unknown to the court and also to the party claiming revision, always provided that such ignorance was not due to negligence. The members of ICJ are elected for nine years.

84. Arrange the following provisions in the chronological order of arrangement in the Consumer Protection Act, 2019.

I. District Consumer Protection Council
II. Central Consumer Protection Council
III. Central Consumer Protection Authorities
IV. Investigation Wing
V. Consumer Mediation Cell

Choose the correct answer from the options given below.

1 II, I, III, IV, V
2 III, II, IV, V, I
3 V, III, II, I, IV
4 IV, II, I, V, III

Ans. (1)

➲ *Exp.* The correct chronological order is II, I, III, IV and V.

Section 3 Central Consumer Protection Council

Section 8 District Consumer Protection Council

Section 10 Establishment of Central Consumer Protection Authorities

Section 15 of Consumer Protection Act provides for Investigation Wing.

Section 74 consumer mediation cell.

85. In which of the following case, the Supreme Court has held that Section 309 of IPC is not unconstitutional and is not violative of Articles 21 and 14 of the Constitution of India?

1 P. Rathinam *v/s* Union of India
2 Aruna Ramchandra Shanbaug *v/s* Union of India
3 MS Dubal *v/s* State of Maharashtra
4 Gian Kaur *v/s* State of Punjab

Ans. (4)

➲ *Exp.* The Supreme Court in Gian Kaur *v/s* State of Punjab upheld the constitutionality of Sections 306 and 309 of the Indian Penal Code, ruling that the right to life does not include the right to die. Consequently, the court dismissed Gian Kaur's appeal and held her accountable for aiding and abetting suicide.

86. Transfer of property between buyer and seller is explained in Chapter III of Sale of Goods Act, 1930.

Arrange the following provisions in the sequence of their appearance in the Act.

I. Property in goods passes when they are ascertained.
II. Property in goods passes when the buyer and seller intend it to pass.
III. In case of specified goods in deliverable state, property in goods passes when contract is made.
IV. Risk prima facie passes with property.

Choose the correct answer from the options given below

1 I, II, III, IV
2 I, III, II, IV
3 IV, II, III, I
4 II, I, III, IV

Ans. (1)

➲ *Exp.* The correct sequence of the provisions is given I, III, II, IV.

Section 18: Goods must be ascertained

Section 19: Property passes when intended to pass

Section 20: Specific goods in a deliverable state.

Section 26: Risk prima facie passes with property.

87. Gap between two consecutive board meeting of a company should not be more than

1 90 days
2 120 days
3 150 days
4 180 days

Ans. (2)

➲ *Exp.* A minimum of four meetings of the Board of Directors is required to be held every year with a gap between the two consecutive meetings not exceeding 120 days. There is no requirement of holding the meeting every quarter; the only requirement is that not more than 120 days shall elapse between two consecutive meetings.

88. Arrange the following International Humanitarian Law Treaties and Conventions in the chronological order of their adoption.

I. Chemical Weapons Convention
II. Arms Trade Treaty
III. International Convention for the Protection of the All Persons from Enforced Disappearance
IV. Geneva Convention
V. Treaty on the Prohibition of Nuclear Weapons

Choose the correct answer from the options given below.

1 II, III, IV, I, V
2 IV, II, III, V, I
3 I, V, IV, III, II
4 IV, I, III, II, V

Ans. (4)

➲ *Exp.* The correct sequence is IV, I, III, II, V.

In 1949, an international conference of diplomats built on the earlier treaties for the protection of war victims, revising and updating them into four new conventions comprising 429 Articles of law-known as the Geneva Conventions on 12th August, 1949.

The Chemical Weapons Convention (CWC) was adopted by the United Nations Conference on Disarmament on 3rd September, 1992 and the treaty was opened to signature by all states on 13th January, 1993. The CWC entered into force on 29th April, 1997.

The International Convention for the Protection of the All Persons from Enforced Disappearance (ICPPED) was adopted by General Assembly resolution A/RES/61/177 in December 2006 and came into force on 23rd December,

2010. Countries that ratify the Convention agree to be legally bound by it and are called State parties.

The Arms Trade Treaty was adopted on 2nd April, 2013 by resolution 67/234B during the 67th session of the General Assembly of the United Nations.

The Treaty on the Prohibition of Nuclear Weapons was adopted by the Conference (by a vote of 122 states in favour, with one vote against and one abstention) at the United Nations on 7th July, 2017 and opened for signature on 20th September, 2017.

89. Which Articles were added to the Constitution of India to facilitate the establishment of specific tribunals to meet the needs of administrative justice?

1 Article 124A   2 Article 233A
3 Articles 323A and 323B
4 Articles 338A and 338B

Ans. *(3)*

Exp. Articles 323A and 323B were added to the Constitution of Indiao facilitate the establishment of specific tribunals to meet the needs of administrative justice.

The 42nd Amendment to the Constitution introduced Part XIV-A, which included Article 323A and 323B providing for the Constitution of tribunals dealing with administrative matters and other issues.

According to these provisions of the Constitution, tribunals are to be organised and established in such a manner that they do not violate the integrity of the judicial system given in the Constitution which forms the basic structure of the Constitution.

90. Match List-I with List-II.

List-I (Types of Governments)	List-II (Name of Countries)
A. Constitutional Monarchy	I. Canada, Australia
B. Dual Federalism	II. United States of America
C. Presidential	III. Denmark, Bhutan, Belgium
D. Parliamentary	IV. India and United Kingdom

Codes

	A	B	C	D		A	B	C	D
1	III	I	II	IV	2	I	III	II	IV
3	III	II	I	IV	4	I	II	III	IV

Ans. *(1)*

Exp. The correct matching is A-III, B-I, C-II, D-IV.

Constitutional Monarchy - Denmark, Bhutan and Belgium
Dual Federalism- Canada, Australia
Presidential - United States of America
Parliamentary - India and United Kingdom

Directions (Q. Nos. 91-95) *Read the passage carefully and answer the questions that follows.*

The Shriram gas leak case pitted the Supreme Court against one of India's largest corporation. CJ Bhagwati presided over the Supreme Court bench and was deeply concerned for safety of citizens. He was anxious to improve plant-safety, a task which the statutory agencies seemed incapable of performing. The Honourable Chief Justice saw in the Oleum case a way of influencing the far more important Bhopal gas leak case. The Shriram case has also raised some important questions concerning the true scope and ambit of Articles 21 and 32 of the Constitution. The case also dealt with principles and norms of determining the liability of large enterprises engaged in manufacturing and sale of hazardous products. It also decided the basis on which damage should be quantified and whether the corporation should be allowed to function from thickly populated areas and if they are allowed what measures should be taken for minimising hazards to workmen. This led the Parliament to enact law and articulate new standard of absolute liability in 1991.

91. The judgement in Shriram gas leak case influenced the decision of

1 Shrimp case   2 Goel Ganga case
3 Bhopal gas leak case   4 Clean Narmada case

Ans. *(3)*

Exp. The judgement in Shriram gas leak influenced the decision of Bhopal gas leak case. In 1988, the Supreme Court's judgement in the Oleum gas leak case held the industries responsible for proper waste treatment and emphasised the importance of environmental protection. The court ordered the establishment of primary treatment plants and held local authorities accountable for prevention.

92. In the Shriram gas leak case, the Chief Justice was mainly concerned with which of the following?

1 Safety of citizen   2 Profit of companies
3 Disaster in community 4 Aftermath of gas leak

Ans. *(1)*

Exp. As given in the passage, the Chief Justice was deeply concerned for the safety of citizen.

93. The Shriram gas leak case did not focus on which of the following issue?

1 Scope of Articles 21 and 32 of Constitution
2 Norms of determining liability of large corporation
3 Basis of quantifying damages
4 Measures of increasing profit of company

Ans. *(4)*

Exp. Shriram case did not focus on measures for increasing the profit of the company.

94. As an effect of Shriram gas leak case, the law enacted by Parliament in 1991 dealt with

1 private liability
2 storage of hazardous substances
3 absolute liability
4 safety of plants and animals

Ans. *(3)*

➲ *Exp.* As an effect of the Shriram gas leak case, the law enacted by the Parliament in 1991 dealt with the concept of absolute liability.

95. Statutory agencies seem incapable of performing which of the following task?

1 Safety of citizen
2 Plant safety
3 Safety of community
4 Prevention of disaster

Ans. *(2)*

➲ *Exp.* As per the given passage, statutory agencies seemed incapable of handling plant safety.

Directions (Q. Nos. 96-100) *Read the passage carefully and answer the questions that follows.*

From the second half of the 19th century to the present, the Geneva Convention, 1864 (revised in 1906, 1929 and 1949) and Hague Convention, 1899 (revised in 1907) comprised one of the most extensive bodies of positive international law outlining constraints on state behaviour. The Geneva and Hague Conventions are noteworthy not only for their content, but also their widespread ratification. Accepting the Conventions was a prestigious symbol of membership in the exclusive 'international society of civilised states' and most states ratified them sooner or later. The conventions gave combatant victims of war-wounded soldiers and POWs-international rights to medical care and humane conditions of incarceration. The Hague Convention was built on a fundamental distinction between combatants and non-combatants, designed to ensure that non-combatants did not become victims of war. Non-combatants were not considered legitimate military targets and military occupation authorities were prohibited from exploiting civilian populations under their control.

96. Which international instrument predominantly ensures that non-combatants did not become victims of war?

1 Positive International Law
2 The Geneva Convention
3 The Hague Convention
4 International Humanitarian Law

Ans. *(3)*

➲ *Exp.* The Hague Convention acted as the international instrument that predominantly ensures that non-combatants did not become victims of war.

97. What was the fundamental distinction on which the Hague Convention was built?

1 Distinction between military occupation and civil population
2 Distinction between positive international law and laws of the war
3 Distinction between combatants and non-combatants
4 Distinction between military targets and military authorities

Ans. *(3)*

➲ *Exp.* The Hague Convention was built on the fundamental distinction between combatants and non-combatants, designed to ensure that non-combatants did not become victims of war.

98. What makes Geneva Convention (1864) noteworthy?

1 It's content alone.
2 It's widespread ratification alone.
3 It's content and its widespread ratification.
4 The new international rights created by the Geneva Convention.

Ans. *(3)*

➲ *Exp.* Geneva Convention is noteworthy for its content and widespread ratification.

99. What motivated the states to ratify the Geneva and Hague Conventions?

1 The Conventions being prestigious symbol of membership in the international society of civilised states.
2 The Conventions being the most extensive body of positive international law.
3 As the Conventions enlist constraints on state behaviour.
4 As the Conventions prescribe international rights of medical care

Ans. *(1)*

➲ *Exp.* The states were motivated to ratify Hague and Geneva Conventions because they were prestigious symbols of membership in the international society of civilised states.

100. What do Hague Convention, 1899 and Geneva Convention, 1864 primarily outline?

1 Human conditions of incarceration
2 Constraints on state behaviour
3 Rights of victims of war
4 Rights of wounded soldiers

Ans. *(2)*

➲ *Exp.* The Hague Convention, 1899 and Geneva Convention, 1864 outlined constraints on state behaviour.

UGC-NET
LAW
SOLVED PAPER 2023 (December)

PAPER II

Direction *This paper contains **hundred** (100) objective type questions of **two** (2) marks each. All questions are compulsory.*

1. As per the provisions of the Hindu Adoption and Maintenance Act, 1956, a bachelor male adopts a child. He subsequently marries a woman shall

1 be the adoptive mother of that adopted child
2 be the step mother of that adopted child
3 be the adoptive mother of that child if the child accepts her as mother
4 be the adoptive mother of that child at her discretion

Ans. (2)

Exp. As per the Section 14(3) of the Hindu Adoption and Maintenance Act, 1956, where a widower or a bachelor adopts a child, any wife whom he subsequently marries shall be deemed to be the step mother of the adopted child.

2. A Hindu male having a Hindu wife, changed his religion and adopts Islam in 2012. He marries again to a Muslim girl in 2013. In 2014, his Hindu wife died. His second marriage is

1 valid as he married after conversion to Islam which permits bigamy
2 valid as his wife died after his marriage to Muslim girl
3 void as he has not taken the consent of his Hindu wife
4 void as his second marriage amounts to bigamy

Ans. (4)

Exp. A Hindu male having a Hindu wife, changed his religion and adopts Islam in 2012. He marries a Muslim girl in 2013. In 2014, his Hindu wife died. His second marriage is void as his second marriage amounts to bigamy. In the landmark judgement of Sarla Mudgal *v/s* Union of India, it was held by the Supreme Court that assuming that a Hindu husband has a right to embrace Islam as his religion, he has no right under the Act to marry again without getting his marriage under the Act dissolved. The second marriage after conversion to Islam would, thus, be in violation of the rules of natural justice and as such would be void.

3. Which one of the following is not a ground for divorce under Section 13 of the Hindu Marriage Act, 1955 ?

1 Respondent is convicted for committing an offence
2 Respondent has renounced the world by entering any religious order
3 Respondent has ceased to be a Hindu by conversion to another religion
4 Respondent has not been heard of as being alive for a period of seven years

Ans. (1)

Exp. Respondent being convicted for an offence has not been provided as a ground for divorce under Section 13 of the Hindu Marriage Act, 1955. As per Section 13(1), any marriage solemnised, whether before or after the commencement of this act, may on a petition presented by either the husband or the wife, be dissolved by a decree of divorce on the ground that the other party.

4. A Muslim can make a bequest of his property without the consent of heirs to the extent of

1 half of his property
2 whole of his property
3 one -fourth of his property
4 one -third of his property

Ans. (4)

Exp. A Muslim testator can make a will of only one-third of his property without the consent of his or her heirs.

5. Which Article in the Constitution of India established National Commission for the Scheduled Castes?

1 Article 335
2 Article 338
3 Article 341
4 Article 342A

Ans. (2)

Exp. Article 338 of the Indian Constitution deals with the National Commission for Scheduled Castes. Article 338 A deals with the National Commission for Scheduled Tribes.

6. Polluter pays principle is also known as ....

1 Principle of Good Neighbourliness
2 Principle of Common Responsibility
3 Principle of Public Liability
4 Principle of Extended Producer Responsibility (EPR)

Ans. (4)

➲ *Exp.* The polluter pays principle is also known as Extended Producer Responsibility (EPR). It is a commonly accepted practice that suggests that those who produce pollution should manage it to prevent damage to human health or the environment. This principle is a part of the 1992, Rio Declaration, which provides broader principles for sustainable development worldwide.

7. Which country does not provide any written constitutional guarantee of fundamental freedoms ?

1 UK 2 UK and USA
3 UK and India 4 USA

Ans. (1)

➲ *Exp.* UK does not provide any written constitutional guarantee of fundamental freedoms. Although, the British Constitution is not codified, the Supreme Court recognises constitutional principles and constitutional statutes, which shape the use of political power. There are at least four main constitutional principles recognised by the courts.

8. Which among the following follow a Parliamentary System of Government ?

1 Only India 2 Only Australia
3 India and Australia 4 UK and USA

Ans. (3)

➲ *Exp.* India and Australia follow a Parliamentary System of Government. A Parliamentary Government is a democratic administration in which the government is formed by the political party that obtains the most seats in the Legislature or Parliament during the federal election.

9. Which among the following countries do not follow the scheme of distribution of power ?

1 India 2 USA 3 UK 4 Canada

Ans. (3)

➲ *Exp.* UK does not follow the scheme of distribution of power. In the UK, there is no written constitutional document that guarantees the rules of the Doctrine and in practice, the functions of the state organs overlap significantly.

10. In which country, the appointment of judges are made through the Parliament ?

1 UK 2 USA 3 India 4 All of these

Ans. (2)

➲ *Exp.* In USA, the appointment of judges are made through the Parliament. All justices are nominated by the President, confirmed by the Senate and hold their offices under life tenure. Since, Justices do not have to run or campaign for re-election, they are thought to be insulated from political pressure when deciding cases.

11. A human being ceases to be a person, in law as in fact ....

1 on being adjudged an insolvent
2 on renunciation of citizenship
3 on conviction
4 at death

Ans. (4)

➲ *Exp.* A human being ceases to be a person, in law as in fact, at death. It is the recognised principle that the personality of a human being commences on his birth and ceases to exist at death. The only exception which we can say is the personality of an unborn child. The rationale behind this rule is that a dead person has no rights and interest.

12. Salmond distinguishes between 'possession in fact' and 'possession in law'. He treated possession in fact as ....

1 a fallacy 2 a fiction
3 a conception 4 a right

Ans. (3)

➲ *Exp.* Salmond distinguishes between possession in fact and possession in law. He treated possession in fact as a conception. Possession in fact or de facto possession is the actual or physical possession. And possession in law or de jure possession is possession in the eye of law, that is, recognised and protected by law. They both most often exist together and must not always.

13. American realist Judge Jerome Frank described his own attitude (towards realism) as one of

1 Decisive cynicism 2 Constructive skepticism
3 Positive evangelism 4 Radical objectivity

Ans. (2)

➲ *Exp.* American realist, Judge Jerome Frank described his own attitude (towards realism) as one of constructive skepticism. He was a constructive legal skeptic who questioned everything and took nothing for granted in everyday terms, as well as holding a traditional understanding of the law. Among his most renowned and controversial works is 'Law and the Modern Mind', in which he introduced the notion of 'legal myth'.

14. The term preferred by Bentham to explain his imperative concept of a law is

1 Firman 2 Mandate 3 Dictate 4 Fiat

Ans. (2)

➲ *Exp.* The term preferred by Bentham to explain his imperative concept of a law is Mandate. Like Austin's theory, Bentham's is an imperative theory of law in which the central concepts are those of sovereign and command and the definitions of both sovereign and command are at first sight very similar in the two authors.

15. With respect to which of the following kind of IPR, there exists a statutory ban for assignment?

1 Patents 2 Trademarks
3 Geographical Indication
4 Layout Designs of Integrated Circuits

Ans. (3)

Exp. There exists a statutory ban on assignment in case of Geographical Indication. Section 24 of the Geographical Indication of Goods Act, 1999 clearly indicates that assignment, transmission, licensing, pledge, mortgage or any such agreement is prohibited by law.

16. 'Moral Right' is a concept prevailing in

1 Industrial Design
2 Geographical Indication
3 Trademark
4 Copyright

Ans. (4)

Exp. 'Moral Right' as a concept, prevails in copyright. Moral rights serve to safeguard the reputation of the author and grant them the authority to alter or remove their work. They provide the author with creative control, ensuring that their expressions or ideas are preserved intact and hence encourages authors to fight for their rights.

17. Which of the following international legal instrument is relating to patent ?

1 Budapest Treaty, 1977
2 Madrid Agreement, 1891
3 Berne Convention, 1886
4 Washington Treaty, 1989

Ans. (1)

Exp. Adopted in 1977, the Budapest Treaty concerns a specific topic in the international patent process: micro-organisms. All states party to the Treaty are obliged to recognise micro-organisms deposited as a part of the patent procedure, irrespective of where the depository authority is located.

18. Which kind of patent is protectable in India ?

1 Design patent
2 Utility patent
3 Process patent
4 Plant Variety patent

Ans. (3)

Exp. Process patent is protected in India. According to Section 48(2) of the Indian Patents Act, 1970, for patents related to a process, the patentee has exclusive rights to prevent unauthorised use of the process and the use, sale or importation of products obtained directly from that process in India.

19. "To protect and improve the natural environment including forest, lakes, rivers and wildlife, and to have compassion for living creatures" is provided under which Part of the Indian Constitution ?

1 Fundamental Rights
2 Fundamental Duties
3 Directive Principles of State Policy
4 Obligation of State

Ans. (2)

Exp. "To protect and improve the natural environment including forests, lakes, rivers and wildlife, and to have compassion for living creatures" is provided under Fundamental Duties, as provided under Article 51 A (g).

20. As per National Green Tribunal Act, 2010, 'Environment' includes water, air and land and other inter-relationship, which exists among and between water, air and land and human beings, other living creatures, plants, micro-organism and ....

1 Ecosystem
2 Biodiversity
3 Property
4 Climate

Ans. (3)

Exp. Section 2(1)(3) of National Green Tribunal Act, 2010, Environment includes water, air and land and other inter-relationship, which exists among and between water, air and land and human beings, other living creatures, plants, micro-organism and property.

21. When an absolute right is violated, the law conclusively presumes damages although the person wronged may have suffered no pecuniary loss. This was decided in case of

1 Rogers *v/s* Rajender Dutt
2 Ashby *v/s* White
3 Winsmore *v/s* Greenbank
4 Tozer *v/s* Child

Ans. (2)

Exp. The court in Ashby *v/s* White recognised the concept of exemplary damages for misfeasance in public office, which aimed to punish and deter harmful conduct by public officers. Lord Holt acknowledged that greater compensatory damages were appropriate in such cases to serve as a punishment and a deterrent against future misconduct by public officers.

22. Red herring prospectus is a prospectus issued

1 prior to the issue of prospectus
2 after the issue of main prospectus
3 with the consent of shareholder
4 on the behest of RoC (Register of Companies)

Ans. (1)

Exp. A red herring prospectus is a preliminary document produced by a company planning to go public through an IPO. It gives detailed information on the company's activities, finances and fund raising objectives, but excludes specifics such as the IPO price and share amount.

23. The term 'Contra Proferentem' means

1 Contradictory contract
2 Standard form contract are to be interpreted legally
3 Limited construction
4 Ambiguity is to be resolved against the party who inserted limiting term

Ans. (4)

Exp. Contra proferentem is a rule of contract interpretation that states an ambiguous contract term should be construed against the drafter of the contract. The term Contra Proferentem is derived from a Latin phrase meaning against the offeror.

24. As per the Partnership Act, 1932 'Partnership' is defined under

1 Section 8 2 Section 7 3 Section 5 4 Section 4

Ans. (4)

Exp. According to Section 4 of the Partnership Act, 'Partnership' is the relation between persons who have agreed to share the profits of a business carried on by all or any of them acting for all.

25. "Consideration is not necessary for creation of Agency." This is provided in

1 Section 185 of the Indian Contract Act, 1872
2 Section 4 of the Partnership Act, 1932
3 Section 4 of the Indian Agency Act, 1950
4 Section 2 of the Companies Act, 2013

Ans. (1)

Exp. According to Section 185 of the Indian Contract Act, 1872 no consideration is necessary to create an Agency.

26. 'A' makes a contract with 'B' to buy B's horse if 'A' survives 'C'.

1 'C' dies in lifetime of 'A' 2 'A' dies in lifetime of 'C'
3 'A' and 'C' both die 4 'B' dies in lifetime of 'A'

Ans. (1)

Exp. According to Section 32 of the Contract Act, Contingent contracts to do or not to do anything if an uncertain future event happens cannot be enforced by law unless and until that event has happened. If the event becomes impossible, such contracts become void. The given question is framed from illustration (1) to Section 32 of Contract Act. Thus, when 'A' makes a contract with 'B' to buy B's horse if 'A' survives 'C', this contract cannot be enforced by law unless and until 'C' dies in lifetime of 'A'.

27. There is no distinction between de facto and de jure recognition for the purpose of giving effect to the internal acts of the recognised authority. This was held so in the case of

1 Mighell *v/s* Sultan of Johore
2 Luther *v/s* Sagor
3 Vavasseur *v/s* Krupp
4 Schooner Exchange *v/s* Mc Faddon

Ans. (2)

Exp. In Luther *v/s* Sagor Case (KB, CoA 1921), the court held that the recognition of the state was retroactive in effect, thus the change of government and the delay in recognising the new government would have no impact before the English courts. The court also observed that there is no distinction between de facto and de jure recognition for the purpose of giving effect to the internal acts of the recognised authority.

28. The Supreme Court of India remarked that "Extradition with foreign states is, except in exceptional case, governed by treaties or arrangements made " in the cases of

1 State of Maharashtra *v/s* Shobha Vitthal Kolte
2 T. Vellaiyan *v/s* The Registrar, SHRC, Chennai
3 State of Madras *v/s* CG Menon
4 NC Dhoundial *v/s* Union of India

Ans. (3)

Exp. In the case of The State of Madras *v/s* CG Menon, it was held that since the Fugitive Offenders Act of 1881 is inapplicable in India, there was a lot of gap felt in the extradition policies. Firstly, the extradition process to Commonwealth countries was not finalised and secondly, the extradition process from Part B States to other foreign countries including Commonwealth countries was again doubtful and unclear. These concerns led the country to develop and work towards a code and a legislation which tackled the matter of extradition effectively on a large scale.

29. "A man's nationality is a continuing legal relationship between the sovereign state on the one hand and the citizen on the other. The fundamental basis of a man's nationality is membership of an independent political community". This definition of nationality is given by the British Mexican Claims Commission in the case of

1 Youman's case 2 Re, Meunier
3 Re, Castioni 4 Re, Lynch

Ans. (4)

Exp. In the words of Lynch, a man's nationality is a continuing legal relationship between the sovereign state on the one hand and the citizen on the other. The fundamental basis of a man's nationality is membership of an independent political community.

30. The General Assembly of the United Nations passed the Uniting for Peace Resolution on

1 10th December, 1948
2 1st August, 1950
3 1st August, 1965
4 3rd November, 1950

Ans. (4)

Exp. On 3rd November, 1950, the General Assembly adopted Resolution 377 A (V), which was given the title 'Uniting for Peace'.

31. The Preamble of the Constitution of India

1 can be amended
2 cannot be amended
3 can be amended only by the Supreme Court
4 cannot be amended because it is a part of the basic feature of the Constitution

Ans. (1)

Exp. The Preamble of the Constitution of India can be amended. It has been clarified by the Supreme Court of India that, being a part of the Constitution, the Preamble can be subjected to Constitutional Amendments exercised under Article 368, however, the basic structure cannot be altered.

32. According to Kaushal Kishore *v/s* State of UP (2023) the Fundamental Right under Article 19 is available against

1 State actors only
2 Non-state actors only
3 State as well as non-state actors
4 State under Article 12 only

Ans. (3)

Exp. According to Kaushal Kishore *v/s* State of UP (2023), the Fundamental Right under Article 19 is available against state as well as non-state actors. The Court held that a Fundamental Right under Article 19 to 21 can be enforced even against persons other than the State or its instrumentalities.

33. In which of the following cases has it been held that the doctrine of basic features does not constitute a limitation on the legislature while enacting ordinary legislation?

1 Indira Gandhi *v/s* Raj Narain
2 Swadeshi Industries *v/s* Workmen
3 Royappa *v/s* State of Tamil Nadu
4 Kishor *v/s* State of Rajasthan

Ans. (1)

Exp. In the case of Indira Gandhi *v/s* Raj Narain, it was held that the doctrine of basic features does not constitute a limitation on the legislature while enacting ordinary legislation. This was a significant precedent set by the Apex Court, which not only upholds the doctrine of basic structure again but also states that the powers of Parliament are not unfettered or unlimited and that they are subject to certain exceptions. The Supreme Court upheld the supremacy of the Constitution and laid down that the Constitution is above all and that the judiciary is the protector and guarantor of the Constitution. This case also sustained the two important principles of the Constitution, which are the separation of powers and judicial review.

34. Which among the following provisions of the Constitution of India mandates criminalisation of prohibited conduct?

1 Article 17 only
2 Article 23 only
3 Article 17 and 23 only
4 Article 17, 23 and 24

Ans. 3

Exp. Criminalisation of prohibited conduct is given in Articles 17 and 23 of the Constitution. The two Articles prohibited human trafficking and forced labour. Option (3) is the right answer.

35. Mens rea does not include

1 intention
2 knowledge
3 reason to believe
4 motive

Ans. (4)

Exp. Mens rea does not include motive. It is not a type of mens rea. It is the reason or the driving force behind doing a particular act. A motive may be good or bad. Therefore, the motive is not necessarily bad or guilty always.

36. The right of private defence extends to causing death under which provision of IPC

1 Section 100 only
2 Section 100 and 103 only
3 Section 103 only
4 Section 100, 103, 105

Ans. (2)

Exp. Section 100 and 103 of IPC allow for the right of private defence to cause death. Section 100 covers the right of private defence of the body, which means a human body. It recognises this right in the seven most brutal forms of acts to the extent of even causing death of the assailant but subject to the restrictions contained under Section 99.

Section 103 enumerates the cases in which the right of defence of property may extend to the causing of death.

37. A_1 and A_2 plan to commit robbery. Mere agreement to commit this offence is punishable under which provision of IPC?

1 120-B
2 107 (2)
3 120-B and 107 (2)
4 Without actus reus it is not possible at all

Ans. (1)

Exp. When A_1 and A_2 plan to commit robbery, mere agreement to commit this offence is punishable under Section 120-B of IPC. Section 120-B of the IPC defines criminal conspiracy as an agreement between two or more persons to commit an illegal act or a legal act by illegal means. The essence of this offence lies in the agreement and the intention to commit the act.

38. A is lawfully arrested by Z who is a police officer. A loses his self-control by grave and sudden provocation due to arrest and kills Z. A shall be punished under

1 Section 304 of IPC
2 Section 302 of IPC
3 Section 304 or 302 of IPC
4 Section 301 read with Section 302 of IPC

Ans. (2)

Exp. In the given situation, if A loses self-control by grave and sudden provocation due to arrest and kills Z. A shall be punished under Section 302 of IPC. Section 302 talks about "Punishment for murder." It states that whoever commits murder shall be punished with death or imprisonment for life and shall also be liable to fine.

39. All sums realised by way of penalties under the Competition Act, 2002 are credited to

1 Competition Fund
2 Consolidated Fund of India
3 Finance Account of Ministry of Commerce
4 PM Relief Fund

Ans. (2)

Exp. All sums realised by way of penalties under the Competition Act, 2002 are credited to the Consolidated Fund of India. According to Section 47 of Competition Act, all sums realised by way of penalties and recovery of legal costs by the Commission under this Act shall be credited to the Consolidated Fund of India.

40. Central Consumer Protection Council is headed by a Chairperson who is

1 Retired judge of the Supreme Court of India
2 Minister-in-charge of Department of Consumer Affairs in Central Government
3 President of India or his nominee
4 Head of Competition Commissions of India

Ans. (2)

Exp. Central Consumer Protection Council is headed by a Chairperson who is Minister-in-charge of the Department of Consumer Affairs in Central Government.

According to Section 3(2)(1) of the Consumer Protection Act, 2019, the Central Council shall be an advisory council and consist of the following members, namely

the Minister-in-charge of the Department of Consumer Affairs in the Central Government, who shall be the Chairperson and

such number of other official or non-official members representing such interests as may be prescribed.

41. 'Dominant Position' of an enterprise is reflected in which of the following situations?

I. Position of strength in the relevant international market
II. Enterprise operating independently of market forces in India
III. Affecting competition or consumers of relevant market in India in its favour
IV. Position of strength enjoyed in relevant market in India

Choose the correct answer from the options given below.

1 I, II and III   2 I, III and IV
3 II, I and IV   4 II, III and IV

Ans. (4)

Exp. The dominant position of an enterprise is reflected in the following situations

Enterprise operating independently of market forces in India.

Affecting competition or consumers of relevant market in India in its favour.

Position of strength enjoyed in relevant market in India.

42. What amongst the following are necessary to Constitution a false imprisonment?

I. Total restrain on liberty of a person
II. Detention may be actual or constructive
III. It should be for a period of 2 years atleast
IV. Detention or restrain should be unlawful

Choose the correct answer from the options given below.

1 I, II and III   2 II, III and IV
3 I, II and IV   4 I, III and IV

Ans. (3)

Exp. To constitute the tort of false imprisonment, the following essentials are required.

Total restrain on liberty of a person.

Detention may be actual or constructive.

Detention or restraint must be unlawful.

43. Which amongst the following are necessary characteristics for 'Libel'?

I. It is defamation of permanent form.
II. The burden of proof that the words are false lie upon the plaintiff.
III. No actual damage need to be proved to sustain an action.
IV. Falsity of charge is presumed in favour of plaintiff.

Choose the correct answer from the options given below.

1 I, II and III   2 II, III and IV
3 I, II and IV   4 I, III and IV

Ans. (4)

Exp. To constitute 'Libel', the following conditions need to be fulfilled

It is defamation of permanent form.

No actual damage need to be proved to sustain an action.

Falsity of charge is presumed in favour of the plaintiff.

44. Which of the following are characteristics of a government promissory note?

I. It is a promise of President of India or Governor of a state.
II. It is regulated by the Indian Securities Act, 1886.
III. They are not negotiable instrument.
IV. They can be assigned without endorsement.

Choose the correct answer from the options given below.

1 I and II   2 II and III
3 II and IV   4 III and IV

Ans. (1)

Exp. The following are the essential characteristics of a government promissory note

It is a promise of President of India or Governor of a state.

It is regulated by the Indian Securities Act, 1886.

45. Non-obstnate Clause in Section 145 of the Negotiable Instrument Act, 1881 provides for which of the following?

I. Ddispenses with the procedure under Section 200 of CrPC
II. Procedure of examination of complainant and witness on oath is done away
III. Affidavit of complainant and witness can be accepted
IV. Sworn statement recoding by the magistrate is dispensed with

Choose the correct answer from the options given below.

1 I and II   2 I and III
3 II, III and IV   4 I, II, III and IV

Ans. (4)

➲ *Exp.* According to Section 145(1) of the Negotiable Instruments Act, notwithstanding anything contained in the Code of Criminal Procedure, 1973 (2 of 1974), the evidence of the complainant may be given by him on affidavit and may, subject to all just exceptions be read in evidence in any enquiry, trial or other proceeding under the said Code.

46. Which among the following expressly contain a provision for 'right to bear arms' as Fundamental Right?

I. The Constitution Act, 1867 (Canada)
II. Amendment II of US Constitution
III. Constitution (108th Amendment) Act (India)
IV. Human Rights Act, 1998 (UK)

Choose the correct answer from the options given below.

1 I and II   2 Only I
3 Only II   4 III and IV

Ans. (3)

➲ *Exp.* In the United States, the right to keep and bear arms is a Fundamental Right protected by the Amendment II to the United States Constitution. It states "A well regulated Militia, being necessary to the security of a free State, the right of the people to keep and bear arms shall not be infringed."

47. Constitution of which of the country expressly states that the Constitution shall be the supreme law of the land?

I. USA   II. South Africa
III. India   IV. UK

Choose the correct answer from the options given below.

1 I and II   2 II and III   3 I and III   4 II and IV

Ans. (1)

➲ *Exp.* The Constitutions of USA and South Africa expressly states that the Constitution shall be the supreme law of the land.

48. Consider the following statements.

I. Fundamental Rights are expressly provided in the US Constitution.
II. Restrictions on Fundamental Rights are expressly provided in the US Constitution.
III. Fundamental Rights and Human Rights are same in India.
IV. Directive Principles in Indian Constitution are not enforceable by courts.

Choose the correct answer from the options given below.

1 I, III and IV   2 I and IV
3 I, II, III and IV   4 I, II and IV

Ans. (2)

➲ *Exp.* Statements I and IV are correct.

Fundamental Rights are expressly provided in the US Constitution.

Directive Principles in Indian Constitution are not enforceable by courts.

Statements II and III is incorrect because the restrictions on Fundamental Rights are not expressly provided in the US Constitution, but in the Indian Constitution.

Fundamental Rights and Human Rights are not same in India.

49. Which among the following makes a distinction between common intention and similar intention?

I. Mahbub Shah *v/s* Emperor (1945)
II. Barendra Kumar Ghosh *v/s* Emperor (1925)
III. Jagmohan Singh *v/s* State of Uttar Pradesh (1973)
IV. Balwant Singh *v/s* State of Punjab (1995)
V. Badri *v/s* State of Rajasthan (1995)

Choose the correct answer from the options given below.

1 I and II   2 Only I
3 Only II   4 II, III, IV and V

Ans. (2)

➲ *Exp.* The difference between common intention and similar intention was highlighted in the case of Mahbub Shah *v/s* Emperor (1945). The judgement in Mahbub Shah *v/s* Emperor is pivotal in distinguishing between 'same intention' and 'common intention'. This distinction is crucial for determining liability in crimes involving multiple actors. The ruling underscores the necessity for a clear, shared intent to jointly execute a criminal act, as mere similarity of intentions among individuals does not suffice to meet the threshold of common intention under Section 34 of the IPC. This case remains significant in the jurisprudence relating to collective criminal actions.

50. Consider the following statements relating to death penalty.

I. Death sentence follows deterrence theory.
II. The Parliament of India wants to remove death sentence.
III. Recent amendments in IPC and other proposals have added new offences with death sentence.
IV. The Parliament wants harsh punishment for heinous offences through capital punishment.
V. After rarest of the rare doctrine, the number of capital punishment is reduced.

Choose the correct answer from the options given below.

1 I, III, IV and V   2 I, II, III, IV and V
3 I, II, III and IV   4 II, IV and V

Ans. (1)

➲ *Exp.* Statements I, III, IV and V are correct. Death sentence follows deterrence theory. Recent amendments in IPC and other proposals have added new offences with death sentences. The Parliament wants harsh punishment for heinous offences through capital punishment. Further, after the rarest of the rare doctrine, the number of capital punishments was reduced.

51. The following Articles in the Indian Constitution deal with protection of Environment and / or places.

I. Article 51A (g) II. Article 40
III. Article 48A IV. Article 51A (j)
V. Article 49

Choose the correct answer from the options given below.

1 I, III and V 2 I, II and III
3 III, IV and V 4 I, III and IV

Ans. (1)

Exp. Article 51A (g) which deals with Fundamental Duties of the citizens states, "it shall be the duty of every citizen of India to protect and improve the natural environment including forests, lakes, rivers and wildlife, and to have compassion for living creatures."

Article 48A of the Constitution says that "the state shall endeavour to protect and improve the environment and to safeguard the forests and wildlife of the country".

Article 49 of the Constitution of India contains provisions relating to the state's obligation to protect cultural heritage.

52. In respect of which of the following items India does not have legislations to specifically cover them as Intellectual Property?

I. Traditional Knowledge II. Street Art
III. Publicity Right IV. Celebrity Right
V. Computer Programme

Choose the correct answer from the options given below.

1 II, IV and V 2 III, IV and V
3 I, II, III and IV 4 II, III, IV and V

Ans. (3)

Exp. India does not have legislations to specifically cover the following as Intellectual Property

Traditional Knowledge Street Art
Publicity Right Celebrity Right

53. Which of the following is part of first generation of Human Rights?

I. Right to Social Security
II. Right to Liberty
III. Equality Before Law
IV. Right to Self-determination
V. Right to Life

Choose the correct answer from the options given below.

1 I, II and IV 2 II, III and V
3 III, IV and V 4 I, III and V

Ans. (2)

Exp. The following can be considered to be a part of the first generation of Human Rights.

Right to Liberty
Equality Before Law
Right to Life

54. Which of the following provisions in the Information Technology Act, 2000 prescribe punishment for offences?

I. Section 65 II. Section 66-D
III. Section 67-B IV. Section 52
V. Section 62

Choose the correct answer from the options given below.

1 I, II and III 2 III, IV and V
3 II, III and V 4 I, II and IV

Ans. (1)

Exp. Sections 65, 66-D and 67-B of IT Act provide for punishment for different offences.

Section 65 dealt with Tampering with computer source documents.

Section 66-D deals with Punishment for cheating by personation by using computer resource.

Section 67-B of the Information Technology (IT) Act, 2000 is an Indian law that criminalises the publishing, transmitting or causing the transmission of sexually explicit content depicting children.

55. Which of the following statements given below are correct?

I. A wrong is an act contrary to the rule of right and justice.
II. A moral or natural wrong is an act which is morally or naturally wrong being contrary to the rule of natural justice.
III. A legal wrong is an act which is legally wrong, being contrary to the rule of legal justice and a violation of the law.
IV. A legal wrong is always a moral wrong and a moral wrong is always a legal wrong.
V. Natural and legal wrongs cannot form intersecting circles.

Choose the correct answer from the options given below.

1 I, II and III 2 I, IV and V
3 II, III and IV 4 II, IV and V

Ans. (1)

Exp. Statements I, II and III are correct. A wrong is an act contrary to the rule of right and justice. A moral or natural wrong is an act which is morally or naturally wrong being contrary to the rule of natural justice. A legal wrong is an act which is legally wrong, being contrary to the rule of legal justice and a violation of law.

56. Which of the following statements in relation to the dissenting judgement of Dr. Radha Vinodpal in the Tokyo Trial can be correctly attributed to him?

I. War is beyond the scope of International law.
II. Conduct of war is within the scope of the rules of International law.
III. The Pact of Paris brought about no change in the status of war.

IV. International law has developed so much so as to make war a crime.

V. Conspiracy is an independent crime under International law.

Choose the correct answer from the options given below.

1 I, II and III 2 III, IV and V
3 II, III and V 4 I, II and IV

Ans. (1)

Exp. Statements I, II and III are correct. The following statements in relation to the dissenting judgement of Dr. Radha Vinodpal in the Tokyo Trial can be correctly attributed to him

War is beyond the scope of International law.

Conduct of war is within the scope of the rules of International law.

The Pact of Paris brought no change in the status of war.

57. The Nuremberg Trial classified the crimes punishable under International law into the categories of

I. Genocide

II. Crimes against women and children

III. Crimes against peace

IV. War crimes

V. Crimes against humanity

Choose the correct answer from the options given below.

1 I, III and V 2 II, III and IV
3 III, IV and V 4 I, II and IV

Ans. (3)

Exp. During the Nuremberg Trials from 1945 to 1946, Nazi Germany leaders stood trial for crimes against peace, war crimes, crimes against humanity and conspiracy to commit any of the foregoing crimes.

58. Which of the following statements are correct?

I. In SS Lotus case, the Permanent Court of International Justice (PCI) defined International Law as "principles which are in force between all independent nations" .

II. Professor Dias suggests that International law can never be called a 'Law'.

III. Lord Halsbury, when he was the Prime Minister of England, one remarked, "It was a misnomer to call International law as 'Law'. It should be better described as a branch of ethics".

IV. Russel has defined International Law as "the aggregate of the rules to which the nations have agreed to conform to their conduct towards one another".

V. According to Austin, International Law is set and enforced by political sovereign authority.

Choose the correct answer from the options given below.

1 I, II and III 2 I, III and IV
3 II, III and V 4 II, IV and V

Ans. (2)

Exp. Statements I, III and IV are correct.

In SS Lotus case, the Permanent Court of International Justice (PCI) defined International Law as "principles which are in force between all independent nations" .

Lord Halsbury, when he was the Prime Minister of England, one remarked, "It was a misnomer to call International law as 'Law'. It should be better described as a branch of ethics".

Russel has defined International Law as "the aggregate of the rules to which the nations have agreed to conform to their conduct towards one another".

Statements II and V are incorrect because law consists largely of ought (normative) propositions prescribing how people ought to behave the 'ought' of laws are variously dictated by social, moral, economic, political and other purposes.

According to Austin "Law is a command of the sovereign backed by a sanction". The simple meaning of 'Sovereign' is an individual or group of people having the highest possible authority and not controlled by any other country or independent. Similarly sovereignty is a signature feature of modern politics.

59. According to Austin's definition of ownership, the attributes of ownership are

I. Indefinite user

II. Plenary control over an object

III. Unrestricted disposition

IV. Bundle of rights

V. Unlimited duration

Choose the correct answer from the options given below.

1 I, III and V 2 II, IV and V
3 I, III and IV 4 I, II and IV

Ans. (1)

Exp. Austin defined ownership as "a right indefinite in point of user, unrestricted in point of disposition and unlimited in point of duration". His definition thus implies three attributes *viz*

Indefinite user – The owner of a thing is free to use or misuse the thing in a way he likes.

Unrestricted disposition – The power of disposition of the owner is unhampered by law meaning that he is absolutely free to dispose of it to anyone.

Unlimited duration – The ownership of a person cannot be cut short and the owner can continue to be the owner as long as he likes.

60. Article 19 of the Constitution of India is automatically suspended if the Proclamation of Emergency is declared on the ground of

I. War

II. External aggression

III. Armed rebellion

IV. Failure of Constitution machinery in the state

Choose the correct answer from the options given below.

1 I and II   2 I, II and III
3 I, II, III and IV   4 I, III and IV

Ans. (1)

Exp. According to Article 358I, while a Proclamation of Emergency declaring that the security of India or any part of the territory thereof is threatened by war or by external aggression is in operation, nothing in Article 19 shall restrict the power of the State as defined in Part III to make any law or to take any executive action which the State would but for the provisions contained in that Part be competent to make or to take, but any law so made shall, to the extent of the incompetency, cease to have effect as soon as the Proclamation ceases to operate, except as respects things done or omitted to be done before the law so ceases to have effect.

61. Fundamental Duties in the Constitution of India under Article 51A

I. can be enforced by the Supreme Court
II. can be used by the Supreme Court in interpretation
III. can be amended by the states
IV. has been amended by the Parliament only once

Choose the correct answer from the options given below.

1 II and IV   2 I, II and IV
3 II, III and IV   4 I, II and III

Ans. (1)

Exp. Fundamental Duties in the Constitution under Article 51 A can be used by the Supreme Court in interpretation and has only been amended by the Parliament once.

The 42nd Amendment Act of 1976 added 10 Fundamental Duties to the Indian Constitution. The 86th Amendment Act 2002 later added the 11th Fundamental Duty to the list. The Fundamental Duties are dealt with in Article 51A under Part IV A of the Indian Constitution.

62. Article 163 of the Constitution of India says that there shall be Council of Minister along with Chief Minister to aid and advise the Governor in exercise of his functions except so far he is required by the Constitution to exercise his functions or any or them in his discretion. Under what circumstances Governor can be called to exercise his discretion?

I. Appointment of Chief Minister
II. Dismissal of Ministry or Dissolution of Assembly
III. Submitting report to President for proclamation under Article 356
IV. Appointment of High Court judges

Choose the correct answer from the options given below.

1 I, II and III   2 II, III and IV
3 IV, III and I   4 IV, I and II

Ans. (1)

Exp. The Governors of states can act at their situational discretion in the following instances

When he has to appoint a Chief Minister after no party has a clear majority in the election or when the incumbent dies in office.

When he dismisses the council of ministers on an inability to prove confidence in the state legislative assembly.

When he dissolves the state legislative assembly on time when it loses its majority.

63. Article 28 of the Constitution of India mentions four types of educational institution given below. In which of the following institution religious instruction can be imparted with the consent of individual or otherwise?

I. Institution wholly maintained by the state
II. Institution recognised by the state
III. Institution that receive aid out of state fund
IV. Institution that are administered by the state but established under any trust or endowment

Choose the correct answer from the options given below.

1 I, II and III   2 II, III and IV
3 I, III and IV   4 I, II and IV

Ans. (2)

Exp. Article 28 Freedom as to attendance at religious instruction or religious worship in certain educational institutions

No person attending any educational institution recognised by the state or receiving aid out of state funds shall be required to take part in any religious instruction that may be imparted in such institution or to attend any religious worship that may be conducted in such institution or in any premises attached thereto unless such person or, if such person is a minor, his guardian has given his consent thereto.

No religious instruction shall be provided in any educational institution wholly maintained out of state funds.

Nothing in clause (1) shall apply to an educational institution which is administered by the state but has been established under any endowment or trust which requires that religious instruction shall be imparted in such institution.

64. Section 7 of the Hindu Marriage Act, 1955 provides that a Hindu marriage may be solemnised in accordance with the customary rites and ceremonies of either party thereto. Consider the following situations and decide in which case the marriage is validly solemnised?

I. At the time of marriage all essential shastric ceremonies are performed.
II. At the time of marriage all customary rites and ceremonies of bride's family are performed.

III. At the time of marriage half of the ceremonies of bride's family and other half of the bridegroom's family are performed.
IV. Bride and bridegroom decided to perform the simple ceremonies of exchange of rings.
V. Bride and bridegroom started living together as husband and wife without performing any ceremony.

Choose the correct answer from the options given below.

1 I and II 2 I, II and III
3 II, III and IV 4 II, III, IV and V

Ans. (1)

Exp. Section 7 of Hindu Marriage Act provides for ceremonies for a Hindu marriage.

I. A Hindu marriage may be solemnised in accordance with the customary rites and ceremonies of either party thereto.
II. Where such rites and ceremonies include the Saptapadi (that is, the taking of seven steps by the bridegroom and the bride jointly before the sacred fire), the marriage becomes complete and binding when the seventh step is taken.

65. Under the Hindu Marriage Act, 1955 Sapinda relationship and degrees of prohibited relationship include relationship by

I. Full, half and uterine blood
II. Adoption
III. Legitimate blood
IV. Fosterage relations
V. Illegitimate blood relations

Choose the correct answer from the options given below.

1 I, II, III and IV 2 I, II, III and V
3 II, III, IV and V 4 I, III, IV and V

Ans. (2)

Exp. Under the Hindu Marriage Act, 1955, Sapinda relationship and degrees of prohibited relationship include relationship by

Full, half and uterine blood
Adoption
Legitimate blood
Illegitimate blood relations

66. Match List-I with List-II.

	List I (Enactment)		List II (Year)
A.	The Civil Rights Act	I.	1955
B.	The Probation of Offenders Act	II.	1956
C.	The Immoral Traffic (Prevention) Act	III.	1958
D.	The Medical Termination of Pregnancy Act	IV.	1971

Codes

	A	B	C	D		A	B	C	D
1	II	IV	III	I	2	I	III	IV	II
3	I	III	II	IV	4	II	IV	I	III

Ans. (3)

Exp. The correct matching is A-I, B-III, C-II, D-IV.

The Civil Rights Act, 1955 is a law that prohibits the practice of untouchability and prescribes punishment for those who inforce it.

The Probation of Offenders Act, 1958 is an act to provide for the release of offenders on probation on after due admonition and for matters connected therewith.

The Immoral Traffic (Prevention) Act, 1956 is an act to provide in pursuance of the international convention signed at New York on the 9th May, 1950 for the prevention of immoral traffic.

The Medical Termination of Pregnancy Act, 1971 is an act to provide for the termination of certain pregnancies by registered Medical Practitioners and for the matters connected therewith or incidental thereto.

67. Match List-I with List-II.

	List-I (Case)		List-II (Year of Reporting)
A.	Hussainara Khatoon *v/s* State of Bihar	I.	1981
B.	Kadra Phadia *v/s* State of Bihar	II.	1980
C.	MH Hoskot *v/s* State of Maharashtra	III.	1979
D.	Khatri *v/s* State of Bihar	IV.	1978

Codes

	A	B	C	D		A	B	C	D
1	III	I	II	IV	2	IV	III	II	I
3	I	II	III	IV	4	III	II	IV	I

Ans. (4)

Exp. The correct matching is A-III, B-II, C-IV, D-I.

Hussainara Khatoon *v/s* State of Bihar, 1979
Kadra Phadia *v/s* State of Bihar, 1980
MH Haskot *v/s* State of Maharashtra, 1978
Khatri *v/s* State of Bihar, 1981

68. Match List-I with List-II.

	List-I (UN Days relating to IPR and Biological Diversity)		List-II (Days)
A.	World Intellectual Property Day	I.	23rd April
B.	World Book and Copying Day	II.	22nd May
C.	International Day for Biological Diversity	III.	21st April
D.	World Creativity and Innovation Day	IV.	26th April

Codes

	A	B	C	D		A	B	C	D
1	IV	II	I	III	2	IV	I	II	III
3	I	II	III	IV	4	III	I	IV	II

Ans. (2)

Exp. The correct matching is A-IV, B-I, C-II, D-III.

World Intellectual Property Day is celebrated on 26th April.

World Book and Copyright Day is celebrated on 23rd April.

International Day for Biological Diversity is celebrated on 22nd May.

World Creativity and Innovation Day is celebrated on 21st April.

69. Match List-I with List-II

	List-I (Provision from IT Act)		List-II (Section)
A.	Secure Electronic Record	I.	16
B.	Security Procedures and Practices	II.	15
C.	Secure Electronic Signature	III.	14
D.	Attribution of Electronic Record	IV.	11

Codes

	A	B	C	D		A	B	C	D
1	III	I	II	IV	2	I	III	IV	II
3	IV	II	III	I	4	III	II	I	IV

Ans. (1)

Exp. The correct matching is A-III, B-I, C-II, D-IV.

Section 14 of IT Act provides for secure electronic record. It states that where any security procedure has been applied to an electronic record at a specific point of time. Then such record shall be deemed to be a secure electronic record from such point of time to the time of verification.

Section 16 of IT Act provides for security procedures and practices. It states that the Central Government may for the purposes of Sections 14 and 15 prescribe the security procedures and practices.

Section 15 provides for secure electronic signature. It states that an electronic signature shall be deemed to be a secure electronic signature if the signature creation data, at the time of affixing signature, was under the exclusive control of signatory and no other person.

Section 11 of IT Act provides for attribution of electronic record. It states that an electronic record shall be attributed to the originator.

if it was sent by the originator himself;

by a person who had the authority to act on behalf of the originator in respect of that electronic record; or

by an information system programmed by or on behalf of the originator to operate automatically.

70. Match List-I with List-II.

	List-I (Schedule)		List-II (Description)
A.	Fifth Schedule	I.	Languages
B.	Eight Schedule	II.	Provisions of disqualification on ground of defection
C.	Tenth Schedule	III.	Administration and control of Scheduled Area and Scheduled Tribe
D.	Fourth Schedule	IV.	Allocation of seats in Council of States

Codes

	A	B	C	D		A	B	C	D
1	I	II	IV	III	2	III	I	II	IV
3	II	IV	III	I	4	IV	III	I	II

Ans. (2)

Exp. The correct matching is A-III, B-I, C-II, D-IV.

Fifth Schedule- Administration and control of Scheduled Areas and Scheduled Tribes

Eighth Schedule- Languages

Tenth Schedule-Provisions of disqualification on grounds of defection

Fourth Schedule- Allocation of seats in Council of States

71. Match List-I with List-II.

	List-I (Case)		List-II (Issue/Concept/ Principle)
A.	Linkletter *v/s* Walkar	I.	Prospective overruling in the context of constitutional interpretation
B.	Golak Nath *v/s* State of Punjab	II.	Right to register a "none of above" vote
C.	Jolly George Varghese *v/s* Bank of Cochin	III.	Importation of provision from ICCPR into Indian Constitutional law
D.	People's Union for Civil Liberties *v/s* Union of India	IV.	Prospective overruling in the context of criminal procedure

Codes

	A	B	C	D		A	B	C	D
1	II	I	IV	III	2	I	IV	II	III
3	IV	II	III	I	4	IV	I	III	II

Ans. (4)

Exp. The correct matching is A-IV, B-I, C-III, D-II.

Linkletter *v/s* Walker Prospective overruling in the context of criminal procedure. Prospective overruling allows the Court to return to the original meaning while incurring smaller reliance costs.

The Doctrine of Prospective Overruling was for the first time adopted in the case of **Golak Nath *v/s* State of Punjab** by the Supreme Court of India. The Court had put forward certain provisions to stop the use of the doctrine in the Indian system.

Jolly George Verghese *v/s* Bank of Cochin Importation of provision from ICCPR into the Indian Constitutional law. The court granted the appeal, holding that incarceration cannot be justified by simply failing to pay off a debt. The court emphasised that in addition to the present ability to pay, the law needs proof of some bad faith or refusal to pay.

People's Union for Civil Liberties *v/s* Union of India Right to register a "none of the above" vote. NOTA was used for the first time in the 2013 Assembly elections in five states of Chhattisgarh, Mizoram, Rajasthan, Delhi and Madhya Pradesh and later in the 2014 General Elections. It was introduced into the electoral process following the 2013 Supreme Court directive in the PUCL Union of India Case.

72. Match List-I with List-II.

List-I	List-II
A. Malice in Law	I. Commission of an unlawful act which are actionable perse
B. Malfeasance	II. Improper performance of a lawful act
C. Misfeasance	III. Omission to perform an act when there is obligation to perform it
D. Non-feasance	IV. International doing of a wrongful act and improper motive

Codes

	A	B	C	D
1	IV	I	II	III
2	I	II	III	IV
3	III	IV	I	II
4	II	III	IV	I

***Ans.** (1)*

Exp. The correct matching is A-IV, B-I, C-II, D-III.

Malice in law is a legal term which refers to a party's intention to do injury to another party. Malice is either expressed or implied.

Malfeasance is an act that is illegal and causes physical or monetary harm to someone else. Malfeasance is intentional conduct that is wrongful or unlawful, especially by officials or public employees.

Misfeasance is the act of engaging in an action or duty but failing to perform the duty correctly. Misfeasance refers to an action that is unintentional. However, malfeasance is the willful and intentional act of doing harm.

Non-feasance can more loosely be defined as "not doing something which you ought to do." The term "non-feasance" commonly appears in the areas of contract and tort law.

73. Match List-I with List-II.

List-I	List-II
A. Producer Companies	I. Do not necessarily require Memodrandum of Association
B. Statutory Companies	II. Association not for profit
C. Section 8 Company	III. Formed to convert cooperative into a company
D. Small Company	IV. Paid up share capital is between 50 lakh -5 crore and turnover is between 2 crore - 20 crore

Codes

	A	B	C	D
1	I	II	IV	III
2	III	I	II	IV
3	IV	III	I	II
4	II	IV	III	I

***Ans.** (2)*

Exp. The correct matching is A-III, B-I, C-II, D-IV.

Producer Companies formed to convert cooperative into a company.

Statutory Companies do not necessarily require memorandum of association.

Section 8 Company Association not for profit.

Small Company paid up share capital is between 50 lakh-5 crore and turnover is between 2 crore - 20 crore.

74. Match List-I with List-II.

List-I (Subject)	List-II (Section of Indian Penal Code)
A. Punishment for extortion	I. Section 403
B. Attempt to commit robbery	II. Section 409
C. Dishonest misappropriation of property	III. Section 384
D. Criminal breach of trust by public servant	IV. Section 393

Codes

	A	B	C	D
1	II	III	I	IV
2	III	II	I	IV
3	III	IV	I	II
4	IV	II	I	III

***Ans.** (3)*

Exp. The correct matching is A-III, B-IV, C-I, D-II.

The order has been mentioned below

Section 384 - Punishment for extortion

Section 393 - Attempt to commit robbery

Section 403 - Dishonest misappropriation of property

Section 409 - Criminal breach of trust by a public servant

75. Match List-I with List-II.

List-I (Name of the Case)	List-II (Subject Matter)
A. Gita Hariharan *v/s* Reserve Bank of India	I. Maintenance Rights of Muslim women
B. Sarla Mudgal *v/s* Union of India	II. Guardianship of a minor child
C. Danial Latifi *v/s* Union of India	III. Compulsory registration of marriages

D.	Seema v/s Ashwani Kumar	IV.	Validity of second marriage of a Hindu male after his conversion to Islam

Codes

	A	B	C	D		A	B	C	D
1	II	IV	I	III	2	I	II	III	IV
3	II	IV	III	I	4	IV	III	II	I

Ans. 1

Exp. The correct matching is A-II, B-IV, C-I, D-III.

Gita Hariharan v/s Reserve Bank of India It held that both the father and mother are natural guardians of a minor Hindu child, and the mother cannot be said to be natural guardian only after the death of the father as that would not only be discriminatory but also against the welfare of the child, which is legislative intent of HMGA, 1956.

Sarla Mudgal v/s Union of India Validity of second marriage of Hindu male after his conversion to Islam. The Supreme Court decided that every bigamous marriage of a Hindu convert to Islam would be void and therefore punishable under the Indian Penal Code.

Daniel Latifi v/s Union of India The court held that a divorced Muslim woman is entitled to fair and reasonable maintenance for her future, which extends beyond the iddat period.

Seema v/s Ashwani Kumar In this case, the Court directed that marriages of all persons who are citizens of India belonging to various religions should be made compulsorily registrable in their respective states.

76. Arrange the names of the following jurists in terms of chronological order of their birth.

I. Jeremy Bentham II. John Austin
III. Sir Henry Maine IV. Hans Kelson
V. Immanuel Kant

Choose the correct answer from the options given below.

1 I, II, III, IV, V 2 V, I, II, III, IV
3 I, II, III, V, IV 4 IV, V, II, I, III

Ans. (2)

Exp. The names of the jurists in terms of chronological order of their birth are

Immanuel Kant (born Emanuel Kant; 22nd April, 1724 – 12th February, 1804) was a German philosopher and one of the central enlightenment thinkers. Born in Königsberg, Kant's comprehensive and systematic works in epistemology, metaphysics, ethics, and aesthetics have made him one of the most influential and controversial figures in modern Western philosophy, being called the "father of modern ethics", the "father of modern aesthetics", and for bringing together rationalism and empiricism earned the title of "father of modern philosophy".

Jeremy Bentham (born on 15th February, 1748 – 6th June, 1832) was an English philosopher, jurist, and social reformer regarded as the founder of modern utilitarianism.

John Austin (3rd March, 1790 – 1st December, 1859) was an English legal theorist who posthumously influenced British and American law with an analytical approach to jurisprudence and a theory of legal positivism.

Sir Henry James Sumner Maine (15th August, 1822 – 3 February, 1888), was a British Whig comparative jurist and historian. He is famous for the thesis outlined in his book Ancient Law that law and society developed "from status to contract."

Hans Kelson (11th October, 1881 – 19th April, 1973) was an Austrian jurist, legal philosopher and political philosopher. He was the principal architect of the 1920 Austrian Constitution, which with amendments is still in operation.

77. Arrange the following in the chronological order of its sequence in the Parents Act.

I. Consequence of secrecy directions
II. Grant of patent III. Date of patent
IV. Term of patent V. Rights of patentee

Choose the correct answer from the options given below.

1 III, V, II, IV, I 2 II, III, V, IV, I
3 I, II, III, V, IV 4 II, V, IV, I, III

Ans. (3)

Exp. The correct sequence as per the Patents Act is I, II, III, V, IV.

Section 37 : Consequence of secrecy directions
Section 43 : Grant of patent
Section 45 : Date of patent
Section 48 : Rights of patentee
Section 53 : Term of patent

78. Arrange the following cases in the sequence in which they were decided.

I. Gloucester Grammar School Case
II. Donoghue v/s Stevenson Case
III. Ashby v/s White case
IV. Rylands v/s Fletcher Case

Choose the correct answer from the options given below.

1 I, III, IV, II 2 II, III, IV, I
3 III, IV, II, I 4 II, I, IV, III

Ans. (1)

Exp. The correct sequence is I, III, IV, II.

The Gloucester Grammar School Case of 1410 is a significant legal landmark in the realm of Damnum Sine Injuria.

Ashby v/s White 92 ER 126 is a foundational case in UK constitutional law and English tort law. It concerns the right to vote and misfeasance of a public officer.

Rylands v/s Fletcher LR 3 HL 330 is a leading decision by the House of Lords which established a new area of English tort law. It established the rule that one's non-natural use of their land, which leads to another's land being damaged as a result of dangerous things emanating from the land, is strictly liable.

Donoghue v/s Stevenson (1932) AC 562 was a landmark court decision in Scots delict law and English tort law by the House of Lords. It laid the foundation of the modern law of negligence in common law jurisdictions worldwide, as well as in Scotland, establishing general principles of the duty of care.

79. Arrange the following cases in sequences of year they were decided.

I. Ashbury Rly Carriage Co. Ltd. *v/s* Riche
II. Royal British Bank *v/s* Turquand
III. Mohori Bibee *v/s* Dharmodas Ghosh
IV. State trading Corporaton of India Ltd. *v/s* CTO, Visakhapatnam
V. Salomon *v/s* Salomon Co. Ltd.

Choose the correct answer from the options given below.

1 II, I, V, III, IV   2 I, II, III, V, IV
3 III, IV, I, II, V   4 II, III, V, I, IV

Ans. *(1)*

➲ *Exp.* The correct sequence is II, I, V, III and IV.

Royal British Bank v/s Turquand 6 E and B 327 is a UK company law case that held people transacting with companies are entitled to assume that internal company rules are complied with, even if they are not. This "indoor management rule" or the "Rule in Turquand's Case" is applicable in most of the common law world.

Ashbury Railway Carriage and Iron Co Ltd v/s Riche LR 7 HL 653 is a UK company law case, which concerned the objects clause of a company's memorandum of association.

Salomon v/s A Salomon and Co. Ltd (1896) UKHL 1, (1897) AC 22 is a landmark UK company law case. The effect of the House of Lords' unanimous ruling was to uphold firmly the doctrine of corporate personality.

Mohori Bibee v/s Dharmodas Ghose, (1903) UKPC 12 is a major Indian contract law case decided by the Judicial Committee of the Privy Council. The case held that a contract entered into by a minor is totally void.

The case of State Trading Corporation of India Limited v/s CTO 1964 concluded that the company though a legal person is not a citizen and can act only through a natural person.

80. Arrange in chronological order the insertion of the following provisions in the Indian Penal Code.

I. Section 124-A   II. Section 153-A
III. Section 120-A   IV. Section 304-B

Choose the correct answer from the options given below.

1 I, II, III, IV   2 I, III, II, IV
3 I, IV, II, III   4 I, IV, III, II

Ans. *(1)*

➲ *Exp.* Here is the chronological order of insertion for these sections.

Section 124-A This section, relating to sedition, was introduced in 1870.

Section 153-A This section, concerning promoting enmity between different groups, was introduced in 1898.

Section 120-A This section, relating to criminal conspiracy, was inserted by the Criminal Law Amendment Act, 1913.

Section 304-B This section, related to dowry death, was added in 1986.

81. Arrange the following cases relating to advice/direction of the Supreme Court to the State to enact a uniform civil code in the chronological order (advice earlier to later) of their pronouncement.

I. Mohd. Ahmed Khan *v/s* Shah Bano Begum.
II. Sarla Mudgal *v/s* Union of India
III. ABC *v/s* State (NCT of Delhi)
IV. Jorden Diengdeh *v/s* SS Chopra
V. ohn Vallamattom *v/s* Union of India

Choose the correct answer from the options given below.

1 I, II, IV, III, V   2 II, IV, I, V, III
3 I, IV, II, V, III   4 V, IV, III, II, I

Ans. *(3)*

➲ *Exp.* The correct chronological order is I, IV, II, V, III.

Mohd. Ahmed Khan v/s Shah Bano Begum (1985) A landmark case concerning maintenance rights for divorced Muslim women, where the Supreme Court highlighted the need for a Uniform Civil Code.

Jorden Diengdeh v/s S.S. Chopra (1985) This case emphasised the need for uniform divorce laws across all religions.

Sarla Mudgal v/s Union of India (1995) The court reiterated the need for a UCC, especially in the context of bigamy and personal laws.

John Vallamattom v/s Union of India (2003) The court commented on the discriminatory provisions in personal laws, stressing again the need for a UCC.

ABC v/s State (NCT of Delhi) (2015) A case involving the rights of an unwed Christian mother, where the court again raised the issue of the Uniform Civil Code.

82. Arrange the following UN Conventions in their chronological order.

I. UN Convention on Biological Diversity
II. UN Convention on Climate Change
III. UN Convention Against transnational Crimes
IV. UN Convention on the Rights of the Child
V. UN Convention on Jurisdictional Immunities of States and Their Property

Choose the correct answer from the options given below.

1 II, III, IV, V, I   2 I, IV, V, III, II
3 IV, II, III, V, I   4 I, IV, III, II, V

Ans. *(1)*

➲ *Exp.* The correct chronological order is IV, I, II, III, V.

The Convention on the Rights of the Child (CRC) was approved by the General Assembly of the United Nations on 20th November, 1989. The Convention was formally opened for ratification on 26th January, 1990, the

Government of India ratified the CRC on 11th December, 1992.

The work on UN Convention on Biological Diversity culminated on 22nd May, 1992 with the Nairobi Conference for the Adoption of the Agreed Text of the Convention on Biological Diversity. The Convention was opened for signature on 5th June, 1992 at the United Nations Conference on Environment and Development (the Rio 'Earth Summit').

The United Nations Framework Convention on Climate Change (UNFCCC) was adopted in 1992 with the ultimate aim of preventing dangerous human interference with the climate system. The 1997 Kyoto Protocol and 2015 Paris Agreement build on the Convention.

The UN Convention on Transnational Crimes was adopted by a resolution of the United Nations General Assembly on 15th November, 2000. The Convention came into force on 29th September, 2003.

On 2nd December, 2004, the UN General Assembly adopted the UN Convention on Jurisdictional Immunities of States and Their Property.

83. Arrange the following cases decided by the Permanent Court of Arbitration in their chronological order.

I. Muscat Dhows case
II. North Atlantic Fisheries case
III. Savarkar's case
IV. Russian Indemnity case
V. The Island of Palmas case

Choose the correct answer from the options given below.

1 I, II, III, IV, V   2 III, IV, II, I, V
3 II, III, IV, I, V   4 III, V, IV, II, I

Ans. *(1)*

Exp. The correct chronological order is I, II, III, IV, V.

Muscat Dhows Case (1905) This case concerned the issue of jurisdiction over vessels of Muscat.

North Atlantic Fisheries Case (1910) A dispute between the United States and Great Britain regarding fishing rights off Newfoundland.

Savarkar's Case (1911) This case involved the legality of the arrest of Indian freedom fighter Vinayak Savarkar in France.

Russian Indemnity Case (1912) This case was regarding the indemnities Russia owed to Turkey after the Russo-Turkish war.

The Island of Palmas Case (1928) A territorial dispute between the United States and the Netherlands over an island in the Pacific.

84. Arrange the following in chronological order of their Enactment.

I. Protection of Human Rights Act
II. National Commission for Women Act
III. 89th Constitutional Amendment Act
IV. National Commission for Minorities Act

Choose the correct answer from the options given below.

1 I, IV, II, III   2 III, II, I, IV
3 IV, III, II, I   4 II, IV, I, III

Ans. *(4)*

Exp. The correct chronological order is II, IV, I, III.

National Commission for Women Act (1990) The objective of the NCW is to represent the rights of women in India and to provide a voice for their issues and concerns. The subjects of their campaigns have included dowry, politics, religion, equal representation for women in jobs and the exploitation of women for labour.

National Commission for Minorities Act (1992) An Act to constitute a National Commission for Minorities and to provide for matters connected therewith or incidental thereto.

Protection of Human Rights Act, 1993 An Act to provide for the Constitution of a National Human Rights Commission, State Human Rights Commissions in States and Human Rights Courts for better protection of human rights and for matters connected therewith or incidental thereto.

The 89th Amendment Act, 2003 of the Indian Constitution established the National Commission for Scheduled Tribes.

85. Arrange the following cases in sequence of their year of verdict.

I. Kesavananda Bharati *v/s* State of Kerala
II. Sankari Prasad *v/s* Union of India
III. Golak Nath *v/s* State of Punjab
IV. Sajjan Singh *v/s* State of Rajasthan

Choose the correct answer from the options given below.

1 II, IV, III, I   2 I, II, III, IV
3 III, IV, II, I   4 I, IV, II, III

Ans. *(1)*

Exp. The correct order is II, IV, III, I.

Sankari Prasad *v/s* Union of India (1951) case was significant in both the development of the basic structure theory and the interpretation of the Indian Constitution.

Sajjan Singh *v/s* State of Rajasthan (1965) dealt with the Constitutional validity of the 17th Constitutional Amendment. The Supreme Court upholding the validity of the 17th Amendment held that the Parliament has the authority to amend any part of the Constitution including any Fundamental Rights.

Golak Nath *v/s* State of Punjab (1967 AIR 1643, 1967 SCR (II) 762), or simply the Golak Nath case, was a 1967 Indian Supreme Court case, in which the Court ruled that Parliament could not curtail any of the Fundamental Rights in the Constitution.

Kesavananda Bharati *v/s* State of Kerala (1973), the majority of the bench wanted to preserve the Indian Constitution by protecting its basic features. So, they decided not to provide unlimited power to amend the Constitution as it can be misused by the government in future. It provided stability to the Constitution.

86. Given below are two statements, one is labelled as Assertion (A) and the other is labelled as Reason (R).

Assertion (A) Highly developed legal systems strive to create an autonomous apparatus of legal concepts, legal techniques and legal norms.

Reason (R) Law needs to be endowed with logical consistency, predictability and stability.

In the light of the above statements, choose the correct answer from the options given below.

1 Both A and R are correct and R is the correct explanation of A.
2 Both A and R are correct, but R is not the correct explanation of A.
3 A is correct, but R is not correct.
4 A is not correct, but R is correct.

Ans. *(1)*

Exp. Both A and R are correct and R is the correct explanation of A.

Highly developed legal systems strive to create an autonomous apparatus of legal concepts, legal techniques and legal norms. This is because law needs to be endowed with logical consistency, predictability and stability.

87. Given below are two statements, one is labelled as Assertion (A) and the other is labelled as Reason (R).

Assertion (A) Trade Secrets Act, 2020 is a legislation enacted in India to provide for confidential information and trade secrets.

Reason (R) India has enacted a number of legislations to create legal framework on Intellectual Property Rights (IPRs).

In the light of the above statements, choose the correct answer from the options given below.

1 Both A and R are correct and R is the correct explanation of A
2 Both A and R are correct, but R is not the correct explanation of A
3 A is correct, but R is not correct
4 (A) is not correct, but (R) is correct

Ans. *(4)*

Exp. A is not correct, but R is correct.

India does not have a specific legislation called the 'Trade Secrets Act, 2020' or any specific trade secrets law.

88. Given below are two statements one is labelled as Assertion (A) and the other is labelled as Reason (R).

Assertion (A) The tests of proportionality, necessity and balancing are found at prominent places in the GATs, the GATT as well as in the SPS and TBT Agreements.

Reason (R) The meaning of these tests and their interrelationship is not always clear.

In the light of the above statements, choose the correct answer from the options given below.

1 Both A and R are correct and R is the correct explanation of A.
2 Both A and R are correct, but R is not the correct explanation of A.
3 A is correct but, R is not correct.
4 A is not correct, but R is correct.

Ans. *(2)*

Exp. Both A and R are correct, but R is not the correct explanation of A.

The tests of proportionality, necessity and balancing are found at prominent places in the GATS and GATT as well as in SPS and TBT agreements.

89. Given below are two statements.

Statement I The doctrine of stare decisis has essentially developed as a result of progress made in law-reporting.

Statement II Since the law in India is mostly based on the English Law, the system of law reporting is fairly developed in India.

In the light of the above statements, choose the correct answer from the options given below.

1 Both Statement I and Statement II are correct.
2 Both Statement I and Statement II are incorrect.
3 Statement I is correct, but Statement II is incorrect.
4 Statement I is incorrect, but Statement II is correct.

Ans. *(1)*

Exp. Both Statement I and Statement II are correct.

The doctrine of stare decisis has essentially developed as a result of progress made in law-reporting. In the beginning, there was no doctrine of stare decisis as there was no reporting of the decisions of the courts in England.

In India, the system of law reporting has developed over time after being introduced by the British in their courts in India.

90. Given below are two statements, one is labelled as Assertion (A) and the other is labelled as Reason (R).

Assertion (A) Mahr (dower) is a sum of money which the Muslim husband agrees to pay to the wife as a mark of respect for her for agreeing to marry him. Since Muslim marriage is a contract, it is necessary that dower must be specified at the time of marriage and if it is not specified it can be presumed.

Reason (R) If not paid earlier, Mahr become due on death of the husband or the dissolution of marriage by divorce.

In the light of the above statements, choose the correct answer from the options given below.

1 Both A and R are correct and R is the correct explanation of A.
2 Both A and R are correct, but R is not the correct explanation of A.

3 A is correct, but R is not correct.
4 A is not correct, but R is correct.

Ans. (1)

Exp. Both A and R are correct and R is the correct explanation of A.

In Islam, a Mahr is the bride's wealth obligation, in the form of money, possessions or teaching of verses from the Quran by the groom, to the bride in connection with an Islamic wedding. If the husband dies, the Mahr that had not been paid to the wife becomes a debt that he still owes; it should be taken from the estate before it is divided among the heirs.

Directions (Q.Nos. 91-95) *Read the passage carefully and answer the questions that follows.*

In India, the protection and enforcement of Human Rights confined to 'Civil and Political Rights' in the form of 'Fundamental Rights' (Part III) and 'Economic, Social and Culture Rights' in the form of 'Directive Principles' (Part IV) in the Constitution of India discusses the vision of the Constitution and its framers of the kind of society they aspired to establish in the country. The framers of the Constitution were quite clear in assigning an equal role to each and every individual in the political process and decision-making. Not only did they provide for universal adult suffrage but they also provide for affirmative steps in the form of seats allocation or reservation in elections bodies for those incapable of competing in political process on equal footing. For effective participation in that process as well as for leading a dignified life, which they did not want to leave to the political process alone or postpone for the future, they also provided for Fundamental Rights and Directive Principles, which have been distinguished as the conscience of the Constitution, and harmony and balance between them, have been found to be among the basic feature to the Constitution. Part IV A of the Constitution of India title 'Fundamental Duties' (Article 51A) provides that every citizen must do his duty towards the nation as well as the fellow citizens.

91. Which Part of the Constitution of India discusses the vision of the Constitution and its framers as to which kind of society they aspired to establish in the country?

1 Article 51A
2 Part III and Part IV
3 Part IV only
4 Part dealing with affirmative steps

Ans. 2

Exp. Part III and Part IV of the Constitution discuss the vision of the Constitution and its framers as to which kind of society they aspired to establish in the country.

92. The notation that every citizens must do his duty towards the nation as well as the fellow citizens is incorporated in the Indian Constitution in ....

1 Part III
2 Part IV
3 Part IV A
4 Preamble

Ans. (3)

Exp. Part IV A provides for the Fundamental Duties. The Fundamental Duties were included in the Constitution with the idea of curbing subversive and unconstitutional activities. Originally, there were no Fundamental Duties in the Constitution. They were added by 42nd and 86th Constitutional Amendment Acts.

93. Which of the following is part of the basic feature of the Constitution?

1 Fundamental Duties
2 Directive policies
3 Political process and decision making
4 Harmony and balance between Part III and Part IV

Ans. (4)

Exp. Self-explanatory, Political process and decision making cannot be considered to be a part of the basic structure of the Constitution.

94. Which is distinguished as the 'Conscience' of the Constitution?

1 Fundamental Duties
2 Preamble
3 Universal adult suffrage
4 Fundamental Rights and Directive Principles

Ans. (4)

Exp. The section on Fundamental Rights has often been referred to as the 'conscience' of the Indian Constitution.

95. The protection and enforcement of Human Rights under Article 32 is confined in India to

1 Fundamental Rights
2 Economic, Social and Culture Rights
3 Fundamental Duties
4 Right to Vote

Ans. (1)

Exp. The Protection and Enforcement of Human Rights under Article 32 is confined in India to Fundamental Rights. Article 32 grants every individual the right to move the Supreme Court for the enforcement of their Fundamental Rights. This means that if someone believes their Fundamental Rights have been violated, they can approach the Supreme Court directly for relief.

Directions (Q.Nos. 96-100) *Read the passage carefully and answer the questions that follows.*

This is the greatest paradox involved in the doctrine of 'basic features', namely, that though it does not constitute a limitation on the legislature while enacting ordinary legislation, it would operate as a limitation on the 'Constituent' body, thought in the same breath it is conceded that the latter is a 'Sovereign' authority while the Legislature is not. This means that while determining the validity of an ordinary law, the court can only look like into express provisions of the Constitution or the necessary implications thereof, but when the validity of a Constitution Amendment Act is challenged, the court may travel behind or beyond the express provisions of the

Constitution to invoke some principles, which are supposed to Constitution the 'norm' behind the specific provisions of the Constitution. In short, it involve an illogical attempt to usher in the doctrines of 'spirit of the Constitution' or of 'natural law', through the backdoor, to circumscribe the Constitution itself, while it had been openly rejected as a limitation upon ordinary legislation.

96. What does the author consider to be the doctrine used to circumscribe the Constitution?

1 Doctrine of 'Spirit of the Constitution' and 'nature law'
2 Doctrine of 'Basic Structure' and of 'grund norms'
3 Doctrine of 'Basic Features' and of 'ultra vires'
4 Doctrine of 'Constituent Body' and of 'Sovereign authority'

Ans. **(1)**

Exp. The author used the doctrine of 'spirit of the Constitution' and 'natural law' to circumscribe the Constitution.

97. What does the author identify as the greatest paradox involved in the doctrine of basic features?

1 The doctrine does not Constitution a limitation on the power of the Parliament, but limits the state legislatures.
2 The doctrine ushers in the concept of natural law through the backdoors, while the judiciary get a free run.
3 The doctrine operates as a limitation on the constituent body as well as legislature when enacting ordinary legislation.
4 The doctrine does not constitute a limitation on the legislature while enacting ordinary legislation but operates as a limitation on the Constitution body though the constituent body is a sovereign authority while the legislature is not.

Ans. **(4)**

Exp. The doctrine does not constitute a limitation on the legislature while enacting ordinary legislation but operates as a limitation on the constituent body though the constituent body is a sovereign authority while the legislature is not.

98. Which of the following options reflect the opinion of the author as can be discerned from the cited paragraph?

1 A critical and negative view of the way the court uses the doctrines of 'Spirit of the Constitution' and of 'natural law' to circumscribe the Constitution itself
2 Admiration of the court's view that legislative power need not be circumscribed
3 Neutral view on the use of basic features by the court to limit the Constitution power and the legislative power
4 Positive view on the use of natural law as a limitation on the legislative power and Constitution power

Ans. **(1)**

Exp. The opinion of the author can best be reflected as a critical and negative view of the way as the Court uses the doctrine of the 'Spirit of the Constitution' and of 'natural law' to circumscribe the Constitution itself.

99. While determining the validity of an ordinary law, what can the court look into?

1 The Court cannot look into the express provisions of the Constitution.
2 The Court can only look into the necessary implications but not the express provisions of the Constitution.
3 The Court can only look into express provisions of the Constitution or the necessary implications thereof.
4 The Court can only look into the express provisions of the Constitution and not the implications thereof.

Ans. **(3)**

Exp. While determining the validity of an ordinary law, the Court can look into the express provisions of the Constitution or the necessary implications thereof.

100. As per the apprehension of the author, when may a court travel beyond the express provisions of the Constitution to invoke some principles superior to the express provisions?

1 While exercising the judicial power to interpret the Constitution.
2 When the court wants to assert the power of judicial review.
3 When the validity of a Constitution Amendment Act is challenged.
4 When the validity of an ordinary legislation is challenged.

Ans. **(3)**

➲ *Exp.* When the validity of a Constitution Amendment Act is challenged, the court may travel beyond the express provisions of the Constitution to invoke some principles superior to the express provisions.

UGC-NET
LAW
SOLVED PAPER 2023 (June)

PAPER II

1 The theory of 'separation of powers' is credited to

1. Aristotle 2. Locke 3. Montesquieu 4. Kelsen

***Ans.* (3)**

Exp. The concept of 'separation of powers' was given by Montesquieu. He described the separation of political power among a legislature, an executive and a judiciary.

2 Who made the statement that "Jurisprudence is the study and systematic arrangement of the general principles of law"?

1. RWM Dias 2. Julius Stone
3. Keeton CG 4. EW Patterson

***Ans.* (3)**

Exp. According to Keeton, "Jurisprudence is the study and systematic arrangement of the general principles of law". Further, jurisprudence deals with the distinction between public and private laws and considers the contents of principal departments of law.

3 "International Law or the Law of the Nations is the name of the body of rules which according to the usual definition regulate the conduct of states in their intercourse with one another," who said it?

1. Oppenheim 2. Lauterpacht
3. Brierly 4. Kelsen

***Ans.* (4)**

Exp. According to Kelsen, "International Law or the Law of Nations is the name of the body of rules which according to the usual definition regulate the conduct of the states in their intercourse with one another.".

4 In case of 'Tort of Trespass', which of the following defence shall not apply?

1. Statutory authority 2. Contributory negligence
3. Private defence 4. Mesne profits

***Ans.* (2)**

Exp. The defence of contributory negligence shall not apply in the case of 'Tort of Trespass'. Contributory negligence is a legal doctrine that prohibits victims from recovering compensation in a personal injury claim if they were even 1% responsible for their own injuries.

5 "I promise to pay ₹ 5000 and to deliver to him my black horse on 1st January next." This is an illustration for which of the following?

1. A valid promissory note
2. An invalid promissory note
3. A valid bill of exchange
4. An invalid bill of exchange

***Ans.* (2)**

Exp. The promise to deliver the horse in addition to the monetary payment makes it invalid as a promissory note. According to Section 4 of the Negotiable Instruments Act, a 'promissory note' is an instrument in writing (not being a bank-note or a currency-note) containing an unconditional undertaking, signed by the maker, to pay a certain sum of money only to, or to the order of, a certain person, or to the bearer of the instrument. The said question has been framed from illustration (h) of Section 4.

6 With respect to 'Daughters' under 'Class I heirs' in the Hindu Succession Act, 1956, which one of the following holds true?

1. 'Daughters' means natural born daughters and not adopted daughters
2. Step daughter is included
3. Daughter includes posthumous daughter
4. Unchasity of daughter is a bar to inheritance

***Ans.* (3)**

Exp. With respect to 'Daughters' under 'Class I heirs' in the Hindu Succession Act, 1956, daughter includes posthumous daughter. Class I heirs include son, daughter, mother, widow and grandchildren, who can claim rights to a property. In the case of multiple surviving heirs, each is given a share of the property. If a widow or brother's widow remarries, then they can't claim any rights to a property.

7 One of the heirs is not included in 'Class I heirs' under the Hindu Succession (Amendment) Act, 2005.

1. Daughter of a pre-deceased daughter of a pre-deceased daughter
2. Daughter of a pre-deceased son of a pre-deceased daughter
3. Son of a pre-deceased son of a pre-deceased daughter
4. Son of a pre-deceased daughter of a pre-deceased daughter

Ans. (3)

Exp. "Son of pre-deceased son of a pre-deceased daughter" as well as "son of a pre-deceased daughter of a pre-deceased son" of the intestate are not added under Class I by the said amendment of 2005. The said relations are also derived through daughter and granddaughter of the intestate.

8 "The Grand function of the Law of Nature was discharged in giving birth to modern International Law" Who said it?

1. Oppenheim
2. Henry Maine
3. Holland
4. HLA Hart

Ans. (2)

Exp. According to Henry Maine, the grandest function of the Law of Nature was discharged in giving birth to modern International Law and to the modern Law of War, but this part of its effects must here be dismissed with consideration very unequal to its importance.

9 The principle of Jus Cogens is incorporated in which Article of the Vienna Convention on Law of Treaties, 1969?

1. Article 25
2. Article 37
3. Article 53
4. Article 63

Ans. (3)

Exp. The principle of Jus Cogens is incorporated under Article 53 of the Vienna Convention of the Law of Treaties. Article 53 of the Vienna Convention is the origin of the principle of Jus Cogens. It states that a treaty is void if, at the time of its conclusion, it conflicts with the peremptory norm of general international law.

10 Which of the following is correct?

1. 'The only right which any man can possess is the right always to do his duty' is Duguit's theory.
2. 'Social Solidarity' a natural principle is given by Jurist Gierke.
3. Pound, legal philosophy is 'Utilitarianism'.
4. Austin said, "Law is Social Engineering".

Ans. (1)

Exp. Only statement (1) is correct. 'In Duguit's theory, the only right which man can possess is the right always to do his duty.'

11 Resale share right in original copies under Section 53A of the Copyright Act, 1957 is not applicable to

1. original copy of painting
2. original copy of sculpture
3. original manuscript of a literary of dramatic work
4. cinematograph film

Ans. (4)

Exp. Section 53 (A) Resale share right in original copies

(1) In the case of resale for a price exceeding ₹ 1000, of the original copy of a painting, sculpture or drawing, or of the original manuscript of a literary or dramatic work or musical work, the author of such work if he was the first owner of rights under Section 17 or his legal heirs shall, not with standing any assignment of copyright in such work, have a right to share in the resale price of such original copy or manuscript in accordance with the provisions of this section provided that such right shall cease to exist on the expiration of the term of copyright in the work.

(2) The share referred to in sub-section (1) shall be such as the Commercial Court may fix.
Provided that the Commercial Court may fix different shares for different classes of work.
Provided further that in no case shall the share exceed 10% of the resale price.

(3) If any dispute arises regarding the right conferred by this section, it shall be referred to the Commercial Court whose decision shall be final.

12 'Voyeurism' for a second or subsequent conviction attracts a punishment of

1. Imprisonment of not less than 1 year but which may extend to 3 years and fine.
2. Imprisonment of not less than 2 years but which may extend to 4 years and fine.
3. Imprisonment of not less than 3 years but which may extend to 7 years and fine.
4. Imprisonment of not less than 5 years but which may extend to 9 years and fine.

Ans. (3)

Exp. As per Section 354C of IPC, any man who watches, or captures the image of a woman engaging in a private act in circumstances where she would usually have the expectation of not being observed either by the perpetrator or by any other person at the behest of the perpetrator or disseminates such image1 shall be punished on first conviction with imprisonment of either description for a term which shall not be less than 1 year, but which may extend to 3 years, and shall also be liable to fine, and be punished on a second or subsequent conviction, with imprisonment of either description for a term which shall not be less than 3 years, but which may extend to 7 years and shall also be liable to fine.

13 The Motor Vehicles Act, 2019 has amended the following Act.

1. The Motor Vehicles Act, 1988
2. The Motor Vehicles Act, 1978
3. The Motor Vehicles Act, 1980
4. The Motor Vehicles Act, 1990

Ans. (1)

Exp. The Motor Vehicles (Amendment) Act of 2019 sought to bring about changes in the Motor Vehicles Act of 1988.

14 Which of the following theories of punishment provides that 'crime is a disease' and the object should be to 'cure disease'?

1. Deterrent theory
2. Reformative theory
3. Expiatory theory
4. Retributive theory

Ans. (2)

➲ *Exp.* According to the reformative theory of punishment, crime is like a disease. This theory maintains that you can cure by killing. The ultimate aim of reformists is to try to bring about a change in the personality and character of the offender, so as to make him a useful member of society.

15 Which of the following legal maxims is not related to tort?

1. Ubi jus ibi remedium
2. Volenti non fit injuria
3. Res ipsa Loquitur
4. Pari delicto

Ans. (4)

➲ *Exp.* The doctrine of pari delicto bars is not related to the tort. It is a party that has been damaged as a result of its own intentional wrongdoing from recovering those damages. This is more frequently related with the Contract Act.

16 Which one of the following is not covered by the schools of Jurisprudence?

1. The Historical school
2. The Realist school
3. The Sociological school
4. The Critical school

Ans. (4)

➲ *Exp.* The Critical school is not covered by the schools of Jurisprudence. There are five major schools of law-Analytical school, Historical school, Sociological school, Philosophical school and lastly Realist school.

17 By which writ, the decision of the highest tribunal of a State can be revised?

1. Mandamus
2. Prohibition
3. Certiorari
4. Quo Warranto

Ans. (3)

➲ *Exp.* Certiorari means 'to be certified' or 'to be informed'. The Writ of Certiorari is issued by the higher court to the lower court directing them to either transfer the pending case to the higher court or to squash the order passed by them in a case.

18 The Berne Convention, 1886 deals with

1. Copyright law
2. Trade Mark law
3. Designs law
4. Geographical indications law

Ans. (1)

➲ *Exp.* The Berne Convention, adopted in 1886, deals with Copyright law, i.e., the protection of works and the rights of their authors. It provides creators such as authors, musicians, poets, painters, etc. With the means to control how their works are used, by whom and on what terms.

19 The 'bailment of the goods,' as security for payment of a debt or performance of a promise, is called

1. Indemnity
2. Guarantee
3. Mortgage
4. Pledge

Ans. (4)

➲ *Exp.* The 'bailment of the goods', as security for payment of a debt or performance of a promise, is called a 'pledge'. The bailor is in this case called the 'pawnor'.

20 The following is known as to 'SAFETY NET' of International Humanitarian Law

1. Leveen Masse
2. Hors De Combat
3. Henry Dunants Clause
4. Martens Clause

Ans. (4)

➲ *Exp.* Named after a Russian diplomat, the Martens Clause Acts as a safety net. It ensures that civilians and combatants remain under the realm of humanity in situations not covered by other treaties or customary laws.

21 The 'Estrada Doctrine' was propounded by Estrada, who was

1. the Foreign Minister of Spain
2. the Foreign Minister of France
3. the Foreign Minister of Mexico
4. the Foreign Minister of Malta

Ans. (3)

➲ *Exp.* The doctrine's name derives from Genaro Estrada, Secretary of Foreign Affairs of Mexico during the presidency of Pascual Ortiz Rubio.

22 With respect to *'Muta* marriage' amongst Muslims, which of the following is/are correct?

1. Spouses have no right of mutual inheritance eyen if one of the spouses dies when if *Muta* is subsisting.
2. The husband has no right of 'talaq' though the parties are free to terminate it by mutual consent.
3. The children of *Muta* marriage are illegitimate.
4. Both (1) and (2)

Ans. (4)

➲ *Exp.* Both the statements (1) and (2) are correct. In *Muta* marriage (temporary marriage in some Shia Muslim traditions), there is generally no right to inheritance between the spouses unless specifically agreed upon in the contract.

Since *Muta* marriage is fixed for a predetermined period, there is no concept of 'talaq' (divorce). However, the marriage can be terminated by mutual consent before the period expires.

Statement (3) is incorrect because the children born out of a *Muta* marriage are legitimate.

23 The owner of the Copyright of the sound recording has which one of the following right, under Section 14 (e) of the Copyright Act, 1957?

1. To encrypt the sound recording
2. To make any adaptation of the sound recording
3. To communicate the sound recording to the public
4. To make any translation of the work recorded in the sound recording

Ans. (3)

➲ *Exp.* According to Section 14 (e) of the Copyright Act, in the case of a sound recording,

(a) To make any other sound recording embodying it including storing of it in any medium by electronic or other means;
(b) To sell or give on commercial rental or offer for sale or for such rental, any copy of the sound recording;
(c) To communicate the sound recording to the public.

24 In which case the 'principle of Prospective Overruling' was laid down?
1. SP Gupta *v/s* Union of India
2. IC Golaknath *v/s* State of Punjab
3. Sunil Batra *v/s* Delhi Administration
4. MC Mejhta *v/s* Union of India

Ans. (2)

➲ *Exp.* The Doctrine of Prospective Overruling was for the first time adopted in the case of IC Golaknath *v/s* the State of Punjab (1967). The court laid down certain provisions restricting the application of the doctrine in the Indian system, which is the Doctrine of Prospective Overruling can be invoked only in matters arising under our Constitution.

25 Who made the following statement "Life of law is not logic, it is experience"?
1. Roscoe Pound
2. H. Kelsen
3. OW Holmes (Jr)
4. John Austin

Ans. (3)

➲ *Exp.* Justice Oliver Wendell Holmes (Jr.) famously maintained that "the life of the law has not been logic it has been experience." Holmes' statement suggests an antecedent question: what is the life of the law?

26 Which one of the following is incorrect?
1. Patents are granted to encourage inventions.
2. Protection and enforcement of patents contribute to technological innovation.
3. Patented invention shall be available at reasonable affordable price.
4. The invention shall be published before applying for patent.

Ans. (4)

➲ *Exp.* Statement (4) is incorrect because the invention cannot be published before applying the patent.

27 Which of the following 'select combination' of words, from the Preamble of the Constitution of India, is in correct order?
1. "Fraternity assuring the integrity"
2. "Fraternity assuring the dignity"
3. "Fraternity assuring the unity"
4. "Fraternity assuring the unity and integrity"

Ans. (2)

➲ *Exp.* The correct order as per the Preamble is "fraternity assuring the dignity of the individual and the unity and integrity of the nation".

28 Who made the following statement?
"Large part and as many would add the best part of Law of England is judge made law, that is to say, consists of rules to be collected from the judgements of the courts".
1. Dicey 2. Lord Denning 3. Bacon 4. Bentham

Ans. (1)

➲ *Exp.* Dicey made the statement "large part and as many would add, the best part of Law of England is judge made law, that is to say, consists of rules to be collected from the judgements of courts."

29 Which of the following case is popularly known as 'Taj Trapezium' case?
1. MC Mehta *v/s* Union of India & Urs (1997) 2 SCC 353
2. Vineet Kumar Mathura *v/s* Union of India (1996) 7 SCC 714
3. Okhla Bird Sanctuary *v/s* Anand Arya (2011) 7 SCC 74
4. MC Mehta *v/s* Union of India (AIR 1987 SC 1086)

Ans. (1)

➲ *Exp.* MC Mehta *v/s* Union of India and Ors (1997) 2 SCC 353 case is popularly known as 'Taj Trapezium' case. The Taj Trapezium case, led by environmentalist MC Mehta in 1985, sought to protect the Taj Mahal from severe pollution-related degradation.

30 Which Jurist gave the classification of the sources of law as (a) Binding and (b) Persuasive?
1. Keeton 2. Salmond
3. Allen 4. Rosco Pound

Ans. (1)

➲ *Exp.* According to Keeton, the sources of law can be classified into two broad categories i.e., Binding sources of law and Persuasive sources.

31 According to Article 80 of the Constitution of India, the respresentatives of each state in the Council of States are elected by
1. elected members of the Legislative Assembly of the state by majority vote through secret ballot.
2. all the members of the Legislative Assembly of the state by majority vote through secret ballot.
3. elected members of the Legislative Assembly of the state in accordance with system of proportional representation by means of the single transferable vote.
4. all the members of the Legislative Assembly of the state in accordance with system of proportional representation by means of the single transferable vote.

Ans. (3)

➲ *Exp.* According to Article 80 (4) of the Constitution of India, the representatives of each state in the Council of States shall be elected by the elected members of the Legislative Assembly of the state in accordance with the system of proportional representation by means of the single transferable vote.

32 Under which of the following principles is the 'Polluter Pays Principle' is envisaged?
1. Principle 15, Earth Summit, 1992
2. Principle 1 & 2, Stockholm Declaration, 1972
3. Principle 16, Rio Declaration, 1992
4. Principle 5, Rio Declaration, 1992

Ans. (3)

➲ *Exp.* 'Polluter Pays Principle' is envisaged under the Principle 16 of Rio Declaration, 1992. The 'Polluters Pays Principle' is a commonly accepted practice that suggests that those who produce pollution should manage it to prevent damage to human health or the environment. This principle is a part of the 1992, Rio Declaration, which provides broader principles for sustainable development worldwide.

33 The strict adherence to the 'rule of Locus standi' was diluted first in
1. DC Wadhwa *v/s* State of Bihar
2. Parmanand Katar *v/s* Union of India
3. Ratlam Municipal Council *v/s* Vardichand
4. Vishakha *v/s* State of Rajasthan

Ans. (3.)

➲ *Exp.* The strict adherence to the 'rule of Locus standi' was first diluted in Ratlam Municipal Council *v/s* Vardichand. The Supreme Court found that a Municipality cannot claim financial inability when it is responsible for preserving public health. The Supreme Court stated, responsible Municipal Council constituted for the precise purpose of preserving public health and providing better finances cannot run away from its principal duty by pleading financial inability. Decency and dignity are non-negotiable facets of Human Rights and are a first charge on local self-governing bodies'.

34 Given below are two statements.

To constitute a tort

Statement I There must be some act or omission on the part of the defendant.

Statement II The act or omission should result in legal damage.

In the light of the above statements, choose the correct answer from the options given below.
1. Both Statement I and Statement II are true.
2. Both Statement I and Statement II are false.
3. Statement I is true, but Statement II is false.
4. Statement I is false, but Statement II is true.

Ans. (1)

➲ *Exp.* Both Statements I and II are true. There must be an omission or some act on the part of the defendant. An act or omission shall be wrong if the person sought to be held liable was under a legal duty. The relevant act or omission should be recognised by law. It should not be a moral or social mistake.

35 Who wrote the book 'Concept of Law'?

1. Paton　　2. Korkunor
3. Salmond　　4. HLA Hart

Ans. (4)

➲ *Exp.* HLA Hart wrote the book 'Concept of Law'. The was Professor of Jurisprudence at Oxford University and the Principal of Brasenose College, Oxford. He authored the Concept of Law, one of the seminal works of English-language jurisprudence.

36 In the light of which of the following Articles of the Constitution of India, the Environment (Protection) Act, 1986 was enacted
1. Article 249
2. Article 250
3. Article 252
4. Article 253

Ans. (4)

➲ *Exp.* In light of Article 253, the Environmental Protection Act, 1986 was enacted. This was enacted in the wake of Bhopal Gas Tragedy.

37 In which of the following cases the Supreme Court observed that the noise pollution cannot be tolerated even if such noise was direct results of and was connected with religious activities?
1. KM Chinappa *v/s* Union of India
2. AP Pollution Control Board *v/s* Prof. MV Naidu
3. Church of God (Full Gospel) in India *v/s* KKR Majestic Colony Welfare Association
4. Common Cause *v/s* Union of India

Ans. (3)

➲ *Exp.* The analysis of Church of God (Full Gospel) in India *v/s* KKR Majestic Colony Welfare Association highlights an individual's right to a serene and noise-free environment.

38 Which of the following Schedules of the National Green Tribunal (NGT) Act provides for the heads of the compensation?
1. Schedule IV
2. Schedule II
3. Schedule III
4. Schedule I

Ans. (2)

➲ *Exp.* Schedule II of the National Green Tribunal Act provides for the heads of compensation under which compensation or relief for damage may be claimed.

39 Section 28 of the Indian Forest Act, 1927 provides for
1. protected areas
2. reserved forest
3. village forests
4. power of forest settlement officer

Ans. (3)

➲ *Exp.* Section 28 of Indian Forest Act, 1927 provides for formation of village forests. According to Section 28(1), the State Government may assign to any or ever village-community the rights of Government to or over any land which has been constituted a reserved forest and may cancel such assignment. All forests so assigned shall be called village-forests.

40 Given below are two statements, one is labelled as Assertion (A) and the other is labelled as Reason (R).

Assertion (A) The polluter pays principle says that the absolute liability for the harm to environment extends not only to compensate the victims of pollution but also to the cost of restoring the environment degradation.

Reason (R) The case MC Mehta *v/s* Kamalnath and other has decided so.

In the light of the above statements, choose the correct answer from the options given below.

1. Both A and R are true and R is the correct explanation of A.
2. Both A and R are true and R is not the correct explanation of A.
3. A is true, but R is false.
4. A is false, but R is true.

***Ans.* (3)**

➲ *Exp.* A is true, but R is false.

The polluter pays principle says that the absolute liability for the harm to environment extends not only to compensate victims of pollution but also to the cost of restoring the environment degradation.

In India, the 'polluter pays principle' was for the first time applied and defined in the 1996 case of Indian Council of Enviro-Legal Action *v/s* Union of India.

41 Asha, a journalist employed, writes a story in the newspaper. Deepak makes a film based on the story. Raghu and Rekha plays the lead role in the film. The dance in the film is choreographed by Ajay.

I. Asha is the author of literary work.

II. Proprietor of the newspaper has copyright on the story, in the absence of a contract regarding copyright.

III. Proprietor of the newspaper has only the publication rights.

IV. Raghu and Rekha have performer's right.

V. Ajay is the author of musical work.

Choose the correct answer from the options given below.

1. I, IV and V
2. I, III and IV
3. Only II
4. I, III, IV and V

***Ans.* (2)**

➲ *Exp.* Statements I, III and IV are correct. In the given situation, the following points are correct

a. Asha is the author of the literary work.

b. Proprietor of the newspaper has only publication rights.

c. Raghu and Rekha have performer's rights.

42 About Administrative Tribunals, Supreme Court recommended in 2010 Madras Bar Association Case.

I. The tribunal should not become post-retirement heaven for Civil Servants.

II. Members of the tribunals should be independent person and not serving Civil Servants.

III. Members of tribunal should retain lien in any government department.

IV. The tribunal should resemble more the Courts and not bureaucratic boards.

V. The tribunals must depend on government for infrastructure facilities.

Choose the correct answer from the options given below.

1. I, II and III
2. I, III and IV
3. III, IV and V
4. I, II and IV

***Ans.* (4)**

➲ *Exp.* Statements I, II and IV are correct.

The question asks about the recommendations made by the Supreme Court in the 2010, Madras Bar Association case regarding Administrative Tribunals.

The Supreme Court emphasised that tribunals should not become a place for post-retirement employment for civil servants.

The Court also highlighted that members should be independent and not currently serving as Civil Servants, to maintain impartiality.

The Court stated that tribunals should operate more like judicial courts and less like bureaucratic bodies, to ensure judicial standards.

Statements III and V are incorrect.

Members of the tribunals should not retain any lien on government departments, as this could lead to conflicts of interest or a lack of independence.

The Court did not state that tribunals must depend on the government for infrastructure, as such dependence could undermine their independence.

43 Consider the following statements.

I. International Law recognises general duty of state in respect of extradition.

II. International Law does not recognise general duty of state in respect of extradition.

III. Extradition depends on the provision of existing extradition treaties.

IV. Countries may grant extradition without a treaty.

V. Customary International Law governs extradition.

Choose the correct answer from the options given below.

1. I, II, IV and V
2. I, III, IV and V
3. II, III and V
4. II, III and IV

***Ans.* (4)**

➲ *Exp.* Statements II, III and IV are correct.

Factor *v/s* Labubenheimer clearly stated that International Law recognises no right to extradition apart from a treaty.

The Extradition Act, 1962 prescribes separate procedures for handling extradition requests from different countries depending on the procedural and evidentiary requirements envisaged in the relevant extradition treaty.

Generally under US Law (18 U.S.C. § 3184), extradition may be granted only pursuant to a treaty. However, some countries grant extradition without a treaty and of those that do, most require an offer of reciprocity.

44 As per Salmond, there are 4 distinct kinds of rights.

I. Liberties
II. Rights
III. Power
IV. Immunities
V. Kindness

Choose the correct answer from the options given below.

1. I and II
2. I, II, III and IV
3. III, IV and V
4. I, II, IV and V

***Ans.** (2)*

➲ *Exp.* Option (2), i.e., I, II, III and IV are correct.

According to Salmond, there are four distinct kind of rights

a. Liberties
b. Rights
c. Power
d. Immunities

45 With respect to valid conditions for Hindu Marriage, u/s 5 of the Hindu Marriage Act, 1955, which of the following are true?

I. Neither party has a spouse living at the time of marriage
II. Mental capacity
III. Ceremonies of marriage
IV. Parties are not within prohibited degree
V. No impotency

Choose the correct answer from the options given below.

1. I, III and IV
2. I, II and IV
3. II, III and V
4. I, II and V

***Ans.** (2)*

➲ *Exp.* According to Section 5 of the Hindu Marriage Act, a marriage may be solemnised between any two Hindus, if the following conditions are fulfilled, namely

(i) neither party has a spouse living at the time of the marriage;
(ii) at the time of the marriage, neither party
(a) is incapable of giving a valid consent to it in consequence of unsoundness of mind; or
(b) though capable of giving a valid consent, has been suffering from mental disorder of such a kind or to such an extent as to be unfit for marriage and the procreation of children; or
(c) has been subject to recurrent attacks of insanity;
(iii) the bridegroom has completed the age of 21 years and the bride has completed the age of 18 years at the time of the marriage;
(iv) the parties are not within the degrees of prohibited relationship unless the custom or usage governing each of them permits of a marriage between the two;
(v) the parties are not sapindas of each other, unless the custom or usage governing each of them permits of a marriage between the two.

46 Consider the following statements.

I. Treaties may be terminated.
II. Treaties cannot be terminated.
III. Treaties may be terminated by (i) operation of law and (ii) by act of state parties.
IV. Importing of performance of a treaty is also a ground for the termination of treaty and the provisions is contained Article 51 of the Vienna Convention of Law of Treaties, 1969.
V. Importing of performance of a treaty is also a ground for the termination of treaty and the provisions is contained Article 57 of the Vienna Convention of Law of Treaties, 1969.

Choose the correct answer from the options given below.

1. I, II, III and V
2. II, III and IV
3. II, III and V
4. II and III

***Ans.** (2) This Question has been dropped by UGC.*

➲ *Exp.* The options given here are incorrect.

Statements I, III and V are correct.

Treaties maybe terminated either by operation of law or by act of parties.

Statement V is also correct because it deals with termination of a treaty by operation of law (which signifies termination of treaty by performance of the obligations therein)

47 Which of the following is true with regards to *Iddat* period?

I. *Iddat* of widowhood is 4 months and 10 days
II. The period of *Iddat* begins from the date when she comes to know of divorce and not from the date when divorce is pronounced.
III. If the marriage is irregular and is consummated, the wife is under obligation to observe *Iddat*.
IV. If the wife observe *Iddat*, husband is bound to maintain the wife during the period on *Iddat*.
V. In case the wife is pregnant, period of *Iddat* extends till the delivery of the child.

Choose the correct answer from the options given below.

1. I, II, IV and V
2. I, III, IV and V
3. II, III, IV and V
4. II and IV

***Ans.** (2)*

➲ *Exp.* Statements I, III, IV and V are correct.

The concept of *Iddat* is very significant in Islamic law. Under Muslim law, it is that period during which a woman is prohibited from remarrying after the dissolution of her marriage and is required to live a simple life.

When a marriage dissolves by the death of the husband, the duration of *Iddat* is 4 months and 10 days.

Under Sunni law, marriage with a woman undergoing *Iddat* is irregular and not void. But under Shia law marriage with a woman who is undergoing *Iddat* is void.

If the wife observes *Iddat*, the husband is bound to maintain the wife during the period of *Iddat*.

If wife is pregnant at the time of husband's death, it continues till the delivery of the child or 4 months 10 days whichever is longer.

48 Consider the following statements.

I. Uniting for peace resolution was passed in 1950.
II. Uniting for peace resolution was passed by the General Assembly.
III. Uniting for peace resolution was passed by the Security Council.
IV. Maintenance of international peace and security is the primary responsibility of the Security Council.
V. Maintenance of international peace and security is the primary responsibility of the General Assembly.

Choose the correct answer from the options given below.

1. I, II and IV
2. I, II, III and IV
3. I, II, IV and V
4. I, II and V

Ans. (1)

➲ *Exp.* Statements I, II and IV are correct. General Assembly resolution 377(V) is known as the Uniting for peace resolution. Adopted in 1950, the resolution resolves that if the Security Council fails to exercise its responsibility to maintain international peace and security, the General Assembly may call an Emergency Special Session.

49 Under Article 51 of the Constitution of India the state is directed to endeavour to

I. promote international peace and security
II. maintain just and honourable relations between nations
III. foster respect for international law and treaty obligations
IV. protect and improve the environment and to safeguard forests
V. encourage settlement of international disputes through arbitration

Choose the correct answer from the options given below.

1. I, II, III and IV
2. I, II, III and V
3. II, III, IV and V
4. I, III, II and IV

Ans. (2)

➲ *Exp.* Statements I, II, III and V are correct.

Under Article 51 of the Constitution, the state is directed to endeavour to

a. promote international peace and security
b. maintain just and honourable relations between nations
c. foster respect for international law and treaty obligations
d. encourage settlement of international disputes through arbitration.

50 Which of the following can be registered as Trade Mark under the Trade Marks Act, 1999?

I. Rasoi for hydrogenated oil
II. Jhoomritalaiya for pens
III. Bank for banking service
IV. Square shape for tyres
V. Obscene matters (things)

Choose the correct answer from the options given below.

1. Only II
2. I, II and IV
3. II and IV
4. III and V

Ans. (3)

➲ *Exp.* Option (3), i.e., II and IV are correct.

Jhoomritalaiya for pens can be registered under Trade Marks Act.

Square shape for tyres can also be registered under the Trade Marks Act.

51 The Corporate Social Responsibility (CSR) Committee of a Company carries out the following functions.

I. To appoint an individual or a firm as an auditor
II. To recommend a CSR policy
III. To recommend the amount of expenditure for the indicated activities
IV. To inspect the books of accounts during business hours
V. To monitor the CSR policy of the company from time to time

Choose the correct answer from the options given below.

1. I, II and III
2. II and IV
3. II, III and V
4. II, III, IV and V

Ans. (3)

➲ *Exp.* Corporate Social Responsibility is rooted in preserving the environment. A company can pursue environmental stewardship by reducing pollution and emissions in manufacturing, recycling materials, replenishing natural resources like trees, or creating product lines consistent with CSR.

Following functions are carried out by the CSR committee

To recommend a CSR policy.

To recommend the amount of expenditure for the indicated activities.

To monitor the CSR policy of the company from time to time.

52 In order to convert a proposal into a promise, the acceptance must be

I. absolute
II. unqualified
III. conditional
IV. random
V. expressed in some usual and reasonable manner

Choose the correct answer from the options given below.

1. I and II
2. I and III
3. I, II and V
4. II, III and IV

Ans. *(3)*

➲ ***Exp.*** According to Section 7 of the Contract Act, in order to convert a proposal into a promise, the acceptance must— (1) be absolute and unqualified; (2) be expressed in some usual and reasonable manner, unless the proposal prescribes the manner in which it is to be accepted.

53 Given below are two statements, one is labelled as Assertion (A) and the other is labelled as Reason (R).

Assertion (A) The Criminal Law Amendment Act, 2013 was a result of the public outrage.

Reason (R) Society forces the law to accept the change.

In the light of the above statements, choose the correct answer from the options given below.

1. Both A and R are true and R is the correct explanation of A.
2. Both A and R are true and A is not the correct explanation of A.
3. A is true, but R is false.
4. A is false, but R is true.

Ans. *(1)*

➲ ***Exp.*** Both A and R are true and R is the correct explanation of A.

The Criminal Law Amendment Act, 2013 was a result of the public outrage. It was passed in the aftermath of the Nirbhaya case wherein a female student was gang-raped in December, 2012. The Act amended several provisions of the Indian Penal Code, Indian Evidence Act and the Criminal Procedure Code.

54 Given below are two statements, one is labelled as Assertion (A) and the other is labelled as Reason (R).

Assertion (A) Rights to pollution free air and clean water are attributes of the right of a dignified life.

Reason (R) These rights are the basic elements that sustain the life.

In the light of the above statements, choose the correct answer from the options given below.

1. Both A and R are true and R is the correct explanation of A.
2. Both A and R are true and A is not the correct explanation of A.
3. A is true, but R is false.
4. A is false, but R is true.

Ans. *(1)*

➲ ***Exp.*** Both A and R are true and R is the correct explanation of A.

Rights to pollution free air and clean water are attributes of the right of a dignified life. This is because the right to live is a Fundamental Right under Article 21 of the Constitution and it includes the right of enjoyment of pollution-free water and air for full enjoyment of life. These are the basic elements that sustain the life.

55 Consider the following statements.

I. For State Legislature, Constitutional provisions for special address of the Governor, is in Article 176.
II. For State Legislature the Constitutional provisions for oath or affirmation by members is in Article 109.
III. For State Legislature the special procedure in respect of Money Bill is covered by Article 198.
IV. For State Legislature provisions as to introduction and passing of bills is given in Article 196.
V. For State Legislature provision for disqualifications for membership are given in Article 190.

Choose the correct answer from the options given below.

1. I, II and III
2. II, III and V
3. I, IV and V
4. I, III and IV

Ans. *(4)*

➲ ***Exp.*** Statements I, III and IV are correct.

Article 176 of the Indian Constitution pertains to the Governor's special address to the State Legislature. It states that the Governor shall address the Legislative Assembly of the State at the commencement of the first session after each general election and the first session of each year.

Article 198 specifies that Money Bills can only be introduced in the Legislative Assembly and not in the Legislative Council. Article 196 provides for provisions as to introduction and passing of bills.

56 The following fall under Chapter IV (General Exceptions) of the Indian Penal Code, 1860.

I. Act done by a person bound, or by mistake of fact believing himself to be bound, by law
II. Act of judge when acting judicially
III. Omission to assist public servant when bound by law to give assistance
IV. International resistance or obstruction by a person to his lawful apprehension
V. Accident in doing a lawful act

Choose the correct answer from the options given below.

1. I and V
2. I and II
3. Only II
4. I, II and V

Ans. *(4)*

➲ ***Exp.*** Statements I, II and V are correct. Of the given options, the following fall under Chapter IV of Indian Penal Code, 1860.

Act done by a person bound, or by mistake of fact believing himself be to bound, by law (Section 76).

Act of judge when acting judicially (Section 77).

Accident in doing a lawful act (Section 80).

57 Consider the following statements.

I. Recognition de jure is final and once given cannot be withdrawn

II. Recognition de jure is not final
III. De facto recognition may be withdrawn
IV. Withdrawal of recognition by a state because that state has ceased to be the state
V. Retroative recognition of a new government does not invalidate the acts of the previous de jure government

Choose the correct answer from the options given below.

1. I, III and V
2. II, III, IV and V
3. I, II, IV and V
4. I, III, IV and V

Ans. *(1)*

Exp. Statements I, III and V are correct. De jure recognition is a legal recognition and permanent recognition that are fixed or permanent that cannot be withdrawn. The de jure government can get membership in the United Nations when most of the people or the majority of the states have recognised that de jure government. De facto recognition may be withdrawn if the circumstances change. Retroactive recognition of a new government does not invalidate the acts of the previous de jure government.

58 Consider the following statements.

I. Article 2(4) of the UN Charter contains the proposition of the unilateral use of force or threat theory by states in their international relations.
II. There are no exception to the above.
III. UN Charter makes an exception to Article 2(4) in individual and collective self-defense as in Article 51.
IV. States may use or encourage the use of economic and political measures to coerce another state.
V. States have a duty to refrain from propaganda for wars of aggression.

Choose the correct answer from the options given below.

1. I, II, IV and V
2. I, III, IV and V
3. I, III and V
4. II, III, IV and V

Ans. *(3)*

Exp. Statements I, III and V are correct. Article 2 (4) of the Charter prohibits the threat or use of force and calls on all Members to respect the sovereignty, territorial integrity and political independence of other States.

59 Consider the following statements.

I. The Preamble of the UN Charter says: 'We the peoples, of the United Nations'.
II. The Preamble of the UN Charter says: 'We the people of the United Nations'.
III. Maintenance of international peace and security is the primary responsibility of the Security Council.
IV. Maintenance of international peace and security is the primary responsibility of the General Assembly.
V. Maintenance of international peace and security is the primary responsibility of the International Court of Justice.

Choose the correct answer from the options given below.

1. II and III
2. I and III
3. I and IV
4. II and V

Ans. *(2)*

Exp. Statements I and III are correct.

The Preamble of the UN Charter reads as follows

"WE THE PEOPLES OF THE UNITED NATIONS DETERMINED to save succeeding generations from the scourge of war, which twice in our lifetime has brought untold sorrow to mankind, and to reaffirm faith in fundamental Human Rights, in the dignity and worth of the human person, in the equal rights of men and women and of nations large and small, and to establish conditions under which justice and respect for the obligations arising from treaties and other sources of international law can be maintained, and to promote social progress and better standards of life in larger freedom,....."

60 Consider the following statements.

I. The International Bank of Reconstruction and Development (IBRD) is also called the World Bank.
II. The International Bank of Reconstruction and Development (IBRD) is also called the International Monetary Fund.
III. The Dunkel Draft Act embodies the results of the Tokyo Round.
IV. The WTO provides for a Secretariat headed by a Director-General.
V. The WTO provides for a Secretariat headed by Secretary General.

Choose the correct answer from the options given below.

1. I, III and V
2. I and V
3. I, III and IV
4. I and IV

Ans. *(4)*

Exp. Statements I and IV are correct.

The International Bank for Reconstruction and Development is also known as the World Bank. The IBRD and its concessional lending arm, the International Development Association (IDA), are collectively known as the World Bank as they share the same leadership and staff.

The WTO Secretariat, based in Geneva, has approximately 620 staff. It is headed by a Director-General, who is supported by four Deputy Directors-General. Since the WTO is run by its member governments, the Secretariat has no decision-making powers.

61 With regards to cruelty under the Hindu Marriage Act, 1955 the following holds true.

I. It is very difficult to define cruelty which can fit in all circumstances.
II. Cruelty can be physical and mental.
III. Intention plays an important role in cases on cruelty.
IV. Cruelty should be aimed at the petitioner.
V. The act complained of must be that of the respondent.

Choose the correct answer from the options given below.

1. I, III and V
2. I and II
3. I, II and IV
4. II, III and IV

Ans. (1)

Exp. Statements I, III and V are correct.

It is very difficult to define cruelty which can fit in all circumstances. This is true as cruelty can manifest in various forms and degrees making it challenging to provides a universally applicable definition.

Intention plays an important role in cases on cruelty while unintentional acts can sometimes constitute cruelty, the intention behind the act is generally considered a significant factor in determining, whether it constitutes cruelty.

62 Under the Hindu Succession Act, 1956, heirs of a Hindu Male fall under following heads.

I. Class I heirs
II. Class II heirs
III. Sharers
IV. Agnates
V. Congnates

Choose the correct answer from the options given below.

1. I, III, IV and V
2. I and V
3. I, II, IV and V
4. I, IV and V

Ans. (3)

Exp. Option (3) i.e., I, II, IV and V are correct.

As per the provisions of the Hindu Succession Act, the heirs of Hindu male fall under the following heads.

a. Class I heirs
b. Class II heirs
c. Agnates; and
d. Cognates

63 Following essentials are to be fulfilled for death to be called 'Dowry death' under Section 304 B of the Indian Penal Code.

I. Death of a women within 10 years of her marriage.
II. Fact of cruelty or harassment by her husband for or in connection with any demand for dowry.
III. Fact of cruelty or harassment by any relative of her husband for or in connection with any demand for dowry.
IV. Death of a women within 7 years of her marriage.
V. Dowry shall have the same meaning as in Section 2 of the Dowry Prohibition Act, 1961.

Choose the correct answer from the options given below.

1. II and IV
2. II, III, IV and V
3. I, II and V
4. II, IV and V

Ans. (2)

Exp. According to Section 304B of IPC, where the death of a woman is caused by any burns or bodily injury or occurs otherwise than under normal circumstances within 7 years of her marriage and it is shown that soon before her death she was subjected to cruelty or harassment by her husband or any relative of her husband for, or in connection with, any demand for dowry, such death shall be called "dowry death", and such husband or relative shall be deemed to have caused her death.

64 Constitutional remedies include

I. Extraordinary remedies under Article 32 and 226
II. Appeals to Supreme Court under Article 132 to 135
III. Appeals to High Court under Article 139 to 139 A
IV. Transfer of cases to Supreme Court under Article 139 B
V. Advisory jurisdiction under Article 143

Choose the correct answer from the options given below.

1. I, III and IV
2. I, II and V
3. II, III and IV
4. III, IV and V

Ans. (2)

Exp. Statements I, II and V are correct. Constitutional remedies include the following.

a. Extraordinary remedies as provided under Article 32 and 226.
b. Appeals to Supreme Court under Article 132 to 135.
c. Advisory jurisdiction under Article 143.

65 Which of the following are Fundamental Rights?

I. Right not to remain employed
II. Right not to remain uneducated
III. Right not to remain unmarried
IV. Right not to be killed without trail
V. Right not to change religion

Choose the correct answer from the options given below.

1. II, IV and V
2. I, III and IV
3. I, IV and V
4. II, III and V

Ans. (1)

Exp. Statements II, IV and V are correct.

Fundamental Rights the following are

a. Right not to remain uneducated as per Article 21A.
b. Right not to be killed without trial as per Article 20.
c. Right not to change religion as per Article 25-28.

66 Match List-I with List-II.

List-I		List-II	
A.	Soundness of mind	I.	Section 14
B.	Fraud	II.	Section 12
C.	Free consent	III.	Section 11
D.	Competency to contract	IV.	Section 17

Codes

	A	B	C	D		A	B	C	D
1.	I	II	III	IV	2.	II	IV	I	III
3.	II	III	I	IV	4.	II	IV	III	I

Ans. (2)

➲ *Exp.* The correct matching is A-II, B-IV, C-I, D-III.

Section 12 Soundness of mind

Section 17 Fraud

Section 14 Free consent

Section 11 Competency to contract

67 Match List-I with List-II.

List-I		List-II	
A.	Equal justice and free legal aid	I.	Article 39A
B.	Promotion of cooperative societies	II.	Article 43
C.	Living wages, etc for workers	III.	Article 43B
D.	Uniform Civil Code for citizens	IV.	Article 44

Codes

	A	B	C	D		A	B	C	D
1.	II	III	I	IV	2	III	I	II	IV
3.	I	III	II	IV	4.	I	II	III	IV

Ans. (3)

➲ *Exp.* The correct matching is A-I, B-III, C-II, D-IV.

Article 39 A deals with equal justice and free legal aid.

Article 43B provides for promotion of cooperative societies.

Article 43 provides for living wages, etc of workers.

Article 44 provides for Uniform Civil Code for citizens.

68 Match List-I with List-II.

List-I		List-II	
A.	Eastern Book Co *v/s* D.B Modak (2006, SC)	I.	Idea expression dichotomy
B.	Bayer Corpn *v/s* Union of India	II.	Minimum of creativity test
C.	RG Anand *v/s* Deluxe Films (1978 SC)	III.	Prior user test
D.	NR Dongre *v/s* Whirlpool Corpn (1996 SC)	IV.	Compulsory license of patents

Codes

	A	B	C	D
1.	I	II	III	IV
2.	II	IV	I	III
3.	IV	I	II	III
4.	III	I	II	IV

Ans. (2)

➲ *Exp.* The matching coding is A-II, B-IV, C-I, D-III.

Eastern Book Company *v/s* **DB Modak** The test for originality in copyright in India was given by EBC *v/s* DB Modak. The court held that a compilation may be copyrightable if it is original in its 'selection, coordination or arrangement of pre-existing data.' For originality, the work must achieve a 'minimum degree of creativity' not in the sense of being 'novel or non-obvious', but in producing a 'substantive variation and not merely a trivial variation'.

Bayer Corporation *v/s* **Union of India** The court in the present case was right in dismissing the petition filed by Bayer Corporation. The judgement very well-clarified that when there the subject matter of the issue in contention is in relation to the public at large then the top most priority is of public interest as it is in the present case.

RG Anand *v/s* **Deluxe Films** The plaintiff RG Anand, contended that it was modeled on the plot of a play Hum Hindustani written and produced by him. The judgement is remarkable for clarifying the concepts of idea-expression dichotomy and copyright infringement under the Indian copyright law.

NR Dongre *v/s* **Whirlpool Corporation** In this landmark case, Whirlpool claimed a mark based on the principle of 'prior use' and its transborder reputation stating that the goods being marketed by using such mark gave the impression that such goods belong to Whirlpool.

69 Match List-I with List-II.

List-I		List-II	
A.	Asymmetric crypto-system	I.	Neighbouring rights
B.	Rome Convention	II.	Industrial property
C.	Paris Convention, 1883	III.	Trademarks
D.	Madrid Protocol	IV.	Digital signature

Codes

	A	B	C	D		A	B	C	D
1.	IV	I	III	II	2.	IV	II	I	III
3.	IV	I	II	III	4.	I	III	II	IV

Ans. (3)

➲ *Exp.* The correct matching is A-IV, B-I, C-II, D-III.

Asymmetric crypto-system Section 2(1)(f) of the IT Act, 2000, defines an asymmetric crypto-system is a system of a secure key pair consisting of a private key for creating a digital signature and a public key to verify the digital signature.

Rome Convention The Rome Convention on related rights is a treaty that was created in 1961 to set minimum standards for the rights of performers, producers and broadcasters. These rights are called neighbouring rights and were not protected under previous copyright conventions.

Paris Convention, 1883 The Paris Convention, adopted in 1883, applies to industrial property in the widest sense, including patents, trademarks, industrial designs, utility models, service marks, trade names, geographical indications and the repression of unfair competition.

Madrid Protocol Protocol is a convenient and efficient way for trademark owners worldwide to file one application to register their trademark in multiple countries.

70 Match List-I with List-II.

List-I		List-II
A. Rule of specialty	I.	Importance of the works of jurists
B. Paquete Habana	II.	Extradition
C. Barcelona Traction case	III.	Sources of International Law are not hierarchical but complimentary and inter-related
D. Nicara Gua *v/s* USA	IV.	Equity and Justice

Codes

	A	B	C	D
1.	II	I	IV	III
2.	III	II	I	IV
3.	II	III	IV	I
4.	II	IV	III	I

Ans. *(1)*

Exp. The correct matching is A-II, B-I, C-IV, D-III.

Rule of specialty The principle of speciality provides that the requesting state is bound to try or punish the extradited offender only for the offence for which he is extradited.

Paquete Habana As stated in the Paquete Habana, "the works of jurists and international law experts are resorted to by judicial tribunals, not for the speculations of their authors concerning what the law ought to be, but for trustworthy evidence of what the law really is."

Barcelona Traction case The Court found that Belgium had no legal standing to exercise diplomatic protection of shareholders in a Canadian company in respect of measures taken against that company in Spain.

Nicara Gua *v/s* **USA** Under the case, sources of international law are not hierarchical but complimentary and inter-related.

71 Match List-I with List-II.

List-I		List-II
A. Kyto Treaty on Climate Change	I.	1995
B. International Convention on the Protection of the Rights of all migrant workers and members of their families	II.	1997
C. SAARC accord on extradition	III.	1990
D. WTO came into force in the year	IV.	1987

Codes

	A	B	C	D
1.	II	III	IV	I
2.	IV	III	II	I
3.	III	IV	II	I
4.	II	I	IV	III

Ans. *(1)*

Exp. The correct matching is A-II, B-III, C-IV, D-I.

The **Kyoto Protocol** is an international treaty adopted in 1997 that aimed to reduce the emission of gases that contribute to global warming.

International Convention on Protection of Rights of all migrant workers and the members of their families (1990) It covers the rights of migrant workers and their families.

SAARC Accord on Extradition (1987) For the purpose of extradition between SAARC Member States, any two or more Contracting States may, by agreement, decide to include any other serious offence involving violence, which shall not be regarded as a political offence or an offence connected with a political offence or an offence inspired by political motives.

World Trade Organisation (WTO) came into force in 1995. The overall objective of the WTO is to help its members use trade as a means to raise living standards, create jobs and improves people's lives. The WTO operates the global system of trade rules and helps developing economies build their trade capacity.

72 Match List-I with List-II.

List-I		List-II
A. Restitution of conjugal rights	I.	Section 10, the Hindu Marriage Act, 1955
B. Judicial separation	II.	Section 12, the Hindu Marriage Act, 1955
C. No petition for divorce within one year of marriage	III.	Section 9, the Hindu Marriage Act, 1955
D. Voidable marriage	IV.	Section 14, the Hindu Marriage Act, 1955

Codes

	A	B	C	D
1.	IV	III	I	II
2.	III	I	IV	II
3.	II	I	III	IV
4.	III	II	IV	I

Ans. *(2)*

Exp. The correct matching is A-III, B-I, C-IV, D-II.

Section 9 of the Hindu Marriage Act provides for restitution of conjugal rights. It states that "When either the husband or the wife has, without reasonable excuse, withdrawn from the society of the other, the aggrieved party may apply, by petition to the District Court, for restitution of conjugal rights and the court, on being satisfied of the truth of the statements made in such petition and that there is no legal ground why the application should not be granted, may decree restitution of conjugal rights accordingly."

Section 10 provides for Judicial Separation. It states that either party to a marriage, whether solemnised before or after the commencement of this Act, may present a petition praying for a decree for judicial separation on any of the grounds specified in Sub Section (1) of Section 13, and in the case of a wife also on any of the grounds specified in Sub-Section (2) thereof, as grounds on which a petition for divorce might have been presented.

Section 14 No petition for divorce to be presented within one year of marriage. It states that notwithstanding anything contained in this Act, it shall not be competent for any court to entertain any petition for dissolution of a marriage by a decree of divorce, unless at the date of the presentation of the petition one year has elapsed] since the date of the marriage.

Section 12 deals with the concept of voidable marriages.

73 Match List-I with List-II.

List-I	List-II
A. State of Rajasthan *v/s* G. Chanda	I. Pith and substance
B. K.T. Moopil Nair *v/s* State of Kerala	II. Colourable Legislation
C. O.N. Mahindroo *v/s* Bar Council of Maharashtra & Goa	III. Repugnancy
D. M. Karunanidhi *v/s* Union of India	IV. Harmonious construction

Codes

	A	B	C	D
1.	I	II	III	IV
2.	II	I	IV	III
3.	IV	III	I	II
4.	I	II	IV	III

Ans. *(4)*

Exp. The correct matching is A-I, B-II, C-IV, D-III.

State of Rajasthan *v/s* **G. Chanda** In this case, the state of Rajasthan made a law restricting the use of sound amplifiers.

K.T. Moopil Nair *v/s* **State of Kerala** The Supreme Court declared the Travancore Cochin Land Tax Act,1955 as invalid. The court said that the Act violated Articles 14 and 19(1) and its provisions were confiscatory in nature.

O.N. Mahindroo *v/s* **Bar Council of Maharashtra and Goa**. The doctrine of harmonious construction is a tool that helps judges and legal experts make sense of conflicting laws or rules.

M. Karunanidhi *v/s* **Union of India** The Court opined that where there is a direct collision between State made law and a parliamentary law, the State Law would be void to the extent of repugnancy.

74 Match List-I with List-II.

List-I	List-II
A. Rule of strict liability	I. Slander
B. Publication of a defamatory statement	II. Rylands *v/s* Fletcher
C. Defamatory representation made in some permanent form	III. Act of God
D. Vis Major	IV. Libel

Codes

	A	B	C	D
1	IV	I	II	III
2.	I	II	III	IV
3.	II	I	IV	III
4.	II	IV	I	III

Ans. *(3)*

Exp. The correct matching is A-II, B-I, C-IV, D-III. [incorrectly given as answer for both B and C would be libel]

The rule of strict liability was propounded in the case of Rylands *v/s* Fletcher. According to this rule, a person can be held liable even there is no negligence on his part.

Publication of a defamatory statement is known as libel. [this option is incorrectly given in the paper since libel is defamation in oral form-its publication in permanent form is slander]

Defamatory representation made in some permanent form is known as libel.

The terms Act of God, natural disaster, and force majeure are synonymous with vis major. These terms are commonly used in contracts to exclude one or both parties from liability and fulfilling their contractual obligations when events beyond their control occur.

75 Match List-I with List-II.

List-I	List-II
A. Natural guardians of a Hindu minor	I. Section 8, Hindu Minority and Guardianship, Act, 1956
B. Powers of natural guardian	II. Section 9, Hindu Minority and Guardianship, Act, 1956
C. Testamentary guardians and their powers	III. Section 6, Hindu Minority and Guardianship, Act, 1956
D. Welfare of minor to be paramount consideration	IV. Section 13, Hindu Minority and Guardianship, Act, 1956

Codes

	A	B	C	D
1.	I	III	II	IV
2.	III	I	II	IV
3.	II	I	III	IV
4.	IV	II	I	III

Ans. *(2)*

Exp. The correct matching is A-III, B-I, C-II, D-IV.

Section 6 of the Hindu Minority and Guardianship Act provides for the natural guardian of a Hindu minor.

Section 8 provides for the powers of the natural guardian. Section 8 (1) provides that the natural guardian of a Hindu minor has power to do all acts which are necessary or reasonable and proper for the benefit of the minor or for the realisation, protection or benefit of the minor's estate. Also, the guardian cannot bind the minor by a personal covenant in any case.

Section 9 provides for testamentary guardians and their powers. It states that a Hindu father entitled to act as the natural guardian of his minor legitimate children, may, by will, appoint a guardian for any of them in respect of the minor's person or in respect of the minor's property (other than the undivided interest referred in Section 12) or in respect of both.

Section 13 provides for welfare of minor to be paramount consideration. It states that in the appointment of declaration of any person as guardian of a Hindu minor by a court, the welfare of the minor shall be the paramount consideration.

76 Which is the correct chronological order (old to new) of the following judgements on appointment and transfer of judges?

A. SP Gupta *v/s* Union of India
II. Sakal Chand Seth *v/s* Union of India
III. Special Reference No 1 of 1998
IV. Supreme Court Advocates on Record Association *v/s* Union of India

Choose the correct answer from the options given below.

1. I, III, II, IV
2. II, I, IV, III
3. IV, II, III, I
4. I, II, III, IV

Ans. (2)

Exp. The correct chronological order is II, I, IV and III.

Sakal Chand Seth *v/s* Union of India (1977) The ruling observed judicial independence from governmental over reach by upholding the rule that High Court judges cannot be transferred without their consent.

SP Gupta *v/s* Union of India (1981) also known as the "Judges Transfer Case" (1981), was a landmark legal case in India.

Supreme Court Advocates on Record Association *v/s* Union of India (1982) The Court held that while it has the inherent power to punish for contempt, including the misconduct of advocates, it does not have the power to debar or suspend an advocate from practicing before it.

Special Reference No. 1 of 1988 This case played a major role in developing the Collegium system as it is in existence today. It stated that the Collegium system would consist of CJI and four most senior most judges of the Supreme Court.

77 Indicate the chronological order of the following.

I. Treaty of Westpholia
II. Kellogg Brand port
III. Brussels Conference
IV. Convention of the statutes of refugees
V. Montevideo Convention

Choose the correct answer from the options given below.

1. I, II, III, V, IV
2. I, V, II, III, IV
3. I, III, V, II, IV
4. I, III, II, V, IV

Ans. (4)

Exp. The correct chronological order is I, III, II, V and IV.

Treaty of Westphalia The Peace of Westphalia is the collective name for two peace treaties signed in October 1648 in the Westphalian cities of Osnabrück and Münster. They ended the Thirty Years' War and brought peace to the Holy Roman Empire, closing a calamitous period of European history that killed approximately eight million people.

Brussels Conference The Brussels Anti-Slavery Conference in 1889–1890 agreed upon a sales ban of modern firearms for large parts of the African continent, a covenant that served joint imperial interests amid the 'Scramble for Africa'.

Kellogg Brand port This is a 1928 international agreement on peace in which signatory states promised not to use war to resolve disputes or conflicts of whatever nature.

Montevideo Convention The Montevideo Convention on the Rights and Duties of States is a treaty signed at Montevideo, Uruguay, on 26th December, 1933 during the Seventh International Conference of American States.

Convention on the status of refugees The 1951 Refugee Convention and its 1967 Protocol are the key legal documents that form the basis of UNHCR's work. They define the term 'refugee' and outline their rights and the international standards of treatment for their protection.

78 Indicate the chronological order in which the following cases were decided.

I. Fisheries jurisdiction (merit) case
II. Island of Palmas arbitration case
III. Nuremberg judgement
IV. Right of pange on Indian testing case
V. SS Lotus case

Choose the correct answer from the options given below

1. II, V, III, IV, I
2. II, III, IV, V, I
3. V, II, III, IV, I
4. V, III, IV, II, I

Ans. (3)

Exp. The correct chronological order is V, II, III, IV and I.

SS Lotus case : The case was accepted and the decision was made by the permanent court of international justice on 7th September, 1927. This case is famous for scrutinising the condition of jurisdiction.

Island of Palmas arbitration case (1928) : It was a territorial dispute over the Island of Palmas (or Miangas) between the Netherlands and the United States which was heard by the Permanent Court of Arbitration. Palmas (Indonesian: Pulau Miangas) was declared to be a part of the Netherlands East Indies and is now part of Indonesia.

Nuremberg judgement On 1st October, 1946, the tribunal convicted 19 of the defendants and acquitted 3. Of those convicted, 12 were sentenced to death.

Right of pange on Indian testing case (1954) : The Court found that Portugal had in 1954 the right of passage claimed by it but that such right did not extend to armed forces, armed police, arms and ammunition, and that India had not acted contrary to the obligations imposed on it by the existence of that right.

Fisheries jurisdiction (merit) case (1974) : The Court held that "The delimitation of sea areas has always an international aspect; it cannot be dependent merely upon the will of the coastal State as expressed in its municipal law".

79 Arrange the correct sequence in which an application for grant of Patent will be considered.

I. Opposition under Section 25 (2) of the Patents Act, 1970
II. Publication of application
III. Filling of claims
IV. Request for examination
V. Grant of patents

Choose the correct answer from the options given below.

1. II, IV, III, I, V
2. II, I, III, IV, V
3. III, II, IV, V, I
4. III, I, II, IV, V

Ans. (3)

Exp. The correct sequence is III, II, IV, V and I.

a. Filling of claims
b. Publication of application
c. Request for examination
d. Grant of patents
e. Opposition under Section 25(2) of Patents Act 1970

80 Indicate the chronological order in which the following cases were decided.

I. ELCAMANN's case
II. Anglo Norwegian fisheries case
III. Anglo Iranian Oil company case
IV. Chorzow Factory case
V. Western Sahara case

Choose the correct answer from the options given below.

1. IV, III, I, II, V
2. IV, II, III, I, V
3. IV, I, III, II, V
4. IV, I, II, III, V

Ans. (2)

Exp. The correct chronological order is IV, II, III, I and V.

Chorzow factory case The Chorzów Factory case was a case heard before the Permanent Court of International Justice in 1927. It was an early authority in international law that established a number of precedents in international law.

Anglo Norwegian fisheries case United Kingdom *v/s* Norway [1951] ICJ 3, also known as the Fisheries Case, was the culmination of a dispute, originating in 1933, over how large an area of water surrounding Norway was Norwegian waters and how much was 'high seas'.

Anglo Iranian Oil company case The United Kingdom *v/s* Iran [1952] ICJ 2 was a public international law dispute between UK and Iran. This case concerned the nationalisation of Iran's oil which had been, in large part, controlled by the United Kingdom since the early 20th century.

ELCAMANN's case The ELCAMANN's case was a legal dispute that was decided by the International Court of Justice (ICJ) in 1955. It involved a dispute between the Netherlands and Belgium over a parcel of land located near the border between the two countries.

Western Sahara case The International Court of Justice Advisory Opinion on Western Sahara was a 1975 advisory, non-binding opinion by the International Court of Justice of two questions presented to it by the UN General Assembly under Resolution 3292 regarding the disputed territory of Western Sahara.

81 Arrange the expiry term of copyright in an ascending order in following cases.

I. A writes a book on 1.10.2000 and dies on 2.10.2001.
II. A book is written by an anonymous author and published on 1.10.2000. The identify of the author is disclosed on 2.11.2000. Author dies on 3.12.2000.
III. A government work is published on 3.12.2000.
IV. Author dies on 3.12.2000 and his work published on 2.1.2003.
V. A cinematograph film was published on 5.1.1999.

Choose the correct answer from the options given below:

1. V, IV, III, II, I
2. V, III, II, I, IV
3. V, I, II, IV, III
4. V, III, I, II, IV

Ans. (*) This question has been dropped by UGC.

Exp. The correct coding would be V III I II IV.

Case I A writes a book on 1.10.2000 and dies on 2.10.2001.

The copyright term is the author's lifetime plus 60 years. So, it expires on 2.10.2061.

Case II A book is written by an anonymous author and published on 1.10.2000. The identity of the author is disclosed on 2.11.2000. The author dies on 3.12.2000.

Since the author's identity is disclosed and he dies on 3.12.2000, the copyright term is the author's lifetime plus 60 years. So, it expires on 3.12.2060.

Case III A government work is published on 3.12.2000.

The copyright term for government work is 60 years from the date of publication. So, it expires on 3.12.2060.

Case IV Author dies on 3.12.2000 and his work is published on 2.1.2003.

The copyright term is the author's lifetime plus 60 years. Since the author dies on 3.12.2000, the copyright expires on 3.12.2060.

Case V A cinematograph film was published on 5.1.1999.

The copyright term for cinematograph films is 60 years from the date of publication. So, it expires on 5.1.2059.

82 Matters covered under List-I of the Schedule VII of the Constitution.

I. Foreign loan
II. Public health
III. Atomic energy
IV. Public order
V. Insurance

Choose the correct answer from the options given below.

1. I, II, and III
2. I, III and V
3. III, IV and V
4. II, III and IV

Ans. (2)

Exp. Option (2) i.e., I, III and V are correct.

The following matters are covered under List-I of Schedule VII of the Constitution.

a.Foreign loan b. Atomic energy c.Insurance

83 Under Article 15 of the Constitution of India, Special provisions can be made about

I. Women and Children
II. Scheduled Tribes
III. Economically backward classes
IV. Socially backward classes
V. Linguistic minorities

Choose the correct answer from the options given below.

1. I, III, II and V
2. II, III, IV and V
3. I, II, III and IV
4. I, II, III and V

Ans. (3)

Exp. While Article 15 prohibits discrimination on the grounds of sex, special provisions for women and children are permissible. State institutions created exclusively for women, or special places reserved for women in public transport or places of entertainment do not violate Article 15.

84 Indicate the chronological order of the following

I. Genocide Convention
II. Warsaw Pact
III. Montreal Convention of Hijacking
IV. UN Convention on the Rights of the Child
V. Vienna Convention on Diplomatic Relations

Choose the correct answer from the options given below.

1. I, III, II, V, IV
2. I, V, II, III, IV
3. I, II, V, III, IV
4. I, II, III, V, IV

Ans. (3)

Exp. The correct chronological order is I, II, V, III and IV.

Genocide Convention The Genocide Convention (1948) is the first Human Rights treaty in the history of the United Nations, adopted on the eve of the Universal Declaration of Human Rights.

Warsaw Pact The Warsaw Pact, formally the Treaty of Friendship, Cooperation and Mutual Assistance, was a collective defence treaty signed in Warsaw, Poland, between the Soviet Union and seven other Eastern Bloc socialist republics of Central and Eastern Europe in May 1955, during the Cold War.

Vienna Convention on Diplomatic Relations The Vienna Convention on Diplomatic Relations of 1961 is an international treaty that defines a framework for diplomatic relations between independent countries.

Montreal Convention on Hijacking (1971) Under this Convention, the State parties have undertaken that they will provide deterrent punishment to the hijackers. Other provisions are similar to that of the Hague Convention.

UN Convention on Rights of Child The Convention on the Rights of the Child (CRC) was approved by the General Assembly of the United Nations on 20th November 1989.

85 Given below are two statements, one is labelled as Assertion (A) and the other is labelled as Reason (R).

Assertion (A) Law may be unjust though being opposed to the divine good; such laws are the laws of tyrants laws of this kind must no wise be observed.

Reason (R) Exterment order is of no effect and its violation is no offence.

In the light of the above statements, choose the correct answer from the options given below.

1. Both A and R are true and R is the correct explanation of A.
2. Both A and R are true and R is not the correct explanation of A.
3. A is true, but R is false.
4. A is false, but R is true.

Ans. (*) This Question has been dropped by UGC.

Exp. Assertion is true but Reason is false.

An order of externment is not an ordinary measure and it must be resorted to sparingly and in extraordinary circumstances.

86 Given below are two statements, one is labelled as Assertion (A) and the other is labelled as Reason (R).

Assertion (A) From a functional point of view 'an administrative tribunal is neither exclusively a judicial body nor exclusively an administrative body but is somewhere between the two'.

Reason (R) An administrative tribunal is not bound by strict rules of evidence and procedure.

In the light of the above statements, choose the correct answer from the options given below.

1. Both A and R are true and R is the correct explanation of A.
2. Both A and R are true and R is not the correct explanation of A.
3. A is true, but R is false.
4. A is false, but R is true.

Ans. (1)

Exp. Both (A) and (R) are true and (R) is the correct explanation of (A).

In the case of PN Sharma, AIR 1965 SC 1595, Supreme Court held that, a Tribunal may possess some but not all trapping of the Court. From a functional point of view and administrative tribunal is neither exclusively a judicial body nor exclusively an administrative body but is somewhere between the two.

An administrative tribunal is not bound by strict rules of evidence and procedure.

87 Given below are two statements, one is labelled as Assertion (A) and the other is labelled as Reason (R).

Assertion (A) Multilateral treaties which declare the established customary international law may bind even non-parties.

Reason (R) Article 38 of the Vienna Convention makes an exception to Article 34 or 37 of the Vienna Convention.

In the light of the above statements, choose the correct answer from the options given below.

1. Both A and R are true and R is the correct explanation of A.
2. Both A and R are true and R is not the correct explanation of A.
3. A is true, but R is false.
4. A is false, but R is true.

Ans. *(1)*

Exp. Both A and R are true and R is the correct explanation of A.

Non-parties may also bind multilateral treaties which declare the established customary international law. This is because Article 38 of the Vienna Convention makes an exception to Article 34 or 37 of the Vienna Convention.

88 Given below are two statements, one is labelled as Assertion (A) and the other is labelled as Reason (R).

Assertion (A) Mr. X hands over a machine to Y, a common carrier to deliver without any delay to the mill of Mr. X. Y unreasonably delays the delivery of the machine despite being informed that the mill is locked due to lack of machine. As a consequence Mr. X lose a government contract. He is entitled to receive compensation that includes the average amount of profit which he would have made during the time for which the delivery was delayed but not the loss sustained through the lose of the government contract.

Reason (R) Compensation for the loss or damage caused by breach of contract is not to be given for any remote and indirect loss or damage sustained due to such breach.

In the light of the above statements, choose the correct answer from the options given below.

1. Both A and R are true and R is the correct explanation of A.
2. Both A and R are true and R is not the correct explanation of A.
3. A is true, but R is false.
4. A is false, but R is true.

Ans. *(1)*

Exp. Both A and R are true and R is the correct explanation of A.

In the given situation, the reasoning given is correct because as per Section 73 of the Contract Act, compensation is not to be given for any remote and indirect loss or damage sustained by reason of the breach. Compensation for failure to discharge obligation resembling those created by contract.

89 Given below are two statements, one is labelled as Assertion (A) and the other is labelled as Reason (R).

Assertion (A) The Supreme Court in Dev Dutta *v/s* Union of India (2008) emphasised that now transparency and good governance have been added as a new dimension to natural justice which includes the duty to give reason.

Reason (R) Reason reassure that discretion has been exercised by the decision maker on relevant grounds and by disregarding extraneous considerations.

In the light of the above statements, choose the correct answer from the options given below.

1. Both A and R are true and R is the correct explanation of A.
2. Both A and R are true and R is not the correct explanation of A.
3. A is true, but R is false.
4. A is false, but R is true.

Ans. *(1)*

Exp. Both A and R are correct and R is the correct explanation of A.

Dev Dutta *v/s* Union of India- The court directs that the 'good' entry of 1993-94 be communicated to the appellant and he should be permitted to make a representation against the same, requesting its upgradation. The petitioner's representation deserves consideration by an authority higher than the Director General, Border Roads.

90 Given below are two statements, one is labelled as Assertion (A) and the other is labelled as Reason (R).

Assertion (A) Article 38(2) of the Statute of the ICJ states, that "Provision in Article 38(1) shall not prejudice the power, of the court to decide a case Ex Aequo et Bono if parties agree thereto."

Reason (R) Ex Aequo et Bono enable the court to decide upon considerations of fair dealing and good faith. Which may be independent or even contrary to law.

In the light of the above statements, choose the correct answer from the options given below.

1. Both A and R are true and R is the correct explanation of A.
2. Both A and R are true and R is not the correct explanation of A.
3. A is true, but R is false.
4. A is false, but R is true.

Ans. (1)

➲ *Exp.* Both A and R are true and R is the correct explanation of A.

Article 38 states the following

The Court, whose function is to decide in accordance with international law such disputes as are submitted to it, shall apply

a. international conventions, whether general or particular, establishing rules expressly recognised by the contesting states;

b. international custom, as evidence of a general practice accepted as law;

c. the general principles of law recognised by civilised nations;

d. subject to the provisions of Article 59, judicial decisions and the teachings of the most highly qualified publicists of the various nations, as subsidiary means for the determination of rules of law".

This provision shall not prejudice the power of the Court to decide a case ex aequo et bono, if the parties agree thereto".

Directions (Q.Nos. 91-95) *Read the passage carefully and answers the questions that follows.*

One is that power should not be exercised arbitrarily. This has meant that it should be exercised for the purpose for which it has been conferred. It also means that power should be exercised within the statutory ambit and purported exercise of it would not just be ultra vires, but in true sense of the term arbitrary. Simple negation of arbitrariness is, however, not enough to preserve the Rule of Law values. Indian Courts have gone further to insists on specific positive content of the Rule of Law obligations. These include the rules of nature justice which have to be followed not just in quasi-judicial action, but often also in purely administrative action. The scope and content of the requirements of natural justice have varied from time to time according to the judicial interpretation, but the board insistence remains. In addition, access to information as to the grounds of decision has remained an important preoccupation of the Indian judiciary. as any impediments to it have the tendency of obstructing judicial review of administrative action.

This means that the courts have from time to time insisted that exercise of administrative power be accompanied by reasons, although the exact status of the obligation to give reason is as yet indeterminate. The Rule of Law notion has been in addition consistently extended to secure for the individual fair dealing by the state in its economic activities.

91 Under what circumstances powers should be exersised arbitrarily?

1. Under limited circumstances
2. Under unlimited circumstances
3. Under no circumstances
4. As per the policy of the government

Ans. (3)

➲ *Exp.* According the given passage, under no circumstances can the powers be exercised arbitrarily.

92 Rule of Law implies

1. No one is above the law
2. Some people are above the law
3. Everybody is above the law
4. Only government is above the law

Ans. (1)

➲ *Exp.* The Rule of Law implies that no one is above the law.

93 Rule of Law is

1. negation of arbitrariness
2. oppsomal of arbitrariness
3. simple negation of arbitrariness
4. violation of natural justice

Ans. (1)

➲ *Exp.* Rule of Law is negation of arbitrariness. It means the exclusion of the existence of arbitrariness on the part of the government.

94 Specific positive content of the Rule of Law is

1. must be complied with
2. may not be complied with
3. complied in limited content
4. complied under modified circumstances

Ans. (1)

➲ *Exp.* Specific positive content of the Rule of Law must be complied with.

95 Rule of Law notion is extended to secure

1. fair dealing by state in limited activities.
2. fair dealing by state in all its activities.
3. fair dealing by state only in the economic activities.
4. State has no concern.

Ans. (2)

➲ *Exp.* Rule of Law notion is intended to secure the fair dealing by state in all its activities.

Directions (Q.Nos. 96-100) *Read the passage carefully and answers the questions that follows.*

"Where a legal wrong or legal injury is caused to a person or to a determinate class of person by reason of violation of any Constitutional or Legal Right and such person or determinate class of persons is by reason of poverty, helplessness or disability or socially or economically disadvantaged position unable to approach the court for relief, any member of the public can maintain an application for an appropriate direction or order or writ in the High Court under Article 226 or in case of breach of any Fundamental Right to this court under Article 32. Where the weaker section of the community are concerned such as undertrial prisoners languishing in jails without a trial, inmates of the protective home in Agra or Harijan workers engaged in road construction in the district of

Ajmer, who are living in poverty and desolation, Who are barely eking out a miserable existence with their sweat and toil, who are helpless victims of an exploitative society and who do not have easy access to justice. The Supreme Court will not insist on a regular writ petition to be filed by the public spirited individual espousing their cause and seeking relief for them. The Supreme Court will readily respond to the letter addressed by such individual acting *pro bono piblico*. It is true that there are rules made by the Supreme Court prescribing the procedure for moving it for relief under Article 32 and they require various formalities to be gone through by a person seeking to approach it. But it must not be forgotten that procedure is but a handmaid of justice and the cause of justice may never be allowed to be wasted by any procedural technicalities. The Court will therefore unhesitatingly cast aside the technical rules of procedure in the exercise of its dispensing power and treat the letter of the public minded individual as a writ-petition and act upon it."

96 Choose the first case in which the Public Interest Litigation (PIL) was invoked.

1. Sheela Barse *v/s* UOI
2. Bandua Mukti Morcha *v/s* UOI
3. PUDR *v/s* UOI
4. Mumbai Kamgar Sabha *v/s* Abdul Bhai

Ans. *(4)*

➲ *Exp.* The first case in which the concept of Public Interest Litigation was invoked was Mumbai Kamgar Sabha *v/s* Abdul Bhai, which concerned the plight of prisoners awaiting trial.

97 PIL cases are

1. Private Interest cases 2. Personal Interest cases
3. Public Interest cases 4. Permanent Interest cases

Ans. *(3)*

➲ *Exp.* PIL cases are Public Interest cases. Public interest means the interest or right belonging to the society, a particular class of the community or a group of people.

98 Under which Article of the Constitution of India, one can maintain an application to the Supreme Court for an appropriate remedy in PIL cases?

1. Article 226 2. Article 21 3 Article 19 4. Article 32

Ans. *(4)*

➲ *Exp.* Article 32 provides that one can maintain an application to the Supreme Court for an appropriate remedy in PIL cases.

99 Article 32 requires various procedural formalities to be gone through by a person seeking to approach the Supreme Court.

I. It is necessary to follow all technical formalities even in PIL cases.
II. It is not necessary to follow the technical formalities in such cases.
III. The Supreme Court may even treat a letter addressed to it as writ petition in PIL.
IV. Rule of locus standi is not relaxed in such cases.

Choose the correct options.

1. Only II is correct
2. Only II and III are correct
3. Only III is correct
4. Only I and IV are correct

Ans. *(2)*

➲ *Exp.* Only Statements II and III are correct. In PIL cases under Article 32, it is not necessary to follow the technical formalities in such cases. Even a letter sent to the Supreme Court may be considered as a writ petition in PIL.

100 In PIL cases the Supreme Court on a regular writ petition has insisted that it should be filed by a public spirited individual espousing the cause. Choose the correct options.

1. Supreme Court will insists always.
2. Supreme Court may waive this.
3. Supreme Court cannot insist.
4. Person filing the petition should be related to the aggrieved party.

Ans. (*) This Question has been dropped by UGC.

➲ *Exp.* Any Indian citizen or organisation can move the court for a public interest/cause by filing a petition:

1. In the SC under Article 32
2. In the High Courts under Article 226

The court can treat a letter as a writ petition and take action on it. The court has to be satisfied that the writ petition complies with the following: 1. the letter is addressed by the aggrieved person or a public-spirited individual or a social action group for the enforcement of legal or constitutional rights to any person who, upon poverty or disability, are not able to approach the court for redress.

The court can also take action based on newspaper reports if it is satisfied with the case.

UGC-NET LAW SOLVED PAPER 2022 (October)

PAPER II

Direction *This paper contains **hundred** (100) objective type questions of **two (2)** marks each. All questions are compulsory.*

1 In the Constitution of India, the principle of rule of law is mainly embodied in

1 Article 14 2 Article 32
3 Article 226 4 Article 227

Ans. (1)

Exp. In the Constitution of India, the principle of rule of law is mainly embodied in Article 14.

Article 14 of the Constitution of India reads as under: "The State shall not deny to any person equality before the law or the equal protection of the laws within the territory of India."

2 In case of theft under IPC, the following ingredients are necessary.

I. Dishonest intention to take the property.
II. The property can be movable or immovable.
III. Property should be taken without the consent of the person.
IV. There must be some removal of the property.
V. The property must be movable property.

Choose the correct answer from the options given below.

1 I, II, III and IV 2 II, III, IV and V
3 I, III, IV and V 4 I, II, III and V

Ans. (3)

Exp. In case of theft under IPC, the following ingredients are necessary

- Dishonest intention to take away the property.
- The property should be taken without the consent of the person.
- There must be some removal of the property.
- The property must be a movable property.

These essentials satisfy the criteria of Section 378 of IPC which defines theft.

3 Which of tho following arc true with regard to the desertion of spouse under the Hindu Marriage Act, 1955?

I. Factum of separation
II. Animus deserendi
III. Prescribed period of two years must have passed before presentation of petition.
IV. With reasonable cause.
V. Without the consent of the petitioner.

Choose the correct answer from the options given below.

1 I, III, IV and V
2 II, III and IV
3 I, II, III and V
4 I, II and IV

Ans. (3)

Exp. Statements I, II, III and V are true with regard to desertion of spouse under the Hindu Marriage Act, 1955. Desertion means withdrawing from matrimonial obligations. It is a negation of living together which is essence of any matrimonial relationship. It is total repudiation of marital obligations. Following are the essential requirements of desertion

- Factum of separation of one spouse from other.
- Animus deserendi, i.e., intention to desert permanently.
- The deserted spouse must not have agreed to the desertion.
- The desertion must be without reasonable cause.
- This state of affairs must have continued for at least two years.

4 Choose the correct chronological order of the jurists from the earliest to the latest.

I. Austin, Bentham, Pound, Holmes
II. Bentham, Holmes, Austin, Pound
III. Bentham, Austin, Pound, Holmes
IV. Holmes, Austin, Bentham, Pound
V. Bentham, Holmes, Pound, Austin

Codes

1 Only II 2 Either I or II
3 Only III 4 Only V

Ans. (3)

➲ *Exp.* The correct chronological order of the jurists from the earliest to the latest are:

- **Bentham** He was an English philosopher, jurist and social reformer. He was trained as a Lawyer but never practised. He was called to the bar in 1769.
- **Austin** He was an English legal theorist who posthumously influenced British and American law with an analytical approach to jurisprudence and a theory of legal positivism. He was appointed as a Professor of Jurisprudence at the University College London in 1826.
- **Pound** He became dean of the University of Nebraska College of Law in 1903.
- **Holmes** He was an American jurist and legal scholar. He served as an associate justice of the Supreme Court of the United States from 1902 to 1932.

5 Given below are two statements.

Statement I The power of legislation carries with it the power to delegate and unless the legislature has completely abdicated or effaced itself, there is no restriction on delegation of legislative powers.

Statement II Parliament can abdicate or efface itself by creating a parallel legislative body.

In light of the above statements, choose the most appropriate answer from the options given below.

1 Both statement I and statement II are correct.
2 Both statement I and statement II are incorrect.
3 Statement I is correct, but statement II is incorrect.
4 Statement I is incorrect, but statement II is correct.

Ans. *(3)*

➲ *Exp.* Statement I is correct but statement II is incorrect. The power of legislation carries with it the power to delegate and unless the legislature has completely abdicated or effaced itself, there is no restriction on the delegation of legislative powers. Power of delegation is thus ancillary to the power of legislation.

Parliament cannot abdicate or efface itself by creating a parallel legislative body.

6 Consider the following statements.

I. An agreement without consideration is a void contract.
II. An agreement in restraint of marriage is a voidable contract.
III. An unmeaning agreement is a void contract.
IV. An agreement to do impossible acts is a voidable contract.
V. An agreement in restraint of legal proceedings is a void contract.

Choose the correct answer from the options given below.

1 I and III 2 II and IV
3 I, III and V 4 Only V

Ans. *(3)*

➲ *Exp.* Statements I, III and V are correct.

Statement I is correct because according to Section 25, an agreement made without consideration is void.

Statement III is correct because an agreement, the meaning of which cannot be ascertained, is void.

Statement V is correct because Section 28 of the Contract Act bars agreements that impose fetters on a party from initiating legal proceedings or enforcing its rights or reduce the period within which such party may enforce its rights.

7 Arrange the following cases chronologically (starting from the earliest to the latest).

I. National Legal Service Authority *v/s* UOI
II. Naz Foundation *v/s* Govt of NCT
III. Navtej Singh Johar *v/s* UOI
IV. Suresh Kaushal *v/s* Naz foundation
V. The cases of Navtej Singh Johar and Suresh Kaushal were decided in the same year.

Codes

1 III, V, II, IV 2 IV, II, I, III
3 II, IV, I, III 4 V, IV, I, II

Ans. *(3)*

➲ *Exp.* The chronological order of the cases is II, IV, I, III.

Naz Foundation *v/s* Govt of NCT (2009)
Suresh Kaushal *v/s* Naz Foundation (2013)
National Legal Service Authority *v/s* UOI (2014)
Navtej Singh Johar *v/s* UOI (2018)

8 When an unmarried woman adopts a child and subsequently marries the person who she subsequently marries, shall be the

1 adoptive father of the child
2 stepfather of the child
3 natural father of the child
4 Either 1 or 2

Ans. *(2)*

➲ *Exp.* When an unmarried woman adopts a child and subsequently marries, the person who she subsequently marries, shall be the stepfather of the child, as per Section 14 of the Hindu Adoptions and Maintenance Act.

9 Choose the correct chronological order of the emergence of the Schools of Jurisprudence (earliest to the latest).

I. Natural, Historical, Analytical Positivism, Realist
II. Historical, Natural, Realist, Analytical Positivism
III. Analytical Positivism, Historical, Realist, Natural
IV. Realist, Historical, Analytical Positivism, Natural
V. Realist, Natural, Historical, Analytical Positivism

Choose the correct answer from the options given below

1 Only I 2 Only II 3 Only III 4 Only IV

Ans. *(1)*

➲ *Exp.* The correct chronological sequence of the emergence of schools of jurisprudence is option I.

Natural law school was the first to emerge followed by historical, analytical positivism and then the realist school emerged.

10 The Consumer Protection Act, 2019 talks about direct selling, e-commerce and electronic service provider

1 True
2 False
3 Consumer Protection Act, 1986 did not provide about this
4 Both 1 and 3

Ans. (4)

Exp. The Consumer Protection Act, 2019 talks about direct selling, e-commerce and electronic service providers. The said statement is true and the earlier 1986 Act did not have this provision.

11 'General principles of law' recognised by civilised states as a source of international law has been applied in following case.

1 Corfu Channel Case
2 Asylum Case
3 Mavrommatis Palestine Concessions Case
4 Reparations Case

Ans. (3)

Exp. In the Mavrommatis Palestine, Concessions Case, the 'General Principles of Law' recognised by civilised states as a source of international law, was applied.

General principles of law are legal norms existing among the majority of nations. Enduring examples of general principles of law, typically followed in most jurisdictions, are the doctrines of good faith, estoppel and equity.

12 Match List I with List II.

	List I		List II
A.	Theory of Justice	I.	David Hume
B.	Idea of Justice	II.	John Rawls
C.	Nicomachean Ethics	III.	Amartya Sen
D.	An Enquiry Concerning the Principles of Morals	IV.	Aristotle

Choose the correct answer from the options given below.

	A	B	C	D		A	B	C	D
1	I	II	III	IV	2	II	III	I	IV
3	II	III	IV	I	4	II	I	III	IV

Ans. (3)

Exp. The correct matching is A-II, B-III, C-IV, D-I.

Theory of Justice is a 1971 work of political philosophy and ethics by the philosopher John Rawls (1921-2002) in which the author attempts to provide a moral theory alternative to utilitarianism and that addresses the problem of distributive justice (the socially just distribution of goods in a society).

Idea of Justice is a 2009 book by the economist Amartya Sen. The work is a critique and revision of the philosopher John Rowls' 'A Theory of Justice (1971)'.

Nicomachean Ethics is Aristotle's best-known work on ethics, the science of the good for human life, which is the goal or end at which all our actions aim. The aim of the inquiry is political science and the master art of politics. It consists of ten books or scrolls, understood to be based on notes from his lectures at the Lyceum. The title is often assumed to refer to his son Nicomachus, to whom the work was dedicated or who may have edited it (although his young age makes this less likely). Alternatively, the work may have been dedicated to his father, who was also called Nicomachus. The work plays a pre-eminent role in explaining Aristotelian ethics.

An Enquiry Concerning the Principles of Moral's is a book by Scottish enlightenment philosopher David Hume. In it, Hume argues that the foundations of morals lie with sentiment, not reason. 'An Enquiry Concerning the Principles of Morals' is the enquiry subsequent to the enquiry concerning human understanding.

13 ……… has to provide by making regulations for any class or class of companies which may file a shelf-prospectus with the Registrar at the stage of first offer of securities.

1 NCLT
2 SEBI
3 IBBI
4 Director of a company

Ans. (2)

Exp. SEBI has to provide by making regulations for any class or classes of companies which may file a shelf-prospectus with the Registrar at the stage of first offer of securities.

14 The following is/are the exceptions to the principle of strict liability

I. Act of God
II. Consent of the plaintiff
III. Intention of the defendant
IV. Act of third party
V. Minority

Choose the correct answer from the options given below.

1 I and II
2 I, II and IV
3 I, III and IV
4 II and V

Ans. (2)

Exp. Act of god, Consent of plaintiff and Act of third party are the exceptions to the principles of strict liability.

15 Restitution of conjugal rights has its genesis under the

1 English law
2 Indian law
3 Jewish law
4 Swedish law

Ans. (1)

Exp. Restitution of conjugal rights has its genesis under the English law, where marriage was considered as a property deal and wife was part of man's possession like other Chattels.

It can also be said to have its roots in the Jewish law and was implemented in India because of the rule of the British in India.

16 Given below are two statements. One is labelled as Assertion (A) and the other is labelled as Reason (R).

Assertion (A) Nothing is an offence which is done in the exercise of right of private defence.

Reason (R) Z is carried off by a tiger. A fires at the tiger knowing that the shot may kill Z. His shot gives Z a mortal wound. A has not committed any offence.

In light of the above statements, choose the correct answer from the options given below.

1 Both A and R are true and R is the correct explanation of A.
2 Both A and R are true, but R is not the correct explanation of A.
3 A is true, but R is false.
4 A is false, but R is true.

Ans. (1)

Exp. Both Assertion (A) and Reason (R) are true and Reason (R) is the correct explanation of Assertion (A). Nothing is an offence, which is done in the exercise of the right of private defence. Right of private defence cannot be said to be an offence in return. The given reason aptly defines the assertion.

17 The Hicklin test under Article 19(2) is related to

1 Defamation
2 Decency and Morality
3 Integrity of India
4 Negligence

Ans. (2)

Exp. The Hicklin test under Article 19(2) is related to decency and morality. This test examines whether the impugned matter tends to "deprave and corrupt those whose minds are open to such immoral influences, and into whose hands a publication of this sort may fall."

18 Consider the following statements.

I. Courts cannot review the question as to what 'aid and advice' is given by the Council of Ministers to the President.
II. The question of 'aid and advice' by the Council of Ministers is a justifiable issue.
III. Article 14 cannot be worked against discrimination made by constitutional provisions.
IV. The question of 'aid and advice' by the Council of Ministers is a non-justifiable issue.
V. Article 14 can be worked against discrimination made by Constitutional provisions.

Choose the correct answer from the options given below.

1 I, II and III 2 I, III and IV
3 II, III and IV 4 III, IV and V

Ans. (2)

Exp. Only statements I, III and IV are correct. Statements II and V are incorrect as the question of 'aid and advice' by council of ministers is not a justifiable issue, rather, is important to ensure that tyranny does not prevail.

Statement V is incorrect because Article 14 does not allow discrimination.

19 Given below are two statements. One is labelled as Assertion A and the other is labelled as Reason R.

Assertion (A) A bigamous marriage is void under Hindu Law.

Reason (R) A child born out of void marriage is legitimate child of his parents.

In light of the above statements, choose the correct answer from the options given below.

1 Both A and R are true and R is the correct explanation of A.
2 Both A and R are true, but R is not the correct explanation of A.
3 A is true, but R is false.
4 A is false, but R is true.

Ans. (2)

Exp. Both Assertion (A) and Reason (R) are true but Reason (R) is not the correct explanation of Assertion (A) because (R) does not explain why a bigamous marriage is void under the Hindu law.

20 Which of the following doctrines is called as 'Doctrine of Non-recognition'?

1 Estrada Doctrine 2 Hallestein Doctrine
3 Franco Doctrine 4 Stimson Doctrine

Ans. (4)

Exp. Stimson Doctrine is also known as 'Doctrine of Non-recognition.' This Doctrine stated that the United States would not recognise any treaty or agreement between Japan and China that violated US rights or agreements to which the United States subscribed.

21 Every decision of the Goods and Services Tax Council shall require it to be taken at a meeting

1 by a majority of not less than two-thirds of the weighted votes of the members present.
2 by a majority of not less than three-fourths of the weighted votes of the members present.
3 by a majority of not less than two-thirds of the weighted votes of all the members of the council.
4 by a majority of not less than three-fourths of the weighted votes of all the members of the council.

Ans. (2)

Exp. Every decision of the GST council is required to be taken at a meeting by a majority of not less than three-fourths of the weighted votes of the members present. Here the Central government would have the weightage of one third of the total vote cast and the State governments would have a weightage of two-third of the total votes cast.

22 Match List I with List II.

List I	List II
A. Mersey Docke *v/s* Proctor	I. Statutory Authority
B. Metropolitan Asylum District *v/s* Hill	II. Vicarious Liability
C. Nichols *v/s* Marsland	III. Inevitable Accident
D. Holmes *v/s* Mather	IV. Act of God

Choose the correct answer from the options given below.

	A	B	C	D		A	B	C	D
1	II	I	IV	III	2	III	II	I	IV
3	I	II	III	IV	4	IV	II	III	I

Ans. (1)

Exp. The correct matching is A-II, B-I, C-IV, D-III.

Merse Docke *v/s* Proctor Vicarious liability. In this case, it was held that the plaintiff had proved negligence on the part of the defendants, which had caused the death, and accordingly set aside the judgment of Branson J and ordered a new trial.

Metropolitan Asylum District *v/s* Hill Statutory authority In this case a local Municipal Corporation had authority to set up a smallpox hospital. It was held that to establish a smallpox hospital in a residential area was a nuisance and the appellants were prevented from constructing the hospital by issuing an injunction. In such cases, the statutory authority is conditional.

Nichols *v/s* Marsland-Act of God It was held that a defendant is not liable for damage caused by an 'act of God', because he cannot be said to have 'caused' the damage.

Holmes *v/s* Mather-Inevitable accident In this case, while the horses of the defendant were guided by his servant on a public highway, the barking of a dog made the horses run away and they became so insurmountable that the servant could not deter them, but could direct them to some extent. It was considered that no action was necessary by the plaintiff for the servant had done his best under the situation.

23 The doctrine, res-ipsa loquitur was applied by the Supreme Court in

1 Alka *v/s* Union of India
2 Asa Ram *v/s* Municipal Corporation of Delhi
3 Municipal Corporation of Delhi *v/s* Subhagwanti
4 Jasbir Kaur *v/s* State of Punjab

Ans. (3)

Exp. The doctrine of res ipsa loquitur was applied by the Supreme Court in the case of Municipal Corporation of Delhi *v/s* Subhagwanti.

In this case, due to the collapse of the Clock Tower situated opposite the Town Hall in the main bazar of Chandni Chowk, Delhi, a number of persons died. The Clock Tower belonged to the Municipal Corporation of Delhi and was exclusively under its control. It was 80 years' old but the normal life of the structure of the top storey of the building, which had fallen, could be 40-45 years, having regard to the kind of mortar used.

24 The Institution of Ombudsman was first developed in

1 India
2 UK
3 France
4 Sweden

Ans. (4)

Exp. The institution of Ombudsman was first developed in Sweden. When Sweden created the office of Ombudsman in the constitution of 1809, the holder of that office was occupied with civil affairs and was appointed by the legislature.

25 Trade secrets do not cover the following information.

1 commercially valuable
2 production methods
3 business plans
4 information discovered by reverse engineering

Ans. (4)

Exp. Trade secrets do not cover information discovered by reverse engineering.

26 Match List I with List II.

List I	List II
A. Post-modernism	I. Grund norm
B. Source of law	II. Ratio decidendi
C. Authority of a decision as a precedent	III. Critical legal studies
D. Analytical school	IV. Volkgeist

Choose the correct answer from the options given below.

	A	B	C	D		A	B	C	D
1	III	IV	II	I	2	IV	III	II	I
3	II	I	III	IV	4	I	II	IV	III

Ans. (1)

Exp. The correct matching is A-III, B-IV, C-II, D-I.

Post-modernism-Critical legal studies Postmodernity affirms the urgent need for a new form of legal reasoning.

Source of law-Volkgeist Volkgeist as a concept believes in the origin of law from customs followed by people in different communities. It means the general or common consciousness or the popular spirit of the people.

Authority of a decision-Ratio decidendi The ratio decidendi is "the point in a case that determines the judgement" or "the principle that the case establishes".

Analytical school-Grund norm The grund norm delegates authority to inferior norms which derives their validity from the norms superior to themselves. The validity of other inferior norms can be defined by testing against grund norm.

27 Match List I with List II.

List I		List II
A. Voluntarily causing grievous hurt by use of acid	I.	354-A, IPC
B. Voluntarily throwing or attempting to throw acid	II.	326-B, IPC
C. Sexual harassment and punishment for sexual harassment	III.	354-D, IPC
D. Stalking	IV.	326-A, IPC

Choose the correct answer from the options given below.

	A	B	C	D		A	B	C	D
1	IV	II	I	III	2	III	II	IV	I
3	II	III	I	IV	4	III	II	I	IV

Ans. (1)

Exp. The correct matching is A-IV; B-II; C-I; D-III.

Voluntarily causing grievous hurt by use of acid, etc. It is related to Section 326A.

It states that fine shall be just and reasonable to meet the medical expenses of the treatment of the victim.

It provided further that any fine imposed under this section shall be paid to the victim.

Voluntarily throwing or attempting to throw acid It is related Section 326B.

This section has provision for punishment with imprisonment of either description for a term which shall not be less than five years but which may extend to seven years, and shall also be liable to fine.

Sexual harassment and punishment for sexual harassment It is related to Section 354A.

This section provides punishment with rigorous imprisonment for a term which may extend to three years, or with fine, or with both.

Stalking It is related to Section 354D.

Under this section, such conduct shall not amount to stalking if the man who pursued it proves that

(i) it was pursued for the purpose of preventing or detecting crime and the man accused of stalking had been entrusted with the responsibility of prevention and detection of crime by the State; or

(ii) it was pursued under any law or to comply with any condition or requirement imposed by any person under any law; or

(iii) in the particular circumstances such conduct was reasonable and justified.

28 Ordinarily, a delegated legislation can be given

1 prospective effect only
2 retrospective effect only
3 Both prospective and retrospective effect
4 effect as the court may decide

Ans. (1)

Exp. Ordinarily, a delegated legislation can be given a prospective effect only. The Supreme Court observed that a rule or law cannot be construed as retrospective unless it expresses a clear or manifest intention to the contrary. In the absence of express statutory authorisation, delegated legislation in the form of rules or regulations, cannot operate retrospectively.

29 Read the following principles of the Rio-Declaration on Environment and Development (1992) and select the correct answer from the given options.

I. Principle 1– Human beings are at the centre of concerns for sustainable development.

II. Principle 16– In order to protect the environment, the precautionary approach shall be widely applied by states according to their capabilities.

III. Principle 14– Environmental impact assessment shall be undertaken for proposed activities that are likely to have a significant adverse impact on the environment.

IV. Principle 20– Women have a vital role in environmental management and development.

V. Principle 24– Peace, development and environmental protection are interdependent and indivisible.

Choose the correct answer from the options given below.

1 I and IV 2 II and III
3 III and V 4 II and V

Ans. (1)

Exp. Statements I and IV are correct with reference to the principles of Rio-Declaration on Environment and development. Principle 1 of the Rio-Declaration states that human beings are the center of concerns for sustainable development. Statement IV is also correct because Principle 20 states that women have a vital role in environmental management and development.

30 Among the Muslims, Sariri is the stage

1 when the boy or the girl is below 10 years of age.
2 when the boy or the girl is above seven years but below fifteen years.
3 when the boy or the girl is above fifteen years of age.
4 when the boy or the girl is above 10 years of age.

Ans. (2)

Exp. Among the Muslims, Sariri is the stage when the boy or the girl is above seven years but below fifteen years. At this stage, the father can give consent for marriage.

31 Match List I with List II.

List I (Provision)		List II (Section)
A. Void marriage	I.	Section 27, Hindu Marriage Act, 1955
B. Divorce by mutual consent	II.	Section 24, Hindu Marriage Act, 1955
C. Maintenance pendente lite	III.	Section 13 B, Hindu Marriage Act, 1955
D. Disposal of property	IV.	Section 11, Hindu Marriage Act, 1955

Choose the correct answer from the options given below.

	A	B	C	D		A	B	C	D
1	I	III	IV	II	2	IV	III	II	I
3	III	II	I	IV	4	II	I	III	IV

Ans. (2)

Exp. The correct matching is A-IV, B-III, C-II, D-I.

Section 11 of Hindu Marriage Act deals with void marriage It states that any marriage solemnized after the commencement of this Act shall be null and void and may, on a petition presented by either party thereto against the other party, be so declared by a decree of nullity if it contravenes any one of the conditions specified in clauses.

Section 13B of Hindu Marriage Act deals with divorce by mutual consent Subject to the provisions of this Act a petition for dissolution of marriage by a decree of divorce may be presented to the district court by both the parties to a marriage together, whether such marriage was solemnized before or after the commencement of the Marriage Laws (Amendment) Act, 1976 (68 of 1976), on the ground that they have been living separately for a period of one year or more, that they have not been able to live together and that they have mutually agreed that the marriage should be dissolved.

Section 24 of Hindu Marriage Act deals with maintenance pendente lite It states that where in any proceeding under this Act it appears to the court that either the wife or the husband, as the case may be, has no independent income sufficient for her or his support and the necessary expenses of the proceeding, it may, on the application of the wife or the husband, order the respondent to pay to the petitioner the expenses of the proceeding, and monthly during the proceeding such sum as, having regard to the petitioner's own income and the income of the respondent, it may seem to the court to be reasonable.

Section 27 of the Hindu Marriage Act deals with disposal of property It states that in any proceeding under this Act, the court may make such provisions in the decree as it deems just and proper with respect to any property presented, at or about the time of marriage, which may belong jointly to both the husband and the wife.

32 A car was sold on 'as is' basis and without any warranty or guarantee whatever. After 5 days of the contract, the engine of the car blew up. Discuss the liability of the seller.

1 He is liable for the damages due to the doctrine of fundamental breach of standard form of contract.
2 The seller is not liable because the car was sold on 'as is' basis and without any warranty or guarantee.
3 The buyer should take care if he buys a second-hand car.
4 Under standard form contract, in this case, contributory negligence is applicable.

Ans. (1)

Exp. In the given situation, the seller is liable for damages due to the doctrine of fundamental breach of standard form of contract.

33 Match List I with List II.

List I	List II
A. Doctrine of Pith and Substance	I. What cannot be done directly, cannot be done indirectly.
B. Doctrine of Incidental Encroachment	II. The part of statute which is bad cannot be severed from the rest.
C. Doctrine of Severability	III. A law is not invalid even though trenched incidentally to another list.
D. Doctrine of Colourable Legislation	IV. True nature and character of the legislation.

Choose the correct answer from the options given below.

	A	B	C	D		A	B	C	D
1	I	II	III	IV	2	IV	III	I	II
3	III	II	IV	I	4	IV	III	II	I

Ans. (4)

Exp. The correct matching is A-IV, B-III, C-II and D-I.

The Doctrine of pith and substance refers to the true nature and character of the legislation.

Doctrine of incidental encroachment states that a law is not invalid even though trenched incidentally through another list.

Doctrine of severability states that the part of the statute which is bad cannot be severed from the rest, letting the remaining part continue to be operative.

Doctrine of colourable legislation states that what cannot be done directly, cannot be done indirectly either.

34 Who defined ownership as 'plenary control over an object'?

1 Roscoe Pound 2 Holmes 3 Holland 4 Paton

Ans. (3)

Exp. Holland defined ownership as 'plenary control over an object.' He says, ownership is exercised, in its primary sense of the term, a man may be owner of a patent for an invention. The object owned is in either case described as 'property'.

35 Under which article of the Constitution of India, it is the duty of the union to protect every State against external aggression and internal disturbance and to ensure that the government of every state is carried on, in accordance with the provisions of the Constitution of India?

1 Article 353 2 Article 354
3 Article 355 4 Article 356

Ans. (3)

Exp. According to Article 355, it shall be the duty of the Union to protect every State against external aggression and internal disturbance and to ensure that the government of every State is carried on in accordance with the provisions of this Constitution.

36 Who said, "A legal person, is any subject matter other than a human being to which law attributes personality"?

1 Salmond | 2 Holmes
3 Jerome Frank | 4 Pound

Ans. (1)

Exp. Salmond said, "A legal person is any subject matter other than a human being to which law attributes personality." It includes an object, a mass of property, an institution, a group of human beings etc. Law treats them as right and duty bearing units or entities like a natural person.

37 Who said that there are two elements of possession, (a) Corpus possessionis and (b) Animus domini?

1 Ihering | 2 Paton
3 Savigny | 4 Salmond

Ans. (3)

Exp. Savigny said that there are two elements of possession i.e., a. Corpus possessionis b. Animus domini

According to Savigny, the essence of possession is to be found in the physical power of exclusion. He maintained that possession is consisted of two elements, namely,

- corpus possessionis, i.e., physical control,
- animus domini, i.e., an intention to hold as owner.

38 Which of the following is incorrect?

1 An agreement not enforceable by law is said to be voidable.
2 An agreement enforceable by law is a contract.
3 Every promise and every set of promises forming the consideration for each other is an agreement.
4 An agreement not enforceable by law is said to be void.

Ans. (1)

Exp. An agreement not enforceable by law is said to be voidable. This statement is incorrect as an agreement not enforceable by law is void and not voidable.

39 The National Green Tribunal Act, 2010 came into force on

1 10th May, 2010 | 2 18th August, 2010
3 10th December, 2010 | 4 18th October, 2010

Ans. (4)

Exp. National Green Tribunal (NGT) came into force on 18th October 2010 under the NGT Act of 2010 as a specialised body for handling any environmental disputes that involve multi-disciplinary issues. It was formed by replacing the National Environment Appellate Authority.

40 The Competition Act, 2002, provides for which of the following?

I. Establishment of a commission to prevent practices having effect on competition.
II. To promote and sustain competition in markets.
III. To protect the interests of consumers.
IV. To ensure freedom of trade carried on by the other participants in the markets.
V. To establish NCLT and NCLAT to decide various matters.

Choose the correct answer from the options given below.

1 I, II, III, IV and V
2 II, III and IV
3 III, IV and V
4 I, II, III and IV

Ans. (4)

Exp. Statements I, II, III, and IV are correct according to competition Act, 2002.

Statement V is incorrect because NCLT and NCLAT have been established under the Companies Act and not under the Competition Act.

41 Arrange in chronological order the case laws pertaining to cruelty under the Hindu Marriage Act, 1955 (year wise from beginning till the latest).

I. Durga Prasanna Tripathy *v/s* Arundhati Tripathy
II. Bhagwat *v/s* Bhagwat
III. Parveen Mehta *v/s* Inderjeet Mehta
IV. Swapan Kumar Das *v/s* Maya Rani Dutta
V. Satendra Kumar Gupta *v/s* Kanchan Gupta and Others

Choose the correct answer from the options given below.

1 II, III, I, IV, V | 2 I, III, II, IV, V
3 III, IV, I, II, V | 4 IV, III, II, I, V

Ans. (1)

Exp. The correct chronological order is II, III, I, IV, V.

Bhagwat *v/s* Bhagwat (2001)

Parveen Mehta *v/s* Inderjeet Mehta (2002)

Durga Prasanna Tripathy *v/s* Arundhati Tripathy (2005)

Swapan Kumar Das *v/s* Maya Rani Dutta (2006)

Satendra Kumar Gupta *v/s* Kanchan Gupta and Others (2015)

42 National Commission for Backward Classes has been created through which Amendment to the Constitution of India?

1 100th Amendment
2 101st Amendment
3 102nd Amendment
4 103rd Amendment

Ans. (3)

Exp. Through the 102nd Amendment Act, the National Commission for Backward classes has been created that provides constitutional status to the National Commission for Backward Classes (NCBC).

43 Consider the following statements.

I. Freedom of trade, commerce and intercourse is covered in Article 301.
II. Restrictions on legislative powers of the union and states with regard to trade and commerce are covered in Article 302.
III. Power of Parliament to impose restrictions on trade, commerce and intercourse is covered in Article 302.
IV. Restrictions on trade, commerce and intercourse among states are covered in Article 304.
V. Appointment of authority for carrying out the purposes of Article 301-304 is enshrined in Article 306.

Choose the correct answer from the options given below.

1 I, II and III
2 II, III and IV
3 I, III and IV
4 II, IV and V

Ans. (3)

➲ *Exp.* Only statements I, III and IV are correct.

Statement II is incorrect because Article 302 provides for Power of Parliament to impose restrictions on trade, commerce and intercourse.

Statement V is incorrect because Article 306 (now repealed) dealt with the power of certain states in Part B of the first schedule to impose restrictions on trade and commerce.

44 Every state and every local authority within the state is required to provide adequate facilities for instruction in the mother-tongue at the primary stage of education to children belonging to linguistic minority groups under.

1 Article 350
2 Article 350 A
3 Article 350 B
4 Article 351

Ans. (2)

➲ *Exp.* Article 350A provides that it shall be the endeavour of every state and of every local authority within the state to provide adequate facilities for instruction in the mother-tongue at the primary stage of education to children belonging to linguistic minority groups. The President may issue such directions to any state as he considers necessary or proper for securing the provision of such facilities.

45 Given below are two statements.

Statement I "All human beings are not legal persons".

Statement II "State is a juristic person".

In light of the above statements, choose the most appropriate answer from the options given below.

1 Both statements I and II are correct.
2 Both statements I and II are incorrect.
3 Statement I is correct, but statement II is incorrect.
4 Statement I is incorrect, but statement II is correct.

Ans. (1)

➲ *Exp.* Both statements I and II are correct.

All human beings are not legal persons. In olden days, the slaves were not considered legal persons. They were treated as chattel of their masters. A person who takes religious or holy order for some purposes is considered to be civilly dead in many societies.

The State is a juristic person under law.

46 Which of the following is false?

1 A contract is frustrated where the actual and specific subject matter of the contract has ceased to exist.
2 A contract will frustrate where circumstances arise which make the performance of the contract impossible in the manner contemplated.
3 A contract which required personal performance by promisor is frustrated on the death of the promisor.
4 Ceasing of subject matter of contract does not frustrate the contract.

Ans. (4)

➲ *Exp.* Statement 4 is false because ceasing of subject matter of contract frustrates the contract.

47 Which of the following is/are not administrative actions?

1 Internment, Externment and Deportation
2 Functions of a Selection Committee
3 Fact-Finding Action
4 Forming Opinion on Objective Satisfaction

Ans. (4)

➲ *Exp.* Forming Opinion on Objective Satisfaction does not constitute an administrative action.

48 Given below are two statements.

Statement I An appeal shall lie in the Supreme Court from any judgement, final order or sentence in a criminal proceeding of a High Court in the territory of India, if the High Court has on appeal reversed an order of acquittal of an accused person and sentenced him to death.

Statement II An appeal shall lie in the Supreme Court from any judgement final order or sentence in a criminal proceeding of a High Court in the territory of India, if the High Court has withdrawn from trial before itself any case from any court subordinate to its authority and has in such a trial convicted the accused person and sentenced him to death.

In light of the above statements, choose the most appropriate answer from the options given below.

1 Both statements I and II are correct.
2 Both statements I and II are incorrect.
3 Statement I is correct, but statement II is incorrect.
4 Statement I is incorrect, but statement II is correct.

Ans. (1)

➲ *Exp.* Both the statements I and II are correct. They are self-explanatory.

49 Pacta Terties Nec Nocent Nec Prosunt means

1 Multilateral treaties prevail over bilateral treaties.
2 Treaties are no binding in case of situations of emergency.
3 Only parties to an international treaty are bound by it.
4 The right of innocent passage cannot be thwarted by bilateral treaties.

Ans. (3)

➲ *Exp.* Pacta Terties Nec Nocent Nec Prosunt means that only parties to an international treaty are bound by it.

50 Greenhouse effect means increase in atmospheric temperature due to the concentration of greenhouse

1 gases in the atmosphere.
2 growing vegetables and flowers in increased temperature.
3 growing food crops in glass houses.
4 photosynthesis in plants grown in sunlight received in the glass house.

Ans. (1)

➲ *Exp.* Greenhouse effect refers to an increase in the atmospheric temperature due to the concentration of greenhouse gases in the atmosphere.

51 Which one of the following is correct?

1 A public company can be formed with a minimum of nine persons.
2 A private company can be formed with two or more persons.
3 Memorandum of Association is not required or registration of a company.
4 Articles of Association is not required for registration of a company.

Ans. (2)

➲ *Exp.* Only statement 2 here is correct. A private company can be formed with just two or more persons.

52 Given below are two statements. One is labelled as Assertion A and the other is labelled as Reason R.

Assertion (A) The ex post-facto laws are law which voided and punished an act that had been lawful when done.

Reason (R) Imposing or increasing a penalty with retrospective affect for violation of a taxing statute does not infringe Article 20(1).

In light of the above statements, choose the correct answer from the options given below.

1 Both A and R are true and R is the correct explanation of A.
2 Both A and R are true, but R is not the correct explanation of A.
3 A is true, but R is false.
4 A is false, but R is true.

Ans. (3)

➲ *Exp.* Assertion (A) is true because an ex post facto law is a law that retroactively changes the legal consequences of actions that were committed, or relationships that existed, before the enactment of the law. Reason (R) is false because imposing or increasing a penalty with retrospective effect does violate Article 20(1) of the Constitution.

53 Match List I with List II.

List I	List II
A. Bonn Convention	I. Protection of the ozone layer.
B. Vienna Convention	II. Control of transboundary movements of hazardous wastes and their disposal.
C. Basel Convention	III. Conservation of migratory species of wild animals.
D. Rotterdam Convention	IV. Prior informed consent procedure for certain hazarduous chemicals and pesticides in international trade.

Choose the correct answer from the options given below.

	A	B	C	D		A	B	C	D
1	II	I	IV	III	2	III	I	II	IV
3	IV	II	I	III	4	I	II	III	IV

Ans. (2)

➲ *Exp.* The correct matching is A-III, B-I, C-II and D-IV.

The Convention on the Conservation of Migratory Species of Wild Animals, also known as the Convention on Migratory Species or the **Bonn Convention**, is an international agreement that aims to conserve migratory species throughout their ranges.

The **Vienna Convention** on the Law of Treaties is an international agreement regulating treaties between states on the protection of ozone layer, known as the "treaty on treaties", it establishes comprehensive rules, procedures, and guidelines for how treaties are defined, drafted, amended, interpreted, and generally operated.

The **Basel Convention** on the Control of Transboundary Movements of Hazardous Wastes and Their Disposal, usually known as the Basel Convention, is an international treaty that was designed to reduce the movements of hazardous waste between nations, and specifically to prevent transfer of hazardous waste from developed to Less Developed Countries (LDCs).

The **Rotterdam Convention** is a multilateral treaty to promote shared responsibilities in relation to importation of hazardous chemicals.

54 Arrange the following in chronological order starting from earlier to later years.

I. The Trade Marks Act II. The Patents Act
III. The Design Act IV. The Copyright Act
V. The Protection of Plant Varieties and Farmers' Rights Act

Choose the correct answer from the options given below.

1 I, II, III, IV, V
2 II, IV, I, V, III
3 IV, II, I, III, V
4 I, II, III, V, IV

Ans. (3)

➲ *Exp.* The correct chronological order for the given legislations is IV, II, I, III, V.

- Copyright Act, 1957.
- Patents Act, 1970.
- Trade Marks Act, 1994.
- Design Act, 2000.
- Protection of Plant Varieties and Farmers' Rights Act, 2001.

55 'Voluntarily' has been defined as an effect caused by means whereby a person intended to cause it or by means at the time of employing those means, to know or had reason to believe to be likely to cause it under

1 Section 35, IPC 2 Section 36, IPC
3 Section 39, IPC 4 Section 40, IPC

Ans. (3)

➲ *Exp.* Section 39, IPC- 'Voluntarily'–A person is said to cause an effect 'voluntarily' when he causes it or by means whereby he intended to cause it, or by means which, at the time of employing those means, he knew or had reason to believe to be likely to cause it.

56 The law relating to armed conflicts of non-international character is governed by

1 Common Article 3 of the Geneva Convention, 1949, or The Additional Protocol I, 1977
2 Common Article 3 of the Geneva Convention, 1949 or the Additional Protocol II, 1977
3 Additional Protocols I and II, 1977
4 only Additional Protocol I, 1977

Ans. (2)

➲ *Exp.* The law relating to armed conflicts of non-international character is governed by common Article 3 of the Geneva Convention 1949 of Addition Protocol II, 1977.

Non-international armed conflicts are provided for and governed by Common Article 3 to the four Geneva Conventions of 1949 and by the Additional Protocol II of 1977 to the Geneva Conventions. This Convention contains twenty-eight articles that complete the guarantees of Common Article 3 for the victims of non-international armed conflicts.

57 Select the right answer from the given options.

I. COP 26 - Glasgow Climate Change Conference
II. COP 25 - Lima Climate Change Conference
III. COP 24 - Marrakesh Climate Change Conference
IV. COP 22 - Katowice Climate Change Conference
V. COP 21 - Paris Climate Change Conference

Choose the correct answer from the options given below.

1 I and V 2 II and III
3 II and IV 4 III and IV

Ans. (1)

➲ *Exp.* Pairs I and V are correctly matched. COP26 relates to Glasgow Climate Change Conference while COP 21 relates to the Paris Climate Change Conference. These conferences are very important in determining the global agenda for sustainable development and climate change.

Pairs II, III and IV are incorrectly matched.

COP 25 is related to Madrid Climate Change Conference.

COP 24 is related to Katowice Climate Change Conference.

COP 22 is related to Marrakesh Climate Change Conference.

58 Who amongst the following can be appointed as the Chairperson of the National Human Rights Commission (NHRC)?

1 Only a person who has been the Chief Justice of the Supreme Court.
2 A person who has been the Chief Justice of the Supreme Court or a Judge of the Supreme Court.
3 A person who has been the Chief Justice of a High Court.
4 A person who has been a Judge of the High court.

Ans. (2)

➲ *Exp.* A person who has been the Chief Justice of the Supreme Court or a Judge of the Supreme Court can be appointed as the chairperson of National Human Rights Commission.

59 Which of the following can be registered as a trade mark?

1 Mark devoid of distinctive character
2 A distinctive mark
3 A mark causing confusion
4 Oval shape or medicinal tablet

Ans. (2)

➲ *Exp.* Out of the given options, only a distinctive mark can be registered as a trade mark. It is a sign capable of distinguishing the goods or services of one enterprise from those of other enterprises.

60 Match List I with List II.

List I	List II
A. Solomon *v/s* Solomon	I. Voting rights
B. Royal British Bank *v/s* Turquand	II. Corporate personality
C. Ashbury Railway Carriage and Iron *v/s* Riche (Ashbury)	III. Doctrine of Ultra Vires
D. Vodafone International Holdings *v/s* UOI	IV. Doctrine of indoor management

Choose the correct answer from the options given below.

	A	B	C	D
1	IV	II	III	I
2	I	II	III	IV
3	I	III	II	IV
4	II	IV	III	I

Ans. (4)

➲ *Exp.* The correct matching is A-II, B-IV, C-III, D-I.

Solomon *v/s* Solomon The court also upheld firmly the doctrine of corporate personality, as set out in the Companies Act 1862, so that creditors of an insolvent company could not sue the company's shareholders to pay up outstanding debts.

Royal British Bank *v/s* Turquand It is a UK company law case that held people transacting with companies are entitled to assume that internal company rules are complied with, even if they are not. This "indoor management rule" or the "Rule in Turquand's Case" is applicable in most of the common law world.

Ashbury Railway Carriage and Iron Co Ltd *v/s* Riche (Ashbury) 7 HL 653 is a UK company law case, which concerned the objects clause of a company's memorandum of association.

Vodafone International Holdings *v/s* UOI The court observed that Section 195 of the Income-tax Act only applies to residents and can't have extraterritorial jurisdiction. The court observed that as the transaction took place between two non-residents companies and that happened outside India thus having no direct nexus or Voting right with India.

61 Which of the following is not correct under the Geographical Indications of Goods (Registration and Protection) Act, 1999?

1 Producer, in case of agricultural goods, includes the person who produces the goods.
2 Producer, in case of agricultural goods, includes the person who packages such goods.
3 Producer, in case of natural goods, includes the person who exploits such goods.
4 Producer in case of handicrafts, includes the person who packages such goods.

***Ans.** (4)*

➲ *Exp.* Option (4) is not correct under the Geographical Indications of Goods (Registration and Protection) Act, 1999. Under the GI Act, producer, in case of handicrafts, does not include the person who packages such goods.

62 Match List I with List II.

List I		List II
A. Application of the act to electronic cheque and truncated cheque	I.	Section 3A
B. Electronic signature	II.	Section 81A
C. Secure electronic record	III.	Section 15
D. Validity of contracts formed through electronic means	IV.	Section 10A

Choose the correct answer from the options given below.

	A	B	C	D		A	B	C	D
1	I	II	III	IV	2	II	I	III	IV
3	II	I	IV	III	4	IV	III	II	I

***Ans.** (2)*

➲ *Exp.* The correct matching is A-II, B-I, C-III, D-IV.

Section 81A The provisions of this Act, for the time being in force, shall apply to, or in relation to, electronic cheques and the truncated cheques subject to such modifications and amendments as may be necessary for carrying out the purposes of the Negotiable Instruments Act, 1881 (26 of 1881), by the Central Government, in consultation with the Reserve Bank of India, by notification in the Official Gazette.

Section 3A Electronic signature

(i) notwithstanding anything contained in section 3, but subject to the provisions of sub-section.
(ii) a subscriber may authenticate any electronic record by such electronic signature or electronic authentication technique which
  (a) is considered reliable; and
  (b) may be specified in the second schedule.

Section 15 Secure electronic signature: An electronic signature shall be deemed to be a secure electronic signature if

(i) the signature creation data, at the time of affixing signature, was under the exclusive control of signatory and no other person; and
(ii) the signature creation data was stored and affixed in such exclusive manner as may be prescribed.

In case of digital signature, the 'signature creation data' means the private key of the subscriber.

Section 10A Validity of contracts formed through electronic means wherein a contract formation, the communication of proposals, the acceptance of proposals, the revocation of proposals and acceptances, as the case may be, are expressed in electronic form or by means of an electronic records, such contract shall not be deemed to be unenforceable solely on the ground that such electronic form or means was used for that purpose.

63 The test of reasonable foresight in determining remoteness of damages was first applied in

1 Re: Polemis
2 Wagon Mound Case
3 Doughty *v/s* Turner Manufacturing Co Ltd
4 SCM (United Kingdom) Ltd *v/s* WJ Whittal and Sons

***Ans.** (2)*

➲ *Exp.* The test of reasonable foresight in determining the remoteness of damages was first applied in Wagon Mound Case. If a foreseeable type of damage is present, the defendant is liable for the full extent of the damage, no matter whether the extent of damage was foreseeable.

64 Given below are two statements.

Statement I Hart deals with primary rules of obligation and secondary rules of recognition.

Statement II Hart has nothing to do with the reformulation of analytical positivism.

In light of the above statements, choose the most appropriate answer from the options given below.

1 Both statement I and statement II are correct.
2 Both statement I and statement II are incorrect.
3 Statement I is correct, but statement II is incorrect.
4 Statement I is incorrect, but statement II is correct.

Ans. (3)

Exp. Statement I is correct but statement II is incorrect. Statement I is self-explanatory. Statement II is incorrect because Hart was one of the founding proponents of analytical positivism.

65 Every partner of a partnership firm is liable for all the acts of the firm done while he is a partner. This doctrine is called

1 the doctrine of holding out
2 the doctrine of restitution
3 the doctrine of estoppel
4 the doctrine of proportionality

Ans. (1)

Exp. The 'Doctrine of holding out' states that every partner of a partnership firm is liable for all the acts of the firm done while he is a partner. This has also been enshrined under the Partnership Act.

66 Nottebohm's case deals with nationality by

1 naturalisation 2 birth
3 resumption 4 subjugation

Ans. (1)

Exp. Nottebohm's case deals with nationality by naturalisation. In this case, the court held that Liechtenstein's claim was inadmissible on grounds relating to Mr. Nottebohm's nationality. It was the bond of nationality between a state and an individual which alone conferred upon the state the right to put forward an international claim on his behalf.

67 Given below are two statements.

Statement I Every public company shall have at least three directors and every private company shall have at least two directors.

Statement II There can be a maximum of 15 directors and for having more than 15 directors, the company may pass a special resolution.

In light of the above statements, choose the most appropriate answer from the options given below.

1 Both statement I and statement II are correct.
2 Both statement I and statement II are incorrect.
3 Statement I is correct, but statement II is incorrect.
4 Statement I is incorrect, but statement II is correct.

Ans. (1)

Exp. In the given statements I and II are correct. The given statements are self-explanatory.

68 Given below are two statements.

Statement I A contract which ceases to be enforceable by law becomes void when it ceases to be enforceable.

Statement II An agreement in restraint of trade is voidable.

In light of the above statements, choose the correct answer from the options given below:

1 Both statement I and statement II are true.
2 Both statement I and statement II are false.
3 Statement I is true, but statement II is false.
4 Statement I is false, but statement II is true.

Ans. (3)

Exp. Statement I is true and self-explanatory, but statement II is false because an agreement in restraint of trade is not voidable, instead, it is void.

69 Given below are two statements.

Statement I Personal rights are inheritable.

Statement II Legal rights are recognised and enforced by law.

In light of the above statements, choose the most appropriate answer from the options given below.

1 Both statement I and statement II are correct.
2 Both statement I and statement II are incorrect.
3 Statement I is correct, but statement II is incorrect.
4 Statement I is incorrect, but statement II is correct.

Ans. (4)

Exp. Statement I is incorrect but statement II is correct. The statement I is incorrect because personal rights are not inheritable. Statement II is correct and it is self-explanatory.

70 Match List I with List II.

List I	List II
A. Judicial review	I. Indira Gandhi *v/s* Raj Narayan
B. Free and fair election	II. Keshavananda Bharati *v/s* State of Kerala
C. Balance between Part III and Part IV of the Constitution	III. SR Bommai *v/s* Union of India
D. Secularism	IV. Minerva Mills Ltd *v/s* Union of India

Choose the correct answer from the options given below.

	A	B	C	D		A	B	C	D
1	I	III	IV	II	2	II	I	IV	III
3	IV	I	III	II	4	III	IV	I	II

Ans. (2)

Exp. The correct matching is A-II, B-I, C-IV and D-III.

Keshavanandha Bharati *v/s* State of Kerala case propounded the feature of judicial review as a part of the basic structure of the Constitution.

Indira Gandhi *v/s* Raj Narayan held that free and fair elections constitute the hallmark of democracy and thus, is a part of the basic structure.

Minerva Mills Ltd and Ors. ***v/s*** **Union Of India and Ors** is a landmark decision of the Supreme Court of India that applied and evolved the basic structure doctrine of the Constitution of India. In the Minerva Mills case, the Supreme Court provided key clarifications on the interpretation of the basic structure doctrine.

SR Bommai ***v/s*** **Union of India** is a landmark decision of the Supreme Court of India, where the court discussed at length provisions of Article 356 of the Constitution of India and related issues. This case had huge impact on Centre-State Relations.

71 Given below are two statements. One is labelled as Assertion A and the other is labelled as Reason R.

Assertion (A) The President of India is a mere constitutional head.

Reason (R) In the parliamentary form of government, the Prime Minister is the head of government.

In light of the above statements, choose the correct answer from the options given below.

1 Both A and R are true and R is the correct explanation of A.
2 Both A and R are true, but R is not the correct explanation of A.
3 A is true, but R is false.
4 A is false, but R is true.

Ans. (2)

Exp. Both Assertion (A) and Reason (R) are true but Reason (R) is not the correct explanation of Assertion (A). The President of India is a mere constitutional head, however, the same is not explained through the reason given here. It is true that the prime minister is the head in the parliamentary form of government but it doesn't explain the Assertion (A).

72 Arrange the following Protocols/Declarations in the correct chronological sequence.

I. Kyoto Protocol
II. Cartagena Protocol on Biosafety
III. Montreal Protocol
IV. Nagoya Protocol
V. Rio Declaration on Environment and Development

Choose the correct answer from the options given below.

1 V, I, II, III, IV
2 V, II, III, IV, I
3 V, III, I, II, IV
4 V, IV, III, II, I

Ans. (*)

Exp. The correct sequence is III, V, I, II, IV.

The **Montreal Protocol** is an international treaty designed to protect the ozone layer by phasing out the production of numerous substances that are responsible for ozone depletion. It was agreed on 16 September 1987, and entered into force on 1 January 1989.

The **Rio Declaration on Environment and Development** was approved by the United Nations during the Conference on Environment and Development held in Rio de Janeiro on June 1992. It was aimed at reaffirming the Declaration of the United Nations Conference on the Human Environment, adopted at Stockholm on June 1972.

The **Kyoto Protocol** (1997) was an international treaty which extended the 1992 United Nations Framework Convention on Climate Change that commits state parties to reduce greenhouse gas emissions, based on the scientific consensus that global warming is occurring and that human-made CO_2 emissions are driving it.

The **Cartagena Protocol on Biosafety** to the Convention on Biological Diversity is an international agreement on biosafety as a supplement to the Convention on Biological Diversity effective since 2003.

The **Nagoya Protocol** on Access to Genetic Resources and the Fair and Equitable Sharing of Benefits Arising from their Utilization to the Convention on Biological Diversity, also known as the Nagoya Protocol on Access and Benefit Sharing is a 2010 supplementary agreement to the 1992 Convention on Biological Diversity.

73 Which of the following is not a ground of divorce available to wife under section 13(2) of the Hindu Marriage Act, 1955?

1 Pre-Act Bigamous marriage of the husband
2 Repudiation of marriage
3 Cruelty by husband
4 Husband guilty of rape, sodomy and bestiality

Ans. (1)

Exp. Pre-Act Bigamous act of the husband will not constitute a ground for divorce under the Hindu Marriage Act, 1955, since the act has a prospective application.

74 Given below are two statements. One is labelled as Assertion A and the other is labelled as Reason R.

Assertion (A) A master is liable for all tortious acts of his servants done in the course of employment.

Reason (R) The representatives of the dead person are in certain cases liable for the acts of the deceased.

In light of the above statements, choose the most appropriate answer from the options given below:

1 Both A and R are true and R is the correct explanation of A.
2 Both A and R are true, but R is not the correct explanation of A.
3 A is false, but R is true.
4 A is true, but R is false.

Ans. (2)

Exp. Both Assertion (A) and Reason (R) are true but Reason (R) is not the correct explanation of Assertion (A).

This is because Reason (R) highlights another legal fact altogether without explaining the reason as to why are masters liable for the acts of their servants.

75 Match List I with List II.

List I		List II
A. Ramsar convention	I.	1992
B. Convention on biological diversity	II.	1994
C. Minamata convention	II.	1991
D. The United Nations convention to combat desertification	IV.	2013

Choose the correct answer from the options given below.

	A	B	C	D		A	B	C	D
1	III	II	IV	I	2	IV	II	III	I
3	III	I	IV	II	4	II	I	IV	III

Ans. (*)

Exp. This question is dropped by NTA.

76 In which one of the following cases, legal aid was held as a Fundamental Right?

1 Sunil Batra case
2 MH Hoskot case
3 Prem Shankar Shukla case
4 Kesavananda Bharati case

Ans. (2)

Exp. In the MH Hoskot case, legal aid was held to be a Fundamental Right for the first time in India, it established the right of prisoners to free legal assistance under Article 21 of the Constitution's liberty provision.

77 Given below are two statements.

Statement I It is the duty of the Prime Minister to communicate to the President all decisions of the Council of Ministers relating to the administration of the affairs of the union and proposals for legislations.

Statement II It is the duty of the Prime Minister to furnish such information relating to the administration of the affairs of the union and proposals or legislation as the President may call for.

In light of the above statements, choose the correct answer from the options given below.

1 Both statement I and statement II are true.
2 Both statement I and statement II are false.
3 Statement I is true, but statement II is false.
4 Statement I is false, but statement II is true.

Ans. (1)

Exp. Both the given statements I and II are correct and they are self-explanatory.

78 Which one of the following is not one of the modes of termination of agency?

1 Insolvency of principal
2 Principal or Agent's death
3 General Lien
4 Revocation

Ans. (3)

Exp. General Lien will not constitute one of the ways to terminate an agency. All the other options are different modes of terminating agency.

79 Given below are two statements.

Statement I A childless stepmother is entitled a claim maintenance under the Hindu Adoption and Maintenance Act, 1956.

Statement II Under the Hindu Adoption and Maintenance Act 1956, if the son is to be adopted, the adoptive father or mother should not have a Hindu son, son's son or son's son's son (whether by legitimate blood relationship or by adoption) living at the time of adoption.

In light of the above statements, choose the most appropriate answer from the options given below.

1 Both statement I and statement II are correct.
2 Both statement I and statement II are incorrect.
3 Statement I is correct, but statement II is incorrect.
4 Statement I is incorrect, but statement II is correct.

Ans. (1)

Exp. Both the given statements I and II are correct and they are self-explanatory.

80 The word 'Environment' has been defined under which of the section of the Environment (Protection) Act, 1986?

1 Section 2(a) 2 Section 2(e)
3 Section 2(d) 4 Section 2(b)

Ans. (1)

Exp. The word 'Environment' has been defined under Section 2(a) of the Environment (Protection) Act, 1986. 'Environment' includes water, air and land and the inter-relationship which exists among and between water, air and land, and human beings, other living creatures, plants, micro-organism and property.

81 Given below are two statements.

Statement I Holland defines ownership as plenary control over an object.

Statement II Ownership is either vested or contingent.

In light of the above statements, choose the most appropriate answer from the options given below.

1 Both statements I and II are correct.
2 Both statements I and II are incorrect.
3 Statement I is correct, but statement II is incorrect.
4 Statement I is incorrect, but statement II is correct.

Ans. (1)

Exp. Both the given statements I and II are correct. The statements are self-explanatory.

82 Given below are two statements.

Statement I Imperative law means 'a concept of the rule of action imposed upon men by some authority which enforces obedience to it'.

Statement II Natural law signifies the principles of natural right and wrong.

In light of the above statements, choose the most appropriate answer from the options given below.

1 Both statements I and II are correct.
2 Both statements I and II are incorrect.
3 Statement I is correct, but statement II is incorrect.
4 Statement I is incorrect, but statement II is correct.

Ans. (1)

Exp. Both the given statements I and II are correct. The statements are self-explanatory.

83 Under Article 338(5) of the Constitution of India, National Commission for Scheduled Castes has

1 the power to issue caste certificates.
2 the power to revoke caste certificates.
3 the power to decide validity of caste certificates.
4 no power to issue/revoke certificates and has no power to decide upon the validity of caste certificates.

Ans. (4)

Exp. Under Article 338(5) of the Constitution, National Commission for Scheduled Castes has no power to issue/revoke certificates and also does not have any power to decide on the validity of caste certificates.

84 In order to establish a cartel, what is not necessary?

1 There should be an agreement.
2 It should be between an association of producers, sellers, distributors, traders or service providers.
3 The objective should be to limit, control or attempt to control the product distribution, sale or price of or trade in goods or provisions of services.
4 Cartels are very good for competition.

Ans. (4)

Exp. To establish a cartel, it is not necessary that Cartel should be very good for competition. It is immaterial whether cartels are good or bad for business.

85 Given below are two statements.

Statement I For judicial review, 'irrationality' means that the decision is so outrageous in its defiance of logic or accepted moral standards, that no sensible person could have arrived at such a decision.

Statement II For judicial review, 'unreasonableness' means either the facts do not warrant the conclusion reached by the authority or the decision is partial and unequal in its operation.

In light of the above statements, choose the most appropriate answer from the options given below.

1 Both statements I and II are correct.
2 Both statements I and II are incorrect.
3 Statement I is correct, but statement II is incorrect.
4 Statement I is incorrect, but statement II is correct.

Ans. (1)

Exp. Both the given statements I and II are correct. The statements are self-explanatory.

86 Given below are two statements.

Statement I A becomes surety to C for B's conduct as a manager in C's bank. Afterwards, B and C contract, without A's consent that B's salary shall be raised and that he shall become liable or one-fourth of the losses on overdrafts. B allows a customer to overdraw and the bank loses a sum of money.

Statement II A is liable a make good the loss as he is a surety a C for B's conduct.

In light of the above statements, choose the most appropriate answer from the options given below.

1 Both statements I and II are correct.
2 Both statements I and II are incorrect.
3 Statement I is correct, but statement II is incorrect.
4 Statement I is incorrect, but statement II is correct.

Ans. (3)

Exp. Statement 1 is correct, but statement II is incorrect because A will not be liable to make good this loss as he is not a surety for this act of C.

87 The children born out of a void Hindu marriage, are in the eyes of law

1 illegitimate
2 legitimate
3 illegitimate, having no rights in the ancestral property.
4 legitimate but having right of inheritance limited to their parent's property only.

Ans. (4)

Exp. Children born out of a void Hindu marriage are legitimate in the eyes of the law but their right of inheritance is limited to their parent's property only.

88 In the light of the Criminal Law (Amendment) Act 2013, which of the following statements is correct?

1 The word 'rape' in section 375 IPC has been replaced with 'sexual assault'.
2 Rape is now a gender-neutral offence.
3 The Amendment has fixed the age for consensual sex as 16 years.
4 The Amendment has fixed the age for consensual sex as 18 years.

Ans. (4)

Exp. In light of Criminal Law (Amendment) Act, 2013, the amendment has fixed the age for consensual sex to be 18 years.

89 Given below are two statements.

Statement I A 'negotiable instrument' means a promissory note, bill of exchange or cheque payable either to order or to bearer.

Statement II Holder means any person who for consideration became the possessor of a promissory note, bill of exchange or cheque, if payable to bearer or the payee or endorsee.

In light of the above statements, choose the most appropriate answer from the options given below.

1 Both statements I and II are correct.
2 Both statements I and II are incorrect.
3 Statement I is correct, but statement II is incorrect.
4 Statement I is incorrect, but statement II is correct.

Ans. (3)

Exp. Statement I is correct and self-explanatory, but II is incorrect because the 'holder' of a promissory note, bill of exchange or cheque means any person entitled in his own name to the possession there of and to receive or recover the amount due there on from the parties there to.

90 Article 13 of the Constitution of India does not apply to

1 any legislation made by the Parliament under Article 245 of the Constitution.
2 any legislation made by the Parliament under Article 253 of the Constitution giving effect to international agreements.
3 any amendment of the Constitution made under Article 368.
4 custom and usage.

Ans. (3)

Exp. Article 13 of the Constitution does not apply to any amendment of the Constitution made under Article 368.

Direction (Q.Nos. 91-95) *Read the given passage carefully and answer the questions that follow.*

The binding force of International Law is based on the supreme fundamental norm or principle known as *Pacta sunt servanda*. This means that agreements entered into by states will be respected and followed by them in good faith. This is a well established and recognised custom of International Law. The customary principle of International Law has now been codified and finds mention in Article 26 of the Vienna Convention on the Law of Treaties, 1969.

The principle of *Pacta sunt servanda* is also based on the actual practice of the states. It emphasises the importance of the agreement entered into by states and regards them as the basis of international law.

There is a view that to assert the binding force of international law is based only on the principle of *Pacta sunt servanda* is far from the truth. It fails to explain the binding force of customary rules of international law which are not based on agreement between States. The realisation that international customary law does not rest on agreements and that the tenet, *Pacta sunt servanda* is itself a rule of customary law, led to new formulations of the basic norm.

Kelsen has decided on a formula which takes into account usage, as the fact which is the origin of the rules of International Law - 'States ought to behave as they have customarily behaved'.

91 The codification of *Pacta sunt servanda* finds a mention in which Article of the Vienna Convention on the Law of Treaties, 1969?

1 It does not find mention in the Vienna Convention on the Law of Treaties, 1969
2 Article 26
3 Article 2
4 Article 47

Ans. (2)

Exp. The codification of *Pacta sunt servanda finds a mention in* Article 26-It is under this very heading that the principle of '*Pacta sunt servanda*' is established. This article is under Part III, section 1 of the Vienna Conventions which lays out all the principles. The party must observe when entering a treaty.

92 To which docs, the passage give primacy, *Pacta sunt servanda* or the principles of Customary International Law?

1 *Pacta sunt servanda.*
2 Principles of customary international law.
3 Both *Pacta sunt servanda* and the principles of customary international law.
4 Neither *Pacta sunt servanda* nor principles of customary international law.

Ans. (2)

Exp. The passage gives primacy to the principles of customary international law over '*Pacta sunt servanda.*'

93 Kelsen focuses on

1 Primacy of *Pacta sunt servanda.*
2 State behaviour being in conformity with customary international law.
3 *Pacta sunt servanda* being responsible for the growth of customary international law.
4 *Pacta sunt servanda* being independent of the principles of customary international law.

Ans. (2)

Exp. Kelsen focuses on state behaviour being in conformity with customary international law. Kelsen's monistic theory of law, according to which international and municipal law have the same subject-matter, paved the way for the dominant contemporary doctrine. International law can encompass every aspect of human life which warrants international legal protection of human rights.

94 Which of the following is correct?

1 *Pacta sunt servanda* is an absolute principle.
2 *Pacta sunt servanda* covers unequal treaties also.
3 *Pacta sunt servanda* is not an absolute principle as it fails to explain the binding force of customary rules of international law.
4 *Pacta sunt servanda* explains the binding force of customary rules of international law.

Ans. (3)

Exp. The '*Pacta sunt servanda*' principle is not correct, because it is deviated by other laws or legal principles.

95 The literal meaning of *Pacta sunt servanda* is

1 Pacts are sacred.
2 Pacts are good servants.
3 Pacts need not be observed.
4 Agreements must be observed.

Ans. (4)

Exp. The literal meaning of *'Pacta Sunt Servanda'* is that agreements must be kept. Without such a rule, no international agreement would be binding or enforceable.

Direction (Q.Nos. 96-100) *Read the given passage carefully and answer the questions that follow.*

"In England justice goes to the people, in India, the people had to come to justice." The litigant had to find his way to his strange tribunal in an unknown land as best he could, in charge of the police, whose tender mercies he dreaded, or alone.

If he went alone, it was not for long. Around the courts were swarms of petty lawyers who had their touts on the roads and in the villages. Longer he came within hail of the court he had been fastened upon by several of these, and persuaded that his only chance of success was to put himself in their hands, say what they bade him, pay what, when, and to whom they told him, and above all, to beware of telling the truth, it would never be believed. In those strange cases there was no common ground. Whatever one side asserted that other denied, all the witnesses were tutored, and whether true or not to begin with the case as presented on both sides was invariably concocted.

I for one came the conclusion that nearly all, save a few of the graver cases, were episodes in some dispute not before the court. The parties were not the real parties, but puppets a others, who remained in the back ground paying for and directing the proceedings. Most of the genuine disputes never reached our courts at all, but were settled at some earlier stage in other ways.

While we dispensed justice as best as we could to those who came before us, we knew that an enormous number of injured persons never came to us at all.

Many were deterred by difficulties in the way, many dared not come for fear of offending the local despot, who by threats of injuries - threats which he could carry out was able to prevent them from complaining and to stop the mouths of their witness.

96 In the passage, it is said that all the genuine disputes never reached the courts.

Choose the correct answer.

1 Most of the genuine disputes never reached the courts.
2 Parties to the cases were not the real parties in many cases.
3 Many witnesses are not the real witnesses.
4 Real parties were puppets of others and not the real parties.

Ans. (1)

Exp. According to the given passage statement (1) is correct answer as most of the genuine disputes never reached the courts.

97 Many injured persons never came to the courts because of the following reason.

1 They were deterred by difficulties in the way.
2 They had no interest.
3 They were not sure to win.
4 They could not arrange witnesses.

Ans. (1)

Exp. Many injured persons never came to the courts because they were deterred by difficulties in the way.

98 What are the chances of success of any litigant?

1 The chance of success work only if he puts the hands of petty lawyers and touts.
2 He need not beware of telling the truth.
3 Cases on both sides were usually not concocted.
4 There were no difficulties and the injured person could approach the court easily.

Ans. (1)

Exp. The chances of success work are only if he puts the hands of petty lawyers and touts into work here as they will know the nuances of the law and help the litigant in securing a verdict in his favour.

99 What are the challenges for a litigant to seek justice in India and England?

1 There are no challenges. The passage is silent about this.
2 There are many challenges that are difficult to summarise.
3 In England, justice goes to the people. In India, the litigant faces many difficulties in approaching the strange tribunal to seek justice.
4 The way to the tribunal is easy and the litigant in India need nor dread at all.

Ans. (3)

Exp. In England, justice goes to the people, in India, the litigant faces many obstacles in approaching the strange tribunal to seek justice.

100 Whether, in the strange cases, there were any common grounds?

1 There was no common ground.
2 All grounds are common.
3 Witnesses were not tutored.
4 All witnesses were tutored.

Ans. (1)

Exp. No, there were no common grounds in the strange cases.

UGC-NET LAW

SOLVED PAPER 2021 (November)

PAPER II

1 "Every man has a property in his own person, he has right to preserve his property, that is, his wife, liberty and estate" ...... is said by

1 Bentham 2 Henry Main
3 Locke 4 Laski

Ans. (3)

Exp. According to Locke "Every man has a property in his own person. Every individual has the right to preserve his property, that is, his wife, liberty and estate."

In a narrower sense, the property includes the proprietary rights of a person and not his rights. Proprietary rights constitute his estate or property, whereas, personal rights include his status or personal condition. If viewed from the lens of a narrower sense, then only land, chattels, shares, and debts are personal property and not his life, liberty or reputation. This is the most commonly used interpretation of property in modern times.

2 Under Muslim law, divorce by common consent is known as

I. Talaq-e-Tafwid II. Khula
III. Lian IV. Mubarat

Choose the correct answer from the options given below

1 Only I, II and IV 2 Only II and IV
3 Only III and IV 4 Only I and II

Ans. (2)

Exp. Under Muslim law, divorce by common consent is known as Khula or Mubarat.

In both these forms, the wife agrees to part or let go of her dower or a part of some other property. As per Muslim Law, in a case of mutual consent divorce, the wife needs to pay some compensation for dissolving the matrimonial union.

3 Amendment in the American Constitution may be proposed by

I. Congress with a two-third majority in both the Houses or Representatives and the Senate.
II. Congress with a 3/4 majority in both the Houses of Representatives and the Senate.
III. Constitutional convention called by two-thirds of State Legislatures.
IV. Constitutional convention called by three-fourth of State Legislatures.

Choose the most appropriate answer from the options given below

1 Only I and III 2 Only II and III
3 Only II and IV 4 Only I and IV

Ans. (1)

Exp. Statements I and III are correct regarding amendments in the American Constitution.

Article V of the Constitution provides two ways to propose amendments to the Constitution. Amendments may be proposed either by the Congress, through a joint resolution passed by two-third vote, or by a convention called by Congress in response to applications from two-thirds of State Legislature.

Statements II and IV are incorrect.

The Constitution provides that an amendment may be proposed either by the Congress with a two-thirds majority vote in both the House of Representatives and the Senate or by a constitutional convention called for by two-thirds of the State legislatures.

According to Article V, The Congress, whenever two thirds of both Houses shall deem it necessary, shall propose Amendments to this Constitution, or, on the application of the Legislatures of two thirds of the several States, shall call a Convention for proposing amendments, which, in either case, shall be valid to all intents and purposes, as part of this Constitution, when ratified by the Legislatures of three fourths of the several States, or by Conventions in three fourths thereof, as the one or the other mode of ratification may be proposed by the Congress.

4 Which one of the following Geneva conventions has the provisions on, "The protection of the victims of maritime warfare"?

1 The Second Geneva Convention, 1949
2 The Third Geneva Convention, 1949
3 The Fourth Geneva Convention, 1949
4 The First Geneva Convention, 1949

Ans. (1)

Exp. The Second Geneva Convention, 1949 has the provisions on "The protection of the victims of maritime warfare". This Convention replaced the Hague Convention of 1907 for the adaptation to maritime warfare of the Principles of the Geneva Convention. It closely follows the provisions of the first Geneva Convention in structure and content. It has 63 articles specifically applicable to war at sea. For example, it protects hospital ships. It has one annex containing a model identity card for medical and religious personnel.

5 Which one of the following is related to Amendment of the U.S. Constitution?

1 Article III 2 Article IV
3 Article V 4 Article VI

Ans. (3)

Exp. Article V is related to the amendment of the US Constitution. Article V of the U.S. Constitution provides two ways of amending our Constitution:

1. Congress proposes amendments and sends them to the States for ratification (this was done with our existing 27 Amendments); or
2. Congress calls a convention for proposing amendments if 2/3rd of the State Legislatures apply for it.

However, Congress has never called a convention under Article V.

6 The National Commission for women shall perform some of the following functions

I. Shall fund litigations involving issues affecting a large body of women.

II. Shall provide, financial assistance to all those who are self-employed.

III. Shall call for specific studies or investigation in to specific problems.

IV. Shall impose punishment to those found involved in discrimination of women.

V. Shall investigate and examine all matters relating to the safeguards provided for women under the Constitution and other laws.

Choose the correct answer from the options given below :

1 I, III and V
2 II, IV and V
3 I, II and IV
4 V, I and II

Ans. (1)

Exp. Statements I, III and V are correct.

The National Commission for women shall perform the following functions:

- It shall fund litigations involving issues affecting a large body of women.
- It shall call for specific studies or investigation in to specific problems.
- It shall investigate and examine all matters relating to the safeguards provided for women under the Constitution and other laws.

Statements I and IV are incorrect.

The Commission cannot inflict punishment. According to Rule 17 of National Commission for Women (Procedure) Regulations, 2005, where the inquiry discloses the commission of violence of any right by a public servant, it may recommend to the concerned government or authority the initiation of proceedings for the prosecution or such other actions as the Commission may deem fit against the concerned person/persons.

7 Chronologically arrange (Article wise) the following provisions of the Constitution of India.

I. Special provisions with respect to the state of Sikkim.

II. Special provisions with respect to the state of Karnataka.

III. Special provisions with respect to the state of Manipur.

IV. Special provisions with respect to the state of Nagaland.

Choose the correct answer from the options given below :

1 III, IV, I, II 2 IV, III, II, I
3 IV, III, I, II 4 III, IV, II, I

Ans. (3)

Exp. The correct chronological order is IV, III, I and II.

Article 371-A makes special provision with respect to the State of Nagaland to protect the Nagas. According to this Article, notwithstanding anything in this Constitution, no Act of Parliament in respect of religious or social practices of the Nagas, Naga customary law and procedure, administration of civil and criminal justice involving decisions according to Naga customary law, ownership and transfer of land and its resources shall apply to the State of Nagaland unless the Legislative Assembly of Nagaland by a resolution so decides.

Article 371-C makes special provisions for Manipur whereby the President is authorised to provide for the creation of a committee of the Manipur Legislative Assembly consisting of the members elected from the Hill Areas of the state.

Article 371-F contains special provisions with respect to Sikkim. The Sikkim Legislative Assembly is to consist of not less than 30 members. One seat is allotted to Sikkim in the Lok Sabha and Sikkim forms one Parliamentary constituency.

Article 371-J contains special provisions with respect to the state of Karnataka. Under Article 371-J, the President is empowered to provide that the Governor of Karnataka would have special responsibility for the reservation in state government posts in the region for persons who belong to the region.

8 Match List I with List II.

List I (Books)	List II (Jurists)
A. The Growth of the Law	I. H. Cairns
B. The Theory of Legal Science	II. Cardozo
C. An Introduction to the Principles of Morals and Legislation	III. John Rawls
D. The Law of Peoples	IV. Jeremy Bentham

Codes

	A	B	C	D
1	I	II	III	IV
2	II	I	IV	III
3	I	III	IV	II
4	II	III	I	IV

Ans. (2)

Exp. The correct matching is A-II, B-I, C-IV, D-III.

The Growth of the Law is a book by Cardozo. In this book, Judge Cardozo discusses the twofold need of law today-first, a scientific restatement that will bring certainty out of the wilderness of precedent; second, a philosophy that will supply a principle of growth.

The Theory of Legal Science is written by H. Cairns. This book is a brilliant statement for the possibilities of the scientific approach in regard to social institutions in general and to the sociology of law in particular. It was originally published in 1941.

An Introduction to the Principles of Morals and Legislation is written by Jeremy Bentham. It was originally printed in 1780, and first published in 1789. This book is Bentham's 'most important theoretical work,' as it is where Bentham developed his theory of utilitarianism and is the first major book on the topic.

The Law of Peoples is a book by John Rawls. He was an American moral and political philosopher. The book was originally published in 1993 but was revisited and expanded in 1999. This book is of particular significance as it played a key part in encouraging others to think about and explore different models of global justice.

9 The distinctive features of 'Rioting' are an activity, which is accompanied by

1 Use of force and violence
2 Causing alarm
3 Violence for a common purpose
4 Use of abusive language

Ans. (1)

Exp. The distinctive features of 'Rioting' are an activity, which is accompanied by the use of force and violence. According to Section 146 of Indian Penal Code, whenever force or violence is used by an unlawful assembly, or by any member thereof, in prosecution of the common object of such assembly, every member of such assembly is guilty of the offence of rioting.

10 Which of the following statements are correct?

I. Global justice inquires about what justice among human beings consists in.
II. Global justice inquiries take individual human beings as of primary concern and seek to give an account of what fairness among such agents involves.
III. In the domain of global justice, theorists seek primarily to define justice between states or nations.
IV. In international justice the nation or state is taken as the central entity of concern and justice among nations or states is the focus.

Choose the correct answer from the options given below

1 I, II and III
2 I, II and IV
3 I, III and IV
4 II, III and IV

Ans. (2)

Exp. Statements I, II and IV are correct.

Statement III is incorrect because in International justice the nation or state is taken as the central entity of concern and justice among nations or states is the focus. In the domain of global justice, by contrast, theorists do not seek primarily to define justice between states or nations.

11 Section 53 of Consumer Protection Act of 2019, provides for establishment of National Consumer Disputes Redressal Commission. It is to be known as

1 National Commission
2 National Council
3 National Dispute Redressal Commission
4 National Dispute Redressal Council

Ans. (1)

Exp. Section 53 of Consumer Protection Act of 2019, provides for establishment of National Consumer Disputes Redressal Commission. It is to be known as National Commission.

According to Section 53 of Consumer Protection Act 2019, the Central Government shall, by notification, establish a National Consumer Disputes Redressal Commission, to be known as the National Commission.

12 Nothing in TRIPS agreement, 1995 shall derogate from the existing obligations prescribed under

I. Paris Convention, 1967
II. Rome Convention, 1961
III. Berne Convention, 1971
IV. Biodiversity Convention, 1992
V. Integrated Circuit Treaty, 1989

Choose the correct answer from the options given below

1 I, II, III, IV 2 II, III, IV, V

3 I, II, III, V 4 V, IV, III, I

Ans. (3)

Exp. Nothing in TRIPS agreement, 1995 shall derogate from the existing obligations prescribed under Paris Convention, 1967, Rome Convention, 1961, Berne Convention, 1971, Integrated Circuit Treaty, 1989.

According to Article 2 of the TRIPS Agreement, nothing in Part I to IV of this Agreement shall derogate from existing obligations that Members may have to each other under the Paris Convention, the Berne Convention, the Rome Convention and the Treaty on Intellectual Property in Respect of Integrated Circuits.

13 The term private key refers to

1 Authentication of any electronic record by a subscriber.

2 Electronic signature certificate issued under Section 35.

3 Key pair in an asymmetric crypto system.

4 Key of key pair used to create a digital signature.

Ans. (4)

Exp. The term private key refers to key of key pair used to create a digital signature.

According to Section 2(n) of the Certification Practice Statement (CPS), 'Private Key' means the key of a key pair used to create a digital signature.

14 'Stalking' (Following a women despite her disinterest, spying, etc) is an offence under

1 Section 354 (1) (ii) IPC

2 Section 354 B IPC

3 Section 354 A (1) (iii)

4 Section 354 D IPC

Ans. (4)

Exp. 'Stalking' (following a woman despite her disinterest, spying, etc) is an offence under Section 354 D of IPC. According to Section 354 D, any man who

(i) follows a woman and contacts, or attempts to contact such woman to foster personal interaction repeatedly despite a clear indication of disinterest by such woman.

(ii) monitors the use by a woman of the internet, email or any other form of electronic communication, commits the offence of stalking.

15 State Emergency or President Rule under Article 356 can be imposed in a State by the President for a maximum period of

1 3 years extendable by 1 year

2 2 years

3 6 months

4 1 year

Ans. (1)

Exp. State Emergency or President Rule under Article 356 can be imposed in a State by the President for a maximum period of 3 years extendable by 1 year.

Article 356 empowers the President of India to issue a proclamation if he is satisfied that administration of a state cannot be carried out in the present circumstance under the constitutional framework. Notably, while issuing such a proclamation, the President can act based upon a report of the Governor or also without any receipt of such a report of the Governor.

16 Which of the following groups of Jurists who consider the law as a command of sovereignty enforced by a superior political authority and accordingly subscribe to the view that International Law is not law as 'properly so called'?

1 Starke, Salmond, Holland

2 Hart, Starke, Oppenheim

3 Holland, Oppenheim, Hart

4 Hobbes, Pufendorf, Austin

Ans. (4)

Exp. Hobbes, Pufendorf and Austin constitute that group of Jurists who consider the law as a command of sovereignty enforced by a superior political authority and accordingly subscribe to the view that International Law is not law as 'properly so called'.

According to Austin, law is the command of the sovereign punished by sanctions in case the command is violated by the individual. There must be a legislative authority enacting the rule of conduct and enforcing physical sanction. So based on what he said, it can be concluded that any rule, which is not enacted by any superior or legislative authority, cannot be regarded as a law and moreover, if laws are violated, sanctions must be imposed.

Hobbes and Pufendorff are also of the view that International Law is not a true law as the law is not truly invested with true legal force and it is not backed by the command of a superior.

17 Given below are two statements

Statement I No person except the father or mother of a child shall have the capacity to give the child in adoption under the Hindu Adoptions and Maintenance Act 1956.

Statement II Under the Hindu Adoptions and Maintenance Act 1956, the same child may not be adopted simultaneously by two or more persons. In the light of the above statements, choose the most appropriate answer from the options given below

1 Both Statement I and Statement II are correct.

2 Both Statement I and Statement II are incorrect.

3 Statement I is correct but Statement II is incorrect

4 Statement I is incorrect but Statement II is correct

Ans. (4)

Exp. Statement I is incorrect but Statement II is correct.

Statement I is incorrect because as per Section 9(1) of the Hindu Adoption and Maintenance Act, no person except the father or mother or the guardian of a child shall have the capacity to give the child in adoption. Thus, by virtue of Section 9 (1) of the Act, only the father or mother or the guardian of a child has the capacity to give the child in adoption.

Under the Hindu Adoptions and Maintenance Act 1956, the same child may not be adopted simultaneously by two or more persons.

18 Arrange the following in chronological order.

I. United Nations Conference on the Human Environment

II. United Nations Conference on Sustainable Development

III. United Nations Conference on Environment and Development

IV. World Commission on Environment and Development

V. United Nations Sustainable Development

Choose the correct answer from the options given below :

1 I, II, III, IV, V
2 II, I, IV, III, V
3 I, IV, III, II, V
4 V, IV, II, III, I

Ans. (3)

Exp. The correct chronological order is I, IV, III, II, V.

The United Nations Conference on the Human Environment was held in Stockholm, Sweden, from 5th-16th June in 1972 when the United Nations General Assembly decided to convene the 1972 Stockholm Conference, taking up the offer of the Government of Sweden to host it.

UNEP succeeded in establishing, through the General Assembly, a World Commission on Environment and Development and in 1988 outlined an environmental program to set priorities for the 1990–95 period. International conferences, such as the United Nations Conference on Environment and Development (the 'Earth Summit'), held in Rio de Janeiro in 1992, have continued to focus attention on environmental issues.

United Nations Conference on Environment and Development (UNCED), byname Earth Summit, conference held at Rio de Janeiro, Brazil (3rd-14th June, 1992), to reconcile worldwide economic development with protection of the environment.

The United Nations Conference on Sustainable Development took place in Rio de Janeiro, Brazil on 20th-22nd June, 2012. It resulted in a focused political outcome document, which contains clear and practical measures for implementing sustainable development.

Originally launched in 2017 by the United Nations Sustainable Development Group (UNSDG), this refreshed version of the Toolkit is designed to provide UN Country Teams, policy experts and Governments with access to existing tools for accelerating progress toward the 2030 Agenda.

The tools can also support immediate socio-economic response to the COVID-19 pandemic, as well as effective recovery planning and implementation. The Toolkit is managed jointly by UNICEF and UNDP under the auspices of the UNSDG Task Team on Integrated Policy Support.

19 'Cyber security' is defined under which section of Information Technology Act, 2000?

1 Section 2 (ua)
2 Section 2 (za)
3 Section 2 (nb)
4 Section 2 (tb)

Ans. (3)

Exp. 'Cyber security' is defined under Section 2(nb) of Information Technology Act, 2000. Accordingly, 'cyber security' means protecting information, equipment, devices computer, computer resource, communication device and information stored therein from unauthorised access, use, disclosure, disruption, modification or destruction.

20 The main purpose of corporation sole is

1 To protect the property of the Government
2 To make the property easily transferable
3 To make the property easily inheritable
4 To make continuity of an office

Ans. (4)

Exp. The main purpose of corporation sole is to make continuity of an office.

Corporation sole is a legal entity consisting of a sole incorporated office, occupied by a single man/woman and it has legal continuity. A corporation sole consists of one person only, and the successors of that person in some particular station or office.

21 Which among the following is the most serious offence, and thus severely punishable?

1 Unlawful Assembly
2 Rioting
3 Affray
4 Assault

Ans. (2)

Exp. Among the given options, Rioting is the most serious offence and is thus severely punishable.

According to Section 146 of Indian Penal Code, whenever force or violence is used by an unlawful assembly, or by any member thereof, in prosecution of the common object of such assembly, every member of such assembly is guilty of the offence of rioting.

22 Removal of members of Company Law Appellate Tribunal can be carried out in consultation by

I. Central Government

II. Chief Justice

III. Chairperson of Appellate tribunal

IV. Auditor General

Choose the correct answer from the options given below :

1 Only I and II
2 I, II and III
3 Only III and II
4 I, II, III and IV

Ans. (1)

Exp. Removal of members of National Company Law Appellate Tribunal can be carried out in consultation by the Central Government and Chief Justice of India.

Section 417(1) of the Companies Act, 2013 provides that the Central Government may, after consultation with the Chief Justice of India, remove from office the President, Chairperson or any Member, who

(a) has been adjudged an insolvent; or
(b) has been convicted of an offence which, in the opinion of the Central Government, involves moral turpitude; or
(c) has become physically or mentally incapable of acting as such President, the Chairperson, or Member; or
(d) has acquired such financial or other interest as is likely to affect prejudicially his functions as such President, the Chairperson or Member; or
(e) has so abused his position as to render his continuance in office prejudicial to the public interest:

Provided that the President, the Chairperson or the Member shall not be removed on any of the grounds specified in clauses (b) to (e) without giving him a reasonable opportunity of being heard.

23 Consumer, Mediation Cell has to hold which of the following documents?

I. List of empanelled mediators
II. List of all cases handled by the cell
III. Records of all proceedings
IV. Information specified by regulations

Choose the correct answer from the options given below :

1 Only I and II 2 Only II and IV
3 Only III and IV 4 I, II, III and IV

Ans. (4)

Exp. Consumer, Mediation Cell has to hold list of empanelled mediators, list of all cases handled by the cell, records of all proceedings and information specified by regulations. Section 74 of the Consumer Protect Act, 2019 deals with the establishment of a Mediation Cell.

It states that :

1. The State Government shall establish, by notification, a consumer mediation cell to be attached to each of the District Commissions and the State Commissions of that State.
2. The Central Government shall establish, by notification, a consumer mediation cell to be attached to the National Commission and each of the regional Benches.
3. A consumer mediation cell shall consist of such persons as may be prescribed.
4. Every consumer mediation cell shall maintain-
   - a list of empanelled mediators;
   - a list of cases handled by the cell;
   - record of proceeding; and
   - any other information as may be specified by regulations.

24 The geographical indications are distinctive signs or indications which identify any goods as

I. Act of unfair competition under Paris Convention, 1967.
II. Originating in a specified territory.
III. Stipulate the misleading test guaranteeing a negative right.
IV. Specific quality, reputation and characteristics.
V. Essentially attributable to origin.

Choose the correct answer from the options given below :

1 I, II and III 2 III, IV and V
3 I, IV and II 4 II, IV and V

Ans. (4)

Exp. The geographical indications are distinctive signs or indications which identify any goods as originating in a specified territory, specific quality, reputation and characteristics and essentially attributable to origin. Geographical indications and trademarks are distinctive signs used to distinguish goods or services in the marketplace. Both convey information about the origin of a good or service in a specified terirtory and enable consumers to associate a particular quality with a good or service. Trademarks inform consumers about the source of a good or service.

25 Which of the following statement/statements is/are correct?

I. When a State is defeated or conquered, all the citizens acquire the Nationality of the conquering State. This is called 'cession' mode of gain of nationality.
II. When a person gets Nationality of a State in place of the Nationality of another State. This is called 'substitution' mode of loss of nationality.
III. The Public Trustee case is related to statelessness.
IV. The General Assembly decided to convene a conference to conclude, a convention on reduction of statelessness in 1961.

Choose the most appropriate answer from the options given below:

1 Only II and III 2 I, II and III
3 I, III and IV 4 I, II, III and IV

Ans. (1)

Exp. Statements II and III are correct.

Statements I is incorrect as when a state is defeated or conquered, all the citizens acquire the nationality of the conquering state through the mode of 'Subjugation' and not 'cession'.

Statements IV is incorrect because the General Assembly decided to convene a conference to conclude a convention on reduction of statelessness in 1954.

26 Who among the following can remove the name of company from Register of Companies on suo moto basis in terms of Section 248(1) of Companies Act, 2013?

1 Registrar of Companies
2 Securities and Exchange Board of India
3 National Company Law Tribunal
4 Ministry of Corporate Affair

Ans. (1)

Exp. The Registrar of Companies can remove the name of a company from the Register of Companies on suo moto basis in terms of Section 248(1) of Companies Act, 2013. The Companies Act, 2013 provides two modes of strike-off – namely Strike off by the ROC under Section 248(1) of the Companies Act 2013, and Strike off by a company on its own accord under Section 248(2) of the Companies Act, 2013.

27 Match list I with List II.

List I (Definitions of)	List II (Provisions under Information Technology Act, 2000)
A. Computer	I. Section 2 (g)
B. Computer Network	II. Section 2 (k)
C. Certifying Authority	III. Section 2 (j)
D. Computer Resource	IV. Section 2 (i)

Codes

	A	B	C	D
1	I	II	III	IV
2	II	I	IV	III
3	IV	III	I	II
4	III	IV	II	I

Ans. (3)

Exp. The correct matching is A-IV, B-III, C-I, D-II.

Section 2(i) of Information Technology Act, 2000 defines the term 'Computer'. 'Computer' means any electronic, magnetic, optical or other high-speed data processing device or system which performs logical, arithmetic and memory functions by manipulations of electronic, magnetic or optical impulses and includes all input, output, processing, storage, computer software or communication facilities which are connected or related to the computer in a computer system or computer network.

Section 2(j) of Information Technology Act, 2000 defines the term 'Computer network'. 'Computer Network' means the inter-connection of one or more computers or computer systems or communication device through

(i) the use of satellite, microwave, terrestrial line, wire, wireless or other communication media; and
(ii) terminals or a complex consisting of two or more interconnected computers or communication device whether or not the inter-connection is continuously maintained.

Section 2(g) defines 'Certifying Authority'. 'Certifying Authority' means a person who has been granted a licence to issue a [electronic signature] Certificate under section 24.

Section 2(k) deals with the term 'Computer Resource' and states that 'Computer Resource' means computer, computer system, computer network, data, computer data base or software.

28 Which of the following is not correct in relation to rights in its various forms and its correlatives?

1 Right (Strict sense) – Duty
2 Liberty – No right
3 Power – Liberty
4 Immunity – Disability

Ans. (3)

Exp. The combination of Power-Liberty is not correct in relation to rights in its various forms and its correlatives. The correlative of Power is liability. For instance, the correlative of 'X' having the privilege to kill the enemy soldier 'Y' is that 'Y' has 'no-right' to sue 'X' if 'X' uses her privilege. Hence, the correlative of Power is liability. If 'X' has the power to nullify her contract with 'C', then 'C' has the liability that 'X' may nullify the contract.

29 Arrange in chronological order the following judgements on cruelty as a ground of divorce.

I. A. Jaya Chandra Vs. Aneel Kaur
II. Naveen Kohli Vs. Neelu Kohli
III. Dastane Vs. Dastane
IV. Bhagat Vs. Bhagat

Choose the correct answer from the options given below :

1 III, II, IV, I
2 I, III, II, IV
3 III, IV, I, II
4 IV, III, I, II

Ans. (3)

Exp. The correct chronological order is III, IV, I, II.

Dastane Vs. Dastane (1975) case is the one in which the cruelty was discovered as a ground for divorce and a wife who suffers shall be entitled to be maintained by her husband. Even mental agony was covered under the concept of cruelty.

In cases involving mental cruelty, *Bhagat Vs. Bhagat* (1994) is often cited as the judgement that deals in detail with the definition of mental cruelty. The concept has been dealt with in such a way as to appreciate the diverse situations that can fall within its ambit. The realm of cruelty has been called 'wonderful' by Justice Reddy, as it tends to include a situation within its realm in one case but the same might not be included in a different case because of the background of the parties.

In *A. Jaya Chandra Vs. Aneel Kaur* (2004), the apex court held that the decision of the High court is not justified on the ground that it did not discuss the evidence on records on the specious ground that witnesses from the hospital not examined and hence, adverse inference was to be drawn. It also did not discuss that how the evidence on records was insufficient in establishing mental cruelty. Further, it held that the appellant-husband is entitled to a decree of divorce.

In *Naveen Kohli Vs. Neelu Kohli* (2006), the court ruled that the intrigue and clear interest of all the parties concerned, lay in the legal recognition of this fact that despite the wife does not agree to divorce by mutual consent and seems to plan to live in sorrow only to turn the other half's life into a desperate demon is the machinations found in the hidden marriage breakup.

Maintaining marriage fraud is seen by law as increasingly useful for unethical behaviour and tends to be more biased over enthusiasm than marital breakdown. Failure to acknowledge separation in such circumstances was seen as bad for the sessions. If they allow separation, sooner or later, both mentally and internally, they can settle down and start another part of their daily life.

30 Endorsement of Negotiable instrument followed by delivery

I. Transfers the property in instrument to endorsee.

II. Transfers the right of further negotiation to the endorsee.

III. May exclude or restrict the right of further negotiation by endorsee.

IV. May merely constitute the endorsee as an agent.

Choose the correct answer from the options given below :

1 Only I and II
2 Only III and IV
3 Only I, II, III
4 I, II, III and IV

Ans. (4)

Exp. All statements I, II, III and IV are correct.

The endorsement of a Negotiable instrument is followed by delivery transfers to the endorsee the property therein with the right of further negotiation, but the endorsement may by express words, restrict or exclude such right, or may merely constitute the endorsee an agent to endorse the instrument, or to receive its contents for the endorser, or for some other specified person.

31 Originally under the Hindu Marriage Act, 1955, divorce was based on

1 Consent Theory
2 Breakdown Theory
3 Fault Theory
4 Will Theory

Ans. (3)

Exp. Originally under the Hindu Marriage Act, 1955, divorce was based on Fault Theory.

The Hindu Marriage Act, 1955 originally, based divorce on the fault theory, and enshrined grounds in Section 13(1) on which either the husband or wife could sue for divorce and some other grounds in Section 13(2) on which wife alone could seek the divorce.

32 Under the special powers of Rajya Sabha, which of the following resolutions can originate only in Rajya Sabha?

I. Resolution seeking removal of Vice-President.

II. Any resolution seeking creation of one or more all India service.

III. Any resolution seeking legislation on state subject.

IV. Introduction of money bills.

Choose the correct answer from the options given below :

1 Only I and II
2 Only I and III
3 Only IV and II
4 Only I, II, III

Ans. (4)

Exp. Statements I, II and III are correct.

Under the special powers of Rajya Sabha the following resolutions can originate only in Rajya Sabha:

1. Resolution seeking removal of Vice-President
2. Any resolution seeking creation of one or more all India service.
3. Any resolution seeking legislation on state subject.

However, introduction of money bills can only originate in the Lok Sabha.

33 Prof. William Fisher identified four analytical constructs of theories of intellectual property under which of the following sequence?

I. Personality Theory

II. Labour Theory

III. Social Planning Theory

IV. Utilitarian Theory

Choose the correct answer from the options given below

1 II, I, IV, III
2 III, II, I, IV
3 IV, II, I, III
4 I, IV, III, II

Ans. (3)

Exp. The correct sequence is IV, II, I and III.

Prof. William Fisher identified the four analytical constructs of theories of intellectual property in the following sequence:

1. *Utilitarian Theory* : Utilitarianism is an ethical theory that determines right from wrong by focusing on outcomes. It is a form of consequentialism. Utilitarianism holds that the most ethical choice is the one that will produce the greatest good for the greatest number.
2. *Labour Theory* : It postulates that the human beings can use labour to establish their rights over the natural resources which creates a moral obligation upon others to respect these rights.

3. *Personality Theory* : According to this theory, the juristic personality is only a symbol to facilitate the working of corporation. Only the members of the corporation are "persons" in the true sense and round them a bracket is put to indicate that they are to be treated as one unit when they have formed themselves into a corporation.
4. *Social Planning Theory* : Social planning emphasises the application of rational problem-solving techniques and data-driven approaches to identify, determine, and help coordinate services for target populations. Social planning is carried out by a myriad of organisations—from federal agencies to community organisations—attempting to solve problems ranging from child welfare to aging. The advantages and disadvantages of this empirically objective data-driven approach, including different forms, will be discussed along with past, current, and future trends within the field of social work.

34 Match List I with List II.

	List I		List II
A.	Negligence	I.	Ryland Vs. Fletcher
B.	Strict Liability	II.	M. C. Mehta Vs. Union of India
C.	Absolute Liability	III.	Glasgow Corporation Vs. Muir
D.	Nervous Shock	IV.	Bourhill Vs. Young

Codes

	A	B	C	D		A	B	C	D
1	II	I	III	IV	2	I	III	IV	II
3	III	I	II	IV	4	III	II	I	IV

Ans. (3)

Exp. The correct matching is A-III, B-I, C-II, D-IV.

Glasgow Corporation Vs. Muir case is related to Negligence. It is a leading case in the development of the law of negligence and forms part of Scots Delict law and English tort law. It embeds the concept of the reasonable person.

Rylands Vs. Fletcher case is related to Strict Liability. In the case, the defendant got some contractors to construct a reservoir on his land. Due to the negligence of the contractors, water leaked from the reservoir to the plaintiff's coal mine located below the land, thus causing extensive damage to it.

MC Mehta Vs. Union of India case is related to Absolute Liability. Also known as the Oleum Gas Leakage case, this case established the rule of absolute liability by which the wrongdoer is liable even without his fault and with no exceptions.

Bourhill Vs. Young case is related to Nervous Shock. The case involved psychiatric illness liability in tort. It was held that no one can claim the damages for nervous shock if the wrong done to someone else, as it was too remote.

35 Which of the following statement/statements are correct?

I. 'Theft' is defined under section 378 of IPC, as the dishonest removal of movable property out of the possession of any person without his consent.
II. In the offence of extortion punishment is upto 3 years under Section 384 of IPC.
III. The offence of 'Robbery' is defined under Section 391 of IPC.
IV. Dacoity is Robbery committed by five or more persons.
V. The punishment for 'Dacoity' is prescribed under Section 392 of IPC.

Choose the correct answer from the options given below

1 I, II, III, IV Only
2 I, II, IV Only
3 IV, V Only
4 I, II Only

Ans. (2)

Exp. Statements I, II and IV are correct.

Statement III is incorrect because the offence of 'dacoity' is defined under Section 391 of IPC.

Statement V is incorrect because the punishment for 'Dacoity' has been provided under Section 395 of IPC.

36 Which of the following statement/statements is/are correct?

I. The offence of abetment is defined under Section 107 of IPC.
II. The essential ingredient of 'the offence of conspiracy is the agreement to commit an offence'.
III. The punishment of criminal conspiracy is given under Section 120 of IPC.
IV. State of Tamil Nadu through Superintendent of Police, CBI/SIT Vs. Nalini is a case related to offence of Abetment.
V. Abetment in India of offences committed outside of India is punishable under Section 108A of IPC.

Choose the correct answer from the options given below

1 I, II, III, IV and V
2 II, IV, V only
3 I, II, V only
4 II, III only

Ans. (3)

Exp. Statements I, II and V are correct.

Statement III is incorrect because the punishment for criminal conspiracy has been provided under Section 120B of IPC.

Statement IV is incorrect because the State of Tamil Nadu through Superintendent of Police, CBI/SIT Vs. Nalini is a case related to the offence of criminal conspiracy and TADA Act.

37 Arrange the correct sequence in which the liability for tort will arise for the following

I. Damages II. Breach of duty
III. Duty to take care IV. Causation

Choose the correct answer from the options given below

1 I, II, III, IV
2 II, III, I, IV
3 III, II, IV, I
4 III, I, II, IV

***Ans.* (3)**

Exp. The correct sequence in which the liability for torts will arise is III, II, IV, I.

The liability for tort will arise in the given sequence i.e. Duty to take care, Breach of duty, causation and Damages.

38 Which of the following judgement do not deal with the matter of Live-in relationship?

1 Indra Sarma Vs. K.V. Sarma
2 Sharda Vs. Dharmpal
3 S. Khushboo Vs. Kanniammal
4 Chanmuniya Vs. Chanmuniya Kumar Singh

***Ans.* (2)**

Exp. Sharda Vs. Dharmpal does not deal with the matter of Live-in relationships. It dealt with DNA evidence. In this case, the court states that the court uses such power if the applicant has an extreme prima facie case and there sufficient evidence is present before the court. If the court order and respondent refuses to do so then the court can take action which they think is appropriate.

39 Match List I with List II.

List I (Conferences of WTO)	List II (Places where held)
A. Third Ministerial Conference of WTO was held at	I. Hong Kong (China)
B. Sixth Ministerial Conference of WTO was held at	II. Seattle (USA)
C. Fourth Ministerial Conference of WTO was held at	III. Geneva (Switzerland)
D. Seventh Ministerial Conference of WTO was held at	IV. Doha (Qatar)

Codes

	A	B	C	D
1	I	II	III	IV
2	II	I	IV	III
3	II	IV	I	III
4	IV	III	II	I

***Ans.* (2)**

Exp. The correct matching is A-II, B-I, C-IV, D-III.

The *Third Ministerial Conference of the WTO* was held at Seattle, USA from 30th November to 3rd December, 1999. The Conference brought together trade ministers and other officials from the WTO's 135 member countries in an attempt, which proved unsuccessful, to agree on the issues and agenda for a new round of negotiations aimed at further de-regulating international trade, particularly in such controversial areas as agriculture, services and intellectual property.

The *Sixth Ministerial Conference of WTO* was held at Hong Kong, China. The WTO Hong Kong Ministerial Conference was one of the largest international events ever held in Hong Kong. There were about 11,000 participants. Apart from the 148 WTO members, 1000 non-governmental organisations (NGOs) also took part in the meeting.

The *Fourth Ministerial Conference of the WTO* was held at Doha, Qatar from 9th to 14th November, 2001. Officially, this meeting was the Fourth WTO Ministerial Conference. The Ministerial Conference is the organisation's highest-level decision-making body.

The *Seventh Ministerial Conference of the WTO* was held at Geneva (Switzerland). It took place from 30th November to 2nd December, 2009. The general theme for discussion was 'The WTO, the Multilateral Trading System and the Current Global Economic Environment'.

40 In a contract of Guarantee under the Indian Contract Act, 1872 there are

1 Two parties and two contracts
2 Three parties and three contracts
3 Three parties and one contract
4 Two parties and one contract

***Ans.* (2)**

Exp. In a contract of Guarantee under the Indian Contract Act, 1872 there are generally three parties involved and three contracts. A contract of Guarantee is governed by the Indian Contract Act,1872 and includes three parties in which one of the parties acts as the surety in case the defaulting party fails to fulfill his obligations. Contracts of Guarantee are mostly required in cases when a party requires a loan, goods or employment.

41 The Preamble to both Environment (Protection) Act and Air (Prevention and Control of Pollution) Act were passed to implement the decision reached in one of the following

1 San Francisco Conference, 1945
2 United Nations Conference on Environment and Development, 1992
3 United Nations Conference on the Human Environment, 1972
4 United Nations Conference on Environment, 1982

***Ans.* (3)**

Exp. The Preamble to both Environment (Protection) Act and Air (Prevention and Control of Pollution) Act were passed to implement the decision reached in the United Nations Conference on the Human Environment, 1972. The Stockholm Declaration of 1972 is called the 'Magna Carta' of environment protection and its development. Certain environmental laws were in force in India well before the Stockholm Declaration of 1972, such as the Indian Forest Act etc. Besides, this action could also be taken under Sections 268 and 290 IPC against public nuisance relating to the environment.

42 Match List I with List II.

List I	List II
A. Article V	I. Presidential Election, 7th November, 2012
B. Article III	II. Congress on the eve of Presidential Election
C. Chapter V	III. The Judicial Power in American Supreme Court
D Chapter IV	IV Amendment of the Constitution

Codes

	A	B	C	D
1	I	II	IV	III
2	III	I	IV	II
3	IV	III	II	I
4	II	IV	III	I

Ans. (3)

➲ *Exp.* The correct matching is A-IV, B-III, C-II, D-I.

Article V is related to amendment of the Constitution. Article V of the U.S. Constitution gives states the power to call a Convention of States to propose amendments. It takes 34 states to call the convention and 38 to ratify any amendments that are proposed.

Article III is related to the Judicial power in the American Supreme Court. The judicial power of the United States, shall be vested in one Supreme Court and in such inferior courts as the Congress may from time to time ordain and establish. The Judges, both of the Supreme and inferior courts, shall hold their offices during good behaviour and shall, at stated times, receive for their services, a compensation, which shall not be diminished during their continuance in office.

Chapter V is related to Congress on the eve of the Presidential Election. In 2020, the Presidential election occurred simultaneously with elections to the Senate and the House of Representatives. Gubernatorial and legislative elections were also held in several states. For the subsequent election, the United States House will redistribute the seats among the 50 states based on the results of the 2020 United States Census, and the states will conduct a redistricting of Congressional and State Legislative districts.

Chapter IV is related to Presidential Election, 7th November, 2012. Democratic President Barack Obama won election to a second term, though the Republican Party retained control of the House of Representatives.

43 In which of the following cases the Supreme Court observed "There is a thin line between the preparation for and an attempt to commit an offence"?

1 State of Maharashtra Vs. Mohd.Yakul
2 Abhayanand Mishra Vs. State of Bihar
3 Malkiat Singh Vs. State of Punjab
4 Om Parkesh Vs. State of Punjab

Ans. (2)

➲ *Exp.* In the case of Abhayanand Mishra Vs. State of Bihar, the Supreme Court observed "There is a thin line between the preparation for and an attempt to commit an offence." Undoubtedly, a culprit first intends to commit the offence, then makes preparation for committing it and thereafter attempts to commit the offence.

44 'Digital signature' is defined under which section of Information Technology Act, 2000?

1 Section 2 (p)
2 Section 2 (q)
3 Section 2 (r)
4 Section 2 (tb)

Ans. (1)

➲ *Exp.* 'Digital signature' is defined under Section 2(p) of Information Technology Act, 2000. Accordingly, 'Digital signature' means authentication of any electronic record by a subscriber by means of an electronic method or procedure in accordance with the provisions of Section 3.

45 'Computer network' means the inter-connection of one or more computers of computer systems or communication devices through

I. The use of satellite, microwave, terrestrial line, wire, wireless or other communication media.
II. A device or collection of devices including input and output support devices.
III. Any electronic, magnetic, optical and other high speed data processing device.
IV All input, out, processing, storage, computer software or communication facilities.
V. Terminal or a complex consisting of two or more interconnected computers or communication device.

Choose the correct answer from the options given below

1 Only II and III
2 Only IV and III
3 Only V and II
4 Only I and V

Ans. (4)

➲ *Exp.* Statements I and V are correct.

Section 2(j) of the IT Act, 2000 states that 'Computer Network' means the inter-connection of one or more computers or computer systems or communication device through

1. The use of satellite, microwave, terrestrial line, wire, wireless or other communication media; and
2. terminals or a complex consisting of two or more interconnected computers or communication device whether or not the inter-connection is continuously maintained.

46 Which of the following statements are correct?

I. In Canada, the federation was not a voluntary union but was imposed by an Act.
II. In India, the Act of 1935 created autonomous units and forged them into a federation.

III. The American Union was formed by voluntary agreement among a number of sovereign states.
IV. Indian constitution has been framed by the States and not by the people of India.

Choose the correct answer from the options given below :

1 I, II and III
2 I, II and IV
3 I, III and IV
4 II, III and IV

Ans. (1)

Exp. Statements I, II and III are correct.

Statement IV is incorrect because the Indian Constitution has been framed by the people of India and not by the States.

47 Mental condition of a wrongdoer at the time of wrong doing is

1 Relevant in all torts
2 Relevant in torts based on fault
3 Relevant in tort based on strict liability
4 Not relevant at all

Ans. (2)

Exp. Mental condition of a wrongdoer at the time of wrongdoing is relevant in torts based on fault.

A tort exists when any wrongful act on omission occurs by any individual. The term 'act' here must be understood with the broadest view. Therefore, both positive and negative acts and omission must be included. 'Intentionally, deliberately, or emphatically' the action should be done to cause legal damage to the other party. As a result, a legal remedy must be provided to the injured party that is mostly in the form of 'unliquidated' damages.

48 Arrange the provisions of the Indian Contract Act, 1872 in chronological order (Section wise)

I. Who are competent to contract
II. Effect of mistakes as to law
III. What agreements are contracts
IV. Agreement in restraint of marriage is void

Choose the correct answer from the options given below

1 III, I, IV, II
2 I, III, II, IV
3 III, I, II, IV
4 I, III, IV, II

Ans. (3)

Exp. The correct chronological order is III, I, II, IV.

The provisions of the Indian Contract Act, 1872 in chronological order are:

What agreements are contracts (Section 10): All agreements are contracts if they are made by the free consent of parties competent to contract, for a lawful consideration and with a lawful object and are not hereby expressly declared to be void.

Who are competent to contract (Section 11): Every person is competent to contract who is of the age of majority according to the law to which he is subject, and who is of sound mind and is not disqualified from contracting by any law to which he is subject.

Effect of mistakes as to law (Section 21): A contract is not voidable because it was caused by a mistake as to any law in force in India; but a mistake as to a law not in force in India has the same effect as a mistake of fact.

Agreement in restraint of marriage is void (Section 26): Every agreement in restraint of the marriage of any person, other than a minor, is void.

49 Which of the following is not the principal organ of the United Nations?

1 General Assembly
2 Economic and Social Council
3 International Court of Justice
4 International Human Rights Commission

Ans. (4)

Exp. The International Human Rights Commission is not one of the principal organs of the UN.

The United Nations is an international organisation that strives to maintain world peace and ensure security for all mankind. It also strives to foster friendly relations among nations.

The UN functions through its 6 principal organs. They are:

1. General Assembly
2. Security Council
3. Secretariat
4. Economic and Social Council
5. Trusteeship Council
6. International Court of Justice

50 Arrange in chronological order the publication of the books on Jurisprudence

I. A Practical Treatise of Architectural Jurisprudence by James Elmes
II. The Spirit of Common Law by Roscoe Pound
III. World Poverty and Human Rights by Thomas Pogge
IV. Taking Rights Seriously by Ronald Dworkin
V. The Growth of the Law by Benjamin N. Cardozo

Choose the correct answer from the options given below :

1 II, I, III, V, IV
2 V, II, I, III, IV
3 I, II, V, IV, III
4 II, I, V, III, IV

Ans. (3)

Exp. The correct chronological order is I, II, V, IV, III.

A Practical Treatise of Architectural Jurisprudence by James Elmes was published in 1827.

The Spirit of Common Law is one of Roscoe Pound's most notable works. It contains the brilliant lectures he delivered at Dartmouth College in the summer of 1921. It is a seminal book embodying the spiritual essence of sociological jurisprudence by its leading prophet.

The Growth of the Law by Benjamin N. Cardozo was published in 1963.

In *Taking Rights Seriously* (1978), Ronald Dworkin develops his idea of rights as trumps. His main idea is that there are some moral rights against the Government. This means that governments would do wrong to repeal such Fundamental Rights, even if they were persuaded that the majority would be better off that way (idem).

World Poverty and Human Rights: Cosmopolitan Responsibilities and Reforms is a 2002 book by Thomas Pogge. In the book, Pogge explains that the poorest 44% of humankind have 1.3% of global income and their purchasing power per person per day is less than that of $2.15 in the US in 1993; 826 million of them do not have enough to eat.

57 **Given below are two statements, one is labelled as Assertion (A) and the other is labelled as Reasons (R).**

Assertion (A) The right of private defence of body extends to causing of death to the Assailant in case of assault of throwing or administering acid or an attempt to throw or administer acid which may reasonably cause the apprehension that grievous hurt will otherwise be the consequences of such Act.

Reason (R) This provision was inserted under clause (7) of section 100 IPC by Act 13 of 2013 in view of increasing cases of acid throwing on the girls and women in India.

In the light of the above statements, choose the correct answer from the options given below.

1 Both (A) and (R) are correct and (R) is the correct explanation of (A).

2 Both (A) and (R) are correct and (R) is not the correct explanation of (A)

3 (A) is correct but (R) is not correct.

4 (A) is not correct but (R) is correct.

Ans. (1)

Exp. Both (A) and (R) are correct and (R) is the correct explanation of (A).

The right of private defence of the body extends, under the restrictions mentioned in the last preceding section, to the voluntary causing of death or of any other harm to the assailant, if the offence which occasions the exercise of the right be of any of the descriptions mentioned in this Section. An act of throwing or administering acid or an attempt to throw or administer acid which may reasonably cause the apprehension that grievous hurt will otherwise be the consequence of such act was inserted in clause 7 of Section 100 of IPC by Act 13 of 2013 in view of increasing cases of acid throwing on the girls and women in India.

52 **Match List I with List II.**

List I	List II
A. National Human Rights Commission	I. Article 338
B. National Commission for Backward Class	II. State to introduce regulatory regime in the National Interest
C. National Commission for Minorities	III. Power to recommend payment of compensation
D. National Commission for Scheduled Caste	IV. Article 338-B

Codes

	A	B	C	D
1	I	II	III	IV
2	III	IV	II	I
3	IV	III	II	I
4	IV	II	I	III

Ans. (2)

Exp. The correct matching is A-III, B-IV, C-II and D-I.

National Human Rights Commission is related to power to recommend payment of compensation. The National Human Rights Commission or NHRC is a standalone entity of the Government of India with the mission of promoting and protecting human rights. It is a statutory body mentioned in the Constitution of India that was established in 1993 under the 'Protection of Human Rights Act.' This act was further amended in 2006.

National Commission for Backward Class is related to Article 338-B. Article 338-B deals with the structure, duties, and powers of the National Commission for Backward Classes (NCBC). Article 342-A deals with the power of the President of India to notify a particular caste as a Socially and Educationally Backward Class (SEBC) and the power of the Parliament to change the list.

In *National Commission for Minorities* State introduce regulatory regime in the National Interest. Under the National Commission for Minorities Act, 1992 the government formed the National Commission for Minorities (NCM) which consist of Chairperson, a Vice-Chairperson and five Members. The five Members including the Chairperson shall be from amongst the minority communities.

National Commission for Scheduled Castes (SCs) was formed under Article 338 of the Indian Constitution. National Commission for Scheduled Castes is committed to the full implementation of various Acts like the PCR Act, 1955 and SC and ST (POA) Act, 1989 etc.

53 Indicate the chronological order of the years of the following cases as decided by the Supreme Court :

I. State of T.N. Vs. Balkrishna
II. Mangesh Vs. State of Maharashtra
III. Ram Kumar Vs. State of M.P.
IV. K.M. Nanavati Vs. State of Maharashtra
V. Mahesh Chander Vs. State of Delhi

Choose the correct answer from the options given below

1 I, II, III, IV, V 2 V, III, II, IV, I
3 IV, I, II, III, V 4 III, IV, I, II, V

Ans. (3)

Exp. The correct chronological order is IV, I, II, III, V.

The given cases in correct chronological order of the years decided is as follows :

1. KM Nanavati Vs. State of Maharashtra
2. State of Tamil Nadu Vs. Balkrishna
3. Mangesh Vs. State of Maharashtra
4. Ramkumar Vs. State of MP
5. Mahesh Chander Vs. State of Delhi

54 Section 8(1) of the RTI Act provides how many exemptions from the disclosure of information?

1 7 2 8
3 9 4 10

Ans. (4)

Exp. Section 8(1) of the RTI Act, provides 10 exemptions from the disclosure of information. It states that notwithstanding anything contained in this Act, there shall be no obligation to give any citizen,

(a) information, disclosure of which would prejudicially affect the sovereignty and integrity of India, the security, strategic, scientific or economic interests of the State, relation with foreign State or lead to incitement of an offence;

(b) information which has been expressly forbidden to be published by any court of law or tribunal or the disclosure of which may constitute contempt of court;

(c) information, the disclosure of which would cause a breach of privilege of Parliament or the State Legislature;

(d) information including commercial confidence, trade secrets or intellectual property, the disclosure of which would harm the competitive position of a third party, unless the competent authority is satisfied that larger public interest warrants the disclosure of such information;

(e) information available to a person in his fiduciary relationship, unless the competent authority is satisfied that the larger public interest warrants the disclosure of such information;

(f) information received in confidence from foreign Government;

(g) information, the disclosure of which would endanger the life or physical safety of any person or identify the source of information or assistance given in confidence for law enforcement or security purposes;

(h) information which would impede the process of investigation or apprehension or prosecution of offenders;

(i) cabinet papers including records of deliberations of the Council of Ministers, Secretaries and other officers: Provided that the decisions of Council of Ministers, the reasons thereof, and the material on the basis of which the decisions were taken shall be made public after the decision has been taken, and the matter is complete, or over: Provided further that those matters which come under the exemptions specified in this section shall not be disclosed;

(j) information which relates to personal information the disclosure of which has no relationship to any public activity or interest, or which would cause unwarranted invasion of the privacy of the individual unless the Central Public Information Officer or the State Public Information Officer or the appellate authority, as the case may be, is satisfied that the larger public interest justifies the disclosure of such information: Provided that the information which cannot be denied to the Parliament or a State Legislature shall not be denied to any person.

55 Indicate the correct chronological order of years the following cases they were decided:

I. Case concerning the Temple of Preah Vihear
II. Frontier Dispute (Burkina Faso Vs. Mali)
III. The Caroline case
IV. R.V. Keyn
V. Chorzow factory (Indemnity) case

Choose the correct answer from the options given below

1 I, II, III, IV, V 2 V, IV, III, II, I
3 III, IV, V, I, II 4 II, III, IV, V, I

Ans. (3)

Exp. The correct chronological order is III, IV, V, I, II.

The Caroline case : It was a diplomatic crisis beginning in 1837 involving the United States, Britain and the Canadian independence movement. It began in 1837 when William Lyon Mackenzie and other Canadian rebels, with support from US citizens, fled to an island in the Niagara River, in the ship Caroline. British forces crossed the Niagara River, to board and capture the vessel where it was moored, at Schlosser's Landing, in US territory. Shots were exchanged and one U.S. citizen, a watchkeeper, was killed. British forces set fire to the Caroline and set it adrift in the Niagara River, about two miles above Niagara Falls. Sensationalised accounts of the affair were published by contemporary newspapers.

R.V. Keyn (1876) : It is also known as the Franconia case. The case involved a question of criminal jurisdiction, the right of an English Court to try a foreigner for an offence committed on the high seas, but within British territorial waters, which at this time, were taken to extend three miles out to the sea. This issue arose out of a collision which took place on the 17th February 1876.

Chorzow factory (Indemnity) case (1928, Germany Vs. Poland): This case involved a general principal of law as well as International law, that any breach of agreement creates an obligation to make reparation.

Case concerning the Temple of Preah Vihear (1962) : On 15th June, 1962, the ICJ ordered the jurisdiction in favour of Cambodia and affirmed that the judgment was based on valid maps created during the 1904 and 1907 border agreement which precisely show the temple in the Cambodian territory.

Frontier Dispute (Burkina Faso Vs. Mali) (1986): In this case, it was held that states are bound by the terms of unilateral declarations made by head of state only when the intention confers on the declaration, the character of a legal undertaking. It is left for the court to "form its own view of the meaning and scope intended by the author of a unilateral declaration which might create a legal obligation." In this case, nothing holds the parties back from entering into a formal agreement. Hence, there is no basis to interpret the Mali Head of State's declaration as a unilateral act with legal implications since no such agreement was entered into.

56 According to Prof. Lon L Fuller

I. Law is the enterprise of subjecting human conduct to the governance of rules.

II. The morality of law has two aspects, external and internal.

III. External morality is the morality of aspiration, ideas from which it is possible to derive a procedural version of natural law.

IV. Internal morality of law is a 'substantive version of natural law'.

Choose the correct answer from the options given below

1 Only I and II
2 II, III and IV
3 I, III and IV
4 I, II and III

Ans. (1)

Exp. Statements I and II are correct.

According to Fuller, all purported legal rules must meet eight minimal conditions in order to count as genuine laws. The rules must be:

1. sufficiently general,
2. publicly promulgated,
3. prospective (i.e., applicable only to future behaviour, not past),
4. at least minimally clear and intelligible,
5. free of contradictions,
6. relatively constant, so that they don't continuously change from day to day,
7. possible to obey, and
8. administered in a way that does not wildly diverge from their obvious or apparent meaning.

These are Fuller's 'principles of legality.' Together, he argues, they guarantee that all law will embody certain moral standards of respect, fairness and predictability that constitute important aspects of the rule of law.

57 "The courts have created new torts by the gradual and sometimes almost imperceptible extension of old tort". Who said the given statement?

1 Professor Good Hart
2 Sir Frederick Pollock
3 Clerk and Lindsell
4 Salmond

Ans. (1)

Exp. Professor Good Hart said "The courts have created new torts by the gradual and sometimes almost imperceptible extension of old tort." Professor Hart not only puts to good use some of their characteristic techniques of analysis, but also stresses the importance of rules in social life.

58 Where the money received from a third party by the firm, in ordinary course of business, is misapplied by one of the partners to his own use, then :

1 Defaulting partner alone is liable for the same
2 Third party has no remedy
3 Firm is liable for the same
4 Firm is not liable for the same

Ans. (3)

Exp. Where the money received from a third party by the firm, in ordinary course of business, is misapplied by one of the partners to his own use, then Firm is liable for the same. According to Section 27 of Partnership Act, where

(a) a partner acting within his apparent authority receives money or property from a third party and misapplies it, or

(b) a firm in the course of its business receives money or property from a third party, and the money or property is misapplied by any of the partners while it is in the custody of the firm, the firm is liable to make good the loss.

59 In case of unascertained goods, the property in goods passes

1 When goods are ascertained
2 When the parties intend the property in goods to pass
3 As soon as the contract of sale is signed
4 After the payment of goods is received by the seller

Ans. (1)

Exp. In case of unascertained goods, the property in goods passes when goods are ascertained. In case of unascertained goods, the property in goods does not pass unless and until the goods are ascertained.

60 Given below are two statements.

Statement I Dominant position means position of strength enjoyed by an enterprise in relevant market in India which enables it to operate independently of operative forces and affects competitors and consumers in its favour.

Statement II No enterprise shall abuse its dominant position.

In the light of the above statements, choose the correct answer from the options given below.

1 Both Statement I and Statement II are true
2 Both Statement I and Statement II are false
3 Statement I is true but Statement II is false
4 Statement I is false but Statement II is true

Ans. (1)

Exp. Both Statement I and Statement II are true.

Section 4 of the Competition Act prohibits abuse of dominant position by any enterprise. Such abuse of dominant position, inter alia, includes imposition, either directly or indirectly, of unfair or discriminatory purchase or selling prices or conditions, including predatory prices of goods or service, limiting market access, making the conclusion of contracts subject to acceptance by other parties of supplementary obligations and using dominant position in one market to enter into or protect other market.

The term dominant position means a position of strength, enjoyed by an enterprise, in the relevant market in India. Such a position enables a firm to:

(i) operate independently of competitive forces prevailing in the relevant market; or (ii) affect its competitors or consumers or the relevant market in its favour.

Thus, both statements are correct.

61 Which of the following judgement does not deal with the need of enactment of 'Uniform Civil Code' in India?

1 Mohd. Ahmad Khan Vs. Shah Bano Begum
2 Ashok Hurra Vs. Rupa
3 Sarla Mudgal Vs. Union of India
4 John Vallamatton Vs. Union of India

Ans. (2)

Exp. Ashok Hurra Vs. Rupa case judgement does not deal with the need for enactment of 'Uniform Civil Code' in India. The Supreme Court declared on 10th April, 2002, in its five-judge decision in the Rupa Ashok Hurra case that "it is a settled position in law that no judicial order passed by any superior court in judicial proceedings can be said to violate any of the Fundamental Rights enshrined in Part III" of the Constitution.

62 Given below are two statements.

Assertion (A) The rule making power of the Supreme Court for regulating the practice and procedure of the court is not subject to any law made by the Parliament of India.

Reason (R) Only an impartial and independent judiciary can protect the right of individual without fear or favour.

In the light of the above statements, choose the correct answer from the options given below.

1 Both (A) and (R) are true and (R) is the correct explanation of (A).
2 Both (A) and (R) are true and (R) is not the correct explanation of (A).
3 (A) is true but (R) is false.
4 (A) is false but (R) is true.

Ans. (4)

Exp. (A) is false but (R) is true.

(A) is false as the law declared by the Supreme Court becomes binding on all courts within India and also by the union and state governments because as per Article 142 of the Constitution, it is the duty of the President to enforce the decrees of the Supreme Court.

Only an impartial and independent judiciary can protect the right of individual without fear or favour.

63 Motor vehicle Amendment Act of 2019 refer to the earlier Motor vehicle Act of 1988 as

1 Earlier Act
2 Old Act
3 Adapted Act
4 Principal Act

Ans. (4)

Exp. Motor Vehicle Amendment Act of 2019, refers to the earlier Motor Vehicle Act of 1988 as Principal Act. In addition to this, Amendment of 2019 aims at setting testing standards and bringing the agencies issuing automotive approvals under the Motor Vehicles Act. Another major feature of this Act is the provision for setting up of a National Road Safety Board under the Central government.

64 Examine the relevancy of class action suit and choose the correct answer:

I. A class action would measurably assist in securing redress in Environmental cases.
II. Monetary recoveries from the tort feasors in environmental cases can only be obtained through a suit.
III. The writ procedure appears more suited than the class action procedure.
IV. The most obvious use of class action is in the mass disasters of the sort that occurred in Bhopal.

Choose the most appropriate answer from the options given below.

1 Only I, II, IV
2 Only I, III, IV
3 Only II, III, IV
4 Only I, II, III

Ans. (1)

Exp. Statements I, II and IV are correct.

Statement III is incorrect because the domain of operation of the writ procedure and the class action procedure are generally different. We cannot really compare the efficacy of one with the other.

65 Which of the following statements are correct?

I. The Preamble contains in nutshell ideals and aspirations of the Constitution.

II. The Preamble is the key to open the minds of the Constitution makers.

III. The Preamble to the Constitution of India is solemnly resolved to secure to its citizens justice and equity.

IV. The Preamble is not the part of the Constitution.

Choose the correct answer from the options given below.

1 Only I and II
2 Only III and IV
3 Only I and III
4 Only I and IV

Ans. (1)

Exp. Statements I and II are correct.

Statement III is incorrect because the Preamble to the Constitution of India is solemnly resolved to secure to its citizens to constitute India into a Sovereign Socialist Secular Democratic Republic.

Statement IV is incorrect because the Preamble is a part of the Constitution.

66 The right to Information Act, 2005 explains the meaning of information under

1 Section 2 (e)
2 Section 2 (f)
3 Section 2 (g)
4 Section 2 (h)

Ans. (2)

Exp. The right to Information Act, 2005 explains the meaning of information under Section 2(f). 'Information' means any material in any form, including records, documents, memos, e-mails, opinions, advices, press releases, circulars, orders, logbooks, contracts, reports, papers, samples, models, data material held in any electronic form and information relating to any private body which can be accessed by a public authority under any other law for the time being in force.

67 Match List I with List II.

List I (Definitions of)	List II (Provisions of Indian Penal Code)
A. Solitary confinement	I. Section 95 IPC
B. Act of a child under seven years of age	II. Section 93 IPC
C. Communication made in good faith	III. Section 73 IPC
D. Act causing slight harm	IV. Section 82 IPC

Choose the correct answer from the options given below

Codes

	A	B	C	D		A	B	C	D
1	III	IV	II	I	2	I	II	III	IV
3	IV	II	III	I	4	II	III	IV	I

Ans. (1)

Exp. The correct matching is A-III, B-IV, C-II, D-I.

Section 73, of IPC is related to Solitary Confinement. According to section 73 of Indian Penal Code, whenever any person is convicted of an offence for which under this Code the Court has power to sentence him to rigorous imprisonment, the Court may, by its sentence, order that the offender shall be kept in solitary confinement for any portion or portions of the imprisonment to which he is sentenced, not exceeding three months in the whole, according to the following scale, that is to say:

1. a time not exceeding one month if the term of imprisonment shall not exceed six months;
2. a time not exceeding two months if the term of imprisonment shall exceed six months and shall not exceed one year;
3. a time not exceeding three months if the term of imprisonment shall exceed one year.

Section 82 of IPC exempt the wrongful act of a child under seven years from criminal liability. It is presumed that a child below the age of seven years is doli incapax. It means that such a child is incapable of doing a criminal act and cannot form the necessary mens rea to commit a crime.

Section 93 is related to communication made in good faith. It says no communication made in good faith is an offence by reason of any harm to the person to whom it is made, if it is made for the benefit of that person.

Section 95 of IPC is related to act causing slight harm. Says nothing is an offence by reason that it causes, or that it is intended to cause, or that it is known to be likely to cause any harm, if that harm is so slight that no person of ordinary sense and temper would complain of such harm.

68 The validity of contracts formed through electronic means is contained under which section of Information Technology Act, 2000?

1 Section 3A
2 Section 6A
3 Section 7A
4 Section 10A

Ans. (4)

Exp. The validity of contracts formed through electronic means is contained under Section 10A of Information Technology Act, 2000. Under the provisions of the Information Technology Act, 2000 particularly, Section 10-A, an electronic contract is valid and enforceable. The only essential requirement to validate an electronic contract is compliance with the necessary prerequisites provided under the Indian Contract Act, 1872.

69 In determining relevant geographic market, competition commission shall keep in mind which of the following factors?

I. Regulatory trade barriers and natural procurement policies.
II. Language and local specification requirement.
III. Consumer preference and regular supply and after sale service.
IV. Transport and distribution factors.

Choose the correct answer from the options given below.

1 I, II and III
2 I, II and IV
3 IV, III and II
4 I, II, III and IV

Ans. (4)

Exp. Statements I, II, III and IV are all correct.

As per Section 19 of Competition Act, 2002 in determining relevant geographic market, the competition commission shall keep in mind of the following factors

1. Regulatory trade barriers and natural procurement policies.
2. Language and local specification requirement.
3. Consumer preference and regular supply and after sale service.
4. Transport and distribution factors.

70 Which one of the following is not the functions of Human Rights Council?

1 To promote Human Rights education and learning as well as advisory services.
2 To decide issues without making any recommendations to the General Assembly.
3 To work in close cooperation with the Government regional organisation, National Human Rights institutions and civil society.
4 To serve as forum for dialogue on thematic issues on all Human rights.

Ans. (2)

Exp. To decide issues without making any recommendations to the General Assembly is not one of the functions of the Human Rights Council. The Human Rights Council is an inter-governmental body within the United Nations system responsible for strengthening the promotion and protection of human rights around the globe and for addressing situations of human rights violations and making recommendations on them. It can only make recommendations.

71 Which of the following statements are true under the Constitution of India?

I. Article 61 deals with procedure for impeachment of the President.
II. Article 142 provides that law declared by the Supreme Court shall be biding on all courts.
III. Article 122 provides that courts shall not inquire into proceedings of Parliament.
IV. Article 163 deals with the extent of executive power of State.

Choose the correct answer from the options given below

1 I, II and III
2 Only II and III
3 Only I and III
4 I, III and IV

Ans. (3)

Exp. Statements I and III are correct.

Statement II is incorrect because Article 141 provides that law declared by the Supreme Court shall be binding on all courts.

Statement IV is incorrect because Article 162 deals with the extent of executive power of State.

72 In which of the following cases the duties are not specifically enforced in respect of the act done?

I. The liability of a borrower to repay a debt barred by statute of limitation.
II. The liability of a borrower to repay the money borrowed by him.
III. To refrain the wrongdoer from publication when a libel has already been published.
IV. To refrain the wrong doer to continue the commission of a nuisance.

Choose the correct answer from the options given below

1 Only I and II
2 Only I and III
3 Only II and III
4 Only II and IV

Ans. (2)

Exp. Statements I and III are correct.

The duties are not specifically enforced in respect of the following cases

1. The liability of a borrower to repay a debt barred by statute of limitation.
2. To refrain the wrongdoer from publication when a libel has already been published.

73 Which of the following are fault grounds of divorce under the Hindu Marriage Act, 1955?

I. Desertion
II. Cruelty
III. Consent obtained by force or fraud
IV. Conversion to non-Hindu religion

Choose the most appropriate answer from the options given below.

1 Only I and II
2 II, III and IV
3 Only I and III
4 I, II and IV

Ans. (4)

Exp. Statements I, II and IV are correct.

Section 13(1) states that any marriage solemnised, whether before or after the commencement of this Act, may, on a petition presented by either the husband or the wife, be dissolved by a decree of divorce on the ground that the other party

(i) has, after the solemnisation of the marriage, had voluntary sexual intercourse with any person other than his or her spouse; or

(a) has, after the solemnisation of the marriage, treated the petitioner with cruelty; or

(b) has deserted the petitioner for a continuous period of not less than two years immediately preceding the presentation of the petition; or

(ii) has ceased to be a Hindu by conversion to another religion; or

(iii) has been incurably of unsound mind, or has been suffering continuously or intermittently from mental disorder of such a kind and to such an extent that the petitioner cannot reasonably be expected to live with the respondent.

74 The Supreme Court of India recognised the significance of Intergenerational equity and held a government department's approval to establish forest based industry to be invalid in one of the following case :

1 State of Himachal Pradesh Vs. Ganesh Wood Products
2 Vellore Citizen's Forum Vs. Union of India
3 Dr. B.L. Wadehra Vs. Union of India
4 M.C Metha Vs. Union of India

Ans. (1)

Exp. The Supreme Court of India recognised the significance of Intergenerational equity and held a government department's approval to establish forest based industry to be invalid in the case of State of Himachal Pradesh Vs. Ganesh Wood Products. In the State of Himachal Pradesh Vs. Ganesh Wood Products, AIR 1996 SC 149, the Supreme Court invalidated forest-based industry, recognising the Principle of Intergenerational equity as being central to the conservation of forest resources and sustainable development.

75 The Lokpal and Lokayukta Act 2013 came into force in

1 March 2013
2 February 2013
3 January 2013
4 August 2013

Ans. (*)

Exp. The bill received assent from the President on 1st January, 2014 and came into force on 16th January, 2014 under the name 'The Lokpal and Lokayukta Act 2013'. After the introduction of the Lokpal and Lokayukta Act 2013, a bill was passed by Parliament in July 2016 which amended the Lokpal and Lokayukta Act, 2013.

76 Besides providing for a functional government and consequential growth in the administrative process, the Constitution has provided elaborate control mechanism so that water may not over-run beyond banks. This has been ensured in which of the following articles of the Constitution?

1 Article 32,226,227
2 Article 14, 21 and 41
3 Article 15,16 and 17
4 Article 246, 247, 248

Ans. (1)

Exp. Besides providing for a functional government and consequential growth in the administrative process, the Constitution has provided elaborate control mechanisms so that water may not over-run beyond banks. This has been ensured in Articles 32,226,227 of the Constitution.

Article 32 of the Indian Constitution gives the right to individuals to move to the Supreme Court to seek justice when they feel that their right has been 'unduly deprived'.

As per the powers conferred under Article 226 of Indian Constitution, High courts have the power to issue directions, orders, writs to any person or authority or any governmental authorities (in appropriate cases). Fundamental Rights frame the rampart of The Constitution of India. Each of these rights is sacrosanct.

Article 227 of the Indian Constitution is a supervisory provision that allows the High court to exercise revisional powers over subordinate courts, among other powers.

77 Vice President of India on expiry of his term:-

1 Vacates his office
2 Gets a mandatory extension of 2 months
3 Continues to hold office until successor enters upon office
4 Elects his successor before relinquishing office

Ans. (3)

Exp. Vice President of India on expiry of his term continues to hold office until successor enters upon office. Article 67 deals with the term of office of the Vice President. The Vice President holds office for a term of five years from the date on which he enters upon his office. He can hold office beyond the term of five years until his successor assumes charge.

78 Which of the following statement/statements, is/are correct?

I. De Jure Recognition is final whereas De-facto Recognition is provisional.

II. De-Facto Recognition can be withdrawn but De-Jure Recognition is irrevocable.

III. De-Facto Recognition has retrospective operation as exactly as, in the case of De-Jure recognition.

IV There is no distinction between De-Jure and de Facto recognition for the purpose of giving effects to the internal acts of the Recognised authority.

Choose the most appropriate answer from the options given below

1 I, II and IV 2 II, III and IV
3 I, II and III 4 I, II, III and IV

Ans. (1)

Exp. Only Statements I, II and IV are correct.

Statement III is incorrect because De Facto recognition is the primary step to grant De Jure recognition. De Jure recognition can directly be granted without De Facto recognition.

79 The World Court refused to give its Advisory opinion in which of the following case?

1 The Genocide Convention case
2 The legality of the use by a State of Nuclear weapons in Armed conflict
3 Interpretation of Peace Treaties case
4 Legality of the Threat or use of Nuclear weapons case

Ans. (2)

Exp. The World Court refused to give its Advisory opinion in the case of legality of the use by a State of Nuclear weapons in Armed conflict. There has been no refusal, based on the discretionary power of the Court, to act upon a request for advisory opinion in the history of the present Court; in the case concerning the Legality of the use by a State of Nuclear Weapons in Armed Conflict, the refusal to give the World Health Organisation the advisory opinion requested by it was justified by the Court's lack of jurisdiction in that case.

80 According to Pound, law is

1 The statement of circumstances in which the public force will be brought to bear upon men through courts.
2 A social institution to satisfy social wants.
3 Aggregate of rules set by men as politically superior or sovereign, to men as politically subject.
4 A crystallised common sense of communities.

Ans. (2)

Exp. According to Pound, law is a social institution to satisfy social wants. Pound defines law as a social institution to satisfy social wants. He says law is social engineering, which means that law is an instrument to balance between competing or conflicting interests.

81 Which of the following statement/statements is/are correct?

I. On 16th June, 1987 the foreign secretaries of South Asian Regional Countries entered into agreement on Extradition.
II. Hongkong Pact on Extradition with India was entered in the middle of June 1980.
III. India and Germany signed an Extradition Treaty on 27th June, 2001.
IV. India and France signed an Extradition Treaty on 24th June, 2002.

Choose the most appropriate answer from the options given below.

1 I, II and IV 2 II, III and IV
3 I and III 4 I, II, III and IV

Ans. (3)

Exp. Only Statements I and III are correct.

Statement II is incorrect because before Hongkong became a part of China, Hongkong and India entered into a treaty on extradition in the middle of June, 1997.

Statement IV is incorrect because India, France signed extradition treaty in Paris on 24th January, 2003.

82 Match List I with List II.

	List I		List II
A.	Section 162 of the Indian Contract Act, 1872	I.	Pledge by Mercantile Agent
B.	Section 178 of the Indian Contract Act, 1872	II.	Bailor's duty to disclose faults in goods bailed
C.	Section 214 of the Indian Contract Act, 1872	III.	Termination of gratuitous bailment by death
D.	Section 150 of the Indian Contract Act, 1872	IV.	Agent's duty to comunicate with principal

Choose the correct answer from the options given below.

Codes

	A	B	C	D		A	B	C	D
1	I	IV	III	II	2	II	I	IV	III
3	IV	II	I	III	4	III	I	IV	II

Ans. (4)

Exp. The correct matching is A–III, B–I, C–IV, D–II.

Section 162 of the Indian Contract Act is related to termination of gratuitous bailment by death. A gratuitous bailment is terminated by the death either of the bailor or of the bailee.

Section 178 of Indian Contract Act is related to pledge by Mercantile Agent. As per the Section, where a mercantile agent is, with the consent of the owner, in possession of goods or the document of title to goods, any pledge made by him, when acting in the ordinary course of business of a mercantile agent, shall be as valid as if he were expressly authorised by the owner of the goods to make the same; provided that the pawnee acts in good faith and has not at the time of the pledge notice that the pawnee has not authority to pledge.

Section 214 of Indian Contract Act is related to agent's duty to communicate with principal. It is the duty of an agent, in cases of difficulty, to use all reasonable diligence in communicating with his principal and in seeking to obtain his instructions.

As per the *Section 150 of the Indian Contract Act* the bailor is bound to disclose to the bailee faults in the goods bailed, of which the bailor is aware and which materially interfere with the use of them, or expose the bailee to extraordinary risks; and if he does not make such disclosure, he is responsible for damage arising to the bailee directly from such faults.

If the goods are bailed for hire, the bailor is responsible for such damage, whether he was or was not aware of the existence of such faults in the goods bailed.

83 **Match List I with List II.**

	List I		List II
A.	Section 13 of CPC	I.	Foreign court
B.	Section 2(5) of CPC	II.	Presumption as to foreign judgements
C.	Section 2 (6) of CPC	III.	When foreign judgement not conclusive
D.	Section 14 of CPC	IV.	Judgement of a foreign court

Codes

	A	B	C	D
1	I	II	IV	III
2	III	I	IV	II
3	III	I	II	IV
4	II	IV	III	I

***Ans.* (2)**

Exp. The correct matching is A–III, B–I, C-IV, D–II.

Section 13 of CPC is related with the extent of conclusiveness of foreign judgements in India. A foreign judgement shall be conclusive as to any matter thereby directly adjudicated upon between the same parties or between parties under whom they or any of them claim litigating under the same title except-

(a) where it has not been pronounced by a Court of competent jurisdiction;

(b) where it has not been given on the merits of the case;

(c) where it appears on the face of the proceedings to be founded on an incorrect view of international law or a refusal to recognise the law of 1[India] in cases in which such law is applicable;

(d) where the proceedings in which the judgement was obtained are opposed to natural justice;

(e) where it has been obtained by fraud;

(f) where it sustains a claim founded on a breach of any law in force in 1[India].

Section 2(5) of CPC is related to Foreign Court. It says 'Foreign Court' means a Court situate outside India and not established or continued by the authority of the Central Government.

Section 2(6) of CPC is related to judgement in a foreign Court. 'Foreign Judgement' means the judgement of a foreign Court.

Section 14 of CPC is related to presumption as to foreign judgements. The Court shall presume upon the production of any document purporting to be a certified copy of a foreign judgement that such judgement was pronounced by a Court of competent jurisdiction, unless the contrary appears on the record; but such presumption may be displaced by proving want of jurisdiction.

84 **Under the provisions of the Hindu Succession Act, 1956**

I. Son of a predeceased daughter is class I heir

II. Widow of a predeceased son of a pre-deceased son is class II heir

III. Mother's mother is class I heir

IV Mother's father is class II heir

Choose the most appropriate answer from the options given below.

1 I, II and III
2 Only I and IV
3 Only II and IV
4 II, III and IV

***Ans.* (2)**

Exp. Statements I and IV are correct.

Under the provisions of the Hindu Succession Act, 1956, son of a predeceased daughter is class I heir and mother's father is class II heir.

Statement II is incorrect because the Widow of a predeceased son of a predeceased son is class I heir.

Statement III is incorrect because Mother's mother is Class II heir.

85 **Which one of the following is 'not' a primary source of Muslim Law?**

1 Sunnah
2 Ijma
3 Urf
4 Qiyas

***Ans.* (3)**

Exp. Urf (Custom) is not a primary source of Muslim Law. Islamic law is primarily derived from the Quran and Sunnah according to the consensus of the Muslim scholars.

86 **Which of the following statement/statements is/are correct?**

I. The offence of 'sedition' is defined under section 124A of IPC.

II. The Supreme Court in Kedar Nath Singh Vs. State of Bihar held that section 124A IPC is not unconstitutional.

III. State (NCT. of Delhi) Vs. Navjot Sandhu Afsan Guru is a case related to sedition.

IV. Mohd. Arif Vs. State of NCT of Delhi is also known as Mumbai Terror Attack case.

V. Waging or attempt to wage war or abetting waging of war against the Government of India is an offence under section 121 IPC.

Choose the correct answer from the options given below

1 I, II, III and IV
2 II, III, IV and V
3 I, II and V
4 Only IV and V

***Ans.* (3)**

Exp. Only Statements I, II and V are correct.

Statement III is incorrect because this Case is commonly known as the Parliament Attack Case. This remarkable case was tried speedily in the Special Court by Shri. S.N. Dhingra. The 4 main accused of this case were, Mohammad Afzal Guru, Shaukat Hussain Guru, S.A.R. Gilani and Afsan Guru (Navjot Sandhu) wife of Shaukat Guru.

Statement IV is incorrect because Mohd. Arif Vs. State of NCT of Delhi is also known as Delhi riots case. The case involved the murder of Head Constable Ratan Lal in the Delhi riots, which was caused by an unlawful assembly protesting against the CAA and NRC. Mohd Arif (petitioner) along with four other persons were the main accused in this case. The charge sheet was filed and the matter was pending in the trial court. Many bail applications, followed by interim bail applications were filed and were rejected by the Court after which, the petitioner approached the Supreme Court for relief.

87 Given below are two statements, one is labelled Assertion (A) and the other is labelled as Reasons (R).

Assertion (A) Under the Companies Act of 2013 Central Government is authroised to implement a facility to file documents in electronic form.

Reason (R) Central Government is authorised to make rules to implement this facility and Section 398, 401 and 402 have been incorporated in the Act of 2013.

In the light of the above statements, choose the correct answer from the options given below.

1 Both (A) and (R) are true and (R) is the correct explanation of (A).
2 Both (A) and (R) are true and (R) is not the correct explanation of (A).
3 (A) is true but (R) is false.
4 (A) is false but (R) is true.

Ans. (1)

Exp. Both (A) and (R) are true and (R) is the correct explanation of (A).

Under the Companies Act of 2013 Central Government is authorised to implement a facility to file documents in electronic form. For eg, Section 398 deals with Provisions relating to filing of applications, documents, inspection, etc., in electronic form, as per Section 401 the Central Government may provide such value added services through the electronic form and levy such fee thereon and 402 deals with application of provisions of Information Technology Act, 2000.

88 The trend towards codification of the British Constitution in whole or in part is a movement during the past decade from eminent quarters. Arrange them in chronological order:

I. Northern Ireland Act
II. Referendum Act
III. Scotland Act
IV. European Communities Act

Choose the correct answer from the options given below

1 I, IV, III, II
2 II, III, I, IV
3 IV, I, II, III
4 III, II, IV, I

Ans. (3)

Exp. The correct chronological order is IV, I, II, III.

The European Communities Act (1972) was the instrument whereby the UK Parliament effected the changes required by the Treaty of Accession by which the UK joined the European Union (then known as the European Communities).

The Northern Ireland Act (1998) is an Act of the Parliament of the United Kingdom, which established a devolved legislature for Northern Ireland, the Northern Ireland Assembly, after decades of direct rule from Westminster .

The Referendum Act 1998 is an act of the Oireachtas which modified how referendums are carried out in Ireland. The act was necessary following the McKenna case in which the Supreme Court of Ireland held that the spending of public money in support of the campaign for a government-approved outcome of a constitutional referendum was unconstitutional. To rectify the imbalance, this act was introduced. Its main provision was to provide for the establishment of a Referendum Commission prior to each future referendum.

The Scotland Act 2016 is an act of the Parliament of the United Kingdom. It sets out amendments to the Scotland Act 1998 and devolve further powers to Scotland. The legislation is based on recommendations given by the report of the Smith Commission, which was established on 19th September, 2014 in the wake of the Scottish independence referendum.

89 The Government of India's policy on abatement of pollution adopted certain guiding principles in the year 1992. Which of the following is not covered under the said guiding principles?

1 Prevention of pollution at source
2 Adoption of best available technology
3 Involvement of NGO's for all purposes
4 Public participation in decision making

Ans. (3)

Exp. The Government of India's policy on abatement of pollution adopted certain guiding principles in the year 1992. Involvement of NGOs for all purposes is not covered under the said guiding principles.

90 Match List I with List II.

List I	List II
A. Art 326 of the Constitution	I. Chief Election Commission shall act as the Chairman of the Election Commission
B. Art 324 (3) of the Constitution	II. Ban to interference by courts in electoral matters
C. Art 328 of the Constitution	III. Elections to be on the basis of adult suffrage
D. Art 329 of the Constitution	IV. Power of Legislature of a state to make provisions with respect to elections to such Legislature

Choose the correct answer from the options given below

Codes

	A	B	C	D		A	B	C	D
1	II	IV	I	III	2	III	IV	I	II
3	III	I	IV	II	4	I	II	IV	III

Ans. (3)

Exp. The correct matching is A-III, B-I, C-IV, D-II.

Article 326 of Constitution says that elections to the House of the People and to the Legislative Assemblies of States to be on the basis of adult suffrage.

Article 324(3) of Constitution says that when any other Election Commissioner is so appointed the Chief Election Commissioner shall act as the Chairman of the Election Commission.

Article 328 of Constitution is related to power of Legislature of a State to make provisions with respect to elections to such Legislature. It states that Subject to the provisions of this Constitution and in so far as provision in that behalf is not made by Parliament, the Legislature of a State may from time to time by law make provision with respect to all matters relating to, or in connection with, the elections to the House or either House of the Legislature of the State including the preparation of electoral rolls and all other matters necessary for securing the due Constitution of such House or Houses.

Article 329 of Constitution is related to ban to interference by courts in electoral matters. It states that notwithstanding anything in this Constitution.

1. The validity of any law relating to the delimitation of constituencies or the allotment of seats to such constituencies, made or purporting to be made under Article 327 or Article 328, shall not be called in question in any court;
2. No election to either House of Parliament or to the House or either House of the Legislature of a State shall be called in question except by an election petition presented to such authority and in such manner as may be provided for by or under any law made by the appropriate Legislature.

Directions (Q. No. 91-100) *Read the given passage and answer the questions that follow* :

Privacy of the individual is an essential aspect of dignity. Dignity has both an intrinsic and instrumental value. As an intrinsic value, human dignity is an entitlement or a constitutionally protected interest in itself. In its instrumental facet, dignity and freedom are inseperably intertwined, each being a facilitative tool to achieve the other. The ability of the individual to protect a zone of privacy enables the realisation of the full value of life and liberty. Liberty has a broader meaning of which privacy is a subset. All liberties may not be exercised in privacy. Yet others can be fulfilled only within a private space. Privacy enables the individual to retain the autonomy of the body and mind. The autonomy of the individual is the ability to make decisions on vital matters of concern to life. Privacy has not been couched as an independent Fundamental Right. But that does not detract from the constitutional protection afforded to it, once the true nature of privacy and its relationship with those Fundamental Rights which are expressly protected is understood. Privacy lies across the spectrum of protected freedoms.

91 The referred paragraph is a part of the judgement delivered by

1 Justice Chelameshwar
2 Justice D.Y. Chandrachud
3 Justice S.A. Bobde
4 Justice F.M. Nariman

Ans. (2)

Exp. The referred paragraph is a part of the judgement delivered by Justice D.Y. Chandrachud.

92 The referred paragraph is taken from the judgement of the Supreme Court in

1 A.D.M. Jabalpur Vs. S. Shukla
2 Mohini Jain Vs. State of Karnataka
3 Maneka Gandhi Vs. Union of India
4 Justice K.S. Puttaswamy (Retd.) and another Vs. Union of India and others

Ans. (4)

Exp. The referred paragraph is taken from the judgement of the Supreme Court in the case of Justice K.S. Puttaswamy (Retd.) and another Vs. Union of India and others.

93 In which of the following case it was held that right to privacy is not protected as a Fundamental Right under the Constitution?

1 M.P Sharma Vs. Satish Chandra, District Magistrate, Delhi
2 Govind Vs. State of M.P.
3 R. Rajagopal Vs. State of Tamil Nadu
4 K.S. Puttaswami Vs. Union of India

Ans. (1)

Exp In the case of M.P Sharma Vs. Satish Chandra, District Magistrate, Delhi, held that the right to privacy is not protected as a Fundamental Right under the Constitution. Given that the 1954 case of M.P. Sharma et al. Vs. Satish Chandra, District Magistrate, Delhi et al. holding that privacy is not a right guaranteed by the Indian Constitution was decided by an eight judge bench, a larger bench of nine Supreme Court justices was convened to determine whether the rationale of the M.P. Sharma's judgement and others which similarly found that the Indian Constitution does not guarantee a right of privacy was based on 'jurisprudential correctness.'

94 Which one of the following statement is correct?

1 Right to privacy is expressly provided as a Fundamental Right under the Constitution.
2 Right to privacy is protected as a Fundamental Right under Article 21 of the Constitution.

3 Right to privacy is not protected as a Fundamental Right under Article 21 of the Constitution.
4 Article 21 of the Constitution protects the life and personal liberty only from executive action.

***Ans.* (2)**

Exp. Only Statement 2 is correct, i.e, Right to privacy is protected as a Fundamental Right under Article 21 of the Constitution.

Article 21 of the Constitution of India states that 'No person shall be deprived of his life or personal liberty except according to the procedure established by law'.

95 In which of the following case it was held that the procedure established by law means the procedure must be just, fair and reasonable?

1 Kharak Singh Vs. State of U.P
2 A.K. Gopalan Vs. Union of India
3 Maneka Gandhi Vs. Union of India
4 Govind Vs. State of M.P.

***Ans.* (3)**

Exp. In the case of Maneka Gandhi Vs. Union of India, it was held that the procedure established by law means the procedure must be just, fair and reasonable. In Maneka Gandhi Vs. Union of India case (1978) SC held that procedure established by law' within the meaning of Article 21 must be right, just and fair and 'not arbitrary, fanciful or oppressive' otherwise, it would be no procedure at all and the requirement of Article 21 would not be satisfied.

96 Which one of the following statements is not correct?

1 Starke and Kelsen contend that there is both legislation and law enforcement in international law.
2 According to Starke, legislation being provided by multilateral treaties in international law.
3 According to Kelsen, sanctions are provided by the right of self-help and war in international law.
4 Treaties and self-help can qualify as legislation and law-enforcement in a positivist sense.

***Ans.* (4)**

Exp. Statement 4 is incorrect because self-help is generally regarded by authorities as a legal recourse under customary international law for the enforcement of treaty obligations.

97 According to Austin, the positive law has following three attributes

1 Command, Sovereign, Obedience
2 Command,Sovereign, Sanction
3 Command, Obedience, Sanction
4 Sovereign,Obedience, Sanction

***Ans.* (2)**

Exp. According to Austin, the positive law has the following three attributes-Command, Sovereign and Sanction. According to him, positive law has three main features: (i) It is a type of command, (ii) It is laid down by a political sovereign, and (iii) It is enforceable to sanction. Thus, every law is a species of command and prescribes a course of conduct.

98 The view that international law consisted of the precepts dictated to States by natural law was advanced by

1 Kelsen	2 Vattel
3 HLA Hart	4 Salmond

***Ans.* (2)**

Exp. The view that international law consisted of the precepts dictated to States by natural law was advanced by Vattel. In 1758, Emerich de Vattel published 'Le Droitdes Gens' and became one of the most important and controversial theorists in the history of international legal thought. The purpose of this paper is to examine the influence of contemporary legal theory and political realities on Vattel; specifically to examine the effect on Vattel of the 'enlightened' natural-law theory of international law and the erosion of that theory in the 18th century by the political realities of *raison d'etat,* and by the systems beyond natural law which were offered in an attempt to regulate the anarchy which the *raison d'etat* philosophy produced.

99 Who defines law 'as a body of rules for human conduct within a community, which by common consent of this community shall be enforced by external power'?

1 Oppenheim	2 Austin
3 Bentham	4 Friedman

***Ans.* (1)**

Exp. Oppenheim defines law 'as a body of rules for human conduct within a community, which by common consent of this community shall be enforced by external power.' This definition of Oppenheim has three main parts: there must be a community; there shall be a body of rules to govern the community and thirdly, common consent among the community for the rules to be enforced power must be present.

100 Which one of the following statements is not correct?

1 Hart's analysis of law suggests that international law consists of legal rules forming not a system but a set of rules.
2 The absence in international law of any basic rules of recognition prevents its being unified into a system.
3 International law remains a mere set of separate rules.
4 Many of the rules of international law rest on treaty, not on custom.

***Ans.* (4)**

Exp. Statement 4 is incorrect because many of the rules of international law rest on customs and conventions and not on treaties.

UGC-NET
LAW
SOLVED PAPER 2020 (September)
PAPER II

1 "The movement of progressive societies has hitherto been a movement from status to contract." The statement has been made by

1 Savigny 2 Puchta 3 Maine 4 Burke

Ans. *(3)*

Exp. The given statement has been made by Henry Maine. Henry Maine is best known for the proposition advanced in Ancient Law that "the movement of the progressive societies has hitherto been a movement from status to contract."

As he explained, the ancient law recognized and dealt with the relationships among extended families, not individuals. Individual members of a family were subject to the control of the family head.

2 Which of the following statements describes the relationship between law and morality among non-positively legal theorists?

1 Law is always in advance of moral ideas.
2 Morality is generally in advance of the law.
3 The law is inextricably bound up with morals.
4 There is no relationship between law and morality.

Ans. *(3)*

Exp. According to non-positively legal theorists', the law is inextricably bound up with morals. This position the been well-expressed by Nigel Simmons who said that "law is an intrinsically moral idea, and that inquiry into the nature of law is ultimately a form of moral enquiry and that system specific debates about law's content can never wholly be separated from the philosophical inquiry into the nature of law as such."

3 The main purpose of 'Corporation Sole' is to

1 make the property easily inheritable.
2 make the property easily transferable.
3 maintain continuity of an office.
4 protect the property of state.

Ans. *(3)*

Exp. The main purpose of 'Corporation Sole' is to maintain the continuity in office.

Corporation sole is an incorporated series of successive persons. It consists of a single person who is personified and regarded by law as a legal person. A corporation sole is perpetual. Examples of Corporation Sole are Public Trustee, Comptroller and Auditor-General of India, the President of India etc. The sole purpose of the corporation is to maintain the continuity of an office.

4 "The real relation of Jurisprudence to Law depends not upon what law is treated, but how Law is treated" is said by

1 Gierke 2 Gray 3 Rawls 4 Duguit

Ans. *(2)*

Exp. 'The real relation of Jurisprudence to Law depends not upon what Law is treated, but how law is treated' is said by Gray.

According to Gray, Jurisprudence is the science of Law, the statement and systematic arrangement of the rules followed by the court and the principles involved in those rules. This was criticised by Stone and he said that Gray has failed to determine any province of Jurisprudence rather he has reduced Jurisprudence to merely a matter of arrangement of rules.

5 In which case the Supreme Court held that the Preamble does form part of the Constitution?

1 Re Berubari Union and Exchange of Enclaves
2 Minerva Mills Vs. Union of India
3 Keshavananda Bharti Vs. State of Kerala
4 S R Bommai Vs. Union of India

Ans. *(3)*

Exp. In Keshvananda Bharti Vs. State of Kerala, Supreme court held that the Preamble does form the part of Constitution.

In this case SC rejected the opinion given in Berubari case and held that the Preamble is a part of Constitution. It observed that the Preamble is of extreme importance and the Constitution should be read and interpreted in the light of grand and noble vision expressed in the Preamble. Supreme Court also said that Preamble may not be essential part of the ordinary statute, but it is an essential part of Constitutional law.

In the 1995 case of Union Government Vs LIC of India also, the Supreme Court has once again held that Preamble is the integral part of the Constitution but is not directly enforceable in the Court of Justice in India.

6 Under Article 14 of the Indian Constitution, the term 'Equal Protection of the Laws' has been taken from the

1 American Constitution 2 British Constitution
3 Australian Constitution 4 Canadian Constitution

Ans. (1)

Exp. Under Article 14 of the Indian Constitution the term 'Equal Protection of the Laws' has been taken from the American constitution.

'Equal Protection of Law' which has been given in Article 14 of Indian constitution has been taken from Section 1 of the 14th Amendment Act of the Constitution of the United States.

7 Article 72 of the Indian Constitution makes a provision for

1 discharge of the President's functions in other contingencies.
2 power of President to grant pardons etc, and to suspend, remit or commute sentences in certain cases.
3 extent of Executive power of Union.
4 Council of Ministers to aid and advise the President.

Ans. (2)

Exp. Article 72 of the Indian Constitution makes a provision for power of President to grant pardons etc. and to suspend, remit or commute sentences in certain cases.

According to Article 72, the president shall have the power to grant pardons, reprieves, respites or remissions of punishment or to suspend remit, remit or commute the sentence of any person convicted of any offence

- in all cases where the punishment or sentence is by a Court Martial
- in all cases where the punishment or sentence is for an offence against any law relating to a matter to which the executive power of the Union extends,
- in all cases where the sentence is a sentence of death.

8 In which case, in respect of natural justice, Lord Denning said that "With a good man in the saddle, the unruly horse can be kept under control. It can jump over obstacles. It can leap fences put up by fictions and come down on the other side of justice."?

1 Enderby Town Football Club Ltd. Vs. Football Association Ltd.
2 Canara Bank Vs. Debasis Das
3 R V Hendon Rural District Council
4 American Cyanamide Co. Vs. Federal Trade Commission

Ans. (1)

Exp. Lord Denning in Enderby Town Football Club Ltd Vs. The Football Association Ltd. Case said that "With a good man in the saddle, the unruly horse can be kept under control. It can jump over obstacles. It can leap fences put up by fictions and come down on the other side of justice.". It is an English contract law case, concerning the scope of contracts and association rules that can be contrary to public policy and illegal.

9 The words 'International Law' were used for the first time by which one of the following eminent Jurists?

1 Openheim 2 W Friedmann
3 Austin 4 Jermy Bentham

Ans. (4)

Exp. The words 'International Law' were used for the first time by Jermy Bentham.

International law, also known as public international law and law of nations, is the set of rules, norms and standards generally recognised as binding between nations.

The term was coined by the English philosopher Jeremy Bentham (1748–1832). According to Jermy Bentham, International Law is a collection of rules governing relation between states.

10 Which of the following chapters of the United Nations Charter deals with pacific settlement of disputes?

1 Chapter VI 2 Chapter VII
3 Chapter III 4 Chapter II

Ans. (1)

Exp. Chapter VI of United Nations Charter deals with the pacific settlement of disputes.

The Charter of the United Nations is the founding document of the United Nations. It was signed on 26th June 1945, in San Francisco, at the conclusion of the United Nations Conference on International Organization, and came into force on 24th October 1945.

Chapter VI deals with the practice of the Security Council aimed at promoting and implementing recommendations and methods or procedures for the peaceful settlement of disputes within the framework of Articles 33-38 of Chapter VI and Articles 11 and 99 of the Charter of the United Nations. Overall, Chapter VI of the Charter contains various provisions according to which the Security Council may make recommendations to the parties to a dispute or situation.

11 In which of the following cases, the rule, that "there is no distinction between 'de facto' and 'de jure' recognition for the purpose of giving effect to the internal acts of the recognised authority" was not applied?

1 Bank of Ethiopia Vs. National Bank of Egypt
2 Luther Vs. Sagor
3 Bank of China Vs. Wells Fargo Bank and Union Trust
4 The Arantzazu Mendi Case

Ans. (2)

Exp. In Luther Vs. Sagor case, the rule, that "there is no distinction between 'de facto' and 'de jure' recognition for the purpose of giving effect to the internal acts of the recognised authority" was not applied.

In Luther Vs. Sagor case, it was held that once a government is recognised, its acts will be granted as valid (by de-facto recognition), even those prior to its recognition, known as the retrospective effect.

12 Which of the following provision of the Statute of International Court of Justice lists "General Principles of Law Recognised by Civilised States" as the third source of International Law?

1 Article 38 (a)
2 Para (1) (c) of Article 38
3 Article 38 (b)
4 Para (3) (c) of Article 38

Ans. (2)

Exp. Para (1)(c) of Article 38 of the Statute of International Court of Justice lists "General Principles of Law Recognised by Civilised States" as the third source of International Law.

General Principles of Law are basic rules whose content is very general and abstract, sometimes reducible to a maxim or a simple concept. Unlike other types of rules such as enacted law or agreements, General Principles of Law have not been "posited" according to the formal sources of law.

13 'A' an officer of a court of justice, being ordered by the court to arrest, 'Y', and after due enquiry, believing 'Z' to be 'Y', arrests 'Z', 'A' has committed

1 an offence of wrongful confinement.
2 an offence of wrongful restraint.
3 an offence of criminal trespass.
4 no offense.

Ans. (4)

Exp. 'A' an officer of a court of justice, being ordered by the court to arrest 'Y' and after due enquiry, believing 'Z' to be 'Y' arrests 'Z'. In this case 'A' has committed no offence.

According to Section 76 of IPC, nothing is an offence which is done by a person who is, or who by reason of a mistake of fact and not by reason of a mistake of law in good faith believes himself to be, bound by law to do it.

14 Section 102 of the Indian Penal Code deals with the provision relating to

1 the right of private defence of property extends to causing death.
2 the right of private defence against deadly assault when there is risk of harm to an innocent person.
3 commencement and continuance of a right of private defence of the body.
4 the right of private defence of the body extends to causing death.

Ans. (3)

Exp. Section 102 of the Indian Penal Code deals with the provision relating to commencement and continuance of a right of private defence of the body.

The right of private defence of the body commences as soon as a reasonable apprehension of danger to the body arises from an attempt or threat to commit the offence though the offence may not have been committed; and it continues as long as such apprehension of danger to the body continues.

15 The provision regarding 'selling minors for purposes of prostitution etc' is given in Indian Penal Code under

1 Section 372
2 Section 373
3 Section 370 A
4 Section 371

Ans. (1)

Exp. The provision regarding 'selling minors for purposes of prostitution etc' is given in Indian Penal Code under Section 372.

According to Section 372, whoever sells, lets to hire, or otherwise disposes of any person under the age of eighteen years with intent that such person shall at any age be employed or used for the purpose of prostitution or illicit intercourse with any person or for any unlawful and immoral purpose, or knowing it to be likely that such person will at any age be employed or used for any such purpose, shall be punished with imprisonment of either description for a term which may extend to ten years, and shall also be liable to fine.

16 Section 376 DB of Indian Penal Code provides for the

1 Punishment for gang rape of woman under sixteen years of age.
2 Punishment of rape of woman under twelve years of age.
3 Punishment for gang rape of woman under twelve years of age.
4 Punishment of causing death of resulting in a persistent vegetative state of the victim.

Ans. (3)

Exp. Section 376 DB provides for the punishment for gangrape of woman under twelve years of age.

It says where a woman under twelve years of age is raped by one or more persons constituting a group or acting in furtherance of a common intention, each of those persons shall be deemed to have committed the offence of rape and shall be punished with imprisonment for life, which shall mean imprisonment for the remainder of that person's natural life, and with fine, or with death.

17 According to whom is it 'Law of Tort and not Law of Torts?

1 Winfield
2 Pollock
3 Fraser
4 Salmond

Ans. (1)

Exp. According to Winfield, it is 'Law of Tort not Law of Torts'.

Winfield is the chief supporter of this theory. He says, all injuries done to another person are torts, unless there is some justification recognized by law. Law of tort is a general liability which originates from the violation of duty determined by law. Winfield while supporting this theory comes to the conclusion that law of tort is growing and from time-to-time courts have created new torts. Tortious liability arises from the breach of a duty primarily fixed by law. This duty is towards persons generally and its breach is redressable by an action for unliquidated damages.

18 "A tort is a civil wrong for which, the remedy is an action for damages and which not exclusively breach of contract or breach of trust or breach of merely equitable obligation." The above definition was given by

1 Salmond
2 Winfield
3 Fraser
4 Clerk and Lindsell

Ans. (1)

Exp. "A tort is a civil wrong for which, the remedy is an action for damages and which is not exclusively breach of contract or breach of trust or breach of merely equitable obligation". Salmond has given the above-mentioned definition.

A tort, as per English common law, is a civil wrong that causes a claimant to suffer loss or harm resulting in legal liability for the person who commits the tortuous act.

19 When two motorists coming from opposite directions in their cars collide with each other and in the process, they injure seriously a person who was standing on the roadside, the two motorists are

1 Independent tortfeasors
2 Participate in contributory negligence
3 Two negligent persons
4 Joint tortfeasors

Ans. (1)

Exp. When two motorists coming from opposite directions in their cars collide with each other and in the process, they injure seriously a person who was standing on the roadside, the two motorists are Independent tortfeasor.

Those people who caused the same damage by independent wrongful acts are Independent tortfeasor. In case of Joint tortfeasor the parties must act together in committing the wrong, or their acts, if independent of each other, must unite in causing a single injury.

20 The maxim "Salus Populi Suprema Lex" means

1 welfare of people is Supreme law.
2 increasing population is the supreme cause of concern.
3 no man is above law.
4 whatever the public collectively say, is the law.

Ans. (1)

Exp. Tha maxim "Salus Populi Suprema Lex" means 'welfare of people is Supreme law'.

It is a recognition that laws and rules derive their value from how well they serve their purpose of protecting and promoting the public good.

21 "Threatening to commit certain acts forbidden by Indian Penal Code" to induce a person to enter into a contract is associated with

1 Undue influence
2 Coercion
3 Criminal intimidation
4 Threat

Ans. (2)

Exp. "Threatening to commit certain acts forbidden by Indian Penal Code" to induce a person to enter into a contract is associated with Coercion.

According to section 15 of Indian Contract Act, 1872, 'Coercion' is the committing, or threatening to commit, any act forbidden by the Indian Penal Code (45 of 1860) or the unlawful detaining, or threatening to detain, any property, to the prejudice of any person whatever, with the intention of causing any person to enter into an agreement.

22 "An offer cannot be accepted unless it was brought to the knowledge of the person to whom it is made." This was laid down in the case of

1 Lalman Shukla Vs. Gauri Dutt
2 Balfour Vs. Balfour
3 Mcgregor Vs. Mcgregor
4 Carlill Vs. Carbolic Smoke Ball Co

Ans. (1)

Exp. In Lalman Shukla Vs. Gauri Dutt it was laid down by the court that "An offer cannot be accepted unless it was brought to the knowledge of the person to whom it is made". This case projected light on the important term and explanation of the General offer.

Balfour Vs. Balfour is a leading English contract law case. It held that there is a rebuttable presumption against an intention to create a legally enforceable agreement when the agreement is domestic in nature.

In Mcgregor Vs. Mcgregor case, it was held that the Precedent does not apply if the married couple are separated when the agreement is made.

Carlill Vs. Carbolic Smoke Ball Co, was an English Contract Law decision by the court of appeal which held that an advertisement containing certain terms to get a reward constituted a binding unilateral offer that could be accepted by anyone who performed its terms.

23 Frustration of a contract occurs in two conditions. Firstly, where the contract has become physically impossible and secondly, where the object has failed. The above was laid down in the case of

1 Krell Vs. Henry
2 Paradine Vs. Jane
3 Taylor Vs. Caldwell
4 Komal Rani Vs. Chandram

Ans. (1)

Exp. In Krell Vs. Henry, it was laid down that frustration of a contract occurs in two conditions. Firstly, where the contract has become physically impossible and secondly, where the object has failed.

Section 56 of Indian contract Act talks about frustration of contract. Frustration of contracts refers to a particular way in which contractual obligations can be discharged. A contract is frustrated where further performance of the contract becomes impossible due to an unforeseen event, or series of events, taking place through no fault of the parties to the agreement.

24 A party who suffers loss as a result of a breach of contract can in the usual course claim

1 Ordinary damages
2 Special damages
3 Exemplary damages
4 Penal damages

Ans. (1)

Exp. In usual course, Ordinary damages can be claimed by the party who suffers loss as a result of a breach of contract.

Ordinary damages are damages which fairly and reasonably be considered as arising naturally and directly in the usual course of things from the breach of contract itself.

Special Damages is the term used to refer to any actual financial losses incurred as a direct result of the breach. Damages awarded in addition to actual damages when the defendant acted with recklessness, malice, or deceit is known as Exemplary damages.

When liquidated damages aren't proportionate to the real or anticipated loss, the courts can decide their penalty and they are known as Penal damages.

25 Which one of the following is not an 'Ancient Source' of Hindu Law?

1 Smriti
2 Precedents
3 Digests
4 Shruti

Ans. (2)

Exp. 'Precedents' are not the ancient source of Hindu Law.It is a modern source of Hindu Law.

Ancient sources of Hindu Law are-

Shrutis The word 'Shruti' is derived from the root word 'shru' which means 'to hear' and the term refers to the four Vedas. Vedas originated by the opinion of individual sages and imparted by oral tradition to the families and disciples.

Smritis The second source of Hindu law is a collection of manuals collectively known as smritis authored by 'rishis or sages, the philosophers, social thinkers and teachers. Smritis have the entire code of conduct of life that was proposed by sages in the form of dharma covering all the aspects of life behaviour.

Commentaries and digests Gradual development of society gives rise to complex situations and thus necessitated the need for codified laws. Vedas didn't contain positive laws but hymns only. The need for uniform and clear laws resulted in the writing of commentaries on the sacred text or smritis.

Customs Customs are described as the parent of all laws in society as the origin of all laws can be traced in the roots of customs. Customs are the primary source of law since they're well embedded in society. In order to become a law a custom must be ancient, reasonable, certain, uniform, obligatory, ongoing without interruption, should not be immoral, or opposed to public policy.

26 Which of the following is not a feature of 'Mitakshara Coparcenary'?

1 Unobstructed heritage
2 Obstructed heritage
3 Unpredictable and fluctuating interest
4 Community of interest and unity of possesion

Ans. (2)

Exp. Obstructed heritage is not the feature of 'Mitakshara Coparcenary'.

Under the Mitakshara Corparcenary a son has a right over the joint family property. Following are the characteristic features of Mitakshara Coparcenary:

- Unobstructed heritage
- Unity of Ownership
- Indeterminability of shares
- Community of interest
- Devolution by survivorship
- Right of Maintenance

27 Rules relating to 'Sapinda Relationship' are based on the principle of

1 Endogamy
2 Polyandary
3 Polygyny
4 Exogamy

Ans. (4)

Exp. Rules relating to 'Sapinda Relationship' are based on the principle of Exogamy.

Exogamy is also known as an out-marriage. It is a custom that promotes marriage outside a person's own group. In a few cases, the exogamy rules may also state an outside group to which marriage can be done.

Sapinda relationship with reference to any person extends as far as the third generation (inclusive) in the line of ascent through the mother, and the fifth (inclusive) in the line of ascent through the father, the line being traced upwards in each case from the person concerned, who is to be counted as the first generation. It is mentioned in Section 3(f) of Hindu Marriage Act.

28 A Bigamous Hindu marriage is

1 void but not punishable
2 void and punishable
3 voidable
4 valid

Ans. (2)

Exp. A Bigamous Hindu marriage is void and punishable. Bigamy is prohibited in India under Section 494 of Indian Penal Code. Section 494 of IPC says, "Whoever, having a husband or wife living, marries in any case in which such marriage is void by reason of its taking place during the life of such husband or wife, shall be punished with imprisonment of either description for a term which may extend to seven years, and shall also be liable to fine"

Also, Section 17 of Hindu Marriage Act, 1955 says, "Any marriage between two Hindus (including Buddhist, Jaina or Sikh) solemnized after the commencement of this Act is void if at the date of such marriage either party had a husband or wife living; and the provisions of Sections 494 and 495 of the Indian Penal Code (45 of 1860) shall apply accordingly."

29 National Commission of Minorities was established under which of the following provisions?

1 Article 328 of the Constitution
2 Article 328A of the Constitution
3 Section 3 of National Commission of Minorities Act, 1992
4 Article 280 of the Constitution of India

Ans. *(3)*

➲ *Exp.* Under Section 3 of National Commission of Minorities Act, 1992 the National Commission of Minorities was established.

Section 3 of the Act says, The Central Government shall constitute a body to be known as the National Commission for Minorities to exercise the powers conferred on, and to perform the functions assigned to it under this Act.

Six religious communities viz. Muslims, Christians, Sikhs, Buddhists, Zoroastrians (Parsis) and Jains have been notified in Gazette of India as minority communities by the Union Government all over India.

30 The Chairperson of National Human Rights Commission shall be

1 Chief Justice of the Supreme Court
2 Chief Justice of a High Court
3 Judge of the Supreme Court
4 Chairperson of National Commission of Women

Ans. *(1)*

➲ *Exp.* The Chairperson of the National Human Rights Commission shall be the Chief Justice of the Supreme Court.

Under Section 3(2) of Protection of Human Rights Act, 1993, the Commission shall consist of—

(a) a Chairperson who has been a Chief Justice of the Supreme Court;

(b) one Member who is, or has been, a Judge of the Supreme Court;

(c) one Member who is, or has been, the Chief Justice of a High Court;

(d) two Members to be appointed from amongst persons having knowledge of, or practical experience in, matters relating to human rights.

31 The Commission on Sustainable Development was established in which year?

1 1972 2 1982 3 1992 4 2002

Ans. *(3)*

➲ *Exp.* United Nations Commission on Sustainable Development (CSD) was established by the UN General Assembly in December, 1992 to ensure effective follow-up of United Nations Conference on Environment and Development (UNCED), also known as the Earth Summit. The United Nations Commission on Sustainable Development (CSD) was a body under the UN Economic and Social Council (ECOSOC) tasked with overseeing the outcomes of the 1992 United Nations Conference on Environment and Development/Earth Summit.

32 The legally binding limit to carbon emission was laid down in

1 Kyoto Protocol on Global Warming, 1997.
2 Copenhagen Summit on Climate Change, 2009.
3 Durban Conference on Climate Change, 2009.
4 Lima Conference on Climate Change.

Ans. *(1)*

➲ *Exp.* Legally binding limit to carbon emission was laid down in Kyoto Protocol on Global Warming, 1997.

The Kyoto Protocol was an international treaty which extended the 1992 United Nations Framework Convention on Climate Change (UNFCCC) that commits state parties to reduce greenhouse gas emissions, based on the scientific consensus that global warming is occurring and that human-made CO_2 emissions are driving it. The Kyoto Protocol was adopted in Kyoto, Japan, on 11 December, 1997 and entered into force on 16th February, 2005.

33 The provision relating to 'legal recognition of electronic signatures' is contained under which section of Information Technology Act, 2000?

1 Section 3 2 Section 3-A
3 Section 4 4 Section 5

Ans. *(4)*

➲ *Exp.* Section 5 of Information Technology Act, 2000 talks about legal recognition of electronic signature.

It says, where any law provides that information or any other matter shall be authenticated by affixing the signature or any document shall be signed or bear the signature of any person, then, notwithstanding anything contained in such law, such requirement shall be deemed to have been satisfied, if such information or matter is authenticated by means of electronic signature affixed in such manner as may be prescribed by the Central Government.

34 What is a Whistle-blower?

1 A person who signals illegal or unethical practice to a prescribed body.
2 Usually a disgruntled ex-employee.
3 A subversive person spying on a company.
4 An investigative journalist.

Ans. *(1)*

➲ *Exp.* Whistle-blower is a person who signals illegal or unethical practice to a prescribed body.

In other words, a whistle-blower is a person, who could be an employee of a company, or a government agency, disclosing information to the public or some higher authority about any wrongdoing, which could be in the form of fraud, corruption, etc.

The Whistle-blower Protection Act, 2014 establish a mechanism to receive complaints relating to disclosure on any allegation of corruption or wilful misuse of power or wilful misuse of discretion against any public servant and to inquire or cause an inquiry into such disclosure and to provide adequate safeguards against victimisation of the person making such complaints

35 When the biological resources are accessed for commercial utilisation or the bio-survey and bio-utilisation leads to commercial utilisation, the applicant shall have the option to pay the benefit-sharing ranging from

1 0.1 to 0.2
2 0.1 to 0.3
3 0.1 to 0.4
4 0.1 to 0.5

Ans. (4)

Exp. When the biological resources are accessed for commercial utilisation or the bio-survey and bio-utilisation leads to commercial utilisation, the applicant shall have the option to pay the benefit-sharing ranging from 0.1 to 0.5. Section 21 of Biodiversity Act, 2002 talks about determination of equitable benefit sharing by National Biodiversity Authority. The National Biodiversity Authority shall while granting approvals under Section 19 or Section 20 of the act ensure that the terms and conditions subject to which approval is granted secures equitable sharing of benefits arising out of the use of accessed biological resources, their by-products, innovations and practices associated with their use and applications and knowledge relating thereto in accordance with mutually agreed terms and conditions between the person applying for such approval, local bodies concerned and the benefit claimers.

36 By which amendment, the third and fourth schedules of the IT Act were omitted?

1 Act 10 of 2009
2 Act 55 of 2002
3 Act 66 of 2009
4 Act 09 of 2009

Ans. (1)

Exp. By Act 10 of 2009, the third and fourth schedules of IT Act were omitted.

Third and fourth schedules are omitted by the Information Technology (Amendment) Act, 2008 (Act 10 of 2009), with effect from 27th October, 2009.

The primary objectives of the IT Act, 2000 are Granting legal recognition to all transactions done through electronic data exchange, other means of electronic communication or e-commerce in place of the earlier paper-based communication.

37 In a Parliamentary Form of Government, the British convention of 'Ministerial Responsibility' has been explicitly codified in the Indian Constitution under

1 Article 74 (1)
2 Article 74 (2)
3 Article 75 (2)
4 Article 75 (3)

Ans. (3)

Exp. In Parliamentary Form of government, the British convention of 'Ministerial Responsibility' has been explicitly codified in the Indian constitution under Article 75(3).

Article 75(3) says, Council of Minister shall be collectively responsible to the house of people.

38 Which one of the following is the mandatory minimum requirement for a functional federation?

1 States should be represented in the Upper House of the National Legislature.
2 Judicial review.
3 Distribution of Legislative and Administrative powers between the two sets of Governments-National and State, so as to ensure the independence of the Government within their respective spheres.
4 Distribution of Legislative and Administrative powers between the two sets of Governments-National and State, so as to ensure the independent but coordinated exercise of powers of the Government.

Ans. (3)

Exp. Distribution of Legislative and Administrative powers between the two sets of Governments - National and State, so as to ensure the independence of the Government within their respective spheres is the mandatory requirement for a functional federation.

Some other characteristics of functional federation include Supremacy of constitution, distribution of power, supremacy of judiciary and bicameral legislature.

39 In which case, the Supreme Court held that pardoning powers of the President under Article 72 and Governors under Article 161 is subject to the judicial review?

1 Satya Narain Sharma Vs. State of Rajasthan
2 Vineet Narain Vs. Union of India
3 Epuru Sudhakar Vs. State of Andhra Pradesh
4 Chootey Lal Vs. State of Uttar Pradesh

Ans. (3)

Exp. In case of Epuru Sudhakar Vs. State of Andhra Pradesh, the Supreme Court held that pardoning power of the President under Article 72 and Governors under Article 161 is subject to judicial review.

The Supreme Court laid down certain grounds on which can be claimed by the petitioner for judicial review of the clemency power:

- If the order is passed without any application of mind.
- If the order passed is malafide.
- If the order passed on completely irrelevant considerations.
- If the order suffers from arbitrariness.

The Apex Court states that the cases where the delay in mercy petition was unexplained of 6 to 12 years, then in those cases the death sentences must be commuted by life imprisonment.

40 The provision regarding 'legislation for giving effect to international agreements is given in the Indian Constitution under

1 Article 253
2 Article 255
3 Article 251
4 Article 254

Ans. (1)

Exp. Article 253 of the Indian Constitution is the provision regarding 'legislation for giving effect to international agreements'.

This article says that Parliament has power to make any law for the whole or any part of the territory of India for implementing any treaty, agreement or convention with any other country or countries or any decision made at any international conference, association or other body.

41 Which of the following duties have been included by Austin in the category of 'absolute duties'?

I. Duties owed to persons indefinitely
II. Self-regarding duties
III. Duties owed to the sovereign
IV. Duties owed to parents

Choose the correct answer from the options given below.

1 I, II and III
2 II, III and IV
3 I, III and IV
4 I, II, III and IV all

Ans. (1)

Exp. Duties owed to persons indefinitely, self-regarding duties and duties owed to the sovereign have been included by Austin in the category of 'absolute duties'.

Duties owed to persons indefinitely comes under the category of absolute duties. For example, duties toward community i.e., duty not to create nuisance.

Self-regarding duties are duties owed to oneself and comes under the category of absolute duties. For example, duty not to commit suicide and duty not to become intoxicated.

Duties owed to sovereign is absolute duty according to Austin as it is duty toward the state.

Although duty towards parents is not an absolute duty.

42 Which of the following conditions are essential for a custom to be valid?

I. The custom had to possess a sufficient measure of antiquity.
II. The custom must have been enjoyed 'as a right'.
III. The custom need not be consistent with other customs in the same area.
IV. The custom must be certain and precise.

Choose the correct answer from the options given below.

1 I, and II
2 I, II and III
3 I, II and IV
4 I, II, III and IV all

Ans. (3)

Exp. Statement I, II, and IV are correct.

Statement I is correct because it says custom had to possess a sufficient measure of antiquity. A custom must be in existence from time immemorial. English law fixed the year 1189 to test the antiquity of a custom.

Statement II is correct because custom must have been enjoyed as a matter of right. This right should be enforceable. Thus, custom must result in creating obligatory force at the one hand and related claim on the other hand.

Statement IV is correct as it says custom must be certain and precise. Custom must be certain. If the nature of the custom is not certain then it loses its validity.

Statement III is incorrect as a custom must not be in conflict with other prevailing customs. The customs must be in consistency with other custom.

43 Which of the following are the exceptions of the 'specific enforcement rule' of the Theory of Remedial Liability?

I. Imperfects duties
II. Duties that are impossible for specific performance
III. Duties which are inexpedient to enforce specifically

Choose the correct answer from the options given below.

1 I and II
2 I and III
3 II and III
4 I, II and III all

Ans. (4)

Exp. Imperfect duties, duties that are impossible for specific performance and duties which are inexpedient to enforce specifically are the exceptions of the 'specific enforcement rule' of the Theory of Remedial Liability.

The Theory of Remedial Liability lays down that whenever the law creates a duty, it should enforce the specific fulfilment of it. The sole condition of the existence of remedial liability is the existence of a legal duty binding upon the defendant and unfulfilled by him.

To this general principle there are three exceptions:

(i) Duties of imperfect Obligation : The breach of such a duty gives no cause of action creates no liability at all, example a time barred debt is a legal debt, but the payment of it cannot be compelled by any legal proceeding.

(ii) Where the duty violated is in its nature incapable of specific enforcement : There are duties which cannot be specifically enforced, once they are broken. Thus, it is the duty of everyone to refrain from doing anything that is likely to injure the reputation of others. But once a libel on somebody is perpetrated, it becomes impossible in the nature of the things, to enforce specifically on the miscreant the duty of refraining, for the simple reason that it is too late. Wrongs of this nature cannot be remedied; they can only be punished.

(iii) Where the specific enforcement of a duty is inexpedient: There are duties, the specific performance of which the law can but will not enforce, because it is neither advisable nor expedient to do so. Thus, the law will categorically refuse to enforce specifically many contracts, particularly contracts of service and promises of marriage, for obvious reasons. In such cases, it will only provide pecuniary compensation.

44 The provisions given under Article 13 of the Indian Constitution are as follows :

I. All laws in force in the territory of India immediately before the commencement of this Constitution will be void to the extent of the inconsistency.

II. 'Laws in force' includes all laws passed or made by the legislature or other competent authority in the territory of India before the commencement of this constitution and not previously repealed.

III. The state shall not make any law which takes or abridges right conferred by Part III and any law made in the contravention shall be void.

IV. 'Law' does not include any ordinance, order, bye-law, rule, regulation, notification, custom or usage etc.

V. Article 13 shall apply to any amendment of the Constitution made under Article 368.

Choose the correct answer from the options given below.

1 II and IV 2 II and V
3 I and V 4 I, II and III

Ans. *(4)*

➲ *Exp.* Statement I, II and III contains the provisions given under Article 13 of the Indian Constitution.

Article 13(1) directly says, all laws in force in the territory of India immediately before the commencement of this Constitution, in so far as they are inconsistent with the provisions of this Part (part III, fundamental rights), shall, to the extent of such inconsistency, be void.

Article 13 (3) directly says, 'laws in force' includes laws passed or made by Legislature or other competent authority in the territory of India before the commencement of this Constitution and not previously repealed.

Article 13(2) says state shall not make any law which will take away the rights conferred under part III of constitution, in case if any law is made in contravention to fundamental right that law will stand void.

Statement IV and V are incorrect because Article 13(3) says, law includes Ordinance, order, bye law, rule, regulation, notification, custom or usages etc.

Also, the case is opposite as per article 13(4) that says nothing from Article 13 shall apply to any amendment under Article 368.

45 Under Article 30 of the Indian Constitution, the right to minorities are guaranteed as under

I. the right is guaranteed to the religious minorities only.

II. the right is guaranteed or linguistic and religious minorities.

III. right is given only to administer the educational institution.

IV. right is given to minorities to establish and administer the educational institution.

V. the state is prohibited from making discrimination in the matter of grant of aid to any educational institution on the ground that it is managed by a religious minority or linguistic minority.

Choose the correct answer from the options given below.

1 I and V 2 II, and III
3 II, IV and V 4 III and III

Ans. *(3)*

➲ *Exp.* Statement II, IV, and V are correct with respect to the right to minorities guaranteed as under Article 30 of the Indian Constitution.

Article 30 (1) says, all minorities whether based on religion or language shall have the right to establish and administer educational institutions of their choice.

As per article 30 (1) it says right is given to minorities to establish and administer educational institution.

As per Article 30 (2), the state shall not, in granting aid to educational institutions, discriminate against any educational institution on the ground that it is under the management of a minority, whether based on religion or language.

Statement I is incorrect because Article 30 does not talk about the religious minorities only instead it talks about all minorities whether based on religion or language.

Statement III is incorrect because under Article 30 not only administering right is given but the right to both establish and administer educational institution is provided.

46 Which of the following statements are not correct?

I. In the Hague Conference of 1930, a convention on the conflict of Nationality law was signed and adopted.

II. Nottebohm case is related to "Statelessness."

III. On 7th November 1967, the General Assembly of the UN adopted the declaration on elimination of discrimination against women.

IV. The Convention on the Reduction of Statelessness, 1961 came into force on 13th December, 1965.

V. The Convention on the Status of Stateless Persons was adopted on 6th June, 1960.

Choose the correct answer from the options given below.

1 I, III and V 2 II, IV and V
3 II, III and IV 4 I, II and III

Ans. *(2)*

➲ *Exp.* Statement II, IV, and V are not correct.

Instead of "Statelessness" Nottebohm case was related to matter of nationality.

Instead of 13th December, 1965 the Convention on the Reduction of Statelessness 1961, came into force on 13th December, 1975.

The Convention relating to the Status of Stateless Persons was adopted on 28th September, 1954 and entered into force on 6th June, 1960.

Statement I and III are correct as the Convention on certain questions relating to the Conflict of Nationality Laws was a League of Nations convention adopted during the League of Nations Codification Conference, 1930 in the Hague.

The declaration on the elimination of discrimination against women, outlining that body's views on women's rights, was adopted by the General Assembly on 7th November, 1967.

47 Which of the following statements are correct?

I. The Dunkel Draft Text or Dunkel Package or the Dunkel Draft Act embodying the results of Uruguay Round of Multilateral Trade Negotiation, was released on 20th December, 1995.

II. The new World Trade Organisation (WTO) which came into effect on 1st January, 1995, replaced the General Agreement on Tariff and Trade (GATT).

III. The functions of WTO are mentioned in Article III of the Agreement establishing WTO.

IV. The Sixth Ministerial Conference of WTO was held in Hongkong (China) from 13th to 18th December, 2008.

Choose the correct answer from the options given below.

1 Only II, III
2 I, III and IV
3 Only I, II, III
4 I, II, III, IV all

Ans. (1)

Exp. Statement II and III are correct.

The new World Trade Organisation (WTO) which came into effect on 1st January, 1995, replaced the General Agreement on Tariff and Trade (GATT)

The functions of WTO are mentioned in Article III of the Agreement establishing WTO.

Statement I and IV are incorrect because instead of 1995, Dunkel Draft Text was released on 20th December, 1991. Also, instead of 2008, the Sixth Ministerial Conference of WTO was held in Hong Kong from 13th-18th December, 2005.

48 The provision regarding the offences against the Public Tranquility are as follows

I. Whoever, being aware of facts which render any assembly, an unlawful assembly, intentionally joins that assembly, or continues in it, is said to be member of unlawful assembly.

II. When two or more persons, by fighting in a public, disturb the public peace, they are said to 'Commit an affray'.

III. Whoever is a member of an unlawful assembly, shall be punished with imprisonment of either description for a term which may extend to one year.

IV. Whoever commits an affray, shall be punished with imprisonment of either description for a term which may extend to one month or with fine which may extend to one hundred rupees, or with both.

V. Whoever is guilty of rioting shall be punished with fine only.

Choose the correct answer from the options given below.

1 II and III
2 III and IV
3 I, II and IV
4 I and III

Ans. (3)

Exp. Statements I, II and IV contains the provisions regarding the offences against the Public Tranquility.

Section 142 of IPC states that whoever, being aware of facts which render any assembly, an unlawful assembly, intentionally joins that assembly, or continues in it, is said to be a member of an unlawful assembly.

Section 159 of IPC states that when two or more persons, by fighting in a public place, disturb the public peace, they are said to 'Commit an affray'.

According to Section 160 of IPC, whoever commits an affray, shall be punished with imprisonment of either description for a term which may extend to one month, or with fine which may extend to one hundred rupees, or with both.

Statement III and IV are incorrect.

According to Section 143 of IPC, whoever is a member of an unlawful assembly, shall be punished with imprisonment of either description for a term which may extend to six months, or with fine, or with both.

Instead of only fine according to Section 147 of IPC, whoever is guilty of rioting, shall be punished with imprisonment of either description for a term which may extend to two years, or with fine, or with both.

49 The quantum of punishments given under Indian Penal Code are

I. Whoever commits extortion shall be punished with imprisonment of either description for a term which may extend to three years or with fine or with both.

II. Whoever commits criminal breach of trust shall be punished for a term which may extend to seven years.

III. Whoever dishonestly, misappropriates or converts to his own use any movable property, shall be punished with imprisonment of either description for a term which may extend to two years or with fine or with both.

IV. Whoever makes any preparation for committing dacoity shall be punished with fine only.

V. If at the time of attempting to commit robbery or dacoity the offender is armed with deadly weapons, shall be punished for two years.

Choose the correct answer from the options given below.

1 II and III   2 II and IV
3 I, IV and V   4 I and III

Ans. (4)

Exp. Statement I and III contains the quantum of punishments given under Indian Penal Code.

According to Section 384 of IPC, whoever commits extortion shall be punished with imprisonment of either description for a term which may extend to three years, or with fine, or with both.

According to Section 403 of IPC, whoever dishonestly misappropriates or converts to his own use any movable property, shall be punished with imprisonment of either description for a term which may extend to two years, or with fine, or with both.

Statement II, IV and V is incorrect.

According to Section 406 of IPC, whoever commits criminal breach of trust shall be punished with imprisonment of either description for a term which may extend to three years, or with fine, or with both.

According to Section 399 of IPC, whoever makes, any preparation for committing dacoity, shall be punished with rigorous imprisonment for a term which may extend to ten years, and shall also be liable to fine.

According to Section 398 of IPC, if at the time of attempting to commit robbery or dacoity, the offender is armed with any deadly weapon, the imprisonment with which such offender shall be punished shall not be less than seven years.

50 Under Section 361 of Indian Penal Code the "kidnapping from lawful guardianship" is

I. When someone takes or entices any minor without the consent of the guardian.

II. When someone takes or entices any person of unsound mind out of the keeping of lawful guardian without the consent of the guardian.

III. When someone entices or takes away any minor under 16 years of age if male and 18 years of age if female without consent of the guardian.

Choose the correct answer from the options given below.

1 I and II   2 I, II and III
3 I and III   4 II and III

Ans. (4)

Exp. According to Section 361 of IPC, whoever takes or entices any minor under 16 years of age if a male, or under 18 years of age if a female, or any person of unsound mind, out of the keeping of the lawful guardian of such minor or person of unsound mind, without the consent of such guardian, is said to kidnap such minor or person from lawful guardianship.

51 Where does vicarious liability generally arise from?

I. A contract of service

II. A contract for service

III. A contract of service as well as a contract for service

IV. A wrongful act of servant

Choose the correct answer from the options given below.

1 I and IV   2 Only IV
3 I, II and III, all   4 Only II

Ans. (1)

Exp. Vicarious liability generally arises from a contract of service and a wrongful act of servant.

Contract of service is an agreement between an employer and employee and vicarious liability arises from cases where one person is liable for the acts of others.

A wrongful act of a servant also results in arise of vicarious liability. If the wrongful act takes place during employment vicarious liability arises.

Contract for service means an independent contractor, such as a self-employed person or vendor, is engaged for a fee to carry out an assignment or project, in this case vicarious liability does not arises.

In case of both contract of service and contract for service vicarious liability doesn't arise as vicarious liability only arises in case contract of service.

52 A person may be liable in respect of wrongful acts or omission of others in which of the following ways?

I. As having ratified and authorised the particular act.

II. As standing towards the other person in a relation entailing responsibility for wrongs done by that person.

III. As having abetted the tortious acts committed by others.

Choose the correct answer from the options given below.

1 Only I   2 Only II
3 Only III   4 I, II and III all

Ans. (4)

Exp. Statement I, II and III all are correct.

A person may be liable in respect of wrongful acts or omission of others in the following ways:

- As having ratified or authorised the particular act with the full knowledge of it being tortious is one of the situations where person can be held liable for wrongful act done by another. In ratification the relationship can be between any two or more person, it need not be only master-servant relation.

- As standing towards the other person in a relation entailing responsibility for wrongs done by that person. There should be some or the other relationship between the wrong doer and the person who gave the order. Relationship can be that of Master-Servant, Principle-Agent.
- As having abetted the tortious acts committed by others. If the person abetted the wrongful act which is committed by another, he or she will directly come under the ambit where the person can be held liable for the wrongful act of others.

53 Any agreement in respect of production, supply, distribution, storage, acquisition, or control of goods or provision of service which causes or is likely to cause an appreciable adverse effect on competition in India is void. These agreements include

I. Tie in arrangement
II. Exclusive supply agreement
III. Exclusive distribution agreement
IV. Refusal to deal
V. Resale price maintenance

Choose the correct answer from the options given below.

1 I and II
2 III, IV, V
3 I, II and III
4 I, II, III, IV, V all

Ans. (4)

Exp. Section 3 of Competition Act, 2002 talks about anti-competitive agreements.

Section 3(4) of the act specifically says that any agreement amongst enterprises or persons at different stages or levels of the production chain in different markets, in respect of production, supply, distribution, storage, sale or price of, or trade in goods or provision of services, including-

- tie-in arrangement.
- exclusive supply agreement.
- exclusive distribution agreement.
- refusal to deal.
- resale price maintenance, shall be an considered as anti-competitive agreements and hence are void.

54 Which of the following are correct?

I. The Doctrine of Priority of Consideration is applicable in India.
II. The Doctrine of Priority of Consideration is not applicable in India.
III. The Rule of Priority of Contract is applicable in India.
IV. The Rule of Priority of Contract is not applicable in India.

Choose the correct answer from the options given below.

1 I and III
2 II and IV
3 II and III
4 Only III

Ans. (3)

Exp. Statements II and III are correct.

The Doctrine of Priority of Consideration is not applicable in India. The privity of consideration means the consideration should be furnished by the promisee and not by the third person.

The Doctrine of Privity of Contract is applicable in India. The Privity of contract means the stranger to the contract cannot sue against the parties to the contract.

Note This Question was deleted from paper and is not considered.

55 Under Section 5 of the Sale of Goods Act, 1930, a contract for the sale of goods can be made

I. By writing and must be registered.
II. By word of mouth
III. By partly in writing and partly by word of mouth.
IV. By writing or partly in writing and partly by word of mouth.

Choose the correct answer from the options given below.

1 I and III
2 I and IV
3 I and II
4 II and IV

Ans. (4)

Exp. Under Section 5 of the Sale of Goods Act, 1930, a contract for the sale of goods can be made by word of mouth and by writing or partly in writing and partly by word of mouth.

Section 5(2) of Sales of Goods Act 1930 says, subject to the provisions of any law for the time being in force, a contract of sale may be made in writing or by word of mouth, or partly in writing and partly by word of mouth or may be implied from the conduct of the parties.

56 A company can convert into Limited Liability Partnership

I. by complying to requirements of the third schedule of Limited Liability Partnership Act, 2008.
II. it can convert if there is no security interest in its assets subsisting at the time of application.
III. partners of Limited Liability Partnership are the erstwhile shareholders of the company and no one else.
III. all the assets, interests, rights and privileges of the company are transferred to the firm.

Choose the correct answer from the options given below

1 Only I
2 Only II
3 Only III
4 I, II, III, IV all

Ans. (4)

Exp. Statement I, II, III and IV all are correct required conditions for a company to convert into Limited Liability Partnership (LLP).

According to Section 56 of Limited Liability Partnership Act, 2008, a private company may convert into a limited liability partnership in accordance with the provisions of this Chapter and the Third Schedule, of the LLP Act, 2008.

Other requisites that are required for a company to convert into LLP are the company has no security interest in its assets at the time of application. The partners of the LLP will be no one but the erstwhile shareholders of the company and all the assets, interests, rights and privileges of the company to be transferred to firm.

57 Under the Muslim Women (Protection of Rights on Divorce) Act, 1986, a divorced woman shall be entitled to

I. a reasonable and fair provision and maintenance to be made and paid to her within the 'iddat' period by her former husband.

II. maintenance of children by her former husband for a period of three years.

III. get maintenance from her relatives even after her remarriage.

IV. all the properties given to her at any time only by her husband.

V. an amount equal to the sum of 'Mahr' or dower agreed to be paid to her at the time of marriage or at anytime thereafter according to Muslim Law.

Choose the correct answer from the options given below.

1 I and V 2 I, II and V
3 II, III and V 4 I and II

Ans. (1)

Exp. Statement I and V are correct as per Muslim women (Protection of Rights on Divorce Act) 1986.

According to Section 3(a) of the Muslim Women (Protection of Rights on Divorce) Act, 1986 a muslim women shall be entitled to a reasonable and fair provision and maintenance to be made and paid to her within the iddat period by her former husband.

As per Section 3 (c) of the act, an amount equal to the sum of 'Mahr' or dower agreed to be paid to her at the time of her marriage or at any time thereafter according to Muslim law.

Statement II is incorrect as according to Section 3(b) of the act maintenance of children by woman's former husband is to be paid for a period of two years.

Statement III is incorrect as divorced she is not entitled to receive maintenance from her relatives even after remarriage.

Statement IV is incorrect as it only talks about the property received from her husband instead, she is entitled to receive fixed amount that was decided during mahr.

58 Which of the following is not a condition precedent for a valid adoption under the Hindu Adoptions and Maintenance Act, 1956?

I. Adopter must have the capacity and right to take in adoption.

II. The child must be eligible for adoption.

III. The giver must have the capacity and right to give in adoption.

IV. Datta-homam is mandatory.

Choose the correct answer from the options given below.

1 I and II 2 II and IV
3 III and IV 4 I and III

Ans. (3)

Exp. Statement III and IV are correct.

According to Section 6 Hindu Adoption and Maintenance Act 1956, No adoption shall be valid unless-

- the person adopting has the capacity, and also the right, to take in adoption;
- the person giving in adoption has the capacity to do so;
- the person adopted is capable of being taken in adoption; and
- the adoption is made in compliance with the other conditions mentioned in the Act.

59 The responsibilities of Economic and Social regarding improvement and protection of human rights is laid down under which Article of UN Charter?

I. Article 62 (2) II. Article 68
III. Article 76 3 IV. Article 96

Choose the correct answer from the options given below.

1 Only I 2 Only II 3 Only III 4 Only IV

Ans. (2)

Exp. The responsibilities of Economic and Social Council regarding improvement and protection of human rights is laid down under Article 68 of UN Charter. It says that the Economic and Social Council shall set up commissions in Economic and Social fields and for the promotion of human rights, and such other commissions as may be required for the performance of its functions.

60 The provision relating to 'solid waste management' is contained under which Schedule of the Constitution of India?

I. Schedule VII II. Schedule IX
III. Schedule XI IV. Schedule XII

Choose the correct answer from the options given below.

1 Only I 2 Only II
3 Only III 4 Only IV

Ans. (4)

Exp. The provision relating to 'solid waste management' is contained under Schedule XII of the Constitution of India. The XIIth Schedule contains the powers, authority and responsibilities of Municipalities. It was inserted by the 74th Constitutional Amendment Act of 1992.

61 The provision relating to 'drinking water' is contained under which Schedule of the Constitution of India, 1950?

I. Schedule VII II. Schedule IX
III. Schedule XI IV. Schedule XII

Choose the correct answer from the options given below.

1 Only I 2 Only II
3 Only III 4 Only IV

Ans. *(3)*

Exp. The provision relating to 'drinking water' is contained under Schedule XI of the Constitution of India. The XI Schedule of the Indian Constitution was added after the 73rd Constitutional Amendment Act in 1992. The XIth Schedule is related to Panchayati Raj in India.

62 In which of the following cases, the 'minimal creativity test' was laid down?

I. Eastern Book Company Vs. D B Modak
II. R G Anand Vs. Delux Films
III. Amar Nath Sehgal Vs. Union of India
IV. University of London Press Vs. University Tutorial Press

Choose the correct answer from the options given below.

1 Only I 2 Only II
3 Only III 4 Only IV

Ans. *(1)*

Exp. In Eastern Book Company Vs. D B Modak, the 'minimal creativity test' was laid down. In this case, the Supreme Court prompted 'creative originality' and laid down the new test to protect the creation on basis of the minimal creativity. This doctrine stipulates that originality subsists in a work where a sufficient amount of intellectual creativity and judgment has gone into the creation of that work.

63 By which amendment of Information Technology Act, 2000 the third and fourth schedules were omitted?

I. Act 10 of 2009 II. Act 55 of 2009
III. Act 66 of 2009 IV. Act 09 of 2009

Choose the correct answer from the options given below.

1 Only I 2 Only II
3 Only III 4 Only II

Ans. *(1)*

Exp. By Act 10 of 2009, the third and fourth schedule of IT Act, 2000 were omitted.

Schedules mentioned in question are omitted by the Information Technology (Amendment) Act, 2008 (Act 10 of 2009), with effect from 27th October, 2009.

The primary objectives of the IT Act, 2000 are Granting legal recognition to all transactions done through electronic data exchange, other means of electronic communication or e-commerce in place of the earlier paper-based communication.

64 In the Presidential form of government

I. The Chief executive is relatively free from sectional and party disputes.
II. The Chief executive is free to choose his team of ministers from the best talent available.
III. The term of the Chief executive is not fixed.
IV. It discourages the disease of defections.

Choose the correct answer from the options given below.

1 I, II and III
2 I, II and IV
3 II, III and IV
4 I, II, III and IV All

Ans. *(2)*

Exp. Statement I, II and IV are correct in relation to Presidential form of government.

In the Presidential form of government the Chief executive is relatively free from sectional and party disputes. His term is fixed and, thus it ensures stability of the government and President can devote his entire team for the development of the country.

The chief executive in Presidential form of government is free to choose his team of ministers from the best talent available. This choice is not restricted to elected representatives as is the case in Parliamentary system.

The Presidential form of government discourages the disease of defections and maintains discipline among the members of a political party.

Statement III is not correct as the term of Chief Executive is fixed.

65 Read the statements about 'Rule of law'.

I. Rule of law is an important and fundamental pillar of a liberal and substantive democracy.
II. The rule of law is not merely public order, the rule of law is social justice based on public order.
III. The substantive 'Rule of law' is the rule of proper law which balances the needs of the society and the individual.
IV. Substantive and liberal democracy is based solely on formal democracy.

Choose the correct answer from the options given below.

1 I, II and III 2 I, III and IV
3 I, II and IV 4 I, II, III and IV All

Ans. *(1)*

Exp. Statement I, II, and III are correct about 'Rule of law'. Rule of law is an important and fundamental pillar of a liberal and substantive democracy. Our constitution inheres liberal and substantive democracy with the 'Rule of law' as an important and fundamental pillar.

The rule of law is not merely public order, the rule of law is social justice based on public order. The law exists to ensure proper social life. It is the absence of arbitrary powers on the part of the governmental authorities and ensuring equality before law. The substantive 'Rule of law' is the rule of proper law which balances the needs of the society and the individual. Substantive conceptions of the rule of law go beyond this and include certain substantive rights that are said to be based on, or derived from, the rule of law. The rule of law, at its core, requires that government officials and citizens are bound by and act consistent with the law.

Statement IV is incorrect as Substantive and liberal democracy is not based solely on formal democracy.

66 Match List I with List II.

List I	List II
A. Definition of Permanent Lok Adalat	I. Section 22-B
B. Establishment of Permanent Lok Adalat	II. Section 22-C
C. Cognizance by Permanent Lok Adalat	III. Section 22-E
D. Award of Permanent Lok Adalat	IV. Section 22-A

Choose the correct answer from the options given below.

	A	B	C	D		A	B	C	D
1	I	IV	III	II	2	II	III	I	IV
3	III	II	IV	I	4	IV	I	II	III

Ans. (4)

Exp. The correct matching is A-IV, B-I, C-II, D-III.

Section 22-A contains the definition of Permanent Lok Adalat. Permanent Lok Adalat means a Permanent Lok Adalat established under sub-section (1) of Section 22 B.

Section 22-B is related to establishment of Permanent Lok Adalat. According to this Section, the Central Authority or, as the case may be, every State Authority shall, be notification, establish Permanent Lok Adalat at such places and for exercising such jurisdiction in respect of one or more public utility services and for such areas as may be specified in the notification.

Section 22-C is related to cognizance by permanent Lok Adalat. As per this section, any party to a dispute may, before the dispute is brought before nay court, make an application to the Permanent Lok Adalat for the settlement of dispute.

Section 22-E is related to Award of Permanent Lok Adalat. Every award of the Permanent Lok Adalat under this Act made either on merit or in terms of a settlement agreement shall be final and binding on all the parties. Award is deemed to be a decree of civil court.

(All these sections are from The Legal Services Authority Act, 1987)

67 Match List I with List II.

List I (Provision under the Constitution of India)	List II (Article)
A. Special provisions with respect to the State of Manipur.	I. Article 371-F
B. Special provisions with respect to the State of Karnataka.	II. Article 371-G
C. Special provisions with respect to the State of Sikkim.	III. Article 371-C
D. Special provision with respect to the State of Mizoram.	IV. Article 371-J

Choose the correct answer from the options given below.

	A	B	C	D		A	B	C	D
1	II	I	IV	III	2	I	II	III	IV
3	IV	III	II	I	4	III	IV	I	II

Ans. (4)

Exp. The correct matching is A-III, B-IV, C-I, D-II.

Article 371-C of Constitution of India laid down the special provisions with respect to the state of Manipur. The President by order with respect to Manipur can make special rules of business of the government or with regard to legislative assembly or for any other special responsibility of the governor.

Article 371-J of Constitution of India talks about the special provisions with respect to Karnataka. It states that the President may provide for any special responsibility of the Governor for establishment of a separate development board for Hyderabad-Karnataka region with the provision that a report on the working of the board will be placed each year before the State Legislative Assembly; equitable allocation of funds for developmental expenditure over the said region, subject to the requirements of the State as a whole.

Article 371-F of Constitution of India talks about the special provisions with respect to Sikkim. It states that the Legislative Assembly of the State of Sikkim shall consist of not less than thirty members. The Assembly for Sikkim formed as a result of the elections held in Sikkim in April, 1974 with thirty-two members elected in the said elections (herein after referred to as the sitting members) shall be deemed to be the Legislative Assembly of the State of Sikkim duly constituted under this Constitution.

Article 371-G of Constitution of India laid down the special provisions with respect to Mizoram. It provides that no Act of Parliament in respect of religious or social practices of the Mizos, Mizo customary law and procedure, administration of civil and criminal justice involving decisions according to Mizo customary law, ownership and transfer of land, shall apply to the State of Mizoram unless the Legislative Assembly of the State of Mizoram by a resolution so decides.

68 **Match List I with List II.**

List I (Provision)	List II (Article of the Statute of the International Court of Justice)
A. Law applied by the International Court of Justice.	I. Article 36
B. Courts power to allow a state to intervene in a case to which it is not a party	II. Article 38
C. Jurisdiction of the International Court of Justice	III. Article 41
D. Interim Measures or relief by the International Court of Justice.	IV. Article 62

Choose the correct answer from the options given below.

	A	B	C	D
1	I	II	III	IV
2	II	IV	I	III
3	II	III	I	IV
4	IV	II	III	I

Ans. (2)

Exp. The correct matching is A-II, B-IV, C-I, D-III.

Article 38 of Statute of International Court of Justice (ICJ) talks about Law applied by the International Court of Justice and provides that the Court, whose function is to decide in accordance with international law such disputes as are submitted to it, shall apply to international conventions, whether general or particular, establishing rules expressly recognized by the contesting states; international custom, as evidence of a general practice accepted as law; the general principles of law recognized by civilized nations.

Article 62 of Statute of ICJ talks about Courts power to allow a state to intervene in a case in which it is not a party. It reads as follows- Should a state consider that it has an interest of a legal nature which may be affected by the decision in the case, it may submit a request to the Court to be permitted to intervene. It shall be for the Court to decide upon this request.

Article 36 of Statute of ICJ talks about jurisdiction of the international Court of Justice. It provides that the jurisdiction of the Court comprises all cases which the parties refer to it and all matters specially provided for in the Charter of the United Nations or in treaties and conventions in force.

*Article 41*of Statute of ICJ talks about interim measures or relief by the International Court of Justice, wherein the Court shall have the power to indicate any provisional measures which ought to be taken to preserve the respective rights of either party. Pending the final decision, notice of the measures suggested shall forthwith be given to the parties and to the Security Council.

69 **Match List I with List II.**

List I (Provision under Indian Penal Code)	List II (Section)
A. An Act done in good faith for benefit of a person without consent.	I. Section 423
B. Dishonest or fraudulent execution of the deed of transfer containing false statement of consideration.	II. Section 381
C. Voluntarily causing grievous hurt by use of acid etc.	III. Section 92
D. Theft by clerk or servant of property in possession of master	IV. Section 326 A

Choose the correct answer from the options given below.

	A	B	C	D
1	III	I	II	IV
2	III	I	IV	II
3	I	II	III	IV
4	IV	III	II	I

Ans. (2)

Exp. The correct matching is A-III, B-I, C-IV, D-II.

Section 92 of IPC talks about an act done in good faith for the benefit of a person without consent. It states that nothing is an offence by reason of any harm which it may cause to a person for whose benefit it is done in good faith, even without that person's consent, if the circumstances are such that it is impossible for that person to signify consent.

Section 423 of IPC talks about the dishonest or fraudulent execution of the deed of transfer containing false statement of consideration. It states that "Whoever dishonestly or fraudulently signs, executes or becomes a party to any deed or instrument which purports to transfer or subject to any charge any property, containing false statement relating to the consideration for such transfer or charge, shall be punished with imprisonment of either description for a term which may extend to two years, or with fine, or with both."

Section 326 A of IPC talks about voluntarily causing grievous hurt by use of acid etc. It lays down the punishment for acid attacks. The minimum punishment is 10 years imprisonment. It can extend up to life imprisonment with fine.

Section 381 of IPC talks about the theft of a clerk or servant of property in possession of master. It reads as- "Whoever, being a clerk or servant, or being employed in the capacity of a clerk or servant, commits theft in respect of any property in the possession of his master or employer, shall be punished with imprisonment of either description for a term which may extend to seven years, and shall also be liable to fine."

70 **Match List I with List II.**

List I (Jurisdiction)	List II (Section under Consumer Protection Act, 1986)
A. Jurisdiction of District forum	I. Section 11
B. Jurisdiction of State Commission	II. Section 21
C. Jurisdiction of National Commission	III. Section 22A
D. Power of set aside ex parte orders	IV. Section 17

Choose the correct answer from the options given below.

	A	B	C	D		A	B	C	D
1	I	IV	II	III	2	III	II	IV	I
3	II	III	I	IV	4	IV	I	III	II

Ans. *(1)*

Exp. The correct matching is A-I, B-IV, C-II, D-III.

Section 11 mentions the jurisdiction of district forum (Consumer Protection Act, 1986). District Forum shall have jurisdiction to entertain complaints where the value of the goods or services and the compensation, if any, claimed does not exceed rupees twenty lakhs.

Section 17 mentions the jurisdiction of the State Commission. The State Commission shall have jurisdiction to entertain complaints where the value of the goods or services and compensation, if any, claimed exceeds rupees twenty lakhs but does not exceed rupees one crore, and appeals against the orders of any District Forum within the State.

Section 21 of the Act mentions jurisdiction of the National Commission. The National Commission shall have jurisdiction to entertain complaints where the value of the goods or services and compensation, if any, claimed exceeds rupees one crore.

Section 22A of the Act provides power to set aside ex-parte order. It states that where an order is passed by the National Commission ex-parte against the opposite party or a complainant, the aggrieved party may apply to the Commission to set aside the said order in the interest of justice.

71 **Match List I with List II.**

List I (Terms)	List II (Section of Companies Act, 2013)
A. Abridged Prospectus	I. Section 31
B. Deemed Prospectus	II. Section 32
C. Shelf Prospectus	III. Section 2(1)
D. Red herring Prospectus	IV. Section 25

Choose the correct answer from the options given below.

	A	B	C	D		A	B	C	D
1	III	IV	I	II	2	II	III	IV	I
3	I	II	III	IV	4	IV	I	II	III

Ans. *(1)*

Exp. The correct matching is A-III, B-IV, C-I, D- II.

Section 2(1) Companies Act, 2013 talks about Abridged Prospectus. Abridged prospectus means a memorandum containing such salient features of a prospectus as may be specified by the Securities and Exchange Board by making regulations in this behalf.

Section 25 of the Act mentions Deemed Prospectus. It states that "Where a company allots or agrees to allot any securities of the company with a view to all or any of those securities being offered for sale to the public, any document by which the offer for sale to the public is made shall, for all purposes, be deemed to be a prospectus issued by the company".

Section 31 of the Act mentions Shelf Prospectus. It states that any class or classes of companies, as the Securities and Exchange Board may provide by regulations in this behalf, may file a shelf prospectus with the Registrar at the stage of the first offer of securities.

Section 32 of the Act mentions Red herring Prospectus. It states that a company proposing to make an offer of securities may issue a red herring prospectus prior to the issue of a prospectus.

72 **Match List I with List II.**

List I (Provision)	List II (Section under Muslim Woman Protection of Rights on Marriage Act, 2016)
A. Punishment for pronouncing talaq	I. Section 3
B. Offences to be cognisable, compoundable etc	II. Section 7
C. Custody of minor children	III. Section 4
D. Talaq to be void and illegal	IV. Section 6

Choose the correct answer from the options given below.

	A	B	C	D		A	B	C	D
1	I	II	III	IV	2	III	II	IV	I
3	II	IV	III	I	4	IV	I	III	I

Ans. *(2)*

Exp. Exp. The correct matching is A-III, B-II, C-IV, D-I.

Section 4 of Muslim Women Protection of Rights on Marriage Act, 2016 mentions punishment for pronouncing Talaq. Any Muslim husband who pronounces talaq referred to in Section 3 upon his wife shall be punished with imprisonment for a term which may extend to three years, and shall also be liable to fine.

Section 7 of the Act talks about offences to be cognisable, compoundable etc. An offence punishable under this Act shall be compoundable, at the instance of the married Muslim woman upon whom Talaq is pronounced with the permission of the Magistrate, on such terms and conditions as he may determine.

Section 6 talks about custody of minor children. A married Muslim woman shall be entitled to custody of her minor children in the event of pronouncement of Talaq by her husband, in such manner as may be determined by the Magistrate.

Section 3 talks about Talaq to be void and illegal. Any pronouncement of Talaq by a Muslim husband upon his wife, by words, either spoken or written or in electronic form or in any other manner whatsoever, shall be void and illegal.

73 Match List I with List II.

List I (Provision)		List II (Sectional under National Green Tribunal Act, 2010)
A.	Hazardous Substance	I. Section 2 1
B.	Environment	II. Section 2 (e)
C.	Handling	III. Section 2 (f)
D.	Accident	IV. Section 2 (c)

Choose the correct answer from the options given below.

	A	B	C	D
1	I	III	IV	II
2	II	I	IV	III
3	III	IV	II	I
4	IV	III	I	II

Ans. *(3)*

Exp. The correct matching is A-III, B-IV, C- II, D-I

Section 2(f) of National Green Tribunal Act, 2010, talks about Hazardous substance as any substance or preparation which is defined as hazardous substance in the Environment (Protection) Act, 1986, and exceeding such quantity as specified or may be specified by the Central Government under the Public Liability Insurance Act, 1991.

Section 2(c) of the act mentions Environment. "Environment" includes water, air and land and the inter-relationship, which exists among and between water, air and land and human beings, other living creatures, plants, micro-organism and property.

Section 2(e) of the act mentions Handling. 'Handling', in relation to any hazardous substance, means the manufacture, processing, treatment, package, storage, transportation, use, collection, destruction, conversion, offering for sale, transfer or the like of such hazardous substance.

Section 2 (a) of the act mentions Accident. 'Accident' means an accident involving a fortuitous or sudden or unintended occurrence while handling any hazardous substance or equipment, or plant, or vehicle resulting in continuous or intermittent or repeated exposure to death, of, or, injury to, any person or damage to any property or environment but does not include an accident by reason only of war or civil disturbance.

74 Match List I with List II.

List I (Provisions)		List II (Sections of Copyright Act, 1957)
A.	Performer	I. Section 2 (q)
B.	Performer's right	II. Section 38 B
C.	Performance	III. Section 38
D.	Moral Rights of Performer	IV. Section 2 (qq)

Choose the correct answer from the options given below.

	A	B	C	D		A	B	C	D
1	I	III	IV	II	2	II	I	IV	III
3	III	I	II	IV	4	IV	III	I	II

Ans. *(4)*

Exp. The correct matching is A-IV, B-III, C-I, D-II.

Section 2(qq) of the Copyright Act, 1957 mentions Performer. 'Performer' includes an actor, singer, musician, dancer, acrobat, juggler, conjurer, snake charmer, a person delivering a lecture or any other person who makes a performance.

Section 38 of the Act mentions Performer's right. It says "Where any performer appears or engages in any performance, he shall have a special right to be known as the 'performer's right' in relation to such performance. The performer's right shall subsist until fifty years from the beginning of the calendar year next following the year in which the performance is made."

Section 2(q) of the Act mentions Performance. 'Performance', in relation to performer's right, means any visual or acoustic presentation made live by one or more performers.

Section 38 B of the Act mentions Moral rights of performer.

The performer of a performance shall, independently of his right after assignment, either wholly or partially of his right, have the right to claim to be identified as the performer of his performance and to restrain or claim damage in respect of any distortion, mutilation or other modification of his performance that would be prejudicial to his reputation.

75 Match List I with List II.

List I		List II
A.	Murli S. Deora Vs. Union of India	I. Protection against inhuman treatment in Jail.
B.	Sunil Batra Vs. Delhi Administration	II. Protection of Ecology and Environmental Pollution.
C.	Hussainara Khatoon Vs. State of Bihar	III. Ban on smoking in public places.
D.	Rural Litigation and Entitlement Kendra Vs. State of U.P.	IV. Speedy trial is an integral part of the Fundamental Right under Article 21 of the Indian Constitution.

Choose the correct answer from the options given below.

	A	B	C	D		A	B	C	D
1	I	II	III	IV	2	II	I	IV	III
3	III	I	IV	II	4	IV	III	II	I

Ans. (3)

Exp. The correct matching is A-III, B- I, C-IV, D-II.

Murli S. Deora Vs. Union of India case is related to ban on smoking in public places. The Supreme Court found that smoking in public places is injurious to the health of non–smokers and violated their right to life and liberty.

Sunil Batra Vs. Delhi Administration case is related to protection against inhuman treatment in jail. This judgment helped in securing the fundamental right of prisoners. It brought to light a host of issues, including the clashes between various fundamental rights and the Prison Act of 1874.

Hussainara Khatoon Vs. State of Bihar case is related to speedy trial is an integral part of the Fundamental Right under Article 21 of the Indian Constitution. It formed the basis of the concept of the Speedy Trial. It was held that where under trial prisoners have been in jail for duration longer than prescribed, if convicted, their detention in jail is totally unjustified and in violation to Fundamental Rights under Article 21.

Rural Litigation and Entitlement Kendra Vs. State of UP case is related to protection of Ecology and Environmental Pollution. A letter received from the Rural Litigation and Entitlement Kendra Dehradun was treated as a Writ Petition and notices were issued. The main allegations therein related to unauthorised and illegal mining operations carried on in the Mussoorie Hills and the area around adversely affecting the ecology of the area and leading to environmental disturbances.

76 Arrange in chronological order of the publication of the books on Jurisprudence.

I. Province of Jurisprudence Determined by Austin.
II. Concept of Law by HLA Hart.
III. The Province and Function of Law by Julius Stone.
IV. Nature of Judicial Process by Benjamin N Cardozo.
V. Anatomy of Law by Lon L fuller.

Choose the correct answer from the options given below.

1 I, II, III, IV, V   2 II, III, IV, V, I
3 I, IV, III, II, V   4 III, II, V, IV, I

Ans. (3)

Exp. The correct chronological order of the publications of the book on Jurisprudence is I, IV, III, II, V.

- Province of Jurisprudence Determined by Austin (1832)
- Nature of Judicial Process by Benjamin N Cardozo (1921)
- The Province and Function of Law by Julius Stone (1946)
- Concept of Law by HLA Hart (1961)
- Anatomy of Law by Lon Fuller (1968).

77 Arrange chronologically the following cases decided by the Supreme Court year wise.

I. Olga Tellis Vs. Bombay Municipal Corporation
II. Francis Coralie Vs. Union Territory of Delhi
III. Satwant Singh Vs. Assistant Passport officer
IV. Kharak Singh Vs. the State of U P
V. National Legal Services Authority Vs. Union of India

Choose the correct answer from the options given below.

1 III, IV, I, V, II   2 I, II, III, IV, V
3 II, IV, I, V, III   4 IV, III, II, I, V

Ans. (4)

Exp. IV, III, II, I, V is the correct year wise chronological order of the cases decided by the Supreme Court.

In Kharak Singh Vs. State of U.P (1964) case the Supreme Court of India declared the relevant provisions that allowed police to make domiciliary visits to 'habitual criminals' or individuals likely to become habitual criminals as unconstitutional.

In Satwant Singh Vs. Assistant Passport officer (1967) case the Supreme Court held that the expression of personal liberty under article 21 of the Constitution of India, in its ambit includes the right of a person to go abroad and a person cannot be deprived of that right.

Francis Coralie Vs. Union Territory of Delhi (1981) case this case is a landmark judgment to determine the distinction between preventive detention with punitive detention under the scope of Article 21 of the Indian Constitution and determining the constitutional validity of restricting the right of Petitioner to get an interview with their lawyer and contact with their relatives.

In Olga Tellis Vs. Bombay Municipal Corporation (1985) case, the court held that, right to livelihood covered under right to life that is Article 21 of the constitution.

National Legal Services Authority Vs. Union of India (2012) is a landmark decision by the Supreme Court of India, which declared transgender people the 'third gender' and affirmed that the fundamental rights granted under the Constitution of India will be equally applicable to them, and gave them the right to self-identification of their gender as male, female or third gender.

78 Give the chronological order (year wise) of these cases decided by the courts.

I. West Rand Central Gold Mining Company Ltd V R.
II. Portugal Vs. India
III. Burkina Faso Vs. Mali
IV. Mavrommatis Palestine Concessions Case
V. Chorzow Factory (Indemnity) Case

Choose the correct answer from the options given below.

1 I, III, IV, II, V   2 I, II, III, IV, V
3 I, V, II, III, IV   4 I, V, II, IV, III

Ans. (*)

Exp. The correct chronological order of the cases decided by the courts is I, IV, V, II, III.

- West Rand Central Gold Mining Company Ltd V. R (1904)
- Mavrommiatis Palestine Concession Case (1924)
- Chrozow factory (Indemnity) Case (1927)
- Portugal Vs India Case (1957)
- Burkina Faso Vs. Mali (1986)

79 Arrange the provisions of Indian Penal Code in chronological order, section-wise

I. House-trespass in order to commit an offence punishable with imprisonment for life.

II. House-trespass in order to commit an offence punishable with death.

III. Lurking house-trespass or house-breaking in order to commit an offence punishable with imprisonment.

IV. House-trespass in orders to commit an offence punishable with imprisonment.

V. Lurking house-trespass or house-breaking by night in order to commit an offence punishable with imprisonment.

Chose the correct answer from the options given below.

1 V, I, III, II, IV   2 IV, I, V, III, II
3 I, II, III, IV, V   4 II, I, IV, III, V

Ans. (4)

Exp. II, I, IV, III, V is the correct section-wise chronological order of Indian Penal Code (IPC).

- House-trespass in order to commit an offence punishable with death (Section 449)
- House-trespass in order to commit an offence punishable with imprisonment for life (Section 450)
- House-trespass in order to commit an offence punishable with imprisonment (Section 451)
- Lurking house-trespass or house-breaking in order to commit an offence punishable with imprisonment (Section 454)
- Lurking house-trespass or house-breaking by night in order to commit an offence punishable with imprisonment (Section 457)

80 Arrange the following in chronological order (section wise) as stated in the Motor Vehicle Act, 1988.

I. Procedure and Power of Claims Tribunal

II. Award of Claim Tribunal

III. Claim Tribunals

IV. Application for Compensation

Choose the correct answer from the options given below.

1 III, IV, II, I
2 I, II, III, IV
3 II, III, I, IV
4 III, IV, I, II

Ans. (1)

Exp. III, IV, II, I is the correct section wise chronological order as stated in Motor Vehicle Act, 1988.

Claim Tribunals Section 165 provides that a State Government may, by notification in the Official Gazette, constitute one or more Motor Accidents Claims Tribunals for the purpose of adjudicating upon claims for compensation in respect of accidents involving the death of, or bodily injury to, persons arising out of the use of motor vehicles, or damages to any property of a third party so arising, or both.

Application for Compensation As per Section 166, an application for compensation arising out of an accident can be made by the person who has sustained the injury; or by the owner of the property; or where death has resulted from the accident, by all or any of the legal representatives of the deceased; or by any agent duly authorised by the person injured or all or any of the legal representatives of the deceased.

Award of Claim Tribunal Given under Section 168 it provides that "on receipt of an application for compensation made under Section 166, the Claims Tribunal shall, after giving notice of the application to the insurer and after giving the parties (including the insurer) an opportunity of being heard, hold an inquiry into the claim or, as the case may be, each of the claims may make an award determining the amount of compensation which appears to it to be just and specifying the person or persons to whom compensation shall be paid."

Procedure and Power of Claims Tribunal- Provided under Section 169 it provides that "In holding any inquiry under Section 168, the Claims Tribunal may, subject to any rules that may be made in this behalf, follow such summary procedure as it thinks fit."

81 Arrange the provisions of the Indian Partnership Act, 1932 in chronological order (section wise)

I. Partnership at will

II. Mode of determining the existence of the partnership

III. Property of a firm

IV. Duties of a partner

Choose the correct answer from the options given below.

1 II, I, IV, III   2 III, II, I, IV
3 I, III, II, IV   4 IV, I, II, III

Ans. (1)

Exp. II, I, IV, III is the correct section-wise chronological order as stated in Indian Partnership Act, 1932.

Mode of determining the existence of the partnership is mentioned in Section 6 of the Act. It states in determining whether a group of persons is or is not a firm, or whether a person is or is not a partner in a firm, regard shall be had to the real relation between the parties, as shown by all relevant facts taken together.

Partnership at will is mentioned in Section 7 of the Act. Partnership at will is the partnership where no provision is made by contract between the partners for the duration of their partnership, or for the determination of their partnership.

Duties of partner is mentioned in Section 9 of the Act. It states that Partners are bound to carry on the business of the firm to greatest common advantage, to be just and faithful to each other, and to render true accounts and full information of all things affecting the firm to any partner, his heir or legal representative.

Property of a firm is mentioned in Section 14 of the Act. It states that "subject to contract between the partners, the property of the firm includes all property and rights and interest in property originally brought into the stock of the firm, or acquired, by purchase or otherwise, by or for the firm for the purposes and in the course of the business of the firm, and includes also the goodwill of the business".

82 Chronologically arrange the following Judgements of the Supreme Court of India on Uniform Civil Code.

I. Daniel Latifi Vs. Union of India
II. John Vallamatton Vs. Union of India
III. Sarla Mudgal Vs. Union of India
IV. Mohd. Ahmad Khan Vs. Shah Bano Begum

Choose the correct answer from the options given below

1 III, II, IV, I
2 IV, III, II, I
3 IV, III, I, II
4 I, II, III, IV

Ans. *(3)*

Exp. IV, III, I, II is the correct chronological order of the Judgments given by the Supreme Court on Uniform Civil Code.

In the case of Mohd. Ahmad Khan V.S. Shah Bano Begum (1985), the Supreme Court specifically underlined the that Triple Talaq cannot take away the maintenance right of a divorced Muslim women who is not in a condition to maintain herself or her children when she is disowned or divorced by her husband.

Sarla Mudgal Vs. Union of India (1995) judgement in 1995 laid down the principles against the practice of solemnising second marriage by conversion to Islam, with first marriage not being dissolved.

In Daniel Latifi Vs. Union of India (2001) case the Supreme Court, on a creative interpretation of the MWPRDA, 1986, upheld its constitutionality. It held that a Muslim husband is liable to make reasonable and fair provision for the future of his divorced wife extending beyond the iddat period.

In John Vallamattom Vs. Union of India (2003) case, the Supreme Court was solely concerned with the constitutionality of the provisions of Section 118 of the Indian Succession Act, 1925 which deals with bequest to religious or charitable purposes. The court held that Section118 of the Indian Succession Act, 1925 is unconstitutional as it violates Article 14 of the constitution.

83 Arrange the initiatives on climate change in chronological order.

I. Durban conference on climate change
II. Montreal Protocol on climate change
III. Vienna convention on climate change
IV. Copenhagen Summit on climate change
V. Kyoto Protocol on climate changes

Choose the correct answer from the options given below.

1 I, II, III, IV, V
2 II, III, IV, V, I
3 I, IV, III, II, V
4 III, II, V, IV, I

Ans. *(4)*

Exp. III, II, V, IV, I is the correct chronological order regarding the initiative on climate change.

Vienna convention on climate change- The Vienna Convention for the Protection of the Ozone Layer is a multilateral environmental agreement signed in 1985 that provided frameworks for international reductions in the production of chlorofluorocarbons due to their contribution to the destruction of the ozone layer, resulting in an increased threat of skin cancer.

Montreal Protocol on climate change - The 1987 Montreal Protocol on Substances that Deplete the Ozone Layer is a landmark agreement that has successfully reduced the global production, consumption, and emissions of Ozone-Depleting Substances (ODSs).

Kyoto Protocol on climate change - The Kyoto Protocol was adopted in Kyoto, Japan on 11th December,1997. The Kyoto Protocol operationalizes the United Nations Framework Convention on Climate Change by committing industrialized countries and economies in transition to limit and reduce greenhouse gases (GHG) emissions in accordance with agreed individual targets.

Copenhagen Summit on climate change - The 2009 United Nations Climate Change Conference, commonly known as the Copenhagen Summit. It was held at the Bella Centre in Copenhagen, Denmark, between 7 and 18 December. The document recognised that climate change is one of the greatest challenges of the present day and that actions should be taken to keep any temperature increases to below 2 °C.

Durban conference on climate change - The 2011 United Nations Climate Change Conference (COP17) was held in Durban, South Africa, from 28th November to 11 December 2011 to establish a new treaty to limit carbon emissions.

84 Arrange the theories of intellectual property in order of prominence and influence.

I. Personality theory
II. Social Planning theory
III. Labour Theory
IV. Utilitarian Theory

Choose the correct answer from the options given below.

1 I, IV, III, II
2 II, I, III, IV
3 III, II, IV, I
4 IV, III, I, II

Ans. (4)

➲ *Exp.*IV, III, I, II is the correct order of theories of intellectual property in order of prominence and control.

Utilitarian Theory is based on the fact that industrial progress and cultural goods have a beneficial effect on society.

Labour Theory is a theory of value that argues that the economic value of a good or service is determined by the total amount of "socially necessary labour" required to produce it. The main justification behind this theory is that everyone has a right to consider his/ her ideas as natural property right by the reason that the creation originates from the effort, originality and inventiveness of the creator.

Personality Theory is a principle of intellectual property that gives importance to the point of view of the individual inventor, author, or artist rather than that of society as a whole while analysing intellectual-property rights.

In Social Planning Theory intellectual property rights are considered particularly as a part of general property laws and it must be shaped to cultivate the attainment of a fair and attractive culture.

85 Arrange in chronological order, the cases relating to US Constitutional Amendments.

I. Plessy Vs. Ferguson

II. Hawke Vs. Smith

III. Laser Vs. Garnett

IV. U S Vs. Sprague

Choose the correct answer from the options given below.

1 I, II, III, IV   2 I, III, II, IV

3 II, III, IV, I   4 IV, II, III, I

Ans. (1)

➲ *Exp.* I, II, III, IV is the correct chronological order of the cases relating to US Constitutional Amendments.

In Plessy Vs. Ferguson (1896) case, U.S. Supreme Court upheld the constitutionality of racial segregation under the "separate but equal" doctrine. The case stemmed from an 1892 incident in which African American train passenger Homer Plessy refused to sit in a car for Black people.

In Hawke Vs. Smith (1920) case, George Hawke challenged the validity of amendment to the Ohio Constitution and sought to have Smith stop the issuing of ballots. He alleged that the Ohio amendment conflicted with Article Five of the United States Constitution, which specified that amendments would be ratified by state legislatures.

In Laser Vs. Garnett (1922) case, the Supreme Court of the United States held that the Nineteenth Amendment had been constitutionally established.

In US Vs. Sprague (1931) case, the US Supreme court dealt with the Fifth Article of the US Constitution. The defendants had been indicted under the National Prohibition Act and were attempting to quash their indictments, arguing that the Eighteenth Amendment had not been properly ratified.

86 Give below are two statements, one is labelled as Assertion (A) and the other is labelled as Reason (R).

Assertion (A) The Parliament has the power to make the laws for whole or any part of the territory of India and law made by the Parliament would be applicable beyond the territory of India also.

Reason (R) Article 245 Clause (1) of the Constitution of India empowers the Parliament to make the laws for the whole or any part of the territory of India and Article 245 Clause (2) says that no law made by Parliament shall be deemed to be invalid on the ground that it would have extra-territorial operation.

In light of the above statement, choose the correct answer from the options given below.

Codes

1 Both (A) and (R) are true and (R) is the correct explanation of (A)

2 Both (A) and (R) are true, but (R) is not the correct explanation of (A)

3 (A) is true, but (R) is false

4 (A) is false, but (R) is true

Ans. (1)

➲ *Exp.* Both (A) and (R) are true and (R) is the correct explanation of (A).

Article 245 empowers the Parliament to make the laws for whole or any part of the territory of India and these laws are also applicable to territory beyond India.

As per Article 245(1) Parliament may make laws for the whole or any part of the territory of India, and the Legislature of a State may make laws for the whole or any part of the State, and Article 245(2) says no law made by Parliament shall be deemed to be invalid on the ground that it would have extra-territorial operation.

87 Give below are two statements, one is labelled as Assertion (A) and the other is labelled as Reason (R).

Assertion (A) According to Article 7 of the United Nations Charter, the International Court of Justice is one of the principle organs of the United Nations.

Reason (R) The International Court of Justice consists of 15 Judges who are elected by the Security Council.

In light of the above statements, choose the correct answer from the options given below.

Codes

1 Both (A) and (R) are true and (R) is the correct explanation of (A)

2 Both (A) and (R) are true but (R) is not the correct explanation of (A)

3 (A) is true, but (R) is false

4 (A) is false, but (R) is true

Ans. (3)

Exp. (A) is true, but (R) is false.

According to Article 7(1) of UN charter, following are established as the principal organs of the United Nations: a General Assembly, a Security Council, an Economic and Social Council, a Trusteeship Council, an International Court of Justice, and a Secretariat.

Reason given is false as the International Court of Justice is composed of 15 judges elected to nine-year terms of office by the United Nations General Assembly and the Security Council.

88 Give below are two statements, one is labelled as Assertion (A) and the other is labelled as Reason (R).

Assertion (A) Whoever assaults or uses criminal force on any person, in attempting to commit theft on any property which that person is then wearing or carrying, shall be punished with imprisonment of either description for a term which may extend to two years, or with fine, or with both.

Reason (R) Section 356 of Indian Penal Code provides for the punishment of imprisonment of either description for a term which may extend to two years, or with fine, or with both if a person assaults or uses criminal force on any person in attempting to commit theft or any property which that person is wearing or carrying.

In light of the above statement, choose the correct answer from the options given below.

1 Both (A) and (R) are true and (R) is the correct explanation of (A)
2 Both (A) and (R) are true, but (R) is not the correct explanation of (A)
3 (A) is true, but (R) is false
4 (A) is false, but (R) is true

Ans. (1)

Exp. Both (A) and (R) are true and (R) is the correct explanation of (A).

Section 356 of the IPC is related to assault or criminal force in attempt to commit theft of property carried by a person. It states that whoever assaults or uses criminal force to any person, in attempting to commit theft on any property which that person is then wearing or carrying, shall be punished with imprisonment of either description for a term which may extend to two years, or with fine, or with both.

Section 356 of IPC provides for the punishment of imprisonment of either description for a term which may extend to two years, or with fine, or with both if the person assaults or uses criminal force on any person in attempting to theft or any property which that person is wearing or carrying.

89 Give below are two statements, one is labelled as Assertion (A) and the other is labelled as Reason (R).

Assertion (A) If the adoption is of a son, the adoptive Hindu father or mother by whom the adoption is made must not have a Hindu son, son's son or son's son's son (whether by legitimate blood relationship or by adoption living at the time of adoption.

Reason (R) Section 11 (i) of the Hindus Adoptions and Maintenance Act, 1956, which deals with the right of adoptive parents 'under other conditions for a valid adoption' imposes this restriction.

In light of the above statement, choose the correct answer from the options given below

1 Both (A) and (R) are true and (R) is the correct explanation of (A)
2 Both (A) and (R) are true, but (R) is not the correct explanation of (A)
3 (A) is true, but (R) is not false
4 (A) is false, but (R) is true

Ans. (1)

Exp. Both (A) and (R) are true and (R) is the correct explanation of (A).

Section 11(i) of the Hindu Adoption and Maintenance, Act 1956 says that if any adoption is of a son, the adoptive father or mother by whom the adoption is made must not have a Hindu son, son's son or son's son's son (whether by legitimate blood relationship or by adoption) living at the time of adoption.

Section 11 (i) of Hindu Adoption and Maintenance Act,1956 imposes this restrictions mentioned in the Assertion.

90 Give below are two statements, one is labelled as Assertion (A) and the other is labelled as Reason (R).

Assertion (A) Once a performer consents to the incorporation of his performance in a cinematograph film by a written agreement, he/she will not object to the enjoyment of the performers right by the producer in the same film.

Reason (R) The performer is entitled to royalties in case the producer of the film makes use of the performance for commercial use.

In light of the above statement, choose the correct answer from the options given below.

Codes

1 Both (A) and (R) are true and (R) is the correct explanation of (A)
2 Both (A) and (R) are true, but (R) is not the correct explanation of (A)
3 (A) is true, but (R) is false
4 (A) is false, but (R) is true

Ans. (2)

Exp. Both (A) and (R) are true but (R) is not the correct explanation of (A).

According to Section 38A (2) of Copyright Act, 1957, once a performer consents to the incorporation of his performance in a cinematograph film by a written agreement, he/she will not object to the enjoyment of the performers' right by the producer in the same film.

Reason given is true independently but it is not the correct explanation of assertion. It says, the performer is entitled to royalties in case the producer of the film makes use of the performance for commercial use. Section 38, 39 and 39A of Copyright Act, 1957 deals with the provisions related to the performer rights.

Directions (Q. Nos. 91-95) *Read the following paragraph carefully and answer the five questions which as follows:*

The right to live with dignity has been recognised as a human right on the international front and by the number or precedents of this Court and therefore, the Constitutional courts must strive to protect the dignity of every individual, for, without the right to dignity, every other right would be rendered meaningless.

Dignity is an inseparable facet of every individual that invites reciprocative respect from others to every aspect of an individual which he/she perceives as an essential attribute of his/her individuality, be it an orientation or an optional expression of choice.

The Constitution has ladened the judiciary with the very important duty to protect and ensure the right of every individual including the right to express and choose without any impediments so as to enable an individual to fully realise his/her fundamental right to live with dignity.

Sexual orientation is one of the many biological phenomena which is natural and inherent in an individual and is controlled by neurological and biological factors. The science of sexuality has theorised that an individual exerts little or no control over who he/she gets attracted to. Any discrimination on the basis 0' one's sexual orientation would entail a violation of the Fundamental Right of Freedom of Expression.

91 The above paragraph reflects the judgement in case of

1 Navtej Singh Johar Vs. Union of India
2 Machi Singh Vs. State of Punjab
3 State of UP Vs. Ram Swaroop
4 Chairman Railway Board Vs. Chandrima Das

Ans. (1)

Exp. The above paragraph reflects the judgement in case of Navtej Singh Johar V. Union of India.

In this case, the Supreme Court of India unanimously held that Section 377 of the Indian Penal Code, 1860, which criminalized 'carnal intercourse against the order of nature', was unconstitutional in so far as it criminalized consensual sexual conduct between adults of the same sex.

92 Discrimination on the basis of sexual orientation is violative of which of the followings Fundamental Rights?

1 Article 21
2 Article 14, 15
3 Article 15, 19
4 Articles 14, 15, 19, 21

Ans. (4)

Exp. Discrimination on the basis of sexual orientation is violative of Article 14, 15,19, 21 of the constitution.

The paragraph "The constitution has ladened the judiciary with the very important duty to protect and ensures the right to every individual including the right to express and choose without any impediments so as to enable an individual to fully realize his/her fundamental right to live with dignity." is related to the question.

93 The consensual sexual act of an adult is criminalised under which of the following legislations?

1 Indian Penal Code
2 POCSO
3 Criminal Law (Amendment) Act 2013
4 The Hindu Marriage Act, 1955

Ans. (1)

Exp. Consensual sexual act of an adult is criminalised under Section 377 of the Indian Penal Code.

94 Which one of the following judges were part of the judgement referred to in the paragraph?

1 J Deepak Mishra
2 JRF Nariman
3 Dr. DY Chandrachud
4 J Indu Malhotra

Ans. (1)

Exp. Justice Deepak Mishra was the part of Navtej Singh Johar V. Union of India Judgement.

The Supreme Court of India unanimously held that Section 377 of the Indian Penal Code, 1860, which criminalized 'carnal intercourse against the order of nature', was unconstitutional in so far as it criminalized consensual sexual conduct between adults of the same sex

95 The Fundamental Right of the Freedom of Expression is contained in the following Articles of the Indian Constitution.

1 Article 19 (1) (a)
2 Article 19 (1) (f)
3 Article 18 (1)
4 Article 21

Ans. (1)

Exp. Freedom of Expression is contained under Article 19(1)(a) of Constitution.

In India, freedom of press is implied from the freedom of speech and expression guaranteed under Article 19(1)(a) of the Constitution of India. Article 19(1)(a) says that all citizens shall have the right to freedom of speech and expression.

Directions (Q. Nos. 96-100) *Read the following paragraph carefully and answer the five questions which as follows :*

The State of Uttar Pradesh and Uttarakhand have not cooperated with Central Government to constitute a Ganga Management Board. The Uttarakhand High Court in the exercise of its 'Parens Patriae jurisdiction, ordered conversation of Ganga and Yamuna as juristic/legal persons/living entities, having the status of a legal person. The river Ganga and Yamuna are thus legal persons with corresponding rights of a living person. The director NAMAMI Ganga, the Chief Secretary and Advocate General of Uttarakhand States were declared as persons in 'loco parents'.

The division bench of Uttarakhand High Court sharply berated the state terming their Non-cooperation as the 'sign of non-governance'. The deterioration of Ganga and Yamuna is a classic case of 'desperate times, desperate measures', the court granted the juristic entity at par with Hindu idol. The Uttarakhand High Court in another case reiterated the constitution of the Ganga Management Board has become all the more necessary for the purpose of irrigation, water, supply, hydropower generation and navigation.

96 The term 'Parens Patriae' refers to

1 common suit.
2 descent from parent.
3 parent of his/her own country/state.
4 barred by res judicata.

Ans. *(3)*

Exp. The term 'Parens Patriae' refers to parent of his/her own country/state'. Parens Patriae in Latin means "parent of the nation". In law, it refers to the power of the State to intervene against an abusive or negligent parent, legal guardian or informal caretaker, and to act as the parent of any child or individual who is in need of protection.

97 The Uttarakhand High Court in another case reiterated 'the Constitution ______ navigation' as quoted in the paragraph, refers to which one of the following cases?

1 Mohd Salim Vs. State of Uttarakhand
2 Yogendra Nath Vs. Commissioner of Income Tax
3 Ram Jankijee Vs. State of Bihar
4 MC Mehta Vs. Kamal Nath

Ans. *(1)*

Exp. The Uttarakhand High Court in another case reiterated 'the Constitution...navigation' as quoted in the paragraph, refers to Mohd Salim Vs. State of Uttarakhand.

The Court specified that Ganga and Yamuna have a particular significance for Hindus. The Court cited cases stating that a Hindu idol can be held as a juristic entity.

98 Hindu idol is a juristic entity capable of holding property, was laid down in

1 Bengal Immunity Co. Ltd Vs. State of Bihar
2 Yogendra Nath Naskar Vs. Commissioner of Income Tax
3 KM Basheer Vs. Lona Chakola
4 Nanak Chand Vs. State of UP

Ans. *(2)*

Exp. In Yogendra Nath Naskar Vs. Commissioner of Income Tax it was held that, Hindu Idol is a juristic entity capable of holding property.

99 'The division bench of Uttarakhand High Court sharply berated...non-governance' was observed in which of the following cases?

1 Indian Council for Enviro-legal Action Vs. Union of India
2 Rural Litigation and Entitlement Kendra Vs. State of Uttarakhand
3 Divya Pharmacy Vs. Union of India
4 Lalit Miglani Vs. State of Uttarakhand

Ans. *(4)*

Exp. 'The division bench of Uttarakhand High Court sharply berated...non-governance', it was observed in Lalit Miglani Vs. State of Uttarakhand. This case was filed in 2015 as a public interest litigation and its decision was delivered in 2017. In this case, the petitioner sought to declare the "Himalayas, glaciers, streams, water bodies, etc. as juristic persons at par with the pious rivers Ganga and Yamuna."

100 The term 'loco parents' refers to

1 in equal fault
2 in place of parent
3 hizanat period
4 indigent suit

Ans. *(2)*

Exp. The term 'loco parents' refers to in place of parent.

In loco parentis is a Latin term which means "in the place of parent" and is originally derived from the English common law. It is the legal responsibility of a person or organisation to take on some of the functions and responsibility of a pearent. It refers to a relationship in which a person puts himself or herself in the situation of a parent by assuming and discharging the obligations of a parent to a child.

UGC-NET
LAW

SOLVED PAPER 2019 (December)

PAPER II

1 Which of the following statements are correct?

I. Article 353 of Constitution of India deals with effect of Proclamation of Emergency.

II. Article 354 of Constitution of India deals with income generating power of the Governor during Emergency.

III. Article 355 of the Constitution of India deals with duty of Union to protect States against external aggression and armed rebellion.

IV. Article 356 of the Constitution of India deals with imposition of Emergency during Local disturbance by militants or terrorists.

Choose the correct option :

1 I and II 2 I and III
3 II and III 4 III and IV

Ans. (2)

Exp. Statements I and III are correct.

Article 353 of Indian Constitution deals with the effect of Proclamation of Emergency. The Article provides while a Proclamation of Emergency is in operation, the executive power of the Union shall extend to the giving of directions to any State as to the manner in which the executive power thereof is to be exercised.

Article 355 of the Constitution of India places duty upon the Union to protect States against external aggression and armed rebellion and to ensure that the government of every State is carried on in accordance with the provisions of this Constitution.

Statement II and IV are not correct.

Article 354 of Constitution of India deals with application of provisions relating to distribution of revenues while a Proclamation of Emergency is in operation and such power is conferred upon the President, not Governor.

Article 356 of the Constitution of India lists provisions in case of failure of constitutional machinery in State stating that if the President can assume the control of a state if he is satisfied that a situation has arisen in which the government of the State cannot be carried on in accordance with the provisions of this Constitution.

2 'A' in India, instigates 'B', a foreigner in Goa, to commit a murder in Goa. 'A' is guilty of

1 culpable homicide not amounting to murder
2 committing the offence of murder
3 criminal conspiracy
4 abetting the murder

Ans. (4)

Exp. 'A' has abetted the offence of murder by instigating 'B', a foreigner in Goa, to commit murder in Goa.

Section 107 of IPC defines abetment of a thing as a person who instigates any person to do that thing; or engages with one or more other person or persons in any conspiracy for the doing of that thing, if an act or illegal omission takes place in pursuance of that conspiracy, and in order to the doing of that thing; or intentionally aids, by any act or illegal omission, the doing of that thing.

3 Consider the following statements and point out which statements are related to Positivism.

I. Laws are command.

II. Analysis of legal concept is distinct from Sociological and Historical analysis.

III. Decisions can be deducted logically with recourse to morality.

IV. The 'Law as it is' has to be kept separate from 'Law ought to be'.

Choose the correct option:

1 I, II and III 2 I, II and IV
3 II, III and IV 4 I and IV

Ans. (2)

Exp. Statements I, II and IV are related to Positivism.

Legal Positivism, also known as the Analyst school of jurisprudence, supports the idea that the law is a command of the sovereign. It implies that laws are made by the state and serve as commands which are to be strictly followed as they are. The positivists believe that there is no place of fairness or morality in the application of law and the same is a matter of discretion of the state.

It is not relevant to consider how law should be, rather the emphasis is upon what the law is the 'Law as it is' has to be kept separate from 'Law ought to be'.

It is further believed that legal concepts must be analyzed keeping the Sociological or Historical perspectives separately and that these aspects will have no bearing on law.

Statement III is not correct as legal positivism does not consider the moral aspect of law. Instead, the legal positivist accepts approved rules and laws as law, whether or not he or she agrees with them from a moral perspective.

4 Which sections of Hindu Marriage Act, 1955 deal with matrimonial remedy of divorce?

I. Section 13 II. Section 13 (1-A)
III. Section 17 IV. Section 13-B

Choose the correct option :

1 I, III and IV 2 II, III and IV
3 I, II and IV 4 I, II and III

Ans. (3)

Exp. Section 13, Section 13 (1-A) and Section 13-B of Hindu Marriage Act, 1955 deal with matrimonial remedy of divorce.

Section 13 of Hindu Marriage Act, 1955 deals with matrimonial remedy in the form of Divorce. In this section, it is provided that any marriage solemnized may be dissolved on a petition presented by either the husband or the wife on the ground that the other party has committed an act falling under certain conditions such as cruelty, desertion, conversion, etc.

Section 13(1-A) grants right to either party to a marriage to present a petition for the dissolution of marriage on the ground that there has been no resumption of cohabitation or restitution of conjugal rights between the parties for a period of one year or more after the passing of a decree for judicial separation or restitution of conjugal rights.

Section 13-B mentions divorce by mutual consent. According to it, a petition for dissolution of marriage may be presented by both the parties on the ground, inter alia that they have mutually agreed that the marriage should be dissolved.

However, Section 17 is not related to the remedy of divorce but declares bigamy to be void and punishable with reference to Sections 494, 495 of IPC.

5 Given below are two statements. One is labelled as Assertion (A) and the other is labelled as Reason (R).

Assertion (A) Special Provisions in insurance law are required as to compensation in case of hit and run motor accidents.

Reason (R) Section 161 of the Motor Vehicles Act, 1988, makes special provisions for payment or compensation in respect of the death of, or grevious hurt to persons resulting from hit and run motor accidents.

In the light of the above two statements choose the correct option.

1 Both (A) and (R) are true and (R) is not the correct explanation of (A)
2 Both (A) and (R) are true and (R) is the correct explanation of (A)
3 (A) is true, but (R) is false
4 (A) is false, but (R) is true

Ans. (2)

Exp. Both (A) and (R) are true and (R) is the correct explanation of (A).

Section 161 of Motor Vehicle Act, 1988 incorporates special provisions as to compensation in case of hit and run motor accidents. Section 161(1) defines a hit and run motor accident as an accident arising out of the use of a motor vehicle the identity whereof cannot be ascertained in spite of reasonable efforts. Thus, the Assertion is correct.

Section 161 (2) provides that the General Insurance Corporation of India formed under section 9 of the General Insurance Business (Nationalisation) Act, 1972 Act and the insurance companies shall provide for compensation to persons resulting from hit and run motor accidents. Hence, the Reason is correct.

6 Which of the following is/are true about Bill of Exchange?

I. A Bill of Exchange, requires in its inception of two parties.
II. A Bill of Exchange or draft is a written order by the drawer of drawee to pay money to the payee.
III. Bill of Exchange are primarily used in the International trade and are written orders by one person to his bank to pay the bearer a specific sum on a specific date.
IV. Definition of Bill of Exchange is mentioned in the section 6 of the Negotiable Instrument Act.

Choose the most appropriate option :

1 I and IV 2 I, II and IV
3 II and III 4 III and IV

Ans. (3)

Exp. Statements II and III are true about Bill of Exchange.

A Bill of Exchange or draft is a written order by the drawer of drawee to pay money to the payee. Section 5 of the Negotiable Instruments Act, 1885 defines a Bill of Exchange as an instrument in writing containing an unconditional order, signed by the maker, directing a certain person to pay a certain sum of money only to, or to the order of, a certain person or to the bearer of the instrument. So, Statement II is correct but IV is not correct.

Bill of Exchange are primarily used in the International trade and are written orders by one person to his bank to pay the bearer a specific sum on a specific date. Bill of Exchange are primarily found and used in foreign or International trade transactions for the case of export-import related arrangements wherein payments are to be fulfilled either in advance or at the time of compliance of contract. These bills are similar to promissory notes because they can be drawn by individuals or even banks, and may be cleared by endorsements.

Statement I is incorrect as Bill of Exchange generally includes three parties; the drawee is the party that pays the sum, the payee receives that sum, and the drawer is the one that obliges the drawee to pay the payee.

7 Mention the following decisions in a chronological order on Extradition :

I. Mubarak Ali Ahmed Vs. State of Bombay
II. Hans Muller of Nuremberg Vs. Suptt. Presidency Jail Calcutta and Others
III. Ram Babu Saxena Vs. State
IV. State of Madras Vs. C.G. Menon

Choose the correct option :

1 IV, III, I, II 2 III, IV, II, I
3 II, I, IV, III 4 IV, III, II, I

***Ans.* (2)**

Exp. The correct chronological order of decisions on Extradition is III, IV, II and I.

The decision in Ram Babu Saksena Vs. State (1950) states that there is no legal restriction against the trial of the accused for an offence under Section 161, Penal Code, even though Section 161 is not included in the list of extradition offences in the Indian Extradition Act of 1903.

State of Madras Vs. C.G. Menon (1955) declares that the Fugitive Offenders Act, 1881 was violative of Article 14 of the Constitution and remained unenforceable after enforcement of the Constitution.

In Hans Muller of Nuremberg Vs. Supdt. Presidency Jail, Calcutta and Others (1955) the court held that the government has the right to reject a request for extradition.

Mubarak Ali Ahmed Vs. The State of Bombay (1957) declared that a foreign nationalist extradited under relevant procedures, can be tried for an offense other than the one initially deported for.

8 Arrange the provisions of Hindu Succession Act, 1956 in chronological order (Section wise):

I. Presumption in case of simultaneous death
II. Failure of heirs
III. Act not to apply to certain properties
IV. Full blood preferred to half blood

Choose the correct option :

1 I, II, III, IV 2 IV, III, II, I
3 III, IV, I, II 4 IV, I, III, II

***Ans.* (3)**

Exp. The correct chronological order is III, IV, I, II.

Section 5 of Hindu Succession Act, 1956 provides that the Act shall not apply to certain properties. This Act shall not apply to any property succession to which is regulated by the Indian Succession Act, 1925 by reason of the provisions contained in Section 21 of the Special Marriage Act, 1954 etc.

Section 18 of Hindu Succession Act, 1956 provides that heirs related to an intestate by full blood shall be preferred to heirs related by half blood, if the nature of the relationship is the same in every other respect.

Section 21 of Hindu Succession Act, 1956 is related to Presumption in cases of simultaneous deaths. It states that where two persons have died in circumstances rendering it uncertain whether either of them survived the other then, it shall be presumed until the contrary is proved that the younger survived the elder.

Section 29 of Hindu Succession Act, 1956 is related to Failure of heirs. It states that if an intestate has left no heir qualified to succeed to his or her property in accordance with the provisions of this Act, such property shall devolve on the government.

9 Arrange the following enactments in chronological order enacted to provide social justice.

I. Equal Remuneration Act
II. Immoral Traffic (Prevention) Act
III. Medical Termination of Pregnancy Act
IV. Maternity Benefit Act

Choose the correct option :

1 I, II, III, IV 2 II, III, I, IV
3 II, IV, III, I 4 IV, III, II, I

***Ans.* (3)**

Exp. The correct chronological order is II, IV, III, I.

The Immoral Traffic (Prevention) Act, 1956 was made to prohibit immoral traffic among women and children as India had signed the UN International Convention for the "Suppression of Women in Traffic in Persons and of the Exploitation in Others" in New York in 1950.

Maternity Benefit Act, 1961 is to control the employment of women for certain periods before and after child-birth and to provide for legitimate benefits associated with maternity.

The Medical Termination of Pregnancy Act, 1971 permits termination of certain pregnancies by registered medical practitioners and for connected matters.

Equal Remuneration Act, 1976 is an act to provide for the payment of equal remuneration to men and women workers and to prohibit discrimination on the ground of sex for related matters.

10 Section 3(1) of the Trade Marks Act, 1999 deals with the provision relating to:

1 Refusal of registration
2 Application for registration
3 Appointment of Registrar of Trade Marks
4 Correction and amendment in the application

***Ans.* (3)**

Exp. The Section 3 (1) in the Trade Marks Act, 1999 deals with the provision relating to appointment of Registrar of Trade Marks and other officers.

According to the provision, the Central Government may, by notification in the Official Gazette, appoint a person to be known as the Controller-General of Patents, Designs and Trade Marks, who shall be the Registrar of Trade Marks for the purposes of this Act.

11 In which of the following cases our Supreme Court held that so far as the guarantee of equal protection in Article 14 is concerned, any State action-Executive, Legislative or Judicial, which contravenes Article 14 is void?

1 Amir Abbas Vs. State of M.B.
2 Naresh Mirajkar Vs. State of Bihar
3 Budhan Vs. State of Bihar
4 Himmatlal Vs. State of M.P.

Ans. (3)

Exp. In the case of Budhan Vs. State of Bihar (1954), Supreme Court held that so far as the guarantee of equal protection in Article 14 is concerned, any State action-Executive, Legislative or Judicial, which contravenes Article 14 is void. It noted that the Article condemns both discrimination by law and by procedure, but the Constitution "does not assure unanimity of decisions or immunity from merely erroneous action" by courts or by bureaucracy. It meant that the right to equal protection under Article 14 does not entitle a person to claim similar decisions on similar facts decided previously and the same only depends upon the discretion of the court.

This was done to convey that the decision in a particular case is based on circumstances existing at that time, which may change in future and equality must mean similar treatment in similar situations only.

12 Under Muslim Law, marriage with a woman, whose husband is alive, is :

1 Valid 2 Sahih
3 Void 4 Irregular

Ans. (3)

Exp. Under Muslim Law, marriage with a woman, whose husband is alive, is Void.

An agreement between a prospective bride and a groom which does not meet all the essential conditions of a Muslim marriage is a void agreement and any marriage that takes place in furtherance of a void agreement is called a void marriage or Batil nikah.

The following are certain situations, interalia, in which a Muslim marriage is void; when a marriage takes place between persons who are absolutely incapable, when a person marries to the wife of another man (who is alive) when the marriage of the lady was subsisting.

13 Arrange the provisions of Trade Mark Act, 1999 in chronological order (section wise) :

I. classification of goods and services
II. regulation in case of honest concurrent use etc
III. limitation as to colour
IV. absolute grounds for refusal of registration

Choose the correct option :

1 I, II, III, IV 2 I, III, IV, II
3 I, IV, III, II 4 II, III, IV, I

Ans. (3)

Exp. The correct chronological order is I, IV, III, II.

Section 7 of the Trade Mark Act, 1999 provides for classification of goods and services and states the Registrar shall classify goods and service in accordance with the International classification of goods and services.

Section 9 of the Trade Mark Act, 1999 mentions absolute grounds for refusal of registration, providing that the trade marks which are devoid of any distinctive character, designate the kind, quality, quantity, etc. of the goods or service or which have become customary, shall not be registered.

Section 10 of the Trade Mark Act, 1999 imposes limitation as to colour stating that a trade mark may be limited wholly or in part to any combination of colours.

As per Section 12 of the Trade Mark Act, 1999 in the case of honest concurrent use or of other special circumstances, the Registrar may permit the registration by more than one proprietor of trade marks subject to conditions.

14 Which of the following Section of the Patent Act, 1970 provides for the subject matters that are not invention under the Act?

1 Section 7 2 Section 3
3 Section 10 4 Section 11

Ans. (2)

Exp. Section 3 of the Patents Act, 1970 provides for the subject matters that are not invention under the Act.

As per the provision, there are 16 subject-matters that are not invention under the Act.

Some of them are given below :

- An invention which is frivolous or contrary to well established natural laws;
- An invention which causes serious prejudice to human, animal or plant life or health or to the environment,
- mere discovery of a scientific principle or the formulation of an abstract theory, a method of agriculture or horticulture.
- any process for the medicinal, surgical, curative, prophylactic to render free of disease or to increase their economic value or that of their products
- a mathematical or business method or a computer program per se or algorithms.

15 Arrange the following judgements on Torts in chronological order :

I. Asbhy Vs. White
II. MC Mehta Vs. Union of India
III. Ryland Vs. Fletcher
IV. Donoghue Vs. Stevenson

Choose the correct option:

1 II, IV, III, I 2 I, III, IV, II
3 I, III, II, IV 4 IV, II, I, III

Ans. (2)

Exp. The correct chronological order is I, III, IV, II.

In Ashby Vs. White, (1703), it was held that to have a legal action under tort law, violation of legal right is sufficient and there is no need to prove any damage as such.

In Rylands Vs. Fletcher (1868), the court held defendant liable on the principles of strict liability as the defendant brought something onto his land, made a "non-natural use" of his land, the thing was something likely to do mischief if it escaped and it did escape and cause damage.

Donoghue Vs. Stevenson (1932), is a leading case in Western law. The ruling in this case established the civil law tort of negligence and obliged businesses to observe a duty of care towards their customers.

In M.C. Mehta Vs. Union of India and Ors (1986), the court held that an enterprise which was engaged in a hazardous industry owed an absolutely non-delegable duty to the community to ensure that if any harm resulted to anyone, the enterprise had to be absolutely liable.

16 Mention the following cases in a chronological order on Election Commission :

I. Kuldip Nayar Vs. Union of India
II. T.N. Seshan Vs. Union of India
III. People's Union for Civil Liberties Vs. Union of India
IV. S.S. Dhanoa Vs. Union of India

Choose the correct option :

1 II, III, IV, I
2 III, IV, II, I
3 I, IV, II, III
4 IV, II, I, III

Ans. *(4)*

Exp. The correct chronological order is IV, II, I, III.

In S.S. Dhanoa Vs. Union of India (1991), it was held that no member of an institution can ever claim to be higher than the institution that he represents.

In T.N. Seshan Vs. Union of India (1995), it is held that the concept of plurality is writ large on the face of Article 324, clause (2) whereof clearly envisages a multi-member Election Commission comprising the CEC and one or more ECs.

The court in the case of Kuldip Nayar Vs. Union of India (2006) held that it is no part of federal principle that the representatives of state must belong to that state.

As per People's Union of Civil Liberties (PUCL) Vs. Union of India (2013), Indian voters have a right under Article 19(1)1 of the Indian Constitution to obtain information about political candidates.

17 Match the following.

	List I		List II
A.	Exemplary damages	I.	MC Mehta vs Kamalnath
B.	Evaluation of cleanliness of various fuels	II.	Sterlite Industries
C.	Public Trust Doctrine	III.	Intergenerational equity
D.	Right of each generation to benefit from the past generation and to preserve such heritage for future	IV.	Bhurelal Committee

Choose correct option from those given below

	A	B	C	D		A	B	C	D
1	I	II	III	IV	2	II	IV	I	III
3	IV	II	I	III	4	IV	III	I	II

Ans. *(2)*

Exp. The correct matching is A-II, B-IV, C-I, D-III.

The judgment in *Sterlite Industries* Vs. Union of India (2013) set an example for prospective violations of environmental laws, by ordering Sterlite to pay damages of Rs 100 crore for polluting the environment. Exemplary damages consist of excessive amounts of compensation, ordered for setting an example among violators for deterrence.

The *Bhurelal Committee* was based on evaluation of cleanliness of various fuels. It was established under Section 3 of the Environment (Protection) Act, 1986. It was formed to make suggestions to improve climate conditions and is known for many reforms including the conversion of public transport to CNG mode.

In the case of *M. C. Mehta Vs Kamal Nath* (1997), the Public Trust Doctrine was mentioned for the first time. It holds that certain resources like air, sea, waters and forests cannot be a subject of private ownership.

The Principle of *intergenerational equity* is a principle of sustainable development, and implies that each time must use the natural resources in such a manner that their availability and usage are preserved for future generations.

18 Who among the following said that there is in essence, no difference between the legal personality of a company and that of an individual?

1 Maitland
2 Dicey
3 Gierke
4 Kelsen

Ans. *(4)*

Exp. Kelsen in his Theory of Legal Personality mentions that there is in essence, no difference between the legal personality of a company and that of an individual. Personality in the legal sense is only a technical personificaiton of a complex of norms with the assigned rights and duties.

19 "Human dignity is the Quintessence of Human Rights". This has been stated by:

1 Justice V.R. Krishna Iyer
2 Justice J.S. Verma
3 Justice Kuldeep Singh
4 Justice Ranganath Mishra

Ans. *(2)*

Exp. The given statement has been stated by Justice J.S. Verma.

Justice J.S. Verma had delivered the first part of the Dashrathmal Singhvi Memorial Lecture –2002 on "Human Rights–The Essence of Constitutional Governance" on 16th November 2002, in Jodhpur, Rajasthan.

It is during this session that he stated that "Human dignity is the quintessence of human rights". He meant that human dignity is a strong indicator of human right and presence or absence of dignity is directly related to the compliance or violation of human rights.

He also believed that a proper synthesis of dignity and related ideas must take place in order to constitute human rights in a balanced order, which can be done by realizing every factor that contributes to formation of human rights.

20 "In the British Constitution there is no such thing as the absolute separation of Legislative, Executive and Judicial powers. In practice it is inevitable that they overlap. In the Constitution of France and U.S.A. attempts to keep the organs of the government rigidly apart have been made but have proved unsuccessful". This position of doctrine of separation of powers has been summed-up by :

1 Prof. Ullman
2 Prof. K.T. Shah
3 Wade and Phillips
4 Donoghmore Committee

***Ans.* (4)**

Exp. The Donoughmore Committee in its report had remarked that "In the British Constitution there is no such thing as the absolute separation of Legislative, Executive and Judicial powers. In practice it is inevitable that they overlap. In the Constitution of France and U.S.A. attempts to keep the organs of the government rigidly apart have been made but have proved unsuccessful".

Doctrine of separation of powers is not an essential feature of British Constitution.

The Donoughmore Commission is a committee set up by the British government and placed at Ceylon in 1927 to examine its constitution for revision. The committee's recommendations eventually provided the basis for Constitution in 1931.

21 Which of the following statements are correct as per Article 111 of agreements establishing WTO? The main functions of the WTO aro

I. To administer and promote agreements on individual and multinational agreements;
II. To administer the rules and procedures governing the settlement of disputes;
III. To administer the Trade Policy Review Mechanism (TPRM)
IV. To Coordinate IMF, TBRD and World Bank on regional economic policies.

Choose the correct option:

1 I and II
2 I and III
3 II and III
4 III and IV

***Ans.* (3)**

Exp. Statements II and III contains the main functions of WTO.

According to Article 111 (3) of Agreements establishing WTO, the WTO shall administer the Understanding on Rules and Procedures Governing the Settlement of Disputes to the Agreement.

Further, as per clause (4) of Article 111, the WTO shall administer the Trade Policy Review Mechanism (TPRM) to the Agreement.

22 The expression "Minority" is a relative term and is referred to, to represent the linguistic or religious sections or groups forming less than 50% of the total population of the State, stated by the Supreme Court in the following case

1 T.M.A. Pai Foundation Vs. State of Karnatka
2 P.A. Inamdar Vs. State of Maharashtra
3 Islamic Academy of Education Vs. State of Karnataka
4 Usha Mehta Vs. State of Maharashtra

***Ans.* (1)**

Exp. The case titled as TMA Pai Foundation Vs. State of Karnataka (2002), declared that the term "Minority" is a relative term and is referred to represent the linguistic or religious sections or groups forming less than 50% of the total population of the State.

At present, the status of minority needs to be determined on the basis of two factors; religion and language. For the purpose of ascertaining minority, it has to be ensured that the unit will be the state and not the whole of India.

Further, Minorities have to be considered State-wise since the reorganization of the states of India was made on linguistic lines.

23 Section 9 of the Geographical Indication of Goods (Registration and Protection) Act, 1999 provides for

1 Prohibition of Registration of certain geographical indications
2 Registration of Homonymous geographical indications
3 Geographical Indication Registry and Office thereof
4 Register of Geographical Indications

***Ans.* (1)**

Exp. Section 9 of the Geographical Indications of Goods (Registration and Protection) Act, 1999 provides for prohibition Registration of certain geographical indications.

As per the provision, a geographical indication shall not be registered if the use of which would be likely to deceive or cause confusion; or the use of which would be contrary to any law for the time being in force; or which comprises or contains scandalous or obscene matter; or which comprises or contains any matter likely to hurt the religious susceptibilities of any class or section of the citizens of India; or which would otherwise be disentitled to protection in a court; or which are determined to be generic names or indications of goods and are, therefore, not or ceased to be protected in their country of origin, or which have fallen into disuse in that country; or which, although literally true as to the territory, region or locality in which the goods originate, but falsely represent to the persons that the goods originate in another territory, region or locality, as the case may be.

24 The Supreme Court in regard to Section 34 of Indian Penal Code observed that the existence of a common intention among the participants in a crime is the essential element for application of this section. It is not necessary that the act of the several persons charged with commission of an offence jointly must be the same or identically similar. In which of the following case the above observation was made by the Supreme Court?

1 Ashok Kumar Vs. State of Punjab
2 Shankar Narayan Bhadolkar Vs. State of Maharashtra
3 Gurubachan Singh Vs. State of Punjab
4 S.C. Bahri Vs. State of Bihar

***Ans.* (1)**

Exp. It was observed in Ashok Kumar Vs. State of Punjab (1977), the existence of a common intention amongst the participants in a crime is the essential element for application of Section 34 of IPC. It was held that it is also not necessary that acts committed by several persons be same or similar. In fact, the acts may be different from each other and be committed at different times, but the acts would form part of Section 34 if they were committed in pursuance to common intention formed for the purpose of committing the act.

Section 34 of IPC provides when a criminal act is done by several persons in furtherance of the common intention of all, each of such persons is liable for that act in the same manner as if it were done by him alone.

25 Which of the following is not a valid defence in tort?

1 Private Defence
2 Volenti non fit injuria
3 Vis major
4 Ex dolo malo non Oritur actio

***Ans.* (4)**

Exp. The Latin Maxim Ex dolo malo non Oritur actio is not a defense under tort law.

It means 'no right of action can have its origin in fraud' i.e. That, no court will lend its aid to a man who founds his cause of action upon an immoral or an illegal act. The maxim is based on the principle that a cause of action cannot arise out of an act which amounts to moral turpitude or fraudulent in itself, which destroys the very cause of action in legal sense. The maxim is generally applied in contract law in order to declare the contracts invalid on the ground of fraud or contrary to public policy.

26 A valid contract can be entered into between parties under Indian Contract Act. Which of the following gives legal recognition to such contract.

I. Section 10-A of Information Technology Act
II. Section 65-B of Indian Evidence Act
III. Section 1(4) of Information Technology Act
IV. Section 63 of Indian Evidence Act

Choose the correct option :

1 I and IV
2 I and II
3 I and III
4 III and IV

***Ans.* (2)**

Exp. A valid contract can be entered into between parties under Indian Contract Act. Section 10-A of Information Technology Act and Section 65-B of Indian Evidence Act gives legal recognition to such contract.

The Section 10A of the Information Technology Act, 2000 mentions of validity of contracts formed through electronic means. It states that where in a contract formation, the communication of proposals, the acceptance of proposals, the revocation of proposals and acceptances, as the case may be, are expressed in electronic form or by means of an electronic record, such contract shall not be deemed to be unenforceable solely on the ground that such electronic form or means was used for that purpose.

The Section 65B in The Indian Evidence Act, 1872 deals with admissibility of electronic records. According to it, any information contained in an electronic record which is printed on a paper, stored, recorded or copied in optical or magnetic media produced by a computer shall be deemed to be also a document, if the conditions mentioned in this section are satisfied.

27 "The International Court of Justice is indeed a sine qua non for the establishment of Rule of Law in Inter-state relations" is said by:

1 Justice Shigeru Oda
2 Justice Nagendra Singh
3 Justice Dalveer Bhandari
4 Justice R.S. Pathak

***Ans.* (2)**

Exp. The statement that "The International Court of Justice is indeed a sine qua non for the establishment of Rule of Law in Inter-state relations", was said by Justice Nagendra Singh.

Mr. Nagendra Singh was initially an Indian lawyer and subsequently worked as an administrator or civil servant, who also later on served as President of the International Court of Justice from year 1985 to 1988.

It is worth noting that he was one of the only four judges from India to have served as Judges of the International Court of Justice at The Hague.

Apart from him, the people from India who served as judges at ICJ are B. N. Rau (1952–1953), R. S. Pathak (1989–1991) and Dalveer Bhandari (2012–present).

28 Frustation of contract implies:

1 Legal impediment to materialise the contract
2 Commercial hardship
3 Financial constraint to materialise the contract
4 Physical impossibility due to disappearance of the subject matter of contract or object has failed to materialise

Ans. (4)

Exp. Frustation of contract implies physical impossibility due to disappearance of the subject matter of contract or object has failed to materialise. Frustration of contract can be established upon the fulfillment of following conditions :

- Existence of a valid contract between parties.
- The contract is yet to be performed.
- The performance of the contract becomes impossible or unlawful.
- The impossibility to perform is caused by an event which is beyond the control of both the parties.

29 The maxim 'Damnum Sine injuria' means:

1 Infringement of Legal right with damage or loss
2 Damage or loss without infringement of legal right
3 Where there is a right, there is a remedy
4 Infringement of an absolute right without damage or loss

Ans. (2)

Exp. The maxim 'Damnum Sine injuria' means damage or loss without infringement of legal right.

The Latin term 'Damnum Sine Injuria' means damage without injury. According to this, a person cannot initiate legal action and claim damages on the ground that he suffered damage or loss due to an activity of another without having suffered violation of any of his legal rights.

It implies that irrespective of the kind and extent of any damage, a person cannot claim compensation when his legal rights were not infringed by the action of defendants. In other words, mere damage without loss of legal right is not actionable before the court of law.

30 Various legislations relating to Human Rights in India are given below. Arrange them in chronological order since 1955:

1. I. Bonded Labour system (Abolition) Act
II. Protection of Civil Right Act
III. Immoral Trafficking (Prevention) Act
IV. Child Labour (Prohibition and Regulation) Act

2. I. Protection of Civil Rights Act
II. Immoral Trafficking (Prevention) Act
III. Bonded Labour System (Abolition) Act
IV. Child Labour (Prohibition and Regulation Act)

3. I. Child labour (Prohibition and Regulation) Act
II. Bonded Labour System (Abolition) Act
III. Protection of Civil Rights Act
IV. Immoral Trafficking (Prevention) Act

4. I. Bonded Labour System (Abolition) Act
II. Immoral Trafficking (Prevention) Act
III. Protection of Civil Right Act
IV Child Labour Prohibition and Regulation Act

Ans. (2)

Exp. The correct chronological order of various legislations relating to Human Rights in India are provided in option B correctly.

The Protection of Civil Rights Act, 1955 is an Act to prescribe punishment for the practice of "Untouchability" and for matters connected therewith.

The Immoral Trafficking (Prevention) Act, 1956 was enacted for the prevention of immoral traffic and was done in pursuance of the International Convention signed at New York in 1950.

Bonded Labour System (Abolition) Act, 1976 exists to provide for the abolition of bonded labour system with a view to preventing the economic and physical exploitation of the weaker sections.

The Child Labour (Prohibition and Regulation) Act, 1986 prohibits the engagement of children in certain employments and regulates the conditions of work of children in employments.

31 Which of the following statements are correct?

I. Chapter VI of the UN Charter deals with the Pacific Settlement of Disputes
II. The purpose of United Nation Organisation is World Peace
III. The Security Council comprises of 14 members
IV. The non-permanent member are elected by the General Assembly for a period of three years.

Choose the correct option :

1 I and II 2 I and III 3 II and III 4 II and IV

Ans. (1)

Exp. Statement I and II are correct.

The Pacific Settlement of Disputes is found under Chapter VI of the UN Charter. This section deals with the practice of the Security Council aimed at promoting and implementing recommendations and methods or procedures for the peaceful settlement of disputes within the framework of Articles 33-38 of Chapter VI and Articles 11 and 99 of the Charter of the United Nations. Overall, Chapter VI of the Charter contains various provisions according to which the Security Council may make recommendations to the parties to a dispute or situation.

The purpose of United Nation Organisation is World Peace Article 1 of the UN Charter states the following purposes; to maintain international peace and security, to take effective collective measures for the prevention and removal of threats to the peace, and for the suppression of acts of aggression or other breaches of the peace, and to bring about by peaceful means, and in conformity with the principles of justice and international law, adjustment or settlement of international disputes or situations which might lead to a breach of the peace.

Statement III and IV are incorrect as according to Article 23 of the UN Charter, the Security Council shall consist of 15 Members of the United Nations. Also, the non-permanent members of the Security Council shall be elected for a term of two years.

32 Professor Dicey gave following three meanings of Rule of law :

I. Absence of Arbitrary power or supremacy of the law

II. Equality before law

III. The constitution is the result of the ordinary law of land

Out of the above aspects which of the following apply to Indian system :

1 I and II	2 II and III
3 I and III	4 All I, II and III

***Ans.** (1)*

➲ *Exp.* Among the given options, option 1 provides the correct choices.

A.V. Dicey had primarily based his definition of Rule of Law on three pillars namely, Supremacy of Law, Equality before Law and Predominance of Legal Spirit.

India had adopted the idea of Rule of Law from the common law system of justice which had its roots in British Jurisprudence. Rule of law refers to supremacy of law and the law is above all.

In terms of Indian context, supremacy of Law and equality before law are found in constitution and other laws, more so in Article 14 of Indian Constitution.

However, it is incorrect to say that the constitution is the result of an ordinary law of the land. In fact, the constitution was drafted by a Constituent Assembly created for the special purpose and was dissolved after creating the constitution. It cannot be said that the constitution was created just like any other law by the ordinary legislature following the regular process of law.

33 Read the following statement in the light of Hindu Adoption and Maintenance Act, 1956

I. Section 7 deals with capacity of a male Hindu to take in adoption

II. Section 13 deals with valid adoption not to be cancelled

III. Section 12 deals with effect of adoption

IV. Section 15 deals with right of adoptive parents to dispose off their properties

Choose the correct option

1 I and III	2 II and IV
3 II and III	4 I and IV

***Ans.** (1)*

➲ *Exp.* Statement I and III are correct in relation to Hindu Adoption and Maintenance Act, 1956.

Section 7 of Hindu Adoption and Maintenance Act, 1956 deals with the capacity of a male Hindu to take in adoption. It states that any male Hindu who is of sound mind and is not a minor, has the capacity to take a son or a daughter in adoption.

Section 12 of the Act mentions the effect of adoptions. As per it, an adopted child shall be deemed to be the child of his or her adoptive father or mother for all purposes with effect from the date of the adoption and from such date all the ties of the child in the family of his or her birth shall be deemed to be severed and replaced by those created by the adoption in the adoptive family.

Statement II and IV are incorrect as Section 13 deals with the Right of adoptive parents to dispose of their properties. Also, Section 15 tells us that valid adoptions cannot be cancelled.

34 "The provisions of the Constitution are not mathematical formulas having their essence in their form; they are organic living institutions transplanted from English soil. Their significance is vital not formal; it is to be gathered not simply by taking the words and a dictionary, but by considering their origin and the line of their growth".

The above observation is made by:

1 Schwartz	2 Holmes, C.J.
3 S.A. de Smith	4 Lord Russel

***Ans.** (2)*

➲ *Exp.* The above given observation was made by Justice Holmes, C.J. in Gompers Vs. United States (1914).

He said that "The provisions of the Constitution are not mathematical formulas having their essence in their form; they are organic living institutions transplanted from English soil. Their significance is vital not formal; it is to be gathered not simply by taking the words and a dictionary, but by considering their origin and the line of their growth".

He suggested that the provisions are not rigid in form and they must be applied to suit the existing situations which may vary at times. Thus, he opined that a varying application of law is what is expected, rather than rigid and complex application which serves no purpose of justice.

35 Which of the following statements is NOT correct in regard to distinction between Civil and Criminal liability?

1 Civil liability arises when a wrong is against a private individual but Criminal liability arises in case of offence which is a wrong against the society

2 Civil liability entails punishment whereas criminal liability results into damages

3 The procedure for determining Civil and Criminal liability is different

4 In Civil liability, it is the act and not the intention which is taken into consideration whereas in case of Criminal liability, mens rea is the determining factor

***Ans.** (2)*

➲ *Exp.* Statement 2 is not correct in regard to distinction between Civil and Criminal liability. In civil liability, remedy is provided in the form of damages but punishment is provided as a criminal act remedy usually in the form of imprisonment, fine or death sentence, etc.

Since the civil wrong is against a private individual, it can be redressed by compensation for placing the plaintiff in similar position that he enjoyed before the wrong committed against him.

In criminal wrongs, however, the wrong is against the society which cannot be justifiably redressed by mere compensation and needs more serious actions on the part of state to punish and deter people from committing crimes.

36 The Supreme Court or the High Court in exercise of the power of Judicial Review can declare a law passed by the Parliament or State Legislature as invalid on the ground that :

I. It is not within the competence of the Legislature which passed the law

II. It is in contravention of the fundamental rights stipulated in Part III of the Constitution or any other provision of the constitution

III. The Legislature did not apply its mind or it was prompted by some improper motive or it was arbitrary or unreasonable

Choose the correct option :

1 I and III 2 I and II
3 II and III 4 All I, II and III

Ans. *(2)*

Exp. Among the given options, option 2 provides the correct choice.

The power of Judicial Review can be exercised by the High Court or Supreme Court in order to examine the validity of legislative or executive actions. The judiciary can declare such actions to be void or unconstitutional on certain grounds. Such as, when the law made by a Legislature was beyond its competence or authority, and then such a law can be declared as invalid.

Further, the courts can also declare laws to be void it is in contravention of the fundamental rights stipulated in Part III of the Constitution or any other provision of the constitution. Although restrictions can be put upon the exercise of fundamental rights, such restrictions must be reasonable in order to be valid and the courts have authority to examine the reasonability of such restrictions as well.

However, the court is not concerned with the background in which the law was made and cannot inquire about the motives or intentions of the legislature in formulation of the law which is not within the powers of courts and hence, the law cannot be interfered with on such ground. Thus, statement III is incorrect.

37 Which of the following is not correct under Section 8 of Hindu Succession Act, 1956? The property of a Hindu male dying intestate shall devolve :

1 Firstly upon class I heirs of the deceased
2 Secondly upon class II heirs of the deceased
3 Thirdly upon Agnates of all deceased
4 Fourthly upon the government

Ans. *(4)*

Exp. The property of a Hindu male dying intestate shall not devolve on the government in the fourth instance according to Section 8 of the Hindu Succession Act which provides the general rules of succession in case of males.

It states that the property of a male Hindu dying intestate shall devolve according to the provisions of this Chapter, firstly, upon the heirs, being the relatives specified in class I of the Schedule; secondly, if there is no heir of class I, then upon the heirs, being the relatives specified in class II of the Schedule; thirdly, if there is no heir of any of the two classes, then upon the agnates of the deceased; and lastly, if there is no agnate, then upon the cognates of the deceased.

It must be noted that the property does not get transferred to the government merely in the absence of agnates, rather it goes to the cognates of the deceased.

38 Legal sovereignty in India resides in the Constitution itself and not in 'We the People of India'. This idea was expressed in one of the following cases by the Supreme Court of India.

1 Kesavananda Bharati Vs State of Kerala
2 Golaknath Vs State of Punjab
3 State of West Bengal Vs Union of India
4 Sajjah Singh Vs State of Rajasthan

Ans. *(1)*

Exp. The expression "Legal sovereignty in India resides in the Constitution itself and not in 'We the People of India' " was expressed in the landmark case of Kesavananda Bharati v. Union of India.

In this case, the court had considered a question of law relating to status of preamble in the constitution and power or extent of parliament to amend the provisions of constitution.

It was also believed that the constitution was framed by an assembly which was elected indirectly on a limited franchise and the assembly did not represent the vast majority of the people of the country.

39 Following are good defences to an action in tort

I. Act of God

II. Volenti non fit injuria

III. Private defence

IV. Trustee do son tort

Choose the correct option:

1 I, II and IV 2 II, III and IV
3 IV, I and III 4 I, II and III

Ans. *(4)*

Exp. Act of God, Volenti non fit injuria, Private defence are general defences to an action in tort.

When a plaintiff brings an action against the defendant for a tort committed by him, he will be held liable for it, if there exists all the essential ingredients which are required for that wrong. But there are some defences available to him using which he can absolve himself from the liability arising out of the wrong committed. These are known as 'General defences' in the law of tort.

The defences available are as follows:

- Volenti non fit injuria or the defence of 'constent'
- The wrongdoer is the plaintiff
- Inevitable accident
- Act of God.
- Private defence
- Mistake
- Necessity
- Statutory authority

A trustee de son tort is a person who is under legal obligation not to commit a tort as a trustee despite not being conferred that status in legal sense. It is done so based on the conduct performed by a person as a trustee. The term finds relevance under tort law but does not serve as a defense to avoid liability merely on the ground that the person was never appointed a trustee in official capacity. Thus, liability can be imposed on the action or conduct itself. Hence, it is not one of the defences in the law of torts.

40 Match List I with List II

List I (Section of Hindu Marriage Act, 1955)	List II (Provision)
A. Section 5(i)	I. Ceremonies of Hindu Marriage
B. Section 7	II. Marriageable age
C. Section 8	III. Monogamy
D. Section 5(iii)	IV. Registration of Marriage

Choose the correct option from those given below :

	A	B	C	D		A	B	C	D
1	IV	III	II	I	2	III	I	IV	II
3	I	IV	III	II	4	I	IV	II	III

Ans. (2)

➲ *Exp.* The correct matching is A-III; B-I; C-IV; D-II.

Section 5 (i) in The Hindu Marriage Act, 1955 is related to Monogamy and provides for the conditions for a Hindu marriage and says, inter alia, that a marriage may be solemnized between any two Hindus when neither party has a spouse living at the time of the marriage.

Section 7 deals with ceremonies for a Hindu marriage stating that a Hindu marriage may be solemnized in accordance with the customary rites and ceremonies of either party thereto.

Section 8 mentions registration of Hindu marriages, and holds that for the purpose of facilitating the proof of Hindu Marriages, the State Government may make rules providing that the parties to any such marriage may have the particulars relating to their marriage entered in such manner and subject to such conditions as may be prescribed in a Hindu Marriage Register kept for the purpose.

Section 5(iii) deals with marriageable age and mandates that the bridegroom has completed the age of twenty-one years and the bride, the age of eighteen years at the time of the marriage.

41 Given below are two statements. One is labelled as Assertion (A) and the other is labelled as Reason (R).

Assertion (A) Every Hindu is bound to maintain his or her legitimate or illegitimate minor hindu children.

Reason (R) Under section 20(2) of the Hindu Adoptions and Maintenance Act, 1956 a legitimate or illegitimate minor child may claim maintenance from his or her father or mother.

In the light of the above two statements choose the correct option:

1 (A) is true, but (R) is false
2 (A) is false, but (R) is true
3 Both (A) and (R) are true and (R) is the correct explanation of (A)
4 Both (A) and (R) are true and (R) is not the correct explanation of (A)

Ans. (3)

➲ *Exp.* Both (A) and (R) are true and (R) is the correct explanation of (A).

Section 20 of the Hindu Adoptions and Maintenance Act, 1956 deals with maintenance of children and aged parents. According to Section 20 (1), a Hindu is bound to maintain his or her legitimate or illegitimate children and his or her aged or infirm parents. Thus, the Assertion is true.

In accordance with clause (2) of Section 20 of the Hindu Adoptions and Maintenance Act, 1956 a legitimate or illegitimate child may claim maintenance from his or her father or mother so long as the child is a minor. Thus, the Reason is also true.

42 Arrange the following judgements of the Supreme Court on the issue of constitutionality of death penalty in chronological order:

I. Rajendra Prasad Vs. State of UP
II. Machhi Singh Vs. State of Rajasthan
III. Jagmohan Singh Vs. State of UP
IV. Bachan Singh Vs. State of Punjab

Choose the correct option :

1 I, II, III, IV   2 III, II, I, IV
3 IV, III, II. I   4 III, I, IV, II

Ans. (4)

➲ *Exp.* The correct chronological order is III, I, IV, II.

In the case titled as Jagmohan Singh Vs. State of Uttar Pradesh (1973), the court held that capital punishment was not violative of Articles 14, 19 and 21 of Constitution.

In Rajendra Prasad Vs. State of UP (1979), it was held that death penalty is violative of articles 14, 19 and 21. It was made clear that special reason should be recorded for imposing death penalty and it must be imposed only in extraordinary circumstances.

In Bachan Singh V. State of Punjab (1980) the court overruled decision in Rajendra Prasad case. It expressed the view that death penalty is not unreasonable as an alternative punishment for murder and hence complies articles 14, 19 and 21 of the Constitution of India.

Finally, in Machhi Singh Vs. State of Punjab (1983), the court laid down broad outlines of the circumstances known as rarest of rare cases, when death sentence should be imposed.

43 Given below are two statements. One is labelled as Assertion (A) and other is labelled as Reason (R).

Assertion (A) Whoever attempts to commit robbery shall be punished with rigorous imprisonment for a term which may extend to seven years and shall also be liable for fine.

Reason (R) Section 393 of Indian Penal Code provides for rigorous imprisonment which may extends to seven years and fine for the offence of attempt to commit robbery.

In the light of the above two statements choose the correct option:

1 Both (A) and (R) are true and (R) is correct explanation of (A)
2 Both (A) and (R) are true and (R) is not the correct explanation of (A).
3 (A) is true, but (R) is false
4 (A) is false, but (R) is true

Ans. *(1)*

Exp. Both (A) and (R) are true and (R) is correct explanation of (A).

Section 393 in the Indian Penal Code deals with attempt to commit robbery, The provision states that whoever attempts to commit robbery shall be punished with rigorous imprisonment for a term which may extend to seven years, and shall also be liable to fine.

Section 393 of IPC 1860 prescribes punishment for the offence of attempt to commit robbery. The offence under Section 393 is non-bailable and non-compoundable and is triable by magistrate of first class.

44 Which of the following is the composition of the International Bill of Human Rights?

I. Universal Declaration of Human Rights
II. International Covenant of Civil and Political Rights
III. The International Covenant of Economic, Social and Cultural Rights
IV. The Optional Protocol to the International Covenant on Civil and Political Rights

Choose the most appropriate option:

1 I, II and III
2 I and III
3 I, II, III and IV
4 I and IV

Ans. *(3)*

Exp. Among the given options, option (3) provides correct choices.

The International Bill of Human Rights is composed of five treaties with an objective of advancement of core and fundamental human rights.

The Bill contributes in creating impact on organizations that can protect such rights, either by making a law or by conduct.

The International Bill of Human Rights is based on the following five documents:

(i) Universal Declaration of Human Rights
(ii) International Covenant on Economic, Social and Cultural Rights
(iii) International Covenant on Civil and Political Rights
(iv) Optional Protocol to the International Covenant on Civil and Political Rights
(v) Second Optional Procotol to the International Covenant on Civil and Political Rights.

45 "The Law of nations is that collection of usages which civilized states have agreed to observe in their dealings with one another". This definition of International law is given by Lord Coleridge"–in:

1 Queen Vs. Keyn
2 West Rand Central Gold Mining Ltd Co. Vs. King
3 S.S. Lotus Case
4 A.M. Luther Co. Vs. Sugar and Co.

Ans. *(1)*

Exp. In the popular case titled as Queen v. Keyn (1876), Lord Coleridge, C.J. defined International law as "The law of nations is that collection of usages which civilized States have agreed to observe in their dealings with one another". Thus, International Law can be understood as a law in the form of treaties, conventions and customs governing relations of countries with each other and by which the countries have made themselves bound.

The definition provided by Lord Coleridge emphasizes upon agreement between countries to observe certain usages. It implies the discretion and mutual understanding of nations in determining and choosing the standards of behaviour with which they wish to be bound with each other.

46 Match the following.

List I	List II
A. Fisher Vs. Bell	I. Privity of contract
B. Harvey Vs. Facey	II. Minor-contract is void
C. Mohori Bibi Vs. Dharmodas Ghose	III. Invitation to treat
D. Dunlop Tyre Vs. Selfridge and Co.	IV. Quotation of prices

Choose the correct option from those given below :

	A	B	C	D
1	III	IV	II	I
2	I	II	III	IV
3	IV	II	I	III
4	I	III	IV	II

Ans. (1)

Exp. The correct matching is A-III, B-IV, C-II, D-I.

Fisher Vs. Bell (1961) was a case relating to invitation to treat. In this case, the court held that in accordance with the general principles of contract law, the display of goods including knives was not an offer of sale but merely an invitation to treat.

Harvey Vs. Facey (1893) case dealt with quotation of prices. In this case, the Privy Council held that there was no contract concluded between the parties as merely quoting the lowest price of an article does not assure willingness to sell.

Mohori Bibee Vs. Dharmodas Ghose (1903) declared a contract with minors to be void. It was concluded that an agreement involving minors as a party is not valid in terms of law and can be only void from the very time it was formed.

Dunlop Vs. Selfridge (1915) case is based on privity of contract. It was held that only the parties to the contract had capacity to sue or be sued, except when a party represented another as an agent, in which case such other person may sue or be sued.

47 Which one of the following can not be treated as delivery under the Sale of Goods Act, 1930?

1 Doing anything which has the effect of putting goods in possession of legal representatives of seller
2 Doing anything which has the effect of parting goods in possession of any person authorised by the buyer
3 Doing anything which has the effect of putting goods in possession of the buyer
4 Doing anything which the parties agree to be treated as delivery

Ans. (1)

Exp. Doing anything which has the effect of putting goods in possession of legal representatives of seller cane not be treated as delivery under the Sale of Goods Act, 1930

According to Section 33 of the Sale of Goods Act, 1930, delivery of goods sold may be made by doing anything which the parties agree and shall be treated as delivery or which has the effect of putting the goods in the possession of the buyer or of any person authorised to hold them on his behalf.

It can be observed that the provision does not consider it to be valid delivery of goods when goods are put in possession of legal representatives of the seller.

48 In which of the following cases, the Supreme Court of India has specifically said that 'federal structure' is the basic feature of the Constitution?

1 A.K. Gopalan Vs. State of Madras
2 S.R. Bommai Vs. Union of India
3 Govind Vs. State of Madhya Pradesh
4 Maneka Gandhi Vs. Union of India

Ans. (2)

Exp. In the case of S.R Bommai Vs. Union of India (1994), the Supreme Court of India has specifically said that 'federal structure' is the basic feature of the Constitution.

This case aimed to restrict the uncontrolled power of the executive and act as a check against arbitrary exercise. The Court here described Federalism and Secularism as a part of the Basic Structure. The judgement is relevant as it held that federalism, socialism and democracy, being parts of basic structure, place an obligation upon the law through the court to intervene and assure that the state emergency under Article 356 is imposed on just, fair and reasonable grounds.

Therefore, the power of judicial review was extended to president rule to examine its necessity and constitutional validity.

49 Starting from the earliest, arrange the following countries in chronological order where the Office of Ombudsman was created

I. Sweden　　II. United Kingdom
III. New Zealand　　IV. Finland

Choose the correct option :

1 I, II, III, IV　　2 I, IV, III, II
3 I, III, II, IV　　4 I, II, IV, III

Ans. (2)

Exp. The correct chronological order is I, IV, III, II.

The first Ombudsman, as an autonomous institution forming part of parliament's control over the executive, was elected in Sweden in 1810 and served from 1810–1823.

Finland acquired a Parliamentary Ombudsman in 1919 (Oikeusasiamies) based on the inspiratiom drawn from Sweden.

The requirement of having an Ombudsman was gradually felt widely at the beginning of the 1960s and various Commonwealth and European countries established an Ombudsman office. New Zealand created an Ombudsman office in 1962, followed by the United Kingdom in 1967.

50 Match the following sections of Indian Penal Code with provision given here under:

List I		List II	
A.	Section 80	I.	Act done by person justified or by mistake of fact believing himself justified by law
B.	Section 82	II.	Act of a child above Seven and under twelve of immature understanding
C.	Section 83	III.	Act of child under seven years of age
D.	Section 79	IV.	Accident in doing a lawful act

Choose the correct option from those given below :

	A	B	C	D		A	B	C	D
1	IV	II	III	I	2	II	IV	I	III
3	IV	III	II	I	4	III	IV	II	I

Ans. (3)

Exp. The correct matching is A-IV, B-III, C-II, D-I.

Section 80 of IPC mentions accident in doing a lawful act. It states that nothing is an offence which is done by accident or misfortune, and without any criminal intention or knowledge in the doing of a lawful act in a lawful manner by lawful means and with proper care and caution.

Section 82 of IPC is related to Act of a child under seven years of age. It states nothing is an offence which is done by a child under seven years of age.

Section 83 of IPC is related to Act of a child above Seven and under twelve of immature understanding. It states nothing is an offence which is done by a child above seven years of age and under twelve, who has not attained sufficient maturity of understanding to judge the nature and consequences of his conduct on that occasion.

Section 79 of IPC provides for the Act done by person justified or by mistake of fact believing himself justified by law. It states that nothing is an offence which is done by any person who is justified by law, or who by reason of a mistake of fact and not by reason of a mistake of law in good faith, believes himself to be justified by law, in doing it.

51 Which of the following factors are responsible for judicial activism in India?

I. Denial of court access to the poor, down-trodden and underprivileged sections of the society who do not have sufficient means to approach the court

II. Maladministration, misuse of public office and rampant corruption

III. Increasing social problems as environmental pollution, child labour, smoking in public places, pitiable conditions of prisoners and exploitation of women etc.

IV. Gross violation of Human Rights

Choose the correct option

1 I, II and III 2 II, III and IV
3 I, III and IV 4 I, II, III and IV

Ans. *(4)*

➲ *Exp.* Statement I, II, III and IV contains the factors responsible for judicial activism in India.

The term 'judicial activism' refers to the attempts made by judiciary to bring justice in extra ordinary situations, and empathy towards society at large plays a huge role in such process. Justice Krishna Iyer observed 'every judge is an activist either on the forward gear or on the reverse'.

A lot of factors can be said to have existed as causes behind the evolution of judicial activism. The administrative delays, corruption, maladministration, poor delivery of promises by the governments, child labor or exploitation, blatant use of power by authorities and suppression of minorities, or deprived sections of the society where justice is not getting served, are among many other factors that have significantly led to rise of judicial activism in India.

52 Which of the following provision was inserted by Act 22 of 2018 in Indian Penal Code?

1 Punishment for causing death or resulting persistent vegetative state of victim
2 Punishment for rape on women under Twelve Years of age
3 Sexual intercourse by husband upon his wife during separation
4 Sexual intercourse by a person in authority

Ans. *(2)*

➲ *Exp.* The provision on punishment for rape on women under Twelve Years of age was inserted by the Criminal Law (Amendment) Act, No. 22 of 2018 in Indian Penal Code. It was enacted to amend the Indian Penal Code, Indian Evidence Act, 1872, the Code of Criminal Procedure, 1973 and the Protection of Children from Sexual Offences Act, 2012.

It added Section 376AB to IPC, according to which, whoever, commits rape on a woman under twelve years of age shall be punished with rigorous imprisonment for a term which shall not be less than twenty years, but which may extend to imprisonment for life, which shall mean imprisonment for the remainder of that person's natural life, and with fine or with death.

53 Match List I with List II.

List I	List II
A. Article 153	I. Appointment of Governor
B. Article 154	II. Governor of States
C. Article 155	III. Term of office of Governor
D. Article 156	IV. Executive power of state

Choose the correct option from those given below :

	A	B	C	D		A	B	C	D
1	II	I	IV	III	2	II	IV	I	III
3	III	IV	I	II	4	IV	III	II	I

Ans. *(2)*

➲ *Exp.* The correct matching is A-II, B-IV, C-I, D-III.

Article 153 in the Constitution of India 1949 deals with Governors of States. It says that there shall be Governor for each State, also permitting the same person as Governor for two or more States.

Article 154 mentions executive power of State. It provides that the executive power of the State shall be vested in the Governor and shall be exercised by him either directly or through officers subordinate to him in accordance with this Constitution.

Article 155 makes provision for appointment of Governor and states that the Governor of a State shall be appointed by the President by warrant under his hand and seal.

Article 156 provides details of term of office of Governor which are as follows; the Governor shall hold office during the pleasure of the President, the Governor may, by writing under his hand addressed to the President, resign his office, a Governor shall hold for a term of five years from the date on which he enters upon his office.

54 In which of the following situations, the Quasi Contract Doctrine is not applied?

1 In disputes regarding payment for goods delivered or services rendered with a formal contract
2 Where no contract but fictional agreement arise
3 Where there is an unjust enrichment without a formal contract
4 Where there is a liability to pay gratuitous act

Ans. (4)

Exp. The Quasi Contract Doctrine is not applied where there is a liability to pay for a gratuitous act. The Indian Contract Act, 1872 under Section 70 deals with obligation of person enjoying the benefit of the non-gratuitous act.

As per this provision, when a person lawfully does something for another person (may be delivery of goods or extending a service) without intending to do so 'gratuitously', and the other person enjoys the benefit of the delivery of that good or service, the latter is bound to pay back to the former.

A gratuitous act is one that is done for a person by another without the expectation of a return. Thus, it must be noted that a quasi-contract can very well arise in case the delivery of goods or extension of service was made with an intention to receive money or consideration.

55 Choose the correct section of the Competition Act, 2002 which provides that 'No enterprise shall abuse its dominant position':

1 Section 4 2 Section 9
3 Section 8 4 Section 6

Ans. (1)

Exp. Section 4 in the Competition Act, 2002 deals with abuse of dominant position. According to this provision, 'No enterprise shall abuse its dominant position'.

Section 4 of the Competition Act, 2002 prevents any enterprise or group from abusing its dominant position. The Act also provides circumstances under which there is abuse of dominant position.

Section 4(2) of the Act specifies the following practices by a dominant enterprises or group of enterprises as abuses : if an enterprise directly or indirectly, imposes unfair or discriminatory condition in purchase or sale of goods or services; or price in purchase or sale or indulges in practice or practices resulting in denial of market access; among others.

56 Salmond cnumerates five characteristics of legal rights. Four such characteristics are :

I. Subject of right
II. Object of right
III. Content of right
IV. Title of right

The fifth characteristic is :

1 Property in respect of which right is claimed
2 Act or omission required by the right
3 The legal reason for the existence of the right
4 The subject of the corresponding duty

Ans. (4)

Exp. Salmond defines legal right as a legally protected and recognized interest.

According to him, the following are the features of a legal right:-

- The Subject of the Right- The person in whom the right is vested. It is also called the person of inheritance.
- *The Subject of the Duty* – The person against whom the right operates and the one who is expected to respect the said right. It is the subject of corresponding duty.
- *The Content of right* – It is the essence of the right which has an element of advantage that places the possessor of such right at a higher position than the one who does not enjoy such right.
- *The Object of right* – It is the subject-matter of the right and includes the area that the right seeks to cover.
- *The Title of right* – It includes facts or events which was the reason the right has become vested.

57 Match the theories of Jurisprudence with the Jurists associated with it.

List I		List II	
A.	Spirit of people	I.	Savigny
B.	Social Solidarity	II.	Duguit
C.	Dictates of Reasoning	III.	Thomas Acquinas
D.	Social Control	IV.	Ihering

Choose the correct option :

	A	B	C	D		A	B	C	D
1	I	II	III	IV	2	I	II	IV	III
3	IV	III	II	I	4	II	IV	I	III

Ans. (1)

Exp. The correct matching is A-I, B-II, C-III, D-IV.

Spirit of People is associated with Savigny. He was a German philosopher who was also considered to be founding father of the renowned Historical school of jurisprudence. He said that law is based on the spirit of people since it is a manifestation of the will and consciousness of people.

Social Solidarity is associated with Duguit Leon Duguit was a French Jurist who gave the theory of Social Solidarity, which indicates social cooperation and mutual assistance for individual and society needs as a whole.

Dictates of Reasoning is linked with St. Thomas Aquinas. He is known for his theories on natural law and his support for law by reason. He believes Law is a dictate of reason from the ruler for the community he rules and this dictate of reason originates within the ruler's intellect.

Social Control is associated with Ihering. He is better known for his social interest theory, wherein he described that the social interest of a man may be achieved either by the 'principle of reward' or by the 'principle of coercion' but it is usually the latter which is used by the 'State'. Thus, he suggested that the state in the form of command enforces law which he believed was justified.

58 Which one of the following is not within the scope of Implied Authority of a partner?

1 The act done for carrying on the business of the kind carried on by the firm
2 The act should be done in the usual way of business of the firm

3 The act of acquiring immovable property on behalf of the firm
4 The act must be done in the firm name or in any other manner expressing or implying an intention to bind the firm

Ans. (3)

➲ *Exp.* The act of acquiring immovable property on behalf of the firm does not fall within the scope of Implied Immunity of the Partner.

Statement 1,2 and 4 are correct with respect to the scope of Implied Authority of a partner.

Section 19 in the Indian Partnership Act, 1932, deals with implied authority of partner as agent of the firm. It describes that subject to the provisions of Section 22, the act of a partner which is done to carry on, in the usual way, business of the kind carried on by the firm, binds the firm. The authority of a partner to bind the firm conferred by this section is called his "implied authority". So, Statement 1 and 2 are correct.

As per Section 22, in order to bind a firm, an act or instrument done or executed by a partner or other person on behalf of the firm shall be done or executed in the firm name, or in any other manner expressing or implying an intention to bind the firm. Hence, statement 4 is correct.

However, statement 3 is wrong because Section 19(2) (f) provides that implied authority does not include acquiring immovable property on behalf of the firm.

59 Given below are two statements. One is labelled as Assertion (A) and the other is labelled as Reason (R)

Assertion (A) The liability of the surety is co-executive and it can not go beyond the terms of guarantee.

Reason (R) The rights and liabilities of a surety and borrower are different and distinct and everything depends upon its terms of guarantee.

In the light of the above two statements choose the correct option :

Codes

1 Both (A) and (R) are true and (R) is the correct explanation of (A)
2 Both (A) and (R) are true and (R) is not the correct explanation of (A)
3 (A) is true, but (R) is false
4 (A) is false, but (R) is true

Ans. (1)

➲ *Exp.* Both (A) and (R) are true and (R) is not the correct explanation of (A).

The Section 128 of The Indian Contract Act, 1872 mentions Surety's liability. It is provided that the liability of the surety is co-extensive with that of the principal debtor, unless it is otherwise provided by the contract.

This implies that the rights and liabilities of a surety and borrower are different and distinct but everything depends upon its terms of guarantee. This indicates that what will be the nature and extent of rights and liability of parties to the contract of guarantee, may either by provided by the contract itself or may be based on law.

Hence, in the absence of anything contrary in the contract, the law considers surety's liability co-extensive to that of principal debtor.

60 Match the following sections of the Copyright Act, 1957 with provisions given there under :

List I	List II
A. Section 2 (o)	I. Performer Right
B. Section 38	II. Meaning of Literary work
C. Section 37	III. Meaning of sound recording
D. Section 2 (xx)	IV. Broadcast reproduction right

Choose the correct option from those given below:

	A	B	C	D		A	B	C	D
1	II	I	IV	III	2	IV	II	III	I
3	II	III	I	IV	4	I	IV	III	II

Ans. (1)

➲ *Exp.* The correct matching is A-II, B-I, C-IV, D-III.

The *Section 2(o)* of Copyright Act 1957 gives meaning of "literary work". Literary Work include computer programs, tables and compilations including computer.

Section 38 defines a performer's right as where any performer appears or engages in any performance, he shall have a special right to be known as the "performer's right" in relation to such performance.

Section 37 defines a Broadcast reproduction right as every broadcasting organization shall have a special right to be known as "broadcast reproduction right" in respect of its broadcasts.

Section 2(xx) gives us a meaning of sound recording as a recording of sounds from which such sounds may be produced regardless of the medium on which such recording is the method by which the sounds are produced.

61 Match the following cases decided by the Supreme court with the subject given therein:

List I	List II
A. Hussainara Khatoon Vs. State of Bihar	I. Ban on smoking in public places
B. Murli S. Deora Vs. Union of India	II. Protection against inhumane treatment in jail
C. Lakshmi Kant Pandey Vs. Union of India	III. Speedy Trial
D. Sunil Batra Vs. Delhi Administration	IV. Child welfare

Choose the correct option from those given below :

	A	B	C	D		A	B	C	D
1	I	II	III	IV	2	I	III	IV	II
3	III	I	IV	II	4	II	IV	III	I

Ans. (3)

Exp. The correct matching is A-III, B-I, C-IV, D-II.

Hussainara Khatoon and Ors Vs. Union of India (1979) case deals with the right to speedy trial. It is based on interpretation of Article 21, wherein the court said that free legal aid and speedy trial are fundamental rights of every citizen.

Murli S. Deora Vs. Union of India (2001), case deals with ban on smoking in public places. In this case, the Court held that public smoking indirectly and passively interferes with the right to life of those who do not smoke otherwise.

Lakshmi Kant Pandey Vs. Union of India (1984) case deals with child welfare. The Court laid down certain safeguards to protect interest of children adopted by foreign families.

Sunil Batra Vs. Delhi Administration (1978) case deals with protection against inhumane treatment in jail. The court observed that jail authorities had no right to inflict torture upon inmates, and that the courts under Article 32 and 226 possess sufficient powers to intervene any action that detriments safety of prisoners.

62 The concept of Universalism is based on:

I. Natural Theory
II. Theory of Rationalism
III. Theory of Positivism
IV. Theory of Cultural Relativism

Choose the most appropriate option :

1 I and II 2 I, II and III
3 I, II, III and IV 4 III and IV

Ans. (2)

Exp. The concept of Universalism is based on Natural theory, Theory of Rationalism and Theory of Positivism.

According to the concept of Universalism, each human being located in any part of the world, belonging to any background and status or class, intrinsically possesses certain inalienable or inseparable rights and such rights are conferred solely because of the person being born as a human being.

The supporters of this idea claim that certain rights like right to equality, religion, free speech and expression are some of the rights which form part of Universalism.

The concept of Universalism is based on three fundamental theories; the natural law theory, the theory of rationalism, and the theory of positivism, all of which aim to confer some basic or fundamental human rights upon each person and considers it necessary for free development.

However, Cultural relativism is the idea contrary to that of universalism, since the former is dependent upon diverse cultures across all places and varies accordingly. According to it, the traditions, practices, rights or obligations tend to be different for each place. Thus, it is not a part of Universalism.

63 To constitute the offence of kidnapping from lawful guardianship under Section 361 of Indian Penal Code the age of the minor should be :

I. Under eighteen years if male
II. Under sixteen years if male
III. Under eighteen years if female
IV. Under sixteen years if female

Choose the correct option :

1 I and II 2 I and III
3 II and III 4 I and IV

Ans. (3)

Exp. Section 361 in the Indian Penal Code deals with Kidnapping from lawful guardianship. According to the provision, whoever takes or entices any minor under sixteen years of age if a male, or under eighteen years of age if a female, or any person of unsound mind, out of the keeping of the lawful guardian of such minor or person of unsound mind, without the consent of such guardian, is said to kidnap such minor or person from lawful guardianship.

64 Preamble of the National Green Tribunal Act; 2010 (NGT Act) does not mention about:

1 Johannesburg Conference
2 Rio Conference
3 Article 21 of the Constitution of India
4 The Stockholm Conference

Ans. (1)

Exp. The Preamble to the National Green Tribunal Act, 2010 does not mention about Johannesburg Conference.

The Preamble is as follows; "And whereas India is a party to the decisions taken at the United Nations Conference on the Human Environment held at Stockholm in June, 1972 in which India participated calling upon the States to take appropriate steps for the protection and improvement of the human environment,"

"And whereas decisions were taken at the United Nations Conference on Environment and Development held at Reo de Janeiro in June, 1992 in which India participated calling upon the States to provide effective access to judicial and administrative proceedings, including redress and remedy and to develop national laws regarding liability and compensation for the victims of pollution and other environmental damage"

"And whereas in the judicial pronouncement in India, the right to healthy environment has been construed as a part of the right to life under Article 21 of the Constitution."

65 Whoever by words, either spoken or written, or by signs, or by visible representation, or otherwise, brings or attempts to bring in hatred or contempt or excites or attempts to excite disaffection towards, the government established by law in India; amounts to the offence of

1 Defamation 2 Sedition
3 Criminal Conspiracy 4 Assault

Ans. (2)

Exp. The Section 124A of IPC defines offence of Sedition. It says whoever, by words, either spoken or written, or by signs, or by visible representation, or otherwise, brings or attempts to bring into hatred or contempt, or excites or attempts to excite disaffection towards, the Government established by law in India, shall be punished with imprisonment for life, to which fine may be added, or with imprisonment which may extend to three years, to which fine may be added, or with fine.

It is worth noting that the expression "disaffection" includes disloyalty and all feelings of enmity. Comments expressing disapprobation of the measures of the Government with a view to obtain their alteration by lawful means, without exciting or attempting to excite hatred, contempt or disaffection, do not constitute an offence under this section.

66 Section 49 of the Information Technology Act deals with the provision relating to:

1 Establishment of Cyber Appellate Tribunal
2 Qualification for appointment as Chairperson and member of Cyber Appellate Tribunal
3 Composition of Cyber Appellate Tribunal
4 Distribution of business among benches

Ans. (3)

Exp. Section 49 Information Technology Act, 2000 provides for composition of Cyber Appellate Tribunal.

According to this provision, the Cyber Appellate Tribunal shall consist of a Chairperson and such number of other Members, as the Central Government may, by notification in the Official Gazette, appoint.

It is important to note that the selection of Chairperson and Members of the Cyber Appellate Tribunal shall be made by the Central Government in consultation with the Chief Justice of India.

67 The essential characteristics of Federation in USA are :

I. Supremacy of the Constitution
II. Distribution of powers amongst the various organs of the federation and of regional units of the federation by the provision of constitution
III. Judicial review or enforcement of that Supreme constitution as law
IV. The Rule of Law

Choose the correct option :

1 Only I, II and III
3 Only I, II and IV
3 Only II, III and IV
4 All I, II, III and IV

Ans. (1)

Exp. Statements I, II and III include the essential characteristics of Federation in USA.

Supremacy of the Constitution is certainly one of the features of the U.S. Federation and in no case, any action could go beyond what is provided by the Constitution.

The Federation in the USA refers to the division of functions and powers among the levels of government. The regional and national governments have been conferred discretion to perform work suitably within their domains.

The federation also provides for Judicial review wherever a provision of the Constitution tends to violate rights, the same may be examined by appropriate courts.

Statement IV is incorrect as the USA follows due process of law and not Rule of Law.

68 Which one of the following Jurists asserts that 'Law and morality are complementary and supplementary to each other'?

1 John Austin
2 Hans Kelson
3 H.L.A. Hart
4 Devlin

Ans. (3)

Exp. H.L.A Hart asserts that 'Law and morality are complementary and supplementary to each other.'

The idea of Morality is incorporated in Hart's concept of law. It is because of this that Hart's concept of law is viewed both as a positivistic and natural approach towards study of law. He has made attempts to establish connection between law and morality and asserted that law and morality are complementary and supplementary to each other, because each provides a cause for existence of another. They are co-extensive, in the sense, they exist together in most situations.

69 Under the Companies Act 2013, which of the following company is required to constitute a Corporate Social Responsibility Committee?

I. company having net worth of ₹ 500 crore or more
II. company having turnover of ₹ 1000 crore or more
III. company having net profit of ₹ 5 crore or more
IV. company having net profit of ₹ 2 crore or more during any financial year

Choose the most appropriate option:

1 I, II, III and IV
2 I and IV
3 I, II and III
4 I, III and IV

Ans. (3)

Exp. Among the given options, option (3) provides correct choice.

Corporate Social Responsibility (CSR) finds mention in the Section 135 of Companies Act, 2013 (and as amended).

As per Clause (1), every company having net worth of ₹ 500 crore or more, or turnover of ₹ 1000 crore or more or a net profit of ₹ 5 crore or more during the immediately preceding financial year, shall constitute a Corporate Social Responsibility Committee.

Further, that such committee must consist of three or more directors, out of which at least one director shall be an independent director.

70 Which of the following statement/statements are true?

1 In Nicaragua Vs. U.S.A. the World Court by majority has taken the view that the sources of International Law are hierarchical.

2 In Nicaragua Vs. U.S.A. the World Court has taken unanimously the view that the sources of International Law are not hierarchical.

3 In Nicaragua Vs. U.S.A. the World Court by majority has taken the view that the sources of International Law are not hierarchical but are necessarily complementary and inter-related.

4 In Nicaragua Vs. U.S.A. the World Court has taken unanimously the view that the sources of International Law are not hierarchical but are necessarily complimentary and inter-related.

Ans. (3)

Exp. In Nicaragua Vs. USA case, the ICJ had said that the sources of international law are not hierarchical, but are necessarily complementary and inter-related. It was held that use of force had attained the status of customary rule of jus cogen before the advent of UN charter of 1945.

The court here had affirmed the complementary relationship between treaty and international custom. It also shows that treaties have the competence to codify the international customs, and when treaties are abandoned by the parties or are not honored otherwise, a resort may be made back to the international customs.

The court said that the sources of international law are interrelated and in case a conflict arises as to superiority or dominance of one of the sources over another, the ICJ will resolve the conflict by looking at the intent and objective of each source.

71 To constitute the offence of Affray under Section 159 of the Indian Penal code there must be :

I. Only one person

II. Two or more persons

III. Fighting in Public place to disturb public peace

IV. Fighting in private place

Choose the correct option :

1 I and III　　2 II and III

3 II and IV　　4 I and IV

Ans. (2)

Exp. To constitute the offence of Affray under Section 159 of the Indian Penal code there must be two or more persons fighting in public place to disturb public peace.

The Section 159 in The Indian Penal Code defines offence of Affray. It says, when two or more persons, by fighting in a public place, disturb the public peace, they are said to "commit an affray". Hence, it is necessary for this offence that there be at least two or more persons, who would cause disturbance at a public place.

It is important to note that Section 160 provides for punishment for committing affray as imprisonment of either description for a term which may extend to one month, or with fine which may extend to one hundred rupees, or with both.

72 Which of the following could be considered to be advantages of, Legislation over Precedent?

I. Abrogative capability

II. Fore knowledge

III. Prospective application

IV. Systematic arrangement

Choose the correction option :

1 I, II, IV　　2 I, II, III

3 I, II, III and IV　　4 I and III

Ans. (3)

Exp. Among the given options, option (3) provides correct choices.

All the features mentioned can be said to be advantages of Legislation over a Precedent. A legislation has abrogative capability, meaning thereby that a statute can either make or repeal a law. However, Precedent can only constitute a law, and cannot abrogate.

A statute provides Fore knowledge on an area of dispute. It provides pre-existing information or rules governing the dispute which can be easily resorted to for resolution. Precedent cannot provide this as it is created only when the dispute is resolved by the court.

A statute can make rules for the future cases which may arise, in other words, a statute can be laid down law beforehand. A Precedent can lay down a rule when a case comes before it. Thus, its emergence depends on litigation. Due to this, Legislation also has prospective nature as it can govern future cases since it is already in existence, a Precedent cannot always have prospective application unless created beforehand.

Lastly, Legislation have Systematic arragement because it is codified and incorporated in an order with clearly marked provisions, a Precedent on the other hand lacks this order.

73 Given below are two statements. One is labelled as Assertion (A) and the other is labelled as Reason (R).

Assertion (A) Subject to rules of Jus cogens local customary law can supplement or derogate from general custom.

Reason (R) International law does not recognise the concept of local custom.

In the light of the above two statements choose the correct option.

1 Both (A) and (R) are true and (R) is the correct explanation of (A)

2 Both (A) and (R) are true and (R) is not the correct explanation of (A)

3 (A) is true, but (R) is false

4 (A) is false, but (R) is true

Ans. (3)

Exp. (A) is true, but (R) is false.

Jus Cogens are such rules or regulations, which must be observed positively by all parties irrespective of their personal appreciation of the rules. It is because of this, though the local customary law can supplement or derogate from general custom, but cannot deviate from the Jus Cogens.

However, it is wrong to say that International Law does not recognize the concept of Local custom. If that was the case, the International Law would not have allowed local customs to deviate from general custom and at the same time, restrict their deviation from Jus Cogens.

74 Which of the following statements are correct?

I. The Supreme Court of India has Original Jurisdiction in any dispute between the Government of India and one or more States.

II. The Supreme Court of India has Original Jurisdiction in any dispute between Government of India and any State or States on one side and one or more States on other side.

III. The Supreme Court of India has Original Jurisdiction in any dispute between Government of India and any individual on one side and State one or more on the other side.

IV. The Supreme Court of India has Original Jurisdiction in any dispute in India.

Choose the correct option :

1 I and II
2 II and III
3 I and III
4 I and IV

Ans. (1)

Exp. Statement I and II are correct.

The Constitution of India under Article 131 mentions Original Jurisdiction of the Supreme Court. It says, the Supreme Court shall, to the exclusion of any other court, have Original Jurisdiction in any dispute between the Government of India and one or more States or between the Government of India and any State/States on one side and one or more other States on the other.

Apart from it, the Original Jurisdiction also extends to disputes between two or more States, if and in so far as the dispute involves any question (whether of law or fact) on which the existence or extent of a legal right depends.

75 Article 371-F, special provisions with respect to the state of Sikkim was inserted by :

1 The Constitution (Thirty Second Amendment) Act
2 The Constitution (Thirty Third Amendment) Act
3 The Constitution (Thirty Fifth Amendment) Act
4 The Constitution (Thirty Sixth Amendment) Act

Ans. (4)

Exp. Article 371-F was inserted in the Constitution of India by the Constitution (Thirty Sixth Amendment) Act, 1975. It provided for special provisions with respect to the State of Sikkim.

It is mentioned in the provision, inter alia, that the Legislative Assembly of the State of Sikkim shall consist of not less than thirty members; the sitting members shall be deemed to be the members of the Legislative Assembly of the State of Sikkim duly elected under this Constitution; and, that the said Legislative Assembly of the State of Sikkim shall exercise the powers and perform the functions of the Legislative Assembly of a State under this Constitution.

76 Constitution of India requires the State to adopt the Protectionist Policy and Improvinistic Policy. Which one of the following Article declares the above :

1 Article of 51 A(g)
2 Article 38
3 Article 48 A
4 Article 37

Ans. (3)

Exp. The Constitution of India requires the State to adopt the Protectionist Policy and Improvinistic Policy under Article 48 A. Article 48A in Constitution of India, 1949 contains a provision for protection of environment and forests or wildlife.

It is mentioned therein that the State shall endeavour to protect and improve the environment and to safeguard the forests and wildlife of the country.

It can be observed that under Article-48A, the State is required to adopt the Protectionist policy as well as Improvinistic Policy. As a Protectionist policy, the State must take measures to prevent activities leading to environment damage. This can be done by making rules imposing legal prohibition and punishment on such activities.

As an Improvinistic Policy, the State must resort to alternatives to certain activities in order to reduce adverse impact on environment.

77 The word 'Tort' has been derived from the Latin Word :

1 Tortus
2 Tortum
3 Torrent
4 Torture

Ans. (2)

Exp. The word 'Tort' is derived from the Latin term 'Tortum' which means a twisted act or in simple words, a wrong. The term is French equivalent of the English word 'wrong' and the Roman law term 'delict'.

It refers to a conduct which is not rightful and is classified as a tort under law. Such wrong is civil in nature, and remedy in the form of compensation (damages) is provided by an appropriate court of law.

In essence, tort law serves to grant relief to a person who has lost his legal right due to an action or omission by another. The plaintiff can succeed in an action under tort merely on the basis of establishing violation of his legal right, without having to prove any damage.

78 Which of the following is not correct under Muslim Law?

1 In a gift Transaction delivery of posses is necessary, in a Will it is not required
2 Doctrine of Mushaa is also applicable in case of disposition by will
3 Right of Donor to a gift is unrestricted but right of making a bequest is limited in two ways
4 After completion, a gift cannot be revoked unless by a formal decree of a court, a will may be revoked at any time after making of it

Ans. (2)

Exp. The statement 'Doctrine of Mushaa is also applicable in case of disposition by will' is not correct under Muslim Law.

The Doctrine of Mushaa under Muslim Law relates to transfer of property by way of Gift, not a will. Hence, it has no applicability on disposition by will. The word 'Mushaa' refers to an undivided share in a property.

Such property may be movable or immovable. Mushaa is therefore, naturally a property with multiple owners. In other words, the subject matter of Musha is to consist of those properties who are jointly owned by persons.

79 Which one of the following is not a 'Primary Source' of Muslim Law?

1 Qiyas 2 Quran
3 Takhleed 4 Sunnat

Ans. (3)

Exp. Takhleed is not a 'Primary Source' of Muslim Law.

In Islamic law, it refers to the unconditional acceptance or consent to the decisions taken by another. Such acceptance has a legal force of law. However, Takhleed is not a source of law.

The Muslim law has been derived from various primary as well as secondary sources. The Primary sources are such as Sunna or Ahadis, Quran, Ijma, Qiyas.

The Secondary Sources are such as Judicial Decision, Custom, Legislation, Equity, Just and Good Conscience.

80 According to Article 233 of the Constitution of India, appointment of a District Judge shall be made by :

1 Collegium of the State High Court concerned
2 The Governor of the State concerned in consultation with the Chief Justice of India
3 The Governor of the State in Consultation with the High Court exercising Jurisdiction in relation to such State.
4 The President in consultation with the Chief Justice of the High Court exercising Jurisdiction in relation to the State concerned

Ans. (3)

Exp. According to Article. 233 of the Constitution of India, appointment of a District Judge shall be made by the Governor of the State in Consultation with the High Court exercising Jurisdiction in relation to such State.

Further, a person not already in the service of the Union or of the State shall only be eligible to be appointed a district judge if he has been for not less than seven years an advocate or a pleader and is recommended by the High Court for appointment.

81 Right to Education Act seeks to provide free and compulsory education to all children between 6 and 14 years. But a modification in Child Labour Act formalises employment of children 0 and 14 years in the family enterprises. Therefore, which of the following ILO Conventions is violated?

I. Convention 138 II. Convention 182
III. Convention 126 IV. Convention 141

Choose the correct option :

1 I and II 2 III and IV
3 I and IV 4 II and III

Ans. (1)

Exp. The formal employment under Child Labour Act will violate ILO Conventions 138 and 182.

ILO Conventions, 138 and 182 says that the minimum age for employment should not be less than the age of completion of compulsory schooling (14 years of age in India's case) and calls for elimination of the worst forms of child labour respectively.

The Minimum Age Convention, 1973 (No. 138) establishes the minimum age for admission to employment depending upon different age groups. Like, a general age criterion is 15 years (13 for simple or light work) and the minimum age for dangerous work at 18 (16 under certain exceptional conditions). It also provides for the possibility of initially setting the general minimum age at 14 (12 for light work) where the economy and educational facilities are insufficiently developed.

Worst Forms of Child Labour Convention, 1999 (No. 182) defines a 'child' as a person below 18 years of age. It has an objective that party states must eliminate the worst forms of child labour, including slavery of all kinds, the sale and trafficking of children, bondage, forced or compulsory labour of all kinds.

82 In which of the following cases it was held that "there is no distinction between defacto and dejure recognition for the purpose of giving effect to the international acts of the recognised authority"?

1 Luther Vs. Sagar
2 U.S. Vs. Pink
3 Russian Socialist Federated Soviet Republic Vs. Cibrario
4 Guarantee Trust Co. of New York Vs. U.S.

Ans. (1)

Exp. In the case titled as Luther Vs. Sagor (1921), it was held that "there is no distinction between defacto and dejure recognition for the purpose of giving effect to the international acts of the recognised authority".

In Luther Vs. Sagor, a case involving legislation of an unorganised Soviet government, it was established that the courts must give effect only to legislation of a recognised state. While the case was in the lower courts (and the Soviet government at the time was unrecognised), the action was possible and indeed successful. The case could not, however, proceed once the Soviet government had been officially recognised.

83 The provision under Copyright Act is given as under :

I. Section 52 B deals with provision relating to accounts and audit.
II. Section 53 A deals with resale share rights in original copies.
III. Section 52 deals with importation of infringing copies.
IV. Section 53 deals with certain acts not to be infringement of copyright.

Choose the correct option :

1 I and III
2 II and IV
3 I and IV
4 I and II

Ans. (4)

Exp. Among the given options, option (4) provides the correct choices.

Section 52B in the Copyright Act, 1957 deals with provision relating to Accounts and audit. It provides that every copyright society appointed under Section 34A shall maintain proper accounts and other relevant records and prepare an annual statement of accounts, in such form and in such manner as may be prescribed by the Central Government in consultation with the Comptroller and Auditor General of India.

Section 53A in the Act deals with Resale share right in original copies. It is mentioned that in the case of resale for a price exceeding ten thousand rupees, to the original copy of a painting, sculpture or drawing, or of the original manuscript of a literary or dramatic work or musical work, the author of such work if he was the first owner of rights under Section 17 or his legal heirs shall not with standing any assignment of copyright in such work, have a right to share in the resale price of such original copy or manuscript.

84 A malignant act likely to spread infection or disease dangerous to life and making atmosphere noxious to health are punishable offences for environment protection. But the punishment are meagre to meet objectives. Under which of the following law such meagre punishment is given :

1 Environment Protection Act, 1986
2 Indian Penal Code
3 The Air (Prevention and Control of Pollution) Act, 1981
4 The Water (Prevention and Control of Pollution) Act, 1974

Ans. (2)

Exp. Section 270 in Indian Penal Code describes malignant act likely to spread infection of disease dangerous to life and provides that whoever malignantly does any act which is, and which he knows or has reason to believe to be, likely to spread the infection of any disease dangerous to life, shall be punished with imprisonment of either description for a term which may extend to two years, or with fine, or with both.

It is worth mentioning here that the punishment here is of a meagre two years maximum imprisonment, despite the apprehension and possible harm of severe impact.

85 Some of the notification under Environment Protection Act, 1986 is listed below:

Choose the correct option year wise:

1. Notification on
I. Coastal Regulation Zone
II. Environmental Auditing
III. Environmental Impact Assessment
IV. Dumping and Disposal of Fly Ash

2. Notification on
I. Dumping and Disposal of Fly Ash
II. Coastal Regulation Zone
III. Environmental Auditing
IV. Environmental Impact Assessment

3. Notification on
I. Coastal Regulation Zone
II. Dumping and Disposal of Fly Ash
III. Environmental Auditing
IV. Environmental Impact Assessment

4. Notification on
I. Environmental Impact Assessment
II. Coastal Regulation Zone
III. Environmental Auditing
IV. Dumping and Disposal of Fly Ash

Ans. (1)

Exp. Among the given options, option (1) provides the correct order.

The Coastal Regulation Zone (CRZ) notification was issued in 1991 under the Environmental Protection Act, 1986, to govern activities in coastal areas of India and to achieve sustained utilization of the area.

A gazette notification on Environmental Audit (EA) was issued in 1992 (amended in 1993). An EA is an activity for self-analysis as to the potential threat to environment.

The Environment Impact Assessment notification was promulgated in 1994. It mandated Environmental Clearance (EC) for expansion of any activity disclosed earlier. It seeks to control environment impact at an early stage itself.

A notification on Dumping and Disposal of fly ash was made in 1999 to protect the environment, and prevent the dumping and disposal of fly ash discharged from various factories or plants, especially that are coal based.

86 Ownership can be :

I. Legal and vested ownership

II. Legal and equitable ownership

III. Absolute and limited ownership

IV. Trust and beneficial ownership

Choose the correct option :

1 All I, II, III and IV 2 Only II, III and IV

3 Only I, II and III 4 Only I, III and IV

Ans. (1)

Exp. Ownership can be legal and vested ownership, Legal and equitable ownership, Absolute and limited ownership and Trust and beneficial ownership.

Ownership refers to the legal and exclusive right of a person over an object. It may be of the following kinds-

Legal and Vested Ownership is the legal claim or title to an asset or property.

For example: a lender who has lent money for a property is the legal owner of that property.

According to law, Vested ownership has the complete and full ownership of the property.

For example: Two people sharing ownership of a property. If one dies the other gets the gain of vested ownership of the property.

Trust and Beneficial Ownership wherein the object or the property is being used by a person known as trustee for the benefit of another, called a beneficiary.

In *Legal and Equitable Ownership* the former refers to an ownership under law properly, the latter implies ownership under rules of equity, without being recognized under formal law.

Further, in *Absolute and Limited Ownership* the former essentially confers all rights exclusively upon the owner and there is no restriction upon the usage, while in the latter there can be certain restrictions upon the manner in which rights may be enjoyed.

Lastly, in *Vested and Contingent Ownership* the former denotes to a perfect title without any dispute, while the latter only implies imperfect title at the moment, wherein the title may be perfected subsequently.

87 To constitute the offence of theft under Indian Penal code, there must be:

I. taking away of the movable property

II. without the consent of the person

III. taking away of the immovable property

IV. with the consent of person

Choose the correct option :

1 II and III 2 I and II

3 I and IV 4 II and IV

Ans. (2)

Exp. To constitute the offence of theft under Indian Penal code, there must be taking away of the movable property without the consent of the person.

The offence of theft is defined under Section 378 of IPC as, whoever, intending to take dishonestly any moveable property out of the possession of any person without that person's consent, moves that property in order to such taking, is said to commit theft.

It is worth noting that a thing so long as it is attached to the earth, not being movable property, is not the subject of theft; but it becomes capable of being the subject of theft as soon as it is severed from the earth. Thus, an immovable property per se cannot be stolen, but may be stolen when it is firstly converted into a movable property.

88 Which of the following statement/statements are correct?

I. Convention of Nationality was adopted in 1928.

II. Convention of Nationality of Married Women was adopted in 1957.

III. Convention on the Reduction of Statelessness was adopted in 1961.

IV. Convention on the Nationality of newborn child was adopted in 1938.

Select the correct answer using the code given below :

1 I and II 2 II and III

3 I and III 4 II and IV

Ans. (2)

Exp. Statement II and III are correct.

The Convention on the Nationality of Married Women was adopted in New York on 20th February, 1957 and enforced in 1958. The convention exists for the purpose of recognizing threats to nationality of women due to various reasons such as migration, change of husband's place or due to possible discrimination on the ground of sex.

The Convention on the Reduction of Statelessness was adopted on 30th August 1961 but came into force only in 1975. It provides detailed rules and regulations to provide or protect citizenship in case a person loses his resident state.

89 Match List I with List II.

List I	List II
A. United States of America Vs. Italy	I. Legality of use of force
B. El Salvador Vs. Honduras	II. Case concerning Elettronica Sicula S.pA (ELSI)
C. Spain Vs. Canada	III. Land, Island and maritime dispute case
D. Yugoslavia Vs. U.S.A.	IV. Fisheries Jurisdiction

Choose the correct option from those given below

	A	B	C	D
1	II	III	IV	I
2	III	I	IV	II
3	II	IV	I	III
4	IV	III	II	I

Ans. (1)

Exp. The correct matching is A-II, B-III, C-IV, D-I.

United States of America Vs. Italy is the case concerning Elettronica Sicula S.pA (ELSI). In this case, the ICJ held that Article III of the Treaty, the right "to control and manage corporations", had not been violated.

El Salvador Vs. Honduras is Land, Island and maritime dispute case. This case was filed in the International Court of Justice. The court held when territories come into dispute, compromises need to be made, and balance needs to be struck.

Spain Vs. Canada (1998) is the case concerning Fisheries Jurisdiction. It relates to the power of court. Here, the court held that since party had excluded the Court's jurisdiction on disputes arising out of or concerning conservation with respect to vessels fishing, it lacked the power to adjudicate.

Yugoslavia Vs. U.S.A (1999) case is related to legality of use of force. In this case, the Court was concerned with the legality of use of force in Yugoslavia and held that the circumstances of use of force raises very serious issues of international law.

90 Match the following provisions with the Section under Consumer Protection Act, 1986

List I	List II
A. Jurisdiction of the District forum	I. Section 17 B
B. Composition of State Commission	II. Section 20
C. Composition of National Commission	III. Section 16
D. Circuit benches of State Commission	IV. Section 11

Choose the correct option from those given below :

	A	B	C	D		A	B	C	D
1	II	IV	III	I	2	I	II	III	IV
3	III	II	I	IV	4	IV	III	II	I

Ans. *(4)*

Exp. The correct matching is A-IV, B-III, C-II, D-I.

Section 11 of the Consumer Protection Act, 1986 is related to Jurisdiction of District Forum. It provided that the District Forum shall have jurisdiction to entertain complaints where the value of the goods or services and the compensation claimed does not exceed rupees twenty lakhs.

Section 16 of the Act is related to Composition of State Commission. It mentions that each State Commission shall consist of a person who is or has been a Judge of a High Court appointed by the State Government, who shall be its President, and not less than two, and not more than such number of members, as may be prescribed, and one of whom shall be a woman.

Section 20 of the Act mentions about Composition of National Commission. It provides that the National Commission shall consist of a person who is or has been a Judge of the Supreme Court who shall be its President and four other members, one of whom shall be a woman.

Section 17B mentions about Circuit Benches of State Commission. It mentions that the State Commission shall ordinarily function in the State Capital but may perform its functions at such other place as the State Government may, in consultation with the State Commission, notify in the Official Gazette.

Directions (Qs. No. 91-95) *Read the paragraph carefully and answer the following questions.*

The Preamble of the Constitution is an integral part of the Constitution. Democratic form of government, federal structure, unity and integrity of the nation, secularism, socialism, social justice and judicial review are basic features of the Constitution.

The Union of India shall protect the State Government and as corollary under Article 356 it is enjoined that the government of every state should be carried on in accordance with the provisions of the constitution. On receipt of a report from the Governor or otherwise the President (Council of Ministers) on being satisfied that a situation has arisen in which the Government of a State cannot be carried on in accordance with the provisions of the Constitution, is empowered to issue Proclamation under Article 356(1) and impose president's rule in the state in a manner laid down in sub-clause 1 to 3 of Article 356(1) of the Constitution.

The exercise of the power under Article 356 is an extraordinary one and needs to be used sparingly when the situation contemplated by Article 356 warrants to maintain democratic form of government and to prevent paralysing of the political process. Single or individual act or acts of violation of the constitution for good, bad or in different administration does not necessarily constitute failure of constitutional machinery or characterises that a situation has arisen in which the Government of the State cannot be carried on in accordance with the provisions of the constitution. The exercise of power under Article 356 should under no circumstances be for a political gain to the party in power in the Union government. It should be used sparingly and with circumspection that the government of the State functions with responsibility in accordance with the provisions of the constitution.

Rule of law has been chosen as an instrument of social adjustment and resolution of conflicting social problems to integrate diverse sections of the society professing multi-religious faiths, creed, caste or region fostering among them fraternity, transcending social, religious, linguistic or regional barriers.

Citizen is either by birth or by domicile and not as a member of religion, caste, sect, region or language secularism has both positive and negative constants.

91 Article 356(1) (b) provides that :

1. Any proclamation under Article 356(1) may be revoked by a subsequent proclamation
2. Every proclamation under Article 356(1) shall be laid before each House of Parliament
3. A Proclamation under Article 356(1) shall cease to operate on the expiration of six months from the date of issue of proclamation
4. The President may by proclamation under Article 356(1) declare that the powers of the legislature of the state shall be exercisable by or under the authority of Parliament

Ans. *(4)*

➲ *Exp.* Article 356(1) (b) of the Constitution of India provides that the President may by proclamation under Article 356(1) declare that the powers of the legislature of the state shall be exercisable by or under the authority of Parliament.

The effect of this provision brings State under control of Union and all functions are thereby discharged from center only. The imposition of State emergency is also known as Presidential Rule.

92 Which one of the following provisions of the Constitution imposes an obligation on the Union to ensure that the Government of the State is carried on in accordance with the provisions of the constitution?

1 Article 352 2 Article 355
3 Article 356 4 Article 360

Ans. *(2)*

➲ *Exp.* Article 355 in the Constitution of India imposes an obligation on the Union to ensure that the Government of the State is carried on in accordance with the provisions of the constitution.

Article 355 in the Constitution of India deals with duty of the Union to protect States. It says that it shall be the duty of the Union to protect every State against external aggression and internal disturbance and to ensure that the government of every State is carried on in accordance with the provisions of this Constitution.

93 'Rule of law' has been recognised by the constitution of India under :

1 Article 14 2 Article 19
3 Article 21 4 Article 22

Ans. *(1)*

➲ *Exp.* 'Rule of law' has been recognised by the Constitution of India under Article 14.

The concept of 'Rule of Law' implies that the law is above all, and that everyone is equally bound by the law. The term is of British origin and was coined by Dicey. It emphasizes that the law shall treat everyone with equality before it.

94 In the light of the above, answer the following : In which of the following cases, the supreme court held that the Preamble is the part of the Constitution.

1 Buckingham and Carantic Co. Ltd Vs. Venkiah
2 Keshvananda Bharati Case
3 Golaknath Vs. State of Punjab
4 In re Berubari case

Ans. *(2)*

➲ *Exp.* The landmark judgement Kesavananda Bharati Vs. State of Kerala was delivered by the Supreme Court in 1973 by a majority of 7:6 in which the Supreme Court held that the Preamble is a part of the Constitution.

The court found that Preamble is a part of the Constitution and hence, could be amended by virtue of it, as any other part of constitution may be amended by invoking Article 368 of Constitution. However, the court clarified that in the process of amending Preamble, the basic structure of it cannot be amended.

The term basic structure finds no particular mention in the Constitution but is a judicially evolved concept and the court has time to time held that concepts such as, inter alia, sovereignty, secularism, democracy, judicial review are basic structures.

95 On which grounds of the following a restriction can be imposed on freedom of religion under Article 25(1) of the constitution?

1 Public order, decency and morality
2 In the interest of general public
3 Public order, morality and health
4 In the interest of general public and for the protection of the interest or Scheduled

Ans. *(3)*

➲ *Exp.* A restriction can be imposed on freedom of religion under Article 25(1) of the constitution on the grounds of Public order, morality and health.

Article 25 under clause (1) of the Constitution of India grants a fundamental right to religion to every person which includes the freedom to conscience, profess, practice and propagate any religion.

Since no fundamental right is absolute, the State can impose restrictions in reasonable way to control unlawful exercise of any right and it is for this reason, certain grounds have been provided on the basis of which the freedom to exercise religious choice may be curtailed.

Directions (Qs. No. 96-100) *Read the paragraph carefully and answer the following questions.*

Broadly speaking, legal theory involves a study of the characteristic features essential to law and common to legal systems and analysis of the basic elements of law which made it law and distinguish it from other forms of rules and standards, from systems which cannot be described as legal systems and from other social phenomena. In fact, it is not possible to reach our dogmatic answer to the question 'what is law' or provide exclusive answers to many questions which are asked about its essential nature.

The nature of legal theory lies in a study of the right which other theories may shed on distinctive attributes of law, by an examination of the relative merits and demerits of the principal expositions of the subject. In the same strain legal theory is linked at one end, with philosophy and at other end, with political theory. Sometimes the starting point is philosophy and political ideology plays a secondary part.... sometimes the theory of knowledge and political ideology are welded into one coherent system, of course, it is true that some legal philosophies have been philosophizes first and foremost and juristic because they felt the need to express their political thought in legal form .... In short, before the

nineteenth century legal theory was essentially a by-product of philosophy, religion, ethics or politics.

The new era of legal philosophy arises mainly from the confrontation of professional lawyers, in his legal work, with problems of social justice. The modern jurists legal theory, no less than scholastic philosopher is based on ultimate beliefs whose inspiration comes from outside the law itself.

96 Law is always in a state of continual change. This is the basic tenet of :

1 Realist Jurisprudence
2 Sociological Jurisprudence
3 Philosophical Jurisprudence
4 Analytical Jurisprudence

Ans. *(1)*

➲ *Exp.* Law is always in a state of continual change. This is the basic tenet of Realist Jurisprudence.

Realism makes an attempt to study law in terms of practical and useful application, rather than a hard fact existing on a piece of statute of little or no real usage. It is for this reason that the realists seek to avoid focusing on examination of traditional rules, laws and practices of legal nature as they also believe that law is constantly changing based on the society. No law can be good forever or for a very long time.

97 Law must remain free from social sciences, metaphysical, ethical and moral elements. This was propounded by:

1 Austin 2 Pound
3 Kelson 4 Salmond

Ans. *(3)*

➲ *Exp.* Law must remain free from social sciences, metaphysical, ethical and moral elements. This was propounded by Kelson.

Hens Kelson's theory of pure law served as a revival of analytical jurisprudence. He believed that the study of law must not involve external factors such as history, politics, sociology, economics, psychology, ethics within itself, and law must be studied independently.

It is because of this approach that his theory is known as pure theory of law because he separates law from other factors.

Kelson firmly stated that law must be "as it is" and not "ought to be". This further suggests that he emphasized on legal studies without any outside dominance or influence. His ideas provide strength to the analytical school of jurisprudence or the legal positivism and reinforces the notion that law is what is made by the sovereign which is binding on everyone.

98 Who defined jurisprudence as a "formal science of positive law"?

1 Austin 2 H.L.A. Hart
3 Salmond 4 Holland

Ans. *(4)*

➲ *Exp.* Sir Thomas Erskine Holland defines jurisprudence as "the formal science of positive law".

According to him, a positive law essentially implies general rule of external human behavior which is sanctioned or enforced by a sovereign authority which is politically dominant.

Further, the word 'formal science 'denotes jurisprudence as a study covers only the form of law; that is the outer understanding of law, and not the internal content.

In other words, he indicates that the study of law deals with the very legal relations that exist on the face of it, but excludes the study of particular law and their contents specifically.

99 In the Right of above, answer the following. As the science of law or philosophy of law emerged, which of the following approach came into existence?

1 Analytical positivist approach
2 Socio-legal approach
3 Historical approach
4 Realist approach

Ans. *(2)*

➲ *Exp.* As the science of law or philosophy of law emerged, Socio-legal school came into existence.

A Socio-legal approach can be described as a perspective of study of law directed towards analysing laws and their social impact.

It is due to the emergence of science or philosophy of law, that there arose an idea of Socio-legal approach since the science or philosophy of law incorporated within themselves an examination of factors affecting law and its application. They make an effort to find out the real functioning of law and whether it is able to serve its purpose or not, and hence by taking into account the Socio-legal approach, it can be ascertained very well.

100 Who, among the following jurists, says "legal theory is linked at one end with philosophy and, at other end, with political theory"?

1 John D. Finch 2 Friedman
3 Wayne Morrison 4 Jeremy Bentham

Ans. *(2)*

➲ *Exp.* Friedman has said that "legal theory is linked at one end with philosophy and at the other end, with political theory".

This is to suggest that the study of legal theory or jurisprudence includes examination of law and political sanction. It means there are two aspects; firstly that to understand the relations of legal nature and secondly, to know who created them or brought into existence. He calls them two edges of jurisprudence or legal theory.

According to him, the law is made by political authority on one hand, which is to be followed or complied with an individual subject to the jurisdiction of such authority on the other hand and the examination of legal relations is complete only when these two aspects are covered.

UGC-NET
LAW
SOLVED PAPER 2019 (June)
PAPER II

1 "The law of every modern state shows as at a thousand points the influence of both the accepted social morality and wider moral ideals. These influences enter into law either abruptly and avowedly through legislation, or silently and piecemeal through the judicial process." Who said this?

1 Bentham 2 Gray
3 Hart 4 Karkunov

Ans. (3)

Exp. The above given statement is said by Hart. He always has backed law with morality. According to him, both, law and morality have a common object or end in so far as both of them direct the actions of men in such a way as to produce maximum social and individual good. Both, law and morality are backed by social or external sanction.

2 Which of the following statement/statements is/are not correct?

I. According to Article 16 of the Universal Declaration of Human Rights, 'Everyone has a right to seek and enjoy in other countries asylum from prosecution'.

II. In 1967, United Nations Declaration on Territorial Asylum was unanimously adopted by the General Assembly.

III. The Convention on the Status of Refugees, 1951 entered into force on 24th April, 1956.

IV. In the Asylum Case (Colombia V. Peru), the International Court of Justice explained the distinction between territorial asylum and diplomatic asylum.

Select the correct answer from the codes given below

1 Only I 2 I and II
3 I and III 4 All of these

Ans. (3)

Exp. Statement I and III are incorrect.

According to Article 14 of the Universal Declaration of Human Rights, 'Everyone has a right to seek and enjoy in other countries asylum from prosecution'. According to Article 16 of Universal Declaration of Human Rights, Men and Women of full age, without any limitation due to race, nationality or religion, have the right to marry and to found a family. They are entitled to equal rights as to marriage, during marriage and at its dissolution.

The Convention on the Status of Refugees, 1951 which is in today's date is the centre piece of refugee protection entered into force on 22nd April, 1954.

3 'A citizen has a fundamental right to use the best means of imparting and receiving information and as such to have an access to telecasting for the purpose' is the observation of the Supreme Court in

1 Ministry of Information and Broadcasting, Government of India Vs. Cricket Association of Bengal (1995)
2 Prabhu Dutt Vs. Union of India (1982)
3 Dinesh Trivedi Vs. Union of India (1977)
4 Pramati Educational and Cultural Trust Vs. Union of India (2014)

Ans. (1)

Exp. In case titled, Ministry of Information and Broadcasting, Government of India Vs. Cricket Association of Bengal (1995), Apex Court held that, as right to impart and receive information is a specie of the right to freedom of speech and expression guaranteed by Article 19(1)(a) of the Constitution. A citizen has a fundamental right to use the best means of imparting and receiving information and as such to have an access to telecasting for the purpose. Therefore, the government has no monopoly on electronic media and that a citizen under Article 19(1)(a) has a right to telecast and broadcast to the viewers, listeners through electronic media, television or radio any important event.

4 The prohibition of registration of geographical indication under the GIG Act, 1999 contains as many as

1 four grounds 2 five grounds
3 six grounds 4 seven grounds

Ans. (4)

Exp. Prohibition of registration of certain geographical indications under the GIG Act, 1999 has seven grounds. A geographical indication cannot be registered in following conditions :

- the use of which would be likely to deceive or cause confusion;
- the use of which would be contrary to any law for the time being in force;
- which comprises or contains scandalous or obscene matter;
- which comprises or contains any matter likely to hurt the religious susceptibilities of any class or section of the citizens of India;
- which would otherwise be disentitled to protection in a court;
- which are determined to be generic names or indications of goods and are, therefore, not or ceased to be protected in their country of origin, or which have fallen into disuse in that country; or
- which, although literally true as to the territory, region or locality in which the goods originate, but falsely represent to the persons that the goods originate in another territory, region or locality, as the case may be, shall not be registered as a geographical indication.

5 Match List I with List II.

List I	List II
A. Bentham	I. Historical School
B. Puchta	II. Sociological School
C. Herbert Spencer	III. Analytical School
D. Gary	IV. The Realist School

Select the correct answer from the codes given below

	A	B	C	D		A	B	C	D
1	III	I	II	IV	2	I	II	III	IV
3	II	IV	III	I	4	IV	III	I	II

***Ans.* (1)**

Exp. The correct matching is A-III, B-I, C-II, D-IV

Bentham is the founder of the Analytical School of jurisprudence. The basic idea of Analytical school of jurisprudence is to deal with law that exists in its present form. Analytical school believes that law is the direction of the Sovereign. Thus, it is also termed as an imperative school. This school of jurisprudence gained prominence in the 19th century.

Puchta was a great jurist of the Historical School of jurisprudence. He was a disciple of Savigny, who improved upon his views and made them more rational. He traced the development and evolution of law from the very beginning. The main concept of Puchta's ideas was that "neither the people nor the state alone can make and formulate laws". Both State and individual are the sources of law.

Herbert Spencer was an important figure of the Sociological School of jurisprudence. He gave a scientific exposition of the organic theory of society. In his famous work named "Principles of Sociology", Spencer traced this theory of the origin of law. To him law arises from four sources: inherited usages with quasi-religion sanctions, injunctions of deceased leaders, the will of the predominant man and collective opinion of the community.

Gary is a prominent jurist of the Realist School of jurisprudence. The Realist School of jurisprudence is the combination of the Analytical and Sociological school of jurisprudence.

6 In which of the following cases, the Supreme Court said that 'Fundamental Rights and Directive Principles' aim at the same goal of bringing about a social revolution and establishment of a welfare state and they can be interpreted and applied together and they are supplementary and complementary to each other?

1 Maneka Gandhi Vs. Union of India
2 Re Kerala Education Bill
3 Minerva Mills Vs. Union of India
4 Kesvananda Bharati Vs. State of Kerala

***Ans.* (4)**

Exp. In Kesvananda Bharati Vs. State of Kerala, Supreme Court has adopted the view that the 'Fundamental Rights and Directive Principles' are complementary to each other and they are supplementing the other's role with the aim of establishing the welfare state by the social means.

7 Which one of the following is not an essential of Parliamentary form of government?

1 The presence of a nominal executive head of the State who acts exclusively on the advice of Cabinet
2 The Cabinet, which is the real executive, consists of leaders of a party, who have the support of the majority in the legislature
3 The responsibility of the Cabinet is collective
4 The President appoints ministers and assigns to them their offices

***Ans.* (4)**

Exp. In a Parliamentary form of government, it is not essential for the President to appoint ministers and assign them to their offices.

Parliamentary form of Government is the system of government in which there exists an intimate and harmonious relationship between the executive and the legislative departments, and the stability and efficacy of the executive department depend on the legislature.

Some of the features of a Parliamentary system are as follows :

- Existence of a Titular/Constitutional Head.
- The Lower House plays a vital role in the formation of the Ministry.
- The Cabinet or Ministry has to remain responsible to the legislature for all its activities and policies.

8 Which of the following is a leading case on trespass abinitio?

1 Goldsmith V. Sperring Ltd.
2 Dumbell V. Roberts
3 Bird V. Jones
4 Six carpenters' case

Ans. *(4)*

Exp. Six carpenters' case is a leading case on trespass abinitio. It lays down three major points-

- If a man abuses an authority given to him by the law, he becomes a trespasser abinitio.
- In an action of trespass, if the authority is pleaded, the subsequent abuse may be replied.
- A mere nonfeasance does not amount to such an abuse as renders a man a trespasser abinitio.

9 'Test of control' deals with

1 master and servant relationship
2 measures of damages
3 course of employment
4 implied authority

Ans. *(1)*

Exp. 'Test of control' deals with master and servant relationship. The control test which deals with master servant relationships is developed by courts. According to the test, a person is said to be a servant if his employer retains a right to control not only the work that he does, but also the way in which he does it.

In a Master-Servant relationship, the master employs the services of the servant and he works on the command of master and thus, a special relation exists between the two and in case of a tort (wrongful act) committed by the servant, his master is also held liable.

10 Sedition means

1 expressing disapprobation of the measure of the government with a view to obtain their alteration
2 advocacy of boycott of foreign goods as a means of helping Indian industries
3 exciting or attempting to excite hatred towards the government through a writing which remains with the author unpublished
4 bringing or attempting to bring the government into hatred through words, signs or visible representation

Ans. *(4)*

Exp. Sedition means bringing or attempting to bring the government into hatred through words, signs or visible representation

Section 124-A of IPC defines Sedition in the following words- "Whoever, by words, either spoken or written, or by signs, or by visible representation, or otherwise, brings or attempts to bring into hatred or contempt, or excites or attempts to excite disaffection towards, the Government established by law in India, shall be punished with imprisonment for life, to which fine may be added, or with imprisonment which may extend to three years, to which fine may be added, or with fine.

11 Which section of the Companies Act, 2013 deals with Corporate Social Responsibility?

1 Section 133
2 Section 134
3 Section 135
4 Section 136

Ans. *(3)*

Exp. Section 135 of Companies Act, 2013 talks about Corporate Social Responsibility (CSR) which says, every company having net worth of rupees five hundred crore or more, or turnover of rupees one thousand crore or more or a net profit of rupees five crore or more during the immediately preceding financial year shall constitute a Corporate Social Responsibility Committee of the Board consisting of three or more directors, out of which at least one director shall be an independent director.

Corporate Social Responsibility (CSR) is a self-regulating business model that helps a company be socially accountable to itself, its stakeholders, and the public.

12 Which of the following statement/statements is/are correct?

I. The operation of the doctrine of forum prorogation has not been envisaged under the UN Charter or the Statute of the International Court of Justice.
II. The doctrine of forum prorogatum may not operate where the court already has jurisdiction ratione personae.
III. The doctrine of the forum prorogatum affords an informal way for a state to express consent to the jurisdiction of the court.
IV. The principle underlying doctrine of forum prorogatum was enunciated by the Permanent Court of International Justice in the Island of Palm Case (1928).

Select the correct answer from the codes given below

1 Only I
2 I and III
3 II, III and IV
4 All of these

Ans. *(2)*

Exp. Statements I and III are correct.

The operation of the doctrine of forum prorogation has not been envisaged under the UN Charter or the Statute of the International Court of Justice. Doctrine of forum prorogation is nowhere formally mentioned under the UN Charter or the Statute of International Court of Justice.

The doctrine of forum prorogatum affords an informal way for a state to express consent to the Court's jurisdiction. As understood, this doctrine refers to the extension of a court's jurisdiction by agreement of the parties to a case after proceedings have been instituted.

Statement II and IV are incorrect.

If a State has not recognized the jurisdiction of the Court at the time when an application instituting proceedings is filed against it, that State has the possibility of subsequently accepting such jurisdiction to enable the Court to entertain the case, the Court thus has jurisdiction as of the date of acceptance under the forum prorogatum rule.

Instead of the Island of Palm Case, doctrine of forum progatum was enunciated in Corfu Channel Case by the Permanent Court of International Justice.

13 The inadequacy of consideration will be taken into account by a court of law

1 when the promisor expresses his desire to get maximum return for his promise
2 when the promisor performs his promise
3 when fraud, coercion or undue influence in the formation of the contract is pleaded
4 always at the discretion of the court

Ans. (3)

Exp. The inadequacy of consideration will be taken into account by a court of law when fraud, coercion or undue influence in the formation of the contract is pleaded.

Section 25, Explanation 2, of Indian Contract Act says that, an agreement to which the consent of the promisor is freely given is not void merely because the consideration is inadequate; but the inadequacy of the consideration may be taken into account by the Court in determining the question whether the consent of the promisor was freely given. It should be free from fraud, coercion or undue influence.

14 The liability has been defined as 'the bond of necessity that exists between the wrongdoer and the remedy of the wrong' by

1 Austin 2 Bentham
3 Salmond 4 Holland

Ans. (3)

Exp. Salmond has defined the liability as 'the bond of necessity that exists between the wrongdoer and the remedy of the wrong'.

When a person has committed a wrong, he is said to be liable. Thus, liability is the condition of person who has committed the wrong. Salmond defines 'liability' as the bond that exists between the wrong doer and the remedy of the wrong. Law is not only about laying down the rights and duties, it has to ensure the protection, enforcement and redress also.

15 Who among the following stated that 'postmodernism is a notoriously ambiguous concept'?

1 Llyod 2 Toynbee
3 Someervell 4 Bentham

Ans. (1)

Exp. According to Llyod, 'postmodernism is a notorious and ambiguous concept' which does not have a clear definition. Postmodernism is largely a reaction to the assumed certainty of scientific, or objective, efforts to explain reality.

16 Which of the following statement/statements is/are correct?

I. If the other House does not pass an ordinary Bill and more than six months have passed, the President may summon a Joint Session of both the Houses.
II. At the Joint Session of two Houses, new amendment can be proposed in the Bill with the permission of the Presiding Officer (Speaker of the Lok Sabha).
III. The Lower House has exclusive power over Money Bills.
IV. Money and Financial Bills can be only introduced in the Lok Sabha and with prior recommendations of the President.

Select the correct answer from the codes given below

1 Only I 2 I and III
3 I, III and IV 4 All of these

Ans. (3)

Exp. Statements I, III and IV are correct.

According to Article 108(1)(c) of the Constitution, if the other house does not pass the ordinary bill and more than six months have passed, the President may summon a Joint session of both the Houses.

According to Article 109 of the Constitution, the House of People has more power over the money bill. Money bills can't be introduced in the Council of States.

According to Article 109 and 117, Money Bill and Financial Bills can be only introduced in the Lok Sabha and with prior recommendations of the President.

Statement II is false because in a joint sitting, a new amendment cannot be proposed in the Bill with the permission of the Presiding Officer (Speaker of the Lok Sabha). Instead according to Article 108(4)(a), if the Bill, having been passed by one House, has not been passed by the other House with amendments and returned to the House in which it originated, no amendment shall be proposed to the Bill other than such amendments (if any) as are made necessary by the delay in the passage of the Bill.

17 The Constitution of India incorporates the 'Rule of Law' in

1 Article 14 2 Article 19
3 Article 21 4 Article 32

Ans. (1)

Exp. Article 14 of the Constitution of India incorporates the concept of 'Rule of Law'. It means that no man is above law and also that every person is subject to the jurisdiction of ordinary courts of law irrespective of their position and rank. Rule of law, the mechanism, process, institution, practice, or norm that supports the equality of all citizens before the law, secures a non-arbitrary form of government, and prevents the arbitrary use of power.

18 Whoever counterfeits, or knowingly performs, any part of the process of counterfeiting Indian coin under Section 232 by Indian Penal Code shall be punished with

1 imprisonment which may extend to ten years and fine
2 imprisonment which may extend to seven years and fine
3 imprisonment which may extend to five years and fine
4 imprisonment which may extend to three years and fine

Ans. (1)

Exp. Section 232 of IPC says, whoever counterfeits, or knowingly performs any part of the process of counterfeiting Indian coin, shall be punished with imprisonment for life or with imprisonment of either description for a term which may extend to ten years, and shall also be liable to fine.

19 The doctrine of Separation of powers in its strict and technical sense is applied in

1 India 2 UK
3 USA 4 France

Ans. (3)

Exp. The doctrine of Separation of powers in its strict and technical sense is applied in USA.

The doctrine of Separation of power was first given by Montesquieu and the concept is taken from the USA.

Separation of powers, refer to the division of government responsibilities into distinct branches to limit any one branch from exercising the core functions of another. The intent is to prevent the concentration of power and provide for checks and balances.

The doctrine of Separation of powers forms the foundation on which the whole structure of the American Constitution is based. It has been accepted and strictly adopted in the USA.

20 In which of the following case, it was held that if a person is not a citizen of any state, he will be called 'stateless'?

1 Nottebohm's Case
2 Whicker Vs. Hume
3 Winans Vs. AG
4 Stoeck Vs. The Public Trustee

Ans. (4)

Exp. In Stoeck Vs. The Public Trustee case it was held that if a person is not a citizen of any state, he will be called 'stateless' and this condition is to be called Statelessness. In simple terms, this means that a stateless person does not have a nationality of any country.

21 Which of the following is not the School of Muslim Law?

1 Hanafi 2 Maliki
3 Hanabali 4 Zaida

Ans. (4)

Exp. Zaida is not the school of Muslim law.

Following are the various school of Muslim Law:

Hanafi School derives its name from its founder, Abu Hanafi. This school basically relies on customs and precedents of the Muslim community as the traditions.

Maliki School derives its name from its founder Imam Malik-bin-Anas. The Maliki school originates from Sunna and Hadis. These two important sources give importance to the sayings, teachings, customs and traditions of Prophet Mohammed.

Shafi School originates from Muhammed bin Irdis Shafi, who was a student of both Imam Malik and Imam Hanafi. The Shafi school is basically a combination of the Maliki school and the Hanafi school. Ijma, i.e. the interpretations of jurists is the most important source of law in the Shafi school. It also relies on the customs of the Muslim people. The Qiya source of law, which depends on analogical interpretations by people, originates from this school.

Hanabali School Ahmed bin Hanbal, a disciple of Imam Shafi, was the creator of this school. His theory rejected the Shafi school for relying on Qiya, i.e. the personal analogical reasonings and interpretations of the people. He insisted on going back to Sunna and Hadis to interpret the Quran and other laws.

22 In India, 'the machinery of government is essentially British and the whole collection of British Constitutional Conventions has apparently been incorporated as conventions' is the observation of

1 AV Dicey 2 Sir Ivor Jennings
3 SA de Smith 4 Wade and Phillips

Ans. (2)

Exp. In India, 'the machinery of government is essentially British and the whole collection of British Constitutional Conventions has apparently been incorporated as conventions' is the observation of Sir Ivor Jennings.

Sir William Ivor Jennings was a British lawyer and academician. He was proposed by Jawaharlal Nehru to be the chairman of the drafting committee of the Constitution of India; however, eventually Mahatma Gandhi's candidate, B. R. Ambedkar, was chosen.

23 Which of the following is incorrect regarding meaning of 'Merchantable quality of goods'?

1 The goods are free from patent defects
2 The goods are free from latent defects
3 The goods can be used for the purpose for which they are bought
4 That the goods are marketable at their full value

Ans. (*)

Exp. All four options are correct. (Answer as per the question should be "none of the above")

Goods in order to be of Merchantable quality should fulfil all the above-mentioned conditions i.e. they should be free from latent and patent defect, they can be used for the purpose for which they are brought, and they are to be marketable at their full value.

24 Which section of Indian Penal Code deals with solitary confinement?

1 Section 73 of IPC
2 Section 72 of IPC
3 Section 71 of IPC
4 Section 70 of IPC

Ans. *(1)*

Exp. Section 73 of IPC talks about solitary confinement. In a period of solitary confinement, prisoner lives in complete isolation which deprives him from any type of human contact except from the jail/prison staff. Indian Penal Code, 1860 gives power to keep the prisoner in solitary confinement for a maximum period of three months.

25 The absolute grounds for refusal of registration is contained under which section of the Trademark Act, 1999?

1 Section 7 2 Section 8
3 Section 9 4 Section 10

Ans. *(3)*

Exp. Section 9 of the Trademark Act 1999 lists down the absolute grounds for refusal of registration. If any trademark comes under the grounds listed in this section, it cannot be registered. The absolute grounds for refusing registration are

- Trademarks which do not possess any distinctive character. Distinctive character means trademarks which are not capable of distinguishing the goods or services of one person from those of another.
- Trademarks which exclusively contain marks or indications which serve in trade to define the kind, quality, quantity, intended purpose, values or geographical origin of goods or services rendered.
- Trademarks which exclusively contain marks or indications which have become customary in the current language or the established practices of the trade.
- Trademarks are of such a nature which deceives or cause confusion to the public.
- Trademarks which contain or comprise matter likely to hurt the religious susceptibilities of any class or sections of citizens of India.
- Trademarks which contain or comprise scandalous or obscene matter.
- If the usage of the trademark is prohibited under the Emblems and Names (Prevention of Improper Use) Act, 1950.
- Trademarks which consist of marks of the shape of goods which result from the nature of goods themselves.
- Trademarks which consist of marks of the shape of goods which is necessary to obtain a technical result.
- Trademarks which consist of marks of the shape which gives substantial value to the goods.

26 The communication of an acceptance is complete as against the proposer

1 when it is posted to him
2 when it comes to the knowledge of the proposer
3 when the letter containing acceptance is received by the proposer
4 when it is put in the course of transmission, so as to be out of the acceptor's power

Ans. *(4)*

Exp. According to Section 4 of Indian Contract Act, "the communication of an acceptance is complete as against the proposer, when it is put in a course of transmission to him, so as to be out of the power of the acceptor and as against the acceptor, when it comes to the knowledge of the proposer".

27 Match List I with List II.

	List I (Provisions)		List II (Relevant Supreme Court Cases)
A.	Appointment of judges of Supreme Court	I.	In Re : Vinay Chander Mishra
B.	Jurisdiction of Supreme Court as Court of Record	II.	S C Advocates-on-Record Association V. Union of India
C.	Original jurisdiction of Supreme Court	III.	AR Antulay V. RS Nayak
D.	Power of Supreme Court to withdraw and transfer of cases	IV.	State of Karnataka V. Union of India

Select the correct answer from the codes given below

	A	B	C	D		A	B	C	D
1	II	I	IV	III	2	IV	III	II	I
3	I	IV	III	II	4	I	II	III	IV

Ans. *(1)*

Exp. The correct matching is A-II, B-I, C-IV, D-III.

S C Advocates-on-Record Association Vs. The Union of India case dealt with the appointment of judges of the Supreme Court. The nine Judge Bench not only overruled. S.P. Gupta's case, but also devised a specific procedure for appointment of Judges of the Supreme Court in the interest of "protecting the integrity and guarding the independence of the judiciary." For the same reason, the primacy of the Chief Justice of India was held to be essential.

In Re : Vinay Chander Mishra the Jurisdiction of Supreme Court as Court of Record was determined. In this case an advocate was found guilty of criminal contempt of Court and he was sentenced to undergo simple imprisonment for a period of six years and suspended from practising as an advocate for a period of three years. The punishment of imprisonment was suspended for a period of four years and was to be activated in case of his conviction for any other offence of contempt of Court within the said period.

State of Karnataka Vs. The Union of India case dealt with Original jurisdiction of the Supreme Court. The Court filled the ambiguity and outlined the scope of Article 131 and also laid down the foundation for addressing centre-state disputes.

AR Antulay Vs. RS Nayak Case dealt with the power of the Supreme Court to withdraw and transfer of cases. It is one of the landmark judgments in Indian legal history because it established that corruption matters tried by a Special Court cannot be referred to a High Court judge for a hearing.

28 Human rights are defined in which of the following sections of the Protection of Human Rights Act, 1993?

1 Section 2(a) 2 Section 2(b)
3 Section 2(c) 4 Section 2(d)

Ans. (4)

Exp. Human rights are defined in Section 2(d) of the Protection of Human Rights Act, 1993.

According to Section 2(1)(d) of Protection of Human Rights Act, 1993, 'Human Rights' means the rights relating to life, liberty, equality and dignity of the individual guaranteed by the Constitution or embodied in the International Covenants and enforceable by courts in India.

29 X with the intention to steal ornaments opened Y's box and found it empty. Which of the following statements is correct?

1 X is not liable for attempt to commit theft as the box being empty, commission of theft was impossible.
2 X is not liable for attempt to commit theft as he did not do the penultimate act towards commission of theft
3 X is not guilty of attempt to commit theft as the ornaments were not in the box.
4 X is guilty of attempt to commit theft as he had an intention to commit theft and did an act toward its commission.

Ans. (4)

Exp. In the given case, X is guilty of attempt to commit theft as he had an intention to commit theft and did an act toward its commission.

With reference to Section 511 in the Indian Penal Code, X makes an attempt to steal some jewels by breaking (open) a box, and finds after opening the box, that there is no jewel in it. He has done an act towards the commission of theft, and therefore is guilty under this section.

Section 511 of IPC says "Whoever attempts to commit an offence punishable by this Code with imprisonment for life or imprisonment, or to cause such an offence to be committed, and in such attempt does any act towards the commission of the offence, shall, where no express provision is made by this Code for the punishment of such attempt, be punished with imprisonment of any description provided for the offence, for a term which may extend to one-half of the imprisonment for life or, as the case may be, one-half of the longest term of imprisonment provided for that offence, or with such fine as is provided for the offence, or with both."

30 Two persons are said to be related to each other by what relation when they are descended from a common ancestress but by different husbands?

1 Full blood 2 Half blood
3 Uterine blood 4 Agnate

Ans. (3)

Exp. According to Section 3(d) of Hindu Marriage Act, 1955, two persons are said to be related to each other by Uterine blood when they are descended from a common ancestress but by different husbands.

According to Section 3(c) of Hindu marriage Act, 1955, two persons are said to be related to each other by Full blood when they are descended from a common ancestor by the same wife and by half-blood when they are descended from a common ancestor but by different wives

According to Section 3(1)(a) of the Hindu Succession Act, 1956, one person is said to be an "Agnate" of another if the two are related by blood or adoption wholly through males.

31 A wife has an implied authority of the husband to buy articles of household necessity

1 if the wife is living with her husband in a domestic establishment of their own
2 if the wife is living separately
3 if the wife is living with her husband not in a domestic establishment
4 if the wife is provided a reasonable allowance by the husband for the purchase of household needs

Ans. (1)

Exp. When the wife is living with her husband in a domestic establishment of their own., she has implied an authority to buy the articles of household necessaries.

The following conditions should be satisfied for treating the wife as an agent of the husband:

- The husband and wife are living together in a domestic establishment of their own.
- The wife should be in charge of the domestic establishment.
- The wife must have purchased articles or goods suitable to the style in which the husband chooses to live.

32 Which of the following statement/statements is/are correct?

I. 'Hegel' is one of the chief exponents of the Constitutive Theory' of recognition.
II. Civil Air Transport Incorporated Co. Vs. Central Air Transport Corporation is a leading case on the retrospective effect of recognition.
III. De jure recognition is not final and can be withdrawn.
IV. In Luther Vs. Sagor it was held that there is distinction between de facto and de jure recognition for the purpose of giving effect to the internal acts of the recognised authority.

Select the correct answer from the codes given below
1 Only I is correct 2 I, II and III are correct
3 I, II and IV are correct 4 All are correct

Ans. (3)

Exp. Statement I, III and IV are correct.

Hegel along with Oppenheim and Anzilloti are the chief exponents of 'Constitutive Theory' of recognition. According to this theory the only certificate to issue international personality to a new born state is the consent of the already existing states.

Civil Air Transport Incorporated Co. Vs. Central Air Transport Corporation is a leading case on the retrospective effect of recognition. Recognition de facto as well as de jure has a 'retroactive' effect in the sense that all the acts of newly recognized State are treated valid dating back on the commencement of the activities of the authority thus recognized.

In case of Luther Vs. Sagor it was held that there is distinction between de facto and de jure recognition for the purpose of giving effect to the internal acts of the recognised authority.

Statement III is false as it says De jure recognition is not final and can be withdrawn instead De jure recognition is a final and non-conditional recognition.

33 Which Article of the UN Charter puts the promotion of respect for human rights on the same level as the maintenance of international peace and security as a purpose of the UN?

1 Article 1 2 Article 2
3 Article 3 4 Article 4

Ans. (1)

Exp. Article 1 of UN Charter puts the promotion of respect for human rights on the same level as the maintenance of international peace and security as a purpose of the UN.

According to Article 1 of UN Charter the purposes of the United Nations are:

- To maintain international peace and security, and to that end: to take effective collective measures for the prevention and removal of threats to the peace, and for the suppression of acts of aggression or other breaches of the peace, and to bring about by peaceful means, and in conformity with the principles of justice and international law, adjustment or settlement of international disputes or situations which might lead to a breach of the peace;
- To develop friendly relations among nations based on respect for the principle of equal rights and self-determination of peoples, and to take other appropriate measures to strengthen universal peace;
- To achieve international co-operation in solving international problems of an economic, social, cultural, or humanitarian character, and in promoting and encouraging respect for human rights and for fundamental freedoms for all without distinction as to race, sex, language, or religion; and
- To be a centre for harmonizing the actions of nations in the attainment of these common ends.

34 "Dower may be regarded as consideration for connubial intercourse by way of analogy to the contract for sale."
The above observation has been made is which of the following cases?

1 Abdul Kadir Vs. Salima
2 Zobair Ahmed Vs. Jainandan Prasad
3 Rahana Khattun Vs. Iqtidar-uddin
4 Hamidunissa Bibi Vs. Zaheer Sheik

Ans. (1)

Exp. In the case of Abdul Kadir Vs. Salima, it was observed that "Dower may be regarded as consideration for connubial intercourse by way of analogy to the contract for sale." In the case, the court closely translated a passage in the Hedaya, and it no doubt entitles the wife to resist the claim of the husband for cohabitation with her by pleading the non-payment of her prompt dower, but it proceeds essentially upon the assumption that his right to put forward such claim is antecedent to the plea.

35 In which of the following cases did the Supreme Court of India strike down Section 303 IPC as unconstitutional?

1 Machhi Singh Vs. State of Punjab
2 Bachan Singh Vs. State of Punjab
3 Gian Kaur Vs. State of Punjab
4 Mithu Kaur Vs. State of Punjab

Ans. (4)

Exp. In Mithu Kaur Vs. State of Punjab the Supreme Court of India strike down Section 303 IPC as unconstitutional In Mithu V. State of Punjab, Supreme Court ruled that the mandatory death penalty is unconstitutional. It struck down Section 303 in IPC, which entailed a mandatory death sentence for a person who commits murder while serving a life term in another case.

36 The Cyber Regulations Appellate Tribunal Rule, 2000 has been passed under which Section of the IT Act, 2000?

1 Section 84 2 Section 85
3 Section 86 4 Section 87

Ans. (4)

Exp. The Cyber Regulations Appellate Tribunal Rule, 2000 has been passed under Section 87 of the IT Act, 2000. According to Section 87 (1) of IT Act 2000, The Central Government may, by notification in the Official Gazette and in the Electronic Gazette, make rules to carry out the provisions of this Act. Cyber Regulations Appellate Tribunals Rule, 2000 was established to aid Cyber Appellate Tribunal.

37 Which of the following Articles of Universal Declaration of Human Rights, 1948 deals with civil and political rights?

1 Articles 1 and 2 2 Articles 3 to 21
3 Articles 22 to 27 4 Articles 28 to 30

Ans. (2)

Exp. Article 3-21 of 1948 Universal Declaration of Human Rights talk about civil and political rights. These rights are a class of rights that protect individuals' freedom from infringement by governments, social organizations, and private individuals. They ensure one's entitlement to participate in the civil and political life of society and the state without discrimination or repression.

Civil rights include the ensuring of peoples' physical and mental integrity, life, and safety; protection from discrimination on grounds such as race, gender, sexual orientation, gender identity, national origin, color, age, political affiliation, ethnicity, religion, and disability.

Political rights include natural justice (procedural fairness) in law, such as the rights of the accused, including the right to a fair trial; due process; the right to seek redress or a legal remedy; and rights of participation in civil society and politics such as freedom of association, the right to assemble, the right to petition, the right of self-defence, and the right to vote.

38 Which of the following activities cannot be considered as relating to social responsibility under Section 135 of the Companies Act, 2013?

1 Amount spent on activities which only benefit the employees of the company
2 Amount spent to benefit people who are not economically backward
3 Amount spent on activities which only benefit the consumers of the organisation
4 Amount spent on activities which only benefit the suppliers of the organisation

Ans. (1)

Exp. Amount spent on activities which only benefit the employees of the company cannot be considered as relating to social responsibility under Section 135 of the Companies Act, 2013.

The CSR projects or programs or activities that benefit only the employees of the company and their families shall not be considered as CSR activities in accordance with section 135 of the Act. One-off events such as marathons/ awards/charitable contribution/ advertisement/ sponsorships of TV programmes etc would not be qualified as part of CSR expenditure. The company shall give preference to the local area and areas around where it operates, for spending the amount earmarked for Corporate Social Responsibility activities.

39 Which Article of the Indian Constitution states that "the state shall endeavour to secure for the citizens a Uniform Civil Code throughout the territory of India?"

1 Article 25 of the Constitution
2 Article 37 of the Constitution
3 Article 44 of the Constitution
4 Article 45 of the Constitution

Ans. (3)

Exp. Article 44 of Constitution of India in Part IV of DPSP (Directive Principles of State Policy) states that "The State shall endeavour to secure for the citizens a Uniform Civil Code throughout the territory of India."

The Uniform Civil Code (UCC) essentially calls for the formulation of one law for India, applicable to all religious communities in their personal matters such as marriage, divorce, inheritance, adoption etc.

40 Under which of the following Sections of Code of Civil Procedure (1908) did Indian courts recognise or derecognise the foreign decree of divorce?

1 Section 13 2 Section 12
3 Section 15 4 Section 16

Ans. (1)

Exp. Under Sections 13 of Code of Civil Procedure (CPC)(1908) Indian courts recognise or derecognise the foreign decree of divorce.

According to Section 13 of CPC, a foreign judgment shall be conclusive as to any matter thereby directly adjudicated upon between the same parties or between parties under whom they or any of them claim litigating under the same title except

(a) where it has not been pronounced by a Court of competent jurisdiction;
(b) where it has not been given on the merits of the case;
(c) where it appears on the face of the proceedings to be founded on an incorrect view of international law or a refusal to recognise the law of India in cases in which such law is applicable
(d) where the proceedings in which the judgment was obtained are opposed to natural justice
(e) where it has been obtained by fraud
(f) where it sustains a claim founded on a breach of any law in force in India.

41 Which of the following sections of the Hindu Adoption and Maintenance Act, 1956 deals with the 'rights of adoptive parents to dispose of their properties'?

1 Section 11 2 Section 12
3 Section 13 4 Section 14

Ans. (3)

Exp. Section 13 of the Hindu Adoption and Maintenance Act, 1956 deals with the 'rights of adoptive parents to dispose of their properties.

Section 13 of Hindu Adoption and Maintenance Act, 1956 states that, subject to any agreement to the contrary, an adoption does not deprive the adoptive father or mother of the power to dispose of his or her property by transfer inter vivos or by will.

42 Which one of the following is not a principle which is the very foundation of International Humanitarian Law and which must guide emergency humanitarian actions in armed conflicts?

1 Principle of Humanity
2 Principle of Impartiality
3 Principle of Neutrality
4 Principle of Self-determination

Ans. (4)

➲ *Exp.* Principle of Self-determination is not a principle which is the very foundation of International Humanitarian Law (IHL) which is the law of war or law of armed conflicts.

This principle stands on the virtue that people have the right to freely determine their political status and freely pursue their economic, social and cultural development. It is based on the right of people to decide upon its own political status or form of government, without outside influence.

Few principles on which very foundation of International Humanitarian Law is based on

- The distinction between civilians and combatants.
- The prohibition to attack those hors de combat (i.e., those not directly engaged in hostilities).
- The prohibition to inflict unnecessary suffering.
- The principle of necessity.
- The principle of proportionality.
- Principle of impartiality
- Principle of neutrality.

43 In which one of the following cases, it has been held that Section 9 of Civil Procedure Code, 1908, which enables a civil court to try all suits of civil nature, impliedly confers jurisdiction to apply the law of torts as principles of justice, equity and good conscience?

1 Union Carbide Corporation Vs. Union of India
2 Gujarat State Road Transport Corporation Vs. Ramanbhai Prabhatbhai
3 Rohtas Industries Ltd. Vs. Rohtas Industries Staff Union
4 Waghela Rajsanji Vs. Shekh Masludin

Ans. (1)

➲ *Exp.* In Union Carbide Corporation Vs. Union of India, the court said that Section 9 of CPC, 1908 enables a civil court to try all suits of civil nature & implies jurisdiction to apply the law of torts as principles of justice, equity and good conscience. This case is also known as the Bhopal Gas Tragedy case where the issue of absolute liability was raised.

44 Given below are two statements. One is labelled as Assertion (A) and the other is labelled as Reason (R).

Assertion (A) International Humanitarian Law (IHL) is the law that regulates the conduct of war (jus in bello). It is that branch of international law which seeks, to limit the efforts of armed conflicts by protecting persons who are not participating in hostilities and by restricting and regulating the means and methods of warfare available to combatants.

Reason (R) International Humanitarian Law (IHL) is inspired by considerations of humanity and the mitigation of human sufferings.

Codes

1 Both (A) and (R) are true and (R) is the correct explanation of (A)
2 Both (A) and (R) are true, but (R) is not the correct explanation of (A)
3 (A) is true, but (R) is false
4 (A) is false, but (R) is true

Ans. (1)

➲ *Exp.* Both (A) and (R) are true and (R) is the correct explanation of (A).

International Humanitarian Law (IHL) is the law that regulates the conduct of war (jus in bello). IHL is the branch of Human rights law which is applicable to international armed conflict. In absence of IHL the atrocities, cruelty and sufferings during the war will be limitless.

Reason (R) given in the question perfectly explains the assertion given as International Humanitarian Law (IHL) is inspired by the consideration of humanity, it regulates the conduct of war in such way that there will be a mitigation of human sufferings by protecting the interest of person who are not participating in hostilities.

45 Which of the following statements correctly reflects the cardinal principle, 'Actus non facit reum nisi means sit rea'?

1 Mens rea is an essential element of a crime and there cannot be a crime without mens rea
2 Criminal liability under Indian law always implies mens rea
3 To constitute a crime there must be actus reus and mens rea
4 Actus reus is not always necessary to constitute a crime

Ans. (3)

➲ *Exp.* The statement 'To constitute a crime there must be actus reus and mens rea' correctly reflects the cardinal principle, 'Actus non facit reum nisi mens sit rea'.

'Actus non facit reum nisi mens sit rea' means an act does not make anyone guilty unless there is a criminal intent or a guilty mind. We can also say any act to be illegal in nature must be done with a guilty mind. Thus, to convict the defendant, it must be proved that the criminal act was carried out with a criminal intent.

There are four elements which go to constitute a crime, which are

- Human Being.
- Mens rea or guilty intention.
- Actus reus or illegal act or omission.
- Injury to another human being.

46 Possession through an agent or servant is an example of

1 corporeal possession
2 incorporeal possession
3 mediate possession
4 immediate possession

Ans. (3)

➲ *Exp.* Possession through an agent or servant is an example of mediate possession. Mediate possession of an object is the possession of a thing through a mediator (middleman) like an agent, friend or servant or we can also say that possession held by one man through another is termed as mediate possession. It is also called indirect possession.

47 In which year the Commission on Status of Women was established by Economic and Social Council?

1 1946 2 1947 3 1948 4 1949

Ans. (1)

➲ *Exp.* The Commission on the Status of Women (CSW)was established by Economic and Social Council (ECOSOC) on 21st June, 1946. It is the principal global intergovernmental body exclusively dedicated to the promotion of gender equality and the empowerment of women.

48 Bayer Corporation V. Union of India, 2011 case is dealing on which subject matters?

1 Evergreening of patent
2 Grant and sealing of patent
3 Working of patenting process
4 Surrender and revocation of patent

Ans. (3)

➲ *Exp.* Bayer Corporation V. Union of India, 2011 case dealt with the working of the patenting process.

In this case, the Supreme court upheld the decision of the Intellectual Property Appellate Board and the Bombay High Court, sanctioning the grant of a compulsory license for Bayer's anti-cancer drug 'Nexavar'. Through this case, the Supreme Court also restored the uncertainty that was always attributed to the grant of Compulsory License in India.

49 The remedies for the violation of Sections 3 and 4 of the Competition Act have been laid down under

1 Section 26 2 Section 27
3 Section 42A 4 Section 43A

Ans. (2)

➲ *Exp.* The remedies for the violation of Section 3 and 4 of the Competition Act have been laid down under Section 27 of the Act.

Section 27 says that where after inquiry the Commission finds that any agreement referred to in Section 3 or action of an enterprise in a dominant position, is in contravention of Section 3 or Section 4, as the case may be, it may pass all or any of the following orders, namely :

(a) direct any enterprise or association of enterprises or person or association of persons, as the case may be, involved in such agreement, or abuse of dominant position, to discontinue and not to re-enter such agreement or discontinue such abuse of dominant position, as the case may be.
(b) impose such a penalty, as it may deem fit.
(c) award compensation to parties in accordance with the provisions contained in Section 34
(d) direct that the agreements shall stand modified to the extent and in the manner as may be specified in the order by the Commission;
(e) direct the enterprises concerned to abide by such other orders as the Commission may pass and comply with the directions, including payment of costs, if any.
(f) recommend to the Central Government for the division of an enterprise enjoying dominant position;
(g) pass such other orders as it may deem fit.

50 Judicial review of an administrative action means

1 review by the Parliament
2 review by the Government
3 review by the Legislative Assembly
4 review by the Judiciary

Ans. (4)

➲ *Exp.* Judicial review of an administrative action means review by the Judiciary.

Judicial review is the power of the Supreme Court and the High Courts to examine the constitutionality of the Acts of the Parliament and the state legislatures and executive orders both of the centre and state governments.

Judicial review is the power of courts to decide the validity of acts of the legislative and executive branches of government. If the courts decide that a legislative act is unconstitutional, it is nullified, and same goes with administrative action. The concept of judicial review has been taken from USA.

51 A servant collected money from the debtor of his master as authorised by him. The servant retained the money because it was due to him as wages. He commits

1 criminal breach of trust 2 theft
3 no offence 4 criminal misappropriation

Ans. (1)

➲ *Exp.* In the given case, the servant commits criminal breach of trust.

Section 405 of Indian Penal Code talks about criminal breach of trust, it says : Whoever, being in any manner entrusted with property, or with any dominion over property, dishonestly misappropriates or converts to his own use that property, or dishonestly uses or disposes of that property in violation of any direction of law prescribing the mode in which such trust is to be discharged, or of any legal contract, express or implied, which he has made touching the discharge of such trust, or wilfully suffers any other person so to do, commits "criminal breach of trust".

52 'We have to evolve new principles and lay down new norms which will adequately deal with new problems which arise in a highly industrialised society' was laid down in

1 Common Cause Vs. Union of India
2 MC Mehta Vs. Union of India
3 Invercargill City Council Vs. Hamlin
4 Union of India Vs. Sat Pal Dharam Vir

Ans. (2)

➲ *Exp.* In the case of MC Mehta V. Union of India, the court observed that 'We have to evolve new principles and lay down new norms which would adequately deal with the new problems which arise in a highly industrialised society.'

This case is also famously known as Shriram Industries Case. The court introduced a new "no fault" liability standard (absolute liability). An industry engaged in hazardous activities which poses a potential danger to health and safety of the persons working and residing near these establishments owes an absolute and non-delegable duty to the community to ensure that there should be no harm to anyone. It also held that as new situations arise, the law has to be evolved in order to meet the challenge of such new situations. Law cannot afford to remain static.

53 In which section of the Partnership Act it is laid down that there can be a partnership in a single or particular business venture?

1 Section 8 2 Section 9
3 Section 10 4 Section 11

Ans. (1)

➲ *Exp.* Section 8 of Indian Partnership Act talks about Particular Partnership which means a person can become a partner with another person in a single or particular business ventures or undertakings. In other words, a partnership can be formed for carrying on continuous business, or it can be formed for one particular venture or undertaking. If the partnership is formed only to carry out one business venture or to complete one undertaking such a partnership is known as a Particular partnership.

54 Given below are two statements. One is labelled as Assertion (A) and the other is labelled as Reason (R).

Assertion (A) Under the Indian Constitution, an Amendment Bill passed by both Houses of Parliament by required majority shall be presented to the President who shall give his assent and there upon the Constitution shall stand amended.

Reason (R) The President is bound to give his assent to the Bill.

Codes

1 Both (A) and (R) are right and (R) is the correct explanation of (A)
2 Both (A) and (R) are right, but (R) is not the correct explanation of (A)
3 (A) is right, but (R) is wrong
4 (A) is wrong, but (R) is right

Ans. (1)

➲ *Exp.* Both (A) and (R) are right and (R) is the correct explanation of (A)

According to Article 368(2) of Constitution of India, an amendment to Constitution may be initiated only by the introduction of a Bill for the purpose in either House of Parliament, and when the Bill is passed in each House by a majority of the total membership of that House present and voting, it shall be presented to the President who shall give his assent to the Bill and thereupon the Constitution shall stand amended in accordance with the terms of the Bill.

55 Regulation of Access to Biological Diversity is described under which one of the following Chapters of the Biological Diversity Act, 2002?

1 Chapter I 2 Chapter II
3 Chapter III 4 Chapter IV

Ans. (2)

➲ *Exp.* Chapter II of Biological Diversity Act, 2002 talks about Regulation of Access to Biological Diversity.

This act talks about conservation of biological diversity, sustainable use of its components and fair and equitable sharing of the benefits arising out of the use of biological resources, knowledge and for matters connected therewith or incidental thereto.

56 An accident is 'one out of ordinary course of things, something so unusual as not to be looked for by a person of ordinary prudence', is said to be

1 negligence
2 inevitable accident
3 act of god
4 damnum sine injuria

Ans. (2)

➲ *Exp.* An accident is 'one out of ordinary course of things, something so unusual as not to be looked for by a person of ordinary prudence', is said to be inevitable accident.

An inevitable accident is one of the general defences against tortious liability. Inevitable accident is accident that was not intended, and which, under all the circumstances, could not have been foreseen or prevented by the exercise of reasonable precautions.

57 Given below are two statements, one is labelled as Assertion (A) and the other is labelled as Reason (R).

Assertion (A) The Council of Ministers is the hub of the Parliamentary form of government.

Reason (R) The Council of Ministers (Cabinet) is constituted from the majority party.

Codes

1 Both (A) and (R) are right and (R) is the correct explanation of (A)
2 Both (A) and (R) are right, but (R) is not the correct explanation of (A)
3 (A)is right, but (R) is wrong
4 (A) is wrong, but (R) is right

Ans. (2)

➲ *Exp.* Both (A) and (R) are right, but (R) is not the correct explanation of (A).

The Council of Ministers is the hub of the Parliamentary form of government. The Council of Ministers aid and advise the Prime Minister in the exercise of his functions. Even the Cabinet members are generally chosen from the Council of Ministers itself. They are, in the real sense, the hub of the Parliamentary form of government. Thus, the Assertion is correct.

The Council of Ministers (Cabinet) is constituted from the majority party. This statement is correct, however, it does not prescribe the reason for considering the Council of Ministers as the hub of Parliamentary form of government. It is the role of the Council that makes it the hub of the Parliamentary system. Thus, though R is correct, it is not the right explanation of A.

58 'Uninsured vehicles are also within the scope of Section 165 of the Motor Vehicles Act' was held in

1 LIC of India Vs. Raj Kumari Mittal (1985)
2 Kamal Kusha Vs. Kripal Singh (1988)
3 Permanand Thakur Vs. Commissioner, Coal Mines (1988)
4 New India Assurance Co. Ltd. Vs. Nakul Gurung (2010)

Ans. *(3)*

Exp. 'Uninsured vehicles are also within the scope of Section 165 of the Motor Vehicles Act' was held in the case of Permanand Thakur Vs. Commissioner, Coal Mines (1988).

The primary question which arose in this case was whether the Motor Accident Claims Tribunal constituted under Section 165 of the Act had the jurisdiction to adjudicate upon the claim of compensation in respect of accidents involving the death or bodily injury to a person arising out of the use of a motor vehicle not covered by a policy of insurance. The court held that an uninsured vehicle is also covered under the meaning of motor vehicle under Section 165.

59 In which of the following cases the Supreme Court held that 'the Audi Alteram Partem rule, in essence enforces the equality clause in Article 14 and it is applicable not only to quasi-judicial bodies but also to administrative order adversely affecting the party in question'?

1 UP Warehousing Corporation Vs. Vijay Narain
2 Delhi Transport Corporation Vs. DTC Majdoor Union
3 A K Gopalan Vs. State of Madras
4 Gullapalli Nageshwar Rao Vs. APSRTC

Ans. *(2)*

Exp. In Delhi Transport Corporation Vs. DTC Majdoor Union case, constitutional validity of the right of the employer to terminate the services of permanent employees without holding any inquiry in certain circumstances was questioned. The SC in this case held, that "the Audi Alteram Partem rule, in essence enforces the equality clause in Article 14 and it is applicable not only to quasi-judicial bodies but also to administrative orders adversely affecting the parties in question."

The cardinal rule of justice administration envisaged in the term 'Audi Altrem Partem' which means no one should be condemned unheard. In simpler words, it means "let the other side be heard as well". This rule ensures free and impartial administrative process.

60 The NGT Act, 2010 contains how many schedules?

1 One
2 Two
3 Three
4 Four

Ans. *(3)*

Exp. The NGT Act 2010, contains three schedules and talks about amendment to certain enactments.

NGT act provides effective and expeditious disposal of cases relating to environmental protection and conservation of forest and other natural resources including enforcement of any legal right relating to environment and giving relief and compensation for damages for the matters connected therewith or thereto.

61 The principle 'Restitution stops where repayment begins' can be applied against

1 an alien enemy only
2 minors only
3 lunatics and idiots only
4 an incapable person

Ans. *(2)*

Exp. The principle 'Restitution stops where repayment begins' can be applied against minors only.

If a minor wrongfully obtains an undue advantage from the other party and the same is traceable and in his possession, the minor can be compelled under this doctrine to restore the benefit so received. However, if the minor has sold the goods or converted them, he cannot be compelled to pay the value of such goods because it will amount to enforcing a void contract. Thus, it follows that the doctrine is not applicable to money for it is not possible to identify the money and ask a minor to return the exact same.

62 Which one of the following is not correct?

1 Judicial review tends to elevate the judiciary to the rank of super legislature
2 The scope of judicial review is limited as it emphasises on the 'procedure established by law' rather than 'due procedure of law'
3 Judicial review is indispensable to a federal system of government
4 Judicial review does not include judicial competence to review executive enforcement of legislative enactments

Ans. *(4)*

Exp. Statement 4 is incorrect as it says Judicial review does not include judicial competence to review executive enforcement of legislative enactments instead judicial review includes judicial competence to review executive enforcement of legislative enactments.

63 Which of the following is correct?

1 Administrative Law is a branch of Public Law and is only a part of Constitutional Law. It cannot control the Constitutional Law
2 Administrative Law is a branch of Private Law
3 Administrative Law is independent to the Constitutional Law
4 Administrative Law is neither the branch of Public Law nor of Private Law but a part of Constitutional Law

Ans. *(1)*

Exp. The statement 'Administrative law is a branch of public law and is only a part of constitutional law. It cannot control the constitutional law', is correct.

Administrative law is the body of law that governs the activities of administrative agencies of the government. Activities of government agencies include rule making, adjudication, and the enforcement of a regulatory agenda. Administrative law is considered a branch of public law. Constitutional law regulates those that do the delegating, i.e. institutions whose powers are not delegated but are, as it is sometimes put, inherent or original. Administrative law regulates institutions whose powers are delegated.

64 How many core principles are laid down in United Nations Declaration of Permanent Sovereignty over Natural Resources?

1 Five core principles
2 Six core principles
3 Seven core principles
4 Eight core principles

Ans. *(4)*

Exp. United Nations Declaration of Permanent Sovereignty has eight core principles. This declaration conducts a full survey of the status of permanent sovereignty over natural wealth and resources as a basic constituent of the right to self-determination, with recommendations, where necessary, for its strengthening, and decided further that, in the conduct of the full survey of the status of the permanent sovereignty of people and nations over their natural wealth and resources.

These principles are set out in eight articles concerning, inter alia, the exploration, development and disposition of natural resources, nationalization and expropriation, foreign investment, the sharing of profits, and other related issues.

65 In which one of the following cases, the Supreme Court held that 'the federalism in India, is not a matter of administrative convenience, but one of principle'?

1 SR Bommai Vs. Union of India (1994)
2 Raja Ram Pal Vs. Hon'ble Speaker, Lok Sabha (2007)
3 Madras Bar Association Vs. Union of India (2014)
4 State of West Bengal Vs. Committee for Protection of Democratic Rights, West Bengal (2010)

Ans. *(1)*

Exp. SR Bommai Vs. Union of India was a landmark judgment where the Supreme Court held that 'federalism in India, is not a matter of administrative convenience, but one of the principles.' In this case, the Court discussed at length the provisions of Article 356 of the Constitution of India and other related issues. This case had a huge impact on Centre-State Relations.

66 Which of the following statement/statements is/are not correct?

I. The declaration of national emergency on the ground of 'Armed Rebellion' was inserted by the Constitutional (42nd Amendment) Act, 1976.
II. President shall not issue a proclamation under Clause (1) Article 352 unless the decision of the Union Cabinet (the Prime Minister and his Council of Ministers) is communicated to him in writing.
III. A resolution approving the proclamation of national emergency must be passed by special majority.
IV. A proclamation of emergency once approved by the Parliament shall remain in force until the emergency ceases.

Select the correct answer from the codes given below

1 Only I
2 I and IV
3 II, III and IV
4 All of these

Ans. *(2)*

Exp. Statements I and IV are incorrect.

The declaration of national emergency on the ground of 'Armed rebellion' was inserted by the Constitutional (44 Amendment) Act, 1978 and not by the 42nd Amendment.

A Proclamation of Emergency once approved by the Parliament shall remain in force for a further period of 6 months unless revoked earlier.

67 The Preamble to Agreement on Trade Related Aspects of Intellectual Property Rights (TRIPS) lays down

I. public policy objectives of national system.
II. special needs of the least developed countries.
III. resolving IP disputes through multilateral procedures.
IV. establishing mutually supportive relationship between WTO and WIPO.

Which of the following statement(s) given above is/are true?

1 Only I is true
2 Only I and II are true
3 Only I, II and III are true
4 I, II, III and IV are true

Ans. *(4)*

Exp. All the above mentioned statements are true as Preamble of TRIPS contain all of them.

The Preamble to Agreement on Trade Related Aspects of Intellectual Property Rights (TRIPS) lays down
- public policy objectives of national system.
- special needs of the least developed countries.
- resolving IP disputes through multilateral procedures.
- establishing mutually supportive relationship between WTO and WIPO.

The Agreement on Trade-Related Aspects of Intellectual Property Rights (TRIPS) is an international legal agreement between all the member nations of the World Trade Organization (WTO). The TRIPS Agreement is a minimum standards agreement, which allows Members to provide more extensive protection of intellectual property if they so wish. Members are left free to determine the appropriate method of implementing the provisions of the Agreement within their own legal system and practice.

68 'A Statutory Board conducting examinations is not a service provider and does not offer services to candidates while conducting an examination' was held by the Supreme Court in

1 Buddhist Mission Dental College and Hospital Vs. Bhupesh Khurana (2009)
2 Bihar School Examination Board Vs. Suresh Prasad Sinha (2009)
3 Madan Kumar Singh Vs. District Magistrate, Sultanpur (2009)
4 UT Chandigarh Administration Vs. Amarjeet Singh (2009)

Ans. *(2)*

Exp. The above-mentioned statement was observed by Supreme court in Bihar School Examination Board Vs. Suresh Prasad Sinha (2009).

In this case court held that, Board is not a 'service provider' and a student who takes an examination is not a 'consumer' hence, 'A Statutory Board conducting examinations is not a service provider and does not offer services to candidates while conducting an examination'.

69 "If one's artistic expressions are synonymous with one's personality, then they are deserving of protection just as much as the physical person."
The above observation is true about which theory of intellectual property?

1 Moral desert theory 2 Personality theory
3 Utilitarian theory 4 Libertian theory

Ans. *(2)*

Exp. The above given observation is true about Personality theory.

Personality theory is a principle of intellectual property that gives importance to the point of view of the individual inventor, author, or artist rather than that of society as a whole while analyzing intellectual-property rights. It holds that personal expression is a form of self- actualization that gives the creator inalienable moral rights in the creations.

70 The Sapinda relationship on the line of ascent under the Hindu Law extends

1 three degree through the father and two degree through the mother
2 four degree through the father and three degree through the mother
3 five degree through the father and three degree through the mother
4 seven degree through the father and five degree through the mother

Ans. *(3)*

Exp. The Sapinda relationship on the line of ascent under the Hindu Law extends five degree through the father and three degree through the mother.

Section 3(f) of Hindu Marriage Act mentioned Sapinda Relationship. Sapinda relationships are prohibited under Hindu Marriage Act. A sapinda is someone who is within or has a common ancestor relative within three generations above you on your mother's side of the family and within or has a common ancestor relative within five generations above you on your father's side of the family.

71 'Public health, sanitation conservancy and solid waste management' is inserted to the Schedule of the Constitution by which of the following Constitutional Amendments?

1 42nd Constitutional Amendment
2 44th Constitutional Amendment
3 73rd Constitutional Amendment
4 74th Constitutional Amendment

Ans. *(4)*

Exp. Twelfth schedule was added by the 74th Amendment Act of 1992. 18 items covered under the twelfth schedule of the Indian Constitution including Public Health sanitation, conservancy and solid waste management.

72 Which of the following is an essential condition in Marz-ul-Maut?

1 A malady which makes it impossible for the patient to move
2 It must be continued for more than a year
3 There must be apprehension of death
4 A malady which causes problem with heart

Ans. *(3)*

Exp. An apprehension of death is an essential condition in Marz-ul-Maut.

Marz-ul-Maut means death-bed gift. It is based on the principle of mortis causa meaning in contemplation of approaching death. The rules concerning Marz-ul-Maut inculcate the ideas of the gift as well as will.

In Marz-ul-maut there should be genuine apprehension of death. In case a person does not die, the will made, will be null and void. Mere apprehension of death due to old age is not a ground for Marz-ul-Maut. Thus, a man dying from natural causes due to old age does not come under the purview of this concept.

73 The accused at the time of committing the act because of unsoundness of mind is incapable of knowing

I. the nature of the act.
II. that the act is wrong or contrary to law.
III. that the act is unethical and wrong.
IV. that the act is morally wrong but not contrary to law.

To claim the benefit of Section 84 of IPC which of the above needs to be proved? Give the correct answer

1 I and IV 2 I and II
3 II and III 4 III and IV

Ans. (2)

Exp. The accused at the time of committing the act because of unsoundness of mind is incapable of knowing the nature of the act and that act is wrong or contrary to law.

According to Section 84 of Indian Penal Code, nothing is an offence which is done by a person who, at the time of doing it, by reason of unsoundness of mind, is incapable of knowing the nature of the act, or that he is doing what is either wrong or contrary to law.

74 Holbeck Hotel Ltd. V. Scarborough Borough Council is a leading case on

1 negligence 2 nuisance
3 trespass 4 defamation

Ans. (2)

Exp. Holbeck Hotel Ltd. Vs. Scarborough Borough Council is a leading case on the tort of nuisance.

In this case, Stuart Smith LJ observed: "the law must take account of the fact that the occupier on whom the duty is cast has, ex hypothesi, had this hazard thrust upon him through no seeking or fault of his own. His interest, and his resources, whether physical or material, may be of a very modest character either in relation to the magnitude of the hazard, or as compared with those of his threatened neighbour. A rule which required him in such unsought circumstances in his neighbour's interest a physical effort of which he is not capable, or an excessive expenditure of money, would be unenforceable or unjust."

75 The institution of ombudsman was firstly initiated in the year 1809 by

1 France 2 USA
3 UK 4 Sweden

Ans. (4)

Exp. Institution of Ombudsman was firstly initiated in the year 1809 by Sweden.

The word 'Ombudsman' originated from the Swedish word 'ombuds' that means an officer or commissioner. In its special sense, it is a quasi-judicial administrative authority i.e., the official who has the duty of investigating and reporting to Parliament on citizens complaints against the public servants or public agencies. He performs the duty of inquiry and investigation to deal with the specific complaints from the public against administrative injustice and maladministration.

76 In which of the following cases the Supreme Court said that Governor cannot exercise his power of suspension of the sentence under Article 213 of the Constitution of India, for the period when the Supreme Court is seized of the case. The order of the Governor could only operate until the matter became subjudice in the Supreme Court and it becomes so on the filing of the petition for special leave to appeal?

1 Satpal Dang Vs. State of Punjab
2 DC Wadhwa Vs. State of Bihar
3 KM Nanavati Vs. State of Bombay
4 AK Roy Vs. Union of India

Ans. (3)

Exp. In the case of KM Nanavati Vs. State of Bombay it was observed that Governor cannot exercise his power of suspension of the sentence under Article 213 of the Constitution of India, for the period when the Supreme Court is seized of the case. The order of the Governor could only operate until the matter became subjudice in the Supreme Court and it became so on the filing of the petition for special leave to appeal.

In this case, the court held that the conduct of the accused clearly shows that the murder was a deliberate and calculated one and the facts of the case do not attract the provisions of Exceptions 1 of Sec 300 of IPC as the accused also failed to bring the case under General Exception of IPC by adducing evidence. As a result, the conviction of the accused under Section 302 of IPC was upheld and he was sentenced to imprisonment for life.

77 Every offence punishable under Section 147 of the Negotiable Instruments Act, 1818 is

1 compoundable 2 non-compoundable
3 cognisable 4 Both 2 and 3

Ans. (1)

Exp. Every offence punishable under Section 147 of the Negotiable Instruments Act, 1818 is compoundable. Compoundable offences are those offences where, the complainant (one who has filed the case, i.e. the victim), enter into a compromise, and agrees to have the charges dropped against the accused. Section 147 of Negotiable Instruments Act says that Notwithstanding anything contained in the Code of Criminal Procedure, 1973 (2 of 1974), every offence punishable under this Act shall be compoundable.

78 Match List I with List II.

	List I	List II
A.	Date and year of establishment of United Nations	I. 2nd May, 1981
B.	The first security council came into being	II. 1st January, 1992
C.	Paris Declaration on Sanctions against South Africa	III. 12th January, 1946
D.	Mr Boutros Boutros-Ghali took over as Secretary General of the UN	IV. 24th October, 1945

Select the correct answer from the codes given below

	A	B	C	D		A	B	C	D
1	I	II	III	IV	2	III	I	IV	II
3	IV	II	III	I	4	IV	III	I	II

Ans. *(4)*

➲ *Exp.* The correct matching is A-IV, B-III, C-I, D-II.

Date and year of establishment of the United Nations is *24th October, 1945.* United Nations Day, on 24th October, marks the anniversary of the day in 1945 when the UN Charter entered into force. UN Day, celebrated every year, offers the opportunity to amplify our common agenda and reaffirm the purposes and principles of the UN Charter that have guided us for the past 76 years.

The first security council came into being on *12th January, 1946.* The UN Charter gives the Security Council primary responsibility for maintaining international peace and security. The Council may convene at any time, whenever peace is threatened. In contrast to the decisions made by the General Assembly, all Member States are obligated under the UN Charter to carry out the Security Council's decisions.

Paris Declaration on sanctions against South Africa came into force on *2nd May, 1981.* The apartheid policies of South Africa and ways to bring them to an end remained under active consideration during 1981 in several United Nations bodies (see below). The General Assembly continued to urge the imposition of mandatory sanctions and the Security Council denounced South Africa's bantustanization policy.

Mr. Boutros Boutros-Ghali took over as Secretary General Of UN on *1st January, 1992.* He was an Egyptian politician and diplomat who was the sixth Secretary-General of the United Nations from January 1992 to December 1996.

79 'Cyber security' according to the IT Act, 2000 means

1 a device and collection of devices, including input and output support devices and excluding calculations which are not programmable and capable of being used
2 any electronic, magnetic, optical or other high speed data processing device or system which performs logical, arithmetic and memory functions by manipulation of electronic, magnetic or optical impulse
3 protecting information, equipment, devices, computer, computer resources, communication device and information stored therein from unauthorised access, use, disclosure, disruption, modification or destruction
4 affixing with its grammatical variations and cognate expressions means adoption of any methodology or procedure by a person for the purpose of authenticating an electronic record

Ans. *(3)*

➲ *Exp.* Section 2(1) (nb) of IT Act, 2000 talks about "cyber security" and it means protecting information, equipment, devices computer, computer resource, communication device and information stored therein from unauthorised access, use, disclosure, disruption, modification or destruction.

80 'A legal person is any subject matter other than a human being to which law attributes personality', is statement of

1 Blackstone   2 Salmond
3 Holland   4 Bentham

Ans. *(2)*

➲ *Exp.* 'A legal person is any subject matter other than a human being to which law attributes personality', is statement of Salmond.

According to Salmond, a legal person is any subject matter other than a human being to which law attributes personality. It includes an object, a mass of property, an institution, a group of human beings etc. Law treats them as right and duty bearing units or entities likes a natural person. It is by a fiction of law that they are treated as persons. The law in creating legal persons personifies some real thing or object and then confers upon it a fictitious personality. The former can be called the corpus and the latter the animus of the legal personality.

81 "Decision making process of those authorities being transparent must result in a reasoned conclusion which is reflective of a due application of mind to the diverse concerns arising from a project such as the present." This has been observed regarding Environment Impact Assessment Law in which of the following cases?

1 Utkarsh Mandal Vs. Union of India
2 Deepak Kumar Vs. State of Haryana
3 Gram Panchayat Navlakh Umbre Vs. Union of India
4 Tehri Bandh Virodhi Sangharsh Samiti Vs. State of UP

Ans. *(3)*

➲ *Exp.* In case of Gram Panchayat Navlakh Umbre Vs. Union of India, the above-mentioned observation was made regarding Environment Impact Assessment Law.

Environmental Impact Assessment (EIA) is a process of evaluating the likely environmental impacts of a proposed project or development, taking into account inter-related socio-economic, cultural and human-health impacts, both beneficial and adverse. In 1994, for the first time under the Environment Protection Act, 1986, the EIA notification was formulated in India.

It made environmental clearance mandatory for expansion, modernisation and setting up of new projects.

82 Which of the following are the chief exponents of the 'Theory of Consent' regarding basis of international law?

1 Anzilotti, Triepel, Oppenheim
2 Starke, Smith, Brierly
3 Fawett, Jellinck, Pollock
4 Kelson, Hart, Edward Collins

Ans. *(1)*

Exp. Anzilloti, Triepel, Oppenheim are the chief exponents of 'Theory of Consent' regarding basis of international law.

Theory of consent says "Common consent" is the basis of international law as a legal system. The common consent is not consent to particular rules but to the express or tacit consent of states to the body of rules comprising international law as a whole at any particular point of time. The common consent to internationally valid rules regarding important matters such as international civil aviation, the use of international water bodies.

83 Which of the following articles provides coverage for the intervention in domestic jurisdiction for the enforcement of human right?

1 Article 2(5) of UN Charter
2 Article 2(6) of UN Charter
3 Article 2(7) of UN Charter
4 Article 2(8) of UN Charter

Ans. (3)

Exp. Article 2(7) of UN Charter provides coverage for the intervention in domestic jurisdiction for the enforcement of human right.

Article 2 (7) states that the United Nations has no authority to intervene in matters which are within the domestic jurisdiction of any State, while this principle shall not prejudice the application of enforcement measures under Chapter VII of the Charter. Chapter VII talks about action with respect to threats to the peace, breaches of the peace, and acts of aggression.

84 Which of the following actions can be taken when an issue is made under the provisions of Section 42 of the Companies Act, 2013?

1 An advertisement can be issued in a local newspaper having city coverage
2 The money payable towards subscription can be received in cash
3 The share can be allotted within sixty days of the date of offer
4 The offer can be made to a maximum of fifty people

Ans. (4)

Exp. When an issue is made under the provisions of Section 42 of the Companies Act, 2013 the offer can be made to a maximum of fifty people.

According to Section 42(2) of Companies Act 2013, A private placement shall be made only to a select group of persons who have been identified by the Board whose number shall not exceed fifty or such higher number as may be prescribed [excluding the qualified institutional buyers and employees of the company being offered securities under a scheme of employees stock option in terms of provisions of clause (b) of sub-section (1) of section 62], in a financial year subject to such conditions as may be prescribed.

85 Which of the following provisions of the Indian Constitution have been extended to Jammu and Kashmir state by Presidential Order?

I. Provisions relating to freedom of trade, commerce and intercourse, services and citizenship.
II. Provisions relating to elections.
III. Provision relating to financial emergency under Article 360 of the Constitution of India.
IV. Power of High Courts to issue writs for "Any other purpose".

Select the correct answer from the codes given below

1 Only I 2 III and IV
3 I and II 4 All of these

Ans. (3)

Exp. Statement I and II contain the provisions of the Indian Constitution that have been extended to Jammu and Kashmir state by Presidential Order.

Article 370(1)(d) states that other provisions of the Constitution can be made applicable to J&K with such "modifications as the President may by order specify. Provisions relating to freedom of trade, commerce, intercourse services and citizenship and provision relating to elections have been extended to Jammu and Kashmir state by Presidential Order.

86 Which of the following is not a constituent of tort?

1 Wrongful act 2 Damage
3 Remedy 4 Mens rea

Ans. (4)

Exp. Mensrea is not a constituent of tort. There are three constituents of tort:

- *Wrongful Act :* There must be a wrongful act committed by a person, that is, the defendant.
- *Legal Damage :* The wrongful act must give rise to legal damage to a person, that is, the plaintiff.
- *Legal Remedy :* The wrongful act must be of such a nature so as to give a rise to legal remedy in the form of an action for damages.

87 The Sustainable Development Goals (SDGs) committed to provide

I. universal access to affordable, reliable and modern energy services.
II. improving the share of renewable energy.
III. doubling of energy efficiency by 2030.
IV. protection of ocean and wetland.

Select the correct answer from the codes given below

1 I, II and III are true
2 I, III and IV are true
3 II, III and IV are true
4 I, II and IV are true

Ans. (1)

Exp. Statements I, II and III are true with respect to Sustainable Development Goals (SDGs).

The Sustainable Development Goals (SDGs) are committed to provide universal access to affordable, reliable and modern energy services, improving the share of renewable energy and doubling of energy efficiency by 2030.

The concept of Sustainable Development was described by the 1987 Brundtland Commission Report as "development that meets the needs of the present without compromising the ability of future generations to meet their own needs".

Statement IV is incorrect because protection of ocean and wetlands is dealt with under Agenda 21 of the United Nations Conference on Environment and Development ("the Earth Summit").

88 Who among the following has defined jurisprudence as "the knowledge of things divine and human, the science of right and wrong?"

1 Blackstone 2 Hobbes
3 Salmond 4 Ulpian

Ans. (4)

Exp. The Roman Jurist Ulpian defined jurisprudence as "the knowledge of things divine and human, the science of right and wrong". He mainly emphasized on observing the surrounding circumstances and then to come to a conclusion of how nature works to prevail just and unjust.

89 UN Commissioner for human rights is appointed by

1 General Assembly
2 Security Council
3 Secretary General
4 Human Rights Council

Ans. (3)

Exp. The Secretary General appoints the UN Commissioner for Human rights on the approval of the General Assembly. On 1st September, 2018 Michelle Bachelet assumed her functions as the United Nations High Commissioner for Human Rights. The Office of the High Commissioner for Human Rights was established in 1993 and Ms. Bachelet is the seventh Commissioner.

90 Macleods Pharmaceuticals Ltd. V. Tidal Laboratories Pvt. Ltd. (2011) is a case on which subject of intellectual property rights?

1 Patent 2 Trademark
3 Design 4 Geographical indications

Ans. (2)

Exp. Macleods Pharmaceuticals Ltd. V. Tidal Laboratories Pvt. Ltd (2011) case deals with Trademark.

In this case, the Plaintiffs were seeking an injunction from the court to restrain the defendant from using the impugned trademark named 'Rabemase' or any other mark deceptively similar to the plaintiff's trademark which is 'Rabemac'.

91 'Right to Environment' discourse includes

I. Right to Health
II. Right to Sanitation
III. Right to Clean Technology
IV. Right to Free Speech

Select the correct answer from the codes given below

1 I, II and III are true
2 II, III and IV are true
3 I, III and IV are true
4 I and II are true whereas III and IV are false

Ans. (1)

Exp. Right to Environment falls under the ambit of Right to Life under Article 21, a Fundamental Right. It includes:

1. Right to Health
2. Right to Sanitation
3. Right to Clean Technology.

Right to Free Speech will not come under the ambit of Article 21 as it is covered under the Fundamental Freedoms given under Article 19.

92 Which of the following statement/statements is/are correct?

I. WTO was established as a result of the culmination of Uruguay Round of GATT.
II. The new World Trade Organisation (WTO) came into effect on 1st January, 1995.
III. At the time of establishment, WTO had 88 members.
IV. The 7th Ministerial Conference of WTO was held in Marrakesh (Morocoo) from 30th November to 2nd December, 2008.

Select the correct answer from the codes given below

1 Only I 2 II and III
3 I and II 4 All of these

Ans. (3)

Exp. Statement I and II are correct.

World Trade Organisation (WTO) was established after the Uruguay Round of GATT. The new WTO came into effect on 1st January 1995.

Statement III and IV are incorrect as World Trade Organization (WTO), came into force on 1st January 1995 with 128 original Members.

Also the 7th Session of the WTO Ministerial Conference took place in Geneva, Switzerland, from 30th November to 2nd December 2009.

93 X, with the intention to cause miscarriage administered a drug to a pregnant lady, Y. The child in the womb died. X is guilty of

1 murder
2 culpable homicide not amounting to murder
3 no offence
4 causing miscarriage

Ans. (4)

Exp. In the given case, X is guilty of causing miscarriage. According to Section 312 of Indian Penal Code, whoever voluntarily causes a woman with child to miscarry, shall, if such miscarriage be not caused in good faith for the purpose of saving the life of the woman, be punished with imprisonment of either description for a term which may extend to three years, or with fine, or with both; and, if the woman be quick with child, shall be punished with imprisonment of either description for a term which may extend to seven years, and shall also be liable to fine.

94 "Nobody can be above the institution which he is supposed to serve. He is merely the creature of the institution, he can exist only if the institution exists. To protect the individual as mighter than the Constitution would be grave injustice." In which of the following cases the Supreme Court, through Chief Justice Sikri has observed this?

1 SS Dhannoa Vs. Union of India
2 TN Seshan Vs. Union of India
3 In Presidential Reference, 2000
4 AC Jose Vs. Sivan Pillai

Ans. (2)

Exp. The the case of TN Seshan Vs. Union of India, the Chief Justice Sikri observed that"Nobody can be above the institution which he is supposed to serve. He is merely the creature of the institution, he can exist only if the institution exists. To protect the individual as mighter than the Constitution would be grave injustice." This case revolved around Article 324 that deals with the Election Commission.

Two issues were to be decided in this case :

- Whether the appointment of the other election commissioners was intra-vires the constitution of India;
- The constitutional validity of the Ordinance and thereafter the Act, and the orders thereto.

95 Chandra Vs. Suresh AIR 1971 Delhi 208 deals with

1 maintenance
2 custody of children
3 Hindu undivided family
4 decree of judicial separation

Ans. (4)

Exp. Case of Chandra Vs. Suresh AIR 1917 Delhi 208 deals with decree of judicial separation.

Section 10 of the Hindu Marriage Act, 1955 provides the Judicial Separation for both the spouse, those who are married under the Hindu Marriage Act, 1955. They can claim the relief of Judicial Separation by filing a petition. Once the order is passed, they are not bound to have cohabitation.

96 Match List I with List II.

List I	List II
A. Fighting by two or more persons in public place	I. Abetment
B. Intentional aiding in commission of an offence	II. Sedition
C. Violence is caused by five or more persons	III. Affray
D. Offence committed against state by words, signs or visible representation	IV. Riot

Select the correct answer from the codes given below

Codes

	A	B	C	D		A	B	C	D
1	III	II	IV	I	2	III	I	IV	II
3	IV	III	II	I	4	I	IV	II	III

Ans. (2)

Exp. The correct matching is A-III, B-I, C-IV, D-II.

Fighting by two or more persons in public place is related to the offence of Affray. Section 159 of IPC states that when two or more persons, by fighting in a public place, disturb the public peace, they are said to "commit an affray"

Intentional aiding in commission of an offence is related to offence of Abetment. The definition of Abetment under Section 107, IPC requires a person to abet the commission of an offence. This abetment may occur in any of the three methods that the provision prescribes.

Violence is caused by five or more persons is linked with the offence of Riot. Section 146 of IPC states that whenever force or violence is used by an unlawful assembly, or by any member thereof, in prosecution of the common object of such assembly, every member of such assembly is guilty of the offence of rioting.

Offence committed against state by words, sign or visible representation is related to the offence of Sedition. Section 124 A of IPC defines Sedition in the following words : "Whoever, by words, either spoken or written, or by signs, or by visible representation, or otherwise, brings or attempts to bring into hatred or contempt, or excites or attempts to excite disaffection towards, the Government established by law in India, shall be punished with imprisonment for life, to which fine may be added, or with imprisonment which may extend to three years, to which fine may be added, or with fine."

97 Given below are two statements, one is labelled as Assertion (A) and the other is labelled as Reason (R).

Assertion (A) Article 38 of the statue of International Court of Justice lists International Conventions, whether general or particular, establishing rules expressly recognised by the contesting states as the first source of international law.

Reason (R) In modern period, international treaties are the most important sources of international law.

Codes

1 Both (A) and (R) are correct and (R) is the correct explanation of (A)
2 Both (A) and (R) are correct, but (R) is not the correct explanation of (A)
3 (A) is correct, but (R) is wrong
4 (A) is wrong, but (R) is correct

Ans. *(1)*

Exp. Both A and R are correct and R is the correct explanation of A.

Article 38 of the Statute of International Court of Justice lists International Conventions, whether general or particular, establishing rules expressly recognised by the contesting states as the first source of international law. The term "international conventions", concentrates upon treaties as a source of contractual obligation but also acknowledges the possibility of a state expressly accepting the obligations of a treaty to which it is not formally a party. Thus, the Assertion is true.

In the modern period, international treaties are the most important sources of international law. This has also been mentioned in Article 38 (1)(a) and thus, is the right explanation for the Assertion.

98 In which of the cases did Supreme Court hold that a relationship in the nature of marriage under the Domestic Violence Act, 2005 must also fulfill some basic criteria, merely spending weekends together or one right would not make it a domestic relationship?

1 Payal Katara Vs. Supt. Nari Niketan and other
2 D Velusamy Vs. D Patchaiammal
3 Bharati Matha and others Vs. R Vijaya Ranganathan and other
4 S Khushboo Vs. Kanniammal and others

Ans. *(4)*

Exp. In the case of D Velusamy Vs. D Patchaiammal, the court held that a relationship in the nature of marriage should fulfil following conditions:

- The couple must hold themselves out to society as being akin to spouses.
- They must be of legal age to marry.
- They must be otherwise qualified to enter into a legal marriage, including being unmarried.
- They must have voluntarily cohabited and held themselves out to the world as being akin to spouses for a significant period of time.

Further, the parties must have lived together in a 'shared household' as defined in Section 2(s) of the Act. Merely spending weekends together or a one-night stand would not make it a 'domestic relationship.'

99 Match List I with List II.

List I	List II
A. A right which although, recognised by law, is not enforceable	I. Proprietory Right
B. A person's right in relation to his property	II. Personal Right
C. A person's right relating to status and that arising out of contract	III. Imperfect Right
D. A right which does not create an immediate interest	IV. Contingent Right

Select the correct answer from the codes given below

Codes

	A	B	C	D
1	I	II	III	IV
2	III	I	II	IV
3	II	III	IV	I
4	IV	II	I	III

Ans. *(2)*

Exp. The correct matching is A-III, B-I, C-II, D-IV.

Imperfect Right is a right which although recognised by law, is not enforceable.

Proprietary Right is a person's right in relation to his property.

Personal Right is a person's right relating to status and that arising out of contract.

Contingent Right is a right which does not create an immediate interest.

100 Super Cassettes Industries Ltd. Vs. Myspace Inc. 2011 is a leading case on the Copyright Act, 1957 dealing with which Section of the Act?

1 Section 14
2 Section 22
3 Section 30
4 Section 51

Ans. *(4)*

Exp. Super Cassettes Industries Ltd. Vs. Myspace Inc. is a leading case on the Copyright Act, 1957 dealing with Section 51 of the act.

Section 51 of Copyright Act, 1957 talks about the cases where copyright in a work shall be deemed to be infringed. According to Section 51 of the Act, Copyright is deemed to be infringed if:

- A person without obtaining the permission of the copyright holder does any act which only the copyright holder is authorised to do.
- A person permits the place to be used for communication, selling, distribution or exhibition of an infringing work unless he was not aware or has no reason to believe that such permission will result in the violation of copyright.
- A person imports infringing copies of a work
- A person without obtaining the authority from the copyright holder reproduces his work in any form.

UGC-NET LAW

SOLVED PAPER 2018 (July)

PAPER II

1 Which of the following is not included in the definition of law under Article 13 of the Constitution of India?

1 Legislation
2 Customs
3 Usage having no force of law
4 Ordinance

***Ans.* (3)**

Exp. The term "usage having no force of law" is not mentioned under Article 13 of the Constitution of India.

The definition of Law as found under Article 13 is reproduced as "In this article unless the context otherwise requires law includes any Ordinance, order, bye law, rule, regulation, notification, custom or usages having in the territory of India the force of law".

The 'usage' ordinarily refers to a customary/traditional practice done so long that it has acquired the force of law. It can be observed that usages are also included within the definition of law.

2 Which of the following Article of the Constitution uses the term 'martial law' ?

1 Article 33 2 Article 34
3 Article 352 4 Article 353

***Ans.* (2)**

Exp. Article 34 of Constitution of India mentions the term 'martial law'.

Article 34 provides for the restrictions on fundamental rights while martial law is in force in any area whithin the territory of India. The expression 'martial law' has not been defined anywhere in the Constitution but literally, it means 'military rule'.

The martial law is imposed under extraordinary circumstances like war, invasion, insurrection, rebellion, riot or any violent resistance to law.

Article 34 empowers the Parliament to indemnify (compensate) any government servant or any other person for any act done by him in connection with the maintenance or restoration of order in any area where martial law was in force. The Act of Indemnity made by the Parliament cannot be challenged in any court on the ground of contravention of any of the fundamental rights.

3 Given below are two statements. One is labelled as Assertion (A) and the other is labelled as Reason (R).

Assertion (A) A person shall be disqualified for being chosen as, and for being, a member of either House of Parliament if he holds any office of profit under the Government.

Reason (R) If 'pecuniary gain' is receivable in connection with the office. Then it shall not become an office of profit, irrespective of whether such gains are actually promised or not.

Codes

1 Both (A) and (R) are correct and (R) is the correct explanation of (A)
2 Both (A) and (R) are correct, but (R) is not the correct explanation of (A)
3 (A) is correct and (R) is incorrect
4 (A) is incorrect, but (R) is correct

***Ans.* (3)**

Exp. (A) is correct and (R) is incorrect.

The disqualification rules for member of parliament are found in Article 102 of the Constitution, and for a Member of Legislative Assembly in Article 191.The members are subject to disqualification for a) Holding an office of profit under government of India or State government; b) Being of unsound mind; c) Being an undischarged insolvent; d) Not being an Indian citizen or for acquiring citizenship of another country. Thus, the Assertion is correct in itself.

An office of profit is an office which is capable of yielding a profit or pecuniary gain. Hence, 'pecuniary gain' is an essential feature for an office of profit. Therefore, the Reason is incorrect in itself.

4 Which of the following statement/statements is/are incorrect?

I. The election of the President shall be held in accordance with the system of proportional representation by means of single non-transferable vote.

II. The President may resign, by writing under his hand addressed to the Chief Justice of India.

III. No resolution to remove the Vice-President of India from his office, shall be moved unless at least 30 days notice has been given to him.

IV. Vice-President shall, not with standing the expiration of his term, continue to hold office until his successor enters upon his office.

Select the correct answer from the codes given below :

1 I, II, III and IV are incorrect
2 I, II and III are incorrect
3 I and II are incorrect
4 I is incorrect

Ans. *(2)*

➲ *Exp.* Statements I, II and III are incorrect.

As per Article 55(3) of the Constitution of India, the election of the President shall be held in accordance with the system of proportional representation by means of the single transferable vote and the voting at such election shall be by secret ballot.

According to Article 56(1)(a), the President may, by writing under his hand addressed to the Vice President, resign his office and any such resignation addressed to the Vice President shall forthwith be communicated by him to the Speaker of the House of the People in terms of Article 56(2).

As per Article 67(b), the Vice President may be removed from his office by a resolution of the council of States but no resolution for the purpose of this clause shall be moved unless at least fourteen days notice has been given of the intention to move the resolution.

Statement-IV is correct as according to Article 67(c) of the Constitution of India, Vice-President shall, not with standing the expiration of his term, continue to hold office until his successor enters upon his office.

5 Match List I (Name of the case) with List II (Related subject) and give correct answer by using the codes below.

List I	List II
A. K.M. Nanavati Vs. State of Bombay	I. Right to Life
B. Ram Prasad Vs. State of U.P.	II. Power to Pardon
C. Lily Thomas Vs. Union of India	III. Fundamental Duties
D. Dr. P. Naller Thampy Terah Vs. Union of India	IV. Disqualification of Members

Codes

	A	B	C	D		A	B	C	D
1	II	III	IV	I	2	I	II	III	IV
3	III	IV	I	II	4	IV	I	II	III

Ans. *(1)*

➲ *Exp.* The correct matching is A-II, B-III, C-IV, D-I.

K. M. Nanavati Vs. State of Bombay (1961) is related to power to pardon. It is a popular case wherein Nanavati, a Naval Commander, was punished for the murder of a man having an affair with his wife. He was pardoned by Governor of Maharashtra. The Supreme Court held that the Governor's power to suspend sentence under Article 161 is subject to the rules made by the Supreme Court under Article 145 for disposal of pending appeals before it.

Ram Prasad Vs. State of Uttar Pradesh (1988), case is related to Fundamental Duties. In this case, while stating that the respondents failed to perform their fundamental duties, said "By Constitution 42nd Amendment Article 51A, has been inserted under Part IVA. 'The fundamental duties' which provides inter alia, that it shall be the duty of every citizen of India to strive towards excellence in all spheres of individual and collective activity, so that the, nation constantly rises to higher levels of endeavour and achievement".

Lily Thomas Vs. Union of India (2013) is related to disqualification of members. In this case, the Supreme Court decided that Members of Parliament, Legislative Councils and Legislative Assemblies who were convicted of crimes and awarded a minimum sentence of two years imprisonment would cease to be members of the house to which they were elected.

Dr. P. Naller Thampy Terah Vs. Union of India (1984) is related to Right to Life. In this case, the court held that Indian Railways provided socialized public utility service necessary for life on monopoly basis and constituted the common man's mode of transport.

6 Which of the following case is not related to 'Theory of Basic structure' under Article 368 of the Constitution?

1 Minerva Mills Vs. Union of India
2 Waman Rao Vs. Union of India
3 L. Chandra Kumar Vs. Union of India
4 T.K. Rangarajan Vs. Government of Tamil Nadu

Ans. *(4)*

➲ *Exp.* The T.K Rangarajan Vs. Government of Tamil Nadu case is not related to 'Theory of Basic structure' under Article 368 of the Constitution.

In the case titled as T.K. Rangarajan Vs. Government of Tamil Nadu, the Supreme Court examined the constitutionality of the legislation limiting the right to strike of government employees in India.

The court validated dismissal of government employees by the Tamil Nadu Government and held that there is no fundamental right to strike under the Indian Constitution. Also, that there is no moral, legal or fundamental right to strike as far as the government employees are concerned. The court also cited decisions in

All India Bank Employees' Association Vs. National Industrial Tribunal and others and Kameshwar Prasad Vs. State of Bihar to come to the aforesaid conclusion.

The Basic structure doctrine is a common law legal doctrine that the constitution of a sovereign state has certain characteristics that cannot be erased by its legislature. This was upheld in the Kesavananda Bharati Case.

7 Which of the following is incorrect in relation to the declaration of financial emergency by the President under Article 360 of the Constitution?

1 It shall cease to operate at the expiration of one month unless approved by both Houses of Parliament
2 Salary and allowances of persons serving in connection with affairs of state may be reduced
3 It may be revoked or varied by a subsequent proclamation by President
4 Salary and allowances of the Judges of Supreme Court and High Courts may be reduced

***Ans.* (1)**

Exp. Statement 1 is incorrect in relation to the declaration of financial emergency by the President under Article 360 of the Constitution. According to the Article 360(2)(c), an Emergency shall cease to operate at the expiration of two months unless before the expiration of that period it has been approved by resolutions of both Houses of Parliament.

8 Which of the following statement/statements is/are correct?

I. An ordinary Bill can only originate in council of states.
II. A Bill pending in House of people shall not lapse by reason of the prorogation of the House.
III. A Bill pending in the council of state which has not been passed by the House of people shall not lapse on a dissolution of the House of the people.
IV. A Bill pending in the House of people shall not lapse by reason of the dissolution of the House.

Select the correct answer from the codes given below

1 I and II are correct
2 II and III are correct
3 I and IV are correct
4 II and IV are correct

***Ans.* (2)**

Exp. Statements II and III are correct.

In terms of Article 107(3), an ordinary Bill pending in Parliament shall not lapse by reason of the prorogation of the House.

Article 107(4) provides that an ordinary Bill pending in the Council of States which has not been passed by the House of the People shall not lapse on dissolution of the House of the People

Statement I and IV are not correct.

According to Article 107 (1) of Constitution of India, an ordinary Bill may originate in either House of Parliament; Lok Sabha or Rajya Sabha.

According to Article 107(5), an ordinary Bill which is pending in the House of the People, or which having been passed by the House of the People is pending in the Council of States lapse on a dissolution of the House of the People.

9 In which of the following case, the Parliament has no power to legislate on the state list?

1 Consent of two states
2 Implementing international agreements
3 Emergency is in operation
4 In the public interest if so declared by council of states

***Ans.* (4)**

Exp. In the public interest if so declared by the council of states, the Parliament has no power to legislate on the state list.

According to Article 249, if the Council of States has declared by resolution supported by not less than two-thirds of the members present and voting that it is necessary or expedient in the national interest that Parliament should make laws with respect to [goods and services tax provided under article 246A or] any matter enumerated in the State List specified in the resolution, it shall be lawful for Parliament to make laws for the whole or any part of the territory of India with respect to that matter while the resolution remains in force.

It must be noted that this law making needs to be in "national interest", rather than "public interest".

Under Article 250, Parliament has the power to make laws with respect to all matters in the State List while the proclamation of national emergency is in operation.

As per Article 252, if the legislature of two or more states passes a resolution to the effect that it is desirable to have a law passed by the Parliament on any matters in the State List, then the Parliament can make laws for regulating that matter.

Article 253 empowers the Parliament to make any law for the whole or any part of the territory of India for implementing treaties and international agreements and conventions.

10 Match List-I (Name of case) with List-II (Related subject) and give correct answer by using the codes below

List I	List II
A. Union of India Vs. Sankalchand Seth	I. Power to do complete justice
B. Leila David Vs. State of Maharashtra	II. Foreign precedent
C. B.S.E.S. Ltd. Vs. Fenner India Ltd.	III. Power to punish for contempt
D. Darsan Gupta Vs. Radhika Gupta	IV. Appointment/Transfer of Judges

Codes

	A	B	C	D		A	B	C	D
1	IV	III	II	I	2	I	II	III	IV
3	II	I	IV	III	4	III	IV	I	II

Ans. (1)

Exp. The correct matching is A-IV, B-III, C-II, D-I.

The case *Union of India Vs. Sankalchand Seth* (1977) is related to Appointment/Transfer of judges. The Supreme Court ruled that the President had the power to transfer judges with neither their consent nor the 'concurrence' of the Chief Justice of India (CJI).

The case titled as *Leila David Vs. State of Maharashtra* (2009) is based on power to punish for contempt. The court held throwing of chappal at the Judges be treated as contempt of court as it is demeaning the paramount authority of law.

The case titled *B.S.E.S. Ltd. Vs. Fenner India Ltd.* (2006) pertains to foreign precedents, wherein the court held "Whatever may be the law, as to the encashment of bank guarantees in other jurisdictions, when the law in India is clear, settled and without any deviation whatsoever, there is no occasion to rely upon foreign case law."

Darsan Gupta Vs. Radhika Gupta, (2013), is related to power to do complete justice. In this case, the court held that the court cannot grant divorce to parties on a ground of irretrievable breakdown of marriage, which is not found as a listed ground under the relevant laws. It cannot apply the said ground to grant divorce merely in order to do "complete justice" under Article 142 of the Constitution of India.

11 Which of the following case is not related to the Parliamentary privileges?

1 M.S.M. Sharma Vs. Sri Krishna Sinha
2 State of Karnataka Vs. Union of India
3 Jatish Chandra Ghose Vs. Harisadhan Mukherjee
4 State of Tamil Nadu Vs. K. Shyam Sunder

Ans. (4)

Exp. State of Tamil Nadu Vs. K. Shyam Sunder case is not related to Parliamentary privileges.

In the State of Tamil Nadu Vs. K. Shyam Sunder (2011) case the Supreme Court held that the political party coming to power after an act or law has already been made enforceable, and is operating at the moment when it came to power, should not make attempt to modify or change the law unreasonably. This case pertained to The Tamil Nadu Uniform System of School Education Act, 2010 which was passed to implement the common syllabus, distribute the textbooks printed under the uniform system of education.

12 Which of the following statement/statements is/are correct?

I. It shall be the duty of every citizen to respect the country and abide by the constitution.
II. All minorities, whether based on religion or language, shall have the right to establish and administer educational institutions of their choice.
III. The State shall in particular, take steps for preserving and improving the breeds, and prohibiting the slaughter of cows and calves and other milch and draught cattle.
IV. No law here after enacted by the legislature of Jammu and Kashmir shall be void on the ground that it is inconsistent with any rights conferred on other citizens of India by any provision of Part III of the Constitution.

Select the correct answer from the codes given below

1 Only I and II are correct
2 Only III and IV are correct
3 I, II and III are correct
4 I, II, III and IV are correct

Ans. (4)

Exp. All statements I, II, III and IV are correct.

According to Article 51-A (a), it shall be the duty of every citizen of India to abide by the Constitution and respect its ideals and institutions, the national Flag and the National Anthem.

Article 30(1) says that all minorities, whether based on religion or language, shall have the right to establish and administer educational institutions of their choice.

Article 48 which is based on directive principle of state policy, says that the State shall endeavour to organise agriculture and animal husbandry on modern and scientific lines and shall in particular, take steps for preserving and improving the breeds, and prohibiting the slaughter of cows and calves and other milch and draught cattle.

Article 35-A provided that no law here after enacted by the legislature of Jammu and Kashmir shall be void on the ground that it is inconsistent with any rights conferred on other citizens of India by any provision of Part-III of the Constitution.

13 Which one of the following Jurists distinguished between 'expositorial' jurisprudence (What the law is) and 'Censorial' jurisprudence (What the law ought to be)?

1 John Austin
2 Hans Kelsen
3 Jeremy Bentham
4 H.L.A. Hart

Ans. (3)

Exp. In his famous work, 'Introduction to the Principles of Morals and Legislation', Bentham discussed the branches of jurisprudence. He distinguished between "expository" ('expositorial') and "censorial" jurisprudence saying that the former implies "what the law is", and the latter, means "what the law ought to be". He meant that expository law is what is made by the state, whether such law is appreciated or not. While the censorial law puts emphasis upon the fairness or reasonability of the law as well.

14 'Now, natural law is not considered as absolute but as relative. It is natural law with variable contents.' This observation specifically relates to

1 Dabin
2 Stammler
3 Finnis
4 Acquinas

Ans. (2)

Exp. The given observation specifically relates to Stammler. Stammler believed and asserted that a just law was the supreme most expression of man's social life and aims at protection of liberty of individuals. The fundamental principles necessary for a just law were described by him as: (i) Principle of respect and (ii) Principle of community participation.

In order to stress upon the distinction of revived natural law from the old one, he called the revived natural law as 'natural law with variable content'. He also believed that it is not really possible to formulate principles of law having universal validity.

Further, the nature of law is constant unlike the principles of law. Therefore, he insisted "law is the law of nature with a variable content".

15 According to Professor Hart, the meaning of the term 'Positivism' includes

I. Laws are commands.
II. The analysis of legal concepts is distinct from sociological and historical inquiries.
III. Moral judgements cannot be established or defended by rational argument, evidence or proof.
IV. The law as it is actually laid down, has to be kept separate from the law that ought to be.

Select the correct answer from the codes given below

1 Only I and III are correct
2 Only I, II and IV are correct
3 Only I, III and IV are correct
4 I, II, III and IV all are correct

Ans. (4)

Exp. Statements I, II, III and IV contain the meaning of the term 'Positivism'.

The legal positivist writer in English; H.L.A. Hart, who found common application of 'Positivism' used in relation to law which is composed of the following contentions that laws are commands.

He contended strongly that analysis of legal concepts is of significance and needs to be distinguished from history or sociology of law, from critical enquiry of law. The analysis of legal concepts is distinct from sociological and historical inquiries.

There is no necessary connection between law on one side and morality on the other; between law as it is and as it ought to be. The law as it is actually laid down, has to be kept separate from the law that ought to be.

Also, he has opined that moral judgments, which are based on one's personal opinions or assumptions of ethics/righteousness, unlike statements of fact, cannot be uniformly or universally proven or disproven by even any credible evidence. Moral judgements cannot be established or defended by rational argument, evidence or proof.

16 Match List-I with List-II and give the correct answer by using the codes given below

List I (Theory)	List II (Jurist)
A. Theory of social solidarity	I. Ehrlich
B. Theory of Categorical Imperative	II. Duguit
C. Imperative theory of law	III. John Austin
D. Theory of living law	IV. Immanuel Kant

Codes

	A	B	C	D		A	B	C	D
1	IV	I	III	II	2	II	IV	I	III
3	II	IV	III	I	4	I	III	IV	III

Ans. (3)

Exp The correct matching is A-II, B-IV, C-III, D-I.

Theory of Social Solidarity was given by Duguit. Leon Duguit's Social Solidarity, explains the interdependence on men from his other fellow men. No one can remain without depending on other men. Therefore, social interdependence and cooperation are very important for human existence.

Theory of Categorical Imperative was given by Immanuel Kant. The Categorical imperative is a system used to determine whether an act is morally right or wrong. Under Immanuel Kant's theory or Kantianism, the moral rule is something absolute, there are no exceptions, no matter who is performing the act or under what circumstances the actions is performed.

Imperative theory of law was given by John Austin, an American legal philosopher who has been a huge influence on modern-day understanding of Law. His ideas about Law form the basis of defining and understanding law. Imperative Theory of Law in its simplest terms can be defined as "command of the sovereign backed by sanction". It says that law is whatever the political sovereign of a certain state says law is. This law needs to be backed by legitimate sanction, that is punishment or penalty for violation.

Theory of living law was given by Ehrlich. The 'living law' as conceived by Ehrlich is the 'inner order of associations' that is the law practiced by society as opposed to law enforced by the State.

17 Match List I with List II and give the correct answer by using the codes given below

List I (Book)	List II (Author)
A. The Growth of the Law	I. Gray
B. Foundations of Jurisprudence	II. R. Dworkin
C. The Nature and Sources of Law	III. Cardozo
D. Taking Rights Seriously	IV. Jerome Hall

Codes

	A	B	C	D		A	B	C	D
1	I	II	III	IV	2	III	IV	I	II
3	II	III	I	IV	4	IV	I	II	III

Ans. (2)

Exp. The correct matching is A-III, B-IV, C-I, D-II.

The *Growth of the Law* is work of American lawyer, Jurist and Justice Benzamin N. Cardozo, published in 1924. He had previously shared his views on development of law in 'The Nature of the Judicial Process' in 1921. His lectures on the science and philosophy of law were then published under the title of 'The Growth of the Law'.

The book *Foundations of Jurisprudence* was published by Jerome Hall in 1973. In this book, he criticized an extreme reliance upon legal positivism and pointed out the need to have moral or ethical elements in the study of law.

The Nature and Sources of the Law was first published in 1909 by John Chipman Gray. He discouraged isolated study of jurisprudence and said that judges are the ones who actually make law.

Taking Rights Seriously is a book published in 1977 on the philosophy of law by Ronald Dworkin. He advocated that individuals have legal rights such as political and moral rights against the state which are even beyond the ones laid down in statutes.

18 Which one of the following are the two main theories of legal right?

1 Interest Theory and Fiction Theory
2 Realist Theory and Will Theory
3 Bracket Theory and Interest Theory
4 Interest Theory and Will Theory

Ans. (4)

Exp. The two main theories of the legal rights are Interest theory and Will theory.

The Will theory, as propounded by HLA Hart, provides that the objective of a right is to confer with its holder control over another's duty. Freedom is the most fundamental of all rights. For instance, one's right to a land is his freedom to do with it as he desires. Everyone commits a wrong by interfering with this freedom unless assigned with a right. Hence, if someone uses another's land without having a right, he is free to allow it, or to disallow it.

The Interest theory, initiated by Jeremy Bentham, differs in this respect. A person would have a right to something, against another, if that person had a legal duty to provide the first person with that thing. For instance, a person has a right to vote if someone is legally required to provide him with the opportunity to vote.

19 Which of the following is not a theory relating to corporate personality?

1 Fiction Theory
2 Realistic Theory
3 Purpose Theory
4 Functional Theory

Ans. (4)

Exp. Functional Theory is not related to corporate personality.

There are five principal theories, which are used to explain corporate personality, namely, the Fiction theory, Realist theory, the Purpose theory, the Bracket theory and the Concession theory.

As per the Fiction theory, a corporation exists only as an outcome of fiction and metaphor. So, the personality that is attached to these corporations is done purely by legal fiction.

As per the Realist theory, there is really no distinction between a natural person and an artificial person. So a corporate entity is as much a person as a natural person.

Purpose theory is based on the fundamental principle that corporations can be treated as persons for certain specific purposes.

Bracket theory is one of the more famous and feasible theories of corporate personality. The bracket theory is also known as the symbolist theory which states that a corporation is created only by its members and its agents.

Concession theory is similar to Fiction theory. However, it states that the legal entity has been given a corporate personality or a legal existence by the functions of the State.

20 Match List I with List II and give the Jural correlatives by using the codes given below

List I	List II
A. Claim	I. No claim
B. Liberty	II. Disability
C. Power	III. Duty
D. Immunity	IV. Liability

Codes

	A	B	C	D		A	B	C	D
1	II	III	I	IV	2	III	I	IV	II
3	IV	III	II	I	4	I	II	III	IV

Ans. (2)

Exp. The correct matching is A-III, B-I, C-IV, D-II.

Claim implies the existence of a correlative duty, since it has no content apart from the duty.

Liberty also means no claim. It is defined as the exercise of a right without the interference of law. By adding all the rights and duties across relationships, the degree of liberty can be determined. A perfect liberty is one where no one has any exclusive right to restrain the occurrence of a given act.

Power's correlative is liability. It is susceptibility to someone's exercising of power. It is the position of one whose legal rights may be altered by the exercise of a power.

Immunity's correlative is disability. Disability, the correlative of immunity, is better known as inability and signifies the absence of power. The legal maxim 'Nemo dat quod non habet' means that no person can transfer a better title in property than what is possessed by oneself, is an expression of disability.

21 'X', a servant, finds a bag at the basement of the shop. He hands it over to 'Y', the owner of the shop, who asks him to place it in the almirah. Now, the bag is in possession of

1 'X', because he was the finder
2 'Y', because he was the owner of the shop
3 'Y', because in him there was corpus and animus
4 'X', because he kept it in the almirah

***Ans.* (3)**

Exp. 'X', a servant, finds a bag at the basement of the shop. He hands it over to 'Y', the owner of the shop, who asks him to place it in the almirah. Now, the bag is in possession of 'Y', because in him there was corpus and animus.

The term 'Possession' in general means having physical control over an object. In law, it includes not only physical control but also an intention to exercise such control over an object. According to Svigny, there are two elements necessary to constitute possession; corpus possessionis and animus domini, while the former refers to exercising control over an object and the latter implies an intention to hold the object.

In the given case, X found the bag and handed over to Y, and placed in an almirah as per the directions of Y. The property has transferred to the control of Y, who also has an intention to keep it as is evident.

22 Given below are two statements. One is labelled as Assertion (A) and the other is labelled as Reason (R).

Assertion (A) Laws are valid only if they are just.

Reason (R) The aim of law is to secure justice.

Codes

1 Both (A) and (R) are true and (R) is the correct explanation of (A)
2 Both (A) and (R) are true, but (R) is not the correct explanation of (A)
3 (A) is true, but (R) is false
4 (A) is false, but (R) is true

***Ans.* (4)**

Exp. (A) is false, but (R) is true.

Legal Positivism advocates that laws need to be followed even if they do not appear to be just. According to the positivist approach, law is a command of the sovereign which is binding in all circumstances and the fairness of law on grounds of morality or ethics is not relevant. Thus, a law can be valid even if it is not just. So, Assertion (A) is false.

The aim of the law is to secure justice. It is based on the idea of Ethical Jurisprudence, which investigates the purpose of law and states that law and justice are closely related. It holds that law is a means to attain justice. Thus, Reason (R) is true.

23 Given below are two statements. One is labelled as Assertion (A) and the other is labelled as Reason (R).

Assertion (A) Judges must follow authoritative precedents.

Reason (R) Authoritative precedents derive their authority from basic postulates of the legal system itself.

Codes

1 Both (A) and (R) are true and (R) is the correct explanation of (A)
2 Both (A) and (R) are true, but (R) is not the correct explanation of (A)
3 (A) is true, but (R) is false
4 (A) is false, but (R) is true

***Ans.* (1)**

Exp. Both (A) and (R) are true and (R) is the correct explanation of (A).

Judges must follow authoritative precedents. The Judicial Precedent means that a subsequent decision by court of law must be based on an earlier decision on similar issue. One of the types of Precedents is authoritative precedents which makes it binding for a judge lower in hierarchy or strength to mandatorily follow an earlier decision by higher court/bench. This has to be done irrespective of the belief of the judge subsequently deciding the matter. Thus, Assertion is correct in itself.

The authoritative precedent is based on and derives its authority from the principle of Stare Decisis which means to "stand by the decision made already" which is an essential and basic postulate of legal system. Hence, the Reason is correct in itself, also is a valid explanation behind the Assertion.

24 Which of the following statement/statements is/are correct?

I. Hobbes, Austin and Pufendorf subscribe to the view that 'law properly so called' in command of the sovereign and enforced by a superior political authority and hence deny legal character of international law.

II. Oppenheim has remarked that international law is the vanishing point of Jurisprudence.

III. Holland subscribes to the view that international law is really law.

IV. Starke has expressed the view that international law is a 'Weak law'.

Select the correct answer from the codes given below

1 Only I is correct
2 I and IV both are correct
3 I, II and III are correct
4 I, II, III and IV all are correct

Ans. (2)

Exp. Statements I and IV are correct.

The term 'law properly so called' refers to legal and political sanction of law which is made by sovereign and hence, law is considered a command. This view was supported by John Austin, Thomas Hobbes and Samuel Pufendorf. They all believed that since International Law does not have such a legal sanction by a politically superior authority, it lacks the character of law.

J G Starke has opined that International Law is a 'Weak law' since it does not have legal sanction equivalent to a local or municipal law which is otherwise made by a competent legislature.

Statement II and III are incorrect.

The statement 'international law is the vanishing point of jurisprudence' was said by Sir Eriskine Holland. He meant that there is no relation between both and hence jurisprudence does not include examination of international law as an ordinary law.

Oppenheim believed International Law to be really law.

25 'Triepel' and 'Anzilotti' are the exponents of which of the following theory of Relationship between International law and Municipal law?

1 Monism
2 Dualism
3 Specific Adoption Theory
4 Delegation Theory

Ans. (2)

Exp. 'Triepel' and 'Anzilotti' are the exponents of Dualism theory of relationship between International law and Municipal law.

According to Dualistic theory, Law of nations or international law and municipal laws of individual states are two different and self-contained legal systems. Thus, international Law does not form part of the domestic/local law of a state. This theory was developed by renowned German scholar Triepel in 1899.

The theory was subsequently adopted by Italian jurist Anzilotti. This theory does not recognize supremacy of one law over another, since they share no similarity. Apart from this, there is also Monism theory, according to which only one kind of legal system in the form of domestic law prevails. It is maintained here that International law is not distinct from municipal law. This theory was shaped by Austrian jurist Kelson.

26 Which one of the following is one of the Chief Exponents of 'Constitutive Theory' of Recognition?

1 Pit corbett 2 Kelson 3 Hegel 4 Hall

Ans. (3)

Exp. Hegel is one of the Chief Exponents of 'Constitutive Theory' of Recognition.

International law is influenced by two opposing theories for state recognition; declaratory and constitutive theories. State recognition refers to the process of granting statehood or sovereignty to a territory. While the Constitutive theory maintains that a state does not acquire statehood by default. Rather, only when other already existing states recognize the existence of claimant state in legal sense. Hegel, Oppenheim and Anzilotti are chief exponents of this theory.

The other related notion is Declaratory theory which argues that the status of statehood is based on fact, not on individual state discretion. It implies that the claimant state does not need to have consent of other states for its independent status, and that it always has a right to defend its sovereignty. Hall, Wagner, Fisher and Brierly are the chief exponents of this theory.

27 Which of the following statement/statements is/are not correct?

I. In accordance with the provisions of Article 7 of the United Nations Charter, the Security Council is one of the Principal organs of the United Nations.

II. The First Security Council came into being on 12th January, 1946.

III. At Dumharton proposals, it was finally decided to establish such as an organ in the form of the Security Council.

IV. Ten non-permanent members of the Security Council are elected by the General Assembly for 5 years.

Select the correct answer from the codes given below

1 Only III is not correct
2 III and IV are not correct
3 I, II and III are not correct
4 I, II, III and IV all are not correct

Ans. (2)

Exp. Statements III and IV are not correct.

The Dumbarton Proposals were made at the Dumbarton Oak Conference between 21st August to 7th October, 1944, held in Georgetown, Washington, D.C., where representatives from China, the Soviet Union, the United States, and the United Kingdom drafted proposals for creating a world organization which went on to become the basis for the United Nations.

However, the entire structure of UN existing at present was not finalized there and The Charter of the United Nations was signed on 26th June, 1945, in San Francisco, at the conclusion of the United Nations Conference on International Organization, and came into force on 24th October, 1945 which brought Security Council into force among other organs.

Further, there are 15 members of the Security Council inclusive of permanent and non-permanent members. Five of these members; China, France, the Russian Federation, the United Kingdom and the United States are permanent members. Whereas, rest of the ten non-permanent members are elected by the General Assembly for a period of two-years only.

28 Match List-I with List-II and give the correct answer by using the codes given below

List I (Provisions)		List II (Articles of Statute of Court of International Justice)
A. Law applied by the International Court of Justice	I.	Article 41
B. Binding force of the decision of International Court of Justice	II.	Article 62
C. Interim Measures or Relief	III.	Article 38
D. International court's power to allow a state to intervene, in case to which it is not a party	IV.	Article 59

Codes

	A	B	C	D		A	B	C	D
1	III	IV	I	II	2	I	II	III	IV
3	II	III	IV	I	4	IV	I	II	III

***Ans.* (1)**

➲ *Exp.* The correct matching A-III; B-IV; C-I; D-II.

As per *Article 38* of the Statute of the International Court of Justice, the Court shall apply primary sources of law such as international conventions, international custom, the general principles of law recognized by civilized nations, and secondary sources such as judicial decisions and the teachings of the most highly qualified publicists of the various nations for the determination of rules of law.

Under *Article 59* the decision of the International Court of Justice has not been made binding except between the parties and in respect of the particular case.

As per *Article 41* of the Statute of the International Court of Justice, the Court has been conferred power to recommend any provisional or interim measures needed to be taken to preserve the rights of either party involved.

Article 62 is related to International Court's power to allow a state to intervene, in case to which it is not a party. As per the Article, if a state considers that it has an interest of a legal nature which may be potentially affected by the decision in the case, it may submit a request to the Court to be permitted to intervene.

29 Match List I with List II and give the correct answer by using the codes given below

List I (Modes)	List II (Provision)
A. Cession	I. Acquisition of Nationality
B. Reprisal	II. Loss of Nationality
C. Good offices	III. Pacific means of settlement of International Disputes
D. Substitution	IV. Coercive means of settlement of International Disputes

Codes

	A	B	C	D		A	B	C	D
1	I	IV	III	II	2	II	III	IV	I
3	III	II	I	IV	4	IV	I	II	III

***Ans.* (1)**

➲ *Exp.* The correct matching is A-I, B-IV, C-III, D-II.

Cession is related to acquisition of nationality. It is an arrangement within international law by which a territory may stand transferred from one State to another with the prior consent of both States. It is one of the modes of lawful acquisition of territory. When a state is ceded in another State, all the people of the territory acquire nationality of the State in which their territory has been merged.

Reprisal is a punitive act on the part of a state targeted against another for settling disputes initiated by the latter's unlawful act. When states do not succeed in resolving international disputes by peaceful means, they generally adopt coercive methods.

Good offices is a pacific means of settlement of International disputes. It is a method of peaceful settlement of an international dispute, wherein a third party acts friendly in the capacity of an intermediary but with the consent of disputing states. It is important to note that the third party only encourages disputing parties to negotiate and settle but does not take part in negotiations itself.

Substitution is one of the many ways of losing Nationality. When the nationality of a citizen within a state is terminated or cancelled due to the citizen acquiring nationality of a state in place of other states, it is known as Substitution.

30 Given below are two statements. One is labelled as Assertion (A) and the other is labelled as Reason (R).

Assertion (A) Article 10 of the UN Charter confers upon the General Assembly very wide deliberative functions except in respect of those matters which are being considered by the Security Council.

Reason (R) The Resolutions or declarations of the General Assembly are not binding upon the states. They are merely recommendations.

Codes

1 Both (A) and (R) are correct and (R) is the correct explanation of (A)

2 Both (A) and (R) are correct, but (R) is not the correct explanation of (A)

3 (A) is correct and (R) is wrong

4 (A) is wrong, but (R) is correct

***Ans.* (2)**

➲ *Exp.* Both (A) and (R) are correct, but (R) is not the correct explanation of (A).

The General Assembly under Article 10 of UN Charter may discuss any matters relating to the powers and functions of any organs and may make recommendations to the Members of the United Nations and to the Security Council. However, the General Assembly shall not make any recommendation with regard to a dispute or situation when the Security Council is exercising the functions assigned to it in respect of that dispute or situation, unless the Security Council (SC) so requests. Thus, the Assertion is correct in itself.

Also, it can be observed that under Article 10, the General Assembly may only make recommendations which amount to mere advisories, and hence are not binding upon member states. The Reason is correct in itself, but, the given reason is not appropriate for the Assertion made, because it provides no reason as to why the General Assembly cannot make recommendations to Supreme Court.

31 Which of the following statement/statements is/are correct?

I. All members of the United Nations are ipso facto the members of the statute of the International Court of Justice.

II. The International Court of Justice consists of 25 judges which are elected by the General Assembly.

III. The judges of the International Court of Justice are elected for a term of 5 years.

IV. All the decisions of the International Court of Justice are on the basis of the majority of judges.

Select the correct answer from the codes given below

1 Only I is correct
2 I and II are correct
3 I and IV are only correct
4 I, II, III and IV all are correct

Ans. *(3)*

Exp. Statement I and IV are correct.

According to the Article 93 in Chapter XIV of UN Charter, all Members of the United Nations are ipso facto parties to the Statue of the International Court of Justice (ICJ).

As per Article 55 of the Statute of ICJ, all decisions of ICJ shall be decided by a majority of the judges present and in the event of an equality of votes, the President or the judge who acts in his place shall have a casting vote.

Statement II and III are incorrect as the ICJ is composed of 15 judges elected to nine-year terms of office by the United Nations General Assembly and the Security Council. Also, in order to ensure a degree of continuity, one third of the Court is elected every three years.

32 Given below are two statements. One is labelled as Assertion (A) and the other is labelled as Reason (R).

Assertion (A) When a state behaves in discourteous manner with another state, International law confers right upon the state affected to resort to 'retorsion' which means retaliation.

Reason (R) If the International disputes are not resolved through 'peaceful' means, then the states resort to compulsive or coercive means.

Codes

1 Both (A) and (R) are correct and (R) is correct explanation of (A)
2 Both (A) and (R) are correct, but (R) is not correct explanation of (A)
3 (A) is correct and (R) is wrong
4 (A) is wrong, but (R) is correct

Ans. *(1)*

Exp. Both (A) and (R) are correct and (R) is correct explanation of (A).

An international dispute refers to a conflict of legal views or of interest between the States. Such a disagreement may be resolved either by peaceful or compulsive means. Compulsive or Coercive means are non-peaceful methods for the settlement of the disputes. This includes, among other things, 'retorsion' as retaliation against a discourteous act of a state. It is an action performed by a state identical in nature and treatment to that performed by another state previously. Thus, the Assertion is correct in itself.

However, the non-peaceful methods are applied when the dispute cannot be solved through peaceful means which include practices such as negotiation, good offices, mediation, arbitration, etc. Hence, Reason is correct in itself and is also correct explanation of given Assertion.

33 The 'UN Commission on Human Rights' was established in 1946 by

1 General Assembly
2 Security Council
3 Economic and Social Council
4 International Court of Justice

Ans. *(3)*

Exp. The United Nations Commission on Human Rights (UNCHR) was established by the United Nations Economic and Social Council (ECOSOC) in 1946, and acted as a subsidiary to the council.

It used to be a body operating under the scope of United Nations from 1946, but stood abolished and got replaced with the United Nations Human Rights Council in 2006. It was the United Nation's significant entity concerned primarily with the promotion, maintenance and protection of human rights.

34 Under Hindu law, the persons descended from a common ancestor but by different wives, are known as

1 Full Blood Relations
2 Half Blood Relations
3 Uterine Blood Relations
4 No Blood Relations

Ans. *(2)*

Exp. Under Hindu law, the persons descended from a common ancestor but by different wives, are known as Half blood relations.

According to Section 3(c) of the Hindu Marriage Act, 1955, two persons are related to each other by Half blood when they are descended from a common ancestor but by different wives and by full blood when they are descended from a common ancestor by the same wife.
Also, in clause (d) of Section 3 of the Act, two persons are related to each other by Uterine blood when they are descended from a common ancestress but by different husbands. The above definitions are also provided under Section 3(1)(e) of the Hindu Succession Act, 1956.

35 Match List I with List II and give the correct answer by using the codes given below

List I		List II	
A.	Agnate	I.	What was heard
B.	Shruti	II.	Related wholly through males
C.	Cognate	III.	What has been remembered
D.	Smriti	IV.	Related not wholly through males

Codes

	A	B	C	D		A	B	C	D
1	I	IV	II	III	2	II	I	IV	III
3	II	IV	III	I	4	III	IV	I	II

***Ans.* (2)**

Exp. The correct matching is A-II; B-I; C-IV; D-III.

Section 3 (1) (a) of the Hindu Succession Act, 1956 states that one person is said to be an *agnate* of another if the two are related by blood or adoption wholly through males.

Shruti literally means what was heard, referring to the four Vedas. It is a primary and significant source of Hindu law which is believed to be the words of the divine revelation through the sages.

Section 3(1)(b) of the Hindu Succession Act, 1956 states that one person is said to be a *cognate* of another if the two are related by blood or adoption but not wholly through males.

Smriti means what has been remembered. It is one of the primary sources of Hindu Law. It is a written manual of the knowledge of the sages. Many sages, from time to time, have written the concepts specified in Vedas.

36 If the condition laid down under Section 5(iii) of the Hindu Marriage Act, 1955 is violated, such marriage under the Act is

1 void but not punishable
2 valid and not punishable
3 void and punishable
4 valid but punishable

***Ans.* (4)**

Exp. If the condition laid down under Section 5(iii) of the Hindu Marriage Act, 1955 is violated, such marriage under the Act is valid but punishable.

The Section 5 of Hindu Marriage Act, 1955 lists certain conditions for a valid marriage under the law. One such condition under Section 5(iii) provides that at the time of the marriage, the bridegroom must have completed the age of twenty-one years and the bride the age of eighteen years.

Also, as per Section 18 of the Act, every person who procures a marriage of himself or herself to be solemnized in contravention of the conditions specified in clause (iii) as stated, shall be punished with rigorous imprisonment which may extend to two years or with fine which may extend to one lakh rupees, or with both.

It is significant to note that Sections 11 and 12 of the said Act respectively define void and voidable marriages but neither of these definitions includes marriage in contravention of Section 5(iii) of the Act.
Thus, it is clear that a violation of the condition in Section 5(iii) renders the marriage neither void nor voidable. Hence, the marriage in such a case remains valid but is made punishable as explained above.

37 Under Section 2 of the Dissolution of Muslim Marriages Act, 1939, the following grounds of divorce are available to a wife

I. Whereabouts of the husband have not been known for a period of four years.
II. Four years imprisonment of the husband.
III. Husband has treated her with cruelty.
IV. The husband has neglected her or has failed to pay her maintenance for a period of two years.

Select the correct answer from the codes given below

1 I, III and IV
2 II, IV, III and I
3 IV, III, II and I
4 I, IV, II and III

***Ans.* (1)**

Exp. Statement I, III and IV are correct in relation to Section-2 of the Dissolution of Muslim Marriages Act, 1939.

The Section 2 of the Dissolution of Muslim Marriages Act, 1939 provides grounds for decree for dissolution of marriage to a woman. The relevant grounds are as follows;

- Section 2(i), when the whereabouts of the husband have not been known for a period of four years.
- Under clause (ii) of Section 2 a ground is available when the husband has neglected or has failed to provide for her maintenance for a period of two years.
- The woman can also seek divorce under clause (viii) of the Section 2 when the husband treats her with cruelty.
- Statement-II is not correct because as per clause (iii) of Section 2 a ground of divorce is available only when husband has been sentenced to imprisonment for a period of seven years or upwards, as against four years mentioned therein.

38 Given below are two statements. One is labelled as Assertion (A) and the other is labelled as Reason (R).

Assertion (A) No person except the father or mother or guardian of a Hindu child has the capacity to give such child in adoption.

Reason (R) No re-adoption may take place under the Hindu Adoptions and Maintenance Act, 1956.

Codes

1 (A) is correct, but (R) is incorrect
2 (A) is incorrect and (R) is correct
3 Both (A) and (R) are correct
4 Both (A) and (R) are incorrect

Ans. (3)

Exp. Both (A) and (R) are correct.

According to Section 9(1) of the Hindu Adoptions and Maintenance Act, 1956, no person except the father or mother or the guardian of a child shall have the capacity to give the child in adoption.

No re-adoption may take place under the Hindu Adoptions and Maintenance Act, 1956. According to Section 15, no adoption which has been validly made can be cancelled by the adoptive father or mother or any other person, nor can the adopted child renounce his or her status as such and return to the family of his or her birth.

39 Match List I with List II in the light of the Hindu Adoptions and Maintenance Act, 1956 and give correct answer by using the codes given below.

List I (Section)	List II (Provision)
A. Section 18	I. Maintenance of dependants
B. Section 19	II. Amount of maintenance
C. Section 22	III. Maintenance of wife
D. Section 23	IV. Maintenance of widowed daughter-in-law

Codes

	A	B	C	D		A	B	C	D
1	III	IV	II	I	2	III	IV	I	II
3	I	III	II	IV	4	IV	III	I	II

Ans. (2)

Exp. The correct matching is A-III; B-IV; C-I; D-II.

Section 18 of the Hindu Adoptions and Maintenance Act, 1956 is related to maintenance of wife. It provides that a Hindu wife shall be entitled to be maintained by her husband during her lifetime.

Section 19 of Hindu Adoptions and Maintenance Act, 1956 is related to maintenance of widowed daughter-in- law. According to Section 19, a Hindu wife shall be entitled to be maintained after the death of her husband by her father-in-law.

Section 22 of the Act is related to maintenance of dependants. As per Section 22, the heirs of a deceased Hindu are bound to maintain the dependants of the deceased out of the estate inherited by them from the deceased.

Section 23 of the Act is related to the amount of maintenance, provided that it shall be at the discretion of the court to determine whether any, and if so what, maintenance shall be awarded under the provisions of this Act.

40 "Marriages of all persons who are citizens of India belonging to various religions should be made compulsorily registrable in their respective states where the marriage is solemnized". This was ruled by the Supreme Court in which of the following case?

1 Sarla Mudgil Vs. Union of India
2 Gurupad Vs. Hirabai
3 Shastri Vs. Muldass
4 Seema Vs. Ashwani Kumar

Ans. (4)

Exp. In Seema Vs. Ashwani Kumar (2006), the Supreme Court held that "Marriages of all persons who are citizens of India belonging to various religions should be made compulsorily registrable in their respective states where the marriage is solemnized".

This was done since the Registration of Marriage, if made compulsory, can help in reducing the menace of Child Marriage which was prevalent at that time. The Court also directed the States and Union Territories to respective States to notify the procedure of marriages within three months.

41 Give the correct answer with the help of codes given below.

'Muta' marriage is

I. A temporary marriage
II. Recognised under sunni law
III. Recognised under shia law
IV. A marriage for a fixed period

Select the correct answer from the codes given below

1 I, II, III and IV
2 II, III and IV
3 I, III and IV
4 I, II and IV

Ans. (3)

Exp. 'Muta' marriage is a temporary marriage, for a fixed period which is recognised under Shia law.

The word 'muta' literally means 'enjoyment or use'. It is a 'marriage for pleasure' for a fixed period of time, and hence is also known as temporary marriage. The institution of muta is not recognized by any school of Muslim law in India, except the Shia school.

42 Match List I with List II in the light of the Hindu Marriage Act, 1955, and give correct answer with the help of codes given below.

List I (Section)	List II (Provision)
A. Section 14	I. Alternative relief in divorce proceedings
B. Section 13 A	II. Restitution of conjugal rights
C. Section 9	III. Judicial separation
D. Section 10	IV. No petition for divorce within one year of marriage

Codes

	A	B	C	D		A	B	C	D
1	IV	I	II	III	2	I	IV	III	II
3	IV	III	II	I	4	II	III	I	IV

Ans. *(1)*

Exp. The correct matching is A-IV, B-I, C-II, D-III.

As per *Section 14* of the Hindu Marriage Act, 1955, it shall not be competent for any court to entertain any petition for dissolution of a marriage by a decree of divorce, unless at the date of the presentation of the petition one year has elapsed since the date of the marriage.

As per *Section 13A* of the Act, the court may provide an alternate relief in divorce proceeding by passing a decree for judicial separation instead of a divorce.

The *Section 9* of Act provides for restitution of conjugal rights and states that when either the husband or the wife has, without reasonable excuse, withdrawn from the society of the other, the aggrieved party may apply for restitution of conjugal rights and the court may decree restitution of conjugal rights accordingly.

Section 10 of the Act is related to Judicial separation. It provides that either party to a marriage may present a petition praying for a decree for judicial separation on specified grounds. It shall no longer be obligatory for the petitioner to cohabit with the respondent upon a decree by court to that effect.

43 Given below are two statements. One is labelled as Assertion (A) and the other is labelled as Reason (R).

Assertion (A) A proposal may be revoked at any time before the communication of its acceptance is complete as against the proposer, but not afterwards.

Reason (R) Section 5 of the Indian Contract Act, 1872, deals with the revocation of proposals and acceptances.

Codes

1 Both (A) and (R) are correct, but (R) is not related to (A)
2 (A) is correct, but (R) is wrong
3 (A) is wrong, but (R) is correct
4 Both (A) and (R) are correct and (R) is the correct explanation of (A)

Ans. *(4)*

Exp. Both (A) and (R) are correct and (R) is the correct explanation of (A).

The Section 5 of Indian Contract Act, 1872 provides that a proposal may be revoked at any time before the communication of its acceptance is complete as against the proposer, but not afterwards.

Further, an acceptance may be revoked at any time before the communication of the acceptance is complete as against the acceptor, but not afterwards.

For instance, 'A' proposes, by a letter sent by post, to sell his house to 'B'. 'B' accepts the proposal by a letter sent by post. A may revoke his proposal at any time before or at the moment when 'B' posts his letter of acceptance, but not afterwards. 'B' may revoke his acceptance at any time before or at the moment when the letter communicating it reaches 'A'. Thus, the Assertion and Reason are true in themselves and the statement in Reason is correct for the Assertion made.

44 Which of the following statement(s) is/are correct?

Consideration is

I. a price for any promise.
II. only a moral obligation.
III. a motive for any promise.
IV. something of value in the eye of law.

Select the correct answer from the codes given below

1 I and III are correct
2 I and IV are correct
3 II, III and IV are correct
4 III and IV are correct

Ans. *(2)*

Exp. Consideration is a price for any promise. It is something of value in the eye of law.

Consideration' means "something in return", i.e. quid pro quo that is something for something. It is an essential of a valid contract. An agreement without consideration is void and thus not enforceable by law except under certain circumstances.

According to Section 2(d) of the Indian Contract Act "when at the desire of the promisor, promisee or any other person has done or abstained from doing or does or abstains from doing or promises to do or to abstain from doing something, such act or abstinence, or promise is called a consideration for the promise".

According to Sir Frederick Pollock "Consideration is the price for which the promise of the other is bought, and the promise thus given for value is enforceable."

In Currie v. Misa, it was defined, "A valuable consideration in the sense of the law may consist either in some right, interest, forbearance, detriment, loss or responsibility, given, suffered or undertaken by the other."

45 Consider the following statements and give correct answer with the help of codes given below.

The case of Mohori Bibee Vs. Dharmodas Ghose

I. has laid down that a minor's contract becomes valid when he attains majority.
II. is the decision of the Supreme Court of India regarding minor's contract.
III. is the decision of Privy Council regarding voidness of minor's contract.
IV. has laid down that contract without consideration is void.

Select the correct answer from the codes given below
1 III and IV are correct, but I and II are incorrect
2 I and II are correct, but III and IV are incorrect
3 III is correct, but I, II and IV are incorrect
4 II and IV are correct, but I and III are incorrect

Ans. (3)

Exp. Statement III is correct, but I, II and IV are incorrect.

The case Mohori Bibee Vs. Dharmodas Ghose (1903) was decided by Privy Council and discusses the voidness of minor's agreement. It was held that the minors have no competence to enter into a contract under Section 11 of the Indian Contract Act, 1872, which says that "every person is competent to contract who is of the age of majority according to the law to which he/she is subjected to". Hence, any contract with a minor is void ab initio. Therefore, only the statement-III is correct.

46 Given below are two statements. One is labelled as Assertion (A) and the other is labelled as Reason (R).

Assertion (A) Acceptance is to offer what a lighted match is to a train of gun powder.

Reason (R) Acceptance cannot be separated from offer.

Codes
1 (A) is true, but (R) is false
2 (A) is false, but (R) is true
3 Both (A) and (R) are true and (R) is the correct explanation of (A)
4 Both (A) and (R) are true, but (R) is not the correct explanation of (A)

Ans. (1)

Exp. (A) is true, but (R) is false.

Acceptance is to offer what a lighted match is to train of gunpowder is related to revocation of proposal or acceptance as described by Anson in English law in the following manner referring to gunpowder as an offer and lighted match stick as an acceptance. This implies when the lighted match comes in contact with gun powder, there is a result in the form of explosion which cannot be undone. The statement aims to suggest that once there is an offer and an acceptance, a valid contract is made. Thus, Assertion (A) is true.

Reason (R) is false because an acceptance can be separated from an offer as long as there is no contract by revocation of offer or acceptance in accordance to the rules provided. It is only when there is a contract, acceptance cannot be separated from offer and the given statement does not seem to suggest that.

47 The defence of 'non est factum' is available to the contracting party who has committed mistake as to the
1 identity of the other contracting party
2 nature of contract
3 quality of the subject matter of the contract
4 quality of the promise made by the other party

Ans. (2)

Exp. The defence of 'non est factum' is available to the contracting party who has committed mistake as to the nature of contract.

The Latin phrase 'non est factum' literally means "it is not his/her deed." It is a special kind of defence in contract law to avoid liability in a contract that a person may have agreed because of certain reasons such as mistake as to the kind of contract.

Under contract law, the person who has agreed, under the mistaken impression as to the very nature of the agreement, might be able to plead 'non est factum' in a court and on that basis seek avoidance of the contract.

For instance, a person's signing the deed to a house, under impression that the document signed was only a guarantee for another person's debt. This refers to a mistake regarding nature of the contract and therefore, the person under mistaken belief could be able to avoid the performance of contract.

48 Under the Indian Contract Act, 1872 which one of the following does not fall in the meaning of fraud?
1 Active concealment of a fact
2 Suggestion, as a fact, of that which is not true, by one who does not believe it to be true
3 Positive assertion of unwarranted statements
4 A promise made without any intention of performing it

Ans. (3)

Exp. Positive assertion of unwarranted statements does not fall in the meaning of fraud.

The Section 17 of Indian Contract Act, 1872 defines 'Fraud' as "Fraud means and includes any of the following acts committed by a party to a contract, or with his connivance, or by his agent, with intent to deceive another party thereto or his agent, or to induce him to enter into the contract:

- The suggestion, as a fact, of that which is not true, by one who does not believe it to be true;
- The active concealment of a fact by one having knowledge or belief of the fact
- A promise made without any intention of performing it;
- Any other act fitted to deceive;
- Any such act or omission as the law specially declares to be fraudulent.

49 Special damages will be awarded in case of a breach of contract
1 only when the contracting parties express the same specifically as the terms of the contract
2 always in the special circumstances leading to the formation of the contract
3 only when the court of law thinks fit in the special circumstances of the case
4 only when the special circumstances causing loss of profit resulting from the breach of contract were brought to the notice of the party committing breach at the time of formation of the contract

Ans. (4)

Exp. Special damages will be awarded in case of a breach of contract only when the special circumstances causing loss of profit resulting from the breach of contract were brought to the notice of the party committing breach at the time of formation of the contract.

Special damages are awarded in a contract to cover losses due to a breach of contract. They don't just relate to losses incurred under the contract. They can also include things such as loss of business reputation and loss of profit.

There are broadly two categories of damages: Compensatory and Punitive Damages. Further, there are two kinds of compensatory damages : General Damage (that cover the loss directly and necessarily incurred by the breach of contract) and Special damages (that cover any loss incurred by the breach of contract because of special circumstances or conditions that are not ordinarily predictable).

To obtain Special damages, the non-breaching party must prove that the breaching party was already aware of the special arrangement/circumstances at the time when the contract was made.

For instance, if Company 'A' knew that Company 'B' needed a new building on a particular day because its old building was already sold, the damages for breach of contract could payment for Company B's expense in renting a building until the desired one is allotted.

The Punitive damages, on the other hand, are awarded to punish or set an example of a wrongdoer who has acted willfully, maliciously or fraudulently by providing excessive compensation.

50 Which of the following statement/statements is/are correct?

I. Tort is a civil wrong for which remedy is a common law action.

II. Tort is exclusively a breach of contract or breach of trust.

III. Tort is an infringement of a right in rein of a private individual.

IV. Tort is violation of a legal duty owed to people generally for maintenance of law and order.

Select the correct answer from the codes given below

1 Only II and IV are correct
2 Only II and III are correct
3 Only I and III are correct
4 Only I and IV are correct

Ans. (3)

Exp. Statements I and III are correct.

Tort is a civil wrong for which remedy is a common law action. It is a civil wrong committed by a person against another wherein the aggrieved can sue for damages. The tort law is largely uncodified and hence is not normally found in any statute. The decision for such cases is based on the common law principles such as justice, equity, good conscience and balance of probabilities.

Tort is an infringement of a right in rein of a private individual. It is a violation of a right in rem, i.e., of a right vested in some determinate person, either personally or as a member of the community, and available against the world at large.

Statement II and IV are incorrect.

Remedy in tort is independent of any contract. This implies that a claim under tort is maintainable even without having a contract between the parties.

Also, in the case of a tort, the duty is one imposed by the law but is not for the purpose of maintenance of law and order, since that is an area of concern for criminal law. Rather, the duty is to simply respect the rights of others in general.

51 Match List-I (Name of case) with List-II (Name of defense) and give the correct answer by using the codes given below

List I	List II
A. Samira Kohli Vs. Prabha Manchanda	I. Plaintiff a wrong-doer
B. Sodan Singh Vs. New Delhi Municipal Committee	II. Leave and licence
C. Bird Vs. Holbrook	III. Act of God
D. Kallulal Vs. Hemchand	IV. Necessity

Codes

	A	B	C	D		A	B	C	D
1	II	IV	I	III	2	I	II	IV	III
3	II	I	III	IV	4	III	I	II	IV

Ans. (1)

Exp. The correct matching is A-II, B-IV, C-I, D-III.

Samira Kohli Vs. Prabha Manchanda (2008) was a case relating to leave and license. In this case, the Supreme Court held that when the consent by the patient is for a particular operative surgery; it cannot be treated as consent for an unauthorized additional procedure.

Sodan Singh Vs. New Delhi Municipal Committee (1989) was related to necessity. In this case, the Constitution Bench held that the right to carry on trade or business mentioned in Article 19(1)(g) of the Constitution of street hawkers is subject to reasonable restrictions and the State has the power to impose all necessary limitations on the exercise of such rights in cases of necessity.

Bird Vs. Holbrook (1825) was a case of the plaintiff being the wrongdoer. The defendant had installed a spring gun to guard against trespass without putting up any warning signs of a gun. A 19-year-old boy came into the garden in order to catch a peafowl and was shot. The court decided in favor of the plaintiff saying that if a person sets a gun as a trap without putting up any notice, he will be liable for the damages.

Kallulal Vs. Hemchand (1957) was a case on defence of the Act of God. In this case, the wall of a building collapsed due to normal rainfall of about 2.66 inches. The court held that the defence of the Act of God cannot be pleaded as that much rainfall was normal and something extraordinary was required to plead the defence.

52 Which of the following is correctly matched in relation to the defences of tort of defamation?

1 Fair comment – An expression of statement of fact rather than expression of opinion
2 Absolute privilege – Statements made by the members of either House of Parliament in the House or outside the House
3 Justification by truth – It is enough if the statement is substantially true and may not be mathematically accurate
4 Consent – Plaintiff has not consented to the publication of defamatory words by the defendant

Ans. (3)

Exp. Among the given choices, option (3) is correctly matched in relation to the defences of tort of defamation.

In Justification by truth it is enough if the statement is substantially true and may not be mathematically accurate.

Truth is a complete defense to defamation, but there is no need to prove the truth in its entirety. Rather, the suit is decided based on the doctrine of substantial truth in which, a defamatory statement is protected if it is factually very similar to the alleged truth in its substance, though may not be true totally.

Fair comment is referred to as honest comment and applies where the defamatory words are an expression of opinion and not a statement of fact.

The term 'Privilege', or 'Immunity' is also a defense against a claim of defamation. Absolute privilege protects members of legislative bodies from charges of defamation for statements made "on the floor or inside" of their legislative bodies. The Consent of person who allegedly has been defamed is always a complete defense in the event of a defamation claim.

53 Which of the following case is not related to 'Remoteness of Damage' ?

1 Scott Vs. Shepherd
2 In re an Arbitration between Polemis and Furness, Withy and Co.
3 Sirros Vs. Moore
4 Overseas Tankship Ltd. Vs. Morts Dock and Engineering Co.

Ans. (3)

Exp. The case titled as Sirros Vs. Moore, is not based upon 'Remoteness of Damage'.

It is 1975 decision made by Queen's Bench, U.K. wherein it was held that despite acting mistakenly, a judge and police officers acting on his instruction are immune from liability if the acts complained of are carried out by the judge when he acts in his capacity of a judge and does so in good faith.

Lord Denning MR discussed the immunity of judges from suit: "The words which a judge speaks are protected by an absolute privilege. The orders which he gives, and the sentences which he imposes, cannot be made the subject of civil proceedings against him. No matter that the judge was under some gross error or ignorance, or was actuated by envy, hatred and malice, and all uncharitableness, he is not liable to an action".

54 Which of the following tort is not related to nuisance based on 'Physical discomfort' or interference with another's health and safety?

1 Obstruction of light
2 Injury to property
3 Noise pollution
4 Pollution of water and air

Ans. (2)

Exp. Injury to property is not related to nuisance based on 'Physical discomfort' or interference with another's health and safety.

The Nuisance under tort law is generally of two kinds on the basis of injury : Damage to property and Physical discomfort. The nuisance falling under the head of damage to property must result in causing some damage or loss to any property, whether movable or immovable. Damage to adjacent walls, cracks in the houses, ete. are some of the examples.

However, in the case of Physical discomfort, the act complained of must be in excess of the natural and ordinary course of enjoyment of the property materially interfering with the ordinary comforts of human existence. Such nuisance disturbs the human health, such as carrying any trade causing nuisance resulting in pollution of water, or noise pollution, obstruction of light. ete.

55 Match List I (Name of case) with List II (Capacity to sue) and give the correct answer by using the codes given below

	List I		List II
A.	State of Saurashtra Vs. Memon Haji Ismail	I.	No right to sue as an un-incorporated association
B.	Delhi Transport Corporation Vs. Kumari Lalita	II.	Municipal law does not apply
C.	Brown Vs. Lewis	III.	Suit against corporation
D.	Campbell Vs. Paddington	IV.	Suit by minor

Codes

	A	B	C	D		A	B	C	D
1	II	IV	I	III	2	I	II	IV	III
3	III	I	II	IV	4	IV	III	I	II

Ans. (1)

Exp. The correct matching is A-II; B-IV; C-I; D-III.

State of Saurashtra Vs. Memon Haji Ismail (1959) dealt with matters where municipal law does not apply. In this case, it was held that the essence of an act of State is the exercise of its sovereign power and that is done on principles either outside or paramount to the municipal law. It indicated that municipal or local law is not applicable to judge an action of a sovereign.

Delhi Transport Corporation Vs Kumari Lalita (1982), involved entertaining a suit by a minor. In this case it was held that a judge should only find a child guilty of contributory negligence if he or she is of such an age as to be expected to take precaution for his or her own safety.

Brown Vs. Lewis is a case which provided that an un-incorporated association did not have a right to sue. It was held that an un-incorporated association is not a legal entity and does not have limited liability. Also, it has no right to sue as an un-incorporated association. Clubs and charities are often constituted as un-incorporated associations.

Campbell Vs. Paddington was a suit against a corporation. In this case, it was held that the Metropolitan Borough (the government corporation) was not entitled to erect a stand causing obstruction of view and held to be a nuisance for the plaintiff who was found to be entitled to recover the profit who had sued the corporation for damages.

56 Given below are two statements. One is labelled as Assertion (A) and the other is labelled as Reason (R).

Assertion (A) Negligence means a conduct which creates a risk of causing damage, rather than a state of mind.

Reason (R) It is safe to start a bus before passengers completely get into it.

Codes

1 Both (A) and (R) are correct and (R) is the correct explanation of (A)
2 Both (A) and (R) are correct, but (R) is not the correct explanation of (A)
3 (A) is incorrect, but (R) is correct
4 (A) is correct and (R) is incorrect

Ans. *(4)*

Exp. (A) is correct and (R) is incorrect.

Negligence is that conduct which involves an unreasonably great risk of causing damage. Due care is conduct which does not involve such a risk. According to Henry T. Terry, Negligence is a conduct, not a state of mind. It is most often caused by carelessness or heedlessness; the actor does not advert properly to the consequences that may follow his conduct, and therefore fails to realize that his conduct is unreasonably danger. Hence, Assertion (A) is correct.

Further, it is negligence to start a bus before passengers get into it. In Ishwar Devi Vs. Union of India (2010), it was observed that "the safety of the public who travel by public conveyances like the bus in question is the primary concern of the conductor and the driver, who are in charge of public conveyances". The court held when the conductor saw the deceased was boarding the bus and was still on the foot board, he should not have given the bell for the starting of the bus, but should have waited till he got inside the bus, the failure of which amounts to negligent act. Thus, the Reason (R) is not correct.

57 Which of the following statement is correct in relation to Consumer Courts?

1 National Commission has power to transfer a pending complaint from a District Forum to another in the same State
2 State Commission has power to transfer a pending complaint from a District Forum to another in the same State
3 National Commission can not have circuit benches except the permanent bench at New Delhi
4 State Commission cannot have circuit benches but can have two State Commissions

Ans. *(2)*

Exp. Statement 2 is correct in relation to Consumer Courts.

State Commission has power to transfer a pending complaint from a District Forum to another in the same State. As per Section 48 of the amended Consumer Protection Act, 2019, on the application of the complainant or of its own motion, the State Commission may, at any stage of the proceeding, transfer any complaint pending before a District Commission to another District Commission within the State if the interest of justice so requires.

Statement 1,3 and 4 are incorrect.

The National Commission may transfer any complaint pending before the District Commission of one State to a District Commission of another State or before one State Commission to another State Commission.

As per Section 53 (1), the Central Government shall establish a National Consumer Disputes Redressal Commission, to be known as the National Commission and the Central Government may establish regional Benches of the National Commission at such places as it deems fit.

Further, as per Section 42, the State Government shall, by notification, establish a State Consumer Disputes Redressal Commission to be known as the State Commission in the State. The State Government may also establish regional benches of the State Commission, at such places, as it deems fit.

58 Point out the correct statement.

1 Crime is necessarily an immoral act
2 Crime is necessarily an anti-social act
3 Crime is necessarily an anti-communal act
4 Crime is necessarily an anti-religious act

Ans. *(2)*

Exp. Statement 2 is correct as a crime is necessarily an anti-social act since every crime is said to be against the society on the whole, and the state prosecutes the doers of criminal wrongs.

Statement 1,3 and 4 are incorrect.

A crime is not necessarily immoral since it is made by the sovereign based on the notion as to what is good or bad for the society.

Also, it is wrong to say that crime is necessarily an anti communal act, because crimes are of diverse nature and kinds, and anti-communal act only forms a part of them.

Similarly, a crime is not necessarily an anti-religious act because the scope of crime is broad enough to cover variety of crimes within its ambit.

59 Four accused with common intention to kill, shot one B in the bona fide belief that B was A. In this case,

1 none of them is liable for the offence of murder
2 all accused are guilty of causing death
3 Section 34 of Indian Penal Code does not apply
4 all accused are guilty of causing death without invoking Section 34

Ans. *(2)*

Exp. Four accused with common intention to kill, shot one 'B' in the bona fide belief that 'B' was 'A'. In this case, all accused are guilty of causing death. Their liability lies under Section 300 in the Indian Penal Code which says that culpable homicide is murder, if the Act by which the death is caused is done with the intention of causing death.

60 Under Section 65 of Indian Penal Code, 1860, sentence of imprisonment for non-payment of fine shall be limited to

1 one-half of the maximum term of imprisonment fixed for the offence
2 one-third of the maximum term of imprisonment fixed for the offence
3 one-fourth of the maximum term of imprisonment fixed for the offence
4 one-fifth of the maximum term of imprisonment fixed for the offence

Ans. *(3)*

Exp. Section 65 of Indian Penal Code, 1860 provides a limit to imprisonment for non-payment of fine, when imprisonment and fine are awardable.

According to it, the term for which the Court directs the offender to be imprisoned in default of payment of a fine shall not exceed one-fourth of the term of imprisonment which is the maximum fixed for the offence, if the offence be punishable with imprisonment as well as fine.

For instance, if the maximum term of imprisonment provided for an offence is one year, the term of imprisonment in default of payment of fine can never exceed three months which is one-fourth of one year.

61 Under which of the following sections of the Indian Penal Code, 1860, promoting enmity between different groups on grounds of religion, race, place of birth, residence, language etc. and doing acts prejudicial to maintenance of harmony is dealt with?

1 Section 153   2 Section 153 A
3 Section 153 AA   4 Section 153 B

Ans. *(2)*

Exp. Under Section 153 A of IPC, 1860 promoting enmity between different groups on grounds of religion, race, place of birth, residence, language etc. and doing acts prejudicial to maintenance of harmony is dealt with.

Section 153A of IPC provides that whoever promotes or attempts to promote, on grounds of religion, race, place of birth, residence, language, caste or community or any other ground whatsoever, disharmony or feelings of enmity, hatred or ill-will between different religious, racial, language or regional groups or castes or communities, or commits any act which is prejudicial to the maintenance of harmony between different religious, racial, language or regional groups that are likely to disturb the public tranquility, shall be punished with imprisonment which may extend to three years, or with fine, or with both.

62 'A' instigates 'B' to murder 'D'. 'B' in pursuance of the instigation stabs 'D'. 'D' recovers from the wound. Here, 'A' is guilty of

1 instigating B to commit murder
2 instigating B to commit attempt to murder
3 instigating B to commit grievous hurt
4 no offence

Ans. *(1)*

Exp. 'A' instigates 'B' to murder 'D'. 'B' in pursuance of the instigation stabs 'D'. 'D' recovers from the wound. Here, 'A' is guilty of instigating 'B' to commit murder.

Section 107 of IPC defines abetment of a thing as a person abets the doing of a thing, who instigates any person to do that thing; or engages with one or more other person or persons in any conspiracy for the doing of that thing, if an act or illegal omission takes place in pursuance of that conspiracy, and in order to the doing of that thing; or intentionally aids, by any act or illegal omission, the doing of that thing.

Section 108 provides that to constitute the offence of abetment it is not necessary that the act abetted should be committed, or that the effect requisite to constitute the offence should be caused.

It is clear that to be held liable under the above provision, the completion of desired objective is not necessary. Thus, even if 'D' did not die, 'A' shall still be liable for abetment as stated.

63 Under which of the following provisions of the Indian Penal Code, 1860, an assault or criminal force used in attempting to commit theft of property is punishable?

1 Section 356   2 Section 378
3 Section 379   4 Section 384

Ans. *(1)*

Exp. Under Section 356 of the Indian Penal Code, 1860, an assault or criminal force used in attempting to commit theft of property is punishable.

According to Section 356 of IPC, whoever assaults or uses criminal force to any person, in attempting to commit theft on any property which that person is then wearing or carrying, shall be punished with imprisonment of either description for a term which may extend to two years, or with fine, or with both.

Some of the other related provisions are Section 378 [Theft], Section 379 [Punishment for theft] and Section 384 [Punishment for extortion].

64 'X' gives grave and sudden provocation to 'Y'. 'Y' on this provocation, fires a pistol at 'X', neither intending nor knowing himself to be likely to kill 'Z', who is near him, but out of sight. 'Y' kills 'Z'. Here, 'Y' has committed

1 death by negligence
2 murder
3 culpable homicide not amounting to murder
4 no offence

The exception-1 to Section 300 of IPC states that culpable homicide is not murder if the offender, whilst deprived of the power of self-control by grave and sudden

***Ans.** (3)*

Exp. 'X' gives grave and sudden provocation to 'Y'. 'Y' on this provocation, fires a pistol at 'X', neither intending nor knowing himself to be likely to kill 'Z', who is near him, but out of sight. 'Y' kills 'Z'. Here, 'Y' has committed culpable homicide not amounting to murder.

Exception 1 to Section 300 IPC provides for cases when culpable homicide is not murder and states that Culpable homicide is not murder if the offender, whilst deprived of the power of self-control by grave and sudden provocation, causes the death of the person who gave the provocation or causes the death of any other person by mistake or accident.

65 Match List I with List II and give the correct answer by using the codes given below.

List I	List II
A. Dishonest taking of property	I. Criminal breach of trust
B. Dishonestly inducing any person to deliver property	II. Extortion
C. Entrustment of property	III. Criminal misappropriation
D. Conversion of property	IV. Theft

Codes

	A	B	C	D		A	B	C	D
1	I	II	III	IV	2	IV	II	I	III
3	III	IV	II	I	4	II	III	I	IV

***Ans.** (2)*

Exp. The correct matching is A-IV, B-II, C-I, D-III.

Section 378 of IPC defines *theft* as whoever, intending to take dishonestly any moveable property out of the possession of any person without that per-son's consent, moves that property in order to such taking, is said to commit theft.

Section 383 of IPC defines *extortion* as whoever intentionally puts any person in fear of any injury to that person, or to any other, and thereby dishonestly induces the person so put in fear to deliver to any person any property or valuable security, or anything signed or sealed which may be converted into a valuable security, commits "extortion".

Section 405 of IPC defines *Criminal breach of trust* as "whoever, being in any manner entrusted with property, or with any dominion over property, dishonestly misappropriates or converts to his own use that property, or dishonestly uses or disposes of that property in violation of any direction of law prescribing the mode in which such trust is to be discharged, or of any legal contract, express or implied, which he has made touching the discharge of such trust, or wilfully suffers any other person so to do, commits "criminal breach of trust".

Section 403 of IPC is related *Criminal misappropriation*. It provides whoever dishonestly misappropriates or converts to his own use any movable property, shall be punished with imprisonment of either description for a term which may extend to two years, or with fine, or with both.

66 Given below are two statements. One is labelled as Assertion (A) and the other is labelled as Reason (R).

Assertion (A) Nothing is an offence which is done by a person who, at the time of doing it, by reason of unsoundness of mind, is incapable of knowing the exact nature of the act.

Reason (R) Mistake of fact is a good defence and mistake of law is no defence.

Codes

1 Both (A) and (R) are true and (R) is the correct explanation of (A)
2 Both (A) and (R) are true, but (R) is not the correct explanation of (A)
3 (A) is true and (R) is false
4 (A) is false, but (R) is true

***Ans.** (2)*

Exp. Both (A) and (R) are true, but (R) is not the correct explanation of (A).

According to Section 84 of IPC nothing is an offence which is done by a person who, at the time of doing it, by reason of unsoundness of mind, is incapable of knowing the nature of the act, or that he is doing what is either wrong or contrary to law. Thus, Assertion is correct in itself.

Section 76 of the IPC states that nothing is an offence which is done by a person who is, or who by reason of a mistake of fact and not by reason of a mistake of law in good faith believes himself to be, bound by law to do it. The statement in Reason is correct in itself but is not the accurate reason for assertion.

The appropriate reason should be the absence of mens rea on the part of an accused of unsound mind while committing an act, since such person does not understand the consequences of his actions, he lacks mens rea which is an essential for a crime.

67 Match List-I with List-II and give the correct answer by using the codes given below.

List I	List II
A. Mehboob Shah Vs. Emperor	I. Mens rea
B. State of Maharashtra Vs. M.H. George	II. Intoxication
C. Director of Public Prosecutions Vs. Beard	III. Common Intention
D. R.V. Dudley Vs. Stephens	IV. Necessity

Codes

	A	B	C	D		A	B	C	D
1	I	II	III	IV	2	II	IV	I	III
3	III	I	II	IV	4	IV	II	III	I

Ans. (3)

Exp. The correct matching is A-III, B-I, C-II, D-IV.

Mehboob Shah Vs. Emperor (1945), is related to common intention. In this case, the court held that in order to invoke Section 34, it must be shown that the criminal act complained against was done by one of the accused persons in the furtherance of the common intention of all. Thus, the appellant could not be convicted under Section 34 of the IPC.

State of Maharashtra Vs. M.H. George is related to mens rea. In this case, the court said that the express words of the statute can exclude the mens rea as an essential ingredient of the crime. This may be done for various reasons, for instance, to promote public welfare and activities or to eradicate social evils.

Director of Public Prosecutions Vs Beard mentions intoxication. In this case, the court while rejecting voluntary intoxication as a defense upheld the principle that a man who by his own voluntary act debauches under intoxication and destroys his will power shall be no better situated in regard to criminal acts than a sober man.

R V. Dudley Vs Stepens case is related to necessity. In this case it was held that a man who, in order to escape death from hunger, kills another for the purpose of eating his flesh.

68 Match List I with List II and give the correct answer by using the codes given below.

List I (Provisions for)	List II (Sections of IPC)
A. Punishment for causing death or resulting in persistent vegetative state of victim	I. Section 376 D
B. Sexual intercourse by husband upon his wife during separation	II. Section 376 B
C. Sexual intercourse by a person in authority	III. Section 376 A
D. Gang rape	IV. Section 376 C

Codes

	A	B	C	D		A	B	C	D
1	I	II	III	IV	2	II	IV	I	III
3	III	II	IV	I	4	IV	I	III	II

Ans. (3)

Exp. The correct matching is A-III, B-II, C-IV, D-I.

Section 376 A of IPC provides whoever, commits rape and in the course of such commission inflicts an injury which causes the death of the woman or causes the woman to be in a persistent vegetative state, shall be punished with rigorous imprisonment for a term which shall not be less than twenty years, but which may extend to imprisonment for life, or with death.

Section 376 B provides whoever has sexual intercourse with his own wife, who is living separately without her consent, shall be punished with imprisonment of either description for a term which shall not be less than two years but which may extend to seven years, and shall also be liable to fine.

Section 376 C provides whoever commits rape, being in a position of authority or in a fiduciary relationship; or a public servant; or superintendent or manager of a jail, etc. or on the management of a hospital or being on the staff of a hospital shall be punished with rigorous imprisonment of either description for a term which shall not be less than five years, but which may extend to ten years, and shall also be liable to fine.

Section 376 D of IPC mentions gang rape, it states where a woman is raped by one or more persons constituting a group or acting in furtherance of a common intention, each of those persons shall be deemed to have committed the offence of rape and shall be punished with rigorous imprisonment for a term which shall not be less than twenty years, but which may extend to life and with fine.

69 Give the correct answer by using the codes given below

I. The workman has a right to approach the Labour Court directly without waiting for the conciliation proceedings and government reference.

II. The appropriate government in respect of Corporations and Public Sector undertakings owned or controlled by the Central Government will be the central government.

III. Every industry employing 20 or more workmen is under legal obligation to Constitute and have a Grievances Redressal Committee.

IV. The award passed by the Labour Court can be transmitted to a Civil Court for the effective enforcement of the award.

Select the correct answer from the codes given below

1 Only I and II are correct
2 Only III and IV are correct
3 Only I, II and III are correct
4 I, II, III and IV all are correct

Ans. (4)

Exp. Statements I, II, III and IV all are correct.

Section 2A(2), Industrial Dispute Amendment Act, 2010 states any such workman may make an application directly to the Labour Court or Tribunal for adjudication of the dispute referred to therein after the expiry of forty-five days from the date he has made the application to the Conciliation Officer. Thus, Statement-I is correct.

As per Section 2(a), an appropriate Government means Central government in relation to any industrial dispute concerning any industry or corporation carried on by or under the authority of the Central Government. Thus, Statement-II is also correct.

As per Section 9C, every industrial establishment employing twenty or more workmen shall have one or more Grievance Redressal Committee for the resolution of disputes arising out of individual grievances. Thus, Statement-III is correct.

Section 10 provides that the Labour Court or Tribunal or National Tribunal, as the case may be, shall transmit any award, order or settlement to a Civil Court having jurisdiction and such Civil Court shall execute the award, order or settlement as if it were a decree passed by it. Hence, Statement-IV is correct.

70 Given below are two statements. One is labelled as Assertion (A) and the other is labelled as Reason (R).

Assertion (A) The strike or lockout as the weapon has to be used sparingly for redressal of urgent and pressing grievances when no means are available or when available means have failed to resolve it.

Reason (R) The employment that workmen get and the profit the employer earns are both generated by utilisation of the resources of the society in one form or other and they are to act as Trustees of the said resources.

Codes

1 Both (A) and (R) are true and (R) is the correct explanation of (A)
2 Both (A) and (R) are true, but (R) is not the correct explanation of (A)
3 (A) is false, but (R) is true
4 (A) is true and (R) is false

Ans. *(1)*

Exp. Both (A) and (R) are true and (R) is the correct explanation of (A).

In the decision of Syndicate Bank Vs. Umesh Nayak (1960)etc., it was held that when there is a machinery for settlement of disputes but employees or employers resort to strike or lock-out without having recourse to the prescribed means, strike or lock-out is unjustified and when there is a breach of rules, it would be illegal.

Therefore, the strike or lock out as a weapon has to be used sparingly for redressal of urgent and pressing grievance when either no means are available or the available means have failed. Thus, Assertion is correct in itself.

The statement in Reason is also correct and supports the Assertion because the employees and employers utilize resources of society and an occurrence of strike adversely affects them, which in turn causes loss to the public at large. Strike must be used as a last resort considering it.

71 Match List I with List II and select the correct answer by using the codes given below.

	List I		List II
A.	A strike could be legal or illegal and illegal strike could be justified one	I.	Award
B.	Right of the workmen to approach the Labour Court directly within a period of three years	II.	Bharat Singh Vs. Management of New Delhi Tuberculosis Centre
C.	Right of the workmen to payment of full wages pending proceedings in the High Court	III.	Justice V. R. Krishna Iyer
D.	An interim or a final determination of any industrial dispute	IV.	Section 2 A(2) Industrial Dispute (Amendment) Act, 2010

Codes

	A	B	C	D		A	B	C	D
1	III	IV	II	I	2	I	II	III	IV
3	II	III	IV	I	4	IV	II	I	III

Ans. *(1)*

Exp. The correct matching is A-III; B-IV; C-II; D-I.

"A strike could be legal or illegal and an illegal strike could be justified" was stated by Justice V.R. Krishna Iyer in the case of Crompton Greaves Ltd Vs. The Workmen. He further noted that "It is well settled that in order to entitle the workmen to wages for the period of strike, the strike should be legal as well as justified. A strike is legal if it does not violate any provision of the statute. Again, a strike cannot be said to be unjustified unless the reasons for it are entirely perverse or unreasonable."

Right of the workmen to approach the Labour Court directly within a period of three years has been provided under Section 2A(2) of Industrial Dispute Amendment Act, 2010. It states any such workman may make an application directly to the Labour Court or Tribunal for adjudication of the dispute referred to therein after the expiry of forty-five days from the date he has made the application to the Conciliation Officer.

Right of the workmen to payment of full wages pending proceedings in the High Court was dealt with in the case of Bharat Singh Vs. Management of New Delhi Tuberculosis Centre. It was held where an award directs reinstatement of workman and the employer prefers any proceedings against such award in a High Court or the Supreme Court, the employer shall be liable to pay such workman, during the period of pendency of such proceedings in the High Court or the Supreme Court, full wages last drawn by him.

An interim or final determination of any industrial dispute is called an award. According to Section 2(b) of the Industrial Disputes Act, 1947, an 'Award' means an interim or a final determination of any Industrial Dispute or of any question relating thereto by any Labour Court, Industrial Tribunal or National Industrial Tribunal and includes an arbitration award made under Section 10A.

72 "Although the Judicial interpretation given to the expression 'Industry' by Supreme Court in Bangalore Water Supply Case was intended to settle the test to determine its scope, judicial trends point out that it has done more damage than good, not merely to organisations but also to employees by curtailment of employment opportunities". The above trend is reflected through one of the following case

1 Corporation of City of Nagpur Vs. Employees
2 State of Bombay Vs. Hospital Mazdoor Sabha
3 Coir Board, Ernakulam, Cochin and another Vs. Indira Devi PS and other
4 Madras Gymkhana Club Employees Union Vs. Gymkhana Club

Ans. *(3)*

Exp. In the decision of Coir Board, Ernakulam Cochin and another Vs. Indira Devi PS and other (1992), the court held that the experience of the last two decades did not appear to be entirely happy. Instead of leading to industrial peace and welfare of the community (which was the avowed purpose of artificially extending the definition of industry), the application of the Industrial Disputes Act to organisations which were, quite possibly, not intended to be so covered by the machinery set up under the Industrial Disputes Act, might have done more damage than good, not merely to the organisations but also to employees by the curtailment of employment opportunities.

73 Answer the following using the codes given below

The condition precedent to the order of Reference under Section 10(1) of the Industrial Disputes Act is the satisfactions of the appropriate government to the following

I. Existence of Industrial Dispute

II. Apprehension of Industrial Dispute

Select the correct answer from the codes given below

1 Both I and II are correct
2 I alone is correct
3 II alone is correct
4 Both I and II are wrong

Ans. *(1)*

Exp. Section 10 in The Industrial Disputes Act, 1947 mentions reference of disputes to Boards, Courts or Tribunals. It can be done where the appropriate Government is of opinion that any industrial dispute exists or is apprehended.

The order may refer the dispute to a Board for promoting a settlement thereof; or refer any matter appearing to be connected with or relevant to the dispute to a Court for inquiry; or refer the dispute or any matter appearing to be connected with, or relevant to, the dispute, if it relates to any matter specified in the Second Schedule, to a Labour Court and in the Second Schedule or the Third Schedule to a Tribunal for adjudication.

74 Given below are two statements. One is labelled as Assertion (A) and the other is labelled as Reason (R).

Assertion (A) The unrecognised union has right to meet and discuss with the employer the grievances of Individual workman with the employer and to appeal and participate in a Domestic Departmental Enquiry in which its member is involved.

Reason (R) This is a statutory recognition of a unrecognised Union.

Codes

1 Both (A) and (R) are true and (R) is the correct explanation of (A)
2 Both (A) and (R) are true, but (R) is not the correct explanation of (A)
3 (A) is false, but (R) is true
4 (A) is true and (R) is false

Ans. *(1)*

Exp. Both (A) and (R) are true and (R) is the correct explanation of (A).

Section 22 of Maharashtra Recognition of Trade Union Act and Prevention of Unfair Labour Practices Act, 1971 provide for Rights of unrecognised unions.

It is stated that such officers, members of the office staff and members of any union (other than a recognised union) as may be authorised by or under the rules made in this behalf by the State Government shall, in such manner and subject to such conditions as may be prescribed, have a right-

- to meet and discuss with an employer or any person appointed by him in that behalf, the grievances of any individual member relating to his discharge, removal, retrenchment, termination of service and suspension;
- to appear on behalf of any of its members employed in the undertaking in any domestic or departmental inquiry held by the employer.

Thus, the Assertion and Reason are true and the Reason supports the Assertion as stated.

75 Answer the following using the codes given below

The following are the pre-condition for acquiring Jurisdiction by the National Tribunal under the Industrial Disputes Act

I. Industrial Dispute must involve question of National importance in the opinion of the Central Government.

II. Industrial Dispute must involve question of State importance in the opinion of the State Government.
III. Industrial Disputes must be of such a nature that Industries situated in more than one State and are likely to be interested in or affected by such disputes.
IV. Industrial Disputes must be of such a nature that Industries situated in more than five States and are likely to be interested in or affected by such disputes.

Codes
1 I and IV are correct
2 I and III are correct
3 II and IV are correct
4 IV alone is correct

Ans. (2)

Exp. Statement I and III are correct.
Industrial Disputes Act, 1947 through Section 7B provides for National Tribunals. According to it, the Central Government may constitute National Industrial Tribunals for the adjudication of industrial disputes which, in the opinion of the Central Government, involve questions of national importance or are of such a nature that industrial establishments situated in more than one State are likely to be interested in, or affected by, such disputes.

76 Given below are two statements. One is labelled as Assertion (A) and the other is labelled as Reason (R).

Assertion (A) Administrative law is a branch of public law in contradiction to private law.

Reason (R) Administrative law primarily deals with the relationship of individuals inter se.

Codes
1 Both (A) and (R) are correct and (R) is the correct explanation of (A)
2 Both (A) and (R) are correct, but (R) is not the correct explanation of (A)
3 (A) is correct and (R) is incorrect
4 (A) is incorrect, but (R) is correct

Ans. (3)

Exp. (A) is correct and (R) is incorrect.
The Assertion is correct in itself since the Administrative Law is a branch of public law in contradiction with a private law which deals with the relationship of individuals interests.
Administrative Law primarily deals with the structure and functions of administrative and quasi administrative agencies. Since it involves study of administrative bodies, the relationship of individuals is beyond its scope and hence, the reason is incorrect in itself.
It is worth mentioning that the study includes not only administrative agencies but also the quasi-judicial agencies such as corporation, boards, universities, independent domestic agencies and the like.

77 Match List I (Name of case) with List II (Principle of natural justice) and give correct answer by using the codes given below

List I	List II
A. Hira Nath Mishra Vs. Rajindra Medical College	I. Right to notice or requirement of notice
B. Union of India Vs. Mohd. Ramzan Khan	II. No evidence should be taken at back of the other party
C. Maneka Gandhi Vs. Union of India	III. Report of the enquiry to be shown to the other party
D. Union of India Vs. Narendra Singh	IV. Reasoned decision or speaking orders

Codes

	A	B	C	D
1	III	IV	I	II
2	IV	III	II	I
3	I	II	III	IV
4	II	III	IV	I

Ans. (4)

Exp. The correct matching is A-II, B-III, C-IV, D-I.
Hira Nath Mishra Vs. Rajindra Medical College held that no evidence should be taken at the back of the other party. The two relevant principles of natural justice are audi alteram partem (both parties be heard) and nemo debet esse propria causa (no one shall be a judge in his own cause). In this case of Hiranath Mishra Vs. Rajendra Medical. College Ranchi, the Supreme Court observed that the rules of natural justice were flexible enough to sustain an order of expulsion without the other party being present and copies of individual statements in exceptional conditions.
Union of India Vs . Mohd. Ramzan Khan (1993) dealt with the showing of the report of the inquiry to the other party. It was held that the delinquent is entitled to a copy of such a report holding the delinquent guilty of all or any of the charges with a proposal for any particular punishment.
The case of *Maneka Gandhi Vs. The Union of India* dealt with reasoned decisions or speaking orders. In this case, the court said that section 10(3)(c) of Passport Act, 1967 is void as it violates Article 14 of constitution since it doesn't provide for an opportunity for the aggrieved party to be heard. No sufficient reason was provided for the impounding of the passport.
Union of India Vs. Narendra Singh dealt with the right to notice or requirement of notice. It was held that it is necessary that before an action is taken and a person is actually reverted, he must be given an opportunity to show cause why the proposed action should not be taken against him.

78 Match List I (Name of case) with List II (Name of writ) and give correct answer by using codes given below

List I	List II
A. Sunil Batra Vs. Delhi Administration	I. Quo Warranto
B. U.N.R. Rao Vs. Indira Gandhi	II. Habeas Corpus
C. Gujarat State Financial Corporation Vs. Lotus Hotels	III. Certiorari
D. Nalini Ranjan Vs. Annada Shankar	IV. Mandamus

Codes

	A	B	C	D		A	B	C	D
1	III	IV	I	II	2	IV	III	II	I
3	II	I	IV	III	4	I	II	III	IV

Ans. (3)

Exp. The correct matching is A-II, B-I, C-IV, D-III.

In the decision of *Sunil Batra Vs. Delhi Administration* a letter petition was converted into a "Writ of Habeas Corpus" proceeding in front of the Court under Article 32 of the Constitution. The court expressed its concern for prisoner reform and implementation of necessary provisions.

In *U.N.R. Rao Vs. Indira Gandhi* a writ of Qua Warranto was sought to be issued to the respondent, Smt. Indira Gandhi, for declaration that the respondent has no constitutional authority to the office of and to function as Prime Minister of India. The court held that in th Indian constitutional scheme the President cannot act without the aid and advice of the Council of Ministers, even if the Lok Sabha is dissolved.

In *Gujarat State Financial Corporation Vs. Lotus Hotels Pvt. Ltd.* it was held by Writ of Mandamus that the State cannot commit breach of a solemn undertaking on which the other side has acted.

In *Nalini Ranjan Vs Annada Shankar* it was held that the alternative remedy cannot stand in the way of the writ of Certiorari being issued in the case if there is found to be an absence of or excess of jurisdiction in the Commissioner of Workmen's Compensation in dealing with the matter in question.

79 In which of the following case, the Supreme Court of India ruled that when the selection process consists of only a viva-voce test without any written examination no limit need be imposed on prescribing marks for the interview?

1 A.K. Roy Vs. Union of India
2 A.P. State Financial Corporation Vs. C.M. Ashok Raju
3 Sambhu Nath Sarkar Vs. State of W.B.
4 P. Lakhanpal Vs. Union of India

Ans. (2)

Exp. In A.P State Financial Corporation Vs. CM Ashok Raju the Supreme Court of India ruled that when the selection process consists of only a viva-voce test without any written examination no limit need be imposed on prescribing marks for the interview.

In A.P. State Financial Corporation Vs. C.M. Ashok Raju (1994), the posts of Managers in the A.P.Financial Corporation were to be filled by interview without a written test. The Corporation approved the promotion criteria by viva voce without a written test and allocated marks under various heads; among them for interview 25% and for length of service 15% marks were prescribed.

A Division Bench of the High Court while upholding the allocation of marks under various heads, reduced the percentage of marks for interview from 25% to 15% and increased percentage of marks for length of service from 15% to 25%.

On appeal, the Supreme Court held that the High Court fell into patent error in reaching the conclusion that 25% marks for interview were, in the facts of that case, excessive. It was observed that no limit could be imposed for prescribing the marks for interview.

80 Which of the following statement/statements is/are correct?

I. Absolute discretion is a ruthless master.
II. Where reasonable conduct of government official is expected, the criterion of reasonableness is subjective and not objective.
III. Every action of the executive government must be informed with excuse and should be arbitrary.
IV. Exercise of discretion is an inseparable part of sound administration.

Select the correct answer from the codes given below.

1 Only I and II are correct
2 Only III and IV are correct
3 Only II and IV are correct
4 Only I and IV are correct

Ans. (4)

Exp. Statement I and IV are correct.

Justice William Douglas of the US Supreme Court had said "Law has reached its finest moments when it has freed men from the unlimited discretion of some ruler, some civil or military official, some bureaucrat. Where discretion is absolute, man has always suffered." This suggests that absolute power is a ruthless master and it can go in any direction to any extent if not controlled. Thus, Statement-I is correct.

Justice Bhagwati in R. D. Shetty Vs. International Airport Authority of India in the obiter dicta has said that, "exercise of discretion is an inseparable part of sound administration and, therefore, the State which is itself a creation of Constitution, cannot shed its limitation at any sphere of state activity." Thus, Statement-IV is also correct.

Statement II and III are incorrect because the criterion of reasonableness is objective and not subjective where reasonable conduct of government officials is expected. Also, every action of the executive government must be informed without excuse and should not be arbitrary.

81 Which of the following Acts shall be amended as per Section 58 of the Lokpal and Lokayukta Act, 2013?

I. Commission of Inquiry Act
II. Central Vigilance Commission Act
III. Code of Civil Procedure
IV. Central Bureau of Investigation Act

Select the correct answer from the codes given below

1 I and II are correct
2 III and IV are correct
3 I and IV are correct
4 II and III are correct

Ans. *(1)*

➲ *Exp.* The Section 58 of the Lokpal and Lokayukta Act, 2013 makes the following amendments;

- *Amendment to the Commissions of Inquiry Act, 1952-* In Section 3, in sub-section (1), for the words "The appropriate Government may", the words and figures "Save as otherwise provided in the Lokpal and Lokayuktas Act, 2013, the appropriate Government may" shall be substituted.
- *Amendments to the Central Vigilance Commission Act, 2003-* Among others, in Section 2, after clause (d), the following clause shall be inserted, namely-(da) "Lokpal" means the Lokpal established under sub-section (1) of Section 3 of the Lokpal and Lokayuktas Act, 2013.

Apart from the aforesaid, Amendments were also made to the Delhi Special Police Establishment Act, 1946, Prevention of Corruption Act, 1988, Amendment to the Code of Criminal Procedure, 1973, Amendment to the Code of Criminal Procedure, 1973.

82 Which one of the following is incorrect?

1 Montreal protocol is related to Hazardous Waste
2 The Precautionary Principle and Polluter Pays Principle are essential features of the principles of sustainable development
3 The Stockholm Declaration of 1972 has been described as the Magna Carta of our environment
4 No state has a right to use or permit the use of its territory so as to cause injury by fumes in the territory of another

Ans. *(1)*

➲ *Exp.* Among the given statements, statement 1 is incorrect.

The Montreal Protocol on Substances that Deplete the Ozone Layer is a multilateral environmental agreement that regulates the production and consumption of nearly 100 man-made chemicals referred to as Ozone Depleting Substances (ODS).

Adopted on 15th September 1987, the Protocol is ratified by all 198 UN Member States.

Under this treaty, developing and developed countries have equal but differentiated responsibilities, but most importantly, both groups of countries have binding, time-targeted and measurable commitments.

83 "The State is the trustee of all natural resources which are by nature meant for public use and enjoyment and that Indian legal system includes the Public Trust Doctrine as a part of its jurisprudence".

The Supreme Court of India has observed the above in one of the following case

1 T.N. Godavarman Thirumulpad Vs. Union of India
2 Indian Council for Enviro-Legal Action Vs. Union of India
3 M.C. Mehtha Vs. Union of India
4 Shri Sachidananda Pandey Vs. State of West Bengal

Ans. *(1)*

➲ *Exp.* In T.N. Godavarman Thirumulpad Vs. Union of India case, the Supreme Court held that "The State is the trustee of all natural resources which are by nature meant for public use and enjoyment and that Indian legal system includes the Public Trust Doctrine as a part of its jurisprudence".

In T.N. Godavarman Thirumulpad Vs. Union of India (1947), the Court reiterated the decision of M.C.Mehta Vs. Kamal Nath & Ors., that it is the duty of the State to preserve the natural resources. The Doctrine of Public Trust was also discussed. It was highlighted that the Doctrine of Public Trust is based on the understanding that certain common properties such as rivers, seashore, forest and the air were held by the Government trusteeship for free and undisturbed usage of the general public.

It was reiterated that the Doctrine of Public Trust is a part of jurisprudence. The State is believed to be the trustee of all natural resources which are naturally meant for public use and enjoyment.

84 Match List I with List II and give correct answer by using the codes given below

	List I		List II
A.	No state has a right to use or permit the use of its territory so as to cause injury by fumes in the territory of another	I.	Basel Convention
B.	The Economic Benefit must substantially exceed its Environmental Cost	II.	Trial Smelter Case
C.	The present generation has no right to deplete all the existing forest and leave nothing for the Assessment next and future generation	III.	Environment Impact Assessment
D.	Transboundary Movements of Hazardous Wastes and their Disposal	IV.	Inter Generational Equity

Codes

	A	B	C	D		A	B	C	D
1	I	III	IV	II	2	III	II	IV	I
3	II	III	IV	I	4	I	II	III	IV

Ans. (3)

Exp. The correct matching is A-II; B-III; C-IV; D-I.

The United States Vs. Canada (*Trail Smelter Case*), held that no state has the right to use or permit the use of the territory in a manner as to cause injury by fumes in or to the territory of another or the properties or persons therein as stipulated under the United States laws and the principles of international law.

The *Environmental Impact Assessment* (EIA) aims to foresee climate related impacts at an early stage during project conception/planning and design, and works to find ways and means to reduce harmful effects, suggests design of projects to present the options to decision-makers. According to EIA, the Economic Benefit must substantially exceed its Environmental Cost.

Inter Generational Equity states that the present generation has no right to deplete all the existing forest and leave nothing for the Assessment next and future generation. It incorporates recognised principles of international environmental law providing for the protection of natural resources for the benefit of future generations. It forms a substantial objective of Sustainable development having its origins in the 1972 Stockholm Declaration.

The *Basel Convention* on the Control of Trans-boundary Movements of Hazardous Wastes and their Disposal was adopted on 22nd March, 1989 by the Conference of Plenipotentiaries in Basel, Switzerland. The primary purpose of the Basel Convention is to safeguard human health and the environment from the harmful effects of hazardous wastes. It is related to the transboundary movements of hazardous wastes and their disposal.

85 Given below are two statements. One is labelled as Assertion (A) and the other is labelled as Reason (R).

Assertion (A) It is the duty of the state to devise and implement a coherent and co-ordinated programme to meet its obligation of Sustainable Development.

Reason (R) Adherence to the principle of Sustainable Development is now a Constitutional requirement.

Codes

1 Both (A) and (R) are correct and (R) is the correct explanation of (A)
2 Both (A) and (R) are correct, but (R) is not the correct explanation of (A)
3 (A) is correct, but (R) is wrong
4 (A) is wrong, but (R) is correct

Ans. (1)

Exp. Both (A) and (R) are correct and (R) is the correct explanation of (A).

The doctrine of 'Sustainable Development' was discussed for the first time in the Stockholm Declaration of 1972. In 1992, Rio Declaration on Environment and Development codified the principle of Sustainable Development.

In Indian Council of Enviro-Legal Action Vs. Union of India, the Apex Court held "while economic development should not be allowed to take place at the cost of ecology or by causing widespread environment destruction and violation; at the same time, the necessity to preserve ecology and environment should not hamper economic and other developments". It is suggestive that proper mechanism must be prepared to battle the climate related damage. Hence, the Assertion is correct.

In T.N. Godavaraman Thirumulpad Vs. Union of India, the Supreme Court said "as a matter of preface, we may state that adherence to the principle of Sustainable Development is now a constitutional requirement. How much damage to the environment and ecology occurs has got to be decided on the facts of each case". The Reason is correct in itself and provides true support to Assertion as the state will have a duty to protect environment legally in the presence of constitutional duty.

86 Which of the following do not come under the powers and functions of the Central Board as provided Under the Air (Prevention and Control of Pollution) Act, 1981 ?

1 Planning and execution of National programme for prevention, control and abatement of Air Pollution
2 Co-ordinating activities of State Boards and resolving disputes among them
3 Fixing standards of Quality of Air
4 Making recommendations to the State government for removal of State Board which is defaulter in discharging its duties under the Act

Ans. (4)

Exp. Making recommendations to the State government for removal of State Board which is defaulter in discharging its duties under the Act which do not come under the powers and functions of the Central Board as provided Under the Air (Prevention and Control of Pollution) Act, 1981.

According to Section 18 of Air Prevention and Control of Pollution Act, 1981 states that where the Central Government is of the opinion that any State Board has defaulted in complying with any directions given by the Central Board under sub-section (1) and as a result of such default a grave emergency has arisen and it is necessary or expedient so to do in the public interest, it may, by order, direct the Central Board to perform any of the functions of the State Board in relation to such area, for such period and for such purposes, as may be specified in the order.

Section 16(2)(b) provides for planning and cause to be executed of nation-wide programme for the prevention, control or abatement of air pollution.

Section 16(2)(c) provides to co-ordinate the activities of the State and resolve disputes among them.

Section 16(2)(h) lays down standards for the quality of air.

87 In which one of the following case, the Supreme Court of India held that right to access to drinking water is fundamental to life and it is the duty of the State under Act 21 to provide clean drinking water to its citizens?

1 Vellore Citizens Welfare forum Vs. Union of India
2 A.P. Pollution Control Board Vs. M.V. Nayadu
3 M.C. Mehtha Vs. Union of India
4 Karnataka Industrial Area Development Board Vs. Shri C. Kenchappa

Ans. (2)

Exp. In the decision of A.P. Pollution Control Board Vs. M.V. Nayadu (1999), the court held that drinking water is of primary importance in any country.

In fact, India is a party to the Resolution of the UNO passed during the United Nations Water Conference in 1977 as under: "All people, whatever their stage of development and their social and economic conditions, have the right to have access to drinking water in quantum and of a quality equal to their basic needs."

Thus, the right to access to drinking water is fundamental to life and there is a duty on the State under Article 21 to provide clean drinking water to its citizens.

88 Given below are two statements. One is labelled as Assertion (A) and the other is labelled as Reason (R).

Assertion (A) The provisions concerning Human Rights run throughout the UN Charter 'like a golden thread'.

Reason (R) Much of the credit for this goes to the determined lobbying by non-governmental organisations at San Francisco Conference.

Codes

1 Both (A) and (R) are correct and (R) is the correct explanation of (A)
2 Both (A) and (R) are correct, but (R) is not the correct explanation of (A)
3 (A) is correct, but (R) is wrong
4 (A) is wrong, but (R) is correct

Ans. (1)

Exp. Both (A) and (R) are correct and (R) is the correct explanation of (A).

The decision of the San Francisco Conference, 1945 led to the establishment of the United Nations Organization. International concern for human rights was woven into the United Nations (U.N.) Charter, 1945 'like a golden thread'.

To implement the provisions of the U.N. Charter, 1945 concerning human rights, the General Assembly of the United Nations decided to prepare an International Bill of Human Rights.

With a view to achieve this, the General Assembly of the United Nations requested the Economic and Social Council on 29th January, 1946 to prepare a report on the study conducted by the Commission on Human Rights. The Commission began to work since January 1947, under the Chairmanship of Mrs. Franklin D. Roosevelt.

In its first session a committee has been appointed known as Drafting Committee for the preparation of the draft: International Bill of Rights. Hence, the Assertion and Reason are correct with the reason supporting the Assertion.

89 Under its terms of reference, the UN Commission on Human Rights was directed to prepare recommendations and reports on

I. An International Bill on Human Rights.
II. International Conventions or declarations on civil liberties; the status of woman, freedom of information and similar other matters.
III. The protection of Minorities.
IV. The prevention of discrimination on the basis of race, sex, language or religion and other matters concerning Human Rights.

Which of the following statement(s) is/are correct?

1 Only I is correct
2 Only II and III are correct
3 Only I, II and III are correct
4 I, II, III and IV all are correct

Ans. (4)

Exp. Statements I, II, III and IV all are correct.

At its first session, in 1946, the General Assembly considered a draft Declaration on Fundamental Human Rights and Freedoms and transmitted for reference to the Commission on Human Rights for consideration in its preparation of an international bill of rights. Statement-I is correct. As a part of commission's report, international Covenant on Civil and Political Rights, adopted in 1966.

The Article 3 provides the States Parties to the present Covenant undertake to ensure the equal right of men and women to the enjoyment of all civil and political rights set forth in the present Covenant.

Article 19 states that everyone shall have the right to freedom of expression; this right shall include freedom to seek, receive and impart information and ideas of all kinds.

Article 27 provides that minorities shall not be denied the right, in community with the other members of their group, to enjoy their own culture, to profess and practise their own religion, or to use their own language.

Article 26 holds that the law shall prohibit any discrimination and guarantee to all persons equal and effective protection against discrimination on any ground such as race, colour, sex, language, religion, political or other opinion, national or social origin, property, birth or other status.

90 Match List-I with List-II and give the correct answer by using the codes given below

	List I	List II
A.	Human Rights Council	I. 1993
B.	The Universal Declaration of Human Rights	II. 2006
C.	The International Covenant on Civil and Political Rights	III. 1948
D.	World Conference on Human Rights, Vienna	IV. 1966

Codes

	A	B	C	D		A	B	C	D
1	I	II	III	IV	2	IV	III	II	I
3	II	III	IV	I	4	III	I	II	IV

Ans. (3)

Exp. The correct matching is A-II; B-III; C-IV; D-I.

The *Human Rights Council* is an inter-governmental body within the United Nations system for strengthening the promotion and protection of human rights around the world. It was created by the United Nations General Assembly on 15th March 2006 by resolution.

The Universal Declaration of Human Rights (UDHR) was proclaimed by the United Nations General Assembly in Paris on 10th December 1948 as a common standard of achievements for all peoples and all nations.

The International Covenant on Civil and Political Rights ICCPR is an international human rights treaty adopted in 1966. It grants people rights relating to freedom from torture and other cruel, inhuman or degrading treatment or punishment, fair trial rights, freedom of thought and non-discrimination, etc.

The *World Conference on Human Rights* took place in Vienna, Austria from 14th-25 June 1993. The Vienna Declaration and Programme of Action a common plan for the strengthening of human rights work around the world, was its outcome.

91 Which of the following statement/statements is/are not correct?

I. The position of U.N. High Commissioner for Human Rights was created by the Economic and Social Council.

II. The High Commissioner was to be appointed by the Secretary. General subject to approval by the General Assembly.

III. The term of office of High Commissioner was five years.

IV. The High Commissioner's principal location would be in New York.

Select the correct answer from the codes given below

1 Only IV is not correct
2 I, III and IV all are not correct
3 I, II and III are not correct
4 I, II, III and IV all are not correct

Ans. (2)

Exp. Statements I, III and IV are not correct.

The UN General Assembly established the Office of the High Commissioner for Human Rights in December 1993 through its resolution. Thus, Statement-I is wrong.

In accordance with General Assembly resolution 48/141, the United Nations High Commissioner for Human Rights is appointed by the Secretary-General of the United Nations and approved by the General Assembly, with due regard to geographical rotation for a fixed term of four years with a possibility of one renewal for another fixed term of four years. Thus, statement II is correct but III is wrong.

The office is headed by the High Commissioner for Human Rights, who co-ordinates human rights activities throughout the United Nations System and acts as the secretariat of the Human Rights Council in Geneva, Switzerland. Thus, Statement-IV is incorrect.

92 Which of the following statement/statements are correct?

I. The Chairperson of the National Human Rights Commission shall be who has been the Chief Justice of Supreme Court.

II. The Chairperson and the other Members of National Human Rights Commission are appointed by the President of India after consultation with Prime Minister.

III. Chairperson and other Members of National Human Rights Commission are eligible for re-appointment.

IV. The Chairperson and the other Members of the Commission can be removed on the Recommendation of the Law Minister of India.

Select the correct answer from the codes given below

1 Only I is correct
2 I and III are correct
3 I, II and III are correct
4 I, II, III and IV all are correct

Ans. (1)

Exp. Section 3(2) (a) of The Protection of Human Rights Act, 1993 provides that the chairperson of the NHRC is a person who has been a Chief Justice of the Supreme Court. Hence, Statement -I is correct.

Statement II, III and IV are incorrect.

As per Section 4, the Chairperson and other Members shall be appointed by the President after obtaining the recommendations of a Committee consisting of the Prime Minister, Speaker of the House of the people, Minister in-charge of the Ministry of Home affairs in the Government of India member, etc. Thus, Statement-II is incorrect.

Section 6(1) provides that a person appointed as Chairperson shall hold office for a term of five years or till age of seventy years, whichever is earlier. Further, section 6(2) provides that a person appointed as a Member be eligible for re-appointment for another term of five years. Since, the chairperson was not eligible for reappointment under the previous law. Thus, Statement-III is incorrect.

Section 5 (2) states that the Chairperson or any Member shall only be removed from his office by order of the President of India on the ground of proved misbehaviour or incapacity. Thus, Statement IV is incorrect.

93 Match List I with List II and give the correct answer by using the codes given below

List I (Provisions)	List II (Sections of the Protection of Human Rights Act, 1993)
A. Constitution of National Human Rights Commission	I. Section 10
B. Constitution of State Human Rights Commission	II. Section 12
C. Functions of the National Human Rights Commission	III. Section 3
D. Procedure of the Commission	IV. Section 21

Codes

	A	B	C	D		A	B	C	D
1	I	II	III	IV	2	II	III	IV	I
3	IV	I	II	III	4	III	IV	II	I

Ans. (4)

Exp. The correct matching is A-III; B-IV; C-II; D-I.

Section 3 of Human Rights Act, 1993 provides for the Constitution of a National Human Rights Commission consisting of a Chairperson, four other Members.

Section 21 provides for the constitution of State Human Rights Commissions, consisting of a Chairperson and four other members.

Section 12 provides functions of the Commission which include inquiry into complaints of-(i) violation of human rights or abatement thereof; or (ii) negligence in the prevention of such violation, by a public servant.

Section 10 mentionsprocedure to be regulated by the Commission and states that the Commission shall meet at such time and place as the Chairperson may think fit. Also, the commission shall regulate its own procedure.

94 Under the Partnership Act, a minor who has been admitted to partnership when attains majority should adhere to the following Which one of the following statement(s) is incorrect?

1. Issue a public notice that he has elected to become or that he has elected not to become a partner
2. Option must be exercised within 2 months on attaining majority
3. When the minor opted to become a partner his rights and liabilities as a minor continue upto the date on which he becomes a partner
4. When the minor opted not to become a partner his rights and liabilities shall continue upto the date on which he gives a public notice

Ans. (2)

Exp. Statement 2 is incorrect.

Section 30(5) of the Partnership Act, 1932 provides that at any time within six months of his attaining majority, or of his obtaining knowledge that he had been admitted to the benefits of partnership, whichever date is later, such person may give public notice that he has elected to become or that he has elected not to become a partner in the firm, and such notice shall determine his position as regards the firm. However, if he fails to give such notice, he shall become a partner in the firm on the expiry of the said six months.

95 Match List I with List II and select the correct answer using the codes given below.

List I	List II
A. Mutual Rights and Liabilities of Partners	I. Section 34 of Partnership Act
B. Dissolution of Partnership	II. Section 13 of Partnership Act
C. Retirement of a Partner	III. Section 39 of Partnership Act
D. Insolvency of a Partner	IV. Section 32 of Partnership Act

Codes

	A	B	C	D		A	B	C	D
1	I	II	IV	III	2	II	III	IV	I
3	III	II	I	IV	4	I	II	III	IV

Ans. (2)

Exp. The correct matching is A-II; B-III; C-IV; D-I.

Section 13 of Partnership Act 1932 provides for mutual rights and liabilities of partners. It is stated that a partner is not entitled to receive remuneration for taking part in the conduct of the business and that the partners are entitled to share equally in the profits earned, and shall contribute equally to the losses sustained by the firm.

Section 39 of Partnership Act mentions the dissolution of a partnership between all the partners of a firm which is called the 'dissolution of the firm'.

Section 32 of Partnership Act, contains rules relating to retirement of a partner and states that a partner may retire with the consent of all the other partners, or in accordance with an express agreement by the partners, among others.

Section 34 of Partnership Act is related to insolvency of a partner. It states that where a partner in a firm is adjudicated an insolvent, he ceases to be a partner on the date on which the order of adjudication is made, whether or not the firm is thereby dissolved.

96 Given below are two statements. One is labelled as Assertion (A) and the other is labelled as Reason (R).

Assertion (A) The surety has no right to restrain execution against him until the creditor exhausted all his remedies against the Principal Debtor.

Reason (R) The Liability of the surety is co-extensive with that of the Principal Debtor, unless it is otherwise provided by contract.

Codes

1 (A) and (R) are true and (R) is the correct explanation of (A)
2 (A) and (R) are true, but (R) is not the correct explanation of (A)
3 (A) is false, but (R) is true
4 (A) is true, but (R) is false

***Ans.* (1)**

Exp. (A) and (R) are true and (R) is the correct explanation of (A).

Section 128 of Indian Contract Act provides for Surety's liability. The liability of the surety is co-extensive with that of the principal debtor, unless it is otherwise provided by the contract. This implies that the creditor can sue either the principal debtor or the surety in case of any default.

The effect of this is that the creditor is not bound to exhaust his remedy against the principal before suing the surety, and a suit may be maintained against the surety though the principal has not been sued.

97 Under the Sale of Goods Act, to make the buyer liable for neglecting or refusing delivery of goods the following conditions must be fulfilled.

Which one of the following statements is incorrect?

1 The seller was ready and willing to deliver the goods
2 The seller requested the buyer to take delivery
3 The seller informed the buyer to ignore the delay and take delivery
4 The buyer did not, within a reasonable time after such request take delivery of the goods

***Ans.* (3)**

Exp. Section 44 of the Sale of Goods Act 1930 provides that when the seller is ready and willing to deliver the goods and requests the buyer to take delivery, and the buyer does not within a reasonable time after such request take delivery of the goods, he is liable to the seller for any loss occasioned by his neglect or refusal to take delivery and also for a reasonable charge for the care and custody of the goods.

It is important to note here that nothing in this section shall affect the rights of the seller where the neglect or refusal of the buyer to take delivery amounts to a repudiation of the contract. Thus, due to this reason Statement 3 is incorrect here.

98 Given below are two statements. One is labelled as Assertion (A) and the other is labelled as Reason (R).

Assertion (A) Under the Company Law, though any outsider is presumed to be aware of the documents which are publicly accessable, but not the internal proceedings of which he can not reasonably aware of, because those are not accessible to the public.

Reason (R) The Doctrine of indoor management evolved as a partial exception to the Doctrine of Constructive Notice and the rule was laid down in Royal British Bank V. Turquand.

Codes

1 Both (A) and (R) are correct and (R) is the correct explanation of (A)
2 Both (A) and (R) are correct, but (R) is not the correct explanation of (A)
3 (A) is true, but (R) is false
4 (A) is false, but (R) is true

***Ans.* (1)**

Exp. Both (A) and (R) are correct and (R) is the correct explanation of (A).

The doctrine of indoor management implies that every person has knowledge of the contents of the Memorandum of Association, Articles of Association and every other document such as special resolutions as it is filed with the Registrar and available for public view. Thus, Assertion is correct.

This doctrine had originated out of the popular case titled as Royal British Bank Vs. Turquand (1856). It was held here that, the company shall be liable since the person dealing with the company is entitled to assume that there has been necessary compliance with regards to the internal management. Thus, Reason is correct in itself and the Reason is well supporting the Assertion.

99 Which one of the following is incorrect?

Any mis-statement made in the prospectus would attract the liability of the following persons under the Companies Act

1 Every person who is a director of the company at the time of the issue of the prospectus
2 Every person who has authorised himself to be named and is named in the prospectus either as director or as having agreed to become a director either immediately or after an interval of time
3 Every person who is a promotor of the company
4 An expert, whose consent has not been endorsed to the registration and liable in respect of every content in the prospectus

***Ans.* (4)**

➲ *Exp.* Section 35 of the Companies Act, 2013 imposes Civil liability for misstatements in prospectus and states that where a person has subscribed for securities of a company acting on any statement included, or the inclusion or omission of any matter, in the prospectus which is misleading and has sustained any loss or damage as a consequence thereof, the following persons shall be liable to pay compensation; the company and every person who is a director of the company at the time of the issue of the prospectus or has authorised himself to be named in the prospectus as a director of the company, or has agreed to become such director or is a promoter of the company or has authorised the issue of the prospectus; and is an expert.

No person shall be liable if he proves that, having consented to become a director of the company, he withdrew his consent before the issue of the prospectus, and that it was issued without his authority or consent. Since consent under above clause must have been taken to attract liability. Thus, due to this reason, Statement 4 is incorrect here.

100 Which one of the following is not the essential requirement to fulfil an instrument intended to be a Promissory Note?

1 The instrument must contain a promise to pay
2 A mere acknowledgement of indebtedness is sufficient
3 The sum of money to be paid must be certain
4 Promise to pay must be unconditional

***Ans.* (2)**

➲ *Exp.* Statement 2 is not the essential requirement to fulfil an instrument intended to be a Promissory Note.

Section 4 of Negotiable Instruments Act, 1881 defines "Promissory note" as an instrument in writing (not being a bank-note or a currency-note) containing an unconditional undertaking, signed by the maker, to pay a certain sum of money only to, or to the order of, a certain person, or to the bearer of the instrument.

UGC-NET
LAW
SOLVED PAPER 2017 (November)
PAPER II

1 Read Assertion (A) and Reason (R) and answer using the code given below.

Assertion (A) The Preamble to the Constitution of India clearly indicates the ideals set before the Nation.

Reason (R) The ideals set before the Nation are Justice, Equity, Fraternity of the individual and unity and integrity of the Nation.

Codes

1 Both (A) and (R) are true and (R) is the correct explanation of (A)
2 Both (A) and (R) are true, but (R) is not the correct explanation of (A)
3 (A) is true, but (R) is false
4 (A) is false, but (R) is true

Ans. *(3)*

Exp. (A) is true, but (R) is false

The Preamble sets out the aims and objectives that the Constitution seeks to achieve. It is a keynote to the minds of the makers of the Constitution and contains their ideals and aspirations. The Preamble to the Constitution of India clearly indicates the ideals set before the Nation.

Reason (R) is false because the Preamble does not merely specify Justice, Equity, Fraternity of the individual and unity and integrity of the Nation as the ideals of the Constitution. It also seeks to constitute India into a Sovereign, Socialist, Secular, Democratic Republic and to secure to all its citizens-Justice, Liberty, Fraternity and Unity and Integrity of the nation.

2 Arrange the following leading cases in order, pronounced by the Supreme Court by using the codes given below.

I. Selvi Vs. State of Karnataka
II. Official Liquidator Vs. Dayananda
III. I.R. Coelho Vs. State of Tamil Nadu
IV. P.A. Inamdar Vs. State of Maharashtra

Codes

1 IV, I, III, II
2 IV, III, II, I
3 III, II, IV, I
4 II, III, IV, I

Ans. *(2)*

Exp. The correct chronological order is IV, III, II, I.

P.A. Inamdar Vs. State of Maharashtra (2005) case judgement was unanimous and discussed the issue (inter alia) of reservation policy in the unaided minority and non-minority institutions. The judgement was given to clear the mist of doubts arising from the previous judgement of the Supreme court in T.M.A. Pai Foundation and Ors. Vs. State of Karnataka and Ors.

I.R. Coelho Vs. State of Tamil Nadu (2007) is one of the most important judgments of the Supreme Court of India to date. It determined the importance of judicial review and the powers of the judiciary in this aspect. The supremacy of the judiciary as the final interpreter of law was finally restored in this case.

In Official Liquidator Vs. Dayananda (2008) case the Court of Appeal declared that the Minister had acted unlawfully in abridging the fundamental right of a citizen to become a member of the trade union. The House of Lords approved the judgment of the Court of appeal and held that such a right could not be taken away without consulting the concerned civil servant. In India, the Courts have gradually recognized that while administering the affairs of the State, the Government and its departments are expected to honour the policy statements and treat the citizens without any discrimination.

Selvi Vs. State of Karnataka (2010) case has given a good fight on behalf of humanity against technology. The judgement delivered by the then Hon'ble Chief Justice himself and two of his other companion judges rendered the practise of narco analysis, brain mapping, FMRI and polygraph test to be unconstitutional and void.

3 Which of the following statement is correct?

1 The Fundamental Duties are mandatory on all the persons
2 The Fundamental Duties have always been a part of the Constitution of India

3 The Fundamental Duties have been added through an amendment to the Constitution of India
4 The Fundamental Duties can be enforced by Writs

Ans. (3)

Exp. Statement 2 is correct in relation to Fundamental Duties.

The Fundamental Duties of citizens were added to the Constitution by the 42nd Amendment in 1976, upon the recommendations of the Swaran Singh Committee that was constituted by the Government.

4 Read Assertion (A) and Reason (R) and answer using the code given below.

Assertion (A) No person is eligible for appointment as Governor unless he is a citizen of India and has completed the age of Thirty Five Years.

Reason (R) He is debarred from holding any other office of profit during his term of office.

Codes

1 Both (A) and (R) are true and (R) is the correct explanation of (A)
2 Both (A) and (R) are true, but (R) is not the correct explanation of (A)
3 (A) is true, but (R) is false
4 (A) is false, but (R) is true

Ans. (2)

Exp. Both (A) and (R) are true, but (R) is not the correct explanation of (A).

According to Article 157, No person shall be eligible for appointment as Governor unless he is a citizen of India and has completed the age of thirty five years.

Article 158 lays down the conditions for Governor's office. Article 158(2) of the Constitution states that the Governor shall not hold any other office of profit. Therefore, Reason given is correct in itself, however, it does not really explain the age criteria for being appointed to the office of Governor in a state.

5 Which one of the following pairs is correctly matched with regard to the provisions of the Constitution of India ?

1 Article 352–Effect of proclamation of Emergency
2 Article 353–Application of provisions relating to distribution of revenues while a proclamation is in operation
3 Article 354–Determination of executive powers of the Union, during emergency
4 Article 355–Duty of the Union to protect States against external aggression and internal disturbance

Ans. (4)

Exp. Article 355-Duty of the Union to protect States against external aggression and internal disturbance is the correctly matched.

Article 355 states that "It shall be the duty of the Union to protect every State against external aggression and internal disturbance and to ensure that the Government of every State is carried on in accordance with the provisions of this Constitution."

Article 352 – Proclamation of Emergency

Article 353 – Effect of Proclamation of Emergency

Article 354 –Application of provisions relating to distribution of revenues while a Proclamation of Emergency is in operation.

Article 355–Duty of the Union to protect states against external aggression and internal disturbance.

6 Which one of the following pairs is not correctly matched with regard to constitutional amendment?

1 The Constitution (Seventh Amendment) Act–1956.
2 The Constitution (Fourteenth Amendment) Act–1962.
3 The Constitution (Thirty First Amendment) Act–1973.
4 The Constitution (Forty Second Amendment) Act–1975.

Ans. (4)

Exp. The Constitution (Forty Second Amendment) Act came into force on 2nd November, 1976.

The 42nd amendment, officially known as The Constitution Act, 1976, was enacted during the Emergency by the Indian National Congress government headed by Indira Gandhi. The 42nd Amendment changed the description of India from a "sovereign democratic republic" to a "sovereign, socialist secular democratic republic", and also changed the words "unity of the nation" to "unity and integrity of the nation".

7 Match List I with List II and give the correct answer by using the codes given below the lists.

	List I		List II
A.	The principles of constructive res judicata are also applicable to writ petition	I.	Woman's Education Trust Vs. State of Haryana
B.	Writ petition dismissed for want of prosecution can be restored	II.	M. Nagabhushana Vs. State of Karnataka
C.	Direction given by the High Court under Article 226 cannot be altered by the State Government	III.	Ratan Singh Vs. State of Rajasthan
D.	The disposal of several writ petitions in a batch by a single order would be permissible if facts of all cases are similar or almost similar	IV.	V. Porukutty Mannadissior Vs. State of Kerala

Codes

	A	B	C	D		A	B	C	D
1	II	III	IV	I	2	III	IV	I	II
3	II	I	IV	III	4	IV	III	I	II

Ans. (2)

Exp. The correct matching is A-III, B-IV, C-I, D-II.

In *Ratan Singh Vs. State of Rajasthan*, it was mentioned that the principles of constructive res judicata are also applicable to writ petition. In this case, it was held that a Matter which might or ought to have been raised in an earlier proceeding will not be raised if the principle of constructive res judicata is applicable.The doctrine of constructive res judicata applies to writ proceedings and when any point which might and ought to have been taken but was not taken in earlier proceedings cannot be taken in a subsequent proceeding.

In *V. Porukutty Mannadissior Vs. State of Kerala* it was mentioned that the writ petition dismissed for want of prosecution can be restored. In this case, The High Court, in an appeal against a decision of the Forest Tribunal, under the provisions of the Kerala Forests (Vesting and Assignment) Act, 1971, held that 92 acres of forest land were to be given back to the appellants. Accordingly,the Forest Department returned certain lands. Later on, they realised that the lands constituted thick forests and had valuable trees thereon and refused the timber transit permits applied for by the appellants.

In *Women's Education Trust Vs. State of Haryana* it was mentioned that the direction given by the High Court under Article 226 cannot be altered by the State Government. Article 226 of the Constitution of India refers to the power of High Court's to issue certain writs throughout the territory in relation to which it exercises jurisdiction.

In *M. Nagabhushana Vs. State of Karnataka* it was mentioned that the disposal of several writ petitions in a batch by a single order would be permissible if facts of all cases are similar or almost similar. It was held that the general principle underlying the doctrine of res judicata is ultimately based on considerations of public policy. One important consideration of public policy is that the decisions pronounced by courts of competent jurisdiction should be final, unless they are modified or reversed by appellate authorities; and the other principle is that no one should be made to face the same kind of litigation twice over, because such a process would be contrary to considerations of fair play and justice.

8 "Judges do not make law, but only declare what has always been law." This statement is of

1 Salmond
2 Blackstone
3 Willis
4 Allen

Ans. (2)

Exp. "Judges do not make law, but only declare what has always been law." This statement is of Blackstone.

Judges, through the rules of precedent, merely discover and declare the existing law and never make 'new' law. A judge makes a decision, 'not according to his own private judgment, but according to the known laws and customs of the land; not delegated to pronounce a new law, but to maintain and expound the old one'.

9 Which of the following statements is/are correct in regard to a valid custom ?

I. The custom has to possess a sufficient measure of antiquity.
II. The custom must have been enjoyed 'as of right'.
III. The custom need not to be consistent with other custom in the same area.
IV. The custom must be certain and precise.

Codes

1 Only I and II are correct
2 Only I, II and III are correct
3 Only I, II and IV are correct
4 I, II, III and IV all are correct

Ans. (3)

Exp. Only Statement I, II and IV are correct in regard to a valid custom.

Statement III is incorrect as a custom must be consistent with other customs in the same area in order to be valid. This is one of the essentials of a valid custom.

Following are the essentials of a valid custom:

- The custom has to possess a sufficient measure of antiquity. A custom must be existence from time immemorial. Indian law doesn't fix any particular years to test the antiquity of custom.
- The custom must have been enjoyed as a matter of right. The right should be enforceable.
- The custom must be certain and precise. It must be certain. If the nature of the custom is not certain, then it loses its validity.
- Custom must be practiced without interruption. Continuity is an essential feature of custom.
- Custom must be in consistency with other custom. It must not be in conflict with other prevailing custom.

10 Match List I with List II and select the correct answer using the codes given below.

List I (Theory)		List II (Jurist)
A. Scientific Positivism	I.	Herbert Spencer
B. Social Solidarity	II.	Gierke
C. Organic Theory of Society	III.	Auguste Compte
D. Theory of reality of group personality	IV.	Duguit

Codes

	A	B	C	D		A	B	C	D
1	I	IV	II	III	2	III	IV	I	II
3	II	IV	III	I	4	IV	II	I	III

Ans. (2)

Exp. The correct matching is A-III, B-IV, C-I, D-II.

Scientific Positivism theory was given by August Compte. Positivism is the name for the scientific study of the social world. Its goal is to formulate abstract and universal laws on the operative dynamics of the social universe. A law is a statement about relationships among forces in the universe. In positivism, laws are to be tested against collected data systematically.

Social solidarity theory was given by Duguit. Social solidarity emphasises the interdependence between individuals in a society, which allows individuals to feel that they can enhance the lives of others. It is a core principle of collective action and is founded on shared values and beliefs among different groups in society.

Organic Theory of Society was given by Herbert Spencer. According to Herbert Spencer, society is not merely a collection of individuals, it is more than that; just as an organism is more than a mere collection of cells. He established the hypothesis that society is like a biological organism.

Theory of reality of group personality is given by Gierke. According to this theory, a legal person is a real personality in an extra juridical and pre-juridical sense of the word. It also assumes that the subjects of rights need not belong merely to human beings but to every being which possesses a will and life of its own.

11 Match List I with List II and select the correct answer using the codes given below.

List I	List II (Jural correlatives)
A. Right	I. Liability
B. Privilege	II. Disability
C. Power	III. Duty
D. Immunity	IV. No-right

Codes

	A	B	C	D		A	B	C	D
1	I	II	III	IV	2	III	IV	I	II
3	III	II	IV	I	4	IV	I	III	II

***Ans.* (2)**

Exp. The correct matching is A-III, B-IV, C-I, D-II.

Duty is the jural correlative of right. Whenever there is a right there is a duty.

No-right is the jural correlative of Privilege. Privilege means the freedom a person has to do or not to do something.

Liability is the jural correlative of power.

Disability is the jural correlative of immunity. Disability refers to no-power. Thus, when a person exercises immunity in a legal relationship with another, the latter has no power over the legal relation.

12 "Ownership denotes the relation between a person and an object forming the subject matter of his ownership." This observation was made by :

1 Salmond
2 Pound
3 Holland
4 Savigny

***Ans.* (1)**

Exp. "Ownership denotes the relation between a person and an object forming the subject-matter of his ownership." This observation was made by Salmond.

It consists in a complex of rights, all of which are rights in rem, being good against the entire world and not merely against specific persons. The term 'property' also includes goodwill of a business, which is an intangible asset. It includes not only immovable and movable objects, but also patents, copyrights, shares, claims etc. According to Salmond, ownership of corporal property is a general, permanent and inheritable right of the user of a thing.

13 Read the following statements and give the correct answer by using the code given below.

Assertion (A) A perfect duty is one which a person not merely ought to perform, but may be justly compelled to perform.

Reason (R) A perfect duty is one which is not merely recognised by law but enforceable.

Codes

1 (A) and (R) both are correct and (R) is the correct explanation of (A)
2 (A) and (R) both are correct and (R) is not the correct explanation of (A)
3 (A) is correct, but (R) is incorrect
4 (A) is incorrect but (R) is correct

***Ans.* (1)**

Exp. (A) and (R) both are correct and (R) is the correct explanation of (A).

A perfect duty is one which a person not merely ought to perform, but may be justly compelled to perform. A perfect duty is one which law not merely recognizes but also enforces. For e.g. an adult male's duty to maintain his old parents is a perfect duty enforceable against the son.

A perfect duty is one which is not merely recognised by law but enforceable by law. Perfect duties are considered as the pillars of law.

14 In which of the following cases, Judge Alvarez has aptly remarked, "The fundamental principles of international law are passing through a serious crisis and this necessitates its reconstruction. A new international law is developing which embodies not only this reconstruction but also some entirely new elements"?

1 Anglo - Norwegian Fisheries Case
2 Aegean Sea Continental Shelf Case
3 Conditions of admission of a State to the United States
4 International Status of South West Africa

***Ans.* (3)**

Exp. In the case of Conditions of admission of a State to the United States, Judge Alvarez has aptly remarked, "The fundamental principles of international law are passing through a serious crisis and this necessitates its reconstruction. A new international law is developing which embodies not only this reconstruction but also some entirely new elements."

The requisite conditions are five in number. To be admitted to membership in the United Nations, an applicant must (1) be a State; (2) be peace-loving; (3) accept the obligations of the Charter; (4) be able to carry out these obligations; and (5) be willing to do so.

15 Which of the following statement/statements is/are not correct ?

I. The words 'International Law' were used for the first time by eminent British Jurist, Jermy Jentham in 1780.

II. J.S. Starke has remarked that international law is a "living and expanding code."

III. Prof. Oppenheim has remarked that international law is the vanishing point of jurisprudence.

IV. Holland has viewed that International law is mere a positive morality.

Codes

1 Only III is incorrect
2 I and IV both are incorrect
3 II, III and IV are only incorrect
4 I, II, III and IV all are incorrect

Ans. *(3)*

Exp. Statements II, III and IV are incorrect.

The remark that International law is a "living and expanding code" was made by Lord Chancellor Sankey in the case Re Piracy Jure Gentium (1934).

Holland has remarked that international law is the vanishing point of jurisprudence.

Austin stated that international law is merely a positive morality.

16 Which of the following is not a theory of relationship between international law and municipal law?

1 Specific Adoption Theory 2 Delegation Theory
3 Declaratory Theory 4 Monism

Ans. *(3)*

Exp. Declaratory theory is not a theory of relationship between international law and municipal law.

Declaratory theory deals with the recognition of new states and authority of governments representing them. According to this theory, existence of statehood is independent of recognition and recognition is merely an acknowledgement of certain facts which already exist.

17 Match List I with List II and give the correct answer by using the code given below the lists.

	List I		List II
A.	Decision given by the Permanent Court of Arbitration	I.	The Right of Minorities in the upper Silesia (Minority schools)
B.	The principle/doctrine of Forum Prorogatum was enunciated in the case	II.	Pious Fund case
C.	A leading case on "reprisal" is :	III.	The Asylum (Colombia Vs. Peru) case
D.	Case decided by International Court of Justice under 'Contentious Jurisdiction'	IV.	Naulilaa Incident

Codes

	A	B	C	D		A	B	C	D
1	II	I	IV	III	2	I	II	III	IV
3	III	IV	I	II	4	IV	III	II	I

Ans. *(1)*

Exp. The correct matching is A-II, B-I, C-IV, D-III.

The decision was given by the Permanent Court of Arbitration in Pious fund case. This dispute arose between the U.S.A and the Republic of Mexico when the latter refused the abide by the arbitral award of 1875 after it was amended. The award had ordered Mexico to pay the Catholic church of California the interest on the capital of funds. The US claimed on the behalf of the church the remaining installments of the payments. The Tribunal held in favour of the USA that its claim was governed by the principle of res judicata which applied to the international arbitration in the same manner as it applied to the judgements of national courts. It ordered Mexico to both extinguish the accrued debt and continue to pay the annual allowance in perpetuity.

The principle/doctrine of Forum Prorogatum was enunciated in the case The Right of Minorities in the upper Silesia (Minority schools). The case of minorities in the upper Silesia dealt with rights of minorities in the connection of public school in the upper Silesia. Doctrine of Forum Prorogatum affords an informal way for a state to express consent to the court's jurisdiction.

A *leading case on "reprisal" is* Naulilaa Incident. In terms of international law, a reprisal is the forcible taking in time of peace, by the government of one country of the property or territory belonging to another country or belonging to the citizens of the other country as redress intended to satisfy a claim. Reprisals in international law contexts were clearly defined in the Naulilaa case/incident (Portugal Vs. Germany). A reprisal is an act of self-help by the insured state, responding after an unsatisfied demand to an act contrary to international law committed by the offending state.

A Case decided by International Court of Justice under 'Contentious Jurisdiction' is the Asylum (Colombia Vs. Peru) case. The contentious jurisdiction is jurisdiction over matters in controversy between parties, in contradistinction to voluntary jurisdiction, or that exercised upon matters not opposed or controverted. The Asylum case was decided by the ICJ under contentious jurisdiction. The court held that "protection from the operation of regular legal proceedings" was not justified under diplomatic asylum.

18 Which of the following cases are not related to "recognition" ?

I. Civil Air Transport Incorporated Co. Vs. Central Air Transport Corporation

II. The Azantzazu Mendi case

III. Barcelona Traction case

IV. United States Vs. Schooner

Codes

1 Only IV 2 Only I, II and III
3 Both III and IV 4 I, II, III and IV

Ans. (3)

Exp. Barcelona Traction case and United States Vs. Schooner, both the cases are not related to the "recognition".

Barcelona Traction case deals with the concept of corporate personality and use of this principle of procedure as a 'General Principle' recognised by all civilised states as a source of law.

United States Vs. Schooner case deals with treaty law.

Recognition is a process whereby certain facts are accepted and endowed with a certain legal status, such as statehood, sovereignty over newly acquired territory, or the international effects of the grant of nationality.

19 Which of the following statement/statements is/are correct ?

I. The most important purpose of the United Nations is to maintain international peace and security.

II. The principles of the United Nations are provided under Article 2 of the U. N. Charter.

III. Section 6 of the U. N. Charter provides for provisions to withdraw of a Member-Slate from the United Nations.

IV. There are five (5) principal organs of the United Nations.

Codes

1 Only I is correct
2 I, II and III are correct
3 I, II, III and IV all are correct
4 Only I and II are correct

Ans. (4)

Exp. Only statement I and II are correct.

Statement III is incorrect because Section 6 of the UN Charter states that a Member of the United Nations which has persistently violated the Principles contained in the present Charter may be expelled from the Organization by the General Assembly upon the recommendation of the Security Council.

Statement IV is incorrect because there were six principal organs of the UN : the General Assembly, the Security Council, the Economic and Social Council, the Secretariat, the Trusteeship Council and the International Court of Justice. However, since the task of Trusteeship Council has been done with, we now have 5 principal organs only.

20 In which of the following cases, the Supreme Court held that "it is now well established that in the absence of any rule of Hindu Law, the court have authority to decide cases on the principle of justice, equity and good conscience" ?

1 Gurunath Vs. Kamlabai
2 Lohar Amrit Vs. Doshi Janti Lal
3 Sarastivali Vs. Jagadammbai
4 Munna Lal Vs. Rajkumar

Ans. (1)

Exp. The court in the case of Gurunath Vs. Kamlabai (1955 AIR 206), the court said that, "It is well known that in the absence of any clear Shastric text the courts have authority to decide cases on principles of justice, equity and good conscience and it is not possible to bold that the reasons stated in support of the rule are not consistent with these principles."

21 Match List I with List II and indicate the correct answer using the code given below.

List I	List II
A. Vishwanath Agrawal Vs. Sarla Agrawal	I. Divorce by mutual consent
B. Geeta Maugalani Vs. Jagdesh Maugalani	II. Saptapadi
C. Manish Goel Vs. Rohni Goel	III. Cruelty
D. Vishnu Prakash Vs. Sheela Devi	IV. Desertion

Codes

	A	B	C	D		A	B	C	D
1	II	IV	III	I	2	I	III	IV	II
3	III	IV	I	II	4	I	IV	III	II

Ans. (3)

Exp. The correct matching is A-III, B-IV, C-I, D-II.

Vishwanath Agrawal Vs. Sarla Agrawal case is related to Cruelty. In this case court observed that mental cruelty is considered as one of the grounds of divorce and it comes under the ambit of Section 13.

Geeta Maugalani Vs. Jagdesh Maugalani case is related to Desertion. In this case, court observed that when either of the parties have no intention of living together, and they have been living separately, this will amount to desertion and is a valid ground for divorce.

Manish Goel Vs. Rohni Goel case is related to Divorce by mutual consent. This case talks about the mutual consent as the right to divorce. Divorce by mutual consent can be obtained within six months, but no petition in such a case can be filed within first year of marriage.

Vishnu Prakash Vs. Sheela Devi case is related to Saptapadi. Saptapadi is an essential ritual under Hindu law. The word, 'Saptapadi' means 'Seven steps'.

22 A Hindu contracting second marriage during pendancy of appeal against the decree of divorce is:

1 Valid
2 Invalid
3 Factum valid
4 Void

Ans. (4)

Exp. A Hindu contracting second marriage during pendency of appeal against the decree of divorce is void.

Section 15 of the Hindu Marriage Act, 1955, allows remarriage only after the dismissal of appeal against a decree of divorce, but no consequences for contravention of the provision are provided in the Act.

23 A Married Hindu contracting second marriage after professing Islam, would be guilty of offence punishable under :

1 Section 17 HM Act, 1955 only
2 Section 494 IPC only
3 Section 17 HM Act read with S.494 IPC
4 Neither S.17 nor S.494.IPC

Ans. (3)

Exp. A Married Hindu contracting second marriage after professing Islam, would be guilty of offence punishable under Section 17 HM Act read with S.494 IPC.

A married Hindu male cannot escape liability under Section 17 of Hindu Marriage Act and Section 494 of IPC merely by professing Islam at a later date. In the Sarla Mudgal case, it was held by the apex court that a Hindu husband cannot marry second time simply by embracing Islam without lawfully dissolving the first marriage.

24 Which is not the modern source of Hindu Law ?

1 Precedent
2 Legislation
3 Dharamshastra
4 Justice, equity and good conscience

Ans. (3)

Exp. Dharamshastra is not the modern source of Hindu law. It is an ancient source of Hindu law.

Modern sources of Hindu law are: Principles of equity, justice and good conscience, precedents and legislations.

25 In which of the following case, the Supreme court held that "Triple Talaq" would be treated as a "Single Talaq" and not a valid talaq?

1 Bai Tahira Case
2 Fazlunbi Case
3 Mohd Ahmad Khan Case
4 Shamim Ara Case

Ans. (4)

Exp. In Shamim Ara Case, the Supreme Court held that "Triple Talaq" would be treated as a "Single Talaq" and not a valid talaq.

Shamim Ara Vs. State of U.P. and Anr. is a family law case decided by the Supreme Court of India in 2002. The Court held for the third option, concluding that Talaq outside of the wife's presence and delivered to her later by writing is so inequitable to Muslim wives as to be without legal sanction.

26 Read Assertion (A) and Reason (R) and answer by using code given below

Assertion (A) An agreement would be void if both the parties to the agreement were under a mistake as to a matter of fact not essential to the agreement.

Reason (R) Because Section 20 of the Indian Contract Act so provides.

Codes

1 (R) is correct , but (A) is incorrect
2 (A) is correct, but (R) is incorrect
3 Both (A) and (R) are correct
4 Both (A) and (R) are incorrect

Ans. (4)

Exp. Both (A) and (R) are incorrect.

Assertion (A) is incorrect because where both parties to an agreement are under a mistake as to a matter of fact essential to the agreement, the agreement is void and it is considered essential to an agreement.

Reason (R) is incorrect because Section 20 reads as, "Where both the parties to an agreement are under a mistake as to a matter of fact, essential to the agreement, the agreement is void."

27 Match List I with List II and select the correct answer using the code given below.

List I		List II
A. Lapse of offer	I.	Week Vs. Tybald
B. General offers	II.	Henthon Vs. Fraser
C. Communication of proposal	III.	Coffee Board Vs. CCT
D. Implied proposal	IV.	Lalman Shukla Vs. Gauri Datt

Codes

	A	B	C	D		A	B	C	D
1	IV	III	I	II	2	II	I	III	IV
3	II	I	IV	III	4	I	II	IV	III

Ans. (3)

Exp. The correct matching is A-II, B-I, C-IV, D-III.

Henthon Vs. Fraser is related to lapse of offer. The issue in the Henthron Vs. Fraser case concerned the revocation of the offer. This was completed before the postal acceptance of the offer was received. It was for the court to decide wheather the acceptance of the offer was valid if the contract had been revoked successfully before the acceptance.

Week Vs. Tybald was related to General offers. General offer means an offer made to the world at large. It can be accepted by any person having notice of the offer by doing what is required under the offer. Thus, it follows that an offer need not be made to an ascertained person but it must be accepted by a definite purpose. In Week Vs Tybald (1605) parties not bound by general words in relation to purported marriage agreement.

Lalman Shukla Vs. Gauri Dutta is related to communication of proposal. The communication of proposal is complete when it comes to the knowledge of the person to whom it is made. There can be acceptance only when there is knowledge of the offer. It should be brought to the knowledge of the person to whom it is made. The case of Lalman Shukla vs Gauri Dutt is a popular case related to the acceptance of a contract and communication of proposal.

Coffee Board Vs. CCT is related to implied proposal. Some contracts are not written. They are implied and this type of contract happens when no written contract is present, but circumstances may cause one person to become unjustly enriched as a result of their actions or an understanding exists. It comes under two forms implied in fact and implied in Law. Coffee Board Vs. CCT deals with the extent and scope the expression 'Sale'. The question of law is whether mandatory sale to the board warrants taxes or is under the course of import and thus exempt from all taxes under Article 286 of the Constitution. The Coffee Act made in mandatory upon coffee growers to deliver its produce to the coffee Board, who was under compulsion to purchase the coffee.

28 "Consideration is the recompense given by the party contracting to the other" : Above definition is attributed to ______.

1 Pollock 2 Justice Patterson
3 Cheshire and Fifoot 4 Blackstone

Ans. (4)

Exp. Consideration is the recompense given by the party contracting to the other". This definition is attributed to Blackstone.

According to section 2(d) of the Indian Contract Act "when at the desire of the promisor, promisee or any other person has done or abstained from doing or does or abstains from doing or promises to do or to abstain from doing something, such act or abstinence, or promise is called a consideration for the promise."

29 Which of the following statement is correct ?

1 Acceptance may be made in the manner prescribed or indicated by the offerer.
2 Acceptance has to be made in the manner prescribed or indicated by the offeree.
3 Acceptance has to be made in the manner prescribed or indicated by the offerer.
4 Acceptance need not be made in the manner prescribed or indicated by the offerer.

Ans. (3)

Exp. Acceptance has to be made in the manner prescribed or indicated by the offeror is the correct statement.

Section 7(2) of Indian Contract Act says that the offeror has to prescribe any mode of acceptance and it is accepted in that prescribed manner only, but when no mode of acceptance is prescribed by the offeror, it will not come under reasonable manner.

30 In which of the following cases, law of frustration was applied? Answer using code given below :

I. Paradine Vs. Jane
II. Taylor Vs. Caldwell
III. Krell Vs. Henry
IV. Cricklewood Property and Investment Trust Ltd. Vs. Leighton's Investment Trust Ltd.

Codes

1 Only I 2 Only I and II
3 Only I, II and III 4 I, II, III and IV

Ans. (4)

Exp. In all the mentioned cases, law of frustration was applied.

The doctrine of frustration basically talks about the impossibility of performance of the contract. It means a contract cannot be executed because of an incident beyond the control of parties. The performance of such a contract becomes frustrated i.e. it becomes complicated, impossible or even illegal.

31 Which one of the following cases enshrine the present position of the doctrine of public policy in India?

1 Ramchand Hirachand Vs. Askar Nawaz Jung
2 Gherulal Parakh Vs. Mahadeodas
3 Muniammal Vs. Raja
4 Geeta Satish Gokarna Vs. Satish Shankarrao Gokarna

Ans. (2)

Exp. Gherulal Parakh Vs. Mahadeodas enshrine the present position of the doctrine of public policy in India.

In the case of Gherulal Parakh Vs. Mahadeodas, the honourable apex court has said that any agreement which tends to be injurious to/against interest or conscience of the public at large is said to be opposed to public policy. It is a branch of common law and unless a particular principle of public policy is recognized by that law, Courts cannot invent a new head of public policy. The ordinary function of the Court is to rely on the well settled heads of public policy and to apply them to varying situations unless harm to public interest is substantially incontestable.

The court, ultimately held that partnership agreement formed with the object of entering into wagering transactions is enforceable, valid and subsisting for its object of wagering isn't unlawful under Section 23 of the Indian Contract Act 1872, because it is neither forbidden by law, nor opposed to public policy, and nor immoral.

32 Read Assertion (A) and Reason (R) and answer using code given below.

Assertion (A) A contract is a property in the nature of a promise supported by some consideration upon which either the remedy of specific performance or that of damages is available.

Reason (R) Above principle is laid down in Sunrise Associates Vs. Govt. of NCT of Delhi.

Codes

1 Both (A) and (R) are correct
2 Both (A) and (R) are incorrect
3 (A) is correct, but (R) is incorrect
4 (R) is correct, but (A) is incorrect

Ans. (2)

Exp. Both (A) and (R) are incorrect.

Assertion is incorrect because a contract is not a property. It is only a promise supported by some consideration upon which either the remedy of specific performance or that of damage is available. The party who is injured by the breach of a contract may bring an action for the damages. The term 'Damages' means compensation in terms of money for the loss suffered by the injured party. Burden lies on the injured party to prove his loss.

Reason is incorrect because the case of Sunrise Associates Vs. Govt. of NCT of Delhi had laid down the opposite of what the Assertion states.

33 Which of the following statement/s is/are correct? Answer by using the code below.

I. In tort, duty is imposed by law and is owed to the community at large.

II. A tort is founded upon consent of parties.

III. A tort is civil wrong for which the remedy is a common law action for liquidated damages.

IV. In tort 'motive' for the violation of right is immaterial.

Codes

1 Only I is correct
2 I and II are correct
3 I, II and III are correct
4 I, II, III and IV are correct

***Ans.* (1)**

Exp. Only Statement I is correct.

In tort, duty is imposed by law and is owed to the community at large. In tort law, a duty of care is a legal obligation which is imposed on an individual, requiring adherence to a standard of reasonable care while performing any acts that could foreseeably harm others.

Statement II, III and IV are incorrect.

In a tort, the obligation arises independently of any consent, that is consent is not required to form any action under the tort.

A tort is civil wrong for which the remedy is a common law action for unliquidated damages.

Motive is generally irrelevant in tort law, just like intention. Motive leads to intention formation, which is the ultimate cause.

34 Match List I (Name of defence) with List II (Related case) and give the answer by using the code given below.

List I	List II
A. Plaintiff a wrongdoer	I. Nichols Vs. Marsland
B. Act of God	II. Bird Vs. Holbrook
C. Inevitable accident	III. Consolidated Co. Vs. Curtis
D. Mistake	IV. Stanley Vs. Powell

Codes

	A	B	C	D		A	B	C	D
1	IV	III	II	I	2	III	IV	I	II
3	II	I	IV	III	4	I	II	III	IV

***Ans.* (3)**

Exp. The correct matching is A-II, B-I, C-IV, D-III.

The defence *Plaintiff a wrongdoer* is related to Bird Vs. Holbrook case. Plaintiff the wrongdoer is based on the principle of 'ex-turpi causa mon-ortitur actio' meaning that 'out of a wrongful cause, no action arises. In such a case, the plaintiff has no legal recourse since the harm caused to him was a result of some wrong of his own doing. In case of Bird Vs. Holbrook, court held that no man can do indirectly that which he is forbidden to do directly.

The defence *Act of God* is related to Nichols Vs. Marsland case. The courts have recognised various events as acts of God-tornadoes, earthquakes, tides, winds and floods. Many insurance policies for property damage exclude from their protection damage caused by acts of God. In this case, the defendant created an artificial lake on his land by collecting water from natural streams and they overflowed due to the weather. The court held that the defendants were not liable as the same was due to the Act of God.

The defence *Inevitable accident* is related to Stanley Vs. Powell case. In the case of Stanley Vs. Powell, the defendent, Mr. Powell, is a member of the shooting party, fired at a pheasant but the pellet from gun glanced off a tree and accidentally wounded Stanley, another member of the party. It was held that Powell was not liable. If the act is wilful or negligent, the defendent would be liable and there is no negligent.

The defence *Mistake* is related to Consolidated Co. Vs. Curtis case. In this case, an auctioneer auctioned some goods of his customer, believing that the goods belonged to him, but then the true owner filed a suit against the auctioneer for the tort of conversion. The court held auctioneer liable and mentioned that the mistake of fact is not a defence that can be pleaded here.

35 Read Assertion (A) and Reason (R) and give correct answer with the help of code given below.

Assertion (A) The relations of partners inter se is that of principal and agent.

Reason (R) The rules of the law of agency does not apply in case of their liability.

Codes

1 Both (A) and (R) are true and (R) is the correct explanation of (A)
2 Both (A) and (R) are true, but (R) is not the correct explanation of (A)
3 (A) is right, but (R) is wrong
4 (A) is wrong, but (R) is right

***Ans.* (3)**

Exp. (A) is right, but (R) is wrong.

The relations of partners inter se is that of principal and agent. A partner needs to play the role of a principal as well as the agent of a business firm. When the partner acts in his interest in the common goal of a firm, he is playing the role of a principal. On the other hand, when he is acting as per the interest of the co partners, he is an agent.

Reason is wrong because rules of agency apply in cases of liability as every partner is liable, jointly with all the other partners and also severally, for all acts of the firm done while he is a partner.

36 A servant is engaged by the master under ________.

1 Contract of service
2 Contract for services
3 Contract from services
4 Contract in services

Ans. (1)

Exp. A servant is engaged by the master under contract of service.

A contract of service is different from a contract for service. In a contract of service the employer normally enjoys the power of control over the work of the servant and the servant is bound to obey the orders/instructions of the master. Contract of service denotes a master-servant relationship in which master not only controls 'What' is to be done but also 'how' is to be done.

37 Match List I (Name of Rule) with List II (Related case) and give correct answer by using code given below.

List I	List II
A. Last opportunity	I. Bernina Mills Vs. Armstrong
B. Apportionment of damages	II. Davies Vs. Mann
C. Alternative danger	III. Shyam Sunder Vs. State of Rajasthan
D. Identification	IV. Vidya Devi Vs. M.P. Road Transport Corporation

Codes

	A	B	C	D		A	B	C	D
1	II	IV	III	I	2	I	III	II	IV
3	III	II	I	IV	4	IV	I	II	III

Ans. (1)

Exp. The correct matching is A-II, B-IV, C-III, D-I.

Rule of last opportunity is related to Davies Vs. Mann case. In this case, the court ruled that since the defendant had an opportunity to avoid the accident by driving with reasonable care, it was the defendant's negligence that really caused the accident.

Appointment of damages is related to Vidya devi Vs. MP Road Transport Corporation. The tribunal held that the claimants failed to prove negligence on the part of the driver of the bus and the facts and circumstances of the case established that the deceased himself was negligent.

Alternative danger is related to Shyam Sunder Vs. State of Rajasthan. The Supreme Court held that the District Judge correctly held the driver liable for negligence in putting a vehicle, not road-worthy, on the road which consequently caught fire.

Identification is related to Bernina Mills Vs. Armstrong. In this case, two ships, the SS Bushire and SS Bernina, collided because of the mutual negligence of those in charge of and operating each ship. The trial court imputed the contributory negligence of those in charge of the SS Bushire to the employees of the SS Bushire (Plaintiffs) so as to bar their recovery under the traditional law.

38 Which of the following is an exception to the rule of strict liability?

1 Defendant's own fault 2 Statutory authority
3 Consent of third party 4 Act of defendant

Ans. (2)

Exp. Statutory authority is an exception to the rule of strict liability.

If any act done under the authorization of the law/statute like the government of a country or a state government causes any damage to a person, it acts as a defence to an action for tort. Statutory authority however cannot be pleaded as a defence when there is negligence.

39 Match the appropriate statements with that of its authors.

List I (Statement)	List II (Author)
A. The behaviour as criminal is part of the political process	I. Klare H. J.
B. Disobedience of law may be termed as a crime	II. Huda
C. Crime is not absolute like sin	III. Terence Morris
D. Crime is an act committed or omitted in violation of a public law	IV. Blackstone

Codes

	A	B	C	D		A	B	C	D
1	IV	III	II	I	2	II	III	I	IV
3	I	IV	II	III	4	I	II	III	IV

Ans. (1)

Exp. The correct matching is A-IV, B-III, C-II, D-I.

Blackstone gave the statement 'The behaviour as criminal is part of the political process'. The Blackstone principle instructs that in distributing errors in criminal punishment, our justice system should strive to minimize false convictions, even at the expense of creating more false acquittals and more errors overall.

Terence Morris gave the statement 'Disobedience of law may be termed as a crime'. According to Terence Morris, "Crime is what society says is crime by establishing that an act is a violation of the criminal law. Without law there can be no crime at all, although there may be moral indignation which results in law being enacted."

Huda gave the statement 'Crime is not absolute like sin'. Crime is not absolute like sin, that can be defined and have an existence beyond the limits of what men may say and do. It is essentially a relative definition of behaviour that is constantly undergoing change.

Klare H. J. gave the statement 'Crime is an act committed or omitted in violation of a public law'. Crime is defined as an act committed or omitted in violation of a public law forbidding or commanding it; a wrong which the Government notices as injurious to the public and punishes in what is called a criminal proceeding in its own name.

40 In the absence of any evidence as to the mens rea, in which of the cases the criminal liability can be fixed upon a person?

1 Where the consequences are not so harmful to the society.
2 Where there is no violent presumption.
3 The intended consequence is not injurious but conjointly injurious on other facts.
4 Where an act is not performed wantonly.

Ans. *(3)*

Exp. In the absence of any evidence as to the mens rea, the criminal liability can be fixed upon a person when, the intended consequence is not injurious but conjointly injurious on other facts.

Mens rea is the mental element of a person's intention to commit a crime; or knowledge that one's action or lack of action would cause a crime to be committed. It is a necessary element of many crimes.

41 In the application of the principle 'Nemo debet proeadem causa bis vexari', what enquiries are relevant?

1 Whether the accused is not in jeopardy on the first indictment?
2 Whether there was final verdict?
3 Whether the previous charge was not the same as that of the present one ?
4 Whether the statute directs not to have a second trial?

Ans. *(2)*

Exp. "Whether there was final verdict?" is a type of enquiry which is relevant in the application of the principle 'Nemo debet proeadem causa bis vexari'.

The principle 'Nemo debet proeadem causa bis vexari'. means no one should be tried twice in respect to the same matter. This is a Latin saying that expresses what in criminal law is known as the rule against double jeopardy, ie the notion that a person should not be "vexed" or have to answer for themselves by being tried or punished more than once for any particular accusation brought against them.

42 Read the following statements and state where the principles of joint liability is applied instantly flowing from mens rea?

1 When he himself commits a crime.
2 When he shares in the commission of crime.
3 When he, with a view to the commission of crime, sets some third agency to work.
4 When he helps the offender after commission of the crime in screening the offence.

Ans. *(2)*

Exp. In case 'when he shares in the commission of crime' is the scenario where the principles of joint liability is applied instantly flowing from mens rea.

The concept of joint liability comes under Section 34 of IPC which states that "when a criminal act is done by several persons, in furtherance of the common intention of all, each of such persons is liable for that act in the same manner as if it were done by him alone."

43 Acts done in moments of delusion are protected because

1 By virtue of absence of free will.
2 Lack of intelligence to distinguish between good and evil.
3 Expediency grounds says so.
4 Circumstances are such that they are incompatible to the existence of Mens rea.

Ans. *(4)*

Exp. Acts done in moments of delusion are protected because circumstances are such that they are incompatible with the existence of Mens rea.

Section 84 of the Indian Penal Code protects a person of unsound mind from prosecution if he was of unsound mind at the time of the commission of crime. It says that nothing is an offence committed by someone who is currently unable to know the nature of the act or does what is wrong or contrary to legislation due to a lack of a sound mind.

44 Which of the factors are essential for fixing criminal liability on importing girls from different territory other than India for seduction?

1 That girl must be below the age of 21 years.
2 That imported girl must be from Indian origin irrespective of age.
3 That girl must be from Jammu and Kashmir or any other UN recognised country and is brought forcefully to render domestic help.
4 That girl is on a tourist Visa and above 21 years and is likely that she will be forced to illicit intercourse.

Ans. *(1)*

Exp. The factor that is essential for fixing criminal liability on importing girls from different territory other than India for seduction is that the girl must be below the age of 21 years.

Section 366B of IPC says that whoever imports into India from any country outside India, any girl under the age of twenty-one years with intent that she may be, or knowing it to be likely that she will be, forced or seduced to illicit intercourse with another person, shall be punishable with imprisonment which may extend to ten years and shall also be liable to fine.

45 Read Assertion (A) and Reason (R) and answer using the code given below.

Assertion (A) There is a more continuous and systematic surveillance over industrial disputes on the part of the government by resorting to compulsory adjudications as the tradition of free collective bargaining has always been weak in India.

Reason (R) With respect to the merits and demerits of collective bargaining Vis-a-Vis compulsory adjudications there is a serious conflict and over lapping of views .

Codes

1 Both (A) and (R) are true and (R) is the correct explanation of (A)
2 Both (A) and (R) are true and (R) is not the correct explanation of (A)
3 (A) is true, but (R) is false
4 (A) is false, but (R) is true

Ans. *(1)*

Exp. Both (A) and (R) are true and (R) is the correct explanation of (A).

Assertion is true because the collective bargaining system in India is weak in nature therefore the government keeps watch over industrial disputes. The Labour Court or to the Industrial tribunal for promoting a settlement of the dispute.

Harmonious employer-employee relationship in industry and uninterrupted production is essential both for the industry and the labour to prosper. To achieve this objective, 'the concept of compulsory adjudication of industrial disputes was statutorily ushered in with a view to providing a forum and compelling the parties to resort to the forum for arbitration so as to avoid confrontation and dislocation in the industry.

Reason is true because collective bargaining is a weak system due to the lapping views.

Further, Section 10 of the Industrial Disputes Act provides for reference of disputes to Boards, Courts or Tribunals. It says that where the appropriate Government is of opinion that any industrial dispute exists or is apprehended, it may at any time, by order in writing,-

(a) refer the dispute to a Board for promoting a settlement thereof; or
(b) refer any matter appearing to be connected with or relevant to the dispute, to a Court for inquiry; or
(c) refer the dispute or any matter appearing to be connected with, or relevant to, the dispute, if it relates to any matter specified in the Second Schedule, to a Labour Court for adjudication; or
(d) refer the dispute or any matter appearing to be connected with, or relevant to, the dispute, whether it relates to any matters specified in the Second Schedule or the Third Schedule, to a Tribunal for adjudication:

46 Match List I with List II and select the correct answer using the code given below the list.

List I	List II
A. Food Corporation of India staff union Vs. Food Corporation of India and others	I. Settlements are the "live wires" of the Act for ensuring industrial peace and prosperity.
B. Virudhachalam Vs. Management of Lotus Mills	II. An unregistered trade union or trade union whose registration has been cancelled has no right.
C. B. Srinivasa Reddy Vs. Karnataka Water Supply and Drainage Board Employees Association	III. Reflection of recent judicial trends on the interpretation of definition of industry.
D. Coir Board, Ernakulam, Cochin and another Vs. Indira Devi P.S. and others	IV. Norms and procedure to be followed for assessing the representative character of Trade Union by a secret ballot system.

Codes

	A	B	C	D		A	B	C	D
1	IV	I	II	III	2	I	II	III	IV
3	III	II	I	IV	4	II	I	IV	III

Ans. *(1)*

Exp. The correct matching is A-IV, B-I, C-II, D-III.

In *Food Corporation of India staff union Vs. Food Corporation of India and others*, the Supreme Court laid down norms and procedure to be followed for assessing the representative character of trade unions by the 'Secret Ballot' system. All eligible workers of an establishment may vote for their chosen union, elections to be conducted by a neutral agent, generally the Registrar of Unions.

In *Virudhachalam Vs. Management of Lotus Mills*, it was mentioned that settlements are the "live wires" of the Act for ensuring industrial peace and prosperity. In this case the court said that, the section 102 of the industrial dispute act highlights the position where if the dispute between the two parties arises then in that case the parties can go to the various bodies and courts mentioned under the act for the settlement of the dispute.

In *B. Srinivasa Reddy Vs. Karnataka Water Supply and Drainage Board Employees Association*, it was mentioned that an unregistered trade union or trade union whose registration has been cancelled has no right. In this case court held that, the unregistered trade unions, per se, have no rights except to represent their members. In cases where the union has a considerable number of workmen as its members, they can raise industrial disputes and put forth their negotiations.

In *Coir Board, Ernakulam, Cochin and another Vs. Indira Devi P.S. and others*, it was mentioned that reflection of recent judicial trends on the interpretation of definition of industry. This case talks about the recent trends that were adopted court for interpreting the definition of industry. Section 2(j) of industrial dispute act defines industry as any business, trade, undertaking, manufacture or calling of employers and includes any calling, service, employment, handicraft, or industrial occupation or avocation of workmen.

47 Which one of the following is wrong?

1 The right to strike or declare lock-out may be controlled or restricted by appropriate industrial legislation.
2 The conciliation officers under the industrial disputes Act are charged with the duty of adjudication of disputes.
3 An interim award is like a preliminary decree within the meaning of Section 2 (2) of Code of Civil Procedure.
4 The Works Committee is not authorised to consider real or substantial changes in the conditions of service.

Ans. *(2)*

➲ *Exp.* Statement 2 is wrong because conciliation officers are not charged with the duty to adjudicate the dispute but the Conciliation Officer makes efforts to resolve the dispute through settlement between the workmen and the management. The duties of Conciliation Officers have been laid down under Section 12 of the Industrial Disputes Act.

48 The Fifth Schedule, under the Industrial Disputes Act contains several unfair labour practices. In which of the conditions of category I, it is required to establish that Employer Sponsored Trade Union of workmen is said to be Unfair Labour Practice?

1 Employees or their Trade Union
2 Employee only
3 Employers or their Trade Union
4 Employer and Employee Collectively

Ans. *(3)*

➲ *Exp.* The Fifth Schedule, under the Industrial Disputes Act contains several unfair labour practices.

There are two parts to the 5th Schedule of Industrial Dispute Act, 1948. Clause (ra) of Section 2 of the Industrial disputes act defines unfair labour practice to mean the practices specified in the fifth schedule and the fifth schedule was also inserted by the said Amending act. The Fifth schedule has two parts. Part I refers to unfair labour practices on the part of the employers and trade union of employers and the Part II refers to unfair labour practices on the part of the workmen and trade union of workmen.

49 When a party to dispute under the Industrial Disputes Act is prevented from appearing at the hearing, due to sufficient cause and is faced with exparte award, the Industrial Tribunal has

1 no power to set aside the exparte award.
2 only duty to set aside the exparte award.
3 both power and duty to set aside the exparte award which is based on the rule of statutory construction.
4 express provision in the Act or rules giving the tribunal the jurisdiction to set aside the award.

Ans. *(3)*

➲ *Exp.* When a party to dispute under the Industrial Disputes Act is prevented from appearing at the hearing, due to sufficient cause and is faced with ex-parte award, the Industrial Tribunal has both power and duty to set aside the ex-parte award which is based on the rule of statutory construction.

Clause 9 to Section 10B of the Industrial Disputes Act, 1947 says that in case any party defaults or fails to appear at any stage, the Labour Court, Tribunal or National Tribunal, as the case may be, may proceed with the reference ex parte and decide the reference application in the absence of the defaulting party. Provided that the Labour Court, Tribunal or National Tribunal, as the case may be, may on the application of either party filed before the submission of the award revoke the order that the case shall proceed ex-parte, if it is satisfied that the absence of the party was on justifiable grounds.

50 "The concept of compulsory adjudication of industrial disputes was statutorily ushered with a view to providing a forum and compelling the parties to resort to the forum for arbitration, so as to avoid confrontation and dislocation in industry." The above observation was made by one of the justice in a case decided by the Supreme Court :

1 Justice V.R. Krishna Iyer
2 Justice O. Chinnappa Reddy
3 Justice Desai
4 Justice Gajendragadkar

Ans. *(3)*

➲ *Exp.* "The concept of compulsory adjudication of industrial disputes was statutorily ushered with a view to providing a forum and compelling the parties to resort to the forum for arbitration, so as to avoid confrontation and dislocation in industry." This observation was made by Justice Desai. Justice D.A. Desai has very aptly described the nature and philosophy of compulsory adjudication in this judgement.

PAPER III

1 Answer the following by using code given below. 'Economic Justice' is one of the objectives of the Constitution of India. It has been provided in

I. Preamble
II. Fundamental Rights
III. Directive Principles of State Policy
IV. Fundamental Duties

Codes

1 I and II are correct
2 I and III are correct
3 II and III are correct
4 II, III and IV are correct

Ans. *(2)*

Exp. 'Economic Justice' is one of the objectives of the Constitution of India, has been provided under Preamble and Directive Principles of State Policy.

The expression 'Economic Justice' has been envisaged in the Preamble of the Indian Constitution. Economic Justice means equitable distribution of wealth, economic equalities, the end of monopolistic control over means of production and distribution, decentralisation of economic resources and securing of adequate opportunities to all for earning their living. Article 38(1) states "The state shall strive to promote the welfare of the people by securing and protecting as effectively as it may a social order in which justice, social, economic and political shall inform all the institutions of the national life". (Directive Principle of State Policy).

2 Arrange the following decided cases in a chronological order and answer by using the code given below.

I. Union of India Vs. N.S. Rathnam and others
II. Basawaraj Vs. Special Land Acquisition Officer
III. Usha Mehta Vs. Government of A.P
IV. City Industrial Development Vs. Platinum Entertainment

Codes

1 III, II, IV, I
2 II, III, IV, I
3 IV, II, III, I
4 II, III, I, IV

Ans. *(1)*

Exp. The correct chronological order is III, II, IV, I.

In *Usha Mehta Vs. Government of A.P.* (2012) case, the Government observed that the grant of lease in favour of her is unauthorised; that the entire transaction is the result of fraud and collusion between her and Sri Venkata Rao, the then Inspector of Estate Officer, Secunderabad; that any claim based on forged document should not be accepted much less acted upon; and that Sri R.D. Bhoopal, Sri K.P. Rao and Dr. Usha Mehta have no locus standi to claim the land. Therefore, the Government holds that the parties have no claim of any kind of land in question and that it is a Government land. Accordingly their claim petitions are dismissed.

In *Basawaraj Vs. Special Land Acquisition Officer* (2013), it was stated that it is a settled legal proposition that law of limitation may harshly affect a particular party but it has to be applied with all its rigour when the statute so prescribes. The Court has no power to extend the period of limitation on equitable grounds. A result flowing from a statutory provision is never an evil. A Court has no power to ignore that provision to relieve what it considers a distress resulting from its operation. The statutory provision may cause hardship or inconvenience to a particular party but the Court has no choice but to enforce it giving full effect to the same. The legal maxim 'dura lex sed lex' which means 'the law is hard but it is the law', stands attracted in such a situation. It has consistently been held that, 'inconvenience is not' a decisive factor to be considered while interpreting a statute.

In *City Industrial Development Vs. Platinum Entertainment* (2014), it was held that a rational policy of allotting land on the basis of individual applications cannot de hors an invitation or advertisement by the State or its instrumentality, bringing it to the knowledge of public at large so that the eligible persons should not be excluded from lodging their competitive claims.

In *Union of India Vs. N.S. Rathnam and others* (2015), it was held that the extent of reasonableness of any taxation statute lies in its efficiency to achieve the object sought to be achieved by the statute. Thus, the classification must bear a nexus with the object sought to be achieved.

3 Read Assertion (A) and Reason (R) and answer using the code given below.

Assertion (A) The Constitution of India under Article 40 states that The State shall take steps to organise village panchayats and endow them with such powers and authority as may be necessary to enable them to function as units of self-government.

Reason (R) This directive gives an assurance that every village where maximum people live, has to be made an autonomous republic, self-sufficient, self-sustaining and capable of managing its own affairs.

Codes

1 Both (A) and (R) are true and (R) is the correct explanation of (A)
2 Both (A) and (R) are true and (R) is not the correct explanation of (A)
3 (A) is true, but (R) is false
4 (A) is false, but (R) is true

Ans. *(1)*

➲ Exp. Both (A) and (R) are true and (R) is the correct explanation of (A).

Article 40 of Constitution states that the state shall take steps to organise village panchayats and endow them with such powers and authority as may be necessary to enable them to function as units of self-government.

This article gives an assurance that every village where maximum people live, has to be made an autonomous republic, self-sufficient, self-sustaining and capable of managing its own affairs.

4 Which of the following statements are correct? Answer by using the code given below.

I. "Persons in Govt/Judicial service need not resign to participate in District Judge selection process" held in Vijay Kumar Misra and another Vs. High court of Judicature at Patna by the Supreme Court of India

II. The Supreme Court of India held in S. Kazi Vs. Muslim education society that "All Tribunals are not necessary parties to the proceedings where legality of its orders challenged"

III. The Supreme Court of India observed in Cardamom Marketing Corporation and others Vs. State of Kerala and others that "Social Security to the legal profession becomes an essential part of legal system"

IV. The Supreme Court of India held in "Union of India v. Rajasthan High Court and others that High Court Judges are exempted from Airport frisking".

Codes

1 Only II is correct
2 I, II and III are correct
3 II, III and IV are correct
4 I, II and IV are correct

Ans. (2)

➲ Exp. Statement I, II and III are correct.

In Vijay Kumar Misra and another Vs. High Court of Judicature at Patna, the Supreme Court of India held that persons in Govt/Judicial service need not resign to participate in District Judge selection process.

The Supreme Court of India held in S. Kazi Vs. Muslim education society that "All Tribunals are not necessary parties to the proceedings where legality of its orders challenged".

The Supreme Court of India in Cardamom Marketing Corporation and others Vs. State of Kerala and others held that "Social Security to the legal profession becomes an essential part of legal system."

Statement IV is incorrect because in "Union of India Vs. Rajasthan High Court and others, the Supreme Court held that High Court Judges are not exempted from Airport frisking.

5 Which one of the following pairs is correctly matched with regard to the provisions of the Constitution of India?

1 Article 118 – Duration of parliament
2 Article 119 – Restriction on discussion in Parliament
3 Article 120 – Language to be used in Parliament
4 Article 121 – Courts not to inquire into the Proceedings of Parliament

Ans. (3)

➲ Exp. Article 120 talks about the language to be used in Parliament, it says that business in Parliament shall be transacted in Hindi or in English, provided that the Chairman of the Council of States or Speaker of the House of the People, or Person acting as such, as the Case may be, may permit any member who cannot adequately express himself in Hindi or in English to address the House in his mother tongue.

Article 118 deals with the rules of Parliamentary Procedure. Article 119 deals with the Regulation by law of procedure in Parliament in relation to financial business while Article 121 deals with Restriction on discussion in Parliament.

6 Match List I with List II and select the correct answer using the code given below.

List I (Constitutional Provision)	List II (Subject)
A. Article 249	I. Power of Parliament to legislate for two or more States by consent and adoption of such legislation by any other State
B. Article 250	II. Power of Parliament to legislate with respect to any matter in the State List if a Proclamation of Emergency is in operation
C. Article 252	III. Legislation for giving effect to international agreements
D. Article 253	IV. Power of Parliament to legislate with respect to a matter in the State List in the national interest

Codes

	A	B	C	D		A	B	C	D
1	I	II	III	IV	2	IV	II	I	III
3	III	II	IV	I	4	II	III	I	IV

Ans. (2)

➲ Exp. The correct matching is A-IV, B-II, C-I, D-III.

Article 249 of the Indian Constitution deals with Power of Parliament to legislate with respect to a matter in the State List in the national interest. It states that if the Council of States has declared by resolution supported by not less than two-thirds of the members present and voting that it is necessary in the national interest that Parliament should make laws with respect to any matter enumerated in the State List specified in the resolution, then parliament can do so.

Article 250 deals with Power of Parliament to legislate with respect to any matter in the State List if a Proclamation of Emergency is in operation. It states that Parliament shall, while a Proclamation of Emergency is in operation, have power to make laws for the whole or any part of the territory of India with respect to any of the matters enumerated in the State List.

Article 252 deals with Power of Parliament to legislate for two or more States by consent and adoption of such legislation by any other State. It states if the legislatures of the two or more states pass resolutions to the effect that it is desirable to have a parliamentary law regulating any of the matters included in the state list, then it is lawful for parliament to make laws on regulation of such matter.

Article 253 deals with Legislation for giving effect to international agreements. It states that Parliament has power to make any law for the whole or any part of the territory of India for implementing any treaty, agreement or convention with any other country or countries or any decision made at any international conference, association or other body.

7 Which of the following statements is/are correct regarding Constitutional Amendment Bill? Give correct answer by using the code given below.

I. Prior permission of President is required before introducing the constitutional Amendment Bill in Parliament

II. Constitutional Amendment Bill can be introduced in either House of Parliament.

III. President is bound to give his assent to the Bill if duly passed by both Houses of Parliament and ratified, if required, by the Legislatures of not less than one-half of the States

IV. President may return the Bill to the Houses for reconsideration

Codes

1 Only I, II and III are correct
2 Only II and III are correct
3 Only II, III and IV are correct
4 I, II, III and IV all are correct

***Ans.** (2)*

Exp. Only statement II and III are correct.

A Constitution Amendment Bill under Article 368 can be introduced in either House of Parliament and has to be passed by each House by special majority.

When bill has been passed by both houses following the described process, it is sent to the President for his approval per Article 111. The President can assent or withhold his assent to a bill or he can return a bill, other than a money bill which is recommended by the President himself to the houses. However, President is bound to give his assent to the Bill if duly passed by both Houses of Parliament and ratified, if required, by the Legislatures of not less than one-half of the States.

Statement I and IV are incorrect.

Prior permission of the President is not required to introduce a constitutional amendment bill in the parliament. An amendment of the Constitution can be initiated only by the introduction of a bill for the purpose in either House of Parliament and not in the state legislatures. The bill can be introduced either by a minister or by a private member and does not require prior permission of the President.

When a Bill amending the Constitution passed by each House with the requisite majority is presented to the President, he shall give his assent thereto and he or she cannot return it for reconsideration.

8 Match List I with List II and select the correct answer using the code given below.

List I	List II
A. Article 324(1)	I. Composition of Election Commission
B. Article 324(2)	II. Appointment of Regional Commissioners
C. Article 324(4)	III. Powers vested in the Election Commission
D. Article 324(5)	IV. Conditions of service and tenure of office of Election Commission

Codes

	A	B	C	D		A	B	C	D
1	III	I	II	IV	2	I	II	III	IV
3	II	IV	I	III	4	IV	II	III	I

***Ans.** (1)*

Exp. The correct matching is A-III, B-I, C-II, D-IV.

Article 324(1) of Indian Constitution deals with Powers vested in the Election Commission. It provides that the superintendence, direction and control of the preparation of the electoral rolls for, and the conduct of, all elections to Parliament and to the Legislature of every State and of elections to the offices of President and Vice President held under this Constitution shall be vested in Election Commission.

Article 324(2) deals with composition of Election Commission. It states that the Election Commission shall consist of the Chief Election Commissioner and such number of other Election Commissioners, if any, as the President may from time to time fix.

Article 324(4) deals with appointment of Regional Commissioners. It provides that before each general election to the House of the People and to the Legislative Assembly of each State, and before the first general election and thereafter before each biennial election to the Legislative Council of each State having such Council, the President may also appoint after consultation with the Election Commission such Regional Commissioners as he may consider necessary to assist the Election Commission.

Article 324(5) deals with conditions of service and tenure of office of Election Commission. It provides that the conditions of service and tenure of office of the Election Commissioners and the Regional Commissioners shall be such as the President may by rule determine.

9 Administrative Law as a separate branch of legal discipline, especially in India, came to be recognised in the middle of :

1 17th century
2 18th century
3 19th century
4 20th century

Ans. *(4)*

➲ ***Exp.*** Administrative Law as a separate branch of legal discipline, especially in India, came to be recognised in the middle of 20th century.

Administrative law is the law that governs the administrative actions. It includes law relating to the rule-making power of the administrative bodies, the quasi-judicial function of administrative agencies, legal liabilities of public authorities and power of the ordinary courts to supervise administrative authorities.

10 Read Assertion (A) and Reason (R) and answer using code given below.

Assertion (A) Natural justice is justice of the nature where the lion devours the lamb and the tiger feeds upon the antilope.

Reason (R) Above statement is taken from Union of India Vs. Tulsiram Patel

Codes

1 Both (A) and (R) are correct
2 (A) is correct, but (R) is incorrect
3 (R) is correct, but (A) is incorrect
4 Both (A) and (R) are incorrect

Ans. *(4)*

➲ ***Exp.*** Both (A) and (R) are incorrect.

Natural justice is an expression of English common law, which involves a procedural requirement of fairness. It is an important concept in administrative law. Natural justice ensures fairness in social and economic activities of the people and also acts as shield to individuals' liberty against the arbitrary action. This is the base for principle of Natural Justice. It is not based on the analogy of tiger and lion given in the statement.

In Union of India Vs. Tulsiram Patel case, it involved the interpretation of Articles 309, 310 and 311 of the Constitution and in particular the second proviso to clause (2) of Article 311 after its amendment by the Constitution (Forty-second Amendment) Act, 1976. It does not deal with the principle of Natural justice.

11 In which of the following cases, underwritten quotation is taken from?
"Principles of natural justice must be read into the provision of law".

1 State of U.P. Vs. Vijay Kumar Tripathi
2 P. Satyanarayana Vs. Land Reforms Tribunal
3 I.T.C. Vs. State of Madras
4 Manjula Manjari Devi Vs. Director of Public Instruction

Ans. *(1)*

➲ ***Exp.*** "Principles of natural justice must be read into the provision of law" is taken from State of U.P. Vs. Vijay Kumar Tripathi.

In State of UP Vs. Vijay Kumar Tripathi the normal rule enunciated by Court was that wherever it is necessary to ensure against the failure of justice, principles of natural justice must be read into a provision. It was further held that awarding censure without affording an opportunity to the effected employee to explain the material on the basis of which the penalty of censure is proposed to be awarded is violative of the principles of natural justice.

12 Match List I (Name of Principle) with List II (Related Case) and answer by using the code below.

List I	List II
A. Res judicata	I. S.P. Gupta Vs. Union of India
B. Legitimate expectation	II. Motilal Padampat Sugar Mills Vs. State of Uttar Pradesh
C. Promissory estoppel	III. Daryao Vs. State of Uttar Pradesh
D. Locus standi	IV. Monnet Ispat and Energy Ltd. Vs. Union of India

Codes

	A	B	C	D		A	B	C	D
1	II	IV	III	I	2	III	IV	II	I
3	I	III	IV	II	4	IV	III	II	I

Ans. *(2)*

➲ ***Exp.*** The correct option is A-III, B-IV, C-II, D-I.

Res judicata is related to Daryao Vs. State of Uttar Pradesh. The term 'res judicata' means 'thing already decided by a competent court'. It states that no court shall try any suit or issue in which the issue directly and substantially, in a former suit, between the same parties or their representatives, in a competent court, has been heard and finally decided by such court.

Legitimate expectation is related to Monnet Ispat and Energy Ltd. Vs. Union of India. 'Legitimate expectation' is a judicial innovation that provides locus standi to a person who though does not have a legal right, does have an expectation of the concerned authority behaving in a certain way.

Promissory estoppel is related to Motilal Padampat Sugar Mills Vs. State of Uttar Pradesh. Promissory estoppel is the legal principle that a promise is enforceable by law, even if made without formal consideration when a promisor has made a promise to a promisee who then relies on that promise to his subsequent detriment.

Locus standi is related to S.P. Gupta Vs. Union of India. 'Locus standi' is Latin for 'place to stand'. It is the ability of a party to demonstrate to the court sufficient connection to and harm from the law or action challenged to support that party's participation in the case.

13 Which of the following is a ground for judicially attacking the exercise of administrative discretion? Answer by using code below.

I. Ultra vires the law II. Mala fide intent
III. Arbitrariness IV. Irrelevant considerations

Codes

1 I and II are correct
2 II and III are correct
3 I, II and III are correct
4 I, II, III and IV are correct

***Ans.* (4)**

Exp. Ultra vires the law, Mala fide intent, arbitrariness, irrelevant considerations are the grounds for judicially attacking the exercise of administrative discretion.

Grounds for judicial review of administrative discretion are :

- Excess or failure to exercise the jurisdiction
- Violation of natural justice rules such as right of notice and hearing
- Violation of fundamental rights or statutory provisions of laws.
- Finding of facts which no person would have reached to the conclusion.

14 "Writ of certiorari can be issued to quash actions which are administrative in nature". Above principle was laid down in :

1 Indian Rly. Construction Co. Ltd Vs. Ajay Kumar
2 A.K. Kraipak Vs. Union of India
3 Union of India Vs. Bashyan
4 Rajesh Kumar Vs. C.I.T.

***Ans.* (2)**

Exp. Writ of certiorari can be issued to quash actions which are administrative in nature". This principle was laid down in A.K. Kraipak Vs. Union of India.

The Writ of Certiorari is issued by the Supreme Court to some inferior court or tribunal to transfer the matter to it or to some other superior authority for proper consideration.

15 Which is the qualification of a judicial member of Lokpal?

1 A member of Parliament
2 A member of State Legislature
3 A retired High Court Judge
4 A retired Chief Justice of a High Court

***Ans.* (4)**

Exp. A retired Chief Justice of a High Court is the qualification of a judicial member of Lokpal.

According to Section 3(3) (a) of Lokpal and Lokayukta Act, 2013, a person shall be eligible to be appointed as a Judicial member if he is or has been a Judge of the Supreme Court or is or has been a Chief Justice of a High Court.

Lokpal consists of a chairperson and eight members, half of whom are judicial members who are or have been a Judge of the Supreme Court or a Chief Justice of a High Court and the other half being non-judicial members are people of impeccable integrity and outstanding ability having special knowledge and expertise of not less than twenty-five years in the matters relating to anti-corruption policy, public administration, vigilance, finance including insurance and banking, law and management.

16 "I think adherence to precedent should be the rule and not the exception". This statement is of :

1 Keeton 2 Blackston
3 Cardozo 4 Paton

***Ans.* (3)**

Exp. "I think adherence to precedent should be the rule and not the exception". This statement is of Cardozo.

Cardozo is known for his significant influence on the development of American common law in the 20th century. Generally a liberal, he was less concerned with ideology than with the nature of the judicial process; largely for this reason, his importance—while universally conceded—is difficult to fix precisely.

17 Which one of the following jurists was hostile to the natural law school?

1 Emmanuel Kant 2 John Rawls
3 Jeremy Bentham 4 Stammeler

***Ans.* (3)**

Exp. Jeremy Bentham was hostile to the natural law school.

The focus of historians of political thought on canonical figures like, Jeremy Bentham, John Austin, and John Stuart Mill, all of whom were antagonistic to the natural law and rights tradition has led them to fail to appreciate not only the continued role of natural law and rights but its development of a post enlightenment accommodation with positive law, resulting in a more pragmatic understanding of natural law.

18 Match List I with List II and select the correct answer using the code given below.

List I		List II	
A.	Utilitarian Individualism	I.	Pound
B.	Social Utilitarian	II.	Bentham
C.	Scientific Positivism	III.	Ihering
D.	Social Engineering	IV.	Compte

Codes

	A	B	C	D		A	B	C	D
1	I	II	III	IV	2	II	III	IV	I
3	III	II	IV	I	4	II	IV	III	I

***Ans.* (2)**

Exp. The correct matching is A-II, B-III, C-IV, D-I.

The legal theory of *Utilitarian Individualism* was propounded by Jeremy Bentham. Bentham's legal philosophy is called Utilitarian Individualism. He said that the function of law is to emancipate the individual from the bondage and restraint upon the freedom.

Social Utilitarianism theory was given by Ihering. According to him, the social activities of individuals can be controlled by the state by means of coercion, reward and duty for achieving social control for the welfare of society.

Scientific Positivism is related to Compte. Positivism is the name for the scientific study of the social world. Its goal is to formulate abstract and universal laws on the operative dynamics of the social universe. A law is a statement about relationships among forces in the universe. In positivism, laws are to be tested against collected data systematically.

Social Engineering is related to Pound. According to Pound, 'Law is social engineering which means a balance between the competing interests in society', in which applied science are used for resolving individual and social problems.

19 Which one of the following sources of law has the basis under Article 141 of the Constitution of India?

1 Supreme legislation
2 Subordinate legislation
3 Colonial legislation
4 Precedent

***Ans.** (4)*

Exp. Precedent is one of the sources of law that has the basis under Article 141 of the Constitution of India.

Article 141 of the Constitution of India stipulates that the law declared by the Supreme Court shall be binding on all Courts within the territory of India. Thus, the general principles laid down, by the Supreme Court are binding on each individual including those who are not a party to an order.

20 Which one of the following jurists is not related to Historical school?

1 Savigny
2 Ehrlich
3 Henry Main
4 Hegel

***Ans.** (2)*

Exp. Ehrlich is the jurist who is not related to Historical school.

Historical School of Jurisprudence describes the origin of law. This school argues that the law was found not made. The main source of law is Kings Judgement, Customs and habits. Jurists like Montesquieu, Savigny, Sir Henry Maine, and Georg Friedrich Puchta are the supporter of the Historical School of Jurisprudence.

21 Read Assertion (A) and Reason (R) and give the correct answer using codes given below.

Assertion (A) A legal right is a legally protected interest

Reason (R) An element of advantage is essential to constitute right

Codes

1 Both (A) and (R) are right and (R) is the correct explanation of (A)
2 Both (A) and (R) are right and (R) is not the correct explanation of (A)
3 (A) is right, but (R) is wrong
4 (A) is right, but (R) is wrong

***Ans.** (3)*

Exp. (A) is right but (R) is wrong.

Assertion (A) is right because legal rights are those bestowed onto a person by a given legal system (they can be modified, repealed, and restrained by human laws). It is essentially a legally protected interest.

Reason (R) is wrong because an element of advantage is not essential to constitute a right. It is a claim recognized and delimited by law for the purpose of securing it.

22 Match List I with List II and select the correct answer by using the code given below.

List I	List II
A. Inner morality of Law	I. Maine
B. Minimum content of law	II. Stammler
C. Law with a variable Content	III. Fuller
D. 'Status to contract' Theory	IV. Hart

Codes

	A	B	C	D
1	I	II	III	IV
2	III	IV	II	I
3	I	IV	II	III
4	III	II	IV	I

***Ans.** (2)*

Exp. The correct matching is A-III, B-IV, C-II, D-I.

Inner morality of Law is related to Fuller. He formulated principles of what he called "the inner morality of law", principles requiring that laws be general, public, prospective, coherent, clear, stable, and practicable and also argued that these were indispensable to law-making.

Minimum content of Law is related to Hart. In advancing his minimum content of natural law, Hart "simply offers a very human set of assertions, of them made as empirical generalisations, not a priori truths, about limited altruism, vulnerability, approximate equality and limited resources".

Law with a variable content is related to Stammler. He defined law as, "species of will, others-regarding, self-authoritative and inviolable". With a view to distinguishing the new revived Natural Law from the old one, he called the former as 'Natural Law with variable content'.

Theory of *Status to contract* was given by Henry Maine. In the ancient world individuals were tightly bound by status to traditional groups, while in the modern one, in which individuals are viewed as autonomous agents, they are free to make contracts and form associations with whomever they choose.

23 Match List I with List II and select the correct answer using the code given below.

List I (Theory)	List II (Subject)
A. Will Theory	I. Legal Person
B. Concession Theory	II. Analytical School
C. Declaratory Theory	III. Legal Right
D. Command Theory	IV. Precedent

Codes

	A	B	C	D		A	B	C	D
1	III	I	II	IV	2	I	III	II	IV
3	III	I	IV	II	4	I	II	III	IV

Ans. (3)

Exp. The correct matching is A-III, B-I, C-IV, D-II.

Will Theory is related to Legal Right. According to this theory, the purpose of the law is to grant to the citizen the means of free expression of his will. Limiting anyone's freedom always requires the authorization of others' rights, and the subjects of rights remain free to "claim" them or not.

Concession Theory is related to Legal Person. It says that any legal personality can take birth from law itself. It is concession or grant from the side of law that legal personality is created and recognized. At certain point this theory is correct because any right or any recognition to any personality would flow from the law.

Declaratory Theory is related to Precedent. The declaratory theory of law represents one side of a debate about whether judges actually make law when they produce judicial decisions or merely declare what the existing law is. The declaratory theory in its starkest form says that 'the judge is no more than the voice of an autonomous legal system that she/he, through her/his legal training, is able to gain access to but is in no way able to influence.

Command Theory is related to Analytical School. The purpose of the Analytical School of jurisprudence is to analyze the first principles of law. The analytical school takes law as the command of the sovereign. It puts emphasis on legislation as the source of law. The whole system is based on its concept of law.

24 The Self evident principle of criminal justice is based on

1 Nullum crimen sine lege, nulla poena sine lege
2 Perils of his life and liberty on refusal of bail
3 Simple Principles based on corrective law
4 To avoid purposeless cruelty

Ans. (1)

Exp. The self-evident principle of criminal justice is based on Nullum crimen sine lege, nulla poena sine lege. Nullum crimen sine lege is sometimes called the legality principle. It is also interchangeable with "nullum poena sine lege."

Nulla poena sine lege is a legal principle which states that one cannot be punished for doing something that is not prohibited by law. This principle is accepted and codified in modern democratic states as a basic requirement of the rule of law.

25 What is the basic justification on the law of conspiracy?

1 It does not allow a preventive action because an act of conspiracy is derived when the crime results
2 It dispenses the difficult requirement of proximity in attempt
3 The momentum justifies punishment
4 The object is simply to make of a crime

Ans. (2)

Exp. The basic justification on the law of conspiracy is that it dispenses the difficult requirement of proximity in attempt.
In criminal law, a conspiracy is an agreement between two or more persons to commit a crime at some time in the future.

26 Which one of the expressive factors does not constitute sedition?

1 Disapprobation of the government
2 Excite disrespect against government
3 Commenting on administrative actions of the government
4 Attempting to excite disaffection against government

Ans. (3)

Exp. Commenting on administrative actions of the government does not constitute sedition.
Under Section 124A of IPC, the offence of sedition is committed when any person by words or otherwise brings or attempts to bring into hatred or contempt, or excites or attempts to excite disaffection towards the government established by law.

27 The right to private defence against an act done by a public servant is not available :

1 When it is discharged in good faith
2 When it is attempted to be done by him
3 When it was done while he was not in his office
4 When it is strictly to be justifiable by law

Ans. (2)

Exp. The right to private defence against an act done by a public servant is not available when it is attempted to be done by him.
Section 99 of IPC says there is no right of private defence against an act which does not reasonably cause the apprehension of death or of grievous hurt, if done, or attempted to be done, by a public servant acting in good faith under colour of his office, though that act, may not be strictly justifiable by law.

28 Which of the conditions are essential for enhanced punishment to an offender with previous conviction?

1 The previous conviction must have been for not less than 3 years of imprisonment
2 The subsequent offence is not punishable with imprisonment for more than 3 years

3 The offence must be an offence relating to property or coin or government stamp
4 The previous conviction was not in India

Ans. (3)

Exp. The conditions that is essential for enhanced punishment to an offender with previous conviction is that the offence must be an offence relating to property or coin or government stamp.

Chapter 12 is related to offences relating to coin and government stamps.

29 Non-Compos mentis denotes

1 Every person is considered to be sane unless contrary is proved
2 When a criminal act is performed during derrangement
3 When the cognitive facilities are such that he does not know what he has done
4 Non-serene memory not from birth

Ans. (3)

Exp. Non-Compos mentis denotes when the cognitive facilities are such that he does not know what he has done.

Non compos mentis is a Latin legal phrase that translates to "of unsound mind", non ('not') prefaces compos mentis, meaning "having control of one's mind". This phrase was first used in thirteenth-century English law to describe people afflicted by madness, the loss of memory or ability to reason.

30 In which of the conditions, the act will not be wrongful confinement?

1 Circumscribing limits
2 Malice
3 Moral force
4 Mistaken exercise of power

Ans. (2)

Exp. Malice is defined as an evil intent on the part of a person who commits a wrongful act injurious to others. This act does not constitute wrongful confinement as it is a deliberate attempt to cause harm.

The term 'Wrongful confinement' is defined in Section 340 of the IPC that says whoever wrongfully restrains any person in such a manner as to prevent that person form proceeding beyond certain circumscribing limits, is said 'wrongfully to confine' that person.

31 Which of the following statement is correct?

1 A publisher is responsible for publishing a defamatory statement for first time only and not for repeating it
2 Only editor and not printer and publisher are responsible for that defamatory statement in the newspaper
3 Defamatory imputation concerning any person may be conveyed obliquely or indirectly, or by way of question, conjecture, exclamation or by irony
4 The court does not distinguish between "character" and "reputation" for fixing liability against defamation

Ans. (3)

Exp. Statement 3 that says defamatory imputation concerning any person may be conveyed obliquely or in directly, or by way of question, conjecture, exclamation or by irony is correct.

Statement 1, 2 and 4 are incorrect.

A publisher is responsible for publishing a defamatory statement for the first time as well as for repeating it. A fresh cause of action arises everytime a publication is made of the defamatory statement.

Both editor and printer and publisher are responsible for that defamatory statement in the newspaper.

The courts often draw up the difference between "character" and "reputation" for fixing liability against defamation. This is because the truth about a person's character can be used as a defence against defamation.

32 Read Assertion (A) and Reason (R) and answer using the code given below.

Assertion (A) Redemption of the damaged environment is a part of the process of sustainable development and as such polluter in liable to pay the cost of the individual sufferers as well as the cost of reversing the damaged ecology

Reason (R) 'Polluter pays principle' is part of the environmental jurisprudence of this country

Codes

1 Both (A) and (R) are correct and (R) is the correct explanation of (A)
2 Both (A) and (R) are correct and (R) is not the correct explanation of (A)
3 (A) is true, but (R) is false
4 (A) is false, but (R) is true

Ans. (1)

Exp. Both (A) and (R) are correct and (R) is the correct explanation of (A).

The 'polluter pays' principle is the commonly accepted practice that those who produce pollution should bear the costs of managing it to prevent damage to human health or the environment. The Environment is polluted and the only way to redeem it is to sustain the factors affecting the environment, thus sustainable development is seen as a way to do so therefore it was concluded that it is only fair that whoever pollutes has to pay the price of redemption.

'Polluter pays' principle is one of the tenets of environmental jurisprudence in India. In India according to Section 20 of National Green Tribunal Act, the tribunal can apply for the principles of sustainable development, the polluter pays principles and precautionary principle while passing any order, award or decision for balanced development without harming the mother earth.

33 Which one of the following principle is associated with 'Trial Smelter' case?

1 Principle of sustainable development
2 No state has a right to use or permit the use of its territory so as to cause injury by fumes in the territory of another
3 Redemption of the damaged environment is a part of the process of sustainable development
4 Placing a duty on the State to hold environmental resources in trust for the benefit of public

Ans. (2)

➲ *Exp.* The principle that says no state has a right to use or permit the use of its territory so as to cause injury by fumes in the territory of another is related to 'Trial Smelter case.

In the 'Trail Smelter' case it was held that no State has the right to use or permit the use of its territory in such a manner as to cause injury by fumes in or to the territory of another or the properties or persons therein, when the cause is of serious consequence and the injury is established by clear and convincing evidence.

34 Match List I with List II and give the correct answer by using the code given below.

List I (Theory)	List II (Subject)
A. National Environmental Tribunal	I. Basel Convention, 1989
B. "Doctrine of Sic utere tuo ut alienum non leadas"	II. Rio Declaration
C. To stop and prevent the international traffic in dumping and resultant accumulation of toxic and dangerous products and wastes	III. Kyoto Protocol, 1997
D. Convention or climate change strengthened	IV. Principle 21 and 22 of Stockholm Declarations

Codes

	A	B	C	D		A	B	C	D
1	I	III	IV	II	2	IV	II	I	III
3	II	IV	I	III	4	III	II	I	IV

Ans. (3)

➲ *Exp.* The correct matching is A-II, B-IV, C-I, D-III.

The *National Environment tribunal* came as a result of the Rio Declaration. The Rio Declaration was a short document produced at the 1992 United Nations "Conference on Environment and Development", informally known as the Earth Summit.

"Doctrine of Sic utere tuo ut alienum non leadas" is related Principle 21 and 22 of Stockholm Declarations. The maxim 'sic utere tuo ut alienum non laedas' (use your own property in such a manner as not to injure that of another) stands for the proposition that one State's sovereign right to use its territory is circumscribed by an obligation not to cause injury to, or within, another State's territory.

To stop and prevent the international traffic in dumping and resultant accumulation of toxic and dangerous products and wastes is mentioned in Basel convention, 1989. Basel Convention, is an international treaty that was designed to reduce the movements of hazardous waste between nations, and specifically to prevent transfer of hazardous waste from developed to less developed countries.

Convention on climate change strengthened due to Kyoto Protocol, 1997. Due to Kyoto protocol convention on climate change was strengthened. The parties under the Kyoto Protocol commits to reduce greenhouse gas emissions, based on the scientific consensus that global warming is occurring and that human-made CO_2 emissions are driving it.

35 Which one of the following statement is wrong?

1 Every person enjoys the right to a wholesome environment which is a facet of the right to life guaranteed under Art 21 of the Constitution of India
2 The power confered under an Environmental Statute may be exercised only to advance Environment Protection and not for a purpose that would defeat the object of the law
3 Financial constraints of the government may be a reasonable factor to exonorate the Government/ Municipal bodies from performing its statutory liability
4 Precautionary principle imposes the onus of proof on the developer to show his or her action is environmentally benign

Ans. (3)

➲ *Exp.* Statement 3 is incorrect as the financial inconsistencies or constraints is no factor that can absolve the civic authorities of their liabilities. The civil authorities including the Municipal and the Central Government bodies would continue to be liable.

The Supreme Court in Municipal Council, Ratlam Vs. Vardhichand case observed that, "the issue of pollution should not be resolved at the cost of the poor people's livelihood."

36 The Supreme Court in which one of the following cases observed that, "the issue of pollution should not be resolved at the cost of the poor people's livelihood"?

1 Indian Council for Enviro Legal Action Vs. Union of India
2 Municipal Council, Ratlam Vs. Vardichand
3 M.C. Metha Vs. Union of India
4 T.N. Godavarman Thimmulpaad Vs. Union of India

Ans. (3)

➲ *Exp.* In M.C. Mehta Vs. Union of India it was held that "the issue of pollution should not be resolved at the cost of the poor people's livelihood". It was specially addressed towards the Oleum gas disaster leakage and also drew conclusions from the Union carbide disaster in Bhopal.

37 Under the Wild Life Protection Act, the boundaries of a National Park shall be made in one of the following way :

1 By passing a resolution in the Parliament
2 By passing a resolution in the Legislature of a State
3 By passing a resolution both in the Parliament and State Legislature
4 By passing a resolution in the Municipal Body and State Legislature

Ans. (2)

Exp. Under the WildLife Protection Act, the boundaries of a National Park shall be made by passing a resolution in the Legislature of a State.

Section 35(5) of the wildlife Protection Act states no alteration of the boundaries of a National park shall be made except on a resolution passed by the Legislature of the State.

38 'Basel Convention' is associated with one of the following conventions on :

1 International Trade in Endangered Species of Wild Fauna and Flora
2 The control of transboundary movements of Hazardous Wastes and their disposal
3 Climate Change
4 Protection of the ozone layer

Ans. (2)

Exp. 'Basel Convention' is associated with the control of transboundary movements of Hazardous Wastes and their disposal.

Basel Convention is an international treaty that was designed to reduce the movements of hazardous waste between nations, and specifically to prevent transfer of hazardous waste from developed to less developed countries. It does not, however, address the movement of radioactive waste.

39 Which of the following jurists deny legal character of international law?

I. Hobbes   II. Pufendorf
III. Oppenheim   IV. Starke

Codes

1 Only I
2 Both I and II
3 Only I, II and III
4 I, II, III and IV all

Ans. (2)

Exp. Hobbes and Pufendorf are the jurists who deny the legal character of international law.

According to them there is no positive law of nations properly invested with true legal force and binding as the command of a superior. As per a leading English Jurist, John Austin, International law is not a true law, but a code of rules of conduct of moral force only. Basis of Austin's view is that International law has no command of the sovereign.

40 In which of the following cases, the world court by majority has taken the view that the sources of law are not hierarchal but are necessarily complimentary and inter related?

1 Nicaragua Vs. U.S.A
2 Frontier Dispute (Burkina Faso Vs. Mali)
3 Portugal Vs. India
4 Case concerning the Temple of Preah Vihear

Ans. (1)

Exp. In Nicaragua Vs. U.S.A, the world court by majority has taken the view that the sources of law are not hierarchal but are necessarily complimentary and inter related.

The Nicaragua case involved military and paramilitary activities carried out by the United States against Nicaragua from 1981 to 1984. Nicaragua asked the Court to find that these activities violated international law. It was held that the sources of law are not hierarchal but are necessary complementary and inter related.

41 Who of the following has viewed that there is legal duty on the part of the existing states to recognise any community that has in fact acquired the characteristics of Statehood?

1 Oppenheim   2 Lauterpacht
3 Philip C. Jessup   4 Anzilloti

Ans. (2)

Exp. Lauterpacht has viewed that there is legal duty on the part of the existing states to recognise any community that has in fact acquired the characteristics of Statehood.

Lauterpacht argued that the doctrine of the inherent limitations of the judicial function was inconsistent with general principles of law and with a view of public international law as a legal system. Obligatory judicial settlement should therefore be regarded as inherent.

42 Which of the following statement/statements is/are correct?

I. In Nottelohm's case the International Court of Justice held that in respect of grant of nationality there is no obligation of the states if that man has no relationship with the State of Naturalisation
II. In famous Re lynch case it was held that if a person is not a citizen of any state he will be called Stateless
III. Nationality is the principal link between an individual and international law
IV. The Convention on the Reduction of Statelessness was adopted in 1959 by the General Assembly

Codes

1 Only I is correct
2 Only I, II and III are correct
3 Only II, III and IV are correct
4 Only I and III are correct

Ans. (4)

Exp. Statements I and III are correct.

Statement II is incorrect because in Re Lynch case, the Court considered an appeal from an order terminating parental rights brought on behalf of a parent. It was held that statlessness shall not be adopted as a penalty for a crime.

Statement IV is incorrect because the Convention on the Reduction of Statelessness was adopted on 30th August, 1961.

43 Read both Assertion (A) and Reason (R) and give the correct answer by using the code given below.

Assertion (A) It is a very important principle of International Law that extradition for political crimes is not allowed.

Reason (R) Stoeck Vs. The Public Trustee is a leading case relating to non-extradition of political criminals.

Codes

1 Both (A) and (R) are correct and (R) is the correct explanation of (A)
2 Both (A) and (R) are correct, but (R) is not the correct explanation of (A)
3 (A) is right, but (R) is wrong
4 (A) is wrong, but (R) is right.

***Ans.* (3)**

Exp. (A) is right, but (R) is wrong.

The given Assertion is right as extradition is violative of the principle of international law. The consensus in international law is that a state does not have any obligation to surrender an alleged criminal to a foreign state, because one principle of sovereignty is that every state has legal authority over the people within its borders.

Reason (R) is wrong because Stoeck Vs. The Public Trustee is not related to extradition. This case gave the definition of 'stateless' and it was held that if a person is not a citizen of any state, he will be called 'stateless'.

44 Which of the following statement/statements is/are not correct?

I. United Nations Declaration on Territorial Asylum was unanimously adopted in 1977 by the General Assembly
II. Article 14 of the 1948 Universal Declaration of Human Rights (UDHR) makes obligatory by states to grant Asylum
III. The international court of justice explained the distinction between 'Territorial asylum' and 'diplomatic asylum' in the Colombia Vs. Perus
IV. The Convention on the status of Refugees, 1951 entered into force on 22nd April, 1954

Codes

1 Only I is not correct
2 Only I and IV are not correct
3 I, II and III all are not correct
4 I, II, III and IV all are not correct

***Ans.* (3)**

Exp. Statement I, II and III all are not correct.

The UN Declaration on Territorial Asylum was adopted in 1967.

Article 14 does not make it mandatory to grant any type of political asylum. Article 14 of the Universal Declaration of Human Rights simply gives everyone a right "to seek and enjoy asylum" but does not make it obligatory upon the states to grant asylum.

The international court of justice did not explain the distinction between 'Territorial asylum' and 'diplomatic asylum' in the Colombia Vs. Perus. In Asylum case (Columbia Vs. Peru 1950) the International court of Justice discussed whether there exist any local custom in Latin American countries to grant asylum in embassies.

The Convention on the status of Refugees, 1951 entered into force on 22nd April, 1954.

45 Which of the following statement/statements is/are correct?

I. The General Assembly consists of all the members of the United Nations. Each member may not have not more than five representatives in the General Assembly
II. China, Russia, America, Britain and Italy are the permanent members of the security Council
III. The members of the Economic and Social Council are elected by the security council, one - third of its members are elected every year by the security council for a term of five years
IV. All members of the United Nations are ipso facto the members of the Statute of International Court of Justice

Codes

1 Only I and IV are correct
2 Only I, II and III are correct
3 Only II, III and IV are correct
4 I, II, III and IV all are correct

***Ans.* (1)**

Exp. Only Statement I and IV are correct.

The General Assembly consists of all the members of the United Nations. Each member may not have not more than five representatives in the General Assembly.

The International Court of Justice was established by the Charter of the United Nations, which provides that all Member States of the United Nations are ipso facto parties to the Court's Statute.

Statement II and III are incorrect.

The permanent members of the United Nations Security Council (also known as the Permanent Five, Big Five, or P5) are the five sovereign states to whom the UN Charter of 1945 grants a permanent seat on the UN Security Council and they are China, France, Russia, the United Kingdom, and the United States.

Members of economic and social council are elected by the General Assembly for three-year terms.

46 Advisory opinion can be given by the International Court of Justice on legal question :

1 On the request of Security Council only
2 On the request of the General Assembly only
3 On the request of General Assembly or the Security Council both
4 On the request of the Economic and Social Council if authorised by the Security Council

Ans. (3)

Exp. Advisory opinion can be given by the International Court of Justice on legal question on the request of General Assembly or the Security Council both.

Advisory proceedings begin with the filing of a written request for an advisory opinion addressed to the Registrar by the United Nations Secretary-General or the director or secretary-general of the entity requesting the opinion. In urgent cases the Court may do whatever is necessary to speed up the proceedings.

In order that it may be fully informed on the question submitted to it, the Court is empowered to hold written and oral proceedings. So, it is only on the request of General Assembly or the Security council both that the International Court of Justice can exercise Advisory opinion.

47 Read both Assertion (A) and Reason (R) and answer using the code given below.

Assertion (A) In Mithila, a widow cannot adopt at all, not even if she has the express authority of her husband.

Reason (R) A widow may adopt under the authority from her husband.

Codes

1 Both (A) and (R) are correct and (R) is the correct explanation of A
2 Both (A) and (R) are correct and (R) is not correct explanation of (A)
3 A is true, but (R) is false
4 A is false ,but (R) is true

Ans. (1)

Exp. Both (A) and (R) are correct and (R) is the correct explanation of (A).

In case of Mithila school the assent of the husband is required according to Vachaspati Misra at the time of adoption. Obviously, a widow cannot get such consent since her husband is dead. So, according to the Mithila School a widow cannot make an adoption. So, in isolation a widow cannot adopt at all in Mithila School. However, if the authority has been sanctioned from the side of the husband, the adoption can be made.

48 In which of the following cases, the Supreme Court held that "We are not prepared to express any definite opinion on the question whether there can be two Karta of a Joint Hindu Family".

1 Moraka Properties Vs. Biharilal Moraka
2 Union of India Vs. Sree Ram Bohra
3 Nopany Investment Vs. Santosh Singh
4 Commissioner of Income Tax Vs. Govindram Sugar Mills

Ans. (1)

Exp. In case of Moraka Properties Vs. Biharilal Morarka, the Supreme Court held that "We are not prepared to express any definite opinion on the question whether there can be two Karta of a Joint Hindu Family." The Court held that the family became divided in status sometime before 1932. In any event the division's status was effected in 1932. Even if there was a joint family in existence, since the transactions were for the benefit of the family, the other coparceners cannot challenge its validity.

49 In which of the following case, the court held that, "Divorce is good in law though bad in Theology"?

1 Shah Bano case
2 Bai Tahira case
3 Shamim Ara case
4 Sarabai case

Ans. (4)

Exp. In Sarabai case, it was held that, "Divorce is good in law though bad in Theology".

In Sarabai Vs Rabiabai (Sarabai case) it was held that there can be no doubt that a talak-ul-bidaat (or irregular divorce) is good in law, though bad in theology.

Talaq-e-biddat or instantaneous triple talaq has been set aside. Thus, in effect, it is the practice of divorce by the consecutive utterance of talaq three times that has been deemed invalid. However, a man continues to be free to utter talaq three times over three months, in order for the divorce to be effective.

50 In Muslim law 'Hizanat' related to :

1 Father's custody of child
2 Brother's custody of child
3 Mother's custody of child
4 Sister's custody of child

Ans. (3)

Exp. In Muslim law "Hizanat" related to Mother's custody of child.

The first and foremost right to have the custody of children belongs to the mother and she cannot be deprived of her right so long as she is not found guilty of misconduct. Mother has the right of custody so long as she is not disqualified.

This right is known as right of hizanat and it can be enforced against the father or any other person. The mother's right of hizanat was solely recognised in the interest of the children and in no sense it is an absolute right".

51 Match the List I with List II and indicate the correct answer using the code given below.

List I	List II
A. Nijhawan Vs. Nijhawan	I. Dowry
B. Daniel Latifi Vs. Union of India	II. Uniform civil code
C. Husain Ara Vs. Zubaida Begum	III. Cruelty
D. Gujarat Woman Workers Association Case	IV. Maintenance

Codes

	A	B	C	D		A	B	C	D
1	III	IV	I	II	2	I	III	II	IV
3	III	II	I	IV	4	II	IV	III	I

***Ans.* (1)**

Exp. The correct matching is A-III, B-IV, C-I, D-II.

Nijhawan Vs. Nijhawan case is related to Cruelty. Cruelty which is a ground for dissolution of marriage may be defined as wilful and unjustifiable conduct of such character as to cause danger to life, limb or health, bodily or mental, or as to give rise to a reasonable apprehension of such a danger.

Daniel Latifi Vs. *Union of India* case is related to Maintenance. In this case, the Constitutionality of the Muslim Women (Protection of Rights On Divorce) Act, 1986 was challenged. It was held that there is no discrimination when the state has made a specific provision for a particular community that is equally or more beneficial than the general law.

Husain Ara Vs. *Zubaida Begum* case is related to Dowry Under the Muslim law, Mehr (dower) means money or property which the wife is entitled to receive from the husband in consideration of the marriage.

Gujarat Woman Workers Association case is related to Uniform Civil Code. The Uniform Civil Code (UCC) essentially calls for the formulation of one law for India, applicable to all religious communities in their personal matters such as marriage, divorce, inheritance, adoption etc.

52 Read Assertion (A) and Reason (R) and answer using the code given below.

Assertion (A) 'Option of Puberty' is an easy process to repudiate the marriage under Hindu Law.

Reason (R) "Option of Puberty" is not an easy process to repudiate the marriage under Muslim Law.

Codes

1 Both (A) and (R) are correct and (R) is the correct explanation of (A)

2 Both (A) and (R) are correct and (R) is not the correct explanation of (A)

3 (A) is true, but (R) is false

4 (A) is false, but (R) is true

***Ans.* (2)**

Exp. Both (A) and (R) are correct and (R) is not the correct explanation of (A).

Assertion (A) is correct because under the Hindu Marriage Act 1955 the option of puberty could be exercised by the wife for a divorce.

Reason (R) is correct because in Muslim law in certain unusual situations, the wife has the means to dissolve the marriage unilaterally. One of them is called the 'option of puberty'. This is where the girl is married before puberty. When she reaches puberty, she has the right to accept or reject the marriage.

53 The Dissolution of Muslim Marriages Act, 1939 brought various grounds for dissolution of marriage based on the principles of

1 Shia Schools
2 Hanafi School
3 Shafai School
4 Maliki School

***Ans.* (4)**

Exp. The Dissolution of Muslim Marriages Act, 1939 brought various grounds for dissolution of marriage based on the principles of Maliki School.

The Dissolution of Muslim Marriages Act, 1939 was brought under the Maliki School. It is one of the four major madhhabs of Islamic jurisprudence within Sunni Islam. The principles of the Maliki school were sought into in drafting the Dissolution of Muslim Marriages Act, 1939 that brought various grounds for dissolution of marriage.

54 A muslim husband has E-mailed Talaq letter writing "I divorce you, I divorce you, I divorce you," without the signature of witnesses, Talaq will be :

1 Valid

2 Voidable

3 Void

4 Neither valid nor void or no talaq

***Ans.* (4)**

Exp. A muslim husband has E-mailed Talaq letter writing "I divorce you, I divorce you, I divorce you," without the signature of witnesses, then in this case Talaq will be neither valid nor void or no talaq.

Islamic seminaries in Deoband have stated that triple talaq over the phone is valid. The fatwa says that triple talaq can be pronounced through emails would not be void ab initio neither is it no talaq. It is just not recognized. It is neither illegal nor voidable.

55 Sec 2(d) of 'The protection of Human Rights Act, 1993 defines," human rights" means the rights relating to ________ of the individual guaranteed by the Constitution or embodied in the International Covenants and enforceable by courts in India. Fill in the blank.

1 Life, Liberty, Equality and Dignity
2 Life, Equality, Liberty and Dignity
3 Life, Equality, Dignity and Liberty
4 Life, Liberty, Dignity and Equality

***Ans.* (1)**

Exp. Section 2 (d) of the Protection of Human Rights Act 1993 acts as the base for all individual liberty and equality. According to this act "human rights" means the rights relating to life, liberty, equality and dignity of the individual guaranteed by the Constitution or embodied in the International Covenants and enforceable by courts in India.

56 Which one of the following pairs is correctly matched with regard to National Human Rights Commission of India, under the Protection of Human Rights Act, 1993?

1 Section 3 – Appointment of chairperson and other members
2 Section 4 – Removal of a member of the commission
3 Section 5 – Member to act as chairperson in certain times
4 Section 6 – Term of office of members

***Ans.* (4)**

Exp. Section 6 in the Protection of Human Rights Act, 1933 talks about term of office of Chairperson and Members. It says a person appointed as Chairperson shall hold office for a term of five years from the date on which he enters upon his office or until he attains the age of seventy years, whichever is earlier. A person appointed as a Member shall hold office for a term of five years from the date on which he enters upon his office and shall be eligible for re-appointment for another term of five years. Provided that no Member shall hold office after he has attained the age of seventy years.

On ceasing to hold office, a Chairperson or a Member shall be ineligible for further employment under the Government of India or under the Government of any State.

Section 3 of the Act talks about Constitution of a National Human Rights Commission.

Section 4 of the Act talks about appointment of chairperson and other members.

Section 5 of the Act talks about resignation and removal of chairperson and Members.

57 Which one of the following pairs is not correctly matched with regard to the duration of the position of the members/chairpersons of N.H.R.C of India?

1 Justice S. Rajendra Babu - 02.04.2007 to 31.05.2009
2 Justice K.G. Bala Krishnan - 07.06.2010 to 11.05.2015
3 Justice Ms.M. Fathima Beevi - 03.11.1993 to 24.01.1997
4 Justice V.S. Malimat - 05.08.1994 to 12.10.1998

***Ans.* (4)**

Exp. Justice Shri Vs. Malimath held the post of chairperson of NHRC from 14.09.1994 to 11.06.1999. Previously he was the Chief Justice, High Court of Kerala and Karnataka. He headed the Committee on Reform of Criminal Justice System and was instrumental in bringing about several changes in the Criminal Law System.

58 Match List I with List II and give the correct answer by using the code given below.

List I	List II
A. Optional Protocol to the Convention on the Elimination of All Forms of Discrimination against Women	I. Proclaimed by the U.N General Assembly resolution 3318 (XXIX) of 14th December, 1974
B. Declaration on the Elimination of violence against women	II. Adopted and opened for signature, ratification and accession by the U.N. General Assembly resolution 34/180 of 18th December, 1979
C. Convention on the Elimination of All forms of Discrimination against Women	III. Proclaimed by the U.N General Assembly resolution 48/104 of 20 December, 1993
D. Declaration on the protection of women and children in Emergency and Armed Assembly conflict	IV. Adopted by the U.N General Resolution 54/4 of 6th October, 1999 and opened for signature, ratification and accession on 10th December, 1999

Codes

	A	B	C	D		A	B	C	D
1	IV	III	II	I	2	IV	I	II	III
3	II	IV	I	III	4	III	IV	I	II

***Ans.* (1)**

Exp. The correct matching is A-IV, B-III, C-II, D-I.

Optional Protocol to the Convention on the Elimination of All Forms of Discrimination against Women was adopted by the U.N General Resolution 54/4 of 6th October, 1999 and opened for signature, ratification and accession on 10th December, 1999. The Optional Protocol to the Convention on the Elimination of All Forms of Discrimination against Women is an international treaty which establishes complaint and inquiry mechanisms for the Convention on the Elimination of All Forms of Discrimination Against Women.

Declaration on the Elimination of violence against women was proclaimed by the U.N General Assembly resolution 48/104 of 20th December, 1993. For the purposes of this

Declaration, the term "violence against women" means any act of gender-based violence that results in, or is likely to result in, physical, sexual or psychological harm or suffering to women, including threats of such acts, coercion or arbitrary deprivation of liberty, whether occurring in public or in private life.

Convention on the Elimination of All forms of Discrimination against Women was adopted and opened for signature, ratification and accession by the U.N. General Assembly resolution 34/180 of 18th December, 1979. The Convention provides the basis for realizing equality between women and men through ensuring women's equal access to, and equal opportunities in, political and public life including the right to vote and to stand for election as well as education, health and employment.

Declaration on the protection of women and children in Emergency and Armed Assembly conflict was proclaimed by the U.N General Assembly resolution 3318 (XXIX) of 14th December, 1974. The Declaration states that women and children suffer victimization during armed conflict due to "suppression, aggression, colonialism, racism, alien domination and foreign subjugation". The Declaration specifically prohibits attacks and bombing of civilian populations.

59 Which of the following statement/statements is/are incorrect?

I. Optional Protocol to the Convention on the Rights of the Child on the involvement of Children in Armed Conflict was adopted and opened for signature, ratification and accession by the United Nations General Assembly resolution 54/263 of 25th May, 2000

II. Worst forms of Child Labour Convention, 1999 (No.182) was adopted on 15th June, 1999 by the General Conference of the International Labour Organisation at its eighty - seventh session

III. Minimum Age Convention, 1973 (No. 138) was adopted on 26th August, 1973 by the General Conference of the International Labour Organisation at its Fifty Eighth session

IV. Convention on the Rights of the Child was adopted and opened for signature, ratification and accession by the United Nations General Council Resolution 44/25 of 20th November, 1989.

Codes

1 Only I, II and III are incorrect
2 Only II, III and IV are incorrect
3 Only I and II are incorrect
4 I, II, III and IV all are incorrect

Ans. *(2)*

Exp. Statements II, III and IV are incorrect.

The Worst Forms of Child Labour Convention, was adopted by the International Labour Organization (ILO) on 17th June 1999 as ILO Convention No 182.

The Convention concerning Minimum Age for Admission to Employment was adopted on 26th June 1973 by the International Labour Organisation.

The convention on the Rights of the Child was adopted on 2nd September 1990.

60 The division of Human Rights into three generations was initially proposed in 1979 by one of the following Czech Jurist at the International Institute of Human Rights in Strasbourg?

1 Karel Vasak 2 Charles O. Lee
3 Maurice Cranston 4 Frederic Bastial

Ans. *(1)*

Exp. The division of Human Rights into three generations was introduced in 1979 by Czech Jurist Karel Vasak. The three categories align with the three tenets of the French Revolution: liberty, equality, and fraternity. He classified human rights into First Generation human rights, Second Generation human rights and Third Generation human rights.

61 Arrange the following decided cases on the right to health in a chronological order and choose the answer by using the code given below.

I. Pascim Banga Khet Mazdoor Samiti Vs. State of West Bengal
II. Parmanand Katara Vs. Union of India
III. Social Jurists Vs. Govt. of NCT of Delhi
IV. Sahara House Vs. Union of India

Codes

1 II, I, III, IV 2 IV, I, II, III
3 II, IV, III, I 4 III, IV, I, II

Ans. *(1)*

Exp. The correct chronological order is II, I, III, IV.

In Parmanand Katara Vs. Union of India (1989), the Petitioner, Parmanand Katara was a human rights activist who filed a writ petition in the Supreme Court of India on the basis of a published newspaper report in the Hindustan Times in 1988, concerning the death of a scooter driver who was knocked down by a speeding car.

In Paschim Banga Khet Mazdoor Samiti Vs. State of West Bengal (1996) the Court stated that denial of timely medical treatment necessary to preserve human life in government-owned hospitals is a violation of this right.

In Social Jurists Vs. Govt of NCT Delhi (2007) the Social Jurist (a civil society organisation) filed a Public Interest Litigation to highlight the deficiency of requisite teaching aids for children with disability and non-availability of special teachers, in unaided and aided private schools of Delhi, and its consequences upon students. The petitioner sought directions from the Court to ensure all recognised aided and unaided private schools in Delhi made provisions for the education of children with disabilities.

In Sahara House Vs. Union of India (2012) the Supreme Court after in taking note of the irrational prescription of treatment and medicines by private doctors, the Court ordered the Medical Council of India to ensure that all private sector health care facilities followed NACO protocol guidelines. It also ordered all health care providers to submit quarterly reports on the treatment provided to PLHIV, in a format that could be made available by NACO on its website.

62 Which of the following statement(s) is/are correct with regard to 'absolute liability' principle laid down in MC Mehta Vs. Union of India. Answer by using the code below.

I. The principle was approved except as to quantum of damages in Charan Lal Sahu Vs. Union of India

II. The principle in determining compensation was applied in Union Carbide Corporation Vs. Union of India

III. The compensation to be awarded must have some broad correlation not only with magnitude and capacity of the enterprise but also with the harm caused by it was held in Deepak Nitrite Vs. State of Gujarat.

IV. The principle is not followed in India because Parliament could not pass yet Public Liability Insurance Bill, 1991

Codes

1 Only I is correct
2 Only I and II are correct
3 Only I, II and III are correct
4 I, II, III and IV are correct

Ans. (3)

Exp. Statement I, II and III are correct.

MC Mehta Vs. Union of India case is the famous tort law case which brought in the principle of absolute liability. It observed that "the development and the protection of environments are not enemies. If without degrading the environment or minimising adverse effects thereupon by applying stringent safeguards, it is possible to carry on development activity applying the principles of sustainable development, in that eventuality, the development has to go on because one cannot lose sight of the need for development of industries, projects, etc. including the need to improve employment opportunities and the generation of revenue. A balance has to be struck. Thus, the Supreme court of India fixed the liability in this case to the supplier. The first three statements naturally follow from the case while the fourth statement is incorrect.

63 Which of the following pair is correctly matched?

1 Defamation published in permanent form-Slander
2 Libel is recognised as offence-England
3 Truth of defamatory matter is no defence-Civil law
4 Action lies for defamatory statement-Absolute Privilege

Ans. (2)

Exp. Libel is recognised as offence-England is correctly matched.

The crime of scandalum magnatum (spreading false reports about the magnates of the realm) was established by the Statute of Westminster 1275, but the first fully reported case in which libel is affirmed generally to be punishable at common law is one tried in the Star Chamber in the reign of James I.

English law allows actions for libel to be brought in the High Court for any published statements which are alleged to defame a named or identifiable individual (or individuals; under English law companies are legal persons, and allowed to bring suit for defamation) in a manner which causes them loss in their trade or profession, or causes a reasonable person to think worse of him, her or them.

64 Read Assertion (A) and Reason (R) and give correct answer by using the codes given below.

Assertion (A) The existence of a duty to take care is essential before a person can be held liable in negligence.

Reason (R) The standard of care required is not a matter of law and does vary according to the individuals although it does not vary according to the circumstances.

Codes

1 Both (A) and (R) are true and (R) is the correct explanation of A
2 Both (A) and (R) are true and (R) is not the correct explanation of (A)
3 (A) is right, but (R) is wrong
4 (A) is wrong, but (R) is right

Ans. (3)

Exp. (A) is right, but (R) is wrong.

Assertion (A) is right because the existence of a duty to take care is essential before a person can be held liable in negligence.

Reason (R) is wrong because a duty of care is a legal obligation which is imposed on an individual requiring adherence to a standard of reasonable care while performing any acts that could foreseeably harm others. It is the first element that must be established to proceed with an action in negligence. The second statement is incorrect as a reasonable standard of care should be exercised. Hence, the standard of care is a matter of law.

65 Match List I with List II with regard to tort of nuisance and answer by using codes given below.

List I	List II
A. Burden of proof, once nuisance is proved	I. Prescription
B. Remedy for the private nuisance	II. Occupier

List I	List II
C. Right to action for nuisance of a temporary nature	III. Abatement
D. Right to commit a private nuisance may be acquired	IV. Defendant

Codes

	A	B	C	D		A	B	C	D
1	III	II	IV	I	2	II	IV	III	I
3	I	II	III	IV	4	IV	III	II	I

Ans. *(4)*

Exp. The correct matching is A-IV, B-III, C-II, D-I.

Burden of proof, once nuisance is proved is related to Defendant. Burden of proof can define the duty placed upon a party to prove or disprove a disputed fact, or it can define which party bears this burden.

Remedy for the private nuisance is related to Abatement. There are three possible remedies where a defendant is found to have committed a nuisance; injunctions, damages and abatement.

Right to action for nuisance of a temporary nature is related to Occupier. Occupier can take action against the nuisance if any damage to the property takes place.

Right to commit a private nuisance may be acquired is linked with Prescription. A person may obtain a prescriptive right to commit nuisance if he has been committing it continuously for 20 years or more, then the person will be deemed to obtain a prescriptive right to commit nuisance and law cannot stop them on committing so.

66 Read Assertion (A) and Reason (R) and give correct answer by using codes given below.

Assertion (A) According to the 'law of tort' every wrongful act for which there is no justification or excuse to be treated as a tort.

Reason (R) Theory of 'pigeon-hole' was propounded by Salmond.

Codes

1 Both (A) and (R) are true and (R) is the correct explanation of (A)
2 Both (A) and (R) are true but (R) is not the correct explanation of (A)
3 (A) is right, but (R) is wrong
4 (A) is wrong, but (R) is right

Ans. *(2)*

Exp. Both (A) and (R) are true but (R) is not the correct explanation of (A).

Assertion (A) is true because according to Winfield's law of 'tort' theory, all the unjustifiable harm for which there is no excuse will be treated as a tort.

Reason (R) is true because Theory of 'pigeon-hole' was propounded by Salmond. According to Salmond if one person commits any wrong and that wrong can be placed in a pigeon hole or he opined that there is no general principle and if the plaintiff can by any mean put that wrong in the pigeon-hole which has all the labelled torts, then the plaintiff could succeed.

67 The provisions of the Consumer Protection Act shall be

1 Only in derogation of other law
2 No addition to other law
3 Not in addition and in derogation of other law
4 In addition to and not in derogation of other law

Ans. *(4)*

Exp. The provisions of the Consumer Protection Act shall be in addition to and not in derogation of other law.

Section 3 of the Consumer Protection Act provides that, the provisions of this Act shall be in addition to and not in derogation of the provisions of any other law for the time being in force.

68 Section 19-A of the Consumer Protection Act provides that State and National Commissions shall hear as expeditiously as possible and an endeavour shall be made to finally dispose of the appeal within ninety days from the date of its admission. The Section further empowers the Commissions to make following orders ; answer by using code below.

I. Ordinarily grant no adjournment unless sufficient cause
II. To impose costs occasioned by adjournment
III. Record the reason for delay while disposing of the appeal
IV. Dispose of the appeal ex parte

Codes

1 Only I and II are correct
2 Only I, II and III are correct
3 Only I, II and IV are correct
4 Only II, III and IV are correct

Ans. *(2)*

Exp. Statement I, II, and III are correct.

Section 19 A of the Consumer Protection Act provides further that the State Commission or the National Commission, as the case may be, shall make such orders as to the costs occasioned by the adjournment as may be provided in the regulations made under this Act. It is empowered to impose costs that are occasioned by adjournment.

Also it is bound to record the reason for delay while disposing off the appeal. Provided also that in the event of an appeal being disposed of after the period so specified, the State Commission or, the National Commission, as the case may be, shall record in writing the reasons for the same at the time of disposing of the said appeal.

69 Read Assertion (A) and Reason (R) and give correct answer using code below.

Assertion (A) Where a bill is unintentionally cancelled by the holder or his agent and the cancellation is not apparent thereon, the bill is discharged.

Reason (R) Above principle is laid down in Section 82 of the Negotiable Instruments Act.

Codes

1 Both (A) and (R) are wrong
2 Both (A) and (R) are right
3 (A) is right, but (R) is wrong
4 (A) is wrong, but (R) is right

Ans. *(1)*

➲ *Exp.* Both (A) and (R) are wrong.

Both assertion and reason are wrong because Section 82 of the Negotiable Instruments act states that discharge from liability that the maker, acceptor or endorser respectively of a negotiable instrument is discharged from liability thereon

(a) by cancellation to a holder there of who cancels such acceptor's or indorser's name with intent to discharge him, and to all parties claiming under such holder;

(b) by release to a holder thereof who otherwise discharges such maker, acceptor or indorser, and to all parties deriving title under such holder after notice of such discharge;

(c) by payment to all parties thereto, if the instrument is payable to bearer, or has been indorsed in blank, and such maker, acceptor or indorser makes payment in due course of the amount due thereon.

70 Match List I with List II and select the correct answer using the code given below.

List I		List II
A. Partnership not created by status	I.	CST Vs. K. Kelukutty
B. Essentials of partnership	II.	Kshetra Mohan Vs. Commr. of Excess Profit Tax
C. Joint Hindu Family and partnership	III.	Rakesh Kumar Dinesh Kumar Vs. U.G. Hotels and Resorts Ltd.
D. Partnership between outsiders and joint family	IV.	Ganpat Vs. Annaji

Codes

	A	B	C	D		A	B	C	D
1	III	I	IV	II	2	I	III	IV	II
3	III	I	II	IV	4	IV	II	I	III

Ans. *(1)*

➲ *Exp.* The correct matching is A-III, B-I, C-IV, D-II.

Partnership not created by status is related to Rakesh Kumar Dinesh Kumar Vs. U.G. Hotels and Resorts Ltd. Partnership is the result of a contract. It does not arise from status, operation of law or inheritance. Section 5 of the act says so.

Essentials of partnership is related to CST Vs. K. Kelukutty. To determine whether a partnership exists, its essential elements are:

1. sharing of profit or losses.
2. joint ownership of the business.
3. an equal right to be involved in the management of the business. Joint ownership of property does not in and of itself create a partnership, as intentions are key.

Joint Hindu Family and partnership is related to Ganpat Vs. Annaji. The members of a Hindu Undivided Family (HUF) carrying on a family business cannot be called partners for their relation arises not from any contract but from status.

Partnership between outsiders and joint family is related to Kshetra Mohan Vs. Commr. of Excess Profit Tax. By entering into an agreement, partnership between outsiders and joint family can be established.

71 Match List I with List II and select the correct answer using the code given below.

List I (Duties of partners)		List II (Relevant section under the Indian Partnership Act)
A. Duty of absolute good faith	I.	Section 16 (b)
B. Duty not to compete	II.	Sections 12 (b) and 13 (f)
C. Duty of due deligence	III.	Section 10
D. Duty to indemnify for fraud	IV.	Section 9

Codes

	A	B	C	D		A	B	C	D
1	I	IV	II	III	2	IV	I	II	III
3	IV	I	III	II	4	II	III	I	IV

Ans. *(2)*

➲ *Exp.* The correct matching is A-IV, B-I, C-II, D-III.

Duty of absolute good faith is related to Section 9. As per section 9 of the act, partners are bound to carry on the business of the firm to greatest common advantage, to be just and faithful to each other, and to render true accounts and full information of all things affecting the firm to any partner, his heir or legal representative.

Duty not to compete is related to Section 16(b) If a partner carries on any business of the same nature as and competing with that of the firm, he shall account for and pay to the firm all profits made by him in that business as he has the duty of absolute good faith.

Duty of due diligence is related to Sections 12 (b) and 13 (f). As per Section 12 (b), every partner is bound to attend diligently to his duties in the conduct of the business and as per Section 13(f), a partner shall indemnify the firm for any loss caused to it by his wilful neglect in the conduct of the business of the firm.

Duty to indemnify for fraud is related to Section 10. As per Section 10 every partner shall indemnify the firm for any loss caused to it by his fraud in the conduct of the business of the firm.

72 Read Assertion (A) and Reason (R) and give correct answer using code given below.

Assertion (A) 'Goods' means every kind of movable property including actionable claims and money and excludes stock and shares, growing crops, grass and things attached to or forming part of the land which are agreed to be severed before sale or under the contract of sale.

Reason (R) Above principle is laid down in Section 2 (7) of the Sale of Goods Act.

Codes

1 Both (A) and (R) are right
2 Both (A) and (R) are wrong
3 (A) is wrong, but (R) is right
4 (A) is right, but (R) is wrong

Ans. *(2)*

Exp. Both (A) and (R) are wrong.

Assertion (A) is wrong because 'Goods' is defined as per Section 2 (7) of the 'Act' as "Every kind of movable property other than actionable claims and money; and includes stock and shares, growing crops, grass, and things attached to or forming part of the land which are agreed to be severed before sale or under the contract of sale." Hence the given Assertion is wrong because, the statement uses the term 'exclude' and Section 2(7) of the Sale of Goods Act does not say so.

Reason (R) is wrong because principle mentioned is not given by Section 2(7).

73 Which of the following statement is correct?

1 Notwithstanding any express contract the seller of goods is not bound to deliver them until the buyer applies for delivery
2 Apart from any express contract, the seller of goods is not bound to deliver them until the buyer applies for delivery
3 Apart from any express contract the seller of goods is bound to deliver them until the buyer applies for deliver
4 Apart from any express contract, the buyer of goods is bound to deliver them when the seller applies for delivery

Ans. *(2)*

Exp. Only statement 2 is correct.

Section 35 of Sale of Goods Act states that apart from any express contract, the seller of goods is not bound to deliver them until the buyer applies for delivery. While an express contract is a contract in which all elements are specifically stated (offer, acceptance, consideration), and the terms are stated, as compared to an 'implied' contract in which the existence of the contract is assumed by the circumstances.

74 "Directors are agents of the company". In which of the following cases above principle was laid down. Answer using code given below :

I. Ferguson Vs. Wilson
II. Elkington and Co. Vs. Harter
III. Hampshire Land Co, re
IV. Allen Vs. Hyatt

Codes

1 Only I
2 Only I and II
3 Only I, II and III
4 I, II, III and IV

Ans. *(4)*

Exp. The principle "Directors are agents of the company" is laid down in all the given cases.

A Director is an agent of the Company for the conduct of the business of the company. Directors of a company have fiduciary relationship with the company as well as the shareholders when he acts as an agent or officers of a company.

In Ferguson Vs. Wilson, the court clearly recognised that directors are in the eyes of law, agents of the company.

In Elkington and Co. Vs. Hurter, where the plaintiff supplied certain goods to a company through its chairman, who promised to issue him a debenture for the price, but never did so and company went into liquidation, he was held not liable to the plaintiff.

In Hampshire Land Company, Re case, the rule of law that information held by an agent in the worse of his agency is to be imputed to his principal has an exception where the agent is committing a proud on his principal.

In Allen Vs. Ayatt, 1914, the court considered the duties of directors toward shareholders in circumstances of them making representations to secure options to purchase shares of shareholders and undertaking to self-shares of shareholders in agency capacity.

75 Which of the following case is about doctrine of ultravires?

1 Royal British Bank Vs. Turquand
2 Premier Industrial Bank Ltd. Vs. Carlton Mfg. Co. Ltd.
3 Rajendra Nath Dutta Vs. Shibendra Nath Mukherjee
4 Attorney General Vs. Great Eastern Railway Co.

Ans. *(4)*

Exp. Attorney General Vs. Great Eastern Railway Co is about doctrine of ultravires. In this case the doctrine of ultravires was given a liberal and reasonable interpretation and it was said that whatever may fairly be regarded as incidental or consequential upon those things specified in the memorandum of association as object ought not to be held ultravires unless expressly prohibited.

UGC-NET
LAW
SOLVED PAPER 2017 (January)
PAPER II

1. The Preamble to Constitution of India proclaims that, 'We, the People of India,' have established

1 A Sovereign, Socialist, Democratic, Republic only
2 A Sovereign, Secular, Democratic, Republic only
3 A Secular, Socialist, Democratic, Republic only
4 A Sovereign, Socialist, Secular, Democratic Republic

***Ans.* (4)**

➲ *Exp.* The Preamble to Constitution of India proclaims that, 'We, the People of India,' have established a Sovereign, Socialist, Secular, Democratic Republic.

Preamble declares India to be a Sovereign, Socialist, Secular and Democratic Republic. The objectives stated by the Preamble are to secure justice, liberty, equality to all citizens and promote fraternity to maintain unity and integrity of the nation.

2. Match List I with List II and select the correct answer by using the codes given below.

List I	List II
A. Article 16(3) amended by	I. 1st Amendment
B. Article 19(5) amended by	II. 17th Amendment
C. Article 19(6) amended by	III. 7th Amendment
D. Article 31A(2)(a) amended by	IV. 44th Amendment

Codes

	A	B	C	D		A	B	C	D
1	III	IV	I	II	2	III	I	II	IV
3	I	II	IV	III	4	II	III	I	IV

***Ans.* (1)**

➲ *Exp.* The correct matching is A-III, B-IV, C-I, D-II

Article 16(3) was amended by the 7th Amendment. In this amendment, Article 16(3) was amended. The 7th Amendment of Indian Constitution was needed to implement the recommendations of the States Reorganisation Commission regarding the reorganisation of the states on a linguistic basis.

Article 19(5) was amended by the 44th Amendment. The 44th Amendment of 1978 removed the right to property from the list of fundamental rights. A new provision, Article 300-A, was added to the constitution, which provided that "no person shall be deprived of his property save by authority of law". The right to property, which has been the occasion for more than one amendment of the Constitution, would cease to be a Fundamental Right and become only a legal right. Necessary amendments for this purpose are being made to Article 19 and Article 31 is being deleted.

Article 19(6) was amended by the 1st Amendment. The main objectives of this Bill are to amend Article 19 and to insert provisions fully securing the constitutional validity of zamindari abolition laws in general and certain specified State Acts in particular.

Article 31 A (2) (a) was amended by the 17th Amendment. This amendment talks about securing the constitutional validity of acquisition of estates and placing land acquisition laws in Schedule 9 of the Constitution.

3. Read Assertion (A) and Reason (R) and select the correct answer with the help of codes given below.

Assertion (A) Under Article 226 of the Constitution of India the High Court has discretionary remedy to issue writs.

Reason (R) If the High Court is satisfied that the aggrieved party can have an adequate remedy elsewhere it can refuse to grant writ.

Codes

1 (A) and (R) are true and (R) is the correct explanation of (A)
2 (A) and (R) are true, but (R) is not the correct explanation of (A)
3 (A) is true, but (R) is false
4 (A) is false, but (R) is true

***Ans.* (1)**

➲ *Exp.* (A) and (R) are true and (R) is the correct explanation of (A).

Under Article 226 of the Constitution of India the High Court has discretionary remedy to issue writs. Article 226 of the Constitution empowers the Hon'ble High Courts to exercise power through issuance of writs : habeas corpus, mandamus, quo warranto, prohibition and certiorari or any appropriate writ.

If the High Court is satisfied that the aggrieved party can have an adequate remedy elsewhere it can refuse to grant writ. Issuance of writs is the discretionary power of courts, and it correctly explains the given Assertion.

4. Match List I with List II and select the correct answer using the codes given below.

List I (Cases)	List II (Principles)
A. Indira Nehru Gandhi Vs. Raj Narain	I. Departmental bias
B. Gullapalli Nageswara Rao Vs. APSRTC	II. Preventive detention
C. Fagu Shaw Vs. State of WB	III. Rights of inmates of protective homes
D. Upendra Baxi Vs. State of UP	IV. Rule of law

Codes

	A	B	C	D		A	B	C	D
1	IV	I	II	III	2	I	IV	II	III
3	IV	I	III	II	4	II	III	I	IV

Ans. (1)

Exp. The correct matching is A-IV, B-I, C-II, D-III.

Indira Nehru Gandhi Vs. Raj Narain laid down the principle of Rule of law. In this case, Rule of law was discussed and upheld the same. Rule of law is a principle under which all persons, institutions, and entities are accountable to laws.

Gullapalli Nageswara Rao Vs. APSRTC laid down the principle of Departmental bias. This case discussed the principle of Departmental bias. It is popularly known as the rule against bias. The problem of departmental bias is something which is inherent in the administrative process, and if it is not effectively checked, it may negate the very concept of fairness in the administrative proceeding.

Fagu Shaw Vs. State of WB laid down the principle of Preventive detention. In this case principle of Preventive detention was laid down, which is the practice of incarcerating accused individuals before trial on the assumption that their release would not be in the best interest of society.

Upendra Baxi Vs. State of UP talks about the Rights of inmates of protective homes. In this case Rights of inmates of protective homes were discussed. Article 21 of constitution implicitly talks about the right of inmates, for example right to speedy trial, right to fair trial.

5. "The Fundamental Duties incorporated in Article 51A of the Constitution of India are mere reminder to the citizens, with no enforceability, to ensure their compliance" was said by

1 Justice JS Verma
2 Justice O Chinnapa Reddy
3 Justice YV Chandrachud
4 Justice PN Bhagwati

Ans. (1)

Exp. "The Fundamental Duties incorporated in Article 51A of the Constitution of India are mere reminder to the citizens, with no enforceability, to ensure their compliance" was said by Justice JS Verma.

The Fundamental Duties are defined as the moral obligations of all citizens to help promote a spirit of patriotism and to uphold the unity of India. These duties set out in Part IV–A of the Constitution, concern individuals and the nation.

6. Justice Mukherjee CJ speaking for the court, stated "that though the executive power is vested in the President, the President is only a formal or constitutional head of the executive. The real power is vested in the Council of Ministers on whose aid and advise the President acts in the exercise of his functions," in the following case

1 UNR Rao Vs. Indira Gandhi
2 Ram Jawaya Kapur Vs. State of Punjab
3 Jayantilal Amratlal Shodan *Vs.* FN Rao
4 Sardarilal Vs. Union of India

Ans. (2)

Exp. Justice Mukherjee CJ speaking for the court, stated "that though the executive power is vested in the President, the President is only a formal or constitutional head of the executive. The real power is vested in the Council of Ministers on whose aid and advise the President acts in the exercise of his functions," in the case of Ram Jawaya Kapur Vs. State of Punjab.

Article 74(1) of Constitution provides that there shall be a Council of Ministers with Prime Minister at the head, to aid and advise President in exercise of his functions.

7. The right of a person to be appointed as a guardian of his minor children under the personal law is not a Fundamental Right was decided by the Supreme Court in one of the following cases

1 Mohd-Aslam Vs. Union of India
2 Sahifzada Saiyed Muhammed Amirabbas Abbasi Vs. State of Madhyabharat
3 Khatri Vs. State of Bihar
4 Mohd Faruk Vs. State of MP

Ans. (2)

Exp. The right of a person to be appointed as a guardian of his minor children under the personal law is not a Fundamental Right was decided by the Supreme Court in Sahifzada Saiyed Muhammed Amirabbas Abbasi Vs. State of Madhyabharat.

It was held that the Court can exercise jurisdiction under Article 32 of the Constitution only in enforcement of the Fundamental Rights guaranteed by Part III of the Constitution. Where on account of the decision of a court of competent jurisdiction, the right alleged by the petitioner does not exist and therefore its infringement cannot arise, this Court cannot entertain a petition under that Article for protection of the alleged right.

8. According to Austin, the positive law has following three attributes.

1 Command, sovereign, obedience
2 Command, sovereign, sanction
3 Command, obedience, sanction
4 Sovereign, obedience, sanction

***Ans.* (2)**

Exp. According to Austin the positive law has three attributes namely command, sovereign, sanction.

As per his definition of law, it was command of a political superior to his political inferiors which we in general call it as the command of sovereign backed by sanction or it is a guidance of an intelligence being to an intelligent being having power over him, and breach of these command by sovereign will lead to sanction.

9. "The movement of progressive societies has hitherto been a movement from status to contract." This statement is of

1 Hegel 2 Savigny
3 Henry Maine 4 Puchta

***Ans.* (3)**

Exp. "The movement of progressive societies has hitherto been a movement from status to contract." This statement is given by Henry Maine.

Henry Sumner Maine characterises the evolution towards progressive societies as a passage from status(an ascribed position) to contract (a voluntary stipulation). According to Maine, most of the ancient communities are founded on a patriarchal pattern wherein the eldest male parent called the paterfamilias dominated the entire family. With the march of time the institution of paterfamilias withered away and now rights and obligations were dependent on individual contracts and free negotiation between persons.

10. Match List I with List II and select the correct answer by using the codes given below.

List I	List II
A. The Concept of Law	I. Austin
B. The Province of Jurisprudence Determined	II. Bentham
C. Some Reflections on Jurisprudence	III. Hart
D. Limits of Jurisprudence Defined	IV. Buckland

Codes

	A	B	C	D		A	B	C	D
1	III	II	I	IV	2	III	I	IV	II
3	I	II	III	IV	4	IV	I	II	III

***Ans.* (2)**

Exp. The correct matching is A-III, B-I, C-IV, D-II

The Concept of Law-Hart.

The Concept of Law is a 1961 book by the legal philosopher HLA Hart and his most famous work. The Concept of Law presents Hart's theory of legal positivism.

The Province of Jurisprudence Determined is a book written by John Austin and first published in 1832. In this book, he sets out his theory of law generally known as the 'Command theory'.

Some Reflections on Jurisprudence is the book by Buckland. In the book', the author writes, Jurisprudence is a most hospitable word. It can be understood to include not only the analysis of legal concepts, but also all those topics which are discussed under the rubric 'philosophy of law'.

Limits of Jurisprudence Defined is a book by Bentham. Jeremy Bentham was an English philosopher, jurist and social reformer regarded as the founder of modern utilitarianism.

11. Which one of the following is not a theory of corporate personality?

1 Fiction Theory 2 Interest Theory
3 Bracket Theory 4 Will Theory

***Ans.* (*)**

Exp. Will theory and Interest theory are not the theory of Corporate personality.

Corporate personality is the fact stated by the law that a company is recognised as a legal entity distinct from its members. A company with such personality is an independent legal existence separate from its shareholders, directors, officers and creators. Fiction theory, concession theory, realist theory and bracket theory are the theories of Corporate personality.

Interest theory and Will theory are theories on legal rights.

12. 'A' has a house and nobody should interfere with the enjoyment of proprietary right over the house. This right is called

1 Personal right 2 Imperfect right
3 Right in rem 4 Right in personam

***Ans.* (3)**

Exp. 'A' has a house and nobody should interfere with the enjoyment of proprietary right over the house. This right is called Right in rem.

As per the law of the land, every person entering into a contract has rights in rem. This is right available to him or her against the entire world or public at large. It protects a person's property from the entire world.

13. Match List I with List II and select the correct answer by using the codes given below.

List I	List II
A. Theory of Volksgeist	I. Bentham
B. Theory of Social Interest	II. Ihering
C. Theory of Utilitarian Individualism	III. Burke
D. Gradual and Organic Process Theory	IV. Savigny

Codes

	A	B	C	D		A	B	C	D
1	I	II	III	IV	2	IV	II	III	I
3	IV	II	I	III	4	III	I	IV	II

Ans. (3)

Exp. The correct matching is A-IV, B-II, C-I, D-III.

Theory of Volksgeist or The Volksgeist theory was coined by Von Savigny (1778-1861) which stated that the nature of any particular system of law was a reflection of the spirit of the people who evolved it. The broad principles of the system are to be found in the spirit of the people and they must manifest themselves in customary rules.

Theory of Social Interest was given by Ihering. Ihering stressed that law does not exist for the individual as an end in himself, but serves his interest while taking into consideration the good of society. If the society is happy, so will the individual.

Theory of Utilitarian Individualism was given by Jeremy Bentham who was a philosopher, economist, jurist, and legal reformer and the founder of modern utilitarianism, an ethical theory holding that actions are morally right if they tend to promote happiness or pleasure (and morally wrong if they tend to promote unhappiness or pain) among all those affected by them.

Gradual and Organic Process Theory was given by Burke. According to the Gradual and Organic Process Theory by Burke, the society as an organism that emerges and evolves gradually over time in order to meet the needs of its members.

14. Who has remarked that "It is both practically inconvenient and also contrary to the best juristic thought to deny its (International law) legal character"?

1 HLA Hart
2 JG Starke
3 Edward Collins
4 JL Brierly

Ans. (4)

Exp. JL Brierly remarked that "It is both practically inconvenient and also contrary to the best juristic thought to deny its (International law) legal character".

International law is based on rules made by states for states. States are sovereign and equal in their relations and can thus voluntarily create or accept to abide by legally binding rules, usually in the form of a treaty or convention. According to Brierly, "The Law of Nations or International Law may be defined as the body of rules and principles of action, which are binding upon civilised states in their relations with one another."

15. Read both Assertion (A) and Reason (R) and select the correct answer by using the codes given below.

Assertion (A) 'Res Judicata', 'estoppel' etc are examples of the General Principles of Law recognised by civilised states.

Reason (R) In the case of diversion of water from Muese, the Permanent Court of International justice applied 'Res Judicata' and 'Estoppel'.

Codes

1 Both (A) and (R) are correct and (R) is the correct explanation of (A)
2 Both (A) and (R) are true, but (R) is not correct explanation of (A)
3 (A) is true, but (R) is false
4 (A) is false, but (R) is true

Ans. (1)

Exp. Both (A) and (R) are correct and (R) is the correct explanation of (A).

Assertion (A) says, 'Res Judicata', 'estoppel' etc are examples of the General Principles of Law recognised by civilised states. Article 38 of the International Court of Justice Statute talks about "General Principles of Law recognised by civilized nations" (i.e. general principles of fairness and justice which are applied universally in legal systems around the world) and Principle of Res Judicata and Estoppel are applicable worldwide.

In the case of diversion of water from Muese, the Permanent Court of International justice applied 'Res Judicata' and 'Estoppel' is true and correctly explains the given Assertion as the case applied the general principle recognised by civilized nations.

16. Which of the following is not a 'theory' propounded to explain the relationship between International Law and Municipal Law ?

1 Transformation Theory
2 Delegation Theory
3 Fiction Theory
4 Specific Adoption Theory

Ans. (3)

Exp. Fiction Theory is not a 'theory' propounded to explain the relationship between International Law and Municipal Law.

As per the Fiction Theory, a corporation exists only as an outcome of fiction and metaphor. So, the personality that is attached to these corporations is done purely by legal fiction. The legal person is created only in the eyes of the law for a specific purpose.

17. Which of the following statement/s is/are correct? Answer by using the codes below

I. The Charter of the United Nations came into force on 24th October, 1945.
II. The purposes of the United Nations are enshrined in Article 2 of the Charter.
III. The seventh and the last principle of the United Nations states that nothing contained in present Charter shall authorise the United Nations to intervene in matters which are essentially within domestic jurisdiction of any state.
IV. The provision relating to suspension of a member finds mention in Article 3 of the charter.

Codes
1 Only I and III are correct
2 Only I, II and III are correct
3 Only II, III and IV are correct
4 Only I, II, III and IV all are correct

***Ans.** (1)*

Exp. Statements I and III are correct.

Statement I is correct because the Charter of the United Nations came into force on 24th October, 1945.

Statement II is incorrect because Article 1 of the Charter talks about the purpose of United Nations.

Statement III is correct because the seventh and the last principle of the United Nations states that nothing contained in the present Charter shall authorise the United Nations to intervene in matters which are essentially within the domestic jurisdiction of any state.

Statement IV is incorrect because Article 5 of the Charter is the provision relating to the suspension of a member.

18. Which of the following statement/s is/are correct? Answer by using the codes below

I. 'Mediation' is not 'pacific means' of settlement of International Disputes.
II. 'Pious Fund Case' is an important decision given by the Permanent Court of Arbitration.
III. 'Retorsion' is a compulsive or 'coercive' means of settlement of International Disputes.
IV. A leading case on 'Reprisal' is the 'Naulilaa Incident'.

Codes
1 Only II is correct
2 Only I, II and III are correct
3 Only II, III and IV are correct
4 I, II, III and IV all are correct

***Ans.** (3)*

Exp. Statements II, III and IV are correct.

Statement II is correct because 'Pious Fund Case' is an important decision given by the Permanent Court of Arbitration.

Statement III is correct because 'Retorsion' is a compulsive or 'coercive' means of settlement of International Disputes.

Statement IV is correct because, a leading case on 'Reprisal' is the 'Naulilaa Incident'.

Statement I is incorrect because 'Mediation' is a pacific means of settlement of International Disputes.

19. Which of the following statement/s is/are incorrect? Answer by using the codes below

I. The Commission on Human Rights was established by the Economic and Social Council in February, 1946.
II. The General Assembly decided to replace UN Human Right Commission by Human Right Council Vide Resolution 60/251 of 15th March, 2006.
III. The Human Right Council concluded its first session at Hague on 30th June, 2007.
IV. The Universal Declaration of Human Rights was adopted by the General Assembly by a vote of 48 to nil with eight abstentions.

Codes
1 Only III is incorrect
2 Only I, II and III are incorrect
3 Only II, III and IV are incorrect
4 I, II, III and IV all are incorrect

***Ans.** (1)*

Exp. Only statement III is incorrect.

Statement III is incorrect because The Human Right Council concluded its first session at Hague on 30th June, 2006.

The United Nations Commission on Human Rights (UNCHR) was a functional commission within the overall framework of the United Nations from 1946 until it was replaced by the United Nations Human Rights Council in 2006. It was a subsidiary body of the UN Economic and Social Council (ECOSOC), and was also assisted in its work by the Office of the United Nations High Commissioner for Human Rights (UNOHCHR). It was the UN's principal mechanism and international forum concerned with the promotion and protection of human rights.

20. Read the following statements and answer with the help of codes given below

I. Two persons are said to be related to each other by full blood when they are descended from a common ancestor by the same wife.
II. Two persons are said to be related to each other by uterine blood when they are descended from a common ancestress but by different husbands.
III. Two persons are said to be related to each other by half blood when they are descended from a common ancestor by the same wife.
IV. Two persons are said to be related to each other by half blood when they are descended from a common ancestor but by different wives.

Codes
1 I and II are correct, but III and IV are incorrect
2 I, II and IV are correct, but III is incorrect
3 IV and II are correct, but III and I are incorrect
4 II and III are correct, but I and IV are incorrect

***Ans.** (2)*

Exp. Statements I, II and IV are correct, but III is incorrect.

Statement I is correct because it says two persons are said to be related to each other by full blood when they are descended from a common ancestor by the same wife and Section 3 of Hindu Marriage Act, 1955 talks about the same.

Statement II is correct because it says two persons are said to be related to each other by uterine blood when they are descended from a common ancestress but by different husbands and Section 3 (d) of The Hindu Marriage Act, 1955 talks about the same.

Statement IV is correct because it says two persons are said to be related to each other by half-blood when they are descended from a common ancestor but by different wives and Section 3 of Hindu Marriage Act talks about the same.

Statement III is incorrect because two persons are said to be related to each other by half-blood when they are descended from a common ancestor by the different wife. This has been provided under Section 3(c) of the Hindu Marriage Act.

21. A person shall not be treated as Buddhist under Section 21 of the Hindu Marriage Act, 1955, if

1 Both of his parents were Buddhists.
2 His father was Christian, mother was Buddhist and he was brought up as Buddhist child.
3 His father was Christian, mother was Buddhist and he was brought up as Christian child.
4 He was a Muslim and has converted to Buddhist religion.

Ans. *(3)*

Exp. A person shall not be treated as Buddhist under Section 21 of the Hindu Marriage Act,1955, if his father was Christian, mother was Buddhist and he was brought up as a Christian child.

The explanation to Section 2 of the Hindu Marriage Act says that the following persons are Hindus, Buddhists, Jainas or Sikhs by religion, as the case may be:

(a) any child, legitimate or illegitimate, both of whose parents are Hindus, Buddhists, Jainas or Sikhs by religion;
(b) any child, legitimate or illegitimate, one of whose parents is a Hindu, Buddhist, Jaina or Sikh by religion and who is brought up as a member of the tribe, community, group or family to which such parent belongs or belonged; and
(c) any person who is a convert or re-convert to the Hindu, Buddhist, Jaina or Sikh religion.

22. Ancient sources of Hindu law are

1 Custom, Shruti, Precedent
2 Shruti, Vedas, Custom, Legislation
3 Smritis, Custom, Precedent
4 Shruti, Smritis, Custom, Digests etc

Ans. *(4)*

Exp. Ancient sources of Hindu law are Shruti, Smritis, Custom, Digests, etc.

Shruti: The word is derived from the root 'shru' which means 'to hear'. In theory, it is the primary and paramount source of Hindu law and is believed to be the language of the divine revelation through the sages. The material heard by people constitute Shruti.

Smritis: The word Smriti is derived from the root 'smri' meaning 'to remember'. Traditionally, Smritis contain those portions of the Shrutis which the sages forgot in their original form and the idea whereby they wrote in their own language with the help of their memory.

Customs: Customs are a principle source and their position is next to the Shrutis and Smritis but usage of custom prevails over the Smritis. It is superior to written law. One of the requirements for a custom to take force of law in Hindu Law is that it should be ancient apart from being certain, uninterrupted and not opposed to public policy.

Commentaries and Digests: Commentaries (Tika or Bhashya) and Digests (Nibandhs) covered a period of more than thousand years from 7th century to 1800 A.D. In the first part of the period most of the commentaries were written on the Smritis but in the later period, the works were in the nature of digests containing a synthesis of the various Smritis and explaining and reconciling the various contradictions.

23. The Muslim Personal Law (Shariat) Application Act, 1937 is applicable to all kinds of property except

1 Agricultural land, testamentary succession and Charities other than wakfs.
2 Testamentary succession and charities other than wakfs only.
3 Agricultural land and testamentary succession only.
4 Agricultural land and charities other than wakfs only.

Ans. *(1)*

Exp. The Muslim Personal Law (Shariat) Application Act, 1937 is applicable to all kinds of property except Agricultural land, testamentary succession and Charities other than wakfs.

Agricultural lands, charities and charitable endowments, being provincial (State) subjects, had to be expressly excluded from Section 2 of the Act. The result is that the courts cannot apply Muslim law on these questions under the authority of the Shariat Act.

24. Match List I with List II under the Hindu Marriage Act, 1955 and select the correct answer using the codes given below.

List I	List II
A. Age of marriage	I. Section 13(1-A)
B. Breakdown grounds of marriage	II. Section 8
C. Overriding effect of Act	III. Section 5(iii)
D. Registration of marriage	IV. Section 4

Codes

	A	B	C	D		A	B	C	D
1	I	III	II	IV	2	III	I	IV	II
3	II	III	IV	I	4	IV	III	I	II

Ans. *(2)*

Exp. The correct matching is A-III, B-I, C-IV, D-II.

Age of marriage is related to Section 5 (iii). Section 5(iii) of Hindu Marriage Act, 1955 says that the bridegroom must complete the age of twenty-one years and the bride must have completed the age of eighteen years at the time of the marriage.

Breakdown grounds of marriage is related to Section 13 (1-A). This section says any marriage solemnised, whether before or after the commencement of the Act, may, on a petition presented by either the husband or the wife, be dissolved by a decree of divorce on the ground that the other party has, after the solemnisation of the marriage, treated the petitioner with cruelty.

Overriding effect of Act is related to Section 4. It says any text rule or interpretation of Hindu law or any custom or usage as part of that law in force immediately before the commencement of this Act shall cease to have effect with respect to any matter for which provision is made in this Act; and any other law in force immediately before the commencement of this Act shall cease to have effect in so far as it is inconsistent with any of the provisions contained in this Act.

Registration of marriage is related to Section 8. The Act provides that a Hindu Marriage shall be compulsorily registered if the State Governments have made rules regarding them. The State Governments also give an option to make rules and conditions for registering the marriages in a register called Hindu Marriage Register.

25. Presently the Hindu Marriage Act, 1955 recognises the following theories of divorce

1 Fault and Mutual Consent
2 Mutual Consent and Breakdown of Marriage
3 Fault, Breakdown of Marriage, Mutual Consent and Customary
4 Fault, Irretrievable Breakdown of Marriage and Mutual Consent

***Ans.** (3)*

Exp. Presently the Hindu Marriage Act, 1955 recognises Fault, Breakdown of Marriage, Mutual Consent and Customary as theories of divorce.

Theories for divorce are fault theory, mutual consent theory and irretrievable breakdown of marriage theory. Under the Fault theory or the offences theory or the guilt theory, marriage can be dissolved only when either party to the marriage has committed a matrimonial offence.

Another theory of divorce is that of mutual consent. The underlying rationale is that since two persons can marry by their free will, they should also be allowed to move out of the relationship of their own free will. The third theory relates to the irretrievable breakdown of the marriage. The breakdown of marriage is defined as "such failure in the matrimonial relationships or such circumstances adverse to that relationship that no reasonable probability remains for the spouses again living together as husband and wife." Such marriage should be dissolved with maximum fairness and minimum bitterness, distress and humiliation.

26. Talaq ahsan is

1 Irrevocable
2 Revocable during the tuhr in which it has been pronounced
3 Revocable until the next successive tuhr
4 Revocable during the period of iddat

***Ans.** (4)*

Exp. Talaq ahsan is revocable during the period of iddat. The duration of the 'iddat' is ninety days or three menstrual cycles or three lunar months. If the couple resumes cohabitation or intimacy, within the period of 'iddat', the pronouncement of divorce is treated as having been revoked. Therefore, 'talaq-e-ahsan' is revocable.

27. Match List I with List II and select the correct answer using the codes given below.

List I	List II
A. Proposal	I. Grainger and Son Vs. Gough
B. Invitation to make an offer	II. Maharashtra Rajya Sahakari Kappas Utpadak Panan Mahasabha Ltd. Vs. Manga Bhaga Chaudhary
C. Communication of acceptance of offer by acceptor himself	III. Henthorn Vs. Fraser
D. Revocation of offer	IV. Powell Vs. Lee

Codes

	A	B	C	D		A	B	C	D
1	II	I	IV	III	2	I	II	IV	III
3	II	I	III	IV	4	IV	III	I	II

***Ans.** (1)*

Exp. The correct matching is A-II, B-I, C-IV, D-III.

Proposal is related to Maharashtra Rajya Sahakari Kappas Utpadak Panan Mahasabha Ltd. Vs. Manga Bhaga Chaudhary. In the mentioned case, the term Proposal was discussed. According to the Indian Contract Act 1872, Proposal is defined in Section 2(a) as "when one person will signify to another person his willingness to do or not do something (abstain) with a view to obtain the assent of such person to such an act or abstinence, he is said to make a proposal or an offer.

Invitation to make an offer is related to Grainger and Son Vs. Gough. This case discussed an invitation to offer. In an invitation to offer, no specific party has the intention to enter into a contract. The seller may enter into a contract with anybody from the public who makes the best offer to him. So, the essence of an invitation to offer is that the offer is actually made by the seller.

Communication of acceptance of offer by acceptor himself is related to Powell Vs. Lee case. It was an English contract law case. The ruling established that acceptance of an offer must be communicated to the offeror by the offeree himself or authorised agent.

Revocation of offer is related to Henthorn Vs Fraser case. It is a decision of the Court of Appeal of England and Wales dealing with the postal rule in English law of contract formation. In this case, Lord Herschell argued: "Where the circumstances are such that it must have been within the contemplation of the parties that, according to ordinary usage of mankind, the post might be used as a means of communicating the acceptance of an offer, the acceptance is complete as soon as it is posted."

28. Read Assertion (A) and Reason (R) and select the correct answer using codes given below.

Assertion (A) An agreement made with consideration is void unless it is in writing and registered.

Reason (R) Because Section 25(1) of the Indian Contract Act stipulates so.

Codes

1 Both (A) and (R) are true and (R) is correct explanation for (A)
2 Both (A) and (R) are false
3 (A) is true, but (R) is false
4 (R) is true, but (A) is false

***Ans.* (2)**

Exp. Both (A) and (R) are false.

Assertion (A) is false because Section 25 of the Indian Contract Act says that an agreement without consideration is void unless it is in writing and registered, or is a promise to compensate for something, or is a promise to pay debt time-barred by the limitation law.

Reason (R) is false because none of the section stipulates the mentioned Assertion.

29. In which one of the following cases doctrine of frustration was laid down?

1 BOI Finance Ltd. Vs. Custodian
2 Odisha Textile Mills Ltd. Vs. Ganesh Das
3 Sachidananda Patnaik Vs. GP and Co.
4 Taylor Vs. Caldwell

***Ans.* (4)**

Exp. In Taylor Vs. Caldwell, doctrine of frustration was laid down.

Taylor Vs. Caldwell is a landmark English contract law case, with an opinion delivered by Mr Justice Blackburn which established the doctrine of frustration. The doctrine of frustration basically talks about the impossibility of performance of the contract. It means a contract cannot be executed because of an incident beyond the control of parties. The performance of such a contract becomes frustrated i.e. it becomes complicated, impossible or even illegal.

30. Which of the following statement is correct ?

1 A person who wrongfully rescinds a contract is entitled to compensation for any damage which he has sustained through the non-fulfilment of the contract
2 A person who rightfully rescinds a contract is not entitled to compensation for any damage which he has sustained through the non-fulfilment of the contract
3 A person who rightfully rescinds a contract is entitled to compensation for any damage which he has sustained through the non-fulfilment of the contract
4 A person who rightfully rescinds a contract is entitled to compensation for any damage which he has not sustained through the non-fulfilment of the contract

***Ans.* (3)**

Exp. Statement 3 is correct.

According to Section 75 of the Contract Act, a person who rightfully rescinds a contract is entitled to compensation for any damage which he has sustained through the non-fulfilment of the contract.

31. Every person is competent to contract

1 who is of the age of minority according to law to which he is subject and who is of sound mind and is not disqualified from contracting by any law to which he is subject
2 who is of the age of majority according to law to which he is not subject and who is of sound mind, and is not disqualified from contracting by any law to which he is subject
3 who is of the age of majority according to law to which he is subject, and who is of sound mind, and is not qualified from contracting by any law to which he is subject
4 who is of the age of majority according to law to which he is subject, and who is of sound mind, and is not disqualified from contracting by any law to which he is subject

***Ans.* (4)**

Exp. According to Section 11 of Indian Contract Act 1872, "Every person is competent to contract who is of the age of majority according to law to which he is subject, and who is of sound mind, and is not disqualified from contracting by any law to which he is subject".

32. Match List I with List II and select the correct answer using the codes given below.

List I (Types of Vitiating elements of a contract)	List II (Relevant case-law)
A. Undue influence	I. Nursey SPG and Wvg. Co. Ltd., Re
B. Misrepresentation	II. Jaggan Nath Vs. Secy of State for India
C. Fraud	III. Lancashire Loans Vs. Black
D. Mistake	IV. Derry Vs. Peek

Codes

	A	B	C	D		A	B	C	D
1	II	IV	III	I	2	I	III	IV	II
3	III	I	IV	II	4	III	I	II	IV

***Ans.* (3)**

Exp. The correct matching is A-III, B-I, C-IV, D-II.

Undue influence is mentioned in Lancashire Loans Vs. Black. In this case undue influence was discussed. In this case, when a girl just before her marriage entered in a money lending transaction as surety for her mother, it was held to be entered under undue influence.

Misrepresentation was discussed in Nursery SPG and Wvg Co. Ltd. Re. This case discussed the concept of misrepresentation under a contract.

Fraud is related to Derry Vs. Peek. This is a case on English contract law, fraudulent misstatement, and the tort of deceit.

Mistake is related to Jaggan Nath Vs. Secy of State for India This case discussed the concept of mistake under contract. 'Mistake' is related to can be defined as any action, decision or judgement that produced an unwanted and unintentional result. A Mistake is said to have occurred where parties intending to do one thing by error do something else.

33. Read Assertion (A) and Reason (R) and select the correct answer using codes given below.

Assertion (A) Compensation is recoverable for any loss or damage which the parties knew at the time of the contract as unlikely to result from the breach of the contract.

Reason (R) Because above rule is laid down in Hadley Vs. Baxendale case.

Codes

1 Both (A) and (R) are correct and (R) is correct explanation for (A)
2 Both (A) and (R) are false
3 (A) is true, but (R) is false
4 (R) is true, but (A) is false

***Ans.* (2)**

Exp. Both (A) and (R) are false.

Assertion (A) is false because Section 73 in The Indian Contract Act, 1872 provides for compensation for loss or damage caused by breach of contract. It reads as, "When a contract has been broken, the party who suffers by such breach is entitled to receive, from the party who has broken the contract, compensation for any loss or damage caused to him thereby, which naturally arose in the usual course of things from such breach, or which the parties knew, when they made the contract, to be likely to result from the breach of it. Compensation is not to be given for any remote and indirect loss or damage sustained by the reason of the breach."

Reason (R) is false because in Hadley Vs. Baxendale, it was held that consequential damages can be claimed by the non-breaching party only if both the parties to the contract were aware of the possibility of such losses arising from the breach of contract.

34. Match List I (Name of case) with List II (Decision of case) by using codes below.

List I (Name of case)	List II (Decision of cases)
A. Manju Bhatia Vs. New Delhi Municipal Corporation	I. Liability of owner of tree for an injury caused by its falling.
B. Municipal Corporation Delhi Vs. Sushila Devi	II. Legal duty of Railway to assure reasonable safety at railway level crossing.
C. Union of India Vs. Lalman	III. Teacher's duty of case towards children when they are taken out on a picnic for fun and swim.
D. M.S. Grewal Vs. Deepchand Sood	IV. Liability of builder towards purchasers of flats.

Codes

	A	B	C	D		A	B	C	D
1	II	I	III	IV	2	I	II	IV	III
3	III	IV	I	II	4	IV	I	II	III

***Ans.* (4)**

Exp. The correct matching is A-IV, B-I, C-II, D-III.

Manju Bhatia Vs. New Delhi Municipal Corporation is related to Liability of builder towards purchasers of flats.

Municipal Corporation Delhi Vs. Sushila Devi is related to Liability of owner of tree for an injury caused by its falling.

Union of India Vs. Lalman is related to Legal duty of Railway to assure reasonable safety at railway level crossing.

M.S. Grewal Vs. Deepchand Sood is related to Teacher's duty of case towards children when they are taken out on a picnic for fun and swim.

35. Read Assertion (A) and Reason (R) and answer using codes given below.

Assertion (A) Acts of state are directed against another sovereign state or its sovereign personally or its subjects.

Reason (R) Acts of executive government in the name of President in normal course of administration are acts of state and are not open to judicial scrutiny.

Codes

1 Both (A) and (R) are correct and (R) is correct explanation of (A)
2 Both (A) and (R) are correct, but (R) is not correct explanation of (A)
3 (A) is true, but (R) is false
4 (R) is true, but (A) is false

***Ans.* (3)**

Exp. (A) is true, but (R) is false.

Assertion (A) is true because Acts of state are directed against another sovereign state or its sovereign personally or its subjects. The Madras High Court in Secretary of State Vs. Hari Bhanjj (1882) held that immunity of East India Company extended only to 'Acts of the State'. The defence of an act of State is not available against a citizen. Acts of State are directed against another sovereign State or its sovereign personally or its subjects and being based on policy consideration and not on law administered by Municipal Courts.

Reason (R) is false because Acts of executive government in the normal course of administration are open to judicial scrutiny. An administrative action is a legal action which is concerned with the conduct of a public administrative body. This kind of action can compel an authority to take a certain action. It does not decide a right though it might affect a right. The principles of natural justice cannot be ignored while exercising 'administrative powers'.

36. Which of the following is correct? Answer using the codes given below.

I. Corporation is vicariously liable for acts done by its employees.

II. Minor is liable for the torts committed by him.

III. Wife is liable under law of torts to her husband if she negligently fractures his legs.

IV. Tort committed by any partner in the ordinary course of business of firm all other partners are liable.

Codes

1 I, II, III and IV   2 I, II and III
3 I, II and IV   4 I and IV

Ans. (3)

Exp. Statements I, II and IV are correct.

Statement I is correct because a corporation is vicariously liable for acts done by its employees as companies are made criminally liable for the offences committed by its employees within the scope of their employment.

Statement II is correct because there is no minimum age for the existence of tortious liability. A minor can be very well sued like an adult, if the action committed by him is in contrast with the reasonable action expected from the child of that age in a particular situation.

Statement IV is correct because for the tort committed by any of the partners of the company, all partners will be held liable for the damages. In a Partnership firm each partner acts on behalf of other partner or on behalf of partnership. Hence, a partnership can be held vicariously liable for negligence committed by a partner.

Statement III is incorrect because under common law, there could be no action between husband and wife for tort.

37. In which case the principle 'ubi jus ibi remedium' was recognised?

1 Rylands Vs. Flecher
2 Ashby Vs. White
3 Ashdown Vs. Samuel Williams
4 Pema Chibber Vs. Union of India

Ans. (2)

Exp. In Ashby Vs. White, the principle of 'ubi jin ibi remedium' was recognised.

In Ashby Vs. White, the plaintiff was a qualified voter and he was detained from giving a vote in a parliamentary election by the defendant who was a police officer. The party to whom he wanted to vote had won the election and the plaintiff filed a suit against the defendant stating that he was detained from giving a vote and his right to vote was infringed and also claimed a certain amount of compensation for the damage caused to him. The defendant in his defence said that the party to whom he wanted to vote had won the election and therefore no damage and injury was caused to him.

The court held that no damage or injury was caused as the candidate for whom the plaintiff wanted to vote had won the election but his right to vote was violated. To restrain a person from giving vote is a civil wrong and therefore the plaintiff had the right to seek remedy from the court of law. The maxim 'ubi jus ibi remedium' was applied in this case and the plaintiff was awarded some amount of compensation.

38. State Government may notify that State Commission may perform its function at other places other than state capital. Who needs to be consulted by the State Government for such notification under Consumer Protection Act?

1 Central Government
2 National Commission
3 State Commission
4 State Commission and High Court

Ans. (3)

Exp. "State Government may notify that State Commission may perform its function at other places other than state capital". State commission needs to be consulted by the State Government for the mentioned notification under Consumer Protection Act.

Section 42 of the Consumer Protection Act, 2019 [new Act has repealed the old one] says that the State Government shall, by notification, establish a State Consumer Disputes Redressal Commission, to be known as the State Commission, in the State.

It also says that the State Commission shall ordinarily function at the State capital and perform its functions at such other places as the State Government may in consultation with the State Commission notify in the Official Gazette.

39. Who among the following cannot file a complaint before the District Forum under Section 12 of the Consumer Protection Act?

1 One consumer and not more than one consumer
2 Any recognised consumer association
3 Central and State Government
4 One or more consumers

Ans. (1)

Exp. One consumer and not more than one consumer cannot file a complaint before the District Forum under Section 12 of the Consumer Protection Act.

Section 35 of the Consumer Protection Act 2019 says that a complaint, in relation to any goods sold or delivered or agreed to be sold or delivered or any service provided or agreed to be provided, may be filed with a District Commission by—

(a) the consumer

(i) to whom such goods are sold or delivered or agreed to be sold or delivered or such service is provided or agreed to be provided; or

(ii) who alleges unfair trade practice in respect of such goods or service;

(b) any recognised consumer association, whether the consumer to whom such goods are sold or delivered or agreed to be sold or delivered or such service is provided or agreed to be provided, or who alleges unfair trade practice in respect of such goods or service, is a member of such association or not;

(c) one or more consumers, where there are numerous consumers having the same interest, with the permission of the District Commission, on behalf of, or for the benefit of, all consumers so interested; or

(d) the Central Government, the Central Authority or the State Government, as the case may be.

40. 'The degree of cogence need not reach certainty but it must carry a high degree of probability.'
As per the statement answer using codes as to in which of the situations, in sequential order the principle of natural justice is applied

I. Alibi
II. Self-incrimination
III. Presumption of innocence
IV. Strict liability

Codes

1 I, II, III, IV   2 IV, III, I, II
3 III, II, I, IV   4 II, III, IV, I

***Ans.* (2)**

Exp. The correct order is IV, III, I, II.

Following are the situations in sequential order in which the principle of natural justice is applied:

1. Strict liability
2. Presumption of innocence
3. Alibi
4. Self incrimination.

Natural justice is technical terminology for the rule against bias (nemo iudex in causa sua) and the right to a fair hearing (audi alteram partem). The mere fact that a decision affects rights or interests is sufficient to subject the decision to the procedures required by natural justice.

41. The principle of 'Quod necessitas non-habet leegen' is applied in circumstances of

1 an act done in order to avoid consequence
2 in a little harm that resulted in the consequence
3 a harm resulted in order to do another evil
4 self-preservation

***Ans.* (4)**

Exp. The principle of 'Quod necessitas non-habet leegen' is applied in circumstances of self-preservation. It means "Act likely to cause harm, but done without criminal intent, and to prevent other harm".

Law protects public necessity and not private necessity i.e. to save your own life you cannot take away the life of others. Public necessity refers to prevention of public harm or any threat inflicted to public which may affect the public at large on the other hand private necessity focuses more on individual interest than public interest. However, public necessity is an absolute defence but in case of private necessity one cannot take defence because in order to protect one's interest, another's interest cannot be overridden.

42. Aggravated abetment can be found within the public

1 when the act was done by any one of the ten or more members present
2 when the act was done by one of the seven members while collecting funds from other public
3 while a person affixing a poster on the wall specially called attention of an assembly of five persons to protest against police excesses
4 when an un-named member of a fluctuating population incite others to undertake a strike to stop train movement

***Ans.* (1)**

Exp. Aggravated abetment can be found within the public when the act was done by any one of the ten or more members present.

If an individual abets another in the commission of an offense and the chief goes further from there on and accomplishes something more which has an alternative outcome from that planned by the abettor and makes the offense an aggravated one, the abettor is liable for the consequences of the acts of his principal.

43. In which of the matters it was held that disclosure of identity of victim either by printing or publishing will not amount to penal liability?

1 In a judgement given by the Session's Judge on the ground of social victimisation.
2 In a judgement given by the High Court on the ground of Ostracism.
3 In a judgement given either by High Court or Supreme Court on the ground of preventing social victimisation or contracism
4 In a judgement given by the Supreme Court on the ground of prevention from social victimisation

***Ans.* (3)**

Exp. In a judgement given either by High Court or Supreme Court on the ground of preventing social victimisation or contracism, it was held that disclosure of identity of victim either by printing or publishing will not amount to penal liability.

Section 228A(1) of IPC states that "Whoever prints or publishes the name or any matter which may make known the identity of any person against whom an offence under Section 376, Section 376A, Section 376B, Section 376C or Section 376D is alleged or found to have been committed (hereafter in this section referred to as the victim) shall be punished with imprisonment of either description for a term which may extend to two years and shall also be liable to fine".

44. Read Assertion (A) and Reason (R) and answer the reasonableness using the 'codes' given below.

Assertion (A) Section 304-A is directed at offences outside the range of Sections 299 and 300.

Reason (R) It contemplates those acts into which neither intention nor knowledge enters.

Codes

1 Both (A) and (R) are correct as the act results from rash and negligence act

2 (A) is correct as certain acts are unjustifiable while (R) is not the correct reason as it falls short of culpable homicide

3 (R) is correct while (A) is incorrect application to the rule of culpable homicide to cause murder

4 Both (A) and (R) are incorrect statement as to imposing penalty

Ans. *(1)*

➲ *Exp.* Both (A) and (R) are correct as the act results from rash and negligence act.

Assertion is correct as according to Section 304-A "Whoever causes the death of any person by doing any rash or negligent act not amounting to culpable homicide, shall be punished with imprisonment of either description for a term which may extend to two years, or with fine, or with both".

Reason (R) is correct because to constitute an offence under Section 304 A, knowledge and intentions are not required.

45. Read Assertion (A) and Reason (R) and answer using codes given below.

Assertion (A) Multiple Trade Unions in industries and the consequential necessity for selecting one as the recognised union by the management devising a method on democratic principles is necessary.

Reason (R) The Union which represents the largest number of workmen working in the undertaking must acquire the status as that would be in tune with the concept of Industrial democracy.

Codes

1 (A) and (R) are correct and (R) is the correct explanation of (A)

2 (A) and (R) are correct and (R) is not the correct explanation of (A)

3 (A) is true, but (R) is false

4 (A) is false, but (R) is true

Ans. *(1)*

➲ *Exp.* (A) and (R) are correct and (R) is the correct explanation of (A).

Assertion is correct because Multiple Trade Unions in industries and the consequential necessity for selecting one as the recognised union by the management devising a method on democratic principles is necessary and also the recognised unions gain important rights.

Reason is correct because the union which represents the largest number of workmen working in the undertaking must acquire the status as that would be in tune with the concept of Industrial democracy and this also correctly explains the given Assertion.

46. "The working class unfamiliar with the sophistications of definitions and shower of decisions, unable to secure expert legal opinion, what with poverty pricing them out of justice market and denying them the staying power to withstand the multi-decked litigative process, defacto is denied social justice if legal drafting is vagarious, definitions indefinite and court rulings contradictory."

The above remarks were made in support of an expensive definition of 'Industry' by one of the following justice

1 Justice O Chinnappa Reddy

2 Justice VR Krishna Iyer

3 Justice Gajendragadkar

4 SP Bharucha

Ans. *(2)*

➲ *Exp.* "The working class unfamiliar with the sophistications of definitions and shower of decisions, unable to secure expert legal opinion, what with poverty pricing them out of justice market and denying them the staying power to withstand the multi-decked litigative process, defacto is denied social justice if legal drafting is vagarious, definitions indefinite and court rulings contradictory." These remarks were made in support of an expensive definition of 'Industry' by Justice VR Krishna Iyer.

Krishna Iyer J. made this remarkable remark in the Bangalore Water Supply case, and at various places in his opinion, expressed that the attempt made by the Court to impart definite meaning to the words in the wide definition of 'industry' is only a workable solution until a more precise definition is provided by the legislature. He said that, "Our judgment here has no pontifical flavour but seeks to serve the future hour till changes in the law or in industrial culture occur."

47. Which one of the following is incorrect ?

1 Workman whose name is borne on the muster rolls of an industrial establishment and who has completed one year of continuous service under an employer is laid off, whether continuously or intermittently shall be paid by the employer for all days during which he is so laid off except for such weekly holidays.

2 Termination on the ground of misconduct or continued ill health of a workman is not a retrenchment.

3 Lock-out means the permanent closing of a place of employment, or the total suspension or the refusal by an employer to continue to employ any number of persons employed.

4 The right to close down the business, trade or undertaking is subject to payment of compensation to the workers engaged in the business immediately before the closure.

Ans. (3)

Exp. Statement 3 is incorrect.

Section 2(1) of the Industrial Disputes Act, 1947 defines 'Lock-out' as "the temporary closing of employment or the suspension of work, or the refusal by an employer to continue to employ any number of persons employed by him".

48. Match List I with List II and select the correct answer using the codes given below.

List I	List II
A. Kalinga Tubes Ltd. Vs. Their workmen	I. Deduction of wages for the period of strike
B. Bank of India Vs. TS Kelawala and others	II. Closure has to be genuine and bonafide
C. Bombay Union of Journalist Vs. State of Bombay	III. Definition of Industry
D. Coir Board Vs. Indira Devi PS and others	IV. Condition precedent to retrenchment of workman

Codes

	A	B	C	D		A	B	C	D
1	III	II	I	IV	2	II	I	IV	III
3	I	II	IV	III	4	IV	II	III	I

Ans. (2)

Exp. The correct matching is A-II, B-I, C-IV, D-III.

Closure has to be genuine and bonafide is related to Kalinga Tubes Ltd. Vs. Their workmen. It was held that the measure of compensation payable when an undertaking is closed down for any reason whatsoever is different as provided in sub-s. (1) which refers to the provisions of S. 25F as if the workmen had been retrenched.

Deduction of wages for the period of strike is related to Bank of India Vs. TS Kelawala and others. The Court opined that "Go-slow which is a picturesque description of deliberate delaying of production by workmen pretending to be engaged in the factory is one of the most pernicious practices that discontented or disgruntled workmen sometimes resort to. It would not be far wrong to call this dishonest."

Condition precedent to retrenchment of workmen is related to Bombay Union of Journalist Vs. State of Bombay. It was held that when the appropriate Government considers the question as to whether any industrial dispute should be referred for adjudication or not, it may consider, prima facie, the merits of the dispute and take into account other relevant considerations which would help it to 'decide whether making a reference would be expedient or not.

Definition of Industry is related to Coir Board Vs. Indira Devi PS and others. A Full Bench of the Kerala High Court considered the question of application of the Industrial Disputes Act to the appellant-Coir Board along with a similar question raised in respect of a large number of Government Departments, Government Companies, other statutory corporations and local bodies, in the impugned judgment. After extensively dealing with the various decisions of this Court on what is an 'industry' and who is a 'workman' under the Industrial Disputes Act, the High Court has come to the conclusion, inter alia, that Coir Board is an 'industry' as defined in the Industrial Disputes Act. Hence Chapter V-A of the Industrial Disputes Act would be applicable in respect of termination of the services of its temporary clerks and typists.

49. Reference of an Industrial Dispute, the subject matter of which is covered by a settlement as defined in Section 2(P) of the Act would be

1 valid during the operation of such settlement
2 invalid during the operation of such settlement
3 valid and subject to the importance of Industrial Dispute
4 voidable at the option of the parties to the dispute during the operation of such settlement

Ans. (2)

Exp. Reference of an Industrial Dispute, the subject matter of which is covered by a settlement as defined in Section 2(p) of the Act would be invalid during the operation of such settlement.

According to Section 2(p), 'settlement' means a settlement arrived at in the course of conciliation proceeding and includes a written agreement between the employer and workmen arrived at otherwise than in the course of conciliation proceeding where such agreement has been signed by the parties thereto in such manner as may be prescribed and a copy thereof has been sent to an officer authorised in this behalf by the appropriate Government and the conciliation officer.

50. Read Assertion (A) and Reason (R) and answer using codes given below.

Assertion (A) The retention of Industrial Adjudication is necessary till all Trade Unions attain sufficient strength to bargain with employers, from a position of equality.

Reason (R) Collective Bargaining presently provides only lip services, whereas in practice it has perpetuated Adjudication.

Codes

1 (A) and (R) are correct and (R) is the correct explanation of (A)
2 (A) and (R) are correct, but (R) is not the correct explanation of (A)
3 (A is true, but (R) is false
4 (A is fasle, but (R) is true

Ans. (1)

Exp. (A) and (R) are correct and (R) is the correct explanation of (A).

Assertion is correct because it says the retention of Industrial Adjudication is necessary till all Trade Unions attain sufficient strength to bargain with employers, from a position of equality.

Reason says Collective Bargaining presently provides only lip services, whereas in practice it has perpetuated Adjudication is correct and explains the assertion.

PAPER III

1. Match List I with List II and select the correct answer by using codes given below the lists.

List I	List II
A. Kesavananda Bharati Vs. State of Kerala	I. Basic structure doctrine new dimensions added
B. Indira Nehru Gandhi Vs. Raj Narain	II. Basic structure doctrine created
C. Minerva Mills Vs. Union of India	III. Basic structure doctrine strengthened
D. IR Coelho Vs. State of Tamil Nadu	IV. Basic structure doctrine crystallised

Codes

	A	B	C	D		A	B	C	D
1	II	III	IV	I	2	II	IV	I	III
3	IV	I	II	III	4	III	IV	II	I

Ans. (1)

Exp. The correct matching is A-II, B-III, C-IV, D I.

Kesavananda Bharati Vs. State of Kerala also known as the Kesavananda Bharati judgement, is a landmark decision of the Supreme Court of India that outlined the basic structure doctrine of the Indian Constitution.

Indira Nehru Gandhi Vs. Raj Narain is related to Basic structure doctrine. Here, the SC applied the theory of Basic structure and struck down Clause(4) of Article 329-A, which was inserted by the 39th Amendment in 1975 on the grounds that it was beyond the Parliament's amending power as it destroyed the Constitution's basic features.

In the *Minerva Mills Vs. Union of India* case, the Supreme Court provided key clarifications on the interpretation of the basic structure doctrine. The court ruled that the power of the parliament to amend the constitution is limited by the constitution.

In *IR Coelho Vs. State of Tamil Nadu* Basic structure doctrine new dimensions added. In the judgement, the court held that Article 368 confers vast power to the legislature to amend all the parts of the Constitution as long as it does not damage or destroy the essential elements or basic structure of the Constitution. In this case, the doctrine of basic structure came into existence in India.

2. Read Assertion (A) and Reason (R) and select the correct answer with the help of codes given below.

Assertion (A) A State made law on any matter of Concurrent List prevails not-withstanding any repugnancy with an earlier law made by the Parliament.

Reason (R) The Parliament can make a law, on any matter in the Concurrent List that prevails over any repugnant state law.

Codes

1 (A) and (R) are true and (R) is the correct explanation of (A)
2 (A) and (R) are true, but (R) is not the correct explanation of (A)
3 (A) is false, but (R) is true
4 (A) is true, but (R) is false

Ans. (1)

Exp. (A) and (R) are true and (R) is the correct explanation of (A).

Assertion says a state made law on any matter of Concurrent List prevails not withstanding any repugnancy with an earlier law made by the Parliament and it is backed by Article 254 of the Constitution.

Reason says that the Parliament can make a law, on any matter in the Concurrent List that prevails over any repugnant state law is the correct explanation of given Assertion. According to Article 254(1), if any provision of a state law is repugnant to a provision in a law made by the Parliament, which the Parliament is competent to enact, or with any existing law regarding any matter in the Concurrent List, then the Parliamentary law would prevail over the State law.

3. Read Assertion (A) and Reason (R) and select the correct answer with the help of codes given below.

Assertion (A) The President of India has a right to seek advisory opinion of the Supreme Court of India on a question of law or fact has arisen or likely to arise, which is of such nature and of such public importance.

Reason (R) The Constitution of India makes it obligatory for the President to accept the advice rendered by the Supreme Court of India.

Codes

1 (A) and (R) are true and (R) is the correct explanation of (A)
2 (A) and (R) are true, but (R) is not the correct explanation of (A)
3 (A) is true, but (R) is false
4 (A) is false, but (R) is true

Ans. (3)

Exp. (A) is true, but (R) is false

Assertion is true because Article 143 of the Constitution authorises the President to seek the opinion of the Supreme court in the two categories of matters: On any question of law or fact of public importance which has arisen or which is likely to arise.

Reason is false because it is completely at the discretion of the President to follow the advice rendered by Supreme Court or not.

4. Match List I with List II and select the correct answer by using codes given below the lists.

	List I		List II
A.	Article 136	I.	Appellate jurisdiction of Supreme Court in regard to criminal matters.
B.	Article 134	II.	Seat of Supreme Court
C.	Article 131	III.	Special leave to appeal jurisdiction of the Supreme Court over any court or administrative tribunal.
D.	Article 130	IV.	Original jurisdiction of the Supreme Court.

Codes

	A	B	C	D		A	B	C	D
1	IV	I	III	II	2	I	III	IV	II
3	II	IV	I	III	4	III	I	IV	II

***Ans.* (4)**

➲ ***Exp.*** The correct matching is A-III, B-I, C-IV, D-II.

Article 136 is related to Special leave to appeal jurisdiction of the Supreme Court over any court or administrative tribunal. Under this article, the Supreme Court may, in its discretion, grant special leave to appeal from any judgment, decree, determination, sentence or order in any cause or matter passed or made by any court or tribunal in the territory of India.

Article 134 is related to Appellate jurisdiction of Supreme Court in regard to criminal matters. Under this article, an appeal shall lie to the Supreme Court from any judgement, final order or sentence in a criminal proceeding of a High Court in the territory of India if the High Court has on appeal reversed an order of acquittal of an accused person and sentenced him to death; or has withdrawn for trial before itself any case from any court subordinate to its authority and has in such trial convicted the accused person and sentenced him to death.

Article 131 is related to Original jurisdiction of the Supreme Court. Under this article, the Supreme Court shall have Original jurisdiction in any dispute between the Government of India and one or more States; or between the Government of India and any State or States on one side and one or more other States on the other; or between two or more States.

Article 130 is related to seat of Supreme Court. This article talks about seat of SC and says that the Supreme Court shall sit in Delhi or in such other place or places, as the Chief Justice of India may, with the approval of the President, from time to time, appoint.

5. Match List I with List II and select the correct answer by using codes given below the lists.

	List I		List II
A.	Article 221	I.	Transfer of a Judge from one High Court to another
B.	Article 222	II.	Appointment of acting Chief Justice of a High Court
C.	Article 223	III.	Appointment of additional and acting Judges of the High Court
D.	Article 224	IV.	Salaries etc of High Court Judges

Codes

	A	B	C	D		A	B	C	D
1	IV	I	II	III	2	II	IV	I	III
3	III	IV	II	I	4	III	I	IV	II

***Ans.* (1)**

➲ ***Exp.*** The correct matching is A-IV, B-I, C- II, D-III.

Article 221 is related to salaries etc of High Court Judges. Article 221 says, there shall be paid to the Judges of each High Court such salaries as may be determined by Parliament by law and, until provision in that behalf is so made, such salaries as are specified in the Second Schedule.

Article 222 is related to transfer of a Judge from one High Court to another. Article 222 of the Constitution makes provision for the transfer of a Judge (including Chief Justice) from one High Court to any other High Court. The initiation of the proposal for the transfer of a Judge should be made by the Chief Justice of India whose opinion in this regard is determinative.

Article 223 is related to appointment of acting Chief Justice of a High Court. This article says, when the office of Chief Justice of a High Court is vacant or when any such Chief Justice is, by reason of absence or otherwise, unable to perform the duties of his office, the duties of the office shall be performed by such one of the other Judges of the Court as the President may appoint for the purpose.

Article 224 is related to appointment of additional and acting Judges of the High Court. When any Judge of a High Court other than the Chief Justice is by reason of absence or for any other reason unable to perform the duties of his office or is appointed to act temporarily as Chief Justice, the President may, in consultation with the National Judicial Appointments Commission, appoint a duly qualified person to act as a Judge of that Court until the permanent Judge has resumed his duties.

6. Read Assertion (A) and Reason (R) and select the correct answer with the help of codes given below.

Assertion (A) An accused person is guaranteed under the Constitution of India the right to be informed of the nature and cause of his accusation.

Reason (R) The accused person has to be produced before the nearest District Judge within twenty four hours.

Codes

1 (A) and (R) are true and (R) is the correct explanation of (A)
2 (A) and (R) are true, but (R) is not the correct explanation of (A)
3 (A) is false, but (R) is true
4 (A) is true, but (R) is false

***Ans.* (4)**

Exp. (A) is true, but (R) is false.

Assertion says an accused person is guaranteed under the Constitution of India the right to be informed of the nature and cause of his accusation is true, because it is the fundamental right of accused person to know about the nature and cause of his accusation.

Reason is false because under Article 22(2) of the Constitution any person arrested and detained in custody must be produced before the nearest Magistrate within 24 hours of his arrest and no person can be detained beyond the period of 24 hours without the authority of the Magistrate.

7. Read Assertion (A) and Reason (R) and select the correct answer with the help of codes given below.

Assertion (A) Subject to anything in this Constitution, Parliament may in exercise of its constituent power amend by way of addition, variation or repeal any provision of this Constitution in accordance with the procedure laid down in this article.

Reason (R) Above statement is Article 368(1) of the Indian Constitution.

Codes

1 Both (A) and (R) are correct and (R) is correct explanation of (A)
2 Both (A) and (R) are false
3 (A) is false, but (R) is true
4 (R) is false, but (A) is true

***Ans.* (2)**

Exp. Both (A) and (R) are false.

Assertion (A) is false because Article 368 (1) of the Constitution of India grants constituent power to make formal amendments and empowers Parliament to amend the Constitution by way of addition, variation or repeal of any provision according to the procedure laid down therein, which is different from the procedure for ordinary legislation.

Reason (R) is false because Article 368(1) doesn't support the statement mentioned in assertion.

8. Read Assertion (A) and Reason (R) and select the correct answer with the help of codes given below.

Assertion (A) No person to be eligible for election in, or to claim to be included in a special electoral roll on grounds of religion, race, caste or sex.

Reason (R) Above statement is title of Article 325 of the Indian Constitution.

Codes

1 Both (A) and (R) are correct and (R) is correct explanation for (A)
2 Both (A) and (R) are false
3 (A) is false, but (R) is true
4 (R) is false, but (A) is true

***Ans.* (2)**

Exp. Both (A) and (R) are false.

Assertion is false because according to Article 325, "No person to be ineligible for inclusion in, or to claim to be included in a special, electoral roll on grounds of religion, race, caste or sex. There shall be one general electoral roll for every territorial constituency for election to either House of Parliament or to the House or either House of the Legislature of a State and no person shall be ineligible for inclusion in any such roll or claim to be included in any special electoral roll for any such constituency on grounds only of religion, race, caste, sex or any of them."

Reason is false because the assertion statements is not the title of Article 325 of the Indian Constitution.

9. Discretion, when applied to a court of justice, means sound discretion guided by law. It must be governed by rule, not by humour; it must not be arbitrary, vague and fanciful but legal and regular. This observation was made in

1 Union of India Vs. Kuldeep Singh
2 Reliance Airport Developers (P) Ltd. Vs. Airports Authority of India
3 Maneka Gandhi Vs. Union of India
4 National Insurance Co. Ltd Vs. Keshav Bahadur

***Ans.* (2)**

Exp. Discretion, when applied to a court of justice, means sound discretion guided by law. It must be governed by rule, not by humour; it must not be arbitrary, vague and fanciful but legal and regular. This observation was made in Reliance Airport Developers (P) Ltd. Vs. Airports Authority of India.

In this case, the decision taken by a group of Ministers in a matter of joint venture partnership as a part of the privatisation policy of the Government of India was assailed before the High Court.

10. Under which of the following condition(s) a writ of mandamus can be granted? Give correct answer using the codes:

I. There must be a public duty.
II. There must be a specific demand and refusal.
III. There must be a clear right to enforce the duty.
IV. The right must be subsisting on the date of the petition.

Codes
1 All I, II, III and IV are correct
2 Only I, II and III are correct
3 Only I and III are correct
4 Only I and II are correct

Ans. (1)

➲ *Exp.* All the given statements I, II, III and IV are correct.
'Mandamus' means 'we command'. It is issued by the Court to direct a public authority to perform the legal duties which it has not or refused to perform. It can be issued by the Court against a public official, public corporation, tribunal, inferior court or the government.

It can be granted in following conditions:
(i) There must be a public duty
(ii) There must be a specific demand and refusal
(iii) There must be a clear right to enforce the duty.
(iv) The right must be subsisting on the date of the petition.

11. In which one of the following cases, the Supreme Court made it explicit that 'even when the authority has statutory power to take action without hearing, it would be arbitrary to take action without hearing and, thus, violative of Article 14 of the Constitution'?
1 AK Kraipak Vs.Union of India
2 Union of India Vs. Satish Chandra
3 AK Roy Vs. State of Punjab
4 HL Trehan Vs. Union of India

Ans. (4)

➲ *Exp.* In the case of HL Trehan Vs. Union of India, the Supreme Court made it explicit that 'even when the authority has statutory power to take action without hearing, it would be arbitrary to take action, without hearing and thus, violative of Article 14 of the Constitution'.

Article 311 embodies the right to hearing as a basic principle of natural justice. Under Article 19(2) to (6) reasonable restrictions can be imposed on the right to carry on trade and business which include procedural restrictions also. In determining the validity of reasonable restrictions, courts have referred to the principles of natural justice. Duty to act fairly is a part of the fair procedure envisaged under Article 14 and 21.

12. Match List I with List II and select the correct answer using the codes given below.

List I	List II
A. Personal bias	I. Jeejebhoy Vs. Collector
B. Pecuniary bias	II. Krishna Bus Service (P) Ltd. Vs. State of Haryana
C. Subject-matter bias	III. Manak Lal Vs. Dr. Prem Chand
D. Departmental bias	IV. G. Nageswara Rao Vs. APSRTC

Codes

	A	B	C	D		A	B	C	D
1	I	II	III	IV	2	III	I	IV	II
3	III	II	IV	I	4	IV	I	II	III

Ans. (2)

➲ *Exp.* The correct matching is A-III, B-I, C-IV, D-II.
The concept of *Personal bias* was discussed in Manak Lal Vs. Dr. Prem Chand case. Personal bias arises from a relation between the party and deciding authority which lead the deciding authority in a doubtful situation to make an unfair activity and give judgement in favour of his person. Such equations arise due to various forms of personal and professional relations.

The concept of *Pecuniary bias* was discussed in Jeejeebhoy Vs. Collector case. In judicial approach unanimous and decisive on the point that any financial interest, howsoever small it may be, would vitiate administrative action. The disqualification will not be avoided by non-participation of the biased member in the proceedings if he was present when the decision was reached.

The concept of *Subject-matter bias* was discussed in G. Nageswara Rao Vs. APSRTC case. Those cases fall within this category where the deciding officer is directly, or otherwise, involved in the subject-matter of the case. Here again mere involvement would not vitiate the administrative action unless there is a real likelihood of bias.

The concept of *Departmental bias* was discussed in Krishna Bus Service (P) Ltd. Vs. State of Haryana case. The rule against bias strikes against those factors which may improperly influence a judge against arriving at a decision in a particular case. The problem of departmental bias arises in different context-when the functions of judge and prosecutor are combined in the same department.

13. Read the Assertion (A) and Reason (R) and select the correct answer with the help of codes given below.

Assertion (A) A writ of prohibition can be issued on the same grounds on which the writ of certiorari can be issued except in case of an error of law apparent on the face of the record.

Reason (R) A writ of certiorari is issued at a stage when proceedings are in progress, to forbid the authority from continuing the proceedings whereas a writ of prohibition is issued at a stage when the authority has given a final decision, to quash the decision.

Codes
1 Both (A) and (R) are true and (R) is the correct explanation of (A)
2 Both (A) and (R) are true, but (R) is not the correct explanation of (A)
3 (A) is true, but (R) is false
4 (A) is false, but (R) is true

Ans. (3)

Exp. (A) is true, but (R) is false.

Assertion says a writ of prohibition can be issued on the same grounds on which the writ of certiorari can be issued except in case of an error of law apparent on the face of the record is true because a writ of prohibition is a writ directing a subordinate to stop doing something that the law prohibits.

Reason is false because the writ of certiorari is issued after the case is heard and decided. And writ of prohibition is issued prohibiting the proceedings in the lower court which acts without or in excess of jurisdiction while the case is pending before it.

14. Match List I with List II and select the correct answer using the codes given below.

	List I (Subject)		List II (Provision of the Lokpal and Lokayuktas Act, 2013)
A.	The composition of Lokpal	I.	Section 3(2)
B.	Establishment of Lokayukta	II.	Section 6
C.	Term of office of Chairperson and Members of Lokpal	III.	Section 37
D.	Removal of Chairperson and Members of Lokpal	IV.	Section 63

Codes

	A	B	C	D		A	B	C	D
1	I	II	III	IV	2	I	IV	II	III
3	II	III	I	IV	4	I	II	IV	III

Ans. (2)

Exp. The correct matching is A-I, B-IV, C-II, D-III.

Section 3(2) of the Act discuss about the compostion of Lokpal. Section 3(2) states that the Lokpal shall consist of a chairperson, who is or has been a Chief Justice of India, or is or has been a Judge of the Supreme Court or an eminent person who fulfills the eligibility specified in clause (b) of sub-section (3).

Section 63 discuss about establishment of Lokayukta. It says, every State shall establish a body to be known as the Lokayukta for the State, if not so established, constituted or appointed, by a law made by the State Legislature, to deal with complaints relating to corruption against certain public functionaries, within a period of one year from the date of commencement of this Act.

Section 6 discuss about term of office of Chairperson and Members of Lokpal. It says, the Chairperson and every Member shall, on the recommendations of the Selection Committee, be appointed by the President by warrant under his hand and seal and hold office as such for a term of five years from the date on which he enters upon his office or until he attains the age of seventy years, whichever is earlier.

Section 37 talk about removal of Chairperson and Members of Lokpal-Section 37. Section 37(2) says that the Chairperson or any Member shall be removed from his office by order of the President on grounds of misbehaviour after the Supreme Court, on a reference being made to it by the President on a petition signed by at least one hundred Members of Parliament has, on an inquiry held in accordance with the procedure prescribed in that behalf, reported that the Chairperson or such Member, as the case may be, ought to be removed on such ground.

15. The appointment of Chairperson of Lokpal shall be made by the President after obtaining the recommendation of a selection committee consisting of

1 The Prime Minister, the Speaker of the House of the People and the Chief Justice of India
2 The Prime Minister, the Speaker of the House of the People, the leader of opposition in the House of the people
3 The Prime Minister, The Leader of opposition in the House of the People and one eminent jurist to be nominated by the President
4 The Prime Minister, the Speaker of the House of the People, the Leader of opposition in the House of the People, the Chief Justice of India or a Judge of the Supreme Court nominated by him and one eminent jurist to be nominated by the President

Ans. (4)

Exp. The appointment of Chairperson of Lokpal shall be made by the President after obtaining the recommendation of a selection committee consisting of the Prime Minister, the Speaker of the House of the People, the Leader of opposition in the House of the People, the Chief Justice of India or a Judge of the Supreme Court nominated by him and one eminent jurist to be nominated by the President.

According to Section 4(1) of Lokpal and Lokyukta Act, 2013, The Chairperson and Members shall be appointed by the President after obtaining the recommendations of a Selection Committee consisting of

(a) the Prime Minister—Chairperson;
(b) the Speaker of the House of the People—Member;
(c) the Leader of Opposition in the House of the People—Member;
(d) the Chief Justice of India or a Judge of the Supreme Court nominated by him—Member;
(e) one eminent jurist, as recommended by the Chairperson and Members referred to in clauses (a) to (d) above, to be nominated by the President—Member.

16. "Law is not only a set of rules but is a method or technique for harmonising conflicting interests." This statement is of

1 Auguste Comte
2 Herbert Spencer
3 Roscoe Pound
4 Leon Duguit

Ans. (3)

➲ *Exp.* "Law is not only a set of rules but is a method or technique for harmonising conflicting interests." This statement is of Roscoe Pound.

Roscoe Pound has criticised the definition of Salmond as reducing law to a mass of isolated decisions and the law in that sense to be an organic whole.

17. Match List I with List II and select the correct answer by using the codes given below.

List I (Meaning)	List II (Jurists Associated With)
A. Jurisprudence is a science of just and unjust	I. Salmond
B. Jurisprudence is the science of the first principle of civil law	II. Gray
C. Jurisprudence is the philosophical aspect of knowledge of law	III. Ulpian
D. Jurisprudence is in truth no more a formal science than physiology	IV. Cicero

Codes

	A	B	C	D		A	B	C	D
1	I	II	III	IV	2	III	I	IV	II
3	II	III	I	IV	4	III	IV	II	I

Ans. (2)

➲ *Exp.* The correct matching is A-III, B-I, C-IV, D-II.

Ulpian gave the definition "Jurisprudence is a science of just and unjust." Ulpian termed jurisprudence as observation of things or divine, the knowledge of the just and unjust. Thus, at that time was mixed up with theology.

Salmond gave the definition, " Jurisprudence is the science of the first principle of civil law". Thus, he points out that jurisprudence deals with a particular species of law namely; civil law or the law of the State. The civil law consists of rules applied by courts in the administration of justice.

Cicero gave the definition, "Jurisprudence is the philosophical aspect of knowledge of law". In Cicero's words, True law is the right reason in agreement with nature. In his opinion nature is the highest manifestation of right reason. It is universal application, unchanging and everlasting; it summons to duty by its commands and averts from wrongdoing by its prohibitions.

Gray gave the definition, "Jurisprudence is in truth no more a formal science than physiology". He opined that "Jurisprudence is the science of law, the statement and systematic arrangement of the rules followed by the courts and the principals involved in those rules."

18. Which one of the following requisites is not necessary to be fulfilled for a custom to be valid and operative as a source of law?

1 Reasonableness
2 Conformity with statute law
3 Immemorial antiquity
4 May not have been practiced continuously

Ans. (4)

➲ *Exp.* The requisite that is not necessary to be fulfilled for a custom to be valid and operative as a source of law is 'may not have been practiced continuously'.

Essentials of a valid legal custom are:

Antiquity: A custom to be recognized as law must be proved to be in existence from time immemorial.

Continuity: It must have been practised continuously.

Reasonableness: A custom must be reasonable.

19. Match List I with List II and select the correct answer by using the codes given below.

List I (Theory)	List II (Jurist Associated with)
A. Inner Morality	I. Compte
B. Concept of living law	II. Fuller
C. Organic concept of society	III. Burke
D. Gradual and organic process	IV. Ehrlich

Codes

	A	B	C	D		A	B	C	D
1	II	IV	I	III	2	III	IV	I	II
3	II	III	IV	I	4	I	II	III	IV

Ans. (1)

➲ *Exp.* The correct matching is A-II, B-IV, C- I, D-III.

Inner Morality is related to Fuller. He argues that law is subject to an internal morality consisting of several principles.

Concept of living law is related to Ehrlich. The living law is the law which dominates life itself even though it has not been posited in legal propositions. The source of our knowledge of this law is, first, the modern legal document; secondly, direct. observation of life, of commerce, of customs and usages and of all.

Organic concept of society is related to Compte. The concept says society grows rather than being constructed and as an evolving organism it ought not to be subjected to sudden and drastic changes, which may weaken or destroy it.The goals of the society are set by the state, which leads society toward fulfiling those goals.

Gradual and Organic Process is related to Burke. The concept says society is considered as an organism that emerges and evolves gradually over time in order to meet the needs of its members.

20. If 'A' leaves his car with the driver, the driver's possession will be

1 Immediate whereas that of 'A' would be mediate
2 Mediate whereas that of 'A' would be immediate
3 Incorporeal whereas that of 'A' would be corporeal
4 Corporeal whereas that of 'A' would be incorporeal

Ans. (1)

Exp. If 'A' leaves his car with the driver, the driver's possession will be immediate whereas that of 'A' would be mediate.

Mediate Possession is when a person who is legally entitled to hold/possess it through somebody else. Immediate possession is the person who holds a thing on behalf of someone else.

21. Read Assertion (A) and Reason (R) and answer using the codes given below.

Assertion (A) The legislature can forge a sledge-hammer capable of cracking open the corporate shell.

Reason (R) Corporate personality cannot be used as a shield to harm national interest.

Codes

1 Both (A) and (R) are true and (R) is the correct explanation of (A)

2 Both (A) and (R) are true, but (R) is not the correct explanation of (A)

3 (A) is true, but (R) is false

4 (A) is false, but (R) is true

Ans. (1)

Exp. Both (A) and (R) are true and (R) is the correct explanation of (A).

Assertion (A) says that, the legislature can forge a sledge-hammer capable of cracking open the corporate shell, is true because every incorporated company has separate legal entity, and even without statutory assistance, the courts have often been ready to draw aside the veil and impose legal liability on members and directors.

Reason (R) says corporate personality cannot be used as a shield to harm national interest is true and explains the assertion correctly as in case of need corporate veil can be lifted, and real culprit behind the veil must be held liable.

22. Read the Assertion (A) and Reason (R) and select the correct answer with the help of codes given below.

Assertion (A) The most important power of an owner is the right to exclude others.

Reason (R) The owner may grant to another many of his rights and yet remain owner.

Codes

1 Both (A) and (R) are true and (R) is the correct explanation of (A)

2 Both (A) and (R) are true, but (R) is not the correct explanation of (A)

3 (A) is true, but (R) is false

4 (A) is false, but (R) is true

Ans. (2)

Exp. Both (A) and (R) are true, but (R) is not the correct explanation of (A).

Assertion (A) is true because the owner has the exclusive right to enjoy his or her property. The labour theory primarily believes that property can be claimed on the exclusive basis of one's work, which produced that property. It recognises the role of labour for adequate rewards. When a person acquires property, he is entitled to hold it exclusively.

Reason (R) is true because the owner of a property can grant rights to another regarding their property, however the final discretion always remains with the owner, as they have the right to exclude others from their property.

23. "Law is a social engineering to remove the existing imbalance and to further the progress, serving the needs of the Socialist Democratic Bharat under the rule of Law." This was the observation of Justice K Ramaswami in

1 Delhi Transport Corp. Vs. DTC Mazdoor Congress

2 Indra Sawhney Vs. Union of India

3 State of Karnataka Vs. Appa Balu Ingale

4 Parmanand Kataria Vs. Union of India

Ans. (1)

Exp. "Law is a social engineering to remove the existing imbalance and to further the progress, serving the needs of the Socialist Democratic Bharat under the rule of Law." This was the observation of Justice K Ramaswami in Delhi Transport Corp. Vs. DTC Mazdoor Congress.

Social engineering is based on the notion that Laws are used as a means to shape society and regulate people's behaviour. According to Pound, 'Law is social engineering which means a balance between the competing interests in society, in which applied science are used for resolving individual and social problems'.

24. In which of the crimes retributive theory strikes the moral blameworthiness of the offender to punish him ?

1 Clamping prohibitory orders

2 Sexual harassment at workplace

3 Wilful attempt to defame

4 Common intention to commit riot

Ans. (2)

Exp. In crime of sexual harassment at workplace retributive theory strikes the moral blameworthiness of the offender to punish him.

Retributive justice is a theory of punishment that when an offender breaks the law, justice requires that they suffer in return, and that the response to a crime is proportional to the offence.

25. In which of the circumstances the defense of necessity involves a collusion of interest and the consequential judgement of values ?

1 Stealing to avert hungers

2 Absolute necessity for self-preservation

3 Private homicide for keeping up the honour

4 Acts done against anarchy

Ans. (4)

Exp. In acts done against anarchy the defense of necessity involves a collusion of interest and the consequential judgement of values.

The defense of necessity recognises that there may be situations of such overwhelming urgency that a person must be allowed to respond by breaking the law. Necessity is an affirmative defense that a defendant invokes the defense against the torts of trespass to chattels, trespass to land or conversion.

26. Read Assertion (A) and Reason (R) and using the codes given below choose the appropriate answer.

Assertion (A) The apprehension of use of criminal force must emanate from the gesture of a person to attract punishment.

Reason (R) Mere advancing with a threatening attitude will not amount to criminal force.

Codes

1 Both (A) and (R) are contradictory to each other
2 (A) is correct while (R) is not the cause of it
3 (A) is incorrect while (R) is appropriate
4 (A) is correct while (R) is the cause of it

Ans. *(2)*

Exp. (A) is correct while (R) is not the cause of it.

Assertion (A) is true as Section 351 of IPC states that whoever makes any gesture, or any preparation intending or knowing it to be likely that such gesture or preparation will cause any person present to apprehend that he who makes that gesture or preparation is about to use criminal force to that person, is said to commit an assault. Thus, the apprehension of use of criminal force must emanate from the gesture of a person to attract punishment is correct because the right to protect oneself and use self-defence arises as soon as reasonable apprehension arises.

Reason (R) says mere advancing with a threatening attitude will not amount to criminal force is correct but does not explain the assertion completely as all the essentials of Assault are not fulfilled.

27. Read Assertion (A) and Reason (R) and using the codes given below write the correct answer.

Assertion (A) In a case of attempt to rape there must be an indecent assault or action with any resistance from the victim.

Reason (R) There was some action which shows that he was going to have sexual connection with her.

Codes

1 (R) is correct explanation of (A) and both (A) and (R) are complementary to each other
2 (A) is correct but (R) is not complementary to (A)
3 (A) and (R) have no legal standing in view of change of burden of proof
4 (R) is essential to formulate (A) otherwise there may not be a crime

Ans. *(1)*

Exp. (R) is the correct explanation of (A) and both (A) and (R) are complementary to each other.

Assertion (A) is true because in the case of Koppula Venkat Rao Vs. State of A.P, (2004) 3 SCC 602, it was observed that in order to find an accused guilty of an attempt with intent to commit rape, court has to be satisfied that the accused, when he laid hold of the prosecutrix, not only desired to gratify his passions upon her person, but that he intended to do so at all events, and notwithstanding any resistance on her part. Indecent assaults are often magnified into attempts at rape. In order to come to a conclusion that the conduct of the accused was indicative of a determination to gratify his passion at all events, and in spite of all resistance, materials must exist. Surrounding circumstances many times throw beacon light on that aspect.

Reason (A) says there was some action which shows that he was going to have sexual connection with her is also true in light of the reasoning given above. Thus, both (A) and (R) complement each other.

28. Which of the factors fall under the limits within which the right of private defense should be exercised ?

1 Where there is time to have recourse to the protection of the public authorities
2 When a public servant performs an act in good faith
3 An act committed strictly in conformity with law
4 Where the act was irregular and outside the scope of power

Ans. *(3)*

Exp. An act committed strictly in conformity with law falls under the limits within which the right of private defense should be exercised. Section 96 talks about things done in private defence and states that nothing is an offence, which is done in the exercise of the right of private defence.

Right of private defence cannot be said to be an offence in return. The right of self-defence under Section 96 is not absolute but is clearly qualified by Section 99 which says that the right in no case extends to the inflicting of more harm than it is necessary for the purpose of defence.

29. Dacoity with murder creates co-extensive responsibility of each participant because

1 Collective liability is the core-essence whether it was culminated suddenly or not
2 Mere non-participation in dacoity will not exempt from criminal liability since there was pre-concert
3 Planning was to commit only dacoity, but another person, for earlier enemity, abetted to commit murder while there was no common object
4 There must be one or more participants for the constructive action by each member

Ans. *(1)*

Exp. Dacoity with murder creates co-extensive responsibility of each participant because collective liability is the core-essence whether it was culminated suddenly or not.

Section 396 talks about dacoity with murder, if anyone of five or more persons, who are conjointly committing dacoity, commits murder in so committing dacoity, every one of those persons shall be punished with death, or imprisonment for life, or rigorous imprisonment for a term which may extend to ten years, and shall also be liable to fine.

30. What offence, if any, has been committed by a married woman giving free consent to her own abduction ?

1 Abetting her own abduction
2 Criminal conspiracy for abduction
3 No criminal liability against her as the acts was not committed in deceitful manner
4 Attempt to abduction when there was failure to obtain clear consent

Ans. *(3)*

Exp. If a married woman gives free consent to her own abduction that will amount to no criminal liability against her as the acts was not committed in deceitful manner.

Criminal liability law also recognises situations in which the person who personally and directly engaged in the criminal act should not be held liable for the crime.

31. A young man waves a currency note of rupees one thousand in front of a woman as if he offers the money for an indecent favour from the woman, he may be criminally booked under

1 Section 506 of IPC
2 Section 507 of IPC
3 Section 508 of IPC
4 Section 509 of IPC

Ans. *(4)*

Exp. A young man waves a currency note of rupees one thousand in front of a woman as if he offers the money for an indecent favour from the woman, he may be criminally booked under Section 509 of IPC.

Section 509 of IPC says, whoever, intending to insult the modesty of any woman, utters any word, makes any sound or gesture, or exhibits any object, intending that such word or sound shall be heard, or that such gesture or object shall be seen, by such woman, or intrudes upon the privacy of such woman, shall be punished with simple imprisonment for a term which may extend to one year, or with fine, or with both.

32. Which one of the following International Convention is not related to wildlife conservation?

1 Convention on International Trade in endangered species of wild Fauna and Flora
2 Convention on Environmental Impact Assessment in Transboundary Context
3 Convention on Migratory Species of Wild Animals
4 Convention on International Union for Conservation of Nature and Natural Resources

Ans. *(2)*

Exp. Convention on Environmental Impact Assessment in Transboundary Context is not related to wildlife conservetion.

The Convention on Environmental Impact Assessment in a Transboundary Context is a United Nations Economic Commission for Europe convention signed in Espoo, Finland, in 1991 that entered into force in 1997. This convention sets out the obligations of Parties to assess the environmental impact of certain activities at an early stage of planning.

33. The Montreal Protocol is related to

1 Transboundary Air pollution
2 Ozone Layer
3 Climate change
4 Hazardous waste

Ans. *(2)*

Exp. The Montreal Protocol is related to Ozone layer.

The Montreal Protocol on Substances that deplete the Ozone Layer (the Montreal Protocol) is an international agreement made in 1987. It was designed to stop the production and import of ozone depleting substances and reduce their concentration in the atmosphere to help protect the earth's ozone layer.

34. Read both Assertion (A) and Reason (R) and select the correct answer by using the codes given below.

Assertion (A) Over 200 Central and State Statutes which have atleast some concern with environmental protection, either directly or indirectly have unfortunately not resulted in preventing environmental degradation, on the contrary has increased over the years.

Reason (R) Unless the government policy is backed by adequate budgetary allocation, changes to the statutory regime and a bureaucratic will, the government's intention are apt to remain on paper.

Codes

1 Both (A) and (R) are correct and (R) is the correct explanation of (A)
2 Both (A) and (R) are correct, but (R) is not the correct explanation of (A)
3 (A) is true, but (R) is false
4 (A) is false, but (R) is true

Ans. *(1)*

Exp. Both (A) and (R) are correct and (R) is the correct explanation of (A).

The Supreme Court in Indian Council for Enviro-Legal Action Vs. The Union of India said that if the mere enactment of laws relating to protection of environment was to ensure a clean and pollution free environment, then India would perhaps, be the least polluted country in the world. But this is not so. There are stated to be more than 200 Central and State Statutes which have at least some concern with environment protection, either directly or indirectly. The plethora of such enactments has unfortunately not resulted in preventing environment degradation, which on contrary, has increased over the years.

Unless the government policy is backed by adequate budgetary allocation, changes to the statutory regime and a bureaucratic will, the government's intention are apt to remain on paper.

35. Match List I and List II and select correct answer by using codes given below.

List I	List II
A. Public Liability	I. MC Metha and Another Vs. Union of India and Others
B. Sustainable Development	II. Narmada Bachao Andolan Vs. Union of India
C. Wildlife protection	III. State of Bihar Vs. Murad Ali Khan
D. Hazardous waste material	IV. Research Foundation for Science Vs. Union of India and Others

Codes

	A	B	C	D		A	B	C	D
1	I	III	IV	II	2	II	IV	I	III
3	II	III	IV	I	4	IV	II	III	I

***Ans.* (*)**

Exp. The correct matching is A-II, B-I, C-III, D-IV.

Narmada Bachao Andolan Vs. Union of India is related to Public Liability. Sardar Sarovar Dam was constructed on Narmada river that runs in four States (Gujarat, Madhya Pradesh, Maharashtra and Rajasthan) in India starting in 1987. In April 1994, Narmada Bachao Andolan filed a writ petition inter alia praying that the Union of India and other respondents should be restrained from proceeding with the construction of the dam and they should be ordered to open the aforesaid sluices. Narmada Bachao Andolan cited displacement and rehabilitation problems that the project would cause. It had also argued for reduction in the height of the dam so as to reduce the extent of submergence and the consequent displacement.

Research Foundation for Science Vs. Union of India and Others is related to hazardous waste material. The basic grievance of the Writ Petitioner was with regard to the import of toxic wastes from industrialized countries to India, despite such wastes being hazardous to the environment and life of the people of this country. The Writ Petitioner sought to challenge the decision of the Ministry of Environment and Forests permitting import of toxic wastes in India under the cover of recycling, which, according to the Petitioner, made India a dumping ground for toxic wastes. It was alleged that these decisions were contrary to the provisions of Articles 14 and 21 of the Constitution and also Article 47, which enjoins a duty on the State to raise the standards of living and to improve public health. In the writ petition it was also contended that Article 48A provides that the State shall endeavour to protect and improve the environment and to safeguard the forests and wildlife of the country.

MC Mehta and Another Vs. Union of India and Others is related to Sustainable Development. The Court held that the incorporation of protection of environment as an obligation of the State in the Directive Principles and the mandate in Article 51-A to the citizens of India as part of fundamental duty are indications of the Constitutional recognition of the importance of the environment of life-both the flora and the fauna.

State of Bihar Vs. Murad Ali Khan is related to wildfle protection. This case dealt with the provisions of the Wildlife Protection Act, 1972. It specifically dealt with the hunting of elephants and whether the hunting of elephants is justified under the provisions of the Indian Penal Code and the necessary provisions of the Wildlife Protection Act.

36. Give correct answer by using codes given below. The Environmental approach has led the Supreme Court to derive, adopt and apply a range of principles to guide the development of environmental jurisprudence. Notable amongst the fundamental norms recognised by the court are

I. Every person enjoys the right to a wholesome environment, which is a facet of the right to life guaranteed under Article 21 of the Constitution.

II. Enforcement agencies are under an obligation to strictly enforce environmental laws.

III. Government agencies may not plead non-availability of funds, inadequacy of staff or other insufficiencies to justify the non-performance of their obligations under environmental laws.

IV. Stringent action ought to be taken against contumacious defaulters and persons who carry on industrial or development activity for profit without regard to environmental laws.

Codes

1 Only I and II
2 Only I, II and III
3 I, II, III and IV
4 Only I

***Ans.* (3)**

Exp. Statements I, II, III and IV are correct.

The Environmental approach has led the Supreme Court to derive, adopt and apply a range of principles to guide the development of environmental jurisprudence. Notable amongst the fundamental norms recognised by the court are

I. Every person enjoys the right to a wholesome environment, which is a facet of the right to life guaranteed under Article 21 of the Constitution.

II. Enforcement agencies are under an obligation to strictly enforce environmental laws.

III. Government agencies may not plead non-availability of funds, inadequacy of staff or other insufficiencies to justify the non-performance of their obligations under environmental laws.

IV. Stringent action ought to be taken against contumacious defaulters and persons who carry on industrial or development activity for profit without regard to environmental laws.

37. In which of the following case the Supreme Court after referring to International Covenant of Civil and Political Rights and Universal Declaration of Human Rights observed that, "It is almost an accepted proposition of law that rule of customary international law which are not contrary to the Municipal Law shall deemed to be incorporated in the domestic law" ?

1 MC Mehta Vs. Union of India
2 Rural Litigation and Entitlement Kendra Vs. State of UP
3 PUCL Vs. Union of India
4 Church of God (Full Gospels) in India Vs. KKR Majestic Colony Welfare Association

Ans. (3)

Exp. In PUCL Vs. Union of India, the Supreme Court after referring to International Covenant of Civil and Political Rights and Universal Declaration of Human Rights observed that, "It is almost an accepted proposition of law that rule of customary international law which are not contrary to the Municipal Law shall deemed to be incorporated in the domestic law."

38. Which one of the following is correct ?

The Air (Prevention and Control of Pollution) Act of 1981 was enacted

1 by the Parliament under Article 252 1 of the Constitution after securing enabling resolution from the States
2 by the Parliament invoking the power under Article 253 to make laws implementing decisions taken at International Conferences
3 by the states, as the executive functions under the Air Act are carried out by the State Pollution Control Board
4 by the Parliament based on the directions given by the Supreme Court

Ans. (2)

Exp. The Air (Prevention and Control of Pollution) Act of 1981 was enacted by the Parliament invoking the power under Article 253 to make laws implementing decisions taken at International Conferences.

The Air (Prevention and Control of Pollution) Act, 1981 is an Act of the Parliament of India to control and prevent air pollution in India. The law was amended in 1987. This was the first attempt by the government of India to combat air pollution.

39. Which of the following pair/pairs is/are correctly matched ? Give correct answer by using the codes given below.

I. JG Starke – An Introduction to International Law
II. Hackworth – Digest of International Law
III. JL Brierly – The Changing Structure of International Law
IV. W Friedman – The Basis of Obligation in International Law

Codes

1 Only II
2 Only I and II
3 Only I, II and III
4 I, II, III and IV

Ans. (2)

Exp. Pair I and II are correctly matched.

JG Starke written the book named 'An Introduction to International Law'

Hackworth written the book named 'Digest of International Law'

The Changing Structure of International Law' is a 1964 book written by Wolfgang Friedmann.

'The Basis of Obligation in International Law' is written by JL Brierly.

40. In which of the following cases the International Court of Justice pointed out that when in regard to any matter or practice, two states follow it repeatedly for a long time, it becomes a binding customary rule?

1 West Rand Central Gold Mining Company Ltd., VR Case
2 South West Africa Case
3 Right of Passage over Indian Territory Case (Portugal Vs. India)
4 North Sea Continental Shelf Case

Ans. (3)

Exp. In Right of Passage over Indian Territory Case (Portugal Vs. India), the International Court of Justice pointed out that when in regard to any matter or practice, two states follow it repeatedly for a long time, it becomes a binding customary rule.

States are typically bound by customary international law regardless of whether the states have codified these laws domestically or through treaties.

41. In International law a good example of the application of the principle sovereignty is the 'Theory of Auto Limitation'. According to this theory, states follow International law because they have by their consent reduced their powers. This principle is based on the principle of state sovereignty. The chief exponent of this principle was

1 Only Anzilotti
2 Anzilotti and Triepel both
3 Salmond
4 Max Huber

Ans. (2)

Exp. In International law a good example of the application of the principle sovereignty is the 'Theory of Auto Limitation'. According to this theory, states follow International law because they have by their consent reduced their powers. This principle is based on the principle of state sovereignty. The chief exponent of this principle was Anzilotti and Triepel both.

42. Which of the following statement/statements is/are incorrect ? Give correct answer by using the codes given below.

I. 'Subjugation' is a mode of 'acquisition' of Nationality under the International Law.

II. Stock Vs. The Public Trustee is a case related to Double Nationality.

III. Articles 3 to 6 of the Hague Convention of 1930 provide the provisions for solving the problem of Double Nationality of married women.

IV. 'Cession' is a mode of 'Loss' of Nationality under the International Law

Codes

1 Only II is incorrect
2 Only I, II and III are incorrect
3 Only II, III and IV are incorrect
4 I, II, III and IV all are incorrect

Ans. (3)

Exp. Statements II, III and IV are incorrect.

Statement II is incorrect because Stock Vs. The Public Trustee case is related to statelessness.

Statement III is incorrect because Articles 3 to 6 of the Hague Convention of 1930 talks about nationality in general.

Statement IV is incorrect because 'cessation' is a mode of assignment of property (e.g. Land) of another entity. It is an understanding under international law by which territory is transferred from one State to another with the consent of both States.

43. Read Assertion (A) and Reason (R) both and select the correct answer by using the codes given below.

Assertion (A) The General Assembly is one of the principal organ of the United Nations which consists of all the members of United Nations.

Reason (R) The Resolutions or Declaration of the General Assembly are not binding upon the States. They are merely recommendations.

Codes

1 Both (A) and (R) are correct and (R) is the correct explanation of (A)
2 Both (A) and (R) are correct individually, but (R) is not correct explanation of (A)
3 (A) is true, but (R) is false
4 (A) is false, but (R) is true

Ans. (2)

Exp. Both (A) and (R) are correct individually, but (R) is not correct explanation of (A).

Assertion (A) says that the General Assembly is one of the principal organs of the United Nations which consists of all the members of United Nations is correct because the General Assembly is the main deliberative, policymaking and representative organ of the UN. All 193 Member States of the UN are represented in the General Assembly, making it the only UN body with universal representation.

Reason (R) says that the Resolutions or Declaration of the General Assembly are not binding upon the States. They are merely recommendations is correct individually but does not explain the given assertion.

44. Match List I with List II and select the correct answer by using the codes given below the lists.

List I (Jurisdiction of the International Court of Justice)	List II (Cases decided)
A. Case decided under contentious jurisdiction	I. Nicaragua Vs. United States of America
B. Under Advisory Jurisdiction	II. North Sea Continental Shelf Case
C. Courts' competence in respect of determination of its own jurisdiction	III. Western Sahara Case
D. Transferred Jurisdiction	IV. Anglo-Iranian Oil Company Case

Codes

	A	B	C	D		A	B	C	D
1	IV	I	II	III	2	I	II	III	IV
3	II	III	IV	I	4	III	IV	I	II

Ans. (1)

Exp. The correct matching is A-IV, B-I, C-II, D-III.

Anglo Iranian Oil Company is the case decided under contentious jurisdiction. In the exercise of its jurisdiction in contentious cases, the International Court of Justice settles disputes of a legal nature that are submitted to it by States in accordance with international law.

Nicaragua Vs. United States of America is the case under Advisory Jurisdiction. In accordance with Article 96, paragraph 1, of the Charter of the United Nations the General Assembly or the Security Council may request the International Court of Justice to give an advisory opinion on any legal question.

North Sea Continental Shelf Case is related to Courts' competence in respect of determination of its own jurisdiction. The doctrine of competence-competence states that the Arbitral Tribunal has the jurisdiction to determine the scope and ambit of its own powers, i.e., the tribunal has the 'competence' to decide its own 'competence'.

Western Sahara Case is related to transferred Jurisdiction. Transferred jurisdiction is transfer of case from one court to another.

45. Which of the following pair/pairs is/are not correctly matched ? Give correct answer by using the codes given below.

I. Composition of the Security Council of U.N. – Article 23 of the UN Charter

II. Composition of the Economic and Social Council – Article 61 of the UN Charter

III. Composition of the General Assembly of the United Nations – Article 86 of the UN Charter

IV. Composition of Trusteeship Council – Article 28 of the UN Charter

Codes

1 Only IV
2 Only III and IV
3 Only I, II and III
4 I, II, III and IV all

Ans. *(2)*

➲ *Exp.* Pair III and IV are incorrectly matched.

Article 9 of the UN Charter talks about the composition of the General Assembly. It states that The General Assembly shall consist of all the Members of the United Nations. Each Member shall have not more than five representatives in the General Assembly.

Article 86 talks about the composition of the trusteeship council. Article 86 reads as follows:

1. The Trusteeship Council shall consist of the following Members of the United Nations:
   (a) those Members administering trust territories;
   (b) such of those Members mentioned by name in Article 23 as are not administering trust territories; and
   (c) as many other Members elected for three-year terms by the General Assembly as may be necessary to ensure that the total number of members of the Trusteeship Council is equally divided between those Members of the United Nations which administer trust territories and those which do not.
2. Each member of the Trusteeship Council shall designate one specially qualified person to represent it therein.

46. Match List I and List II and find correct answer by using the codes given below.

List I (Case Law)		List II (Decision)
A.	Saroj Rani Vs. Sudarshan Kumar	I. Uniform Civil Code
B.	Jorden Diengdeh Vs. SS Chopra	II. Meaning of Hindu
C.	Russel Vs. Russel	III. Constitutionality of Section 9 of Hindu Marriage Act, 1955
D.	Shastri Vs. Muldas	IV. Meaning of Cruelty

Codes

	A	B	C	D		A	B	C	D
1	II	III	I	IV	2	IV	II	III	I
3	III	I	IV	II	4	I	IV	III	II

Ans. *(3)*

➲ *Exp.* The correct matching is A-III, B-I, C-IV, D-II.

Saroj Rani Vs. Sudarshan Kumar case is related to constitutionality of Section 9 of Hindu Marriage Act, 1955. Section 9 of the Hindu Marriage Act, 1955, deals with restitution of conjugal rights which reads: "When either the husband or the wife has, without reasonable excuse, withdrawn from the society of the other, the aggrieved party may apply, by petition to the district court, for restitution of conjugal rights."

Jorden Diengdeh Vs. SS Chopra case is related to Uniform Civil Code. Uniform Civil Code is a proposal in India to formulate and implement personal laws of citizens which apply on all citizens equally regardless of their religion. Currently, personal laws of various communities are governed by their religious scriptures.

Russel Vs. Russel case is related to meaning of Cruelty. Cruelty may consist of physical violence; other conduct that endangers the life or safety of the complaining spouse; abusive or derogatory language; neglect; humiliation; threats of violence, etc. A single act of cruelty must generally be extreme to be sufficient for filing a divorce complaint.

Shastri Vs. Muldas case is related to meaning of Hindu. A person can be a Hindu by religion in any of its forms or developments, including a Virashaiva, a Lingayat or a follower of the Brahmo, Prarthana or Arya Samaj, (b) to any person who is a Buddhist, Jaina or Sikh by religion.

47. A marriage solemnised between any two Hindus who are Sapindas of each other shall be

1 Valid, if the custom or usage governing any of them permits a marriage between the two
2 Valid, if the custom or usage governing each of them permits a marriage between the two
3 Voidable, if the custom or usage governing each of them permits a marriage between the two
4 Void, if the custom or usage governing each of them permits a marriage between the two

Ans. *(2)*

➲ *Exp.* As per Section 5 of the Hindu Marriage Act, 1955 a marriage solemnised between any two Hindus who are Sapindas of each other shall be valid, if the custom or usage governing each of them permits a marriage between the two.

Sapinda relationships are prohibited under Hindu marriage law. A sapinda is someone who is within or has a common ancestor relative within three generations above you on your mother's side of the family. within or has a common ancestor relative within five generations above you on your father's side of the family.

48. Read the following and select correct answer with the help of codes given below:
A married Hindu female can adopt a child

I. Only with the consent of her husband.
II. In case of void marriage, consent of husband is necessary.
III. In case of voidable marriage, consent of husband is not necessary.
IV. If husband has converted to Muslim religion, his consent is not necessary.

Codes
1 I and IV are correct, but II and III are incorrect
2 I, III and IV are correct, but II is incorrect
3 II and IV are correct, but I and III are incorrect
4 IV and II are correct, but III and I are incorrect

Ans. (1)

Exp. Statement II and IV are correct. but II and III are incorrect.

Statement I is correct because as per Section 7 of Hindu Adoption and Maintenance Act, 1956, a married Hindu female can adopt a child only with the consent of her husband.

Statement IV is correct because as per Section 8 of the referred act if husband has converted to Muslim religion, his consent is not necessary.

Statement II is incorrect because in case of void marriages, there is no husband, and consent is not required to adopt the child.

Statement III is incorrect because a voidable marriage is a valid marriage until a decree of annulment is not obtained from the Court of law. So, consent of husband is necessary in this case.

49. Which of the following is not a ground of divorce available to wife under Section 13 (2) of the Hindu Marriage Act, 1955 ?

1 Pre-Act bigamy of the husband
2 Repudiation of marriage
3 Cruelty by the husband
4 Husband is guilty of rape, sodomy and bestiality

Ans. (3)

Exp. Cruelty by the husband is not a ground of divorce available to the wife under Section 13 (2) of the Hindu Marriage Act, 1955.

Section 13(2) of the referred act talks about the ground available for a wife to file for divorce. It states that-A wife may also present a petition for the dissolution of her marriage by a decree of divorce on the following ground,.

(i) in the case of any marriage solemnised before the commencement of this Act, that the husband had married again before such commencement or that any other wife of the husband married before such commencement was alive at the time of the solemnisation of the marriage of the petitioner: Provided that in either case the other wife is alive at the time of the presentation of the petition; or

(ii) that the husband has, since the solemnisation of the marriage, been guilty of rape, sodomy or bestiality; or

(iii) that in a suit under section 18 of the Hindu Adoptions and Maintenance Act, 1956 , or in a proceeding under section 125 of the Code of Criminal Procedure, 1973 [or under the corresponding section 488 of the Code of Criminal Procedure, 1898 (5 of 1898)], a decree or order, as the case may be, has been passed against the husband awarding maintenance to the wife notwithstanding that she was living apart and that since the passing of such decree or order, cohabitation between the parties has not been resumed for one year or upwards; or

(iv) that her marriage (whether consummated or not was solemnised before she attained the age of fifteen years and she has repudiated the marriage after attaining that age but before attaining the age of eighteen years.

50. Read the following statements and select correct answer with the help of codes given below.

I. A Muslim woman can marry a Kitabi.
II. A Shia male can contract 'Muta' with a fire worshipper.
III. Marriage of a Muslim woman with a Hindu would be irregular.
IV. A Muslim man cannot marry with his niece.

Codes
1 I and II are correct, but III and IV are incorrect
2 II and III are correct, but I and IV are incorrect
3 III and IV are correct, but I and II are incorrect
4 II and IV are correct, but I and III are incorrect

Ans. (4)

Exp. Statements II and IV are correct, but I and III are incorrect.

Statement II is correct because a Shia male can contract 'Muta' with a fire worshipper. A male shia may contract a Muta marriage with a woman professing the Mahomedan, Christian or Jewish religion, or even with a woman who is a fire worshipper but not with any woman following any other religion.

Statement IV is correct because a muslim man cannot marry with his niece because under Muslim law marriage between aunt and nephews and uncle and nieces are strictly forbidden.

Statement I is incorrect because a muslim woman cannot marry a kitabi. Islamic Law permits a Muslim man to marry non-Muslim women provided that they are from among the People of the Book (i.e. female Christians or female Jews).

Statement III is incorrect because an irregular marriage is one which can be validated by some post of the parties. However, a Muslim woman's marrige to a fire worshipper (e.g. a Hindu) is invalid and cannot be a regularised.

51. Read the following statements in the light of Hindu Adoptions and Maintenance Act, 1956 and select correct answer with the help of codes given below.

I. The obligation of husband to maintain his wife is co-extensive with his property.

II. Sec 18(2) provides for maintenance and separate residence of wife in some conditions.

III. Father-in-law's obligation to maintain widowed-daughter-in-law is a personal obligation

IV. An unchaste and non-Hindu wife is not entitled to maintenance.

Codes

1 I and IV are correct, but II and III are incorrect
2 II and IV are correct, but I and III are incorrect
3 III and IV are correct, but I and II are incorrect
4 I and III are correct, but II and IV are incorrect

Ans. (2)

Exp. Statement II and IV are correct, but I and III are incorrect

Statement II is correct because Section 18(2) provides for maintenance and separate residence of wife in some conditions. It cannot be applicable to the case of the wife who lives with her husband.

Section IV is correct because an unchaste and non-Hindu wife is not entitled to maintenance. This general disqualification is laid down in Section 24.

Statement I is not correct as the obligation of the husband to maintain his wife is not subject or co-extensive with his property.

Statement III is not correct as Father-in-law's obligation to maintain widowed-daughter-in-law is not his personal obligation but the statutory obligation under the Hindu Adoption and Maintenance Act, 1956.

52. Which of the following is not a ground of divorce under Section 2 of the Dissolution of Muslim Marriage Act, 1939?

1 7 years imprisonment to the husband
2 Failure of the husband to pay maintenance for the last two years
3 Whereabouts of the husband have not been known for a period of 3 years
4 Failure of the husband to perform, without reasonable cause, his marital obligations for a period of three years

Ans. (3)

Exp. If whereabouts of the husband have not been known for a period of 3 years, is not a ground of divorce under Section 2 of the Dissolution of Muslim Marriage Act, 1939.

According to Section 2(i) of the Dissolution of Muslim Marriage Act, 1939, if the whereabouts of husband is not known for the period of four years, then that will be considered as the valid ground for divorce.

53. Which of the following are not available to a Hindu husband as grounds of Judicial Separation?

I. Extra marital sex by wife.

II. Conversion of wife to a non-Hindu religion.

III. Wife's pre-marriage pregnancy.

IV. Non-consummation of marriage owing to impotence of wife.

Codes

1 Only I and II
2 Only II and III
3 Only IV and I
4 Only III and IV

Ans. (4)

Exp. Wife's pre-marriage pregnancy and non-consummation of marriage owing to impotence of wife are not available to a Hindu husband as grounds of Judicial Separation.

A judicial separation is a legal process by which a married couple is formally separated, despite being legally married. The separation is granted in the form of a court order.

54. Which Article of the UN Charter charges the UN to promote "Universal respect for and observance of, human rights and fundamental freedoms for all without distinction as to sex, race, language or religion"?

1 Article 56
2 Article 55(c)
3 Article 62
4 Article 76(c)

Ans. (2)

Exp. Article 55(c) of the UN Charter charges the UN to promote "Universal respect for and observance of, human rights and fundamental freedoms for all without distinction as to sex, race, language or religion".

55. Match List I and List II and select the correct answer by using the codes given below.

	List I	List II
A.	The Commission on Human Rights was established by the Economic and Social Council on	I. 15th December, 1989
B.	The General Assembly created the position of UN High Commissioner for Human Rights on	II. 20th December, 1993
C.	The General Assembly adopted Second Optional Protocol to the International Covenant on Civil and Political Rights on	III. February, 1946
D.	The Optional Protocol to the International Law on Civil and Political Rights, 1966 came into force on	IV. 23rd March, 1976

Codes

	A	B	C	D		A	B	C	D
1	III	II	I	IV	2	IV	III	II	I
3	III	IV	II	I	4	II	I	IV	III

Ans. (1)

Exp. The correct matching is A-III, B-II, C-I, D-IV.

The *Commission on Human Rights* was established by the Economic and Social Council on February, 1946. The United Nations Commission on Human Rights was a functional commission within the overall framework of the United Nations from 1946 until it was replaced by the United Nations Human Rights Council in 2006.

The *General Assembly* created the position of UN High Commissioner for Human Rights on 20th December, 1993. This position promote and protect human rights that are guaranteed under international law and stipulated in the Universal Declaration of Human Rights of 1948.

The *General Assembly* adopted Second Optional Protocol to the International Covenant on Civil and Political Rights on 15th December, 1989. The Second Optional Protocol to the International Covenant on Civil and Political Rights, aiming at the abolition of the death penalty, is a subsidiary agreement to the International Covenant on Civil and Political Rights. It was created on 15 December 1989 and entered into force on 11th July, 1991.

The *Optional Protocol* to the International Law on Civil and Political Rights, 1966 came into force on 23rd March, 1976. An Optional Protocol is a legal instrument related to an existing treaty that addresses issues that the parent treaty does not cover or does not cover sufficiently. It is usually, although not always, open to ratification or accession only by States that are parties to the parent treaty.

56. Which of the following pair/pairs is/are not correctly matched ? Give the correct answer by using the codes given below.

I. The World Conference on Human Rights was held at Vienna–Year 1993

II. International Conference on Human Rights at Tehran was held–Year 1958

III. First World Conference on Women was held in Beijing in–1975

IV. International Convention on Elimination of all forms of Racial Discrimination–1963

Codes

1 Only II
2 I and II
3 II, III and IV
4 I, II, III and IV

Ans. *(3)*

Exp. Pair II, III and IV are not correctly matched.

The International Conference on Human Rights at Tehran was held in year 1968. It was attended by representatives of 84 States and by representatives or observers from a number of United Nations bodies and specialised agencies, regional inter-governmental organisations and non-governmental organisations.

The First World Conference on Women was held in Mexico in year 1975. It was the first international conference held by the United Nations to focus solely on women's issues and marked a turning point in policy directives.

International Convention on Elimination of all forms of Racial Discrimination was adopted in 1965. The Convention which entered into force on 4th January, 1969 has three signatories, and 182 countries have ratified or acceded to it, including India.

57. Which of the following has commented on the legal significance of the Universal Declaration of Human Rights thus, "The declaration is merely a statement of principles, not a legally binding instrument, but it has become one of the best known international documents and it has been often referred to in resolutions of the UN, the specialised agencies, regional arrangements and other International Organisations and in national constitutions, legislation and court decision. It is a beacon light for all mankind even though it has been honoured more often in the breach than in the observance"?

1 Starke
2 H. Lauterpacht
3 Oppenheim
4 Palmer and Perkins

Ans. *(4)*

Exp. Palmer and Perkins has commented on the legal significance of the Universal Declaration of Human Rights thus, "The declaration is merely a statement of principles, not a legally binding instrument, but it has become one of the best-known international documents and it has been often referred to in resolutions of the UN, the specialised agencies, regional arrangements and other International Organisations and in national constitutions, legislation and court decision. It is a beacon light for all mankind even though it has been honoured more often in the breach than in the observance".

58. Read both Assertion (A) and Reason (R) and select the correct answer by using the codes given below.

Assertion (A) The Universal Declaration of Human Rights does not define the term 'Human Rights'. It refers them as "the equal and inalienable rights of all members of the Humanity".

Reason (R) The framers of the Indian Constitution were influenced by the concept of Human Rights and guaranteed most of the Human Rights contained in the Universal Declaration of Human Rights.

Codes

1 Both (A) and (R) are correct and (R) is the correct explanation of (A)
2 Both (A) and (R) are correct, but (R) is not the correct explanation of (A)
3 (A) is true, but (R) is false
4 (A) is false, but (R) is true

Ans. (2)

Exp. Both (A) and (R) are correct, but (R) is not the correct explanation of (A).

Assertion is correct as Universal Declaration of Human Rights (UNDHR) does not define human rights. It declares that human rights are universal–to be enjoyed by all people, no matter who they are or where they live. The Universal Declaration includes civil and political rights, like the right to life, liberty, free speech and privacy.

The Reason is also correct as India was a signatory to the Universal Declaration of Human Rights. The Indian constitution was adopted by the Constituent Assembly on 26th December, 1949, which came into force from 26th January, 1950. Our Indian constitution was greatly influenced by the Universal Declaration of Human Rights, 1948. However this is not the reason as to why UDHR does not define the term 'Human Rights'.

59. To which of the following International Conventions on Human Rights, India has become party to such conventions ? Give correct answer with the help of codes given below.

I. Convention on the Political Rights of Women.
II. Convention on the Right of the Child.
III. Convention for the Suppression of the Traffic in Person and of exploitation of the prostitution of others.
IV. Convention on International Recovery of Child Support and Other Forms of Family Maintenance.

Codes

1 Only I
2 Only I and IV
3 Only I, II and III
4 I, II, III and IV

Ans. (3)

Exp. Statement I, II and III are correct.

International Conventions on Human Rights, India has become party to such conventions. Human rights protect human beings and their dignity in war and in peacetime. These rights are protected under international law and it is the duty of states to ensure they are respected, protected and fulfilled. To this end, the United Nations has developed a body of binding conventions, all stemming from the 1948 Universal Declaration of Human Rights.

The conventions are :

Convention on the Political Rights of Women : It was approved by the United Nations General Assembly during the 409th plenary meeting, on 20th December 1952, and adopted on 31st March 1953. The Convention's purpose is to codify a basic international standard for women's political rights.

Convention on the Right of the Child : The United Nations Convention on the Rights of the Child is an international human rights treaty which sets out the civil, political, economic, social, health and cultural rights of children.

Convention for the Suppression of the Traffic in Person and of exploitation of the prostitution of others : It was approved by the United Nations General Assembly on 2nd December, 1949 and entered into force on 25th July, 1951.

60. Match List I and List II and select the correct answer by using the codes given below.

List I (Provisions of Protection of Human Rights Act, 1993)	List II (Relevant Sections)
A. Removal of a Member of the Commission	I. Section 12
B. Functions of the Commission	II. Section 4
C. Procedure with respect to Armed Forces	III. Section 5
D. Appointment of Chairperson and other members	IV. Section 19

Codes

	A	B	C	D
1	II	IV	I	III
2	I	II	III	IV
3	III	I	II	IV
4	IV	III	I	II

Ans. (*)

Exp. The correct matching is A-III, B-I, C-IV, D-II.

Section 5 is related to removal of a Member of the Commission. According to Section 5(1), the Chairperson or any Member may, by notice in writing under his hand addressed to the President of India, resign his office.

Section 12 is related to functions of the Commission. It states that the Commission shall perform all or any of the following functions, namely:

(a) inquire, *suo motu* or on a petition presented to it by a victim or any person on his behalf 1[or on a direction or order of any court], into complaint of
  (i) violation of human rights or abetment thereof; or
  (ii) negligence in the prevention of such violation, by a public servant;
(b) intervene in any proceeding involving any allegation of violation of human rights pending before a court with the approval of such court;

Section 19 is related to procedure with respect to Armed Forces. Section 19 (1) states that notwithstanding anything contained in this Act, while dealing with complaints of violation of human rights by members of the armed forces, the Commission shall adopt the following procedure, namely

(a) it may, either on its own motion or on receipt of a petition, seek a report from the Central Government;
(b) after the receipt of the report, it may, either not proceed with the complaint or, as the case may be, make its recommendations to that Government.

Section 4 is related to appointment of Chairperson and other members. Section 4(1) states that the Chairperson and the Members shall be appointed by the President by warrant under his hand and seal.

61. In which among the following cases malice becomes relevant to determine a person's liability in law of torts? Answer using codes below :

I. Malice may result in aggravation of damages.
II. In torts of decit and conspiracy one of the essential is malice.
III. When act is lawful, intention can be gathered from past circumstances.
IV. Causing of personal comfort by lawful means may turn lawful act into a tort.

Codes
1 Only I and II
2 Only I and III
3 Only I, II and III
4 I, II, III and IV

***Ans.* (1)**

➲ ***Exp.*** Statement I and II are correct.

Aggravated damages will arise where the defendant has acted with malice that increased the injury to the plaintiff. The malice may be established by intrinsic evidence derived from the libellous statement itself and the circumstances of its publication, or by extrinsic evidence pertaining to the surrounding circumstances which demonstrate that the defendant was motivated by an unjustifiable intention to injure the plaintiff.

Malice is essential in the torts of deceit, conspiracy, malicious prosecution and injurious falsehoods.

62. Match List I with List II and select correct answer by using codes given below.

List I (Maxims)	List II (Cases)
A. Damnum sine injuria	I. Padmavati Vs. Dugganika
B. Injuria sine damno	II. Vishnu Datt Vs. Board of Higher Secondary and Intermediate Education, UP
C. Volenti non fit injuria	III. Bindra Devi Chauhan Vs. State of HP
D. Res ipsa loquitor	IV. Bhim Singh Vs. State of Jammu and Kashmir

Codes

	A	B	C	D
1	II	IV	III	I
2	II	III	I	IV
3	II	IV	I	III
4	I	II	IV	III

***Ans.* (3)**

➲ ***Exp.*** The correct matching is A-II, B-IV, C-I, D-III.

Vishnu Datt Vs. Board of Higher Secondary and Intermediate Education, UP is related to Damnum sine injuria. Damnum sine Injuria is a legal maxim which refers to as damages without injury or damages in which there is no infringement of any legal right which are vested with the plaintiff. It is an implied principle in law that there are no remedies for any moral wrongs, unless and until any legal right has been infringed.

Bhim Singh Vs. State of Jammu and Kashmir is related to Injuria sine damno. It is injury without damage or infringement of an absolute private right without any actual loss or damage.

Padmavati Vs. Dugganika is related to Volenti non fit injuria. Volenti non fit injuria is Latin for "to a willing person, it is not a wrong." This legal maxim holds that a person who knowingly and voluntarily risks danger cannot recover for any resulting injury.

Bindra Devi Chauhan Vs. State of HP is related to Res ipsa loquitor. Res ipsa loquitur is a doctrine in the Anglo-American common law and Roman Dutch law that says in a tort or civil lawsuit a court can infer negligence from the very nature of an accident or injury in the absence of direct evidence on how any defendant behaved.

63. In which of following cases originator of defamatory statement will be liable for the damage resulting from repetitive publication by third persons?

I. He himself authorised repetition.
II. Repetition was the natural and probable consequence of his act.
III. There was immoral obligation on the person in whose presence the slander was made to repeat it.
IV. There was moral obligation on the person in whose absence the slander was made to repeat it.

Codes
1 Only I and II
2 Only I and III
3 Only I and IV
4 Only II and IV

***Ans.* (1)**

➲ ***Exp.*** Statement I and II are correct.

A person who is privileged to repeat a statement—for example, a person testifying in a court of law or a reporter relying on a public document or public official is not liable for the any harm resulting from repeating a defamatory statement. Likewise, if the repetition is authorized by the originator of the defamatory statement, the person repeating the statement is not liable. In both of these situations the originator of the statement would be liable to the person who was defamed.

Criminal intent may also be presumed from the commission of the act. That is, the prosecution may rely on the presumption that a person intends the Natural and Probable Consequences of his or her voluntary acts.

64. Which of the following is true in relation to nuisance?

1 An action for nuisance is actionable per se and no special damage need to be proved.
2 It can be committed through the medium of intangible objects.
3 It is direct interference with the possession of plaintiff
4 There is no interference with plaintiff's use or enjoyment of land.

Ans. (2)

Exp. Nuisance can be committed through the medium of intangible objects is true in relation to nuisance.

Nuisance is an injury to the right of a person's possession of his property to undisturbed enjoyment of it and results from an improper usage by another individual.

65. Read Assertion (A) and Reason (R) and answer by using codes below.

Assertion (A) The law takes no cognisance of carelessness in the abstract.

Reason (R) Cause of action for negligence accrues when damage that is real damage is suffered.

Codes

1 Both (A) and (R) are true and (R) is right explanation of (A)
2 Both (A) and (R) are true, but (R) is not right explanation of (A)
3 (A) is true, but (R) is false
4 (A) is false, but (R) is true

Ans. (1)

Exp. Both (A) and (R) are true and (R) is right explanation of (A).

Assertion (A) is true because carelessness shall not be considered as an excuse to escape any liability. It concerns itself with carelessness only where there is a duty to take care and where failure in that duty has caused damage. In such circumstances carelessness assume the legal quality of negligence

Reason (R) says that cause of action for negligence accrues when damage that is real damage is suffered is true because every negligent act in order to be considered as a crime should result in damage. A prospective loss, alone, is not enough, and a cause of action of negligence will accrue when the plaintiff first suffers any actual damage.

66. Which of the following is not correct in relation to the Consumer Protection Act ?

1 It extends to whole of India except the State of Jammu and Kashmir
2 It shall come into force on such date as the Central Government may by notification appoint
3 This Act shall be in addition to and not in derogation of provisions of any other law for the time being in force
4 This Act shall overside the provisions of Sale of Goods Act

Ans. (4)

Exp. Consumer Protection Act shall overside the provisions of Sale of Goods Act is not correct in relation to Consumer Protection Act.

The Consumer Protection Act, 1986 seeks to provide for better protection of the interests of consumers and for the purpose, to make provision for the establishment of Consumer councils and other authorities for the settlement of consumer disputes and for matter connected therewith.

67. What is the period of limitation to file a complaint before the Consumer Dispute Redressal Agencies ?

1 Within one year from the date of cause of action
2 Within two years from the date of cause of action
3 Within three years from the date of cause of action
4 No limitation period to file a complaint

Ans. (2)

Exp. The period of limitation to file a complaint before the Consumer Dispute Redressal Agencies is within two years from the date of cause of action.

The District Forum, the State Commission or the National Commission shall not admit a complaint unless it is filed within two years from the date on which the cause of action has arisen.

68. Read Assertion (A) and Reason (R) and answer by using codes below.

Assertion (A) Salary drawn by a partner from the firm for his services rendered to it has been treated different from his right to get an additional amount in the form of salary as his share of the firm's profit.

Reason (R) Because RM Chidambaram Pillai Vs. Commissioner of Income tax case laid down above principle.

Codes

1 Both (A) and (R) are correct and (R) is correct explanation for (A)
2 Both (A) and (R) are false
3 (A) is true, but (R) is false
4 (R) is true, but (A) is false

Ans. (2)

Exp. Both (A) and (R) are false.

Assertion (A) is false because the salary drawn by a partner from the firm for his services rendered to it has not been treated as something different from his right to get an additional amount in the form of salary as his share of the firm's profits.

Reason (R) given is false because the case held the exact opposite statement given in Assertion

69. Match List I with List II and select the correct answer using the codes given below.

List I (Principles of mutual rights and liabilities of partners)	List II (Relevant case-law)
A. Remuneration to a partner in absence of an agreement on this matter	I. Md. Abdul Sattar Vs. State of Andhra Pradesh
B. Fixation of remuneration by agreement in respect of a partner does not alter his status as a partner	II. Ghisulal Vs. Gambirmal
C. Interest on the capital of a partner	III. Shelat Brothers Vs. Nanalal Harilal Shelat
D. Action against a partner for balance due to another	IV. Bhagchand Vs. Kaluram @ Moolchand

Codes

	A	B	C	D		A	B	C	D
1	IV	II	I	III	2	III	I	II	IV
3	I	III	IV	II	4	III	I	IV	II

Ans. (4)

Exp. The correct matching is A-III, B-I, C-IV, D-II

Shelat Brothers Vs. Nanalal Harilal Shelat is related to Remuneration to a partner in absence of an agreement on this matter.

Md. Abdul Sattar Vs. State of Andhra Pradesh is related to fixation of remuneration by agreement in respect of a partner does not alter his status as a partner

Bhagchand Vs. Kaluram and Moolchand and others is related to interest on the capital of a partner.

Ghisulal Vs. Gambirmal is related to action against a partner for balance due to another.

70. Read Assertion (A) and Reason (R) and answer using codes given below.

Assertion (A) Partner of an erstwhile unregistered partnership firm can bring a suit to enforce a right arising out of a contract falling within the ambit of Section 69 of the Indian Partnership Act.

Reason (R) Because Judgement in case of Loonkaran Sethia Vs. Ivan E. John laid down above judicial principle.

Codes

1 Both (A) and (R) are correct and (R) is correct explanation for (A)
2 Both (A) and (R) are false
3 (A) is true, but (R) is false
4 (A) is false, but (R) is true

Ans. (2)

Exp. Both (A) and (R) are false.

Assertion (A) is false because unregistered partnership firm cannot bring a lawsuit because as per Section 69 of the partnership act if the firm is unregistered it cannot be treated as a separate entity and no suit can be brought by it. Reason (R) is false because the said assertion was not laid down in mentioned case.

71. Which of the following statement is correct according to Section 2(9) of the Sale of Goods Act?

'Mercantile Agent' means a mercantile agent

1 having in the usual course of business as such seller authority either to sell goods, or to consign goods for the purpose of sale, or to buy goods, or to distribute money for security of goods
2 having in the customary business as such agent power either to sell goods, or to mortgage goods for purpose of sale
3 having in the customary course of business as such agent authority to sell goods
4 having in the normal course of business as such agent authority to confine goods or to raise goods for purpose of the security of money

Ans. (3)

Exp. 'Mercantile Agent' means a mercantile agent having in the customary course of business as such agent authority to sell goods.

Section 2(9) of the act talks about the mercantile agents. It says 'mercantile agent' means 'a mercantile agent having in the customary course of business as such agent authority either to sell goods, or to consign goods for the purposes of sale, or to buy goods, or to raise money on the security of goods.'

72. Which of the following statements are correct?

I. Ascertainment of goods for sale is done by buyer.
II. Appropriation of goods for sale is done by seller.
III. Distinction between ascertainment of goods and appropriation of goods that former involves "the element of common intention between buyer and seller", whereas later can be a unilateral act by buyer.
IV. Property in goods does not pass to buyer till appropriation.

Codes

1 Only I, III and IV are correct
2 Only II is correct
3 Only IV is correct
4 Only III is correct

Ans. (3)

Exp. Statement IV is correct.

Property in goods does not pass to buyer till appropriation. According to Sale of Goods Act, 1930, Sale of unascertained goods and appropriation are :

(i) Where there is a contract for the sale of unascertained or future goods by description and goods of that description and in a deliverable state are unconditionally appropriated to the contract, either by the seller with the assent of the buyer or by the buyer with the assent of the seller, the property in the goods thereupon passes to the buyer. Such assent may be expressed or implied, and may be given either before or after the appropriation is made.

(ii) Delivery to carrier where, in pursuance of the contract, the seller delivers the goods to the buyer or to a carrier or other bailee (whether named by the buyer or not) for the purpose of transmission to the buyer, and does not reserve the right of disposal, he is deemed to have unconditionally appropriated the goods to the contract.

73. Which of the following are presumptions as to a negotiable instrument under Section 118 of the Negotiable Instruments Act?

I. Presumption of contractual capacity
II. Presumption of consideration
III. Presumption of maturity of instrument
IV. Presumption of date

Codes

1 Only I and III 2 Only II and IV
3 Only I and IV 4 Only I and II

***Ans.* (2)**

Exp. The presumptions as to a negotiable instrument under Section 118 of the Negotiable Instruments Act are Presumption of consideration and Presumption of date.

According to section 118, in the Negotiable Instruments Act, 1881 presumptions as to negotiable instruments are:

(i) Presumption of consideration that every negotiable instrument was made or drawn for consideration, and that every such instrument, when it has been accepted, indorsed, negotiated or transferred, was accepted, indorsed, negotiated or transferred for consideration;

(ii) Presumption of as to date that every negotiable instrument bearing a date was made or drawn on such date.

74. Which of the following statement is correct?

I. Doctrine of indoor management apply in case of knowledge of irregularity in company.
II. Doctrine of indoor management does not apply in case of suspicion of irregularity.
III. Doctrine of indoor management apply in case of forgery.
IV. Doctrine of indoor management does not apply if the act of an officer of a company is one which would ordinarily be beyond the powers of such an officer.

Codes

1 Only I is correct 2 Only II is correct
3 Only III is correct 4 Only IV is correct

***Ans.* (4)**

Exp. Statement IV is correct.

Doctrine of indoor management does not apply if the act of an officer of a company is one which would ordinarily be beyond the powers of such an officer. The doctrine of indoor management was evolved 150 years ago. It is also known as Turquand's rule. The role of the doctrine of indoor management is opposed to the role of the doctrine of constructive notice. The doctrine of constructive notice protects the company against outsiders whereas the doctrine of indoor management protects outsiders against the actions of the company. This doctrine also is a possible safeguard against the possibility of abusing the doctrine of constructive notice.

75. Find answer by using codes given below

Director may be removed by

I. Other Directors
II. Creditors
III. Central Government
IV. Shareholders in a general meeting

Codes

1 I and II are correct 2 II and III are correct
3 III and IV are correct 4 IV and I are correct

***Ans.* (3)**

Exp. Directors can be removed by Central Government and shareholders in a general meeting.

A Company has the authority to remove a director by passing an Ordinary Resolution, given the Director was not appointed by the Central Government or the Tribunal. A Board Meeting will be called by giving seven days' notice to all the directors. They can be removed before the expiry of their tenure except for those directors who are appointed by Tribunal or Government.

The Central Government has power to remove managerial personnel on the recommendations of the National Company Law Tribunal.

UGC-NET
LAW
SOLVED PAPER 2016 (July)
PAPER II

1 In Golaknath Vs. State of Punjab, Justice K Subba Rao observed

1 The Preamble contains in a nutshell ideals and aspirations of the Constitution
2 The Preamble is the key to open the minds of the Constitution makers
3 The Preamble is enforceable by the Judiciary
4 The Preamble of our Constitution is of great importance and it should be implemented

***Ans.* (1)**

Exp. In Golaknath Vs. State of Punjab, Justice K Subba Rao observed that the Preamble contains in a nutshell ideals and aspirations of the Constitution.

The Judgement of Subba Rao, CJ Shah, Sikri, Shelat and Vaidialingam JJ was delivered by Subba Rao. According to this Judgement:

(i) the power to amend the Constitution is not to be found in Article 368, but in Article 245, 246 and 248 read with Entry 97 of List 1.
(ii) the amending power cannot be used to abridge or take away the Fundamental Rights guaranteed in Part III of the Constitution.
(iii) a law amending the Constitution is 'Law' within the meaning of Article 13(2).
(iv) the First, Fourth and Seventeenth Amendments though they abridged Fundamental Rights were valid in the past on the basis of earlier decisions of this court and continue to be valid for the future.

2 The Five Judges Constitution Bench held that 'Imparting Education cannot be treated as a Trade or Business' in which of the following cases?

1 Unnikrishanan Case
2 Mohini Jain Case
3 Dinesh Kumar Case
4 PA Inamdar Case

***Ans.* (1)**

Exp. In Unnikrishanan Case, the court held that commercialisation of education cannot and should not be permitted. The Parliament as well as State Legislatures have expressed this intention in unmistakable terms. Both in the light of our tradition and from the stand-point of interest of general public, commercialisation is positively harmful; it is opposed to public policy. Therefore, 'Imparting Education cannot be treated as a trade, business or profession.

3 As per the Constitution of India, which of the following statement(s) is/are correct?

I. The state may make provision for securing just and humane conditions of work
II. The state shall endeavour to provide early childhood care and education for all the children until they complete the age of six years
III. The state shall not endeavour to secure for the citizens a Uniform Civil Code in the territory of India
IV. The state shall endeavour to protect and improve the environment and to safeguard the forests and wildlife of the country

Codes

1 I, II and III
2 II, III and IV
3 II and IV
4 III and IV

***Ans.* (3)**

Exp. As per the Constitution of India; Statements II and IV are correct.

According to Article 45, the state shall endeavour to provide early childhood care and education for all the children until they complete the age of six years.

According to Article 48A, the state shall endeavour to protect and improve the environment and to safeguard the forests and wildlife of the country.

Statement I and III are incorrect.

According to Article 42, the state shall make provision for securing just and humane conditions of work and for maternity relief.

As per Article 44 of Indian Constitution, the state shall endeavour to secure for the citizens a Uniform Civil Code (UCC) throughout the territory of India.

4 Read Assertion (A) and Reason (R) and answer using the codes given below.

Assertion (A) No minimum age is prescribed for appointment as a Judge of the Supreme Court of India nor is there any fixed period of office.

Reason (R) The original jurisdiction of the Supreme Court is dealt within Article-132 of the Constitution of India.

Codes

1 (A) and (R) are right and (R) is the correct explanation of (A)
2 (A) and (R) are right, but (R) is not the right explanation of (A)
3 (A) is right, but (R) is wrong
4 Both (A) and (R) are wrong

Ans. *(3)*

Exp. (A) is right, but (R) is wrong.

Article 124 of the Constitution of India lays down the provisions for establishment and constitution of Supreme Court. This article has only mentioned an age for compulsory retirement. However, the article has not fixed the tenure of a judge of the Supreme Court

According to Article 124(3):

"A person shall not be qualified for appointment as a Judge of the Supreme Court unless he is a citizen of India and

(a) has been for at least five years a Judge of a High Court or of two or more such Courts in succession; or
(b) has been for at least ten years an advocate of a High Court or of two or more such Courts in succession; or
(c) is, in the opinion of the President, a distinguished jurist."

The Article has not prescribed a minimum age for appointment as a Judge of the Supreme Court of India. Therefore, Assertion is right.

Original Jurisdiction of Supreme Court is dealt within Article 131. Article 132 deals with Appellate jurisdiction of the Supreme Court in appeals from High Courts in certain cases. Therefore, Reason is wrong.

5 In which one of the following cases, the Supreme Court of India had invalidated a Constitutional Amendment for non-compliance with the procedure contained in the provision to Clause (2) of Article-368 ?

1 Kihoto Hollohan Vs. Zachilhu and others
2 Keshavanand Bharati Vs. State of Kerala
3 Golaknath Vs. State of Punjab
4 State of West Bengal Vs. Union of India

Ans. *(1)*

Exp. In Kihoto Hollohan Vs. Zachilhu and others the Supreme Court of India had invalidated a Constitutional Amendment for non-compliance with the procedure contained in the provision to Clause (2) of Article-368.

In this case, it was by majority held that the Amendment in terms and in effect brings about a change in the operation and effect of the Articles 136 and 226 and thus requires ratification under the Clause (2) of the Article 368.

6 If the President of India is satisfied that a grave emergency exists whereby the security of India or any part of the territory thereof is threatened, whether by war or external aggression or armed rebellion, he may by proclamation, make a declaration to that effect. Here the 'satisfaction' of the President of India means

1 The personal satisfaction of the President of India
2 The personal satisfaction of the Prime Minister and all the Council of Ministers and informing to the President of India
3 The decision of the Union Cabinet that such a proclamation may be issued, has been communicated to him in writing
4 The decision of the Union Cabinet, that such a proclamation may be issued, has been communicated to him in writing along with 2/3rd Parliament Member's signature

Ans. *(3)*

Exp. If the President of India is satisfied that a grave emergency exists whereby the security of India or any part of the territory thereof is threatened, whether by war or external aggression or armed rebellion, he may by proclamation, make a declaration to that effect. Here the 'satisfaction' of the President of India means the decision of the Union Cabinet that such a proclamation may be issued, has been communicated to him in writing.

Article 352 lays down the provision for proclamation of national emergency. Article 352 (1) states "If the President is satisfied that a grave emergency exists whereby the security of India or of any part of the territory thereof is threatened, whether by war or external aggression or armed rebellion, he may, by Proclamation, made a declaration to that effect in respect of the whole of India or of such part of the territory thereof as may be specified in the proclamation.

Article 352 (3) of the Indian Constitution says, "The President shall not issue a Proclamation under clause (I) or a Proclamation varying such Proclamation unless the decision of the Union Cabinet that such a Proclamation may be issued has been communicated to him in writing."

7 Match List I with List II and select the correct answer using the codes given below.

List I	List II
A. Hari Krishna Bhargav Vs. Union of India	I. Conditional legislation
B. Godfrey Philips India Ltd. Vs. State of UP	II. Principles of interpretation to avoid overlapping
C. KC Gajapati Narayan Deo Vs. State of Odisha	III. Power of Parliament to levy taxes on income other than agricultural income
D. In Re : The Delhi Laws Act	IV. Colourable Legislation

Codes

	A	B	C	D		A	B	C	D
1	III	II	IV	I	2	II	III	I	IV
3	III	IV	II	I	4	II	III	IV	I

Ans. (1)

Exp. The correct matching is A-III, B-II, C-IV, D-I.

Hari Krishna Bhargav Vs. Union of India case in related to Power of Parliament to levy taxes on income other than agricultural income. In this case, the court held that the Parliament has by Article 246 read with Entry 82 in List I of the Seventh Schedule Power to levy "taxes on income other than agricultural income".

Godfrey Phillips India Ltd. Vs. State of UP case is related to Principles of interpretation to avoid overlapping. In this case, the court held that there should be no overlapping in the taxable events specified in taxing entries in the Constitution, and the Court should adopt an interpretation which does not allow any kind of overlapping.

KC Gajapati Narayan Deo Vs. State of Odisha case is related to Colourable Legislation. In this case, the court held that the doctrine of colourable legislation depends upon the competency of the legislature to enact that law, the procedure followed and not merely on the motive of the body in passing such law. The maxim asserts, "You cannot do indirectly what you cannot do directly."

In Re : The Delhi Laws Act case is related to Conditional legislation. In this case, the court held that essential delegations cannot be delegated by the legislature in any condition. This case laid down that because of the difference in the Constitution, the British model of delegated legislation cannot be implemented in India. This case defined the scope of delegated legislation.

8 "The task of social engineering is to build as efficient structure of the society as possible with minimum friction and waste." This statement is of

1 Kelsen
2 Roscoe Pound
3 Savigny
4 Karl Marx

Ans. (2)

Exp. The above given statement was given by Roscoe Pound.

Roscoe Pound was one of the greatest leaders of the sociological school of jurisprudence. American Jurist Roscoe Pound is considered as the father of 'Sociological School' of jurisprudence and is credited with the theory of 'Social Engineering' as a purpose of law.

9 Ratio decidendi may be defined as

1 Statement of law applied to the legal problems disclosed by facts
2 Finding of material facts, direct and inferential, based on earlier case law
3 The rule of law which others regard as being of binding authority
4 All of the above

Ans. (4)

Exp. All the given statements are true.

Ratio decidendi means 'the rule in a decision'. This is a crucial part of the understanding of the way in which the common law works. 'Ratio decidendi' can be defined as statement of law applied to the legal problems disclosed by facts which includes finding of material facts, direct and inferential, based on earlier case law. It is the rule of law which others regard as being of binding authority.

10 Which one of the following groups indicate the four sanctions as enumerated by Bentham for various kinds of pleasure and pain ?

1 Physical, Moral, Ethical and Political
2 Physical, Political, Moral and Religious
3 Moral, Social, Legal and Political
4 Legal, Ethical, Moral and Social

Ans. (2)

Exp. Bentham in his book, 'An Introduction to the Principles of Morals and Legislation' cites the four sanctions from which pleasure and pain usually flows as Physical, Political, Moral and Religious.

'An Introduction to the Principles of Morals and Legislation,' by Jeremy Bentham, was first printed in 1780 then revised until 1823. Bentham used this text to outline a process of moral decision-making that depends only on the consequences of actions.

11 The three defects in the simple social structure of primary rules as enunciated by Hart are

1 Their inadequacy, immobility and efficiency
2 Their uncertainty, static and inefficiency
3 Their mobility, easiness and simplicity
4 Their abnormality, violability and unsoundness

Ans. (2)

Exp. The three defects in the simple social structure of primary rules as enunciated by Hart are their uncertainty, static and inefficiency.

In Hart's view, a society might live only by primary rules of obligation, but will suffer from three defects: there will be uncertainty as to what the rules are and their scope; the rules will be static insofar as there is no means of deliberately eliminating or introducing rules and, the social pressure by which rules are maintained will be inefficient because there is no agency for finally settling disputes over violations of the primary rules.

12 Match List I with List II and select the correct answer using the codes given below.

List I (Book)	List II (Author)
A. The Concept of Law	I. Gray
B. The Nature and Sources of the Law	II. Julius Stone
C. Some Reflections on Jurisprudence	III. Buckland
D. The Province and Function of Law	IV. HLA Hart

Codes

	A	B	C	D
1	IV	I	III	II
2	IV	II	I	III
3	IV	I	II	III
4	I	III	IV	II

Ans. (1)

Exp. The correct matching is A-IV, B-I, C-III, D-II.

The book *The Concept of Law* was written by HLA Hart in 1961. It is compiled of several lectures on legal positivism that Hart delivered in 1952 on the subjects of sovereignty, legal validity, etc. The book addresses a number of traditional jurisprudential topics such as the nature of law, whether laws are rules, and the relation between law and morality.

The book *The Nature and Sources of the Law* was written by Gray in 1909. The book is divided into two parts which respectively look at 'Nature' and 'Sources'. In Part I, Gray warns that the study of jurisprudence, in isolation, could lead to dogmatism. Rather, he advocates the structure offered by common law with its reliance on flexible interpretations of statutes, the use of all relevant cultural inputs and a highly adaptable approach to the resolution of disputes. Gray, in Part II, turns his attention to sources of the law, and begins with statutes. Here, he asserts that judges are the ones who actually turn into law, going against the conventional scholarship that judges merely interprets statutes. He also extensively examines the influence of tradition and the common law.

The book *Some Reflections on Jurisprudence* was written by Buckland in 1945. Buckland was a primary supporter of the analytical school of law and the same has also been highlighted in this book.

The book *The Province and Function of Law* was written by Julius Stone in 1946. This study is also called the "greatest juristic volume of the twentieth century."

13 Which one of the following is not a theory of the nature of 'Legal Persons' ?

1 Purpose Theory　　2 Fiction Theory
3 Interest Theory　　4 Bracket Theory

Ans. (3)

Exp. Interest Theory is not a theory of the nature of 'Legal Persons'.

Interest Theory is a theory of function of legal rights. According to this, the function of a legal right is to further the right-holder's interests. Major exponents of Interest theory of legal rights are Bentham, Ihering, Austin, etc.

There are five principal theories, which are used to explain corporate personality, namely the Fiction theory, Realist theory, the Purpose theory, the Bracket theory and the Concession theory.

14 "International law must be continuously developed by revision in content, expansion of scope and improvement of the means of securing compliance, so that it is kept in accordance with the changing needs of the international community." This statement is made by

1 Starke　　2 Edward Collins
3 L Oppenheim　　4 W Friedman

Ans. (2)

Exp. The given statement is made by Edward Collins in his book 'International law in a changing world'.

According to Edward Collins, "International law is a constantly evolving body of norms that are commonly observed by the members of the international community in their relation with one another. These norms confer rights and impose obligation upon the states and to a lesser extent upon international organization and individuals."

15 Which of the following statement(s) is/are not correct ?

I. Decisions or determinations of the organs of International Institution does not find mention in Article-38 of the Statute of the International Court of Justice.
II. West Rand Central Gold Mining Company Ltd. V R is related to general principles of law recognised by civilized states.
III. Frontier Dispute (Burkina Faso Vs. Mali) is a case related to International customs as a source of law.
IV. The importance of the works of the jurists has been stressed by Justice Gray in Barcelona Traction Case.

Codes

1 I, II and III are not correct
2 II, III and IV are not correct
3 III and IV are not correct
4 I, II, III and IV all are not correct

Ans. (2)

Exp. Statements II, III and IV are not correct.

In West Rand Central Gold Mining Company Ltd. V R, the court held that the Sovereign of a conquering State was not liable for the obligations of the conquered, in the absence of stipulation or convention; international law formed part of the law of England to the extent that it had received the common consent of civilised nations. Such rules of international law must be shown to have been actually accepted as binding between nations by satisfactory evidence of international agreement or usage ; that acts of State are not cognisable by the English Courts.

Frontier Dispute (Burkina Faso Vs. Mali), also known as 'upper volta,' is related to the importance of the principles of uti possidetis juris and the intangibility of borders.

Justice Gray, in Barcelona Traction Case, highlighted the importance of the legal problems raised by the allegation, which is at the root of the Belgian claim for reparation, concerning the denials of justice allegedly committed by organs of the Spanish State.

16 Read the following statements and give the correct answer by using the codes given below

Assertion (A) According to the exponents of Monism Theory, law is a unified branch of knowledge, no matter whether it applies on persons or other entities.

Reason (R) In view of the Monistic writers, in the ultimate analysis of the law we find that man is at the root to all laws.

Codes

1 (A) and (R) both are correct and (R) is the correct explanation of (A)
2 (A) and (R) both are correct, but (R) is not the correct explanation of (A)
3 (A) is correct, (R) is wrong
4 (A) is wrong, (R) is correct

Ans. (1)

➲ *Exp.* (A) and (R) both are correct and (R) is the correct explanation of (A).

According to the exponents of Monism Theory, law is a unified branch of knowledge, no matter whether it applies on persons or other entities. As per this theory, man lies at the root of all laws.

The Monism theory maintains that the subject of two systems of law, i.e., International Law and Municipal Law are essentially one as much as the former law is essentially a command binding upon the subjects of the law independent of their will, which is in one case is the state and in the other individuals.

17 Which of the following statement(s) is/are correct ?

I. According to the Constitutive theory of recognition, statehood or the authority of the new government exists as such prior to and independently of recognition.
II. De Jure recognition is by nature provisional and may be made dependent on conditions with which the new entity has to comply.
III. The principle that there is no distinction between de facto and de jure recognition for the purpose of giving effect to the internal acts of the recognised authority was laid down in Luther Vs. Sagar.
IV. De jure recognition is final and once given cannot be withdrawn.

Codes

1 II is correct
2 I, II and III are correct
3 II, III and IV are correct
4 I, II, III and IV all are correct

Ans. (3)

➲ *Exp.* Among the following statements, Statement II, III and IV are correct.

Statement I is incorrect because according to Constitutive Theory, it is the act of recognition alone which creates statehood or which clothes a new government with any authority or status in the international sphere. According to Declaratory theory, statehood or the authority of a new government exists as such prior to and independently of recognition.

18 The principle of self-determination has been incorporated in the Charter of United Nations under

1 Article 2(7) 2 Article 5
3 Article 6 4 Articles 1(2), 55 and 56

Ans. (4)

➲ *Exp.* The principle of self-determination has been incorporated in the Charter of United Nations under Articles 1 (2), 55 and 56.

Article 1(2) of the Charter of United Nations states that to develop friendly relations among nations based on respect for the principle of equal rights and self-determination of people and to take other appropriate measures to strengthen universal peace.

Article 55 states that with a view to the creation of conditions of stability and well-being which are necessary for peaceful and friendly relations among nations based on respect for the principle of equal rights and self-determination of people, the United Nations shall promote:

(i) higher standards of living, full employment, and conditions of economic and social progress and development;
(ii) solutions of international economic, social, health and related problems and international cultural and educational cooperation and
(iii) universal respect for and observance of, human rights and fundamental freedoms for all without distinction as to race, sex, language, or religion.

Article 56 states that all Members pledge themselves to take joint and separate action in co-operation with the organisation for the achievement of the purposes set forth in Article 55.

19 The Commission on Human Rights was replaced by Human Rights Council by the General Assembly vide its Resolution

1 60/251 of 15th March, 2006
2 61/260 of 15th March, 2008
3 60/251 of 20th March, 2006
4 60/251 of 30th March, 2006

Ans. (1)

➲ *Exp.* The Commission on Human Rights was replaced by Human Rights Council by the General. Assembly vide its Resolution 60/251 of 15th March, 2006. The Council is made up of 47 United Nations Member States which are elected by the UN General Assembly.

20 'Sapinda Relationship', which prohibits marriage among Hindus with near relatives on paternal and maternal sides, is based on the principle of

1 Monogamy 2 Endogamy
3 Exogamy 4 Polygamy

Ans. (3)

➲ *Exp.* 'Sapinda Relationship', which prohibits marriage among Hindus with near relatives on paternal and maternal sides, is based on the principle of Exogamy.

Exogamy means marrying outside one's community/family. Therefore, marrying within the Sapinda relationship is prohibited thus promoting Exogamy. Under Hindu law, 'Sapinda relationship' extends to 5 generations on the line of ascent of father's side and 3 generations on the line of ascent of mother's side.

21 Match List I with List II under the Hindu Marriage Act, 1955 and select the correct answer with the help of codes given below.

List I	List II
A. Ceremonies for a Hindu marriage	I. Sec. 15
B. Restitution of Conjugal Rights	II. Sec. 7
C. Remarriage of divorced persons	III. Sec. 16
D. Legitimacy of Children	IV. Sec. 9

Codes

	A	B	C	D		A	B	C	D
1	I	III	II	IV	2	II	IV	I	III
3	IV	II	III	I	4	III	IV	II	I

***Ans.* (2)**

Exp. The correct matching is A-II, B-IV, C-I, D-III.

Provision for *ceremonies for a Hindu marriage* is stated under Section 7 of the Hindu Marriage Act.

Provision for *Restitution of Conjugal Rights* is stated under Section 9 of the Hindu Marriage Act.

Provision for *remarriage of divorced persons* is stated under Section 15 of the Hindu Marriage Act.

Provision for *legitimacy of children* is stated under Section 16 of the Hindu Marriage Act.

22 Read the following statements and answer with the help of the codes given below : The guilt theory of divorce, on the one hand, implies a guilty party and on the other, it implies that the other party is innocent. In view of this which of the following is/are correct ?

I. If cruelty is provoked, divorce will be refused.

II. If innocent party condones the acts of the guilty party, no divorce can be granted.

III. If both parties were guilty, divorce would not be granted to either.

IV. Unreasonable delay in filing petition is no bar for the relief of divorce.

Codes

1 I and III are correct 2 II and III are correct

3 I, II and III are correct 4 III and IV are correct

***Ans.* (3)**

Exp. Statements I, II, III are correct.

It is a settled principle that a party shall not be allowed to take benefit from its wrong. Hence, if cruelty is provoked then it is not a ground of divorce for the party alleging cruelty.

If innocent party condones that acts of the guilty party, no divorce can be guaranteed. According to guilty theory of divorce, condonation acts as a bar for granting the relief of divorce.

Guilt theory requires existence of one guilt party and one innocent party, if both parties are guilty then according to this theory none is entitled for the refief of divorce.

Statement IV is incorrect because any unnecessary or improper delay in instituting the proceeding is a bar to relief of divorce. Section 23 of the Hindu Marriage Act states that the court shall decree such relief if the court is satisfied that there has not been any unnecessary or improper delay in instituting the proceeding.

23 Match List I with List II and select the correct answer using the codes given below.

List I (Veda)	List II (Deals with)
A. Yajurveda	I. Praise of forces of nature
B. Samaveda	II. Magic, Spell and Incantation
C. Atharvaveda	III. Rituals
D. Rigveda	IV. Dance

Codes

	A	B	C	D		A	B	C	D
1	I	II	IV	III	2	II	IV	I	III
3	IV	II	III	I	4	III	IV	II	I

***Ans.* (4)**

Exp. The correct matching is A-III, B-IV, C-II, D-I.

Yajurveda deals with rituals. Yajurveda is about 'Knowledge of the Sacrificial formulas', for liturgy. It is the Veda primarily of prose mantras for worship rituals. Yajurveda is one of the four Vedas, and one of the scriptures of Hinduism.

Samaveda deals with dance. Samaveda is about 'Knowledge of the Melodies', for chanting. The Samaveda, is the Veda of melodies and chants. It is an ancient Vedic Sanskrit text, and part of the scriptures of Hinduism. One of the four Vedas, it is a liturgical text which consists of 1,875 verses.

Atharvaveda deals with magic spell and incantation. Atharvaveda is about 'Knowledge of the Magic formulas', named after a kind of group of priests. The Atharvaveda is the "knowledge storehouse of atharvaas, the procedures for everyday life". The text is the fourth Veda, but has been a late addition to the Vedic scriptures of Hinduism. The language of the Atharvaveda is different from Vedic Sanskrit, preserving pre Vedic Indo-European archaisms. It is a collection of 730 hymns with about 6,000 mantras, divided into 20 books.

Rigveda deals with praises of forces of nature. Rigveda is about 'Knowledge of the Hymns of Praise', for recitation. The Rigveda or Rig Veda is an ancient Indian collection of Vedic Sanskrit hymns (suktas). It is one of the four sacred canonical Hindu texts known as the Vedas. The Rigveda is the oldest known Vedic Sanskrit text.

24 Which of the following statement(s) is/are correct in relation to 'muta' marriage?

I. It is a temporary marriage.

II. It is recognised under Sunni law.

III. It is recognised under Shia law.

IV. It is a marriage for a fixed period.

Codes
1 I, III and IV are correct
2 II, III and IV are correct
3 Only II is correct
4 All are correct

Ans. *(1)*

Exp. Statements I, III and IV are correct.

Muta marriage is a temporary marriage for a fixed period which is recognised under Shia law.

Statement II is incorrect because muta marriage is recognised under Shia law and not by Sunni law.

25 Read Assertion (A) and Reason (R) and answer using the codes given below.

Assertion (A) The Shariat Act, 1937 makes Muslim law applicable expressly to all Muslims.

Reason (R) The Act has abrogated almost all the customs (except relating to agricultural land) applicable to Muslims.

Codes
1 (A) is right, but (R) is wrong
2 Both (A) and (R) are wrong
3 (R) is right, but (A) is wrong
4 Both (A) and (R) are right and (R) is the correct reason of (A)

Ans. *(4)*

Exp. Both (A) and (R) are right and (R) is the correct reason of (A).

The Shariat Act, 1937 is an Act to make provision for the application of the Muslim Personal Law (Shariat) to all Muslims in India. The Act has abrogated almost all the customs (except relating to agricultural land) applicable to Muslims.

26 The remedy of Restitution of Conjugal Rights has its roots in
1 Jewish Law
2 French Law
3 English Law
4 Indian Law

Ans. *(1)*

Exp. The remedy of Restitution of Conjugal Rights is a new notion in Indian matrimonial jurisprudence that finds its origin in the Jewish laws.

The remedy of Restitution was unknown to Hindu law till the British introduced it in the name of social reforms.

27 Read Assertion (A) and Reason (R) and answer using the codes given below.

Assertion (A) A juvenile delinquent may have physical capacity to commit crime, while he has no contractual capacity to do so.

Reason (R) According to Section-11 of the Indian Contract Act, a juvenile has no contractual capacity to commit crime.

Codes
1 Both (A) and (R) are right and (R) is correct answer for (A)
2 Both (A) and (R) are wrong
3 (A) is wrong, but (R) is right
4 Both (A) and (R) are right, but (R) is not correct answer for (A)

Ans. *(2)*

Exp. Both (A) and (R) are wrong.

According to Section 11 of the Contract Act, every person is competent to contract who is of majority according to the law to which he is subject and who is of sound mind and is not disqualified from contracting by any law to which he is subject. Since both (A) and (R) are in contradiction to this. Section 11 of the Indian Contract Act deals with a minor's capacity to contract. It does not deals with the capacity to commit crime.

28 "Consideration means a reasonable, equivalent or other valuable benefit passed on by the transferor to the transferee. Similarly, when the word 'consideration' was qualified by the word 'adequate', it makes the consideration stronger so as to make it sufficient and valuable having regard to the facts, circumstances and necessities of the case." Above Principle was laid down in
1 Sonia Bhatia Vs. State of UP
2 LIC of India Vs. Pushpa P Mansukhani
3 Dipraich Sugar Mills Ltd. Vs. Mazdoor Union
4 ABC Laminart Pvt. Ltd. Vs. AP Agencies, Salem

Ans. *(1)*

Exp. In the case of Sonia Bhatia Vs. State of UP, the court held that "consideration means a reasonable equivalent or other valuable benefit passed on by the promisor to the promisee or by the transferor to the transferee. Similarly, when the word 'consideration' is qualified by the word 'adequate', it makes consideration stronger so as to make it sufficient and valuable having regard to the facts, circumstances and necessities of the case."

29 Which of the following statements is right ?
1 An agreement not to do an impossible act in itself is void
2 An agreement to do a possible act is void
3 An agreement to do an act impossible in itself is void
4 A contract to do an act, which after the contract is made, becomes impossible, or, by reason of some event which the promisor could not prevent to be unlawful, becomes valid, when the act becomes impossible or unlawful

Ans. *(3)*

Exp. Statement 3 is right.

Section 56 states that an agreement to do an act impossible in itself is void. It also states that a contract to do an act which, after the contract is made, becomes impossible, or, by reason of some event which the promisor could not prevent, unlawful, becomes void when the act becomes impossible or unlawful.

30 Match List I with List II and select the correct answer using the codes given below.

	List I		List II
A.	Remoteness of damage	I.	Chief Secretary, State of Gujarat Vs. Kothari and Associates
B.	Proof of loss to be given to claim special damages	II.	Madras Railways Co. Vs. Govind Rau
C.	Loss of profit is special loss	III.	Karsandas H. Thacker Vs. Saran Engg. Co. Ltd.
D.	Consequences of delays in transit	IV.	Union of India Vs. Steel Stock Holders

Codes

	A	B	C	D		A	B	C	D
1	I	II	IV	III	2	II	I	III	IV
3	II	III	I	IV	4	IV	I	III	II

Ans. *(2)*

Exp. The correct matching is A-II, B-I, C-III, D-IV.

Madras Railways Co. Vs. Govind Rau case is related to remoteness of damage. The court held that"recovery of a sum on account of estimated profits by the plaintiff were too remote and do not fall within the purview of Section 73 of the Contract Act".

Chief Secretary, State of Gujarat Vs. Kothari and Associates case mentions the proof of loss to be given to claim special damages. It was held that it is essential that a person who claims damages for breach of a contract should have performed or was ready to perform his part of the obligations arising under the contract. It is the fundamental principle of damages for breach of contract that these are awarded to place the injured party in the same position in which he would have been, had he not sustained the injury of which he complains. Hence, the damages must be commensurate with the injury sustained.

Karsandas H. Thacker Vs. Saran Engg. Co. Ltd. case mention the Loss of profit is special loss. It was held that on a breach of contract by one party, the other party is entitled to receive compensation for any loss caused to him which naturally arose in the usual course of business from such breach or which the party knew when they made the contract to be likely to result from the breach of it. Remote or indirect loss or damage sustained by reason of the breach will not entitle the party to receive any compensation on that score.

Union of India Vs. Steel Stockholders case mention the consequence of delays in transit. The court held that it is clear that there is no question of Section 73 of the Contract Act overriding the provisions of the Interest Act, because in the instant case the Interest Act has no application at all in as much as no interest is claimed by the plaintiff at all but interest has been used as a measure to determine the compensation which the plaintiff could seek against the appellant for its negligence in causing inordinate delay in the delivery of the goods.

31 Which of the following aspects are the parts of undue influence?

I. Inability to dominate will of other.

II. A party unduly influencing and another party being unduly influenced are on equal footing.

III. A relationship involving trust and confidence.

IV. In a relationship, one party is a person in mental distress.

Codes

1	I and II	2	II and III
3	III and IV	4	I and IV

Ans. *(3)*

Exp. Only III and IV are correct.

Section 16 of ICA states that 'a contract is said to be induced by undue influence where the will of the party consenting is able to be dominated by the other one due to the existence of the relation subsisting between them.'

One party influences the other while the contract is formed to get an unfair advantage over the other. It further qualifies that a person is able to dominate the will of the other if he:

- Has a real or apparent authority arising out of fiduciary relations (relationship of trust) between them, or
- Forms the contract with a person whose mental capacity, due to illness or age or due to mental distress is temporarily or permanently affected.

32 Which of the following statements are wrong?

I. Fraud renders a contract void.

II. Misrepresentation renders a contract voidable.

III. Misrepresentation is more or less an intentional wrong, whereas fraud may be quite innocent.

IV. Damages for loss caused by innocent misrepresentation are assessed on the same principles as in the case of a deliberate fraud.

Codes

1	I and III	2	II and IV
3	I and IV	4	I and II

Ans. *(1)*

Exp. Statements I and III are wrong.

As per Section 19 of the Indian Contract Act, 1872, "when consent to an agreement is caused by coercion, fraud or misrepresentation, the agreement is a contract voidable at the option of the party whose consent was so caused."

A misrepresentation is a false statement of fact made by one party to another, which, whilst not being a term of the contract, induces the other party to enter the contract. Fraud can never be unintentional while misrepresentation can.

33 Which one of the following statements is correct in relation to the law of torts in India ?

1 It is based on morality that no one has a right to injure or harm other intentionally or even innocently

2 It is a civil wrong for which remedy is a common law action for liquidated damages

3 It is based on law which in the constitutional context means judicially developed equity, covers everything which is covered by a statute

4 It is an act and not omission suffered by a determinate person

Ans. (1)

➲ *Exp.* Statement 1 is correct in relation to the law of torts in India.

Statement 2, 3 and 4 are incorrect.

A tort is a civil wrong for which the legal remedy is an action brought by means of civil proceedings by or on behalf of the injured party for damages or some other legal remedy desired by the person who has suffered the wrong.

The law of torts is based on the principles of 'common law.' Law of torts generally covers all those civil wrongs which are not covered by any statute for the time being.

Tort is an act or omission suffered by another. It needs not necessarily be a determinate person.

34 Match List I with List II and select the correct answer using the codes given below.

List I (Defences in Tort)	List II (Related Cases)
A. Volenti non fit injuria	I. Olga Tellis Vs. Municipal Corporation, Bombay
B. Judicial acts	II. Samira Kohli Vs. Prabha Manchanda
C. Acts of State	III. Anwar Hussain Vs. Ajoy Kumar
D. Necessity	IV. Vinod Kumar Shantilal Gosalia Vs. Gangadhar Narsinghadas Agarwal

Codes

	A	B	C	D		A	B	C	D
1	II	III	IV	I	2	II	I	IV	III
3	IV	III	I	II	4	I	II	III	IV

Ans. (1)

➲ *Exp.* The correct matching is A-II, B-III, C-IV, D-I.

Samira Kohli Vs. Prabha Manchanda case deal with the maxim Volenti non fit injuria. In this case, a doctor removed the uterus and ovaries of a woman when she was still under general anaesthesia and without any medical emergency. In this case, the court mainly discussed the importance of the consent of patient and the actions that can be initiated within the purview of the given consent.

Anwar Hussain Vs. Ajoy Kumar case deal with maxim Judicial acts. In this case, the court held that Judges enjoy absolute protection under the Judges (Protection) Act, 1985. This protection is not just available to the sitting Judge but also to an Ex-Judge in respect of the actions taken or words spoken by him while discharging his official or judicial functions.

Vinod Kumar Shantilal Gosalia Vs. Gangadhar Narsingdas Agarwal case is related to maxim Acts of State. It was held by the Court that the mere fact that the old laws were continued did not mean that the rights under those laws were recognised by the Government of India and, therefore, the petitioner was not entitled to seek recognition of his import licences from the Government of India.

Olga Tellis Vs. Municipal Corporation, Bombay case deals with the maxim of Necessity. In this case, the court held that if the State were obliged to provide citizens with adequate means of subsistence and the right to work, it would be quite irreproachable to exclude the right to subsistence from the content of the right to life. The State cannot, by positive action, be obliged to provide adequate means of subsistence or work to the citizens. However, anyone deprived of their right to a means of subsistence, except in accordance with the just and fair procedure established by law, may challenge deprivation as a violation of the right to life conferred by Article 21.

35 The police officers failed to observe the provisions of UP Police Regulations in taking care of the gold seized. The injury had been committed by the employees of the state during the course of its employment, but the employment was in special category of sovereign power, so the claim was not sustainable. It was held by the Supreme Court in

1 Mohammad Murad Vs. Govt. of UP

2 Kasturilal Ralia Ram Jain Vs. State of UP

3 State of UP Vs. Hindustan Lever Ltd

4 State of UP Vs. Tulsiram

Ans. (2)

➲ *Exp.* In Kasturilal Ralia Ram Jain Vs. State of UP, the court held that the police officers failed to observe the provisions of UP Police Regulations in taking care of the gold seized. The injury had been committed by the employees of the state during the course of its employment, but the employment was in special category of sovereign power, so the claim was not sustainable.

The Supreme Court in this case has followed the rule laid down in PSO Steam Navigation Case by distinguishing Sovereign and non-Sovereign functions of the state and held that the act of police officers is a Sovereign sct, therefore the state is not liable.

36 In which of the following cases the Supreme Court of India applied the principle of absolute liability?

I. MC Mehta Vs. Union of India

II. Charan Lal Sahu Vs. Union of India

III. Indian Council for Enviro Legal Action Vs. Union of India

IV. MC Mehta Vs. State of MP

Codes

1 I, II, III and IV 2 II, III and IV

3 III and IV 4 I, II and III

Ans. (4)

➲ *Exp.* Principle of absolute liability is followed in case of MC Mehta Vs. Union of India, Charan Lal Sahu Vs. Union of India and Indian Council for Enviro Legal Action Vs. Union of India.

Under the principle of absolute liability, a party/company in a hazardous industry cannot claim any exemption. It has to mandatorily pay compensation, whether or not the disaster was caused by its negligence.

37 What remoteness of damage mean in relation to liability of defendant?

1 The defendant is not liable for all direct consequences of the tortuous acts if he could foresee them
2 Forseeability is no test of remoteness of damages
3 Liable in Law only for consequences which are not remote
4 Directness of the consequences is the only test for the remoteness of the damages

Ans. (3)

Exp. The principle of remoteness of damages states that the damage must be direct and the natural result of the consequence of the act of the defendant. Otherwise, the plaintiff will not succeed. Tortuous liability exists for all direct and reasonably foreseeable consequences of tortuous act.

38 Andhra Pradesh State Road Transport Corporation Vs. K Hemlatha and Municipal Corporation Greater Bombay Vs. Laxman Iyer are important cases decided by the Supreme Court on the rule of

1 Act of God
2 Contributory Negligence
3 Nuisance
4 Trespass

Ans. (2)

Exp. Andhra Pradesh State Road Transport Corporation Vs. K Hemlatha and Municipal Corporation Greater Bombay Vs. Laxman Iyer are important cases decided by the Supreme Court on the rule of Contributory Negligence.

In the above cases, the court has held that where a person suffers injury, partly due to the negligence on the part of another person or persons, and partly as a result of his own negligence, then the negligence on the part of the injured which contributed to the accident is referred to as his Contributory Negligence.

39 Read the following principle "There is always an imposed duty on a person to act on moral necessity to preserve one's life, yet there may be justifiable occasions of causing harm on innocent persons." In the light of the above, in which of the following circumstances the accused can claim doctrine of self-preservation under the provisions of Section 81 of IPC?

1 When necessity is pleaded as a means of defence under Sections 96 to 106
2 Self-preservation is not an absolute necessity, so killing the weaker is justifiable by the stronger
3 Arresting a drunken person moving in great danger at a public place
4 When there is no choice of evil affecting the accused

Ans. (3)

Exp. The accused can claim the doctrine of self-preservation under the provisions of Section 81 of IPC in the case of arresting a drunk person moving in great danger at a public place.

Section 81 of the IPC states "Nothing is an offence merely by reason of its being done with the knowledge that it is likely to cause harm, if it be done without any criminal intention to cause harm, and in good faith for the purpose of preventing or avoiding other harm to person or property."

In the given scenario, a drunken person moving in great danger in public place is likely to cause harm to himself or to others, hence arresting such a person to prevent any such harm entails protection of Section 81 IPC.

40 In the absence of any cogent definition of unsoundness of mind, the world wide acceptance of its equivalent to insanity was propounded by

1 Stephan
2 Harris
3 Kenny
4 Davis

Ans. (1)

Exp. In the absence of any cogent definition of unsoundness of mind, the world wide acceptance of its equivalent to insanity was propounded by Stephan.

According to Stephan, the law recognises nothing but incapacity to realise the nature of the act and presumes that where a man's mind or his faculties of ratiocination are sufficiently dim to apprehend what he is doing, he must always be presumed to intend the consequence of the action he takes.

41 The underlying principle covering the law on 'consent' is based on absolute and unconditional prohibition on the gravity of the offence relating to

1 Simple hurt
2 Death
3 Theft from an unlocked house
4 Submission for detaining indecent liberties

Ans. (2)

Exp. The underlying principle covering the law on 'consent' is based on absolute and unconditional prohibition on the gravity of the offence relating to death.

42 The right of private defence is not allowed in which of the facts leading to

1 The death was consequence of the assault
2 More harm was done than necessary
3 When the fact is clearly based on conjectures
4 When the fact reveals about imminent danger to self or property

Ans. (2)

Exp. The right of private defence is not allowed when more harm was done than necessary.

IPC Section 96 to 106 of the Penal Code states the law relating to the right of private defence of person and property. The provisions contained in these sections give authority to a man to use necessary force against an assailant or wrong-doer for the purpose of protecting one's own body and property and also another's body and property when immediate aid from the state machinery is not readily available and in doing so, he is not answerable in law for his deeds.

43 When a person tries to escape from lawful custody while being taken to a Magistrate to furnish security for good behaviour could be punished under the provision of

1 Section 224 of IPC 2 Section 225 of IPC
3 Section 225A of IPC 4 Section 225B of IPC

Ans. (4)

Exp. When a person tries to escape from lawful custody while being taken to a Magistrate to furnish security for good behaviour could be punished under Section 225B of IPC.

Section 225B of the IPC states the punishment for resistance or obstruction to lawful apprehension, or escape or rescue in cases not otherwise provided for.

It states that whoever, in any case not provided for in Section 224 or Section 225 or in any other law for the time being in force, intentionally offers any resistance or illegal obstruction to the lawful apprehension of himself or of any other person, or escapes or attempts to escape from any custody in which he is lawfully detained, or rescues or attempts to rescue any other person from any custody in which that person is lawfully detained, shall be punished with imprisonment of either description for a term which may extend to six months, or with fine, or with both.

44 The distinction between intentional killing in hot blood and intentional killing when the blood was cool may be inferred through

1 Provocation 2 Self-control
3 Passion 4 Resentment

Ans. (1)

Exp. The distinction between intentional killing in hot blood and intentional killing when the blood was cool may be inferred through Provocation.

Provocation can be defined as conduct by which one induces another to do a particular deed; the act of inducing rage, anger, or resentment in another person that may cause that person to engage in an illegal act. Provocation may be alleged as a defense to certain crimes in order to lessen the severity of the penalty normally imposed.

45 Read Assertion (A) and Reason (R) and answer using the codes given below.

Assertion (A) In an illegal termination of workman, the reinstatement of workman in service does not appear to be an acceptable option in all cases. The monetary compensation may sufficiently meet the ends of justice.

Reason (R) The compensation in lieu of reinstatement is the normal rule.

Codes

1 Both (A) and (R) are true and (R) is the correct explanation of (A)
2 (A) and (R) are true, but (R) is not the correct explanation of (A)
3 (A) is true, but (R) is false
4 (A) is false, but (R) is true

Ans. (1)

Exp. Both (A) and (R) are true and (R) is the correct explanation of (A)

In an illegal termination of workman, the reinstatement of workman in service does not appear to be an acceptable option in all cases. Clause (b) of Section 25F of the Industrial Disputes Act 1947 says that while effecting retrenchment of the workmen, it is obligatory on the part of the employer to pay retrenchment compensation at the rate of 15 days wages (for every completed year) to be calculated at the last drawn salary of an employee.

The calculation of compensation is to be based from the date of appointment and in case an employee has completed 240 days, he will be entitled to 15 days retrenchment compensation besides one month's notice or salary in lieu thereof as if he has worked for one year. 240 days includes Sundays or off days as well as festivals or national holidays.

The monetary compensation may sufficiently meet the ends of justice. The compensation in lieu of reinstatement is the normal rule.

46 An arbitration award is binding on

1 All parties to the dispute
2 All the workmen employed on the date of dispute and subsequent to the dispute
3 The parties to the arbitration agreement
4 All parties summoned to appear as parties to the dispute

Ans. (3)

Exp. An arbitration award is binding on all the parties to the arbitration agreement.

Section 35 of the Arbitration and Conciliation Act, states that an arbitral award shall be final and binding on the parties and persons claiming under them respectively.

Arbitration is the submission of a dispute to an unbiased third person designated by the parties to the controversy, who agree in advance to comply with the award a decision to be issued after a hearing at which both parties have an opportunity to be heard.

47 The Supreme Court referred the ILO instruments to reiterate the workers' participation in the industrial process as enshrined in the Constitution and other labour legislations in one of the following case

1 Chandra Bhavan Boarding and Lodging, Bangalore Vs. State of Mysore
2 Monogram Mills Ltd. Vs. State of Gujarat
3 University of Delhi Vs. Ramnath
4 KVS Ravi Vs. Bangalore Metropolitan Transport Corporation

Ans. (2)

Exp. In Monogram Mills Ltd. Vs. State of Gujarat, the Supreme Court referred the ILO instruments to reiterate the workers' participation in the industrial process as enshrined in the Constitution and other labour legislations.

It was held that if the impugned legislation, in pith and substance, relates to subjects which are within the competence of the State Legislature, the fact that there is an incidental encroachment on matters which are the subject- matter of Entries in List-I, would not affect the legislative competence of the State Legislature to pass the impugned legislation.

48 Where an undertaking is closed for any reason whatsoever, every workman is entitled to compensation if such workman has been in the continuous service

1 for not less than 90 days
2 for not less than 6 months
3 for not less than one year
4 for not less than two years

Ans. (3)

Exp. Section 25FFF in the Industrial Disputes Act states that where an undertaking is closed down for any reason whatsoever, every workman who has been in continuous service for not less than one year in that undertaking immediately before such closure shall, subject to the provisions of sub-section (2), be entitled to notice and compensation in accordance with the provisions of Section 25F, as if the workman had been retrenched.

49 "A strike could be legal or illegal and an illegal strike could be a justified one" was opined by Justice VR Krishna Iyer in one of the following case.

1 Bharat Kumar K Palicha Vs. State of Kerala
2 Gujarat Steel Tubes Vs. Its Majdoor Sabha
3 Monogram Mills Ltd. Vs. State of Gujarat
4 University of Delhi Vs. Ramnath

Ans. (2)

Exp. "A strike could be legal or illegal and an illegal strike could be a justified one" was opined by Justice VR Krishna Iyer in Gujarat Steel Tubes Vs. Its Mazdoor Sabha case. He further stated that the right to strike is recognized by the concept of social justice and industrial jurisprudence. Further, Justice Krishna Iyer had opined that "a strike could be legal or illegal and even an illegal strike could be a justified one in this case and it is thus beyond doubt that the Industrial Disputes Act, 1947 recognizes a right to strike."

50 A Seven Judges Bench of the Supreme Court exhaustively considered the scope of the definition 'Industry' and laid down the 'Triple test' in one of the following case.

1 State of Bombay Vs. Hospital Mazdoor Sabha
2 University of Delhi Vs. Ramnath
3 Management of Safdurjung Hospital, Delhi Vs. Kuldip Singh
4 Bangalore Water Supply Vs. A Rajappa

Ans. (4)

Exp. In the landmark judgment of Bangalore Water Supply Vs. A. Rajappa, the Supreme Court exhaustively considered the scope of 'Industry' and laid down the 'triple test', to ascertain what an industry is.

Section 2(j) of Industrial Disputes Act, 1947 gives the definition of industry, which was elaborated by the Supreme Court in this case by giving the term 'industry' a wide scope and according to it any activity will be industry if it satisfies the 'Triple test'.

It was stated that where there is a (i) systematic activity, (ii) organised by co-operation between employer and employee, (iii) for the production and/or distribution of goods and services calculated to satisfy human wants and wishes, prima facie, there is an 'industry' in that enterprise.

PAPER III

1 Which of the following statements are correct?

I. The 'Basic Structure' of the Constitution of India cannot be amended.
II. Parliamentary Democracy is included in the list of 'Basic structure' of the Constitution of India.
III. According to convention of Parliamentary Democracy, the Prime Minister has to be from the House of People.
IV. Article 83 of the Constitution of India deals with the duration of Houses of Parliament.

Codes

1 I, II and III are correct
2 I, III and IV are correct
3 II, III and IV are correct
4 All are correct

Ans. (4)

Exp. All the given statements are correct.

In the Kesavananda Bharati case, it was held that Parliament can amend any part of the constitution as long as it did not alter or amend the basic structure of the constitution.

The judgement listed some basic structures of the constitution as: Supremacy of the Constitution, Unity and sovereignty of India, Democratic and republican form of government, Federal character of the Constitution, Secular character of the Constitution, Parliamentary Democracy, Separation of power, Individual freedom Over time, many other features have also been added to this list of basic structural features.

A Prime Minister must be a member of the Lok Sabha or the Rajya Sabha. If the person choosen as the Prime

Minister is neither a member of the Lok Sabha nor the Rajya Sabha at the time of selection, he/she must become a member of either of the houses within six months.

Article 83 of the Constitution of India deals with the duration of Houses of Parliament. Rajya Sabha is a permanent house and is not subject to dissolution. However, one-third members of Rajya Sabha retire after every second year. A member who's elected for a full term serves for a period of six years.

2 From the following statements, select the correct answer using the codes given below.

I. In India at the head of the entire judicial system stands the Supreme Court of India.

II. Under the Supreme Court of India stands the high courts of various states.

III. District and Sessions Court functions under the concerned high court.

Codes

1 I and II 2 II and III
3 I and III 4 I, II and III

***Ans.* (4)**

Exp. Statements I, II and III are correct.

In India at the head of the entire judicial system stands the Supreme Court of India. Under the Supreme Court of India stand the high courts of various states. District and Sessions Court functions under the concerned high court. Articles 124 to 147 of the Constitution lay down the composition and jurisdiction of the Supreme Court.

3 Match List I with List II and select the correct answer using codes given below.

List I	List II
A. Article 13	I. Protection in respect of conviction for offences.
B. Article 15	II. Prohibition of traffic in human beings and forced labour.
C. Article 20	III. Prohibition of discrimination on grounds of religion, race, caste, sex or place of birth.
D. Article 23	IV. Laws inconsistent with or in derogation of fundamental rights.

Codes

	A	B	C	D		A	B	C	D
1	IV	II	I	III	2	II	I	IV	III
3	III	II	I	IV	4	IV	III	I	II

***Ans.* (4)**

Exp. The correct matching is A-IV, B-III, C-I, D-II.

Article 13 in the Constitution of India, 1949 is related to Laws inconsistent with or in derogation of the fundamental rights. Clause (1) states that all laws in force in the territory of India immediately before the commencement of this Constitution, in so far as they are inconsistent with the provisions of this Part, shall, to the extent of such inconsistency, be void.

Article 15 in the Constitution of India 1949 is related to Prohibition of discrimination on grounds of religion, race, caste, sex or place of birth. Clause (1) states that the State shall not discriminate against any citizen on grounds only of religion, race, caste, sex, place of birth or any of them.

Article 20 in the Constitution of India 1949 is related to Protection in respect of conviction for offences. Clause (1) states that no person shall be convicted of any offence except for violation of the law in force at the time of the commission of the act charged as an offence, nor be subjected to a penalty greater than that which might have been inflicted under the law in force at the time of the commission of the offence.

Article 23 in the Constitution of India, 1949 is related to Prohibition of traffic in human beings and forced labour. Traffic in human beings and beggar and other similar forms of forced labour are prohibited and any contravention of this provision shall be an offence punishable in accordance with law.

4 Which one of the following Parliamentary Committees in India, acts as 'watch dog' on departmental expenditure and irregularities ?

1 Committee on public undertakings
2 Committee on public assurances
3 Estimates Committee
4 Public Accounts Committee

***Ans.* (4)**

Exp. Public Accounts Committee is a Parliamentary committee in India, which acts as 'watch dog' on departmental expenditure and irregularities. This Committee consists of 15 members elected by the Lok Sabha and 7 members of the Rajya Sabha are associated with it. The term of the Committee is one year.

The main duty of the Committee is to ascertain whether the money granted by Parliament has been spent by Government 'within the scope of the Demand'. The Appropriation Accounts of the Government of India and the Audit Reports presented by the Comptroller and Auditor General mainly form the basis for the examination of the Committee. Cases involving losses, nugatory expenditure and financial irregularities come in for severe criticism by the Committee. The Committee is not concerned with questions of policy. It is concerned only with the execution of the policy laid down by Parliament and its results.

5 Read Assertion (A) and Reason (R) and answer using the codes given below.

Assertion (A) Both houses of Parliament as well as of a State Legislature have similar privileges under the Constitution of India.

Reason (R) In general the position of the Speaker is similar to that of the Speaker of English House of Commons.

Codes

1 Both (A) and (R) are true and (R) is the correct explanation of (A)

2 Both (A) and (R) are true, but (R) is not the correct explanation of (A)

3 (A) is true, but (R) is false

4 (A) is false, but (R) is true

Ans. *(2)*

Exp. Both (A) and (R) are true, but (R) is not the correct explanation of (A).

Both Houses of Parliament as well as of a State Legislature have similar privileges under the Constitution of India. Article105 and Article 194 grants privileges or advantages to the members of the parliament so that they can perform their duties or can function properly without any hindrances. Such privileges are granted as they are needed for democratic functioning.

Some of the privileges are freedom of speech and publication under parliamentary authority, power to make rules etc.

In general the position of the Speaker is similar to that of the Speaker of English House of Commons. However, a British-type convention of 'once a Speaker, always a Speaker', is yet to be established in India and sitting Speakers have been seeking re-election on party tickets subjecting themselves to the compulsions of party-politics. Indeed, the position of the Indian Speaker is paradoxical: he has to contest election on a party ticket but is expected to conduct himself in a non-partisan manner once elected.

6 Which of the following are included in the list of Fundamental Duties in the Constitution of India? Answer using the codes given below.

I. To uphold and protect the sovereignty, unity and integrity of India and the states

II. To defend the country and render national service when called upon to do so

III. To value and preserve the rich heritage of our composite culture

IV. To develop the scientific temper, humanism and the spirit of inquiry and reform

Codes

1 I, II and III   2 I, II and IV

3 II, III and IV   4 I, III and IV

Ans. *(3)*

Exp. Statement II, III and IV are included in the list of Fundamental Duties in the Constitution of India.

The Fundamental Duties are defined as the moral obligations of all citizens to help promote a spirit of patriotism and to uphold the unity o India. Article 51A, Part IVA of the Indian Constitution, specifies the list of fundamental duties of the citizens. It says 'it shall be the duty of every citizen of India'

(i) to abide by the Constitution and respect its ideal and institutions;

(ii) to cherish and follow the noble ideals which inspired our national struggle for freedom;

(iii) to uphold and protect the sovereignty, unity and integrity of India;

(iv) to defend the country and render national service when called upon to do so;

(v) to promote harmony and the spirit of common brotherhood amongst all the people of India transcending religious, linguistic and regional diversities, to renounce practices derogatory to the dignity of women;

(vi) to value and preserve the rich heritage of our composite culture;

(vii) to protect and improve the natural environment including forests, lakes, rivers, and wild-life and to have compassion for living creatures;

(viii) to develop the scientific temper, humanism and the spirit of inquiry and reform;

(ix) to safeguard public property and to abjure violence;

(x) to strive towards excellence in all spheres of individual and collective activity, so that the nation constantly rises to higher levels of endeavour and achievement.

(xi) who is a parent or guardian , to provide opportunities for education to his child, or as the case may be, ward between the age of six and fourteen years.

7 Match List I with List II and select the correct answer using the codes given below the lists.

	List I (Articles)		List II (Provisions)
A.	Article 40	I.	Separation of judiciary from executive
B.	Article 42	II.	Organisation of village panchayats
C.	Article 44	III.	Provision for just and human conditions of work and maternity relief
D.	Article 50	IV.	Uniform civil code

Codes

	A	B	C	D		A	B	C	D
1	I	II	IV	III	2	II	III	IV	I
3	II	IV	I	III	4	III	IV	I	II

Ans. *(2)*

Exp. The correct matching is A-II, B-III, C-IV, D-I.

Article 40 in the Constitution of India 1949, talks about the organisation of village panchayats. It states that the State shall take steps to organise village panchayats and endow them with such powers and authority as may be necessary to enable them to function as units of self government.

Article 42 in the Constitution of India 1949, talks about the provision for just and human conditions of work and maternity relief. It lays down the provision for just and human conditions of work and maternity relief. The article states that the State shall make provision for securing just and humane conditions of work and for maternity relief.

Article 44 in the Constitution of India 1949, mention the Uniform Civil Code. It states that the State shall endeavour to secure for the citizens a Uniform Civil Code for the citizens throughout the territory of India.

Article 50 in the Constitution of India 1949, talks about the separation of judiciary from executive. It states that the State shall take steps to separate the judiciary from the executive in the public services of the State.

8 Which one of the following was not a recommendation of the Dinesh Goswami Committee on electoral reforms ?

1 State assistance to national political parties for elections
2 Maintenance of proper accounts of elections
3 Strict enforcement of model code of conduct
4 Video coverage of polling booths to check booth capturing

Ans. (4)

Exp. "Video coverage of polling booths to check booth capturing" is not one of the recommendations of the Dinesh Goswami Committee on electoral reforms.

Following are the recommendation of the Dinesh Goswami Committee on electoral reforms are:

(i) State assistance to national political parties for elections
(ii) Maintenance of proper accounts of elections
(iii) Strict enforcement of model code of conduct

9 Read the Assertion (A) and Reason (R) and answer by using the codes given below

Assertion (A) The system of Droit Administrative is not at all based on the doctrine of separation of powers.

Reason (R) The most original aspect of the French Administrative Law is the independence of the administration from judicial control.

Codes

1 Both (A) and (R) are true and (R) is the correct explanation of (R)
2 Both (A) and (R) are true, but (R) is not the correct explanation of (A)
3 (A) is true, but (R) is false
4 (A) is false, but (R) is true

Ans. (4)

Exp. (A) is false, but (R) is true.

The system of Droit Administrative is the system of administrative law prevalent in France. It is based on strict separation of power between the administration and courts.

However, in the French administration system, the interference of the administrative courts with that of ordinary courts is also not permitted. Administrative independence from judicial control is the most original aspect of the French Administrative Law.

10 Which of the following is not an essential element of the doctrine of audi alteram partem ?

1 Person affected adversely must be heard
2 Fair and transparent procedure must be provided by authority
3 Reasoned decision must not be based on the satisfaction of the concerned authority
4 Authority concerned must dispose off the matter by a speaking order

Ans. (3)

Exp. Reasoned decision must not be based on the satisfaction of the concerned authority is not an essential elements of the doctrine of audi alteram partem.

The maxim 'audi alteram partem' means 'hear the other side' or no man should be unheard, both the parties have an opportunity of being heard. It is one of the principles of natural justice.

The essentials of the principle include: persons affected adversely must be heard; fair and transparent procedure must be provided by authority; authority concerned must dispose off the matter by a speaking order.

11 Match List I with List II and select the correct answer using the codes given below.

	List I (Name of Case)		List II (Decision)
A.	Hira Nath Mishra Vs. Rajendra Medical College	I.	The inquiry was vitiated as class IV employee has to defend himself against officers, hence denial of principles of natural justice.
B.	Bhagat Ram Vs. State of HP	II.	Principle of natural justice can be exempted for the security of girl students and girls could be testified in the absence of miscreants.
C.	AK Roy Vs. Union of India	III.	No deprivation of existing right enjoyed by government servant without giving him opportunity of being heard.
D.	HL Trehan Vs. Union of India	IV.	Principles of natural justice are not rigid norms of unchanging context, they have to be tailored to suit the nature of the proceeding.

Codes

	A	B	C	D		A	B	C	D
1	II	I	IV	III	2	I	II	III	IV
3	IV	III	II	I	4	II	I	III	IV

Ans. (1)

Exp. The correct matching is A-II, B-I, C-IV, D-III.

In *Hira Nath Mishra Vs. Rajendra Medical College*, the court held that the principle of natural justice can be exempted for the security of girl students and girls could be testified in the absence of miscreants.

In *Bhagat Ram Vs. State of HP*, the court held that the inquiry was vitiated as class IV employee has to defend himself against officers, hence denial of principles of natural justice.

In *AK Roy Vs. Union of India*, the court held that principles of natural justice are not rigid norms of unchanging context, they have to be tailored to suit the nature of the proceeding.

In *HL Trehan Vs. Union of India*, the court held that no deprivation of existing right enjoyed by government servant without giving him opportunity of being heard.

12 A statute confers discretionary powers on an official for his use, by denoting expressions like

I. Reasonable II. Appropriate
III. Equitable IV. Sufficient

Codes

1 Only I is correct
2 I and II are correct
3 I, II and III are correct
4 I, II, III and IV are correct

Ans. (4)

Exp. A statute confers discretionary powers on an official for his use, by denoting expressions like (i) reasonable, (ii) appropriate (iii) equitable (iv) sufficient.

All these words whenever they appear in a statute give scope to the official/authority to exercise discretion.

13 Read the Assertion (A) and Reason (R) and answer by using the codes given below.

Assertion (A) The court can direct competent authority to exercise discretion in accordance with law, but court cannot direct to exercise the discretion in a particular manner.

Reason (R) The Supreme Court strikes down a decision of competent autority on ground of 'extraneous consideration' and 'improper purpose'.

Codes

1 Both (A) and (R) are true and (R) is the correct explanation of (A)
2 Both (A) and (R) are true, but (R) is not the correct explanation of (R)
3 (A) is true, but (R) is false
4 (A) is false, but (R) is true

Ans. (1)

Exp. Both (A) and (R) are true and (R) is the correct explanation of (A).

The court can direct competent authority to exercise discretion in accordance with law, but court cannot direct to exercise the discretion in a particular manner. The authority in which discretion is vested can be compelled to exercise it, but not to exercise it in a particular manner. When a discretionary power is conferred on an authority, the said authority must excercise that power after applying its mind to the fact and circumstances in hand. Thus, where a authority abdicates its power e.g. abdication of functions, acting under dictation,etc there is a failure to exercise discretion.

The Supreme Court strikes down a decision of competent authority on ground of 'extraneous consideration' and 'improper purpose' is true and is the correct explanation of Assertion.

14 What is the objective of the Lokpal and Lokayukta Act, 2013 ?

1 To investigate the charges of corruption against public and private companies
2 To substitute the Central Vigilance Commission by the institution of Lokpal
3 To repeal the Lokayukta and establish Lokpal
4 To inquire into allegations of corruption against public functionaries

Ans. (4)

Exp. The Lokpal and Lokayukta Act established statutory bodies which perform the function of an 'ombudsman' and inquire into allegations of corruption against certain public functionaries and for related matters.

The Lokpal and Lokayukta Act, 2013 provided for the establishment of Lokpal for the Union and Lokayukta for States. These institutions are statutory bodies without any constitutional status.

15 Which of the following declarations relating to assets and liabilities by a public servant are to be made under the Lokpal and Lokayukta Act, 2013? Answer by using the codes given below

I. Assets of which he, his spouse and his dependent children are jointly or severally, owner or beneficiary.
II. Assets of which he, his parents and children are owner or beneficiary.
III. His liabilities and that of his spouse and his dependent children.
IV. His liabilities and that of his spouse, parents and children.

Codes

1 I and II 2 III and IV
3 I and III 4 II and IV

Ans. (3)

Exp. Statements I and III are correct.

The Lokpal and Lokayukta Act, 2013 seeks to provide for the establishment of Lokpal for the Union and Lokayukta for States to inquire into allegations of corruption against certain public functionaries and for related matters. The act extends to the whole of India, including Jammu and Kashmir and is applicable to 'public servants' within and outside India.

Section 44 of the Act mentions about declaration of assets. As per the Act, every public servant shall make a declaration of his assets and liabilities in the manner as provided by or under this Act.

Also, a public servant shall, within a period of thirty days from the date on which he makes and subscribes an oath or affirmation to enter upon his office, furnish to the competent authority the information relating to

- the assets of which he, his spouse and his dependent children are, jointly or severally, owner or beneficiaries;
- his liabilities and that of his spouse and his dependent children.

16 Which one of the following statements is incorrect ?

1 In Jurisprudence, we are concerned to derive rules from authority and apply them to problems

2 In Jurisprudence, we are concerned to reflect on the nature of legal rules

3 In Jurisprudence, we are concerned on the underlying meaning of legal concepts

4 In Jurisprudence, we are concerned on the essential features of legal systems

***Ans.** (1)*

➲ *Exp.* Statement 1 is incorrect as in Jurisprudence, we are concerned on the underlying meaning of legal concepts and essential features of legal systems.

Jurisprudence has its own intrinsic interest and value because this is a subject of serious scholarship and research; researchers in Jurisprudence contribute to the development of society by having repercussions in the whole legal, political and social school of thoughts.

One of the tasks of this subject is to construct and elucidate concepts serving to render the complexities of law more manageable and more rational. It is the belief of this subject that the theory can help to improve practice.

17 Which of the following requisites are necessary to be fulfilled for a custom to be valid source of law?

I. Reasonableness, antiquity and conformity with statute law.

II. Immemorial antiquity, conformity with statute law and observance as of right.

III. Specificity, efficacy and reasonableness.

Codes

1 I and III	2 I, II and III
3 II and III	4 I and II

***Ans.** (4)*

➲ *Exp.* Statements I and II contains the requisites which are necessary to be fulfilled for a custom to be valid source of law.

For a custom to take the force of law, it must have following ingredients :

(i) *Antiquity*–The custom must be ancient.

(ii) *Certainty*–If a custom is vague and ambiguous, so that no uniform observance of it exists, it is not a valid custom.

(iii) *Reasonableness* A custom is treated to be unreasonable, if it is opposed to the principles of justice, equity and good conscience and hence invalid.

(iv) *Compulsory Observance* For a custom to take the force of law it must enjoy compulsory observance in the region and community it is observed.

(v) *Conformity with statute law* Those customs are apposed to public policy or are entirely opposed to statue law are not valid customs.

18 Read the Assertion (A) and Reason (R) and select the correct answer with the help of codes given below.

Assertion (A) Judges must follow authoritative precedents.

Reason (R) Authoritative precedents derive their authority from basic postulate of the legal system itself.

Codes

1 Both (A) and (R) are true and (R) is the correct explanation of (A)

2 Both (A) and (R) are true, but (R) is not the correct explanation of (A)

3 (A) is true, but (R) is false

4 (A) is false, but (R) is true

***Ans.** (1)*

➲ *Exp.* Both (A) and (R) are true and (R) is the correct explanation of (A).

Judges must follow authoritative precedents. Authoritative precedent or decision (a binding decision) is one which judges must follow whether they approve it or not. It is also known as mandatory precedent or binding authority. As per the doctrine of stare decisis, a court lower in the hierarchy follows and honours the findings of law made by a court higher in the hierarchy.

Authoritative precedents derive their authority from basic postulate of the legal system itself. The decisions of lower courts are not binding on courts higher in the system. Lower courts are bound by precedent (that is, prior decided cases) of higher courts within their region.

19 Read the Assertion (A) and Reason (R) and give the correct answer using the codes given below

Assertion (A) A person in possession of a thing is deemed to be the owner of the thing possessed.

Reason (R) Possession is as good as ownership.

Codes

1 Both (A) and (R) are true and (R) is the correct explanation of (A)

2 Both (A) and (R) are true, but (R) is not the correct explanation of (A)

3 (A) is true, but (R) is false

4 (A) is false, but (R) is true

***Ans.** (3)*

➲ *Exp.* (A) is true, but (R) is false.

Salmond defines possession (in legal terms) as the continuous exercising of a claim, to the exclusive use of an object or a thing constitutes possession of the object. In simpler words, if a person has apparent control of an object and apparent power to exclude others from the use of the object, then we can say he has possession. A person in possession of a thing is deemed to be the owner of the thing possessed. Thus, Assertion is true.

However, the possessor has a better claim to the title of the object than anyone, except the owner himself. Therefore, it does not indicate the right to ownership. Thus, Reason is false.

20 Read the Assertion (A) and Reason (R) and select the correct answer with the help of codes given below.

Assertion (A) A claim to recover a debt barred by lapse of time is an imperfect right

Reason (R) The statute of limitations does not provide that after a certain time a debt shall become extinct

Codes

1 Both (A) and (R) are true and (R) is the correct explanation of (A)
2 Both (A) and (R) are true, but (R) is not the correct explanation of (A)
3 (A) is true, but (R) is false
4 (A) is false, but (R) is true

***Ans.* (3)**

Exp. (A) is true, but (R) is false.

Imperfect rights are those rights which are recognised but are unenforceable. Debts barred by the lapse of time is an imperfect right. Hence, Assertion is true.

Item 26 of the Schedule of the Limitation Act provides that the limitation period for money payable to the plaintiff for money found to be due from the defendant to the plaintiff on accounts stated between them is three year. This means that a debt expires after three years. Therefore, Reason is false.

21 The fundamental principle of legal positivism is to draw a clearcut demarcation between law and morals, between law as it is and law as ought to be wherein the former is essential in the nature of 'command' and latter being merely

1 Routine and normal
2 Persuasive and non-obligatory
3 Non-persuasive and obligatory
4 Directive and non-persuasive

***Ans.* (2)**

Exp. The fundamental principle of legal positivism is to draw a clear-cut demarcation between law and morals, between law as it is and law as ought to be wherein the former is essential in the nature of 'command' and latter being merely Persuasive and non-obligatory.

22 Which one of the following is not a theory of corporate personality?

1 Fiction theory
2 Will theory
3 Realist theory
4 Bracket theory

***Ans.* (2)**

Exp. Will theory is not a theory of corporate personality. It is a theory of function of legal rights. According to this, the function of a legal right is to give its holder control over another's duty. For example if a person 'A' has a right (ownership) over the house he has given to person 'B' on rent. Then, person 'A' has control over the duties person 'B' has towards 'A' in relation to his use of A's house. Hart is one of the most prominent 'will' theorist. Fiction theory, Realist theory, Bracket theory are concerned with 'Corporate Personality'.

23 Match List I with List II and give the correct answer by using the codes given below the lists

List I (Theory)	List II (Jurist associated with)
A. Interest theory of legal rights	I. Duguit
B. Realist theory of corporate personality	II. Ihering
C. Doctrine of social solidarity	III Gierke
D. Doctrine of social engineering	IV Pound

Codes

	A	B	C	D		A	B	C	D
1	III	II	I	IV	2	II	III	I	IV
3	IV	I	III	II	4	III	I	II	IV

***Ans.* (2)**

Exp. The correct matching is A-II, B-III, C-I and D-IV.

Interest theory of legal rights was propounded by Ihering. The true position as per Ihering is that law is a process to achieve a proper balance between social and individual interests.

Realist theory of corporate personality was propounded by Gierke. Realist theory is also known as "Organic Theory". This theory was propounded by Gierke and Maitland was the supporter of this theory. This theory says that a corporation has all the characteristics just like a natural person. So, he opines that a legal or juristic person is really just like human beings. It further says that juristic persons are not fictitious and also do not require the recognition of the State.

Doctrine of social solidarity was propounded by Duguit. He was greatly inspired by Auguste Comte and Durkheim. He gave the theory of social solidarity, which describes the social cooperation between individuals for their need and survival. Social Solidarity is the spirit of oneness.

The *Doctrine of social engineering* was propounded by Pound. He was one of the greatest leaders of the sociological school of jurisprudence. He introduced the doctrine of "social engineering" which aims to build an efficient structure of society resulting in the satisfaction of maximum wants with the minimum of friction and waste.

24 Doli Capax is the principle which decides

1 Immunity from punishment as there is no understanding of the consequences
2 That there was discern between good and evil for which punishment would be justified
3 Proof of innocence would ipso facto be an answer for imposing a sentence
4 Before punishing a person his immaturity of intellect is to be assessed

Ans. *(2)*

➲ *Exp.* 'Doli capax' it the principle which decides that there was discern between good and evil for which punishment would be justified.

'Doli Capax' is a Latin term that means 'incapable of doing harm'. This term has been used to describe a presumption of innocence for children in Criminal law in most countries. The basis of this presumption lies in the theory of criminal responsibility.

A person is considered to be Doli Capax if he is beyond such tender age as to have sufficient capacity to form an intention to commit a tort or a crime.

25 The law is clear that consent of the party becomes immaterial when the very act itself is unlawful. In which of the cases there could be an exception ?

1 Prize fight
2 Advantage taken in a game of fencing
3 Aiding and abetting in a game of boxing
4 Negligent while sky-diving

Ans. *(1)*

➲ *Exp.* The law is clear that consent of the party becomes immaterial when the very act itself is unlawful. However, it can be an exception in the case of prize fights.

'Prize fight' means an encounter or fight with fists, hands or feet between two persons who have met for that purpose by previous arrangement made by or for them, but does not include :

- a contest between amateur athletes in a combative sport with fist, hands or feet in a province if the sport is on the programme of the International Olympic Committee.
- a contest between amateur athletes in a combative sport with fists, hand or feet held in a province if the sports has been designated by the province's lieutenant governor in council.
- a boxing contest or mixed martial art contest held in a province with the permission or under the authority of an athletic board.

26 The apprehension of the use of criminal force must be from the person making the gesture, but if it arises from some other person, then what offence, if any, has been caused ?

1 Common intention to cause assault
2 Common object to cause assault
3 Criminal force
4 No offence

Ans. *(4)*

➲ *Exp.* According to Section 351 of IPC, "whoever makes any gesture, or any preparation intending or knowing it to be likely that such gesture or preparation will cause any person present to apprehend that he who makes that gesture or preparation is about to use criminal force to that person is said to commit an assault".

Therefore, the apprehension of the use of criminal force must be from the person making the gesture, but if it arises from some other person, then it amounts to no offence.

27 For convicting a person the state must rule out the possibility of an accidental death in a case of dowry harassment because the law requires

1 That the death occurred otherwise than in normative circumstances
2 The demand for dowry is not evidenced as the following consequence of death
3 The mitigating factors of death do not reveal any demand as to dowry but there was breach of promise to provide dowry
4 The rule of presumption, in the absence as to the demand of dowry provides contrary jurisprudence for convicting the accused

Ans. *(1)*

➲ *Exp.* For convicting a person the state must rule out the possibility of an accidental death in a case of dowry harassment because the law requires that the death occurred otherwise than in normative circumstances.

Section 304B (1) states that 'Where the death of a woman is caused by any burns or bodily injury or occurs otherwise than under normal circumstances within seven years of her marriage and it is shown that soon before her death she was subjected to cruelty or harassment by her husband or any relative of her husband for, or in connection with, any demand for dowry, such death shall be called "dowry death", and such husband or relative shall be deemed to have caused her death.'

28 In the eventuality of grievous hurt becomes culpable homicide not amounting to murder the injury which is actually found should itself be such that it may put the life of the injured in danger, was decided in the case of

1 Maung Po Yi. Vs. Mo E Tin
2 Government of Bom. Vs. Abdul Wahab
3 Muhammad Rafi Vs. King
4 Bishnovnam Surma Vs. King

Ans. (2)

Exp. In Government of Bom. Vs. Abdul Wahab, the court held that in the eventuality of grievous hurt becomes culpable homicide not amounting to murder the injury which is actually found should itself be such that it may put the life of the injured in danger.

29 A snatcher cut the nostrils of a woman and committed grievous hurt and later she died. What offence if any, he has committed ?

1 Voluntary causing grievous hurt of serious nature
2 Grievous hurt and murder
3 Accidental death while extortion was committed
4 No knowledge as to the condition of the deceased, so offence

Ans. (1)

Exp. A snatcher cut the nostrils of a woman and committed grievous hurt and later she died. He has committed the offence of voluntary causing grievous hurt of serious nature.

Section 326 of the Indian Penal Code states: "whoever, except in the case provided for by Section 335, voluntarily causes grievous hurt by means of any instrument for shooting, stabbing or cutting, or any instrument which, used as a weapon of offence, is likely to cause death, or by means of fire or any heated substance, or by means of any poison or any corrosive substance, or by means of any explosive substance, or by means of any substance which it is deleterious to the human body to inhale, to swallow, or to receive into the blood, or by means of any animal, shall be punished with imprisonment for life, or with imprisonment of either description for a term which may extend to ten years and shall also be liable to fine"

Therefore, it is clear that the snatcher had caused grievous hurt.

30 The restrainment of a person in a place or compelling the person to go in a particular direction with an exterior motive will amount to

1 Visit to shrine
2 Custodial imprisonment
3 Wrongful confinement
4 Confinement against the will of a person to administer enema by the doctor

Ans. (3)

Exp. The restrainment of a person in a place or compelling the person to go in a particular direction with an exterior motive will amount to wrongful confinement.

Section 340 of the Indian Penal Code 1860, defines wrongful confinement as "whoever wrongfully restrains any person in such a manner as to prevent that person from proceeding beyond certain circumscribing limits, is said wrongfully to confine that person."

31 Which offence is outside the range of culpable homicide in view of the fact that the accused had neither intention nor knowledge about the consequence, yet it is punishable ?

1 When the injury results due to carelessness
2 When the mishap happens due to rash and negligent act
3 When the contributory act was voluntarily done
4 When the act resulted in course of exaseperation

Ans. (2)

Exp. When the mishap happens due to rash and negligent act, it is an offence outside the range of culpable homicide in view of the fact that the accused had neither intention nor knowledge about the consequence, yet it is punishable.

Section 299 of the Indian Penal Code defines culpable homicide as " whosoever causes death by doing an act with the intention of causing death or with the intention of causing such bodily injury as it is likely to cause death or with the knowledge that he is likely by such act to cause death , commits the offence of culpable homicide ."

32 The total forest cover in our country is far less than the ideal minimum of 1/3 of the total land. Therefore, the Parliament by 42nd Amendment to the Constitution has added two more Articles to ensure improvement of environment and impose duty on every citizen. They are

1 Article 31 C and 51 A (a)
2 Article 48 A and 51 A (g)
3 Article 39 A and 51 A (b)
4 Article 31 D and 51 A (d)

Ans. (2)

Exp. The Parliament by 42nd Amendment to the Constitution has added two more Articles to ensure improvement of environment and impose duty on every citizen. They are Article 48 A and Article 51 A (g). Article 48A has been added in the directive principles of state policy and Article 51A (g) has been added in the list of Fundamental Duties in our Constitution.

Article 48-A of our Constitution, which states as follows "The State shall endeavour to protect and improve the environment and to safeguard the forests and wildlife of the country".

Article 51 A(g) of our Constitution states as follows "It shall be the duty of every citizen of India to protect and improve the natural environment including forests, lakes, rivers and wildlife and to have compassion for living creatures."

33 The Supreme Court held that, "the precautionary principle has no applicability in this case as the gains and losses of building a big dam are predictable and certain", in one of the following case

1 MC Mehta Vs. Union of India
2 Narmada Bachao Andolan Vs. Union of India
3 State of MP Vs. Krishna Das Tuka Ram
4 S Jaganath Vs. Union of India

Ans. (2)

Exp. In Narmada Bachao Andolan Vs. Union of India, the court held that "the precautionary principle has no applicability in this case as the gains and losses of building a big dam are predictable and certain."

The object of this principle is to make the polluter liable for the compensation to the victims as also for the cost of restoring environmental degradation.

34 Which one of the following has been described as the 'Magna-Carta' of the environment ?

1 Rio declaration
2 Tbilisi declaration
3 The Stockholm declaration
4 Environment product declaration

Ans. (1)

Exp. The Rio Declaration has been described as the 'Magna-Carta' of the environment.

The Rio Declaration on environment and development was approved by the United Nations during the Conference on Environment and Development held in Rio de Janeiro on June 1992. It was aimed at reaffirming the Declaration of the United Nations Conference on the Human Environment, adopted at Stockholm on June, 1972.

The Declaration adopted a set of principles to guide the future development. These principles define the right of people to development, and their responsibilities to safeguard the common environment. The Rio Declaration states that the only way to have long term economic progress is to link it with environmental protection. This will only happen if nations establish a new and equitable global partnership involving governments, their people and key sectors of societies.

35 Match the item in List I with the item in List II using the codes given below.

	List I		List II
A.	No reason to compel non-smokers to be helpless victims of air pollution	I.	Church of God (Full Gospel) in India Vs. KKR Majestic Colony Welfare Association
B.	Noise pollution cannot be tolerated even if such noise was a direct result of and was connected with religious activity	II.	S Jaganath Vs. Union of India
C.	Duty to protect the natural resources applying the principle of public trust	III.	Murli Deora Vs. Union of India
D.	Pay compensation for reversing the ecology and compensate the individual for loss suffered	IV.	MC Mehta Vs. Kamalnath and others

Codes

	A	B	C	D		A	B	C	D
1	III	I	IV	II	2	I	III	II	IV
3	II	IV	I	III	4	IV	I	III	II

Ans. (1)

Exp. The correct matching is A-III, B-I, C-IV and D-II.

In *Church of God (Full Gospel) in India Vs. KKR Majestic Colony Welfare Association*, the court held that noise pollution cannot be tolerated even if such noise was a direct result of and was connected with religious activity.

In *S Jaganath Vs. Union of India*, the court held that the party shall pay compensation for reversing the ecology and compensate the individual for loss suffered.

In *Murli Deora Vs. Union of India*, the court held that there was no reason to compel non-smokers to be helpless victims of air pollution.

In *MC Mehta Vs. Kamalnath and others*, the court held that regarding duty to protect the natural resources applying the principle of public trust.

36 The Supreme Court constituted Bhure Lal Committee to examine and report the low sulphur diesel as a clean fuel to be used by vehicles in one of the following case

1 Research Foundation for Science, Technology and Natural Resources Policy Vs. Union of India
2 MC Mehta Vs. Kamalnath
3 MK Sharma Vs. BEL
4 MC Mehta Vs. Union of India and others

Ans. (4)

Exp. In MC Mehta Vs. Union of India and others, the court constituted Bhure Lal Committee to examine and report the low sulphur diesel as a clean fuel to be used by vehicles.

The Committee was established under Section 3 of the Environment (Protection) Act, 1986. It was based on recommendations of this committee that a time-frame for switching over to CNG fuel for Government and Public transport was fixed.

37 Read the Assertion (A) and Reason (R) and answer by using codes given below.

Assertion (A) All natural resources are held in trust by the government. The doctrine enjoins upon the government to protect the resources for the enjoyment of general public rather than to permit their use for private ownership or commercial purpose.

Reason (R) The public has a right to expect certain lands and natural resources to retain their natural characteristic in finding its way into the law of the land.

Codes

1 Both (A) and (R) are true and (R) is the correct explanation of (A)
2 Both (A) and (R) are true, but (R) is not the correct explanation of (A)
3 (A) is true, but (R) is false
4 (A) is false, but (R) is true

Ans. (1)

Exp. Both (A) and (R) are true and (R) is the correct explanation of (A).

The public trust doctrine refers to the duty of sovereign states to hold and preserve certain resources including wildlife, for the benefit of its citizens. Described simply, the doctrine provides that natural resources belong to the whole public; private owners may not deprive the public of access the state has legal authority to pursue causes of action for damages and injunctive relief against parties responsible for the pollution of natural resources.

The Public Trust Doctrine is a common-law customized by each state, which establishes public rights in navigable waters and on their shores. Historically, the purpose of the public trust doctrine was to protect water resources for navigation and to commence when waterways were the principal means of transportation and a source of food. Thus, the doctrine originally evolved to allow recovery by the state in cases involving discharges into navigable waterways and tidelands.

38 "Cases involving issues of environmental pollution, ecological destruction and conflict over natural resources are on the increase and hence setting up of environmental courts on the regional basis with one professional judge and two experts drawn from Ecological Science Research Group is necessary", was observed in one of the following case

1 MC Mehta Vs. Union of India
2 Bittu Sehgal Vs. Union of India
3 TN Godavarman Thirulmulpad Vs. Union of India
4 AP Pollution Control Board Vs. Prof. MV Nayudu

Ans. (2)

Exp. In Bittu Sehgal Vs. Union of India, the court held that "cases involving issues of environmental pollution, ecological destruction and conflict over natural resources are on the increase and hence setting up of environmental courts on the regional basis with one professional judge and two experts drawn from Ecological Science Research Group is necessary."

It took a Public Interest Petition filed by environmentalist and editor of Sanctuary magazine, Bittu Sehgal, in the Supreme Court to set matters right. The Court directed the National Environmental and Engineering Institute (NEERI) to prepare a report on the issues raised in the petition.

39 Who has remarked that International Law is the vanishing point of Jurisprudence because in his view, rules of International Law are followed by courtesy and hence they should not be kept in the category of law ?

1 Prof HLA Hart 2 JG Starke
3 Louis Henkin 4 Holland

Ans. (4)

Exp. Holland remarked that International Law is the vanishing point of Jurisprudence because in his view, rules of International Law are followed by courtesy and hence they should not be kept in the category of law.

According to Holland, International law is the vanishing point of jurisprudence. By using the words 'vanishing point' in relation to international law and jurisprudence, he meant that international law and jurisprudence are parallel to each other, and they therefore are distinct and separate though it might be appearing that they are one and the same at vanishing point. Vanishing point is a point at which parallel lines in the same plane appears to meet. Thus, international law cannot be kept in the category of law mainly because there is neither any sovereign authority nor exists sanctions if its rules are violated.

40 In which of the following cases, the World Court by majority has taken the view that the sources of international law are not hierarchical but are necessarily complementary and inter-related ?

1 Nicaragua Vs. USA
2 In North Sea Continental Shelf case
3 In the Barcelona Traction case
4 Frontier dispute (Burkina Faso Vs. Mali)

Ans. (1)

Exp. In Nicaragua Vs. USA case, the World Court by majority has taken the view that the sources of international law are not hierarchical but are necessarily complementary and inter-related.

It was a case where the International Court of Justice (ICJ) held that the U.S. had violated international law by supporting the Contras in their rebellion against the Sandinistas and by mining Nicaragua's harbors. The case was decided in favor of Nicaragua and against the United States with the awarding of reparations to Nicaragua.

41 Who has remarked that the wide acceptance of declaratory theory is due to the reaction against the traditional conception of recognition as a political act purely and simply. There is a legal duty on the part of the state to recognise any community that has in fact acquired the charactoristics of statehood ?

1 L Oppenheim 2 Hans Kelson
3 Lauterpacht 4 Anzilloti

Ans. (3)

Exp. Lauterpacht remarked that the wide acceptance of declaratory theory is due to the reaction against the traditional conception of recognition as a political act purely and simply. There is a legal duty on the part of the state to recognise any community that has in fact acquired the characteristics of statehood.

Lauterpacht accepts that statehood and personality under international law is conferred on communities through recognition by existing states. Thus, recognition has a legal effect and he adopts a form of constitutive theory.

42 In which of the following cases, the Supreme Court clarified the distinction between 'expulsion' and 'extradition' following international norms ?

1 Mobarak Ali Ahmad Vs. State of Bombay
2 Hans Muller of Nurenburg Vs. Supdt, Presidency Jail, Calcutta and Others

3 Dharam Teja's case
4 Ram Babu Saxena Vs. State

Ans. (2)

Exp. In Hans Muller of Nurenburg Vs. Supdt, Presidency Jail, Calcutta and Others the Supreme Court clarified the distinction between 'expulsion' and 'extradition' following international norms.

In Hans Muller of Nurenburg Vs. Supdt, Presidency, Jail, Calcutta and Others, a West German citizen was detained by Govt. of West Bengal for his expulsion from India consequent to appropriate orders made in that regard by the Central Government. The distinction between extradition and expulsion was clarified in this case. Extradition requires a requisition from a foreign state whereas expulsion does not require any such request. A sovereign state can expel a foreigner suo motu according to the laws framed by it in this regard.

43 Which of the following statement/statements is/are correct?

I. By asylum we mean shelter and active protection extended to a political refugee from another state which admits him on his request.

II. Under Article 14 of the Universal Declaration of Human Rights, Right to asylum is recognised.

III. International Court of Justice explained the distinction between territorial and extraterritorial asylum in the Asylum Case (Colombia Vs. Perus).

IV. In 1966, the United Nations declaration on territorial asylum was unanimously adopted by the General Assembly.

Codes

1 Only I is correct
2 I, II and III are correct
3 III and IV both are correct
4 All are correct

Ans. (2)

Exp. Statements I, II and III are correct.

The term 'asylum' generally means, the protection granted to a foreign citizen against his own country by the state. The person who is seeking asylum is named the asylee. The asylum seeker has to apply for asylum in a particular country in which they want to take asylum.

Article 14 of the Universal Declaration of Human Rights states that everyone has the right to seek and to enjoy in other countries asylum from persecution. This right may not be invoked in the case of prosecutions genuinely arising from non-political crimes or from acts contrary to the purposes and principles of the United Nations.

The International Court of Justice explained the distinction between territorial and extra territorial asylum in the Asylum Case (Colombia Vs. Perus).

Statement IV is incorrect because the United Nations declaration on territorial asylum was unanimously adopted by the General Assembly at the 1631st plenary meeting, 14th December, 1967.

44 Which of the following statement/statements is/are not correct in reference to the Economic and Social Council (ECOSOC) ?

I. The Economic and Social Council (ECOSOC) consists of 54 members which are elected by General Assembly.

II. Half of its members are elected each year for a term of two years.

III. India is one of the members of the council.

IV. President of ECOSOC is elected for two year term.

Codes

1 Only IV is not correct
2 II and IV both are not correct
3 I, II and III are not correct
4 All are not correct

Ans. (2)

Exp. Statement II and IV are not correct in reference to the Economic and Social Council (ECOSOC).

The Economic and Social Council (ECOSOC) consists of 54 members are elected by the General Assembly for overlapping three-year terms.

The Economic and Social Council elects a new Bureau, a President and four Vice-presidents, at the first meeting of the new session of the council, typically in July. These officials are chosen at large from among the representatives of the council's members for one-year terms.

45 Under which Article of the United Nations Charter, the Security Council is empowered to implement the judgements of the World Court in case one of the parties fails to implement it and other party to the dispute brings the matter to the Security Council ?

1 Article 94
2 Article 96
3 Article 62
4 Article 36(5)

Ans. (1)

Exp. Under Article 94 of the United Nations Charter, the Security Council is empowered to implement the judgements of the World Court in case one of the parties fails to implement it and other party to the dispute brings the matter to the Security Council.

Article 94 of the United Nations Charter states that:

- Each Member of the United Nations Charter undertakes to comply with the decision of the International Court of Justice in any case to which it is a party.
- If any party to a case fails to perform the obligations incumbent upon it under a judgment rendered by the Court, the other party may have recourse to the Security Council, which may, if it deems necessary, make recommendations or decide upon measures to be taken to give effect to the judgement.

46 Read the following propositions and give correct answer with the help of codes given below.

Propositions are

I. A voidable Hindu marriage is regarded as a valid marriage until a decree annulling it has been passed by a competent court.

II. A void Hindu marriage is never a valid marriage and there is no necessity of any decree annulling it.

III. A void Hindu marriage remains valid until a decree annulling it has been passed by a competent court.

IV. Children of void and voidable Hindu marriages are legitimate.

Codes

1 Only I and II are correct, but IV is incorrect
2 I, II and IV are correct, but III is incorrect
3 I, II, III and IV are correct
4 I and IV are correct, but II and III are incorrect

Ans. (2)

Exp. Statement I, II and IV are correct, but III is incorrect.

Statement III is incorrect because the term void means null. A void marriage is null ab initio and the parties don't have the position of husband and wife in a void marriage.

47 Match List I with List II and find correct answer by using the codes given below

List I (Case Law)	List II (Decision)
A. Seema Vs. Ashwani	I. Cruelty as a ground of divorce
B. Githa Hariharan Vs. Reserve Bank of India	II. Maintenance of Muslim wife
C. Vs. Bhagat Vs. D Bhagat	III. Compulsory registration of marriages
D. Mohd. Ahmad Khan Vs. Shah Bano	IV. Mother as natural guardian

Codes

	A	B	C	D		A	B	C	D
1	II	I	III	IV	2	I	III	IV	II
3	III	IV	I	II	4	IV	II	I	III

Ans. (3)

Exp. The correct matching is A-III, B-IV, C-I, D-II.

Seema Vs. Ashwani case is related to compulsory registration of marriages. In this case, the court directed the States and the Central Government to notify the procedure for registration of marriage within three months from today.

Githa Hariharan Vs. Reserve Bank of India case mentions mother as natural guardian. In this case, the court established for the first time that a natural guardian referred to in the HMGA, 1956 can be a father or a mother, whoever is capable of and available for taking care of the child and is deeply interested in the welfare of the child, and that need not necessarily be the father.

Vs. Bhagat Vs. D Bhagat case declared cruelty as a ground of divorce. In this case, husband sued for divorce on the ground that the wife was guilty of mental cruelty.

Mohd. Ahmad Khan Vs. Shah Bano case is related to maintenance of Muslim wife. In this case, the court favoured maintenance given to an aggrieved divorced Muslim woman.

48 Which of the following is not a condition for a marriage under Section 5 of the Hindu Marriage Act, 1955 ?

1 No Sapinda and prohibited degree relationship
2 Mental capacity
3 Monogamy
4 Free consent of the parties

Ans. (4)

Exp. Free consent of the parties is not a condition for a marriage under Section 5 of the Hindu Marriage Act, 1955.

Section 5 of the Hindu Marriage Act, 1955 lays down the condition of a valid Hindu marriage. It states:

"A marriage may be solemnised between any two Hindus, if the following conditions are fulfilled, namely

(i) neither party has a spouse living at the time of the marriage;

(ii) at the time of the marriage, neither party—

(a) is incapable of giving a valid consent to it in consequence of unsoundness of mind.

(b) though capable of giving a valid consent, has been suffering from mental disorder of such a kind or to such an extent as to be unfit for marriage and the procreation of children.

(c) has been subject to recurrent attacks of insanity.

(iii) the bridegroom has completed the age of twenty-one years and the bride, the age of eighteen years at the time of the marriage.

(iv) the parties are not within the degrees of prohibited relationship unless the custom or usage governing each of them permits of a marriage between the two.

(v) the parties are not sapindas of each other, unless the custom or usage governing each of them permits of a marriage between the two"

49 Read the following and answer with the help of codes given below

A married Hindu male can adopt a child

I. Only with his wife's consent.

II. If he has more than one wife, consent of all the wives is necessary.

III. In case of void marriage, consent of wife is necessary.

IV. In case of voidable marriage, the wife's consent is necessary.

Codes
1 I, II and IV are correct, but III is incorrect
2 I and II are correct
3 II, III and IV are correct, but I is incorrect
4 I, II and IV are correct, but II is incorrect

Ans. (1)

➲ *Exp.* I, II and IV are correct, but III is incorrect.

Section 7 lays down the capacity of a male Hindu to take in adoption. It states that: "Any male Hindu who is of sound mind and is not a minor has the capacity to take a son or a daughter in adoption. Provided that, if he has a wife living, he shall not adopt except with the consent of his wife unless the wife has completely and finally renounced the world or has ceased to be a Hindu or has been declared by a court of competent jurisdiction to be of unsound mind."

Statement III is incorrect as a void marriage is void ab initio i.e. it is not recognised as a marriage in the eyes of the law and parties to such a marriage have no legal relation as husband and wife. Hence, in case of such a marriage no consent of wife is required for a valid adoption.

50 The most proper or approved form of divorce among Muslims is

1 Triple talaq 2 Ahsan talaq
3 Hasan talaq 4 Talak-al-biddat

Ans. (2)

➲ *Exp.* Ahsan Talaq is considered to be the most proper or approved form of divorce among Muslims because of two reasons single pronouncement of talaq and revocability.

In Ahsan Talaq, the husband is required to pronounce talaq only once during the period of tuhr (purity) of wife and then abstain from revocation,whether express or implied for the entire period of iddat.

51 Which of the following is not a ground of divorce under the Hindu Marriage Act, 1955 ?

1 Leprosy 2 Insanity
3 Epilepsy 4 Veneral disease

Ans. (3)

➲ *Exp.* Section 13 of the Hindu Marriage Act lays down the following grounds for divorce: Adultery, cruelty, conversion, desertion, insanity, leprosy, renunciation, venereal disease and presumption of death.

Epilepsy was earlier a ground for annulment of marriage, but it was ommitted by Marriage Laws (Amendment) Act, 1999, w.e.f. 29-12-1999.

52 In default of the mother and female relatives, the following persons are entitled to the custody of a Muslim child

I. Nearest paternal grandfather
II. Father
III. Full brother
IV. Consanguine brother etc.

Among the aforesaid the correct order of priority is

Codes
1 I, II, III, IV 2 II, I, III, IV
3 IV, I, II, III 4 III, IV, I, IV

Ans. (2)

➲ *Exp.* The correct order of priority is II, I, III, IV.

Under Muslim law, right to custody of child is called Hizanat and it primarily belongs to the mother. Mother, if not disqualified by misconduct or some other disability cannot surrender this right in favour of any one including her husband. Father's right of Hizanat commences upon the expiry of this right in favour of the mother. Apart from father, certain other male relations are also entitled to custody in a hierarchical order :

(i) Nearest paternal grandfather
(ii) Full brother
(iii) Consanguine brother
(iv) Full brother's son
(v) Consanguine brother's father
(vi) Full brother of the father
(vii) Consanguine brother of the father
(viii) Father's full brother's son
(ix) Father's consanguine brother's son

53 Under the Muslim Women (Protection of Rights on Divorce) Act, 1986, besides the former-husband of Muslim woman, the following relatives etc. are also liable to pay maintenance to her

I. Children
II. Other relatives
III. State Wakf Bord
IV. Parents

Give the correct order of liability of the above with the help of codes given below

Codes
1 IV, II, III, I 2 I, III, II, IV
3 I, II, IV, III 4 I, IV, II, III

Ans. (4)

➲ *Exp.* The correct order of liability is I, IV, II, III.

As per section 3 and 4 of the Muslim Women (Protection of Rights on Divorce) Act, besides the former-husband of Muslim woman, the following relatives etc. are also liable to pay maintenance to her in the following order

(i) Children
(ii) Parents
(iii) Other relatives
(iv) State Wakf Board

54 The Vienna Declaration and Programme of Action on Human Rights was adopted by the World Conference on

1 25th June, 1993 2 10th June, 1994
3 15th June, 1995 4 25th June, 1996

Ans. (1)

➲ *Exp.* The Vienna Declaration and Programme of Action on Human Rights was adopted by the World Conference on 25th June, 1993. It was the first human rights conference held since the end of the cold war. The main result of the conference was the Vienna Declaration and Programme of Action.

55 Which one of the following slogans was adopted for the 50th Anniversary of UDHR ?

1 All Human Rights for All
2 Save the Child
3 Women Empowerment
4 Clean Environment For All

Ans. *(1)*

Exp. The slogan 'All Human Rights for all' was adopted for the 50th Anniversary of UDHR.

On 10th December, 1948, the United General Assembly adopted the Universal Declaration of Human Rights as 'a common standard of achievement for all people and all nations.' This Declaration was the starting point for the development of modern international human rights law and procedures and the massive human rights movement of today.

56 Which one of the following countries originally suggested the idea of an International Treaty on the Rights of the Child ?

1 U.S.A 2 China
3 Poland 4 India

Ans. *(3)*

Exp. Poland originally suggested the idea of an International Treaty on the Rights of the Child.

In 1978, Poland suggested the idea of a Convention of the Rights of the Child that would be legally binding for all nations.

The bill consisted of nineteen articles, of which ten are legislative, and nine procedural. In contrast to the prior Geneva Declaration, this Convention is supposed to be binding for states.

57 "It is my aspiration that health will finally be seen not as a blessing to be wished for, but as a Human Right to be fought for". It was said by

1 Dr Lee Jong-Wook 2 Dr Boutros Boutros Ghali
3 Barack Obama 4 Kofi Annan

Ans. *(4)*

Exp. "It is my aspiration that health will finally be seen not as a blessing to be wished for, but as a Human Right to be fought for," was said by Kofi Annan.

58 Match List I with List II and select the correct answer using the codes given below

	List I		List II
A.	Convention Relating to the Status of Refugees	I.	1948
B.	American Convention on Human Rights	II.	1969
C.	American Declaration of the Rights and Duties of Man	III.	1951
D.	International Convention on the Elimination of All Forms of Racial Discrimination	IV.	1969

Codes

	A	B	C	D		A	B	C	D
1	III	IV	I	II	2	II	III	IV	I
3	I	III	II	IV	4	IV	II	III	I

Ans. *(1)*

Exp. The correct matching is A-III, B-IV, C-I, D-II.

The Convention Relating to the Status of Refugees, also known as the 1951 Refugee Convention was signed on 28th July, 1951. It is also known as the 1951. It is the United Nation Multilateral treaty that defines who is refugee and sets out the rights of individuals who are granted asylum and the responsibilities of nations that grant asylum.

The *American Convention on Human Rights* was signed on 22nd November, 1969. The American Convention on Human Rights, also known as the Pact of San José, is an international human rights instrument. It was adopted by many countries in the Western Hemisphere in San José, Costa Rica, on 22nd November, 1969. It came into force after the eleventh instrument of ratification (that of Grenada) was deposited on 18 July, 1978.

The *American Declaration of the Rights and Duties of Man* was signed in April, 1948. Also known as the Bogota Declaration, it was the world's first international human rights instrument of a general nature, predating the Universal Declaration of Human Rights by less than a year.

The *International Convention on the Elimination of All Forms of Racial Discrimination* was effective from 4th January, 1969. It remains the principal international human rights instrument defining and prohibiting racial discrimination in all sectors of private and public life.

59 The General Assembly of the United Nations created the office of UN High Commissioner for Human Rights in the year

1 1993 2 1994
3 1995 4 1996

Ans. *(1)*

Exp. The General Assembly of the United Nations created the office of UN High Commissioner for Human Rights in the year 1993.

The post of UN High Commissioner for Human Rights was established by General Assembly resolution 48/141 of 20th December, 1993. The Office of the UN High Commissioner for Human Rights (OHCHR) provides support for UN human rights activities, including providing secretariat support for all UN human rights bodies and maintaining the specialised human rights document databases.

60 Under Section 3(2) of the Protection of Human Rights Act, 1993, the Chairperson shall be

1 one who has been a Chief Justice of the Supreme Court
2 one who has been a Chairperson of a National Tribunal or Commission
3 an eminent jurist in the field of Human Rights
4 a judge of the Supreme Court who served not less than five years

Ans. (1)

Exp. Under Section 3(2) of the Protection of Human Rights Act, 1993, the Commission shall consist of a Chairperson:

(i) who has been a Chief Justice of the Supreme Court;
(ii) one Member who is or has been a Judge of the Supreme Court;
(iii) one Member who is or has been the Chief Justice of a High Court;
(iv) two Members to be appointed from amongst persons having knowledge of, or practical experience in matters relating to human rights.

61 Match List I with List II and select the correct answer using the codes given below

List I (Case)	List II (Maxim)
A. Bhim Singh Vs. State of J and K	I. Damnum sine injuria
B. Municipal Corporation of Delhi Vs. Subhagwanti	II. Injuria sine damnum
C. Nichols Vs. Marsland	III. Res ipsa loquitor
D. Mogul Steamship Co. Vs. McGregor Gow and Co.	IV. Vis major

Codes

	A	B	C	D		A	B	C	D
1	I	II	III	IV	2	IV	III	II	I
3	II	III	IV	I	4	II	I	IV	III

Ans. (3)

Exp. The correct matching is A-II, B-III, C-IV, D-I.

Bhim Singh Vs. State of J and K is related to the maxim Injuria sine damnum. In this case, Mr. Bhim Singh, an MLA of Jammu and Kashmir was arrested and detained in police custody and was deliberately prevented from attending the sessions of the legislative assembly to be held on 11th September, 1985.

Municipal Corporation of Delhi Vs. Subhagwanti is related to maxim Res ipsa loquitur. In this case, the MCD owed a responsibility of maintenance of a tower clock on a traffic square of the city, escaped from maintaining it properly because of which it fell and caused the death of many, including the plaintiff. Court held the corporation liable for not maintaining the clock tower.

Nichols Vs. Marsland is related to maxim Vis major. It was held that the defendant could not have anticipated the exceptional flood which caused her dam to break; no conduct of hers was a proximate cause of the plaintiff's damage.

Mogul Steamship Co. Vs. McGregor Gow and Co. is related to maxim Damnum sine injuria. It was held that Competition, however severe and egotistical, if unattended by circumstances of dishonesty, intimidation, molestation, or such illegalities gives rise to no cause of action at common law.

62 Read Assertion (A) and Reason (R) and answer using the codes given below.

Assertion (A) Making statement of fact on matters of public interest is a defence to an action for defamation.

Reason (R) If defendant in a newspaper publishes a statement of facts making serious allegations of dishonesty against the plaintiff, and subsequently could not prove the truth, the plea of fair comment shall fail as based on untrue facts.

Codes

1 Both (A) and (R) are true and (R) is the correct explanation of (A)
2 Both (A) and (R) are true, but R is not correct explanation of (A)
3 (A) is true, but (R) is false
4 (A) is false, and (R) is true

Ans. (4)

Exp. (A) is false, but (R) is true.

Merely making a statement of fact on matters of public interest is not a defence to an action for defamation. Statements of facts should also be true. A publisher cannot put up the defence that he published defamatory material against plaintiff believing the material to be true and that he had no intention to defame. If defendant in a newspaper publishes a statement of facts making serious allegations of dishonesty against the plaintiff, and subsequently could not prove the truth, the plea of fair comment shall fail as based on untrue facts.

63 The prescriptive right of easement of access and use of light and air can be acquired if it has been

I. Enjoyed with interruption
II. As a matter of concession
III. Enjoyed without interruption as right
IV. For twenty years

Codes

1 I and II are incorrect and III and IV are correct
2 I and IV are incorrect and II and III are correct
3 I and III are correct and II and IV are incorrect
4 II and I are correct and IV and III are incorrect

Ans. (1)

Exp. Statements I and II are incorrect and III and IV are correct.

Statements I and II are incorrect because Section 16 of the Indian Easement Act, 1882 states that the access and use of light or air to and for any building have been peaceably enjoyed therewith, as an easement, without interruption, and for twenty years.

64 Which of the following is not true about the slander form of defamation ?

1 Statement is made in some transient form
2 It is addressed to ear
3 Slander is always a criminal offence
4 It is not actionable in absence of proof of actual damage

Ans. (3)

➲ *Exp.* Statement 3 is not true because under the Law of torts, slander is not a criminal offence but a civil one. Slander is a species of defamation. In India defamation can be both civil and criminal offence depending upon the action brought by plaintiff. It is incorrect to hold that a slander is always a criminal offence.

65 Arrange the following cases in the chronological order by using the codes.

I. Municipal Corporation of Delhi Vs. Sushila Devi
II. Shyam Sunder Vs. State of Rajasthan
III. Pushpabai Vs. Ranjit Ginning and Pressing Co.
IV. Syad Akbar Vs. State of Karnataka

Codes

1 IV, I, II and III
2 II, III, IV and I
3 II, I, III and IV
4 I, II, III and IV

Ans. (2)

➲ *Exp.* The correct chronological is II, III, IV, I.
Shyam Sunder Vs. State of Rajasthan–1974
Pushpabai Vs. Ranjit Ginning and Pressing Co.–1977
Syad Akbar Vs. State of Karnataka–1979
Municipal Corporation of Delhi Vs. Sushila Devi–1999

66 What are the rights of consumers which are to be protected and promoted by Consumer Councils under the Consumer Protection Act? Answer by using codes below

I. Protection against marketing of goods and services which are hazardous to life and property.
II. Information about quality, quantity and price of goods and services.
III. Access to a variety of goods and services at competitive prices.
IV. Consumer education.

Codes

1 Only I is correct
2 II and III are correct
3 I, II and III are correct
4 I, II, III and IV are correct

Ans. (4)

➲ *Exp.* Statements I, II, III, and IV are correct.
The Consumer Protection Act postulates establishment of Consumer Protection Councils at the Central and State levels for the purpose of spreading consumer awareness. The objects of the Councils, as per the Act, shall be to promote and protect the rights of the consumers such as:

(i) The right to be protected against the marketing of goods and services which are hazardous to life and property.
(ii) The right to be informed about the quality, quantity, potency, purity, standard and price of goods or services, as the case may be so as to protect the consumer against unfair trade practices.
(iii) The right to be assured, wherever possible, access to a variety of goods and services at competitive prices.
(iv) The right to be heard and to be assured that consumer's interests will receive due consideration at appropriate forums.
(v) The right to seek redressal against unfair trade practices or restrictive trade practices or unscrupulous exploitation of consumers.
(vi) The right to consumer education.

67 If a complaint is found frivolous or vexatious under the Consumer Protection Act, complainant shall pay to opposite party the cost

I. As specified by orders of the court.
II. Dismissal of complaint without any cost.
III. Not exceeding ten thousand rupees.
IV. One-tenth of the amount claimed as relief.

Codes

1 I and III are correct
2 III and IV are correct
3 II and IV are correct
4 I and II are correct

Ans. (1)

➲ *Exp.* If a complaint is found frivolous or vexatious under the Consumer Protection Act, complainant shall pay to opposite party the cost as specified by orders of the court and not exceeding ten thousand rupees.
Section 26 in the Consumer Protection Act, 1986 lays down the provision for dismissal of frivolous or vexatious complaints. It states that: "Where a complaint instituted before the District Forum, the State Commission or, as the case may be, the National Commission is found to be frivolous or vexatious, it shall, for reasons to be recorded in writing, dismiss the complaint and make an order that the complainant shall pay to the opposite party such cost, not exceeding ten thousand rupees, as may be specified in the order of the court."

68 Read Assertion (A) and Reason (R) and answer using the codes given below

Assertion (A) It shall not be a defence in a prosecution for an offence under Section 138 of the Negotiable Instrument Act that the drawer had no reason to believe when he issued the cheque that the cheque may be dishonoured on presentment for the reason stated in that Section.

Reason (R) Above assertion is laid down in Section 140 of the Negotiable Instrument Act.

Codes

1 Both (A) and (R) are false
2 Both (A) and (R) are right and (R) is correct explanation of (A)
3 (A) is true, but (R) is false
4 (A) is true, but (R) is false

Ans. (2)

➲ *Exp.* Both (A) and (R) are right and (R) is correct explanation of (A).

Section 140 of the Negotiable Instrument Act lays down the provision for defence which may not be allowed in any the prosecution under section 138. It states that "It shall not be a defence in a prosecution for an offence under section 138 that the drawer had no reason to believe when he issued the cheque that the cheque may be dishonoured on presentment for the reasons stated in that Section."

69 Match List I with List II and select the correct answer using the codes given below.

List I (Consequences of ultra vires transaction)	List II (Judgement)
A. Right of a member of company to get injunction against ultra vires transaction	I. Jehangir R Modi Vs. Shamji Ladha
B. Personal liability of directors	II. Attorney General Vs. Great Eastern Railway Company
C. Breach of warranty of authority to induce a third party to enter into ultra vires transaction with company	III. Coltman Vs. Coltman
D. Ultra vires acquired property	IV. Weeks Vs. Propert

Codes

	A	B	C	D
1	II	I	IV	III
2	I	II	IV	III
3	II	I	III	IV
4	IV	III	I	II

***Ans.* (1)**

➲ *Exp.* The correct matching is A-II, B-I, C-IV, D-III.

In *Attorney General Vs. Great Eastern Railway Company* case, it was held that it is the right of a member of company to get injunction against ultra vires transaction. In this case, a company was given permission to construct a railway through an act of the parliament. However, when two other companies collaborated with the first one to provide rolling stock for the railway, an injunction was brought to stop the same. The court held that a company was given permission to construct a railway through an act of the parliament. However, when two other companies collaborated with the first one to provide rolling stock for the railway, an injunction was brought to stop the same.

Jehangir R Modi Vs. Shamji Ladha case is related to personal liability of directors. In this case, the court held that shareholder can maintain an action against the directors without impleading the company to compel them to restore to the company, the funds of the company that have been employed in transactions that they have no authority to enter into.

In *Weeks Vs. Propert*, the issues related to breach of warranty of authority to induce a third party to enter into ultra vires transaction with company was discussed.

In *Coltman Vs. Coltman*, the court held that all contracts which were ultra vires were not necessarily illegal. The case is related to ultra vires acquired property.

70 Match List I with List II and select the correct answer using the codes given below

List I (Exceptions to doctrine of indoor management)	List II (Judgement)
A. Knowledge of irregularity	I. TR Pratt Ltd. Vs. MT Ltd.
B. Suspicion of irregularity	II. Ruben Vs. Great Fingall Consolidated
C. Forgery	III. Anand Behari Ltd. Vs. Dinshaw and Co.
D. Acts outside apparent authority	IV. Morris Vs. Kanssen

Codes

	A	B	C	D
1	II	III	I	IV
2	IV	I	III	II
3	I	IV	II	III
4	IV	I	II	III

***Ans.* (4)**

➲ *Exp.* The correct matching is A-IV, B-I, C-II, D-III.

Morris Vs. Kanssen is related to 'knowledge of irregularity'. In this case, a director could not defend an allotment of shares to him as he participated in the meeting, which made the allotment. His appointment as a director also fell through because none of the directors appointed him was validly in office.

TR Pratt Ltd. Vs. MT Ltd. is related to 'Suspicion of irregularity'. In this case, Company A had lent money to Company B for mortgaging its assets. The procedure for the same which was laid down in the Articles for such nature of transactions were not complied with. The Directors of both the companies were the same. It was held by the Court that the lender was aware of such an irregularity and hence the transaction was not binding.

Ruben Vs. Great Fingall Consolidated is related to Forgery. In this case, the plaintiffs advanced in good faith a sum of money which they had borrowed from their bankers to the Secretary of the defendant-company for their own purposes on the security of a share certificate issued to them by the Secretary which in accordance with the Articles of Association of the Company purported to be signed by two Directors, to bear the Company's seal, and to be countersigned by the Secretary. It turned out as a matter of fact that the signatures of the Directors were forgeries, and that the seal had been fraudulently affixed by the Secretary without any authority from the defendant-company.

The court held that the defendant-company were stopped by the certificate issued by their Secretary from disputing the right of the plaintiffs to have the names of their tankers registered as owners of the shares.

Anand Behari Ltd. Vs. Dinshaw and Co. is related to acts outside apparent authority. On an action brought by him for breach of contract, the court held the transfer to be void. It was observed that the power of transferring immovable property of the company could not be considered within the apparent authority of an accountant.

71 Read Assertion (A) and Reason (R) and answer using the codes given below

Assertion (A) Payer alone, whether a corporeal person or incorporeal person, shall be competent in case of dishonour of cheque.

Reason (R) Because Section 138 of Negotiable Instrument Act mandates so.

Codes

1 Both (A) and (R) are true and (R) is correct explanation of (A)
2 Both (A) and (R) are false
3 (A) is false, but (R) is true
4 (A) is true, but (R) is false

Ans. *(2)*

Exp. Both (A) and (R) are false.

According to Section 138 of Negotiable Instruments Act, payee or the holder in due course both are competent to sue the drawer of the cheque in case of dishonour of cheque.

Section 138 of Negotiable Instrument Act provides that: "Where any cheque drawn by a person on an account maintained by him with a banker for payment of any amount of money to another person from out of that account for the discharge, in whole or in part, of any debt or other liability, is returned by the bank unpaid, either because of the amount of money standing to the credit of that account is insufficient to honour the cheque or that it exceeds the amount arranged to be paid from that account by an agreement made with that bank, such person shall be deemed to have committed an offence and shall, without prejudice to any other provisions of this Act, be punished with imprisonment for 19 [a term which may be extended to two years], or with fine which may extend to twice the amount of the cheque, or with both: Provided that nothing contained in this section shall apply unless

(a) the cheque has been presented to the bank within a period of six months from the date on which it is drawn or within the period of its validity, whichever is earlier.
(b) the payee or the holder in due course of the cheque, as the case may be, makes a demand for the payment of the said amount of money by giving a notice in writing, to the drawer of the cheque, 20 [within thirty days] of the receipt of information by him from the bank regarding the return of the cheque as unpaid.
(c) the drawer of such cheque fails to make the payment of the said amount of money to the payee or, as the case may be, to the holder in due course of the cheque, within fifteen days of the receipt of the said notice."

72 Which of the following statements is correct ?

1 A condition is a stipulation essential to any purpose of the contract
2 A warranty is a stipulation collateral to any purpose of the contract
3 When a buyer waives a warranty, it becomes a condition
4 Where a contract of sale is not severable and the buyer has accepted the goods or part thereof, the breach of any condition to be fulfilled by the seller can only be treated as a breach of warranty and not as a ground for rejecting the goods and treating the contract as repudiated, unless there is a term of the contract, express or implied to that effect.

Ans. *(4)*

Exp. Statement 4 is correct because Section 13(2) of The Sale of Goods Act states that: "Where a contract of sale is not severable and the buyer has accepted the goods or part thereof, the breach of any condition to be fulfilled by the seller can only be treated as a breach of warranty and not as a ground for rejecting the goods and treating the contract as repudiated, unless there is a term of the contract, express or implied, to that effect."

73 Match List I with List II and select the correct answer using the codes given below

List I	List II
A. Goods in sale of goods	I. Bhopal Sugar Industries Ltd. Vs. STO
B. Consideration for a sale of goods	II. Instalment Supply Ltd. Vs. STO
C. Sale and agreement to sale	III. R.D. Goyal Vs. Reliance Industries Ltd.
D. Difference between contract of sale and contract of agency	IV. Aldridge Vs. Johnson

Codes

	A	B	C	D		A	B	C	D
1	III	IV	II	I	2	IV	III	II	I
3	III	IV	I	II	4	II	I	IV	III

Ans. *(1)*

Exp. The correct matching is A-III, B-IV, C-II, D-I.

R.D. Goyal Vs. Reliance Industries Ltd. is related to goods in sale of goods.

Aldridge Vs. Johnson is related to consideration for a sale of goods.

Instalment Supply Ltd. Vs. STO is related to sale and agreement to sale.

Bhopal Sugar Industries Ltd. Vs. STO is related to difference between contract of sale and contract of agency.

74 Which of the following partnerships are legal ? Answer using the codes given below

I. Twelve members forming a banking firm

II. A partnership to create a monopoly

III. Twenty members forming a firm for tea trade on a railway platform

IV. Trustees carry on business of a firm in their own name

Codes

1 I, II, III and IV 2 II, III and IV

3 II and III 4 III and IV

Ans. *(4)*

Exp. Statement III and IV contains the conditions for the legal partnerships.

Statement I is not correct as in a legal partnership the maximum number of partners required to start a business firm is 10.

Statement II is not correct as the purpose of the partnership to create a monopoly is unlawful.

75 Read Assertion (A) and Reason (R) and answer using codes given below

Assertion (A) Notwithstanding a contract between the partners, a partner shall not indemnify the firm for any loss caused to it by his wilful neglect in the conduct of the business of the firm.

Reason (R) Because Section 13(f) of Indian Partnership Act stipulates so.

Codes

1 Both (A) and (R) are true and (R) is correct explanation of (A)

2 Both (A) and (R) are false

3 (A) is true and (R) is false

4 (R) is true and (A) is false

Ans. *(2)*

Exp. Both (A) and (R) are false.

Section 13(f) of the Indian Partnership Act states that a partner shall indemnify the firm for any loss caused to it by his willful neglect in the conduct of the business of the firm.

UGC-NET
LAW

SOLVED PAPER 2015 (December)

PAPER II

1 Read Assertion (A) and Reason (R) and select the correct answer using the codes given below.

Assertion (A) The Preamble of the Constitution of India defines the ideal philosophy of Indian democracy and its key-concepts are laid down as justice, liberty, equality and fraternity.

Reason (R) A democracy to be real must be characterised by two features.

Codes

1 Both (A) and (R) are true and (R) is the correct explanation of (A)
2 Both (A) and (R) are true, but (R) is not the correct explanation of (A)
3 (A) is true, but (R) is false
4 (A) is false, but (R) is true

Ans. *(3)*

Exp. The Assertion (A) is true, but the Reason (R) is false. The Preamble of the Constitution of India defines the ideal philosophy of Indian democracy and its key-concepts are laid down as justice, liberty, equality and fraternity. It is also considered to be the key to the minds of the makers of the Constitution. Thus, the Assertion is true.

However, a democracy to be real, must not be characterised by two features only. A real democracy must fulfill all the philosophies mentioned in the Preamble. Hence, the Reason is false.

2 Which of the following statements is wrong to issue Writ of Quo-warranto?

1 The office in question should be a public office
2 The office should be held by an usurper without legal authority
3 The petition is barred by res-judicate
4 It is necessary for the petitioner to show that he himself suffered a personal injury nor it is necessary to show that he is seeking redress of a personal grievance

Ans. *(4)*

Exp. Only Statement 4 is incorrect to issue Writ of Quo-warranto.

A Writ of Quo-warranto is not a petition, but a notice of demand, issued by a demandant, to a respondent claiming some delegated power and filed with a court of competent jurisdiction, to hold a hearing within 3 to 20 days, depending on the distance of the respondent to the court, to present proof of his authority to execute his claimed powers. It was held in the case of Bindra Ban Vs. Sham Sundar that it is not necessary for the petitioner to show that he himself suffered a personal injury or it is necessary to show that he is seeking redress of a personal grievance, to issue a Writ of Quo-warranto.

3 Match List I with List II and select the correct answer using the codes given below the list.

List I	List II
A. SR Chaudhary Vs. State of Punjab	I. Ban on smoking at public places
B. Murali S Deora Vs. Union of India	II. Two extra increments to the existing employees on earning Higher Qualification
C. Food Corporation of India Vs. Bharatiya Khadya Nigam Karmachari Sangh	III. Classifications based on the number of children for elected post in Panchayat
D. Javed Vs. State of Haryana	IV. Non-member cannot be re-appointed as minister if he fails to get elected within six months

Codes

	A	B	C	D		A	B	C	D
1	IV	I	II	III	2	IV	II	I	III
3	II	II	IV	I	4	III	II	IV	I

Ans. *(1)*

Exp. The correct matching is A-IV; B-I; C-II; D-III.

SR Choudhary Vs. State of Punjab is the case in which the Court held that a Non-member cannot be re-appointed as minister if he fails to get elected within six months. Further, the Supreme Court, after a combined reading of Articles 75 and 88, held that "The combined effect of these two articles is that a person not being a Member of either house of Parliament can be a Minister up to a period of six months. Though he would not have any right to vote, he would be entitled to participate in the proceedings thereof."

Murali S Deora Vs. Union of India case dealt with ban on smoking at public places. The Supreme Court found that smoking in public places is injurious to the health of non-smokers and violated their right to life and liberty.

Food Corporation of India Vs. Bharatiya Khadya Nigam Karmachari Sangh case dealt with providing two extra increments to the existing employees on earning Higher Qualification. The main grievance in this petition was that the employees were unable to exercise their option to receive a sanctioned monthly pension before the cut-off date.

Javed Vs. State of Haryana case dealt with classifications based on the number of children for elected post in Panchayat. The court upheld the provision of the Haryana Panchayati Raj Act, 1994 while citing the reason that the Act is made for the benefits of the general public.

4 Which of the following statements are correct?

Freedom of press includes

I. Right to print and publish news
II. Distribution of printed matter
III. Criticism of public affairs
IV. Pre-censorship

Codes

1 I, II, III and IV
2 I, II and III
3 I, III and IV
4 II, III and IV

Ans. (2)

Exp. Freedom of press includes the right to print and publish news, to distribute the printed matter and to criticise public affairs.

However, pre-censorship is actually a tool to curtail freedom of speech instead of pushing it forward.

5 During a Financial Emergency, the executive authority of the union exercises control over state finances through the following measures

I. It can issue directions to states to observe certain cannons of financial propriety.
II. It can ask the states to reserve their Money Bills for the consideration of the President
II. It can direct the states to reduce the salaries and allowances of all the persons serving in connection with the affairs of the states, including the judges of the Supreme Court and High Courts.

Codes

1 I and II 2 I and III
3 II and III 4 I, II and III

Ans. (4)

Exp. All the given statements are correct.

By virtue of Clause 3 of Article 360, the executive authority of the Union has the power to issue directions to states to observe certain cannons of financial propriety.

It can also ask the states to reserve their Money Bills for the consideration of the President.

Further, it can also direct the states to reduce the salaries and allowances of all the persons serving in connection with the affairs of the states, including the judges of the Supreme Court and High Courts.

6 Justice Pasayat held that 'pardon obtained on the basis of manifest mistake or fraud can be rescinded or cancelled' in which of the case?

1 G Krishta Goud Vs. State of AP
2 Maru Ram Vs. Union of India
3 Epuru Sudhakar Vs. Government of AP
4 Kehar Singh Vs. Union of India

Ans. (3)

Exp. Justice Pasayat held that 'pardon obtained on the basis of manifest mistake or fraud can be rescinded or cancelled' in the case of Epuru Sudhakar Vs. Government of AP.

In this case, the immunity of the pardoning power of the Governor from judicial review had come up. Supreme Court set aside a decision of the then Andhra Pradesh Governor Sushil Kumar Shinde, remitting the sentence of a Congress activist who faced ten years in prison in connection with the killing of two persons including a TDP activist, the Supreme Court bench of Justices S H Kapadia and Arijit Pasayat warned that the exercise of the power would be tested by the court against the maintenance of Rule of Law.

7 Given below are two statements. One is labelled as Assertion (A) and the other is labelled as Reason (R).

Assertion (A) The administrative control over the Subordinate Judiciary in the State lies with the Governor.

Reason (R) The High Court has a power of Superintendence over all courts and tribunals throughout the territory in relation to which it exercises jurisdiction, except military court and tribunals.

Codes

1 Both (A) and (R) and true and (R) is the correct explanation of (A)
2 Both (A) and (R) are true, but (R) is not the correct explanation of (A)
3 (A) is true, but (R) is false
4 (A) is false, but (R) is true

Ans. (4)

➲ *Exp.* The Assertion (A) is false, but the Reason (R) is true.

The Administrative control over the Subordinate Judiciary in the State lies with the High Court and not the governor. The High Court, being at the helm of the judiciary of the state, has administrative control over the subordinate judiciary of the state in respect of certain matters. This is in addition to the appellate and superintending jurisdiction.

According to Article 227 of the Constitution, the High Court has a power of Superintendence over all courts and tribunals throughout the territory in relation to which it exercises jurisdiction, except military court and tribunals.

8 Who has described Jurisprudence as "The lawyer's extraversion. It is lawyer's examination of the precepts, ideals and techniques of the law in the light derived from present knowledge in disciplines other than the law"?

1 Paton　　2 Holland
3 Austin　　4 Julius Stone

Ans. (4)

➲ *Exp.* Julius Stone has described Jurisprudence as "The lawyer's extraversion. It is a lawyer's examination of the precepts, ideals and techniques of the law in the light derived from present knowledge in disciplines other than the law."

The term 'jurisprudence' has been subjected to different meanings at different times. This variation is due to the different methods of inquiry and approach to the study of this subject. For instance, in England during the formative era, the term 'jurisprudence' was being used in a generic sense to include the study of various facets of law.

9 Who may be regarded as the leading contemporary representative of British Positivism?

1 Holland　　2 Salmond
3 Hart　　4 Hohfeld

Ans. (3)

➲ *Exp.* Hart may be regarded as the leading contemporary representative of British Positivism.

He revolutionized the methods of jurisprudence and the philosophy of law. Hart authored 'The Concept of Law' and made major contributions to political philosophy. He is regarded as the leading contemporary representative of British positivism. From his book it shows that he is a linguist, philosopher, barrister and a jurist. To Hart, law is a system of rules. According to him, "Where there is law, the human conduct is non-optional or obligatory.

10 Match List I with List II and select the correct answer by using the codes given below.

List I	List II
A. Justice is realised only through good law	I. Jerome Hall
B. Moral value needs to be included in a definition of positive law	II. John Finnis
C. Natural law with a variable content	III. Morris
D. A sophisticated version of Natural Law has been put forward in the tradition of Aristotle and Aquinas	IV. Stammler

Codes

	A	B	C	D		A	B	C	D
1	II	IV	I	III	2	I	II	III	IV
3	III	I	IV	II	4	IV	III	II	I

Ans. (1)

➲ *Exp.* The correct matching is A-II; B-IV; C-I; D-III.

Justice is realised only through good law is given by John Finnis. Finnis notion of justice consists of three components: general justice, distributive justice and commutative justice. The underlying principle behind any unjust law for Finnis is that a basic good must not be directly attacked by a law or in the alternative the common good must be favoured, fostered, or respected by a law. Deviations from this negative or positive test result in injustice in the law.

Moral value needs to be included in a definition of positive law is given by Stammler. According to him, law should be seen as one of the regulating standards for the social economy, in which people cooperate to meet their needs through production and exchange of goods and services.

Natural law with a variable content is given by Jerome Hall. He found partial truths and also certain fallacies in the dominating legal philosophies such as legal positivism, natural law, and sociology of law. He delineated the salient features of his "integrative jurisprudence" in which the basic concept was "law-as-action."

A sophisticated version of Natural Law has been put forward in the tradition of Aristotle and Aquinas is given by Morris. Aristotle's association with natural law may be due to the interpretation given to his works by Thomas Aquinas. But whether Aquinas correctly read Aristotle is in dispute.

11 According to whom, whenever a person looked like an owner in relation to a thing, he had possession of it, unless possession was denied him by special rules based on practical convenience. The 'Animus' element was simply an intelligent awareness of the situation?

1 Salmond　　2 Pollock
3 Ihering　　4 Savigny

Ans. (3)

➲ *Exp.* According to Ihering, whenever a person looked like an owner in relation to a thing, he had possession of it, unless possession was denied him by special rules based on practical convenience. The 'Animus' element was simply an intelligent awareness of the situation.

Ihering (1818-1892) was a German jurist. He is known as the 'Father of Modern Sociological Jurisprudence'. Possession, according to him, is more objective and it presents a sociological approach to possession. It was stated by him that whenever a person looked like an owner in relation to a thing, he had possession of it unless possession was denied to him by rules of law based on practical convenience.

12 Match List I with List II and select the correct answer by using the codes given below.

List I	List II
A. Social Solidarity	I. Roscoe Pound
B. Social Utilitarian	II. Grotius
C. Social Engineering	III. Duguit
D. Social Contract	IV. Ihering

Codes

	A	B	C	D		A	B	C	D
1	I	I	III	IV	2	II	III	IV	I
3	IV	I	II	III	4	III	IV	I	II

***Ans.* (4)**

Exp. The correct matching is A-III; B-IV; C-I; D-II.

Social solidarity theory is given by Duguit. The theory of Social Solidarity describe the social cooperation between individuals for their need and survival.

Social utilitarian is associated with Ihering.He was inspired by Bentham and Mill's utilitarianism for he defines 'interest' in terms of pleasure and pain. However, he rejected their ideas of individualism.

Social engineering theory was given by Roscoe Pound. His social engineering theory is an American correlation to the interests of German jurisprudence.

Social contract theory was given by Grotius. Hugo Grotius was of the opinion that the social contract theory is a historical fact. He argued that by entering into a social contract, the people are forfeiting their right to punish the rule, however bad his government may be.

13 Match List I with List II and select the correct answer by using the codes given below.

List I	List II
A. Legal right means, "A capacity residing in one man of controlling with the assent and assistance of the state, the acts of the other".	I. Gray
B. 'Right' is not the interest by itself but it is a mean by which enjoyment of interest in secured.	II. Holland
C. 'Right' is power over an object which by means of this right he subjected to will of the person enjoying the right	III. Duguit
D. No one has any other 'right' than always to do his duty	IV. Pachta

Codes

	A	B	C	D		A	B	C	D
1	IV	III	I	II	2	I	II	III	IV
3	III	I	II	IV	4	II	IV	I	III

***Ans.* (1)**

Exp. The correct matching is A-IV, B-III, C-I, D-II.

According to *Pachta* legal right means, "A capacity residing in one man of controlling with the assent and assistance of the state, the acts of the other". This theory was widely accepted by the jurists in Germany.

According to *Duguit*, 'Right' is not the interest by itself but it is a means by which enjoyment of interest is secured. He emphasised on the concept of duty which is the basis of co-operation and rejected the abstract concept of right which is the source of conflict.

According to *Gray*, 'Right' is power over an object which by means of this right he subjected to the will of the person enjoying the right. His definition is criticised on the ground that he is not concerned with the nature of law rather than its Purposes and Ends.

According to *Holland*, no one has any other 'right' than always to do his duty. He emphasised on the enforcement of legal rights.

14 Who has state that "As a matter of fact international law is neither a myth on the one hand nor a penacea on the other, but just one institution among other which we can use for the building of a better international order"?

1 Professor Louis Henkin 2 JL Brierly
3 JG Starke 4 Oppenheim

***Ans.* (2)**

Exp. JL Brierly stated that, "As a matter of fact international law is neither a myth on the one hand nor a panacea on the other, but just one institution among other which we can use for the building of a better international order."

Brierly was a British lawyer and a professor of international law. There have been varied definitions of international law by different jurists.

According to Prof. L. Oppenheim Law of Nations or International Law is the name for the body of customary and conventional rules which are considered legally binding by the civilised states in their intercourse with each other.

15 Which one of the following sources of International Law does not find or mention in Article 38 of the statute of the International Court of Justice but it has now become a well recognised source?

1 International conventions
2 General principles of law recognised by civilised nations
3 Decisions of Judicial or arbitral tribunals and juristic works
4 Decision or determination of the organs of International Institutions

***Ans.* (4)**

Exp. Article 38(1) of the ICJ statute recognises international conventions, international customs, general principles of law and judicial decisions and the teachings of the most highly qualified publicists of the various nations as sources of international law.

However, the decision or determination of the organs of International Institutions does not find a mention in Article 38 but has now become an effective source of international law as well.

16 Which of the following statements is/are correct?

I. Custom is the oldest and the original source of International as well as of law in general.

II. In Barcelona Traction case, the International Court applied the general rule of subrogation.

II. In Chorzow factory (Indemnity) case the Permanent court of Justice ruled that' the International law is based on justice, equity and good conscience.

IV. In Nicaragua Vs. USA the World Court has taken the view that the sources of International law are not hierarchial but are necessarily complementary and inter related.

Codes

1 Only I is correct
2 I, II and III are correct
3 Both I and IV are correct
4 I, II, III and IV all are correct

Ans. (3)

Exp. Statements I and IV are correct.

Custom is one of the oldest and well-recognised sources of international law and law in general.

Nicaragua Vs. The USA case was decided in favour of Nicaragua and against the United States with the awarding of reparations to Nicaragua.

Statement II and III are incorrect.

The Barcelona Traction case is a well-recognised case in public international law concerning the abuse of rights and not the general rule of subrogation.

In the Crew Factory case, it was held that reparations were to be made for violations of international law as a general principle.

17 Which of the following statement(s) is/are incorrect?

I. There are five prominent theories of relationship between International law and Municipal law.

II. According to Dualism Theory law is a unified branch of knowledge.

III. 'Mosism' and 'Dualism' are diametrically opposed to each other.

IV. Wright, Kelson and Duguit are prominent exponents of Dualism Theory.

Codes

1 II and IV are incorrect
2 I, II and IV are incorrect
3 Only IV is incorrect
4 I, II, III and IV all are incorrect

Ans. (1)

Exp. Statements II and IV are incorrect.

According to Dualism theory, the system of International Law and Municipal Law are separate and self-contained to the extent that the rules of the one are not expressly or tacitly received into the other system.

Wright, Kelson and Duguit are some of the prominent exponents of Monism theory and not of Dualism theory.

18 Match List I with List II and select the correct answer by using the codes given below the list.

List I (Provisions)	List II (Articles of Statute of International Court)
A. Law applied by the International Court of Justice	I. Article 62
B. Transferred Jurisdiction	II. Article 59
C. Court power to allow a state to intervene in case to which if is not party	III. Article 38
D. Binding force of the decisions of the International Court of Justice	IV. Article 36 (5)

Codes

	A	B	C	D		A	B	C	D
1	I	II	III	IV	2	IV	III	II	I
3	III	IV	I	II	4	II	I	IV	III

Ans. (3)

Exp. The correct matching is A-III; B-IV; C-I; D-II.

Article 38 mention that law to be applied by the International Court of Justice when deciding cases within its jurisdiction. It is generally considered to be the most authoritative enumeration of the sources of International Law.

Article 36(5) mention the Transferred jurisdiction. Declarations made under Article 36 of the Statute of the Permanent Court of International Justice and which are still in force shall be deemed, as between the parties to the present Statute, to be acceptances of the compulsory jurisdiction of the International Court of Justice for the period which they still have to run and in accordance with their terms.

Article 62 mention that Court has power to allow a state to intervene in a case to which it is not a party. It shall then be upon the Court to decide on this request.

Article 59 mention about the binding force of the decisions of the International Court of Justice. It states that the decision of the Court has no binding force except between the parties and in respect of that particular case.

19 Given below are two statements. One is labelled as Assertion (A) and the other is labelled as Reason (R).

Assertion (A) When a state wants to delay the de jure recognition of any state, it may, in the first stage grant de-facto recognition.

Reason (R) There is no distinction between 'de facto' and 'de jure' recognition for the purpose of giving effect to the internal acts of the recognised authority.

Use the codes below and select the correct answer.

Codes

1 Both (A) and (R) are true and (R) is the correct explanation of (A)
2 Both (A) and (R) are true, but (R) is not the correct explanation of (A)
3 (A) is true (R) is false
4 (A) is false (R) is true

Ans. (2)

Exp. Both (A) and (R) are true, but (R) is not the correct explanation of (A).

According to Prof. G. Schwarzenberger, "When a state wants to delay the de jure recognition of any state, it may, in the first stage grant de facto recognition." Thus, Assertion is correct.

In the case of Luther v. Sagor, it was that there is no distinction between 'de facto' and 'de jure' for the purpose of giving effect to the internal acts of the recognised authority. Thus, R is correct but it is not the correct explanation to the Assertion which talks about the stages in granting recognition to a state.

20 Two person are said to be related to each other by uterine blood when they are descended from

1 a common ancestor by the same wife
2 a common ancestor by the different wives
3 a common ancestress by the same husband
4 a common ancestress but the different husbands

Ans. (4)

Exp. Section 3(e)(ii) of the Hindu Succession Act, 1956 provides that two persons are said to be related to each other by uterine blood when they are descended from a common ancestress but by different husbands.

21 Match the List I with List II under the Hindu Marriage Act, 1955 and select the correct answer with the help of codes given below.

List I	List II
A. Restitution of Conjugal Rights	I. Section 5
B. Marriageable Age	II. Section 29 (2)
C. Customary Divorce	III. Section 9
D. Ceremonies of Marriage	IV. Section 7

Codes

	A	B	C	D		A	B	C	D
1	IV	I	II	III	2	III	II	I	IV
3	III	I	II	IV	4	I	II	III	IV

Ans. (3)

Exp. The correct matching is A-III; B-I; C-II; D-IV.

Restitution of conjugal rights is mentioned in Section 9 of Hindu Marriage Act, 1955. It states when either the husband or the wife has, without reasonable excuse, withdrawn from the society of the other, the aggrieved party may apply, by petition to the district court, for restitution of conjugal rights and the court, on being satisfied of the truth of the statements made in such petition and that there is no legal ground why the application should not be granted, may decree restitution of conjugal rights accordingly.

Marriageable age is mentioned in Section 5 of Hindu Marriage Act, 1955. It states a marriage may be solemnised between any two Hindus, if the conditions given in this Section are fulfilled.

Customary Divorce is mentioned in Section 29(2) of Hindu Marriage Act. It states nothing contained in this Act shall be deemed to affect any right recognised by custom or conferred by any special enactment to obtain the dissolution of a Hindu marriage, whether solemnized before or after the commencement of this Act.

Ceremonies of marriage is mentioned in Section 7 of Hindu Marriage Act. It states a Hindu marriage may be solemnized in accordance with the customary rites and ceremonies of either party thereto.

22 In which of the following cases, a child could be a Hindu? Answer with the help of codes

I. Only one parent is a Hindu and the child was brought up as a Hindu
II. Only one parent is a Hindu and the child was not brought up as a Hindu
II. If after the birth of child, father converts to non-Hindu religion
IV. Both the parents are Hindu

Codes

1 I, III and IV
2 II, III and IV
3 I and IV
4 III and IV

Ans. (1)

Exp. Statements I, III and IV are correct.

Statement II is incorrect as according to explanation of Section 2 (1) (b) a person is Hindu, Buddhist, Jains or Sikh by religion if any child, legitimate or illegitimate, one of whose parents is a Hindu, Buddhist, Jaina or Sikh by religion and who is brought up as a member of the tribe, community, group or family to which such parent belongs or belonged.

23 Under the provision of the Hindu Marriage Act, 1955, the degree of Judicial Separation

I. dissolve the marriage.
II. does not dissolve the marriage bond but only suspends marital rights and obligations during the subsistence of the decree.

III. the parties continue to be husband and wife but not obligated to live together and neither party is free to marry.

IV. if after a decree of judicial separation the parties have not resumed cohabitation for a period of one year, either party may seek divorce.

Codes

1 I, II and III 2 II, I and IV
3 II, III and IV 4 I, II, III and IV

***Ans.* (3)**

Exp. Statements II, III and IV are correct.

Statement I is incorrect because judicial separation does not dissolve the marriage per se but only suspends the marital rights and obligations. Reference can be made to Section 10 of the Hindu Marriage Act, 1955.

24 Read Assertion (A) and Reason (R) and select the correct answer with the help of codes given below.

Assertion (A) The Muslim Personal Law (Shariat) Application Act, 1937 makes Muslim Law applicable expressly to all Muslims.

Reason (R) The Muslim Personal Law (Shariat) Application Act, 1937 has abrogated the customs and restores to Muslims their own personal law in almost all cases.

Codes

1 (A) and (R) are true and (R) is the correct explanation of (A)
2 (A) is true but (R) is false
3 (A) is false but (R) is true
4 Both (A) and (R) are false

***Ans.* (1)**

Exp. Both (A) and (R) are true and (R) is the correct explanation of (A).

It was through the Muslim Personal Law (Shariat) Application Act, 1937 that the Act was expressly made applicable to all Muslims. This Act deals with marriage, succession, inheritance and charities among Muslims.

The Muslim Personal Law (Shariat) Application Act, 1937 has abrogated the customs and restores to Muslims their own personal law in almost all cases. The objective of this Act was to restore the personal Muslim laws to the Muslims in almost all cases. So, (R) is the correct explanation of (A).

25 Observance of 'Iddat' is necessary

1 where Cohabitation is lawful i.e. consummation of marriage
2 where Cohabitation is unlawful i.e. illicit intercourse and the pregnancy follows the illicit intercourse
3 In Both (1) and (2)
4 Only in (1) and not in (2)

***Ans.* (3)**

Exp. Observance of 'Iddat' is necessary where cohabitation is lawful i.e. consummation of marriage and where cohabitation is unlawful i.e. illicit intercourse and the pregnancy follows the illicit intercourse.

Iddah or 'Iddat' is an Arabic term which means period of waiting and is observed by Muslim women. A marriage with a woman who is undergoing iddat is termed as irregular marriage.

26 Modern sources of Hindu law are

1 Legislation, Precedents and Digests
2 Legislation, Precedents, Equity
3 Precedents, Smritis and Legislation
4 Legislation, Customs, Precedents and Commentaries

***Ans.* (2)**

Exp. Precedents, Legislations and Equity are the modern sources of Hindu Law.

Legislations are Acts of Parliament, which have been playing a paramount role in the formation of Hindu Law. Shrutis, Smritis, Customs, Digests and Commentaries are traditional sources of Hindi law.

27 Match List I with List II and select the correct answer using the codes given below.

List I (Heads of Public Policy)	List II (Case-Law)
A. Trading with enemy	I. Girdhari Singh Vs. Neeladhar Singh
B. Trafficking in public offices	II. Espostiv Vs. Bowden
C. Interference with administration of justice	III. Shivsaran Lal Vs. Keshav Prasad
D. Marriage brokage contracts	IV. Nand Kishore Vs. Kunj Behari Lal

Codes

	A	B	C	D		A	B	C	D
1	I	IV	II	III	2	IV	I	II	III
3	IV	I	III	II	4	II	III	I	IV

***Ans.* (2)**

Exp. The correct matching is A-IV; B-I; C-II; D-III.

Nand Kishore Vs. Kunj Behari Lal is related to trading with enemy. This case was a second appeal by the defendants against the concurrent decrees of the two lower courts.

Girdhari Singh Vs. Neeladhar Singh case is related to trafficking in public offices.

Espostiv Vs. Bowden is related to interference with the administration of justice. It was held that if performance of a contract becomes illegal by English law the contract is discharged.

Shivsaran Lal Vs. Keshav Prasad is related to Marriage brokerage contracts. In this case the defendant had applied for a certificate that the case complied with the requirements of Section 110 of the Code of Civil Procedure.

28 Read Assertion (A) and Reason (R) and select the correct answer using the codes given below

Assertion (A) Compensation is recoverable for any loss or damage arising unnaturally in the unusual course of things from breach of contract, or which the parties did not know at the time of the contract as likely to result from the breach.

Reason (R) Because Section 73 of the Indian Contract Act stipulates so.

Codes

1 Both (A) and (R) are true and (R) is correct explanation for (A)
2 Both (A) and (R) are false
3 (A) is true, but (R) is false
4 (R) is true, but (A) is false

Ans. (2)

Exp. Both Assertion (A) and Reason (R) are false.

Section 73 of the Indian Contract Act, provides for Compensation of loss or damage caused by breach of contract and states that "When a contract has been broken, the party who suffers by such breach is entitled to receive, from the party who has broken the contract, compensation for any loss or damage caused to him thereby, which naturally arose in the usual course of things from such breach, or which the parties knew, when they made the contract, to be likely to result from the breach of it." Since the Assertion states the opposite of what has been stated in Section 73, it is false.

29 Doctrine of frustration was laid down for the first time in

1 Krell Vs. Henry
2 Taylor Vs. Caldwell
3 Paradine Vs. Jane
4 Cricklewood Property and Investment Trust Ltd. Vs. Leighton's Investment Trust Ltd

Ans. (2)

Exp. The Doctrine of frustration was laid down for the first time in the case of Taylor Vs. Caldwell.

The case is related to a music hall which was destroyed by fire, without fault of either party and both the parties were excused, as it was held that the performance under the contract depended upon the existence of the hall. In India, this doctrine finds its application under Section 56 of the Contract Act.

30 Which of the following statements is correct?

1 A contract is voidable because it was caused by a mistake as to any law in force in India
2 A mistake as to law not in force in India has the same effect as a mistake of fact
3 A contract is voidable merely because it was caused by one of the parties to it being under a mistake as to a matter of fact
4 Where both the parties to an agreement are under a mistake as to a matter of fact essential to the agreement is not void

Ans. (2)

Exp. Statement 2 is correct by virtue of Section 21 of the Indian Contract Act which provides for the effect of mistakes as to law. It states that a contract is not voidable because it was caused by a mistake as to any law in force in India; but a mistake as to a law not in force in India has the same effect as a mistake of fact.

31 An agreement without consideration is valid, unless

1 It is in writing and registered
2 Is a promise to compensate for something done
3 It is made by two minors
4 Is a promise to pay a debt barred by limitation law

Ans. (3)

Exp. An agreement without consideration is valid, unless it is made by two minors.

All other conditions given in question are mentioned under Section 25 of the Indian Contract Act, which provides for cases where agreements without consideration are not void. According to the Indian law, an agreement with a minor/ between two minors is void-ab-initio.

32 A proposal is revoked

1 by the notice of revocation of the proposal
2 by the lapse of a reasonable time if time is prescribed in the proposal
3 by acceptance of a condition precedent to acceptance
4 by the death or insanity of the proposer, if the fact of his death or insanity comes to the knowledge of the acceptor before acceptance

Ans. (4)

Exp. A proposal is revoked by the death or insanity of the proposer, if the fact of his death or insanity comes to the knowledge of the acceptor before acceptance.

As per Section 6 of the Indian Contract Act, a proposal is revoked in the following cases:

(a) by the communication of notice of revocation by the proposer to the other party;
(b) by the lapse of the time prescribed in such proposal for its acceptance, or, if no time is so prescribed, by the lapse of a reasonable time, without communication of the acceptance;
(c) by the failure of the acceptor to fulfil a condition precedent to acceptance; or
(d) by the death or insanity of the proposer, if the fact of his death or insanity comes to the knowledge of the acceptor before acceptance.

33 In order to bring an action for tort, the plaintiff has to prove that

1 There has been a legal damage caused to him
2 Violation of a legal right not vested in him
3 There has been no legal damage caused to him
4 Violation of no legal right and has not resulted in harm to him

Ans. (1)

Exp. In order to bring an action for tort, the plaintiff has to prove that there has been legal damage caused to him.

In other words, there must be the existence of injuria sine damnum (injury without damage) to enable an action under tort law. It is injuria sine damnum and not damnum sine injuria that is actionable under the tort law.

34 In which case it was held by the Supreme Court that state was not liable on the ground that police were acting in discharge of statutory powers and power of the police in keeping the property in the police Malkhana was a sovereign power?

1 Ramawati Kaur Vs. State Bihar
2 Radha Aggarwal Vs. State of UP
3 Kasturi Lal Vs. State of UP
4 State of Bihar Vs. Rameshwar Prasad

Ans. (3)

Exp. In the case of Kasturi Lal Vs. State of UP the Supreme Court held that the state was not liable on the ground that police were acting in discharge of statutory powers and power of the police in keeping the property in the police Malkhana was a sovereign power.

The Court distinguished between the Sovereign and non-Sovereign functions of the state and held that since the act of police officers is a Sovereign act, the State is not liable.

35 Match the List I with List II and select the correct answer by using the codes given below.

List I (Name of defence)		List II (Name of Case-Law)
A.	Act of State	I. Buron Vs. Denman
B.	Consent	II. Hail Vs. Brookland and Auto Racing Club
C.	Statutory authority	III. Metropolitan Asylum Board Vs. Hills
D.	Act of God	IV. Nicholas Vs. Marsland

Codes

	A	B	C	D		A	B	C	D
1	III	II	I	IV	2	I	II	IV	III
3	III	I	II	IV	4	I	II	III	IV

Ans. (4)

Exp. The correct matching is A-I; B-II; C-III; D-IV.

Buron Vs. Denman is related to Act of State. It was held that if a servant of the Crown commits a wrongful act against an alien, and the Crown authorised such act, or subsequently ratified it, it is an act of State and no action will lie in respect of it against such servant (Act of State as a general defence).

Hail Vs. Brookland and Auto Racing Club is related to Consent. It is a landmark case of Volenti non fit injuria which means to voluntarily give consent to take the risk of injury. It is one of the general defences against the claim of tort.

Metropolitan Asylum Board Vs. Hills is related to Statutory authority. The authority to construct a hospital by the local authority was construed as impliedly conditional only, i.e. to erect the hospital provided that the hospital authorities selected a site where no injurious results were likely to be caused to others.

Nicholas Vs. Marsland is related to Act of God. The defendant was held not liable under Rylands Vs. Fletcher as the cause of the flood was an act of God.

36 In which of the following cases, is the occupier of a house liable for 'negligence?

1 Keeping a dog, which may bite trespassers
2 Fixing broken glass pieces on the top of a wall to prevent trespassers
3 Setting spring guns in the premises to prevent trespassers
4 Constructing a compound wall to prevent trespassers

Ans. (3)

Exp. The occupier of a house can be held liable for 'negligence' in case if they set up spring guns in the premises to prevent trespassers.

In the case of Katko Vs. Briney, two homeowners were held liable for injuries caused to a trespasser who set off a spring gun set as a mantrap in an abandoned house on the homeowners' property.

37 Read Assertion (A) Reason (R) and select the correct answer with the help of codes given below.

Assertion (A) Mental element is a essential element in most of the torts.

Reason (R) State of mind of the defendant is not relevant to ascertain his liability in all branches of law of torts.

Codes

1 Both (A) and (R) are true and (R) is the correct explanation of (A)
2 Both (A) and (R) are true, but (R) is not the correct explanation of (A)
3 Both (A) and (R) are true
4 Both (A) and (R) and false

Ans. (4)

Exp. Both (A) and (R) are false.

Unlike criminal law, both intention and mens rea are not important grounds to constitute a tort in most of the cases. It is the act and not the motive for the act that must be regarded to constitute a tort. Thus, Assertion is false. However, it cannot be said that the defendant's state of mind is irrelevant in all cases of torts. Torts like defamation, malicious prosecution will require the presence of a guilty intention. Thus, Reason is false.

38 Which one of the following is not an exception to the rule of Volenti non-fit injuria?

1 Surgeon amputates a limb of a patient to save his life
2 Injury is caused while play-fighting with naked swords at a religion function
3 Injury is caused while doing lawful acts under contract
4 Injury is cause to a player in football match

Ans. (4)

➲ *Exp.* Injury caused to a player during a football match is not an exception to the rule of Volenti non fit injuria, rather it comes within the ambit of this rule.

A player, while playing a match, is well-aware of the risks associated with it and thus voluntarily consents to his suffering of the same.

39 Which of the facts do not include within the principle of joint liability?

1 The actuated act need not be a crime or when it was foisted
2 An act done in a pre-arranged plan between more than one person
3 More participation in some manner in the act constituting the offence
4 An act done in furtherance of a intention to cause harm

Ans. (1)

➲ *Exp.* The actuated act need not be a crime or when it was foisted do not include within the principle of joint liability. Section 34 of the Indian Penal Code lays down a principle of joint criminal liability which is only a rule of evidence but does not create a substantive offence. It states that when a criminal act is done by several persons in furtherance of the common intention of all, each of such persons is liable for that act in the same manner as if it were done by him alone. Section 34 only comes into the picture for acts that are offences at the time they were foisted.

40 'Imposing punishment implies that some one should be legally authorised to impose it upon the offender'. In which of the following cases a private person can impose such punishment?

1 Where the law recognises moral blame worthiness
2 Where there is justification for punishing any person provided the offender had broken a law
3 Where one can establish the connection between punishment and crime
4 Where the act falls within a retroactive penal legislation

Ans. (2)

➲ *Exp.* When there is a justification for punishing any person provided that the offender had broken a law, a private person can impose a punishment on him. This holds relevance especially in cases/situations where an individual has no option but to exercise his right of private defence since resorting to the concerned authorities might not be possible in that situation.

41 The Apex court has shown as to how compromise is not a free choice of the rape survivor but a hidden secret of law where justice is reduced to a bargain between the victim's kin, state authorities and the accused. Identify the case law

1 Ravindra Vs. State of MP
2 Shraya Singhal Vs. Union of India
3 Sanskar Marathe Vs. State of Maharashtra
4 Khursheed Ahmed Khan Vs. State of UP

Ans. (1)

➲ *Exp.* In the case of Ravindra Vs. State of MP the Apex Court has shown that compromise is not a free choice of the rape survivor, rather a hidden secret of law where justice is reduced to a bargain between the victim's kin, state authorities and the accused.

The proviso to Section 376(2)(g) of IPC was invoked in this case for awarding a lesser sentence, as the incident was 20 years old and the fact that the parties are married and have entered into a compromise, were the adequate and special reasons.

42 There is a specific provision that the intention to screen the offender must be primary and the role object of the accused. This provision is provided in ________.

1 Section 202 2 Section 201
3 Section 199 4 Section 203

Ans. (2)

➲ *Exp.* There is a specific provision that the intention to screen the offender must be primary and the role object of the accused. This provision is provided in Section 201 of IPC. Section 201 of IPC, provides for the punishment for causing disappearance of evidence of offence, or giving false information to screen offenders. This section makes causing disappearance of evidence of an offence, or giving false information to screen an offender of an offence.

43 Which of the following offences fall under causing hurt as well as assault?

1 Digging a pit in the public path
2 Flinging boiling water over a person
3 Mixing deleterious poison in a liquid and placing the same on another table
4 Pulling hair of a woman

Ans. (2)

➲ *Exp.* Flinging boiling water over a person fall under causing hurt as well as assault

Section 319 with Section 351 of the IPC help us to understand that the act of flinging boiling water over a person would constitute both-an act of assault and an act of hurt (if it does cause bodily injury to a person).

The other options mentioned here will only constitute assault and not hurt since they are preparatory gestures and no hurt is actually caused yet.

44 There must be dishonest intention which should co-exist while taking a thing for an offence of theft. In which of the following situations it will not amount to theft?

1 Taking a stick from the person to beat him
2 Taking a sugar packet from another person in good faith while his own packet was at the shop

3 A senior student snatching some books from a junior student with promise to return on the next day
4 Not finding the helmet hanged on a bike, a person takes away a similar helmet from the adjacent bike, but afterwards repenting on his fault returns the same to the owner

Ans. (1)

Exp. In the situation given, taking a stick out of someone's possession to beat him will not be considered as theft since it will be returned to him after the act.

Section 378 of the Indian Penal Code states theft as- "whoever, intending to take dishonestly any moveable property out of the possession of any person without that person's consent, moves that property in order to such taking, is said to commit theft".

45 The Constitution of Works Committee under the Industrial Disputes Act is to

1 remove causes of friction between the employer and workmen in the day to day waking of the establishment
2 remove causes of friction between the employer and workmen relating to wage settlement
3 remove causes of fiction between the employer and workmen relating to standing orders
4 remove causes of friction between the employer and workmen relating to implementation of awards

Ans. (1)

Exp. The Constitution of Works Committee under the Industrial Disputes Act is to remove causes of friction between the employer and workmen in the day to day waking of the establishment.

Section 3 of the Industrial Disputes Act, 1947 provides for the Constitution of a Works Committee. Sub-Section 2 provides that it shall be the duty of the Works Committee to promote measures for securing and preserving amity and good relations between the employer and workmen and, to that end, to comment upon matters of their common interest or concern and endeavour to compose any material difference of opinion in respect of such matters.

46 Under the Industrial Disputes Act, a reference to an Industrial tribunal will be

1 Only where both the parties to an Industrial Dispute apply for such reference
2 Only where the appropriate government considers it expedient to do so
3 Only where both the parties to an Industrial Dispute apply for such reference and also where the appropriate government considers it expedient to do so
4 Only where the affected party to the dispute apply for such reference

Ans. (3)

Exp. Section 10 (1A) and (2) of the Industrial Disputes Act provide that a reference to an Industrial Tribunal will lie where both the parties to an Industrial Dispute apply for such reference, and also where the appropriate Government considers it expedient to do so.

An award of a Tribunal may be enforced either wholly or in part by the appropriate Government for a period not exceeding one year.

47 To which settlement machinery can the Central Government refer the dispute under Rule 81-A?

1 Conciliation
2 Arbitration
3 Adjudication
4 Supreme Court

Ans. (3)

Exp. Under Rule 81-A, the Central Government can refer the dispute for adjudication.

The underlying objective is that where a dispute has been referred to conciliation for adjudication, a strike or lock-outing furtherance thereof, would be both unnecessary and inexpedient.

48 A settlement under the Industrial Disputes Act arrived at in the course of conciliation proceeding, between the employer and a recognised majority union will be binding on

1 parties to the settlement
2 all workmen of the establishment
3 all workmen of a recognised majority union
4 all workmen of a registered Trade Union

Ans. (2)

Exp. Section 10 of the Industrial Disputes Act provides that a settlement under the Industrial Disputes Act arrived at in the course of conciliation proceeding, between the employer and a recognised majority union will be binding on all the workmen of the establishment where they are the parties to an industrial dispute or have been summoned to appear in the proceedings as parties to the dispute.

49 The permission applied for by the government shall be deemed to have granted if the appropriate government does not communicate the order under ID Act, granting or refusing to grant permission within a period of

1 15 days
2 30 days
3 60 days
4 90 days

Ans. (3)

Exp. The permission applied for by the government shall be deemed to have granted if the appropriate government does not communicate the order under ID Act, granting or refusing to grant permission within a period of 60 days.

Section 25N(4) of the Industrial Disputes Act, 1947 provides that where an application for permission has been made under sub-section (1) and the appropriate Government or the specified authority does not communicate the order granting or refusing to grant permission to the employer within a period of 60 days from the date on which such application is made, the permission applied for shall be deemed to have been granted on the expiration of the said period of sixty days.

50 "The right to strike may be controlled or restricted by appropriate industrial legislation and the validity of such legislation would have to be tested not with reference to the criteria laid down in clause (4) of Article 19 but by totally different considerations", was observed by the Supreme Court in

1 Syndicate Bank Vs. Umesh Nayak
2 All India Bank Employees Association Vs. I.T.
3 Management of Churakulam Tea Estate (P) Led Vs. The workmen and another
4 Ramnagar cane and sugar Co. Vs. Jatin Chalin

Ans. (2)

Exp. In the case of All India Bank Employees Association Vs. National Industrial Tribunal the Court observed that the right to strike or "the right to declare a look-out may be controlled or restricted by appropriate industrial legislation, and the validity of such legislation would have to be tested not with reference to the criteria laid down in clause (4) of Article 19 but by totally different considerations".

PAPER III

1 Match List I and List II and select the correct answer by using codes given below.

	List I		List II
A.	To renounce practices the derogatory to dignity of women	I.	Surya Narain Choudhary Vs. Union of India
B.	Mandamus cannot be sought against an individual who does not observe a fundamental duty	II.	Union of India Vs. Naveen Jindal
C.	Respect to National Anthem	III.	Bijoe Emmanuel Vs. State of Kerala
D.	Respect and dignity of National Flag	IV.	Union of India Vs. Naveen Jindal

Codes

	A	B	C	D		A	B	C	D
1	I	II	III	IV	2	II	I	III	IV
3	II	I	IV	III	4	III	IV	I	II

Ans. (2)

Exp. The correct matchin is A-II; B-I; C-III; D-IV.

In *Union of India v. Naveen Jindal* it was mentioned that to renounce practices derogatory to the dignity of women.

The Supreme Court held that Fundamental Duties may serve as a guide to the interpretation of the Constitution and legal issues. Although if, Parliament enacts a law through amendment then, these duties can be enforced.

In the case of *Surya Narayan Choudhary Vs. Union of India* Rajasthan Court held that the duties under Part IVA are the duties of individual citizens and thus, Mandamus cannot be sought against those individuals who did not observe his duties under Article 51A.

Bijoe Emmanuel Vs. State of Kerala is related to respect for the National Anthem. This case was significant because it affirmed that no one can be legally compelled to violate his conscientiously held religious beliefs.

Union of India Vs. Naveen Jindal is related to respect and dignity of the National Flag. The Supreme Court held that Fundamental Duties may serve as a guide to the interpretation of the Constitution and legal issues.

2 Match List I with List II according to the provisions of the Constitution of India. Select the correct answer by using the codes given below.

	List I (Provisions)		List II (Articles)
A.	Power of Parliament to legislate with respect to a matter in the state list in the national interest	I.	Articles 253
B.	Legislation for giving effect to international agreements	II.	Article 247
C.	Power of Parliament to provide for the establishment of certain additional courts	III.	Article 252
D.	Power of Parliament to legislate for two or more states by consent	IV.	Article 249

Codes

	A	B	C	D		A	B	C	D
1	IV	I	II	III	2	I	II	III	IV
3	IV	III	I	II	4	I	II	IV	III

Ans. (1)

Exp. The correct matching is A-IV; B-I; C-II; D-III.

Power of Parliament to legislate with respect to a matter in the state list in the national interest is stated under Article 249. Clause (1) states that "Notwithstanding anything in the foregoing provisions of this Chapter, if the Council of States has declared by resolution supported by not less than two thirds of the members present and voting that it is necessary or expedient in national interest that Parliament should make laws with respect to any matter enumerated in the State List specified in the resolution, it shall be lawful for Parliament to make laws for the whole or any part of the territory of India with respect to that matter while the resolution remains in force."

Legislation for giving effect to international agreements is stated under Article 253. It states that "Notwithstanding anything in the foregoing provisions of this Chapter, Parliament has power to make any law for the whole or any part of the territory of India for implementing any treaty, agreement or convention with any other country or countries or any decision made at any international conference, association or other body."

Power of Parliament to provide for the establishment of certain additional courts is stated under Article 247. It states that "Notwithstanding anything in this Chapter, Parliament may by law provide for the establishment of any additional courts for the better administration of laws made by Parliament or of any existing laws with respect to a matter enumerated in the Union List."

Power of Parliament to legislate for two or more states by consent is stated under Article 252. Clause (1) states that "if it appears to the Legislatures of two or more States to be desirable that any of the matters with respect to which Parliament has no power to make laws for the States except as provided in Articles 249 and 250 should be regulated in such States by Parliament by law, and if resolutions to that effect are passed by all the House of the Legislatures of those States, it shall be lawful for Parliament to pass an Act for regulating that matter accordingly, and any Act so passed shall apply to such States and to any other State by which it is adopted afterwards by resolution passed in that behalf by the House or, where there are two Houses, by each of the Houses of the Legislature of that State."

3 Read Assertion (A) and Reason (R) and select the correct answer using the codes given below.

Assertion (A) The rule making power of the Supreme Court of India is not subject to any law made by the Parliament.

Reason (R) Only an impartial and independent judiciary can protect the rights of Individual without fear or favour.

Codes

1 Both (A) and (R) are correct and (R) is correct explanation of (A)
2 Both (A) and (R) are correct, but (R) is not the correct explanation of (A)
3 (A) is false, but (R) is true
4 (A) is true, but (R) is false

Ans. *(3)*

Exp. (A) is false, but (R) is true.

The rule making power of the Supreme Court must not be ultra vires to its own powers. The term 'Ultra Vires' implies absence of capacity or power of the person to do any act. Hence, the Assertion is false.

Only an impartial and independent judiciary can protect the rights of individuals without fear or favour. This is why an independent judiciary is the hallmark of any democracy. Thus, the Reason is correct.

4 Who among the following shall be disqualified as a member of either House of Parliament?

I. Who is not a citizen of India.
II. Who has acquired the citizenship of a foreign state.
III. Who is under any acknowledgement to a foreign state.
IV. Who is under acknowledgement of adherence to a foreign state.

Codes

1 Only I	2 I and II
3 I, II and III	4 All of these

Ans. *(4)*

Exp. Statement I, II, III contains the conditions for disqualification as a member of either House of Parliament.

Article 102 of the Constitution provides for the disqualification of membership on any of the following grounds :

(a) if he holds any office of profit under the Government of India or the Government of any State, other than an office declared by Parliament by law not to disqualify its holder;
(b) if he is of unsound mind and stands so declared by a competent court;
(c) if he is an undischarged insolvent;
(d) if he is not a citizen of India, or has voluntarily acquired the citizenship of a foreign State, or is under any acknowledgement of allegiance or adherence to a foreign State;
(e) if he is so disqualified by or under any law made by Parliament.

For the purposes of this clause a person shall not be deemed to hold an office of profit under the Government of India or the Government of any State by reason only that he is a Minister either for the Union or for such State;

(f) if he is disqualified under the Tenth Schedule.

5 Under Article 324 of the Constitution the Election Commission of India shall be responsible to conduct elections to

I. Parliament and State Legislature
II. President and Vice-President
III. Zila Parishad and Panchayats
IV. Municipal Corporations and Municipal Committees

Codes

1 I, II, III and IV	2 I, II and III
3 I and II	4 I, III and IV

Ans. *(3)*

Exp. Under Article 324 of the Constitution the Election Commission of India shall be responsible to conduct elections to Parliament and State Legislature and President and Vice-President.

According to Article 324(1), the superintendence, direction and control of the preparation of the electoral rolls for, and the conduct of, all elections to Parliament and to the Legislature of every State and of elections to the offices of President and Vice President held under this Constitution shall be vested in a Commission.

6 Who among the following can establish additional court for better administration of any existing law with respect to a matter concerned in Union List?

1 Chief Justice of India
2 Parliament
3 The Concerned State Legislature
4 High Court of the State Concerned

Ans. (2)

Exp. Parliament can establish additional court for better administration of any existing law with respect to a matter concerned in Union List.

Article 247 of the Constitution provides for the Power of Parliament to provide for the establishment of certain additional courts. It states that "Notwithstanding anything in this Chapter, Parliament may by law provide for the establishment of any additional courts for the better administration of laws made by Parliament or of any existing laws with respect to a matter enumerated in the Union List."

7 Which one of the following statements is correct? Article 368 of the Constitution of India lays down

1 Procedure for Amendment of the Constitution only
2 Power of Parliament to amend the Constitution only
3 Power of Parliament to amend the Constitution and procedure therefore
4 Limitation on the power of the Parliament to amend the Constitution

Ans. (3)

Exp. Article 368 of the Constitution lays down the power of the Parliament to amend the Constitution and the procedure therefore.

Clause (1) states that "Notwithstanding anything in this Constitution, Parliament may in exercise of its constituent power amend by way of addition, variation or repeal any provision of this Constitution in accordance with the procedure laid down in this article."

8 In which one of the following cases the Supreme Court held that, "No election can be challenged on the ground of defect in electoral rolls"?

1 Inderjit Barua Vs. Election Commission of India
2 NP Ponnuswami Vs. Returning Officer
3 Kalyan Lal Omar Vs. RK Trivedi
4 Mohinder Singh Gill Vs. Chief Election Commissioner

Ans. (1)

Exp. In the case of Inderjit Barua Vs. Election Commission of India, the Supreme Court had held that "No election can be challenged on the ground of defect in electoral rolls."

This case challenged the validity of the elections to the Assam Legislative Assembly held in February, 1983.

9 Who defined administrative law as, "Law relating to the Administration. It determines the organisation, powers and duties of administrative authorities"?

1 Sir Ivor Jennings
2 AV Dicey
3 Kenneth Culp Davis
4 Griffith and Strut

Ans. (1)

Exp. Sir Ivor Jenning defined administrative law as, "Law relating to the Administration. It determines the organisation, powers and duties of administrative authorities".

It includes law relating to the rule-making power of the administrative bodies, the quasi-judicial function of administrative agencies, legal liabilities of public authorities and power of the ordinary courts to supervise administrative authorities.

10 What was specifically declared by the Supreme Court in the Delhi Laws Act case?

I. Legislature should not delegate its essential function.
II. Excessive delegation of powers can be struck down by courts.
III. Extension of laws with certain modification and by changing the underlying policy of legislation is allowed.
IV. Legislature should itself lay down standard in the delegating act learning the delegate with the power to make rules to execute the policy laid down in the Legislation.

Codes

1 I, III and IV
2 II, IV and I
3 IV, III and II
4 I, II and IV

Ans. (4)

Exp. The Delhi Laws Act is a landmark judgment of the 7 Judge Bench of the Supreme Court wherein each judge had a difference of opinion. The following points were specifically stated in this case :

- Legislature should not delegate its essential function. (Statement I)
- Excessive delegation of powers can be struck down by courts. (Statement II)
- Legislature should itself lay down standards in the delegating act, learning the delegate with the power to make rules to execute the policy laid down in the Legislation. (Statement IV)

11 Which of the following is not true regarding the application of 'Doctrine of Promissory Estoppel'?

1 The court may refuse to apply promissory estoppel against the government if the 'public interest' suffers in fulfilling the promise
2 The government cannot be compelled to carry out a promise which falls outside its power and contrary to law

3 The promise in question may be tentative or uncertain and it need not to be unambiguous and unequivocal
4 There can be no promissory estoppel against the Legislature in the exercise of its legislative functions

Ans. (3)

Exp. Statement 3 is not true regarding the application of 'Doctrine of Promissory Estoppel' because the promise in question must be clear and unambiguous and not uncertain or tentative in nature.

'The Doctrine of Promissory Estoppel' works on the principle of equity, fairness and moral conscience. It means when an individual with an intention of forming a relationship which is lawful makes a clear promise to another individual and the latter individual acts on it, that promise becomes an obligation for the individual who made the promise.

12 Match List I with List II in the light of cases decided by the Supreme Court and select the correct answer using the codes given below.

List I (Case Law)		List II (Principles)
A. Canara Bank Vs. VK Awasthy (2005)	I.	Duty to act fairly-in administrative functions as well
B. Gullapalli Nageswara Rao Vs. AP State Road Transport Corporation, 1959	II.	Post decisional hearing
C. Swadeshi Cotton Mills Vs. Union of India (1981)	III.	Exclusion of rule of hearing
D. AK Kraipak *Vs.* Union of India (1970)	IV.	One who decides must hear

Codes

	A	B	C	D		A	B	C	D
1	I	II	III	IV	2	IV	III	I	II
3	II	IV	III	I	4	III	IV	II	I

Ans. (3)

Exp. The correct matching is A-II; B-IV; C-III; D-I.

Canara Bank Vs. *VK Awasthy* (2005) case deal with the principle post-decisional hearing. It was held that post-decisional hearing can obliterate the procedural deficiency of a pre-decisional hearing.

Gullapalli Nageswara Rao Vs. *AP State Road Transport Corporation,* 1959 case deal with the principle one who decides must hear. This principle with reference to hearing by a quasi judicial forum is not applicable to all situations in the hearing of the suit. "Hearing of the suit" as understood is not confined to oral hearing.

Swadeshi Cotton Mills Vs. *Union of India* (1981) case deal with the principle exclusion of rule of hearing. The primary question here was whether the principle of audi alteram partem be implied while construing Section 18AA of the Industries (Development and Regulation) Act, 1951.

AK Kraipak Vs. *Union of India* (1970) case deal with the principle duty to act fairly- in administrative functions as well. The Court held that a person who sits on a Committee for selection of candidates for a certain job must not be a candidate himself for the job. The logic is that Judges could be impartial and neutral. He must be free from any controversy, suspicion of bias in rendering Justice.

13 Read Assertion (A) and Reason (R) and select the correct answer using the codes given below.

Assertion (A) A High Court may decline to exercise its extraordinary jurisdiction under Article 226 and dismiss the writ summarily or in limine.

Reason (R) It would be proper for the High Court to dispose of the petition summarily or in limine, when no important question of law are raised in a writ petition.

Codes

1 Both (A) and (R) are true and (R) is correct explanation of (A)
2 Both (A) and (R) are true, but (R)is not correct explanation of (A)
3 (A) is true, but (R) is false
4 (A) is false, but (R) is true

Ans. (1)

Exp. Both (A) and (R) are true and (R) is correct explanation of (A).

The High Court in exercise of judicial discretion declines to exercise its extraordinary jurisdiction under Article 226 where the petition is frivolous, vexatious or prima facic unjust or may not be appropriately tried in extraordinary jurisdiction. Thus, the Assertion is true.

It would also be proper for the High Court to dispose of the petition summarily or in limine, when no important question of law is raised in a writ petition, as per Article 226. Thus, the Reason is also true.

14 When a writ is issued to a public authority in respect of any type of administrative, legislative, Quasi-judicial or judicial functions, it is called a writ of

1 Mandamus
2 Quo - warranto
3 Certiorari
4 Prohibition

Ans. (1)

Exp. When a writ is issued to a public authority in respect of any type of administrative, legislative, Quasi-judicial or judicial functions, it is called a writ of Mandamus.

Mandamus is used to enforce the performance of public duties by public authorities. However, it is not issued when the Government is under no duty under the law.

15 Read Assertion (A) and Reason (R) and select the correct answer using codes given below.

Assertion (A) In judicial review of administrative actions, generally the court would not interfere with the merits of the case by embarking upon inquiry into the facts.

Reason (R) Courts can review the procedure through which a decision has been taken by the administrative authority but courts cannot supplement its own decision and act as appellate court over the administrative authority.

Codes

1 Both (A) and (R) are true and (R) is the correct explanation of (A)
2 Both (A) and (R) are true, but (R) is not correct explanation of (A)
3 (A) is true, but (R) is false
4 (A) is false, but (R) is true

Ans. (1)

Exp. Both (A) and (R) are true and (R) is the correct explanation of A.

In judicial review of administrative actions, generally the court would not interfere with the merits of the case by embarking upon inquiry into the facts. Judicial investigation of administrative decisions would not extend far as reviewing the actions on merit. Thus, Assertion is true.

Courts can review the procedure through which a decision has been taken by the administrative authority but courts cannot supplement its own decision and act as appellate court over the administrative authority as it would be a violation of the basic feature of separation of powers. Hence, Reason is true as well.

16 "The polemical version of legal realism has wielded enormous influence on the entire judicial system". Who propounded such philosophy?

1 Gray
2 Holmes
3 Salmond
4 Waismann

Ans. (2)

Exp. According to Holmes, "The polemical version of legal realism has wielded enormous influence on the entire judicial system." This is the theory that all law is in reality judge made.

Holmes's understanding of legal realism shows his relationship to the natural law and natural rights traditions. For Holmes, law and society are always in flux, and courts adjudicate with an eye to law's practical effects.

17 The liberam arbitrium of the courts depends upon what is right, justice, equitable or reasonable and is dependent upon

1 Evidence and demonstration of public
2 Arguments submitted with reason
3 Discovering the right or justice of the matter
4 Pure intellectual process

Ans. (2)

Exp. The liberum arbitrium of the courts depends upon what is right, justice, equitable or reasonable and is dependent upon the arguments submitted with reason. Liberum arbitrium is a faculty of reason and will, by which good is chosen with the assistance of grace, or evil, when grace is not there to assist.

18 Obiter dicta has no binding authority but it helps to

1 rationalise legal sanctions
2 encourages providing solution to future litigations
3 it allows greater prestige to the judge
4 it makes the acceptability of precedents more flexible

Ans. (1)

Exp. Obiter dicta has no binding authority but it helps to rationalise legal sanctions.

Obiter dicta means "things said (dicta) by the way (obiter)". They are without binding authority, but are nonetheless important because not only do they help to rationalize the law but they also serve to suggest solutions to problems not yet decided by the courts.

19 The statement 'equitable ownership of a legal right is different from the ownership of an equitable right' shows that law and equity differ with regard to

1 Only the existence of right
2 Only the ownership of rights
3 Both existence and ownership of rights
4 The existence of a right but not regarding the consistency of a right

Ans. (3)

Exp. The statement 'equitable ownership of a legal right is different from the ownership of an equitable right' shows that law and equity differ with regard to both the existence as well as the ownership of rights.

At common law, a person who holds legal title to a property has rights in relation to that property against the entire world–thus, it is said that the common law acts in rem. In equity, however, equitable rights are only enforceable against a particular person.

20 Read Assertion (A) and Reason (R) and select the correct answer using codes given below.

Assertion (A) The relation of morality to a concept of law cannot be stated simply in the form of a stark alternative that the former is either externally or internally related to the later.

Reason (R) It is depending upon time-frame of reference

Codes

1 Both (A) and (R) are false
2 Both (A) and (R) are true and (R) is correct explanation of (A)
3 (A) is false, but (R) is true
4 (A) is true, but and (R) is false

Ans. (2)

Exp. Both (A) and (R) are true and (R) is correct explanation of (A).

The relation of morality to a concept of law cannot be stated simply in the form of a stark alternative that the former is either externally or internally related to the later. It depends upon the time frame of reference. While positivists have strongly contended that law should be studied in complete isolation from ideas such as that of morality, there is a general agreement amongst law-makers regarding the important part played by morals in effective law-making.

21 The House of Lords upheld the Attorney General's political discretion in refusing to invoke the law in face of a threatened criminal offence in deliberate defiance of an Act of Parliament, in the case of

1 Gouriet Vs. Union of Post Office Workers
2 Francome Vs. Mirror Group Newspaper Ltd.
3 R. Vs. Bourne
4 Johnson Vs. Phillips

Ans. (1)

Exp. The House of Lords upheld the Attorney General's political discretion in refusing to invoke the law in face of a threatened criminal offence in deliberate defiance of an Act of Parliament, in the case of Gouriet Vs. Union of Post Office Workers. The case raised the question of how far the Rule of Law operates in contemporary Britain.

22 Modern doctrine of bindingness of precedents was first laid down in

1 London Transways Co. Vs. LCC
2 Young Vs. Bristol Aeroplane Co. Ltd.
3 Mirehouse Vs. Rennel
4 Sirros Vs. Moore

Ans. (3)

Exp. Modern doctrine bindingness of precedents was first laid down in the case of Mirehouse Vs. Rennel.

The Modern doctrine of bindingness came into existence only when the hierarchy of courts got settled. In England it assumed its present shape in the Judicature Acts 1873-1875 which is now modified by the Courts Act 1971. The Judicature Acts reorganised the courts into a unified structure surmounted by the House of Lords as the ultimate appellate court.

23 Read Assertion (A) and Reason (R) and select the correct answer using the codes given below.

Assertion (A) Shareholders are not, in the eye of law, part owners of a company. The company is something different from the totality of the shareholders.

Reason (R) Shareholders are collective owners of the company.

Codes

1 Both (A) and (R) are true and (R) is correct explanation of (A)
2 Both (A) and (R) are false
3 (A) is true, but (R) is false
4 (R) is true, but (A) is false

Ans. (1)

Exp. Both (A) and (R) are true and (R) is correct explanation of (A).

Shareholders are not, in the eye of law, part owners of a company. The company is something different from the totality of the shareholders. The company has a separate legal existence from its owners and is capable of suing and being sued in its own name. A shareholder or stakeholder is an individual or institution that legally owns a share of stock in a public or private corporation. Unlike the owners of sole proprietorships or partnerships, corporate shareholders are not personally liable for the company's debts and other obligations.

The shareholders own the shares of the company and therefore are the collective owners (also called members) of the company.

24 An idea of inducement by exciting hope or desire on the other is known as ______ .

1 Seduction
2 Enticing
3 Inciting
4 Abduction

Ans. (2)

Exp. An idea of inducement by exciting hope or desire on the other is known as Enticing.

It refers to the act of persuading someone to do something by offering them something pleasant. In legal perspective, the act of enticing is to wrongly indulge someone in committing wrongful act by persuading, procuring unwanted things that in beginning or ultimately harms him/her.

25 'A' takes his own suit from the tailor without his knowledge but had the intention of returning it to the tailor later. What offence, if any has been committed by 'A'?

1 Stealing
2 Dishonest taking
3 Theft
4 Unlawful retention

Ans. (3)

Exp. 'A' takes his own suit from the tailor without his knowledge but had the intention of returning it to the tailor later. 'A' has committed the offence of theft.

Section 378 of IPC defines theft as "whoever, intending to take dishonestly any moveable property out of the possession of any person without that person's consent, moves that property in order to such taking, is said to commit theft."

26 Read Assertion (A) and Reason (R) and select the correct answer using the codes given below.

Assertion (A) That the act is imminently dangerous or that in all probability it will cause death.

Reason (R) Such specific principle apply to punish a person although there is no intention to cause death.

Codes

1 Both (A) and (R)are concurrent as per Section 299(c) and 300 respectively
2 Both (A) and (R) are intravivos as per Section 300 and Section 302
3 Both (A) and (R) are dependant upon facts based as per Section 299(b) and Section 302
4 Both (A) and (R) must co-exist as per Section 300(2) and Section 301

***Ans.* (1)**

Exp. Both (A) and (R) are concurrent as per Section 299(c) and 300 respectively.

Section 299 of IPC deals with the offence of culpable homicide and states that "whoever causes death by doing an act with the intention of causing death, or with the intention of causing such bodily injury as is likely to cause death, or with the knowledge that he is likely by such act to cause death, commits the offence of culpable homicide."

Explanation 1 to Section 299(c) in IPC states that a person who causes bodily injury to another who is labouring under a disorder, disease or bodily infirmity, and there by accelerates the death of that other, shall be deemed to have caused his death.

Further, the fourth clause to Section 300 states that if the person committing the act knows that it is so imminently dangerous that it must, in all probability, cause death or such bodily injury as is likely to cause death, and commits such act without any excuse for incurring the risk of causing death or such injury as aforesaid.

27 The aggravated form of perjury is known from

1 False statement on oath
2 False evidence in a judicial proceeding
3 Administering oath to speak truth
4 False affidavit before honorary Magistrate

***Ans.* (2)**

Exp. The aggravated form of perjury is known from false evidence in a judicial proceeding.

According to Section 193, IPC, "whoever intentionally gives false evidence in any stage of a judicial proceeding, or fabricates false evidence for the purpose of being used in any stage of a judicial proceeding, shall be punished with imprisonment of either description for a term which may extend to seven years, and shall also be liable to fine, and whoever intentionally gives or fabricates false evidence in any other case, shall be punished with imprisonment of either description for a term which may extend to three years, and shall also be liable to fine."

28 Which of the following is not a crime in order to provide protection to currency?

1 A war medal
2 Gold Mohur
3 Current Coin
4 Genuine specimen of antique coin

***Ans.* (3)**

Exp. The use of a current coin in circulation will not be considered to be a crime to provide protection to currency. However, the use of war medal, gold mohur or a genuine specimen of an antique coin can be considered to be a crime to provide protection to currency.

29 Which of the following cases does not amount to robbery?

1 Taking away ornaments from the body of a lady while she was in coma
2 Removal of ornaments after death of a lady
3 Voluntary disposition of valuables
4 While theft is committed along with assault

***Ans.* (2)**

Exp. Removal of ornaments after death of a lady does not amount to robbery because after her death those valuables may be collected by the next of Kin of the deceased or those become the family asset.

30 Criminal liability for abandonment of a child is based on the principle of loco-parentis. Who else could be responsible for that offence?

1 Adoptive father before the completion of formalities of adoption
2 When a mother leaves the house for her husband's ill-treatment and abandons the children to the care of husband
3 When the school master who has been teaching infants placed under him for education
4 A mother leaves a blind child on a foot path promising to return after fetching food but never returned

***Ans.* (3)**

Exp. Options 1, 2 and 4 list down the situations wherein criminal liability can be imposed for the abandonment of a child. However, when a child is placed under a schoolmaster for education, it will not amount to abandonment of a child. The term 'in loco-parentis' means in the place of parent' refers to the legal responsibility of a person or organisation to take on some of the functions and responsibilities of a parent.

31 Which of the following do not constitute an offence of forgery?

1 The intention to induce a belief that the document was duly signed
2 The intention to induce a belief that the document was duly sealed
3 The intention to induce a belief that the document was executed by the authority of a person
4 Knowingly makes false entries initially in the public record on his own authority by a public officer

***Ans.* (1)**

Exp. If a public officer makes false entries in a public record under his own authority, he can be tried under Section 167, IPC (Public servant framing an incorrect document with intent to cause injury) and not under forgery.

Section 463 of IPC defines forgery as "whoever makes any false document or false electronic record or part of a document or electronic record with intent to cause damage or injury, to the public or to any person, or to support any claim or title, or to cause any person to part with property, or to enter into any express or implied contract, or with intent to commit fraud or that fraud may be committed, commits forgery".

32 "Where directive principles have found statutory expression in do's and dont's the court will not sit idle and allow government to become a statutory mockery for protection of environment. The law will relentlessly be enforced and the plea of poor finance will be poor alibi when people in misery cry for justice". The above was observed in Municipal Council of Ratlam Vs. Vardhichand by

1 Justice Chinnappa Reddy
2 Justice VR Krishna Iyer
3 Justice PN Bhagavati
4 Justice Ranganath Misra

Ans. (2)

Exp. It was Justice VR Krishna Iyer, who, in the case of Municipal Council of Ratlam Vs. Vardhichand said that "Where directive principles have found statutory expression in do's and don'ts the court will not sit idle and allow government to become a statutory mockery for protection of environment.

The law will relentlessly be enforced and the plea of poor finance will be a poor alibi when people in misery cry for justice". This case pertained to the tackling of environmental issues and establishment of the obligation of statutory bodies using the public nuisance doctrine in the CrPC.

33 Protection and Improvement of Environment and safeguarding forest and wildlife is

1 a Fundamental Right
2 one of the Directive Principles of State Policy
3 one of the Fundamental Duties
4 Both Directive Principles of State Policy and Fundamental Duty

Ans. (4)

Exp. Protection and Improvement of Environment and safeguarding forest and wildlife is both a Directive Principles of State Policy (DPSP) under Article 48A and a Fundamental Duty under Article 51A(f).

Article 48 A states that "the State shall endeavour to protect and improve the environment and to safeguard the forests and wildlife of the country."

Article 51A(f) states that "we must value and preserve the rich heritage of our composite culture."

34 In which of the following cases, the Supreme Court directed closing down and demolition of shrimp Industries in coastal regulation zone and implement the 'Precautionary principle' and 'the polluter pays principle' and held them liable for payment of compensation for reversing the ecology and compensate the individual for loss suffered?

1 MC Mehta Vs. Union of India
2 S Jagannath Vs. Union of India
3 Church of God (Full Gospels) in India Vs. KKR Majestic Colony Welfare Association
4 Vellore Citizen's Welfare Forum Vs. Union of India

Ans. (2)

Exp. The case of S Jagannath Vs. The Union of India dealt with the ecological and social implications of commercial shrimp farming in India. The court had directed the Central Government to constitute an authority with all the powers necessary to protect the ecologically fragile coastal areas and also directed for closing down and demolition of shrimp industries in coastal regulation zone. The authority had to implement 'the Precautionary principle' as well as 'the Polluter pays principle'.

35 Read Assertion (A) and Reason (R) and select the answer by using the codes given below.

Assertion (A) The right to clean drinking water and right to pollution free air to breath are attributes of 'Right to Life'.

Reason (R) Because they are the basic elements which sustain life

Codes

1 Both (A) and (R) are true (R) is correct explanation of (A)
2 Both (A) and (R) are true, but (R) is not a correct explanation of (A)
3 (A) is true, but (R) is false
4 (A) is false, but (R) is true

Ans. (1)

Exp. Both (A) and (R) are true and (R) is the correct explanation of (A).

The right to clean drinking water and pollution free air would come under the ambit of 'Right to life' under Article 21, which is a fundamental right under Part-III. The rationale is that these are the basic amenities that one needs to sustain life.

36 In which of the following cases the Supreme Court applied the doctrine of public trust that the state as a trustee of all natural resources is under a legal duty to protect the natural resources. These natural resources are meant for public use and cannot be converted into private ownership?

1 MC Mehta Vs. Union of India (Ganga Water Pollution Case)
2 MC Mehta Vs. Kamalnath and Others
3 MC Mehta Vs. Union of India (Replacing diesel vehicles by CNG vehicles)
4 Rural Litigation and Entitlement Kendra Vs. State of UP

Ans. (2)

Exp. MC Mehta Vs. Kamalnath and Others the Supreme Court applied the doctrine of public trust that the state as a trustee of all natural resources is under a legal duty to protect the natural resources.

The case of MC Mehta Vs. Kamal Nath whose judgment (1996) was one of the landmark cases in the history of environmental law in India. This case mainly set a precedent as to how the doctrine of public trust must be applied with respect to the protection of natural resources in India.

37 What is the main objective of the Prohibition of Employment as Manual Scavengers and their Rehabilitation Act, 2013?

I. To prohibit employment of manual scavengers
II. To rehabilitate manual scavengers
III. To rehabilitate manual scavengers and their families
IV. To rehabilitate manual scavengers only and not their families

Codes

1 Only I
2 I, II and III
3 I and II
4 All of these

Ans. (2)

Exp. Statements I, II and III are correct.

The primary objectives of Prohibition of Employment as Manual Scavengers and their Rehabilitation Act, 2013 are

- To prohibit the employment of manual scavengers.
- To ensure the rehabilitation of manual scavengers.
- To rehabilitate manual scavengers and their families.

Statement IV is incorrect as rehabilitation of both manual scavengers and their families is an objective of the Act.

38 Which one of the following is the main objective of the Wildlife (Protection) Act, 1972 as amended upto 2003?

1 To check on poaching and illegal trade in domestic and wild animals
2 To check on poaching and on illegal trade in ivory
3 To check on poaching and legal trade in dog
4 To check on hunting and legal trade in elephant

Ans. (1)

Exp. Wildlife (Protection) Act, 1972 was one of the first environment-based Acts that helped lay down the foundation of Environmental law in India. The primary objective of the Act was to check on poaching and illegal trade in domestic and wild animals.

39 Whose observations are these on the point that whether International law is a mere positive Morality?

"If International Law were only a kind of morality, the framers of state papers concerning foreign policy would throw all their weight on moral arguments. But, as a matter of fact, this is not what they do. They appeal not to the general feeling of moral rightness, but to precedents, to treaties and to opinion of specialists".

1 HLA Hart
2 Oppenheim
3 Edward Collins
4 Frederick Pollock

Ans. (4)

Exp. Sir Frederick Pollock has observed that "If International Law were only a kind of morality, the framers of state papers concerning foreign policy would throw all their weight on moral arguments. But, as a matter of fact, this is not what they do. They appeal not to the general feeling of moral rightness, but to precedents, to treaties and to opinion of specialists" He wrote that the only essential conditions for the existence of law are the existence of the political community and the recognition by its members of settled rules binding upon them in that capacity.

40 Which of the following statement(s) is/are not correct?

I. Principle of law which is recognised by domestic law of a large number of states does not automatically become a 'Principle' of International Law.
II. Para 1 (G) of Article 38 of the Statute of International Court of justice lists "general principles of law recognised by civilised states" as the second source of International Law.
III. General principles of law recognised by civilised states include only substantive principles provided they have received general recognition of civilised states.
IV. The development of general principles of law recognised by civilised states as an important source of law, has given a death-knell to the positivism.

Codes
1 Only II is incorrect
2 Both II and III are incorrect
3 I, II and III are incorrect
4 All of the above are incorrect

Ans. (2)

Exp. Statements II and III are incorrect.

Statement II is incorrect because Article 38(1)(c) provides that the general principles of law recognised by civilised states to decide disputes submitted before the ICJ. There is no (g) to Article 38(1) of the ICJ.

Statement III is incorrect because Article 38 of ICJ provides that the Statute of International Court of Justice lists general principles of law recognised by civilised States as the third source of international law.

41 Which one of the following cases is not a case on the point that there is no distinction between 'De Facto' and 'De-Jure' recognition for the purpose of giving effect to the internal acts of the recognised authority?

1 Bank of Ethopia Vs. National Bank of Egypt and Liquori
2 Luther Vs. Sagor
3 Civil Air Transport Incorporated Co. Vs. Central Air Transport Corporation
4 The Arantzazu Mendi Case

Ans. (3)

Exp. Civil Air Transport Incorporated Co. Vs. Central Air Transport Corporation is not a case on the point that there is no distinction between 'De Facto' and 'De-Jure' recognition for the purpose of giving effect to the internal acts of the recognised authority.

Civil Air Transport Incorporated Co. Vs. Central Air Transport Corporation provided for the concept of Retroactive effect of recognition and not for the distinction between 'De jure' and 'De facto' recognition.

42 In which one of the following cases the International Court of Justice has held that in respect of grant of nationality there is no obligation of the states if a man has no relationship with the state of Naturalisation and the court has applied the 'Principle of effective nationality'?

1 Re Lynch Case
2 Stoeck Vs. The Public Trustee
3 Nottebohm's Case
4 Paneyezys Soldutisk

Ans. (3)

Exp. In the Nottebohm's Case, the International Court of Justice has held that in respect of grant of nationality there is no obligation of the states if a man has no relationship with the state of Naturalisation and the court has applied the 'Principle of effective nationality.' In this case, Liechtenstein sought a ruling to force Guatemala to recognize Friedrich Nottebohm as a Liechtenstein national. This case has been cited in many definitions of nationality.

43 Which one of the following institution is not authorised for requesting for, 'Advisory Opinion' of the International Court of Justice?

1 Economic and Social Council
2 The Trusteeship Council
3 The International Atomic Energy Agency
4 Secretariat

Ans. (4)

Exp. Secretariat is not authorised for requesting for, 'Advisory Opinion' of the International Court of Justice. Article 96 of the UN Charter authorises the General Assembly and the Security Council to seek the advice of the ICJ. Pursuant to Article 96(2) of the UN Charter, the ECOSOC and Trusteeship Council to seek ICJ's advice.

44 Read both Assertion (A) and Reason (R) and select the correct answer by using the codes given below.

Assertion (A) International Law is not potent enough to restrain a powerful state which has no respect for public opinion.

Reason (R) Sanctions behind International Law are weak.

Codes
1 Both (A) and (R) are true and (R) is the correct explanation of (A)
2 Both (A) and (R) are true, but (R) is not the correct explanation of (A)
3 (A)is true, but (R) is false
4 (A) is false, but (R) is true

Ans. (1)

Exp. Both (A) and (R) are true, but (R) is not the correct explanation of (A).

International Law is not potent enough to restrain a powerful state which has no respect for public opinion. Due to the absence of poor sanctions backing the international law, it is not strong enough to act as a deterrent factor for countries that violate its standards.

45 Consider the following.

The Recommendation of the Security Council made to the member under Article 42 of UN Charter becomes an obligation for them which one can shirk?

I. If the Security Council decides to take action, no time is given for further declarations by the General Assembly.

II. When the Security Council decides for taking enforcement measures, it also determines the part to be played by each member state.

III. All or only some members may be requested to participate but every member is to join in mutual assistance.

IV. The legal requirements for military action are still not satisfied even after the council has acted.

Which of the above statement(s) is/are correct

1 I, II, IV are correct
2 II, III and IV are correct
3 I, II and III are correct
4 III, IV and I are correct

Ans. (3)

Exp. Statements I, II and III are correct.

Article 42 of the UN Charter states as follows-

"Should the Security Council consider that measures provided for in Article 41 would be inadequate or have proved to be inadequate, it may take such action by air, sea, or land forces as may be necessary to maintain or restore international peace and security. Such action may include demonstrations, blockade, and other operations by air, sea, or land forces of Members of the United Nations."

Statement IV is incorrect as it states the opposite of what Article 41 provides.

46 Match List I with List II and select the correct answer by using the codes given below.

List I (Provisions)	List II (Article of UN Charter)
A. Voting procedure of the General Assembly	I. Article 23
B. Composition of Security Council	II. Article 86
C. Composition of Trusteeship Council	III. Article 4
D. Provisions regarding membership in the United Nations	IV. Article 18

Codes

	A	B	C	D
1	II	III	IV	I
2	I	II	III	IV
3	III	I	II	IV
4	IV	II	I	III

Ans. (*)

Exp. The correct matching is A-IV; B-I; C-II; D-III.

Voting procedure of the General Assembly is stated under Article 18 of United Nations Charter. It states that each member of the General Assembly shall have one vote.

Composition of Security Council is stated under Article 23. It states that the Security Council shall consist of eleven Members of the United Nations. The Republic of China, France, the Union of Soviet Socialist Republics, the United Kingdom of Great Britain and Northern Ireland, and the United States of America shall be permanent members of the Security Council.

Composition of Trusteeship Council is stated under Article 86. It states that the Trusteeship Council shall consist of the following Members of the United Nations: (a) those Members administering trust territories; (b) such of those Members mentioned by name in Article 23 as are not administering trust territories; and (c) as many other Members elected for three-year terms by the General Assembly as may be necessary to ensure that the total number of members of the Trusteeship Council is equally divided between those Members of the United Nations which administer trust territories and those which do not.

Provisions regarding membership in the United Nations is stated under Article 4. It states that Membership in the United Nations is open to all other peace-loving states which accept the obligations contained in the present Charter and, in the judgment of the Organisation, are able and willing to carry out these obligations.

47 Which of the following is not a ground of Judicial Separation under the Hindu Marriage Act, 1955?

1 Renunciation of the world
2 Seven years absence
3 Conversion to Non - Hindu religion
4 Desertion for one year

Ans. (4)

Exp. Desertion for one year is not a ground of Judicial Separation under the Hindu Marriage Act, 1955.

Section 10 of the Hindu Marriage Act provides for the concept of judicial separation on the grounds specified in Section 13(1). Among a few certian grounds given in Section 13(1) of Hindu Marriage Act, 1955, deserting for a continuous period of not less than two years by husband or wife legally enables him/her to obtain a decree of judicial separation.

48 Grounds of divorce meant exclusively for wife under Section 13(2) of the Hindu Marriage Act, 1955 are

I. Pre-Act bigamy by Husband.
II. Husband is guilty of rape, sodomy and bestiality.
III. Non-payment of maintenance and no cohabitation for one year or upwards.
IV. Repudiation of marriage by wife.

Codes

1 I, II and IV
2 I, II, III and IV
3 II, III and IV
4 I, II and III

Ans. (2)

Exp. Statement I, II, III and IV contains the grounds of divorce meant exclusively for wife under Section 13(2) of the Hindu Marriage Act, 1955.

Section 13(2) provides for the grounds of divorce meant exclusively for the wife.

Accordingly, a wife can present a petition for dissolution of marriage on any of the following grounds:

(i) the husband had married again before the commencement of the Act or that any other wife of the husband married before such commencement was alive at the time of the solemnization of the marriage of the petitioner

(ii) that the husband has, since the solemnization of the marriage, been guilty of rape, sodomy or bestiality; or

(iii) that in a suit under Section 18 of the Hindu Adoptions and Maintenance Act, 1956 (78 of 1956), or in a proceeding under section 125 of the Code of Criminal Procedure, 1973 (2 of 1974) (or under the corresponding Section 488 of the Code of Criminal Procedure, 1898 (5 of 1898), a decree or order, as the case may be, has been passed against the husband awarding maintenance to the wife notwithstanding that she was living apart and that since the passing of such decree or order, cohabitation between the parties has not been resumed for one year or upwards;

(iv) that her marriage (whether consummated or not) was solemnized before she attained the age of fifteen years and she has repudiated the marriage after attaining that age but before attaining the age of eighteen years.

49 Under the provisions of the Hindu Adoptions and Maintenance Act, 1956 an adopted child

I. can be given in adoption generally.
II. cannot be given in adoption.
III. can be given in adoption with the consent of natural parents.
IV. can be given in adoption only with the prior permission of the court.

Codes

1 II and IV are correct, but I and III are incorrect
2 IV is correct and I, II and III are incorrect
3 II is correct and I, III and IV are incorrect
4 I and II are correct and III and IV are incorrect

Ans. (3)

Exp. Statement II is correct and I, III and IV are incorrect.

The adopted parents cannot give the adopted child in adoption. A child once given in adoption cannot further be given in adoption. The Hindu Adoptions and Maintenance Act of 1956 deals specifically with the legal process of adopting child by a Hindu adult.

50 Match List I with List II in relation to the Hindu Adoptions and Maintenance Act, 1956 and select the correct answer by using the codes given below the lists.

	List I		List II
A.	Maintenance of wife	I.	Section 19
B.	Maintenance of widowed daughter-in- law	II.	Section 22
C.	Maintenance of parents and children	III.	Section 18
D.	Maintenance of dependants	IV.	Section 20

Codes

	A	B	C	D		A	B	C	D
1	III	I	IV	II	2	I	III	II	IV
3	IV	II	I	III	4	II	I	IV	III

Ans. (1)

Exp. The correct matching is A-III; B-I; C-IV; D-II.

Maintenance of wife has been provided under Section 18. It states that a Hindu wife, whether married before or after the commencement of this Act, shall be entitled to be maintained by her husband during her lifetime.

Maintenance of widowed daughter-in-law has been provided under Section 19. It states that a Hindu wife, whether married before or after the commencement of this Act, shall be entitled to be maintained after the death of her husband by her father-in-law

Maintenance of parents and children has been provided under Section 20. It states that a Hindu is bound, during his or her life-time, to maintain his or her legitimate or illegitimate children and his or her aged or infirm parents.

Maintenance of dependants has been provided under Section 22. It states that the heirs of a deceased Hindu are bound to maintain the dependants of the deceased out of the estate inherited by them from the deceased.

51 After the petition is presented under Section 13(B) of Hindu Marriage Act, 1955, the parties have to wait for a minimum period of

1 One year
2 Eighteen months
3 Two years
4 Six months

Ans. (4)

Exp. After the petition is presented under Section 13(B) of Hindu Marriage Act, 1955, the parties have to wait for a minimum period of Six months.

According to Section 13B(2), on the motion of both the parties made not earlier than six months after the date of the presentation of the petition referred to in sub-section (1) and not later than eighteen months after the said date, if the petition is not withdrawn in the meantime, the court shall, on being satisfied, after hearing the parties and after making such inquiry as it thinks fit, that a marriage has been solemnised and that the averments in the petition are true, pass a decree of divorce declaring the marriage to be dissolved with effect from the date of the decree.

52 Talaq 'ahsan' is

1 Revocable during the tuhr in which it has been pronounced
2 Revocable until the next successive tuhr
3 Revocable during the period of iddat
4 Irrevocable

Ans. (3)

Exp. Talaq 'ahsan' is revocable during the period of iddat.

Talaq 'ahsan' is a single pronouncement of 'talaq' by the husband followed by a period of abstinence called iddat. The duration of the 'iddat' is ninety days or three menstrual cycles (in case, where the wife is menstruating). However, it is revocable during the period of iddat.

53 Match List I with List II in the light of the Dissolution of Muslim Marriage Act, 1939 and select the correct answer by using the codes given below.

List I (Provision)	List II (Section)
A. Notice to heirs of the husband when his where about are not known	I. Section 4
B. Effect of conversion to another faith	II. Section 3
C. Rights to dower not to be affected	III. Section 2 (v)
D. Impotence of the husband as a ground of divorce	IV. Section 5

Codes

	A	B	C	D		A	B	C	D
1	I	III	II	IV	2	II	I	IV	III
3	IV	II	I	III	4	III	I	IV	II

Ans. *(2)*

➲ *Exp.* The correct matching is A-II; B-I; C-IV; D-III.

Notice to the heirs of the husband when his where about are not known is stated under Section 3 of the Dissolution of Muslim Marriages Act, 1939. Clause (a) states that the names and addresses of the persons who would have been the heirs of the husband under Muslim law if he had died on the date of the filing of the plaint shall be stated in the plaint.

Effect of conversion to another faith is stated under Section 4. It state that the renunciation of Islam by a married Muslim woman or her conversion to a faith other than Islam shall not by itself operate to dissolve her marriage.

Rights to dower not to be affected is stated under Section 5. It states that nothing contained in this Act shall affect any right which a married woman may have under Muslim law to her dower or any part thereof on the dissolution of her marriage.

Impotence of the husband as a ground for divorce is stated under Section 2(v). It states that a women married under Muslim law shall be entitled to obtain a decree for the dissolution of her marriage if the husband was impotent at the time of the marriage and continues to be so is a valid ground for divorce.

54 Match List I with List II under the Hindu Minority and Guardianship Act, 1956 and select the correct answer with the help of the codes given below.

List I (Provision)	List II (Section)
A. Testamentary guardian and their powers	I. Section 6
B. Natural guardians of a Hindu Minor	II. Section 9
C. Welfare of minor to be paramount consideration	III. Section 11
D. De facto guardian not to deal with minor's property	IV. Section 13

Codes

	A	B	C	D		A	B	C	D
1	II	I	IV	III	2	I	IV	III	II
3	IV	II	I	III	4	III	I	IV	II

Ans. *(1)*

➲ *Exp.* The correct matching is A-II; B-I; C-IV; D-III.

Testamentary guardian and their powers is stated under Section 9 of Hindu Minority and Guardianship Act, 1956. It states that a Hindu father entitled to act as the natural guardian of his minor legitimate children may, by will appoint a guardian for any of them in respect of the minor's person or in respect of the minor's property (other than the undivided interest referred to in Section 12) or in respect of both.

Natural guardians of a Hindu minor is stated under Section 6. For instance, in the case of a boy or an unmarried girl-the father, and after him, the mother: provided that the custody of a minor who has not completed the age of five years shall ordinarily be with the mother.

Welfare of minor to be of paramount consideration is stated under Section 13. It states that no person shall be entitled to the guardianship by virtue of the provisions of this Act or of any law relating to guardianship in marriage among Hindus, if the court is of opinion that his or her guardianship will not be for the welfare of the minor.

De facto guardian not to deal with minor's property is stated under Section 11. It states that after the commencement of this Act, no person shall be entitled to dispose of, or deal with, the property of a Hindu minor merely on the ground of his or her being the de facto guardian of the minor.

55 Read both Assertion (A) and Reason (R) and select the correct answer by using the codes given below.

Assertion (A) The member State of United Nations Organisation have committed to promote and the respect for observance of Human Rights.

Reason (R) The Human Rights are Inalienable, Natural, Interdependent and Indivisible. They are means to achieve human dignity.

Codes

1 Both (A) and (R) are true and (R) is not the correct explanation of (A)

2 Both (A) and (R) are true and (R) is the correct explanation of (A)

3 (A) is false, but (R) is true

4 (A) is true, but (R) is false

Ans. *(2)*

➲ *Exp.* Both (A) and (R) are true and (R) is the correct explanation of (A).

The member State of United Nations Organisation have committed to promote and the respect for observance of Human Rights. The Human Rights are Inalienable, Natural, Interdependent and Indivisible. They are means to achieve human dignity.

Towards the end of the Second World war, the United Nations Charter was debated, drafted, and ratified to reaffirm faith in fundamental human rights, and dignity and worth of the human person and commit all member states to promote universal respect for, and observance of, human rights and fundamental freedoms for all without distinction as to race, sex, language, or religion.

56 The International Covenant on Economic, Social and Cultural Rights came into force on

1 3rd January, 1976 2 13th January, 1976
3 30th June, 1977 4 13th June, 1977

Ans. (1)

Exp. The International Covenant on Economic, Social and Cultural Rights (ICESCR) came into force 3rd January, 1976. It is a multilateral treaty adopted by the United Nations General Assembly on 16th December 1966, through the General Assembly Resolution 2200A (XXI).

57 UNICEF was created by the UN General Assembly to help

1 Children after World War I
2 Children after World War II in Europe
3 Children of third world countries
4 Children of suffering from malnutrition

Ans. (2)

Exp. UNICEF was created by the UN General Assembly to help children after World War II in Europe.

UNICEF was founded in the aftermath of World War II. The General Assembly of the United Nations voted to establish the United Nations International Children's Emergency Fund (UNICEF) as an organization to help provide relief and support to children living in countries devastated by the war.

58 Match List I with List II and select the correct answer using the codes given below.

List I	List II
A. Mr. Jose Ayala Lasso	I. President International Court of Justice
B. Justice Nagendra Singh	II. Secretary General UNO
C. Kofi Annan	III. Chairperson Commission on human Rights
D. Mrs FD Roosevelt	IV. UN High Commissioner for Human Rights

Codes

	A	B	C	D		A	B	C	D
1	IV	I	II	III	2	II	IV	III	I
3	III	II	I	IV	4	III	II	IV	I

Ans. (1)

Exp. The correct matching is A-IV; B-I; C-II; D-III.

Mr. Jose Ayala Lasso served as a UN High Commissioner for Human Rights. He became the first United Nations High Commissioner for Human Rights on 5th April, 1994. He was appointed for a four-year term by the Secretary-General of the United Nations.

Justice Nagendra Singh served as a President of the International Court of Justice. Sri Nagendra Singh (18th March, 1914 – 11th December, 1988) was an Indian lawyer and administrator who served as President of the International Court of Justice from 1985 to 1988.

Kofi Annan served as a Secretary General UNO. He was the seventh Secretary-General of the United Nations, served from 1997 to 2006 and was the first to emerge from the ranks of United Nations staff.

Mrs FD Roosevelt served as a Chairperson of Commission on Human rights. She was an American political figure, diplomat and activist. She served as the first lady of the United States from 1933 to 1945, during her husband President Franklin D. Roosevelt's four terms in office, making her the longest-serving first lady of the United States.

59 The Universal Declaration of Human Rights 1948 contains provisions relating to

1 Operationalisation of Human Rights
2 Establishment of Human Rights Institutions
3 Establishment of Human Rights Committee
4 Conceptualisation of Human Rights

Ans. (1)

Exp. The Universal Declaration of Human Rights 1948 contains provisions relating to the operationalisation of Human Rights.

The Universal Declaration of Human Rights (UDHR) is an international document adopted by the United Nations General Assembly that enshrines the rights and freedoms of all human beings. It was accepted by the General Assembly as Resolution 217 during its third session on 10th December, 1948 at the Palais de Chaillot in Paris, France.

60 Which of the following statements is correct?

1 The UN Convention on Elimination of all Forms of Discrimination Against Women (CEDAW) was adapted by the General Assembly in 1979 but, India ratified it in June, 1993
2 The UN Convention on Elimination of all Forms of Discrimination Against Women (CEDAW) was adapted by the General Assembly in 1979 but, India ratified it in December, 1997
3 The UN Convention on Elimination of all Forms of Discrimination Against Women (CEDAW) was adapted by the General Assembly in 1981 but India ratified it in June, 1993
4 The UN Convention on Elimination of all Forms of Discrimination Against Women (CEDAW) was adapted by the General Assembly in 1981 but, India ratified it in December, 1997

Ans. (1)

Exp. The UN Convention on Elimination of all Forms of Discrimination Against Women (CEDAW) was adopted by the General Assembly in 1979 but, India ratified it in June, 1993. It is also defined as the international bill of rights for women.

The Convention defines discrimination against women was adopted as " any distinction, exclusion or restriction made on the basis of sex which has the effect or purpose of impairing or nullifying the recognition, enjoyment or exercise by women, irrespective of their marital status, on a basis of equality of men and women, of human rights and fundamental freedoms in the political, economic, social, cultural, civil or any other field."

61 The correct chronological order of the following Human Rights documents be choosen using the codes given below.

I. International Covenant on Civil and Political Rights.
II. Convention on the Elimination of all Forms of Discrimination Against Women.
III. Universal Declaration of Human Rights.
IV. Convention on the Rights of the Child.

Codes

1 III, II, I and IV
2 III, I, II and IV
3 IV, III, I and II
4 III, IV, II and I

Ans. (2)

Exp. The correct chronological order is III, I, II and IV.

The Universal Declaration of Human Rights (1948) is the parent human right document that is also called the Internal Bill of Rights. It was accepted by the General Assembly as Resolution 217 during its third session on 10 December 1948 at the Palais de Chaillot in Paris, France.

The International Covenant on Civil and Political Rights was adopted in 1966. It came into force on 23rd March 1976. The treaty commits its parties to respect the civil and political rights of individuals including, freedom of religion, right to life, freedom of assembly, electoral rights and rights to due process and a fair trial. About 173 countries are parties to the Covenant.

The Convention on the Elimination of all Forms of Discrimination Against Women was adopted in 1979. It was adopted by the General Assembly in 1979 but India ratified it in June, 1993. It is also defined as the international bill of rights for women.

The Convention on the Rights of the Child was adopted in 1989. The Convention on the Rights of the Child is part of the legally binding international instruments for the guarantee and the protection of Human Rights. Its objective is to protect the rights of all children in the world.

62 Who defined law of tort as "tortious liability arises from the breach of a duty primarily fixed by the law: this duty is towards persons generally and its breach is redressible by an action for unliquidated damages"?

1 Salmand
2 Lord Denning
3 Fraser
4 Winfield

Ans. (4)

Exp. Winfield defined law of tort as "tortious liability arises from the breach of a duty primarily fixed by the law. This duty is towards persons generally and its breach is redressible by an action for unliquidated damages". Thus, according to his theory, all the unjustifiable harm for which there is no excuse will be treated as a tort.

63 Which of the following is not a form of damnum sine injuria?

I. There is no right of action for damages for contempt of court.
II. Loss inflicted on individual traders by competition.
III. Damage is done by a man acting under necessity to prevent a greater evil.
IV. Damage caused by defamatory statements made on any occasion.

Codes

1 I, II, III and IV
2 II and IV
3 I and II
4 None of the above

Ans. (3)

Exp. To constitute an action under tort, there must be a legal injury that is suffered by the plaintiff. Damage without injury is not actionable under tort law. Damnum sine injuria means damage without injury. Statements I and II refer to situations wherein a damage has been caused but there is no legal injury, hence, they are not actionable.

64 Facts : "The defendant was a plaintiff's landlord and was living in the same building on the floor above him. Some rats damaged a rain water box maintained by the defendant for the benefit both of himself and plaintiff and the water running through injured plaintiff's goods below." What action can be taken on the above mentioned facts in view of the exceptions to the theory of 'strict liability'?

1 No action lie because of plaintiff's own fault
2 Action lie because it is not act of God
3 No action lie because of the consent of plaintiff
4 Action lie because it is not an act of stranger

Ans. (3)

Exp. According to the facts given here, the defence that can be taken under the rule of strict liability is that no action can lie since the plaintiff gave his consent. The plaintiff can be construed to have consented to any harm that arises out of the flow of the rain water box that was maintained by the defendant since he had been living in the same building, knowing that the box is maintained by the defendant.

65 Read Assertion (A) and Reason (R) and select the correct answer with the help of codes given below.

Assertion (A) A master is liable for the torts committed by his servant while not acting in the course of his employment.

Reason (R) Liability of the master for the act of his servant is based on the maxim respondent superior.

Codes

1 Both (A) and (R) are true and (R) is the correct explanation of (A)
2 Both (A) are (R) are true, but (R) is not the correct explanation of (A)
3 (A) true, but (R) is false
4 (A) is false, but (R) is true

Ans. *(4)*

Exp. (A) is false, but (R) is true.

The Liability of the master for the act of his servant is based on the maxim respondent superior. Thus, the reason is correct. However, the master will only be liable for those acts of the servant which are done within the course of his employment and not beyond. Thus, the Assertion is incorrect.

66 Match List I with List II and select the correct answer by using the codes given below.

	List I (Case Laws)		List II (Principles)
A.	Re Polemis and Furners, Wilhy and Co. Ltd	I.	Vicariom liability of the state
B.	Saheli Vs. Commissioner of Police, Delhi	II.	Remoteness of damages
C.	Municipal Corporation of Delhi Vs. Subhagwanti	III.	Duty of case of plaintiff
D.	South Wales Miners Federation Vs. Glamorgan Coal Company	IV.	Malice in Fact

Codes

	A	B	C	D		A	B	C	D
1	II	I	III	IV	2	I	II	IV	III
3	I	II	III	IV	4	II	III	I	IV

Ans. *(1)*

Exp. The correct code is A-II; B-I; C-III; D-IV.

Re Polemis and Furners, Wilhy and Co. Ltd case deal with remoteness of damage. The Court of Appeal held that a defendant can be deemed liable for all consequences flowing from his negligent conduct, regardless of how unforeseeable such consequences are. It is an example of a case of strict liability.

Saheli Vs. Commissioner of Police, Delhi case deal with vicarious liability of the state. The State was held liable for the death of a nine-year-old child by Police assault and beating. Delhi Administration was ordered to pay compensation of Rs. 75000.

Municipal Corporation of Delhi Vs. Subhagwanti case deal with duty of case of plaintiff. The doctrine of res ipsa loquitur was applicable to the circumstances of the present case.

South Wales Miners Federation Vs. Glamorgan Coal Company case deal with malice in fact. It is a part of an infamous three tort cases that imposed liability on trade unions for going on strike.

67 What is the period of limitation under Section 24 A of the Consumer Protection Act, 1986 (as amended w.e.f 18.6.1993)for filling a complaint from the date of the cause of action?

1 No period of limitation
2 Three years
3 Two years
4 One year

Ans. *(3)*

Exp. Section 24A of the Consumer Protection Act, 1986 provides for the Limitation period and stated that the District Forum, State Commission or the National Commission (as the case may be) shall not admit a complaint if it has been filed after two years from the date on which cause of action has arisen.

68 Match the List I with List II and select answer by using the codes given below.

	List I (Name of Case Law)		List II (Principle)
A.	Tolley Vs. JS Fry and Sons Ltd.	I.	Publication of statement
B.	Williamson Vs. Frier	II.	Innuendo
C.	Alexander Vs. North Eastern Railway	III.	Fair comment
D.	Merivale Vs. Carson	IV.	Defence of truth

Codes

	A	B	C	D		A	B	C	D
1	II	I	IV	III	2	I	II	III	IV
3	IV	I	II	III	4	III	II	I	IV

Ans. *(1)*

Exp. The correct matching is A-II; B-I; C-IV; D-III.

Tolley Vs. JS Fry and Sons Ltd case is related to innuendo. It was held that since the publication could have the meaning alleged by the claimant, the caricature was capable of constituting defamation.

Williamson Vs. Frier case is related to publication of statement. Publication can also occur where a third party intercepts the communication, even if it was not intended by the original publisher.

Alexander Vs. North Eastern Railway case is related to defence of truth. For the defence of justification to apply, the statements or imputations complained of must be 'substantially true'.

Merivale Vs. Carson case is related to fair comment. The defence of fair comment is open to a commentator however prejudiced he might be, and however exaggerated or obstinate his views.

69 Match List I with List II and select the correct answer using the codes given below.

List I	List II
A. Kundan Lal Rallaram Vs. custodian	I. Presumption under Section 118 of the Negotiable Instrument Act arises only if the execution of the document is proved as true
B. CT Joseph Vs. IV Phillip	II. Burden of proof of failure of consideration for a negotiable instrument
C. AV Murthy Vs. BS Nagabasavanna	III. A negotiable instrument is presumed to be drawn for consideration
D. Beni Madhavnath Vs. Jugandra Nath Balwan	IV. The statutory presumption envisaged under Section 118 (a) of the Negotiable Instrument Act is rebuttable

Codes

	A	B	C	D		A	B	C	D
1	II	I	III	IV	2	I	II	III	IV
3	II	IV	I	III	4	III	I	IV	II

***Ans.* (1)**

Exp. The correct matching is A-II; B-I; C-III; D-IV.

Kundan Lal Rallaram Vs. custodian case mention the burden of proof of failure of consideration for a negotiable instrument. The burden of proof as a question of law rests, therefore, on the plaintiff; but as soon as the execution is proved.

Section 118 of the Negotiable Instruments Act imposes a duty on the court to raise a presumption in his favour that the said instrument was made for consideration.

CT Joseph Vs. IV Phillip case mention that the presumption under Section 118 of the Negotiable Instrument Act, arises only if the execution of the document is proved as true. The case dealt with whether presumption under Section 118 read with Section 139 NI Act can be raised in the favour of complainant in the present case.

In *AV Murthy Vs. BS Nagabasavanna* case a negotiable instrument is presumed to be drawn for consideration. Under Section 118 of the Act, there is a presumption that until the contrary is proved, every negotiable instrument was drawn for consideration.

Beni Madhavnath Vs. Jugandra Nath Balwan case mention that the statutory presumption envisaged under Section 118 (a) of the Negotiable Instrument Act is rebuttable. As per section 118(g) of the Negotiable Instrument Act says that unless contrary is proved the holder of a negotiable instrument is a holder in due course.

70 Which of the following statements is incorrect?

1 A cheque is a bill of exchange, but every bill of exchange is not a cheque
2 A cheque is always payable on demand
3 A cheque is a conditional order from the drawer of a cheque to the drawee bank to make payment of money only
4 A post dated cheque cannot be considered as a valid cheque till the date of maturity

***Ans.* (3)**

Exp. Statement 3 is incorrect.

As per Section 6 of the Negotiable Instruments Act, 1881, a "cheque" is a bill of exchange drawn on a specified banker and not expressed to be payable otherwise than on demand and it includes the electronic image of a truncated cheque and a cheque in the electronic form.

71 Which of the following cases is about doctrine of indoor management?

1 Ashbury Railway Carriage and Iron Co. Ltd. Vs. Riche
2 Rama Corpn. Vs. Proved tin and General Investment Co
3 London Country Council Vs. Attorney - General
4 A Lakshmana Swamy Mudaliar Vs. LIC

***Ans.* (2)**

Exp. Rama Corpn. Vs. Proved tin and General Investment Co. is a case on the doctrine of indoor management that evolved 150 years ago. It is also known as Turquand's rule.

The doctrine of indoor management lays down that persons dealing with a company having satisfied themselves that the proposed transaction is not in its nature inconsistent with the memorandum and articles, are not bound to inquire the regularity of any internal proceeding.

The role of the doctrine of indoor management is opposed to the role of the doctrine of constructive notice.

72 Read Assertion (A) and Reason (R) and select the correct answer using codes given below.

Assertion (A) For the proper exercise of the functions of a director, it is essential that he be disinterested, that is, be free from any conflicting interest.

Reason (R) Conflict is injurious to mental and physical health.

Codes

1 Both (A) and (R) are true and (R) is correct explanation of (A)
2 (A) is true, but (R) is false
3 Both (A) and (R) are false
4 Both (A) and (R) are true, but (R) is not correct legal explanation of (A)

Ans. (4)

➲ *Exp.* Both (A) and (R) are true but (R) is not the correct explanation of (A) because (R) defines conflict in terms of its adverse impacts on health, whereas the Assertion deals with the independence of Directors under the Companies Act. For the proper exercise of the functions of a director, it is essential that he be disinterested, i.e. be free from any conflicting interest. When a director befalls himself into the tangle of any conflict, he cannot dischage his duties properly as a director.

Conflict is injurious to mental and physical health because conflict always remains to be a factor behind deterioration of mental and physical health.

73 Which are essentials of a partnership?

I. A contract of two or more competent persons

II. Agreement to share profits

III. Mutual agency

IV. Lawful business

Codes

1 I, II and III 2 I, II and IV

3 II, III and IV 4 All of these

Ans. (4)

➲ *Exp.* According to Section 4 of the Partnership Act, 1932, "Partnership" is the relation between persons who have agreed to share the profits of a business carried on by all or any of them acting for all. 'Persons' here imply people who are competent to contract under the Indian Contract Act, 1872.

Following are the essentials of a partnership :

- A contract of two or more competent persons
- Agreement to share profits
- Mutual agency
- Lawful business

74 Match List I with List II and select the correct answer using the codes given below.

List I	List II
A. Section 54 of the Sale of Goods Act	I. Risk where goods are delivered at distant place
B. Section 40 of the Sale of Goods Act	II. Delivery of wrong quantity
C. Section 37 of the Sale of Goods Act	III. Sale by description
D. Section 15 of the Sale of Goods Act	IV. Rights of unpaid seller against the goods

Codes

	A	B	C	D
1	I	IV	II	III
2	IV	I	II	III
3	IV	I	III	II
4	II	III	I	IV

Ans. (2)

➲ *Exp.* The correct matching is A-IV; B-I; C-II; D-III.

Section 54 of Sale of Goods Act is related to rights of unpaid seller against the goods. It stated that subject to the provisions of this section, a contract of sale is not rescinded by the mere exercise by an unpaid seller of his right of lien or stoppage in transit.

Section 40 of Sale of Goods Act is related to risk where goods are delivered at distant place. It stated that where that seller of goods agrees to deliver them at his own risk at a place other than that where they are when sold, the buyer shall, nevertheless, unless otherwise agreed, take any risk of deterioration in the goods necessarily incident to the course of transit.

Section 37 of Sale of Goods Act is related to delivery of wrong quantity. It stated that where the seller delivers to the buyer a quantity of goods less than he contracted to sell, the buyer may reject them, but if the buyer accepts the goods so delivered he shall pay for them at the contract rate.

Section 15 of Sale of Goods Act is related to sale by description. It stated that where there is a contract for the sale of goods by description, there is an implied condition that the goods shall correspond with the description; and, if the sale is by sample as well as by description, it is not sufficient that the bulk of the goods corresponds with the sample if the goods do not also correspond with the description.

75 Which of the following cases is about performance of contract?

1 Maruti Udyog Ltd. Vs. Susheel Kumar Gabgetra

2 Great Northern Railway Co. Vs. Harrison

3 Joyce Vs. Swann

4 Behn Vs. Burness

Ans. (2)

➲ *Exp.* Great Northern Railway Co. Vs. Harrison is the case on performance of contract. In this case, it was held that a tender is a continuing offer to supply goods or services, which can be accepted by the other party at any time while the offer is open.

UGC-NET LAW

SOLVED PAPER 2015 (June)

PAPER II

1 Which of the following statement(s) is/are incorrect?

I. In Keshavananda Bharati case, the Supreme Court has said that the Preamble of the Constitution is a key to open the mind of the makers.

II. 'Socialist and Secular' words were added to the Preamble by 44th Amendment of the Constitution.

III. Preamble can only be amended if it violates the Basic Structure of the Constitution.

IV. Since Preamble is not articled, so it is not the part of Constitution.

Codes

1 Only II　　2 III and IV

3 I, II and III　　4 I, II, III and IV all are incorrect

Ans. *(4)*

Exp. Statements I, II, III and IV all are incorrect.

Statements I, III and IV are incorrect as in the Keshavananda Bharati case, the Supreme Court has said that the Preamble of the Constitution is a part of the Constitution and can be amended, but the Basic Structure of the Constitution cannot be amended. The Preamble is a key to open the minds of the framers was said in the Re Berubari judgement (1960).

Statement II is incorrect as the words Socialist, Secular, and Integrity were not in the original Constitution and have been inserted by 42nd Amendment Act, 1976.

2 Match List I with List II and select the correct answer by using the codes given below the lists

List I	List II
A. Article 329	I. Golaknath Vs. State of Punjab
B. 10th Schedule Part-7	II. Keshavananda Bharati Vs. State of Kerala
C. Article 31(C)	III. Indira Nehru Gandhi Vs. Raj Narain
D. Article 13(2)	IV. Kihota Vs. Zachilhu

Codes

	A	B	C	D		A	B	C	D
1	II	I	III	IV	2	III	IV	II	I
3	IV	III	I	II	4	I	II	IV	III

Ans. *(2)*

Exp. The correct matching is A-III; B-IV; C-II; D-I.

Article 329 is related to case Indira Nehru Gandhi Vs. Raj Narain (1975). The majority decision in Indira Nehru Gandhi Vs. Raj Narain (1975) adjudged the impugned Clause 4 of Article 329 as unconstitutional based on the doctrine of Basic Structure. The verdict was delivered by the Constitutional bench with a 3-2 majority, with Justice Chandrachud, Justice Mathew, and Chief Justice Ray being in favour of declaring the clause as unconstitutional.

10th Schedule Part-7 is related tp the case Kihota Vs. Zachilhu and others (1992). In this case the court held that the Speakers/Chairman hold a pivotal position in the scheme of Parliamentary democracy and are guardians of the rights and privileges of the House. They are expected to and do take far reaching decisions in the Parliamentary democracy. Vestiture of power to adjudicate questions under the Tenth Schedule in them should not be considered exceptionable.

Article 31(C) is related to the case Keshvananda Bharati Vs. State of Kerala (1973). Five of the majority judges in Kesavananda Bharati Vs. State of Kerala (1973) held that the entirety of Article 31(C), which was added to the Constitution by the 25th Amendment, was void. Justice Reddy separated parts of the same Article to hold it valid, and only Justice Khanna held that the first part of Article 31(C) was valid while the second part was void.

Article 13(2) is related to the case Golaknath Vs. State of Punjab (1967). The majoritarian bench in Golaknath Vs. State of Punjab (1967) remained of the opinion that since the 1950's there have been several instances where the Parliament missed the powers conferred by Article 368 and infringed the Fundamental Rights of the people. The court felt that if not stopped, the autocratic actions of the Parliament will know no bounds.

3 **"If I was asked to name any particular Article in this Constitution as the most important an Article without which this Constitution would be a nullity I could not refer to any other Article except this one (Article 32) .... It is the soul of the Constitution and the very heart of it".**

Whose observations are these?

1 Justice PN Bhagwati
2 Dr BR Ambedkar
3 Justice VR Krishna Iyer
4 Pandit Jawahar Lal Nehru

Ans. *(2)*

Exp. The given observation was made by Dr. B R Ambedkar.

During the Constituent Assembly debate, Dr. B.R Ambedkar had said that Article 32 is the heart and soul of the Constitution, and rights given through it will always be exercised in the Supreme Court unless any amendment has been made in the Constitution.

Article 32 i.e., 'Right to Constitutional Remedies' was made to deal to ensure that no citizen stays deprived of using their Fundamental Rights and gives the power to the citizens of India to go directly to the Supreme Court of India if they feel that any of their Fundamental Rights have been violated.

4 **Which of the following statement(s) is/are incorrect?**

I. Chapter III on Fundamental Rights of the Constitution is based upon Bill of Rights of the USA.

II. 'Right to die' is a Fundamental Right under Article 21 of the Constitution.

III. Indian Constitution is a complete Federal Constitution.

IV. Fundamental Rights can be waived under the Indian Constitution.

Codes

1 Only II	2 III and IV
3 II and III	4 II, III and IV

Ans. *(4)*

Exp. Statements II, III and IV are incorrect.

Statement II is incorrect because 'Right to Die' is not a Fundamental Right under Article 21.The court in Gian Kaur Vs. State of Punjab overruled the P. Ratinam's case and held that Right to Life under Article 21 of the Constitution does not include Right to die or Right to be killed and there is no ground to hold that the Section 309 of IPC is constitutionally invalid.

Statement III is incorrect because the Indian Constitution is not a completely Federal. Constitution. It is at best quasi-federal in nature since it has a federal structure with unitary features. Thus, it cannot be called a complete federation like the USA. Throughout the Constitution, emphasis is laid on the fact that India is a single United Nation. It is described as a Union of States constituted into a Sovereign, Secular, Socialist and Democratic Republic.

Statement IV is incorrect because Fundamental Rights cannot be waived by a person. Behram Khurshed Pesikaka Vs. The State of Bombay, 1954, wherein, it was observed that Fundamental Rights are a matter of public policy and the same cannot be waived. The doctrine of waiver has no application on law enacted as a matter of Constitutional policy.

5 **Match List I with List II and select the correct answer by using the codes given below the lists.**

List I (Principles)	List II (Case Law)
A. Equal work for Equal pay	I. RD Shetty Vs. The International Airport Authority of India
B. 'Agencies or Instrumentalition' of the State are covered under the definition of state under Article 12 of the Constitution	II. Rudul Sah Vs. State of Bihar
C. Fundamental Rights and Directive Principles of state policy are supplementary and complimentary to each other	III. Randhir Singh Vs. Union of India
D. Damages can be awarded for violation of Fundamental Rights under Article 21 of the Constitution	IV. Unni Krishnan Vs. State of AP

Codes

	A	B	C	D		A	B	C	D
1	III	I	IV	II	2	I	II	III	IV
3	IV	III	I	II	4	II	IV	III	I

Ans. *(1)*

Exp. The correct matching is A-III, B-I, C-IV, D-II.

Randhir Singh Vs. Union of India is related to principle equal work for equal pay. The Supreme Court first constitutionalised the right to equal pay for equal work [Article 39(d)] in a 1982 judgement called Randhir Singh Vs. Union of India. The Court grounded equal pay for equal work in Article 14 of the Constitution, and observed that in cases where all "relevant considerations are the same", the government could not deny equal pay simply by performing the bureaucratic manoeuvre of splitting the workforce into different posts, or different departments.

RD Shetty Vs. The International Airport Authority of India is linked with 'Agencies or Instrumentalities' of the State which are covered under the definition of state under Article 12 of the Constitution. The Court, in this case, had laid down a 5-pointer test to determine the test of instrumentality to bring an organisation within the ambit of 'State' under Article 12 of the Constitution.

Unni Krishnan Vs. State of A.P (1993) iselated to the principle that Fundamental Rights and Directive Principles of State Policy are supplementary and complementary to each other. The Court also held that the Fundamental Rights must be construed in the light of the Directive Principles.

Rudul Sah Vs. State of Bihar (1983) is related to the principle that damages can be awarded for violation of Fundamental Rights under Article 21 of the Constitution. It is a landmark judgement in the jurisprudence of state liability. It is considered particularly important as it led to the emergence of compensatory jurisprudence for the violation of Fundamental Rights under the Constitution.

6 Match List I with List II and select the correct answer by using the codes given below the lists.

List I (Added/Amended Provisions)	List II (Amendment)
A. Article 15 clause (4) providing for special provisions for socially and educationally backward classes.	I. 24th Amendment Act, 1971
B. Article 13 clause (4) providing for nothing shall apply to any constitutional amendment.	II. Constitution (85th Amendment) Act, 2001
C. Article 16 clause (4 A) providing for Consequential Seniority with promotion to SC/ST.	III. Constitution (86th Amendment) Act, 2002
D. Article 21A providing for right to Education as Fundamental Right.	IV. Constitution (1st Amendment) Act, 1951

Codes

	A	B	C	D		A	B	C	D
1	I	II	III	IV	2	IV	I	II	III
3	III	IV	I	II	4	II	III	IV	I

Ans. *(2)*

Exp. The correct matching is A-IV, B-I, C-II, D-III.

The Constitution (1st Amendment) Act, 1951 amended Article 15 of the Constitution to add clause (4) stating that nothing in this article or in clause (2) of Article 29 shall prevent the State from making any special provision for the advancement of any socially and educationally backward classes of citizens or for the Scheduled Castes and the Scheduled Tribes. The State under Article 15 cannot discriminate against any citizen on grounds only of religion, race, caste, sex, place of birth or any of them.

According to the 24th Amendment Act, 1971, in Article 13 of the Constitution, after clause (3), the clause (4) was inserted stating that nothing in this article shall apply to any amendment of this Constitution made under Article 368. As per Article 13, all laws in force in the territory of India immediately before the commencement of this Constitution, in so far as they are inconsistent with the provisions of this Part, shall, to the extent of such inconsistency, be void.

In the *85th Amendment Act, 2001* Parliament amended Article 16(4A) and introduced the principle of Consequential Seniority to promoted SC/ST candidates. Subsequently, the text of Article 16 (4A) was amended such that 'in matters of promotion to any class' became 'in matters of promotion, with consequential seniority to any class.'

Article 21A was added in part III by the Constitution *(86th Amendment) Act*, 2002 and stated that every child has a right to full time elementary education of satisfactory and equitable quality in a formal school which satisfies certain essential norms and standards.

7 Given below are two statements, one is labelled as Assertion (A) and other as Reason (R) and select the correct answer from the codes given below.

Assertion (A) Powers and functions are distributed between the two tiers of government under the written Constitution in India.

Reason (R) Union and the States are completely independent of each other under the Indian Constitution.

Codes

1 (A) is true and (R) is the correct explanation of (A)
2 (A) is true, but (R) is not the correct explanation of (A)
3 (A) is true, but (R) is false
4 (A) is false, but (R) is true

Ans. *(3)*

Exp. (A) is true, but (R) is false.

The Indian Constitution has divided the powers between the centre and the state in terms of union list, state list and the concurrent list as mentioned in Schedule VII. The Indian Constitution is the supreme law of the land which means all the authorities of the Union and the State are subject to the authority of the Indian Constitution. Thus, the Assertion is correct.

The Reason is incorrect because the Union and the States are not completely independent of each other under the Indian Constitution. List III of the Seventh Schedule provides for those matters where both the Union as well as the States can legislate. Further, the Centre has the power to make laws on State list in cases of emergency. Thus, they are not independent of each other and the given Reason is incorrect.

8 Which of the following school in jurisprudence encompasses the 'Functional approach'?

1 Philosophical school 2 Natural school
3 Sociological school 4 Historical school

Ans. *(3)*

Exp. Sociological school in jurisprudence encompasses the 'Functional approach'.

The Sociological School of Law lays more emphasis on the functional aspect of law rather than its abstract content. They consider law as a social institution essentially interlinked with other scientists and the direct impact of the law on society with its formation according to social needs.

9 A legal system which works to ensure a fair division of social benefits and burdens among the member of community. It serves to secure a balance and equilibrium among the members of the society. What is the name of this legal system?

1 Distributive Justice 2 Corrective Justice
3 Remedial Justice 4 Adversarial justice

***Ans.* (1)**

Exp. The name of the legal system described is Distributive Justice.

Distributive Justice is concerned with the fair allocation of resources among diverse members of a community. Fair allocation typically takes into account the total amount of goods to be distributed, the distributing procedure, and the pattern of distribution that results.

10 Which of the following is not correct regarding Legislation and Precedent?

1 Legislation reflects the formal will of the state and precedent has its source in Judgement of court
2 Legislation is the formal expression of new laws by legislature and precedent is the creation of law by recognition
3 Legislation is general declaration of law in abstract form and precedent is the manifestation of law in action
4 Legislations are based on the minority opinion and precedents are created or based for future decisions

***Ans.* (4)**

Exp. Statement 4 in incorrect as Legislations are not based on the minority opinion.

'Legislation' refers to the codification of law by the parliament or any other similar body, while 'Precedent' is the interpretation and declaration of a law by the court of law that subsequently applies to lower courts as well.

11 Read Assertion (A) and Reason (R) and select the correct answer from the codes given below.

Assertion (A) A person in possession of a thing is deemed to be the owner of the thing possessed.

Reason (R) Possession is as good as ownership.

Codes

1 (A) and (R) are true and (R) is the correct explanation of (A)
2 (A) and (R) are true, but (R) is not the correct explanation of (A)
3 (A) is true, but (R) is false
4 (A) is false, but (R) is true

***Ans.* (3)**

Exp. (A) is true, but (R) is false.

Possession is one of the most essential concepts in human life. It is legal as well as a factual concept, which makes it difficult to define. The literal meaning of possession is to have physical control over something materialistic. According to Salmond, "possession is the continuing exercise of a claim to the exclusive use of an object." Thus, the Assertion is true.

However, possession is not as good as ownership, as in the former the rights are limited as against the latter, wherein there is an absolute authority over the object owned. Thus, the Reason is false.

12 Which of the following is not a 'kind of possession'?

1 De facto and De jure
2 Concurrent and duplicate
3 Corporeal and immediate
4 Infinity and antiquity

***Ans.* (4)**

Exp. Infinity and antiquity do not constitute any 'kind of possession'.

'Possession' means physical control over an object or thing. Following are the important types of possession:

1. Corporeal possession
2. Incorporeal Possession
3. Mediate possession
4. Immediate possession
5. Constructive possession
6. Adverse possession
7. De facto possession
8. De jure possession

13 Which of the following are elements of legal right?

1 Responsibility, liability and power
2 Subject, object and title
3 Liability, title and accountability
4 Accountability, responsibility and impartiality

***Ans.* (2)**

Exp. Among the given choices, Subject, object and title are elements of a legal right.

According to Salmond every legal right has the following five elements or characteristics:

1. Person of inherence
2. Person of incidence
3. Contents of the Right
4. Subject matter of the Right
5. Title of the right

14 "International Law or the Law of Nations is the name of body of rules which according to the usual definition regulate the conduct of the states in their intercourse with each another". Who has given this definition?

1 Hack Warth
2 Charles G Fenwick
3 Gray
4 Whiteman

***Ans.* (3)**

Exp. The provided definition was given by Justice Gray.

Gray said that "International Law or the Law of Nations is the name of a body of rules which according to the usual definitions regulate the conduct of States in their intercourse with each other."

The term 'International law', also referred to as Laws of Nations was first coined by Jeramy Bentham in 1780. Every country is referred to as a 'state' in International Law.

15 In which of the following cases the Permanent Court of International Justice applied the general principle of Subrogation?

1 Chorzow Factory (indemnity case)
2 Case concerning the Temple of Preah Vihar
3 Barcelona Traction Case
4 Mavrommatis Palestine Concessions Case

Ans. (4)

➲ *Exp.* In the case titled as Mavrommatis Palestine Concessions (Greece Vs. Great Britain) (1924 – 27), the general principle of Subrogation was applied.

Subrogation refers to substitution of one person into another's place in regards to a legal right, demand, or other lawful claim. The individual who takes another's place by subrogation incurs the rights of the original party in the matter. Subrogation is most commonly seen in insurance claims, where an insurance company, having made payment to its insured, steps into the insured's shoes and in pursuit of payment from a third party.

16 In which of the following cases Justice Gray remarked "International law is a part of our law and must be ascertained and administered by the courts of justice of appropriate jurisdiction as often as questions of rights depending on it are duly presented for administration."

1 Nicaragua Vs. US
2 Paquete Habana case
3 US Vs. Schooner
4 US Vs. Canada

Ans. (2)

➲ *Exp.* The given remark was made by Justice Gray in the Paquete Habana case. In this case, it was held that "International law is part of our law, and must be ascertained and administered by the courts of justice of appropriate jurisdiction as often as questions of rights depending upon it are duly presented for their determination". For this purpose, where there is no treaty and no controlling executive or legislative act or judicial decision, resort must be had to the customs and usages of civilised nations, and, as evidence of these, to the works of jurists and commentators, not for the speculations of their authors concerning what the law ought to be, but for trustworthy evidence of what the law really is.

17 Match List I with List II and select the correct answer by using the codes given below the lists.

List I (Charter of the United Nations Titles)	List II (Number of the Chapter)
A. Membership	I. Chapter XIV
B. The Security Council	II. Chapter II
C. The International Court of Justice	III. Chapter V
D. The General Assembly	IV. Chapter IV

Codes

	A	B	C	D
1	I	II	III	IV
2	II	III	IV	I
3	II	III	I	IV
4	IV	I	II	III

Ans. (3)

➲ *Exp.* *Chapter II* of the United Nations charter deals witht members of the UN organisation. Membership is open to the signatoires and 'all other peace loving states which accept the obligations contained in the present charter.

Chapter V of the United Nations Charter contains provisions establishing the United Nations Security Council that is estabilisehed with the coposition of 5 permanent members and 10 non-permanent members. The non-permanent members are elected for a tern of 2 years by the General Assembly.

Chapter XIV of the United Nations charter deals with International Court of Justice. It is the principal judicial organ of the UN.

Chapter IV of the United Nations charter contains the charter's provisions dealing with the Charter's Provisions dealing with UN General Assembly, specially its composition, functions, power, voting and procedures.

18 Who has observed, "De Facto recognition is by nature provisional and may be made dependent upon conditions which the new entity has to comply. It differs form De Jure recognition, in that there is not yet a formal exchange of diplomatic representatives. De Jure recognition .... is complete, implying full and normal diplomatic relations."

1 Lauterpacht
2 Philip C Jessup
3 Oppenheim
4 Schwarzenberger

Ans. (4)

➲ *Exp.* Schwarzenberger has observed "De facto recognition is by nature provisional and may be made dependent upon conditions which the entity has to comply with. It differs form De Jure recognition, in that there is not yet a formal exchange of diplomatic representatives. De Jure recognition is complete, implying full and normal diplomatic relations.

A De-facto Recognition is extended where a government has not acquired sufficient stability. It is a temporary or conditional recognition. Three conditions for giving de-facto recognition are

- permanence
- the government commands popular support
- the government fulfils international obligations.

19 Given below are two statements, one is labelled as Assertion (A) and other as Reason (R) and select the correct answer from the codes given below.

Assertion (A) International customs used to be the most important source of International Law in the past.

Reason (R) The development of custom is very slow and as compared to it rapid changes made through Treaties.

Codes

1 Both (A) and (R) are true and (R) is the correct explanation of (A)
2 Both (A) and (R) are true, but (R) is not the correct explanation of (A)
3 (A) is true, but (R) is false
4 (A) is false, but (R) is true

Ans. (2)

Exp. Both (A) and (R) are true, but (R) is not the correct explanation of (A).

Sources of INternational law include treaties, international customs, general principles of lw as recognised arond the world, decisions of national and lower courts. Custom, whose importance reflects the decentralised nature of the international system, involves two fundamental elements: the actual practice of states and the acceptance by states of that practice as law. Thus, the Assertion is correct.

The development of custom is very slow and as compared to it rapid changes made through Treaties. This is correct, however, it does not state the reason for considering custom to be an important source of law.

20 Marriage under the Hindu Marriage Act, 1955 is

1 Purely contract
2 Purely sacramental
3 Semblance of contract and sacrament
4 Neither contract nor sacrament

Ans. (3)

Exp. The marriage under Hindu Marriage Act, 1955 is a semblance of a contract and sacrament. The Hindu marriage contemplated by the Act hardly remains sacramental.

The Act has brought in some changes of far reaching consequences which have undermined the sacramental nature of marriage and rendered it contractual in nature to a great extent.

21 Match the List I with List II under the Hindu Marriage Act, 1955 and select the correct answer using the codes given below.

List I	List II
A. Monogamy	I. Section 10
B. Judicial separation	II. Section 5
C. Void marriage	III. Section 11
D. Divorce by Mutual Consent	IV. Section 13-B

Codes

	A	B	C	D		A	B	C	D
1	II	I	III	IV	2	I	III	IV	II
3	II	III	IV	I	4	IV	III	I	II

Ans. (1)

Exp. The correct matching is A-II, B-I, C-III, D-IV.

Section 5 of the Act is related to Monogamy. According to Section 5(i) of the Hindu Marriage Act, a marriage may be solemnised between any two Hindus, if neither party has a spouse living at the time of the marriage.

Section 10 is related to Judicial separation. As per the Section 10. Either party to a marriage, whether solemnized before or after the commencement of this Act, may present a petition praying for a decree for judicial separation on any of the grounds specified in sub-section (1) of Section 13, and in the case of a wife also on any of the grounds specified in sub-section (2) thereof, as grounds on which a petition for divorce might have been presented.

Section 11 is related to void marriage. Any marriage solemnised after the commencement of this Act shall be null and void under Section 11 if it contravenes any one of the conditions specified in clauses (i) , (iv) and (v) of Section 5 of the Act.

Section 13 B is related to divorce by mutual constent. As per Section 13-B, a petition for dissolution of marriage by a decree of divorce may be presented to the district court by both the parties to a marriage together on the ground that they have been living separately for a period of one year or more, that they have not been able to live together and that they have mutually agreed that the marriage should be dissolved.

22 Which of the following are fault grounds of divorce under the Hindu Marriage Act, 1955?

I. Extra marital sex
II. Consent obtained by force or fraud
III. Desertion
IV. Conversion to Non-Hindu religion

Codes

1 I, II and III
2 II, III and IV
3 II, I and IV
4 I, III and IV

Ans. (4)

Exp. The factors like extra marital sex, desertion and conversion to Non-Hindu religion are fault grounds of divorce under the Hindu Marriage Act, 1955.

Section 13 of the Hindu Marriage Act, 1955 and Section 27 of the Special Marriage Act, 1954 state the grounds and reasons for divorce which are as follows:

- Adultery which is the act of indulging in sexual intercourse outside marriage is termed as adultery. Adultery is counted as a criminal offence and substantial proofs are required to establish it. An amendment to the law in 1976 states that one single act of adultery is enough for the petitioner to get a divorce.

If one of the spouses voluntarily abandons his/her partner for at least a period of two years, the abandoned spouse can file a divorce case on the ground of desertion.

In case either of the two converts himself/herself into another religion, the other spouse may file a divorce case based on this ground.

23 A Muslim male is prohibited from marrying the following relations

I. Mother, Grandmother (how high so ever)
II. Daughter, Granddaughter (how low so ever)
III. Aunt, Great aunt (how high so ever, whether paternal or maternal)
IV. Niece, Grand niece (how low so ever)

Codes

1 I, III and IV
2 IV, II and I
3 II, III, IV and I
4 III, II and IV

Ans. (3)

Exp. A Muslim male is prohibited from marrying any of the following-

(a) his mother
(b) his grandmother or upwards, whether on the side of his father or his mother, and her ascendants, (how high so ever)
(c) his daughter and his granddaughter
(d) his sister of the same parents, or
(e) his sister of the same father; or
(f) his sister of the same mother;or
(g) the daughter of his brother or sister, niece, grand niece.
(h) his aunt on his father's side or on his mother's side.

24 The Dissolution of Muslim Marriage Act, 1939 makes available the following grounds of divorce to a Muslim woman married under Muslim Law

I. Seven years imprisonment of the husband.
II. No maintenance by husband for two years.
III. Where abouts of the husband are not known for a period of four years.
IV. Failure of husband to perform marital obligation for a period of three years.

Codes

1 III, II and IV
2 I, II, III and IV
3 II, III and I
4 I, II and IV

Ans. (2)

Exp. The Dissolution of Muslim Marriage Act, 1939 makes available all the given grounds of divorce to a Muslim woman married under Muslim Law. She shall be entitled to obtain a decree for the dissolution of her marriage on any one or more of the following grounds, namely;

- that the whereabouts of the husband have not been known for a period of four years,
- that the husband has neglected or has failed to provide for her maintenance for a period of two years,
- that the husband has been sentenced to imprisonment for a period of seven years or upwards,
- that the husband has failed to perform, without reasonable cause, his marital obligations for a period of three years,
- that the husband has impotent at the time of the marriage and continues to be so,
- that the husband has been insane for a period of two years or is suffering from leprosy or a virulent venereal disease,
- that she, having been given in marriage by her father or other guardian before she attained the age of fifteen years, repudiated the marriage before attaining the age of eighteen years.

25 The ancient sources of Hindu Law include

I. Shruti
II. Smriti
III. Customs
IV. Digests and commentaries

Codes

1 II, III and IV
2 IV, I and II
3 I, II and III
4 I, II, III and IV

Ans. (4)

Exp. The ancient sources of Hindu Law include Shruti, Smriti, Customs and Digests and Commentaries.

- *Shruti*: The word Shruti means; 'what was heard' and Hindu law is considered as revelation by God, which is contained in Shruti. Shruti is divided into Vedas, Brahmanas, Aranyak and Upanishad.
- *Smriti:* The word Smriti means 'What has been remembered'. The era of this is accepted to be 800 BC to 600 AD, this is also known as the golden era of Hindu law. Both Shruti and Smriti refer to the words and principles of the Almighty, which have been heard and remembered respectively, and handed down by the Sages from generation to generation.
- *Customs:* Customs are the most significant and the oldest form of law making. Customs mean the traditions, practices, activities, which have been followed by the people from ages and overtime recognised as law.
- *Digest and Commentaries:* Later sages started to interpret the verses of Manu Smriti. The commentaries and digest cover a period of one thousand year from 700 BC to 700 AD.

26 Originally under the Hindu Marriage Act, 1955, divorce was based on

1 Fault theory only
2 Breakdown theory
3 Consent theory
4 Fault and consent theories

Ans. (1)

Exp. Originally under the Hindu Marriage Act, 1955, divorce was based on Fault theory only.

The Hindu Marriage Act, 1955 originally, based divorce on the fault theory, and enshrined grounds in Section 13(1) on which either the husband or wife could sue for divorce, and some other grounds in Section 13(2) on which wife alone could seek the divorce.

27 "A grocer supplied goods worth ₹ 6000 on credit to 'A'. In addition the grocer solicited a donation of ₹ 2000 for his sons education to which 'A' consented. Later 'A' refused to pay both sums as the lost money on stock transaction". Which one of the following is correct while deciding the liability of 'A'?

I. 'A' has already availed of the benefits in terms of goods supplied, hence consideration between the two binds 'A' to pay.
II. 'A' is not bound to pay ₹ 2000 as it a gift which is not enforceable in Law.
III. 'A' is liable to pay both sums as it is a promise between 'A' and grocer.
IV. 'A' is not liable to pay either of the sums as both of them are joint and not separate.

Codes

1 I and II 2 I and III
3 II and IV 4 III and IV

Ans. (1)

Exp. In the given case, the grocer sold goods worth ₹ 6,000 which is the true consideration and that alone needed to be paid in accordance with the law of contract. The amount of ₹ 2,000 was a mere donation promised, which falls within the category of a gift without consideration and the same is not enforceable in itself in the absence of any consideration arising out of it.

So, 'A' has already availed of the benefits in terms of goods supplied, hence consideration between the two binds 'A' to pay. Also, 'A' is not bound to pay ₹ 2000 as it a gift which is not enforceable in Law.

28 'X' makes an offer to 'Y'. 'X' dies the next day, but 'Y' does not know of the death. 'Y' sends a communication to the address of 'X' accepting the offer. Is the agreement formed between the parties? Select the correct answer.

I. Requirements of offer followed by acceptance are met.
II. Absence of knowledge of death will not invalidate the agreement.
III. No meeting of minds which does not render it to agreement.
IV. Death of the offerer reduces it to nullity.

Codes

1 I and II 2 I and II
3 III and IV 4 II and IV

Ans. (2)

Exp. Among the given statements, only I and II are true.

A contract is started with the offer which means that when one person signifies to another person his willingness to do or not to do something with a view to obtain the assent of another person then this is said to be offer or proposal. When this offer is accepted by another person then it is called acceptance

The word 'acceptance' is broadly defined under our Indian Contract Act, 1872 under Article 2(b), which states that when the person to whom the proposal is made signifies his assent to the proposal is said to be accepted.

The communication of a proposal is complete when it comes to the knowledge of the person to whom it is made.

The communication of an acceptance is complete, as against the proposer, when it is put in a course of transmission to him so as to be out of the power of the acceptor; as against the acceptor, when it comes to the knowledge of the proposer.

In the given case, when acceptance was dispatched, it became complete as against the proposer and a binding obligation arises against him. This consequence is not dependent upon the living status of proposer at that moment as the contract had arisen at the stage of transmission of acceptance.

The statements III and IV are incorrect because the moment acceptance was communicated, there arose a meeting of mind which created a contract and death of the proposer did not affect formation of contract.

29 Match items of List I with List II and select the correct answer using the codes given below the lists.

List I	List II
A. Food Corporation of India Vs. Ram Keshav Yadav	I. Impossibility of performance
B. Kedar Nath Bhattacharji Vs. Gori Mohammed	II. Capacity of minor to enter into contract
C. K. Balakrishnan Vs. K Kamalam	III. Offer and acceptance
D. Satyabrata Goshe Vs. Mugneeram Bangar and Co.	IV. Consideration

Codes

	A	B	C	D		A	B	C	D
1	IV	II	III	I	2	IV	III	II	I
3	III	IV	II	I	4	I	II	III	IV

Ans. (3)

Exp. The correct matching is A-IV, B-III, C-II, D-I.

Food Corporation of India Vs. Ram Keshav Yadav is related to consideration. The Supreme Court in Food Corporation of India v. Ram Kesh Yadav and Another (2007), upheld the direction for grant of employment only because of the acceptance of an interlinked conditional offer.

It the case, Sri Ram keshav Yadav appealed in consideration of his retirement on medical ground that Since his health did not allow him to continue his service of such a hard work, his son may paease beprovided with an "employement in his place.

Kedar Nath Bhattacharji Vs. Gori Mohammed was realted to offer and acceptance. As per the case of Kedarnath Bhattacharji v. Gorie Mohomed, (1886), suit would lie for the recovery of a promised subscription where on the faith of the promisee, the promiser entered into a contract with a contractor.

The case *K.Balakrishnan Vs. K.Kamalam. and Ors* (2003) held that where a gift is made in favour of a child of the donor, who is the guardian of the child, the acceptance of gift can be presumed to have been made by him or on his behalf without any overt act signifying acceptance by the minor.

The Supreme Court in *Satyabrata Ghose Vs. Mugneeram Bangur* (1954) stated that the principles of Frustration of Contract in English law, as per the judgment passed by the High Court, were not relevant in the statutory provisions of the Indian Contract Act. Besides this, the court also affirmed that the execution of the contract did not become impossible.

30 Agreement without consideration is valid under Indian Law. Among the following statements select the one which is against this rule.

1 When agreements written exist on account of natural love and affection
2 When the consideration is too inadequate
3 Where the consideration is past one
4 Where the consideration is from third party

Ans. (2)

➲ *Exp.* Agreement without consideration is invalid unless it is in writing and registered or is a promise to compensate for something done or is a promise to pay a debt barred by limitation law. If the consideration is too inadequate, it will be considered against this rule.

As per Section 25 of the Indian Contract Act, 1872, an agreement without consideration is void, unless:

- it is in writing and and registered under the law for the time being in force for registration and is made on account of natural love and affection between parties standing in a near relation to each other; or
- it is a promise to compensate, wholly or in part, a person who has already voluntarily done something for the promisor, or something which the promisor was legally compellable to do; or
- it is a promise, made in writing and signed by the person to be charged therewith or by his agent generally or specially authorized in that behalf, to pay wholly or in part a debt of which the creditor might have enforced payment but for the law for the limitation of suits.

31 Select the incorrect combination.

1 Proposal + Acceptance = Promise
2 Promise + Consideration = Agreement
3 Agreement + Enforceability = Contract
4 Proposal + Consideration = Acknowledgement

Ans. (4)

➲ *Exp.* Among the given combinations, Proposal + Consideration = Acknowledgment is the incorrect combination.

According to Section 2(a) of the Indian Contract Act, 1872, when one person signifies to another his willingness to do or to abstain from doing anything, with a view to obtaining the assent of that either to such act or abstinence, he is said to make a proposal. A proposal, when accepted, becomes a promise under Section 2(b) and thus, does not constitute acknowledgement.

32 Match the List I with List II and select the correct answer using the codes given below.

List I	List II
A. Doctrine of unjust enrichment	I. Section 11 of Contract Act
B. Doctrine of absolute contract	II. Section 56
C. Doctrine of Estoppel	III. Section 72
D. Doctrine of Pari Delicto	IV. Section 23

Codes

	A	B	C	D		A	B	C	D
1	I	III	II	IV	2	II	III	I	IV
3	III	II	I	IV	4	IV	II	III	I

Ans. (3)

➲ *Exp.* The correct matching is A-III, B-II, C-I, D-IV.

Section 72 is related to Doctrine of unjust enrichment. It states that "A person to whom money has been paid, or anything delivered, by mistake or under coercion, must repay or return it."

Section 56 is related to Doctrine of absolute contract. It states that an agreement to do an act impossible in itself is void.

Section 11 is related to Doctrine of Estoppel. It prevents a party from stating something which contradicts his previous statements. Thus, the minor is not estopped from presenting the defense of infancy. The reason is, there can be no estoppel against a statutory provision given by law.

Section 23 is related to Doctrine of Pari Delicto.

It states that "The consideration or object of an agreement is lawful, unless— it is forbidden by law; or is of such a nature that, if permitted, it would defeat the provisions of any law; or is fraudulent; or involves or implies, injury to the person or property of another; or the Court regards it as immoral, or opposed to public policy". In each of these cases, the consideration or object of an agreement is said to be unlawful. Every agreement of which the object or consideration is unlawful is void.

33 "Just as the criminal law consists of a body of rules establishing specific offence, so the law of torts consists of a body of rules establishing specific injuries". Who stated this?

1 Austin
2 Salmond
3 Winfield
4 Pollock

Ans. (2)

➲ *Exp.* The given statement was made by Salmond.

Sir John Salmond defined 'Tort' as a civil wrong for which the remedy is common law action for unliquidated damages and which is not exclusively the breach of contract or the breach of trust or other merely equitable obligation. Torts are of three types: Intentional Torts, Negligence, Strict Liability.

34 Consider the following elements.

I. Infringement of a legal right
II. Any damage
III. Existence of a legal right
IV. Legal damages

Right to claim damages in tort would arise only if

1 IV, II and I are present
2 II and IV are present
3 I, III and IV are present
4 II, III and I are present

Ans. (3)

Exp. Right to claim damages in tort would arise only if there is infringement of a legal right, existence of a legal right and legal damages.

In order for a right to arise to claim damages for a wrong, it is necessary that there must be the existence of a right in the first place. Then, such a right must be violated by another. This is also known as Injuria Sine Damnum, which simply means damages will be awarded in an actionable claim when there is a legal injury, that is a violation of right.

However, damage is not a necessary ingredient and a right to claim damages may arise with or without any damage, as long as a legal right is violated.

35 Given below are two statements, one is labelled as Assertion (A) and other as Reason (R) and select the correct answer from the codes given below.

Assertion (A) 'X' opens a food court in front of Y's 'food joint'. All the customers of 'Y' patronise 'X'. 'Y' can not claim damages from 'X'.

Reason (R) There is a Latin Maxim 'damnum since injuria'.

Codes

1 (A) is true, but (R) is false
2 (A) is false, but (R) is true
3 Both (A) and (R) are true, but (R) is not the correct explanation of (A)
4 Both (A) and (R) are true and (R) is the correct explanation of (A)

Ans. (4)

Exp. Both (A) and (R) are true and (R) is the correct explanation of (A).

In this case 'Y' cannot claim the damage caused by 'X' because it is a case of damnum since injuria.

This legal maxim refers to damages without injury or damages in which there is no infringement of legal right. Since there is no infringement of legal right so no cause of action arises in the cases of damnum sine injuria. In the given situation, it is not relevant that customers started going to another shop leaving the previous one, because no violation of legal right was caused and it only amounted to damage which is not actionable in itself.

36 In contributory negligence

1 Only one party is negligent and other has not taken due care
2 Both parties have contributed to negligence equally
3 Lack of care is equal on both sides
4 One party is negligent resulting in injury while the other has taken due care

Ans. (1)

Exp. In contributory negligence, only one party is negligent and the other party has not taken due care.

The concept of contributory negligence is used to characterize conduct that creates an unreasonable risk to one's self. The idea is that an individual has a duty to act as a reasonable person. When a person does not act this way and injury occurs, that person may be held entirely or partially responsible for the resulting injury, even though another party was involved in the accident. It is thus wrong to say that in contributory negligence, there is an equal amount of fault involved from all parties. Such participation may or may not be equal, depending on the facts and circumstances of the case.

37 Match List I with List II and select the correct answer using the codes given below.

List I (Principle)	List II (Associated Case)
A. Absolute Liability	I. Gloucester Grammar School
B. Damnum sine injuria	II. Ashby Vs. White
C. Injuria sine damnum	III. Stanley Vs. Powell
D. Inevitable accident	IV. Ryland Vs. Fletcher

Codes

	A	B	C	D		A	B	C	D
1	I	II	III	IV	2	II	III	IV	I
3	IV	II	I	III	4	III	I	II	IV

Ans. ()

Exp. The correct matching is A-III; B-I; C-II; D-IV.

Absolute Liability is associated with the case Stanley Vs Powell. Stanley Vs. Powell In this case the defendant and the plaintiff had gone for a shooting party. The defendant fired a shot at a distance but the bullet glanced off a tree and injured the plaintiff. It was held that this was just an accident which was inevitable, and the defendant was not held liable.

Damnum Sine Injuria is associated with the case Gloucester Grammar School. In this case, it was held that no suit could lie as the defendant wasn't liable. Compensation is not the ground of action despite the fact that the monetary loss is caused but if no right is violated. The defendant had lawfully established his school and didn't violate any legal rights of the plaintiff in doing so.

Injuria Sine Damnum is associated with the case Ashby Vs. White. In this case, it was held that it is an infringement of a legal private right without any actual loss or damage. In such a case, the person whose right has been infringed has a good cause of action. It is not necessary for him to prove any special damage because every injury imports a damage when a man hinders his right.

Inevitable accident Stanley Vs. Powel is associated with the cash Ryland Vs. Flethern It established a rule that the person who for his own purposes brings on his lands and collects and keeps there anything likely to do mischief if it escapes, must keep it in at his peril, and, if he does not do so, is prima facie answerable for all the damage which is the natural consequence of its escape.

38 Which one of the following is not a valid defence in tort?

1 Vis major
2 Volenti non fit injuria
3 Inevitable accident
4 Scienti non fit injuria

Ans. (4)

➲ *Exp.* Scienti non fit injuria is not a valid defence in tort.

An act of God is a general defense used in cases of torts when an event over which the defendant has no control over occurs and the damage is caused by the forces of nature.

The principle of Volenti non-fit injuria states that if one voluntarily takes the risk of something then he may not claim a suit of action if such risk leads to injury.

Inevitable Accident is a defence that can be claimed under a situation where in spite of taking reasonable care and protection the harm could not be averted.

39 Fill in the gap

The actus reus of omission commands ________ .

1 There must be moral duty
2 There should be legal duty to act
3 The state has option to fix criminal liability
4 The act performed is due to unavoidable accident

Ans. (2)

➲ *Exp.* The actus reus of omission commands there should be a legal duty to act.

According to Section 33 of IPC, the word "act" denotes as well a series of acts as a single act: the word "omission" denotes as well as a series of omissions as a single omission.

40 Several persons can be vicariously liable for the criminal act of another provided there is prior meeting of mind between the persons. Which of the objectives of Criminal Law is applied in such a case?

1 A pre-arranged plan with intention of performing the act
2 A pre-arranged plan for causing injury
3 A pre-arranged plan to kill the deceased whether fatal blow was given by that accused or not
4 The pre-arranged plan must be incompatible with the innocence of the accused

Ans. (3)

➲ *Exp.* The objective of Criminal Law is that a pre-arranged plan to kill the deceased whether fatal blow was given by that accused or not.

Section 34 of IPC states the Acts done by several persons in furtherance of Common intention. The section explains that "When a criminal act is done by several persons in furtherance of the common intention of all, each of such persons shall be liable for that act in the same manner as if it were done by him alone."

41 The applicability of the principle on common object has two essential features. One purpose is that the object must import a high degree of probability; while the other purpose is

1 An act committed immediately connected to the common object of the assembly
2 The member must have prior knowledge that there is possibility of happening of the act
3 The Co-accused knows that, he will be responsible for offence that is likely to be committed
4 The object was to cause simple injury but a fatal injury resulted

Ans. (1)

➲ *Exp.* The applicability of the principle on common object has two essential features. One purpose is that the object must import a high degree of probability; while the other purpose is an act committed immediately connected to the common object of the assembly.

Section 149 lays down the principle of constructive liability on the basis of common object. It states that if an offence is committed by any member of an unlawful assembly in prosecution of the common object of that assembly, or such as the members of that assembly knew to be likely to be committed in prosecution of that object, every person who, at the time of the committing of that offence, is a member of the assembly, is guilty of that offence.

42 In which of the cases the measures of self-defence is considered to be proportionate to the quantum of force by the person accused for an offence?

1 Aggression
2 Accident
3 Apprehension
4 Assault of harmless nature

Ans. (3)

➲ *Exp.* The apprehension is a factor on the basis of which the measures of self-defence is considered to be proportionate to the quantum of force by the person accused for an offence.

Section 102 of IPC is the relevant provision here which states that the right of private defence of the body commences as soon as a reasonable apprehension of danger to the body arises from an attempt or threat to commit the offence though the offence may not have been committed; and it continues as long as such apprehension of danger to the body continues.

43 Ignorance of law does not permit acquittal as it is built against justification of a crime, while in extreme cases it allows

1 Pardon 2 Suspended sentence
3 Deferred sentence 4 Paper sentence

Ans. (1)

Exp. Ignorance of law does not permit acquittal as it is built against justification of a crime, while in extreme cases it allows Pardon.

A pardon, in the most comprehensive sense-including all of its forms is any relief from the penalty for crime enforceable by law. While ignorance of the law is no legal defense and does not touch the essence of the offense, yet in a case of this sort it may be that the lesson will be taught more effectively by an enforcement of the law in mercy than in rigor.

44 In which of the circumstances an inchoate instigation to commit a crime is said to be incomplete?

1 Withdrew from the act after instigation
2 The letter posted could not reach the person so sent
3 When the purported crime is different from that of instigation
4 When the crime results through the conspiracy of another person

Ans. (3)

Exp. When the purported crime is different from that of instigation an inchoate instigation to commit a crime is said to be incomplete.

The word 'inchoate' denotes something that has 'just begun' or is 'underdeveloped', 9 'partially completed' or 'imperfectly formed'. Inchoate offences are thus incomplete offences, which are deemed to have been committed despite the fact that the substantive offence, that is, the offence whose commission they were aiming at, is not completed and the intended harm is not realized.

45 Given below are two statements, one is labelled as Assertion (A) and other as Reason (R) and select the correct answer from the codes given below.

Assertion (A) Managers collectively bargain with labourers to get cheapest labour rates and derive maximum benefit from labourers.

Reason (R) Management must manage to maximise profits for company and give maximum dividend to shareholders. Management must be economically sound.

Codes

1 Both (A) and (R) are true and (R) is correct explanation of (A)
2 (A) is true, but (R) is false
3 (A) is false, but (R) is true
4 Both (A) and (R) are true, but (R) is not the correct explanation for (A)

Ans. (3)

Exp. (A) is false, but (R) is true.

Collective bargaining is the process in which working people, through their unions, negotiate contracts with their employers to determine their terms of employment, including pay, benefits, hours, leave, job health and safety policies, ways to balance work and family, and more. However, the purpose is not to get the cheapest labour, but to have employment at mutually acceptable prices. Thus, the Assertion is false.

The primary goal of management through corporate finance is to maximize shareholder value and it deals with the monetary decisions that business enterprises make. Managerial finance is interested in the internal and external significance of a firm's financial figures. The terms corporate finance and corporate financier are also associated with investment banking. Thus, Reason is true.

46 An Independent Industrial Relation Commission to provide labour welfare in India was recommended by

1 Ramanujam Committee 2 Madhavan Committee
3 Vasudevan Committee 4 Santhanam Committee

Ans. (1)

Exp. An Independent Industrial Relation Commission to provide labour welfare in India was recommended by Ramanujam Committee.

The Ministry of Labour and Employment has always been striving to promote harmonious industrial relations in the country. Based on the recommendations of the Ramanujam Committee and subsequent deliberations held thereon at different fore, a Bill for amending the Trade Unions Act, 1926 was drawn up in consultation with the Ministry of Law.

47 Match List I with List II using the codes given below. Answer in the context of right and liabilities of trade unions.

List I	List II
A. Conway Vs. Wade	I. Role and right of minority trade unions
B. Rohtas Industries Staff Union Vs. Bihar	II. Inducement to break a contract without violence is permissible
C. Chairman, SBI Vs. Orissa Bank Association	III. Amplification of scope of immunity provisions for striking employees
D. Food Corporation of Indian Staff Union Vs. FCI	IV. Secret ballot is valid as a credible system for determining the representative character of a Trade Union in a multi union establishment

Codes

	A	B	C	D		A	B	C	D
1	III	II	I	IV	2	II	III	I	IV
3	III	II	IV	I	4	I	IV	II	III

Ans. (2)

Exp. The correct matching is A-II, B-III, C-I, D-IV.

Conway Vs. Wade (1909) case is stated as Inducement to break a contract without violence is permissible.

The House of Lords held that a jury was entitled to find that the conduct of an individual in attempting to induce an employer to dismiss an employee was not conduct in 'contemplation or furtherance of a trade dispute' and provided guidance as to the meaning of those words.

Rohtas Industries Staff Union Vs. Bihar (1963) us related to Amplification of scope of immunity provisions for striking employees.The Court quashed the award of the arbitrator and held that employers had no right of civil action for damages against the employees participating in an illegal strike within the meaning of section 24 of the Industrial Disputes Act, 1947.

SBI Vs. Odisha Bank Association (2003) is related to Role and right of minority trade unions. The court held that denying a right of representation to the minority union, when such a right is not conceded even to the majority union, amounts to discrimination requiring redressal at the hands of the High Court.

Food Corporation of India Staff Vs. Food Corporation of India (FCI) (1995) mentions that secret ballot is valid as a credible system for determining the representative character of a Trade Union in a multi union establishment. The court observed that as agreed to by the parties the relative strength of all the eligible unions by way of secret ballot be determined under the overall supervision of the Chief Labour Commissioner (Central) (CLC).

48 Read Assertion (A) and Reason (R) and select the answer using codes given below.

Assertion (A) Civil servants are engaged in the task of sovereign and regal task of the government and as such they can be included with the definition of 'workman' in an 'industry' as contemplated in Section 2(s) and 2(j) of the Industrial Disputes Act.

Reason (R) Because Tamil Nadu, NGO Union Vs. Regisrar of Trade Unions decided so.

Codes

1 (A) and (R) are true and (R) is the correct explanation of (A)
2 (A) and (R) are true, but (R) is not the correct explanation of (A)
3 (A) is true, but (R) is false
4 Both (A) and (R) are false

Ans. (4)

Exp. Both (A) and (R) are false.

According to the Tamil Nadu Non-Gazetted officers Vs. The Registrar of Trade Unions (1961), the civil services being integrated with the inalienable and regal functions of Government; those aspects of Governmental activities cannot be an 'industry'; nor can such civil servants be 'workmen'. Thus, Assertion is false.

Under Article 310 of the Constitution, even in the country, the tenure of office of a civil servant is during the pleasure of the Head of the Union or the State, as the case may be, and Article 311 provides for statutory safeguards against certain penalties, such as dismissal, removal or reduction in rank.

To such a relationship, the concept of "Collective bargaining" is utterly inappropriate and foreign. "Collective bargaining" is a right conceded to Labour Organisations within the contractual field of the employer and employee relationship. Therefore, it may be observed that civil servants cannot be termed as workmen within the Industrial Disputes Act. Thus, Reason is also false.

49 Which of the following statements, is correct?

1 A Trade Union cannot constitute a separate or political fund under Section 6(1) of the Trade Union Act
2 The general fund of a Trade Union cannot be utilised for the purpose stipulated in Section 15 of Trade Union Act
3 Trade Unions are not immune from civil and criminal liability
4 Certain officers of Trade Union, who are styled as protected workmen, are given certain safeguards in the matter of alteration of service conditions and termination of service during the pendency of any proceeding in respect of an industrial dispute

Ans. (4)

Exp. Certain officers of Trade Union, who are styled as protected workmen, are given certain safeguards in the matter of alteration of service conditions and termination of service during the pendency of any proceeding in respect of an industrial dispute.

According to Section 33(3) of the Industrial Disputes Act, 1947, no employer shall, during the pendency of any such proceeding in respect of an industrial dispute, take any action against any protected workman concerned in such dispute by altering, to the prejudice of such protected workman, the conditions of service applicable to him immediately before the commencement of such proceedings; or by discharging or punishing, whether by dismissal or otherwise, such protected workman, save with the express permission in writing of the authority before which the proceeding is pending.

50 Which of the following is incorrect?

1 An Employee having less than one year of continuous service will not be retrenched
2 One months notice with reasons and one months wages in lieu of such notice is necessary
3 Employee is entitled to compensation equivalent to 15 days average pay for every completed one year
4 Serving of notice to appropriate government or any such authority is not mandatory

Ans. (4)

Exp. It is incorrect that serving of notice to the appropriate government or any such authority is not mandatory.

Section 25F of the Act provides for the employer to fulfill certain conditions before retrenching any employee. It states that no workman employed in any industry who has been in continuous service for not less than one year under an employer shall be retrenched by that employer until the workman has been given one month's notice in writing indicating the reasons for retrenchment and the period of notice has expired, or the workman has been paid in lieu of such notice, wages for the period of the notice; the workman has been paid, at the time of retrenchment, compensation which shall be equivalent to fifteen days average pay for every completed year of continuous service or any part thereof in excess of six months; and notice in the prescribed manner is served on the appropriate Government or such authority as may be specified by the appropriate Government by notification in the Official Gazette.

PAPER III

1 Through 42nd Amendment to the Constitution which of the following 'Expressions' were added to the Preamble?

I. Sovereign　　II. Socialist

III. Secular　　IV. Integrity

Codes

1 I, II and III　　2 I, III and IV

3 II, III and IV　　4 I, II, III and IV

Ans. (1)

Exp. As per 42nd Constitution Amendment, two changes were made in the Preamble. Firstly, the characterization of India as "Sovereign Democratic Republic" has been changed to "Sovereign Socialist, Secular Democratic Republic" and Secondly, the words "unity of nation" were changed to "unity and integrity of the nation".

2 Match List I with List II and select the correct answer by using the codes given below the lists.

List I	List II
A. Compensation to persons killed in 'Fake Encounter'	I. Delhi Domestic Working Women's forum Vs. Union of India
B. Compensation to Rape Victims	II. Bodhisattwa Gautam Vs. Subhra Chakraborty
C. Interim Compensation to Rape Victims	III. People's Union for Civil liberties Vs. Union of India
D. Protection against illegal arrest, detentions and custodial deaths.	IV. Joginder Kumar Vs. State of UP

Codes

	A	B	C	D		A	B	C	D
1	IV	III	II	I	2	III	I	II	IV
3	II	IV	I	III	4	I	II	III	IV

Ans. (2)

Exp. The correct matching is A-III, B-I, C-II, D-IV.

People's Union for. Civil liberties Vs. Union of India (1997) is related to Compensation to persons killed in 'Fake Encounter'. The Supreme Court observed in relation to the fake encounter that the question of granting of compensation to the dependents of the deceased would depend upon the facts and circumstances of each case and it shall be determined by NHRC. However, in every case of a person being killed by the police party in the course of an encounter, the compensation granted must necessarily be at least the same as that granted to the dependents of a police officer killed by terrorists in the course of duty by the Government.

Delhi Domestic Working Women's Vs. Union of India and Others (1994) is related to compensation to rape victims. It was held that compensation for rape victims shall be awarded by the court on conviction of the offender and by the Criminal Injuries Compensation Board whether or not a conviction has taken place. The Board will take into account pain, suffering and shock as well as loss of earnings due to pregnancy and the expenses of child birth if this occurred as a result of the rape.

Bodhisattwa Gautam Vs. Miss Subhra Chakraborty (1996) is related to interim compensation to victims of rape. It was based on the rationale that if the Court has the jurisdiction to grant compensation after conviction of the offender, the grant to interim compensation would also fall within its overall jurisdiction.

Joginder Kumar Vs. State of Uttar Pradesh (1994) is related to protection against illegal arrest, detentions and custodial deaths. The Court held that "No arrest can be made because it is lawful for the Police Officer to do so. The existence of the power to arrest is one thing. The justification for the exercise of it is quite another.

3 Match List I with List II and select the correct answer by using the codes given below the lists

List I	List II
A. Right to speak includes Right not to speak	I. R Rajagopal Vs. State of TN
B. Government has no monopoly on electronic media	II. Tata Press Ltd. Vs. Mahanagar Telephone Nigam Ltd.
C. Commercial Advertisement is part of Freedom of Speech and Expression	III. Secretary, Ministry of I and B Vs. Cricket Association of Bengal (WB)
D. Government cannot impose prior restraint on publication of defamatory material against its officials	IV. Bijjoe Emmanuel Vs. State of Kerala

Codes

	A	B	C	D		A	B	C	D
1	IV	III	II	I	2	III	II	I	IV
3	I	IV	III	II	4	II	I	IV	III

***Ans.* (1)**

Exp. The correct matching is A-IV, B-III, C-II, D-I.

Bijjoe Emmanuel Vs. State of Kerala (1978) is related to right to speak includes Right not to speak. The Court observed that there was no provision of law which obliged anyone to sing the National Anthem nor was it disrespectful to the National Anthem if a person who stood up respectfully when the National Anthem was sung did not join the singing.

Secretary, Ministry of I and B Vs. Cricket Association of Bengal (WB) (1995) state that Government has no monopoly over electronic media. It was held that a diversity of opinions, views and ideas cannot be provided by a medium controlled by a monopoly, whether the monopoly is of the State or any other individual, group or organization.

Tata Press Vs. Mahanagar Telephone Nigam Limited (1995) states that Commercial Advertisement is part of Freedom of Speech and Expression. The Court maintained and upheld the integrity of one of the most basic rights in the form of Article 19(1)(a) of the Constitution. It gave a lucid example of a brief interpretation of freedom of speech and expression.

R. Rajagopal Vs. State of Tamil Nadu (1994) mentions that Government cannot impose prior restraint on publication of defamatory material against its officials. The Court explained that it was important to strike a balance between the freedom of the press and the right to privacy.

4 Which of the following statement/statements is/are correct?

I. Fundamental Rights are not absolute. They are subject to reasonable restrictions.

II. Freedom of Press is implict in Article 19 of the Constitution.

III. Socially and economically backward classes of persons are entitled to get benefit under clause (4) of Article 15 of the Constitution.

IV. 'Equal protection of laws' under Article 14 of the Constitution is based upon English law.

Codes

1 I and II are correct 2 I, II and III are correct
3 III and IV are correct 4 All of these

***Ans.* (1)**

Exp. Among the given statements, only I and II are correct.

The Fundamental Rights are not absolute rights and will be subjected to reasonable restrictions. The state can impose reasonable restrictions to protect the legitimate interest of the state. Any law passed by the state or action that results in an infringement of the rights will be subjected to judicial review. Thus, statement I is correct.

In India, Freedom of Press is implied from the freedom of speech and expression guaranteed under Article 19(1)(a) of the Constitution of India. Article 19(1)(a) says that all citizens shall have the right to freedom of speech and expression. Thus, statement II is correct.

Statement III is incorrect because Article 15(4) allows the state to form special provision for the advancement of any socially and educationally (not economically) backward classes of citizens or for the Scheduled Castes and the Scheduled Tribes.

Statement IV is also incorrect since the term 'equal protection of law' as found in Article 14 of Indian Constitution has been taken from the American Constitution.

5 Match List I with List II and select the correct answer by using the codes given below the lists.

List I	List II
A. Parliamentary form of government	I. The USA Constitution
B. Directive Principles of State Policy	II. German Constitution
C. Fundamental Rights	III. United Kingdom Constitution
D. Emergency Provisions	IV. Constitution of Ireland

Codes

	A	B	C	D		A	B	C	D
1	IV	III	I	II	2	III	IV	I	II
3	I	II	III	IV	4	II	I	IV	III

***Ans.* (2)**

Exp. The correct matching is A-III, B-IV, C-I, D-II.

United Kingdom Constitution is based on Parliamentary form of government. It is also called the ministerial or cabinet system. Cabinet or parliamentary form of government is that in which Legislature and executive are closely related and share powers with each other.

Directive Principles of State Policy are mentioned in Constitution of Ireland. These are guidelines or principles given to the central and state governments and are fundamental in the governance of the country.

Fundamental Rights are mentioned in US Constitution. The very idea of Fundamental Rights was borrowed from America's Bill of Rights. Even the preamble, which begins with "We the people" a phrase which confers ideas of equality, came from the US Constitution.

Emergency Provisions German Constitution. The need to include emergency provisions arose in the context of an unusual political situation in India.

6 In which of the following cases the Supreme Court held that Article 31-C was beyond the amending power of the Parliament and was void since, it destroyed the basic features of the Constitution. The court observed that the Constitution is founded on the bed rock of the balance between Part III and Part IV. To give absolute primary to one over the other is to disturb the harmony of the Constitution which is essential feature of the basic structure.

1 Minerva Mills Vs. Union of India
2 In Re Kerala Education Bill Case
3 Keshavananda Bharati Vs. State of Kerala
4 Sarla Mudgal Vs. Union of India

Ans. (1)

➲ *Exp.* The given observation was made in the Minerva Mills Ltd. Vs. Union Of India (1980).

The Parliament by 42nd Amendment widened the scope of the Fundamental Rights. However, in the Minerva Mills case, the Supreme Court struck down these provisions. On the ground that it changed the basic structure of the Constitution. The Supreme Court held that the Constitution exists on the balance of Part III and Part IV. Giving absolute primacy to one over other will disturb the harmony of the Constitution.

This took the Article 31(C) to its prior condition that " a law would be protected by Article 31(C) only if it has been made to implement the directive in Article 39(b) and (c) and not any of the Articles included in Part IV. After the Minerva Mills Case, the Supreme Court to the view that there is no conflict between the Fundamental Rights and the DPSP and they were complementary to each other. There was no need to sacrifice one for the sake of the other. If there is a conflict it should be avoided as far as possible.

7 Match List I with List II and select the correct answer by using the codes given below the lists

	List I		List II
A.	Original Jurisdiction of the Supreme Court	I.	Article 143
B.	Advisory Jurisdiction	II.	Article 136
C.	Appeal by Special leave	III.	Article 132
D.	Appellate Jurisdiction	IV.	Article 131

Codes

	A	B	C	D		A	B	C	D
1	II	III	IV	I	2	I	II	III	IV
3	IV	I	II	III	4	III	IV	I	II

Ans. (3)

➲ *Exp.* The correct matching is A-IV, B-I, C-II, D-III.

Article 131 is related to Original Jurisdiction of Supreme Court. It states that the Supreme Court shall, to the exclusion of any other court, have original jurisdiction in any dispute between the Government of India and one or more States; or between the Government of India and any State or States on one side and one or more other States on the other; or between two or more States.

Article 143 is related to Advisory Jurisdiction. According to Article 143, if at any time it appears to the President that a question of law or fact has arisen, or is likely to arise, which is of such a nature and of such public importance that it is expedient to obtain the opinion of the Supreme Court upon it, he may refer the question to that Court for consideration and the Court may, after such hearing as it thinks fit, report to the President its opinion thereon.

Article 136 is related to appeal by Special Leave. The Supreme Court may, under Article 136, in its discretion, grant special leave to appeal from any judgment, decree, determination, sentence or order in any cause or matter passed or made by any court or tribunal in the territory of India.

Article 132 is related to appellate Jurisdiction. As per Article 132, an appeal shall lie to the Supreme Court from any judgement, decree or final order of a High Court in the territory of India, whether in a civil, criminal or other proceeding, if the High Court certifies under Article 134A that the case involves a substantial question of law as the interpretation of this Constitution.

8 Which of the following statement/statements is/are correct?

I. Pre-dominance is given to the Union List under Article 246 (1) of the Constitution.
II. Residuary powers are given to states under the Indian Constitution.
III. 'Pith and Substance' means 'the true object of the legislation or a statute'.
IV. 'Colourable Legislation' means 'what you can do directly you can also do indirectly'.

Codes

1 I and III are correct
2 I, II and III are correct
3 II, III and IV are correct
4 All of the above

Ans. (1)

➲ *Exp.* Among the given statements, only I and III are true.

Statement I is correct as per-dominance is given to the union List under Article 246(1) of the constitution. The legislative field of the Parliament and the state Ligislatures has been specified in Article 276 of the constitution. Article 246(1) states tat, the parliament has exclusive power to make laws with respect to any of the matters enumerated in List I or the Union List in the Seventh schedule.

Statement III is correct because 'Pith and Substance' denotes the true nature of law. The doctrine places emphasis on the fact that it is the real subject matter which is to be challenged and not its incidental effects on another field.

Statement II is incorrect because the residuary powers are vested in the Union under Article 248 of the Constitution.

Statement IV is incorrect as the doctrine of 'colourable legislation' is based on the maxim that "what cannot be done directly cannot also be done indirectly".

9 Administrative law primarily does not concern itself with which of the official functions?

1 Rule - making
2 Rule - application
3 Quasi - judicial action
4 Private law

Ans. (4)

➲ *Exp.* Administrative law primarily does not concern itself with Private Law.

Administrative law involves the administration and regulation of federal and state government agencies. Government agencies have purview over a wide variety of economic functions, such as telecommunications, the financial market, and social issues, such as instances of racial discrimination. Administrative law is an arm of public law and is also known as "regulatory law."

10 Which of the following is not an exception to the principles of natural justice?

1 Impracticability 2 Legislative action
3 Rule against dictation 4 Statutory necessity

Ans. (3)

Exp. The Rule against dictation is not an exception to the principles of natural justice.

The requirements of procedural fairness are on first appearance applicable to Judicial, Quasi-Judicial and Administrative Proceedings, however, the decision maker may be exempted from all or some of the procedural safeguards that would otherwise be required.

Several factors may be identified as capable of excluding the normal procedural fairness requirements in Common Law Courts are; exclusion in case of emergency, express statutory exclusion, Where discloser would be prejudicial to public interests, Where prompt action is needed, where it is impracticable to hold hearing or appeal, exclusion in case of purely administrative matters, where no right of person is infringed, the procedural defect would have made no difference to the outcome, exclusion on the ground of 'no fault' decision maker.

11 Match the List I with List II and select the correct answer of using codes given below

List I	List II
A. Ram Jawaya Kapur Vs. State of Punjab	I. Doctrine of post decisional hearing
B. Maneka Gandhi Vs. Union of India	II. Doctrine of public accountability
C. Vineet Narain Vs. Union of India	III. Doctrine of separation of powers
D. Union of India Vs. Hindustan Development Corporation	IV. Doctrine of legitimate expectation

Codes

	A	B	C	D		A	B	C	D
1	III	I	II	IV	2	IV	II	I	III
3	I	IV	III	II	4	I	II	III	IV

Ans. (1)

Exp. The correct matching is A-III, B-I, C-II, D-IV.

Ram Jawaya Kapur Vs. State of Punjab (1955) is related to doctrine of separation of powers. The Supreme Court held that "Indian Constitution has not indeed recognized the doctrine of separation of powers in its absolute rigidity but the functions of the different parts or branches of the government have been sufficiently differentiated and consequently it can be very well said that our Constitution does not contemplate assumption by one organ or part of the State of functions that essentially belong to another."

Maneka Gandhi Vs. Union of India (1978) is related to doctrine of post decisional hearing. Post decisional hearing is a hearing which occurs after a provisional decision is reached. The logic behind introducing the post-decisional hearing is to increase and maintain administrative fairness. Post decisional hearing takes place where it may not be feasible to hold pre-decisional hearing.

Vineet Narain and Others Vs. Union of India and another (1997) is related to doctrine of public accountability. It is known for effectively addressing public corruption is essential for the sustainable realisation of economic and social rights since the impact of corruption often overlaps with violations of economic and social rights.

Union of India Vs. Hindustan Development Corporation and Ors. (1994) is related to doctrine of legitimate expectation. It is a concept evolved by the courts in order to review the actions of administrative authorities. It must be restricted to the general legal limitations applicable and binding the manner of the future exercise of administrative power in a particular case.

12 Read Assertion (A) and Reason (R) and answer using the codes given below

Assertion (A) It is true that in any intensive form of government, the government cannot function without the exercise of some discretion by its official.

Reason (R) Giving discretion to government officials is necessary for the welfare of people.

Codes

1 (A) and (R) are true and (R) is the correct explanation of (A)
2 (A) and (R) are true, but (R) is not the correct explanation of (A)
3 (A) is true, but (R) is false
4 Both (A) and (R) are false

Ans. (2)

Exp. Both (A) and (R) are true, and (R) is the correct explanation of (A).

It is true that in any intensive form of government, the government cannot function without the exercise of some discretion by the officials. It is necessary not only for the individualisation of the administrative power but also because it is humanly impossible to lay down a rule for every conceivable eventuality in the complex art of modern government.

Giving discretion to government officials is necessary for the welfare of people. In most administrative actions, the power to act or not to act in one way or another is called discretionary power.

13 Which of the following is correct in relation to the functioning of the institution of Lokayukta in Indian States?

1 Provided with independent investigating agency
2 They have not been given constitutional status
3 Prosecution and final punishment power vested with them
4 Their decision are final and not recommendentary in nature

Ans. (2)

➲ *Exp.* In relation to the functioning of the institution of Lokayukta in Indian States, it is true that they have not been given constitutional status.

The Lokpal and Lokayukta Act, 2013 provided for the establishment of Lokpal for the Union and Lokayukta for States.These institutions are statutory bodies without any constitutional status. They perform the function of an 'ombudsman' and inquire into allegations of corruption against certain public functionaries and related matters.

The Lokpal is not given any constitutional backing and there is no adequate provision for appeal against the Lokpal. The specific details in relation to the appointment of Lokayukta have been left completely on the States.

14 Which of the following is not considered 'irrational', basing upon the Wednesburg principles laid down in Associated Provincial Picture House Ltd. Vs. Wednesburg Corporation, 1948 (KB)?

1 Without the authority of law
2 Based on no evidence
3 It has sanction of law
4 It is unreasonable

Ans. *(3)*

➲ *Exp.* The sanction of law is not considered 'irrational', basing upon the Wednesburg principles.

Associated Provincial Picture Houses Ltd. Vs. Wednesbury Corporation (1948) is an English law case that sets out the standard of unreasonableness of public-body decisions that would make them liable to be quashed on judicial review, known as Wednesbury unreasonableness.

The court gave three conditions on which it would intervene to correct a bad administrative decision in making the decision; the defendant took into account factors that ought not to have been taken into account, or the defendant failed to take into account factors that ought to have been taken into account, or the decision was so unreasonable that no reasonable authority would ever consider imposing it.

15 On which of the following ground writ of certiorari cannot be issued?

1 Abuse of jurisdiction
2 Exercise of jurisdiction
3 Violation of principles of natural justice
4 Error of law apparent on the face of the record

Ans. *(2)*

➲ *Exp.*A writ of certiorari cannot be issued on the ground of exercise of jurisdiction.

Certiorari is a command or order to an inferior Court or tribunal to transmit the records of a cause or matter pending before them to the superior Court to be dealt with there and if the order of inferior Court is found to be without jurisdiction or against the principles of natural justice, it is quashed. The writ of certiorari can be issued on the following grounds: want of jurisdiction, excess of jurisdiction, abuse of jurisdiction, absence of jurisdiction, violation of Natural justice, fraud, error on the face of records.

16 Which of the following is not a jural postulate of the legal system of a society as propounded by Roscoe Pound. So in a civilised society men must be able to assume

1 That these will be no intentional aggression
2 That members of society will act in good faith
3 That people will control for their beneficial use, what they have created
4 That people will cause injury to others during their course of work

Ans. *(4)*

➲ *Exp.* The statement that People will cause injury to others during their course of work is not a jural postulate of the legal system of a society as propounded by Roscoe Pound.

Pound believes that the first problem in confronting society is the establishment of his theory of interests as a functioning part of the legal order. The development of this theory occurred in two steps: the formulation of the jural postulates, in 1919, followed by the announcement of a classification or scheme of interests two years later. Pound claims this to be his most valuable contribution to jurisprudence. While recognising certain valid criticisms, he has defended it vigorously as the most workable means yet devised for sound social engineering.

17 Who said that customs are superior to the legislation. Therefore, legislations should not abrogate the customs rather synthesise them with the common consciousness of the people and society?

1 Henry Maine 2 HLA Hart
3 Savigny 4 Hans Kelson

Ans. *(3)*

➲ *Exp.* The given observation was made by Freidrich Karl Von Savigny.

Freidrich Karl Von Savigny, a German jurist and legal scholar, was one of the founders of the dominant 'historical school' of jurisprudence. He says that customs are superior to the legislation. He propounds that the proper form of law is custom (Gewohnheit). He speaks of law generally, although his focus is on private law, which he assumes (as in Roman law) to be fundamental.

According to Savigny, custom is a safeguard against Willkiir (arbitrariness or despotic caprice) and of course, people are against that.

18 Who among the following is not the exponent of Philosophical school?

1 Hegel 2 Kant
3 Puchta 4 Holland

Ans. *(4)*

➲ *Exp.* Among the given choices, Holland is not considered to be the exponent of Philosophical school.

Kant, Hegel, G.G Puchta and Sebelling are considered to be the main exponents of the ethical or Philosophical school of jurisprudence. According to the exponents of this school, legal philosophy must be based on ethical values so as to motivate people for an up-right living.

19 According to Honfield table of jural relations the jural correlative of right is duty. What are the jural correlatives of Liberty, Power and Immunity respectively?

1 No claim, Liability and Power
2 No claim, Responsibility and Liability
3 No claim, Duty and Liberty
4 No claim, Liability and Disability

Ans. (4)

Exp. No claim, Liability and Disability are the jural correlatives of Liberty, Power and Immunity respectively. Wesley Newcomb Honfield, late professor of law in Yale University, was widely known among his professional colleagues as a successful teacher and a keen analyst of legal problems. The jural correlatives of Liberty, Power and Immunity according to the Honfield System of Fundamental Legal Concepts, is set as No claim (Right), Liability and Disability.

20 'The Limits of Jurisprudence Defined' was published in 1945. It was written in 1782 by

1 Bentham 2 Blackstone
3 Hobbes 4 Locke

Ans. (1)

Exp. The limits of jurisprudence defined was written in 1782 by Bentham.

Jeremy Bentham, an author of 'The Limits of Jurisprudence Defined', was a British philosopher, jurist and social reformer. He is regarded as the founder of modern utilitarianism. Written in 1782 and published by Columbia University Press in 1945, 'The Limits of Jurisprudence Defined' deals mainly with penal law was edited and co-authored by Charles Warren Everett.

21 Who among the following has not associated his theory of the state with 'Social Contract'?

1 Hobbes 2 Locke
3 Henry Maine 4 Rousseau

Ans. (3)

Exp. Henry Maine has not associated his theory of the state with 'Social Contract'.

The Social Contract theory is a most important theory of the state. According to this theory the origin of the state is the result of the agreement by the people voluntarily to form a civilised society. This theory implies two things, first it seeks to explain the origin of state, it attempts to define the relationship between the rulers and rule. Thus, it is a theory both about the origin and nature of the state.

22 Read Assertion (A) and Reason (R) and give the correct answer with the help of codes given below

Assertion (A) Criminal is a victim of circumstances, he is sick so he requires treatment.

Reason (R) Prison reforms and juvenile schools are established to reform the criminals.

Codes
1 (A) and (R) are true and (R) is the correct explaination of (A)
2 (A) and (R) are true, but (R) is not the correct explaination of (A)
3 A is true, but R is false
4 A is false, but R is true

Ans. (2)

Exp. Both (A) and (R) are true, but (R) is not the correct explanation of (A).

Criminal is a victim of circumstances, he is sick so he requires treatment. Society plays a huge role in determining an individual's mindset and often the situations surrounding a person contribute to the commission of a crime. Thus, Assertion is true.

The purpose behind prison reforms and juvenile schools is to reform the criminals. This statement is true, however, it is not the right reason for given Assertion.

23 Match List I with List II and select the correct answer using the codes given below

List I	List II
A. Right of a person not to be assaulted	I. Right in re-propria
B. Right of a person in his own property	II. Right in rem
C. Right of a person to enjoy his premises	III. Right in personam
D. Right of a person in the property of someone else	IV. Right in re-aliena

Codes

	A	B	C	D		A	B	C	D
1	II	I	III	IV	2	IV	III	I	II
3	I	II	IV	III	4	III	IV	II	I

Ans. (1)

Exp. The correct matching is A-II, B-I, C-III, D-IV.

A right in rem is a right of a person not to be assaulted. Rights in rem refer to a legal action directed towards property, rather than towards a particular person, allowing the owner of the right the opportunity to recover, possess or enjoy a specific object. These rights may apply to trade marks or designs.

Right in re-propria is the right of a person in his own property. These rights are immaterial forms of Property. These are a product of human skill and labour. Patents, copyrights and commercial goodwill may be included under this category.

Right in personam is the right of a person to enjoy his premises. This right is applicable against a particular person or entity.

Right in re aliena is the right of a person in the property of someone else. They are also sometimes referred to as encumbrances. These are the rights of a specific user. These prevent the owner from exercising some definite right in reference to his Property. Lease, security and trust may be included under this category.

24 Read the following situations and state which combination is correct to claim benefit under the broad concept of unsoundness of mind

I. Extreme Anger II. Somnambulism
III. Irresistible impulse IV. Hallucination

Codes

1 Both I and II 2 Both I and III
3 Both II and III 4 Both II and IV

Ans. (4)

Exp. Somnambulism and Hallucination are correct to claim benefit under the broad concept of unsoundness of mind

Somnambulism does not enjoy the free and rational exercise of his understanding and is more or less unconscious of his outward relations; none of his acts can rightfully by imputed to him as crimes." Hallucinations can cause one to detach from reality and to see or hear things that do not exist. To qualify for benefits, the claimant will have to prove that he/she suffers from severe hallucinations or conditions that result in hallucinations, such as Schizophrenia.

Irresistible impulse, mental agitation, annoyance and fury all merely indicate loss of control and not indicative of soundness of mind. Every minor mental aberration is not insanity and the circumstances indicating a mere probability of legal insanity cannot however be sufficient to discharge the onus of the accused to establish the plea of insanity.

25 Read the following situations and select the correct one, where right of private defence is available

1 Against an act done or attempted to be done by a public servant
2 Where there is time available to have recourse to state authorities
3 Where there is a reasonable apprehension of causing injury to third person
4 Where harm caused in no case should exceed the quantum of harm

Ans. (3)

Exp. The right of private defense is available where there is a reasonable apprehension of causing injury to a third person. The expression 'private defence' that has been used in the Indian Penal Code, 1860, has not been defined therein. Thus, it has been the prerogative of the judiciary to evolve a workable framework for the exercise of the right. Thus in India, the right of private defence is the right to defend the person or property of himself or of any other person against an act of another, which if the private defence is not pleaded would have amounted to a crime.

26 Match List I with List II and select the correct answer by using the codes given below the lists

List I	List II
A. KN Mehra Vs. State of Rajasthan	I. Section 300
B. Aruna Ramchandra Shanbaugh Vs. Union of India	II. Section 120-A
C. State (NCT of Delhi) Vs. Navjot Sandhuaka Afsana Guru	III. Section 309
D. Virsa Singh Vs. State of Punjab	IV. Section 378

Codes

	A	B	C	D
1	I	III	IV	II
2	I	III	II	IV
3	IV	III	II	I
4	III	IV	II	I

Ans. (3)

Exp. The correct matching is A-IV, B-III, C-II, D-I.

Section 378 is related to KN Mehra Vs. State of Rajasthan (1957). The alleged theft was of an aircraft, which belonged to the government (Indian Air Force Academy). Two youngsters, Mehra and Phillips, were cadets on training in the Indian Air Force at Jodhpur. It was held that the fact that they took off Harvard T-22 plane rather than the allowed Dakota, and left India at 5 am instead of the scheduled time of 6 am, without waiting for Om Prakash, and that they also refused to respond to the wireless messages from Indian aerodrome authorities at 11 am, showed that they had the dishonest intention to take off a Harvard T-22 plane necessary to constitute offence of theft.

Section 309 is related to Aruna Ramachandra Shanbaug Vs. Union of India (2011). The court discussed the issue of euthanasia within Section 309 of IPC at length and allowed passive euthanasia. It defined 'passive euthanasia' and held that passive euthanasia is allowed if the doctors act on the basis of notified medical opinion and withdraw life support in the patient's best interest.

Section 120A is related to State (NCT of Delhi) Vs. Navjot Sandhu (2005). It was held that "a few bits here and a few bits there on which the prosecution relies cannot be held to be adequate for connecting the accused in the offence of criminal conspiracy under Section 120-A."

Section 300 is related to Virsa Singh Vs. The State Of Punjab (1958). It was held that even if the intention of accused was limited to the infliction of a bodily injury sufficient to cause death in the ordinary course of nature, and did not extend to the intention of causing death, the offence would be murder in Section 300 of IPC.

27 Criminal Law (Amendment) Act 2013, seems to have determined quantum of punishment proportionate to the severity of offence. Following are two sets of offences and punishment. Match the correct ones and select appropriate answer using the codes.

List I (Offences)	List II (Maximum Punishment)
A. Voluntarily causing grevious hurt by acid attack	I. Life imprisonment (Remainder of the period of life)
B. Stalking	II. 3 years
C. Gang Rape	III. Life imprisonment and fine
D. Sexual intercourse by husband upon his wife during separation	IV. 7 years and fine

Codes

	A	B	C	D		A	B	C	D
1	II	III	I	IV	2	III	II	I	IV
3	I	II	III	IV	4	I	III	II	IV

Ans. (2)

Exp. The correct matching is A-III, B-II, C-I, D-IV.

According to Section 326A, whoever causes permanent or partial damage or deformity to, or burns or maims or disfigures or disables, any part or parts of the body of a person or causes grievous hurt by throwing acid on or by administering acid to that person, or by using any other means with the intention of causing or with the knowledge that he is likely to cause such injury or hurt, shall be punished with imprisonment of either description for a term which shall not be less than ten years but which may extend to imprisonment for life, and with fine.

The Section 354D defines Stalking as any man who follows a woman and contacts, or attempts to contact such woman to foster personal interaction repeatedly despite a clear indication of disinterest by such woman; or monitors the use by a woman of the internet, email or any other form of electronic communication, commits the offence of stalking. Whoever commits the offence of stalking shall be punished on first conviction with imprisonment of either description for a term which may extend to three years, and shall also be liable to fine.

As per Section 376D, where a woman is raped by one or more persons constituting a group or acting in furtherance of a common intention, each of those persons shall be deemed to have committed the offence of rape and shall be punished with rigorous imprisonment for a term which shall not be less than twenty years, but which may extend to life which shall mean imprisonment for the remainder of that person's natural life, and with fine.

The Section 376B says whoever has sexual intercourse with his own wife, who is living separately, whether under a decree of separation or otherwise, without her consent, shall be punished with imprisonment of either description for a term which shall not be less than two years but which may extend to seven years, and shall also be liable to fine.

28 'X' a servant committed theft of Mobile phone of his master 'M' and ran away from home. While travelling the said mobile phone was taken away by 'Y' a co-traveller without the knowledge of 'X'. Decide the liability of 'Y', select correct one among the following

1 Criminal mis-appropriation as the phone was lying on the seat of 'X'
2 Criminal Breach of Trust-as they were co-travellers
3 Theft-as property in possession of 'X' was taken without his consent
4 Cheating as the method adopted was dubious

Ans. (3)

Exp. In the given situation, 'Y' is liable for theft, as property in possession of 'X' was taken without his consent.

The offence of theft is defined under Section 378 and states that whoever, intending to take dishonestly any moveable property out of the possession of any person without that per-son's consent, moves that property in order to such taking, is said to commit theft.

It may be observed that 'Y' had taken the property out of 'X's possession with dishonest intention and without consent, thereby committing theft. It is not relevant as to whether 'X' had a rightful possession over the property or not. As long as essentials of theft are fulfilled, the offence is said to be committed.

29 Certain factors are essential to get Extortion converted to Robbery. Following are a few given factors, select the correct one which is not required for the said conversion

1 Dishonesty
2 Removal of property from the possession of another, by putting him in fear
3 It is immaterial whether the person putting another in fear must be in the immediate presence or far away
4 Such fear should result in the delivery of property

Ans. (3)

Exp. The factor that it is immaterial whether the person putting another in fear must be in the immediate presence or far away is not an essential to get extortion converted to Robbery.

As per Section 390 of IPC, Extortion is "robbery" if the offender, at the time of committing the extortion, is in the presence of the person put in fear, and commits the extortion by putting that person in fear of instant death, of instant hurt, or of instant wrongful restraint to that person or to some other person, and, by so putting in fear, induces the person so put in fear then and there to deliver up the thing extorted.

The offender is said to be present if he is sufficiently near to put the other person in fear of instant death, of instant hurt, or of instant wrongful restraint.

30 'There are two facets to the definition of dishonesty and it is sufficient to establish the existence of anyone of them. There is no requirement in Law to establish both'. Select the correct case among the following in which the above statement of Supreme Court has been laid down as ratio.

1 Tulsi Ram Vs. State of Uttar Pradesh
2 Hari Sao Vs. State of Bihar
3 Gurdatta Mal Vs. State of Uttar Pradesh
4 State of Bihar Vs. Nathu Pandey

Ans. (1)

Exp. In the case of Tulsi Ram Vs. State of Uttar Pradesh (1962), the given statement of Supreme Court has been laid down as ratio.

The court observed inter alia that to establish that the accused had dishonestly induced another to part with property within the meaning of Section 420, Indian Penal Code, it was not necessary to prove both wrongful gain and wrongful loss. Wrongful gain and wrongful loss were two facets of the definition of dishonesty and it was enough to establish the existence of one of them.

In the case referred by the court, the appellants had made wrongful gain to themselves by obtaining credits by unlawful means and even if no wrongful loss was caused to the banks, the appellants were guilty of cheating.

31 Following are given some Provisions of Law (IPC). Select the odd one out.

1 Section 149 2 Section 141
3 Section 34 4 Section 147

Ans. (4)

Exp. Among the given Provisions of law, Section 147 (Punishment for rioting and states) is the odd one out. This is because the other Sections do not lay down any punishment and provide definitions for certain offences while Section 147 lays down punishment.

Sections 34 and 149 define joint and constructive liability respectively while Section 141 defines unlawful assembly.

32 Which one of the following institutions gave suggestion for imposing environmental tax?

1 Amnesty International
2 World Water Institute
3 UNESCO
4 United Nations

Ans. (2)

Exp. World Water Institute gave suggestion for imposing environmental tax.

The world water institute imparts education on our contributions to understanding of water hed health and all pertaining to utilisation and preservation of water besides doing research to help address critical water management issues related to flood damage reduction and natural resource enhancement.

33 Under the Environment (Protection) Act, the term 'environment' does not include

1 Water, air and land
2 Inter -relationship which exists between water, air and land and human beings
3 Inter-relationship which exists between water, air and land and plants
4 Environment at work place

Ans. (4)

Exp. Under the Environment (Protection) Act, the term 'environment' does not include environment at workplace.

According to Section 2 of Environmental Protection Act, 1986, 'Environment' includes water, air and land and the inter-relationship which exists among and between water, air and land, and human beings, other living creatures, plants, micro-organism and property.

34 Match List I with List II and select the correct answer using the codes given below.

	List I		List II
A.	Power of Central Government to take measures to protect and improve environment	I.	Section 6 of Environment (Protection) Act
B.	Constitution of Central Pollution Control Board	II.	Section 3 of Environment (Protection)Act
C.	Power of Central Government to make rules to regulate environmental pollution	III.	Section 3 of the Water (Prevention and Control of Pollution) Act
D.	Gaseous of liquid pollutants in the atmosphere injurious to human beings	IV.	Section 2(a)of the Air (Prevention and Control of Pollution) Act

Codes

	A	B	C	D		A	B	C	D
1	I	III	IV	II	2	II	IV	I	III
3	II	III	I	IV	4	III	IV	II	I

Ans. (3)

Exp. The correct matching is A-II, B-III, C-I, D-IV.

Section 3 of Environment (Protection) Act discuss about Power of Central Government to take measures to protect and improve environment. According to Section 3 in The Environment (Protection) Act, 1986, the Central Government shall have the power to take all such measures as it deems necessary or expedient for the purpose of protecting and improving the quality of the environment and preventing, controlling and abating environmental pollution.

Section 3 of Water (Prevention and Control of Pollution) Act mention about Constitution of Central Pollution Control Board. It states that the central Government shall, with effect from such date as it may, by notification in the official Gazette, appoint, Constitute a Central Board to be called Central Pollytion control Board to exercise the powers conferred on and perform the functions assigned to that that Board under this Act.

Section 6 of Environment (Protection) Act discuss about Power of Central Government to make rules to regulate environmental pollution. The Central Government may in accordance with Section 6 in The Environment (Protection) Act, 1986, by notification in the Official Gazette, make rules in respect of all or any of the matters referred. In particular, and without prejudice to the generality of the foregoing power, such rules may provide for all or any of the following matters, namely, inter alia, the standards of quality of air, water or soil for various areas and purposes, the maximum allowable limits of concentration of various environmental pollutants (including noise) for different areas.

Section 2(a)of the Air (Prevention and control of pollution) Act is related to gaseous or liquid pollutants in the atmosphere injurious to human beings. It says 'air pollutant' means any solid, liquid or gaseous substance (including noise) present in the atmosphere in such concentration as may be or tend to be injurious to human beings or other living creatures or plants or property or environment.

35 Match List I with List II and select the correct answer using the codes given below

List I	List II
A. Rylands Vs. Fletcher	I. Principle of public trust for ecological protection
B. Indian Council for Environment Legal Action Vs. Union of India	II. Precautionary Principle
C. Vellore Citizens Welfare Forum Vs. Union of India	III. Principle of Polluter pays
D. MC Mehta Vs. Kamal Nath	IV. Principle of strict liability

Codes

	A	B	C	D		A	B	C	D
1	IV	III	II	I	2	I	II	IV	III
3	II	IV	III	I	4	I	II	III	IV

Ans. (1)

Exp. The correct matching is A-IV, B-III, C-II, D-I.

Rylands Vs. Fletcher (1868) is related to Principle of strict liability. It established a rule that the person who for his own purposes brings on his lands and collects and keeps there anything likely to do mischief if it escapes, must keep it in at his peril, and, if he does not do so, is prima facie answerable for all the damage which is the natural consequence of its escape.

Indian Council for Enviro-legal Action and others Vs. Union of India and others (1996) is related to Polluter pays principle. The Court endorsed the polluter pays principle, under which the financial costs of preventing or remedying damage lie with those who cause the pollution.

Vellore Citizens Welfare Forum Vs. Union Of India and ors (1996) is related to Precautionary principle. It was held that under Environmental Measures, state governments, as well as other statutory bodies, must anticipate future environmental degradation and take action to prevent it.

M.C. Mehta Vs. Kamal Nath and Ors (1997) is related to Public Trust doctrine. The Court categorically asserted that the Public Trust doctrine was a part of the Indian legal system. It further held that in its role as a public trustee of natural resources, the government was bound by three different restrictions: one, the trust property must be available for public use, two, the same cannot be sold at any price, three, the trust must be maintained for only certain uses.

36 Which one of the following statements is incorrect?

1 The Public Liability Insurance Act was enacted to provide immediate relief to the victims of an accident involving a hazardous substance
2 The Public Liability Insurance Act imposes 'no fault' liability upon the owner of the hazardous substance and requires the owner to compensate the victims irrespective of any neglect or default on his part
3 The Public Liability Insurance Act, does not provide for maximum compensation for injury or death of the victims
4 The Public Liability Insurance Act obligates every owner to take out an insurance policy covering potential liability from an accident

Ans. (3)

Exp. The statement that the Public Liability Insurance Act does not provide for maximum compensation for injury or death of the victims is incorrect.

The Public Liability Insurance Act of 1991 is an Act of Parliament of India to provide for immediate relief to the persons affected by accidents occurring while handling any hazardous substance. This act is related to immediate relief and not compensation.

37 Read Assertion (A) and Reason (R) and select the correct answer using codes given below

Assertion (A) Polluter pays principle means polluters should internalise the costs of their pollution, control it at its source, and pay for its effects, including remedial or cleanup costs, rather than forcing other states or future generations to bear such costs.

Reasons (R) Vellore Citizen's Welfare Forum Vs. Union of India decided so.

Codes

1 (A) is true, but (R) is false
2 Both (A) and (R) are true and (R) is the correct explaination of (A)
3 Both (A) and (R) are false
4 Both (A) and (R) are true, but (R) is not the correct explaination of (R)

Ans. (2)

Exp. Both (A) and (R) are true and (R) is the correct explanation of (A).

The 'polluters pay' principle is the commonly accepted practice that those who produce pollution should bear the costs of managing it to prevent damage to human health or the environment. For instance, a factory that produces a potentially poisonous substance as a by product of its activities is usually held responsible for its safe disposal.

In Vellore Citizen Forum Vs. Union of India, the Supreme Court of India recognised the Principle of polluter pays and sustainable development as a basis for balancing ecological imperatives with development goods.

38 Match List I with List II and select the correct answer using the codes given below

List I	List II
A. Rural Litigation and Entitlement Kendra, Dehradun Vs. State of Uttar Pradesh	I. Grant of a lease of land or its renewal without the approval of the Central Government is void.
B. Samatha Vs. State of Andhra Pradesh	II. Balancing environmental and ecological integrity against industrial demands on forest resources.
C. KV Shanmugam Vs. State of Tamil Nadu	III. Renewal of lease on forest land is not a vested right.
D. State of Himachal Pradesh Vs. Ganesh Wood Products	IV. Forest- based industries do not have an absolute or an unrestricted right to operate their units where forest resources are scarce.

Codes

	A	B	C	D		A	B	C	D
1	II	III	I	IV	2	I	IV	II	III
3	II	III	IV	I	4	I	II	III	IV

Ans. (1)

Exp. The correct matching is A-II, B-III, C-I, D-IV.

Rural Litigation and Entitlement Kendra Dehradun and others Vs. State of U.P. and others (1985) is state that Balancing environmental and ecological integrity against industrial demands on forest resources.It was held that lime-stone quarrying and excavation of the lime-stone deposits seemed to affect the perennial water springs. The environmental disturbance was however to be weighed in the balance against the need of lime-stone quarrying for industrial purposes in the country.

Samatha Vs. State of A.P. (1997) states that renewal of lease on forest land is not a vested right. The Court, by full bench decided in favour of the tribals and held that Government lands, forest lands and tribal lands in the Scheduled area cannot be leased out to non-tribals or to private industries.

K.V. Shanmugam Vs. State of Tamil Nadu (1997) concluded that grant of a lease of land or its renewal without the approval of the Central Government is void. It was held that no State. Government or any other authority have power to grant lease of any area from the reserve forest or any portion thereof without the prior approval of the Central Government.

State of Himachal Pradesh Vs. Ganesh Wood Products states that forestbased industries do not have an absolute or an unrestricted right to operate their units where forest resources are scarce. It was held that insofar as forest-based industries are concerned, there is no absolute or unrestricted right to establish industries notwithstanding the policy of liberalisation announced by the Government of India.

39 Who of the following has remarked that International law is a 'Living and Expanding Code'?

1 Judge Alvarez
2 Lord Chancellor Sankey
3 JG Starke
4 Prof Lissitzyn

Ans. (2)

Exp. In Re Piracy Jure Gentium, Lord Chancellor Sankey remarked that International Law is a 'Living and Expanding Code'.

In view of the changing character and expanding scope of International Law today, international organizations, some non-State entities and individuals have also become the legitimate subjects of International Law.

40 Which of the following statement/statements is/are incorrect?

I. Long duration is an essential element for International Custom.

II. The custom should be completely uniform and consistent to be an International custom.

III. In an International custom, universality of practice is not necessary, the practice should have been generally observed or repeated by numerous states.

IV. Opinio Juris is present, that is to say, customary pratice to be a International custom, must be recognised as being required by International law.

Codes

1 Only I is incorrect
2 Only I and II are incorrect
3 II, III and IV are incorrect
4 I, II, III, IV all are incorrect

Ans. (2)

Exp. Statement I and II are incorrect.

According to Article 38(1) of the Statute of International Court of Justice, International Customs are recognized as an important source of International Law. The Statute recognizes general customs but in practice, Courts accept local or regional customs amongst a group or between two or more countries. Local customs may supplement or derogate from general customs.

A Valid Custom should be; Reasonable and be in Conformity with Statute Law. The Essential features of Customs are; Reasonableness, Confirmatory with Statue Law, Uniformity, Immemorial antiquity (Long duration).

41 Match List I with List II and select the correct answer by using the codes given below the lists.

List I (Topics)	List II (Related Cases)
A. Sources of International law	I. Haya Dela Torra Case
B. Recognition	II. Re Castioni Case
C. Extradition	III. The Arantzazu Mendi Case
D. Asylum	IV. United States Vs. Schooner

Codes

	A	B	C	D		A	B	C	D
1	IV	III	II	I	2	III	II	IV	I
3	IV	III	I	II	4	II	IV	III	I

Ans. (1)

➲ *Exp*. The correct matching is A-IV, B-III, C-II, D-I.

United States Vs. Schooner Peggy (1801) case mention the sources of international law. The court ruled that the treaty was applicable as law and should apply retroactively to all seized vessels whose sentence was not yet final. Since the seizure of the vessel was on appeal to the Supreme Court at the time the treaty was ratified, the seizure was not final.

The Arantzazu Mendi Case (1939) deals with Recognition. It was held in this case that a de facto government has control over state assets within the territory it controls. A de jure government has control even of overstate assets abroad.

Re Castioni (1891) is related to Extradition. The Divisional Court in Re Castioni stated that fugitive criminals are not to be surrendered for extradition crimes, if those crimes were incidental to and formed a part of political disturbances.

Haya De la Torre Case is related to Asylum. The relevant treaties cited by Colombia in the case titled as Colombia Vs Peru (1950) (also called asylum case) were not ratified by Peru, and it was not found that the custom of Asylum was uniformly or continuously executed sufficiently to demonstrate that the custom was of a generally applicable character.

42 Which one of the following cases is not a case decided by permanent court of International Justice?

1 Movrommatis Palestine Concessions Case
2 SS Wimbledon Case
3 Anglo Norwegian Fisheries Case
4 Chorzow Factory (Indemnity) Case

Ans. (3)

➲ *Exp*. The Anglo Norwegian Fisheries Case is not a case decided by permanent court of International Justice.

Anglo Norwegian Fisheries Case also known as the United Kingdom Vs. Norway (1951) was the culmination of a dispute, originating in 1933, over how large an area of water surrounding Norway was Norwegian waters (that Norway thus had exclusive fishing rights to) and how much was 'high seas' (that the UK could thus fish).

The UK on 24th September, 1949, made a plea that the International Court of Justice determine how far Norway's territorial claim extended to sea, and to award the UK damages in compensation for Norwegian interference with UK fishing vessels in the disputed waters, claiming that Norway's claim to such an extent of waters was against international law.

43 Read both statements (A) and (R) and give the correct answer by using the codes given below.

Assertion (A) By the term 'Asylum' we generally mean the shelter and active protection which is extended to a political refugee from another state, by a state which admits him on his request.

Reason (R) Everyone has a right to seek and enjoy in other countries, an asylum from prosecution.

Codes

1 Both (A) and (R) are true and (R) is the correct explanation of (A)
2 Both (A) and (R) are true, but (R) is not correct explanation of (A)
3 (A) is true, but (R) is false
4 (A) is false, but (R) is true

Ans. (1)

➲ *Exp.* Both (A) and (R) are true and (R) is the correct explanation of (A).

Asylum, in international law is the protection granted by a state to a foreign citizen against his own state. The person for whom asylum is established has no legal right to demand it, and the sheltering state has no obligation to grant it. The right of asylum falls into three basic categories: territorial, extraterritorial, and neutral.

Article 14 of Universal Declaration of Human Rights (1948) provides that everyone has the right to seek and to enjoy in other countries asylum from persecution. This right may not be invoked in the case of prosecutions genuinely arising from non-political crimes or from acts contrary to the purposes and principles of the United Nations.

44 Which of the following is the only Principal organ of the UNO which consists of all the members of United Nations?

1 Security Council
2 General Assembly
3 The Economic and Social Council
4 Trusteeship Council

Ans. (2)

➲ *Exp.* The General Assembly is the only Principal organ of the UNO which consists of all the members of United Nations.

The UN General Assembly (UNGA) is the main policy-making organ of the organisation. Comprising all Member States, it provides a unique forum for multilateral discussion of the full spectrum of international issues covered by the Charter of the United Nations. Each of the 193 Member States of the United Nations has an equal vote.

The UNGA also makes key decisions for the UN, including:appointing the Secretary-General on the recommendation of the Security Council electing the non-permanent members of the Security Council approving the UN budget.

45 Match List I with List II and give the correct answer by using the codes given below.

List I (Provisions)	List II (Articles of UN Charter)
A. Suspension of members	I. Article 5
B. Veto Power	II. Article 97
C. Appointment of Secretary General	III. Article 27
D. Composition of Trusteeship council	IV. Article 86

Codes

	A	B	C	D		A	B	C	D
1	I	III	II	IV	2	IV	III	II	I
3	III	II	IV	I	4	II	I	III	IV

Ans. (1)

Exp. The correct matching is A-I, B-III, C-II, D-IV.

Article 5 of UN Charter says that a Member of the United Nations against which preventive or enforcement action has been taken by the Security Council may be suspended from the exercise of the rights and privileges of membership by the General Assembly upon the recommendation of the Security Council. The exercise of these rights and privileges may be restored by the Security Council.

Article 27 of the charter is related to veto power. It provides that each member of the Security Council shall have one vote. Decisions of the Security Council on procedural matters shall be made by an affirmative vote of nine members. Decisions of the Security Council on all other matters shall be made by an affirmative vote of nine members including the concurring votes of the permanent members; provided that, in decisions under Chapter VI, and under paragraph 3 of Article 52, a party to a dispute shall abstain from voting.

Article 97 says that the Secretariat shall comprise a Secretary-General and such staff as the Organisation may require. The Secretary-General shall be appointed by the General Assembly upon the recommendation of the Security Council. He shall be the chief administrative officer of the organisation.

Article 86 is related to composition of Trusteeship council. It mentions that the Trusteeship Council shall consist of the following Members of the United Nations: those Members administering the trust territories; such of those Members mentioned by name in Article 23 as are not administering trust territories; and as many other Members elected for three-year terms by the General Assembly as may be necessary to ensure that the total number of members of the Trusteeship Council is equally divided between those Members of the United Nations which administer trust territories and those which do not.

46 Which is not the official language of the United Nations?

1 Russian 2 Japenese 3 Spanish 4 Arabic

Ans. (2)

Exp. Japanese is not the official language of the United Nations.

There are six official languages of the UN. These are Arabic, Chinese, English, French, Russian and Spanish. The correct interpretation and translation of these six languages, in both spoken and written form, is very important to the work of the Organisation, because this enables clear and concise communication on issues of global importance.

47 The offence of bigamy is not committed under the Hindu Marriage Act, 1955 if a person marries during life time of his or her spouse provided

I. The first marriage is null and void

II. The first marriage was performed without ceremonies

III. The first marriage is voidable and decree annulling it has not been passed

IV. The first marriage is valid

Codes

1 I and III 2 I and II

3 II and III 4 II and IV

Ans. (2)

Exp. Among the given statements, only I and II are true.

The case of bigamy is dealt in section 5, 11 and 17 of the Hindu Marriage Act, 1955.

Section 5 (i) prohibits bigamy or polygamy.

Section 11 make a bigamous marriage void and section 17 makes it a penal offence for both Hindu males and females under Section 494 and 495 of IPC.

As per Section 494, IPC, whoever, having a husband or wife living, marries in any case in which such marriage is void by reason of its taking place during the life of such husband or wife, shall be punished with imprisonment of either description for a term which may extend to seven years, and shall also be liable to fine.

This section does not extend to any person whose marriage with such husband or wife has been declared void by a Court of competent jurisdiction, nor to any person who contracts a marriage during the life of a former husband or wife, if such husband or wife, at the time of the subsequent marriage, shall have been continually absent from such person for the space of seven years, and shall not have been heard of by such person as being alive within that time provided the person contracting such subsequent marriage shall, before such marriage takes place, inform the person with whom such marriage is contracted of the real state of facts so far as the same are within his or her knowledge.

48 A marriage under the Hindu Marriage Act 1955, must be solemnised in accordance with the customary rites and ceremonies of

1 The bridegroom

2 The bride

3 Either bride or bridegroom

4 Both bride and bridegroom

Ans. (3)

Exp. According to Section 7 of the Hindu Marriage Act, 1955, a marriage under the Hindu Marriage Act, 1955, must be solemnised in accordance with the customary rites and ceremonies of either bride or bridegroom.

Such rites and ceremonies must include the saptpadi (that is, the taking of seven steps by the bridegroom and the bride jointly before the sacred fire), the marriage becomes complete and binding when the seventh step is taken.

49 The absence of witnesses make a Muslim marriage

1 Irregular under Sunni law, but void under Shia law

2 Irregular under Sunni and Shia law

3 Valid under Sunni law, but irregular under Shia law

4 Valid under Shia law, but irregular under Sunni law

Ans. (4)

➲ *Exp.* The absence of witnesses make a Muslim marriage valid under Shia law, but irregular under Sunni law.

Marriage/Nikah as per Muslim Law is a contract underlying a permanent relationship based on mutual consent. There are certain preconditions for solemnisation of marriage of a Muslim couple. Besides other preconditions, there is also a condition of witnesses.

Under the Sunni Law, the proposal and acceptance (in Nikah) must be made in presence of two males or one male and two female witnesses who should be sane, adult and Muslim. On the contrary, under Shia Law, witnesses are not necessary at the time of marriage. They are required at the time of dissolution of marriage.

50 Section 14 of the Hindu Marriage Act, 1955 enacts a 'fair trial' rule, according to which a person

1 can petition for divorce within one year of marriage
2 cannot petition for divorce within one year of marriage except in exceptional cases
3 cannot petition for judicial separation within one year of marriage
4 can petition for restitution of Conjugal Rights within one year of marriage

Ans. (2)

➲ *Exp.* Section 14 of the Hindu Marriage Act, 1955 enacts a 'fair trial' rule, according to which a person cannot petition for divorce within one year of marriage except in exceptional cases.

The court may, upon application made to it in accordance with such rules as may be made by the High Court in that behalf, allow a petition to be presented before one year has elapsed since the date of the marriage on the ground that the case is one of exceptional hardship to the petitioner or of exceptional depravity on the part of the respondent, but if it appears to the court at the hearing of the petition that the petitioner obtained leave to present the petition by any misrepresentation or concealment of the nature of the case, the court may, if it pronounces a decree, do so subject to the condition that the decree shall not have effect until after the expiry of one year from the date of the marriage or may dismiss the petition without prejudice to any petition which may be brought after the expiration of the said one year upon the same or substantially the same facts as those alleged in support of the petition so dismissed.

51 With the help of codes given below mark the incorrect statement in the light of the Hindu Adoptions and Maintenance Act, 1956

I. Permission of the court is not necessary except when guardian gives the child in adoption.
II. An adoption once made is revocable by natural parents only.
III. Mother may give the child in adoption with the consent of father.
IV. Performance of 'datta homam' ceremony is essential for a valid adoption.

Codes

1 III and IV 2 IV and II
3 II and III 4 I and IV

Ans. (2)

➲ *Exp.* Among the given statements, only IV and II are incorrect.

Under the previous law, it was not well-settled whether the ceremony of datta homam (i.e., oblations of clarified butter to fire) was essential to the validity of a Hindu adoption. Section 11 now lays down, in express terms, that performance of datta homam is not essential for a valid adoption.

As per Section 15, no adoption which has been validly made can be cancelled by the adoptive father or mother or any other person, nor can the adopted child renounce his or her status as such and return to the family of his or her birth.

52 Abstinence from sexual intercourse for a period of not less than four months pursuant to a vow is called

1 Divorce in hasan form
2 Divorce in ahsan form
3 Divorce by Zihar
4 Divorce of Ila

Ans. (4)

➲ *Exp.* Abstinence from sexual intercourse for a period of not less than four months pursuant to a vow is called divorce of Ila.

In Ila, the husband takes an oath not to engage in sexual intercourse with his wife.

Following this oath, if the husband has abstained from sexual intercourse there is no consummation for a period of four months, then after the expiry of the fourth month, the marriage dissolves irrevocably. But if the husband resumes cohabitation within four months, Ila is cancelled and the marriage does not dissolve.

53 In which of the following cases the Supreme Court of India has not addressed the issue of Uniform Civil Code?

1 Sarla Mudgal Vs. Union of India
2 John Vallamattom Vs. Union of India
3 Romesh Chander Vs. Savitri
4 John Deingdeh Vs. SS Chopra

Ans. (3)

➲ *Exp.* In the case of Romesh Chander Vs. Savitri (1995), the Supreme Court has not addressed the issue of Uniform Civil Code.

The instant case presented the special features warranting the exercise of such power. Since, the court has been exercising the power under Article 142 of the Constitution for dissolution of marriage where the Court finds that marriage is totally unworkable, emotionally dead and has broken down irretrievably, even if the facts of the case do not provide a ground in law on which the divorce could be granted, decree of divorce has been granted to resolve all cases between the parties to save them from further agony.

54 Answer using the following codes

Hindu wife is entitled to claim maintenance from her husband under the provisions of the Hindu Adoption and Maintenance Act, 1956 if,

I. She is unchaste, but living with her husband.
II. She is unchaste, but not living with her husband.
III. She is living separate on any ground mentioned under section 18(2) of the Act.
IV. She has converted to Muslim religion.

Codes

1 I and III 2 I and II
3 II and III 4 III and IV

Ans. (1)

Exp. Among the given statements, statements I and III are correct.

According to Section 18 (3), a Hindu wife shall not be entitled to separate residence and maintenance from her husband if she is unchaste or ceases to be a Hindu by conversion to another religion.

If a Hindu wife is living separately, she is also entitted to elaim her maintenance for her husband on any ground mentioned in Section 18(2) of the Act.

55 Which of the following statements is wrong? Answer using codes given below

I. Human Rights are essentially a product of bureaucracy.
II. Human Rights are a reaction to tyranny.
III. Primitive man could move all over world, without any restriction.
IV. All women are born free, but everywhere they are in chains.

Codes

1 I 2 II 3 III 4 IV

Ans. (1)

Exp. Among the given statements, it is wrong to say that Human Rights are essentially a product of bureaucracy.

Human rights are rights inherent to all human beings, regardless of gender, nationality, place of residency, sex, ethnicity, religion, colour and other categorization. Thus, human rights are non-discriminatory, meaning that all human beings are entitled to them and cannot be excluded from them. Of course, while all human beings are entitled to human rights, not all human beings experience them equally throughout the world. Many governments and individuals ignore human rights and grossly exploit other human beings.

Human rights emerged as a result of strong opposition to suppressing and exploitative practices of bureaucracy. The primitive men were able to travel anywhere without any restrictions as limitations on travel and related formalities came into picture only due to civilization once the legal machinery took shape. Also, though women are born free, but their living conditions are still not at par with men in terms of liberty and choice.

56 Read Assertion (A) and Reason (R) and answer using codes given below.

Assertion (A) In the exercise of his rights and freedoms, no one shall be subjected only for such limitations as are determined by law solely for the purpose of securing due recognition and respect for the rights and freedoms of others and of meeting the just requirements of morality, public order and the general welfare in a democratic society.

Reason (R) Because Article 29(2) of the Universal Declaration of Human Rights states so.

Codes

1 Both (A) and (R) are true and (R) is correct explanation of (A)
2 (A) is true, but (R) is false
3 (A) is false, but (R) is true
4 Both (A) and (R) are false

Ans. (4)

Exp. Both the (A) and (R) are false.

Article 29 of Universal Declaration of Human Rights provides that everyone has duties to the community in which alone the free and full development of his personality is possible.

In the exercise of his rights and freedoms, everyone shall be subject only to such limitations as are determined by law solely for the purpose of securing due recognition and respect for the rights and freedoms of others and of meeting the just requirements of morality, public order and the general welfare in a democratic society.

These rights and freedoms may in no case be exercised contrary to the purposes and principles of the United Nations.

57 Section 3 of the Protection of Civil Rights Act, 1955 prescribes punishment for

1 Enforcing economic disabilities
2 Civil disobedience
3 Enforcing religions disabilities
4 Enforcing political disabilities

Ans. (3)

Exp. Section 3 in the Protection of Civil Rights Act, 1955 prescribes punishment for enforcing religions disabilities.

The provision says that whoever on the ground of 'untouchability' prevents any person from entering any place of public worship which is open to other persons professing the same religion or any section thereof, as such person; or from worshipping or offering prayers or performing any religious service in any place of public worship, or bathing in, or using the waters of any sacred tank, well, spring or water-course, river or lake or bathing at any ghat of such tank, water-course, river or lake in the same manner and to the same extent as is permissible to other persons professing or any section thereof, as such the same religion, (i) or any section there of, as such person; (ii) shall be punishable with imprisonment for a term of not less than one month and not more than six months and also with fine which shall be not less than one hundred rupees and not more than five hundred rupees.

58 Article 6 of the Universal Declaration of Human Rights provides for

1 Right to life
2 Prohibition of slavery
3 Right to be recognised as a person before law
4 Equality before law

Ans. (3)

Exp. Article 6 of Universal Declaration of Human Rights provides that everyone has the right to recognition everywhere as a person before the law.

The Preamble describes objectives of declaration of human rights as whereas recognition of the inherent dignity and of the equal and inalienable rights of all members of the human family is the foundation of freedom, justice and peace in the world, whereas disregard and contempt for human rights have resulted in barbarous acts which have outraged the conscience of mankind, and the advent of a world in which human beings shall enjoy freedom of speech and belief and freedom from fear and want has been proclaimed as the highest aspiration of the common people.

59 Match List I with List II in the light of Geneva Convention relating to the Treatment of Prisoners of War, and select the answer using codes given below.

	List I		List II
A.	Categories of Prisoners to be treated as prisoner of war	I.	Article 13
B.	Prisoners of war to be humanely treated	II.	Article 91
C.	No Physical or mental torture	III.	Article 4
D.	Escape of prisoner of war	IV.	Article 17

Codes

	A	B	C	D		A	B	C	D
1	I	III	II	IV	2	I	III	IV	II
3	III	I	II	IV	4	III	I	IV	II

Ans. (4)

Exp. The correct matching is A-III, B-I, C-IV, D-II.

Article 4 - is related to Categories of Prisoners to be treated as prisoners of war. As per Article 4 of the Geneva Convention relative to the Treatment of Prisoners of War (1950), Prisoners of war, are persons belonging to one of the following categories, who have fallen into the power of the enemy:

(a) Members of the armed forces of a Party to the conflict as well as members of militias or
(b) volunteer corps forming part of such armed forces, Members of other militias and members of other volunteer corps, including those of organized resistance movements, belonging to a Party to the conflict and operating in or outside their own territory.

Article 13 is related to Prisoners of war to be humanely treated. Any unlawful act or omission by the Detaining Power causing death or seriously endangering the health of a prisoner of war in its custody is prohibited, and will be regarded as a serious breach of the present Convention.

Article 17 mention about no physical or mental torture, nor any other form of coercion, may be inflicted on prisoners of war to secure from them information of any kind whatever. Prisoners of war who refuse to answer may not be threatened, insulted, or exposed to any unpleasant or disadvantageous treatment of any kind as described under Article 17.

Article 91 is related to Escape of prisoner of war. It shall be deemed to have succeeded as per Article 91 when he has joined the armed forces of the Power on which he depends, or those of an allied Power, he has left the territory under the control of the Detaining Power, or of an ally of the said Power; he has joined a ship flying the flag of the Power on which he depends, or of an allied Power, in the territorial waters of the Detaining Power, the said ship not being under the control of the last named Power.

60 Match List I with List II in the light of Human Rights under the Constitution of India.

	List I (Case Law)		List II (Principles)
A.	East Coast Railway Vs. Madhav Appa Rao	I.	Freedom of expression
B.	LIC Vs. Professor Manubhai D Shah	II.	Equality
C.	Vakil Prasad Singh Vs. State of Bihar	III.	Religious instructions
D.	Aruna Roy Vs. Union of India	IV.	Speedy trial

Codes

	A	B	C	D		A	B	C	D
1	II	I	IV	III	2	I	II	IV	III
3	I	II	III	IV	4	II	I	III	IV

Ans. (1)

Exp. The correct matching is A-II, B-I, C-IV, D-III.

East Coast Railway Vs. Madhav Appa Rao (2010) is related to the principle Equality. It was observed that the rule of law above all rests upon the principle of legal certainty, which will be considered here, along with a principle which is partly but not wholly contained within the rule of law, namely, the principle of equality, or equal treatment without unfair discrimination.

Life Insurance Corporation of India Vs. Prof. Manubhai D. Shah (1992) is related to the principle Freedom of expression. It stated that the restriction had to be interpreted strictly and narrowly. Such restrictions are bound to be viewed as anathema, inasmuch as they are in the nature of curbs or limitations on the exercise of the right and are, therefore, bound to be viewed with suspicion, thereby throwing a heavy burden on the authorities who seek to impose them.

Vakil Prasad Singh Vs. State of Bihar (2009) - Speedy trial. It was held that it is well settled that the right to speedy trial in all criminal prosecutions is an inalienable right under Article 21 of the Constitution. This right is applicable not only to the actual proceedings in court but also includes within its sweep the preceding police investigations as well.

Ms. *Aruna Roy and others Vs. Union of India and Others* (2002) is related to the Principle Religious instructions. It was held that no person attending any educational institution recognised by the State or receiving aid out of State funds could be compelled to take part in any religious instruction that may be imparted in such institution or to attend any religious worship that may be conducted in such institution.

61 State of Kerala Vs. NM Thomas is about

1 Religious minorities 2 Linguistic minorities
3 Area wise reservation 4 Backward class

Ans. (4)

Exp. The case titled as State of Kerala and Anr Vs. N M Thomas and Ors (1975) is about backward class.

In this case, a governmental order granted provisional promotions to members of Scheduled Castes and Scheduled Tribes who did not have the requisite qualifications to be eligible for such promotion, along with a two year grace period for them to gain such qualifications. This was challenged.

The key contention of the aggrieved parties was that the classification was clearly void under Articles 16(1) and (2) and not covered by Article 16(4). Under existing precedent, this ought to have been a simple case. If Article 16(4) did not apply, then special provisions for SCs and STs clearly did violate Articles 16(1) and (2).

The Supreme Court did extend the benefit of reservations to promotions while upholding the rule that gave further exemption of two years to SC/ST candidates in passing the tests.

62 The main aims of Law of tort are

I. Punishment
II. Deterrence to wrong doers
III. Restoration of original position
IV. Damages to victims

Codes

1 I and III 2 III and II
3 II and IV 4 III and IV

Ans. (4)

Exp. The main aims of law of tort are deterrence to wrong doers and damages to victims. Tort is concerned with civil wrongs caused by individuals and other legal entities. Tort has two main objectives. One is to offer compensation to the victims of civil wrongs for the loss, damage or injury that they have suffered. The most common remedy for tortious conduct is money, referred to as damages. Another type of remedy is an injunction, where the court orders a person not to do something, for example, not to publish an article in a newspaper. It may also be used to compel a person to do something, although this is less common.

Punishment and deterrence to wrong doers are identified as objectives under the criminal law, rather than a civil law like tort.

63 The 'Absolute Liability' theory on the basis of pollution causing industrial injuries was propounded by

1 VR Krishna Iyer, J 2 PN Bhagwati, CJ
3 Kuldip Singh, J 4 MN Venkatachaliah, CJ

Ans. (2)

Exp. The 'Absolute Liability' theory on the basis of pollution causing industrial injuries was propounded by PN Bhagwati' CJ.

The rule of 'absolute liability' took birth through one of the most intriguing sets of events for the Indian jurisprudence. The rule was propounded by the then Chief Justice of India P.N. Bhagwati. This rule has also led to the revolutionizing of the entire aspect of environmental protection laws in India. After the Bhopal gas tragedy in 1984 followed by the Oleum Gas Leak Case in 1986, the judiciary felt the need for enforcement of absolute liability into the Indian Context. In the case of M.C.Mehta Vs Union of India, a landmark judgement was passed under which not only the scope of Article 21 was expanded to include the Right to human health and a healthy environment but also the rule of absolute liability was introduced in the Indian jurisprudence.

64 Defence of absolute privilege in case of defamation is available in which of the following cases?

I. Parliamentary Proceedings
II. Publication of matters of public interest
III. State of Communications
IV. Judicial Proceedings

Codes

1 I, II and III 2 II, III and IV
3 I, II and IV 4 IV, III and I

Ans. (4)

Exp. Defence of absolute privilege in case of defamation is available in such cases as Judicial proceedings, State of communications and Parliamentary proceedings.

Privilege, or immunity, is also a defence against a claim of defamation. Absolute privilege is an old common-law privilege that protects members of lawmaking bodies from charges of defamation for statements made on the floor of their legislative bodies, without regard for whether the words are stated in good faith. In addition, reports of proceedings of legislative bodies have absolute privilege, as do communications as part of a trial.

65 The essential ingredients of the tort of negligence are

I. One owes a duty of care towards the other
II. One commits a breach of that duty
III. The other person suffers damage as a consequence there of

Select your correct answer with the help of codes given below.

1 Only the first is an essential ingredient
2 None of them is an essential ingredient
3 All of them are essential ingredients
4 Even if the first is absent the tort of negligence is committed

Ans. (3)

Exp. All the given ingredients are essential for the tort of negligence.

One of the essential conditions of liability for negligence is that the defendant owed a legal duty towards the plaintiff. It is not sufficient that the defendant owed a duty to take care. It must also be established that the defendant owed a duty of care towards the plaintiff. Another essential condition for the liability in negligence is that the plaintiff must prove that the defendant committed a breach of duty to take care or he failed to perform that duty.

The last essential requisite for the tort of negligence is that the damage caused to the plaintiff was the result of the breach of the duty. The harm may fall into following classes; physical harm, i.e. harm to body, harm to reputation, harm to property, i.e. land and buildings and rights and interests pertaining thereto, and his goods, economic loss; and mental harm or nervous shock.

66 Negligence is failure in duty of taking due care. The expression 'duty' means

1 A legal duty
2 A legal as well as moral duty
3 A legal as well as social duty
4 A specific legal duty

Ans. (4)

Exp. The expression 'duty' means a specific legal duty.

In tort law, a duty of care is a legal obligation which is imposed on an individual requiring adherence to a standard of reasonable care while performing any acts that could foreseeably harm others. It is the first element that must be established to proceed with an action in negligence.

Such duty of care must be specifically recognized by law and cannot depend solely on the basis of individual cases. Unless the duty is specified as a legal duty either by legislation, or a precedent or through any other formal source of law, the same is not relevant for determination of tortuous liability.

67 There is no qualitative difference between a medical practitioner and an advocate, ... from the point of view of his status, duties and regulatory control by a statutory body. Hence, there is no reason why the legal practitioner should be excluded from the purview of Consumer Protection Act. From the following, select the correct decision in which it has been held?

1 K Vishnu Vs. National Consumer Dispute Redressal Commission and others
2 Joshi Vs. Motor industries Co.
3 Charan Singh Vs. Healing touch Hospital
4 Arvind Mills Ltd Vs. Associated Roadways

Ans. (1)

Exp. The given observation was made in the case of K Vishnu Vs. National Consumer Dispute Redressal Commission and others (2000).

It was held that the scope for suing a legal practitioner for negligence may be more limited than what it is in the case of a medical doctor. Even this will make no real difference. The fact that the Advocates are governed by the statutory enactments and the rules framed there under and are subject to the disciplinary control of a statutory body does not in our view, take them out of the net of Consumer Protection Act.

68 Read Assertion (A) and Reason (R) and answer using codes given below.

Assertion (A) Consumer Act is made to simplify the procedure and avoid the complexity, so that an ordinary citizen can file a complaint without a difficulty.

Reason (R) It intends to protect a large body of consumers from exploitation.

Codes

1 (A) and (R) are true and (R) is the correct explanation for (R)
2 Both (A) and (R) are false
3 (A) is true, but (R) is false
4 (R) is true, but(A) is false

Ans. (1)

Exp. Both (A) and (R) are true and (R) is the correct explanation for (A).

The purpose of the Consumer Protection Act is to promote protection of consumers with respect to safety, quality, purity, potency, healthfulness, durability, performance, repair ability, effectiveness, truthfulness, dependability, availability and cost of any real or personal property or tangible or intangible goods, services, or credit. Preservation of consumer choice and a competitive market price and adequacy of supply of goods and services, Prevention of unfair or deceptive trade practices. Thus, Assertion is true.

It is the purpose of Section 24 of this Act to establish a means for estimating in advance the consumer cost and benefits of Federal legislation or rules that have substantial economic impact and to prevent the adoption of Government programs whose costs to consumers outweigh their benefits. Thus, R is true.

69 Which are essentials of sale of goods? Answer using codes given below

I. Contractual capacity
II. Bilateral contract
III. Profit for seller
IV. Mutual and free consent of parties to the contract of sale of goods

Codes

1 I, II and III
2 I, II and IV
3 II, III and IV
4 I, III and IV

Ans. (2)

Exp. Contractual capacity, Bilateral contract and mutual and free consent of parties to the contract of sale of goods are essentials of sale of goods.

Contractual capacity refers to the ability of a contracting party to enter into legally binding relations.

A bilateral contract is the type of agreement most people regard a traditional contract as a mutual exchange of promises among the parties. Mutual and free consent of parties to the contract of sale of goods means a legally enforceable agreement between two or more parties with mutual obligations.

There is no essential condition for a contract of sale that the seller must derive profit, which may or may not be there or vary in amount depending upon each kind of transaction.

70 Read Assertion (A) and Reason (R) and answer using codes given below.

Assertion (A) Every partner is an agent of the other partner.

Reason (R) Partnership is agency.

Codes

1 Both (A) and (R) are false
2 (A) is true, but (R) is false
3 (A) is false, but (R) is true
4 Both (A) and (R) are true and (R) is correct explanation of (A)

Ans. *(4)*

Exp. Both (A) and (R) are true and (R) is the correct explanation of (A).

Section 18 of the Partnership Act, states that Subject to the provisions of this Act, a partner is the agent of the firm for the purposes of the business of the firm. Thus, Assertion is true.

This is because every Partnership is considered to be an agency where the Partners act as their agents. Thus, Reason is true.

71 Match List I with List II and select the correct answer using the codes given below.

List I	List II
A. Instalment Supply Ltd. Vs. STO	I. Conditions applied by trade usage
B. Gardiner Vs. Gray	II. Nemo dat quo non habet
C. Peter Darlington Partners Ltd. Vs. Gesho Co. Ltd	III. Sale by description
D. Farquharson Bros Vs. King and Co.	IV. Difference between sale and agreement to sale

Codes

	A	B	C	D		A	B	C	D
1	III	IV	II	I	2	III	IV	I	II
3	IV	III	I	II	4	IV	III	II	I

Ans. *(3)*

Exp. The correct matching is A-IV, B-III, C-I, D-II.

Instalment Supply Ltd. Vs. STO Ahmedabad (1974) case is mentioned about the difference between sale and agreement to sale. It was held that a contract of sale should be distinguished from a contract of hire-purchase. A contract of hire-purchase is properly speaking a contract of hire by which the hirer is granted an option to buy but is not, as under a contract of sale, under a legal obligation to do so.

Gardiner Vs. Gray (1815) case is related to Sale by description. The buyer bought 12 bags of 'waste silk' which turned out to be unmerchantable. Lord Ellenborough said that where there is no opportunity to inspect the commodity, the maxim of caveat emptor does not apply.

Peter Darlington Partners Ltd Vs. Gosho Co Ltd (1964) case is related to conditions applied by trade usage. A contract for the sale of canary seeds was subjected to the custom of trade and held that if there exist any impurities in the seeds the buyer will get a rebate on the price but he would not reject the goods. However, a custom which is unreasonable will not affect the parties' contract.

Farquharson bros Vs. King and Co. (1923) case is related to Nemo dat quod non habet. The plaintiff delivered his car to a mercantile agent to sell it for not less than 575 pounds. But the mercantile agent sold it to the defendant for pound 140 and misappropriated the amount. In an action by the plaintiff it was held that the defendant (buyer) had a good title to the goods.

72 Which one statement is correct from the following statements?

1 A director of a company as a director is a servant of the company
2 A director is an agent of his company
3 A director is not a fiduciary person of his company
4 A director is master of his company

Ans. *(2)*

Exp. A director is an agent of his company is the correct statement.

A company acts as a legal entity. However, it requires the assistance of human agency. Therefore, a company acts through directors who are essentially elected representatives of shareholders and make decisions for their benefit. By the basic definition, an agent is someone who acts on behalf of the principal; thereby ensuring that the third party can hold only the principal and not the agent liable for any wrong. Hence, directors do act as agents as they act on behalf of the company and cannot be held personally liable for company's default.

73 Match List I with List II and select the correct answer using codes given below. Answer in context of the Negotiable Instruments Act.

List I	List II
A. Time and place of presentment	I. Section 19
B. Cheques are payable in demand	II. Section 8
C. Holder of a negotiable instrument	III. Section 61
D. Fictitious drawer or payee	IV. Section 42

Codes

	A	B	C	D		A	B	C	D
1	I	IV	II	III	2	III	II	IV	I
3	II	III	IV	I	4	II	III	I	IV

Ans. (*)

Exp. The correct matching is A-III, B-I, C-II, D-IV.

Section 61 provides that a bill of exchange payable after sight must, if no time or place is specified therein for presentment, be presented to the drawee thereof for acceptance, if he can, after reasonable search, be found, by a person entitled to demand acceptance, within a reasonable time after it is drawn, and in business hours on a business day.

Section 19 says a promissory note or bill of exchange, in which no time for payment is specified and a cheque, are payable on demand.

Section 8 is related to holder of a megotiable instrument. It states that the 'holder' of a promissory note, bill of exchange or cheque means any person entitled in his own name to the possession thereof and to receive or recover the amount due thereon from the parties thereto. Where the note, bill or cheque is lost or destroyed, its holder is the person so entitled at the time of such loss or destruction.

Section 42 is related to fictitious drawee or payee. It states that an acceptor of a bill of exchange drawn in a fictitious name and payable to the drawer's order is not, by reason that such name is fictitious, relieved from liability to any holder in due course claiming under an indorsement by the same hand as the drawer's signature, and purporting to be made by the drawer.

74 Which of the following statements is correct?

1 Open cheques are those which cannot be directly presented to the drawee bank for payment across the counter
2 A 16 year old girl can draw a cheque
3 Indorsement is written on front of a cheque
4 Indorsement cannot be made by the holder of a negotiable instrument

Ans. (2)

Exp. Statement 2 is correct as 16 year old girl can draw a cheque.

A Cheque may be defined as an unconditional order drawn upon a specified banker, signed by the maker, directing the banker to pay on demand a certain sum of money only to the order of a person or to be the bearer of the instrument.

There are three parties in cheque these are (i) Drawer; the person who draws the cheque is known as the drawer. The person whose name the account stands is the drawer. (ii) Drawee; the bank on which the cheque is drawn is known as the drawee, (iii) Payee; the person in whose favour the cheque is made payable is the payee. If the cheque is drawn payable to self, the drawer himself would be the payee of the cheque.

75 Which of the following statement (s) is/are incorrect? Answer using codes given below.

I. In Attorney General Vs. Great Eastern Railway Co. the House of Lords observed that the doctrine of ultra vires as it was explained in the Ashbury case, should not be maintained.
II. Section 13 (i) (c) of the Companies Act provides incidental objects which need not be stated in the memorandum.
III. If incidental objects are not stated in the memorandum, they would not be allowed by the principle of reasonable construction.
IV. The doctrine of indoor management operates to protect insiders against the company.

Codes

1 I and II	2 II and III
3 I, II and III	4 All of these

Ans. (4)

Exp. All the given statements are incorrect.

The House of Lords in Attorney General Vs. Great Eastern Railway (1880) case, relied upon the decision of the Ashbury case, that if a contract or act is done beyond the provisions of the object clause of the memorandum then it is considered as a void act.

Section 13 of Companies Act 2013 regulates the process of amendment in Memorandum of Association is applicable to all companies. All clauses of Memorandum except Capital clause can be altered by following the provisions of Section 13 of Companies Act, 2013 by passing special resolution. For alteration of any of the clauses of Memorandum, consent of members by way of Special Resolution is required.

The objects must be distinguished from powers. and objects must be stated in the memorandum, but not powers. Even if the powers are stated, they can be used only to effectuate the objects of the company.

The doctrine of indoor management, also known as Turquand rule is a 150-year old concept, which protects the outsiders against the actions done by the company. Any person who enters into a contract with the company shall ensure that the transaction is authorised by the articles and memorandum of the company.

UGC-NET
LAW
SOLVED PAPER 2014 (December)
PAPER II

1 Which of the following statements is right?

1 Law consist of rules in accordance with reason and nature has formed the basis of imperative law
2 Natural law is a type of command
3 Law, according to positivist, is made through medium of courts
4 Hart talks in terms of conduct supplemented by an attitude of mind to the effect that the conduct in question is obligatory because it is required by rule

***Ans.* (4)**

Exp. Statement 4 that says Hart talks in terms of conduct supplemented by an attitude of mind to the effect that the conduct in question is obligatory because it is required by rule, is right.
Hart states that primary rules are social rules imposing obligations not because of any attitudes toward them on the part of citizens, but because they are the valid rules of the system in that they satisfy all the criteria provided by the secondary rule of recognition which must be accepted by the legal officials.

2 Right in re aliena means a right over

1 his own property
2 a property of someone else
3 property situated in a foreign country
4 property situated in one's own country

***Ans.* (2)**

Exp. Right in re aliena means a right over a property of someone else.
For eg: if 'A' leases his property to 'B', then 'A' is the owner of the house and 'B' is the temporary occupier of the house. In this case, the right of temporary detachment of the ownership is called as Right in re aliena.

3 Given below are two statements. One is labelled as Assertion (A) and the other is labelled as Reason (R).

Assertion (A) A perfect duty is one which a man not merely ought to perform, but may be justly compelled to perform.

Reason (R) A perfect duty is one which is not merely recognised by law but enforced.

Codes

1 (A) is true, but (R) is false
2 (A) is false, but (R) is true
3 Both (A) and (R) are true
4 Both (A) and (R) are false

***Ans.* (3)**

Exp. Both (A) and (R) are true
A perfect duty is one in which a man not merely ought to perform, but may be justly compelled to perform. A perfect duty is one which is not merely recognised by law but is also enforced. In a fully developed legal system, there are rights and duties which, though recognised by law, are not perfect in nature. Both are important but we need not take action to enforce them.

4 Possession is prima facie evidence of title of ownership. Hence

1 long adverse possession confers title even to a property which originally belonged to another
2 in all cases possession leads to ownership
3 transfer of possession is not a mode of transferring ownership
4 long possession do not confer title to the property which originally belonged to government

***Ans.* (1)**

Exp. Possession is prima facie evidence of title of ownership. Hence, long adverse possession confers title even to a property which originally belonged to another.
Possession is the the prima facie evidence of ownership, and is also called as nine out of ten points of law, meaning that there is a presumption that the possessor of a thing is the owner of it and the other claimants in order to have that thing must prove their title or better possessory right.

5 Who among the following said that there is in essence no difference between the legal personality of a company and that of an individual ?

1 Maitland
2 Dicey
3 Gierke
4 Kelsen

Ans. (4)

Exp. Kelsen said that there is in essence no difference between the legal personality of a company and that of an individual.

Hans Kelsen was great jurist of the analytical school, who gave a theory "the Pure Theory of Law". Pure theory says that that law should operate, and be studied, free of moral, economic or other influences. Law is seen as a series of norms arising from a foundational Grundnorm (Basic norm).

6 Ownership of Goodwill of a business is

1 Limited ownership 2 Corporeal ownership
3 Incorporeal ownership 4 Beneficial ownership

Ans. (3)

Exp. Ownership of Goodwill of a business is incorporeal ownership.

The ownership of right is called incorporeal ownership. Patent, copyright, right of lease are examples of incorporeal ownership. For example, if you own piece of land, that is corporeal ownership. But if you own a right of way on that piece of land, that is incorporeal ownership.

7 It was remarked in 'Golaknath Vs. State of Punjab' that our 'Preamble to the Constitution contains in a nutshell its ideals and aspirations' by one of the judges ?

1 Justice Vs. Krishna Iyer
2 Justice K Subba Rao
3 Justice AN Ray
4 Justice HR Khanna

Ans. (2)

Exp. The above mentioned remark was made in 'Golaknath Vs. the State of Punjab' in 1967, by Justice K Subba Rao.

In this case, the Court ruled that Parliament could not curtail any of the Fundamental Rights in the Constitution. The Fundamental Rights were transcendental and inviolable and the Parliament of India had no power to take away or abridge any of the Fundamental Rights guaranteed by the Constitution by way of the Constitutional amendments.

8 Right of eligible employees to be considered for promotion is virtually a part of Fundamental Right of employees, was decided by the Supreme Court in

1 Union of India Vs. Hemraj Singh Chauhan
2 Supreme Court Employees Association Vs. Union of India
3 John Vallamattam Vs. Union of India
4 St Stephens College Vs. University of Delhi

Ans. (1)

Exp. In Union of India Vs. Hemraj Singh Chauhan, the Supreme Court said that right of eligible employees to be considered for promotion is virtually a part of Fundamental Right of employees.

In this case, Supreme Court has ruled that a Government employee has a Fundamental Right to be considered for promotion and it is mandatory for the Centre and States to carry out cadre review of eligible officers for promotion to the Indian Administrative Service(IAS). The right of eligible employees to be considered for promotion is virtually a part of their Fundamental Right guaranteed under Article 16 (Equality of opportunity in matter of public employment) of the Constitution.

9 In Vishram Singh Raghubanshi Vs. State of Uttar Pradesh (AIR2011 SC2275) the court held that

1 It is the duty of Superior Courts to protect the reputation of judicial officers of Subordinate courts
2 Procedure laid down in the appointment of officers of subordinate courts
3 Procedure laid down in the salaries and service conditions of the judicial officers of the lower judiciary
4 Transfer of the Judges of the High Court.

Ans. (1)

Exp. In Vishram Singh RaghuBanshi Vs. State of Uttar Pradesh (AIR 2011 SC 2275) the court held that it is the duty of Superior Courts to protect the reputation of judicial officers of Subordinate courts.

In the given case, the Supreme Court, in exercise of contempt jurisdiction, held that Superior courts have duty to protect judicial officers of Subordinate courts, taking note of growing tendency of maligning reputation of judicial officers by unscrupulous practising advocates who either fail to secure desired orders or do not succeed in browbeating for achieving ulterior purpose. It also held that any violation of professional ethics by an advocate is unfortunate and unacceptable, and that the dangerous trend of making false allegations against judicial officers and humiliating them should be curbed with heavy hands.

10 In which of these cases, Fundamental Duties are judicially invoked ? Answer using codes given below

I. Prem Prakash Vs. Punjab University
II. Suresh Koshy George Vs. University of Kerala
III. Rural Litigation and Entitlement Kendra Vs. State of Uttar Pradesh
IV. Shri Sachidanand Pandey Vs. State of West Bengal

Codes

1 I and II are correct
2 II and III are correct
3 III and IV are correct
4 All of the above

Ans. (3)

Exp. In Rural Litigation and Entitlement Kendra Vs. State of Uttar Pradesh and Shri Sachidanand Pandey Vs. State of West Bengal cases, Fundamental Duties are judicially invoked.

In Rural Litigation and Entitlement Kendra Vs. State of Uttar Pradesh, it was held that 'Forest' was initially a State subject covered by Entry 19 in List II of the Seventh

Schedule. In 1976, under the 42nd Amendment the Entry was deleted and Entry 17-A in the concurrent List was inserted. The change from the State List to the Concurrent List was brought about following the realisation of the Central Government that 'forests' were of national importance and should be placed in the Concurrent List to enable the Central Government to deal with the matter. The same Amendment of the Constitution brought in Article 48A and Article 51A(g) is Part IVA.

In Shri Sachidanand Pandey Vs. State of West Bengal, it was held that whenever a problem of ecology is brought before the Court, the Court is bound to bear in mind Article 48A of the Constitution the Directive Principle which enjoins that "The State shall endeavour to protect and improve the environment and to safeguard the forests and wildlife of the country," and Article 51A(g) which proclaims it to be the Fundamental Duty of every citizen of India "to protect and improve the natural environment including forest, lakes, rivers and wildlife, and to have compassion for living creatures."

11 Match List I with List II and select the correct answer by using codes given below.

List I	List II
A. Executive power must be exercised in accordance with the Constitution.	I. HH Maharajadhiraja Madhav Rao Jivaji Rao Scindia Bahadur Vs. Union of India
B. Executive power is the residue of functions of government, which are not legislative or judicial	II. Maganbhai Ishwarbhai Patel Vs. Union of India
C. Executive power may be exercised without prior legislative support	III. Kehar Singh Vs. Union of India
D. The President is not bound to hear a petitioner for mercy before he rejects the petition	IV. A Sanjeevi Naidu Vs. State of Madras

Codes

	A	B	C	D		A	B	C	D
1	IV	I	II	III	2	I	IV	II	III
3	IV	I	III	II	4	II	III	I	IV

Ans. (1)

Exp. The correct matching is A-IV, B-I, C-II, D-III.

In *A Sanjeevi Naidu* Vs. *State of Madras* case it was mentioned that the Executive power must be exercised in accordance with the Constitution. In this case, it was held that the Governor is essentially a constitutional head and the Government is run by the Council of Ministers. All the matters in which the Governor is specifically required to act in his discretion have to be decided by the Council of Ministers.

In *HH Maharajadhiraja Madhav Rao Jivaji Rao Scindia Bahadur* Vs. *Union of India* case it was mentioned that the Executive power is the residue of functions of government, which are not legislative or judicial. In this case, the Court held that the action of the President withdrawing recognition of all Rulers is ultra vires Article 366(22) and a nullity. Article 366(22) neither expressly nor by implication places the power in the hands of the President to say that although a ruler is in existence or a successor is available there shall be no ruler of any particular state. The definition contemplates the existence of the Ruler "for the time being".

In *Maganbhai Ishwarbhai Patel* Vs. *Union of India* it was mentioned that the Executive power may be exercised without prior legislative support. The Court while deciding on the issue said that the case deals with international law as well as domestic law. Therefore, it discussed provisions from various other countries like the United States of America, England, and France to support the view that the Indian Constitution does not provide any clear direction towards enforcement of treaties as provided under the Constitution of America and France.

In *Kehar Singh* Vs. *Union of India* it was held that the President is not bound to hear a petitioner for mercy before he rejects the petition. In this case, The President refused to grant pardon, with the reasoning that they cannot go into the merits of the case that has been finally decided by the Highest Court. The petitioner was also not granted an oral hearing. The main issue raised is whether the President is precluded from entering into the merits of a case finally decided by the Supreme Court.

12 The Supreme Court has laid down guidelines for imposing emergency under Article 356 in one of the following cases

1 AK Roy Vs. Union of India
2 SR Bommai Vs. Union of India
3 State of Rajasthan Vs. Union of India
4 Rameswar Prasad Vs. Union of India

Ans. (2)

Exp. In case of SR Bommai Vs. Union of India, the Supreme Court has laid down guidelines for imposing emergency under Article 356.

It was a landmark judgment of the Supreme Court of India, where the Court discussed at length provisions of Article 356 of the Constitution of India and related issues. This case had huge impact on Centre-State Relations.

13 By which constitutional amendment "The total number of ministers, including the Prime Minister, in the Council of Ministers shall not exceed fifteen percent of the total number of members of the House of the people" ?

1 Ninety First
2 Ninety Second
3 Ninety Third
4 Ninety Fifth

Ans. (1)

Exp. By Ninety First constitutional amendment the mentioned provision is added.

Article 75(1A) of the constitution says, "the total number of Ministers, including the Prime Minister, in the Council of Ministers shall not exceed fifteen percent of the total number of members of the House of the People."

14 Match List I with List II and select the correct answers by using the codes given below.

List I (Principles applied by the Courts)	List II (Cases)
A. Law must be based on justice, equity and good conscience	I. RV Keyn
B. Subrogation	II. Chorzaw Factory (Indemnity) Case
C. Res-Judicata	III. Mavrommatis Palestine Concessions Case
D. Estoppel	IV. Barcelona Traction Case

Codes

	A	B	C	D		A	B	C	D
1	I	II	IV	I	2	I	III	II	IV
3	II	IV	III	II	4	I	II	III	IV

Ans. (2)

Exp. The correct matching is A-I, B-III, C-II, D-IV.

R V. Keyn in the case in which law must be based on justice, equity and good conscience. In this case, Franconia, a German ship, collided with a British vessel within the British Maritime Belt. The British Vessel sank and one person died. The British Court convicted the master of the German ship for manslaughter. Questions arose about the jurisdiction of the Court as the incident had happened within the British territorial waters. The House of Lords, held that the English Court was bound by Municipal Law and Municipal Law had not provided for the Jurisdiction hence no jurisdiction.

Mavrommatis Palestine Concessions Case deals with the principle of Subrogation. The Mavrommatis dispute was about the fate of conflicting concessions for the supply of water and electricity and associated economic and political control over Palestine in the interwar period. Both water and electricity were essential to the aspirations of the Jewish people to create a homeland in this inhospitable part of the world.

Chorzow Factory (Indemnity) Case deals with the principle of Res Judicata. In this case, it was held that the Permanent Court of International Justice had its jurisdiction to try the case. Poland had violated the international agreement between Germany and Poland. Poland would be liable to repair any loss suffered by Germany due to the forfeit of that two companies as they violated that international agreement.

Barcelona Traction Case deals with the principle of Estoppel. In this case, the court observed that adoption of the theory of diplomatic protection of the shareholders would open the doors to competing claims on the part of different States, which would create an atmosphere of insecurity in international economic relations. Thus, the court held that the Belgium government did not have the jus standi in the present case and therefore it did not find any reason to examine other aspects of the case.

15 Who is not the exponent of the Constitutive Theory of 'Recognition' ?

1 Hegel 2 Oppenheim
3 Hall 4 Anzilloti

Ans. (3)

Exp. Hall is not the exponent of Constitutive Theory of 'Recognition.'

The Constitutive Theory, holds that "a state is and becomes an international person through recognition only and exclusively." This means that states are essentially non-existent and do not possess any legal rights until recognized by other states.

16 Match List I with List II and select the correct answer by using the codes given below.

List I (Sources of Public International Law)	List II (Case-related)
A. General principles of law recognised by the civilised countries	I. North Sea Continental Self Case
B. Juristic Work	II. Burkina Faso Vs. Mali
C. International Customs	III. Portugal Vs. India
D. Justice and Equity	IV. Paquete Habana Case

Codes

	A	B	C	D		A	B	C	D
1	I	II	III	IV	2	II	III	IV	I
3	III	IV	I	II	4	IV	I	III	II

Ans. (4)

Exp. The correct matching is A-IV, B-I, C-III, D-II.

General principles of law recognised by the civilised countries is related to Paquete Habana Case. It was a landmark decision of the United States Supreme Court concerning the applicability and recognition of international law by the United States. The Court held that the capture of fishing vessels as prizes of war violated customary international law, which is integrated with U.S. law and binding as such.Paquete Habana influenced subsequent court decisions that incorporated international law regarding other matters. The case is also notable for citing a wide breadth of historical and international sources, including jurists from around the world and foreign state practices going back centuries.

Juristic Work is related to North Sea Continental Shelf Case. this case, the court held that the passage of a considerable period of time was unnecessary (i.e. duration) for the formation of a customary law.

International Customs is related to Portugal Vs. India. The Portuguese possessions in India included the two enclaves of Dadra and Nagar-Haveli which, in mid-1954, had passed under an autonomous local administration. Portugal claimed that it had a right of passage to those enclaves and between one enclave and the other to the extent necessary for the exercise of its sovereignty and subject to the regulation and control of India. It also claimed that, in July 1954, contrary to the practice previously followed, India had prevented it from exercising that right and that situation should be redressed. It was held that a right of passage for non-military civilians exists as a rule of regional customary international law between India and Portugal.

Justice and Equity is related to Burkina Faso Vs. Mali case. In the case of frontier dispute between Burkina Faso Vs. Mali, for the first time a chamber of the court, rather than the court itself, ordered interim measures, having confirmed its authority to do so.

17 Statement I Subject to Rules of Jus Cogens, local customary law can supplement or derogate from general custom.

Statement II International law does not recognise the concept of local custom.

Codes

1 Both the statements are individually true and Statement II is the correct explanation of statement I
2 Both the Statements are individually true but Statement II is not the correct explanation of Statement I
3 Statement I is true, but Statement II is false
4 Statement I is false, but Statement II is true

***Ans.* (3)**

Exp. Statement I is true, but statement II is false.

Statement I true because it is a fundamental and overriding principle of international law. It is a Latin phrase that translates to 'compelling law'. It is absolute in nature which means that there can be no defence for the commission of any act that is prohibited by Jus Cogens.

Statement II is false because customary international law can be general or particular. Particular customary law embodies local or regional customs. This type doesn't bind all States; but, binds some States that share a common interest or that are in a similar geographical location.

18 Using the codes given below, indicate the chronological sequence in which of the following judgements were delivered by the International Court of Justice?

I. Right of passage over Indian Territory case
II. South-West Africa case
III. Frontier Dispute
IV. Temple of Preah Vihear

Codes

1 I, II, III and IV
2 II, IV, I and III
3 I, IV, II and III
4 III, II, IV and I

***Ans.* (3)**

Exp. The correct chronological sequence is I, IV, II and III.

Right of passage over Indian Territory case (1957). The Portuguese possessions in India included the two enclaves of Dadra and Nagar Haveli which, in mid-1954, had passed under an autonomous local administration. Portugal claimed that it had a right of passage to those enclaves and between one enclave and the other to the extent necessary for the exercise of its sovereignty and subject to the regulation and control of India; it also claimed that, in July 1954, contrary to the practice previously followed, India had prevented it from exercising that right and that situation should be redressed. It was held that a right of passage for non-military civilians exists as a rule of regional customary international law between India and Portugal.

Temple of Preah Vihear (1962) case is related to territorial dispute between Cambodia and Thailand over the Preah Vihear Temple located in disputed area between Preah Vihear Province of Cambodia and Sisaket Province of Thailand which Thai authority stationed troops there since 1954. Cambodia complained International Court of Justice (ICJ) in 1959 and it given judgement in 1962 that the temple is situated in Cambodion territory.

In South-West Africa case (1966), the Court found that Ethiopia and Liberia could not be considered to have established any legal right or interest appertaining to them in the subject-matter of their claims, and accordingly decided to reject those claims.

Frontier Dispute (2013) case was a public international law case with the International Court of Justice served by the West African states of Burkina Faso and Niger, which share a border. Both nations submitted a border dispute to the court in 2010. The court delivered its judgement in 2013, and the parties implemented it in 2015 and 2016.

19 Match List I with List II and select the correct answer by using the codes given below.

List I (Provisions under Statute of International Court of Justice)	List II (Related Articles)
A. Binding force of decrees of International Court of Justice	I. Article 65
B. Methods of conferring Jurisdiction upon the court	II. Article 62
C. Advisory Jurisdiction of the Court	III. Article 59
D. Courts power to allow a state to intervene in case to which it is not a party	IV. Article 36

Codes

	A	B	C	D		A	B	C	D
1	III	IV	I	II	2	II	III	IV	I
3	IV	II	III	I	4	I	II	III	IV

***Ans.* (1)**

Exp. The correct matching is A-III, B-IV, C-I, D-II.

Binding force of decrees of International Court of Justice is stated under Article 59 of statute of International Court of Justice. It states that the decision of the Court has no binding force except between the parties and in respect of that particular case.

Methods of conferring Jurisdiction upon the court is stated under Article 36. It states that the jurisdiction of the Court comprises all cases which the parties refer to it and all matters specially provided for in the Charter of the United Nations or in treaties and conventions in force.

Advisory Jurisdiction of the Court is stated under Article 63. It states that the court may give an advisory opinion on any legal question at the request of whatever body may be authorised by or in accordance with the Charter of the United Nations to make such a request.

Courts power to allow a state to intervene in case to which it is not a party is stated under Article 62. It states that, should a state consider that it has an interest of a legal nature which may be affected by the decision in the case, it may submit a request to the Court to be permitted to intervene. It shall be for the Court to decide upon this request.

20 In which of the following cases, a child could not be a 'Hindu' under the Hindu Marriage Act, 1955 ?

I. Only one parent is a Hindu and the child was brought up as a Hindu.

II. If after the birth of a child both the parents convert to Buddhism.

III. Only one parent is Jain and the child was not brought up as a Jain.

IV. If after the birth of a child both the parents convert to Muslim religion and in the exercise of parental right the child is also converted to Muslim religion.

Codes

1 I, II and IV
2 III and IV
3 II and I
4 I, II and III

Ans. (2)

Exp. Statements III and IV contains the conditions when a child could not be a 'Hindu' under the Hindu Marriage Act, 1955.

Section 2 of the Hindu Marriage Act, states that the following persons are Hindus, Buddhists, Jainas or Sikhs by religion, as the case may be:

- any child, legitimate or illegitimate, both of whose parents are Hindus, Buddhists, Jainas or Sikhs by religion;
- any child, legitimate or illegitimate, one of whose parents is a Hindu, Buddhist, Jaina or Sikh by religion and who is brought up as a member of the tribe, community, group or family to which such parent belongs or belonged; and
- any person who is a convert or re-convert to the Hindu, Buddhist, Jaina or Sikh religion.

21 When two Hindus are descendants of a common ancestress but by different husbands, they are said to be related to each other by

1 Uterine Blood
2 Half Blood
3 Full Blood
4 Fosterage

Ans. (1)

Exp. When two Hindus are descendants of a common ancestress but by different husbands, they are said to be related to each other by Uterine blood.

Section 3(1)(e) of the Hindu Succession Act 1956, says that two persons are said to be related to each other by Uterine blood when they are descended from a common ancestor but by different husbands.

22 A 'Muta' marriage is

I. a temporary marriage.

II. recognised under Sunni law.

III. recognised under Shia law.

IV. for a fixed period.

Codes

1 I and IV
2 I, II, III and IV
3 I, III and IV
4 II and III

Ans. (3)

Exp. A 'Muta' marriage is a temporary marriage, recognised under Shia law, for a fixed period.

Muta is a distinct kind of marriage recognised only by the Shias. Muta may be defined as a temporary union of male and female for specified duration, on payment of some consideration. As against the permanent or a regular marriage (Nikah), the Muta may be regarded as a temporary marriage.

Literal meaning of the Arabic word 'Muta' is 'enjoyment'; therefore, it may also be regarded as 'marriage for pleasure'.

23 A decree of judicial separation

I. dissolve the matrimonial bond.

II. does not dissolve the matrimonial bond but merely suspends marital rights and obligations during the subsistence of the decree.

III. mandates that the parties still continue to be husband and wife but not obliged to live together.

IV. provides that if the parties have not resumed cohabitation for a period of one year either party may seek divorce.

Codes

1 I, II and IV
2 I, II, III and IV
3 I and IV
4 II, III and IV

Ans. (4)

Exp. Statement II, III and IV are correct.
Judicial separation is a decree, through which either party to the marriage seeks to remove the obligation of co-habitation with the other, not necessarily proving that their marriage has irretrievably broken down. It is a legal way to live separately from the spouse, without obtaining a decree of divorce. It also provides that if the parties have not resumed cohabitation for a period of one year either party may seek divorce.

24 Match List I with List II and select the correct answer with the help of codes given below.

List I	List II
A. Ijma	I. Cancellation of marriage
B. Faskh	II. Opinion of one individual only
C. Mahr-ul-misl	III. Collective opinion of commentators
D. Qiyas	IV. Customary power

Codes

	A	B	C	D		A	B	C	D
1	III	I	IV	II	2	I	II	III	IV
3	III	IV	II	I	4	IV	I	II	III

Ans. (1)

Exp. The correct matching is A-III, B-I, C-IV, D-II.

Ijma is related to collective opinion of commentators. Ijma in Islamic law is the universal and infallible agreement of either the Muslim community as a whole or Muslim scholars in particular.

Faskh is related to cancellation of marriage. 'Faskh' means the cancellation, abolition, revocation, annulment. Before the passing of the dissolution of Marriage Act, Muslim women could only apply for the dissolution of their marriage under the doctrine of Faskh.

Mahr-ul-misl is related to customary dower. In fixing the Proper dower (Mahr-ul-misl), the Court is guided by the amount of dower settled upon the other female members of the family of the wife's father, as for instance, the father's sisters.

Qiyas is related to opinion of one individual only. Qiyas, in Islamic law is an analogical reasoning as applied to the deduction of juridical principles from the Quran and the Sunnah.

25 Rules relating to Sapinda relationship are based on the principle of

1 Polygyny 2 Endogamy 3 Exogamy 4 Polyandry

Ans. (3)

Exp. Rules relating to Sapinda relationship are based on the principle of Exogamy.

Sapinda relationships are prohibited under Hindu marriage law. A sapinda is someone who is within or has a common ancestor relative within three generations above you on your mother's side of the family, within or has a common ancestor relative within five generations above you on your father's side of the family.

26 Divorce by Zihar is a species of

1 actual divorce 2 inchoate divorce
3 khula divorce 4 constructive divorce

Ans. (2)

Exp. Divorce by Zihar is a species of inchoate divorce.

Zihar is illegal and considered an insult in the Islamic law. It implies that the man, declaring his wife akin to his mother, is guilty of the sin of forbidding the lawful things. It has been proscribed by law and the act does not ensue in divorce. It is condemned in the law.

27 For a valid contract acceptance should be

1 absolute and qualified
2 partial but unqualified
3 absolute and unqualified
4 absolutely qualified

Ans. (3)

Exp. For a valid contract acceptance should be absolute and unqualified.

Section 7 in the Indian Contract Act, 1872 says contract must be absolute and unqualified, and it must be expressed in some usual and reasonable manner, unless the proposal prescribes the manner in which it is to be accepted.

28 According to Explanation 2 to Section 25 of the Indian Contract Act, which of the following statements are correct ?

I. An agreement to which the consent of the promisor is not freely given is valid because consideration is adequate.
II. An agreement to which the consent of the promisor is not freely given is valid even if consideration is inadequate.
III. Consideration must be legal.
IV. Consideration can be illegal.

Codes

1 I and II are correct
2 II and III are correct
3 III and IV are correct
4 I and IV are correct

Ans. (2)

Exp. Statement II and III are correct.

According to Section 25 explanation 2 of the Indian Contract Act, an agreement to which the consent of the promisor is freely given is not void merely because the consideration is inadequate, but the inadequacy of the consideration may by taken into account by the Court in determining the questions, whether the consent of the promisor was freely given.

29 In Jyotindra Bhattacharjee Vs. Mrs. Sona Balon Bora, it was held that

1 the onus of proving soundness of mind of a person always rests upon a person who alleges such state of mind of another person
2 the onus of proving unsoundness of mind of a person always rests upon a person who alleges such state of mind of another person
3 the onus of proving unsoundness of mind rests upon person of unsound mind
4 the onus of proving unsoundness of mind is on the judge deciding the case involving person of unsound mind

Ans. (2)

Exp. In Jyotindra Bhattacharjee Vs. Mrs. Sona Balon Bora, it was held that the onus of proving unsoundness of mind of a person always rests upon a person who alleges such state of mind of another person.

Section 105 of Indian Evidence Act says, when a person is accused of any offence, the burden of proving the existence of circumstances bringing the case within any of the General Exceptions in the Indian Penal Code, (45 of 1860), or within any special exception or proviso contained in any other part of the same Code, or in any law defining the offence, is upon him, and the Court shall presume the absence of such circumstances.

30 Read Assertion (A) and Reason (R) and select the correct answer with the help of codes given below.

Assertion (A) Agreement is void when both parties are under mistake as to the matter of law.

Reason (R) Parties entering into a contract are legally obliged to know the law relating to the contract.

Codes

1 Both (A) and (R) are true and (R) is correct explanation for (A)
2 (A) is true, but (R) is false
3 (R) is true, but (A) is false
4 Both (A) and (R) are false

Ans. (4)

Exp. Both (A) and (R) are false.

Assertion is false because Section 21 of the Indian Contract Act, says that a contract is not voidable because it was caused by a mistake as to any law in force in India, but a mistake as to a law not in force in India has the same effect as a mistake of a fact.

Reason is false because Section 20 of the Act deems a contract void when both parties are under mistake of fact essential to the contract.

31 Where, a law promulgated after the contract is made, makes the performance of the agreement impossible, the agreement becomes

1 Voidable
2 Valid
3 Void
4 Absolutely binding

Ans. (3)

Exp. Where, a law promulgated after the contract is made, makes the performance of the agreement impossible, the agreement becomes void. This scenario comes under the frustration of contract by virtue of legislation.

Section 56 of the Indian Contract Act, 1872 says that a contract to do an act which, after the contract is made, becomes impossible, or, by reason of some event which the promisor could not prevent, unlawful, becomes void when the act becomes impossible or unlawful.

32 Match List I with List II and select the correct answer using the codes given below.

	List I		List II
A.	Damages arising in the usual course of things	I.	Ghaziabad Dev Authority Vs. Union of India
B.	Compensation for mental anguish	II.	Hadley Vs. Baxendale
C.	Measure of damages	III.	M/s. Ganga Maruthi Vs. Nagaraj
D.	Compensation for breach of contract where penalty is stipulated for	IV.	Jamal Vs. Moolla Dawood

Codes

	A	B	C	D		A	B	C	D
1	II	I	IV	III	2	I	II	IV	III
3	II	I	III	IV	4	IV	III	I	II

Ans. (1)

Exp. The correct matching is A-II, B-I, C-IV, D-III.

Hadley Vs. Baxendale case is related to damages arising in the usual course of things. The Bench held that Hadley cannot recover the loss of profits from Baxendale as the shutting down of the mill was not contemplated as a consequence of the breach of contract by the breaching party. Hadley at the time of contracting did not mention that the mill will be non-operational till the new crankshaft is installed. A party cannot be expected to compensate for what he was not able to reasonably contemplate at the time of entering into a contract.

Ghaziabad Dev Authority Vs. Union of India case is related to compensation for mental anguish. The High Court has held that the term of the brochure to be unconscionable and arbitrary and hence violative of Article 14 of the Constitution. The High Court has directed the amount due and payable to be refunded with interest calculated at the rate of 12 per cent per annum from the date of deposit to the date of refund.

Jamal Vs. Moola Dawood case is related to measure of damages. The Privy Council observed that Section 73 is declaratory of the common law as to damages.

M/s. Ganga Maruthi Vs. Nagaraj case is related to compensation for breach of contract where penalty is stipulated for. It was held that it is a well settled principle of law if there are material documents which may throw light on the question involved and the documents are in possession of a party proceedings and that party in possession of such material does not produce the adverse presumption that has to be raised against that party.

33 Who is the propounder of 'Pigeon hole' theory?

1 Winfield
2 Salmond
3 Flemming
4 Paton

Ans. (2)

Exp. Salmond is the propounder of 'Pigeon hole' theory. According to Salmond, the law of torts may be described as a "a neat set of pigeon hole,each containing a specific labelled tort." Also he propounded that "just as the criminal law consists of a body of rules establishing specific offences, so the laws of torts consists of a body of rules establishing specific injuries."

34 The owner of the bus instructed the driver not to race and compete with other omnibuses on a particular route. Driver still tried to obstruct a rival omnibus and caused an accident. What shall be the nature of liability ?

1 The driver shall be liable for the accident because he did not follow the instructions of his owner
2 It shall be the liability of the owner of bus because he has no authority to give instruction to his driver and his act was totally wrong
3 The owner of the bus shall be vicariously liable for the accident committed by his driver during the course of employment
4 Neither owner nor driver shall be liable

Ans. (3)

Exp. In the given case, the owner of the bus shall be vicariously liable for the accident committed by his driver during the course of employment.

Vicarious liability is a situation in which one party is held partly responsible for the unlawful actions of a third party. The third party also carries his or her own share of the liability.

35 Which of the following is not a sovereign function of the State?

1 Construction of military road
2 Injury to the plaintiff during the lathi-charge by the police to disperse the unlawful crowd
3 A Government jeep being taken from the workshop to the collector's bungalow for his use
4 Distribution of meals to army personnel

Ans. (3)

Exp. A Government jeep being taken from the workshop to the collector's bungalow for his use is not an example of sovereign function of the state.

Sovereign function of the state can be defined as those functions where the state is not answerable before the court of law for their performance. These functions are mainly concerned about the defence of the country, maintenance of the armed forces of the country, and maintenance of peace in the territory.

36 Given below are two statements. One is labelled as Assertion (A) and the other is labelled as Reason (R).

Assertion (A) A wooden chair while being used by a guest, caused an injury to him due to defective manufacture. The guest is entitled to claim damages from the manufacturer.

Reason (R) The manufacturer owes a duty to take care only towards the lawful buyer under the Consumer Protection Act.

Codes

1 Both (A) and (R) are true and (R) is the correct explanation of (A)
2 Both (A) and (R) are true, but (R) is not the correct explanation of (A)
3 (A) is true, but (R) is false
4 (A) is false, but (R) is true

Ans. (3)

Exp. (A) is true, but (R) is false.

In the law of product's liability, a manufacturing defect is a defect in a product that was not intended. This kind of defect occurs when a product departs from its intended design and is more dangerous than consumers expect the product to be.

The term 'product liability' has been defined under the Consumer Protection Act, 2019 as the "responsibility of a product manufacturer or product seller, of any product or service to compensate for harm caused to a consumer by such defective product manufactured or sold by or by deficiency in services relating thereto". Therefore, here, in this case, the manufacturer is liable for the injury caused to the consumer due to the manufacturing defect in the chair.

Reason (R) is false as according to Law of Torts, it is the sole responsibility and duty to take care while making any product, towards the ultimate user.

37 If a journalist publishes an article in a leading newspaper that all lawyers were thieves, no particular lawyer could sue him unless there is something to point to the particular individual. It refers to

1 Defamation of a company
2 Innuendo
3 Defamation of public figures
4 Defamation of class of persons

Ans. (4)

Exp. The given scenario talks about the defamation of a class of persons.

Defamation is the act of making untrue statements about another which damages his/her reputation. If the defamatory statement is printed or broadcasted over the media it is libel and, if only oral, it is slander. When particular words spoken are referred to a group of individuals or a class of persons, then no single person of that group or class can sue unless he proves that the words could reasonably be considered to be referring to him. So, in this case, if the journalist had written that all lawyers of the Bar Council of XYZ were thieves, then the members of such a bar would have a cause of action against the journalist.

38 Match the List I (Name of Case) with List II (Name of Court) and select the correct answer by using the codes given below:

List I	List II
A. Municipal Corporation Vs. Subhagwanti	I. High Court of Madhya Pradesh
B. Roop Lal Vs. Union of India	II. High Court of Jammu and Kashmir
C. State Vs. Chironji Lal	III. High Court of Calcutta
D. Rural Transport Service Vs. Bezlum Bibi	IV. Supreme Court

Codes

	A	B	C	D		A	B	C	D
1	IV	II	I	III	2	II	I	IV	III
3	III	IV	II	I	4	IV	I	III	II

Ans. (1)

Exp. The correct matching is A-IV, B-II, C- I, D-III.

Municipal Corporation Vs Subhagwanti case was held in Supreme Court. The Supreme Court held that the principle of res ipsa loquitur applied to the case. The Supreme Court considered that it was the duty of the Municipal Committee to carry out a periodical examination for the purpose of determining whether deterioration had taken place in the structure and whether any precaution was necessary to strengthen the building.

Roop Lal Vs Union of India case was held in High Court of Jammu and Kashmir. It was held that the act of the jawans fell within the course of employment and the Union of India was liable for the same.

State Vs Chironji Lal case was held in High Court of Madhya Pradesh. The Court held that "Where the driver of a jeep, owned and maintained by the State of Rajasthan for the official use of the Collector of a district, drove it rashly and negligently, while bringing it back from the workshop after repairs and knocked down a pedestrian and fatally injured him."

Rural Transport Service Vs Bezlum Bibi case was held in High Court of Calcutta. In this case, the conductor allowed the people to travel on the roof of the bus. During the journey, one of the passengers got hit by a branch of a tree and as a result, fell from the bus and got injured. The court mentioned that the conductor was liable as : firstly, the act of allowing people to travel on the top of the bus was rash and negligent. He should have stopped people from traveling on the roof. Inviting them to travel on the roof of an overloaded bus proved his negligence.

Secondly, the person who consented to travel on the top of the bus contributed to the accident. Hence, it was contributory negligence. The consequences of an act were foreseeable.

39 The Revenue Inspector knowingly disobeys the direction to conduct enquiry at a place for demarcation, what offence, if any, has been caused by him under IPC ?

1 An offence as per Section 166-A
2 For continuing to remain in an unlawful assembly as per Section 145
3 For touching any point material as per Section 199
4 For giving false information as per Section 201

Ans. (1)

Exp. In the given scenario, the revenue inspector has committed an offence as per Section 166-A.

Section 166-A of the Indian Penal Code states that whoever, being a public servant knowingly disobeys any direction of the law which prohibits him from requiring the attendance at any place of any person for the purpose of investigation into an offence or any other, or knowingly disobeys, to the prejudice of any person, any other direction of the law regulating the manner in which he shall conduct such investigation, or fails to record any information given to him under sub-section (1) of Section 154 of the Code of Criminal Procedure, 1973, shall be punished with rigorous imprisonment for a term which shall not be less than six months but which may extend to two years, and shall also be liable to fine.

40 A man has committed physical contact involving unwelcome sexual overture against a female. What offence has been caused by him under IPC?

1 Requesting for sexual favour as per Section 354-A (1)(ii)
2 Sexual harassment as per Section 354(1)(i)
3 Out-raging of modesty as per Section 354
4 Attempt to rape as per Section 370(A)

Ans. (2)

Exp. In this case, the man has committed sexual harassment as per Section 354(1)(i).

According to Section 354A of Indian Penal Code as follows:

1. A man committing any of the following acts:
   (i) physical contact and advances involving unwelcome and explicit sexual overtures; or
   (ii) a demand or request for sexual favours; or
   (iii) showing pornography against the will of a woman; or
   (iv) making sexually coloured remarks, shall be guilty of the offence of sexual harassment.
2. Any man who commits the offence specified in clause (i) or clause (ii) or clause (iii) of sub-section (1) shall be punished with rigorous imprisonment for a term which may extend to three years, or with fine, or with both.
3. Any man who commits the offence specified in clause (iv) of sub-section (1) shall be punished with imprisonment of either description for a term which may extend to one year, or with fine, or with both.

41 Read the Assertion (A) and the Reason (R) given below to answer the correct explanation using the codes given below.

Assertion (A) The legal right involves freedom from penalty.

Reason (R) A legal right is one which is either enforceable or recognised.

Codes

1 Both (A) and (R) are true, but (R) is not the correct explanation of (A)
2 Both (A) and (R) are true and (R) is the correct explanation of (A)
3 Assertion (A) is correct, but Reason (R) is false.
4 Assertion (A) is incorrect because Reason (R) fixes liability when not enforceable or derecognised

Ans. (2)

Exp. Both (A) and (R) are true and (R) is the correct explanation of (A).

Assertion is true because a legal right is an interest accepted and protected by law and it is free of penalty. According to Salmond, A legal right is an "interest which is protected and recognized by the rule of law. It is an interest which has its duty and disregard of which is wrong".

Reason is true as in legal terms a right is an interest recognised and protected by the State and enforceable through the court of law. A right is enforceable only to the extent it is protected by the state.

42 The maxim 'ream linguam non facit nisi mens rea' is propounded by

1 Coke 2 Lord Kenyon
3 Augustine 4 Lord Arbinger

Ans. (3)

Exp. The maxim 'ream linguam non facit nisi mens rea' is propounded by Augustine.

Actus non facit reum nisi mens sit rea is an old maxim. The origin of the maxim was traced by Justice Coke from the sermons of Augustin as 'ream linguam non facit nisi mens rea'. 'Mens rea' means guilty mind, without which there cannot be committed any crime.

43 Fill in the gap.
Disobedience of law is not ordinarily a crime unless that act is declared as crime by some ——— .

1 law 2 method
3 society 4 All of these

Ans. (1)

Exp. Disobedience of law is not ordinarily a crime unless that act is declared as a crime by some law.

Under Section 40 of the Indian Penal Code, the word 'offence' has been extensively defined. It says that "Except in the Chapters and sections mentioned in clauses 2 and 3 of this section, the word 'offence' denotes a thing made punishable by this Code".

44 The Indian Penal Code prohibits fixing of liability on a person so long he is authorised or gives assent to it. But there is an exceptional situation arising out of

1 Libel 2 Public nuisance
3 Contempt of Court 4 All of these

Ans. (4)

Exp. The Indian Penal Code prohibits fixing of liability on a person so long he is authorised or gives assent to it. But there is an exceptional situation arising out of Libel, Public nuisance, Contempt of Court.

Section 499 of IPC states that "whoever, by words either spoken or intended to be read, or by signs or by visible representations, makes or publishes any imputation concerning any person intending to harm, or knowing or having reason to believe that such imputation will harm, the reputation of such person, is said, except in the cases hereinafter expected, to defame that person."

45 Who among the following moved a resolution in the Central Legislative Assembly recommending that the Government should introduce a legislation for registration and protection of Trade Union in the year 1921 ?

1 BP Wadia 2 MN Joshi
3 NM Lokhanddey 4 VV Giri

Ans. (2)

Exp. MN Joshi moved a resolution in the Central Legislative Assembly recommending that the Government should introduce a legislation for registration and protection of Trade Union in the year 1921.

After some cases in various High Courts in India, it was felt that some legislation for the protection of trade unions was necessary. In March, 1921, Shri N. M. Joshi, then General Secretary of the All India Trade Union Congress, successfully moved a resolution in the Central Legislative Assembly recommending that the Government should introduce legislation for the registration and protection of trade unions. Opposition from employers to the adoption of such a measure was, however, so great that it was not until 1926 that the Indian Trade Unions Act, was passed.

46 "Works Committee under the Industrial Disputes Act should be substituted by an 'Industrial Relations Committee' to promote in-house dispute settlement." This recommendation was made by

1 Royal Commission on Labour
2 National Commission on Labour 1969
3 National Commission on Labour 2002
4 National Commission for enterprises in the Unorganised Sector

Ans. (3)

Exp. The mentioned recommendation was made by the National Commission on Labour 2002.

The National Commission on Labour, 2002, in Chapter XI of its recommendations, submitted that, "The Works Committee to be constituted under Section 3 of the Industrial Disputes Act (IDA) should be substituted by an 'Industrial Relations Committee' to promote in-house dispute settlement and resolve all the differences at the unit level as far as practicable."

47 Who is a protected workman under the Industrial Disputes Act ? Answer from the codes given below

I. A workman who is a member of a registered Trade Union.
II. Recognised by the Registrar of the Trade Union as protected workman.
III. A workman who is a member of the Executive or other office bearer of a registered Trade Union connected with the establishment.
IV. Recognised as protected workman under the rules applicable to the establishment.

Codes

1 I and II	2 II and IV
3 III and IV	4 I and III

Ans. *(3)*

Exp. Statement III and IV are correct.

According to the explanation of Section 33(3) of Industrial Disputes Act, 1947, a "protected workman", in relation to an establishment and means a workman who, being a member of the executive or other office bearer of a registered trade union connected with the establishment, is recognised as such in accordance with rules made in this behalf."

48 Failure of the conciliation proceedings under the Industrial Disputes Act leads to refer the matter to adjudication by

1 the conciliation officer
2 both employer and employee
3 the employer
4 the appropriate government

Ans. *(4)*

Exp. Failure of the conciliation proceedings under the Industrial Disputes Act leads to refer the matter to adjudication by the appropriate government.

Section 4 of Industrial Disputes Act, 1947 empowers the appropriate government to appoint such number of persons as may be deemed necessary by notification in the official gazette as conciliation officers, for discharging the responsibility of mediating in and promoting the settlement of industrial disputes.

49 The power of the Government to refer a Dispute under the Industrial Disputes Act is

1 Mandatory
2 Discretionary
3 Recommendatory
4 Either mandatory or discretionary

Ans. *(2)*

Exp. The power of the Government to refer a Dispute under the Industrial Disputes Act is discretionary.

Under Section 10 of the Industrial Disputes Act, where the appropriate Government is of opinion that any industrial dispute exists or is apprehended, it may at any time, by order in writing as

- refer the dispute to a Board for promoting a settlement thereof; or
- refer any matter appearing to be connected with or relevant to the dispute to a Court for inquiry; or
- refer the dispute, if it relates to any matter specified in the Second Schedule, to a Labour Court for adjudication; or
- refer the dispute, whether it relates to any matter specified, in the Second Schedule or the Third Schedule, to a Tribunal for adjudication.

50 Read the Assertion (A) and Reason (R) and select the correct answer using the codes given below.

Assertion (A) The conciliation officer has no power under the Industrial Disputes Act when neither industrial disputes exists or apprehended.

Reason (R) Conciliation officer only investigates the Industrial disputes which exists or apprehended.

Codes

1 Both (A) and (R) are false
2 Both (A) and (R) are true
3 (A) is true and (R) is false
4 (A) is false and (R) is true

Ans. *(2)*

Exp. Both (A) and (R) are true.

The conciliation officer has no power under the Industrial Disputes Act when neither industrial disputes exists or apprehended. If no dispute exists or apprehended there is no requirement of a conciliation officer. Section 12 of the Industrial Disputes Act, 1947 talks about the duties of a conciliation officer. It says that where any industrial dispute exists or is apprehended, the conciliation officer may, or where the dispute relates to a public utility service and a notice under Section 22 has been given, shall hold conciliation proceedings in the prescribed manner.

A conciliation officer can only function if any dispute exists or apprehended. Section 12 states that the conciliation officer shall, for the purpose of bringing about a settlement of the dispute, without delay, investigate the dispute and all matters affecting the merits and the right settlement thereof and may do all such things as he thinks fit for the purpose of inducing the parties to come to a fair and amicable settlement of the dispute. He shall also, whether a settlement is arrived at or not, submit a report to the appropriate government within 14 days of the end of proceedings and the appropriate government can then refer the dispute to adjudication.

PAPER III

1 Read Assertion (A) and Reason(R) and select the answer using the codes given below.

Assertion (A) The writ of Habeas Corpus can be granted to enable the detainee to argue his case in person.

Reason (R) Because R Vs. Secretary of State for Home Department ex parte Wynne (1992) decided so.

Codes

1 (A) and (R) are right and (R) is right reason for (A)
2 (A) is right, but (R) is wrong
3 (A) is wrong, but (R) is right
4 Both (A) and (R) are wrong

Ans. (4)

Exp. Both (A) and (R) are wrong

'Habeas Corpus' literally means "to have a body of". This writ is used to release a person who has been unlawfully detained or imprisoned. By virtue of this writ, the Court directs the person so detained to be brought before it to examine the legality of his detention.

In the mentioned case it was held that, a Legislature could so provide even though it interfered with the right of access to the courts. Courts should be very reluctant to take cases which appeared to be merely hypothetical.

2 Which of the following are matched incorrectly?

I. Habeas Corpus – 'To produce the body'
II. Quo warranto – 'Issued to a lower court to stop proceedings in a case'.
III. Prohibition – 'Issued to a lower court quashing a decision or order'
IV. Mandamus – 'Commands a person to perform a public duty'.

Codes

1 I, II and III 2 II and III
3 II, III and IV 4 II and IV

Ans. (2)

Exp. II and III are incorrectly matched.

Quo warrant to means 'by what warrant'. Through this writ, the court calls upon a person holding a public office to show under what authority he holds that office.

Prohibition is a writ issued by a superior court to lower court or a tribunal forbidding it to perform an act outside its jurisdiction.

3 Article 51 A of the Constitution of India is confined to

1 All citizens of India
2 All persons of India
3 All Non-Residents of India
4 All students of India

Ans. (1)

Exp. Article 51 A of the Constitution of India is confined to all citizens of India.

Fundamental duties are defined under Article 51A of the Constitution. The Fundamental Duties are dealt with Article 51A under Part-IV A of the Indian Constitution. The fundamental duties were added by the 42nd Amendment Act of the Constitution in 1976.

4 Read Assertion (A) and Reason (R) and select the correct answer by using codes given below.

Assertion (A) Code of conduct has statutory force.

Reason (R) Because Article 102 of the Constitution says so.

Codes

1 (A) and (R) are true and (R) is correct explanation for (A)
2 Both (A) and (R) are false
3 (A) is true, but (R) is false
4 (R) is true, but (A) is false

Ans. (2)

Exp. Both (A) and (R) are false.

Assertion is false because every code of conduct doesn't have statutory force. A code of conduct is a set of rules outlining an individual party or an organisation's norms, rules and responsibilities or proper practices. However, it is specific to any organisation and does not have a statutory force.

Reason is false because Article 102 says that a person shall be disqualified for being chosen as, and for being, a member of either House of Parliament if he holds any office of profit under the Government of India or the Government of any State, other than an office declared by Parliament by law not to disqualify its holder; if he is of unsound mind and stands so declared by a competent court, if he is an undischarged insolvent; if he is not a citizen of India, or has voluntarily acquired the citizenship of a foreign State, or is under any acknowledgment of allegiance or adherence to a foreign State; if he is so disqualified by or under any law made by Parliament.

5 Read Assertion (A) and Reason (R) to answer using codes given below.

Assertion (A) One of the two Acts enacted under List I Entry 66 and the other under List III Entry 25 can be repugnant to each other.

Reason (R) Because in Annamalai University Vs. Secretary of Information and Tourism Department decided so.

Codes
1 (A) and (R) are true and (R) is correct explanaction for (A).
2 (A) is true, but (R) is false
3 (A) is false, but (R) is true
4 Both (A) and (R) are false

Ans. *(4)*

Exp. Both (A) and (R) are false.

Assertion is false because List I Entry 65 provides for Union agencies and institutions. List II Entry 25 provides for Gas and gas-works. Thus, they cannot be repugnant to each other.

Reason is false because Decision of the Court in Annamalai University had examined the interplay between the provisions of the UGC Act and Indira Gandhi National Open University Act, 1985 (for short, referred to as Open University Act) and the purported repugnance between the two.

6 If the Government is defeated on the floor of Rajya Sabha, what is the consequence ?
1 Parliament is dissolved
2 Prime Minister has to submit his resignation
3 President's rule is imposed immediately
4 Nothing happens

Ans. *(4)*

Exp. If the government is defeated on the floor of Rajya Sabha then nothing happens.

The Rajya Sabha or Council of States is the upper house of the bicameral Parliament of India. The potential seating capacity of the Rajya Sabha is 250 (238 elected, 12 appointed), according to Article 80 of the Indian Constitution.

7 Read Assertion (A) and Reason (R) and select the answer by using the codes given below.

Assertion (A) The power under 368 of the Constitution is a constituent power subject to the constitutional scheme as to distribution of legislative power according to entries in the Seventh Schedule.

Reason (R) Because Sasanka Sekhar Maity Vs. Union of India decided so.

Codes
1 Both (A) and (R) are false
2 Both (A) and (R) are true, but (R) is not correct explanation for (A)
3 (A) is true and (R) is false
4 (A) is false and (R) is true

Ans. *(1)*

Exp. Both (A) and (R) are false.

Assertion is false because Article 368 with its marginal note "Procedure for amendment of the Constitution" dealt only with the procedure for amendment. Amendment was a legislative process and the power of Parliament to make amendments was contained in Article 248 and Entry 97 in List I of the Seventh Schedule (the Union List) which confer residuary legislative powers on the Union Parliament.

Reason is false because in the case of Sasanka Sekhar Maity Vs. UOI it was said that the power under 368 of the Constitution is a constituent power subject to the constitutional scheme as to distribution of legislative power according to entries in the Seventh Schedule.

8 Using codes given below, find out correct answers.

Administrative Law deals with
I. the powers of constitutional authorities
II. the powers of judicial authorities
III. the powers of the administrative authorities
IV. the powers of the legislative authorities

Codes
1 I and II are correct
2 II is correct
3 III is correct
4 All of these

Ans. *(3)*

Exp. Administrative law deals with the power of administrative authorities.

Administrative law is the division of law that governs the activities of administrative agencies of government. Government agency action can include rule making, adjudication, or the enforcement of a specific regulatory agenda. Administrative law is considered a branch of public law. It does not deal with the constitutional, judicial or legislative authority.

9 Match List I with List II using are correct codes given below.

	List I		List II
A.	There is no rigid formula for principles of natural justice.	I.	RS Dass Vs. Union of India
B.	Choice of application of rules of natural justice.	II.	R Vs. Sussex Justices
C.	Justice should not only be done, but manifestly and undoubtedly be seen to be done.	III.	Union of India Vs. PK Roy
D.	Meaning of bias	IV.	Secretary to Govt. Transport Dept. Vs. Munuswamy

Codes

	A	B	C	D
1	I	II	III	IV
2	III	I	IV	II
3	I	III	II	IV
4	III	I	II	IV

Ans. *(4)*

Exp. The correct matching is A-III, B-I, C-II, D-IV.

In *Union of India Vs. P.K.Roy* case it was mentioned that there is no rigid formula for principles of natural justice. It was observed that "Till very recently it was the opinion of the courts that unless the authority concerned was required by the law under which it functioned to act judicially, there was no room for the application of the rules of natural justice. The validity of that limitation is now questioned. If the purpose of the rules of natural justice is to prevent miscarriage of justice, one fails to see why those rules should be made inapplicable to administrative enquiries."

In *RS Dass Vs Union of India* case is related to choice of application of rules of natural justice. It was held that in the absence of a statutory provision an Administrative Authority is under no legal obligation to record reasons in support of its decision. There is no scope for applying principles of natural justice in matters relating to selection of suitable members of State Service for promotion to a higher service.

In R Vs. Sussex Justices it was mentioned that Justice should not only be done, but manifestly and undoubtedly be seen to be done. The principle of natural justice originated in the case of R Vs. Sussex Justices ('Sussex Justices'). In this case, Mr. McCarthy was riding a motorcycle that collided with another motorcycle driven by Mr. Whitworth. In the sidecar, Mr. Whitworth's wife was accompanying him. The couple suffered injuries. In this regard, criminal action was instituted against McCarthy. Further, Whitworth engaged a firm of solicitors namely M/s. Langham, Son and Douglas to claim civil damages from McCarthy.

Secretary to Govt. Transport Dept. Vs. Munuswamy was related to meaning of bias.

10 Read Assertion (A) and Reason (R) and find out correct answer using codes given below.

Assertion (A) Legitimate expectation does not grant an absolute right to a claimant.

Reason (R) Legitimate expectation protects the right of fair hearing before a decision which results in negating a promise or withdrawing an undertaking is taken.

Codes

1 (A) and (R) are true and (R) is correct explanation of (A)
2 (A) and (R) are true, but (R) is not correct explanation of (A)
3 (A) is true and (R) is false
4 (A) is false and (R) is true

***Ans.* (1)**

Exp. (A) and (R) are true and (R) is the correct explanation of (A).

Legitimate Expectation means that a person may have a reasonable expectation of being treated in a certain way by administrative authorities owing to some consistent practice in the past or an express promise made by the concerned authority.

Legitimate expectation gives the applicant sufficient locus standi, for judicial review. This doctrine is to be confined mostly to the right of a fair hearing before a decision, which results in negating a promise or withdrawing an undertaking, is taken.

11 Which of the following statements is correct ?

1 Gullappalli Nageswara Rao Vs. State of AP, is about bias
2 KL Tripathi Vs. State Bank of India, is about right of cross examination
3 General Medical Council Vs. Spaekmen, is about irrelevance of principles of natural justice if in reaching a decision, the principles make no difference
4 N Kalindi Vs. Tata Locomotives, is about the right of representation by a lawyer being considered to be a part of natural justice and it can be claimed as of right

***Ans.* (2)**

Exp. KL Tripathi Vs State Bank of India, is about the right of cross examination. In this case, the Investigating officer held that the appellant had committed certain irregularities wilfully, violated the established practices and defied the Bank's instructions. On the basis of the report of the Investigating officer the appellant was served with a charge-sheet.

According to Section 137 of the Indian Evidence Act, the examination of a witness by the adverse party shall be called his cross-examination.

12 Which one of the following is the correct statement?

1 While certiorari can be issued against judicial or quasi-judicial authorities, mandamus can be issued against administrative authorities also
2 Mandamus can be issued for a declaration that an Act is ultra vires the Constitution and certiorari can also be issued for correcting that defect
3 Certiorari can be issued against a quasi-judicial authority to prevent it from exercising jurisdiction not vested in it. Mandamus cannot be issued for that purpose
4 Certiorari cannot be issued against usurping a public officer, but Mandamus can be issued for that purpose

***Ans.* (1)**

Exp. Statement 1 is correct as while certiorari can be issued against judicial or quasi-judicial authorities, mandamus can be issued against administrative authorities also.

The writ of certiorari can be issued by the Supreme Court or any High Court for quashing the order already passed by an inferior court, tribunal or quasi-judicial authority.

Mandamus is a writ issued as a command to an inferior court or ordering a person to perform a public or statutory duty.

13 Abuse of discretion can be inferred from the following circumstances. Find out the answer from the codes given below

I. Non-application of mind.
II. Colourable exercise of power.
III. Non-observance of audi alteram partem.
IV. Irrelevant considerations.

Codes

1 Only I is correct 2 I and II are correct
3 II and III are correct 4 II, III and IV are correct

Ans. (4)

Exp. Abuse of discretion can be inferred from the Colourable exercise of power, Non-observance of audi alteram partem and Irrelevant considerations.

When discretionary power is conferred on an administrative authority, it must be exercised according to law. When the mode of exercising a valid power is improper or unreasonable there is an abuse of the power.

14 What was the principle laid down by the Supreme Court in A K Kraipak Vs. Union of India ?

1 Rule of law is embedded in Article 14 of the Constitution of India
2 Judicial review is a part of basic structure of the Constitution
3 Principles of natural justice are applicable to administrative proceedings
4 Post-decisional hearing would be sufficient for the observance of principles of natural justice

Ans. (3)

Exp. In A K Kraipak Vs Union of India, Supreme Court laid down that principles of natural justice are applicable to administrative proceedings.

Principles of natural justice are those rules which have been laid down by courts as being the minimum protection of the rights of the individual against the arbitrary procedure that may be adopted by a Judicial, Quasi-Judicial and Administrative authority while making an order affecting those rights. These rules are intended to prevent such authority from doing injustice.

15 Find correct answer from the following statements:

1 A quasi-judicial body may never review its own decision unless authorised by the statute
2 A quasi-judicial body may review its own decision if there is grave error of law in it
3 A quasi-judicial body may review its own decision if there is violation of natural justice
4 All tribunals may review their decisions

Ans. (1)

Exp. A quasi-judicial body may never review its own decision unless authorised by the statute is correct.

Quasi-judicial authority has no jurisdiction to review its earlier order. Tribunals have been constituted to lessen the work load accumulated before the High Courts and Supreme Court. If any person aggrieved against the order of a quasi-judicial authority he is to file against the order to the appellate authority.

16 Select the correct answer using the codes given below on the following decided cases about possession.

I. Cartwright Vs. Green
II. R Vs. Hudson
III. Daimler Co. Vs. Continental Tyre and Rubber Co.

Codes

1 Only III 2 II and III
3 I and III 4 I and II

Ans. (4)

Exp. Cartwright Vs. Green and R Vs. Hudson case are related to possession.

In Cartwright Vs Green case a bureau was delivered to the carpenter, and there was money in the secret drawer of the bureau. Carpenter appropriated the money. It was held by the court that animus was lacking in the carpenter therefore money was not in his possession until he found it therefore he was held guilty. Court followed the same principle in Merry Vs. Green (1843).

In R. Vs. Hudson case, Hudson who had a previous record of drug related offences was found not guilty of cultivation but received three years for possession for the purpose of trafficking.

17 Austin described ownership as a right over determinate thing with reference to one of the following. Specify the correct answer.

1 Restricted in point of disposition
2 Indefinite in point of user
3 Unlimited in point of duration
4 Unlimited in point of space

Ans. (2)

Exp. Austin described ownership as a right over determinate thing with reference to indefinite in point of user.

According to Austin, ownership refers to "a right indefinite in point of user, unrestricted in point of disposition and unlimited in point of duration." According to him, ownership is an aggregate of all rights pertaining to the possession, enjoyment and disposition of an object.

18 Consider the following statements regarding vested and contingent rights.

I. A vested right creates an immediate interest and is transferable and heritable.
II. A contingent right creates an immediate interest and is defeated when the required facts have not occurred.

Which of the Statement given above is/are correct ?

1 Only I 2 Only II
3 Both I and II 4 Neither I nor II

Ans. (1)

Exp. Only statement I is correct.

A vested right creates an immediate interest and is transferable and heritable. Vested interest is a transferable and heritable right. It creates a present right that is in effect immediately, although the enjoyment is postponed to the time prescribed in the transfer. It does not entirely depend on the condition as the condition involves a certain event.

Statement II is incorrect because though, contingent interest is a transferable right, whether it is heritable or not, depends upon the nature of such transfer and the condition. It is an interest which is created in favour of a person on a condition of the happening of a specified uncertain event. The person having the contingent interest does not get the possession of that property but has the expectancy to receive it upon happening of that event but will not receive the property if the event does not happen as the condition is not fulfilled.

19 There is a clear cut division between the spheres of legislature and judiciary. The former makes the laws and the latter applies them. Which of the school propounds this doctrine ?

1 Analytical jurisprudence
2 Historical jurisprudence
3 Sociological jurisprudence
4 Philosophical jurisprudence

Ans. *(2)*

Exp. According to the Historical School of Jurisprudence, there is a clear cut division between the spheres of the legislature and the Judiciary. The former makes the laws and the later applies them.

The Historical School of Jurisprudence describes the origin of law. This school argues that the law was found not made. The main source of law is Kings Judgment, Customs and habits. Jurists like Montesquieu, Savigny, Sir Henry Maine, and Georg Friedrich Puchta are supporters of the Historical School of Jurisprudence.

20 In which one of the following cases was it observed by the Supreme Court that precedent should not be petrified nor judicial dicta divorced from the socio-economic mores of the age ?

1 Mamleshwar Vs. Kanahaiya Lal
2 Bengal Immunity Company Ltd. Vs. State of Bihar
3 State of West Bengal Vs. Corporation of Calcutta
4 KC Dora Vs. G Annamanaidu

Ans. *(2)*

Exp. In case of Bengal Immunity Company Ltd. Vs. State of Bihar, the Supreme Court held that precedent should not be petrified nor judicial dicta divorced from the socio-economic mores of the age.

21 Who among the following divided the Sources of Law into Formal sources and Material sources?

1 Gray 2 Keaton 3 Allen 4 Salmond

Ans. *(4)*

Exp. Salmond divided the Sources of Law into Formal sources and Material sources.

Formal sources are those from which law derives its validity and force, that is, the will of the State which is expressed through statutes and judicial decisions.

The Material sources of law are those from which is derived the matter, though not the validity of the law. The matter of law may be drawn from all classes of material sources.

22 According to Professor Goodhart a ratio decidendi of a case is

1 the principle of law laid down in a decision which is the decisive element
2 the conclusion reached by the judge on the basis of the material facts of the case
3 the reason given by the court for its decision
4 any opinion of the court on a question of law

Ans. *(2)*

Exp. According to Professor Goodhart a ratio decidendi of a case is the conclusion reached by the judge on the basis of the material facts of the case.

Ratio decidendi is a Latin phrase meaning "the reason" or "the rationale for the decision". It is a legal phrase which refers to the legal, moral, political and social principles used by a court to compose the rationale of a particular judgment.

23 Read Assertion (A) and Reason (R) and with the help of codes given below find the correct explanation.

Assertion (A) Nullum Crimen is an injunction to the legislature not to implicate all the suspected persons to be prosecuted.

Reason (R) To avoid impossibility and to settle the question, the legislature must have to use administrative ruling.

Codes

1 Both (A) and (R) are true and (R) is correct explanation of (A)
2 Both (A) and (R) are true, but (R) is not correct explanation of (A)
3 (A) is true, but (R) is false
4 (A) is false, but (R) is true

Ans. *(1)*

Exp. Both (A) and (R) are true and (R) is the correct explanation of (A).

Nullum crimen sine lege is Latin for "no crime without law." Nullum Crimen is an injunction to the legislature not to implicate all the suspected persons to be prosecuted.

These principles developed during the enlightenment period as protection against arbitrary acts and extraordinary penalties and state that "substantive crimes (nullum crimen) and punishments (nulla poena) must be enacted before the commission of an offence." To avoid impossibility and to settle the question, the legislature must have to use administrative ruling.

24 Read Assertion (A) and Reason (R) and with the help of codes given below find the correct explanation.

Assertion (A) Participation in some manner in the act constituting the offence of common intention by all the persons to be prosecuted is necessary.

Reason (R) Physical presence at the time of commission of crimes is not mandatory in all cases.

Codes

1 Both (A) and (R) are true, but (R) is not the correct explanation of (A)
2 Both (A) and (R) are true and (R) is the correct explanation of (A)
3 (A) is true, but (R) is false
4 (A) is false, but (R) is true

Ans. (2)

Exp. Both (A) and (R) are true and (R) is the correct explanation of (A).

Assertion is true because according to Section 34, when a criminal act is done by several persons in furtherance of common intention of all, each of such persons is liable for that act in the same manner as if it were done by him alone.

Reason is true because physical presence is not necessary to book the person under crime, even if the person facilitates the act in any way, it will amount to crime.

25 Which of the mitigating factors do not justify the award of death penalty ?

1 Where the murder has been previously planned
2 Such murder involves exceptional depravity
3 When such murder was against a public servant while on duty
4 When the offence was committed by the accused under the influence of extreme mental disturbance

Ans. (4)

Exp. When the offence was committed by the accused under the influence of extreme mental disturbance, it will act as a mitigating factor that do not justify the award of death penalty.

In India, death penalty is awarded in rarest of the rare case. Pre-planned, brutal, cold-blooded and sordid nature of a crime, without giving any chance to the victim, are generally taken into account to decide whether a particular case falls within the parameters of "rarest of rare".

26 Read Assertion (A) and Reason (R) and with the help of codes given below find the correct explanation.

Assertion (A) The gist of conspiracy lies in forming the scheme between two or more persons to perform the overt act.

Reason (R) The alleged agreement must provide circumstantial evidence about the participation by all to establish conspiracy.

Codes

1 Both (A) and (R) are true and (R) is the correct explanation of (A)
2 Both (A) and (R) are true, but (R) is not the correct explanation of (A)
3 (A) is correct, but (R) is false
4 (A) is false, but (R) is true

Ans. (1)

Exp. Both (A) and (R) are true and (R) is the correct explanation of (A).

The gist of conspiracy lies in forming the scheme between two or more persons to perform the overt act. Section 120A talks about conspiracy that says two or more people are involved in an offence of conspiracy to perform an overt act. According to Section 120A, when two or more persons agree to do, or cause to be done- an illegal act, or an act which is not illegal by illegal means, such an agreement is designated a criminal conspiracy: Provided that no agreement except an agreement to commit an offence shall amount to a criminal conspiracy unless some act besides the agreement is done by one or more parties to such agreement in pursuance there of.

Reason is true because when it is proved that two or more people are involved in performing an act it is a conspiracy. The alleged agreement must provide circumstantial evidence about the participation by all to establish conspiracy.

27 Which of these facts do not constitute the degree of knowledge for holding a person to be criminally liable for adducing false evidence ?

1 A statement known to be false
2 A statement believed to be false
3 A statement not believed to be true
4 An offence committed but not affirmed

Ans. (4)

Exp. The fact that "an offence committed but not affirmed" do not constitute the degree of knowledge for holding a person to be criminally liable for adducing false evidence.

28 What offence, if any, has been caused by the accused 'X' in the following facts?
'X' had some verbal wrangle with his wife 'Y' and incourse of that he gave her a blow with great force and after an interval for two hours 'Y' died. Medical evidence provided the causative factor as rapture in the spleen.

1 Culpable homicide not amounting to murder
2 Grievous hurt
3 Homicide
4 Simple hurt

Ans. (2)

Exp. In the following facts, grievous hurt is caused by 'X'. Section 320 if IPC, talks about grievous hurt. The following kinds of hurt only are designated as "grievous":

(i) Emasculation.
(ii) Permanent privation of the sight of either eye.
(iii) Permanent privation of the hearing of either ear,
(iv) Privation of any member or joint.

(v) Destruction or permanent impairing of the powers of any member or joint.
(vi) Permanent disfiguration of the head or face.
(vii) Fracture or dislocation of a bone or tooth.
(viii) Any hurt which endangers life or which causes the sufferer to be during the space of twenty days in severe bodily pain, or unable to follow his ordinary pursuits.

29 Which of the following properties could not be held to be an offence of theft, when committed/taken by a person ?

1 Durga Idol
2 Cooking Gas
3 Running Electricity
4 Forgotten Umbrella

Ans. *(3)*

➲ *Exp.* Running electricity is not taken as an offence of theft when committed/taken by a person.

Section 378 of the IPC defines theft as, "whoever, intending to take dishonestly any movable property out of the possession of any person without that person's consent, moves that property to such taking, is said to commit theft".

30 Read Assertion (A) and Reason (R) and select the correct answer by using the codes given below.

Assertion (A) In criminal breach of trust, there is conversion of property held by a person in a fiduciary capacity.

Reason (R) A person has a right to convert property held by him in a fiduciary capacity.

Codes

1 Both (A) and (R) are true and (R) is correct explanation for (A)
2 (A) is true, but (R) is false
3 (A) is false, but (R) is true
4 Both (A) and (R) are false

Ans. *(2)*

➲ *Exp.* (A) is true, but (R) is false.

In criminal breach of trust, there is an entrustment of property and the property entrusted is converted by a person in fiduciary capacity. According to Section 405 of IPC, whoever, being in any manner entrusted with property, or with any dominion over property, dishonestly misappropriates or converts to his own use that property, or dishonestly uses or disposes of that property in violation of any direction of law prescribing the mode in which such trust is to be discharged, or of any legal contract, express or implied, which he has made touching the discharge of such trust, or wilfully suffers any other person so to do, commits "criminal breach of trust"

Reason is false because a person doesn't have the right to convert the property to someone who is in fiduciary capacity.

31 The main objective of the Air (Prevention and Control of Pollution) Act is

1 To provide for the prevention, control and abatement of air pollution
2 To provide for ensuring standards for emission from automobiles
3 To put restrictions on the establishment of certain industrial plants
4 To establish air laboratory for air quality standards

Ans. *(1)*

➲ *Exp.* The main objective of the Air (Prevention and Control of Pollution) Act is to provide for the prevention, control and abatement of air pollution.

The Indian government enacted specific laws under Article 253 of the Constitution for the preservation of natural resources and the law enacted for air preservation was the Air (Prevention and Control of Air Pollution) Act, 1981. The objectives of the Act is to provide for the prevention, control and abatement of air pollution, for the establishment, with a view to carrying out the aforesaid purposes, of Boards, for conferring on and assigning to such Boards powers and functions relating thereto and for matters connected therewith.

32 The definition of 'environmental pollution' under the Environment (Protection Act) is

1 Any pollution of air, water and soil
2 The presence of any solid, liquid or gaseous substance in the environment that causes injuries to man
3 The presence in the environment of any environmental pollutant
4 Any pollution in land, sea and air

Ans. *(3)*

➲ *Exp.* The definition of 'environmental pollution' under the Environment (Protection Act) is the presence in the environment of any environmental pollutant.

Section 2(b) of the Environment Pollution Act (EPA) says "environmental pollutant" means any solid, liquid or gaseous substance present in such concentration as may be, or tend to be, injurious to environment.

33 Given below are two statements. One is labelled as Assertion (A) and the other is labelled as Reason (R).

Assertion (A) A company was unlawfully polluting streams and rivers by discharging trade effluents which raised pollution level beyond permissible limits.

Reason (R) The court decided that the company could not be held liable under Water Act, 1974.

Codes

1 Both (A) and (R) are true and (R)is the correct explanation of (A)
2 Both (A) and (R) are true, but (R) is not the correct explanation of (A)
3 (A) is true, but (R) is false
4 (A) is false, but (R) is true

Ans. (3)

Exp. (A) is true, but (R) is false.

In the case of Criminal Appeal No.: 112/17 Vs Delhi Pollution Control on 21st November, 2017 Haryana Paneer Bhandar, a manufacturer of sweets and namkeen, was found to be discharging untreated trade effluents into the river.

A complaint was filed in June 2000 against the owner by the Delhi Pollution Control Committee (DPCC) under the relevant provisions of the Water (Prevention and Control of Pollution) Act, 1974 (the Water Act) after inspection of the site. Almost 17 years after the complaint was filed, the additional chief metropolitan magistrate convicted the owner for the offence of discharging untreated waste (pollutants) into the river, and operating without the necessary consent. He was sentenced to three years' imprisonment and fined Rs 2 lakh under the relevant provisions of the Water Act, 1974.

Reason is false because the company will be held liable under Water Act, 1974.

34 The National Environment Tribunal Act provides for compensation on the basis of no fault liability in the cases of

I. Death of any person

II. Injury to any person

III. Death and injury to workman

IV. Damage to any property

Codes

1 I and II are correct

2 II and III are correct

3 IV only is correct

4 I, II and IV are correct

Ans. (4)

Exp. The National Environment Tribunal Act provides for compensation on the basis of no fault liability in the cases of death of any person, injury to any person and damage to any property.

The Rule of Strict Liability also known as 'The Rule of No-Fault Liability' means that the individual might have the liability without being at fault. In the rule of no fault liability the defendant or the doer will be held liable irrespective of presence of any negligence from his part.

35 Arrange the following cases in the chronological order on the basis of the year in which they have been decided by the Supreme Court on Public Trust doctrine under Environment law. Use the code given below

I. MC Mehta Vs. Kamal Nath

II. MI Builders Pvt. Ltd. Vs. Radhey Shyam Sahu

III. Hinch Lal Tiwari Vs. Kamala Devi

IV. Intellectual Forum, Thirupathi Vs. State of Andhra Pradesh

Codes

1 IV, III, I, II   2 III, II, IV, I

3 III, I, IV, II   4 I, II, III, IV

Ans. (4)

Exp. The correct chronological order is I, II, III, IV.

MC Mehta Vs Kamal Nath (1996) was a landmark case in Indian environmental law. In the case, the Supreme Court of India held that the public trust doctrine applied in India.

In *MI Builders Pvt. Ltd. Vs Radhey Shyam Sahu* (1999) case it was held that there was no licence to create another kind of trust which the appellant has sought to create. It cannot be said therefore that there was an irrevocable licence which falls under Section 60(b) of the Act. Even such a licence is deemed to be revoked under Section 62(f) of that Act where the licence is granted for a specific purpose and the purpose is attained or abandoned or becomes impracticable. In the present case the purpose for which the licence was granted has either been abandoned or has become impracticable because of the action of the appellant.

In *Hinch Lal Tiwari Vs. Kamala Devi* (2001) case the Court held that 'the material resources of the community like forests, tanks, ponds, hillocks, mountains etc. are nature's bounty. They maintain delicate ecological balance. They need to be protected for a proper and healthy environment which enables people to enjoy a quality life which is the essence of the guaranteed right under Article 21 of the Constitution.

Land recorded as a pond must not be allowed to be allotted to anybody for construction of a house or any allied purpose. The Governments, including the Revenue Authorities having noticed that a pond is falling in disuse, should have bestowed their attention to developing the same which would, on one hand, have prevented ecological disaster and on the other provided better environment for the benefit of the public at large. For the afore-mentioned reasons, the order of the High Court is set aside, and the order of the Additional Collector dated 25th February, 1999 confirmed by the Commissioner on 12th March, 1999 restored. Consequently, respondents shall vacate the land, which was allotted to them, and the State shall restore the pond, develop and maintain the same as a recreational spot which will undoubtedly be in the best interest of the villagers.

In *Intellectual Forum, Thirupathi Vs. State of Andhra Pradesh* (2006) the Supreme Court stressed that in recent times because of poverty migration of people from rural areas to urban areas was a common phenomenon. Due to the limited infrastructure of the towns the towns were becoming slums. The Supreme Court therefore could not prevent the government from proceeding with the town development in question.

36 **Match items in List I with items in List II and select the correct answer by using the codes given below.**

List I	List II
A. Intergenerational Equity	I. Earth Summit, 1992, Principle 15
B. Sustainable Development	II. Rio Declaration, 1992, Principle 16
C. Precautionary Principle	III. Stockholm Declaration 1972, Principles 1 and 2
D. Polluter Pays Principle	IV. Rio Declaration, 1992, Principle 3

Codes

	A	B	C	D		A	B	C	D
1	IV	III	I	II	2	I	III	II	IV
3	II	IV	I	III	4	III	IV	I	II

Ans. *(4)*

Exp. The correct matching is A-III, B-IV, C-I, D-II.

Intergenerational Equity is related to Principles 1 and 2 of Stockholm Declaration 1972. Principle 1 mentions about Right to Protect Environment and Principle 2 mentions about Management of Natural Resources. Principle of Stockholm Declaration says Human rights must be asserted, apartheid and colonialism condemned. Natural resources must be safeguarded. The Earth's capacity to produce renewable resources must be maintained.

Sustainable Development is mentioned in Principle 3 of Rio Declaration, 1992. Principle 3 states that the right to development must be fulfilled so as to equitable meet developmental and environmental needs of present and future generations. The Principle of Rio declaration says that all States and all people shall cooperate in the essential task of eradicating poverty as an indispensable requirement for sustainable development, in order to decrease the disparities in standards of living and better meet the needs of the majority of the people of the world.

Precautionary Principle is mentioned in Principle 15 of Earth Summit, 1992. The Precautionary Principle enables decision-makers to adopt precautionary measures when scientific evidence about an environmental or human health hazard is uncertain and the stakes are high. To others, it is an approach that protects human health and the environment.

Polluter Pays Principle is mentioned in Principle 16 of Rio Declaration, 1992. The 'Polluter Pays' principle is the commonly accepted practice that those who produce pollution should bear the costs of managing it to prevent damage to human health or the environment. This principle underpins most of the regulation of pollution affecting land, water and air.

37 **For which special purpose a conditional permit for hunting any wild animal, cannot be granted under the Wildlife (Protection) Act?**

1. Preparation of snake venom for manufacturing of life saving drugs
2. Collection of specimen for zoos and museums
3. Scientific research
4. Research in traditional and established universities

Ans. *(4)*

Exp. For the purpose of research in traditional and established universities, a conditional permit for hunting any wild animal, cannot be granted under the Wildlife (Protection) Act.

The Wildlife (Protection) Act, 1972 is an Act of the Parliament of India enacted for protection of plants and animal species. Among other reforms, the Act established schedules of protected plant and animal species; hunting or harvesting these species was largely outlawed.

38 **Under whose specification the recycling of plastic is undertaken as per the Plastic Manufacture, Sales and Usage Rules, 1999 ?**

1. Indian Standard Institution
2. Bureau of Indian Standards
3. Indian Standard Organisation
4. Indian Plastic Bureau

Ans. *(4)*

Exp. Under Indian Plastic Bureau, the recycling of plastic is undertaken as per the Plastic Manufacture, Sales and Usage Rules, 1999.

Recycling of plastics shall be undertaken strictly in accordance with the Bureau of Indian Standards specification: IS 14534: 1998 entitled "The Guidelines for Recycling of Plastics".

39 **"International law may be defined in broad terms as the body of general principles and specific rules which are binding upon the members of the International Community in their mutual relations". Who has given this definition of Public International Law ?**

1. JG Starke
2. Charles G Fenwick
3. Whiteman
4. Torsten Gihl

Ans. *(2)*

Exp. The mentioned definition is given by Charles G Fenwick.

Public International Law is composed of the laws, rules, and principles of general application that deal with the conduct of nation-states and international organisations among themselves as well as the relationships between nation-states and international organisations with persons, whether natural or juridical.

40 Match List I with List II and give the correct answer by using the codes given below.

List I (Name of Cases)	List II (Popular Names)
A. Portugal Vs. India	I. The Asylum Case
B. Burkina Faso Vs. Mali	II. Fisheries Jurisdiction Case
C. Spain Vs. Canada	III. Frontier Dispute Case
D. Columbia Vs. Peru	IV. Right of Passage over Indian Territory Case

Codes

	A	B	C	D		A	B	C	D
1	I	II	III	IV	2	IV	III	II	I
3	II	IV	I	III	4	III	I	IV	II

Ans. *(2)*

Exp. The correct matching is A-IV, B-III, C-II, D-I.

Right of Passage over Indian Territory Case is the popular name of Portugal Vs. India case. In this case, the Court found that Portugal had in 1954 the right of passage claimed by it but that such right did not extend to armed forces, armed police, arms and ammunition, and that India had not acted contrary to the obligations imposed on it by the existence of that right.

Frontier Dispute Case is the popular name of Burkina Faso Vs. Mali case. It was a public international law case with the International Court of Justice served by the West African states of Burkina Faso and Niger, which share a border. Both nations submitted a border dispute to the court in 2010. The court delivered its judgement in 2013, and the parties implemented it in 2015 and 2016.

Fisheries Jurisdiction Case is the popular name of Spain Vs. Canada Case. In this case, the Court held that the essence of the dispute between the Parties was whether the Canadian measures violated Spain's rights under international law and require reparation.

The Asylum Case is the popular name of Columbia Vs. Peru case. It is a public international law case, decided by the International Court of Justice. The ICJ recognised that the scope of Article 38 of the Statute of the International Court of Justice encompassed bi-lateral and regional international customary norms as well as general customary norms, in much the same way as it encompasses bilateral and multilateral treaties. The Court also clarified that for custom to be definitively proven, it must be continuously and uniformly executed.

41 Match List I with List II and select the correct answer by using the codes given below.

List I	List II
A. Recognition clothes the recognised State with rights and duties under International law	I. De Facto Recognition
B. Recognition is merely a formal acknowledgement through which established facts are accepted	II. Constitutive Theory of Recognition
C. State recognised possesses the essential elements of statehood and fit to be subject of international law	III. De-Jure Recognition
D. Recognition is final and once granted cannot be withdrawn	IV. Declaratory Theory of Recognition

Codes

	A	B	C	D		A	B	C	D
1	II	IV	I	III	2	I	II	III	IV
3	III	IV	II	I	4	IV	III	I	II

Ans. *(1)*

Exp. The correct matching is A-II, B-IV, C-I, D-III.

Recognition clothes the recognised State with rights and duties under International law is stated under Constitutive Theory of Recognition. In constitutive theory, an entity must gain formal or implied recognition by other states to become a state.

Recognition is merely a formal acknowledgement through which established facts are accepted is stated under Declaratory Theory of Recognition. According to the Declaratory theory, recognition has no legal effects; statehood or the status of a new government exists as such prior to and independently of recognition. states, rights, duties and obligations of statehood community under International Law is not applicable to it.

State recognised possesses the essential elements of statehood and fit to be subject of international law is stated under De Facto Recognition. It is a provisional recognition of statehood. It is a primary step to de jure recognition. It is a temporary and factual recognition as a state, and it can either be conditional or without any condition. The state having de facto recognition are not eligible for being a member of the United Nations.

Recognition is final and once granted cannot be withdrawn is stated under De-Jure Recognition. It is the recognition of a new state by the existing state when they consider that the new state fulfils all the essential characteristics of a state. The de jure recognition can be granted either with or without granting de facto recognition.

42 The Estrada Doctrine was propounded by

1 The Home Minister of Mexico
2 The Foreign Minister of Mexico
3 The External Secretary of USA
4 The Prime Minister of UK

Ans. *(2)*

Exp. The Estrada Doctrine was propounded by the Foreign Minister of Mexico.

It was named after Genaro Estrada, Secretary of foreign affairs (1930-32). It is believed that foreign government should not judge, positively or negatively, the government or changes in government of other States, as judging them will raise a question mark on their sovereignty.

43 Provision, "that the UNO has no competence to intervene in matters which are essentially within the domestic jurisdiction of any State", has been provided under which Article of UN Charter?

1 Article 1(7) 2 Article 2(7)
3 Article 7(2) 4 Article 98(7)

***Ans.* (2)**

Exp. The mentioned provision is provided under Article 2(7) of UN charter.

Article 2(7) of UN charter says that, nothing contained in the present Charter shall authorise the United Nations to intervene in matters which are essentially within the domestic jurisdiction of any state or shall require the Members to submit such matters to settlement under the present Charter; but this principle shall not prejudice the application of enforcement measures under Chapter VII of UN charter.

44 Match List I with List II and select the correct answer by using the codes given below.

List I (Name of Cases)	List II (Years of decision)
A. Luther Vs. Sagor	I. 1939
B. Bank of Ethiopia Vs. National Bank of Egypt	II. 1942
C. Arantzazu Mendi Case	III. 1937
D. US Vs. Pink	IV. 1921

Codes

	A	B	C	D
1	I	II	III	IV
2	III	IV	II	I
3	II	I	IV	III
4	IV	III	I	II

***Ans.* (4)**

Exp The correct matching is A-IV, B-III, C- I, D-II.

In *Luther Vs. Sagor* (1921) case it was held that the British Government recognized the Government of Russia and the retrospective effect will be applicable for that recognition.

In *Bank of Ethiopia Vs. National Bank of Egypt* (1937) case it was held that the Bank of Ethiopia had been dissolved by the Italian decree it had the authority to bring such action because the government of Italy was a de facto government in entire control of the territory occupied and therefore having complete governmental control over that territory.

In *Arantzazu Mendi Case* (1939) it was held that a de facto government has control over state assets within the territory it controls. A de jure government has control even overstate assets abroad.

US Vs Pink (1942) case was a United States Supreme Court decision related to the Litvinov Assignment, wherein the US government recognised Soviet Russia as the successor of the previous Russian government. The United States sued Louis H. Pink, the Superintendent of Insurance of the State of New York, for claims regarding the First Russian Insurance Company. The court ruled that rights to the property in question passed from the Soviet government to the United States by the Litvinov Assignment.

45 Give the chronological order of the following in which they came into existence.

I. Charter of United Nations.

II. Universal Declaration of Human Rights.

III. International Covenant on Civil and Political Rights.

IV. International Covenant on Economic, Social and Cultural Rights.

Codes

1 I, III, II, IV 2 IV, II, I, III
3 I, II, IV, III 4 III, IV, II, I

***Ans.* (3)**

Exp. The correct chronological order is I, II, IV, III.

The Charter of the United Nations (1945) is the founding document of the United Nations. It was signed on 26th June, 1945, in San Francisco, at the conclusion of the United Nations Conference on International Organisation, and came into force on 24th October, 1945.

The Universal Declaration of Human Rights (1948) is an international document adopted by the United Nations General Assembly that enshrines the rights and freedoms of all human beings.

The International Covenant on Economic, Social and Cultural Rights (1966) is a multilateral treaty adopted by the United Nations General Assembly on 16th December, 1966 through GA. Resolution 2200A (XXI), and came in force from 3rd January, 1976.

International Covenant on Civil and Political Rights (1976) recognizes the inherent dignity of each individual and undertakes to promote conditions within states to allow the enjoyment of civil and political rights.

46 Propositions are

I. A void marriage remains valid until a decree annulling it has been passed by a competent court.

II. A void marriage is never a valid marriage and there is no necessity of any decree annulling it.

III. A voidable marriage is a valid subsisting marriage until a decree annulling it has been passed by a court of competent jurisdiction.

In respect of the aforesaid propositions which is correct ?

1 I and III are correct, but II is incorrect
2 II and III are correct, but I is incorrect
3 I and III are incorrect, but II is correct
4 I and II are incorrect, but III is correct

***Ans.* (2)**

Exp. Proposition II and III are correct, but I is incorrect.

A void marriage is never a valid marriage and there is no necessity of any decree annulling it.

A voidable marriage is a valid subsisting marriage until a decree annulling it has been passed by a court of competent jurisdiction.

Proposition I is incorrect because void marriages are void from the beginning and no decree can make them a valid marriage.

47 As per Section 5 of the Hindu Marriage Act, 1955 the essential conditions of a Hindu Marriage are

I. Monogamy

II. Mental capacity

III. The bridegroom has completed the age of 21 years and the bride of 18 years

IV. No prohibited degree and sapinda relationship unless saved by custom.

Codes

1 I, II and IV	2 II, III, and IV
3 I, II and III	4 I, II, III and IV

Ans. (4)

Exp. I, II, III and IV are the essential conditions of a Hindu Marriage.

Section 5 talks about the conditions for Hindu Marriage. A marriage may be solemnized between any two Hindus, if the following conditions are fulfilled, namely:

(i) neither party has a spouse living at the time of the marriage.

(ii) at the time of the marriage, neither party is incapable of giving a valid consent to it in consequence of unsoundness of mind; or though capable of giving a valid consent, has been suffering from mental disorder of such a kind or to such an extent as to be unfit for marriage and the procreation of children; or has been subject to recurrent attacks of insanity.

(iii) the bridegroom has completed the age of 21 years and the bride, the age of 18 years at the time of the marriage.

(iv) the parties are not within the degrees of prohibited relationship unless the custom or usage governing each of them permits of a marriage between the two; the parties are not sapindas of each other, unless the custom or usage governing each of them permits of a marriage between the two.

48 Section 9 of the Hindu Marriage Act, 1955 was held to be 'intravires' the Constitution by the Supreme Court in the case of

1 T. Sareetha Vs. TV Subbhiah

2 Saroj Rani Vs. Sudarshan

3 Harvinder Kaur Vs. Harmandar Singh

4 Sarla Mudgil Vs. Union of India

Ans. (2)

Exp. Section 9 of the Hindu Marriage Act, 1955 was held to be 'intravires' the Constitution by the Supreme Court in the case of Saroj Rani Vs Sudarshan.

Section 9 of Hindu Marriage Act, talks about restitution of conjugal rights. It states when either the husband or the wife has, without reasonable excuse, withdrawn from the society of the other, the aggrieved party may apply, by petition to the district court, for restitution of conjugal rights and the court, on being satisfied of the truth of the statements made in such petition and that there is no legal ground why the application should not be granted, may decree restitution of conjugal rights accordingly.

49 A Muslim has given Triple Talaq to his wife and now wants to marry her again. He can do so

1 without any restriction

2 only on request of such wife

3 cannot marry her

4 only if such woman marry another man, the marriage is consummated and he has [second Husband] divorced her

Ans. (4)

Exp. A Muslim has given Triple Talaq to his wife and now wants to marry her again. He can do so only if such woman marries another man, the marriage is consummated and he has [second Husband] divorced her.

Nikah halala also known as tahleel marriage is a practice in which a woman, after being divorced by triple talaq, marries another man, consummates the marriage, and gets divorced again in order to be able to remarry her former husband.

50 In giving a child in adoption by the Hindu father, the requirement of the consent of the mother, can be dispensed with if

I. She has been declared to be of unsound mind by the Court of Competent jurisdiction.

II. She has finally and completely renounced the world.

III. She has ceased to be a Hindu.

IV. Her age is less than 18 years.

Codes

1 II, III and IV	2 I, II, III and IV
3 I, II and III	4 I, III and IV

Ans. (3)

Exp. In giving a child in adoption by the Hindu father, the requirement of the consent of the mother, can be dispensed with if she has been declared to be of unsound mind by the Court of Competent jurisdiction. Also, she has finally and completely renounced the world and she has ceased to be a Hindu.

51 "A Hindu mother can be natural guardian of her minor child during the life of father of the child if he is not taking due care of the child." This was held by the Supreme Court of India in case of

1 MM Ganguli Vs. Jayanti Ganguli

2 Jijabai Vs. Pathan Khan

3 Sarla Mudgil Vs. Union of India

4 Githa Hariharan Vs. Reserve Bank of India

Ans. (4)

Exp. In case of Githa Hariharan Vs. Reserve Bank of India, it was held that "A Hindu mother can be natural guardian of her minor child during the life of father of the child if he is not taking due care of the child."

Justice AS Anand has interpreted Section 6 of the Hindu Minority and Guardianship Act liberally holding that the natural guardian of a Hindu minor in respect of the minor's person as well as the minor's property, can be the mother in the absence of the father. The word 'absence' has to be interpreted broadly as meaning the father's absence for any reason whatsoever in the context of taking care of the minor's person or property. If the father is wholly indifferent to the minor even if he/she lives with the mother, or by virtue of a mutual understanding between the father and the mother, the mother is put in exclusive charge of the minor.

52 Match List I with List II in the light of Section 2 of the Dissolution of Muslim Marriage Act, 1939 and select the correct answer using the codes given below.

List I	List II
A. Imprisonment of Husband	I. Section 2(vii)
B. Option of puberty	II. Section 2(iii)
C. Husband missing	III. Section 2(v)
D. Impotency of husband	IV. Section 2(i)

Codes

	A	B	C	D		A	B	C	D
1	II	I	IV	III	2	I	II	III	IV
3	IV	II	I	III	4	III	I	II	IV

Ans. (1)

Exp. The correct matching is A-II, B-I, C-IV, D-III.

Section-2(iii) of Dissolution of Muslim Marriage Act, 1939 mention about the Imprisonment of husband. It stated that a woman married under Muslim law shall be entitled to obtain a decree for the dissolution of her marriage if the husband has been sentenced to imprisonment for a period of seven years or upwards.

Section-2(vii) mention about Option of puberty It stated that a woman married under Muslim law shall be entitled to obtain a decree for the dissolution of her marriage that she, having been given in marriage by her father or other guardian before she attained the age of fifteen years, repudiated the marriage before attaining the age of eighteen years.

Section-2(i) mention about Missing of husband. It stated that a woman married under Muslim law shall be entitled to obtain a decree for the dissolution of her marriage that the whereabouts of the husband have not been known for a period of four years.

Section-2(v) mention about the Impotency of husband. It stated that a woman married under Muslim law shall be entitled to obtain a decree for the dissolution of her marriage if the husband was impotent at the time of the marriage and continues to be so.

53 Which of the following has not yet been statutorily recognised as a theory of divorce under the Hindu Marriage Act, 1955 ?

1 Fault Theory
2 Will Theory
3 Breakdown Theory
4 Mutual Consent Theory

Ans. (2)

Exp. Will theory has not yet been statutorily recognised as a theory of divorce under the Hindu Marriage Act, 1955. The underlying rationale is that since two persons can marry by their free will, they should also be allowed to move out of the relationship of their own free will.

54 Read Assertion (A) and Reason (R) and select the correct answer by using codes given below.

Assertion (A) Human Rights are regarded as those fundamental but alienable rights which are preferred for life as human being.

Reason (R) Change is general rule of life. Therefore, legislatures are free to change human rights according to changing needs and circumstances.

Codes

1 Both (A) and (R) are true and (R) is correct explanation for (A)
2 Both (A) and (R) are true, but (R) is not correct explanation for (A)
3 Both (A) and (R) are false
4 (A) is false, but (R) is true

Ans. (3)

Exp. Both (A) and (R)are false.

Assertion is false because Human rights are fundamental as well as inalienable rights. Human rights are universal and inalienable; indivisible; interdependent and interrelated. They are universal because everyone is born with and possesses the same rights, regardless of where they live, their gender or race, or their religious, cultural or ethnic background.

Reason is false because Human rights are fundamental rights that are inherent in life. Legislature cannot change the human rights as per the changing needs, because they are the basic foundation of life, and cannot be altered.

55 Which of the following statements are wrong ?

I. Human rights are created by legislation.
II. Legal duty to protect human rights is not duty to respect them.
III. International concern with human rights as enshrined in the United Nations Charter is a modern innovation.
IV. A human right violation is now conceived as violation of those personally and directly aggrieved, but not of everyone.

Codes

1 I and II
2 II and III
3 III and IV
4 I, II, III and IV

Ans. (4)

Exp. Statements I, II, III and IV are wrong.

Human Rights were not created by any legislation but were formulated by the Universal Declaration on Human Rights.

States have the legal obligation to respect, protect and fulfil the human rights set out in the international human rights conventions they ratify.

International concern with human rights is not a modern innovation. There was a strong need to recognize them especially in the light of world war atrocities and genocides.

A human right violation is not only conceived as violation of those personally and directly aggrieved, but also of everyone.

56 Read Assertion (A) and Reason (R) and select the correct answer by using codes given below.

Assertion (A) The purpose of the United Nation is to maintain national security and peace.

Reason (R) Because Article–I of the Charter of the United Nations says so.

Codes

1 Both (A) and (R) are true and (R) is correct explanation for (A)
2 Both (A) and (R) are false
3 (A) is true and (R) is false
4 (A) is false and (R) is true

Ans. (2)

Exp. Both (A) and (R) are false.

Assertion is false because the purpose of United Nation (UN) is to maintain international peace and security; develop friendly relations among nations, achieve international cooperation in solving international problems.

Reason is false because Article I of UN charter says that "The purposes of the United Nations are as follows :

- to maintain international peace and security, and to that end: to take effective collective measures for the prevention and removal of threats to the peace, and for the suppression of acts of aggression or other breaches of the peace, and to bring about by peaceful means, and in conformity with the principles of justice and international law, adjustment or settlement of international disputes or situations which might lead to a breach of the peace; To develop friendly relations among nations based on respect for the principle of equal rights and self-determination of peoples, and to take other appropriate measures to strengthen universal peace;
- to achieve international cooperation in solving international problems of an economic, social, cultural, or humanitarian character, and in promoting and encouraging respect for human rights and for fundamental freedoms for all without distinction as to race, sex, language, or religion;
- to be a centre for harmonizing the actions of nations in the attainment of these common ends.

57 Right to nationality, right to marry and to found a family are the rights under

I. Only women rights
II. Social and cultural rights
III. Civil and political rights
IV. Inherent rights

Codes

1 I, II and IV 2 II, III and IV
3 II and III 4 Only III

Ans. (4)

Exp. Right to nationality, right to marry and to found a family are the rights under Civil and political rights.

Civil and political rights are a class of rights that protect individuals' freedom from infringement by governments, social organisations and private individuals, and which ensure one's ability to participate in the civil and political life of the society and state without discrimination or repression.

58 Which of the following court normally is/are notified by the State Governments to act as Human Rights Court for speedy trial of offences violating Human Rights?

I. Munsiff Courts
II. Lok Adalats
III. Senior Civil Judge Court
IV. Sessions Court

Codes

1 I and IV 2 I, III and IV
3 II and IV 4 Only IV

Ans. (4)

Exp. Session courts are notified by the State Governments to act as Human Rights Court for speedy trial of offences violating Human Rights.

Speedy trial is a fundamental right implicit in the guarantee of life and personal liberty enshrined in Article 21 of the Constitution and any accused who is denied this right of speedy trial is entitled to approach Supreme Court under Article 32 for the purpose of enforcing such right.

59 The power of 'enquiry and investigation' was given to Human Rights Commission under the following sections of the protection of Human Rights Act, 1993

I. Section 13 II. Section 14
III. Section 9 IV. Section 10

Codes

1 I and II 2 I and III
3 II and III 4 III and IV

Ans. (1)

Exp. Section 13 and Section 14 of Human rights Act, 1993 talks about the power of 'enquiry and investigation' conferred to Human Rights Commission.

Section 13 of the Act talks about the power relating to enquiries, it says that the Commission shall, while inquiring into complaints under this Act, have all the powers of a civil court trying a suit under the Code of Civil Procedure, 1908.

Section 14 talks about investigations. It says that the Commission may, for the purpose of conducting any investigation pertaining to the inquiry, utilise the services of any officer or investigation agency of the Central Government or any State Government with the concurrence of the Central Government or the State Government, as the case may be.

60 Read Assertion (A) and Reason (R) and select the correct answer by using codes given below.

Assertion (A) A refugee means any person who, owing to well-founded fear of being persecuted for reason of race, religion, nationality, membership of a particular social group or political opinion, is outside the country of his nationality.

Reason (R) Because the United Nations Convention on the Refugees 1951 in its Article 1A says so.

Codes

1 Both (A) and (R) are true and (R) is correct explanation of (A)
2 (A) is false and (R) is true
3 (A) is true and (R) is false
4 Both (A) and (R) are false

Ans. (4)

Exp. Both (A) and (R) are false.

Assertion is false because person who has fear of being persecuted due to various reasons should be within the country of his nationality.

Reason is false because because Article 1 of the convention did not mentioned the definition given in Assertion.

61 Match the List I (Name of Maxim) with List II (Meaning of Maxim) by using the codes given below.

List I	List II
A. Scienti non fit injuria	I. Where there is remedy there is a right
B. Qui facit per alium facit per se	II. He who does an act through another is deemed in law to do it himself
C. Ubi jus ibi remedium	III. No injury is done to one who knowingly does an act
D. Ubi remedium ibi jus	IV. Where there is wrong there is remedy

Codes

	A	B	C	D		A	B	C	D
1	III	IV	I	II	2	IV	III	II	I
3	III	II	IV	I	4	I	II	III	IV

Ans. (3)

Exp. The correct matching is A-III, B-II, C-IV, D-I.

The maxim *Scienti non fit injuria* means 'no injury is done to one who knowingly does an act'. Only having knowledge about the risk is not enough for the application of this defence, it is known as Scienti non fit injuria, which means that mere knowledge does mean consent to the risk.

The maxim *Qui facit per alium facit per se* means 'He who does an act through another is deemed in law to do it himself'. He who acts through another does the act himself. It is a fundamental legal maxim of the law of agency. It is a maxim often stated in discussing the liability of the employer for the act of an employee in terms of vicarious liability.

The maxim *Ubi jus ibi remedium* means 'Where there is wrong, there is remedy'. It postulates that where law has established a right there should be a corresponding remedy for its breach. The right to a remedy is one of the fundamental rights historically recognized in all legal systems.

The maxim *Ubi remedium ibi jus* means 'Where there is remedy, there is a right.' It means where remedy exists, it is because there exists a right.

62 Which of the following is an effective defence in the tort of nuisance?

I. Public good II. Prescription
III. Statutory authority IV. Reasonable care

Codes

1 I and III are correct
2 II and IV are correct
3 II and III are correct
4 I and IV are correct

Ans. (3)

Exp. Prescription and statutory authority is an effective defence in the tort of nuisance.

Prescription is a title acquired by use and time and which is allowed by the law, a person claims any property because his ancestors have had the possession of the property by law. Statutory authority means When a statute authorises the doing of a particular act or the use of land in a way, all the remedies whether by action or indictment or charge, are taken away. Provided that every necessary reasonable precaution has been taken.

63 Given below are two statements. One is labelled as Assertion (A) and the other is labelled as Reason (R).

Assertion (A) Negligence as a tort is the breach of legal duty to take care which results in damage.

Reason (R) In the tort of negligence law takes cognisance of carelessness only if it is supported by the legal duty to care.

Codes

1 Both (A) and (R) are true and (R) is the correct explanation of (A)
2 Both (A) and (R) are true but (R) is not the correct explanation of (A)
3 (A) is true, but (R) is false
4 (A) is false, but (R) is true

Ans. (1)

Exp. Both (A) and (R) are true and (R) is the correct explanation of (A).

Negligence as a tort is the breach of legal duty to take care which results in damage. According to Winfield and Jolowicz "Negligence is the breach of a legal duty to take care which results in damage, undesired by the defendant to the plaintiff."

In the tort of negligence law takes cognisance of carelessness only if it is supported by the legal duty to care. 'Duty of care' means a legal duty rather than mere moral, religious or social duty. In the absence of such legal duty, negligence in the popular sense has no legal consciousness. It is not sufficient to show that the defendant was careless, the plaintiff has to establish that the defendant owed to the plaintiff a legal duty to take care.

64 In the tort of slander it is essential that some special damage has been resulted from the use of word by the defendant. In which of the following case an action of slander may be maintained, without proof of special damage? Answer using the Codes

I. Words imputing criminal offence to the plaintiff.
II. Words imputing to the plaintiff that he has an infectious disease.
III. Words prejudice the plaintiff in his office, profession etc.
IV. Words imputing unchastity to a woman.

Codes

1 I and II are correct
2 I, II and III are correct
3 I, III and IV are correct
4 I, II, III and IV are correct

Ans. (4)

Exp. Statement I, II, III and IV are correct.

In the following cases an action of slander may be maintained, without proof of special damage :

- Accusation of criminal effence,
- Accusation of virulent disease,
- Imputation against office, profession or trade,
- Unchastity in women or girl

65 Which of the following is not an exception to the strict liability principle laid down in Rylands Vs. Fletcher ?

1 Independent contractor
2 Statutory authority
3 Act of God
4 Consent of the plaintiff

Ans. (1)

Exp. Independent contractor is not an exception to the strict liability principle laid down in Rylands Vs. Fletcher.

Strict Liability is a kind of Tort that makes a person or entity responsible for their acts even when the consequences were unintentional. Law also imposes liability only on those actions which it feels are naturally dangerous. Strict Liability is also known as 'no fault liability'.

The rule of strict liability and absolute liability can be seen as exceptions. A person is made liable only when he is at fault. This is known as the principle of "no fault liability." Under these rules, the liable person may not have done the act, but he'll still be responsible for the damage caused due to the acts.

66 Which of the following is the Right of the consumer under Consumer Protection Act, 1986?

I. Right to consumer education
II. Right to seek redressal
III. Access to a variety of goods and services at competitive prices
IV. Take goods and services free of cost

Codes

1 I and III are correct
2 I, II and III are correct
3 I and II are correct
4 All of the above

Ans. (2)

Exp. I, II and III are correct.

Six consumer rights have been defined in the Consumer Protection Act, 1986, including the Right to: (i) be Protected against marketing of goods and services which are hazardous to life and property; (ii) be informed of the quality, quantity, potency, purity, standard and price of goods or services; (iii) be assured of access to a variety of goods or services at competitive prices; and (iv) seek redressal against unfair or restrictive trade practices.

67 What is the pecuniary jurisdiction of the State Commission under the Consumer Protection Act?

1 Exceeds ₹ 50 lakhs but does not exceed rupees one crore
2 Exceeds ₹ 20 lakhs but does not exceed rupees one crore
3 Exceeds ₹ 50 lakhs but does not exceed rupees one crore
4 Exceeds ₹ 1 crore

Ans. (2)

Exp. The State Consumer Dispute Redressal Commission has the pecuniary jurisdiction where the claim exceeds ₹ 20 lakhs but does not exceed ₹ 1 crore.

The Nation Consumer Dispute Redressal Commission has the pecuniary jurisdiction where the claim exceeds the amount of ₹ 1 crore.

68 According to Section 12 of the Partnership Act, any difference arising as to ordinary matters connected with the business of partnership may be decided by

1 the seniormost partner 2 an arbitrator
3 a majority of partners 4 a judge

Ans. (3)

Exp. According to Section 12 of the Partnership Act, any difference arising as to ordinary matters connected with the business of partnership may be decided by the majority of partners.

Section 12 talks about the conduct of business. According to Section 12, subject to contract between the partners,

- every partner has a right to take part in the conduct of the business;
- every partner is bound to attend diligently to his duties in the conduct of the business;
- ny difference arising as to ordinary matters connected with the business may be decided by a majority of the partners, and every partner shall have the right to express his opinion, before the matter is decided, but no change may be made in the nature of the business without the consent of all the partners; and
- every partner has a right to have access to and to inspect and copy any of the books of the firm.

69 Which are essentials of a contract of sale of goods ? Answer using codes given below

I. Offer
II. Acceptance of offer
III. Exchange of goods for money
IV. Transfer of property in goods from seller to buyer

Codes

1 Only I and II 2 Only III and IV
3 Only II and III 4 I, II, III and IV

Ans. (4)

➲ *Exp.* The essential of a contract of sale of goods are : (i) Offer, (ii) Acceptance of offer, (iii) Exchange of goods for money, (iv) Transfer of property in goods from seller to buyer.

70 Read Assertion (A) and Reason (R) and select the correct answer by using the codes below.

Assertion (A) Where under a contract of sale the property in the goods has passed to the buyer and the buyer wrongfully neglects to pay for the goods according to the terms of the contract, the buyer may sue the seller for the price of the goods.

Reason (R) The seller is entitled to get the contractual price.

Codes

1 Both (A) and (R) are correct, and (A) is correct explanation for (A)
2 Both (A) and (R) are wrong
3 (A) is wrong, but (R) is right
4 (R) is wrong, but (A) is right

Ans. (3)

➲ *Exp.* (A) is wrong, but (R) is right.

Assertion is wrong as according to Section 55 in the Sale of Goods Act, 1930, (1) "Where under a contract of sale the property in the goods has passed to the buyer and the buyer wrongfully neglects or refuses to pay for the goods according to the terms of the contract, the seller may sue him for the price of the goods.

The seller is entitled to get the contractual price as per Section 55.

71 Match List I with List II and select the correct answer using the codes given below.

List I	List II
A. Intention of parties to pass property in goods	I. Ghasiram Vs. State of Rajasthan
B. Ascertainment of intention to pass property in goods	II. Badriprasad Vs. State of Madhya Pradesh
C. Passing of property in goods	III. United Breweries Ltd. Vs. State of Andhra Pradesh
D. Specific goods in deliverable State	IV. Usha Beltron Ltd. Vs. State of Punjab

Codes

	A	B	C	D		A	B	C	D
1	II	IV	I	III	2	III	I	II	IV
3	I	III	IV	II	4	III	I	IV	II

Ans. (4)

➲ *Exp.* The correct matching is A-III, B-I, C-IV, D-II.

United Breweries Ltd. Vs. State of Andhra Pradesh case mention the intention of parties to pass property in goods. It was held that the intention of parties to pass property in goods is important.

Ghasiram Vs. State of Rajasthan case mention the ascertainment of intention to pass. It was held that it must be the duty of the Government in such cases to bring to the notice of the Court all orders of detention which might have been passed against the detenu upto the date of the hearing of his petition by the court for release from detention.

Usha Beltron Ltd. Vs. State of Punjab case mention about the passing of property in goods. In this case, the contract provided that property in the goods does not pass till after delivery and after successful testing and takeover.

Badri prasad Vs. State of Madhya Pradesh case mention the specific goods in deliverable State. It was held that the timber was sufficiently identifiable and was therefore specified goods and there was nothing in the contract postponing possession till the other instalments have been paid. The fact that the contract was signed by the Chief Conservator, after fire had broken out has no effect on the validity of the contract, or on the question of delivery of possession or on the passing of property in the timber.

72 Which one statement is correct from the following statements ?

1 If the contract is inconsistent with the public documents, the person contracting will not be prejudiced by irregularities that may be set the outdoor working of the company
2 If the contract is consistent with the public documents, the person contracting will not be prejudiced by irregularities that may be set the indoor working of the company

3 The doctrine of indoor management seeks to protect the company against the outsider
4 The doctrine of ultra vires seeks to protect the outsider against internal irregularities of the company

Ans. (2)

Exp. If the contract is consistent with the public documents, the person contracting will not be prejudiced by irregularities that may be set the indoor working of the company is the correct statement.

The doctrine of indoor management, also known as Turquand rule is a 150-year old concept, which protects the outsiders against the actions done by the company. Any person who enters into a contract with the company shall ensure that the transaction is authorised by the articles and memorandum of the company.

73 Match List I with List II and select the correct answer using the codes given below.

List I	List II
A. Directors with unlimited liability	I. Section 202 and 203 of the Companies Act
B. Prevention of management of a company by undesirable persons	II. Section 312 of the Companies Act
C. A director cannot assign his office in favour of any one	III. Section 322 and 323 of the Companies Act
D. Appointment to a place of profit under the company	IV. Section 314 of the Companies Act

Codes

	A	B	C	D		A	B	C	D
1	I	III	II	IV	2	III	I	II	IV
3	III	I	IV	II	4	II	IV	I	III

Ans. (2)

Exp. The correct matching is A-III, B-I, C-II, D-IV.

Section 322 and 323 of the Companies Act, 1956 deals with Directors with unlimited liability. Section 322 says that in a limited company, the liability of the directors or of any director or of the managing agent, secretaries and treasurers or manager may, if so provided by the memorandum be unlimited.

Section 323 of the Companies Act deals with special resolution of limited company making liability of directors unlimited.

Section 202 and 203 of the Companies Act deals Prevention of management of a company by undesirable persons. Section 202 talks about undischarged insolvent not to manage companies. Section 203 talks about the power to restraint fraudulent person from managing companies.

Section 312 of the Companies Act deals with prohibition of assignment of office by directions. A director cannot assign his office in favour of any one. It says any assignment of his office made after the commencement of this Act by any director of a company shall be void.

Section 314 of the Companies Act deals with Appointment to a place of profit under the company. Section 314 says that the Directors etc not to hold office or place of profit.

74 Match List I with List II and select the correct answer using the codes given below.

List I	List II
A. Inchoate stamped instrument	I. Union Bank of India Vs. Ankur Corp.
B. Liability of acceptor of a negotiable instrument	II. Section 31 of the Negotiable Instrument Act
C. Liability of an endorser	III. Section 35 of the Negotiable Instrument Act
D. Liability of the drawee of a cheque	IV. Section 20 of the Negotiable Instrument Act

Codes

	A	B	C	D		A	B	C	D
1	I	IV	III	II	2	IV	I	III	II
3	IV	I	II	III	4	III	II	I	IV

Ans. (2)

Exp. The correct matching is A-IV, B-I, C-III, D-II.

Section 20 of the Negotiable Instrument Act is related to Inchoate stamped instrument. Section 20 says that where one person signs and delivers to another a paper stamped in accordance with the law relating to negotiable instruments then in force in India, and either wholly blank or having written thereon an incomplete negotiable instrument, he thereby gives prima facie authority to the holder thereof to make or complete, as the case may be, upon it a negotiable instrument, for any amount specified therein and not exceeding the amount covered by the stamp.

Union Bank of India Vs. Ankur Corp is related to liability of the acceptor of a negotiable instrument. An acceptor for honor binds himself to all parties subsequent to the party for whose honor he accepts to pay the amount of the bill if the drawee does not; and such party and all prior parties are liable in their respective capacities to compensate the acceptor for honor for all loss or damage sustained by him in consequence of such acceptance.

Section 35 of the Negotiable Instrument Act mention the Liability of an endorser. Section 35 of the act says that in the absence of a contract to the contrary, whoever indorses and delivers a negotiable instrument before maturity, without, in such endorsement, expressly excluding or making conditional his own liability, is bound thereby to every subsequent holder, in case of dishonour by the drawee, acceptor or maker, to compensate such holder for any loss or damage caused to him by such dishonour.

Section 31 of the Negotiable Instrument Act mention the Liability of the drawee of a cheque. It says that the drawee of a cheque having sufficient funds of the drawer in his hands properly applicable to the payment of such cheque must pay the cheque when duly required so to do, and, in default of such payment, must compensate the drawer for any loss or damage caused by such default.

75 Which of the following statements are correct ? Answer using codes given below.

In order that a person can be called a holder in due course, he must show

I. that he is the drawer of the negotiable instrument.

II. that he has obtained it without consideration.

III. that he has obtained it before the maturity of the negotiable instrument.

IV. that he has obtained the negotiable instrument in good faith.

Codes

1 I and II are correct
2 II and III are correct
3 III and IV are correct
4 I and IV are correct

Ans. *(3)*

Exp. III and IV are correct.

The definition of holder in due course in Section 9 of the Negotiable Instruments Act, 1881 'Holder in due course' means that any person who for the consideration paid becomes the possessor of a negotiable instruments, before its maturity, in good faith and without any sufficient reason to believe that any defect existed in the title of the person from whom he obtained it. In order that a person can be called a holder in due course, he must show :

(i) He must be a holder in due course.

(ii) He must be a holder of valuable consideration.

(iii) He must become a holder of the negotiable instrument before the date of maturity.

(iv) He must become a holder of the negotiable instrument in good faith.

UGC-NET

LAW

SOLVED PAPER 2014 (June)

PAPER II

1 In which of the following cases, the Supreme Court held that "the Preamble is the part of the Constitution"?

1 Berubari union and Exchange of enclave
2 Golaknath Vs. State of Punjab
3 Kesavananda Bharati Vs. State of Kerala
4 None of the above

Ans. (3)

➲ *Exp.* In the case of Kesavananda Bharati Vs. State of Kerala, the Supreme Court held that the Preamble is a part of the Indian Constitution.

The Court held that the Preamble is a part of the Constitution, though not an operative part. It can be amended, however, the fundamental features or the basic structure must remain intact.

2 Clause(5) of Article15 has been added to the Constitution by

1 Constitution (First Amendment) Act
2 Constitution (Seventh Amendment) Act
3 Constitution (Forty-second Amendment) Act
4 Constitution (Ninety-third Amendment) Act

Ans. (4)

➲ *Exp.* Constitution (Ninety-third Amendment) Act, 2005 inserted Clause (5) in Article 15 of the Constitution.
It aims to promote the educational advancement of the socially and educationally backward classes of citizens, the Scheduled Castes and the Scheduled Tribes through special provisions relating to admission of students belonging to these categories in all educational institutions, including private educational institutions, whether aided or unaided by the state.

3 Match List I with List II and select the correct answer using the codes given below the lists.

List I	List II
A. Equal justice and free legal aid	I. Article 44
B. Uniform civil code for citizens	II. Article 48A
C. Protection and improvement of environment and safeguarding of forests and wildlife.	III. Article 39A
D. Promotion of international peace and security	IV. Article 51

Codes

	A	B	C	D		A	B	C	D
1	III	II	IV	I	2	III	I	II	IV
3	I	II	III	IV	4	IV	I	II	III

Ans. (2)

➲ *Exp.* The correct matching is A-III, B-I, C-II, D-IV.

Article 39A of the Constitution of India provides for free legal aid to the poor and weaker sections of the society and ensures equal justice for all.

Article 44 states that the State shall endeavour to secure for the citizens a Uniform civil code throughout the territory of India.

Article 48A lays down the directive principle for protection and improvement of environment and safeguarding of forests and wildlife.

Article 51 says that the State shall promote international peace and security by the prescription of open, just and honourable relations between nations, by the firm establishment of the understandings of international law.

4 Rights of a citizen under Article 19 are automatically suspended during the period of emergency, if emergency under Article 352 is declared on the grounds of

1 war, external aggression or armed rebellion
2 war or armed rebellion
3 external aggression or armed rebellion
4 war or external aggression

Ans. (4)

➲ *Exp.* Rights of a citizen under Article 19 are automatically suspended during the period of emergency, if emergency under Article 352 is declared on the grounds of war or external aggression.

Article 352 talks about Proclamation of Emergency, if the President is satisfied that a grave emergency exists whereby the security of India or of any part of the territory thereof is threatened, whether by war or external aggression he may, by proclamation, make a declaration to that effect in respect of the whole of India or of such part of the territory thereof as may be specified in the proclamation. The Constitution of India has provided for imposition of emergency caused by war, external aggression or internal rebellion. This is described as the National Emergency.

5 In which of the following cases the Supreme Court has held that the word 'law' in Article 21 does not mean merely an enacted piece of law but must be just, fair and reasonable law?

1 AK Gopalan Vs. State of Madras
2 Maneka Gandhi Vs. Union of India
3 Both 1 and 2
4 None of the above

Ans. *(2)*

Exp. In Maneka Gandhi Vs. Union of India case, the Supreme Court has held that the word 'law' in Article 21 does not mean merely an enacted piece of law but must be just, fair and reasonable law.

Maneka Gandhi filed a writ petition under Article 32 of the Constitution in the Supreme Court challenging the order of the Government of India as violating her Fundamental Rights guaranteed under Article 21 of the Constitution.

The main issues before the court in this case were as follows

(i) Whether right to go abroad is a part of right to personal liberty under Article 21.
(ii) Whether the Passport Act prescribes a 'procedure' as required by Article 21 before depriving a person from the right guaranteed under the said Article.
(iii) Whether Section 10(3) (c) of the Passport Act is violative of Article 14, 19(1) (a) and 21 of the Constitution.
(iv) Whether the impugned order of the regional passport officer is in contravention of the principles of natural justice.

6 A distinguished jurist can be appointed as a judge of the

1 High Court only
2 Supreme Court only
3 Both 1 and 2
4 None of these

Ans. *(2)*

Exp. A distinguished jurist can be appointed as a judge of Supreme Court by President.

According to Article 124(3) of Indian Constitution a person shall not be qualified for appointment as a Judge of the Supreme Court unless he is a citizen of India and (a) has been for atleast 5 years a Judge of a High Court or of two or more such courts in succession; or (b) has been for atleast 10 years an advocate of a High Court or of two or more such courts in succession; or (c) is, in the opinion of the President, a distinguished jurist.

7 'Which cannot be done directly, cannot be done indirectly'. This statement epitomises the doctrine of

1 colourable legislation
2 pith and substance
3 harmonious construction
4 eclipse

Ans. *(1)*

Exp. The given statement epitomises the doctrine of colourable legislation.

The literal meaning of colourable legislation is that the 'colour or guise of power conferred for one particular purpose, the legislature cannot seek to achieve some other purpose which it is otherwise not competent to legislate on. This implies that "when anything is prohibited directly, it is also prohibited indirectly". In common parlance, it is meant to be understood as "whatever legislature can't do directly, it can't do indirectly."

8 Match List I with List II by using the codes given below and select the correct answer. Possession must be protected because

List I	List II
A. Kent	I. Man by taking possession has brought the object within his sphere of will.
B. Hegel	II. In possession there is manifestation of individual's will.
C. Hollard	III. Every act of violence is unlawful.
D. Savigny	IV. It is essential for preservation of peace.

Codes

	A	B	C	D		A	B	C	D
1	III	II	IV	I	2	I	IV	II	III
3	II	IV	III	I	4	I	II	III	IV

Ans. *(2)*

Exp. The correct matching is A-I, B-IV, C- II, D-III.

Kent said possession must be protected because man by taking possession has brought the object within his sphere of will. In his discussion of property rights, Kent drew a distinction between the 'sensible' (or 'empirical') possession of an external object and the 'intelligible' (or 'rational') possession of an object.

Hegel said possession must be protected because it is essential for preservation of peace. There are many reasons for the protection of possession: Protection of possession aids the criminal law by preserving peace.

Hollard states that in possession there is manifestation of an individual's will. In his view, the predominant motive that has induced the law to give protection to possession was probably a concern for the preservation of peace. Possession connotes respect for the rightful claim of a person.

Savigny said every act of violence is unlawful. He considers the protection of possession as a branch of the protection of the person.

9 Which one of the following statements is not correct?

1 Austin and Kelson did much to rescue jurisprudence from the so-called confusion of social sciences
2 Historical school of jurisprudence was a reaction against a prior methods of reasoning of eighteen century natural law
3 Cujas and Hugo also applied the historical approach in the study of law
4 Savigny did not discard the principle of natural law

Ans. (4)

Exp. Statement that says, "Savigny did not discard the principle of natural law" is not correct.

Savigny protested against the tradition of natural law, believing that such doctrine prevented nations from securing the free development of legal progress.

10 Match List I (Name of Books) with List II (Name of Writers) and select the correct answer.

List I	List II
A. Pure Theory of Law	I. Hans Kelson
B. Three lectures on Vedanta Philosophy	II. Max Muller
C. Judiciary Attacks and Survivals	III. Justice VD Tulzapurkar
D. The Growth of Law	IV. Justice Cardozo

Codes

	A	B	C	D		A	B	C	D
1	I	II	III	IV	2	IV	III	II	I
3	III	I	IV	II	4	II	IV	I	III

Ans. (1)

Exp. The correct matching is A-I, B-II, C-III, D-IV.

Pure Theory of Law was authored by Hans Kelson. Kelson describes the law as a normative science distinguishing it from natural science. The basic character of the science of law is the knowledge of what "ought to be" as opposed to the nature of normative sciences which are capable of being determined and discovered. Hence, according to Kelson, the science of law is positive law and not an ideal law.

Three lectures on Vedanta Philosophy is the work done by Max Muller. It was delivered at the Royal Institution in March, 1894.

Judiciary Attacks and Survivals is the book written by Justice VD Tulzapurkar. Justice VD Tulzapurkar was a judge of the Supreme Court of India from 30th September 1977 until 9th March, 1986.

The Growth of Law is written by Justice Cardozo. He was a long-time Justice of the Court of Appeals of New York, where his opinions included many declarations that would become famous in legal circles; he was appointed to the Supreme Court of the United States in 1932.

11 The term 'Legal Theory' has been first time coined by

1 Hans Kelson
2 W Friedman
3 Salmond
4 Ronald Dworkin

Ans. (4)

Exp. The term 'Legal Theory' was first coined by Ronald Dworkin.

Legal theory has been an attempt to identify the functions of the positive law in supporting an otherwise unproblematic society. Legal theory refers to the principle under which litigant proceeds, or on which a litigant bases its claims or defences in a case. It can also be the law or body of rules of conduct which are of binding legal force and effect, prescribed, recognised and enforced by a controlling authority.

12 Which of the following statement is not true about the conformity of custom?

1 It should be in conformity with public policy
2 It should be in conformity with statutory law
3 In England, custom will be recognised even if it is in conflict with some fundamental principles of law
4 The custom must not be in conflict with tradition

Ans. (3)

Exp. In England, custom will be recognised even if it is in conflict with some fundamental principles of law. This statement is not true about the conformity of custom. It is because customs must be in conformity with the statute, public policy and tradition, in order to retain their validity.

13 "No one has any other right than always to do his duty." It was stated by

1 Kelson
2 Prof Duguit
3 Holland
4 Salmond

Ans. (2)

Exp. According to Duguit, "No one has any other right than always to do his duty".

According to him, the basis of law is the objective fact of 'social solidarity'. It is social law of social solidarity (mutual interdependence) which alone satisfies individual needs through exchange and division of labour on the basis which each perform their mutual duty in society.

14 Given below are two statements, one is labelled as Assertion (A) and the other is labelled as Reason (R).

Assertion (A) Custom is per se law, independent of its prior recognition by the sovereign or the judge.

Reason (R) Custom is a source of law.

Codes

1 Both (A) and (R) are true and (R) is the correct explanation of (A)
2 Both (A) and (R) are true, but (R) is not the correct explanation of (R)
3 (A) is true, but (R) is false
4 (A) is false, but (R) is true

Ans. (1)

Exp. Both (A) and (R) are true and (R) is the correct explanation of (A).

Custom is per se law, independent of its prior recognition by the sovereign or the judge. The term 'source of law' is used in different senses but in the Indian context the expression 'sources of law' is generally used in two senses. In the first sense, according to Hindu scriptures Duty is the foundation head of all law while according to modern jurisprudence, it is the sovereign from where the law emanates.

In the second sense, the expression means where one must resort to get at law. In the ordinary language, custom is a habitual course of conduct observed uniformly and voluntarily by the people concerned.

Custom is a source of law, which is also correct and explains the given Assertion as custom is the traditional source of Law.

15 Given below are two statements, one is labelled as Assertion (A) and the other labelled as Reason (R).

Assertion (A) According to John Austin, international law is true law and not negative international morality.

Reason (R) Three elements in Austin's definition of law, namely command of the sovereign, duty of inferiors and sanction in case inferior who commit breach of the command are absent in international law.

Codes

1 Both (A) and (R) are true and (R) is the correct explanation of (A)
2 Both (A) and (R) are true, but (R) is not a correct explanation of (A)
3 (A) is true, but (R) is false
4 (A) is false, but (R) is true

***Ans.* (3)**

Exp. (A) is true, but (R) is false.

According to John Austin, international law is true law and not negative international morality, is true. According to him, International Law is not true law, but a code of rules and conduct of moral force only. He holds that International Law is no law as it does not emanate from a law giving authority and has no sanction behind it.

Reason (R) is false because the elements of Austin's definition are not absent in international law. All these features are present in international law.

16 "International law is international morality or ethics, international courtesy or convention in the social sense of the word, comity as distinguished from rule of law." Above statement is attributed to

1 Hobbes 2 Pufendorf
3 Bentham 4 Kelson

***Ans.* (3)**

Exp. The given statement is attributed to Bentham.

International law used Bentham's innovation of 1789, which has found favour with public, instead of the older, more expressive term, law of nations has been variously denounced and praised as international morality or ethics, international courtesy or convention in the social sense of the word. Comity as distinguished from rule of law or merely and finally as the foreign policy such as the Monroe doctrine.

17 Match List I with List II and select the correct answer using the codes given below.

List I	List II
A. International custom	I. Peace keeping
B. United Nations	II. Source of international law
C. Enforcing judgement of International Court of Justice	III. Entry 14, list I read with Article 73
D. Nirmal Bose Vs. Union of India, AIR Calcutta, p.506	IV. Political mechanism

Codes

	A	B	C	D		A	B	C	D
1	II	I	IV	III	2	I	II	IV	III
3	I	II	III	IV	4	IV	II	I	III

***Ans.* (1)**

Exp. The correct matching is A-II, B-I, C-IV, D-III.

International custom is the source of international law. Customary law, also known as the law of nations, applies when no other authority is available to create a law.

United Nations is the international organisation that is engaged in various peacekeeping measures. peacekeeping by the United Nations is a role held by the Department of Peace Operations as "a unique and dynamic instrument developed by the organisation as a way to help countries torn by conflict to create the conditions for lasting peace".

Enforcing judgement of the International Court of Justice is linked with the political mechanism of the respective state. The ICJ is one of the six principal organs of the United Nations. Notably, It is the only UN principal organ not situated in New York.

Nirmal Bose Vs. Union of India deals with Entry 14, list I read with Article 73 that is the executive power of the Union extends to matters concerning which the Parliament can make laws.

18 Estrada doctrine relates to

1 necessity of recognition
2 form of recognition
3 no necessity of recognition
4 recognition is superficial

***Ans.* (3)**

Exp. Estrada doctrine relates to no necessity of recognition. The Estrada doctrine is the name of Mexico's core foreign policy ideal from 1930 to the early 2000s. Its name is derived from Genaro Estrada, Secretary of Foreign Affairs during the presidency of Pascual Ortiz Rubio (1930–1932). Estrada doctrine is the recognition of a government should be based on its de facto existence, rather than on its legitimacy.

19 Principle of United Nation is

1 some sovereigns are more equal than others
2 member nations have rights but no obligations
3 all members shall settle their international disputes by peaceful means
4 all members shall settle their national disputes by peaceful means

Ans. (3)

Exp. Principle of the United Nations is that all members shall settle their international disputes by peaceful means in such a manner that international peace and security and justice are not endangered. This has been laid down under the first Chapter of the UN Charter.

20 Doctrine of forum prorogatum means

1 Jurisdiction cannot be conferred upon an existing tribunal not otherwise competent by the litigants during the proceedings
2 Jurisdiction can be conferred upon an existing tribunal not otherwise competent by the litigants during the proceedings
3 Jurisdiction can be conferred upon an existing tribunal not otherwise competent by the litigants after the proceedings
4 None of the above

Ans. (2)

Exp. Doctrine of forum prorogatum means jurisdiction can be conferred upon an existing tribunal not otherwise competent by the litigants during the proceedings.
The jurisdiction of the International Court of Justice (ICJ) in a contentious case is based entirely on the consent of states. The doctrine of forum prorogatum affords an informal way for a state to express consent to the Court's jurisdiction.

21 Given below are two statements, one is labelled as Assertion (A) and the other labelled as Reason (R).

Assertion (A) Nikah is a regular and permanent form of marriage among Muslims.

Reason (R) Muta is contractual form of marriage and is most uncommon in India.

Codes

1 Both (A) and (R) are correct
2 (A) is correct, but (R) is wrong
3 (R) is correct, but (A) is wrong
4 Neither (A) is correct nor (R) is correct

Ans. (1)

Exp. Both (A) and (R) are correct.
Nikah is a regular and permanent form of marriage among Muslims, is correct. In Islam, the marriage between a bride and groom is a legal contract, known as Nikah. The Nikah ceremony is one part of several steps of a marriage arrangement considered ideal by Islamic tradition.
Muta is a contractual form of marriage and is most uncommon in India, is correct. Muta marriage is a temporary marriage. Muta marriage is recognised in Shia only. Sunni law doesn't recognise muta marriage. The majority of Indian Sunnis are followers of the Hanifi division and thus, Muta is not a common form of marriage in India.

22 Where a Hindu male and Hindu female contract their marriage under the Special Marriage Act, 1954, Hindu personal law

1 applies to such marriage
2 does not apply
3 applies with some modifications
4 applies with Indian Contract Act

Ans. (1)

Exp. Where a Hindu male and Hindu female contract their marriage under the Special Marriage Act, 1954, Hindu personal law applies to such marriage.
The Special Marriage Act, 1954 has been passed to solemnise the inter-religion marriage. As per the Hindu Marriage Act, male and female belonging to the Hinduism alone can marry each other observing Hindu formalities. This applies not only to a Hindu by religion, but also to Buddhist, Jain or Sikh by religion and to any other person who is not a Muslim, Christian, Parsi or Jew by religion. Hindu Marriage Act extends to the whole of India, except the State of Jammu and Kashmir. It extends to the Hindus and others mentioned above, who have domiciled in the territories to which Hindu Marriage Act extends and who are outside India.

23 When two persons are descendants of a common ancestor but by different wives, they are said to be related to each other by

1 Full Blood
2 Uterine Blood
3 Half - Blood
4 None of these

Ans. (3)

Exp. When two persons are descendants of a common ancestor but by different wives, they are said to be related to each other by Half-blood.
When two persons have a common father between them, but have two different mothers then they both are related to each other by half blood.
Suppose, 'A' (male) and 'B' (female) are married, and they have 'C' as their daughter and 'D' as son. 'A' remarries with 'E' and further have their children 'F' as daughter and 'G' as son. Here, we see 'C' and 'F' are half blood sisters or half sisters as they both have a common father 'A', but two different mothers 'B' and 'E'.

24 The term 'Hindu' denotes the persons

I. professing Hindu religion
II. professing Buddhist, Jain or Sikh religion
III. who are not professing Muslims, Christian, Parsi or Jew religion.

In respect of the aforesaid propositions which is correct ?

1 I and II are correct and III is incorrect
2 II and III are correct and I is incorrect
3 I and III are incorrect, but II is correct
4 I, II and III all are correct

Ans. (4)

Exp. The Hindu Marriage Act of 1955 goes in greater detail to define this legal Hindu by stipulating in Section 2 that the Act applies

(i) to any person who is a Hindu by religion in any of its forms and developments, including a Virashaiva, a Lingayat or a follower of the Brahmo, Prarthana or Arya Samaj.

(ii) to any person who is a Buddhist, Jain or Sikh by religion

(iii) to any other person domiciled in the territories to which this Act extends, who is not a Muslim, Christian, Parsi or Jew by religion.

25 Given below are two statements, one is labelled as Assertion (A) and the other labelled as Reason (R).

Assertion (A) 'A' having a wife alive, marries another wife. The marriage is void.

Reason (R) Monogamy is the Law.

Codes

1 Both (A) and (R) are true
2 Both (A) and (R) are false
3 (A) is true, but (R) is false
4 (A) is false, but (R) is true

Ans. (1)

Exp. Both (A) and (R) are true.

'A' having a wife alive, marries another wife. The marriage is void and the statement is correct because it amounts to bigamy. Sections 5 and 11 of the Hindu Marriage Act provides that a subsequent marriage is void, if either party has a spouse alive at the time of the marriage.

Monogamy is the law and it explains the assertion correctly. This is because bigamy is made punishable under the Hindu Law under Section 494 of the Indian Penal Code.

26 A marriage under Muslim law between persons with fosterage relationship is

1 Sahih 2 Batil
3 Fasid 4 None of these

Ans. (2)

Exp. A marriage under Muslim law between persons with fosterage relationship is Batil.

Void Marriage is also known as Batil Marriage. It is an illegal union that does not exist in law. Thus, a marriage in violation of absolute prohibitions or polyandry is a void marriage. No mutual rights or obligations are created for the parties in case of void marriage. The children born to such a couple are deemed illegitimate and the wife has no rights to dower or maintenance.

27 Under the Indian Contract Act, acceptance of proposal should be

1 Conditional or Unconditional
2 Conditional but not absolute
3 Unconditional and absolute
4 Unconditional but not absolute

Ans. (3)

Exp. Under the Indian Contract Act, acceptance of a proposal should be unconditional and absolute.

Section 7(1) of the Contract Act states that in order to convert a proposal into a promise, the acceptance must be absolute and unqualified.

28 In Indian Contract Act, the term voidable contract has been defined under

1 Section 2(e) 2 Section 2(h)
3 Section 2(i) 4 Section 2(g)

Ans. (3)

Exp. In Indian Contract Act, the term voidable contract has been defined under Section 2(i).

According to Section 2(i), an agreement which is enforceable by law at the option of one or more of the parties thereto, but not at the option of the other or others, is a voidable contract.

Thus, a voidable contract is one which is enforceable by law at the option of one of the parties.

29 Contractual liability arises, where

1 there is offer and acceptance only
2 there is intention to create legal relation
3 there is loss to one party
4 the loss of one party is the gain of other party

Ans. (2)

Exp. Contractual liability arises, where there is intention to create legal relations.

Intention to create legal relations is a motion that every contracting party must have the necessary intention to enter into a legally binding contract.

30 There may be a contract without consideration, if

1 agreement is in writing and registered
2 parties to the agreement are in near relationship
3 agreement is made due to natural love and affection
4 All the above elements are present

Ans. (4)

Exp. There may be a contract without consideration, if an agreement is in writing and registered, parties to the agreement are in near relationship, agreement is made due to natural love and affection. Section 25 of the Contract Act reads as Agreements without consideration, void unless it is in writing and registered or is a promise to compensate for something or is a promise to pay a debt barred by limitation law.

31 An agreement of trade combination to regulate legal trade in organised way is

1 Void 2 Voidable 3 Legal 4 Illegal

Ans. (3)

Exp. An agreement of trade combination to regulate legal trade in organised way is legal.

Section 27 of Indian Contract Act, 1872 says that an agreement in restraint of trade is void. Every agreement by which anyone is restrained from exercising a lawful profession, trade or business of any kind, is to that extent void.

32 Which one of the following statements is true?

1 Intimation of minimum price is proposal
2 An agreement against public policy is voidable
3 An agreement, the meaning of which is not certain is void
4 Contingent contracts are illegal

Ans. (3)

➲ *Exp.* Among the given statements, statement 3 is true.

An agreement, the meaning of which is not certain, is void under Section 29 of the Contract Act.

Statement 1 is incorrect because intimation of minimum price is not an offer but an invitation to offer.

Statement 2 is incorrect because an agreement against public policy is not voidable but void under Section 28 of the Contract Act.

Statement 4 is incorrect because contingent contracts are valid under Section 31 of the Act.

33 Which one of the following statements is correct?

1 Damages can be dispensed within tort
2 Damages cannot be awarded in tort when other remedies are provided by a statute
3 A remedy by way of damages is essential ingredient of tort
4 Damages can be awarded only if there is a physical injury

Ans. (3)

➲ *Exp.* Among the given statements, statement 3 is correct.

A remedy by way of damages is an essential ingredient of tort. Damages can only be awarded in case of breach of a legal right.

Statement 1 is incorrect because damages cannot be dispensed within tort. They are one of the major ways of compensation in case of any tortious liability.

Statement 2 is incorrect because Damages can be awarded in tort when other remedies are provided by a statute. They may be limited by a statute but can still be awarded.

Statement 4 is incorrect because damages can be awarded even if there is no physical injury. What matters is that there must be an infringement of a legal right.

34 After considering the following, choose the right choice.

Right to claim damages in tort would arise only if

I. Infringement of a legal right
II. Legal damage
III. Any damage
IV. Existence of a legal right

Choose the most appropriate answer from the options given below.

1 I, II and III are present
2 I, II and IV are present
3 I, III and IV are present
4 All I, II, III and IV are present

Ans. (2)

➲ *Exp.* Right to claim damages in tort would arise only if infringement of a legal right, legal damage and existence of a legal right have taken place.

'Injuria sine damnum' is the principle that governs tortious liability. What is essential to constitute a damage in tort, is the breach of a legal right, even if no actual damage has taken place.

35 Mental condition of the wrong doer is

1 relevant in all torts
2 not relevant in tortious liability
3 relevant in case of strict liability
4 relevant in torts based on fault

Ans. (4)

➲ *Exp.* Mental condition of the wrongdoer is relevant in torts based on fault.

In some torts like assault, deceit and conspiracy, the mental condition is relevant, while in most of the torts, the mental condition of the wrongdoer is irrelevant. So, the mental condition of the wrongdoer depends on the act done by him.

36 'P'voluntarily accepted lift from 'D' who was drunk and driving the car. 'D' was affected by the drink and this was known to 'P'. 'D' caused the accident in which 'P' suffered injury. Here,

1 'D' can escape the liability because 'P' was aware of risk
2 'D' is liable because 'P' did not agree to suffer the harm
3 'D' is not liable because he gave free lift to 'P'
4 'D' is liable because the degree of intoxication was not to such an extent that it can be assumed that there was voluntary assumption of risk by 'P'

Ans. (4)

➲ *Exp.* In the given scenario 'D' is liable because the degree of intoxication was not to such an extent that it can be assumed that there was voluntary assumption of risk by 'P'. Thus, the doctrine of volenti non fit injuria will not be applicable here.

37 A rickshaw was being pulled by the rickshaw puller with three passengers on board, which was against law. A bus was being driven rashly and negligently by its driver. The bus collides with rickshaw resulting into damage to rickshaw and injury to rickshaw passengers. Here

1 passengers cannot claim compensation from bus operator for the injury as they themselves were not acting according to law
2 passengers cannot claim compensation from bus operator as there was contributory negligence on their part
3 passengers can claim full compensation from bus operator as their negligence has not contributed to their injury
4 passengers are entitled for compensation which shall be proportionally reduced taking into account their illegal act

Ans. (3)

➲ *Exp.* In the given scenario, passengers can claim full compensation from bus operator as their negligence has not contributed to their injury.

Section 279 of IPC says, whoever drives any vehicle, or rides, on any public way in a manner so rash or negligent as to endanger human life, or to be likely to cause hurt or injury to any other person, shall be punished with imprisonment of either description for a term which may extend to six months, or with fine which may extend to one thousand rupees, or with both.

38 Consider the following and then select the right code

I. Absolute liability implies liability without fault.

II. In case of absolute liability defendant is liable for the injury if his act is the direct and proximate cause of plaintiff's injury.

III. Absolute liability is the liability of the defendant without any defence.

IV. In absolute liability, defendant can escape the liability if he can prove that the damage was the result of an act of stranger.

Codes

1 I, II and IV are correct 2 II and III are correct

3 I, II and III are correct 4 I and IV are correct

Ans. (3)

➲ *Exp.* Statements I, II and III are correct.

In absolute liability, a person could be guilty even if there was no intention to commit a crime, it implies liability without fault. In case of absolute liability the defendant is liable for the injury if his act is the direct and proximate cause of plaintiff's injury. Absolute liability is the liability of the defendant without any defence.

Statement IV is incorrect because it is a strict liability that the defendant can escape the liability if he can prove that the damage was the result of an act of a stranger.

39 Causing one thing to resemble another thing is known as

1 counterfeit 2 deception

3 cheating 4 All of these

Ans. (1)

➲ *Exp.* Causing one thing to resemble another thing is known as counterfeit.

According to Section 28 of the Indian Penal Code, A person is said to 'counterfeit' who causes one thing to resemble another thing, intending by means of that resemblance to practise deception, or knowing it to be likely that deception will thereby be practised.

40 A private libel is not considered as strict liability because

1 there is no common injury or danger inferred from the facts

2 it was the result of bonafide belief

3 it is not a statutory offence

4 the principles of Ryland Vs Fletcher is not applicable

Ans. (1)

➲ *Exp.* A private libel is not considered as strict liability because there is no common injury or danger inferred from the facts. Libel is concerned with defamatory writings; whereas the law of slander is concerned with defamatory speech. There are some differences in the laws relating to slander and libel. It used to be thought that defamatory statements on a website would always be libellous rather than slanderous.

41 Given below are two statements, one is labelled as Assertion (A) and the other is labelled as Reason (R).

Assertion (A) The principle of common intention applies when a criminal act is done by several persons in furtherance of that intention.

Reason (R) A intentional cooperation for committing an offence culminated from several acts.

Codes

1 (A) is true, but (R) is not the reason

2 Both (A) and (R) are true and (R) is the reasonable explanation of (A)

3 Both are distinctive offences and (A) is not dependent on (R)

4 (A) is false, but (R) is true

Ans. (3)

➲ *Exp.* Both are distinctive offences and (A) is not dependent on (R).

The principle of common intention applies when a criminal act is done by several persons in furtherance of that intention, is an offence.

As per Section 34 of IPC, when a criminal act is done by several persons in furtherance of the common intention of all each of such persons is liable for that act in the same manner as if it were done by him alone.

A intentional cooperation for committing an offence culminated from several acts is a distinct offence. This has been dealt with under Section 37 of the Indian Penal Code.

42 Given below are two statements, one is labelled as Assertion (A) and the other is labelled as Reason (R).

Assertion (A) The right of private defence does not depend upon the actual criminality of the aggressor but on the wrongful character of the act attempted.

Reason (R) Even if an act is treated as offence the right of private defence arises against the author despite his personal incapacity.

Codes

1 (A) is correct principle because (R) is the right reason

2 (A) is untenable under law while (R) is the justifiable cause

3 (A) is the law on an unlawful act while (R) results without mens rea

4 (A) is not true while (R) is false

Ans. (1)

Exp. (A) is the correct principle because (R) is the right reason.

The right of private defence does not depend upon the actual criminality of the aggressor but on the wrongful character of the act attempted is correct. This is because every person has the right to defend his body or property irrespective of the mental state of the aggressor. A person cannot be said to not defend himself if he is attacked by an insane person.

Even if an act is treated as an offence, the right of private defence arises against the author despite his personal incapacity, is correct and explains the assertion. The right of private defence will completely absolve a person from all guilt if the offence committed by the deceased, who occasioned the cause of the exercise of the right of private defence of body and property falls within any one of the six or four categories enumerated in Sections 100 and 103 of the Indian Penal Code.

43 The maxim 'De Minimis non curat' relates to ________.

1 Slight harm
2 Trifles
3 Exhibition of disrespect
4 Annoyance

Ans. (1)

Exp. The maxim 'De Minimis non curat' relates to slight harm.

The maxim 'De Minimis non curat' lex actually means that the law does not take any account of the trivial matters. The principle underlying the maxim is that nothing is a wrong which is trivial in nature and a person of ordinary sense and temper would not complain.

This maxim protects a trivial wrong though infringes legal right of other. But the maxim does not protect a wrongdoer when the wrong is not trivial in nature and a harm is caused or a legal right is infringed. This principle is also recognised in Section 95 of the Indian Penal Code. This Section is intended to prevent the penalisation of negligible wrongs or of an offence of trivial character.

44 Instigating or engaging in a conspiracy or intentionally aiding a person to commit an offence is better known as ________.

1 Principal Crime
2 Second Degree Crime
3 Wilful mis-representation
4 Abetment

Ans. (4)

Exp. Instigating or engaging in a conspiracy or intentionally aiding a person to commit an offence is better known as Abetment.

According to Section 107 of the Indian Penal Code, Abetment is when a person abets the doing of a thing, who

(i) Firstly instigates any person to do that thing.
(ii) Secondly engages with one or more person or persons in any conspiracy for the doing of that thing, if act or illegal omission takes place in pursuance of that conspiracy and in order to the doing of that thing.
(iii) Thirdly, intentionally aids, by any act or illegal omission, the doing of that thing.

45 The First Come Last Go and the Last Come First Go rule is associated with

1 Strike
2 Lock out
3 Retrenchment
4 Closure

Ans. (3)

Exp. The First Come Last Go and the Last Come First Go rule is associated with Retrenchment.

Retrenchment means the termination of services of a workmen by the employer on the ground of redundancy, i.e., when he becomes surplus to the requirements of the employer. In the retrenchment 'Last Come First Go' rule must be followed where any workmen is to be retrenched. The employer shall retrench the workmen who is the last person employed in that particular category of workmen.

46 One of the following is not the duty of Works Committee under the Industrial Disputes Act.

1 To promote measures for securing and preserving amity and good relations between the employees and workmen
2 To form groups among workmen and strengthen mediation between employer and employee
3 To achieve the object, it is their duty to comment upon matter of common interest or concern of employers and workmen
4 To endeavour to compose any material difference of opinion in respect of matters of common interest or concern between employers and workmen

Ans. (2)

Exp. To form groups among workmen and strengthen mediation between employer and employee is not the duty of Works Committee under the Industrial Disputes Act.

According to Section 3(2) of the Industrial Disputes Act, 1947, it shall be the duty of the Works Committee to promote measures for securing and preserving amity and good relations between the employer and workmen and, to that end, to comment upon matters of their common interest or concern and endeavour to compose any material difference of opinion in respect of such matters.

47 An unregistered trade union has one of the following disadvantage

1 It can acquire and hold both movable and immovable property
2 It has no corporate existence
3 It can contract through agents
4 It is a legal entity

Ans. (2)

Exp An unregistered trade union has disadvantage that it has no corporate existence. Disadvantages of unregistered trade union are as follows

(i) An unregistered trade union has no advantages as it is not a juristic person, it is only an association of persons.
(ii) It cannot sue or be sued on its own name.
(iii) It has no perpetual succession.

(iv) It cannot be affiliated to any National or International Union Federation.
(v) It cannot acquire properties in its own name.
(vi) It cannot contract on its own name.
(vii) The employers do not come forward for discussions and collective bargaining with the executives of an unregistered trade union, as it has no legal status.

48 In order to entitle the workmen to wages for the period of strike, the strike should be legal as well as justified. The above principle was laid down in one of the following case by the Apex Court

1 Crompton Greaves Vs. The Workmen AIR 1978 SC
2 Ballarpur collieries Vs. CGIT Dhanbad AIR 1972 SC
3 Management of India Radiatiors Ltd and another Vs. presiding officer and another AIR 2003 II LLJ (Mad)
4 Workmen of Motor Industries Co. Ltd Vs. Management of Motor Industries Co Ltd AIR 1969 SC

Ans. (1)

Exp. Two judge bench of the Supreme Court in Crompton Greaves Vs. The Workment AIR 1978 held that "It is well-settled that to entitle the workmen to wages for the period of strike, the strike should be legal as well as justified. A strike is legal if it does not violate any provisions of the statute. Again, a strike cannot be said to be unjustified unless the reasons for it are entirely perverse or unreasonable. It is also well settled that use of force or violence or acts of sabotage resorted to by the workmen during a strike disentitles them to wages for the strike period.

49 In which of the following case the Supreme Court held that when retrenchment of a workmen is invalid reinstatcment can be ordered?

1 Harindara Singh Vs. Punjab State warehousing Corporation 2010 II LLJ SC
2 Surendra Kumar Verma Vs. Central Govt. India. Tribunal 1981 ILLJ SC
3 Management WB India Ltd Vs. Jagannath AIR 1974 SC
4 Pioneer Ltd Vs. Tajdar Hussain AIR 1974 SC

Ans. (2)

Exp In Surendra Kumar Verma Vs. Central Government of India Tribunal 1981 ILJ SC held that when retrenchment of a workmen is invalid, reinstatement can be ordered. The Court held that the High Court was not justified in denying the back-wages to the appellant altogether, and bearing in mind the circumstances of the case, a lump-sum compensation should be directed to be paid.

50 In which of the following, the members of the registered trade union can claim immunity in criminal cases?

1 The combination of two or more members of a registered Trade Union Act in furtherance of a trade dispute
2 The combination of two or more members of a registered Trade Union Act with an intention to create loss or damage to the properties of the employer
3 The trade union leaders in exercise of the managerial powers direct the workers from abstaining to do the work
4 The members of a Trade Union Act in combination with an intention to coerce the employer to acced to their demands

Ans. (1)

Exp. When the combination of two or more members of a registered Trade Union Act in furtherance of a trade dispute, then the members of the registered trade union can claim immunity in criminal cases.

PAPER III

1 'The Constitution establishes a system of government which is almost quasi-federal ...... a unitary state with subsidiary federal features rather than a federal state with subsidiary unitary features.' This is the opinion of

1 KC Wheare
2 Jennings
3 AV Dicey
4 None of the above

Ans. (1)

Exp. The given statement is the opinion of KC Wheare. KC Wheare generally regarded as the father of contemporary federal theories, defined federalism or federal government, in his famous book; 'Federal Government', as 'the method of dividing power so that general and regional governments are each within a sphere co-ordinate and independent'.

2 Match List I with List II and select the correct answer using the codes given below.

	List I		List II
A.	Appointment of Judges	I.	Article 124
B.	A Court of Record	II.	Article 129
C.	Appeal in civil cases	III.	Article 133
D.	Certificate for appeal to Supreme Court	IV.	Article 134A

Codes

	A	B	C	D		A	B	C	D
1	I	II	III	IV	2	I	III	II	IV
3	I	II	IV	III	4	II	I	IV	III

Ans. (1)

Exp. The correct matching is A-I, B-II, C-III, D-IV

Article 124 provides for the appointment of judges. It says there shall be a Supreme Court of India consisting of a Chief Justice of India and, until Parliament by law prescribes a larger number, of not more than seven other Judges.

Article 129 talks about the court of record. It says the Supreme Court shall be a court of record and shall have all the powers of such a court including the power to punish for contempt of itself.

Article 133 talks about appeal in civil cases. It says that an appeal shall lie to the Supreme Court from any judgement, decree or final order in a civil proceeding of a High Court in the territory of India if the High Court certifies under Article 134A.

Article 134A talks about certificate for appeal to Supreme Court. It says parliament may by law confer on the Supreme Court any further powers to entertain and hear appeals from any judgement, final order or sentence in a criminal proceeding of a High Court in the territory of India subject to such conditions and limitations as may be specified in such law.

3 The Constitution of Election Commission is provided in the Constitution under

1 Article 323
2 Article 324
3 Article 327
4 Article 329

Ans. (2)

Exp. The Constitution of Election Commission is provided in the Constitution under Article 324.

Article 324 of the Constitution provides that the power of superintendence, direction and control of elections to Parliament, State legislatures, the office of President of India and the office of Vice-President of India shall be vested in the Election Commission.

4 Match List I with List II and select the correct answer using the codes given below.

List I	List II
A. Doctrine of Eclipse	I. RMDC Vs. Union of India
B. Doctrine of Severability	II. State of Bombay Vs. FN Balsara
C. Doctrine of Waiver	III. Bhikaji Vs. State of MP
D. Doctrine of Pith and Substance	IV. Bashesher Nath Vs. Income Tax Commissioner

Codes

	A	B	C	D		A	B	C	D
1	III	II	IV	I	2	II	III	I	IV
3	III	I	IV	II	4	IV	II	III	I

Ans. (3)

Exp. The correct matching is A-III, B-I, C-IV, D-II.

Doctrine of Eclipse-Bhikaji Vs. State of MP. There was a detailed discussion on the application of the pre-existing laws, nature and effect of the Constitutional amendments and how the courts must determine the unconstitutionality of a particular law. Under the Motor Vehicles Act, 1939, a State Government is given the power to control the road transport and in pursuance of it, in the State of Madhya Pradesh, the C.P and Berar Motor Vehicles Act was enacted. This case had questioned the constitutional validity of the C.P. and Berar Motor Vehicles (Amendment) Act, 1947 (Act III of 1948) and upheld the impugned Act to be valid.

Doctrine of Severability- RMDC Vs. Union of India. The Doctrine of Severability was considered by the Supreme Court of India in this case and the rules regarding severability was laid down in this case. The intention of the legislature behind this is the determine whether theinvalid portion of the statute can be severed from the valid part or not.

Doctrine of Waiver-Bashesher Nath Vs. Income Tax Commissioner. It was held that the fundamental rights set up by the Constitution are spiritual in nature and enacted public interest, and hence cannot be waived.

Doctrine of Pith and Substance-State of Bombay Vs. FN Balsara. The Bombay Prohibition Act was challenged on the ground that it accidentally encroaches upon import and export of liquor across custom frontier – a central subject. The court while upholding the impugned legislation declared that the Act was in pith and substance a State subject even though it incidentally encroached upon a central subject.

5 In case there is any inconsistency between the laws made by Parliament and the laws made by the State Legislature, which one of the following shall prevail?

1 The law made by Parliament only if it is passed before the law made by State Legislature
2 The law made by Parliament only if it is passed after the law made by State Legislature
3 The law made by Parliament whether it is passed before or after the law made by State Legislature
4 The law made by State if it is passed after the law made by Parliament

Ans. (3)

Exp. In case there is any inconsistency between the laws made by Parliament and the laws made by the State Legislature, the law made by Parliament whether it is passed before or after the law made by State Legislature shall prevail.

It is under Article 254 that the Constitution provides that in case both the Parliament and the state make a law upon a matter in the Concurrent List and the laws are such that they are irreconcilable, then the law made by the Parliament shall prevail and the law made by the state shall be deemed to be repugnant to the extent of its repugnancy with the Central law.

6 Which of the following statements is true?

1 All self-incriminatory statements are valid
2 All self-incriminatory statements are violative of Article 20(3)
3 Self-incriminatory statements furnished under compulsion are violative of Article 20(3)
4 None of the above

***Ans.* (3)**

Exp. Self-incriminatory statements furnished under compulsion are violative of Article 20(3) is a true statement.

Article 20(3) says that no person accused of any offence shall be compelled to be a witness against himself.

7 Given below are two statements, one is labelled as Assertion (A) and the other is labelled as Reason (R).

Assertion (A) Under Article 368, The Parliament can amend any part of the Constitution of India.

Reason (R) The Parliament is supreme legislative body elected by people of India.

Codes

1 Both (A) and (R) are true and (R) is the correct explanation of (A)
2 Both (A) and (R) are true, but (R) is not the correct explanation of (A)
3 (A) is true, but (R) is false
4 (A) is false, but (R) is true

***Ans.* (4)**

Exp. (A) is false, but (R) is true.

Under Article 368, the Parliament can amend any part of the Constitution of India is false because Parliament has limited powers to amend the Constitution. Parliament cannot damage or destroy the basic features of the Constitution.

The Parliament is supreme legislative body elected by people of India is the correct fact because every legislation is formed by Parliament through its legislative powers, hence it is true. The Indian Parliament comprises of the President and the two houses Rajya Sabha and Lok Sabha.

8 Match List I with List II and select the correct answer using the codes given below

	List I	List II
A.	Separation of judiciary from executive	I. Article-51
B.	Promotion of international peace and security	II. Article-48A
C.	Organisation of village panchayats	III. Article-50
D.	Protection and improvement of forests and wildlife	IV. Article-40

Codes

	A	B	C	D		A	B	C	D
1	I	II	III	IV	2	III	I	IV	II
3	III	II	IV	I	4	II	I	III	IV

***Ans.* (2)**

Exp. The correct matching is A-III, B-I, C-IV, D-II.

Article 50 of the Constitution of India is related to Separation of judiciary from executive.

It says that the State shall take steps to separate the judiciary from the executive in the public services of the State.

According to *Article 51*, the State shall endeavour to promote international peace and security; maintain just and honourable relations between nations; foster respect for international law and treaty obligations in the dealings of organised peoples with one another; and encourage settlement of international disputes by arbitration.

As per *Article 40* of the Indian Constitution the State shall take steps to organise village panchayats and endow them with such powers and authority as may be necessary to enable them to function as units of self-government.

Article 48-A states that the State shall endeavour to protect and improve the environment and to safeguard the forests and wildlife of the country.

9 Lokpal or Lokayukta is competent to

1 discharge the functions of administrative officer.
2 investigate complaints involving grievances in respect of administrative actions.
3 conduct inquiry against administrative officer for disciplinary action.
4 give observations and recommendations in respect of administrative actions to the government.

***Ans.* (2)**

Exp. Lokpal or Lokayukta is competent to investigate complaints involving grievances in respect of administrative actions.

The Lokpal has three officials under him- Secretary to Lokpal, Director of Inquiry and Prosecution. After receiving the complaint, the Lokpal will decide whether the inquiry is to be conducted or not. The inquiry wing is headed by the Director of Inquiry, and the function of the inquiry wing is to conduct a preliminary inquiry into the offences alleged to have been committed by the public servants. The inquiry needs to be completed within 90 days.

The Lokpal can also conduct the inquiry through CBI. The report made by the inquiry wing or CBI would place before the Lokpal bench with at least 3 members. Departmental inquiry can also be initiated. If the officer is found to be innocent, then a closure report can be filed and proceed against the complainant for a false complaint. The Lokpal has powers of superintendence, ordering search and seizure, confiscation and attachment of property, recommending transfer or suspension of the accused public servant.

10 Given below are two statements, one is labelled as Assertion (A) and the other is labelled as Reason (R).

Assertion (A) Indian Constitution has not recognised the doctrine of separation of power in its absolute rigidity.

Reason (R) Doctrine of separation of power accommodates a system of checks and balances.

Codes

1 Both (A) and (R) are true and (R) is the correct explanation of (A)
2 Both (A) and (R) are true, but (R) is not the correct explanation of (A)
3 (A) is true, but (R) is false
4 (R) is true, but (A) is false

Ans. *(1)*

➲ *Exp.* Both (A) and (R) are true and (R) is the correct explanation of (A).
Indian Constitution has not recognised the doctrine of separation of power in its absolute rigidity is true because at times executive can declare laws through ordinance and judiciary through precedents as a result it keeps the system of check and balance between the different organs.
Doctrine of separation of power accommodates a system of checks and balances is correct explains the given assertion.
Therefore, Indian Constitution has not recognised the doctrine of separation of power in its absolute rigidity because Doctrine of separation of power accommodates a system of checks and balances.

11 Administrative law is concerned with the operation and control of the powers of administrative authorities with emphasis on functions rather than on structure. This definition was given by

1 KC Davis
2 Jennings
3 AV Dicey
4 Wade

Ans. *(4)*

➲ *Exp.* The definition given in question is given by Wade.
According to Professor HWR Wade a first approximation to a definition of administrative law is to say that it is the law relating to the control of governmental power and as a second approximation to a definition, administrative law may be said to be body of general principles which govern the exercise of powers and duties by public authorities. According to Wade, administrative law relates to the control of government power. In his opinion, the primary objective of administrative law is to keep powers of the government within their legal limits, so as to protect the citizens against their abuse.

12 Which one of the following is not basic source of administrative law?

1 Custom
2 Delegated legislation
3 Ordinance promulgated by Governor
4 Reports of the Committees and Commission

Ans. *(1)*

➲ *Exp.* Custom is not the basic source of administrative law. Statute is the principal source of administrative power. Statute emanates from the Constitution. Under the Constitution, law-making power has been given to Parliament and State Legislatures. Administration is given powers by statutes.

13 Doctrine of pleasure is related to

1 Fundamental Duties
2 Fundamental Rights
3 Directive Principles of State Policy
4 None of the above

Ans. *(4)*

➲ *Exp.* Doctrine of pleasure is not related to any of the given choices.
The Doctrine of Pleasure is one of those concepts which has been introduced in India from British rule. Under this doctrine, the civil servants were regarded as servants of the crown and these civil servants served at their pleasure. Article 310 of the Indian constitution incorporates the common law Doctrine of Pleasure. It expressly provides that all persons who are members of the defence Services or the civil services of the union of the All-India Services hold office during the pleasure of the President and every person who is a member of a civil service of a State or holds any civil post under a State holds office during the pleasure of the Governor of the State.

14 Which of the following statements is true?

1 Mandamus lies against quasi-judicial order
2 Mandamus is issued where inferior court declined jurisdiction
3 Mandamus may be issued, even if alternate remedy is available
4 Mandamus may be issued even no legal right of petitioner subsists.

Ans. *(2)*

➲ *Exp.* Statement 2 that says, Mandamus is issued where inferior court declined jurisdiction is true.
Mandamus is a judicial remedy in the form of an order from a court to any government, subordinate court, corporation, or public authority, to do some specific act which that body is obliged under law to do, and which is in the nature of public duty, and in certain cases one of a statutory duty.
Mandamus lies to secure the performance of a public duty. If the petitioner has sufficient legal interest in the performance, it will issue even if the body against which it is claimed, is not a statutory body. However, it will not lie to secure performance by a company of a duty towards its employees which is not of a public nature.

15 The rule of 'Audi alteram partem' requires reasonable opportunity of hearing. Hearing may be

1 only in writing
2 only orally
3 written or oral
4 Both written and oral

Ans. *(3)*

➲ *Exp.* The rule of 'Audi alteram partem' requires reasonable opportunity of hearing. Hearing may be written or oral. Audi alteram partem is a Latin term that means "Listen to the other side" or "let the other side be heard as well". It is fundamental legal principle in which each party is entitled to a fair hearing and given the opportunity to respond to evidence against them. The rule of fair hearing is a code of procedure, and hence covers every stage through which an administrative adjudication passes, starting from notice to final determination.

16 The high court can exercise the supervisory jurisdiction over the courts and tribunals subordinate to is under

1 Article 32 | 2 Article 226
3 Article 227 | 4 Article 141

Ans. (3)

➲ *Exp.* Under Article 227, the high court can exercise the supervisory jurisdiction over the courts and tribunals subordinate.

Article 227 determines that every High Court shall have superintendence over all courts and tribunals throughout the territories in relation to which it exercises jurisdiction (except a court formed under a law related to armed forces).

The High Court, can, under Article 227

(i) Call for returns from such courts,
(ii) Make and issue general rules and prescribe forms for regulating the practice and proceedings of such courts.
(iii) Prescribe forms in which books, entries and accounts be kept by the officers of any such courts.

17 Fiction theory is related to which one of the following concepts?

1 Ownership | 2 Justice
3 Legal Personality | 4 None of these

Ans. (3)

➲ *Exp.* Fiction theory is related to Legal Personality.

Fiction theory was put forward by Von Savigny, Salmond, Coke, Blackstone and Holland etc. According to this theory, the personality of a corporation is different from that of its members. Savigny regarded corporation as an exclusive creation of law having no existence apart from its individual members who form the corporate group and whose acts are attributed to the corporate entity. As a result of this, any change in the membership does not affect the existence of the corporation.

18 "We must admit openly that precedent makes law as well as declare it ________. Original precedents are the outcome of the international exercise by the courts of their privileges of developing the law at the same time that they administer it." Who said it?

1 Salmond Redcliffe
2 Redcliffe
3 Lord Denning
4 Starke

Ans. (1)

➲ *Exp.* The statement given in question is given by Salmond Redcliffe.

According to Salmond, the doctrine of precedent has two meanings, namely

1. in a loose sense precedent includes merely reported case-law which may be cited and follows by the court,
2. in its strict sense, precedent means that case-law which not only has a great binding authority.

19 Professor Holland distinguishes a legal right from

1 Salmond
2 Redcliffe
3 Lord Denning
4 Starke

Ans. (3)

➲ *Exp* Professor Holland distinguishes a legal right from Lord Denning.

Lord Justice Denning has advocated and has himself adopted a re-classification of the traditional conceptions involved under the general heading of burden of proof and presumptions.

They include the right of attribution, the right to have a work published anonymously or pseudonymously, and the right to the integrity of the work.

20 Match List I with List II and select the correct answer using the codes given below.

List I (Concepts)	List II (Jurists)
A. Minimum content of law	I. Fuller
B. Inner morality of law	II. Hart
C. Law with a variable content	III. Kohler
D. Law as a phenomenon of civilisation	IV. Stammler

Codes

	A	B	C	D		A	B	C	D
1	III	I	II	IV	2	II	III	IV	I
3	II	I	IV	III	4	I	II	III	IV

Ans. (3)

➲ *Exp.* The correct matching is A-II, B-I, C-IV, D-III

Hart adopted the phrase 'minimum content of natural law' to show the bare minimums that any legal system has to have in order to survive.

In his widely discussed 1964 book 'The Morality of Law', *Fuller* argues that all systems of law contain an "internal morality" that imposes on individuals a presumptive obligation of obedience.

Stammler defined law as, "species of will, others- regarding, self-authoritative and inviolable". With a view to distinguishing the new revived Natural Law from the old one, he called the former as 'Natural Law with variable content'

According to *Kohler*, civilisation continually changes, and so must law. Principles and rules of law suitable to one stage of civilisation may not be suitable to the next.

21 The 'Bracket Theory' contemplates

1 The members of the corporation are the only persons who have rights and duties.
2 Law puts a bracket around the persons, by organising juristic personality
3 Only human beings can have personality
4 Group has a real will, read mind and real power of action

Ans. (2)

Exp. The 'Bracket Theory' contemplates law puts a bracket around the persons, by organising juristic personality.

The Bracket theory is also known as the Symbolist theory which states that a corporation is created only by its members and its agents. So, the people who represent the corporation make up the corporation. The law only puts a bracket around them for convenience purposes. This is also similar to the concept of lifting of the corporate veil.

This group believed that the juristic personality is only a symbol to facilitate the working of the corporate bodies. Only the members of the corporation are 'persons' in real sense of the term and a bracket is put around them to indicate that they are to be treated as one single unit when they form themselves into a corporation.

22 Consider the following statements and give the correct answer by using the codes given below

I. Equitable ownership always presupposes the existence of a legal ownership.
II. Where property is given by *A* to *B* for the benefit of *C*. *B* becomes the legal owner and *C* the equitable owner.
III. In many cases, equity recognises ownership whereas law does not recognise ownership owing to some flaw or defect.
IV. Contingent ownership is spes successions.

Codes

1 I, II and III are correct
2 II and III are correct
3 I and II are correct
4 II and IV are correct

Ans. (1)

Exp. Among the given statements, statements I, II and III are correct.

Equitable ownership always presupposes the existence of a legal ownership. Where property is given by *A* to *B* for the benefit of *C*. *B* becomes the legal owner and *C* the equitable owner. In many cases, equity recognises ownership whereas law does not recognise ownership owing to some flaw or defect.

Ownership is the state of owning something. Anything that people own or possess gives them the quality of ownership. Wars are often fought over the ownership of land. When you buy a book, you own it.

Statement IV is incorrect because spes successions is non-transferable.

23 Who defined possession as "to gain possession a man must stand in a certain physical relation to the object and to the rest of world and must have a certain intent" ?

1 Holmes 2 Salmond
3 Pollock 4 Savigny

Ans. (1)

Exp. Holmes defines Possession as, "To gain possession a man must stand in a certain physical relation to the object and to the rest of the world and must have certain intent." The concept of possession is though basic and essential in human life; it is a difficult to define. There is no fixed or precise definition of possession because it is legal as well as factual concept.

24 Statement I Person of inheritance is the owner of the right.

Statement II Inheritance is a means to ownership.

Codes

1 Both Statements I and II are individually true statements and Statement II is the correct explanation of Statement I
2 Both the Statements I and II are individually true, but Statement II is not the correct explanation of Statement I
3 Statement I is true, but Statement II is false
4 Statement I is false, but Statement II is true

Ans. (1)

Exp. Both Statements I and II are individually true statements and Statement II is the correct explanation of Statement I.

Statement I says person of inheritance is the owner of the right, is correct because any person who has a right to inherit can only applicable for inheritance.

Statement II says inheritance is a means to ownership because once the person inherits, he or she becomes the owner of the property that is inherited and provides explanation to statement I.

25 Malum Prohibitum means

1 Intrinsically wrong
2 Course of law has made it otherwise
3 Innocent but made punishable by statute
4 All of the above

Ans. (3)

Exp. Malum Prohibitum means innocent but made punishable by statute.

Malum prohibitum is a Latin phrase used in law to refer to conduct that constitutes an unlawful act only by virtue of statute, as opposed to conduct that is evil in and of itself, or malum in se.

In criminal law, it is one of the collection of crimes which are traditional and not just created by statute, which are "malum prohibitum." Example: murder, rape, burglary and robbery are malum in se, while violations of the Securities and Exchange Act or most "white collar crimes" are Malum Prohibitum.

26 Demolishing a private structure standing encroached on a public street amounts to

1 gain by unlawful means
2 wrongful gain for public purpose
3 wrongful loss by mischief
4 None of the above

Ans. *(3)*

Exp. Demolishing a private structure standing encroached on a public street amount to wrongful loss by mischief.

According to section 425 of IPC whoever with intent to cause, or knowing that he is likely to cause, wrongful loss or damage to the public or to any person, cause the destruction of any property, or any such change in any property or in the situation thereof as destroys or diminishes its value or utility, or affects it injuriously, commits "mischief".

27 Given below are two statements, one is labelled as Assertion (A) and the other is labelled as Reason (R).

Assertion (A) When an act is done dishonestly it does not require deception or concealment as its ingredient.

Reason (R) Dishonesty requires an intention to cause wrongful loss or gain of property.

Codes

1 (A) is true, but (R) is not the reason
2 Both (A) and (R) are true because (R) is the right reason of (A)
3 Both (A) and (R) are distinctive offences
4 (A) is false, while (R) is true

Ans. *(2)*

Exp. Both (A) and (R) are true because (R) is the right reason for (A).

Assertion (A) says when an act is done dishonestly it does not require deception or concealment as its ingredient is true. Section 24 of IPC states that "Whoever does anything with the intention of causing wrongful gain to one person or wrongful loss to another person, is said to do that thing "dishonestly".

Reason (R) says dishonesty requires an intention to cause wrongful loss or gain of property is true.

When an act is done dishonestly, it does not require deception or concealment as its ingredient and reason for this dishonesty, requires an intention to cause wrongful loss or gain of property both are true.

28 Given below are two statements, one is labelled as Assertion (A) and the other is labelled as Reason (R).

Assertion (A) Harbouring includes supplying a person with shelter, food, money or conveyance.

Reason (R) The supply must relate to evading apprehension.

Codes

1 (A)A is correct clarification, but (R) is not the correct reason
2 (A) is not true, while (R) is the correct explanation
3 Both (A) and (R) are correct proposition
4 Only in exceptional situation (R) is the reason of (A)

Ans. *(3)*

Exp. Both (A) and (R) are correct proposition.

Assertion (A) says, harbouring includes supplying a person with shelter, food, money or conveyance is correct. The provision regarding Harbouring offenders is mentioned under section 212 of the Indian Penal Code, 1860.

Reason (R) says the supply must relate to evading apprehension is correct. Harbouring includes supplying a person with shelter, food, money or conveyance and reason for this the supply must relate to evading apprehension, and thus, it is true.

29 The real and abiding concern for the dignity of human life was decided in the case of

1 Rajendra Prasad Vs. State of UP
2 Mohindra Singh Vs. Delhi Administration
3 Javed Ahmed Vs. State of Maharashtra
4 Bachan Singh Vs. State of Punjab

Ans. *(4)*

Exp. The real and abiding concern for the dignity of human life was decided in the case of Bachan Singh Vs State of Punjab. The Apex Court in the landmark case of Bachan Singh Vs. State of Punjab laid down that life imprisonment is the rule and death sentence is an exception and principle of rarest of the rare case is also laid down under this case. The five judges bench laid down that " A real and abiding concern for the dignity of human life postulates resistance to taking a life through law instrumentality.

30 An unlawful assembly is a particular state of activity accompanied by the use of force or violence is riot, but it does not include

1 There must be five or more persons
2 There must be animation by a common object
3 persons assembled for lawful purpose but started quarrelling without any previous intention.
4 All of the above

Ans. *(3)*

Exp. An unlawful assembly is a particular state of activity accompanied by the use of force or violence is riot, but it does not include persons assembled for lawful purpose but started quarrelling without any previous intention.

As provided under Section 146 of the Indian Penal Code, 1860, a riot is simply an unlawful assembly in a particular state of activity, that activity being accompanied by the use of force or violence. It is this use of force or violence that distinguishes rioting from an unlawful assembly.

The word 'violence' in this context is not restricted to force used against persons only, but it extends also in force used against inanimate objects. Thus, if an unlawful assembly came together to for the purpose of pulling down a house or a shop or destroying any other property, it would be enough to show that violence was used.

31 Which of the following statements are not false evidence in discharge of public justice?

1 A false statement given under instigation
2 A statement known to be false
3 A statement not believed to be true
4 None of the above

***Ans.* (1)**

Exp. A false statement given under instigation is not false evidence in discharge of public justice.

Chapter 11 of Indian Penal Code deals with the false evidence and offences against public justice. Section 191 of the Indian Penal Code explains that giving false evidence means a person bound by oath or express provision of law, to tell the truth, makes a false statement or a statement that he doesn't believe to be true or believes to be false. False statement or evidence given by a person can be in written form or otherwise (oral or indicative).

32 A ceremonial pollution is an act relating to unclean worship and is known as the offence of

1 Insult to religion
2 Defilement
3 Anti secularism
4 Religious hatredness

***Ans.* (2)**

Exp. A ceremonial pollution is an act relating to unclean worship and is known as the offence of Defilement.

Section 295 in The Indian Penal Code says whoever destroys, damages or defiles any place of worship or any object held sacred by any class of persons with the intention of thereby insulting the religion of any class of persons or with the knowledge that any class of persons is likely to consider such destruction, damage or defilement as an insult to their religion, shall be punishable with imprisonment of either description for a term which may extend to two years or with fine or with both.

33 One of the following case is popularly known as "Doon Valley Case"

1 Pathumna Vs. State of Kerala AIR 1978, 2 SCC.
2 MC Mehta Vs. Union of India AIR 1987 SC.
3 Unni Krishnan Vs. State of AP AIR 1993, 1 SCC.
4 RL and E Kendra Vs. State of UP AIR 1985 SC.

***Ans.* (4)**

Exp. RL and E Kendra Vs. State of UP AIR 1985 SC, (popularly known as Doon Valley Case) was the first case of its kind in the country involving issues relating to environment and ecological balance which brought into sharp focus the conflict between development and conservation and the court emphasised the need for reconciling the two in the larger interest of the country, mining which denuded the Mussoorie Hills of trees and forests cover and accelerated soil erosion resulting in landslides and blockage of underground water which fed many rivers and springs in the river valley. The court appointed an expert committee to advise the Bench on the technical issues and on the basis of the report of the committee; the court ordered the closure of number of limestone quarries.

34 The polluter pays principle has been incorporated in

1 Principle 15 of the Rio Declaration on Environment and Development
2 Principle 27 of the Rio Declaration on Environment and Development
3 Principle 8 of the Rio Declaration on Environment and Development
4 Principle 16 of the Rio Declaration on Environment and Development

***Ans.* (4)**

Exp. The polluter pays principle has been incorporated in Principle 16 of the Rio Declaration on Environment and Development.

The 'Polluters Pays' principle is the commonly accepted practice that those who produce pollution should bear the costs of managing it to prevent damage to human health or the environment.

For instance, a factory that produces a potentially poisonous substance as a by-product of its activities, is usually held responsible for its safe disposal. This principle underpins most of the regulation of pollution affecting land, water and air. Pollution is defined in UK law as contamination of the land, water or air by harmful or potentially harmful substances.

35 Protection and Improvement of environment and safeguarding forests and wildlife is

1 One of the Directive Principles of State Policy
2 A Fundamental Right
3 Fundamental Duty
4 Both Directive Principles of State Policy and Fundamental Duties

***Ans.* (4)**

Exp. Protection and Improvement of environment and safeguarding forests and wildlife is both Directive Principles of State Policy and Fundamental Duties.

When the Constitution of India was adopted in 1950, the framers had not foreseen the importance of environmental preservation.

This aspect did receive attention later and, in 1976, the 42nd Amendment incorporated protection of wildlife and forests in the Directive Principles. It also included forests and protection of wild animals in the Concurrent List–Seventh Schedule (Article 256) of the Constitution. It is now enshrined in Article 51 A (g) of the Constitution that it shall be the fundamental duty of every citizen to protect and improve the natural environment including forests and wildlife.

In the Directive Principles of State Policy Article 48 A, mandate that the state shall endeavour to protect and improve the environment and to safeguard the forests and wildlife of the country.

36 Two important Amendments were brought in the year 1976. One with reference to Directive Principles of State Policy making the state responsible to protect and improve the environment and safeguard the forests and wild life of the country. The other under Fundamental duties making every citizen to protect and improve the natural environment including forests, lakes, rivers and wildlife and to have compassion for living creatures. The relevant amendment is

1 49th Amendment
2 45th Amendment
3 43rd Amendment
4 42nd Amendment

Ans. (4)

Exp. 42nd Amendment is the relevant amendment here.

The 42nd Constitutional Amendment Act brought a number of changes in the Constitution. The Act inter-alia gave preponderance to the Directive Principles of State Policy over the Fundamental Rights established the supremacy of Parliament and curtailed the powers of Judiciary. The Act was first of its kind. It is the most comprehensive act and touched almost all the sensitive areas of the Constitution. The Amendment was meant to enhance enormously the strength of the Government.

37 Section 19 of the Environment (Protection) Act, 1986 enables a person to file a complaint in a criminal court after giving a notice to the Pollution Control Board. Once a complaint has been made, the board is bound to make available to the complaint all relevant reports to him on demand. The board may also refuse to disclose on public interest.
Similar provisions are also available under

1 Section 49 of the Water Act, 1974 and Section 43 of the Air Act, 1981
2 Section 43 of the Water Act, 1974 and Section 49 of the Air Act, 1981
3 Section 42 of the Water Act, 1974 and Section 46 of the Air Act, 1981
4 Section 41 of the Water Act, 1974 and Section 42 of the Air Act, 1981

Ans. (1)

Exp. Similar provisions as in the question are also available under Section 49 of the Water Act, 1974 and Section 43 of the Air Act, 1981. Both the section talks about the cognizance of offence. Any person who has given notice of not less than sixty days, in the manner prescribed, of the alleged offence and of his intention to make a complaint to the Board or officer authorised as aforesaid, and no court inferior to that of a Metropolitan Magistrate or a Judicial Magistrate of the first class shall try any offence punishable under this Act.

38 The Supreme Court of India ordered conversion from fuel to CNG on 28th July, 1998. It also set up a committee to evaluate the cleanliness of various fuels on 27th April, 2001. The name of the committee is

1 Bhurelal Committee
2 Santhanam Committee
3 Mallimath Committee
4 Madanlal Committee

Ans. (1)

Exp. The name of the committee is Bhurelal Committee.

Bhure lal was the Chairman of the Environment Pollution (Prevention and Control) Authority (EPCA) and a member of the Monitoring Committee on Sealing set up by the Supreme Court. In 1999-2000, he prepared a report on environmental pollution and the ways to curb it. The report was tabled in the court pertaining to pollution levels in Delhi. The court stated that it could be implemented in all Indian cities. According to the Bhurelal report it is important to reduce sulphur and nitrous oxide levels in the atmosphere.

Some of the report's recommendations are to use lead-free fuel, to use more CNG in public transportation, to ensure all old vehicles and two stroke-engines are scrapped from the city, to encourage more public transportation, discourage private vehicles in central business districts, ban trucks from city roads, to implement strict parking norms and to ensure there are signal-free roads. It has been noticed that air pollution is lesser on the ring roads than on city roads. This is because vehicles move at a constant pace on the well-maintained ring roads without signals and speed breakers.

39 "The public trust doctrine primarily rests on the principle that certain resources like air, sea, water and the forests have such a great importance to the people as a whole that it would be wholly injustified to make them a subject of private ownership." The above Doctrine was discussed in detail in one of the following case

1 MC Mehta Vs. Kamalnath 1997 1 SCC.
2 Rural litigation and Environment Kendra Vs. Union of India AIR.1985 SC.
3 Vellore Citizen's welfare Forum Vs. Union of India 1996, 5 SCC.
4 MC Mehta Vs. Union of India AIR. 1987 SC.

Ans. (1)

Exp. In MC Mehta vs Kamalnath 1997 1 SCC, the doctrine of public trust was discussed in detail. The Public Trust Doctrine primarily rests on the principle that certain resources like air, sea, waters and the forests have such a great importance to the people as a whole that it would be wholly unjustified to make them a subject of private ownership. The said resources being a gift of nature, they should be made freely available to everyone irrespective of the status in life. The doctrine enjoins upon the Government to protect the resources as trustees for the enjoyment of the general public rather than to permit their use for private ownership or commercial purposes.

Though traditionally, this doctrine was applied only for the protection of access to the common for public benefit, but now the doctrine is being applied even to prevent over exploitation of the environment.

40 "Form of rules accepted by civilised states as determining their conduct towards each other and each other's subject, is defined as international law."

Above statement is attributed to

1 SS Lotus case
2 West Rand Central Gold Mining Ltd. Co. Vs. King
3 Queen Vs. Keyn
4 L Oppenheim

***Ans.** (2)*

➲ *Exp.* The given statement is attributed to West Rand Central Gold Mining Ltd, Co Vs. King [1905].

In principle, customary international law will be applied in the administration of municipal law. However, a rule of customary international law requires 'the common consent of civilised nations.

41 Given below are two statements, one is labelled as Assertion (A) and the other is labelled as Reason (R).

Assertion (A) International convention is the most important source of law.

Reason (R) International convention has generic wisdom.

Codes

1 Both (A) and (R) are true and (R) is the correct explanation of (A)
2 Both (A) and (R) are true, but (R) is not the correct explanation of (A)
3 (A) is true, but (R) is false
4 (A) is false, but (R) is true

***Ans.** (2)*

➲ *Exp.* Both (A) and (R) are true, but (R) is not the correct explanation of (A)

Assertion (A) that says, international convention is the most important source of law is true because it is considered as one of the modern sources of international law.

Reason (R) here says that international convention has generic wisdom is also true but this reason does not satisfy the given assertion.

42 Which of the following statement is true?

1 The community to be recognised as an international person should be organised one.
2 Control of the community over definite territory is desirable.
3 The control over the territory may be permanent.
4 The community must be independent.

***Ans.** (4)*

➲ *Exp.* Among the given statements, only Statement 4 is true. Community is a group of people living together or in the same locality or who share interests or a sense of identity. The community must be independent. For a state to be recognised internationally, it must be a sovereign i.e. independent. A sovereign state is a political entity that is represented by one centralised government that has sovereignty over a geographic area. International law defines sovereign states as having a permanent population, defined territory, one government and the capacity to enter into relations with other sovereign states.

43 Which of the following statement is correct?

1 Primary responsibility of international peacekeeping and security is on the General Assembly.
2 The Security Council is a deliberative organ.
3 Members may not accept and carry out the advice of the Security Council.
4 Social and economic council is to discharge the responsibility of the states enshrined in Chapter IX from Articles 55-60. This council operates under the authority and supervision of General Assembly.

***Ans.** (4)*

➲ *Exp.* Among the given statements, only statement 4 is true. Social and economic council is to discharge the responsibility of the states enshrined in Chapter IX from Articles 55-60. This council operates under the authority and supervision of General Assembly is true.

This council operates under the authority and supervision of General Assembly. Under the Charter, the council is authorised to make or initiate studies, reports and recommendations on economic, social, cultural, educational, health, and related matters; to make recommendations to promote respect for and observance of human rights; to prepare draft conventions for submission to the General.

44 Match List I with List II and select the correct answer using the codes given below.

List I	List II
A. Doctrine of forum prorogatum	I. Certain expenses case, ICJ Rep. 1962, p. 151
B. Condition of reciprocity	II. Nicaragua Vs. US, ICJ Rep. 1984, pp. 392, 421-26
C. Advisory jurisdiction	III. Interhandel case, ICJ Rep. 1959, p.6
D. Reservations	IV. Corfu channel case, (Preliminary objection), ICJ Rep. 1948, p.28

Codes

	A	B	C	D		A	B	C	D
1	III	IV	I	II	2	IV	III	I	II
3	IV	III	II	I	4	I	II	IV	III

Ans. *(2)*

Exp. The correct matching is A-IV, B-III, C-I, D-II.

Doctrine of forum prorogatum is related to Corfu channel case, (Preliminary objection), ICJ Rep. 1948, p.28.

Consent established subsequent to the initiation of the proceedings is referred to as doctrine of 'Forum Prorogatum'. In the Corfu Channel Case, U.K sought to found jurisdiction in accordance with Article 25 of the Charter.

Condition of reciprocity is related to Interhandel case, ICJ Rep. 1959, p.6 The principle of reciprocity states that favours, benefits, or penalties that are granted by one state to the citisens or legal entities of another, should be returned in kind.

Advisory jurisdiction is related to Certain expenses case, ICJ Rep. 1962, p. 151. The Court's role is to settle, in accordance with international law, legal disputes submitted to it by States and to give advisory opinions on legal questions referred to it by authorised United Nations organs and specialised agencies.

Reservations is related to Nicaragua Vs. US, ICJ Rep. 1984, pp. 392, 421-26. A reservation is a declaration by a state made upon signing or ratifying a treaty that the state reserves the right not to abide by certain provisions of the treaty. Reservations are formally defined in Article 2.1(d) of the 1969 Vienna Convention on the Law of Treaties.

45 Which of the following statement is true?

1 Mere counting of heads is enough to assess the degree of authority and credibility of a resolution of General Assembly
2 Mere counting of heads is not enough to assess the degree of authority and credibility of a resolution of General Assembly
3 Mere counting of heads is enough to assess integrity of General Assembly
4 None of the above

Ans. *(2)*

Exp. Statement 2 is true, as Judge Dillard observed in the fisheries case, the mere counting of heads is not enough to assess the degree of authority and credibility of a resolution of General Assembly.

46 Given below are two statements, one is labelled as Assertion (A) and the other is labelled as Reason (R).

Assertion (A) Recognition of a state is not the same as recognition of its government.

Reason (R) Within existing states, governments come and go and normally the changes raise no question of recognition.

Codes

1 Both (A) and (R) are true and (R) is the correct explanation of (A)
2 Both (A) and (R) are true, but (R) is not the correct explanation of (A)
3 (A) is true, but (R) is false
4 (A) is false, but (R) is true

Ans. *(1)*

Exp. Both (A) and (R) are true and (R) is the correct explanation of (A)

Assertion (A) says recognition of a state is not the same as recognition of its government because recognition of a government means that the recognising state regards it as the sole representative of the given State in international intercourse.

Reason (R) says within existing states, governments come and go and normally the changes raise no question of recognition as states are recognised once when they are formed and provides correct explanation to assertion.

47 A Muslim wife may sue for divorce under the Dissolution of Muslim Marriage Act, 1939 if the husband has been insane for a period of

1 1 year 2 2 years 3 3 years 4 5 years

Ans. *(2)*

Exp. A Muslim wife may sue for divorce under the Dissolution of Muslim Marriage Act, 1939 if the husband has been insane for a period of 2 years.

Section 2 (ii) of the Dissolution of Muslim Marriage Act, 1939 states that a woman married under Muslim law shall be entitle to obtain a decree for the dissolution of her marriage that the husband has been insane for a period of two years.

48 Which of the following is not essential for divorce by mutual consent?

1 They have been living separately for one year
2 They have not been able to live together
3 The wife has not received any maintenance
4 They have mutually agreed that the marriage should be dissolved

Ans. *(3)*

Exp. The wife has not received any maintenance is not essential for divorce by mutual consent.

The ground of divorce by mutual consent was inserted in the Hindu Marriage Act, 1955 by an amendment in 1976, by adding Section 13B. Section 13B of the Hindu Marriage Act, 1955 runs the requirements of divorce by mutual consent.

The requirements which have to be met to seek divorce under Hindu Marriage Act are as follows (i) The parties have been living separately for a period of atleast 1 year. (ii) They have not been able to live together and (iii) They have mutually agreed that marriage should be resolved.

49 That the respondent was, at the time of the marriage, pregnant by some person other than the petitioner, is a ground for voidable marriages under

1 Section 12(1) (a)
2 Section 12(1) (b)
3 Section 12(1) (c)
4 Section 12(1) (d)

Ans. *(4)*

Exp. That the respondent was, at the time of the marriage, pregnant by some person other than the petitioner, is a ground for voidable marriages under Section 12(1) (d).

Section 12 in the Hindu Marriage Act, 1955 deals with Voidable marriages and states (a) that any marriage solemnised, whether before or after the commencement of this Act, shall be voidable and may be annulled by a decree of nullity on any of the following grounds, namely (b) that the marriage has not been consummated owing to the impotence of the respondent; or (c) that the consent of the petitioner, or where the consent of the guardian in marriage of the petitioner was required under Section 5 as it stood immediately before the commencement of the Child Marriage Restraint (Amendment) Act, 1978 (2 of 1978), the consent of such guardian was obtained by force [or by fraud as to the nature of the ceremony or as to any material fact or circumstance concerning the respondent]; or (d) that the respondent was at the time of the marriage pregnant by some person other than the petitioner.

50 A petition for the dissolution of the marriage by a decree of divorce may be presented, if cohabitation as between the parties to the marriage, after the passing of a decree of judicial separation, is not resumed for a period of

1 One year or upwards
2 Two years or upwards
3 Six months or upwards
4 None of the above

Ans. *(1)*

➲ *Exp.* In 1964, Section 13 (1-A) has been inserted containing two clauses under which, non-resumption of cohabitation for one year or upwards after the decree of judicial separation or restitution of conjugal rights was made a ground of divorce. This is a modification of clauses (viii) and (ix) of Section 13 of the Hindu Marriage Act, 1955. By the Marriage Laws (Amendment) Act, 1976, the period of 2 years is reduced to 1 year. Section 13 (1-A) introduced an element of Break-down theory in the Hindu Marriage Act, 1955. Prior to the amendments, the petition for divorce could be filed on the grounds of non-resumption of cohabitation after the decree of judicial separation and restitution of conjugal rights only by the petitioner. After the amendments, either party to the marriage can prefer such petitions.

51 Match List I with List II and select the correct answer using the codes given below.

List I	List II
A. Marriage during Iddat period is	I. Void
B. Marriage with an impotent person is	II. Irregular
C. Marriage below the age of 18 years is	III. Voidable
D. Inter-caste marriage	IV. Valid

Codes

	A	B	C	D		A	B	C	D
1	I	II	III	IV	2	II	I	IV	III
3	III	II	I	IV	4	II	III	I	IV

Ans. *(4)*

➲ *Exp.* The correct matching is A-II, B-III, C-I, D-IV.

Marriage during Iddat period is Irregular. Irregular marriage is also known as Fasid marriage. For example, when a person marries his wife's sister, the marriage is irregular, but he can validate it by pronouncing talaq on his wife.

Marriage with an impotent person is Voidable. Voidable marriages are those which are void at the option of the aggrieved party. Such marriages can be annulled by a decree of nullity.

Marriage below the age of 18 years is Void. A void marriage is a marriage that is unlawful or invalid under the laws of the jurisdiction where it is entered. A void marriage is one that is void and invalid from its beginning. It is as though the marriage never existed and it requires no formality to terminate.

Inter-caste marriage is Valid. A marriage can be said valid, if it fulfils all the required conditions.

52 Where the marriage has not been consummated, Iddat has to be observed in case of

1 Death of husband
2 Divorce
3 Both death and divorce
4 Neither death nor divorce

Ans. *(1)*

➲ *Exp.* Where the marriage has not been consummated, Iddat has to be observed in case of Death of husband.

Iddat refers to the period that a woman undergoes after divorce or the death of her husband. It literally means counting. This period is essential to ascertain whether the wife/widow is pregnant or not. The object of the iddat is firstly to ascertain whether the wife is pregnant, and if so, the paternity of the child. Secondly, in the event of a revocable divorce, it gives the husband the opportunity to return to his wife, and thirdly, it gives a widow the opportunity to mourn the death of her husband.

53 Match List I with List II and select the correct answer using the codes given below:

List I (Cases)	List II (Grounds)
A. Ram Narayan Vs. Rameshwari	I. Insanity
B. Lachman Vs. Meena	II. Cruelty
C. Dastane Vs. Dastane	III. Desertion
D. Mr X Vs. Hospital Z	IV. Venereal Diseases

Codes

	A	B	C	D		A	B	C	D
1	III	I	IV	II	2	II	IV	III	I
3	I	III	II	IV	4	IV	II	I	III

Ans. *(3)*

➲ *Exp.* The correct matching is A-I, B-III, C-II, D-IV

Ram Narayan Vs. Rameshwari case is related to Insanity. Insanity generally includes severe mental illness and incompetence.

Lachman Vs. Meena case is related to Desertion. Section 13(1) (ib) of the Hindu Marriage Act, 1955 deals with desertion as a ground for divorce and the explanation of the same reads: The expression 'desertion' means the desertion of the petitioner by the other party to the marriage without reasonable cause and without the consent of or against the wish of such party.

Dastane Vs. Dastane is related to Cruelty. By 1976 Amendment, the Cruelty was made ground for divorce. The words, which have been incorporated, are "as to cause a reasonable apprehension in the mind of the petitioner that it will be harmful or injurious for the petitioner to live with the other party".

Mr X vs Hospital Z is related to Venereal Diseases. If one of the spouses is suffering from a serious disease that is easily communicable, a divorce can be filed by the other spouse. The sexually transmitted diseases like AIDS are accounted to be venereal diseases.

54 Under the Shia school, what is the chronological order of persons entitled to the 'Hizanat' of a minor child?

I. Father　　II. Mother
III. Grandfather　　IV. Grandmother

Codes

1 II, I, III, IV
2 II, I, IV, III
3 III, II, I, IV
4 IV, III, II, I

Ans. *(1)*

Exp. The correct chronological order of person entitled to the 'Hizanat' of a minor child under the Shia school is following (i) Mother (ii) Father (iii) Grandfather (iv) Grandmother.

55 The solidarity rights, more commonly known as 'Third Generation Human Rights' is based on

1 Independent needs of people
2 Concept of Universalism
3 Right to self-determination
4 Common heritage of mankind

Ans. *(2)*

Exp. The solidarity rights are based on concept of Universalism.

Third generation human rights are sometimes called 'solidarity rights'. The most prominent examples of such alleged rights are the right to peace, the right to development and the right to a clean (healthful) environment.

None of these rights has solid legal foundations in a legal instrument of worldwide applicability. At the regional level, however, the African Charter on Human and Peoples' Rights has proclaimed the right to development and the right to peace and security as well as the right to a 'general satisfactory environment'.

56 "Human rights have two main dimensions. One of them can be called negative freedom in the sense that it is less important, it is negative because such freedom is based on a bedrock of what cannot be done, rather than what can be done." The above is from the thoughts of

1 Kofi Annan　　2 PN Bhagwati
3 Amartya Sen　　4 MN Venkatachaliah

Ans. *(3)*

Exp. The mentioned thought is given by Amartya Sen.

The notion of positive and negative rights may also be applied to liberty rights. Rights considered negative rights may include civil and political rights such as freedom of speech, life, private property, freedom from violent crime, freedom of religion, habeas corpus, a fair trial, freedom from slavery.

57 Match List I containing Human Rights and List II containing related Articles of Universal Declaration of Human Rights, using the codes given below.

	List I		List II
A.	Rights to own property	I.	Article- 18
B.	Freedom of religion	II.	Article-9
C.	Right to liberty and security of person	III.	Article-12
D.	Right to privacy	IV.	Article-17

Codes

	A	B	C	D		A	B	C	D
1	I	III	IV	II	2	I	IV	III	II
3	I	IV	II	III	4	IV	I	II	III

Ans. *(4)*

Exp. The correct matching is A-IV, B-I, C-II, D-III.

Article 17 is related to right to own property. As per this article, Everyone has the right to own property alone as well as in association with others. No one shall be arbitrarily deprived of his property.

Article 18 is related to freedom of religion as per this Article, Everyone has the right to freedom of thought, conscience and religion; this right includes freedom to change his religion or belief, and freedom, either alone or in community with others and in public or private, to manifest his religion or belief in teaching, practice, worship and observance.

Article 9 is related to Right to liberty and security of person. As per this Article, No one shall be subjected to arbitrary arrest, detention or exile.

Article-12 is related to Right to privacy. As per this Article, No one shall be subjected to arbitrary interference with his privacy, family, home or correspondence, nor to attacks upon his honour and reputation. Everyone has the right to the protection of the law against such interference or attacks.

58 Human rights are inscribed in the hearts of the people ; they were there long before law makers drafted their first proclamation. This statement was made by

1 Kofi Annan   2 Krishna Iyer, J
3 Mary Robinson   4 None of these

Ans. (3)

Exp. The given statement is made by Mary Robinson.

Mary Robinson is former United Nations High Commissioner for Human Rights, 1997-2002, and former President of Ireland, 1990-97. She now leads Realising Rights: The Ethical Globalisation Initiative. As former President of Ireland, she was ideally positioned for passionately and eloquently arguing the case for human rights around the world. Over five tumultuous years that included the tragic events of 9/11, she offered moral leadership and vision to the global human rights movement.

59 Human Rights Council has taken the place of

1 Human Right Committee
2 International Human Rights Institute
3 Centre for Human Rights
4 Human Right Commission

Ans. (2)

Exp. Human Rights Council has taken the place of International Human Rights Institute.

The UN Human Rights Council is responsible for promoting universal respect for human rights, addressing situations where human rights are violated and making recommendations to UN member states. The UN Human Rights Council (UNHRC) was established in 2006 following a resolution by the UN General Assembly. At the same time, the UN closed the International Human Rights Institute. The UNHRC meets a number of times each year and is able to deal with emergency situations where human rights are being violated as they arise.

60 Select the correct answer using the codes given below.

The National Human Rights Commission can

I. itself take action and punish those who violate human rights.
II. recommend the government to take action.
III. initiate proceedings in the court.
IV. join as a party to a case in the court involving violation of human rights.

Codes

1 I and II are correct   2 II, III and IV are correct
3 I, II and III are correct   4 III and IV are correct

Ans. (2)

Exp. Among the given statements, Statements II, III and IV are correct.

The National Human Rights Commission can recommend the government to take action,initiate proceedings in the court and join as a party to a case in the court involving violation of human rights.

The National Human Rights Commission performs the following functions, namely Inquire, suo motu or on a petition presented to it by a victim or any person on his behalf, into complaint of

(i) violation of human rights is extremely obvious.
(ii) negligence in the prevention of such violation, by a public servant.
(iii) intervene in any proceeding involving any allegation of violation of human rights pending before a court with the approval of such court.

61 Some of the human rights are contained in the Indian Constitution under

1 Part III and Part IV-A
2 Part III and Part IV
3 Part IV and Part IV-A
4 Part II and Part IV-A

Ans. (2)

Exp. Some of the human rights are contained in the Indian Constitution under Part III and Part IV.

The Indian Constitution guarantees essential human rights under Part III and also Directive Principles of State Policy in Part IV which are fundamental to the governance of the country.

62 Tort is defined as "an infringement of a right in rem of a private individual giving a right of compensation of the suit of the injured party" by

1 Salmond   2 Franger
3 Winfield   4 Flemmings

Ans. (2)

Exp. The statement given in question was made by Franger.

Tort is a civil wrong, or wrongful act, whether intentional or accidental, from which injury occurs to another. Torts include all negligence cases as well as intentional wrongs which result in harm.

Therefore, tort law is one of the major areas of law (along with contract, real property and criminal law), and results in more civil litigation than any other category. Some intentional torts may also be crimes such as assault, battery, wrongful death, fraud, conversion (a euphemism for theft) and trespass on property and form the basis for a lawsuit for damages by the injured party.

Defamation, including intentionally telling harmful untruths about another, either by print or broadcast (libel) or orally (slander), is a tort and used to be a crime as well.

63 Which of the following correctly represent the position under the law of torts?

A person is responsible for

I. all the consequences of his wrongful act.
II. consequences which directly flow from his wrongful act.
III. consequences which are not too remote.
IV. all the consequences which are reasonably foreseeable.

Codes
1 I and II are correct
2 I, II and III are correct
3 II and III are correct
4 II, III and IV are correct

Ans. (4)

➲ *Exp.* Among the following statements, Statement II, III and IV are correct.

Under the law of torts a person is responsible for

(i) consequences which directly flow from his wrongful act.

(ii) consequences which are not too remote.

(iii) all the consequences which are reasonably foreseeable.

64 Which of the following is not necessary in tort of defamation?

1 The statement is defamatory
2 There is intention to refer to the plaintiff
3 The right thinking members in the society infer that the statement refers to plaintiff
4 The statement is made known to other members of society

Ans. (2)

➲ *Exp.* There is intention to refer to the plaintiff is not necessary in tort of defamation.

The essentials of defamation are

(a) Words must be false and defamatory

(b) The said words must refer to the plaintiff.

(c) The words must be published.

65 A film critic in his review of a film comments adversely on the cinematic values and quality of the film. The director of the film sues the film critic for defamation. Which of the following is correct.

I. The film critic is not liable as he can raise the defence of justification.

II. The critic is not liable because it was a fair and bonafide comment in public interest.

III. It was an expression of opinion and not assertion of facts.

IV. It was a fair criticism of a film meant for public entertainment.

Codes
1 I and IV are correct
2 I and II are correct
3 II, III and IV are correct
4 I and III are correct

Ans. (3)

➲ *Exp.* Among the given statements statement II, III and IV are correct.

Following statements are correct regarding film critic

(i) The critic is not liable because it was a fair and bonafide comment in public interest.

(ii) It was an expression of opinion and not assertion of facts.

(iii) It was a fair criticism of a film meant for public entertainment.

66 The 'standard of care' generally used in care of negligence is

1 the care taken by an intelligent and prudent man
2 the skill and care taken by a qualified and competent person
3 the foresight of an adult person
4 the care and skill of a prudent and careful man belonging to defendant's calling for business or skill

Ans. (4)

➲ *Exp.* The 'standard of care' generally used in care of negligence is the care and skill of a prudent and careful man belonging to defendant's calling for business or skill.

Standard of care is the watchfulness, attention, caution and prudence that a reasonable person in the circumstances would exercise. If a person's actions do not meet this standard of care, then his/her acts fail to meet the duty of care which all people (supposedly) have toward others. Failure to meet the standard is negligence and any damages resulting there from may be claimed in a lawsuit by the injured party. The problem is that the 'standard' is often a subjective issue upon which reasonable people can differ.

67 Which one of the following is a good defence for the tort of private nuisance?

1 Plaintiff has come to the place of nuisance
2 Reasonable care was taken to prevent nuisance
3 The activity is for the public benefit
4 The activity is continuing for the past 20 years

Ans. (4)

➲ *Exp.* The activity is continuing for the past 20 years is a good defence for the tort of private nuisance.

Private nuisance is a continuous, unlawful and indirect interference with the use or enjoyment of land, or of some right over or in connection with it. There must be a continuous interference over a period of time with the claimant's use or enjoyment of land.

68 Who is a consumer under the Consumer Protection Act, 1986?

1 A person who gives his pants for stitching to a tailor
2 A person who purchases goods for sale in his shop
3 A person who purchases a car for being used as a taxi in his taxi service
4 A person who avails of medical services free of cost

Ans. (1)

➲ *Exp.* In the given question a person who gives his pants for stitching to a tailor is a consumer.

Section 2 in the Consumer Protection Act, 1986 2(d) 'consumer' means any person who,

(i) buys any goods for a consideration which has been paid or promised or partly paid and partly promised, or under any system of deferred payment and includes any user of such goods other than the person who buys such goods for consideration paid or promised or partly paid or partly promised, or under any system of deferred payment, when such use is made with the approval of such person.

(ii) hires or avails of any services for a consideration which has been paid or promised or partly paid and partly promised or under any system of deferred payment and includes any beneficiary of such services other than the person who, hires or avails of the services for consideration paid or promised or partly paid and partly promised, or under any system of deferred payment, when such services are availed of with the approval of the first mentioned person but does not include a person.

69 Partnership is

1 Trust
2 Company
3 Mutual agency
4 Mutual fund

Ans. (3)

➲ *Exp.* Partnership is mutual agency.

Partnership is the relation between persons who have agreed to share the profits of a business carried on by all or any of them acting for all. Persons who have entered into partnership with one another are called individually partners and collectively a firm and the name under which their business is carried on is called the firm name.

70 Given below are two statements, one is labelled as Assertion (A) and the other is labelled as Reason (R).

Assertion (A) When something of valuable nature is acquired by a partner in breach of his duty in good faith, it is taken to be acquired for the benefit of all the partners and has to be accounted for, to the firm.

Reason (R) Partnership is a trust.

Codes

1 Both (A) and (R) are true and (R) is the correct explanation of (A)
2 Both (A) and (R) are true, but (R) is not the correct explanation of (A)
3 (A) is true, but (R) is false
4 (A) is false, but (R) is true

Ans. (3)

➲ *Exp.* (A) is true, but (R) is false.

Assertion is true as when something of valuable nature is acquired by a partner in breach of his duty in good faith, it is taken to be acquired for the benefit of all the partners and has to be accounted to the firm.

Reason is false because partnership is not a trust but an agency.

71 Arrange the following concepts in which sequentially they appeared, using the codes given below.

I. Damage
II. Breach of terms of agreement of partnership
III. Damaged
IV. Agreement to share profits from business of firm

Codes

1 I, II, IV, III
2 IV, II, I, III
3 II, IV, I, III
4 III, I, IV, IV

Ans. (2)

➲ *Exp.* IV, II, I, III is the correct sequence.

The concepts given in correct sequence in which they sequentially appears are:

(i) Agreement to share profits from business of firm
(ii) Breach of terms of agreement of partnership
(iii) Damage
(iv) Damaged

72 Match items in List I with items in List II using the codes given below and select the correct answer.

List I	List II
A. Liability for misappropriation by a partner	I. Section 26
B. Liability of a partner for torts	II. Section 27
C. Liability of a partner for holding out	III. Section 28
D. Doctrine of implied authority of a partner	IV. Sections 18 and 19

Codes

	A	B	C	D
1	III	IV	I	II
2	II	I	IV	III
3	I	II	III	IV
4	II	I	III	IV

Ans. (4)

➲ *Exp.* The correct matching is A-II, B-I, C-III, D-IV

Liability for misappropriation by a partner is given under Section 27. A firm in the course of its business receives money or property from a third party, and the money or property is misapplied by any of the partners while it is in the custody of the firm the firm is liable to make good the loss.

Liability of a partner for torts is given under Section 26. As per the Section, Where, by the wrongful act or omission of a partner acting in the ordinary course of the business of a firm, or with the authority of his partners, loss or injury is caused to any third party, or any penalty is incurred, the firm is liable therefore to the same extent as the partner.

Liability of a partner for holding out is given under Section 28. As per this Section, Anyone who by words spoken or written or by conduct represents himself or knowingly permits himself to be represented, to be a partner in a firm, is liable as a partner in that firm to anyone who has on the faith of any such representation given credit to the firm, whether the person representing himself or represented to be a partner does or does not know that the representation has reached the person so giving credit.

Doctrine of implied authority of a partner is given under Sections 18 and 19. A partner is the agent of the firm for the purposes of the business of the firm'. There is an implied authority that has been vested on the partner to bind the firm until and unless, there is a clause or a statement that proves otherwise.

73 Which one of the following pairs does match?

1 Definition and essentials of sale–E and S 5 : 02 PM Ruben Ltd. Vs. Faire Bros. (1949)1 KB 254
2 Formalities of sale–Drummond and Sons Vs. Van Ingen, (1887) 12 App. Cases 284
3 Conditions implied by trade and usage–Peter Darlington Partners Ltd. Vs. Gosho Co. Ltd., (1964) 1 Lloyds Rep 149
4 Sale by sample–Rowland Vs. Divall (1923) 2 KB 500, CA.

***Ans.** (3)*

Exp. In Peter Darlington Partners, Ltd Vs. Gosho Co. Ltd. 57 court held that the buyers were liable to reject the goods even though the quality of pure canary seed supplied was of about 98 percent. Since by the custom of the trade, it is impossible to get pure canary seed of 100 per cent quality. However, if a sale is by description as well as by sample, the buyer has a double edged right to reject goods for non-compliance to both.

74 Which one of the following statements is true ?

1 The order contained in the bill of exchange may be conditional.
2 A bill of exchange must contain a request to pay.
3 Every bill of exchange is a promissory note.
4 The payee must be certain.

***Ans.** (4)*

Exp. Among the statements, Statement 4 is true.
The payee must be certain as in the case of maker, the payee of a note must also be certain on the face of the instrument. A note is valid even in conditions wherein the payee is misnamed or indicated by the official designation. A promissory note may be payable to two or more payees jointly.

75 Haward Vs. Patent Ivory Manufacturing Co., (1888) 38 Ch.D. 156 is a case about

1 Doctrine of ultra vires
2 Doctrine of indoor management
3 Doctrine of public notice
4 Doctrine of social responsibility

***Ans.** (2)*

Exp. Haward Vs. Patent Ivory Manufacturing Co. (1888) 38 Ch. D.156 is a case about Doctrine of indoor management.
Basis for Doctrine of Indoor Management are

(i) What happens internal to a company is not a matter of public knowledge. An outsider can only presume the intentions of a company, but not know the information he/she is not privy to.
(ii) If not for the doctrine, the company could escape creditors by denying the authority of officials to act on its behalf.

UGC-NET
LAW
SOLVED PAPER 2013 (December)
PAPER II

1 Social, economic and political justice is

1 an idea enshrined in the Preamble to the Constitution of India
2 guaranteed by Fundamental Rights in the Constitution of India
3 a Directive Principle of State Policy taken into consideration while making enactments
4 guaranteed to the people by the writs issued by the High Courts and Supreme Court

Ans. (1)

Exp. Social, economic and political justice is an idea enshrined in the Preamble to the Constitution of India.

The Preamble mentions, "We the people of India, having solemnly resolved to constitute India into a sovereign, socialist, secular, democratic, republic and to secure to all its citizens; Justice, social, economic and political; Liberty of thought, expression, belief, faith and worship; Equality of status and of opportunity and to promote among them all, Fraternity assuring the dignity of the individual and the unity and integrity of the nation."

2 Without paying proper remuneration, labour taken from the prisoners is 'forced labour' and violation of

1 Article 20 of the Constitution of India
2 Article 21 of the Constitution of India
3 Article 22 of the Constitution of India
4 Article 23 of the Constitution of India

Ans. (4)

Exp. Without paying proper remuneration, labour taken from the prisoners is 'forced labour' and violation of Article 23 of the Constitution of India.

Article 23 in Constitution of India deals with Prohibition of traffic in human beings and forced labour. It provides that Traffic in human beings and beggar and other similar forms of forced labour are prohibited and any contravention of this provision shall be an offence punishable in accordance with law.

Nothing in this Article shall prevent the State from imposing compulsory service for public purpose and in imposing such service the State shall not make any discrimination on grounds only of religion, race, caste or class or any of them.

3 Article 51(A) of the Constitution of India provides for the Fundamental Duties of

1 Citizens of India
2 Public Servants
3 All those who run public and private sectors
4 Prime Minister and his Council of Ministers

Ans. (1)

Exp. Article 51(A), under Part IV(A) of the Indian Constitution, specifies the list of fundamental duties of the citizens of India.

The chapter IV-A was added in the Constitution on Fundamental Duties by 42nd Amendment, 1976. Initially, there were only ten duties, and one more fundamental duty (eleventh) was added to the Indian Constitution by the 86th Amendment of the Constitution in 2002.

The 11th duty provides that one who is a parent or guardian, has to provide opportunities for education to his child, or as the case may be, ward between the age of 6 and 14 years.

4 The appropriate writ issued by Supreme Court to quash the appointment of a person to a public office is

1 Certiorari
2 Mandamus
3 Prohibition
4 Quo-Warranto

Ans. (4)

Exp. The appropriate writ issued by Supreme Court to quash the appointment of a person to a public office is Quo-warranto.

Following are the five types of writs:

- *Habeas Corpus* is a Latin term which literally means 'You may have the body.' The writ is issued to produce a person who has been unlawfully detained , whether by state or a private person.
- *Mandamus* is a Latin word, which means 'We Command'. This writ of command is issued by the Supreme Court or High Court when any government, court, corporation or any public authority has to do a public duty but fails to do so.
- *Certiorari* means 'to be certified'. The writ of Certiorari can be issued by the Supreme Court or any High Court for quashing the order already passed by an inferior court, tribunal or quasi judicial authority.
- *Prohibition* means 'to forbid or to stop' and it is popularly known as 'Stay Order'.The writ of prohibition is issued by any High Court or the Supreme Court to any inferior court, or quasi-judicial body prohibiting the latter from continuing the proceedings in a particular case, where it has no jurisdiction to try.
- *Quo-warranto* The meaning of the writ is 'What is your authority'?. This writ is issued to restrain a person from holding a public office to which he is not entitled to.

5 The Power of the President of India to issue an ordinance is a

1 Legislative power 2 Executive power
3 Quasi-judicial power 4 Judicial power

Ans. (1)

Exp. The Power of the President of India to issue an ordinance is a Legislative power.

Article 123 in the Constitution of India mentions Power of President to promulgate Ordinances during recess of Parliament.

According to the provision, if at any time, except when both Houses of Parliament are in session, the President is satisfied that circumstances exist which render it necessary for him to take immediate action, he may promulgate such Ordinance as the circumstances appear to him to require.

6 The jurisdiction of Supreme Court of India may be enlarged by

1 The President of India
2 The Parliament by resolution
3 The Parliament by Law
4 The President in consultation with the Chief Justice of India

Ans. (3)

Exp. The jurisdiction of the Supreme Court of India may be enlarged by the Parliament by Law.

Article 138 of Constitution mentions Enlargement of the jurisdiction of the Supreme Court. It provides that the Supreme Court shall have such further jurisdiction and powers with respect to any of the matters in the Union List as Parliament may by Law confer.

7 At the first instance, the President can issue a proclamation of financial emergency for a period of

1 Fifteen days 2 Two months
3 One month 4 Six months

Ans. (2)

Exp. At the first instance, the President can issue a proclamation of financial emergency for a period of two months.

Article 360 of Indian Constitution states that if the President is satisfied that a situation has arisen whereby the financial stability or credit of India or of any part of the territory thereof is threatened, he may by a Proclamation make a declaration to that effect. A Proclamation issued under this provision shall cease to operate at the expiration of two months, unless before the expiration of that period it has been approved by resolutions of both Houses of Parliament.

8 Legal Theory is based on

1 a systematic study of positive laws
2 purely logical and empirical study
3 concepts like morality, justice and ethics
4 total exclusion of customary practices, morality and social vagaries

Ans. (3)

Exp. Legal theory is based on concepts like morality, justice and ethics. It aims to provide a backdrop to the legal, moral, philosophical and societal influences impacting the English legal system.

The popular conception of the connection between law and morality is that in some way the law exists to promote morality, to preserve those conditions which make the moral life possible and then to enable men to lead sober and industrious lives.

9 Who separated jurisprudence from religion ?

1 Kant 2 Hugo Grotius
3 Salmond 4 Jethro Brown

Ans. (2)

Exp. Hugo Grotius separated jurisprudence from religion. He defended natural law without appealing to the Bible or organized religion. He insisted it followed from the nature of things, and it was discovered by human reason. He wrote, "Now the Law of Nature is so unalterable, that it cannot be changed even by God himself."

10 Under how many categories the five theories of punishment can be divided ?

1 2 2 4
3 5 4 3

Ans. (4)

Exp. Under 3 categories, the five theories of punishment can be divided.

The five theories of punishment are

1. *Deterrent Theory* believes in the fact that if severe punishments were inflicted on the offender would deter him from repeating that crime.
2. *Retributive Theory* underlines the idea of vengeance and revenge rather than that of social welfare and security. It is the most ancient justification for punishment. This theory insists that a person deserves punishment as he has done a wrongful deed.
3. *Preventive Theory* aims to prevent the crime rather than avenging it suggesting that the need of a punishment for a crime arises out of mere social needs i.e. while sending the criminals to the prisons the society is in turn trying to prevent the offender from doing any other crime.
4. *Reformative Theory* aims at transforming the law-offenders in such a way that the inmates of the correctional institutions can lead a life like a normal citizen.
5. *Expiatory Theory* believed that if the offender expiates or repents and realizes his mistake, he must be forgiven.

11 On which one of the following one can have corporeal ownership ?

1 A right
2 Trademark
3 Movable property
4 A debt

Ans. (3)

➲ Exp. On movable property one can have corporeal ownership.

Corporeal ownership is the right of ownership in material things, such as land, goods, etc. Corporeal ownership is of that object which is tangible in nature. Ownership of a house, a table, etc is corporeal membership.

Ownership of a right is called Incorporeal ownership. For. e.g. ownership of a copyright, a patent or a trademark is incorporeal ownership.

12 "Sovereignty must be determinate, it is essential, is indivisible and is unlimited and illimitable." Who conceived this about the sovereignty ?

1 Hobbes
2 Austin
3 Jean Bodin
4 Plato

Ans. (2)

➲ Exp. Austin conceived the given statement about sovereignty.

Austin places the notion of sovereignty at the basis of his theory of law. Austin's Theory of Law or Imperative Theory of Law suggests following features of a law; (i) it is a type of command, (ii) it is laid down by a political superior, (iii) it is enforced by a sanction.

Austin concept of sovereignty has been discussed in his book, 'Province of Jurisprudence Determined'. He uses the concept of sovereignty to define law and content of jurisprudence.

13 Consider the following statements.

I. Statements, which are not partaking of the character of ratio decidendi can be ignored while deciding the latter case.

II. The ratio decidendi is not the reason of decision.

III. Only that part of the judgement in an earlier decision is binding which constitutes the ratio decidendi of that case.

IV. A judicial decision has a binding force for subsequent cases but the whole judgement is not binding, only a part of it is biding.

Which of the above statement(s) is/are correct ?

1 I, III and IV
2 I, II and III
3 II, III and IV
4 I, II and IV

Ans. (1)

➲ Exp. Among the given statements, only statement I, III and IV are correct.

The literal meaning of 'ratio decidendi' is 'the reason for deciding'. It is the principle or rule of law on which a court's decision is founded. It is a general rule without which a case must have been decided otherwise.

There are two steps involved in the ascertainment of ratio decidendi. First, it is necessary to determine the facts of the case as seen by the judge; secondly, it is necessary to discover which of those facts were treated as material by the judge.

A judicial decision has a binding force for subsequent cases but the whole judgement is not binding. Only a part of judgment is binding. Only that part of the judgement in an earlier decision is binding which constitutes the ratio decidendi of that case. Statement which are not partaking of the characters of ratio decidendi can be ignored while deciding the latter case.

Statement II is incorrect because ratio decidendi is actually the reason behind a particular decision, as it tends to indicate the guiding force behind the decision.

14 "Case law is gold in the mine, a few grains of the precious metal to the tons of useless matter, while statute law is coin of the realm ready for immediate use." Who said these words ?

1 Ihering
2 Austin
3 Kelson
4 Salmond

Ans. (4)

➲ Exp. The given statement "Case law is gold in the mine, a few grains of the precious metal to the tons of useless matter, while statute law is coin of the realm ready for immediate use", is said by Salmond.

Statute law is definite, brief, clear and easily understandable. Therefore, in the form it is superior to precedent, to know principles and rules one will have to look into the details of the case. Salmond puts the same thing in the form of allegory in the statement given in question.

According to Salmond, "Law may be defined as the body of principles recognised and applied by the state in the administration of justice". In other words, law consists of rules recognised and acted upon by the Courts of Justice.

Salmond believed that law may arise out of popular practices and its legal character becomes patent when it is recognised and applied by a Court in the Administration of Justice.

15 Which of the following statements are true ?

I. There is no rule to determine when usage shall give rise to a custom.

II. Customary rules of International law are diminishing and are being replaced by Treaties and Conventions.

III. Treaty contracts are not direct source of International law.

IV. International law is a positive morality.

Codes

1 I, II, III and IV 2 II, III and IV
3 I, II and III 4 I and II

Ans. *(1)*

Exp. Among the given statements, statement I, II, III and IV are correct.

Custom is a habitual course of conduct. Until recently, international law consisted for the most part of customary rules. It is the oldest and the original source, of International as well as of law in general. There is no rule to determine when usage shall give rise to a custom. A customary element has been a feature of the rules of international law from antiquity to modern times.

Customary rules of international law are diminishing and are being replaced by Treaties and Conventions.

The term "treaty" is used as a generic term embracing all kinds of international agreements which are known by a variety of different names such as, conventions, pacts, general acts, charters, statutes, declarations, covenants, protocol, as well as, the name agreements itself. In contrast with the process of creating law through custom, treaties are a more modern, more deliberate and speedy method. They are of growing importance in International Law. Their role in the formation of new rules of International Law increases day after day. Today, the law making treaties are considered the most important primary source of Public International Law.

Treaty contracts are not direct source of International law. Treaties act as a direct source of rights and obligations for the states, they codify the existing customary source of law. According to Austin, law is the command of the sovereign, and the indeterminacy of sovereign at the international level and the lack of coercive force had made him classify international law as mere positive morality.

16 "The law of National or International law may be defined as the body of rules and principles of actions which are binding upon civilised states in their relations with one-another."
This definition of International law was given by

1 JL Brierly 2 Torsten Vitel
3 Hackworth 4 None of these

Ans. *(1)*

Exp. JL Brierly said that "The law of National or International law may be defined as the body of rules and principles of actions which are binding upon civilised states in their relations with one-another."

The definition aims to establish that international law consists of those rules or obligations that states have agreed to be bound by, and pursue in the course of their dealings with each other. It indicates voluntary acceptance of rules by the states, instead of any ordinary law which is made by competent legislature and then imposed upon people, irrespective of their individual desires.

17 Match the following and select the correct answer using codes given below.

List I		List II	
A.	Recognition only and exclusively bestows a state with rights and duties under International Law	I.	De-facto recognition
B.	It is a first step towards final recognition	II.	De-Jure recognition
C.	It is a final recognition by a state	III.	Declaratory Theory
D.	International personality of a state does not depend upon recognition	IV.	Constitutive Theory

Codes

	A	B	C	D		A	B	C	D
1	IV	I	II	III	2	I	II	III	IV
3	IV	III	II	I	4	III	II	I	IV

Ans. *(1)*

Exp. The correct matching is A-IV, B-I, C-II, D-III.

According to *Constitutive Theory* for a state to be considered as an international person, its recognition by the existing states as a sovereign is required. Thus, theory is of the view that only after recognition a State gets the status of an International person and becomes a subject to International Law.

De facto recognition is a first step towards final recognition. It is the process of acknowledging a new state by a non-committal act. De facto recognition is a provisionally grant.

De jure recognition is a final recognition by a state. De jure recognition is the recognition of a new state by existing states when they believe that the new state meets all the basic characteristics of a state. De jure recognition may or may not grant factual recognition. This model of recognition will be granted when the newly established State attains permanent stability and national status.

In *Declaratory Theory* International personality of a state does not depend upon recognition. In the declaratory theory of statehood, an entity becomes a state as soon as it meets the minimal criteria for statehood. Therefore, recognition by other states is purely "declaratory". This theory states that the existence of a new state does not depend on being recognised by the existing state. Even before recognition by other states the new state has the right to defend its integrity and independence under International law.

18 The Charter of the United Nations can be amended by

1 Five-third of the members of General Assembly
2 The Security Council only
3 Two-third of the members of the UN including all permanent members of the Security Council after recommendations by a two-thirds vote of a conference convened for the purpose, is received
4 Two-thirds of the members of the Security Council including five permanent members

Ans. (4)

Exp. The Charter of the United Nations can be amended by two-thirds of the members of the Security Council including five permanent members.

The amendments to the United Nations Charter can be made by a procedure set out in Chapter XVIII of the UN Charter. The UN Charter has been amended five times since 1945. Article 108 provides, Amendments to the present Charter shall come into force for all members of the United Nations when they have been adopted by a vote of two-thirds of the members of the General Assembly and ratified in accordance with their respective constitutional processes by two-thirds of the members of the United Nations, including all the permanent members of the Security Council.

19 In which of the following case, International Court of Justice denied existence of customary rule ?

1 North Sea Continental Shelf Case
2 The Lotus Case
3 Both of the above
4 None of the above

Ans. (3)

Exp. In the North Sea Continental Shelf Case and the Lotus Case, International Court of Justice denied existence of customary rule.

In the popular case North Sea Continental Shelf (1969), the International Court of Justice (ICJ) held that the method of determining boundaries of the continental shelf in such a way that every point of the boundary is equidistant from the nearest points of the baselines from which the breadth of the territorial sea of each State is measured (equidistance method), is not a rule of customary international law and is therefore not applicable as such between the Parties.

The Lotus case (France Vs. Turkey) (1927), gave an important dictum on creating customary international law. France had alleged that jurisdictional questions on collision cases are rarely heard in criminal cases, because States tend to prosecute only before the flag State. France argued that this absence of prosecutions points to a positive rule in customary law on collisions. The Court disagreed and denied existence of any such customary rule.

20 Which organ of the United Nations has been given responsibility of promoting international co-operation in the realisation of human rights ?

1 General Assembly
2 Security Council
3 Both of these
4 None of the above

Ans. (3)

Exp. Both the General Assembly and Security Council have been given responsibility for promoting international co-operation in the realisation of human rights.

The General Assembly is composed of all member states of the United Nations, each state having one vote. Article 13 UN Charter states that one of the functions of the UN General Assembly is to initiate studies and make recommendations for the purpose of 'promoting international co-operation in the economic, social, cultural, educational and health fields and assisting in the realisation of human rights and fundamental freedoms for all without distinction as to race, sex, language or religion'. The Security Council has 15 members, 5 permanent members and 10 elected by the General Assembly for two-year terms. In accordance with Article 24 UN Charter, the Security Council bears primary responsibility for the maintenance of international peace and security. Actions taken by the Security Council will generally impact human rights, as these invariably come to the fore whenever international peace and security are threatened.

21 In which of the following case the Supreme Court held that even the wife of a void marriage is entitled to maintenance ?

1 Amarjeet Kaur Vs. Harbhajan Singh (2003) 10 SCC 228
2 Chand Dhawan Vs. Jawaharlal Dhawan (1993) 3 SCC 406
3 Nirmala Devi Vs. Ram Dass (2001) 2 SCC. 4
4 Ramesh Chandra Vs. Veena Kausal AIR 1978 SC 1807

Ans. (2)

Exp. In the case of Chand Dhawan Vs. Jawaharlal Dhawan (1993) 3 SCC 406, the Supreme Court held that even the wife of a void marriage is entitled to maintenance.

The court held that where the statute expressly codifies the law, the court as a general rule, is not at liberty to go outside the law so created, just on the basis that before its enactment another law prevailed. The wife's claim to maintenance necessarily has then to be agitated under the Hindu Adoptions and Maintenance Act, 1956 which is a legislative measure later in point of time than the Hindu Marriage Act, 1955, though part of the same socio-legal scheme revolutionising the law applicable to Hindus.

Section 18(1) of the Hindu Adoptions and Maintenance Act, 1956 entitles a Hindu wife to claim maintenance from her husband during her life time. Sub-section (2) of Section 18 grants her the right to live separately, without forfeiting her claim to maintenance, if he is guilty of any of the misbehaviours enumerated there in or on account of his being in one of objectionable conditions as mentioned therein. So, while sustaining her marriage and preserving her marital status, the wife is entitled to claim maintenance from her husband.

22 In which of the following case, the court held that "Dower is a sale price of woman" ?

1 Maina Bibi case
2 Humara Bibi case
3 Subrunnisan case
4 Abdul Kadir case

Ans. (3)

Exp. In the Subrunnisan case, the court held that "Dower is a sale price of woman".

The Calcutta High Court in Saburannessa Vs. Sabdu Sheikh and ors (1994) held that the marriage under the Mahomedan law is a civil contract and is like a contract of sale. Sale is a transfer of property for a price. In the contract of marriage the wife is the property and the dower is the price.

23 Read Assertion (A) and Reason (R). Select the correct answer using codes given below.

Assertion (A) 'Option of Puberty' is an easy process to repudiate the marriage under Hindu Law.

Reason (R) 'Option of Puberty' is not an easy process to repudiate the marriage under Muslim Law.

Codes

1 (A) is correct, but (R) is incorrect
2 Both (A) and (R) are correct
3 (R) is correct, but (A) is incorrect
4 (A) and (R) both are incorrect

Ans. (2)

Exp. Both (A) and (R) are correct.

'Option of Puberty' is an easy process to repudiate the marriage under Hindu Law is correct. The amendment in the Hindu Marriage Act, 1955 added a new clause (iv) for divorce under Section 13 of the act, and states "that her marriage(whether consummated or not) was solemnised before she attained the age of fifteen years and she has repudiated the marriage after attaining that age but before attaining the age of eighteen years".

The provision confers the right to repudiate a woman to repudiate marriage on the option of puberty. It is important to note that such repudiation is available without being subjected to consummation. Thus, it is an easier process and provides exercise of rights more conveniently.

'Option of Puberty' is not an easy process to repudiate the marriage under Muslim Law is also correct. Section 2 of the Dissolution of Muslim Marriage Act, 1939 states that the minor has the right to repudiate the marriage contracted by the father, paternal grandfather, or any other grandfather upon reaching the age of puberty provided that the marriage is not consummated. This shows that the right to repudiation in such cases is available only before consummation. This condition makes repudiation quite difficult and does not guarantee an escape in all circumstances.

24 'Tuhr' means

1 Period of menstruation
2 Period of iddat
3 Period between menstruation
4 None of the above

Ans. (3)

Exp. 'Tuhr' means the period between menstruation. It refers to the days of purity between each menstrual cycle. As such, the period of Tuhr is the period during which cohabitation is possible.

25 Match an item in List I with correct answer in List II using the codes given below.

List I	List II
A. Gujarat Women's Workers Association Vs. Union of India	I. Dower
B. Hamira Bibi Vs. Zubaida Bibi	II. Triple Divorce
C. Anwari Begum Vs. Ziauddin	III. Uniform Civil Code
D. Bai Tahira Vs. Ali Hussain Fissalli	IV. Maintenance

Codes

	A	B	C	D		A	B	C	D
1	I	IV	II	III	2	I	II	III	IV
3	II	I	III	IV	4	II	III	IV	I

Ans. (3)

Exp. The correct match is A-II, B-I, C-III, D-IV.

Gujarat Women's Workers Association Vs. Union of India (1997) is related to Triple Divorce. In this case, the petition was filed, inter alia, to declare muslim Personal Law which allows polygamy as void as offending Articles 14 and 15 of the Constitution; to declare Muslim Personal Law which enables a Muslim male to give unilateral Talaq to his wife without her consent and without resort to judicial process of courts as void, offending Articles 14 and 15 of the Constitution.

Hamira Bibi Vs. Zubaida Bibi (1916) is related to Dower. In this case, the Privy Council held that Dower ranks as a debt, and the wife is entitled along with other creditors, to have it satisfied on the death of the husband out of his estate. Her right, however, is no greater than that of any other unsecured creditor, except that if she lawfully with the express or implied consent of the husband, or his other heirs, obtains possession of the whole or part of his estate, to satisfy her claim with the rents and issues accruing there from, she is entitled to retain such possession until it is satisfied.

Anwari Begum Vs. Ziauddin (1981)is related to Uniform Civil Code. The court said that talaq-e-biddat pronounced by the husband without reasonable cause and without being preceded by attempts of reconciliation and without the involvement of arbitrators with due representation on behalf of husband and wife would not lead to a valid divorce. This case reflected the need for a uniform civil code, which would be helpful in eradicating evil religious practices.

Bai Tahira Vs. *Ali Hussain Fissalli* (1978) is related to Maintenance. The SC held that clause (b) of Explanation to Section 125(1) of the Criminal Procedure Code which defines 'wife' as including a divorced wife contains no words of limitation to justify the exclusion of Muslim women from its scope. The court observed that the right of maintenance available under Section 125 is a statutory right and remains unaffected and also overrides the provisions of personal law if there be any conflict between the two.

26 Which form of talaq is revocable during period of 'iddat' ?

1 Talaq-i-Ahsan
2 Talaq-i-Hasan
3 Triple Talaq
4 None of these

Ans. *(1)*

➲ *Exp.* Talaq-i-Ahsan is revocable during period of 'iddat'.

Talaq-i-ahsan is that talaq which is being given to woman by man one by one in three periods of tuhr purification and did not have sexual intercourse in that period.

In Talaq-e-Hasan, talaq is pronounced once a month, over a period of three months. If cohabitation is not resumed during this period, divorce gets formalised after the third utterance in the third month. However, if cohabitation resumes after the first or second utterance of talaq, the parties are assumed to have reconciled.

27 Essentials of valid contract is

1 Meeting of minds
2 Meeting of parties
3 Meeting to discuss consideration
4 Meeting to discuss proposal and acceptance

Ans. *(1)*

➲ *Exp.* Essential elements of a valid contract is meeting of minds.

According to Section 10, all agreements are contract if they are made by the free consent of parties competent to contract for a lawful consideration and with a lawful object and are not expressly declared to be void." Thus, Sections 2(h) and Section 10 of the Act state that there are some essential elements of a valid contract. If any of these elements is not satisfied by an agreement, it will affect the validity and will not form a valid contract.

The meeting of mind is also known as consensus ad idem under contract law, which refers to the necessity of parties arriving at a conclusion with complete information, out of their free will and they must understand the agreement with same thing in same sense.

28 Read Assertion (A) and Reason (R) and with help of codes given below, point out the correct explanation.

Assertion (A) A proposal, when accepted, results in an agreement.

Reason (R) It is only after the acceptance of the proposal that a contract between the two parties can arise.

Codes

1 Both (A) and (R) are true and (R) is correct explanation of (A)
2 Both (A) and (R) are true, but (R) is not a correct explanation of (A)
3 (A) is true, but (R) is false
4 (A) is false, but (R) is true

Ans. *(1)*

➲ *Exp.* Both (A) and (R) are true, and (R) is the correct explanation of (A).

As per Section 2(a), of Indian Contract Act, 1872 when one person signifies to another his willingness to do or to abstain from doing anything, with a view to obtaining the assent of that either to such act or abstinence, he is said to make a proposal. Thus, the Assertion is correct.

Section 2(b) of Indian Contract Act, 1872 says when the person to whom the proposal is made, signifies his assent there to, the proposal is said to be accepted. A proposal, when accepted, becomes a promise and in clause (e), it is stated that every promise and every set of promises, forming the consideration for each other, is an agreement. Thus, an offer once accepted, becomes an agreement.

29 A minor is son of a beggar. He is told by a law professor that he would not be liable for any goods he purchases. The minor purchases a car and a bread loaf. Decide liability for payment of car and bread loaf, using codes given below.

1 The minor is liable to pay price of car and bread loaf
2 The minor is liable to pay reasonable compensation for car
3 The minor is liable to pay price of bread
4 The minor's parent/guardian is liable to pay reasonable compensation for bread loaf

Ans. *(4)*

➲ *Exp.* In the given case, the minor's parent/guardian is liable to pay reasonable compensation for bread loaf.

A guardian of a minor has the powers and responsibilities of a parent who has not been deprived of custody of a minor and unemancipated child, except that a guardian is not legally obligated to provide from the guardian's own funds for the ward and is not liable to 3rd persons by reason of the parental relationship for acts of the ward.

The provision relating to the position of necessaries supplied to a minor occurs under Section 68 of the Indian Contract Act, 1872. Section 68 of Indian Contract Act says "If a person, incapable of entering into contract or anyone whom he is legally bound to support, is supplied by another person with necessities suited to his condition in life, the person who has furnished such supplies is entitled to be reimbursed from the property of such incapable person." The essence of this provision renders the parent/guardian of the child liable to reimburse the reasonable cost of service or benefit granted to the child by a third person.

30 Arrange following concepts in sequence in which they occur, using codes given below.

I. Offer　　II. Acceptance
III. Damage　　IV. Remedies

Codes

1 I, III, II, I　　2 I, II, IV, III
3 I, IV, II, III　　4 I, II, III, IV

Ans. *(4)*

Exp. Among the given choices, the correct sequence is I, II, III and IV.

Offer - In any agreement, there needs to be an offer from a person, which may be accepted by another, resulting in creation of a contract subject to the satisfaction of other essentials.

Acceptance - Section 2(a) of Indian Contract Act, 1872 states that when one person signifies to another his willingness to do or to abstain from doing anything, with a view to obtaining the assent of that either to such act or abstinence, he is said to make a proposal. As per Section 2(b), when the person to whom the proposal is made, signifies his assent thereto, the proposal is said to be accepted. A proposal, when accepted, becomes a promise.

Damage Once the contract has been formed, any party unreasonably or unjustifiably breaches the contract causing damage to the other party, is held liable under the law for a suitable remedy.

Remedies Section 73 of the Act provides for compensation of loss or damage caused by breach of contract. It says that when a contract has been broken, the party who suffers by such breach is entitled to receive, from the party who has broken the contract, compensation for any loss or damage caused to him thereby, which naturally arose in the usual course of things from such breach, or which the parties knew, when they made the contract, to be likely to result from the breach of it. Such compensation is not to be given for any remote and indirect loss or damage sustained by reason of the breach.

31 A contract may be vitiated by

I. Fraud
II. Mistake
III. Frustration
IV. Undue influence

Codes

1 Only I is correct　　2 I and II are correct
3 I, II and III are correct　　4 All are correct

Ans. *(4)*

Exp. A contract may be vitiated by Fraud, Mistake, Frustration and Undue influence.

Section 17 in the Indian Contract Act, 1872 defines 'Fraud' which means and includes any of the following acts committed by a party to a contract, or with his connivance, or by his agent, with intent to deceive another party thereto or his agent, or to induce him to enter into the contract:

- the suggestion as a fact, of that which is not true, by one who does not believe it to be true;
- the active concealment of a fact by one having knowledge or belief of the fact.
- a promise made without any intention of performing it
- any other act fitted to deceive.

As per Section 20, where both the parties to an agreement are under a mistake as to a matter of fact essential to the agreement the agreement is void.

Section 56 provides that an agreement to do an act impossible in itself is void. Contract to do act afterwards becoming impossible or unlawful. A contract to do an act which, after the contract is made, becomes impossible, or, by reason of some event which the promisor could not prevent, unlawful, becomes void when the act becomes impossible or unlawful.

Section 16 defines 'Undue influence' stating that a contract is said to be induced by 'undue influence' where the relations subsisting between the parties are such that one of the parties is in a position to dominate the will of the other and uses that position to obtain an unfair advantage over the other.

32 Match items in List I with items in List II, using codes given below.

	List I		List II
A.	Promise	I.	Section 56
B.	Frustration	II.	Section 2(4)
C.	Effect of refusal to accept offer of performance	III.	Section 26
D.	Agreement in restraint of marriage	IV.	Section 38

Codes

	A	B	C	D		A	B	C	D
1	II	IV	I	III	2	II	I	IV	III
3	I	II	IV	III	4	I	II	III	IV

Ans. *(2)*

Exp. The correct matching is A-II; B-I; C-IV; D-III.

Section 2(4) of Indian Contract Act, 1872 defines a promise and states that when the person to whom the proposal is made, signifies his assent thereto, the proposal is said to be accepted. A proposal, when accepted, becomes a promise.

Section 56 provides that an agreement to do an act impossible in itself is void. Contract to do the act afterwards becomes impossible or unlawful. A contract to do an act which, after the contract is made, becomes impossible, or, by reason of some event which the promisor could not prevent, unlawful, becomes void when the act becomes impossible or unlawful.

In *Section 38*, the effect of refusal to accept an offer of performance is dealt with. It is said that where a promisor has made an offer of performance to the promisee, and the offer has not been accepted, the promisor is not responsible for non-performance, nor does he thereby lose his right under the contract.

Section 26 says every agreement in restraint of the marriage of any person, other than a minor, is void.

33 'P', owner of a car, asked his friend 'Q' to drive the car to Bombay where he would join him. As the car was about five kilometres from Bombay, it hit a pedestrian 'R', on account of Q's negligent driving and injured him seriously. 'R' sued 'P' for damages. In this case

1 P is not liable
2 The liability is solely of 'Q', as 'P' was not accompanying him
3 Since 'Q' was driving P's car was under his authority, 'P' is liable
4 'P' has the defence of inevitable accident

Ans. (3)

➲ *Exp.* In the given case, Since 'Q' was driving P's car under his authority, then 'P' is liable for damages.

According to the rule of agency, the Principal is liable for the act of his agent. In the given case, 'Q' acted as the agent of 'P' when he authorized him to drive the car. Thus, 'P' would be liable for damages under the concept of Principal-Agent relationship.

34 "If it was lawful act, however ill the motive might be, the defendant had a right to do it." This observation was made by the court in one of the following cases

1 Mayor of Bradford Corporation Vs. Pickles
2 Ashby Vs. White
3 Christie Vs. Davey
4 Hollywood Silver Fox Farm Ltd. Vs. Emmet

Ans. (1)

➲ *Exp.* The given observation was made by the court in Mayor of Bradford Corporation Vs. Pickles (1895).

The House of Lords held that the respondent was not liable even though his act which caused harm to the appellant was done maliciously. The respondent's act was a lawful act and if it caused any harm to the appellant then he was not liable.

This is not a case in which the state of mind of the person doing the act can affect the right to do it. If it was a lawful act, however ill the motive might be, he had a right to do it. If it was an unlawful act, however good his motive might be, he would have no right to do it. Motives and intentions in such a question as is now before your Lordships seem to me to be absolutely irrelevant.

35 'P' and 'Q', unknown to 'R', sought and got a lift in R's car, but on account of some mechanical defect in the car, of which 'R' was not aware, one of the front wheels of the car got detached and flew away, and the car toppled. 'P' and 'Q' got serious injuries and later on, 'P' died of his injuries. 'Q' and P's next kin sued 'R' for damages for negligent driving. What defence 'R' has ?

1 Volenti non fit injuria
2 No responsibility towards 'P' and 'Q' who got a free lift
3 Inevitable accident
4 No defence

Ans. (3)

➲ *Exp.* In this case, 'R' can get a defence of an inevitable accident.

The facts disclose that the mechanical defect in the car was not known to 'R' and therefore, it cannot be reasonably expected from him to be in a position to avoid the liability. The defense of inevitable accident applies when the defendant could not have avoided the damage despite taking reasonable care on his part. Here, there is no apparent negligence on the part of driver 'R'.

The defense of Volenti Non Fit Injuria will have no application in this case because one of the essentials of such defense is knowledge of the plaintiff about the possible risk and subsequent consent to it. However, the plaintiff could not reasonably have knowledge of the risk in a given situation as the accident was beyond anticipation.

36 In contributory negligence

1 Both parties have contributed to the negligence equally
2 Only one party is negligent and other has not taken due care
3 One party is negligent resulting in injury while the other has taken due care
4 When lack of care is equal on both sides

Ans. (2)

➲ *Exp.* Contributory negligence occurs when only one party is negligent and other has not taken due care.

In certain circumstances a person who has suffered an injury will not be able to get damages from another for the reason that his own negligence has contributed to his injury; every person is expected to take reasonable care of himself.

Thus, when the plaintiff by his own want of care contributes to the damage caused by negligence or wrongful conduct of the defendant he is considered to be guilty of contributory negligence.

37 'P' shoot at 'Q' with the view to kill him. When 'Q' was being taken to hospital, a tree fell upon 'Q' on the way and 'Q' died in the hospital a few days later. If it was proved that the falling of the tree caused Q's death, then

1 'P' shall be responsible for the death of 'Q'
2 Falling of tree has broken the chain of causation
3 'P' is not liable to pay compensation to the dependents of 'Q'
4 'P' is responsible for the death of 'Q' as Q's death was the direct consequence of P's act

Ans. (2)

Exp. In the given case, if it was proved that the falling of the tree caused Q's death, then falling of tree has broken the chain of causation.

Causation provides a means of connecting conduct with a resulting effect, typically an injury. In criminal law, it is defined as the actus reus (an action) from which the specific injury or other effect arose and is combined with mens rea (a state of mind) to comprise the elements of guilt.

Here, the death was not ultimately caused by accused's actions, rather because of the tree falling on the deceased and hence, there is no direct connection between the act of accused and the result.

38 Which one of the following has been laid down as basis of responsibility by the rule in Rylands Vs. Fletcher?

1 Fault liability
2 Conditional liability
3 Strict liability
4 Insurance liability

Ans. (3)

Exp. Strict Liability has been laid down as the basis of responsibility by the rule in Rylands Vs. Fletcher (1868). It states that any person who keeps hazardous substances on his premises will be held responsible if such substances escape the premises and cause any damage.

The rule of strict liablity makes the defendant liable for accidental harms caused without any intention or negligence on his part.

39 Read Assertion (A) and Reason (R) and with the help of codes given below decide, what offence if any was committed ?

Assertion (A) 'A' and 'Z' agree to fence with each other for a game. But because of foul, despite playing fairly, 'Z' was injured.

Reason (R) :

I. No offence by virtue of consent between 'A' and 'Z'.
II. Consent was obtained in good faith to gain prise, so no offence by 'A'.
III. 'A' is criminally liable because he had knowledge about the likelihood of injury.
IV. Despite implied consent the intention was bad so 'A' is liable.

Codes

1 Reason 'I' is true when 'II', 'III' and 'IV' are not asserted
2 Reason 'II' is true when 'I', 'III' and 'IV' are not asserted
3 Reason 'III' is true when 'I', 'II' and 'IV' are not asserted.
4 Reason 'IV' is true when 'I', 'II' and 'III' are not asserted

Ans. (1)

Exp. Reason 'I' is true when 'II', 'III' and 'IV' are not asserted.

The given statement would amount to no offence by virtue of consent between 'A' and 'Z'.

If there was consent between 'A' and 'Z' for the fencing and injury was caused without intention arising out of foul, then there is no liability, especially when the game was being played fairly at the moment when such injury occurred. It is not relevant as to whether the consent was obtained in good faith or not, as long as there is consent, there will be no offence if harm is caused purely out of a fair play.

40 Read Assertion (A) and Reason (B) and with the help of codes given below select the correct answer.

Assertion (A) Common intention is asserted

Reason (R) :

I. A period which is anterior in time among the offenders
II. From the facts of pre-arranged plan
III. From the act of conduct resulting from prior concert
IV. From the totality of circumstances in which the act was committed

Codes

1 'I' is false because 'II', 'III' and 'IV' do not support it
2 'IV' is true as 'I', 'II' and 'III' support it
3 'III' is true irrespective of support of 'I', 'II' and 'IV'
4 'II' is true being supported by 'I', 'III' and 'IV'

Ans. (2)

Exp. Among the given statements, IV is true as I, II and III support it.

Common intention under Section 34 IPC is a species of constructive liability which renders every member of a group who shares such intention responsible for the criminal act committed by anyone of them when such an act is done in furtherance of the common intention. Common intention, however, cannot be confused with similar intention.

Although accused persons may have similar intention to commit a crime, say murder, until and unless the pre-requisites of:(a) pre-consent, (b) presence and (c) participation, in respect of each accused are established, it cannot be said that they shared common intention and be culpable for the crime committed by any of them in furtherance to such intention.

41 Select the statement that is most suitable in law: Culpable homicide is not murder when one is deprived of the power of self-control resulting from

1 Grave and sudden provocation
2 When death results by voluntary provocation
3 Where death results in course of obedience of law
4 When death results by mistake

Ans. (1)

Exp. Culpable homicide is not murder when one is deprived of the power of self-control resulting from grave and sudden provocation.

In accordance to exception-1 to Section 300 of IPC, Culpable homicide is not murder if the offender, whilst deprived of the power of self-control by grave and sudden provocation, causes the death of the person who gave the provocation or causes the death of any other person by mistake or accident.

The above exception is subject to the following provisos;

(i) that the provocation is not sought or voluntarily provoked by the offender as an excuse for killing or doing harm to any person,

(ii) that the provocation is not given by anything done in obedience to the law, or by a public servant in the lawful exercise of the powers of such public servant,

(iii) that the provocation is not given by anything done in the lawful exercise of the right of private defence.

42 'B' a married man commits sex with 'C', a girl Child of 16 years with her consent. What offence 'B' has committed?

1 Adultery
2 Rape
3 No offence
4 Sexual outraging

Ans. (2)

Exp. 'B' has committed the offence of rape in the given situation.

Section 375 of IPC defines the offence of rape and states under sixth condition that a man is said to commit "rape" who has sexual intercourse with a woman with or without her consent, when she is under eighteen years of age.

The age of the girl was sixteen years, but such consent is not valid in terms of above provision.

Therefore, the man shall be liable.

43 Fill in the blank.
Extortion is ________, when it is committed under fear of instant hurt.

1 theft
2 attempt to steal property
3 robbery
4 wrongful restraint

Ans. (3)

Exp. Extortion is robbery, when it is committed under fear of instant hurt.

Section 390 of IPC, 1860 says Extortion is "robbery" if the offender, at the time of committing the extortion, is in the presence of the person put in fear, and commits the extortion by putting that person in fear of instant death, of instant hurt, or of instant wrongful restraint to that person or to some other person, and, by so putting in fear, induces the person so put in fear then and there to deliver up the thing extorted.

44 What is the distinctive feature between false information and false charging ?

1 Using lawful power to cause annoyance so as to institute a criminal proceeding
2 To omit act which ought not to be done
3 A case for false information can only be started by a complaint while false charge can be initiated by police
4 There is no real distinction

Ans. (2)

Exp. The distinctive feature between false information and false charging is to omit act which ought not to be done. Section 182 of IPC defines False information while Section 211 defines false charge.

The distinction between the two provisions may be observed as under Section 182, it is an offence to make a public servant do or omit to do which he must otherwise not to or omit, if he was not provided with the wrong information.

45 Collective bargaining serves purposes

1 Regulating wages and conditions of service
2 Regulating labour management relations
3 Both 1 and 2
4 None of the above

Ans. (3)

Exp. Collective bargaining regulates wages and conditions of service and also regulates labour management relations.

Collective bargaining is a procedure by which employment related disputes are resolved cordially, peacefully and voluntarily by settlement between labour unions and managements. The collective bargaining in India remained limited in its scope and restricted in its coverage by a well defined legal structure.

According to an ILO Manual in 1960, the Collective Bargaining is defined as; "Negotiations about working conditions and terms of employment between an employer, a group of employees or one or more employers organization on the other, with a view to reaching an agreement."

It is also asserted that "the terms of agreement serve as a code defining the rights and obligations of each party in their employment relations with one another, if fixes large number of detailed conditions of employees and during its validity none of the matters it deals with, internal circumstances give grounds for a dispute counseling and individual workers".

46 In which country where statutes make it obligatory to negotiate non-performance of the obligation invites penalty, failure to carry obligation is treated as unfair labour practice?

1 UK
2 USA
3 France
4 India

Ans. (2)

Exp. In USA, statutes make it obligatory to negotiate non-performance of the obligation invites penalty, failure to carry obligation invites penalty, failure to carry obligation is treated as unfair labour practice.

Title VII of the Civil Service Reform Act of 1978 is also known as the Federal Service Labor-Management Relations Statute or the Statute in USA. The Statute allows certain non-postal federal employees to organize, bargain collectively, and to participate through labor organizations of their choice in decisions affecting their working lives.

The Statute defines and lists the rights of employees, labor organizations, and agencies to reflect the public-interest demand for the highest standards of employee performance and the efficient accomplishment of government operations.

47 In which of the following case, the Supreme Court held that "there was no rule of thumb that in every case of termination of workman's service in violation of Section 25F of ID Act" relief of re-instatement should be granted ?

1 Talwara Co-operative Credit and Service Society Ltd. Vs Sushil Kumar (2009) I LL J 326 SC
2 Gujarat Steel Tubes Ltd. Vs. GST Mazdoor Sabha (1980) I LL J 137 (SC)
3 Mavji C Lakum Vs. Central Bank of India (2008) III LL J1(SC)
4 None of the above

Ans. *(1)*

Exp. In the case of Talwara Co-operative Credit and Service Society Ltd. Vs. Sushil Kumar (2009) the Supreme Court held that, "there was no rule of thumb that in every case of termination of workman's service in violation of Section 25 F of Industrial Disputes Act."

The court said that there is no rule of thumb that in every case where the Industrial Tribunal gives a finding that the termination of service was in violation of Section 25-F of the Act, entire back wages should be awarded. A host of factors like the manner and method of selection and appointment i.e. whether after proper advertisement of the vacancy or inviting applications from the employment exchange, nature of appointment, namely, whether ad hoc, short term, daily wage, temporary or permanent in character, any special qualification required for the job and the like should be weighed and balanced in taking a decision regarding award of back wages.

48 The Registrar to Pensions Appeal Tribunal was appointed as presiding officer of a Labour Court. The appointment is

1 Valid
2 Void
3 Void ab-initio
4 None of these

Ans. *(3)*

Exp. The Registrar to Pensions Appeal Tribunal was appointed as presiding officer of a Labour Court. The appointment is void-ab-initio.

In law, void means of no legal effect. The term void ab initio, means 'to be treated as invalid from the outset'.

Section 7(2) of the Industrial Disputes Act, 1947 says a Labour Court shall consist of one person only to be appointed by the appropriate Government. The clause (3) says a person shall not be qualified for appointment as the presiding officer of a Labour Court, unless he is, or has been, a Judge of a High Court; or he has, for a period of not less than three years, been a District Judge or an Additional District Judge; or he has held any judicial office in India for not less than seven years; or he has been the presiding officer of a Labour Court constituted under any Provincial Act or State Act for not less than five years.

It may be observed that there is no provision for appointment of a Registrar to Pensions Appeal Tribunal as a presiding officer.

49 Match List I with List II and select the correct answer using the codes given below.

List I (Subject)	List II (Provisions of ID Act)
A. Tribunal	I. Section 2(ra)
B. Wages	II. Section 2(r)
C. Unfair Labour Practices	III. Section 2 (rb)
D. Village Industries	IV. Section 2 (rr)

Codes

	A	B	C	D		A	B	C	D
1	I	IV	III	II	2	II	III	I	IV
3	II	IV	I	III	4	I	III	II	IV

Ans. *(3)*

Exp. The correct matching is A-II, B-IV, C-I, D-III.

Section 2(r) of Industrial Disputes Act, 1947 defines 'Tribunal'. It means an Industrial Tribunal constituted under Section 7A and includes an Industrial Tribunal constituted before the 10th day of March, 1957, under this Act. Section 7A provides that the appropriate government may, by notification in the Official Gazette, constitute one or more Industrial Tribunals for the adjudication of industrial disputes relating to any matter.

Section 2(rr) defines wages. It means all remuneration capable of being expressed in terms of money, which would, if the terms of employment, expressed or implied, were fulfilled, be payable to a workman in respect of his employment or of work done in such employment.

Section 2(ra) mentions "unfair labour practice". It means any of the practices specified in the Fifth Schedule which includes, inter alia, activities to interfere with, restrain from, or coerce, workmen in the exercise of their right to organize, form, join or assist a trade union or to engage in concerted activities for the purposes of collective bargaining or other mutual aid or protection, to dominate, interfere with or contribute support, financial or otherwise, to any trade union on the part of employer and to advise or actively support or instigate any strike deemed to be illegal under this Act, to coerce workmen in the exercise of their right to self-organization or to join a trade union or refrain from, joining any trade union on the part of workmen.

Section 2(rb) defines village industries and has the meaning assigned to it in clause (h) of Section 2 of the Khadi and Village Industries Commission Act, 1956, which means any industry located in a rural area which produces any goods or renders any service with or without the use of power and in which the fixed capital investment per head of an artisan or a worker does not exceed one lakh rupees or such other sum as may, by notification in the Official Gazette, be specified from time to time by the Central Government.

50 Read Assertion (A) and Reason (R), using codes given below, select correct answer.

Assertion (A) Strike is individual stoppage of work to press management to get more pay.

Reason (R) Individual has fundamental right of strike.

Codes

1 (A) and (R) are true and (R) is correct explanation of (A)
2 (A) and (R) are true, but (R) is not correct explanation of (A)
3 (A) and (R) are false
4 (A) is true, but (R) is false

Ans. *(3)*

➲ *Exp.* Both the Assertion and Reason are false.

Assertion is false because Strike has been defined in Section 2 (q) of the Industrial Disputes Act, 1947 and it says that strike means a cessation of work by a body of persons employed in any industry acting in combination, or a concerted refusal, or a refusal under a common understanding, of any number of persons who are or have been so employed to continue to work or to accept employment.

Reason is false because Right to strike is not a fundamental right but a legal right and with this right statutory restriction is attached in the Industrial Dispute Act, 1947.

PAPER III

1 Who among the following expressed the view that the Indian Constitution is Federal as much as it establishes what may be called a dual polity ?

1 Dr BR Ambedkar
2 Sir Ivor Jennings
3 Prof KC Wheare
4 Sir BN Rau

Ans. *(1)*

➲ *Exp.* Dr. B.R. Ambedkar said that the Indian Constitution is Federal as much as it establishes what may be called a dual polity.

Dr. B.R. Ambedkar is one of the prime architects of the Constitution. He said in the Constituent Assembly "The Indian Constitution is a federal constitution in as much as it established what may be called a dual polity which will consist of the Union at the centre and the States at the periphery each endowed with sovereign powers to be excercised in the field assigned to them respectively by the Constitution."

2 In which of the following amendment the words "Nothing in Article 13 shall apply to any amendment made under Article 368" were inserted ?

1 22nd Amendment
2 24th Amendment
3 42nd Amendment
4 44th Amendment

Ans. *(2)*

➲ *Exp.* The words "Nothing in Article 13 shall apply to any amendment made under Article 368" were inserted through the Constitution 24th Amendment, 1971.

As per the objectives of the Amendment Act, the Supreme Court in the well-known Golak Nath's case [1967, 2 S.C.R. 762] reversed, by a narrow majority, its own earlier decisions upholding the power of Parliament to amend all parts of the Constitution including Part III relating to fundamental rights. This led to the formulation of the 24th Amendment Act of 1971. Through this amendment, "Nothing in article 13 shall apply to any amendment made under this article" was added as clause 3 of Article 368.

3 The Supreme Court of India held in which of the following case that the views expressed by it in exercise of its advisory jurisdiction are binding on all courts within the territory of India?

1 In Re-Berubari case
2 In Re-Cauvery Water Disputes Tribunal case
3 In Re-Kerala Education Bill
4 In Re-Special Courts Bill

Ans. *(4)*

➲ *Exp.* The Supreme Court in the case titled as Re-Special Courts Bill (1978) held that the views expressed by it in exercise of its advisory jurisdiction are binding on all courts within the territory of India.

The President's reference under Article 143(1) to the Supreme Court in the said case (the special courtsreference) raised important questions of constitutional law. The facts giving rise to the Special Courts Reference were briefly these; when the former Prime Minister, Mrs. Indira Gandhi revoked the emergency after her defeat in the 1977 Parliamentary elections, the overwhelming demand arose in the country for the punishment of Mrs. Gandhi, her son Sanjay and other guilty men. The investigations of the Shah Commission left no doubt that there had been grave abuse of power during the emergency.

Justice to countless victims of the emergency demanded that the guilty should be brought to trial. However, the ordinary process of law is dilatory and Mrs. Gandhi's party made no secret that the weapon of delay would be used to prevent the "guilty men" from being brought to speedy trial. Consequently, a private member, Mr. Ram Jethmalani, introduced in the House of the People (Lok Sabha) a Bill for the setting up of Special Courts on 1st August, 1978 the President acting under Article 143.

4 In which one of the following case has the Supreme Court upheld the Constitutional validity of the Constitution (93rd Amendment) introducing Article 15(5) ?

1 TMA Pai Foundation Vs. State of Karnataka
2 Indra Sawhney Vs. Union of India
3 M Nagaraj and Ors Vs. Union of India
4 Ashok Kumar Thakur Vs. Union of India

***Ans.* (3)**

Exp. The Supreme Court upheld the Constitutional validity of the Constitution (93rd Amendment) introducing Article 15(5) in M Nagaraj and Ors Vs. Union of India (2006).

The Supreme Court held that it is the duty of the State not only to protect human dignity but facilitate it by taking positive steps in that direction. So, Article 15(5) was introduced by the Constitution (93rd Amendment) Act, 2005, so as to bring private unaided institutions into the ambit of reservations.

Article 19(1)(g) says all citizens shall have the right to practice any profession. But, to practice technical professions, you need to have the required educational qualifications. By reserving seats in private educational institutions as well, under Article 15(5), the State has reduced the chances of an individual to get an admission into those courses that would allow him to practice the profession of his will. So, Article 19(1)(g) is exempted to have any bearing on Article 15(5).

5 Match List 'A' with List 'B' and select the correct answer using the codes given below.

List I		List II	
A.	Independence of the Judiciary	I.	Administrative adjudication
B.	Executive Legislation	II.	Parliamentary form of Government
C.	Quasi-Judicial function	III.	Appointment of Judges
D.	Collective responsibility	IV.	Ordinance

Codes

	A	B	C	D		A	B	C	D
1	II	I	IV	III	2	III	IV	I	II
3	II	IV	I	III	4	III	I	IV	II

***Ans.* (2)**

Exp. The correct matching is A-III, B-IV, C-I, D-II.

The Indian Constitution has ensured the *independence of the judiciary* through a number of measures. The legislature is not involved in the process of appointment of judges. In order to be appointed as a judge, a person must have experience as a lawyer and/or must be well versed in law. Political opinions of the person or his/her political loyalty should not be the criteria for appointments to judiciary.

The Indian Constitution outlines a traditional, westminster separation-of-powers model, where the primary law-making responsibility vests in an elected Parliament, and the task of implementing laws is left to the *Executive*. The Constitution authorises both the federal and the state Executives; the President, or the Governor to promulgate ordinances in circumstances where the central Parliament, or the State legislatures, as the case may be, are not in session, and "immediate action" is required.

Quasi-Judicial functions may be defined as the power to perform acts administrative in nature but requiring incidentally the trial and determination of question of fact and law. The term 'administrative decision making' is used synonymously with 'administrative adjudication'. A simpler statement is that where the function of the body is primarily regulatory, and the power to hear and determine is merely incidental to regulatory duty, the function is administrative.

The principle of *Collective responsibility* can be seen in Parliamentary form of government. It represents ministerial accountability to the legislature. In India, the doctrine of collective responsibility of the Union Executive to the House of the People and of the State Executive to the Legislative Assembly is specifically enshrined in the Constitution. Article 75(3) lays down that the Council of Ministers shall be collectively responsible to the Lok Sabha.

6 Read Assertion (A) and Reason (R) and find correct answer using codes given below.

Assertion (A) The Council of Ministers is the hub of the Parliamentary form of Government.

Reason (R) The Government is formed from the majority party.

Codes

1 Both (A) and (R) are true, but (R) is not the correct explanation of (A)
2 Both (A) and (R) are true and (R) is the correct explanation of (A)
3 (A) is true, (R) is false
4 (A) is false, but (R) is true

***Ans.* (1)**

Exp. Both (A) and (R) are true but (R) is not the correct explanation of (A).

The Constitution of India provides for a parliamentary form of government, both at the Centre and in the states. A parliamentary form of government requires a Council of Ministers to aid and advise the Prime Minister in all important matters. Even the cabinet is formed from the Council of Ministers. Thus, the Assertion is true.

The Reason which states that the Government is formed from the majority party is correct. However, this does not define the reason for the Council of Ministers to be of significant importance in a Parliamentary system. Thus, though Reason is correct, it is not the correct explanation for given Assertion.

7 The jurisdiction of the Supreme Court of India may be enlarged by

1 The President of India
2 The President of India in consultation with the Prime Minister and Chief Justice of India
3 The Parliament by resolution
4 The Parliament by law

Ans. (4)

Exp. The jurisdiction of the Supreme Court of India may be enlarged by the Parliament by law.

The Enlargement of the jurisdiction of the Supreme Court by the Parliament by law is provided under Article 138 of the Indian Constitution. It is stated therein that the Supreme Court shall have such further jurisdiction and powers with respect to any of the matters in the Union List as Parliament may by law confer.

The Supreme Court shall have such further jurisdiction and powers with respect to any matter as the Government of India and the Government of any State may by special agreement confer, if Parliament by law provides for the exercise of such jurisdiction and powers by the Supreme Court.

8 What are exceptions to the rule of natural justice?

I. Exclusion by statutory provisions.
II. Exclusion by Constitutional provision.
III. Exclusion in case of legislative act.
IV. Exclusion in public interest.

Codes

1 Only I is correct
2 I and II are correct
3 I, II and III are correct
4 All of these are correct

Ans. (4)

Exp. All the given statements are exceptions to the rule of Natural Justice.

There are various exceptions to the rule of Natural Justice and Courts in India have applied the exceptions in various situations where the principles of Natural Justice can be put aside. Several factors may be identified as capable of excluding the rule of Natural Justice which are as follows: exclusion in case of emergency, where prompt action is needed, where it is impracticable to hold hearing or appeal, exclusion in case of purely administrative matters, where no right of person is infringed, exclusion on the ground of 'no fault' decision maker, exclusion by statutory provisions, exclusion by constitutional provision, exclusion in case of legislative act, exclusion in public interest etc.

9 Read Assertion (A) and Reason (R) and select the correct answer using codes given below.

Assertion (A) In India the order passed in violation of the principles of natural justice is void.

Reason (R) In India there is void in the area of principles of justice by nature.

Codes

1 (A and (R) are true and (R) is correct explanation of (A)
2 (A) and (R) are true, but (R) is not correct explanation of (A)
3 (A) is true and (R) is false
4 (A) is false and (R) is true

Ans. (3)

Exp. The Assertion is true, but the Reason is false.

In India, the situation is so well settled that if an order is passed in violation of the principles of natural justice, it is void. Failure to give reason to the person concerned or the reasons to the court will result in the quashing of the order and the authority is directed by the court to re-examine the case. Thus, Assertion is true.

Reason is false because the principles of natural justice have been firmly incorporated into our Constitution as well, for instance, Articles 14 and 21.

10 In which of the following conditions, the abuse of discretionary power is inferred ?

I. Use for improper purpose
II. Mala fide
III. Relevant consideration
IV. Leaving out irrelevant consideration

Answer using codes given below

Codes

1 Only I is correct
2 I and II are correct
3 I, II and III are correct
4 All of these are correct

Ans. (2)

Exp. Among the given choices, Mala fide and use of improper purpose will fall within the pureview of the abuse of the discretionary powers.

Exercise of discretion is an inseparable part of sound administration and, therefore, the State which is itself a creature of the Constitution, cannot shed its limitation at any time in any sphere of State activity. It is a well-settled rule of administrative law that an executive authority must be rigorously held to the standards by which it professes its actions to be judged and it must scrupulously observe those standards on pain of invalidation of an act in violation of them.

Now-a-days, the administrative authorities are conferred wide discretionary powers. The discretionary power is required to be exercised according to law. When the mode of exercising a valid power is improper or unreasonable, there is an abuse of power.

The various actions that amount to 'abuse' are Mala fides, improper purpose, taking irrelevant considerations, leaving out relevant considerations, colourable exercise of power and unreasonableness among others.

11 Read Assertion (A) and Reason (R) and select the correct answer using codes given below.

Assertion (A) Equality is antithetic to arbitrariness.

Reason (R) Article 14 of the Indian Constitution prevents arbitrary discretion being vested in the executive.

Codes

1 Both (A) and (R) are true and (R) is correct explanation of (A)
2 Both (A) and (R) are true, but (R) is not correct explanation of (A)
3 (A) is true, but (R) is false
4 (A) is false, but (R) is true

Ans. (1)

Exp. Both (A) and (R) are true, and (R) is the correct explanation of (A).

Equality is a dynamic concept with many aspects and dimensions and it cannot be "cribbed, cabined and confined" within traditional and doctrinaire limits. From a positivistic point of view, equality is antithetic to arbitrariness. This statement was made in the case of Ajay Hasia Vs. Khalid Mujib Sehravardi (1980). Article 14 of Indian Constitution indeed strikes at arbitrariness in State action and ensures fairness and equality of treatment.

Further, it was also held in the above mentioned case that wherever there is arbitrariness in State action whether it be of the legislature or of the executive or of "authority" under Article 12, Article 14 immediately springs into action and strikes down such State action.

12 The writ of habeas corpus will be issued if

1 Detention is legal
2 Detention is prima facie legal
3 Detention is prima facie illegal
4 Detention is primarily illegal

Ans. (3)

Exp. The writ of habeas corpus will be issued if the detention is prima facie illegal.

The writ of Habeas Corpus literally means 'to have the body of'. By this writ, the court can cause any person who has been detained or imprisoned to be physically brought before the court.

Such a writ can be issued in following example cases; when the person is detained and not produced before the magistrate within 24 hours, when the person is arrested without any violation of a law, when a person is arrested under a law which is unconstitutional, when detention is done to harm the person or is malafide.

13 Read Assertion (A) and Reason (R) and select the correct answer using codes given below .

Assertion (A) Lokpal is the demand of time.

Reason (R) Lokpal is a time saving institution.

Codes

1 Both (A) and (R) are true and (R) is correct explanation of (A)
2 Both (A) and (R) are true, but (R) is not correct explanation of (A)
3 (A) is true, but (R) is false
4 (A) is false, but (R) is true

Ans. (2)

Exp. Both (A) and (R) are true, but (R) is not correct explanation of (A).

A national anti-corruption ombudsman to look into complaints against public servants as defined under the Lokpal Act, 2013. The office of Lokpal comprises a chairperson and up to eight members. The Lokpal can initiate a preliminary investigation after it receives a complaint under the Prevention of Corruption Act, 1988. Thus, it is true that Lokpal is indeed a demand of the time. Hence Assertion is correct.

The long prevailing issue of corruption needs to be tackled by a dedicated and effective body. The fact that Lokpal is a time saving institution is not the real cause behind creation of Lokpal, though it is a factor that contributes to its significance.

14 "Administrative Law is the law concerning the powers and procedures of administrative agencies, including especially the law governing judicial review of administrative action." This definition of Administrative Law is given by

1 Ivor Jenning
2 Garner
3 KC Davis
4 Wade

Ans. (3)

Exp. The given definition of Administrative Law is given by KC Davis.

Davis believed that the administrative law seeks to cover various functions, powers or processes of administrative agencies which are created by the state for effective discharge of its functions. This also covers within itself review or examination of administrative action which may have been initiated without basis of law or may be simply against the permitted procedures.

15 In which of the following grounds, a writ of certiorari may be issued ?

1 Error of jurisdiction
2 Error apparent on face of record
3 Violation of natural justice
4 All of the above

Ans. (4)

Exp. A writ of certiorari may be issued in all the given circumstances.

Writ of Certiorari means 'to certify'. It is a writ that orders to move a suit from an inferior court to superior court. It is issued by a higher court to a lower court or tribunal either to transfer a case pending with that to itself or quash its order.

This is generally done because superior court believes that either the inferior court had no jurisdiction or committed an error of law. Thus, certiorari is a kind of curative writ. A writ of certiorari may be issued in the following ground; error of jurisdiction, error apparent on face of record, violation of natural justice etc.

16 Who propounded the 'Doctrine of Moral Reasoning'?

1 Kohler
2 Pound
3 HLA Hart
4 Kant

Ans. *(1)*

Exp. Lawrence Kohlberg propounded the 'Doctrine of Moral Reasoning'.

He is a psychologist who has made significant contributions to the field of moral reasoning by creating a theory of moral development. His theory is a "widely accepted theory that provides the basis for empirical evidence on the influence of human decision making on ethical behaviour."

According to his theory, people pass through three main stages of moral development as they grow from early childhood to adulthood. These stages are pre-conventional morality, conventional morality and post-conventional morality.

17 Which of the following avoid any dogmatic formulation and concentrate on the decisions given by law courts ?

1 Realist school
2 Analytical school
3 Philosophical school
4 Sociological school

Ans. *(1)*

Exp. The Realistic School avoids any dogmatic formulation and concentrates on the decisions given by law courts. It is a type of school which focuses on decisions. It is a branch of sociological approach. They believe that law is only on official action.

This school is known as 'realist' because it focuses on an approach that studies law as it is in the actual working and its effects ahead and rejects traditional definition of law and also avoids any dogmatic formulation and fully concentrates on decisions given by the courts.

18 'Jus Civile', 'Jus gentium' and 'Jus naturale' are found in

1 American Law
2 Greek Law
3 Roman Law
4 French Law

Ans. *(3)*

Exp. 'Jus Civile', 'Jus gentium' and 'Jus naturale' are found in Roman Law.

The term 'Roman law' today often refers to more than the laws of Roman society. In the great span of time during which the Roman Republic and Empire existed, there were many phases of legalistic development. During the period of the republic (753–31 BCE), the Jus Civile (civil law) developed. Based on custom or legislation, it applied exclusively to Roman citizens. By the middle of the 3rd century BCE, however, another type of law, Jus gentium (law of nations), was developed by the Romans to be applied both to themselves and to foreigners. Jus gentium was not the result of legislation, but was, instead, a development of the magistrates and governors who were responsible for administering justice in cases in which foreigners were involved. The idea was also linked with the theoretical notion that it was the law common to all peoples and was dictated by nature; Jus Naturale, an idea that the Romans took from Greek philosophy.

19 Match the following and select the correct answer using the codes given below.

List I	List II
A. Ancient theories	I. Grotius, Hobbes and Locke
B. Modern theories	II. Thomas Acquinas
C. Renaissance theories	III. Stammler and Kohler
D. Medieval theories	IV. Socrates, Aristotle and Plato

Codes

	A	B	C	D		A	B	C	D
1	III	IV	II	I	2	I	II	III	IV
3	II	III	IV	I	4	IV	III	I	II

Ans. *(4)*

Exp. The correct matching is A-IV, B-III, C-I, D-II.

Ancient theories were given by Socrates, Aristotle and Plato. Ancient Greek philosophy arose in the 6th century BC and lasted through the Hellenistic period (323 BC-30 BC). Greek philosophy covers an absolutely enormous amount of topics including: political philosophy, ethics, metaphysics, ontology (the study of the nature of being, becoming, existence, or reality), logic, biology, rhetoric, and aesthetics (branch of philosophy dealing with art, beauty, and taste). Socrates born in Athens in 470 BC, is often credited as one of the founders of Western Philosophy. Plato born in 428 BC is known for being the founder of the Academy in athens, the first institution of higher learning in Western World. Aristotle, student of Plato, lived from 384 BC-322BC. He joined Plato's Academy in Athens and remained there until age of thirty-seven.

Modern theories were given by Stammler and Kohler. Rudolf Stammler (1856-1938) was an influential German philosopher of law. Stammler defined law as, "species of will, others- regarding, self-authoritative and inviolable". For him, a just law was the highest expression of man' social life and aims at preservation of freedom of individuals.

Renaissance theories were given by Grotius, Hobbes and Locke. The period of the Renaissance is marked by the emergence of new ideas and rationalism in different fields of knowledge. In Jurisprudence, it can also be considered as the period of the development of natural law. During the 14th and 15th centuries, there was a rapid increase in scientific inventions along with the general awakening of the masses. These all factors resulted in shattering the foundation of established values.

Medieval Theories were given by Thomas Acquinas. Combining the theological principles of faith with the philosophical principles of reason, Saint Thomas Aquinas ranked among the most influential thinkers of medieval Scholasticism.

20 "Law is without doubt a remedy for greater evil, yet it brings with it evils of its own." Who said it ?

1 Blackstone 2 Friedman
3 Salmond 4 Hobbes

Ans. (3)

Exp. Salmond said that Law is without doubt a remedy for greater evil, yet it brings with it evils of its own.

According to Salmond 'Law may be defined as the body of principles recognised and applied by the state in the administration of justice'. In other words, law consists of rules recognised and acted upon by the Courts of Justice.

Salmond believed that law may arise out of popular practices and its legal character becomes patent when it is recognised and applied by a Court in the Administration of Justice. Courts may misconstrue a statute or reject a custom; it is only the Ruling of the Court that has the Binding Force of Law.

21 According to Salmond, every right involves a three fold relation.

I. It is a right against some person or persons.
II. It is a right to some act or omission of such person or persons.
III. It is a right over or to something to which that act or omission relates.

Codes

1 I and II are false 2 I, II and III are true
3 II and III are false 4 Only I is true

Ans. (2)

Exp. Among the given statements, all statements I, II and III are true.

According to Salmond, every right involves a threefold relation in which the owner of it stands, it is a right against some person or persons, it is a right to some act or omission of such person or persons, it is a right over to some thing to which that act or omission relates.

Ownerless rights are not recognised by English law. This is because, there would be nothing to prevent such a concept being used in legal reasoning. Ownership of a right may be merely contingent or uncertain. The owner of it may be a person indeterminate.

Salmond defines legal right as an interest recognized and protected by a rule of justice. The word 'interest' implies any interest, respect for which is a duty and disregard of which is a wrong. This definition contains two essential elements, legal recognition and legal protection. Both these elements should simultaneously and concurrently be present in an interest for its transformation as a legal right. A legal recognition of an interest without legal protection does not make it enforceable in a court of law, as for example, time barred debts. So also legal, protection of an interest without its legal recognition cannot make it a legal right.

22 Read Assertion (A) and Reason (R) and select the correct answer using codes given below.

Assertion (A) Srutis and Smritis form the greatest treasure house of Hinduism.

Reason (R) Srutis and Smritis are considered immemorial, timeless and eternal.

Codes

1 Both (A) and (R) are true, but (R) is not the correct explanation of (A)
2 Both (A) and (R) are true and (R) is the correct explanation of (A)
3 (A) is true, but (R) is false
4 (A) is false, but (R) is true

Ans. (2)

Exp. Both (A) and (R) are true and (R) is the correct explanation of (A).

The basic material or mantra text of each of the Vedas is called 'Samhita'. Some post Vedic texts are also known as 'Samhitas' such as Ashtavakra Gita, Bhrigu Samhita, Brahma Samhita, Deva Samhita, Garga Samhita, Kashyap Samhita, Shiva Samhita and Yogayajnavalkya Samhita.

The Vedic literature is broadly divided into two categories Shruti and Smriti. Shruti describes the sacred texts comprising the central canon of Hinduism viz. Vedas, Brahmanas, Aranyakas and Upanishads.

Smriti literally means that which is remembered, and it is entire body of the post Vedic Classical Sanskrit literature. It comprises Vedanga, Shad Darsana, Puranas, Itihasa, Upveda, Tantras, Agamas, Upangs. There is another post Vedic class of Sanskrit literature called 'Epics' which includes Ramayana and Mahabharta. Srutis and Smritis are considered immemorial, timeless and eternal.

23 Personality is a very vague and wide term and it has a variety of meanings. It is derived from the word 'persona' which is a

1 Latin word 2 French word
3 German word 4 Greek word

Ans. (4)

Exp. Personality is a very vague and wide term and it has a variety of meanings. It is derived from the word 'persona' which is a Greek word.

Personality is a dynamic and organised set of characteristics possessed by a person that uniquely influences their environment, cognitions, emotions, motivations and behaviours in various situations. According to Baron, "Personality is generally defined as an individual's unique and relatively stable patterns of behaviour, thoughts and emotions."

24 Fill in the blank with appropriate offence Extortion is _______, when it is committed under Fear of instant hurt.

1 Theft
2 Attempt to murder
3 Robbery
4 Wrongful restraint

Ans. (3)

Exp. Extortion is Robbery when it is committed under Fear of instant hurt.

According Section 390 of the Indian Penal Code, 1860, Extortion is robbery if the offender at the time of committing the extortion, is in the presence of the person put in fear and commits the extortion by putting that person in fear of instant death or of instant hurt, or of instant wrongful restraint to that person, or to some other person and by so putting in fear, induces the person so put in fear then and there to deliver up the thing extorted.

25 Fill in the blank with suitable statement. 'Z' dies in possession of gold ring, gold chain and a gold wrist watch during the course of an accident. 'A', before anyone entitled to such possession, dishonestly misappropriates the same causing

1 An aggravated form of misappropriation as per Section 404 of IPC
2 A type of possession by some process as per Section 405 of IPC
3 No offence because the property in question was entrusted to A before the death of Z
4 No offence because the property in question was possessed by some casualty

Ans. (1)

Exp. In the given situation, 'A' commits an aggravated form of misappropriation as per Section 404 of IPC.

Section 404 in The Indian Penal Code deals with Dishonest misappropriation of property possessed by deceased person at the time of his death and states that whoever dishonestly misappropriates or converts to his own use property, knowing that such property was in the possession of a deceased person at the time of that person's decease and has not since been in the possession of any person legally entitled to such possession, shall be punished with imprisonment of either description for a term which may extend to three years, and shall also be liable to fine; and if the offender at the time of such person's decease was employed by him as a clerk or servant, the imprisonment may extend to seven years.

26 Fill in the blank with correct proposition of law The malicious injury to property as per maxim *Sic Utre tuo ut allenum non leadas* (to use your own property so as not to injure your neighbour's property) as provided in _______.

1 Damage of property as per Section 427 IPC
2 Mischief as per Section 425 IPC
3 Mischief to cause wrongful restraint as per Section 440 IPC
4 Destruction of landmark as per Section 433 IPC

Ans. (2)

Exp. The malicious injury to property is provided in Mischief as per Section 425 of IPC.

Section 425 of IPC, 1860 states that whoever with intent to cause, or knowing that he is likely to cause, wrongful loss or damage to the public or to any person, causes the destruction of any property, or any such change in any property or in the situation thereof as destroys or diminishes its value or utility, or affects it injuriously, commits 'mischief'.

It is not essential to the offence of mischief that the offender should intend to cause loss or damage to the owner of the property injured or destroyed. It is sufficient if he intends to cause, or knows that he is likely to cause, wrongful loss or damage to any person by injuring any property, whether it belongs to that person or not.

Mischief may be committed by an act affecting property belonging to the person who commits the act, or to that person and others jointly.

27 Read Assertion (A) and Reason (R) and with the help of codes given below write the appropriate answer.

Assertion (A) The distinctive feature between preparation and attempt must be based on.

Reason (R) Preparation consists in devising means necessary for the commission of offence while attempt is the direct movement towards commission.

Codes

1 Both (A) and (R) are true, but (R) is not correct explanation of (A)
2 Both (A) and (R) are true and (R) is the correct explanation of (A)
3 (A) is true, but (R) is false
4 (R) is true, but (A) is only a stage of crime

Ans. (2)

Exp. Both (A) and (R) are true and (R) is the correct explanation of (A).

The distinctive feature between preparation and attempt must be based on it because preparation consists in devising means necessary for the commission of offence while attempt is the direct movement towards commission. Thus, Assertion is true.

Preparation in general is not punishable because without motive mere preparation is a harmless act. Mere preparation does not ordinarily affect the sense of security of an individual or the society at large e.g. purchasing a gun is not punishable unless anyone having procured the gun pursues his enemy and fires without effect. Thus, R is true.

Attempt is the direct movement towards the commission of an offence after preparations have been made. Thus attempt is something more than preparation.

An act of attempt marks the commencement of criminal liability. Since it creates an alarm which of itself is an injury and the moral guilt of the offender is the same as if he had succeeded.

28 The accused caused bodily pain, disease or infirmity. But it is cognizable, bailable or compoundable. What offence, if any, has been committed by the accused ?

1 Voluntary causing grievous hurt as per Section 322 IPC
2 Voluntary causing serious hurt as per Section 325 IPC
3 Voluntary causing grievous hurt by dangerous weapon as per Section 324 IPC
4 Voluntary causing grievous hurt by dangerous weapon as per Section 326 IPC

Ans. (3)

Exp. In the given situation, the accused has committed voluntary causing grievous hurt by dangerous weapon as per Section 324 of IPC.

Section 324 in the Indian Penal Code, states that whoever,except in the case provided for by Section 334, voluntarily causes hurt by means of any instrument for shooting, stabbing or cutting, or any instrument which, used as weapon of offence, is likely to cause death, or by means of fire or any heated substance, or by means of any poison or any corrosive substance, or by means of any explosive substance or by means of any substance which it is deleterious to the human body to inhale, to swallow, or to receive into the blood, or by means of any animal, shall be punished with imprisonment of either description for a term which may extend to three years, or with fine, or with both.

Section 334 of IPC states that whoever voluntarily causes hurt on grave and sudden provocation, if he neither intends nor knows himself to be likely to cause hurt to any person other than the person who gave the provocation, shall be punished with imprisonment of either description for a term which may extend to one month, or with fine which may extend to five hundred rupees, or with both.

29 An individual's act of abridgement of another's right to movement could be an offence of

1 wrongful confinement as per Section 340 IPC
2 an act of abridgement of right to movement was done in good faith and hence no offence
3 the movement route being diverted so assault results
4 wrongful restraint as per Section 329 IPC

Ans. (1)

Exp. An individual's act of abridgement of another's right to movement could be an offence of wrongful confinement as per Section 340 IPC.

Section 340 describes wrongful confinement as whoever wrongfully restrains any person in such a manner as to prevent that person from proceedings beyond certain circumscribing limits, is said "wrongfully to confine" that person.

As an instance, 'A' causes 'Z' to go within a walled space, and locks 'Z' in. 'Z' is thus prevented from proceeding in any direction beyond the circumscribing line of wall. 'A' wrongfully confines 'Z'.

30 Match the statement that mens rea is a loose term of elastic significance with that of the meaning in sequential order.

I. Foresight of the consequences of the act.
II. Criminal intention of deepest dye.
III. An act which is visible.
IV. It depends upon knowledge and belief.

Matching probabilities

1 It is the bare capacity to know in the sequence of I, II, III and IV.
2 It is essential ingredient of criminal offence in the sequence of IV, III, II and I.
3 It is a presumption to fix criminal liability in the sequence of III, II, I and IV
4 Applicability of the principle becomes essential by the sequence of II, I, IV and III

Ans. (4)

Exp. Among the given choices, II, I, IV and III is the correct sequence.

Mens rea is an essential part of deciding whether an act is culpable or not. *Mens rea* displays specific intent by the accused for the commission of the crime for which he is charged.

In Girija Nath Vs. State (1954), it was observed that "*mens rea* is a loose term of elastic signification and covers a wide range of mental status and conditions, the existence of which would give a criminal to live to *actus reus*. Sometimes it is used to refer to foresight of the consequence of the act and at other times to act per se irrespective of its consequences. In some case it stands for a criminal intention of the 'deepest dye' (i.e., a villain or scoundrel of the worst kind) such as is visible in a designed and premeditated murder committed with a full foresight of its fatal consequences.

Therefore, it may be observed that the correct order indicating *mens rea* should be having a criminal intention of deepest dye with a foresight that also contains knowledge of the consequence, and reflected through the actus reus ultimately.

31 Read Assertion (A) and Reason (R) and with the help of codes given below point out the correct explanation.

Assertion (A) Generally, a master is not criminally liable merely because his servant has committed a negligent act.

Reason (R) In ordinary course of employment a master may be criminally liable against the negligent acts of the servant.

Codes

1 Both (A) and (R) are true, but (R) is not the correct explanation of (A)
2 (A) is true and (R) is the genuine reason of (A)
3 (R) is true, but (A) is not absolutely correct
4 (R) is false, but (A) is only an assertion

Ans. (2)

Exp. (A) is true and (R) is the genuine reason of (A).

As a general proposition, a Master will not be held liable for a servant's unauthorized criminal acts if the crimes are those requiring specific intent. Thus, a department store proprietor who tells his chief buyer to get the "best deal possible" on next fall's fashions is not liable if the buyer steals clothes from the manufacturer.

A Master will, however, be liable if the Master directed, approved, or participated in the crime. Cases here involve, for example, a corporate Master's liability for servants' activity in antitrust violations— price-fixing is one such violation.

32 On which date and place the Earth Summit was held at ?

1 6th June, 1997 at Geneva
2 20th June, 1997 at London
3 21st June, 1992 at Rio
4 27th June, 1992 at Rio

Ans. (3)

Exp. The Earth Summit was held on 21st June, 1992 at Rio De Janerio, Brazil.

The United Nations Conference on Environment and Development (UNCED), also known as the 'Earth Summit', was held in Rio de Janeiro, Brazil. This global conference, held on the occasion of the 20th anniversary of the first Human Environment Conference in Stockholm, Sweden, in 1972, brought together political leaders, diplomats, scientists, representatives of the media and non-governmental organizations (NGOs) from 179 countries for a massive effort to focus on the impact of human socio-economic activities on the environment.

A 'Global Forum' of NGOs was also held in Rio de Janeiro at the same time, bringing together an unprecedented number of NGO representatives, who presented their own vision of the world's future in relation to the environment and socio-economic development.

33 "In case of violation of Article 21 by disturbing the environment, the court could award damages not only for the restoration of the ecological balance but also for the victim who have suffered due to that disturbance."

In which case the Supreme Court of India has made above observations ?

1 MC Mehta Vs. Union of India, AIR 1997 SC 734
2 MC Mehta Vs. Kamal Nath, (1997) 1 SCC 388
3 MC Mehta Vs. Kamal Nath AIR 2000 SC 1997
4 MC Mehta Vs. Kamal Nath 2000 (2) SCALE 654

Ans. (4)

Exp. The Supreme Court of India has made these observations in MC Mehta Vs. Kamal Nath 2000 (2) SCALE 654.

The Court held "In case of violation of Article 21 by disturbing the environment, the court could award damages not only for the restoration of the ecological balance but also for the victim who have suffered due to that disturbance."

This decision is related to an earlier decision by the Supreme Court in the same matter. The court had learned that the private company 'Span Motels Pvt. Ltd.' had built a motel on the bank of the River Beas on land leased by the Indian Government in 1981.

The Court analysed the 'polluter pays principle' including its history, international development and implementation in the national legal system. It emphasised that the polluter pays principle was widely accepted as a means of paying for the cost of pollution and control. The wrongdoer, the polluter, was under an obligation to make good the damage caused to the environment.

34 In which of the following case the constitutionality, legal validity, propriety and fairness of the settlement of the claims of the victims in a mass tort action relating to Bhopal Gas Leak Disaster has been challenged in Supreme Court of India ?

1 Union Carbide Corp. Vs. Union of India, AIR 1990 SC 273
2 MC Mehta Vs. Union of India, AIR 1987 SC 1086
3 Union Carbide Corp. Vs. Union of India, AIR 1992 SC 248
4 Charanlal Sahu Vs. Union of India, AIR 1990 SC 1480

Ans. (3)

Exp. The constitutionality, legal validity, propriety and fairness of the settlement of the claims of the victims in a mass tort action relating to Bhopal Gas Leak Disaster had been challenged in Supreme Court of India in the Union Carbide Corp Vs. Union of India, AIR 1992 SC 248.

The Union Carbide Corporation filed an application in revision in the Supreme Court, in terms of Section 155 of the CPC, against the order of the Bhopal District Court, in a claim for damages made by the Union of India on behalf of all the claimants, under the Bhopal Gas Leak Disaster (Processing of Claim) Act, 198. The Union Carbide Corporation as well as the Union of India filed separate appeals in the Supreme Court against the judgement of the Madhya Pradesh High Court, both of which were heard together.

Damages were sought on behalf of victims of Bhopal gas leak disaster. The Court examined the prima facie material for the purpose of quantifying the damages and also the question of domestication of the decree in the United States for the purpose of execution.

The court decided as follows; the Union Carbide Corporation should pay a sum of US Dollars 470 million (Four hundred and seventy million) to the Union of India in full settlement of all claims, rights and liabilities related to and arising out of the Bhopal gas disaster, the Union Carbide Corporation shall pay the aforesaid sum to the Union of India on or before 31st March, 1989, to enable the effectuation of the settlement, all civil proceedings related to and arising out of the Bhopal gas disaster shall there by stand transferred to the Supreme Court and shall stand concluded in terms of the settlement and all criminal proceedings related to and arising out of the disaster shall stand quashed, wherever these may be pending.

35 Under which Article of the Constitution Environment (Protection) Act, 1986 was enacted?

1 Article 253 2 Article 258
3 Article 255 4 Article 254

Ans. (1)

Exp. Under Article 253 of the Constitution, Environment (Protection) Act, 1986 was enacted.

Article 253 states that Parliament has power to make any law for the whole or any part of the country for implementing any treaty, agreement or convention with any other country. In simple words, this Article suggests that in the wake of Stockholm Conference of 1972, Parliament has the power to legislate on all matters linked to the preservation of natural environment.

Most of the environment related laws enacted by the Parliament under Article 253. For e.g. Environment (Protection) Act 1986, The Water (Prevention and Control of Pollution) Act, 1974, The Air (Prevention and Control of Pollution) Act, 1981 was promulgated under Article 253 of Constitution.

36 The problem of the pollution of river Ganga by the inaction of the municipalities was brought to light in which of the following case ?

1 Indian Council for Environmental Legal Action Vs. Union of India, AIR 1996 SC 1446
2 AP Pollution Control Board Vs. MV Nayudu, AIR 1999 SC 812
3 S Jagannath Vs. Union of India, AIR 1997 SC 811
4 MC Mehta Vs. Union of India, AIR 1988 SC 1115

Ans. (4)

Exp. The problem of the pollution of river Ganga by the inaction of the municipalities was brought to light in the case of MC Mehta Vs. Union of India, AIR 1988 SC 1115.

In this case, apart from industries, more than 250 towns and cities have been ordered to put sewage treatment plants. Six hundred tanneries operating in highly congested residential area of Kolkata have been shifted out of the city and relocated in a planned Leather Complex in the State of West Bengal.

A large number of industries were closed down by the Court and were allowed to reopen only after these industries set up effluent treatment plants and controlled pollution. As a result of these directions millions of people have been saved from the effects of air and water pollution in Ganga basin covering 8 states in India.

37 Which one of the following cases relates to Sariska Tiger Park ?

1 Tarun Bharat Sangh Vs. Union of India, AIR 1992 SC 514
2 Consumer Education and Research Society Vs. Union of India, AIR 2000 SC 975
3 Pradeep Krishan Vs. Union of India, AIR 1997 SC 2040
4 Animal and Environmental Legal Defence Fund case, AIR 1997 SC 1070

Ans. (1)

Exp. The Case of Tarun Bharat Sangh Vs. Union of India, AIR 1992 SC 514 relates to Sariska Tiger Park.

The Court observed that the mining activities outside the protected forest areas but within the tiger reserve after 7th May 1992, was illegal. The Court further added that if there was any illegality attached to the mines that came under the tiger reserve but outside the protected forest areas, the concerned mine-owners should approach the Department of forest and Environment, Government of India, for permission to continue mining operations in those mines only.

38 Which of the following case relates to transfer of tribal lands by government to non-tribal people ?

1 Shri Manchegowda Vs. State of Karnataka, AIR 1984 SC 1151
2 Samatha Vs. State of Andhra Pradesh, AIR 1997 SC 3297
3 Suresh Lohiya Vs. State of Maharashtra, (1996) 10 SCC 397
4 Fatesang Gimba Vasava Vs. State of Gujarat, AIR 1987 Guj. 09

Ans. (2)

Exp. The case titled as Samatha Vs. State of Andhra Pradesh, AIR 1997 SC 3297, relates to transfer of tribal lands by government to non-tribal people.

The Supreme Court of India delivered an authoritative verdict in favour of the right to livelihood of the tribals inhabiting the scheduled areas of the country. In this case, the judiciary reached its pinnacle in upholding the rights of the tribal community.

The Samata judgment is an outcome of sustained people's struggle to safeguard their land, resources and livelihood in tribal belts of Andhra Pradesh. It had ramifications across the country.

The petitioning organisation, 'Samata' had been working for the rights of the people for several years and had filed the case to overcome the hurdles created by the state to acknowledge and deliver on issues of fundamental human rights

39 Match List I with List II and select the correct answer using the codes given below.

List I	List II
A. Suspension of Members	I. Article 5
B. Veto power	II. Article 6
C. Appointment of Secretary-General	III. Article 27
D. Objective of the Trusteeship System	IV. Article 76
	V. Article 97

Codes

	A	B	C	D		A	B	C	D
1	I	II	III	IV	2	I	III	IV	V
3	I	III	V	IV	4	III	II	V	I

Ans. *(3)*

Exp. The correct matching is A-I, B-III, C-V, D-IV.

Suspension of Members is mentioned in Article 5 of UN Charter, which states that a member of United Nations against which preventative or enforcement action has been taken by the Security Council may be suspended from the exercise of rights and privileges of membership by the General Assembly upon the recommendation of the Security Council.

Veto power is mentioned in Article 27 of the UN Charter which states that each member of the Security Council shall have one vote. The decisions of the Security Council on all other matters shall be made by an affirmative vote of nine members including the concurring votes of the permanent members.

Appointment of Secretory-General is mentioned in Article 97 of UN Charter. As per Article 97 of the UN Charter, the Secretariat shall comprise a Secretary-General and such staff as the organization may require. The Secretary-General shall be appointed by the General Assembly upon the recommendation of the Security Council. He shall be the chief administrative officer of the Organization.

The basic *objectives of the Trusteeship System* is given under Article 76 of UN Charter, in accordance with the Purposes of the United Nations laid down in Article 1 of the present Charter shall be to further international peace and security, to promote the political, economic, social, and educational advancement of the inhabitants of the trust territories inter alia, to encourage respect for human rights and for fundamental freedoms for all without distinction as to race, sex, language, or religion, and to encourage recognition of the interdependence of the peoples of the world; and to ensure equal treatment in social, economic, and commercial matters for all Members of the United Nations and their nationals.

40 Which of the following Jurist regard the controversy "whether international law is a law, a dispute about words and not things" ?

1 Lawrence
2 Austin
3 Hobbes
4 Hart

Ans. *(1)*

Exp. Jurist Lawrence regarded the controversy as, "whether international law is a law, a dispute about words and not things."

International Law is comprehensive in nature and due to that it is an amalgamation of various sources, there exists no single system of laws which can interpret and extend the law but international law still exists and is ascertainable.

There are 'sources' available from which the rules of international law may be extracted and analyzed. According to Lawrence, if we take the source of law which has all the authority required to give it binding force, then in respect of International Law there is one source of law and that is the consent of Nations. This consent may be either tacit (custom) or express (treaties).

41 What should be the order of the use of material source of International law ?

I. Treaties and Conventions.
II. Customs
III. General principles of law recognised by civilised States.
IV. Judicial decisions and juristic opinion as subsidiary means for the determination of law.

Codes

1 IV, III, II, I
2 II, III, I, IV
3 IV, II, I, III
4 I, II, III, IV

Ans. *(4)*

Exp. Among the given choices, the correct sequence is I, II, III and IV.

Sources of International law includes treaties, international customs, general principles of law recognised by civilised states, judical decisions and juristic opinion as subsidiary means for the determination of law.

Article 38 of the Statute of International Court of Justice provides the Court, whose function is to decide in accordance with international law such disputes as are submitted to it, shall apply: international conventions, whether general or particular, establishing rules expressly recognized by the contesting states, international custom, as evidence of a general practice accepted as law, the general principles of law recognized by civilized nations, judicial decisions and the teachings of the most highly qualified publicists of the various nations, as subsidiary means for the determination of rules of law.

42 Which of the Article of the Statute of International Court of Justice makes it clear that the decision of the court will have no binding force except between the parties and in respect of that particular case only ?

1 Article 60
2 Article 59
3 Article 68
4 Article 38(1)

Ans. *(1)*

Exp. Article 60 of the Statute of International Court of Justice makes it clear that the decision of the court will have no binding force except between the parties and in respect of that particular case only

In the words of Article 59, the decision of the Court has no binding force except between the parties and in respect of that particular case.

As per Article 60, the judgment is final and without appeal. In the event of dispute as to the meaning or scope of the judgment, the Court shall construe it upon the request of any party.

43 Which of the following functions are performed by Economic and Social Council ?

I. It may make or initiate studies with respect to international economic, social, cultural, educational, health and related matters.

II. It may make recommendations for the purpose of promoting respect for and observance of human rights.

III. It may make recommendations to promote friendly relations and understanding amongst member States.

IV. It may prepare draft conventions for submission to the General Assembly on any of the subjects falling within its competence.

Codes

1 I, II, III, IV
2 I, III, II
3 I, II, IV
4 II, III, IV

Ans. (3)

Exp. Statement I, II, IV contains the functions performed by Economic and Social council.

Economic and Social Council consists of 18 members elected by the General Assembly, one-third retiring after every three years. Retiring members are eligible for immediate re-election. All decisions of the Council are taken by a majority of those present and voting.

The Economic and Social Council is responsible under the authority of the General Assembly for performing the following functions :

- It may make or initiate studies with respect to international economic, social, cultural, educational, health and related matters.
- It may make recommendations for the purpose of promoting respect for and observance of human rights.
- It may prepare draft conventions for submission to the General Assembly on any of the subjects falling within its competence.
- It also undertakes and promotes studies and reports on e economic, social, health and cultural matters, makes recommendations to the General Assembly, states and specialised agencies, etc.
- It prepares drafts of conventions and calls conferences of states.

44 Match List I with List II and select the correct answer.

List I	List II
A. The Covenant on Civil and Political Rights	I. 16th December 1966
B. The Declaration on Human Rights	II. 1948
C. Convention on the Rights of Child	III. 1990
D. American Convention on Human Rights	IV. 1969

Codes

	A	B	C	D
1	IV	III	II	I
2	II	III	IV	I
3	I	II	III	IV
4	IV	II	III	I

Ans. (3)

Exp. The correct matching is A-I, B-II, C-III, D-IV.

International *Covenant on Civil and Political Rights* was adopted on 16th December, 1966. The covenant was agreed upon considering inter alia, the principles proclaimed in the Charter of the United Nations, recognition of the inherent dignity and of the equal and inalienable rights of all members of the human family is the foundation of freedom, justice and peace in the world.

The *Universal Declaration of Human Rights* (UDHR) was adopted on 10th December, 1948. It was drafted by representatives with different legal and cultural backgrounds from all regions of the world, and proclaimed by the United Nations General Assembly in Paris on the said date as a common standard of achievements for all peoples and all nations.

Convention on the Rights of the Child was adopted on 20th November, 1989 considering inter alia that, the principles proclaimed in the Charter of the United Nations, recognition of the inherent dignity and of the equal and inalienable rights of all members of the human family is the foundation of freedom, justice and peace in the world.

American Convention on Human Rights: was adopted on 22nd November, 1969 It guarantees, inter alia, the rights to respect for physical, mental and moral integrity and freedom from torture and cruel, inhuman, or degrading punishment or treatment.

45 Read each of the following two statements Assertion (A) and Reason (R) and indicate your answer using the codes given below

Assertion (A) International law is not a law.

Reason (R) It lacks determinate superior political authority to enforce its rules.

Using the codes given below select the correct answer.

Codes

1 Both (A) and (R) are true and (R) is the correct explanation of (A)
2 Both (A) and (R) are true, but (R) is not the correct explanation of (A)
3 (A) is true, but (R) is false
4 (A) is false, but (R) is true

Ans. *(2)*

Exp. Both (A) and (R) are true, but (R) is not the correct explanation of (A).

There had been a great controversy as to the question, whether international law is a law or not.

Some answered the question in affirmative while others in negative. According to Jane Austin, International Law is not true law, but a code of rules and conduct of moral force only. Thus, Assertion (A) is true.

Reason (R) is true because one of the major reasons cited by jurists not in support of international law being a law is the absence of any sanction or superior political authority to enforce its rules, in the sense of any municipal law.

46 The junior widow has adopted a child without the consent of senior widow. Decide the adoption.

1 Valid
2 Void
3 Voidable
4 None of these

Ans. *(3)*

Exp. If the junior widow has adopted a child without the consent of senior widow, then the adoption is voidable.

There is no illegality on a widow's right to take in adoption without consulting her co-widows.

This issue came up for determination in Vijay Lakshmamma Vs. B.T.Shankar (2001), where a senior widow took a male child in adoption without consulting the junior widow. The adoption was challenged as being invalid. It was contended that the stipulation in the proviso to Section 7 in Hindu Adoptions and Maintenance Act, 1956 with the explanation requiring consent of all wives should be read into Section 8 as well which refers to the capacity of a female Hindu to take in adoption.

The court, however, did not accept this plea and held that the deliberate omission as regards requirement of consent from a junior widow was an indication of Parliament's intention to give independent authority to a female in this matter. This is in keeping with the changing social set recognizing equal rights and status for women.

The apex court observed: To subject the exercise of power by senior widow to adopt conditioned upon the consent of the junior widow where the Hindu male died leaving behind two widows with no progeny of his own, would render the exercise of power more cumbersome and paradoxical, leaving at times, such exercise of power to adopt only next to impossibility.

It may be observed that the above position is not applicable in case a Junior widow adopts without the consent of a senior widow, in which case, the adoption will be voidable.

47 In which State, where a widow may adopt a child without an express authority from her husband, before the Hindu Adoptions and Maintenance Act, 1956 ?

1 Bihar and MP
2 UP and Haryana
3 Madras and Bombay
4 Orissa and Andhra Pradesh

Ans. *(3)*

Exp. In the States of Madras and Bombay, a widow may adopt a child without an express authority from her husband, before the Hindu Adoptions and Maintenance Act, 1956.

The Act has considerably simplified the law on the subject furnishing a uniform code for the whole of India. The law as to adoption by a widow is different in different States. In Mithila, a widow cannot adopt at all, even if she has the express authority of her husband. In Bengal, Benares and Madras, a widow may adopt under an authority from her husband in that behalf. In Madras, a widow may also adopt without her husband's authority, provided she had obtained the consent of the husband's sapindas, if the husband had separated at the time of his death, or, with the consent of his undivided coparceners, if the husband was joint. In Bombay, a widow may adopt even without any authority.

48 In ancient Hindu Marriage, which one is not approved form of Marriage ?

1 Brahma
2 Davia
3 Prajapatya
4 Asura

Ans. *(4)*

Exp. In ancient Hindu Marriage, the Asura marriage was not an approved form of Marriage.

Asura form of marriage is not approved, wherein the bridegroom after having given wealth as much as it is within his means to the father and paternal kinsman or to the damsel herself takes her voluntarily as his bride obviously with the consent of her father. This form of marriage has a striking resemblance with a kind of purchase of bride as the father or the girl herself has already taken money and the father or guardian later giving his consent to marry the girl in lieu of money taken. Apart from this, Gandharava, Rakshasa, Paishach are also among the unapproved forms of marriage.

49 Read Assertion (A) and Reason (R) and with the help of codes given below select the correct explanation.

Assertion (A) The Muslim Women (Protection of Divorce Rights) Act, 1986 brought changes like limit the period of maintenance to Muslim divorcee till 'iddat' period and in case of no relatives the liability on Wakf Boards.

Reason (R) The changes were brought under Muslim's pressure.

Codes

1 Both (A) and (R) are true and (R) is correct explanation of (A)
2 Both (A) and (R) are true, but (R) is not correct explanation of (A)
3 (A) is correct, but (R) is false
4 (A) is false, but (R) is true

Ans. (1)

Exp. Both (A) and (R) are true and (R) is the correct explanation of (A).

In the landmark case titled as Mohd. Ahmed Khan Vs. Shah Bano Begum and Others (1985), the Supreme Court held that muslim women were entitled to maintenance after divorce in terms of Section 125, CrPC. This was widely criticized by the muslim community who regarded this judgment as offensive against their religious tenets. This was followed by massive protests and opposition.

In order to pacify the situation, the Parliament in 1986 passed The Muslim Women (Protection of Rights on Divorce) Act , as a Central legislation enacted to safeguard the rights of divorced Muslim women who have been separated from their husband either by themselves or by the husband. The Act was passed to invalidate the decision of the Supreme Court in Shah Bano case.

As per the law, a divorced woman shall be entitled to a reasonable and fair provision and maintenance to be made and paid to her within the 'iddat' period by her former husband , where she herself maintains the children born to her before or after her divorce, a reasonable and fair provision and maintenance to be made and paid by her former husband for a period of two years from the respective dates of birth of such children, an amount equal to the sum of mahr or dower agreed to be paid to her at the time of her marriage or at any time thereafter according to Muslim law ; and all the properties given to her before or at the time of marriage or after her marriage by her relatives or friends or the husband or any relatives of the husband or his friends.

Thus, these changes were brought in on account of public pressure and hence (R) is correct and also the correct explanation of (A).

50 Read Assertion (A) and Reason (R) and with the help of codes given below select the correct explanation.

Assertion (A) The Dissolution of Muslim Marriages Act, 1939 brought different grounds for dissolution of marriage and based on Maliki schools.

Reason (R) The DMM Act, 1939 is brought on the opinion of Ulema (Ijma).

Codes

1 (A) and (R) are true, (R) is correct explanation of (A)
2 (A) and (R) are true, but (R) is not correct explanation of (A)
3 (A) is correct, but (R) is false
4 (A) is false, but (R) is true

Ans. (1)

Exp. Both (A) and (R) are true, and (R) is the correct explanation of (A).

Dissolution of Muslim Marriage Act, 1939 (DMMA) is sole document which is a departure from the Hanafi School of Islamic thought. It is based on the Maliki School of Islamic jurisprudence.

The two main purposes of this document were to grant women more rights which were not there in the Hanafi School of Islamic jurisprudence and to stop women from committing apostasy to get out of their marriage. Thus, Assertion is true.

The DMM Act, 1939 is brought on the opinion of Ulema (Ijma). In Muslim history, Ijma has always referred to consensuses reached in the past, near or remote, and never to contemporaneous agreement. It is thus a part of traditional authority. It also has come to operate as a principle of toleration of different traditions within Islam. It may be observed that the said Act was passed in order to bring marriage as a part of consensus which is necessary for the instrument of marriage on Ijma's consultation. Thus, Reason is true.

51 A Muslim husband has failed to have 'sexual intercourse' continuously for four months with wife. It could be a form of divorce and is called

1 Ila 2 Mubarrah 3 Zihar 4 Khula

Ans. (1)

Exp. A Muslim husband has failed to have 'sexual intercourse' continuously for four months with wife. It could be a form of divorce and is called Ila.

Ila refers to a situation where a husband of sound mind takes a vow that he will abstain from all relationships from his wife. Followed by this dath, there is no consummation for a period of four months. After the expiry of the fourth month the marriage dissolves irrevocably. Zihar, wherein husband is sane and adult and compares his wife to his mother or any other female within the prohibited degrees.

52 Match List I with List II and select correct answer from the codes given below.

List I		List II
A. Judicial separation	I.	Section 9
B. Divorce	II.	Section 10
C. Voidable Marriages	III.	Section 13
D. Restitution of Conjugal Rights	IV.	Section 12

Codes

	A	B	C	D		A	B	C	D
1	I	III	II	IV	2	II	IV	III	I
3	I	II	IV	III	4	II	III	IV	I

Ans. (4)

Exp. The correct matching is A-II, B-III, C-IV, D-I.

The term *Judicial Separation* is found under Section 10 of Hindu Marriage Act, 1956, according to which either party to a marriage may present a petition to the district court praying for a decree for judicial separation on the ground that the other party has, among other grounds, deserted the petitioner or treated with cruelty.

The term *Divorce* is mentioned under Section 13 which provides certain grounds on the basis of which a party to marriage can obtain divorce from the other. Such grounds include adultery, conversion, insanity, renunciation, not heard alive, etc.

The term *Voidable Marriages* is found under Section 12. As per Section 12 any marriage shall be voidable and may be annulled by a decree of nullity if the respondent was impotent at the time of the marriage, the marriage violates clause (ii) of section 5; or the consent was obtained by force or fraud; or the respondent was pregnant by some person other than the petitioner.

Restitution of Conjugal Rights is mentioned under Section 9. As per Section 9, when either the husband or the wife has, without reasonable excuse, withdrawn from the society of the other, the court may decree restitution of conjugal rights if so asked by the other party.

53 Match List I with List II and select correct answer from the codes given below.

List I	List II
A. Impotency of Husband	I. Divorce
B. Marriage within Sapinda Relationship	II. Voidable Marriage
C. Pre-marriage Pregnancy	III. Nullity of Marriage
D. Option of Puberty	IV. Void Marriage

Codes

	A	B	C	D		A	B	C	D
1	IV	III	I	II	2	III	IV	II	I
3	I	III	IV	II	4	II	IV	I	III

Ans. *(2)*

Exp. The correct matching is A-III, B-IV, C-II, D-I.

Impotence of husband can result in nullity of marriage. Section 12 of Hindu Marriage Act, provides for a decree of nullity of marriage, which is voidable, if the marriage has not been consummated owing to the impotence of the respondent.

Marriage with sapinda relationship are declared null and void as per the Hindu Marriage Act, 1955, unless a custom or usage governs it and the party propounding it must prove such a custom or usage.

Pre-marriage pregnancy is related to voidable marriage. Section 12(1) (d) states that a marriage is voidable on ground that the respondent at the time of the marriage was pregnant by some person other than the petitioner.

Option of puberty can result in divorce. According to Section 13(2)(iv), a Hindu wife may petition for divorce on the ground that her marriage was solemnized before she attained the age of fifteen years and she has repudiated the marriage after attaining the age of 15, but before attaining 18 years of age.

54 The Human Rights has been classified into three categories, viz

I. The Human Rights of first generation

II. The Human Rights of Second generation and

III. The Human Rights of third generation, by

Codes

1 Louis II Sohan
2 Theodoor III Bowen
3 R Dworkin
4 Bernard Mayo

Ans. *(1)*

Exp. The Human Rights are classified into three categories viz. the Human Rights of first generation, the Human Rights of second generation and the Human Rights of third generation.

First Generation of Human Rights are the rights that grow in course of a long stretch of the time following the time the history of the Greek City State and created as the Magna Carta, the American affirmation of freedom and rights of man and the French Declaration of the privilege of man and of the Citizen many other legal documents.

Second Generation of Human Rights is covered by international convention on social, economic and cultural rights. The sources for the creation of economic, and social rights are from Russian revaluation 1917, and the peace conference of Paris 1919.

The Paris peace conference known for the further establishment of International Labour Organization which gave more importance or emphasis on the social justiceby proclaiming that "peace can be established only if it is based upon social justice."

Third Generation of Human Rights is known as collective rights. According to B. Soha, every individual is member of this unit or group like religion, family, social, trade, union etc. people, racial, state and nation all are professional union or association. The international law not recognized only by friendly or in alienable rights for the people, but it is recognized by collective rights of the individuals who are grouped into larger communities, including people and nations.

55 "Everyone has the right to recognition everywhere as a person before the law." This has been stated in which of the following Article of Universal Declaration of Human Rights ?

1 Article 6
2 Article 7
3 Article 8
4 Article 9

Ans. *(1)*

Exp. The given statement has been stated in Article 6 of the Universal Declaration of Human Rights (UDHR).

The Article 6 of UDHR says "Everyone has the right to recognition everywhere as a person before the law."

The UDHR is a milestone document in the history of human rights. Drafted by representatives with different legal and cultural backgrounds from all regions of the World, the Declaration was proclaimed by the United Nations General Assembly in Paris on 10th December, 1948.

56 The United Nations High Commission for Refugees was established in which of the following year by the General Assembly ?

1 1951 2 1953 3 1955 4 1957

Ans. (1)

Exp. The United Nations High Commission for Refugees was established on 14th December, 1951 by the United Nations General Assembly.

The agency is mandated to lead and co-ordinate international action to protect refugees and resolve refugee problems worldwide. Its primary purpose is to safeguard the rights and well-being of refugees.

It strives to ensure that everyone can exercise the right to seek asylum and find safe refuge in another State, with the option to return home voluntarily, integrate locally or to resettle in a third country. It also has a mandate to help stateless people.

57 "The most glaring instance of violation of Human Rights is the continuing poverty among masses in the country." This was said by

1 Justice AS Anand
2 Justice N Venkatachalaiah
3 Justice PN Bhagwati
4 Justice Koka Subba Rao

Ans. (1)

Exp. "The most glaring instance of violation of Human Rights is the continuing poverty among masses in the country" was said by Justice AS Anand while making an appeal to eschew hypocrisy in public life.

Addressing a seminar on "Human Rights and Social Justice" at Jaipur on 3rd May 2003, Dr. Justice Anand said the legislation could help ensure equality and justice only in a favourable atmosphere. "Law cannot be self-applied. It needs to be accepted by society with the resolve for bringing about a change for the better," he affirmed.

He also said discrimination against Dalits in public life–with several cases of refusal of entry into temples, stopping them from bathing in public ponds and dismounting them in marriage processions reported in Rajasthan could be stopped by awareness followed by education.

58 Match List I with List II and select the correct answer.

	List I		List II
A.	The Magna Carta	I.	1628
B.	The Petition of Rights	II.	1789
C.	The English Bill of Rights	III.	1215
D.	The US Bill of Rights	IV.	1689

Codes

	A	B	C	D		A	B	C	D
1	III	I	IV	II	2	I	III	IV	II
3	III	II	IV	I	4	III	I	II	IV

Ans. (1)

Exp. The correct matching is A-III, B-I, C-IV, D-II.

Magna Carta is a royal charter of rights agreed by King John of England at Runnymede, near Windsor on 15th June, 2015. The Magna Carta provided the foundation for individual rights in Anglo-American jurisprudence.

The Petition of Rights passed on 7th June, 1628 was a petition sent by the English Parliament to King Charles I complaining of a series of breaches of law. The petition sought recognition of four principles: no taxation without the consent of Parliament, no imprisonment without cause, no quartering of soldiers on subjects, and no martial law in peacetime.

The English Bill of Rights (1689) was an act signed into lawby William III and Mary II, who became co-rulers in England after the overthrow of King James II. The bill outlined specific constitutional and civil rights and ultimately gave Parliament power over the monarchy.

US Bill of Rights (1789) comprises the first ten amendments to the United States Constitution. The amendments, known as Bill of Rights, were designed to protect the basic rights of US citizens.

59 Gurupadaswamy Committee 1979 was constituted to look into the working conditions of

1 Minorities 2 Women
3 Children 4 NGOs

Ans. (3)

Exp. Gurupadaswamy Committee 1979 was constituted to look into the working conditions of children.

In 1979, Government formed the first committee called 'Gurupadaswamy Committee' to study the issue of child labour and to suggest measures to tackle it.

Based on the recommendations of Gurupadaswamy Committee, the Child Labour (Prohibition and Regulation) Act was enacted in 1986. This committee was constituted to look into the working conditions of children. The Act prohibits employment of children in certain specified hazardous occupations and processes and regulates the working conditions in others.

The list of hazardous occupations and processes is progressively being expanded on the recommendation of Child Labour Technical Advisory Committee constituted under the Act.

60 Using codes, arrange following instruments according to sequence of their enactment starting from past towards present

I. The Convention on the Political Rights of Women.
II. The Declaration on the Elimination of Discrimination against Women.
III. The Convention on consent to Marriage, Minimum Age for Marriage and Registration of Marriages.
IV. The Convention on the nationality of married women.

Codes

1 I, IV, III, II 2 IV, III, II, I
3 III, II, I, IV 4 II, I, IV, III

Ans. (1)

Exp. Among the given choices, the correct sequence is I, IV, III, II.

The Convention on the Political Rights of Women was approved by the United Nations General Assembly during the 409th plenary meeting, on 20th December 1952, and adopted on 31st March, 1953. The Convention's purpose is to codify a basic international standard for women's political rights.

The Convention on the Nationality of Married Women is an international convention passed by the United Nations General Assembly in 1957. The Convention was concluded in the light of the conflicts of law on nationality derived from provisions concerning the loss or acquisition of nationality by women as a result of marriage, divorce, or of the change of nationality by the husband during marriage.

The Convention on Consent to Marriage, Minimum Age for Marriage, and Registration of Marriages was drafted by the Commission on the Status of Women and opened for signature and ratification by General Assembly resolution 1763 A (XVII) on 7th November 1962. The Convention reaffirms the consensual nature of marriages and requires the parties to establish a minimum marriage age by law and to ensure the registration of marriages.

The Declaration on the Elimination of Discrimination against Women (abbreviated as DEDAW[1]) is a human rights proclamation issued by the United Nations General Assembly, outlining that body's views on women's rights. It was adopted by the General Assembly on 7th November, 1967.

61 Which one of the following statements is not correct?

1 In tort, there is a breach of duty which is primarily fixed by law
2 In tort, there is a violation of a right in rem
3 In tort, the motive for breach of duty is immaterial
4 In tort, the damages are fixed according to the terms and conditions

Ans. (4)

Exp. Statement 4 is incorrect as in tort, the damages are not fixed according to the terms and conditions.

Damages in tort are generally awarded to place the claimant in the position that would have been taken had the tort not taken place. Damages in tort are quantified under two headings: general damages and special damages.

Statements 1, 2 and 3 are correct because the duty under tort is fixed by law as a civil duty and grants right in rem to all persons against any wrong done by anyone else to them. There is also no relevance of motive in tort law, unlike a criminal wrong.

62 Read Assertion (A) and Reason (R) and with the help of codes given below select the correct explanation.

Assertion (A) A wooden chair while being used by a guest caused injury to him due to defective manufacture. The guest is entitled to claim damages from the maker.

Reason (R) Manufacturer owes a duty of care to the ultimate user.

Select the correct answer using the codes given below

Codes

1 Both (A) and (R) are true and (R) is the correct explanation of (A)
2 Both (A) and (R) are true, but (R) is not the correct explanation of (A)
3 (A) is true, but (R) is false
4 (A) is false, but (R) is true

Ans. (1)

Exp. Both (A) and (R) are true and (R) is the correct explanation of (A).

A wooden chair while being used by a guest caused injury to him due to defective manufacture. The guest is entitled to claim damages from the maker. A manufacturer must take whatever steps are reasonable, given the nature and purpose of the product which he makes, to ensure that the product is safe from the purpose intended.

This is on account of the principle of duty of care under law. Thus, Assertion is true.

Manufacturer owes a duty of care to the ultimate user. The case of Donoghue Vs. Stevenson held that the manufacturer did owe a duty of care to the plaintiff and thus, the Reason is correct as well.

63 In which of the following situations is slander actionable per se in India ?

1 An imputation that a certain female player is of unchaste character
2 An imputation that a certain person is a habitual smuggler
3 An imputation that a certain person is liar
4 An imputation that the wrestler is womaniser

Ans. (1)

Exp. An imputation that a certain female player is of unchaste character is slander actionable per se in India.

Slander is a form of defamation by spoken words or in transient form. Exceptional cases when slander is actionably per se (i.e. without proof of special damage) are the following; imputation of a criminal offence punishable with imprisonment, imputation of a contagious diseases likely to prevent other persons from associating with the plaintiff, imputation of unchastity or adultery to any women or girl, imputation of unfitness, dishonesty or incompetence in any office, profession, calling, trade, or business held or carried on by the plaintiff at the time when the slander was published.

64 Match List I with List II and select the correct answer using the codes given below.

List I	List II
A. A patient is a consumer	I. Vasantha P Nair Vs. Smt. VP Nair
B. Doctor's duty to maintain secrecy	II. K Rangaswami Vs. Jaya Vital and others
C. Free service	III. Indian Medical Association Vs. VP Shantha
D. Contract of personal service	IV. Dr Tokugha Vs. Apollo Hospital Enterprises Ltd.

Codes

	A	B	C	D		A	B	C	D
1	I	II	III	IV	2	IV	II	I	III
3	I	IV	III	II	4	III	II	I	IV

Ans. (3)

Exp. The correct matching is A-I, B-IV, C-III, D-II.

In *Vasantha P. Nair Vs. Smt. V.P. Nair* (1991) The National Commission held a patient to be a 'consumer' and medical assistance a 'service'. A doctor is held liable for only his acts (other than cases of vicarious liability). Vicarious liability arises in case of government hospitals where though the doctor is responsible, the hospital has to pay the compensation.

Dr. Tokugha v. Apollo Hospital Enterprises (2002) is related to Doctor's duty to maintain secrecy. The Indian Supreme Court said the rule of confidentiality is subject to the exception when the circumstances demand disclosure of the patient's health in public interest, particularly to save others from immediate and future health risks.

Indian Medical Association Vs. V.P. Shantha and Ors (1996) is related to free service. The Court concluded that "Service rendered to a patient by a medical practitioner (except where the doctor renders service free of charge to every patient or under a contract of personal service), by way of consultation, diagnosis, and treatment, both medicinal and surgical, would fall within the ambit of 'service' as defined in Section 2(1) (o) of the Consumer Protection Act."

Rangaswamy Vs. Jaya Vittal (1991) is related to contract of personal service. It was held that according to Section 2(1)(o) of the Consumer Protection Act, 1986 the service under a contract of personal service is excluded from the definition of the word service and since the advocate-client relationship falls under this category, it is automatically excluded from the definition of service.

65 State in which of the following cases, it amounts to nuisance ?

1 Planting of trees on another's land
2 When branches of trees project on the land of their neighbour
3 Construction of a pond on the land of another
4 All of the above

Ans. (4)

Exp. In all the given situations, the tort of nuisance arises.

The word 'nuisance' is derived from the French word 'nuire', which means 'to do hurt, or to annoy'. One in possession of a property is entitled as per law to undisturbed enjoyment of it. If someone else's improper use in his property results into an unlawful interference with his use or enjoyment of that property or of some right over, or in connection with it, we may say that tort of nuisance occurred.

In other words, Nuisance is an unlawful interference with a person's use or enjoyment of land, or of some right over, or in connection with it. Nuisance is an injury to the right of a person in possession of a property to undisturbed enjoyment of it and result from an improper use by another person in his property.

66 In which of the following cases, the rule of absolute liability laid down by the Supreme Court of India was followed ?

1 Indian Council for Enviro-Legal Action *Vs.* Union of India, AIR 1996 SC 1446
2 Klaus Mittelbachert *Vs.* East India Hotels Ltd., AIR 1997 Del.201
3 Both 1 and 2 above
4 None of the above

Ans. (3)

Exp. In both the given cases i.e. Indian Council for Enviro-Legal Action *Vs.* Union of India, AIR 1996 SC 1446, and Klaus Mittelbachert *Vs.* East India Hotels Ltd., AIR 1997 Del.201, the rule of absolute liability was followed by Supreme Court.

The court in the case of Indian Council for Enviro-Legal Action Vs. Union of India, (1996) noted the finding in the Oleum Gas Leak Case under which an enterprise that is engaged in a hazardous or inherently dangerous activity, which results in harm to anyone, is strictly and absolutely liable to compensate all those who are affected by the accident. Such liability was not subject to the exceptions of strict liability set forth in Rylands Vs. Fletcher. This rule was suited to conditions of India. The Court also endorsed the polluter pays principle, under which the financial costs of preventing or remedying damage lie with those who cause the pollution.

The court in the case of Klaus Mittelbachert Vs. East India Hotels Ltd., (1997) held that five-star hotels that charge hefty amounts owe a high degree of care to its guests. This was violated by Hotel Oberoi Inter-continental, New Delhi when the defectively designed swimming pool left a man dead. This made the hotel absolutely liable for payment of damages. The hefty amounts taken from the guests by the hotel owners guaranteed them to pay exemplary damages to the deceased or in any such further cases. It was decided that the plaintiff would receive Rs. 50 lakhs for the accident caused.

67 Match List I with List II and select the correct answer using the codes given below.

List I	List II
A. The Wagon Mound case	I. Remote but proximate
B. Re Polemis and Furness Withy and Co. Ltd.	II. The test of reasonable foresight
C. Scott Vs. Shepherd	III. The test of directness
D. Fardon Vs. Harcourt Rivington	IV. Reasonable foresee ability

Codes

	A	B	C	D		A	B	C	D
1	I	II	III	IV	2	II	III	I	IV
3	I	IV	III	II	4	II	I	IV	III

***Ans.* (2)**

Exp. The correct matching is A-II, B-III, C-I, D-IV.

The Wagon Mound case (1961) is related to test of reasonable foresight. It is an appeal from New South Wales, the Privy Council which has recently held that a defendant is liable in negligence only for those consequences of his acts that a reasonable man could have foreseen, and in doing so has repudiated the rule, laid down by the Court of Appeal in Re Polemis and Furness Withy Co. Ltd.,that a defendant is liable for all the direct consequences of his acts, even though unforeseeable.

Re Polemis and Furness, Withy and *Co Ltd* (1921) was related to test of directness. It was held that the defendant was liable for the claimant's loss, irrespective whether the damage caused was not of a kind reasonably expected whether the consequences of a negligent act are reasonably expected is immaterial to the defendant's liability. The only relevant consideration is whether the loss was a direct cause of the defendant's negligence.

Scott Vs. Shepherd (1987) is related to remote but proximate. In this case, 'A' threw a lighted squib into a crowd, it fell upon 'X'. 'X', in order to prevent injury to himself, did the same thing and it fell upon 'Y' and 'Y' in his turn did the same thing and it then fell on 'B', as a result of which 'B' lost one of his eyes. 'A' was held liable to 'B'. His act was the proximate cause of damage even though his act was farthest from the damage insofar as acts 'X' and 'Y' had intervened in between.

Fardon Vs. Harcourt-Rivington (1932) is related to reasonable foreseeability. It was held that people must guard against reasonable probabilities, but they are not bound to guard against fantastic possibilities and because of an inevitable accident there is no liability.

68 Find right answer from following statements.

1 Every partnership is based on mutual agency
2 Every agency is based on mutual partnership
3 Every agent is a partner
4 Every partner is a sleeping partner

***Ans.* (1)**

Exp. Every partnership is based on mutual agency.

The most important element in a partnership is the mutual agency, which states that every partner must be an agent and principal of himself and other partners. It states that business must be carried on by any or all of the partners.

69 Which statements are correct, answer using codes given below :

I. Directors are trustees of company.
II. Directors are mentors of company.
III. Directors are agents of company.
IV. Directors are agents of shareholders.

Codes

1 I and II are correct 2 I and III are correct
3 I and IV are correct 4 II and IV are correct

***Ans.* (2)**

Exp. Among the given statements, only statement I and III are correct..

Directors are trustees of the company's money and property. They safeguard them and use them for and on behalf of the company.

Directors are agents of a company A company is an artificial person and it functions through human agents — the directors. However, directors being agents are not personally liable for their acts unless they contravene the provisions of the Act as specifically-mentioned in it. It is said that the principle of agency operates as alter ego.

Statements II and IV are wrong because the concept of directors is quite distinct from the principle of agency. The acts and intention of its agents are the acts and intention of the body corporate. Even a company can be held liable for the malice contended by its directors. Directors are neither the mentors of the company, nor the agents of the shareholders of the company.

70 Read Assertion (A) and Reason (R) and with help of codes given below, point out the correct explanation.

Assertion (A) The doctrine of indoor management seeks to protect the company against the outsider.

Reason (R) The company has right to privacy.

Codes

1 Both (A) and (R) are true and (R) is correct explanation of (A)
2 Both (A) and (R) are true, but (R) is not correct explanation of (A)
3 (A) is true, but (R) is false
4 (A) is false, but (R) is true

***Ans.* (3)**

Exp. The Assertion is true, but the Reason is false.

The doctrine of indoor management was evolved 150 years ago. It is also known as 'Turquand's rule'. The role of doctrine of indoor management is opposed to the role of doctrine of constructive notice.

The doctrine of constructive notice protects company against outsiders whereas the doctrine of indoor management protects outsiders against the actions of company. This doctrine also is a possible safeguard against the possibility of abusing the doctrine of constructive notice. Thus, Assertion is true.

The rule is based upon obvious reasons of convenience in business relations. Firstly, the articles of association and memorandum are public documents and they are open to the public for inspection. Hence an outsider is presumed to know the Constitution of a company, but what may or may not have taken place within the doors that are closed to him as the company has right to privacy. Thus, Reason is false.

71 Match items in List I with items in List II, using codes given below.

List I	List II
A. Essentials of partnership	I. Section 41
B. Partnership at will	II. Section 4
C. Effect of non-registration of firm	III. Section 7
D. Compulsory dissolution of firm	IV. Section 69

Codes

	A	B	C	D		A	B	C	D
1	I	II	IV	III	2	II	III	IV	I
3	III	IV	I	II	4	I	II	III	IV

Ans. (2)

Exp. The correct matching is A-II, B-III, C-IV, D-I.

Section 4 of Indian Partnership Act, 1932 give definition of partnership and discuss its essentials. It provides Partnership is the relation between persons who have agreed to share the profits of a business carried on by all or any of them acting for all. Persons who have entered into partnership with one another are called individually partners and collectively a firm, and the name under which their business is carried on is called the firm name.

According to *Section* 7, where no provision is made by contract between the partners for the duration of their partnership, or for the determination of their partnership, the partnership is, partnership at will.

Section 69 discuss about effect of non-registration of firm inter alia, no suit to enforce a right arising from a contract or conferred by this Act shall be instituted in any court by or on behalf of any person suing as a partner in a firm against the firm or any person alleged to be or to have been a partner in the firm unless the firm is registered and the person suing is or has been shown in the register of firms as a partner in the firm.

Section 41 mentions about compulsory dissolution of firm. It provides a firm is dissolved by the adjudication of all the partners or of all the partners but one as insolvent, or by the happening of any event which makes it unlawful for the business of the firm to be carried on or for the partners to carry it on in partnership.

72 Find correct answer, using codes given below.

I. Bulk shall correspond with sample, is an implied condition.
II. Buyer shall have a reasonable opportunity of comparing bulk with sample, is an implied condition.
III. Goods should be free from any defect rendering them unmerchantable, is an implied condition.
IV. There is an implied condition that the buyer shall have and enjoy possession of the goods.

Codes

1 I only is correct
2 I and II only are correct
3 I, II and III are correct
4 All of above are correct

Ans. (3)

Exp. Among the given statements, only I, II and III are correct.

According to Section 17 of the Sale of Goods Act, 1930, in the case of sale by sample the bulk of the goods must correspond with the sample in quality because in such cases it is the sample alone which has been held to be representative of the quality of goods to be supplied by the seller and therefore it is but natural that the goods must conform to the sample.

The buyer should get reasonable opportunity of comparing the bulk with the sample. There is some conflict of legal opinion as to whether the whole of the goods conform to the sample. The courts have laid down a rule that goods supplied shall be considered according to the sample if so much of the quantity out of the entire lot is equal to the sample as any standard of fair play and equity prescribes. In other words, it is the discretion of the court to decide whether the goods conform to the sample or not

In the case of sale by sample there is an implied condition that the goods shall be merchantable and free from defects which could not be disclosed by an ordinary examination

Statement IV is incorrect because as per Section 14 of the Act, there is an implied warranty, and not a condition, that the buyer shall have and enjoy quiet possession of the goods.

73 Select correct statement from following.

1 Right against the goods can be exercised only by a paid seller
2 Right against the goods can be exercised only by an unpaid seller
3 Right against the goods can be exercised only by a paid buyer
4 Right against the goods can be exercised only by an unpaid buyer

Ans. (2)

Exp. The 'statement' Right against the goods can be exercised only by an unpaid seller' is correct.

Section 46 of the Sale of Goods Act, 1930 mentions rights of an unpaid seller against the goods.It is stated therein that subject to the provisions of this Act and of any law for the time being in force, notwithstanding that the property in the goods may have passed to the buyer, the unpaid seller of goods, as such, has by implication of law; a lien on the goods for the price while he is in possession of them, in case of the insolvency of the buyer a right of stopping the goods in transit after he has parted with the possession of them, a right of resale as limited by this Act.

74 Match items in List I with items in List II, using codes given below.

	List I		List II
A.	Prabhu Dayal Vs. Jwala Bank, ILR 1938 All. 634	I.	Section 100
B.	Discharge from liability by cancellation	II.	Section 10
C.	Payment in due course	III.	Forgery of signature
D.	Protest	IV.	Section 82

Codes

	A	B	C	D		A	B	C	D
1	I	III	II	IV	2	III	IV	II	I
3	IV	III	II	I	4	II	I	III	IV

Ans. *(2)*

Exp. The correct matching is A-III, B-IV, C-II, D-I.

Forgery of signature - Prabhu Dayal Vs. Jwala Bank ILR 1938 All. 634. In this case, one of the rules of the bank required customers to keep the cheque book under lock and key, otherwise the bank will not be liable in this connection. The customer left his cheque book in an unlocked box. A cheque was stolen from the cheque book, the customer's signature was forged and the cheque was presented and duly paid by the bank. The banker was held liable for the loss. No doubt, the customer was negligent, but his negligence was not the proximate cause of the loss.

As per *Section 82* of the Negotiable Instruments Act, 1881, the maker, acceptor or endorser respectively of a negotiable instrument is discharged from liability thereon by cancellation, by release and by payment.

As per *Section 10* of Negotiable Instruments Act mentions payment in due course means payment in accordance with the apparent tenor of the instrument in good faith and without negligence to any person in possession thereof under circumstances which do not afford a reasonable ground for believing that he is not entitled to receive payment of the amount therein mentioned.

According to *Section* 100 of NI Act, when a promissory note or bill of exchange has been dishonoured by non-acceptance or non-payment, the holder may, within a reasonable time, cause such dishonour to be noted and certified by a notary public. Such a certificate is called a Protest.

75 Find correct legal principle from following statements.

1 While collecting a cheque for a banker, the customer is under an obligation to present it promptly so as to avoid any loss due to change of circumstances

2 While collecting a cheque for a customer, the banker is under an obligation to present it properly so as to avoid any loss due to change of circumstances

3 While collecting a cheque for a customer, the banker is under no obligation to present it properly so as to avoid any loss due to change of circumstances

4 While collecting a cheque for a banker, the customer is under no obligation to present it promptly so as to avoid any loss due to change of circumstances

Ans. *(2)*

Exp. The correct legal principle is, while collecting a cheque for a customer, the banker is under an obligation to present it properly so as to avoid any loss due to change of circumstances.

The protection is available to the collecting bankers under Section 131 of NI Acts 1881, inter alia, only when following conditions are satisfied by the collecting banker; the bank should have collected such cheque for a customer as an agent for collection and not as a holder for a value, the proceeds of the collected cheque are credited to only to the account of the payee or to the account of endorsee if endorsement on the instrument is regular.

The collecting banker must have acted in good faith. Here 'good faith' means banker had no reasonable ground to believe that the customer is not entitled to receive payment of the amount therein mentioned.

The collecting banker should have acted without negligence. 'Without negligence' means the account of the customer on whose behalf cheque is collected, is opened with proper compliance of KYC norms such as verification of identity proof and address proof before opening the account.

UGC-NET
LAW
SOLVED PAPER 2013 (June)
PAPER II

1 "It is likely that free India may be federal India, though in any event there would be a great deal of Unitary Control." This statement was made by

1 Sir Alladi Krishna Swami Iyer
2 Dr BR Ambedkar
3 Pt Jawaharlal Nehru
4 Sardar Vallabh Bhai Patel

Ans. (3)

Exp. "It is likely that free India may be federal India though in any event there would be a great deal of Unitary Control." This statement was made by Pt Jawaharlal Nehru.

The above statement was made in the Lucknow Session of the Congress on 26th December, 1936, in light of the Government of India Act, 1935 that did give the Indians some sort of provincial autonomy but the major powers were still vested with the Centre.

2 Judicial Review in the Constitution of India is based on

1 Precedents and conventions
2 Rule of law
3 Due process of law
4 Procedure established by law

Ans. (4)

Exp. Judicial Review in the Constitution of India is based on 'Procedure established by law'.

Under Judicial Review, the court examines whether the law has been made in accordance with the powers granted by the Constitution to the law-making body and follows the prescribed procedure or not. It gets rejected when it is held to be violative of procedure established by law.

3 The Constitution of India embodies the Parliamentary form of government because

1 The Council of Ministers is collectively responsible to the Lok Sabha
2 The Council of Ministers is responsible to Lok Sabha and Rajya Sabha
3 The President, the head of the executive, is answerable to Parliament
4 The Prime Minister, the Head of the Cabinet, is accountable to Parliament

Ans. (1)

Exp. The Constitution of India embodies the Parliamentary form of government because the Council of Ministers is collectively responsible to the Lok Sabha.

Collective Ministerial Responsibility in the sole crux of Parliamentary democracy. The principle of collective responsibility represents ministerial accountability to the legislature. In India, the doctrine of collective responsibility has been enshrined under Article 75(3) which lays down that the Council of Ministers shall be collectively responsible to the Lok Sabha.

4 The Supreme Court held that Election Commissioners cannot be placed on par with the Chief Election Commissioner in terms of power and authority in the following case

1 SS Dhannoa Vs. Union of India
2 TN Seshan Vs. Union of India
3 AC Jose Vs. Sivan Pillai
4 Venkatachalam Vs. A Swamickan

Ans. (1)

Exp. The Supreme Court of India in SS Dhanoa Vs. Union of India (1991) held that Election Commissioners cannot be placed on par with the Chief Election Commissioner in terms of power and authority.

It was held that when an institution like Election Commission is entrusted with vital functions, to execute them, it is both necessary and desirable that the powers are not exercised by one individual. But the Chief Election Commissioner does not appear to be primus inter pares, i.e. first among equals, but he is intended to be placed in a distinctly higher position.

5 The maximum interval between the two sessions of each House of Parliament is

1 Three months
2 Four months
3 Five months
4 Six months

Ans. (4)

Exp. The maximum interval between the two sessions of each House of Parliament is six months.

According to Article 85(1) of the Indian Constitution, the President shall from time to time summon each House of Parliament to meet at such time and place as he thinks fit, but six months shall not intervene between its lasting sitting in one session and the date appointed for its first sitting in the next session.

6 The Supreme Court observed that "Parliamentary proceedings are not subject to Fundamental Rights" in the following case

1 Keshav Singh Vs. Speaker, UP Assembly
2 Gunapati Vs. Habibul Hasan
3 MSM Sharma Vs. Sri Krishna Sinha
4 State of Punjab Vs. Satpal Dang

Ans. *(3)*

Exp. The Supreme Court observed that "Parliamentary proceedings are not subject to Fundamental Rights" in the case of MSM Sharma Vs. Sri Krishna Sinha (1958).

In this case, proceedings for the breach of privilege had been started against an editor of a newspaper for publishing those parts of the speech of a member delivered in Bihar Legislative Assembly which the Speaker had ordered to be expunged from the proceedings of the Assembly.

The editor in a writ petition under Article 32 contended that the House of Commons had no privilege to prohibit either the publication of the publicly seen and heard proceedings that took place in the House or of that part of the proceedings which had been directed to be expunged. The Supreme Court of India by a majority of four to one rejected the contention of the petitioner.

7 For the purpose of creating a new State in India, an amendment to the Constitution of India must be passed by

1 2/3rd majority of the members of both Houses of Parliament present and voting
2 2/3rd majority of the members of both Houses of Parliament and ratification by not less than 2/3rd majority of the States
3 A simple majority in Parliament and ratification by not less than half of the States
4 A simple majority by the Parliament

Ans. *(4)*

Exp. For the purpose of creating a new State in India, an amendment to the Constitution of India must be passed by a simple majority by the Parliament.

As per Article 3 of the Constitution, Parliament of India can form new States, alter the area, boundaries or names of the existing States by a law passed by a simple majority.

The bills for the formation of new states or alteration of the boundaries or names of the existing states shall be introduced in either House of the Parliament (Lok Sabha or Rajya Sabha), only on the recommendation of the President of India.

The President of India, before introducing the Bill in the Parliament, shall refer it to the concerned State legislature for its opinion within a specified time limit. If the State Legislature does not give its opinion within the specified time limit, the time limit may be extended. The bill may be introduced even if the opinion has not come.

8 Match the following.

List I	List II
A. Perfect right	I. Which has correlative positive duty
B. Negative right	II. Which has a correlative duty that can be legally enforced
C. Imperfect right	III. A has a right to receive damages
D. Positive right	IV. That right which although recognised by State but not enforceable

Codes

	A	B	C	D		A	B	C	D
1	III	IV	I	II	2	II	III	IV	I
3	IV	III	II	I	4	I	II	III	IV

Ans. *(2)*

Exp. The correct matching is A-II, B-III, C-IV, D-I.

A Perfect right has a correlative duty that can be legally enforced. A perfect right is that right which corresponds to a perfect duty. It is recognized as well as enforced by law.

Negative Right has a right to receive damages. A negative right is merely a right to not be harmed and corresponds to a negative duty.

Imperfect Right is the right which is recognised by State but is not enforceable by law. The rights of the subjects against the state can also be classified as imperfect rights as they cannot be enforced.

Positive Right has a correlative positive duty. A positive right is a right to be positively benefited and corresponds to a positive duty.

9 According to which school, "the purpose of jurisprudence is to analyse and dissect the law of the land as it exists today"?

1 Analytical Jurisprudence
2 Historical Jurisprudence
3 Sociological Jurisprudence
4 Philosophical Jurisprudence

Ans. *(1)*

Exp. According to Analytical Jurisprudence, "the purpose of jurisprudence is to analyse and dissect the law of the land as it exists today."

The major premise of Analytical School of Jurisprudence is to deal with law as it exists in the present form. It seeks to analysis the first principles of law as they actually exist in a given legal system. The purpose of this branch of study is to analyse and dissect the law of the land as it exist today. This analysis as to the principal of the law is done without reference to their historical origin or their ethical significance.

10 "The one who holds the property is the owner." Give your correct response from following on the basis of above statement.

1 The holder of property may be mere possessor or bailee
2 The holder of property need not be the owner
3 This statement is not correct
4 This statement is correct

Ans. (2)

Exp. The holder of property need not be the owner is the correct response of the given statement.

Normally ownership implies the following: the right to manage, the right to possess, the right to capital, the right to the income, etc. The owner of a thing has the right to possess it, to the exclusive of all others i.e. the owner has exclusive physical control of a thing.

11 The sources of law have been divided into two classes. These are

1 Divine sources and human sources
2 Formal sources and material sources
3 Natural sources and universal sources
4 1 and 2 both of the above

Ans. (2)

Exp. The sources of law have been divided into two sources: Formal sources and Material sources.

According to Salmond, there are two main sources of law: formal and material. Formal sources are those from which law derives its validity and force, that is, the will of the State which is expressed through statutes and judicial decisions. Material sources are those from which the law derives the matter of which it is composed and not the validity. He subdivided the Material sources into legal sources and historical sources.

12 According to whose theory, "Law is not universal in its nature; like language it varies with people and age"?

1 Bentham's theory
2 Austin's theory
3 Savigny's theory
4 Montesquieu's theory

Ans. (3)

Exp. According to Savigny' theory, "Law is not universal in its nature; like language it varies with people and age."

In Savigny's understanding, in all societies, the law is established like a language. These laws are stamped with a national character. They are the natural manifestations of popular life and are, by no means, a product of a man's free will. Law, language, customs, and government have no separate existence. There is only one force, i.e, the people and they underline all these institutions. Thus, "law is like a language which develops with the life of people".

13 Which one of the following pairs is not correctly matched?

1 Law properly so-called (in regard to notion of law) – Which is distinct from morals.
2 Law improperly so-called (in regard to notion of law) – Other laws
3 Audi alteram partem – Rule of natural justice
4 Conspectus of justice – Justice denied

Ans. (4)

Exp. Among the given pairs, Conspectus of justice with justice denied is not correctly matched pair.

The conspectus of Jurisprudence was laid down and re-laid by not only jurists but also by experts in other disciplines like political science and sociology besides a host of others.

Their approach to the subject from different perspectives was largely felicitated by its uncertain nature. The only thing that is certain is that it is more than mere knowledge of principles of law. It is generally conceded that it is concerned with ascertaining the fundamental principles of which law is founded. It deals with the foundation and not with the superstructure of law.

14 Read each of the following two statements Assertion (A) and Reason (R) and indicate your answer using the codes given below

Assertion (A) The Maneka Gandhi's case is a landmark decision from the point of human rights and remedial jurisprudence.

Reason (R) From the positivist point of view, equality is antithetic to arbitrariness.

Codes

1 Both (A) and (R) are true and (R) is the correct explanation of (A)
2 Both (A) and (R) are true, but (R) is not the correct explanation of (A)
3 (A) is true, but (R) is false
4 (A) is false, but (R) is true

Ans. (2)

Exp. Both (A) and (R) are true, but (R) is not the correct explanation of (A).

In the case titled as Maneka Gandhi Vs. Union of India (1978), the Supreme Court observed that to the extent to which Section 10(3)(c) of the Passport Act, 1967 authorises the passport authority to impound a passport 'in the interest of the general public', it is violative of Article 14 of the Constitution since it confers vague and undefined power on the passport authority.

Section 10(3)(c) is against Articles 19(1)(a) and 19(1)(g) since it permits restrictions to be imposed on the rights guaranteed by these articles even though such restrictions cannot be imposed under Articles 19(2) and 19(6). Thus, the Assertion is correct.

It was further held in the case that from the positivist point of view 'equality is antithetical to arbitrariness'. The Court ruled that the mere existence of an enabling law was not enough to restrain personal liberty. Such a law must also be 'just, fair and reasonable'. Thus, the Reason is also correct.

15 Who among the following said that the law of nation is "the body of legal rules which apply between states and such entities as have been granted international personality"?

1 Fenwick
2 Oppeheim
3 Schwarzenberger
4 Verdoss

Ans. (3)

Exp. Schwarzenberger said that the law of nation is "the body of legal rules which apply between states and such entities as have been granted international personality".

According to Oppenheim, "Law of nations or international law is the name for the body of customary and treaty rules which are considered legally binding by civilized States in their intercourse with each other."

It can be concluded that international law is a body of rules and principles which regulate the conduct and relations of members of the international community. The character of International Law is changing to cover International institutions, organizations, individuals and non-state entities as subjects of International Law.

16 The main difference between De-facto and De-jure recognition is

I. De-facto recognition may be withdrawn while De-jure recognition is full and final.
II. Only De-jure recognised states can represent the old states, for the purpose of state succession.
III. In De-jure recognition, formal diplomatic relations are established while in case of De-facto they may not be entered into.
IV. Former is legal and the latter is a factual recognition.

Codes

1 I, II and III
2 II, III and IV
3 II and III
4 I and II

Ans. (1)

Exp. Among the given choices, option (1) provides the correct choice.

The two Latin expressions, 'De-jure' and 'De-facto' refer to two closely related concepts that are mainly used in political and legal contexts. Though most of us know that the meaning of these two words is contradictory, we are unable to identify the exact meaning of these two terms. The main difference between these two terms is that De-jure means according to law or by rightful entitlement while De-facto refers to a state of affairs in existence that is not sanctioned by law.

De-facto recognition may be withdrawn while De-jure recognition is full and final. Only De-jure recognised states can represent the old states, for the purpose of state succession. In De-jure recognitions, formal diplomatic relations are established while in case of De-facto they may not be entered into.

Statement IV is incorrect because De-facto refers to only by the fact, and not law, while the De-jure refers to by law.

17 A member of the United Nations can be suspended from the exercise of rights and privileges of membership by the

1 General Assembly
2 Security Council
3 General Assembly on the recommendations of the Security Council
4 Secretary General on the recommendations of the Security Council

Ans. (3)

Exp. General Assembly on the recommendations of the Security Council can suspend a member of the United Nations from the exercise of right and privileges of membership.

According to Article 5 of the UN Charter, a Member of the United Nations against which preventive or enforcement action has been taken by the Security Council may be suspended from the exercise of the rights and privileges of membership by the General Assembly upon the recommendation of the Security Council. The exercise of these rights and privileges may be restored by the Security Council.

18 Read Assertion (A) and Reason (R) and with the help of codes given below select the correct answer.

Assertion (A) International Law consists for the most part of customary rules.

Reason (R) Customary rules are the original and oldest source of International Law.

Codes

1 Both (A) and (R) are true and (R) is the correct explanation of (A)
2 Both (A) and (R) are true, but (R) is not the correct explanation of (A)
3 (A) is true, but (R) is false
4 (A) is false and (R) is true

Ans. (2)

Exp. Both (A) and (R) are true, but (R) is not the correct explanation of (A).

Customary international law is an aspect of international law involving the principle of custom. Along with general principles of law and treaties, custom is considered by the International Court of Justice, jurists, the United Nations, and its member states to be among the primary sources of international law. Thus, the Assertion is correct.

The original and the oldest source of Law is known as Custom. The rules of customary International Law involved a long historical process which gained recognition by the entire community. The presence of customary rules can be deduced from state practice and behaviour because it is not a written source of law. Thus, the Reason is correct.

19 Universal Declaration of Human Rights was adopted on

1 10th December, 1948 2 10th November, 1948
3 20th October, 1948 4 21st January, 1948

Ans. (1)

Exp. Universal Declaration of Human Rights was adopted on 10th December, 1948.

The Universal Declaration of Human Rights (UDHR) is a milestone document in the history of human rights. Drafted by representatives with different legal and cultural backgrounds from all regions of the world, the Declaration was proclaimed by the United Nations General Assembly in Paris on 10th December, 1948.

It sets out, for the first time, fundamental human rights to be universally protected and it has been translated into over 500 languages. The UDHR is widely recognized as having inspired, and paved the way for, the adoption of more than seventy human rights treaties, applied today on a permanent basis at global and regional levels (all containing references to it in their preambles).

20 Read Assertion (A) and Reason (R) and with the help of codes given below select the correct answer.

Assertion (A) Human Rights occupy a significant place in the UN Charter.

Reason (R) Members of the UN have committed themselves to promote respect for and observance of human rights and Fundamental Rights.

Codes

1 Both (A) and (R) are individually true and (R) is the correct explanation of (A)
2 Both (A) and (R) are individually true, but (R) is not the correct explanation of (A)
3 (A) is true, but (R) is false
4 (A) is false, but (R) is true

Ans. (2)

Exp. Both (A) and (R) are individually true, but (R) is not the correct explanation of (A).

When states become members of the UN they accept the obligations of the UN Charter that sets out the four main purposes of the UN: to maintain international peace and security; to develop friendly relations among nations; to cooperate in solving international problems and in promoting respect for human rights; and to be a centre for harmonising the actions of nations. Thus, Human Rights occupy a significant place in the UN Charter and the Assertion is correct.

As per the Preamble to Universal Declaration of Human Rights, member States have pledged themselves to achieve, in cooperation with the United Nations, the promotion of universal respect for and observance of human rights and fundamental freedoms. Thus, the Reason is correct.

However, the reason why Human Rights occupy a significant place in the UN Charter is because it is one of the commitments and objectives of the United Nations stated through its Charter. Thus, both (A) and (R) are individually true but (R) is not the correct explanation of (A).

21 Adultery by a Hindu husband is

1 Ground of divorce only
2 Not a ground of divorce
3 Ground of judicial separation
4 None of the above

Ans. (4)

Exp. Adultery by a Hindu husband may be a ground of divorce or judicial separation, as the case may be.

The Supreme Court in Joseph Shine Vs. Union of India (2018) struck down Section 497 of the IPC as unconstitutional, being violative of Articles 14, 15 and 21 and held that Section 198(2) of the CrPC was unconstitutional to the extent that it was applicable to Section 497, IPC. This judgment overruled several previous judgments upholding the criminalization of adultery.

The judgment effectively rendered Adultery as not a crime but made it a ground of divorce or judicial separation under concerned laws.According to Section 497 of IPC, (now repealed),whoever has sexual intercourse with a person who is and whom he knows or has reason to believe to be the wife of another man, without the consent or connivance of that man, such sexual intercourse not amounting to the offence of rape, is guilty of the offence of adultery and shall be punished with imprisonment of either description for a term which may extend to five years or with fine or with both. In such case, the wife shall not be punishable as an abettor.

22 'A' marries 'B', the widow of the elder brother. The marriage is

1 Valid 2 Void
3 Voidable 4 None of these

Ans. (2)

Exp. If 'A' marries 'B', the widow of the elder brother, then the marriage is void.

A marriage, in order to be valid, must not be within the prohibited degrees of relationship. As per Section 3(g) (iii), two persons are said to be within the degrees of prohibited relationship if one was the wife of the brother or of the father's or mother's brother or of the grandfather's or grandmother's brother of the other. Since the given situation falls under this category, the marriage will be void.

23 Marriage with an impotent and has not been consummated. The marriage is

1 Valid 2 Void
3 Nullity 4 Irregular

Ans. (3)

Exp. Marriage with an impotent and has not been consummated. The marriage is nullity.

Courts have opined that Intercourse is one of the foundations of marriage and without vigorous and harmonious sexual activity it would be impossible for any marriage to continue for long. A valid marriage can only be annulled or dissolved provided one or more specified grounds for divorce have been made out. Conjugal intercourse is one of the objects of marriage. When this object is not fulfilled as a result of the impotency of one of the parties, it becomes a ground for dissolution of marriage.

In Dissolution of Muslim Marriage Act, only the wife can file a suit if her husband is impotent. In Parsi Marriage and Divorce Act, either party to the marriage can file a suit and not necessarily the aggrieved party which means the impotent person can also file a suit for annulment of the marriage when the marriage is not consummated owing to his or her impotency. Whereas in Hindu Marriage Act, only the aggrieved party i.e. the person whose marriage is not consummated because of the impotency of his or her spouse, can file a suit.

24 'Khula' is a form of divorce by

1 Sale 2 Purchase
3 Agreement 4 Coercion

Ans. (2)

Exp. 'Khula' is a form of divorce by Purchase.

'Khula' means the separation of the wife in return for a payment; the husband takes the payment and lets his wife go, whether this payment is the mahr which he gave to her or more or less than that.

Khula is the right of a woman in Islam to divorce and it means separation from her husband. After divorce, the husband is responsible for the education and maintenance of the children. The children live with the mother till the age of Hizanat which is seven years for sons and age of puberty for daughters.

25 Mutah marriage could not be dissolved

1 Ipso facto by the efflux of the period
2 by death
3 by divorce
4 by Hiba-i-Mudat

Ans. (3)

Exp. Muta marriage could not be dissolved by divorce.

The Shia law (Ithna Ashari School) recognises two kinds of marriage, namely permanent and muta (literally means enjoyment or use) or temporary. The fundamental difference between the two is that in the former the term is not specified, while in the latter it is the Sunnis who do not recognise such marriage. According to the Muslim Law, Mutah marriage cannot be dissolved by divorce.

26 By which of the following way a Muslim marriage can be dissolved by a Muslim husband?

1 Talaq 2 Illa
3 Zihar 4 All of these

Ans. (4)

Exp. By the ways of Talaq, Illa and Zihar, a Muslim marriage can be dissolved by a Muslim husband.

Talaq in Islamic law means a divorce affected by the husband's enunciation of the word 'talaq', thus constituting a formal repudiation of his wife.

Illa literally means to make a vow and in the Shariah, it means that the husband makes a vow to refrain from his wife for a stipulated period of time.

Zihar signifies a man comparing his wife to any of his female relations, within such prohibited degree of kindred, whether by blood, by fosterage or by marriage, as renders marriage with them invariably unlawful.

27 When a person making a false statement believes the statement to be true and does not intend to mislead to the other party to the contract, it is known as

1 Mistake 2 Fraud
3 Misrepresentation 4 Undue influence

Ans. (3)

Exp. When a person making a false statement believes the statement to be true and does not intend to mislead to the other party to the contract, it is known as Misrepresentation.

As per Section 18 of the Indian Contract Act, 1872, Misrepresentation means and includes the positive assertion, in a manner not warranted by the information of the person making it, of that which is not true, though he believes it to be true, any breach of duty which, without an intent to deceive, gains an advantage of the person committing it, or any one claiming under him, by misleading another to his prejudice, or to the prejudice of any one claiming under him, causing, however innocently, a party to an agreement, to make a mistake as to the substance of the thing which is the subject of the agreement.

28 Read Assertion (A) and Reason (R) and with the help of codes given below, select the correct answer.

Assertion (A) An agreement not enforceable by law is said to be void.

Reason (R) Law has no force.

Codes

1 Both (A) and (R) are true and (R) is good explanation of (A)
2 Both (A) and (R) are true, but (R) is not correct explanation of (A)
3 (A) is true, but (R) is false
4 (A) is false, but (R) is true

Ans. (3)

Exp. The Assertion is true, but the Reason is false.

Void means having no legal value and agreement means arrangement, promise or contract made with somebody. Thus, void agreement means an agreement that has no legal value.

An agreement not enforceable by law is said to be void under Section 2(g) of the Indian Contract Act, 1872. A void agreement has no legal effect. An agreement which does not satisfy the essential elements of contract is void. Void contract confers no rights on any person and creates no obligation. Thus, the Assertion is true.

It is incorrect to say that Law has no force. Law is a rule which is made by a competent authority which has binding effect on the subjects making submission to it. Thus, Reason is false.

29 'A' and 'B' are friends. 'A' told to 'B' to show him a new movie in a posh theatre, upon which 'A' promised to offer him lunch in a 5 star hotel. 'B' showed him a movie in a posh theatre, but 'A' gave lunch to 'B' in a road side dhaba. Decide A's liability using codes given below.

Codes

1 'A' is liable because there was intention to create legal relation between 'A' and 'B'
2 'A' is not liable because there was no intention to create legal relation between 'A' and 'B'
3 'B' was mistaken
4 'A' was mistaken

Ans. *(2)*

Exp. In this case, 'A' is not liable because there was no intention to create a legal relation between 'A' and 'B'.

Intention to create a legal relationship can be explained as intention to enter into a legal contract and fulfil its obligations lawfully. Intention to create legal relationships in a contract is essential as it shows readiness of parties to accept legal sequences of having entered into a contract.

The parties must intend to enter into a legally binding arrangement in which obligations are enforceable. As simple as it seems, the question whether parties in a contract had intention to create a legal relationship is difficult to answer and extremely depends on facts.

There must be an intention on the part of the parties to create a legal relationship between them. Social or domestic types of agreements which are formed with no intention to create legal relationships are not enforceable in court of law and hence they do not result in contracts.

Without an intention to create a legal relation contract would not be considered as enforceable, legal and binding as a result parties in the contract cannot sue each other in case one defaults.

30 Arrange the following concepts in sequence in which they occur, using codes given below.

I. Offer is communicated
II. Counter offer is made
III. Offer is rejected
IV. Counter offer is accepted

Codes

1 I, II, III, IV
2 I, III, II, IV
3 I, IV, II, III
4 II, I, III, IV

Ans. *(2)*

Exp. The correct sequence is I, III, II, IV.

There are few factors for the existence of a contract. Following is the correct sequence in which they occur;

Firstly, an offer is Communicated. An offer can basically be illustrated as a clear statement of the terms on which a party (the offeror) is prepared to make a business with other party (the offeree). In other words, making (by offeror) an offer is promising to do or not to do something which is depending on acceptance by other person (by offeree).

Secondly, the offer is Rejected. The making of a counter offer results in the rejection of the initial offer.

Thirdly, a Counter-Offer may be made, which automatically rejects the offer preceding it.

Fourth, the Counter Offer is accepted by the party making the original offer. These events are important in the context of contract disputes as it is the order of events that determines the extent of any contractual relationship between the parties in the circumstances.

31 Following are essentials of valid contract.

I. Parties to contract should have capacity to contract.
II. Parties to contract should have legal mind.
III. Parties to contract should be intelligent.
IV. Invitation to offer should be accepted.

Find correct answer, using codes given below

1 Only I is correct
2 Only I and IV are correct
3 All of above are correct
4 Only II is correct

Ans. *(1)*

Exp. Among the given statements statement I is correct.

The term 'Contract' has been defined under Section 2 (h) of the Indian Contract Act, 1872. It defines a Contract as an Agreement enforceable by law. An agreement cannot turn into a contract unless it can be enforceable by Law. Section 11 defines who is competent to contract, and states that every person is competent to contract who is of the age of majority and who is of sound mind and is not disqualified from contracting by any law to which he is subject.

Thus, in order to be enforceable, a contract must contain all the essential elements of a valid contract as defined in Section 10 of the Indian Contract Act, 1872.

Statement II, III and IV are incorrect because there is no legal mandate for the parties to an agreement to have legal mind, or be intelligent as long as other essentials are fulfilled. Further, an invitation to offer precedes an offer which may or may not be accepted and the next step after an invitation to offer is an offer, not an acceptance.

32 Match items in List I with items in List II, using codes given below.

	List I		List II
A.	Ambiguous and uncertain agreements	I.	Section 15
B.	Coercion	II.	Section 25(2)
C.	Past consideration	III.	Section 73
D.	Remoteness of damage	IV.	Section 29

Codes

	A	B	C	D		A	B	C	D
1	II	III	IV	I	2	III	II	IV	I
3	III	II	I	IV	4	I	IV	III	II

Ans. (*)

Exp. The correct matching is A-IV; B-I; C-II; D-III.

Section 29 of Indian Contract Act, 1872 is related to Ambiguous and uncertain agreements. It states that Agreements, the meaning of which is not certain, or capable of being made certain, are void.

Section 15 is related to 'Coercion'. 'Coercion' is the committing, or threatening to commit, any act forbidden by the Indian Penal Code (45 of 1860) or the unlawful detaining, or threatening to detain, any property, to the prejudice of any person whatever, with the intention of causing any person to enter into an agreement.

Section 25(2) is related to Past consideration. It states that an agreement made without consideration is void, unless it is a promise to compensate, wholly or in part, a person who has already voluntarily done something for the promisor, or something which the promisor was legally compellable to do; or unless.

Section 73 is related to Remoteness of damage. It states that when a contract has been broken, the party who suffers by such breach is entitled to receive, form the party who has broken the contract, compensation for any loss or damage caused to him thereby, which naturally arose in the usual course of things from such breach, or which the parties knew, when they made the contract, to be likely to result from the breach of it.

33 Which one of the following statements is incorrect?

1 Tort is a civil wrong in which claim for unliquidated damages is made
2 In tort, action lies against the wrong-doer in a civil court
3 For a tortious liability, a jail term can also be awarded
4 In some torts an injunction can also be issued against the wrong-doer

Ans. (3)

Exp. Statement 3 is incorrect as no jail term can be provided for a tortious liability.

The term 'Tort' means a wrongful act committed by a person, causing injury or damage to another, thereby the injured institutes (files) an action in Civil Court for a remedy i.e. unliquidated damages or injunction or restitution of property or other available relief. Unliquidated damages mean the amount of damages to be fixed or determined by the Court.

In general, the victim of a tortious act is the plaintiff in a tort case. As a general rule, all persons have the capacity to sue and be sued in a tort. Tort law provides an avenue for an injured person of a remedy. It does not provide a guarantee of recovery.

34 Which one of the following defences is not available in Law of Tort?

1 Volenti non-fit injuria 2 Act of God
3 Contributory negligence 4 Inevitable accident

Ans. (3)

Exp. Contributory negligence is not available as a defence under Law of torts.

In an action for a tort, the defendant may avoid his liability by taking the plea of some defences. Some of the defences which can be used in torts are as follows; Volenti Non Fit Injuria, Plaintiff is the Wrong doer, Inevitable Accident, Act of God, Private Defence, etc.

Volenti Non Fit Injuria, which means 'voluntary taking of a risk'. It's when a person chooses to be in the situation that causes the injury.

Plaintiff is the Wrongdoer is applicable when the plaintiff did something wrong which caused him the injury. Since the plaintiff did something wrong so he cannot claim damages from someone else for the injury caused to him.

Inevitable Accident arises when an injury is caused to a person by an event that could not be foreseen and avoided despite reasonable care on the part of the defendant, the defence of inevitable accident can be used.

Act of God is applicable when the accident happens to occur because of unforeseen natural event.

Private Defence is available when if one injures someone or something that belongs to someone else, while defending self or own property, then one can be excused if the force used to protect self was reasonable.

35 'Sometimes it happens that the legal right of a person is violated but he does not suffer any harm.' From which one of the following maxim we can attribute it?

1 Damnum sine injuria 2 Injuria sine damnum
3 Volenti non-fit injuria 4 Res ipsa loquitur

Ans. (2)

Exp. The given statement can be attributed to the maxim Injuria sine damnum.

Injuria sine damnum is used in law of torts and is related to damages. The meaning of the maxim is infringement of an absolute private right without any actual loss or damage. Here, the actual damage means physical loss in terms of money, comfort, health, etc.

Damnum sine injuria refers to a legal situation in which plaintiff's right is not respected by another but where the breach of plaintiff's right does not cause damage or at least not a calculable or admissible damage. A finding of damnum sine injuria can be the basis for a finding of nominal damages.

36 The rule of 'absolute liability' was laid down by the Supreme Court of India in which case?

1 Rylands Vs. Fletcher
2 MC Mehta (Sriram Food and Fertiliser Co) Vs. Union of India
3 MC Mehta (CNG Fuel case) Vs. Union of India
4 None of the above

Ans. (2)

Exp. The rule of 'absolute liability' was laid down by the Supreme Court of India in the case titled as MC Mehta (Shriram Food and Fertiliser Co) Vs. Union of India (1986).

The rule Absolute liability was summed up in the following words, "If an enterprise or an organization is engaged with the hazardous activity and causes damages to any one on account of this accident of this hazardous activity, the escape of toxic gas or any dangerous thing, the enterprise or organization is strictly and absolutely liable to compensate the people who have been affected". Further, Absolute liability is not subject to any kind of exceptions like strict liability in Rylands Vs. Fletcher.

37 In which of the following cases did the Supreme Court of India gave the ruling that sovereign immunity of the State is subject to the Fundamental Rights?

1 Kasturilal Ralia Ram Jain Vs. State of UP
2 State of Rajasthan Vs. Vidhyawati
3 People's Union for Democratic Rights Vs. State of Bihar
4 Shyam Sundar Vs. State of Rajasthan

Ans. *(3)*

Exp. In the case of People's Union for Democratic Rights Vs. State of Bihar (1997), the Supreme Court gave the ruling that sovereign immunity of the State is subject to the Fundamental Rights.

The Supreme Court held that in case of violation of fundamental rights by State's instrumentalities or servants, the Court can direct the State to pay compensation to the victim or his heir by way of "monetary amends" and redressal. The principle of "sovereign immunity" shall be inapplicable in such cases. The court also laid down the working principle for the payment of compensation to the victims of ruthless and unwarranted police firing.

38 The rule laid down in Re Polemis case is that the defendant shall be liable for all

1 direct consequences of his act
2 direct consequences of his act, if he could foresee some damage to the plaintiff from his act
3 direct consequences of his act, only if he could foresee the kind of damage which has actually occurred
4 foreseeable damage

Ans. *(*)*

Exp. The rule of reasonable foreseeability was laid down in Re. Polemis case. This rule meant that the defendant was liable for all the consequences of his action regardless of the fact that the damage which occurred was not reasonably foreseeable.

[Note : The correct answer would be for all damage caused]

39 Match List I (Jurists) with List II (Assumptions) and select the correct answer using the codes given below.

List I	List II
A. Lord TB Macauley	I. Preparation of Penal Code of India
B. Jermy Bentham	II. Un-written jurisprudence on Penal principles
C. Kelson	III. Substantive law on rimes
D. Sir Barnes Peacock	IV. Revision of Penal law

Codes

	A	B	C	D		A	B	C	D
1	I	II	III	IV	2	II	I	IV	III
3	III	IV	I	II	4	IV	I	II	III

Ans. *(1)*

Exp. The correct matching is A-I; B-II; C-III; D-IV.

Lord TB Macaulay is related to Preparation of Penal Code of India. The Indian Penal Code (IPC) is the main criminal code of India. It is a comprehensive code intended to cover all substantive aspects of criminal law. The code was drafted in 1860 on the recommendations of the first law commission of India established in 1834 under the Charter Act of 1833 under the Chairmanship of Thomas Babington Macaulay.

Jeremy Bentham mentions about unwritten jurisprudence on Penal principles. In his General View of a Complete Code of Laws, Bentham summarized his arguments against judge-made law. The grand utility of the law is certainty: unwritten law does not it cannot possess this quality; the citizen can find no part of it, cannot take it for his guide; he is reduced to consultations; he assembles the lawyers-he collects as many opinions as his fortune will permit; and all this ruinous procedure often serves only to create new doubts.

Kelson is related to substantive law on crimes. As per Kelson, the development of legal norms applicable prospectively, heralding a federated world state with a permanent compulsory international court adjudicating cases against war criminals, would, he believed, replace ad hoc international justice.

Sir Barnes Peacock is known for revision of Penal Laws. Indian Penal Code was first enacted on 6th October, 1860. Lord Macaulay got the credit for drafting IPC for he was the President of Indian Law Commission then. The draft was presented to the Governor General of India in Council in 1837. It was further revised by Sir Barnes Peacock, Sir J.W. Colville and others. It was completed in 1850 and presented to the Legislative Council in 1856 and passed on 6th October, 1860.

40 Match List I (Objectives) with List II (Propositions) and select the correct answer using the codes given below.

List I	List II
A. Inchoate crime	I. 'Whaton' says it is the beginning but not complete.
B. Attempt	II. It does not act towards the commission of offence.
C. Preparation	III. Culprit commences to do something.
D. Intention	IV. When preparation merges itself with attempt.

Codes

	A	B	C	D		A	B	C	D
1	II	III	IV	I	2	I	II	III	IV
3	III	IV	I	II	4	IV	I	II	III

Ans. *(2)*

Exp. The correct matching is A-I; B-II; C-III; D-IV.

Inchoate crime are also referred to as incomplete crimes, are acts involving the tendency to commit, or to indirectly participate in a criminal offense. In the past, several inchoate crimes used to be regarded as minor offences. 'Wharton' says it is the beginning but not complete.

Attempt a does not act towards the commission of offence. It is defined as an inchoate crime where an individual, with the intent to actually commit a crime, undertakes an action in furtherance of that crime, but ultimately fails.

In *Preparation* culprit commences to do something. Preparation consists in devising means for the commission of an offence. IPC does not punish acts done in the stage of preparation, mere preparation is punishable only in two cases; namely when the preparation is to wage war against the State section 122 or to commit dacoity Section 399 IPC.

In *Intention* preparation merges itself with attempt. Attempt to commit a crime occurs when a person makes a proper mindset to do a criminal act and put a step forward for fulfilling by arranging the means and methods necessary for the commission of that crime but fail to do so.

41 Fill in the blank using appropriate statement. 'Non Compos Mentis' means ________.

1 Not of sound mind
2 Who lacks the requisite mens rea
3 Unable to know that the act is either wrong or contrary to law
4 A concussion of brain

***Ans.* (1)**

Exp. 'Non Compos Mentis' means not of sound mind.

'Non-compos mentis' is a Latin term which means 'not of sound mind'. A person not in control of oneself can be said to be non-compos mentis. A person not capable to go to trial is also non-compos mentis. This term can also be used to describe a person in a confused state or intoxicated.

42 Fill in the blank using appropriate reason. Right to private defence by a friend is generally not available because ________.

1 there was no specified circumstances
2 explanation II of Section 300 IPC is a bar for it
3 the act was not with an intention to protect the friend
4 the offending party was an aggressor

***Ans.* (2)**

Exp. Right to private defence by a friend is generally not available because explanation II of Section 300 IPC is bar for it.

According to exception-II of Section 300, Culpable homicide is not murder if the offender, in the exercise in good faith of the right of private defence of person or property, exceeds the power given to him by law and causes the death of the person against whom he is exercising such right of defence without premeditation, and without any intention of doing more harm than is necessary for the purpose of such defence.

43 Read Assertion (A) and Reason (R) and with the help of codes given below select the correct answer.

Assertion (A) Section 95 of IPC is intended to prevent penalisation of negligible wrongs of trivial character because

Reasons (R) ??

I. The injury is negligible.
II. The victim and the wrongdoer were related to each other.
III. The injured and the offender were not related by circumstances.
IV. The nature of injury was very minor.

Codes

1 I is true and IV is the reason while II and III are not true
2 II is true and III is the reason while I and IV are false
3 III is true and IV is the reason while I and II are not true
4 IV is the only reason while all others I, II and III are false

***Ans.* (1)**

Exp. I is true and IV is the reason while II and III are not true.

As per Section 95 of IPC, nothing is an offence by reason that it causes, or that it is intended to cause, or that it is known to be likely to cause, any harm, if that harm is so slight that no person of ordinary sense and temper would complain of such harm.

The rationale behind the provision is that the law would not entertain disputes of little or no importance and no man of ordinary prudence is expected to take legal action on that basis.

The statements II and III are incorrect because the relation of parties to each other is not relevant for the purpose of fixing liability.

44 Fill in the blank.

Deceiving dishonestly by inducing a person to retain the property is known as _____ offence.

1 Concealment
2 Deception by false pretention
3 Cheating
4 Fraud

***Ans.* (3)**

Exp. Deceiving dishonestly by inducing a person to retain the property is known as offence of Cheating.

According to Section 415 in the Indian Penal Code, whoever, by deceiving any person, fraudulently or dishonestly induces the person so deceived to deliver any property to any person or to consent that any person shall retain any property or intentionally induces the person so deceived to do or omit to do anything which he would not do or omit if he were not so deceived and which act or omission causes or is likely to cause damage or harm to that person in body, mind, reputation or property, is said to 'cheat'. The punishment of Cheating is provided in Section 420 of IPC.

45 Which of the following amount to Industrial Dispute?

1 Any dispute between Employers and Employees
2 Between Employers and Workmen
3 Between Workmen and Workmen
4 All of the above

Ans. (4)

Exp. All the stated kinds of dispute i.e. any dispute between Employers and Employees, between Employers and Workmen, between Workmen and Workmen amount to Industrial Dispute.

According to Section 2 of the Industrial Dispute Act, 1947, 'Industrial dispute means any dispute or difference between employers and employees or between employers and workmen or between workmen and workmen, which is connected with the employment or non-employment or the terms of employment or with the conditions of labour of any person'.

Industrial disputes are of symptoms of industrial unrest in the same way that boils are symptoms of a disordered body. Whenever an industrial dispute occurs, both management and workers try to pressurise each other. The management may resort to lock-out and the workers may resort to strike, gherao, picketing, etc.

46 In which of the following case, the Supreme Court held that "the benefit of running allowance had to be taken into consideration for computing pension only once, at the time of retirement of the employee, not for any future calculation"?

1 UOI Vs. Dhingara and others (2008) I LLJ 867(SC)
2 Bennet Coleman and Co Vs. Punya Priyadas AIR 1970 SC 426
3 State Bank of Patiala. Vs phoolpati (2005) II LLJ 473 (SC)
4 Pearlite Lines Pvt. Ltd. Vs Manorama Sirse (2004) I LLJ 1041 (SC)

Ans. (1)

Exp. The given observation was made by Supreme Court in the case titled as UOI Vs. Dhingara and others (2008) I LLJ 867(SC).

In this case, respondents were railway 'running staff' employees such as drivers, guards, etc. They retired prior to January, 1986. Their pension was computed by taking into account 'running allowance' in their average emoluments. Subsequently, their pension was revised as per recommendations of the 5th Pay Commission. Respondents claimed that running allowance should be included as per rule 2544(g) of the Railway Establishment Code for calculating the revised pension.

The Central Administrative Tribunal upheld their claim. Hence, the Union Government preferred an appeal to the Supreme Court. The Supreme Court observed that the benefit of running allowance had to be taken into consideration for computing pension only once, namely at the time of retirement of the employee, it was not required to be taken into account again for future calculation.

47 Which rights remain unaffected, during the pendency of a proceeding before a court of inquiry under Sections 22, 23 and 33 of the ID Act, 1947?

1 Workmen to go on strike
2 The rights of Employer to dismiss or to punish the workmen
3 Employer to lock-out his business
4 All of the above

Ans. (4)

Exp. All the given rights remain unaffected during the pendency of proceedings before a court of inquiry under Sections 22, 23 and 33 of the ID Act, 1947.

Section 22 of the Industrial Disputes Act, 1947 provides that no person employed in a public utility service shall go on strike in breach of contract, without giving to the employer notice of strike, as hereinafter provided, within six weeks before striking; or within fourteen days of giving such notice, or before the expiry of the date of strike specified in any such notice as aforesaid; or during the pendency of any conciliation proceedings before a conciliation officer and seven days after the conclusion of such proceedings. No employer carrying on any public utility service shall lock-out any of his workmen.

In accordance to Section 23, no workman who is employed in any industrial establishment shall go on strike in breach of contract and no employer of any such workman shall declare a lock-out, inter alia, during the pendency of conciliation proceedings before a Board and seven days after the conclusion of such proceedings.

The Section 33 mentions that during the pendency of any conciliation proceeding before a conciliation officer or a Board or of any proceeding before [an arbitrator or] a Labor Court or Tribunal or National Tribunal in respect of an industrial dispute, no employer shall in regard to any matter connected with the dispute, alter, to the prejudice of the workmen concerned in such dispute, the conditions of service applicable to them immediately before the commencement of such proceeding, or for any misconduct connected with the dispute, discharge or punish, whether by dismissal or otherwise, any workmen concerned in such dispute, save with the express permission in writing of the authority before which the proceeding is pending.

48 Read Assertion (A) and Reason (R), using the codes given below select the correct answer.

Assertion (A) Termination of service does not amount to retrenchment.

Reason (R) Amount of loss of retrenchment is more than amount of termination.

Codes

1 (A) and (R) are true and (R) is correct explanation of (A)
2 (A) and (R) are true, but (R) is not correct explanation of (A)
3 (A) is true, but (R) is false
4 (A) is false, but (R) is true

Ans. (3)

Exp. The Assertion is true, but the Reason is false.

Section 2(oo) of the Industrial Disputes Act, 1947 defines retrenchment to mean the termination by the employer of the service of a workman for any reason whatsoever, otherwise than as a punishment inflicted by way of disciplinary action, but does not include voluntary retirement of the workman; or retirement of the workman on reaching the age of superannuation if the contract of employment between the employer and the workman concerned contains a stipulation in that behalf; or termination of the service of the workman as a result of the nonrenewal of the contract of employment between the employer and the workman concerned on its expiry or of such contract being terminated under a stipulation in that behalf contained therein; or termination of the service of a workman on the ground of continued Ill-health. Thus, Assertion is true.

However, it is wrong to say that the amount of loss of retrenchment is more than the amount of termination because the amount may be the same, similar or even dissimilar or different completely. Thus, Reason is false.

49 Read Assertion (A) and Reason (R) and using the codes given below select the correct answer.

Assertion (A) Strike is stoppage of work by a body of persons employed in any service acting in combination.

Reason (R) Combined work is service oriented.

Codes

1 (A) and (R) are true and (R) is correct explanation of (A)
2 (A and (R) are true but (R) is not correct explanation of (A)
3 (A and (R) are false
4 (A) is true, (R) is false

Ans. (4)

Exp. The Assertion is true but the Reason is false.

As per Section 2(q) of the Industrial Disputes Act, 1947, strike means a cessation of work by a body of persons employed in any industry acting in combination or a concerted refusal, or a refusal under a common understanding, of any number of persons who are or have been so employed to continue to work or to accept employment. Thus, Assertion is true.

However, the combined work is not service oriented as in case of strike, there is opposition of work and eventual cessation of it. Thus, Reason is false.

50 Trade unionism to be fully effective demands

1 Union of trade
2 Trade of union
3 Democratic spirit and education
4 Soul-elevating and democratic spirits

Ans. (3)

Exp. Trade unionism to be fully effective demands of democratic spirit and education.

A trade union is an organisation made up of members (a membership-based organisation) and its membership must be made up mainly of workers. Trade unionism is a collection of labourers who voluntarily form an association which have a common aim to protect their rights. Trade unionism fully demands two things: a democratic spirit and education.

Most unions have democratic structures at least for selecting the leader and sometimes these are seen as providing the only democratic aspects of work. However, unions are not everywhere and not every workplace that lacks a union lacks democracy and not every workplace that has a union necessarily has a democratic way to resolve disputes.

However, some unions have historically been more committed to it than others. The Industrial workers of the world pioneered the archetypal workplace democracy model, the Wobbly Shop, in which recallable delegates were elected by workers and other norms of grassroots democracy were applied. This is still used in some organisations, notably and in the software industry.

PAPER III

1 In EP Royappa case which of the Supreme Court Judge propounded the new concept of Equality as "Equality is a dynamic concept with many aspects and dimensions and it cannot be 'crippled, combined and confined' within traditional and doctrinaire limits"?

1 Justice YV Chandrachud
2 Justice PN Bhagawati
3 Justice VR Krishna Iyer
4 Justice OP Chinnapa Reddy

Ans. (2)

Exp. In EP Royappa case, the Supreme Court judge PN Bhagawati propounded the new concept of equality as "Equality is a dynamic concept with many aspects and dimensions and it cannot be 'crippled, combined and confined' within traditional and doctrinaire limits".

PN Bhagwati speaking for the majority in a five-judge bench decision in E.P. Royappa Vs. State of Tamil Nadu (1974), discarded a 'narrow, pedantic or lexicographical' interpretation to the concept of 'equality' embedded in Article 14 of the Constitution (that had hitherto been confined to the test of 'reasonable classification') and held "In fact equality and arbitrariness are sworn enemies; one belongs to the rule of law in a republic while the other, to the whim and caprice of an absolute monarch. Where an act is arbitrary it is implicit in it that it is unequal both according to political logic and constitutional law and is therefore violative of Article 14."

2 The State shall make provisions for securing just and humane conditions of work and for maternity relief is found

1 As a part of the Preamble to the Constitution of India
2 As a Fundamental Right under Article 21 of the Constitution of India
3 As a Directive Principle of the State Policy
4 As a Fundamental Duty of the State

Ans. (3)

Exp. The State shall make provisions for securing just and humane conditions of work and for maternity relief is found as a Directive Principle of the State Policy.

The Directive Principles of State Policy is contained in Part IV of the Constitution of India. Article 42 requires that the State shall make provision for securing just and humane conditions of work and for maternity relief. Since Article 42 specifically speaks of 'just and humane conditions of work' and 'maternity relief', the validity of any service rule and of an executive or administrative action in denying maternity benefit has to be examined on the anvil of Article 42 which, though not enforceable at law, is nevertheless available for determining the legal efficacy of the service rule and of the action complained of.

3 Fundamental duties under Part IVA was inserted in the Constitution by

1 17th Amendment
2 25th Amendment
3 42nd Amendment
4 44th Amendment

Ans. (3)

Exp. Fundamental duties under Part IVA were inserted in the Constitution by 42nd Amendment 1976.

These provisions were added during the Emergency period under Indira Gandhi's government. It provides for 11 duties that are to be abided by every citizen of the country.

4 The powers of the President of India are

1 Supra-Constitutional
2 Beyond the Constitution
3 In accordance with the Parliament of India
4 In accordance with the Constitution of India

Ans. (4)

Exp. The powers of the President of India are in accordance with the Constitution of India.

The President derives its power from Article 53 which vests in him all the executive authority including the Supreme Command of the Armed forces. There are several other provisions in the Constitution which mention specific functions of the President.

Briefly, the President has the power to appoint all important offices including those of the Prime Minister and other Central Ministers, Governors, Judges of the Supreme Court and the High Courts and even Election Commissioners. He even has the authority to appoint commissions with respect to the administration of scheduled areas.

Most importantly, the President is vested with wide powers during Emergency under Article 352 to 360 of the Constitution including suspension of Fundamental Rights. Moreover, every bill comes to him for his assent and can either refuse to give his assent or send it back for reconsideration.

5 Which one of the following has been considered as authority of power?

1 The Constitution of India
2 The President of India
3 The Parliament of India
4 The Supreme Court of India

Ans. (1)

Exp. The Constitution of India has been considered as authority of power.

The Constitution of India is the Supreme Law of India. It lays down the framework defining fundamental political principles, establishes the structure, procedures, powers and duties of government institutions and sets out Fundamental Rights, Directive Principles and the duties of citizens.

6 In which of the following judgements it was held that according to Article 226, Courts are flooded with large number of PIL, so it is desirable for Courts to filter out frivolous petitions and dismiss them with costs?

1 Deepak Sharma Vs. Vineeta Sharma
2 Dharampal Vs. State of Uttar Pradesh
3 Holicow Pictures Pvt. Ltd. Vs. Prem Chandra Mishra
4 MC Mehta Vs. Union of India

Ans. (3)

Exp. The given judgment was made in Holicow Pictures Pvt. Ltd. v. Prem Chandra Mishra (2007).

In this case, the Supreme Court of India held that when there is material in the PIL to show that a petition styled as a PIL is nothing but a camouflage to foster personal disputes, the said petition is to be thrown out.

The Supreme Court held: "Public Interest Litigation which has now come to occupy an important field in the administration of law should not be 'publicity interest litigation' or 'private interest litigation' or 'politics interest litigation' or the latest trend 'paise income litigation'.

If not properly regulated and abuse averted, it becomes also a tool in unscrupulous hands to release vendetta and wreak vengeance, as well as Public Interest Litigation is a weapon which has to be used with great care and circumspection and the judiciary has to be extremely careful to see that behind the beautiful veil of public interest an ugly private malice, vested interest and/or publicity seeking is not lurking."

7 A resolution for the revocation of the proclamation of National Emergency may be moved by

1 Ten members of Lok Sabha
2 One-fifth of the total membership of the Lok Sabha
3 One-tenth of the total membership of the Lok Sabha
4 One-fifteenth of the total membership of the Lok Sabha

Ans. (3)

Exp. A resolution for the revocation of the proclamation of National Emergency may be moved by one-tenth of the total membership of the Lok Sabha.

In terms of Article 352 of the Constitution, the President shall revoke proclamation of emergency any time if Lok Sabha passes a resolution by simple majority in relation to disapproval of continuation of National Emergency. A notice in writing shall be given to the Speaker of Lok Sabha or to the President if house is not in session and that notice shall be signed by at least one-tenth of total members of Lok Sabha, in relation to their intention to move a resolution to revoke National Emergency.

8 Administrative Law deals with

I. Composition, powers and functions of the administrative authorities.
II. Procedures to be followed by the administrative authorities in the exercise of their powers and functions.
III. Methods of control of powers of the administrative authorities.
IV. Remedies available to a person in case of violation of his rights by the administrative authorities.

Codes

1 Only I is correct
2 Only I and II are correct
3 Only I, II and III are correct
4 All of the above are correct

Ans. (4)

Exp. Statement I, II, III and IV all are correct with repect to Administrative Law.

Administrative law is that law which governs the administrative actions. According to Ivor Jennings, Administrative law is the law relating to administration. It determines the organisation, powers and duties of administrative authorities. It includes law relating to the rule-making power of the administrative bodies, the quasi-judicial function of administrative agencies, legal liabilities of public authorities and power of the ordinary courts to supervise administrative authorities. It also governs the executive and ensures that the executive treats the public fairly.

Thus, Administrative law deals with the following:

- structure, powers and functions of organs of administration
- limits of their powers
- methods and procedures followed by them in exercising their powers and functions;
- methods by which their powers are controlled including legal remedies available to person whose rights are infringed by their operation.

9 Read Assertion (A) and Reason (R) and with the help of codes given below select the correct answer.

Assertion (A) One of the principles of natural justice is, 'No man shall be judge in his own cause'.

Reason (R) Principles of natural justice require fair play in action.

Codes

1 (A) and (R) are true and (R) is the correct explanation of (A)
2 (A) and (R) are true, but (R) is not the correct explanation of (A)
3 (A) is true and (R) is false
4 (A) is false and (R) is true

Ans. (1)

Exp. Both (A) and (R) are true and (R) is the correct explanation of (A).

Natural justice is an expression of English common law, which involves a procedural requirement of fairness. The principles of natural justice are those rules which have been laid down by the courts as being minimum protection of the rights of the individual against the arbitrary procedure that may be adopted by a judicial, quasi-judicial and administrative authority while making an order affecting those rights. One of the basic postulates of natural justice involves a fair trial to everyone wherein no man would be condemned unheard. Thus, the Assertion is correct.

The principles of natural justice not only ensures fairness in social and economical activities of the people but also acts as a shield to individuals liberty against arbitrary action. Thus, Reason is also correct.

10 Match List I with List II and indicate the correct answer using the codes given below.

List I	List II
A. AK Kraipak Vs. Union of India	I. Post-decisional hearing
B. Manak Lal Vs. Dr Prem Chand	II. Personal bias
C. Maneka Gandhi Vs. Union of India	III. Pecuniary bias
D. Olga Tellis Vs. Bombay Municipal Corporation	IV. Reasonable opportunity of hearing

Codes

	A	B	C	D		A	B	C	D
1	I	II	III	IV	2	I	III	IV	II
3	II	III	I	IV	4	III	II	IV	I

Ans. (3)

Exp. The correct matching is A-II; B-III; C-I; D-IV.

AK Kraipak Vs. Union of India (1969) is related to Personal bias. The court held that the selections made by the Selection Committee were in violation of the principles of natural justice because there was a real likelihood of a bias for the mere presence of the candidate on the Selection Board may adversely influence the judgement of other members.

Manak Lal Vs Dr Prem Chand (1957) is related to Pecuniary bias. In this case, the view point test according to which the court was to determine whether under a given set of circumstances "there is a reasonable ground for assuming the possibility of a bias" and whether the assumptions "is likely to produce in the minds of the litigant, or the public at large a reasonable doubt about the fairness of the administration of justice.

Maneka Gandhi Vs. Union of India (1978) is related to Post-decisional hearing. Post decisional hearing as per the case Maneka Gandhi Vs. UOI (1978) is a hearing which occurs after a provisional decision is reached. The logic behind introducing the post-decisional hearing is to increase and maintain administrative fairness.

Olga Tellis Vs. Bombay Municipal Corporation (1985) is related to reasonable opportunity of hearing. It was held that the right to a livelihood was not absolute and deprivation of the right to livelihood could occur if there was a just and fair procedure undertaken according to law. The government's action must be reasonable and any person affected must be afforded an opportunity of being heard as to why that action should not be taken.

11 Answer the following using the codes given below

Which of the following doctrines were developed by the Court to control the administrative actions?

I. Doctrine of Promissory Estoppel
II. Doctrine of Legitimate Expectations
III. Doctrine of Separation of Power and Rule of Law
IV. Judicial Activism

Codes

1 I, II and III are correct
2 II and IV are correct
3 I and III are correct
4 All of the above are correct

Ans. (4)

Exp. All the given doctrines i.e., Doctrine of Promissory Estoppel, Doctrine of Legitimate Expectations, Doctrine of Separation of Power and Rule of Law and Judicial Activism were developed by the Court to control the administrative actions.

The Doctrine of Promissory Estoppel is an equitable doctrine. Like all equitable remedies, it is discretionary, in contrast to the common law absolute right like right to damages for breach of contract. The doctrine has been variously called 'promissory estoppel', 'equitable estoppel', 'quasi estoppel' and 'new estoppel'. It is a principle evolved by equity to avoid injustice and though commonly named 'promissory estoppel', it is neither in the realm of contract nor in the realm of estoppel.

The 'Doctrine of Legitimate Expectation' means as expectation of a benefit, relief or remedy that may ordinarily flow from a promise or established practice. Such expectation should not be based on the strength of sporadic, casual on random acts. Also such expectations should not be unreasonable, illogical or invalid.

The Doctrine of the Separation of Powers refers to the division of a democratic state into three institutions or branches of government: the legislature, the executive and the judiciary. The rationale being that each branch acts as a 'check and balance' on the others, with no one branch exercising more power than either of the other two.

The Rule of Law is the principle that no one is above the law. The objective of this principle is that the governmental authority is legitimately exercised only in accordance with written, publicly disclosed laws adopted and enforced by established procedural steps that constitute due process.

Judicial Activism refers to judicial rulings that are suspected to being based on personal opinion, rather than on existing law. It is sometimes used as an antonym of judicial restraint.

12 Answer the following using the codes given below :

In which of the following grounds the judicial review of an administrative action be made?

I. Abuse of discretion
II. Mala fide or Bad faith
III. Irrelevant consideration
IV. Unreasonableness

Codes

1 I, II and III are correct
2 I and II are correct
3 II and III are correct
4 All I, II, III and IV are correct

Ans. (4)

Exp. The judicial review of an administrative action can be made on the basis of Abuse of discretion, Mala fide or Bad faith, Irrelevant consideration and Unreasonableness.

Judicial review is the basic feature of the Indian Constitution and therefore, cannot be abrogated even by an amendment of the Constitution. It is incorporated in Articles 226 and 227 of the Constitution in so far as the High Courts are concerned. In regard to the Supreme Court Articles 32 and 136 of the Constitution embody the principle of judicial review.

13 A writ of mandamus will not lie against

1 President of India
2 Parliament
3 Local Authorities
4 Courts and Tribunals

Ans. (1)

Exp A writ of mandamus will not lie against President of India.

Mandamus is a Latin word, which means 'We Command'. Mandamus is an order from the Supreme Court or High Court to a lower court or tribunal or public authority to perform a public or statutory duty. This writ of command is issued by the Supreme Court or High Court when any government, court, corporation or any public authority has to do a public duty but fails to do so.

Under Article 361, mandamus cannot be granted against the President or Governor of a State, "for the exercise and performance of the powers and duties of his office or for any act done or purporting to be done by him in the exercise and performance of those powers and duties".

The writ also cannot be issued against a private individual or body, except where the State is in collusion with the private party for contravening a provision of the Constitution or a statute.

14 Match List I with List II and indicate the correct answer using the codes given below.

List I	List II
A. Bring the body before the Court	I. Writ of Mandamus
B. Petitioner's legal right to compel the performance of public duty	II. Writ of Certiorari
C. By what authority a person is holding the public post	III. Writ of Habeas Corpus
D. Action of subordinate Court in violation of the principles of natural justice	IV. Writ of Quo Warranto

Codes

	A	B	C	D		A	B	C	D
1	I	II	III	IV	2	III	I	IV	II
3	III	II	I	IV	4	III	IV	II	I

Ans. *(2)*

Exp. The correct matching is A-III; B-I; C-IV; D-II.

Writ of Habeas Corpus means bring the body before the Court. 'Habeas Corpus' literally means "to have a body of".This writ is used to release a person who has been unlawfully detained or imprisoned.

Writ of Mandamus is related to Petitioner's legal right to compel the performance of public duty. 'Mandamus' means 'we command'. It is issued by the Court to direct a public authority to perform the legal duties which it has not or refused to perform.

Through *Writ of Quo Warranto* the Court calls upon a person holding a public office to show under what authority he holds that office.

Writ of Certiorari is related to action of subordinate Court in violation of the principles of natural justice. 'Certiorari' means to 'certify'. Certiorari is a curative writ. When the Court is of the opinion that a lower court or a tribunal has passed an order which is beyond its powers or committed an error of law then, through the writ of certiorari, it may transfer the case to itself or quash the order passed by the lower court or tribunal.

15 Which one of the following States has not yet established the institution of Lokayukta?

1 Uttar Pradesh 2 Karnataka
3 Uttarakhand 4 None of these

Ans. *(4)*

Exp. All the given states have established the institution of Lokayukta.

The Lokpal is the first institution of its kind in independent India,established under the Lokpal and Lokayuktas Act 2013 to inquire and investigate into allegations of corruption against public functionaries who fall within the scope and ambit of the above Act.

Lokpal is an ombudsman appointed to work on citizens complaints and grievances regarding corruption at the central level. On the other hand, at the state level, Lokayukta is set up to take action against the corruption complaints made by the residents of the state.

As of now, Maharashtra was the first state in India to introduce the idea of Lokayukta in 1971. At present, states like Maharashtra, Orissa, Rajasthan, Bihar, UP, Uttarakhand, Karnataka, Madhya Pradesh, Andhra Pradesh, Gujarat, Kerala, Meghalaya, and Assam have a Lokayukta.

16 "A legal person is any subject matter other than a human being to which law attributes personality." Who said these words?

1 Savigny 2 Bentham
3 Austin 4 Salmond

Ans. *(4)*

Exp. Salmond said that "a legal person is any subject matter other than a human being to which law attributes personality".

A person can be defined as an entity recognised by the law as separate and independent, with legal rights and existence including the ability to sue and be sued, to sign contracts, to receive gifts, to appear in court either by themselves or by lawyer and generally, other powers incidental to the full expression of the entity in law.

Salmond observes that a person is any being whom the law regards capable of rights and duties. Any being that is so capable is a person whether a human being or not. So by this way we can distinguishes persons into two : natural and legal persons.

A natural person is a being to whom the law attributes the personality in accordance with reality and truth.

Legal persons are beings to whom the attributes personality by way of fiction, when there is none in fact.

17 "Pure theory of Law is an exercise in logic and not life." This observation was made by

1 Pound
2 Savigny
3 Maine
4 Harold Laski

Ans. *(4)*

Exp. Harold Laski said that "Pure theory of Law is an exercise in logic and not life."

Laski analyses the legal theory of state. The central theme of the legal theory of rights is that claim rights if those are not recognised by the state. Mere recognition, moreover, is not sufficient for the exercise of rights. The state must, through law and institutions, implement the rights.

If these two conditions, the legal theory asserts, are not fulfilled the individuals will have hardly any opportunity to enjoy rights. This legal theory of rights was propounded by many chief among them are Hobbes and Bentham. Legal theory further states that the law, in fact, determines the character and implementation of rights.

Prof. Laski said that the legal theory is attractive. Various institutions, along with the individuals themselves, always take active interest in the matters of rights. But though attractive, this theory, according to Laski, is highly questionable.

18 "Law is derived from social facts and not dependent on State authority but on social compulsion." Who said this?

1 Putchta
2 Ehrlich
3 Friedman
4 Pound

Ans. (2)

Exp. Ehrlich said that "Law is derived from social facts and not dependent on State authority but on social compulsion."

Ehrlich's experience of Bukovina's legal culture, where Austrian law and sharply contrasting local custom seemed to co-exist, caused him to question the hierarchical notions of law propounded by such theorists as Hans Kelsen. Ehrlich noted that legal theories that recognised law only as a sum of statutes and judgements gave an inadequate view of the legal reality of a community.

19 Which one of the following pairs is not correctly matched?

1 Sie utere tero out alierum non laedas – To use your own property as not to injure your neighbour's right
2 Re Legitima Portis–A person cannot dispose of his entire property
3 Jus turti–To set up title of a third person other than himself or the plaintiff
4 Nec vi nec calur precario-Possession must show to the competitor

Ans. (4)

Exp. Among the given choices, option (4) is incorrectly matched.

In Roman law, possession was termed as a 'Possessio'. The term 'possessio' denoted physical control over things. In legal terminology, there is no word more ambiguous in its meaning than possession whether considered in relation to immovable property. In law, possession means a fact or condition of a person having such control of property that he may legally enjoy it to the exclusion of others except against the true owner or prior possessor.

A person having a possession over a property is deemed to be rightfully using it and he himself need not prove his rights relating to the property.

20 Read each of the following two statements Assertion (A) and Reason (R) and indicate your answer using the codes given below

Assertion (A) In India the distinction between legal and equitable ownership is not recognised.

Reason (R) The trustees are, subject to the law relating to trust and trustees, bound to carry out the trust according to the dictates of the maker of the trust.

Codes

1 Both (A) and (R) are true and (R) is the correct explanation of (A)
2 Both (A) and (R) are true, but (R) is not the correct explanation of (A)
3 (A) is true, but (R) is false
4 (A) is false, but (R) is true

Ans. (2)

Exp. Both (A) and (R) are true, but (R) is not the correct explanation of (A).

Legal ownership is that which has its origin in the rules of common law and equitable ownership is that which proceeds from the rules of equity. In many cases, equity recognises ownership where law does not recognise ownership owing to some legal defect. Legal rights may be enforced in rem but equitable rights are enforced in personam as equity acts in personam. One person may be the legal owner and another person the equitable owner of the same thing or right at the same time. The equitable ownership of a legal right is different from the ownership of an equitable right. The ownership of an equitable mortgage is different from the equitable ownership of a legal mortgage. There is no distinction between legal and equitable estates in India. Thus, Assertion is correct.

Under the Indian Trusts Act, a trustee is the legal owner of the trust property and the beneficiary has no direct interest in the trust property itself. However, he has a right against the trustees to compel them to carry out the provisions of the trust. Thus, Reason is correct but it is not the correct explanation of A.

21 The purpose theory is based on the assumption that "person is applicable only to human beings; they alone can be the subjects of rural relations".
Who developed this theory of Brinz in England?

1 Barker
2 Duguit
3 Salmond
4 Hoffman

Ans. (1)

Exp. Barker developed the theory of Brinz in England.

According to the purpose theory, one of the theories related to corporate personality, law protects certain purposes and the interest of individual beings.

The property supposed to be owned by juristic persons does not belong to anything; but it does belong for a purpose and that is the essential fact about it.

All juristic or artificial persons are merely legal devices for protecting or giving effect to some real purpose, e.g., a trade union is the continuing fund concerned and the purposes for which it is established.

The theory was originally propounded by German Jurist Brinz, and was developed further by Barker in England.

22 "Ownership in its comprehensive signification, denotes the relation between a person and any right that is vested in him. That which a man owns in this sense is in all cases a right."

Who is the exponent of this theory?

1 Miss Tay 2 Maitland
3 Salmond 4 Fuller

Ans. (3)

Exp. Salmond is the exponent of given theory.

According to Salmond, Ownership in wide sense extends to all classes or rights, whether proprietary or personal in rem or in personam, in re propria, or in re aliena; and it applies not only to rights in the strict sense, but to liberties power and immunities of rights, whether proprietary or personal, in rem or in personam, in re-propria or in re-aliena; He adds that it applies not only to rights in the strict sense but also to liberties, powers and immunities.

Salmond is of the view that the real subject matter of ownership is rights. This particular view of Salmond is supported by the common law system.

Thus, according to Salmond ownership vests in the owner a complex of rights which he/she exercises to the exclusion of all others.

23 "Legal rights are institutional rights to decisions in Courts. Institutions about justice pre-suppose a fundamental right, namely, the right to equality, which I call the right to equal concern and respect." Who propounded this theory in relation to natural rights?

1 Dworkin 2 Fuller
3 Jerome Hall 4 Professor Hart

Ans. (1)

Exp. Dworkin propounded the given theory in relation to natural rights.

Dworkin argues that, law as integrity offers a blueprint for adjudicator which directs judges to decide cases by using the same methodology from which integrity was derived viz, constructive interpretation.

24 Fill in the gap that is most appropriate. Who ever entices a girl child of less than 16 years has said to have caused kidnapping out of the keeping of the lawful

1 Parents 2 Foster parents
3 Adopted parents 4 Guardians

Ans. (4)

Exp. Who ever entices a girl child of less than 16 years has said to have caused kidnapping out of the keeping of the lawful guardians.

In the words of Section 361 of IPC, whoever takes or entices any minor under sixteen years of age if a male, or under eighteen years of age if a female, or any person of unsound mind, out of the keeping of the lawful guardian of such minor or person of unsound mind, without the consent of such guardian, is said to kidnap such minor or person from lawful guardianship.

The words "lawful guardian" in this section include any person lawfully entrusted with the care or custody of such minor or other person.

25 Fill in the gap with the offence that the accused has committed. Whoever dishonestly uses any moveable property to his own advantage has committed the offence of ________ .

1 Breach of trust 2 Wrongful gain
3 Misappropriation 4 None of these

Ans. (3)

Exp. Whoever dishonestly uses any moveable property to his own advantage has committed the offence of Misappropriation.

As per Section 403 in the Indian Penal Code, whoever dishonestly mis-appropriates or converts to his own use any movable property, shall be punished with imprisonment of either description for a term which may extend to two years or with fine or with both.

A dishonest misappropriation for a time only is a misappropriation with the meaning of this section. A person who finds property not in the possession of any other person, and takes such property for the purpose of protecting if for, or of restoring it to, the owner does not take or misappropriate it dishonestly, and is not guilty of an offence; but he is guilty of the offence above defined, if he appropriates it to his own use, when he knows or has the means of discovering the owner, or before he has used reasonable means to discover and give notice to the owner and has kept the property a reasonable time to enable the owner to claim it.

26 Read Assertion (A) and Reason (R) and with the help of codes given below point out the correct explanation.

Assertion (A) Moral derangement is a state of will and turns to be the vehicle of vicious actions.

Reason (R) Crime is committed under the influence of instructive and irresistible impulse.

Codes

1 Moral insanity or imbecility are not exempted from criminal liability as per Section 53 of IPC
2 Both (A) and (R) are correct statements to attract criminal liability as per Section 53 IPC as both are diabolical criminal conduct

3 Only by (R) criminal responsibility can be fixed but not with the help of (A)
4 McNaghten's Rule can be applied in (A) but not in (R)

Ans. (2)

Exp. Both (A) and (R) are correct statements to attract criminal liability as per Section 53 IPC as both are diabolical criminal conduct.

The insanity defence is cognitive and focuses on the defendant's awareness, rather than the ability to control conduct. The defence requires two elements. First, the defendant must be suffering from a mental defect at the time he or she commits the criminal act. The mental defect can be called as "defect of reason" or "disease of the mind," depending on the jurisdiction. Second, the trier of fact must find that because of the mental defect, the defendant did not know either the nature and quality of the criminal act or that the act was wrong. The terms "defect of reason" and "disease of the mind" can be defined in different ways, but in general, the defendant must be cognitively impaired to the level of not knowing the nature and quality of the criminal act, or that the act is wrong. Some common examples of mental defects and diseases are psychosis, schizophrenia, and paranoia.

Section 53 in the Indian Penal Code mentions various punishments that can be imposed on the wrongdoer. The punishments to which offenders are liable under the provisions of this code are Death, Imprisonment for life; Imprisonment, Forfeiture of property and Fine.

27 Read Assertion (A) and Reason (R) and with the help of given codes point out the correct explanation.

Assertion (A) Consent of husband or wife of the victim does not grant immunity from the offence of bigamy.

Reason (R) Sexual offence with the consent of one spouse does not fix liability for adultery.

Codes

1 (A) is correct, but not with the (R)
2 (A) is correct, but with the support of (R)
3 (R) is only the correct proposition while (A) is void
4 (R) is valid when (A) is not admissible

Ans. (1)

Exp. The Assertion is correct, but not with the Reason.

Section 494 of the IPC provides about "Bigamy" as thus "Whoever, having a husband or wife living, marries again in any case in which such marriage is void by reason of its taking place during the life of such husband or wife shall be punished with imprisonment of either description for a term which may extend to seven years, and shall also be liable to fine". Thus, the consent of the wife is not relevant and the offence could still be made out provided the other conditions are met.

Adultery is not a crime anymore, it remains a ground of divorce and in that sense, it does impose liability upon the party performing adultery, as it was decriminalised in Joseph Shine v. UOI (2018).

28 Read Assertion (A) and Reason (R) and with the help of codes given below point out the correct explanation.

Assertion (A) To establish a charge of conspiracy, knowledge about indulgence in an illegal act by certain legal means, is necessary.

Reason (R) The normal rule is that when a particular unlawful use being intended has to be inferred from the chain of actions.

Codes

1 (A) is the judicious cause of conspiracy, because (R) is the correct explanation.
2 (R) is more appropriate explanation than merely fixing charge as per (A).
3 (A) is the correct proposition as (R) is optional.
4 (A) is not correct because as per (R) there must be pre-meditation.

Ans. (1)

Exp. (A) is the judicious cause of conspiracy, because (R) is the correct explanation.

In Kehar Singh and Ors. Vs. The State (Delhi Administration), the Supreme Court observed that generally, a conspiracy is hatched in secrecy and it may be difficult to adduce direct evidence of the same. The prosecution will often rely on evidence of acts of various parties to infer that they were done in reference to their common intention. The prosecution will also more often rely upon circumstantial evidence.

The conspiracy can be undoubtedly proved by such evidence direct or circumstantial. Finally, when the ultimate offence consists of a chain of actions, it would not be necessary for the prosecution to establish, to bring home the charge of conspiracy, that each of the conspirators had the knowledge of what the collaborator would do so, so long as it is known that the collaborator would put the goods or service to an unlawful use.

29 Read Assertion (A) and Reason (R) and with the help of codes given below point out the correct explanation.

Assertion (A) Publishing a report of proceedings of a Court will not amount to defamation.

Reason (R) It is an exception to the principle of defamation.

Codes

1 (A) is true, because (R) is the specific objective
2 (A) is true, but (R) is not the correct proposition
3 (R) is always true, because (A) is not dependent
4 (R) is false, because (A) is always independent of criminal liability

Ans. (1)

Exp. The Assertion is true, because Reason is the specific objective.

As per Section 499 of IPC, whoever, by words either spoken or intended to be read, or by signs or by visible representations, makes or publishes any imputation concerning any person intending to harm, or knowing or having reason to believe that such imputation will harm, the reputation of such person, is said, except in the cases herein after expected, to defame that person.

According to the fourth Exception to this provision, it is not defamation to publish a substantially true report of the proceedings of a Court of Justice, or of the result of any such proceedings. A Justice of the Peace or other officer holding an inquiry in open Court preliminary to a trial in a Court of Justice, is a Court within the meaning of the above section. Thus, R is the specific objective for A.

30 Read Assertion (A) and Reason (R) and with the help of codes given below point out the correct explanation.

Assertion (A) Independently putting a person in fear of injury to another is extortion.

Reason (R) It is an exception to the rule of delivering the valuable security.

Codes

1 (A) is true, but (R) is not the correct statement
2 (A) is true, because (R) is the correct proposition
3 Both (A) and (R) are independent of proof
4 Both (A) and (R) are false

Ans. (2)

Exp. The Assertion is true, because Reason is the correct proposition.

Section 383 of IPC defines Extortion as; whoever intentionally puts any person in fear of any injury to that person, or to any other, and thereby dishonestly induces the person so put in fear to deliver to any person any property or valuable security, or anything signed or sealed which may be converted into a valuable security, commits extortion. Thus, it independently puts a person in fear of any injury.

The objective behind it is to create an exception to the rule of delivering valuable security by intentionally putting another person in fear.

31 Read Assertion (A) and Reason (R) and with the help of codes given below find out the correct explanation.

Assertion (A) Disorder of mind which impairs the mental faculties is known as unsoundness of mind as such it acts as defence to a criminal charge.

Reason (R) Insanity is the mental abnormality and when it impairs the cognitive faculty and if an act results during that period criminal liability could be exempted.

Codes

1 By (A) there is transgression of harmful acts while (R) refers to established rules of society for which no prosecution stands
2 Both (A) and (R) are correct explanations as per Section 84 of IPC
3 (R) is more precise while (A) is only a supportive factor
4 The true test of (A) and (R) is to apply Mc Naghten's Rule

Ans. (2)

Exp. Both (A) and (R) are correct explanations as per Section 84 of IPC.

Section 84 in the Indian Penal Code deals with Insanity as a defence and states that act of a person of unsound mind, nothing is an offence which is done by a person who, at the time of doing it, by reason of unsoundness of mind, is incapable of knowing the nature of the act or that he is doing what is either wrong or contrary to law.

Insanity defence is primarily used in criminal prosecutions. It is based on the assumption that at the time of the crime, the defendant was suffering from severe mental illness and therefore, was incapable of appreciating the nature of the crime and differentiating right from wrong behaviour, hence making them not legally accountable for crime. Insanity defence is a legal concept, not a clinical one (medical one). This means that just suffering from a mental disorder is not sufficient to prove insanity. The defendant has the burden of proving the defense of insanity by a "preponderance of the evidence" which is similar to a civil case.

32 The Air prevention and Control of Pollution Act, 1981 and the Environment (Protection) Act, 1986, were passed by the Parliament under

1 Article 252 of the Constitution of India
2 Article 253 of the Constitution of India
3 Article 250 of the Constitution of India
4 None of the above

Ans. (2)

Exp. The Air prevention and Control of Pollution Act, 1981 and the Environment (Protection) Act, 1986, were passed by the Parliament under were passed by Parliament under Article 253 of the Constitution of India.

The Air Act (Prevention and control of Pollution) Act, 1981 is a law passed by the Parliament of India in the 32nd Year of the Republic of India. This law i.e the Air Act was passed to control and prevent the harmful effects caused by air pollution. The objective of this act is to prevent, control, and abate air pollution.

The Environment Protection Act is umbrella legislation enacted to provide for theCentral Government coordination over the central and State authorities established inter-alia under the water Act, 1974 and the Air Act, 1981.

33 Which of the following Judges of the Supreme Court is famously known as the "Green Judge"?

1 Justice VR Krishna Iyer 2 Justice PN Bhagwati
3 Justice Kuldeep Singh 4 Justice BN Kirpal

Ans. (3)

Exp. Justice Kuldeep Singh of the Supreme Court is famously known as the "Green Judge".

Kuldeep Singh (born 1st January, 1932) is an Indian attorney and former member of the Supreme Court of India.

Following his retirement from the court, he headed the 2002-2008 National Delimitation Commission that redistricted all of India after the 2001 Census. Singh received his education from Col. Brown Cambridge School, followed by his first law degree from Punjab University in 1955 and a second one from the University of London in 1958. He served as a barrister-at-law at Lincoln's Inn in London before returning to India in 1959. Singh was appointed to the Supreme Court on 14th December 1988 and retired on 21st December, 1996.

Justice Kuldeep Singh came to be known as the "green judge" after he decided a number of PILs on environmental issues. Till his retirement from the Supreme Court in 1996, he passed crucial judgments on air pollution, including specifying norms for industries around the Taj Mahal.

34 Which of the following Articles of the Constitution of India have been mostly used by the Supreme Court to protect environment?

1 Article 32
2 Article 21
3 Both Article 21 and 32
4 None of the above

Ans. *(3)*

Exp. Both Articles 21 and 32 of the Constitution of India have been mostly used by the Supreme Court to protect environment.

Article 21 of the Constitution of India provides for the right to life and personal liberty. It states that "no person shall be deprived of his life or personal liberty except according to procedure established by law.

"In Rural Litigation and Entitlement Kendra Vs State of UP, also known as the Dehradun quarrying case, the Supreme Court of India has held that pollution caused by quarries adversely affects the health and safety of people and hence, the same should be stopped as being violative of Article 21. In this case, the Supreme Court for the first time held that the right to wholesome environment is a part of right to life and personal liberty guaranteed under Article 21 of the Constitution.

Further, in the case of Subhash Kumar Vs. State of Bihar, again the apex court held that the right to get pollution free water and air is a fundamental right under Article 21. Following this decision, the right to pollution free environment was incorporated under the head of right to life and all the law courts within the Indian territory were bound to follow the same. This laid down the foundation of environmental litigation in India.

Article 32 in the Constitution of India, 1949 provides Remedies for enforcement of rights which are as follows; the right to move the Supreme Court by appropriate proceedings for the enforcement of the rights conferred by this Part is guaranteed. The Supreme Court shall have power to issue directions or orders or writs, including writs in the nature of habeas corpus, mandamus, prohibition, quo warranto and certiorari, whichever may be appropriate, for the enforcement of any of the rights conferred by this Part. Therefore, Article 32 has significantly contributed to the evolution of environmental protection laws and decisions.

35 What is the period of notice required to be served upon the Central Government for filing a criminal complaint by any person, under the provisions of Environment (Protection) Act, 1986?

1 Not less than 30 days 2 Not less than 60 days
3 Not less than 90 days 4 None of these

Ans. *(2)*

Exp. The period of notice required is less than 60 days to be served upon the Central Government for filing a criminal complaint by any person, under the provisions of Environment (Protection) Act, 1986.

According to Section 19 of the Act, no court shall take cognizance of any offence under this Act except on a complaint made by the Central Government or any authority or officer authorised in this behalf by that Government; or any person who has given notice of not less than sixty days, in the manner prescribed, of the alleged offence and of his intention to make a complaint, to the Central Government or the authority or officer authorised as aforesaid.

36 Which one of the following cases is considered as 'High Water-mark case in Forest Protection' decided by the Supreme Court?

1 Salebhai Mulla Mohmadali Vs. State of Gujarat
2 TN Godavarman Thirumulkpad Vs. Union of India
3 Narmada Bachao Andolan Vs. Union of India
4 Samatha Vs. State of Andhra Pradesh

Ans. *(2)*

Exp. The case titled as TN Godavarman Thirumulkpad Vs. Union of India (1995) is considered as 'High Water-mark case in Forest Protection' decided by the Supreme Court.

At the centre of the controversy was a very large project of the Uttar Pradesh government at Noida. According to the petitioners, the project is a 'huge unauthorised construction'. The applicants state that a very large number of trees were cut down for clearing the ground for the project. These trees formed a 'forest' as the term was construed by this Court in its order dated 12th December, 1996 in TN Godavarman Thirumulkpad Vs. Union of India and the action of the Uttar Pradesh Government in cutting down a veritable forest without the prior permission of the Central Government and this Court, was in gross violation of Section 2(ii) of the Forest (Conservation) Act, 1980.

The Central Empowered Committee (CEC) on a consideration of all the materials made available to it, including the report of the FSI held that the project site was not a forest or a deemed forest or a forest-like area in terms of the order of SC, mainly because the trees in the project area that were cut down for making space for the constructions were planted trees and not naturally grown trees and because the area was neither notified as 'forest' nor recorded as 'forest' in the government record.

37 The Parliament enacted the Water (Prevention and Control of Pollution) Act, 1974 for the control of water pollution

1 On the request from States
2 Of his own
3 On the direction of United Nations
4 On the direction of Supreme Court

Ans. (1)

Exp. The Parliament enacted the Water (Prevention and Control of Pollution) Act, 1974 for the control of water pollution on the request from States.

The Water Act, 1974 with certain amendments in 1978 is an extensive legislation with more than sixty sections for the prevention and control of water pollution. Among other things, the Act provides for Constitution of Central and State Boards for preventing water pollution, power to take water samples and their analysis, discharge of sewage or trade effluents, appeals, revision, minimum and maximum penalties, publication of names of offenders, offences by companies and government departments, cognisance of offences, water laboratories, analysis etc. The Parliament enacted the act on the request from states for the control of water pollution.

Prevention and control of water pollution is achieved through a permit or 'consent administration' procedure. Discharge of effluents is permitted by obtaining the consent of the State Water Board, subject to any condition they specify. Any person who fails to comply with a directive of the State cannot, however, entertain in suit under this Act unless the suit is brought by or with the sanction of the State Board.

38 Under which of the following Article of the Constitution of India, the provisions regarding duty of the State "to protect and improvement of environment and safeguard the forest and wildlife", exist?

1 Article 51(g)
2 Article 47
3 Article 48 (A)
4 None of these

Ans. (3)

Exp. The given provisions exist under Article 48-(A) of the Constitution of India.

Article 48(A) in the Constitution of India 1949 deals with Protection and improvement of environment and safeguarding of forests and wildlife. The State shall endeavour to protect and improve the environment and to safeguard the forests and wildlife of the country.

In M.C. Mehta Vs. Union of India (2002), the Supreme Court heard a public interest litigation in the matter of air pollution in Delhi. The Court made the following observations regarding Article 48A and public health: Articles 39, 47 and 48 A by themselves and collectively cast a duty on the State to secure the health of the people, improve public health and protect and improve the environment.

In Sachidanand Pandey and Ors. Vs. The State of West Bengal and Ors. (1987), the Supreme Court held that Article 48 A must be kept in mind whenever a matter regarding maintenance of the ecology is brought before the Court.

39 Read Assertion (A) and Reason (R) and with the help of codes given below write the correct answer.

Assertion (A) Under International law extradition is mostly a matter of bilateral treaties.

Reason (R) There is no general duty of States in respect of extradition of criminals.

Codes

1 Both (A) and (R) are individually true and (R) is the correct explanation of (A)
2 Both (A) and (R) are individually true, but (R) is not the correct explanation of (A)
3 (A) is true, but (R) is false
4 (A) is false, but (R) is true

Ans. (1)

Exp. Both (A) and (R) are individually true, and (R) is the correct explanation of (A).

Between countries, extradition is normally regulated by treaties. Where extradition is compelled by laws, such as among sub-national jurisdictions, the concept may be known more generally as rendition. Thus, A is correct.

However, historically, there was no general duty to extradite. Extradition was often based on informal relations between leaders of sovereign States. Thus, R is correct.

40 Which of the following case does not concern with the judgement that a non-recognised State cannot sue in the courts of the State which was not recognised?

1 Russian Socialist Federated Soviet Republic Vs. Cibraria
2 Guarantee Trust Company of New York Vs. United States
3 US Vs. Pink
4 Bank of Ethiopia Vs. National Bank of Egypt and Liquori

Ans. (4)

Exp. The case titled as Bank of Ethiopia Vs. National Bank of Egypt and Liquori (1937) does not concern with the judgement that a non-recognised State cannot sue in the courts of the State which was not recognised.

In this case, it was held that to be a de facto government that government must have effective control over the territory.

The facts of the case are as follows; an Italian decree promulgated after the capture of Addis Ababa in 1936 purported to dissolve the Bank of Ethiopia. That Bank claimed certain accounts and orders against the National Bank of Egypt and against the liquidator appointed under the Italian decree.

The issues were whether the Bank of Ethiopia had been dissolved or had otherwise ceased to exist and if not, whether it had authorised the bringing of the action

In the decision, it was held that, the Bank of Ethiopia had been dissolved by the Italian decree it had the authority to bring such action.

The reasoning provided was the Government of Italy was a de facto government in entire control of the territory occupied and therefore having complete governmental control over that territory.

41 Match List I with List II and select the correct answer.

List I (Name of the Case)	List II (Principle Propounded)
A. The Caroline case	I. Self-Defence
B. The Nottebohm case	II. Effective Nationality
C. Re Castioni case	III. Non-Extradition of Political Criminals
D. US Vs Rauscher	IV. Rule of Speciality

Codes

	A	B	C	D
1	I	II	III	IV
2	IV	III	II	I
3	III	IV	I	II
4	II	I	IV	III

Ans. (1)

Exp. The correct matching is A-I; B-II; C-III; D-IV.

Caroline Case is related to Self Defence. This case sets out a customary international law definition of the right to self-defence. It originates from a dispute between the British Government and the US Secretary of State regarding the destruction of an American vessel in an American port by British subjects. The reason behind this act was the use of the vessel to transport munitions and groups of Americans, who were conducting attacks on the Canadian territory.

The Nottebohm Case is related to Effective nationality. In international law, the issue of "effective nationality" was famously considered by the International Court of Justice in the Nottebohm case (Liechtenstein Vs. Guatemala) (1955). The Court considered whether Liechtenstein would espouse the case of Mr. Nottebohm, a national of both Liechtenstein and Germany, against Guatemala.

Re Castioni case is related to non-extradition of political criminals. It was the first English case requiring judicial interpretation of the phrase "offence of a political character". The conduct in question must be committed with "reference to the object and intention of [the rising]",as or, phrased differently, the actor must be politically motivated.

US Vs Rauscher is related to Rule of Speciality. As originally formulated by the Supreme Court in 1886 in United States Vs. Rauscher, the doctrine of specialty limits the court's jurisdiction over the defendant, allowing the court to enter judgment only on charges encompassed by the extradition treaty and included in the foreign government's extradition decree.

42 Match List I with List II and select the correct answer.

List I	List II
A. Australia and Prussia exercised joint sovereignty over	I. New Helarides
B. Great Britain and France exercised joint sovereignty over	II. Schleswig Holstein Anenburg
C. Great Britain exercised sovereignty over	III. Germany
D. In 1898 China leased the district of Kiaochow to	IV. Turkish Island

Codes

	A	B	C	D
1	II	I	IV	III
2	I	II	III	IV
3	IV	III	II	I
4	III	IV	I	II

Ans. (1)

Exp. The correct matching is A-II; B-I; C-IV; D-III.

Australia and Prussia exercised joint sovereignty over *Schleswig Holstein Anenberg*. Schleswig-Holstein question, 19th-century controversy between Denmark, Prussia, and Austria over the status of Schleswig and Holstein. At this time the population of Schleswig was Danish in its northern portion, German in the south, and mixed in the northern towns and centre. In an agreement with Prussia under the 1852 protocol, the Danish government in return undertook not to tie Schleswig more closely to Denmark than to its sister duchy of Holstein.

Great Britain and France exercised joint sovereignty over *New Hilarides*. The New Hilarides were officially discovered by the Spanish explorer Pedro Fernandes de Quiros in 1606. Three centuries after de Quiros discovered the islands, by the Convention of October 20, 1906, the United Kingdom and France established a condominium to administer the New Hebrides. The islands were governed as a condominium for seventy-four years.

Great Britain exercised sovereignty over *Turkish islands*. To achieve this, Britain insisted on retaining sovereign bases in Cyprus and safeguarding the rights of both Turkish and Greek Cypriots. Besides, Britain maintained that she should have the right to intervene along with Turkey and Greece, if there was an attempt to alter the agreed state of affairs.

In 1898 China leased the district of Kiaochow to *Germany.* German colonial ambitions eventually extended to East Asia. After occupying Kiaochow Bay, the German Reich concluded an "unequal treaty" with China.

43 Which of the following statements is correct?

A de-facto government is government

1 whose origin and existence is contrary to the Constitutional law of the State concerned and legality is challenged in International law

2 whose origin and existence is in conformity with the Constitutional law of the State represented and whose legality is uncontested in International law
3 which exercise control over a Foreign State
4 which has been forced to leave the territory of its State due to enemy occupation or civil war

***Ans.** (1)*

Exp. A de-facto government is government whose origin and existence is contrary to the Constitutional law of the State concerned and legality is challenged in International law. e.g. a government that has been overthrown and has moved to another state will attain de jure status if other nations refuse to accept the legitimacy of the revolutionary government.

A de-jure government is the legal, legitimate government of a state and is so recognised by other states. In contrast, a de facto government is in actual possession of authority and control of the state.

44 Under which of the following Article of the UN Charter there is an obligation to inform the Security Council if the regional arrangements take any enforcement action for maintenance of peace and security?

1 Article 51 2 Article 54
3 Article 107 4 Article 108

***Ans.** (2)*

Exp. Under Article 54 of the UN Charter there is an obligation to inform the Security Council if the regional arrangements take any enforcement action for maintenance of peace and security.

In the words of Article 54, the Security Council shall at all times be kept fully informed of activities undertaken or in contemplation under regional arrangements or by regional agencies for the maintenance of international peace and security.

45 In which one of the following cases the permanent court of International justice held, "it is a generally acceptable principle of international law that in relations, between powers, who are contracting parties to a treaty, the provisions of the municipal law cannot prevail over the treaty"?

1 Navlilaa Incident Case
2 Greco, Bulgarian Communities Case
3 Panevezys Saldutiskis Railway Case
4 Polish Postal Service Case

***Ans.** (2)*

Exp. The given observation was made in Greco, Bulgarian Communities Case (1930).

In this case, Greece and Bulgaria appeared before the Court. In an Advisory Opinion, the Permanent Court first clarified the concepts, holding that "a community is a group of persons living in a given country or locality having a race, religion, language and tradition of their own and united by this identity of race, religion, language and tradition in a sentiment of solidarity, with a view to preserving their traditions, maintaining their form of worship, ensuring the instruction and upbringing of their children in accordance with the spirit and tradition of their race and rendering mutual assistance to each other." Moreover, the Court held, contrary to the view of the two governments, that the dividing up of the immovable property of the communities was a privilege reserved to the members of such communities and should not be turned over to the respective governments.

46 The wife's sister's daughter's son can be adopted. The adoption is

1 void 2 valid
3 voidable 4 None of these

***Ans.** (2)*

Exp. The wife's sister's daughter's son can be adopted. The adoption is valid.

As per Section 7 of the Hindu Adoptions and Maintenance Act, 1956, any male Hindu who is of sound mind and is not a minor has the capacity to take "a son or a daughter in adoption: provided that, if he has a wife living, he shall not adopt except with the consent of his wife unless the wife has completely and finally renounced the world or has ceased to be a Hindu or has been declared by a court of competent jurisdiction to be of unsound mind."

In the case of Abhiraj Kuer Vs. Debendra Singh (1961), it was held that the adoption of a wife's sister's daughter's son is valid in law. The court said that assuming for the present that it is no longer open to challenge the correctness of this rule at least so far as the Banaras School is concerned, we are still of the opinion that this argument is of no avail, for the simple reason that we see no reason to think that there can be no legally valid marriage between a person and his wife's mister's daughter.

47 Kritrima Adoption is prevalent in which areas of India?

1 Madras 2 Banaras 3 Avadh 4 Mithila

***Ans.** (4)*

Exp. Kritrima Adoption is prevalent in the areas of Mithila of India.

In the ancient time, Hindu law mainly recognised five kinds of adopted son, but they were reduced only to two namely, the Dattaka and the Kritrima. The Dattaka form is prevalent throughout India whereas the Kritrima form is used in Mithila and the adjoining states.

The Dattaka Mimansa and Dattaka Chandrika are two treaties on adoption in early laws, which have come to be regarded as authority where they differed with each other the latter was accepted as an authority in Bengal and Madras, while the former was respected in other schools.

48 In which case the Supreme Court held that "Cohabitation leads to presumption that person are living as husband and wife"?

1 Balasubramanyam Vs. Suruttayan AIR 1992 SC 756
2 Seema Vs. Ashwin Kumar AIR 2006 SC 1158
3 Vishnu Prakash Vs. Sheela Devi (2001) 4 SCC 729
4 None of the above

Ans. (1)

Exp. In the case of Balasubramanyam Vs. Suruttayan AIR 1992 SC756, the Supreme Court held that "Cohabitation leads to presumption that person are living as husband and wife."

The first time when the Supreme Court held the legitimacy of children born out of live-in relationship was in S.P.S. Balasubramanyam Vs. Suruttayan, the Supreme Court had said, "If a man and woman are living under the same roof and cohabiting for some years, there will be a presumption under Section 114 of the Evidence Act that they live as husband and wife and the children born to them will not be illegitimate."

Further, the court interpreted the status and legislation to an extent that it shows conformity from Article 39(f) of the Constitution of India which sets out the obligation of the State to give the children adequate opportunity so that they develop in proper manner and further safeguard their interest.

49 In which of the case, the Supreme Court held that it is desirable that "all marriages should be compulsorily registered in the state, where they are solemnised"?

1 S Nagalingam Vs. Sivagani AIR (2001) SC 3576
2 Shanti Dev Berma Vs KP Devi AIR (1991) SC 816
3 Seema Vs Ashwin Kumar AIR 2006 SC 1158
4 None of the above

Ans. (3)

Exp. In case of Seema Vs. Ashwin Kumar (2006), the Supreme Court held that it is desirable that "all marriages should be compulsorily registered in the state, where they are solemnised."

The Supreme Court, in this case, had directed the states and the Centre that marriages of all persons who are citizens of India belonging to various religious denominations should be made compulsorily Legislation aimed at protecting women registerable. It had also said when the Centre enacts a comprehensive statute, it should be placed before the court for scrutiny.

50 Rules relating to prohibited degrees are based on the principle of

1 Monogamy
2 Polygamy
3 Exogamy
4 Endogamy

Ans. (3)

Exp. Rules relating to prohibited degrees are based on the principle of Exogamy.

Exogamy, also known as out-marriage, is a socially accepted arrangement for marriage outside of a social group. Exogamy is usually associated with kinship and is at times associated with ethnicity, religion and/or class. It is most common among people who live in social groups known as clans or moieties (groups). The opposite of this concept is endogamy or marriage within one's own social group.

51 In Islamic Law, marriage is both 'Ibadt' and 'Mammulat'. Who said this?

1 Amir Ali Justice
2 Dr Fayzee
3 Abdur-Rahim
4 Mahmood Justice

Ans. (3)

Exp. Abdur-Rahim in Islamic Law said that marriage is both 'Ibadat' and 'Muamalat'.

Abdur Rahim, in 'The Principles of Muahmmadan' jurisprudence (1958), said that muslim marriage is both 'Ibadat' and 'Mammulat'. Islamic law divides all legal acts into either ibadat or mammulat. Ibadat are acts of ritual worship such as prayer or fasting, and mammulat are acts involving interaction and exchange among people such as sales and sureties.

The distinction is important because the principle in all matters involving ibadat is that they are not susceptible to innovations or change (ittiba). In mammulat, however, there is considerably more room to develop and change the law to facilitate human interaction and promote justice. There is disagreement among Muslim jurists on whether certain legal acts, such as marriage or divorce, fall under the category of mammulat or ibadat.

52 A Muslim husband can delegate his right of Talaq to

1 Any other person
2 Wife only
3 Both (1) and (2)
4 None of these

Ans. (3)

Exp. A Muslim husband can delegate his right of Talaq to any other person and by only wife.

Talaq means to divorce and Tafwid or Tafweez means to delegate. In Islam a husband can delegate the right of divorce to his wife or any third person. This delegated divorce is known as Talaq-e-Tafweez also spelt as Talaq-i-Tafwid. This delegation can be made at the time of marriage by way of a prenuptial agreement, with or without conditions.

This delegation (Tafwid) can be made either before or after the marriage. Through this delegated divorce generally inserted in as a prenuptial clause in the marriage contract or Nikahnama gets the right of pronouncing divorce upon herself.

53 A Muslim minor wife can cease her right to repudiate the marriage in case

1 when she attained the age of puberty
2 when the marriage was consummated before attaining the age of puberty
3 when she is less than 18 years of age
4 None of the above

Ans. (2)

Exp. A Muslim minor wife can cease her right to repudiate the marriage in case when the marriage was consummated before attaining the age of puberty.

Section 2 (vii) of the Dissolution of Muslim Marriage Act, 1939 only gives the right to the minor wife to repudiate the marriage and does not consider the right of the husband for the same. It is also mentioned in the section that the wife will lose the right to option of puberty if the marriage is consummated.

54 Find correct answer using codes given below Following are main approaches to explain nature and meaning of human rights

I. The scientific right theory
II. The moral right theory
III. The natural right theory
IV. The legal right theory

Codes

1 I and II are correct
2 II and III are correct
3 III and IV are correct
4 IV and I are correct

***Ans.* (3)**

Exp. The natural right theory and legal right theory are main approaches to explain nature and meaning of human rights.

Among the given statements, only C and D are true.

In ancient times, there was a doctrine known as the 'Doctrines of Natural Law'. These doctrines held that because people are creatures of God and nature, they should be able to live their lives based on the rule of God or nature. As time went on, a man by the name of John Locke helped to modify these doctrines of natural law, based on his belief that everyone was naturally good and rational.

As he believed that the government was obligated to serve the people and protect their natural rights, he strived for a government that really represented the people and their interests. This lead to the modern concept of natural rights — not only do we have these rights, but no person or society can violate or take those rights from us.

According to Legal Right theory, rights are created and maintained by the state. The theory further mean that rights are not natural to man. The individual has no rights against state.The theory thus explains that the state is the only source of right and outside the state an individual has no rights at all. Bentham, Ho and Austin are the main exponents of the theory.

Scientific or moral rights theory does not explain the nature of human rights. While the former refers to analytical perspective of laws and their evolution, and the latter deals with ethical perspective of laws and their application, not targeting specifically human rights, but rights and duties of any kind and extent.

55 Read Assertion (A) and Reason (R). Find correct answer using the codes given below.

Assertion (A) The purpose of Human Rights is to provide protection against the abuse of power committed by the organs of State.

Reason (R) Due to absence of Lok Pal the misuse of power by the State cannot be effectively checked.

Codes

1 (A) and (R) are correct and (R) is correct explanation of (A)
2 (A) and (R) are correct, but (R) is not correct explanation of (A)
3 (A) is true and (R) is false
4 (A) is false and (R) is true

***Ans.* (2)**

Exp. Both (A) and (R) are correct, but (R) is not the correct explanation of (A).

One important factor in compliance with human rights is to ensure that those in positions of authority do not abuse their power. Several international human rights documents directly address actors other than governments (corporate bodies or individuals), stipulating correct behaviour in relation to those within their sphere of influence. These instruments, so-called 'codes of conduct' or 'codes of ethics', are written for specific groups of officials or certain professions, directly addressing those individuals who are subject to demands, for example, that they torture people or commit other forms of human rights violations. Thus, A is correct.

The need and purpose of human right protection gets more strength due to the fact that when there is no mechanism to check abuse of power such as a Lokpal, it becomes pertinent to have an alternate system in place which takes care of human rights protection. Thus, though R is correct, it is not the right explanation of A.

56 Match item in List I with items in List II using codes given below.

List I	List II
A. The first generation of Human Rights	I. Idealistic Theory of Law
B. The second generation of Human Rights	II. Collective Rights
C. The third generation of Human Rights	III. Civil and Political Rights
D. Theoretical approach to Human Rights	IV. Economic, Social and Cultural Rights

Codes

	A	B	C	D		A	B	C	D
1	I	III	II	IV	2	III	IV	II	I
3	IV	III	II	I	4	III	IV	I	II

***Ans.* (2)**

Exp. The correct matching is A-III; B-IV; C-II; D-I.

The first generation of Human Rights is Civil and Political Rights. First generation rights can be divided into two sub-categories. The first sub-category relates to norms of "physical and civil security." This includes not committing acts of torture, slavery, or treating people inhumanely.

The second sub-category relates to norms of "civil-political liberties or empowerments." This includes rights such as freedom of religion and the right to political participation.

The second generation of Human Rights is Economic, Social and Cultural Rights. The second generation of rights concern how people live and work together and the basic necessities of life. They are based on the ideas of equality and guaranteed access to essential social and economic goods, services, and opportunities.

The third generation of Human Rights is Collective Rights. The idea at the basis of the third generation of rights is that of solidarity; and the rights embrace collective rights of society or peoples, such as the right to sustainable development, to peace or to a healthy environment. In much of the world, conditions such as extreme poverty, war, ecological and natural disasters have meant that there has been only very limited progress in respect of human rights.

Theoretical approach to Human Rights is the Idealistic theory of law. This theory insists on the inner development of man, on the development of his full potentiality. Hence, it treats the right of personality as a supreme and absolute right.

57 In Indian Constitution, Civil and Political Rights given in its

1 Part II
2 Part III
3 Part IV
4 Part IX

Ans. *(2)*

➲ *Exp.* In Indian Constitution, Civil and Political Rights is given in its Part-III.

Part III (Article III) of the Indian Constitution deals with Fundamental rights. There are six fundamental rights listed in the Constitution of India. In reference to some rights, Article 14 to 18 of the Constitution guarantee the right to equality to every citizen of India. Article 14 embodies the general principle of equality before law and prohibits unreasonable discrimination between persons. Article 14 embodies the idea of equality expressed in the Preamble. The succeeding Articles 15, 16, 17 and 18 lay down the specific application of the general rules laid down in Article 14. Article 15 relates to prohibition of discrimination on the ground of religion race, caste, sex or place of birth. Article 16 guarantees equality of opportunity in matters of public employment. Article 17 abolishes untouchability. Article 18 abolishes title.

Six fundamental rights in the nature of freedoms which are guaranteed to the citizens by Article 19. These fundamental freedoms are freedom of speech, and expression, freedom of assembly, freedom to form associations, freedom of movement, freedom to reside and to settle, freedom of movement, freedom of trade occupation trade or business.

Article 20 provides safeguards to the persons accused of Crimes such as protection against Ex post facto law, Double Jeopardy, Prohibition against self-incrimination. Article 21 of the Constitution says that "No person shall be deprived of his life or personal liberty except according to procedure established by law." The right guaranteed in Article 21 is available to citizens as well as non-citizens.

58 "No one shall be subjected to arbitrary arrest, detention or exile." Above law is in

1 Article 21 of the Indian Constitution
2 Criminal Procedure Code
3 Civil Procedure Code
4 Article 9 of the Universal Declaration of Human Rights

Ans. *(4)*

➲ *Exp.* "No one shall be subjected to arbitrary arrest, detention or exile" is found under Article 9 of the Universal Declaration of Human Rights.

The Universal Declaration of Human Rights provides in Article 9 that "no one shall be subjected to arbitrary arrest, detention or exile". Article 9(1) of the International Covenant on Civil and Political Rights states: "Everyone has the right to liberty and security of person. No one shall be subjected to arbitrary arrest or detention. No one shall be Deprived of his liberty except on such grounds and in accordance with such procedure as are established by law."

59 Read Assertion (A) and Reason (R) and find correct answer using codes given below

Assertion (A) Advancement of rights of women has been the concern of world community since the end of Second World War.

Reason (R) In Second World War, population of men was significantly decreased.

Codes

1 (A) and (R) are true and (R) is correct explanation of (A)
2 (A) and (R) are true, but (R) is not correct explanation of (A)
3 (A) is true and (R) is false
4 (A) is false, but (R) is true

Ans. *(2)*

➲ *Exp.* Both (A) and (R) are true, but (R) is not the correct explanation of (A).

Advancement of women's rights has been the concern of the world community since the end of the Second World War. The enactment of the Universal Declaration Rights of Man and CEDAW are effective steps taken in this direction. Thus, A is true.

The violence and fights associated with the Second World War had reduced the population of males to a significant extent. This was one of the horrors of the Second World War. However, this was not the reason behind the advancement of women rights . Thus, though both (A) and (R) are true, (R) is not the correct explanation of (A).

60 Read Assertion (A) and Reason (R) and find correct answer using codes given below.

Assertion (A) The child must be given the means requisite for his normal development, both materially and spiritually.

Reason (R) Spirituality is material and material is spiritual.

Codes

1 (A) and (R) are true and (R) is correct explanation of (A)
2 (A) and (R) are true, but (R) is not correct explanation of (A)
3 (A) is true, but (R) is false
4 (A) is false, but (R) is true

Ans. (3)

Exp. The Assertion is true, but the Reason is false.

The Geneva Declaration of the Rights of the Child of 1924 deals with equitable treatment with children. As per the preamble, by the present Declaration of the Rights of the Child, commonly known as 'Declaration of Geneva,' men and women of all nations, recognizing that mankind owes to the Child the best that it has to give, declare and accept it as their duty that, beyond and above all considerations of race, nationality or creed. Article 1 states that the child must be given the means requisite for its normal development, both materially and spiritually. Thus, A is correct.

However, Reason given is incorrect as Spirituality refers to a broad set of principles that transcends all religions. Spirituality is about the relationship between humans and something larger. It is not the same as materialism that simply refers to the preoccupation with the material world.

61 State which of the following statements is incorrect?

1 Liability in tort arises from breach of duty primarily fixed by law
2 The duty, breach of which results in tortious liability, is towards the public generally
3 The duty, breach of which results in liability in tort, is towards some person in particular
4 The breach of duty, which results in liability in tort, is redressable by an action for unliquidated damages

Ans. (3)

Exp. The statement 'The duty, breach of which results in liability in tort, is towards some person in particular' is incorrect.

The law of torts provides remedy for a wrong committed against individual. However, the duty owed under torts is not restricted to a person specific, which is otherwise seen in case of contract law wherein the parties have limited duties towards specific persons.

In tort, a person owes a duty against the world at large and such duty is known as a public duty.

62 The plaintiff was watching a cricket match at a stadium organised by the Cricket Club of India. He was seriously injured by a mighty hit from the batsman. In this case, who is liable to pay the damages to the plaintiff?

1 The Batsman
2 The Cricket Club of India
3 Both 1 and 2 above
4 None of the above

Ans. (4)

Exp. Nobody is liable in the given factual situation.

'Volenti non-fit injuria' is one of the major defences in the Law of Torts. This phrase is derived from a latin term which states 'to a willing person, injury is not done,' in simple words, it states that when a person voluntarily consents to a risk, very well knowing the consequences of it, cannot bring claim against the other party, for the injuries suffered by him in tort or delict, e.g., a spectator who is hit by a foul ball while sitting in the stands at a baseball game, cannot recover for injuries because most of the fans know that stray balls in the stands in an inevitable part of the game.

However, this rule has an exception, where this applies only to the risk which a reasonable person would consider them as assumed by their actions. e.g., a soccer player consents to being hit and to the other expected injuries of the game, but does not consent to his opponent punching him or doing any other activity outside the usual terms of the game.

The defence Volenti non-fit injuria is taken into consideration in various contexts viz, employment relations, rescue cases, suicide case, drunk and drive cases, occupiers liability cases and also taken into consideration in the context of sporting events.

63 Which one of the following sets correctly identifies the specific defence available in an action for defamation?

1 Privilege, Truth, Fair comment
2 Privilege, Mistake, Fair comment
3 Truth, Mistake, Fair comment
4 Truth, Privilege, Mistake

Ans. (1)

Exp. Privilege, Truth and Fair comment are valid defenses for a case of defamation.

The law attempts to fulfil the aim of protecting reputation by allowing an action to be brought against the publisher of a defamatory statement. There are, however, a number of defences, which a defendant can raise in response to an action in defamation. For example- the defence of truth, fair comment or privilege.

64 Read Assertion (A) and Reason (R) and with the help of codes given below, point out the correct explanation.

Assertion (A) Pleading lack of intention to defame someone does not absolve one from liability for defamation.

Reason (R) The essence of defamation lies in the lowering a person in the estimation of the right thinking members of the society, even without intention.

Codes

1 Both (A) and (R) are true and (R) is the correct explanation of (A)
2 Both (A) and (R) are true and (R) is not the correct explanation of (A)
3 (A) is true, but (R) is false
4 (A) is false, but (R) is true

Ans. (4)

Exp. The Assertion is false, but the Reason is true.

Assertion is false because Pleading lack of intention to defame someone can absolve one from liability for defamation, if the statement made was true.

But Reason is correct because the insertion of Defamation as a civil as well as a criminal wrong has been made to ensure that a person's reputation does not suffer undue harm for no reason.

65 Read each of the following two statements Assertion (A) and Reason (R) and indicate your answer using the codes given below

Assertion (A) In India, defendants collecting water in reservoirs have not been held liable for damage caused due to the escape of water from these reservoirs in absence of negligence.

Reason (R) The rule of strict liability laid down in Rylands Vs Fletcher case has been held to be not applicable in India.

Codes

1 Both (A) and (R) are true and (R) is the correct explanation of (A)
2 Both (A) and (R) are true, but (R) is not the correct explanation of (A)
3 (A) is true, but (R) is false
4 (A) is false, but (R) is true

Ans. (1)

Exp. Both (A) and (R) are true and (R) is the correct explanation of (A).

The Supreme court of India in M.C. Mehta case stated that "Moreover the principle so established in Ryland Vs. Fletcher of strict liability cannot be used in the modern world, as the very principle was evolved in 19th century, and in the period when the industrial revolution has just begun, this two century old principle of tortuous liability cannot be taken as it is in the modern world without modifications."

Justice Bhagwati also stated that the rule of strict liability was evolved in 19th century, the time when nature industrial developments was at primary stage, in today's modern industrial society where hazardous or inherently dangerous industries are necessary to carry out development programme, thus this old rule cannot be held relevant in present day context. Also one cannot feel inhibited by this rule which was evolved in the context of totally different social and economic structure.

66 Read each of the following two statements Assertion (A) and Reason (R) and indicate your answer using the codes given below.

Assertion (A) In tort of nuisance, interference by the defendant may cause damage to the plaintiff's property or personal discomfort in the enjoyment of property.

Reason (R) Every interference in the use of property is a nuisance.

Codes

1 Both (A) and (R) are individually true and (R) is the correct explanation of (A)
2 Both (A) and (R) are individually true, but (R) is not the correct explanation of (A)
3 (A) is true, but (R) is false
4 (A) is false, but (R) is true

Ans. (3)

Exp. The Assertion is true, but the Reason is false.

A nuisance is an act that is considered to be harmful or even offensive to the general public or a private person. It is an unlawful act against the person's property. Thus, the Assertion is true.

The Reason is false because every interference is not a nuisance until the interference should be unreasonable.

67 Match List I with List II and indicate the correct answer using the codes given below.

List I	List II
A. Composition of the District Forum	I. Section 10, CP Act
B. Complaint to be Accompanied by Court Fee	II. Section 17, CP Act
C. Jurisdiction of the State Commission	III. Section 23, CP Act
D. Appeals from National Commission to the Supreme Court	IV. Section 12(2) CP Act

Codes

	A	B	C	D		A	B	C	D
1	I	II	III	IV	2	I	IV	II	III
3	II	IV	I	III	4	IV	III	II	I

Ans. (2)

Exp. The correct matching is A-I, B-IV, C-II, D-III.

According to Section 10 of the Consumer Protection Act, 1986, each District Forum shall consist of a person who is, or has been, or is qualified to be a District Judge, who shall be its President; two other members, who shall be persons of ability, integrity and standing, and have adequate knowledge or experience of, or have shown capacity in dealing with, problems relating to economics, law, commerce, accountancy, industry, public affairs or administration, one of whom shall be a woman.

As per Section 12(2), every complaint filed under sub-section (1) shall be accompanied with such amount of fee and payable in such manner as may be prescribed.

State Commission under Section 17 shall have jurisdiction to entertain complaints where the value of the goods or services and compensation, if any, claimed exceeds rupee five lakhs but does not exceed rupees twenty lakhs.

As per Section 23, any person aggrieved by an order made by the National Commission in exercise of its power conferred by sub-clause (i) of clause (a) of Section 21, may prefer an appeal against such order to the Supreme Court within a period of thirty days from the date of the order.

68 Find correct legal principle from following statements.

1 A company may do an act which is necessary for or incidental to the attainment of its objects or which is otherwise not authorised by the Act

2 A company may not do an act which is necessary for or incidental to the attainment of its objects which is otherwise not authorised by the Act

3 A company may do an act which is necessary for or incidental to the attainment of its objects or which is otherwise authorised by the Act

4 A company may do an act which is unnecessary for or not incidental to attainment of its goals or which is otherwise barred by the Act

Ans. *(3)*

Exp. A company may do an act which is necessary for or incidental to the attainment of its objects or which is otherwise authorized by the Act. This is in accordance with the Memorandum of Association of the Company, which otherwise acts as the Charter of the Company. A company cannot do an act which is ultra vires its Memorandum of Association.

69 Match items from List I with items in List II, using codes given below.

List I	List II
A. Lakshmi Ratan Cotton Mills Vs JK Jute Mills Co., AIR 1957 AII 311	I. Director's duty of care, diligence and skill
B. Automatic Self-cleansing Filter Syndicate Co. Ltd. Vs. Cuninghame, (1906) 2 Ch.34	II. Statutory protection to Directors against liability
C. G. Ramesh Vs. ROC, (2007) 135 Comp Cas 655	III. Powers of Directors
D. City Equitable Fire Insurance Company, Re, (1924) AII E Rep 485	IV. Scope of authority of Directors

Codes

	A	B	C	D
1	IV	III	II	I
2	III	II	I	IV
3	II	I	IV	III
4	I	IV	III	II

Ans. *(1)*

Exp. The correct matching is A-IV; B-III; C-II; D-I.

Lakshmi Ratan Cotton Mills Vs JK Jute Mills Co., AIR 1957 AII 311 is related to scope of authority of directors. This case discussed the doctrine of indoor management wherein the Court held that the outsider is entitled to presume that all the formalities required for such a transaction are fulfilled, therefore is protected by the doctrine of internal management.

Automatic Self-cleansing Filter Syndicate Co. Ltd. Vs. Cuninghame, (1906) 2 Ch.34 is related to powers of Directors. The Court held that the Articles constituted a contract by which the members had agreed that the Directors alone should manage the affairs of the company unless and until the powers vested in the Directors was taken away by an alteration in the Articles they could ignore the general meeting directives on matters of management.

G. Ramesh Vs. ROC, (2007) 135 *Comp Cas* 655 is related to Statutory protection to directors against liability. It was held that it is a fundamental principle of any jurisprudence that where a notice proposes any corrective action and more so in a case of punitive action, the materials forming the basis of an opinion need to be disclosed thereby their nexus, so that the opportunity granted is realistic in its content and form.

City Equitable Fire Insurance Company, Re, (1924) AII E Rep 485 is related to Director's duty of care, diligence and skill. The Court ruled that only some of the directors did breach their duty towards the company which is the duty of care. However, those directors are not liable to pay or reimburse the money that the company had lost.

70 Read Assertion (A) and Reason (R) and with help of codes given below, point out the correct explanation.

Assertion (A) A contract of sale may be absolute or conditional.

Reason (R) There is no absolute condition for a contract of sale.

Codes

1 Both (A) and (R) are true and (R) is correct explanation of (A)

2 Both (A) and (R) are true, but (R) is not correct explanation of (A)

3 (A) is true, but (R) is false

4 (A) is false, but (R) is true

Ans. *(3)*

Exp. The Assertion is true, but the Reason is false. According to Section 4 of the Sale of goods Act, 1930, a contract of sale of goods is a contract whereby the seller transfers or agrees to transfer the property in goods to the buyer for a price.

There may be a contract of sale between one part-owner and another. A contract of sale may be absolute or conditional. Thus, the Assertion is correct.

It is wrong to say that there is no absolute condition for contract of sale as the laws have been prescribed in regard to contract of sale and the same can be executed only in the given manner. Thus, (R) is false.

71 "Where under a contract of sale the property in the goods is transferred from the seller to the buyer, the contract is called a sale, but where the transfer of the property in the goods is to take place at a future time or subject to some condition thereafter to be fulfilled, the contract is called an agreement to sell." Read above statement and find correct answer, using the codes given below.

1 Contract of sale is conditional
2 Contract of agreement to sell is conditional
3 There is no difference between sale and agreement to sell, as both are contracts
4 Sale is a contract, agreement to sell is not a contract

Ans. *(2)*

Exp. After reading the statement given in question, it can be concluded that Contract of agreement to sell is conditional.

Section 4(3) of the Sale of Goods Act, 1930 reads as: "where the transfer of the property in the goods is to take place at a future time or subject to some condition thereafter to be fulfilled, the contract is called an agreement to sell." In the agreement to sell the parties agree to exchange the goods for a price depending on the fulfilment of certain conditions at a future specified date. The nature of the sale is absolute. The nature of the agreement to sell is conditional. It is an executed contract.

72 Essential features of a partnership is

I. Agreement
II. Object to carry on a business
III. To share profits
IV. Business is to be carried by all or any of them acting for all.

Codes

1 I is correct
2 I and II are correct
3 I, II and III are correct
4 All of above are correct

Ans. *(4)*

Exp. Essential features of a partnership is Agreement, Object to carry on a business, To share profits, Business is to be carried by all or any of them acting for all.

Partnership under Section 4 of the Partnership Act, 1932 is the relation between persons who have agreed to share the profits of a business carried by all or any of them acting for all. A partnership, as defined in the Act, must have three essential three essential elements; there must be an agreement entered into by two or more persons, the agreement must be to share the profits of a business, the business must be carried on by all or any of them acting for all.

The first element shows the voluntary contractual nature of partnership. A partnership can only arise as a result of an agreement, express or implied, between two or more persons. Where there is no agreement there is no partnership. But a partnership cannot be formed with more than ten persons in banking and twenty persons in other types of business.

The second element states the motive underlying the information of a partnership. It also lays down that the existence of a business is essential to a partnership. Business includes any trade, occupation or profession.

The third element is most important features of partnership. It states that persons carrying on business in partnership are agents as well as principals. The business of a firm is carried on by all or by any one or more of them on behalf of all.

73 Find the correct legal statement from following statements.

1 Every partner is liable, severally with all the other partners and jointly for all acts of the firm done while he is a partner
2 Every partner is liable, jointly with all the other partners and severally for all acts of the firm done while he is a partner
3 Every partner is liable only for acts done by him as acts of the firm done while he is a partner
4 Sleeping partner is not liable for acts done by him as acts of the firm done while he is a partner

Ans. *(2)*

Exp. Every partner is liable, jointly with all the other partners and severally for all acts of the firm done while he is a partner is the correct legal statement.

Section 25 of the Indian Partnership Act, 1932, read with Section 42 of the Indian Contract Act, 1872. Order 1 Rule 6, C.P.C. states that, "The plaintiff may at his option, join as parties to the same suit all or any of the persons severally, or jointly and severally, liable on anyone contract, including the parties to bills of exchange, hundis and promissory notes".

Section 25 of the Indian Partnership Act, 1932, states that, "Every partner is liable, jointly with all the other partners and also severally, for all acts of the firm done while he is a partner", Section 42 of the Indian Contract Act states, "When two or more persons have made a joint promise, then, unless a contrary intention appears by the contract, all such persons, during their joint lives, and, after the death of any of them, his representative jointly with the survivor or survivors, and, after the death of the last survivor the representatives of all jointly, must fulfil the promise."

74 Read Assertion (A) and Reason (R) and with help of codes given below, point out the correct explanation.

Assertion (A) It is the duty of the banker to be acquainted with the customer's handwriting.

Reason (R) A banker must be hand writing expert.

Codes

1 Both (A) and (R) are true and (R) is correct explanation of (A)
2 Both (A) and (R) are true, but (R) is not correct explanation of (A)
3 (A) is true, but (R) is false
4 (A) is false, but (R) is true

***Ans.* (3)**

Exp. The Assertion is true, but the Reason is false.

As observed in Bhagwan Das Vs. Creet on (1903), a banker who pays a forged cheque is in general bound to pay the amount again to his customer, because in the first instance he pays without authority. On this principle the two cases which have been cited (sic) decided, because it is the duty of the banker to be acquainted in his customer's handwriting, and the banker, not the customer, suffer if a payment is made without authority. But though that rule is perfectly well established, yet if it is the fault of the customer that the banker pays more than he ought, he cannot be called on to pay again. Thus, A is correct.

However, this does not mean that the Banker needs to be a handwriting expert. He only needs to have some familiarity with the handwriting of his customers. A professional expert on the other hand would be a person engaged in that kind of activity to make a living but that is clearly not the intention of the law. Thus, R is incorrect.

75 When a negotiable instrument is dishonoured, the party liable to pay, becomes bound to pay compensation to

1 The bank
2 The endorser
3 Holder or endorsee
4 The Court

***Ans.* (3)**

Exp. When a negotiable instrument is dishonoured, the party liable to pay becomes bound to pay compensation to Holder or Endorsee.

The liability of endorser has been defined in Section 35 of Negotiable Instruments Act, 1881 which is as follows; in the absence of a contract to the contrary, the endorser of a negotiable instrument, by indorsing it, engages that on due presentment it shall be accepted and paid according to its tenor and that if it be dishonoured he will compensate the holder or subsequent endorser who is compelled to pay it for any loss or damage caused to him by such dishonour.

UGC-NET
LAW
SOLVED PAPER 2012 (December)
PAPER II

1 Clause (4) of Article 15 has been added to the Constitution by

1 The Constitution First Amendment Act
2 The Constitution Second Amendment Act
3 The Constitution Fourth Amendment Act
4 The Constitution Sixth Amendment Act

Ans. *(1)*

➲ *Exp.* Clause (4) of Article 15 has been added to the Constitution by the Constitution (First Amendment) Act, 1951, so as to enable the State to make any special provisions for the advancement of socially and educationally backward classes of citizens.

This clause empowers the Government to establish and run educational institutions, especially for the backward classes of citizens (like special schools for SC, STs).

2 The state shall endeavour to secure for the citizens a Uniform Civil Code throughout the territory of India as per

1 Article 40   2 Article 43
3 Article 44   4 Article 48

Ans. *(3)*

➲ *Exp.* As per Article 44 of the Constitution the State shall endeavour to secure for the citizens a Uniform Civil Code throughout the territory of India.

Uniform Civil Code is a proposal in India to formulate and implement personal laws of citizens which apply on all citizens equally regardless of their religion.

3 In India, sovereignty lies with

1 The Constitution
2 The Supreme Court
3 The Parliament
4 The People

Ans. *(4)*

➲ *Exp.* In India, sovereignty lies with the people.

In India, the supreme power is possessed by the people of the country. The people of the nation elect their representatives to govern them i.e.,the Parliament derives its sovereignty from the people of the nation. The Preamble also begins with "We, the people of India….."

4 The Supreme Court of India formulated the doctrine of eclipse in

1 Bhikaji Narain Dhakras Vs. State of MP
2 Basheshar Nath Vs. Income Tax Commissioner
3 State of WB Vs. Anwar Ali Sarkar
4 Maneka Gandhi Vs. Union of India

Ans. *(1)*

➲ *Exp.* In Bhikaji Narain Dhakras Vs. State of MP, the Supreme Court of India formulated the doctrine of eclipse.

The Doctrine of Eclipse is a doctrinal principle that advocates the concept of fundamental rights being prospective in nature. If any law made by the Legislature is inconsistent with Part III of the Constitution, that law is invalid and inoperative to the extent of it being overshadowed by the Fundamental Rights.

In this case, the MP Government passed an Act in the year 1950 for nationalising the motor transport before commencement of the Constitution. The statute was challenged by the petitioner under Article 19(1)(g). The Central Government Amended Act, 1955 on 27th April, 1955 enabling the state to nationalise motor transport. The SC held that the statute of MP nationalizing the motor transport 1950 was cured by the 4th Amendment Act, 1955 and therefore the Doctrine of Eclipse has been applied and such Act is valid.

5 The satisfaction of the President means the satisfaction of the Council of Ministers and not his personal satisfaction, held in

1 Shamsher Singh Vs. State of Punjab
2 UN Rao Vs. Indira Gandhi
3 Ram Jawaya Kapoor Vs. State of Punjab
4 Sardar Lal Vs. Union Government

Ans. *(1)*

➲ *Exp.* In the case of Shamsher Singh Vs. State of Punjab (1974), it was held that the satisfaction of the President means the satisfaction of the Council of Ministers and not his personal satisfaction.

Further, the Court held that wherever the Constitution requires the satisfaction of President or the Governor for the exercise of any power or function by the President or the Governor, as the case may be, as for example in Articles

123, 213, 311(2) proviso (c), 317, 352(1), 356 and 360, the satisfaction required by the Constitution is not the personal satisfaction of the President or of the Governor, but is the satisfaction of the President or of the Governor in the Constitutional sense under the Cabinet system of Government.

6 "The Concurrent List was described as a 'Twilight Zone', as it were for both the Union and the States are competent to legislate in this field without coming into conflict" is stated by

1 Basu, DD
2 Dicey, AV
3 Pyle, MV
4 Ambedkar, B

Ans. *(3)*

Exp. "The Concurrent List was described as a 'Twilight Zone', as it were for both the Union and the States are competent to legislate in this field without coming into conflict" is stated by Pyle, MV. The Concurrent List was to serve as a device to avoid excessive rigidity to two-list distribution.

The Concurrent List consists of 52 subjects. Both Centre and States can make laws on the subject mentioned in the Concurrent List. But in case of conflict between the Central and the State law on concurrent subjects, the Central law will prevail.

7 Article 360 has been invoked

1 only one time
2 two times
3 three times
4 never

Ans. *(4)*

Exp. Article 360 has never been invoked.

Article 360 of constitution of India talks about Financial Emergency. It can be imposed if the President is satisfied that a situation has arisen whereby the financial stability or credit of India is threatened.

8 "Jurisprudence is concerned primarily with the effects of law upon society and only to a lesser extent with questions about the social determination of law."

Who said it?

1 Roscoe Pound
2 Eugen Ehrlich
3 Emile Durkheim
4 Max Weber

Ans. *(1)*

Exp. Roscoe Pound said that "Jurisprudence is concerned previously with the effects of law upon society and only to a lesser extent with questions, about the social determination of law."

Roscoe Pound belongs to sociological school of jurisprudence and is also famous for giving theory of social engineering.

9 "True law is that which has right reason in agreement with nature" was propagated by

1 Cicero
2 Hart
3 Grotius
4 Salmond

Ans. *(3)*

Exp. "True law is that which has right reason in agreement with nature" was propagated by Grotius.

Grotius concept of natural law had a strong impact on the philosophical and theological debates and political developments of the 17th and 18th centuries.

Among those who were influenced were Samuel Pufendorf and John Locke, and through these philosophers, his thinking became a part of the cultural background of the Glorious revolution in England and the American Revolution. In Grotius understanding, nature was not an entity in itself, but God's creation. As a result, his concept of natural law had a theological foundation.

10 Match List I with List II and select the correct answer using the codes given below the lists.

List I	List II
A. Privilege	I. Gives content to the claim of a person
B. Duty	II. Freedom from claim of another
C. Power	III. Have no correlative claim according to Austin
D. Absolute Duty	IV. Ability of a person to change legal relations

Codes

	A	B	C	D		A	B	C	D
1	III	II	I	IV	2	I	II	III	IV
3	IV	I	II	III	4	II	I	III	IV

Ans. *(2)*

Exp. The correct match is A–I, B–II, C–III, D–IV.

Privilege gives content to the claim of a person. According to Hohfeld, privilege means the freedom which a person has i.e., to do or not to do something. It means what one can do far himself without being prevented by the law. A right implies a correlative duty but a privilege does not. The right can be extinguished without affecting the privilege.

Duty refers to freedom from the claim of another. When the right is given to the person then it is assumed that certain duties are also imposed on the person. The right has its correlative duties. There are two kinds of duties-a) Primary and Secondary duties; b) Positive and negative duties.

Power has no correlative claim according to Austin. Austin has stated that rights are interdependent, not correlative, contrary to Salmond's opinions.

Absolute duty refers to the ability of a person to change legal relations. Austin distinguishes between relative and absolute duties, the former being those which have rights corresponding to them and the latter being those which have none. Austin conceives it to be the essence of a right that it should be vested in some determinate person and be enforceable by some form of legal process instituted by him.

11 'X' a servant finds a bag at the basement of the shop. He hands it over to 'Y' the owner of the shop, who asks him to place it in the almirah. Now, the bag is in possession of

1 'X' because he was the finder
2 Y' because he was the owner of the shop
3 'X' because he has kept it in the almirah
4 'Y' because in him there was union of corpus and animus

Ans. (4)

Exp. 'X' a servant finds a bag at the basement of the shop. He hands it over to 'Y' the owner of the shop, who asks him to place it in the almirah. Now, the bag is in possession of 'Y' because in him there was union of corpus and animus. According to the principles of Criminal Law in order to prove the possession and ownership, both animus corpus and animus intendi should be present. Possession is defined as "it is continuing exercise of a claim to the exclusive use of it." It does not cover incorporeal possession. Possession is different from ownership but normally possession and ownership lie together.

12 Which one of the following jurists emphasised that "we cannot understand what a thing is unless we study what it docs"?

1 Salmond
2 Roscoe Pound
3 Kelsen
4 Austin

Ans. (1)

Exp. Salmond emphasised that, "we cannot understand what a thing is unless we study what it does." For e.g. Law in action. Law is a process of balancing conflicting interests and securing the satisfaction of the maximum of wants with the minimum of friction.

13 Who defines "ownership as planary control over an object"?

1 Austin
2 Salmond
3 Holland
4 Savigny

Ans. (3)

Exp. Holland defines "ownership as planary control over an object."

According to him an owner has three rights on the subject owned

(i) Possession (ii) Enjoyment (iii) Disposition

The concept of the ownership is one of the fundamental juristic concepts common to all system of law. Ownership refers to the legal right of an individual, group, corporation or government to the possession of a thing.

14 Given below are two statements. One is labelled as Assertion (A) and the other is labelled as Reason (R).

Assertion (A) A legal right is a legally protected interest.

Reason (R) An element of advantage is essential to constitute right.

Codes

1 Both (A) and (R) are true, and (R) is the correct explanation of (A)
2 Both (A) and (R) are true, but (R) is not correct explanation of (A)
3 (A) is true, but (R) is false
4 (A) is false, but (R) is true

Ans. (3)

Exp. (A) is true, but (R) is false.

A legal right is a legally protected interest. A legal right is an interest which is protected and recognised by the rule of law. The main objective is to protect the interests of the people and to avoid the conflict between the individual interests.

Reason is false because the element of advantage is not essential to constitute right. A right may confer an advantage on a person but a right can also be the non-interference into someone's life.

15 Given below are two statements. One is labelled as Assertion (A) and the other is labelled as Reason (R).

Assertion (A) International Law Commission has initiated studies and prepared draft codes on diverse fields in International Law.

Reason (R) International Law Commission was established under General Assembly Resolution No. 174 (11) adopted on 21st November, 1947 with an object to promote, progressively develop and codify international law.

Codes

1 Both (A) and (R) are true
2 (A) is true, but (R) is false
3 (R) is true, but (A) is false
4 Both (A) and (R) are false

Ans. (1)

Exp. Both (A) and (R) are true.

Assertion is true as it says that the International Law Commission had initiated studies and prepared draft codes on diverse fields in International Law. For e.g., it has prepared the draft code of crime against peace and security of mankind, and has also prepared a draft statute of international criminal court.

Reason is true as it correctly supports the assertion and it says that International Law Commission was established under General Assembly Resolution No. 174 (11) adopted on 21st November, 1947 with an object to promote, progressively develop and codify international law.

The objective of this commission is to promote the progressive development of international law and its codification.

16 Match List I with List II and select the correct answer using the codes given below the lists.

List I (Declaration/Treaty/ Convention)	List II (Year of Adoption)
A. Universal Declaration of Human Rights	I. 1948
B. International Convention on Civil and Political Rights	II. 1966
C. Convention on the Rights of the Child	III. 2006
D. Convention on the Rights of Persons with Disabilities	IV. 1999

Codes

	A	B	C	D		A	B	C	D
1	I	II	IV	III	2	II	I	IV	III
3	IV	III	II	I	4	III	II	IV	I

***Ans.* (1)**

➲ *Exp.* The correct matching is A–I, B–II, C–IV, D–III.

The *Universal Declaration of Human Rights* was adopted in 1948. It is an international document adopted by the United Nations General Assembly that enshrines the rights and freedoms of all human beings.

The *International Convention on Civil and Political Rights* was adopted in 1966. This multilateral treaty was adopted by United Nations General Assembly Resolution 2200A (XXI) on 16th December 1966, and came into force from 23rd March, 1976 in accordance with Article 49 of the Covenant.

Convention on the Rights of the Child was adopted in 1999. The United Nations Convention on the Rights of the Child is an international human rights treaty which sets out the civil, political, economic, social, health and cultural rights of children.

Convention on the Rights of Persons with Disabilities was adopted in 2006. The Convention on the Rights of Persons with Disabilities is an international human rights treaty of the United Nations that is intended to protect the rights and dignity of persons with disabilities.

17 Jus Cogens means

1 Peremptory norm of international law
2 Norm of international law
3 Peremptory norm which does not permit derogation
4 None of the above

***Ans.* (3)**

➲ *Exp.* Jus Cogens means a peremptory norm which does not permit derogation.

A peremptory norm of general international law (Jus Cogens) is a norm accepted and recognised by the international community of States as a whole, from which no derogation is permitted. It can be modified only by a subsequent norm of general international law having the same character. Examples of Jus Cogens norms include: prohibition on the use of force; the law of genocide; principle of racial non-discrimination; crimes against humanity; and the rules prohibiting trade in slaves or human trafficking.

18 Which one of the following is primary source of international law?

1 Decisions of International Court of Justice.
2 Resolutions of UN General Assembly
3 General Principles of law recognised by Civilised Nations
4 None of the above

***Ans.* (3)**

➲ *Exp.* Among the given options, General Principles of law recognised by Civilised Nations is the primary source of international Law.

Treaties, custom, and principles of law, are sometimes referred to as 'primary sources'. Judicial decisions and the teachings of publicists are sometimes referred to as 'subsidiary' or 'secondary sources' or evidence of international law rules.

19 Which one of the following is not a permanent member of the UN Security Council?

1 UK 2 USA
3 Japan 4 China

***Ans.* (3)**

➲ *Exp.* Japan is not a permanent member of the UN Security Council.

The permanent members of the United Nations Security Council (also known as the Permanent Five, Big Five, or P5) are the five states which the UN Charter of 1945 grants a permanent seat on the UN Security Council (UNSC) namely China, France, Russia (formerly the Soviet Union), the United Kingdom, and the United States.

20 "Recognition operates retroactively not to invalidate the acts of a former government, but to validate the acts of a de facto government which has become the new de jure government," has been held by the court in the case of

1 Civil Air Transport Inc. *Vs* Central Air Transport Corporation
2 AM Luther Vs. Sagar and Co
3 The Arantzazu Mendi
4 Gdynia Ameryka Linie Vs. Boguslawski.

***Ans.* (1)**

➲ *Exp.* The given statement has been held by the court in the case of Civil Air Transport Inc. Vs. Central Air Transport Corporation.

In this case, the parties disputed ownership of 40 aircraft on an airfield at Kai Tak. The object of the suit brought by an American corporation was to recover possession of airplanes in Hong Kong which had been sold by the Nationalist Government of China to the plaintiff corporation's predecessor in December 1949, before the British recognition of the Communist Government.

21 Rules relating to Sapinda relationship are based on

1 Principle of Endogamy 2 Principle of Exogamy
3 Principle of Polygamy 4 Principle of Monogamy

Ans. (2)

Exp. Rules relating to Sapinda relationship are based on the Principle of Exogamy.

Section 3(f) of Hindu Marriage Act, 1955 defines Sapinda relationship by laying down the manner of computing degrees of ascent and relationship for the purpose of marriage. Sapinda relationships are prohibited under Hindu marriage law. A sapinda is someone who is within or has a common ancestor relative within three generations above you on your mother's side of the family or has a common ancestor relative within five generations above you on your father's side of the family.

Principle of Exogamy is the social norm of marrying outside one's social group.

Principle of Endogamy is the practice of marrying within a specific social group, religious denomination, caste, or ethnic group, rejecting those from others as unsuitable for marriage or other close personal relationships.

Principle of Polygamy referred to the practice of keeping multiple spouses.

Principle of Monogamy refers to the practice of having a single spouse.

22 On the ground of barrenness or sterility, marriage can be

1 voidable
2 void
3 Both 1 and 2
4 Neither 1 nor 2

Ans. (1)

Exp. On the ground of barrenness or sterility, marriage can be voidable.

Section 12(1) in the Hindu Marriage Act, 1955 talks about voidable marriage. It provides that any marriage solemnised shall be voidable and may be annulled by a decree of nullity on grounds like if the marriage has not been consummated owing to the impotence of the respondent.

23 Breakdown theory of divorce is reflected in

1 Section 13 (1) of Hindu Marriage Act, 1955
2 Section 13 (2) of Hindu Marriage Act, 1955
3 Section 13 (IA) of Hindu Marriage Act, 1955
4 Section 13 (B) of Hindu Marriage Act, 1955

Ans. (4)

Exp. Breakdown theory of divorce is reflected in Section 13 (B) of Hindu Marriage Act, 1955.

Breakdown theory of divorce is reflected in Section 13(B) of Hindu Marriage Act, 1955. The basic idea behind this theory is if partners have willingly and mutually consented to the marriage, then they can even mutually revoke their consent. Here comes the irretrievable breakdown theory, which says that if the marriage has irretrievably broken down, with not even a slight possibility of conciliation and if it is continued, it will just add to the misery of the partners, then it should be dissolved. But this theory still has not found its way expressly into the personal laws.

Generally, there are three theories in which the grounds for divorce are categorised. They are popularly termed the Offence theory, the Mutual Consent theory and Irretrievable Breakdown of Marriage Theory. In the Hindu Marriage Act, Section 13 (1) and 13 (2) contains the grounds for divorce, most of which are related to the Offence theory.

24 Match List I with List II and select the correct answer using the codes given below.

List I	List II
A. Ashok Hura Vs. Rupa Hura case	I. Restitution of Conjugal Rights
B. Bipin Chandra Vs. Prabhavati	II. Uniform Civil Code
C. Sarla Mudgal Vs. Union of India	III. Desertion
D. T Sareetha Vs. State of AP	IV. Divorce by Mutual Consent

Codes

	A	B	C	D		A	B	C	D
1	I	II	III	IV	2	IV	III	II	I
3	II	III	I	IV	4	IV	II	I	II

Ans. (2)

Exp. The correct matching is A–IV, B–III, C–II, D–I.

Ashok Hura Vs. Rupa Hura case is related to divorce by mutual consent. In this case, it was held that "in exercise of its extraordinary powers under Article 142 of the Constitution, the Supreme Court can grant relief to the parties without even waiting for the statutory period of six months stipulated in Section 13-B of the Act. This doctrine of irretrievable break-down of marriage is not available even to the High Courts which do not have powers similar to those exercised by the Supreme Court under Article 142 of the Constitution."

Bipin Chandra Vs Prabhavati case is related to Desertion. Court elaborated and shed light on the concept of desertion. Section 13(1) (ib) of the Hindu Marriage Act, 1955 deals with desertion as a ground for divorce.

Sarla Mudgal Vs Union of India is related to Uniform Civil Code. The verdict discusses the issue of bigamy, the conflict between the personal laws existing on matters of marriage and invokes. Article 44 of Indian Constitution. It is considered a landmark decision that highlighted the need for a Uniform Civil Code.

T Sareetha Vs. State of AP is related to restitution of Conjugal Rights. It was observed that the remedy of restitution of conjugal rights provided for by Section 9 of the said Act was a savage and barbarous remedy violating the right to privacy and human dignity guaranteed by Article 21 of the Constitution.

25 Arrange the grounds of divorce in the order in which they appear in the Hindu Marriage Act, 1955.

I. Mutual consent
II. Break down
III. Fault
IV. Customary

Codes

1 III, II, I, IV 2 II, III, IV, I
3 I, II, III, IV 4 IV, III, I, II

Ans. (4)

➲ *Exp.* The correct order is IV, III, I, II.

To protect the sacramental aspect of marriage, Hindu Marriage Act, 1955 was enacted which provided certain matrimonial remedies. Following are the grounds of divorce in the order in which they appear in the Hindu Marriage Act, 1955 (i) Customary (ii) Fault iii) Mutual consent (iv) Break down.

26 The petition for divorce by mutual consent may be presented if the spouses have been living separately for a period of

1 One year 2 Two years
3 Three years 4 None of these

Ans. (1)

➲ *Exp.* The petition for divorce by mutual consent may be presented if the spouses have been living separately for a period of one year.

Section 13B of Hindu Marriage Act, 1955 talks about divorce by mutual consent. The parties intending to dissolve marriage have to show that they have been living separately for a period of one year or more before the presentation of the petition for divorce and that during this period of separation they have not been able to live together as husband and wife.

27 An offer and an acceptance to it must be in the

1 same time 2 same place
3 same sense 4 None of these

Ans. (3)

➲ *Exp.* An offer and an acceptance to it must be in the same sense. It needs to be clear that a particular conduct was performed with the absolute intention of accepting the offer.

Presence of consensus ad idem (agreeing on the same thing in the same sense) is one of the essential elements to constitute a contract.

28 Which of the following statements are true?

I. Past consideration is no consideration under Indian and English Law.
II. Past consideration is no consideration under Indian Law.
III. Past consideration is no consideration under English Law.
IV. Past consideration is made in past.

Codes

1 I and III 2 II and III
3 III and IV 4 IV and I

Ans. (3)

➲ *Exp.* Statement III and IV are true.

Statement III and IV are correct as Past consideration is considered as no consideration under English Law and it is made in past only.

Statement I and II are not correct as under Indian law past consideration is considered as consideration but English law does not recognize past consideration. Consideration is anything given or promised by one party in exchange for the promise or action of another.

29 Given below are two statements. One is labelled as Assertion (A) and the other is labelled as Reason (R).

Assertion (A) When subject matter of a contract is destroyed, the contract is frustrated.

Reason (R) Frustration of a contract frustrates a party to the contract.

Codes

1 Both (A) and (R) are true and (R) is the correct explanation of (A)
2 Both (A) and (R) are true, but (R) is not correct explanation of (A)
3 (A) is true, but (R) is false
4 (A) is false, but (R) is true

Ans. (2)

➲ *Exp.* Both (A) and (R) are true, but (R) is not correct explanation of (A).

When subject matter of a contract is destroyed, the contract is frustrated. Frustration or impracticability occurs when a performance would be deemed impractical because of an unforeseen event. Impossibility occurs when a party is not able to complete a contract because of an event that happens after the contract is executed.

Frustration of a contract frustrates a party to the contract, is independently true but not the correct reason of the assertion. Doctrine of frustration occupies a special place in the Law of Contract. Under the doctrine of frustration, a contract may be discharged if after its formation events occur making its performance impossible.

30 Arrange the following concepts in which they appeared.

I. Invitation to offer II. Damage
III. Offer IV. Damages

Codes

1 I, III, II, IV 2 I, III, IV, II
3 III, I, II, IV 4 I, IV, III, II

Ans. (1)

➲ *Exp.* The correct order is I,III, II, IV i.e. Invitation to offer, Offer, Damage and Damages.

Invitation to offer (treat) is inviting someone to make a proposal. An offer is a proposal.

Damage is injury or the breach of legal right or breach of contract. Damages are intended to compensate the injured party for the loss that he has suffered as a result of the breach of contract.

31 Match an item in List I with an item in List II and select the correct answer using the codes given below.

List I	List II
A. Capacity	I. Breach
B. Damages	II. Unruly horse
C. Remedy	III. Compensation
D. Public policy	IV. Sound mind

Codes

	A	B	C	D		A	B	C	D
1	IV	III	II	I	2	I	II	IV	III
3	III	IV	I	II	4	IV	III	I	II

Ans. (4)

Exp. The correct matching is A–IV, B–III, C–I, D–II.

Capacity to enter into a contract requires a person to be of sound mind. Section 11 of the Contract Act, talks about the capacity of parties to enter into a contract.

Damages is another term for compensation. It is a common law remedy that can be claimed as of right by the innocent party. The object of damages is usually to put the injured party into the same financial position he would have been in had the contract been properly performed.

Remedy is available in case of a breach of contract. There are several remedies for breach of contract, such as award of damages, specific performance, rescission, and restitution.

Public Policy was called an Unruly horse by Justice Burrough while deciding the case of Richardson Vs. Mellish. He said that "Public policy is a very unruly horse, and when you get astride, you never know where it will carry you".

32 Which one of the following pairs does not match?

1 Novation of contract- Section 62
2 Agreement in restraint of legal proceedings - Section 29
3 Tender of performance - Section 38
4 Unlawful object and consideration - Section 23

Ans. (2)

Exp. Agreement in restraint of legal proceeding has been provided under Section 28 of the Indian Contract Act. It states that any agreement that restricts an aggrieved party from enforcing his rights to approach a relevant court or tribunal in case of a breach of contract, or limits the time within which he may do so, is a void agreement.

Section 29 of the Indian Contract Act, 1872 deals with agreements which are void because of uncertainty.

33 Which one of the following is not an example of vicarious liability?

1 Liability of the principle for the tort of his agent
2 Liability of partners for each others' tort
3 Liability of the master for the tort of his servant
4 Liability of the parents for the tort of the children

Ans. (4)

Exp. Liability of the parents for the tort of the children is not an example of vicarious liability.

In vicarious liability, the liability of one person for the act of another person, may arise. In order that the liability of A for the act done by B can arise, it is necessary that there should be certain kind of relationship between A and B, and the wrongful act should be, in certain way, connected with that relationship.

The common examples of such a liability are

Liability of the principal for the tort of his agent;

Liability of partners of each other's tort;

Liability of the master for the tort of his servant.

So, Vicarious Liability deals with cases where one person is liable for the acts of others. In the field of Torts, it is considered to be an exception to the general rule that a person is liable for his own acts only.

34 Match List I and List II, select the correct answer by using the codes given below.

List I	List II
A. Injuria sine damnum	I. Rylands *Vs* Fletcher
B. Damnum sine injuria	II. Gloucester's Case
C. Strict liability	III. Volenti non fit injuria
D. Defence of consent	IV. Ashby *Vs* White

Codes

	A	B	C	D
1	IV	II	I	III
2	II	IV	I	III
3	I	II	III	IV
4	IV	III	II	I

Ans. (1)

Exp. The correct matching is A–IV, B–II, C–I, D–III.

Injuria sine damnum was highlighted in the case of Ashby Vs. White. It is used in the law of torts and refers to an infringement of a legal right without any actual loss or damage.

Damnum sine injuria was highlighted in the Gloucter's case. This maxim refers to a damage without injury, where the breach does not cause damage, or at least not a calculable or admissible damage.

Strict liability principle was laid down in the case of Ryland Vs. Fletcher. It states that any person who keeps hazardous substances on his premises will be held responsible if such substances escape the premises and cause any damage.

The *Defence of consent* can be taken in Volenti non fit injuria case. It is a common law doctrine which states that if someone willingly places themselves in a position where harm might result, knowing that some degree of harm might result, they are not able to bring a claim against the other party in tort or delict.

35 Rule of absolute liability was propounded by

1 Justice Bhagwati
2 Justice Sodhi
3 Justice Ahmadi
4 Justice Kuldeep Singh

Ans. (1)

Exp. Rule of absolute liability was propounded by Justice Bhagwati.

The rule of absolute liability, in simple words, can be defined as the rule of strict liability minus the exceptions. In India, the rule of absolute liability evolved in the case of MC Mehta Vs Union of India. This is one of the most landmark judgement which relates to the concept of absolute liability.

According to the rule of absolute liability, if any person is engaged in an inherently dangerous or hazardous activity, and if any harm is caused to any person due to any accident which occurred during carrying out such inherently dangerous and hazardous activity, then the person who is carrying out such activity will be held absolutely liable.

36 Which one of the defence to strict liability is based on the maxim, volenti non fit injuria?

1 Consent of the plaintiff 2 Act of God
3 Act of Third Party 4 Statutory Authority

Ans. (1)

Exp. The defence of Consent of the plaintiff to strict liability is based on the maxim, volenti non fit injuria.

Volenti non fit injuria is Latin for "to a willing person, it is not a wrong." This legal maxim holds that a person who knowingly and voluntarily risks danger cannot recover for any resulting injury.

37 Mental condition of the wrong-doer at the time of wrong doing is

1 relevant in all torts
2 relevant to torts based on fault
3 relevant in torts based on strict liability
4 not relevant in tortious liability

Ans. (2)

Exp. Mental condition of the wrong-doer at the time of wrong doing is relevant to torts based on fault.

In some torts, such as assault, deceit and conspiracy the mental condition of a wrong-doer is relevant while in other torts the mental condition of a wrong-doer is irrelevant.

38 Consider the following set of legal propositions.

I. A person can claim damages for all wrongs he has suffered.
II. A person can claim damages for wrongs only if they are caused intentionally.
III. A person can claim damages for a wrong if it is caused by infringement of the legal right.
IV. A person can claim damages even if he has suffered no loss.

Of these above propositions which are correct?

Codes

1 I and II 2 III and IV
3 I and III 4 II and IV

Ans. (2)

Exp. Statement III and IV are correct because a person can claim damages for a wrong if it is caused by infringement of the legal right is true, and also, a person can claim damages even if he has suffered no loss.

Both the statements are correct based on the maxim "Injuria Sine Damnum". This maxim means violation of a legal right without causing any harm, loss or damage to the plaintiff.

Statement I and II are not correct because a person cannot claim damages for all the wrong, he or she can claim only in case of infringement of legal right. A person can claim damages for wrongs only if they are caused intentionally is not correct, if there is an infringement of legal right, irrespective of intention, damages can be claimed.

39 Which of the meaning given for the maxim "Actus me invito factus non est mens actus" is correct?

1 Merely a voluntary act by me will not be a crime with a criminal intention
2 An act done by me against my will is not my act
3 Neither I nor my person can be held liable for an act done under compulsion
4 All of the above

Ans. (2)

Exp. "Actus me invito factus non est mens actus" means 'an act done by me against my will is not my act.'

The principle underlying this maxim is that if a person is forced to do an Act which he generally would not do, or has no intention to do, but he is being coerced to do the act, then such an act cannot be said to be his own act because it was not a voluntary act.

40 The general principles as to protection of an accused is based on

I. Autrefois acquit and Autrefois convict.
II. Reasonable doubt as to presumption of innocence.
III. Natural Justice.
IV. Conviction cannot be based without proving the guilt even if it was admitted.

Which statement is correct?

Codes

1 I is correct
2 I and II are correct
3 I, II and III are correct
4 I, II, III and IV are correct

Ans. (4)

Exp. The general principles as to protection of an accused is based on:

- Autrefois acquit and Autrefois convict.
- Reasonable doubt as to presumption of innocence.
- Natural Justice.
- Conviction cannot be based without proving the guilt even if it was admitted.

41 Fill in the blanks with appropriate words. The distinctive features of riot and unlawful assembly are an activity which is accompanied by ______.

1 use of force and violence
2 causing alarm
3 violence on a common purpose
4 All of the above

Ans. (1)

Exp. The distinctive features of riot and unlawful assembly are an activity which is accompanied by use of force and violence.

According to Section 146 of IPC, 1860 a riot is simply an unlawful assembly in a particular state of activity, that activity being accompanied by the use of force or violence. It is the use of force and violence that distinguishes rioting from an unlawful assembly. The word 'violence' in this context is not restricted to force used against a person only but it also extends to the force used against inanimate objects.

42 The offence of ______ homicide supposes knowledge of likelihood of causing death.

1 unlawful
2 abnormal
3 culpable
4 All of these

Ans. (3)

Exp. The offence of culpable homicide supposes knowledge of likelihood of causing death.

Culpable homicide is the first kind of unlawful homicide as defined in Section 299, IPC it purports to define and explain as to when an act of causing death constitutes culpable homicide. The important elements are:

(i) Causing of death of a human being.
(ii) Such death must have been caused by an act
  (a) With the intention of causing death.
  (b) With the intention of causing such bodily injury as is likely to cause death.
  (c) With the knowledge that the doer is likely by such an act to cause death.

Simply an act causing death cannot amount to culpable homicide. Person to come under the ambit of culpable homicide must have knowledge of likelihood of causing death.

43 The expression 'Seduced' used in Section 366 (A) of Indian Penal Code means to ______ a woman to submit to illicit intercourse at any time.

1 use of force by stress
2 deceitfully induce
3 willfully influence
4 None of the above

Ans. (2)

Exp. The expression 'Seduced' used in Section 366 (A) of Indian Penal Code means to deceitfully induce a woman to submit to illicit intercourse at any time.

Section 366 (A) of Indian Penal Code, 1860 talks about Procuration of a minor girl.

According to legal provision of Section 366(A) of Indian Penal Code, 1860, this section makes procuration of a minor girl a punishable offence. It states that whoever by any means whatsoever induces any minor girl under the age of eighteen years to go from any place or to do any act with the intention that such girl may be forced or seduced to illicit inter-course with another person or with the knowledge that it is likely that she will be forced or seduced to illicit intercourse with another person, shall be punishable with imprisonment extending up to ten years and shall also be liable to fine.

44 Preparation consists in devising or arranging means necessary for the commission of the offence. Such attempt is not punishable because

I. the motive was harmless.
II. impossibility to reach wrongful end.
III. does not affect the security of any person.
IV. it remained without culmination.

The reasoned answer is

Codes

1 Only I is correct
2 The most probability is I and II
3 There is quite likelihood of I and II
4 All of the above

Ans. (4)

Exp. Preparation consists in devising or arranging means necessary for the commission of the offence. Such attempt is not punishable because the motive was harmless, and due to impossibility to reach wrongful end. Also, it does not affect the security of any person and it remained without culmination.

Preparation is the second stage of crime under IPC, it is at this stage that the person prepares or does acts which will help him in committing the criminal act. Preparation to commit an offence is punishable only when the preparation is to commit offences under Section 122 (waging war against the Government of India) and Section 399 (preparation to commit dacoit).

45 No person employed in a public utility service shall go on strike

I. without giving notice of strike to employer.
II. within 14 days of giving such notice.
III. after expiry of date specified in notice for strike.
IV. within 7 days of conclusion of conciliation proceeding.

Codes

1 I and IV
2 I and III
3 I and II
4 II and III

Ans. (3)

Exp. No person employed in a public utility service shall go on strike, without giving notice of strike to employer and within 14 days of giving such notice.

Strike means a cessation of work by a body of persons employed in any industry acting in combination or a concerted refusal, or a refusal under a common understanding, of any number of persons who are or have been so employed to continue to work or to accept employment.

46 There can be lay-off for

1 One day
2 More than one day
3 Maximum seven days
4 Any period, even less than one day

Ans. (4)

Exp. There can be lay-off for any period, even less than one day.

According to Section 2(kkk) of the Industrial Disputes Act, 1947 'lay off' means the failure, refusal or inability of an employer on account of shortage of coal, power or raw materials or the accumulation of stocks or the breakdown of machinery or natural calamity or for any other connected reason to give employment to a workman whose name is borne on the muster rolls of his industrial establishment.

47 In which of the following cases the court reiterated the well-known legal position that even a temporary worker can claim retrenchment compensation, if he is covered by the provisions of Section 25 (F) of the Industrial Disputes Act, 1947?

1 Tatanagar Foundary Co. Vs. Their Workmen
2 Management of Willcox Buckwell (India) Ltd. Vs. Jagannath
3 Barsi Light Railway Co. Ltd. Vs. Joglekar
4 Modern Stores Vs. Krishandas

Ans. (2)

Exp. In the case of Management of Willcox Buckwell (India) Ltd. Vs Jagannath, the court reiterated the well-known legal position that even a temporary worker can claim retrenchment compensation, if he is covered by the provisions of Section 25 (F) of the Industrial Disputes Act, 1947.

Section 25(F) of the Industrial Disputes Act, 1947 provides the conditions precedent to retrenchment. According to this section no workman employed in any industry who has been in continuous service for not less than one year under an employer shall be retrenched by that employer until:

- The workman has been given one months' notice in writing indicating the reasons for retrenchment and the period of notice has expired.
- The workman has been paid in lieu of such notice, wages for the period of the notice.
- The workman has been paid, at the time of retrenchment, compensation which shall be equivalent to fifteen days average pay [for every completed year of continuous service] or any part thereof in excess of six months.
- Notice in the prescribed manner is served on the appropriate Government [or such authority as may be specified by the appropriate Government by notification in the Official Gazette].

48 Which one of the following statements is true?

1 All Government departments are industries
2 No Government department can be industry
3 Government department carrying on business or trade may be industry
4 Government department carrying on only sovereign function may be industry

Ans. (3)

Exp. Government departments carrying on business or trade may be industry is true.

Section 2 (j) of the Industrial Disputes Act, 1947 defines 'industry' as "any business, trade, undertaking, manufacture, or calling of employers and includes any calling, service, employment, handicraft or industrial occupation or avocation of workmen". Further, this definition was elaborated upon by the Supreme Court in the Bangalore Water Supply and Sewerage Board Vs. R Rajappa. The court held:

(i) Any activity will be industry if it fulfils the 'triple test', as under: Systematic and organised activity with the cooperation between Employers and employees. For the production and distribution of goods and services whether or not capital has been invested for this activity.

(ii) It is immaterial whether or not there is profit motive or whether or not there is capital.

(iii) If the organisation is a trade or business, it does not cease to be one because of philanthropy animating the triple test, cannot be exempted from scope of definition of industry.

49 According to Section 9 (A) of the Trade Union Act, 1926 minimum requirement about membership of a trade union is

1 Seven
2 Ten percent or one hundred of the workmen
3 Ten percent or one hundred of the workmen, whichever is less
4 Ten percent or one hundred of the workmen, whichever is less, subject to minimum seven

Ans. (4)

Exp. According to Section 9 (A) of the Trade Union Act, 1926, minimum requirement about membership of a trade union is ten percent or one hundred of the workmen, whichever is less, subject to minimum seven, engaged or employed in an establishment or industry with which it is connected, as its members.

50 To be a member of Trade Union, a person must attain the age of

1 18 years
2 16 years
3 15 years
4 21 years

Ans. (3)

Exp. To be a member of a Trade Union, a person must attain the age of 15 years, unless the rules of a particular Trade Union provide for a higher age limit. However, for being an office bearer the person has to be above 18 years of age.

PAPER III

1 Democracy and Federalism are essential features of our Constitution and basic feature of its structure. This observation was made in SR Bommai Vs. Union of India by the Judge

1 Justice PB Sawant
2 Justice SR Pandyan
3 Justice JS Verma
4 Justice AM Ahmadi

Ans. (1)

Exp. Democracy and Federalism are essential features of our Constitution and basic feature of its structure. This observation was made in SR Bommai Vs. Union of India by the Judge PB Sawant.

The SR Bommai Vs. UOI, verdict spelt out clearly that the imposition of Article 356 by the President on a state government should not be arbitrary and there should be a solid ground for it. This judgement largely helped put an end to the arbitrary impositions seen until then.

2 According to AV Dicey in India the 'Rule of Law' is embodied in

1 Article 12 of the Constitution of India
2 Article 13 of the Constitution of India
3 Article 14 of the Constitution of India
4 Article 21 of the Constitution of India

Ans. (3)

Exp. According to AV Dicey in India the 'Rule of Law' is embodied in Article 14 of the constitution.

Dicey's theory of 'Rule of Law' consists of three basic principles:

- Supremacy of law.
- Equality before the law.
- The predominance of a legal spirit.

It means that no person is above the law and that every person is subject to the jurisdiction of ordinary courts.

3 When the court declares that certain provisions of the Act as invalid, it does not affect the validity of the Act and it remains as it is. The principle is known as

1 Doctrine of prospective over ruling
2 Doctrine of severability
3 Doctrine of pleasure
4 Doctrine of Eclipse

Ans. (2)

Exp. When the court declares that certain provisions of the Act as invalid, it does not affect the validity of the Act and it remains as it is. The principle is known as Doctrine of Severability or Separability.

The principle states that when a part of the statute is declared unconstitutional, then the unconstitutional part is to be removed and the remaining valid portion will continue to be valid. The idea is to retain the Act or legislation in force by discarding / deleting only the void portion and retaining the rest.

Article 13 of the Indian Constitution provides for the Doctrine of Severability which states that all laws in force in India before the commencement of constitution shall be void in so far they are inconsistent with the provisions of the constitution.

4 Given below are two statements. One is labelled as Assertion (A) and the other is labelled as Reason (R).

Assertion (A) A Bill which contains a taxation clause besides clauses dealing with other matters may also be a Money Bill.

Reason (R) All Bills dealing with taxes are Money Bills.

Codes

1 Both (A) and (R) are true, but (R) is not the correct explanation of (A)
2 Both (A) and (R) are true and (R) is the correct explanation of (A)
3 (A) is false, but (R) is true
4 (A) is true, but (R) is false

Ans. (1)

Exp. Both (A) and (R) are true, but (R) is not the correct explanation of (A).

A Bill which contains a taxation clause besides clauses dealing with other matters may also be a Money Bill. Only those financial bills which contain provisions exclusively on matters listed in Article 110 of the Constitution are called Money Bills.

On this basis, a bill is Money Bill if it results in imposition, abolition, remission, alteration or regulation of any tax at union or state level but not at local level.

All Bills dealing with taxes are Money Bills is true as discussed in assertion but doesn't provide the correct explanation of Assertion because the assertion talks about clauses other than a taxation clause as well.

5 Article 40 of the Constitution of India deals with

1 Provision for Just and humane conditions of work and maternity relief
2 Living wages etc. for workers
3 Duty of the State to raise the level of nutrition
4 Organisation of Village Panchayats

Ans. (4)

Exp. Article 40 of the Constitution of India deals with organisation of village panchayats. As per Article 40, the State shall take steps to organise Village Panchayats and endow them with such powers and authority as may be necessary to enable them to function as units of self-government.

6 Article 20 and Article 21 has been taken from the purview of Article 359 of the Constitution of India by

1 42nd Amendment
2 43rd Amendment
3 44th Amendment
4 59th Amendment

Ans. (3)

Exp. Article 20 and Article 21 has been taken from the purview of Article 359 of the Constitution of India by 44th Amendment. Article 20 is one of those fundamental rights enshrined in our Constitution, which deals with the protection of certain rights in case of conviction for offences while Article 21 deals with the right to life.

7 The Chairperson of Delimitation Commission ______.

1 Justice Kuldeep Singh
2 Justice RS Sarkaria
3 Justice RS Pathak
4 Justice SN Phukan

Ans. (1)

Exp. The Chairperson of Delimitation Commission is Justice Kuldeep Singh.

The Delimitation Commission or Boundary Commission of India is a commission established by the Government of India under the provisions of the Delimitation Commission Act. The main task of the commission is redrawing the boundaries of the various assembly and Lok Sabha constituencies based on a recent census. The representation from each State is not changed during this exercise.

However, the number of SC and ST seats in a state are changed in accordance with the census. The present delimitation of constituencies has been done on the basis of 2001 census under the provisions of Delimitation Act, 2002. The Commission is a powerful and independent body whose orders cannot be challenged in any court of law.

8 Representation of House of People is based on

1 Literacy of State
2 Area of the State
3 Population
4 Community

Ans. (3)

Exp. Representation of House of People is based on Population.

Article 81 of the Indian Constitution requires that each state receive Lok Sabha seats in proportion to its population and allocate those seats to constituencies of roughly equal size. Article 82 of the Constitution calls for the reallocation of seats after every census based on updated population figures.

9 Administrative law is the law relating to the powers and procedures of

1 The Parliament
2 The Legislature
3 The Administrative Authorities
4 Judiciary

Ans. (3)

Exp. Administrative law is the law relating to the powers and procedures of the administrative authorities.

Administrative law is the law that governs the administrative actions. It includes law relating to the rule-making power of the administrative bodies, the quasi-judicial function of administrative agencies, legal liabilities of public authorities and power of the ordinary courts to supervise administrative authorities.

Also, administrative function means the administration of :

(i) a law of the State.
(ii) a law of a political sub division of the State.
(iii) a rule, regulation, or by law of a public body.

10 The principles of natural justice are

I. No person can be judged in his own case.
II. No person shall be condemned unheard.

Codes

1 Only I is correct
2 Only II is correct
3 I and II are correct
4 None of the above are correct

Ans. (3)

Exp. Among the given choices option (3) i.e. I and II are correct.

Two core points in the concept of principles of natural justice are

(i) No one should be made a judge in his own case, or the rule against bias.
(ii) Hear the other party, or the rule of fair hearing, or the rule that no one should be condemned unheard.

11 Find correct answer : Administrative Tribunals exercises

1 Purely Administrative functions
2 Purely Judicial functions
3 Purely Legislative functions
4 Quasi-judicial functions

Ans. (4)

Exp. Administrative Tribunals exercises Quasi-judicial functions.

Administrative Tribunals were set up by Administrative Act, 1985. Administrative Tribunals Section 323 (A) Parliament may, by law, provide for the adjudication or trial by administrative tribunals of disputes and complaints with respect to recruitment and conditions of service of persons appointed to public services and posts in connection with the affairs of the Union or of any State or of any local or other authority within the territory of India or under the control of the Government of India or of any corporation owned or controlled by the Government.

The legislature enacts the laws, the executive implements the laws and the judiciary interprets the laws. Now, when we speak of Administrative Tribunals, we speak of quasi-judicial bodies whose function is two-fold:

- To relieve congestion in the ordinary courts.
- To provide for speedy disposal of disputes relating to service matters.

12 What is the effect of violation of the rule 'Audi Alteram Partem' on an administrative action?

1 Mere irregularity
2 Null and void
3 An illegality
4 Voidable

Ans. (2)

Exp. The effect of violation of the rule 'Audi Alteram Partem' on an administrative action is null and void.

'Audi Alteram Partem' is a latin maxim which means "hear the other side too" or "hear the alternative party too".

'Audi Alteram Partem' is considered a principle of fundamental justice or equity in most legal systems. The principle includes the right of a party to confront the witnesses against him to have a fair opportunity to challenge the evidence presented by the other party to summon one's own witnesses and to present evidence and to have counsel, if necessary, at public expense, in order to make one's case properly. So, if this rule of Audi Alteram is violated, then the decision becomes void.

13 In which of the following cases, the Supreme Court held that the principles of natural justice are applicable to administrative proceedings?

1 MC Mehta Vs. Union of India
2 Maneka Gandhi Vs. Union of India
3 AK Kraipak Vs. Union of India
4 Smt. Indira Nehru Gandhi Vs. Raj Narain

Ans. (3)

Exp. In AK Kraipak Vs. Union of India, the Supreme Court held that the principles of natural justice are applicable to administrative proceedings.

The court held that the selection made by the Selection Committee were in violation of the principles of natural justice because there was a real likelihood of bias for the mere presence of the candidate on selection board and may adversely influence the judgement of other members.

14 The writ of prohibition may be issued, when there is

1 an absence of jurisdiction or abuse of jurisdiction
2 violation of principles of natural justice and fraud
3 any kind of contravention of the law of the land
4 All of the above

Ans. (4)

Exp. Writ of prohibition is generally issued when a lower court or tribunal acts without jurisdiction or in excess of jurisdiction. It is even issued in cases where there is a violation of rules of natural justice or fundamental rights and especially when an action is being carried out under a law which is ultra vires or unconstitutional.

Writ of prohibition means to forbid or to stop and it is popularly known as 'Stay Order'. This writ is issued when a lower court or a body tries to transgress the limits or powers vested in it.

15 The writ of certiorari necessarily implies that

1 An error of fact, cannot corrected
2 An error of law apparent on the face of the record, can be corrected
3 Violation of natural justice
4 None of the above

Ans. (2)

Exp. Writ of certiorari necessarily implies that an error of law apparent on the face of the record, can be corrected. Literally, Certiorari means to be certified. The writ of certiorari can be issued by the Supreme Court or any High Court for quashing the order already passed by an inferior court, tribunal or quasi-judicial authority.

There are several conditions necessary for the issue of writ of certiorari which are as follows :

- There should be court, tribunal or an officer having legal authority to determine the question with a duty to act judicially.
- Such a court, tribunal or officer must have passed order acting without jurisdiction or in excess of the judicial authority vested by law in such court, tribunal or officer.
- The order could also be against the principles of natural justice or the order could contain an error of judgment in appreciating the facts of the case.

16 "Common law is essentially a Judge made law". This opinion was expressed by

1 Pollock   2 Austin
3 Paton   4 Salmond

Ans. (4)

Exp. "Common law is essentially a Judge made law". This opinion was expressed by Salmond.

Salmond on has described various Sources of Law which are as follows :

Formal Sources -A formal source is as that from which rule of law derives its force and validity. The formal source of law is the will of the state as manifested in statutes or decisions of the court and the authority of law proceeds from that.

Material Sources- These are those from which is derived the matter though not the validity of law and the matter of law may be drawn from all kind of material sources

Historical Sources- These are rules that are subsequently turned into legal principles. Such sources are first found in an unauthoritative form. Usually, such principles are not allowed by the courts as a matter of right. They operate indirectly and in a mediatory manner.

17 Match the following and select the correct answer by using the codes given below the lists.

List I	List II
A. Enacted law	I. Legislation
B. Case law	II. Agreement
C. Customary law	III. Precedent
D. Conventional law	IV. Custom

Codes

	A	B	C	D		A	B	C	D
1	I	II	IV	III	2	I	II	III	IV
3	I	III	IV	II	4	III	I	IV	II

Ans. *(3)*

➲ *Exp.* The correct matching is A-I, B-III, C-IV, D- II.

Enacted law is also known as legislation. Legislation, also known as statutory law, is the basic structure of the present legal system of India. Statutory laws are based on the statutes enacted and imposed by the legislature.

Case law is also known as precedent. The term case law refers to law that comes from decisions made by judges in previous cases.

Case law, also known as "common law," and "case precedent," which provides a common contextual background for certain legal concepts, and how they are applied in certain types of cases.

Customary law is also known as custom. Customs are the earliest sources of law and form the basis of the English Common Law system as we see it today. They can be described as cultural practises which have become definite and backed by obligation or sanction just by virtue of widespread practise and continued presence.

Conventional law is also established by agreements. Conventional law originates in agreement.

Agreement is a law for those who make it or it is a law for those who have been a party to it.

18 State the legal status of Hindu Joint family.

1 Hindu Joint family is a legal person
2 Hindu Joint family is a natural person
3 Hindu Joint family is both a legal and natural person
4 None of the above

Ans. *(1)*

➲ *Exp.* Hindu Joint Family is a legal person.

In the Hindu society, there is a presumption that Hindu families are living in a state of union unless the contrary is established. Members of Hindu families are ordinarily joint and undivided in estate, food and worship. The concept of a Hindu Undivided Family (HUF) as understood today, is an integral feature of the Hindu society and is one that has evolved on the basis of customs.

19 "Case-law is gold in the mine-a few grains of precious metal to the tons of useless matter, while the statute law is coin of the state which ready for immediate use". Who gave this statement?

1 Bentham　　2 Salmond
3 Kelson　　4 Holland

Ans. *(2)*

➲ *Exp.* Salmond gave this statement that "Case-law is gold in the mine-a few grains of precious metal to the tons of useless matter, while the statute law is coin of the state which ready for immediate use".

He also said that "case law, with all its imperfections, has at least this merit that it remains in leaving contact with the reason and justice of the matters and draws from this source a flexibility and power of growth and adaptation which are too much wanting in the litera scripta of enacted law."

20 "Law is the guarantee of the conditions of life of society, assured by the states" "power of constraint" who said it?

1 Duguit　2 Ihering　3 Savigny　4 Ehrlich

Ans. *(2)*

➲ *Exp.* Ihering said "Law is the guarantee of the conditions of life of society, assured by the states" "power of constraint".

Rudolf Von Ihering (1818 – 1892) was German jurist. He has been described as the 'Father of Modern Sociological Jurisprudence'. He rejected the analytical and historical jurisprudence as jurisprudence of conceptions.

According to him, law is an instrument for serving the needs of individuals of society. Hence, the law should be studied in terms of purposes or interests which it sub-serves. Ihering views law as an instrument of social control balancing of individual interest with that of the society.

21 Match List I (Legal Right) with List II (Nature of Legal Right) and select the correct answer by using the codes given below the lists.

	List I		List II
A.	Time barred debt	I.	Personal Right
B.	Right to reputation	II.	Right in Personam
C.	Right to physical integrity	III.	Imperfect Right
D.	Right arising out of a contract	IV.	Right in Rem

Codes

	A	B	C	D		A	B	C	D
1	III	IV	II	I	2	III	II	I	IV
3	II	III	I	IV	4	III	IV	I	II

Ans. *(3)*

➲ *Exp.* The correct matching is A-II, B-III, C-I, D-IV.

Time barred debt is a imperfect Right. Imperfect Right is applied to rights and obligations. A man has a right to be relieved by his fellow creatures, when in distress, but this right he cannot enforce by law; hence it is called an 'imperfect right'. On the other hand, we are bound to be grateful for favours received, but we cannot be compelled to perform such imperfect obligations.

Right to reputation is a Right in Rem. Right in Rem is a law suit against an item of property, not against a person (in personam). An action in Rem is a proceeding that takes no notice of the owner of the property but determines rights in the property that are conclusive against the entire world.

Right to physical integrity is a Personal Right. Personal rights refers to the rights which a person has in relation strictly to the duties owed to him by others and the wrongs consequent to the breach or violation of such duties. The following is an example of a case law referring to personal rights: Personal rights are not rights of person.

Right arising out of contract is a Right in Personam. The Indian Contract Act grants Rights in personam to the parties of a contract. So the parties of a contract have these contractual rights only against each other, i.e. jus in personam. Right in personam gives the person rights against one person or party to the contract.

22 Right in re aliena means a right over

1 his own property
2 a property of someone else
3 a property situated in a foreign country
4 a property situated in one's own country

Ans. (2)

Exp. Right in re aliena means a right over a property of someone else. For instance, the right of easement. It is the result of jurisprudence concept of dominant heritage and servient heritage. For eg: if A leases his property to B, then A is the owner of the house and B is the temporary occupier of the house, in this case, the right of temporary detachment of the ownership is called as right in re aliena.

23 The birth and death of legal person is determined by

1 Nature 2 Custom
3 Law 4 Precedent

Ans. (3)

Exp. The birth and death of a legal person is determined by law. Since law is primarily concerned with the regulation of human conduct, the concept of legal personality is an important subject matter of law as rights and duties cannot exist without a person first.

24 Read the following passage and select the correct code.
The social tolerance towards crime establishes the concept of crime. No longer people accept that crime is related to sin by which people feel remorse and undergo penance to seek exoneration from punishment. But there is a general opinion that crime is relatively connected to individual behaviour, which very often changes. To resolve the conflict, the general view is that, anything which is injurious to public welfare is a crime.

I. Russell–Crime is not absolute as it depends upon social tolerance
II. Black Stone–Changing concept of crime as it is related to sin
III. HJ Klare–Crime is known through attributes as it is related to behaviour
IV. GW Patton–Act which does not attract law is not a crime

Codes

1 I 2 II 3 III 4 IV

Ans. (1)

Exp. According to Russell, Crime is not absolute as it depends upon social tolerance.

Russell defined crime as an act punishable by law as forbidden by statute or injurious to the public welfare. It is a very wide definition, anything which is injurious to public welfare is crime, in modern complex society there are many things which are injurious or against the public welfare e.g., selling contaminated food, molestation of young children, etc.

25 Fill in the gap.
Contributory negligence is _______ defense to a criminal charge.

1 genuine 2 accurate
3 sharp 4 no

Ans. (4)

Exp. Contributory negligence is no defense to a criminal charge.

Contributory negligence, in law, is the behaviour that contributes to one's own injury or loss and fails to meet the standard of prudence that one should observe for one's own good. Contributory negligence usually arises in a lawsuit in which a plaintiff has accused a defendant of negligence.

The contributory negligence of any party in a civil action shall not bar such party or such party's legal representative from recovering damages for negligence resulting in death, personal injury, property damage or economic loss, if such party's negligence was less than the causal negligence of the party or parties against whom claim for recovery is made, but the award of damages to any party in such action shall be diminished in proportion to the amount of negligence attributed to such party.

26 The accused fired two shots with a revolver at point blank range at the Acting Governor but the bullets failed to produce the desired result because of some defect in the ammunition or intervention of leather wallet. What offence is caused?

1 Culpable Homicide
2 Attempt to Murder
3 Attempt to harm
4 None of the above

Ans. (2)

Exp. In the given scenario, offence caused is attempt to murder.

Section 307 of IPC mentions attempt to murder, it says that whoever does any act with such intention or knowledge, and under such circumstances that, if he by that act caused death, he would be guilty of murder, shall be punished with imprisonment of either description for a term which may extend to ten years and shall also be liable to fine; and if hurt is caused to any person by such act, the offender shall be liable either to imprisonment for life, or to such punishment as is herein before mentioned.

27 In a case where a minor girl was in the custody of her mother. Later the mother obtained divorce from her husband and thereafter the father forcefully removed the daughter from the school. What offence is created by the father?

1 Abduction
2 Kidnapping
3 Confinement
4 Custody

***Ans.* (2)**

Exp. In the given scenario the father committed Kidnapping, under Section 361, IPC.

Section 361 states that "whoever takes or entices any minor under sixteen years of age if a male, or under eighteen years of age if a female, or any person of unsound mind, out of the keeping of the lawful guardian of such minor or person of unsound mind, without the consent of such guardian, is said to kidnap such minor or person from lawful guardianship."

28 Can a woman be prosecuted for gang rape?

1 Occasionally
2 As the case demands
3 Not at all
4 When she is a party to it

***Ans.* (3)**

Exp. A woman cannot be prosecuted for gang rape, because Rape is a crime committed by a male against the female.

According to Section 375 of the Indian Penal Code, 1860, a man is said to commit "rape", who except in the cases hereinafter excepted, has sexual intercourse with a woman under circumstances falling under any of the six following descriptions namely:

(i) Against her will
(ii) Without her consent
(iii) With her consent, where it has been obtained by putting her or any person, in whom she is interested in fear of death or hurt.
(iv) With her consent, when the man knows that he is not her husband, and her consent is given because she believes that he is another man to whom she is or believes herself to be lawfully married.
(v) With her consent, when, at the time of giving such consent, by reason of unsoundness of mind or intoxication is unable to understand the nature and consequences.
(vi) With or without her consent, when she is under 16 years of age.

So, it is crystal clear from the above section the female or woman can never be prosecuted for gang rape, as it is a crime against women.

29 Criminal breach of trust is an offence which signifies

1 Entrustment
2 Demand
3 Refusal
4 Wrongful intention

***Ans.* (1)**

Exp. Criminal breach of trust is an offence which signifies Entrustment.

According to Section 405 of the Indian Penal Code, 1860 whoever, being in any manner entrusted with property or with any dominion over property, dishonestly misappropriates or converts to his own use that property or dishonestly uses or disposes of that property in violation of any direction of law prescribing the mode in which such trust is to be discharged, commits "criminal, breach of trust".

30 'X' a Police Officer while executing a warrant of arrest against 'Y' asks 'Z' to identify 'Y'. 'Z' knowingly tells that 'M' is 'Y' and consequently 'M' is arrested. What offence is committed by 'Z'?

1 Abetment by Instigation
2 Abetment by Aiding
3 Abetment by False representation
4 Abetment by Mischief

***Ans.* (1)**

Exp. In the given case, Abetment by Instigation is committed by 'Z'.

According to Section 107 of IPC states that a person who, by wilful misrepresentation, or by wilful concealment of a material fact which he is bound to disclose, voluntarily causes or procures, or attempts to cause or procure, a thing to be done, is said to instigate the doing of that thing.

The Illustration to this explanation provides that 'A', a public officer, is authorized by a warrant from a Court of Justice to apprehend 'Z'. 'B', knowing that fact and also that 'C' is not 'Z', wilfully represents to 'A' that 'C' is 'Z', and thereby intentionally causes 'A' to apprehend 'C'. Here 'B' abets by instigation the apprehension of 'C'.

31 A married man commits adultery if he commits sexual intercourse with

1 A teenaged girl
2 An unmarried woman
3 Any woman who is not his wife
4 Married woman

***Ans.* (4)**

Exp. A married man commits adultery if he commits sexual intercourse with married woman.

The primary law that deals with Adultery is Section 497 of the Indian Penal Code. It says, "whoever has sexual intercourse with a person who is and whom he knows or has reason to believe to be the wife of another man, without the consent or connivance of that man, such sexual intercourse not amounting to the offence of rape, is guilty of the offence of adultery and shall be punished with imprisonment of either description for a term which may extend to five years, or with fine, or with both." In such case, the wife shall not be punishable as an abettor.

32 In which of the following cases, the Supreme Court applied the doctrine of public trust that the State as a trustee of all natural resources is under a legal duty to protect the natural resources. These natural resources are meant for public use and cannot be converted into private ownership?

1 MC Mehta Vs. Kamalnath and Others
2 MC Mehta Vs. Union of India (Ganga Water Pollution case)
3 MC Mehta Vs. Union of India (Replacing diesel vehicles by CNG vehicles)
4 Church of God (Full Gospel) in India Vs. KKR Majestic Colony Welfare Association.

Ans. (1)

Exp. In the case of MC Mehta Vs. Kamalnath and Others, the Supreme Court applied the doctrine of public trust that the State as a trustee of all natural resources is under a legal duty to protect the natural resources. These natural resources are meant for public use and cannot be converted into private ownership.

The Doctrine of Public Trust primarily rests on the principle that certain resources like air, sea, water and the forests have such a great importance to the people as a whole that it would be wholly unjustified to make them a subject of private ownership.

33 In which of the following cases, the Supreme Court discussed the development of the precautionary principle?

1 AP Pollution Control Board Vs. MV Nayudu
2 Rural Litigation and Entitlement Kendra Vs. State of UP
3 MC Mehta Vs. Union of India (Ganga Water Pollution case)
4 Olga Tetlis (1986) case

Ans. (1)

Exp. The Supreme Court of India in AP Pollution Control Board Vs. MV Nayudu, discussed the development of the precautionary principle and the Court also referred to the need for establishing Environmental Courts which would have the benefit of expert advice from environmental scientists/ technically qualified persons, as part of the judicial process, after an elaborate discussion of the views of jurists in various countries.

The Supreme Court, referred to the serious differences in the constitution of appellate authorities under plenary as well as delegated legislation and pointed out that except in one State where the appellate authority was manned by a retired High Court Judge, in other States they were manned only by bureaucrats.

34 The term 'environment' under Section 2(a) of the Environment (Protection) Act, 1986 means

1 Air, Water and Land only
2 Water, Air, Land and interrelationship between air, water, and land only
3 Water, Air, Land, and the interrelationship between water, air and land and human beings, other living creatures, plants, micro-organism and property
4 None of the above

Ans. (3)

Exp. The term 'environment' under Section 2(a) of the Environment (Protection) Act, 1986 includes water, air and land and the inter relationship which exists among and between water, air and land, and human beings, other living creatures, plants, micro-organism and property.

35 Given below are two statements. One is labelled as Assertion (A) and the other is labelled as Reason (R).

Assertion (A) The right to clean drinking water and right to free air to breath are attributes of the right to life.

Reason (R) Because they are the basic elements which sustain life.

Codes

1 (A) and (R) are true and (R) is correct explanation of (A)
2 Both (A) and (R) are true, but (R) is not a good explanation of (A)
3 (A) is true, (R) is false
4 (A) is false, (R) is true

Ans. (1)

Exp. (A) and (R) are true and (R) is the correct explanation of (A).

The right to clean drinking water and right to free air to breath are attributes of the right to life. This right is inscribed as fundamental right under Article 21 of the Constitution. Recognising water and sanitation as rights more explicitly and with measures for its assertion in an enforceable way is critical to overall human development. And, with rights come responsibilities towards water and sanitation, which need to be accepted as well.

Water and air are the basic elements which sustain life. In 2002, the apex court validated the Sardar Sarovar dam project on Narmada in 2000 interpreting the right to life article as right to water. Water is the basic need for the survival of human beings and is part of the right to life and human right as enshrined in Article 21 of the Constitution of India and can be served only by providing a source of water where there is none.

36 In which of the following cases, the Supreme Court observed that, "When there is a state of uncertainty due to the lack of data or material about the extent of damage or pollution likely to be caused, then in order to maintain the ecological balance, the burden of proof that the said balance will be maintained must necessarily be on the industry or the unit which is likely to cause pollution"?

1 MC Mehta Vs. Union of India
2 Olga Tellis Vs. Bombay Municipal Corporation
3 Taj Trapezium case
4 None of the above

Ans. (4)

Exp. In none of the given cases, the Supreme Court observed that "When there is a state of uncertainty, due to the lack of data or material about the extent of damage or pollution likely to be caused, then in order to maintain the ecological balance, the burden of proof that the said balance will be maintained must necessarily be on the industry or the unit which is likely to cause pollution." This was held in the case of N.D. Jayal And Anr Vs. Union Of India And Ors on 1st September, 2003

37 In which of the following cases, the Supreme Court directed closing down and demolition of shrimp industries in coastal regulation zone and implement the 'precautionary principle' and 'the polluter pays principle' and held them liable for payment of compensation for reversing the ecology and compensate the individual for loss suffered?

1 S Jagannath Vs. Union of India
2 Vellore Citizens Welfare Forum Vs. Union of India
3 MC Mehta Vs. Union of India
4 Church of God (Full Gospels) in India Vs. KKR Majestic Colony Welfare Association

Ans. (1)

Exp. In the case of the S Jagannath Vs. Union of India, the Supreme court directed the closing down and demolition of Shrimp industries in coastal regulation zone and implement the 'precautionary principle' and 'the polluter pays principle' and held them liable for payment of compensation for reversing the ecology and compensate the individual for loss suffered.

The Central Government shall constitute an authority under Section 3(3) of the Environment (Protection) Act, 1986 and shall confer on the said authority all the powers necessary to the ecologically fragile coastal areas, sea shore, water front and other coastal areas and specially to deal with situation created by the shrimp culture industry in the coastal States and Union Territories. The authority shall be headed by a retired Judge of a High Court. The authority so constituted by the Central Government shall implement 'the Precautionary Principle' and 'the Polluter Pays' principles'.

38 In which of the following cases, the Supreme Court upheld the governmental direction to close down the lime-stone mining operations and quarrying permanently, holding it the duty of the lessee to protest and safeguard the right of the people to live in a healthy environment with minimal disturbance of ecological balance?

1 All India Council for Enviro Legal Action Vs. Union of India
2 Rural Litigation and Entitlement Kendra Vs. State of Uttar Pradesh
3 Vellore Citizens Welfare Forum Vs. Union of India
4 MC Mehta Vs. Union of India

Ans. (2)

Exp. In the case of Rural Litigation and Entitlement Kendra Vs. State of Uttar Pradesh, the Supreme Court upheld the governmental direction to close down the lime-stone mining operations and quarrying permanently, holding it the duty of the lessee to protest and safeguard the right of the people to live in a healthy environment with minimal disturbance of ecological balance.

This case is also famously known as the 'Dehradun Valley litigation'. In Mussoorie hill range of Himalayas, the activity of quarrying was being carried out. Limestone was extracted by blasting out the hills with dynamite. This also resulted in cave-ins and slumping because the mines dug deep into the hillsides, which is an illegal practice per se.

39 Identify the correct one according to List I

List I	List II
The polluter pays principle	1. Each generation should be obligated to conserve the diversity of natural and cultural resources base so that it does not restrict options of the future generations.
	2. Affirmative State Action for efficient management of resources and empowers the citizens to question ineffective management of natural resources
	3. The pollutant not only has an obligation to make good the loss to the victims but has to bear the costs of restoring the environment to its original state
	4. State's obligation to devise and implement a cohesive and coordinated programme to meet its obligation to sustainable development

Ans. (3)

Exp. The polluter pays principle is related to the pollutant who not only has an obligation to make good the loss to the victims but has to bear the costs of restoring the environment to its original state.

The 'polluter pays' principle is the commonly accepted practice that those who produce pollution should bear the costs of managing it to prevent damage to human health or the environment.

40 "If International Law were only a kind of morality, the framers of state papers concerning foreign policy would throw all strength on moral argument. But as a matter of fact, this is not what they do. They appeal not to the general feeling of moral rightness, but to precedents, to treaties, and to opinions of specialists. They assume the existence among statesmen and publicists of a series of legal as distinguished from moral obligations in the affairs of nations."

This observation is made by

1 Frederick Pollock   2 L Oppenheim
3 Hans Kelson   4 PC Corbett

Ans. (1)

Exp. Frederick Pollock had observed that "If International Law were only a kind of morality, the framers of state papers concerning foreign policy would throw all strength on moral argument. But as a matter of fact, this is not what they do. They appeal not to the general feeling of moral rightness, but to precedents, to treaties, and to opinions of specialists. They assume the existence among statesmen and publicists of a series of legal as distinguished from moral obligations in the affairs of nations."

He wrote that the only essential conditions for the existence of law are the existence of the political community and the recognition by its members of settled rules binding upon them in that capacity. International Law seems on the whole to satisfy these conditions.

41 What are essential tests for the existence of International Custom?

1 Uniform practice of States and longevity of time period
2 Uniform practice of States and opinio juris sine necessitatis
3 Uniform practice of States, longevity of time period and opinio juris sine necessitatis
4 None of the above

Ans. (2)

Exp. Uniform practice of States and opinio juris sine necessitatis, is essential test for the existence of International Custom.

Customary international law is comprised of two elements:

- consistent and general international practice by states.
- a subjective acceptance of the practice as law by the international community (opinio juris).

Uniform practice of state means constant and consistent usage. State practice is creative, or expressive, of rules of customary international law, but only in so far as it is undertaken with the conviction that a legal right or obligation is involved opinio juris sine necessitatis means "an opinion of law or necessity."

Opinio juris is described as the psychological component of customary international law because it refers to an attitude that states have towards a behavioural regularity. The idea of opinio juri is mysterious because the legal obligation is created by the state's belief in the existence of the legal obligation.

42 In which of the following cases, Judge Alvarez evolved a doctrine that General Assembly resolutions are virtually binding upon States in a legislative sense?

1 South West Africa Voting Procedure case, ICJ Reports, 1975, p12
2 Western Sahara case, ICJ Reports, 1975, p.12
3 Anglo-Norwegian Fisheries case, ICJ Reports, 1951, p. 152
4 South West Africa Voting Procedure case, ICJ Reports, 1955, p.67

Ans. (3)

Exp. In the case of Anglo-Norwegian Fisheries case, ICJ Reports, 1951, p. 152 Judge Alvarez evolved a doctrine that General Assembly resolutions are virtually binding upon States in a legislative sense.

Although General Assembly resolutions are generally non-binding towards member states, internal resolutions may be binding on the operation of the General Assembly itself, for example with regard to budgetary and procedural matters.

43 Which of the following cases relates to nationality of an individual which is an evidence of the link of an individual with the State?

1 Nottebohm case (Leichtenstein Vs. Guatemala), ICJ Reports, 1955, p.4
2 South West Africa, Advisory Opinion, ICJ Reports, 1971, p.16
3 Reservations to the Genocide Convention case, ICJ Reports, 1951, p.15
4 United States Diplomatic and Consular Staff in Tehran, ICJ Reports, 1980, p.3

Ans. (1)

Exp. The case of Nottebohm case (Leichtenstein Vs .Guatemala), ICJ Reports, 1955, relates to nationality of an individual which is evidence of the link of an individual with the state.

The Court held that Liechtenstein's claim was inadmissible on grounds relating to Mr. Nottebohm's nationality. It was the bond of nationality between a State and an individual which alone conferred upon the State the right to put forward an international claim on his behalf.

44 The non-permanent members of the Security Council of United Nations are elected for a term of

1 Three years   2 Five years
3 One year   4 Two years

Ans. (4)

Exp. The non-permanent members of the Security Council of United Nations are elected for a term of two years.

Each year, the General Assembly elects five non-permanent members (out of ten in total) for a two-years term. The ten non-permanent seats are distributed on a regional basis

- five for African and Asian countries.
- one for Eastern European countries.
- two for Latin American and Caribbean countries.
- two for Western European and other countries.

45 Which of the following has the power to give effect to the judgement of the International Court of Justice if a party to the case fails to perform the obligations incumbent upon it under a judgment?

1 General Assembly
2 Security Council
3 Highest National Court in the concerned state
4 International Court of Justice

Ans. *(2)*

Exp. Security Council has the power to give effect to the judgement of the International Court of Justice if a party to the case fails to perform the obligations incumbent upon it under a judgment.

The relationship between the ICJ and the Security Council and the separation of their powers, was considered by the Court in 1992.

The Court had to consider an application from Libya for the order of provisional measures to protect its rights, which, it alleged, were being infringed by the threat of economic sanctions by the UK and United States. The problem was that these sanctions had been authorised by the Security Council, which resulted with a potential conflict between the Chapter VII functions of the Security Council and the judicial function of the Court.

The Court decided, by eleven votes to five, that it could not order the requested provisional measures because the rights claimed by Libya, even if legitimate under the Montreal Convention, could no longer be upheld since the action was justified by the Security Council. In accordance with Article 103 of the UN Charter, obligations under the Charter took precedence over other treaty obligations.

46 In which of the following cases, International Court of Justice refused to give advisory opinion at the request of World Health Organisation?

1 Legality of the threat of use of nuclear weapons
2 Nicaragua Vs. USA
3 Competence of Assembly regarding admission to United Nations
4 North Sea Continental Shelf cases

Ans. *(1)*

Exp. In the case of legality of the threat of use of nuclear weapons, International Court of Justice refused to give advisory opinion at the request of World Health Organisation (WHO).

On 8th July, 1996, the ICJ ruled that it was unable to comply with a request received on September, 1993 from the World Health Organisation (WHO) to give an advisory opinion on the following question: "In view of the health and environmental effects, would the use of nuclear weapons by a State in war or other armed conflict be a breach of its obligations under international law including the WHO Constitution?"

The Court pointed out that its jurisdiction to provide an advisory opinion in response to a request by a specialised agency requires that: (i) the specialised agency requesting the opinion must be duly authorised, under the UN Charter, to request advisory opinions from the ICJ, (ii) the opinion requested must relate to a 'legal question' within the meaning of the ICJ Statute and the UN Charter and (iii) the opinion requested must relate to a question that arises within the scope of the activities of the specialised agency requesting the opinion.

47 In which of the following case the Supreme Court held that 'The Three Talaqs' would be treated as a 'Single Talaq' and not a valid Talaq?

1 Shamim Ara Vs. State of UP AIR 2002 SCR 4162
2 Mohd Ahmed Khan Vs. Shah Bano AIR 1985 SC 365
3 Bai Tahira Vs. Ali Hussain AIR 1979 SC 362
4 None of the above

Ans. *(1)*

Exp. In the case of Shamim Ara Vs. State of UP AIR 2002 SCR 4162, the Supreme Court held that 'The Three Talaqs' would be treated as a 'Single Talaq' and not a valid Talaq. The Court also held for the third option, concluding that Talaq outside of the wife's presence and delivered to her later by writing is so inequitable to Muslim wives as to be without legal sanction.

48 Ceremonies of Hindu Marriage have been laid down in minute details in

1 Dharma Sutra
2 Dharma Shastra
3 Grhiya Sutra
4 None of these

Ans. *(3)*

Exp. Ceremony of Hindu Marriage have been laid down in minute details in Grhiya Sutras.

The Grihya Sutras are sacred Hindu texts containing information regarding Vedic domestic rites and rituals meant for the householders. They were rendered into compositions probably during the same period when the Dharmashastras or the Hindu law books were composed.

The Grihya Sutras as their name suggests deal with domestic rituals such as conception, birth, initiation (upanayanam), marriage, death etc. The following translations by Hermann Oldenberg (1886) cover four Grihya Sutras, namely Sankhyayana-Grihya-Sutra, Asvalayana-Grihya-Sutra, Paraskara-Grihya-Sutra and Khadia-Grihya-Sutra.

49 To mature as a ground of Divorce the 'Desertion', under the Hindu Marriage Act, 1955, must continue for a minimum period of

1 One year
2 Two years
3 Three years
4 None of these

Ans. *(2)*

Exp. To mature as a ground of Divorce the 'Desertion', under the Hindu Marriage Act, 1955, must continue for a minimum period of two years. It is provided as a basis for divorce under Section 13 (1) (ib) of the Hindu Marriage Act, 1955. It is pertinent to note that desertion can be taken as grounds for divorce only when the abandonment or separation has occurred over a continuous period of two years. There should be no gap, that is, to say that the period of 2 years must be continuous.

50 In which of its following report the Law Commission recommended, the 'Breakdown Principle' to be accepted as the additional ground of Divorce?

1 70th Report
2 71st Report
3 72nd Report
4 None of these

Ans. (2)

Exp. The Law Commission in its 71st report, submitted in 1978, dealt with the concept of irretrievable breakdown of marriage. In this report the Law Commission recommended, the 'Breakdown Principle' to be accepted as the additional ground of Divorce.

The report deals with an important question concerning the Hindu Marriage Act, 1955, whether irretrievable breakdown of marriage can be made a ground for divorce under that Act.

The Law Commission observed that restricting divorce to matrimonial disability results in an injustice in cases where neither party is at fault, or if the fault is of such a nature that the parties do not wish to divulge it and yet the marriage cannot be worked out. It refers to a situation where the emotional and other bonds, which are the essence of marriage, have disappeared and only a facade remains.

The commission concludes that where a marriage has ceased to exist both in substance and in reality, divorce should be seen as a solution and an escape route out of a difficult situation.

51 Which of the following Ceremony/ Ceremonies are obligatory under the Hindu Marriage Act?

1 Kanyadan
2 Panigrahan
3 Saptapadi
4 All of these

Ans. (3)

Exp. Saptapadi is the obligatory ceremony under Hindu Marriage Act.

According to Section 7 of Hindu Marriage Act, 1955, a Hindu marriage may be solemnised in accordance with the customary rites and ceremonies of either party thereto, where such rites and ceremonies include the Saptapadi (i.e., the taking of seven steps by the bridegroom and the bride jointly before the sacred fire), the marriage becomes complete and binding when the seventh step is taken.

52 Children born to annulled voidable marriages or void marriages under Section 11 and 12 of the Hindu Marriage Act are

1 Illegitimate
2 Illegitimate, but can inherit the property of their parents
3 Legitimate and can inherit all family property
4 Legitimate but can inherit only the property of their parents

Ans. (4)

Exp. Children born to annulled voidable marriages or void marriages under Section 11 and 12 of the Hindu Marriage Act are legitimate but can inherit only the property of their parents.

Legitimacy of children under void and voidable marriages are specified under Section 16 of Hindu Marriage Act, 1955.

According to Hindu Marriage Act, 1955, where a decree of nullity is granted in respect of any marriage under Section 11 or Section 12, any child begotten or conceived before the decree is made who would have been the legitimate child of the parties to the marriage if it had been dissolved instead of having been declared null and void or annulled by a decree of nullity shall be deemed to be their legitimate child notwithstanding the decree of nullity.

53 In which of the following cases, the court held that 'Dower (Mehar) is a sale price of women'?

1 Humara Begum case
2 Aziz Bano Vs. Mohammed
3 Shah Bano case
4 Abdul Kadir case

Ans. (4)

Exp. In Abdul Kadir case, the court held that 'Dower (Mehar) is a sale price of women.'

Importance of Dower (Mehar) Marriage in Muslim Law provides an absolute power to the husband to divorce his wife. Therefore, Mehar is very important for balancing the rights of the husband and wife. Mehar is an absolute requirement of a Muslim marriage and so, even if Mehar is not specified at the time of marriage, the law will presume it by virtue of the contract of marriage itself. Even if a woman stipulates to forgo the Mehar, her declaration will be invalid.

In Abdul Kadir Vs Salima AIR 1980, J Mahmood has observed that the marriage contract is easily dissoluble and the freedom of divorce and of polygamy to a husband place the power in the hands of the husband, which the Muslim law intends to restrain by the mechanism of Mahr. Thus, right of wife to her Mahr is a fundamental feature of the marriage contract.

Thus, Mahr serves the following purposes:

- to impose an obligation of husband as a mark of respect to wife.
- to place a check on the power of husband to divorce and polygamy.
- to provide for subsistence of wife in the event she is divorced by the husband.

54 'Iddat' is a period during which a Muslim woman is prohibited from marrying on dissolution of marriage.

1 By Death of husband
2 By Divorce
3 Only 1 and not 2
4 Both 1 and 2

Ans. (4)

Exp. In case of death of husband or by divorce, 'Iddat' period is observed.

Under Muslim law, 'Iddat' is that period during which a woman is prohibited from re-marrying after the dissolution of her marriage. During this period the widow or a divorced wife is required to live a pure and simple life and she cannot marry again. The object of Iddat is to ascertain the paternity of a possible conception by her former husband.

55 Indicate the order in which the following words appear in the definition of 'Human Rights' as given in Section 2(d), of the Protection of Human Rights Act, 1993.

I. Life II. Liberty
III. Equality IV. Dignity

Codes

1 I, III, II and IV 2 II, III, IV and I
3 I, II, IV and III 4 I, II, III and IV

Ans. (4)

Exp. Section 2 (d) in the Protection of Human Rights Act, 1993 'human rights' means the rights relating to life, liberty, equality and dignity of the individual guaranteed by the Constitution or embodied in the International Covenants and enforceable by courts in India.

56 Who is the Chairperson of NHRC?

1 Justice JS Verma
2 Justice KG Balakrishnan
3 Justice AS Anand
4 Justice MN Venkatachalaiah

Ans. (2)

Exp. Konakuppakatil Gopinathan Balakrishnan (KG Balakrishanan), was the Chairperson of the National Human Rights Commission (NHRC) of India. He is a former Chief Justice of India. He was the first judge from the State of Kerala to become the Chief Justice of the Supreme Court.

NHRC is a statutory public body constituted on 12th October, 1993 under the protection of Human Rights Ordinance of 28th September, 1993. Arun Kumar Mishra is the current and eighth chairperson of NHRC.

57 Match List I with List II and select the correct answer with the help of codes given below.

List I		List II	
A.	Magna Carta	I.	1948
B.	International Convention on Civil and Political Rights (ICCPR)	II.	1989
C.	Universal Declaration of Human Rights	III.	1215
D.	Convention on the Rights of Child (CRC)	IV.	1966

Codes

	A	B	C	D		A	B	C	D
1	III	IV	I	II	2	II	III	I	IV
3	I	II	III	IV	4	II	IV	I	III

Ans. (1)

Exp. The correct matching is A-III, B-IV, C-I, D-II.

Magna Carta was introduced in 1215. Magna Carta Libertatum, commonly called Magna Carta, is a royal charter of rights agreed to by King John of England at Runnymede, near Windsor, on 15th June, 1215.

ICCPR is introduced in 1966. The International Covenant on Civil and Political Rights is a multilateral treaty adopted by United Nations General Assembly Resolution 2200A (XXI) on 16th December, 1966, and in force from 23rd March, 1976 in accordance with Article 49 of the covenant. UDHR came into force in 1948.

The Universal Declaration of Human Rights is an international document adopted by the United Nations General Assembly that enshrines the rights and freedoms of all human beings.

CRC came into force in 1989. The United Nations Convention on the Rights of the Child is an international human rights treaty which sets out the civil, political, economic, social, health and cultural rights of children.

58 India is not a party to

1 International Convention on Civil and Political Rights
2 International Convention on Economic, Social and Cultural Rights
3 Convention on the Rights of Child
4 Optional Protocol to International Covenant on Civil and Political Rights

Ans. (4)

Exp. India is not a party to Optional Protocol to the International Covenant on Civil and Political Rights. It was adopted and opened for signature, ratification and accession by General Assembly Resolution 2200A (XXI) of 16th December, 1966 and came into force on 23rd March 1976, in accordance with Article 9.

The State Parties to the present protocol, considering that in order to further achieve the purposes of the International Covenant on Civil and Political Rights (hereinafter referred to as the Covenant) and the implementation of its provisions it would be appropriate to enable the Human Rights Committee set up in Part IV of the Covenant (hereinafter referred to as the Committee) to receive and consider, as provided in the present Protocol. communications from individuals claiming to be victims of violations of any of the rights set forth in the Covenant.

59 The 'Convention on Elimination of All Forms of Discrimination Against Women' was entered into force in the year

1 1979 2 1981
3 1989 4 1992

Ans. (2)

Exp. The 'Convention on the Elimination of All Forms of Discrimination Against Women' (CEDAW) was adopted in 1981 by the UN General Assembly.

It is often described as an International Bill of rights for women. Consisting of a Preamble and 30 Articles, it defines what constitutes discrimination against women and sets up an agenda for national action to end such discrimination.

The Convention defines discrimination against women as, 'any distinction, exclusion or restriction made on the basis of sex which has the effect or purpose of impairing or nullifying the recognition, enjoyment or exercise by women, irrespective of their marital status, on a basis of equality of men and women, of human rights and fundamental freedoms in the political, economic, social, cultural, civil or any other field.'

60 The Committee on Economic, Social and Cultural Rights was established under ECOSOC Resolution No. 17 adopted on

1 28th May, 1985
2 30th May, 1985
3 26th April, 1986
4 24th May, 1986

Ans. (1)

Exp. The Committee on Economic, Social and Cultural Rights was established under ECOSOC Resolution 1985/No. 17 on 28th May, 1985 to carry out the monitoring functions assigned to the United Nations Economic and Social Council (ECOSOC) in Part IV of the Covenant.

The Committee on Economic, Social and Cultural Rights (CESCR) is the body of independent experts that monitors implementation of the International Covenant on Economic, Social and Cultural Rights by its States parties.

61 Which one of the following is the fourth generation of Human Right?

1 Right to Life
2 Right to Health
3 Right to Environment
4 Right to Communication

Ans. (4)

Exp. Rights to Communication is the fourth generation of Human Right.

Several analysts claim that a fourth generation of human rights is emerging. The first paper entitled Communication rights: human rights in the Information Society; from exclusion to inclusion discusses communication rights in the context of the human rights generations.

The author, while illustrating the notion of the three generations of human rights, as a way for categorizing the wide spectrum of human rights, adds that because of the notion of being 'communicative', there should be a fourth generation that studies the communication rights. The author studies the relationship of this new category with the previous generations of rights. The second paper entitled, access to information in human rights: a forgotten concept starts with this famous phrase that information is the oxygen of democracy.

The author discusses the Article 19 of the Universal Declaration of Human Rights and writes that communication rights have been somehow forgotten by the government, and these have always been civil society organizations that have always raised the issue.

62 Which of the following statement is true?

I. Under English Law Libel is actionable per-se.
II. Under Indian Law 'Libel' as well as Slander are actionable per-se.
III. Under English Law, only 'Libel' is a crime.
IV. Under Indian Law both 'Libel' and 'Slander' are crime.

Codes

1 I, II and III are correct
2 I, III and IV are correct
3 II, III and IV are correct
4 I, III and IV are correct

Ans. (1)

Exp. I, II, and III are correct. Following are the correct statements:

Under English Law 'Libel' is actionable per-se. Words are actionable per se if they are obviously insulting and injurious to one's reputation. 'Libel' involves the publication of some defamatory statement in some permanent or visible form.

Under Indian Law 'Libel' as well as Slander are actionable per-se. The Indian law does not make any distinction between the two.

Under English Law, only 'Libel' is a crime. English Law considers defamation through libel only and not through words that are spoken (slander). Slander is just a civil wrong under English law.

63 Match List I with List II and select the correct answer by using the codes given below the list.

List I	List II
A. Deficiency of services	I. Section 12
B. Grounds of making a complaint	II. Section 2(1) (g)
C. Findings of the District Forum and Relief	III. Indian Oil Corporation Vs. Lakshmi Shankar Narain (1999) 9 SCC2
D. An ex-parte unreasoned order can be recalled	IV. Section 14

Note : Section above are from the Consumer Protection Act.

Codes

	A	B	C	D		A	B	C	D
1	I	II	IV	III	2	II	I	IV	III
3	II	I	III	IV	4	II	IV	III	I

Ans. (3)

Exp. The correct matching is A-II, B-I, C-IV, D-III.

Deficiency of services has been provided under Section 2 (1)(g) of Consumer Protection Act, 1986. According to this definition, any fault, shortcomings, inadequacy, and imperfection in the quality, nature or manner of performance of the service is a deficiency. This standard has to be maintained by or under any law for the time being in force.

Grounds for making a complaint have been given under Section 12. It directs such complaints to be made to the District Forum.

Findings of the District Forum and Relief are given under Section 14. In accordance with Section 14 of the Act, the District Forum has the power to grant damages.This can be in the form of compensation, removing defects or deficiencies.

An ex-parte unreasoned order can be recalled was held in the case of Indian Oil Corporation Vs. Lakshmi Shankar Narain (1999) 9 S.C.C.2.

64 Nuisance is a form of Tort

1 which is actionable per-se
2 which is not actionable per-se
3 actionable per-se if plaintiff suffers pecuniary loss
4 None of the above

Ans. (2)

Exp. Nuisance is a form of Tort which is not actionable per-se.

The word 'nuisance' is derived from the French word 'nuire', which means 'to do hurt, or to annoy'. One in possession of a property is entitled as per law to undisturbed enjoyment of it. Nuisance is a form of tort which is not actionable per-se. If someone else's improper use in his property results into an unlawful interference with his use or enjoyment of that property or of some right over, or in connection with it, we may say that tort of nuisance occurred. In other words, Nuisance is an unlawful interference with a person's use or enjoyment of land, or of some right over, or in connection with it.

65 Given below are two statements. One is labelled as Assertion (A) and the other is labelled as Reason (R).

Assertion (A) Services rendered to a patient by a Medical Practitioner, by way of consultation, diagnosis and treatment would fall within the ambit of 'services' as defined, in Section 2(1) (O) of the Consumer Protection Act.

Reason (R) Like other professions, Medical Practitioner should also conduct himself by using of reasonable skill and care.

Find correct answer using codes given below

Codes

1 (A) is true and (R) is false
2 (R) is true, but (A) is false
3 (A) and (R), both are true, but (R) is not correct explanation of (A)
4 (A) and (R) both are true and (R) is correct explanation of (A)

Ans. (3)

Exp. (A) and (R), both are true, but (R) is not correct explanation of (A).

Section 2 (1) (O) gives the definition of services. Services rendered to a patient by a Medical Practitioner, by way of consultation, diagnosis and treatment would fall within the ambit of 'services' as defined, in Section 2(1) (O) of the Consumer Protection Act is true.

Like other professions, Medical Practitioner should also conduct himself by using of reasonable skill and care is true and in itself explains the statement but doesn't explain the assertion.

66 Which of the following is an essential constituent of negligence?

I. Defendant was under a legal duty to exercise due care.
II. This duty was owed to plaintiff
III. Defendant committed breach of such duty.
IV. That the breach of such duty was the direct and proximate cause of the damage alleged.

Codes

1 I, II and III are correct
2 I, II, III and IV are correct
3 II, III and IV are correct
4 I, II and IV are correct

Ans. (2)

Exp. All the given statements are correct.

In order to prove that the defendant was negligent and therefore liable for your injuries, you must prove all of the 'elements.' For instance, one of the elements is 'damages,' meaning the plaintiff must have suffered damages (injuries, loss, etc.) in order for the defendant to be held liable. So, even if you can prove that the defendant indeed acted negligently, you may not collect damages if you didn't suffer any injuries.

In an action for negligence, the plaintiff has to prove the following essentials:

- Duty to take care.
- Duty towards the plaintiff.
- Breach of duty to take care.
- Consequent damages.

67 The Rule of 'Absolute Liability' was laid down in the case

1 MC Mehta Vs. Union of India
2 Madras Railways Co Vs. Zamidar
3 K Nagireddi Vs. State of AP
4 Minu B Mehta Vs. Balakrishna

Ans. (1)

Exp. The Rule of 'Absolute liability' was laid down in the case MC Mehta Vs. Union of India.

Absolute liability is a standard of legal liability found in tort and criminal law of various legal jurisdictions. In case of strict or absolute liability, a person could be held guilty even if there was no intention to commit an act.

68 Consider the following elements.

I. Infringement of a legal right

II. Legal damage

III. Any damage

IV. Existence of legal right

Right to claim damages in Tort would arise only if

Codes

1 I and II are present

2 I, II and IV are present

3 I, III and IV are present

4 III and IV are present

Ans. (2)

Exp. I, II and IV are present.

In Right to claim damages in Tort would arise only if infringement of a legal right, legal damage and existence of legal right are present. Thus, damages can also be claimed when there is injuria sine damnum (injury without damage) but not in cases where there is damnum sine injuria (damage without injuria). The existence of a legal right and its subsequent breach are the primary conditions to bring about an action in tort law.

69 Which statements are correct?

Directors are

I. Trustees of Company

II. Managers of Company

III. Agents of Company

IV. Owners of Company

Codes

1 I and II are correct
2 II and III are correct
3 III and IV are correct
4 I and III are correct

Ans. (4)

Exp. Directors are the Trustees of company as well as the Agents of the company.

A company director is one of the employees within a group of managers who maintains a prolific role within an organisation and usually has the higher role within an organisation.

Directors are trustees and agents of company. This is mainly because they decide on how to control the business and also make the final and key decisions.

The company director(s) is mainly responsible for:

- Ensuring the company's strategic objectives and plans which have been set are being met.
- Analysing and monitoring the progress of its employees towards achieving the objectives and targets set.
- Appointing or hiring senior managers for certain departments such as Finance and Marketing.

70 Which one of the following is correct statement?

1 Every agency is partnership

2 Every partnership is agency

3 Every partnership is limited company

4 Every private limited company is partnership

Ans. (2)

Exp. Every partnership is agency is the correct statement. Right of all partners in a partnership to act as agents for the normal business operations of the partnership and their responsibility for their partners' business related (but not personal) actions.

71 Read the following passage and match the column.

No suit to enforce a right arising from a contract shall be initiated in any court by any person suing as a partner in a non-registered firm. Registration of firms is not compulsory. There is no penalty for non-registration. An unregistered firm cannot sue any third person for the enforcement of any right arising from contract.

Column P		Column Q	
A.	Registration	I.	No penalty
B.	Non-registration	II.	Optional
C.	Partner of a registered firm	III.	Unenforceability of his rights
D.	Partner of a non-registered firm	IV.	Can sue

Codes

	A	B	C	D		A	B	C	D
1	I	II	III	IV	2	II	I	IV	III
3	II	I	III	IV	4	I	III	II	IV

Ans. (2)

Exp. The correct matching is A-II, B-I, C-IV, D-III.

Registration of partnership firm is optional.

Non-registration of partnership firm attracts no penalty.

Partnership of a registered firm can sue as it is considered separate legal entity.

Partner of a non-registered firm cannot avail any right.

72 Given below are two statements. One is labelled as Assertion (A) and the other is labelled as Reason (R).

Assertion (A) Doctrine of Indoor Management protects an outsider dealing with a company from irregularities inside a company.

Reason (R) Doctrine of ultra vires protects an outsider dealing with a company for corporate capacity not mentioned in the objects clause.

Codes

1 (A) is true, but (R) is false

2 (A) is false, but (R) is true

3 (A) and (R) are true, but (R)is not an explanation of (A)
4 (A) and (R) are true, and (R) is an explanation of (A)

Ans. *(3)*

Exp. (A) and (R) are true, but (R) is not an explanation of (A).

Doctrine of Indoor Management protects an outsider dealing with a company from irregularities inside a company, is true. It is a common law doctrine which protects outsiders who have entered into the contract with the company, by placing the parties in the first place and company's policy behind it. It is also known as Turquand Rule.

Doctrine of ultra vires protects an outsider dealing with a company for corporate capacity not mentioned in the objects clause, is true because Memorandum of Association of a company defines the powers of a company. Any act done contrary to or in excess of the scope of the activity of the company as laid down by its memorandum of association is ultra-vires the company, i.e., beyond the legal powers and authority of the company and shall be wholly void and not binding on the company but this reason is individually true but doesn't explain the assertion.

Doctrine of ultra vires may be a principle which is related to an action taken by a private in reference to an organization or an organization which is beyond the authority of a corporation or a corporation which is incapable of ratification. Whereas intra vires is that the principle where an action taken by a private in reference to an organization or a corporation is outside the authority of director but inside the authority of the corporate and it can be ratified.

73 Match items in Column P with items in Column Q, according to provisions of the Negotiable Instrument Act.

Column P	Column Q
A. Definition of Promissory note	I. Section 30
B. Drawer of cheque	II. Section 45(-A)
C. Holder's right to duplicate	III. Section 135
D. Dishonour	IV. Section 4

Codes

	A	B	C	D		A	B	C	D
1	II	IV	I	III	2	IV	II	III	I
3	IV	I	III	II	4	IV	I	II	III

Ans. *(3)*

Exp. The correct matching is A-IV, B-I, C-II, D-III.

Section 4 in the Negotiable Instruments Act, 1881, is related to the definition of 'Promissory note'. A 'Promissory note' is an instrument in writing (not being a bank-note or a currency-note) containing an unconditional undertaking signed by the maker, to pay a certain sum of money only to, or to the order of, a certain person, or to the bearer of the instrument.

Section 30 in the Negotiable Instruments Act, 1881, talks about Liability of drawer. The drawer of a bill of exchange or cheque is bound in case of dishonour by the drawee or acceptor thereof, to compensate the holder, provided due notice of dishonour has been given to, or received by, the drawer as hereinafter provided.

Section 45 (A) in the Negotiable Instruments Act, 1881, is related to Holder's right to duplicate of lost bill, It provides, as where a bill of exchange has been lost before it is over-due, the person who was the holder of it may apply to the drawer to give him another bill of the same tenor, giving security to the drawer, if required, to indemnify him against all persons whatever in case the bill alleged to have been lost shall be found again.

Section 135 in the Negotiable Instruments Act, 1881, is related to Law of place of payment that governs dishonour. It provides where a promissory note, Bill of exchange or cheque is made payable in a different place from that in which it is made or indorsed, the law of the place where it is made payable determines what constitutes dishonour and what notice of dishonour is sufficient. A Bill of exchange drawn and indorsed in India, but accepted payable in France, is dishonoured.

74 Which statements are correct?

I. Partners have right to profit.
II. Partners have right to attend general meeting.
III. Partners have right to interest.
IV. Partners have right to appoint proxy.

Codes

1 I and II are correct
2 II and III are correct
3 III and IV are correct
4 I and III are correct

Ans. *(4)*

Exp. Statement I and IV are correct.

Duties and rights of each partner are provided in Section 12 and Section 13 of the Partnership Act.

They are

(i) every partner has a right to take part in the conduct of the business, and to share profit as well as interest.
(ii) every partner is bound to attend diligently to his duties in the conduct of business.
(iii) any difference arising as to ordinary matters connected with the business may be decided by a majority of partners and no change in the nature of the business shall be made without the consent of all the partners,
(iv) every partner has a right to have access to and to inspect and copy any books of the firm
(v) a partner is not entitled to receive remuneration for taking part in the conduct of the business.

75 **Match an item in List P with an item in List Q.**

	List P		List Q
A.	Prohibition of assignment of office by Director	I.	Section 267
B.	Appointment of alternate Director	II.	Section 312
C.	Disqualifications to be a Director	III.	Section 5
D.	Officer who is in default	IV.	Section 313

Codes

	A	B	C	D		A	B	C	D
1	IV	II	I	III	2	II	IV	I	III
3	II	IV	III	I	4	II	III	I	IV

Ans. (2)

Exp. The correct matching is A-II, B-IV, C-I, D-III.

Section 312 of compaines Act, 1956 discuss about prohibition of assignment of office by director. This section now imposes total prohibition against, any assignment of his office by a Director.

Section 313 of the Act mentions appointment of alternate director. The Board of directors of a company may authorised by its articles or by a resolution passed by the company in general meeting, appoint an alternate director to act for a director.

Section 267 mentions about disqualification to be a director. Section 267 talks about who should not be appointed as the managing director.

Section 5 of the Act mentions officer who is in default. As per Section 5 of the act, if any officer contravenes the act, that officer is said to be an 'officer in default'.

UGC-NET
LAW
SOLVED PAPER 2012 (June)
PAPER II

1 The Supreme Court held in which of the following cases that Preamble is not the part of the Constitution of India

1 Berubari case 2 AK Gopalan case
3 Balaji Case 4 Minerva Mill's case

Ans. *(1)*

Exp. In Re. Berubari Union and Exchange of Enclaves (AIR 1960 SC 845) case (also known as Berubari case) the Supreme Court held that the Preamble is not a part of the Constitution and thus cannot be amended.

The Supreme Court held that though the Preamble is not a part of the Constitution, it is a key to open the mind of framers and it can be referred to for any clarification in the event of an ambiguity.

The position was changed in the Kesavananda Bharati Vs. State of Kerala (1973), when the court held Preamble to be a part of Constitution and capable of being amended, subject to that no amendment is made to Basic Structure.

2 Article 16(4A) which gives power to the State to make laws regarding reservation in favour of Scheduled Castes and Scheduled Tribes was added by the

1 75th Amendment to the Constitution of India
2 76th Amendment to the Constitution of India
3 77th Amendment to the Constitution of India
4 78th Amendment to the Constitution of India

Ans. *(3)*

Exp. Article 16(4A) which gives power to the State to make laws regarding reservation in favour of Scheduled Castes and Scheduled Tribes was added by the 77th Amendment to the Constitution of India.

The Constitution (77th Amendment) Act, 1955 was introduced in the Lok Sabha on 31st May, 1995. This Act extended reservations for women in employment for Scheduled Castes and Tribes. This amendment inserted a new clause (4A) to the Article 16 which States that "Nothing in this article shall prevent the state from making any provision for reservation in matters of promotion to any class or classes of posts in the services under the State in favour of the Scheduled Castes and Scheduled Tribes, which in the opinion of the State, are not adequately represented in the services under the state."

3 The protection and improvement of environment including forests and wildlife of the country is

1 Directive Principle of State Policy
2 Fundamental National Policy
3 Fundamental Duty of a Citizen
4 Both Directive Principle of State Policy and Fundamental Duty of a Citizen

Ans. *(4)*

Exp. The protection and improvement of environment including forests and wildlife of the country is both a Directive Principle of State Policy and Fundamental Duty under Article 48A and 51A(g).

Article 48A in the Constitution of India 1949 provides that the State shall endeavour to protect and improve the environment and to safeguard the forests and wildlife of the country.

Article 51A(g), a fundamental duty in the Constitution 1949 provides to protect and improve the natural environment including forests, lakes, rivers and wildlife, and to have compassion for living creatures.

4 Originally, the Supreme Court consisted of a Chicf Justicc and

1 Seven other judges 2 Twelve other judges
3 Thirteen other judges 4 Fifteen other judges

Ans. *(1)*

Exp. Originally, the Constitution of India envisaged a Supreme Court with a Chief Justice and Seven other Judges.

Article 124(1) in the Constitution of India, 1949 provides that there shall be a Supreme Court of India constituting of a Chief Justice of India and, until Parliament by law prescribes a larger number, of not more than seven other Judges. The Supreme Court (Number of Judges) Amendment Act, 2019 has increased total number of judges to 34 including Chief Justice of India.

5 A resolution passed under Clause (1) of Article 249 shall remain in force for such period not exceeding

1 Three months 2 Six months
3 Nine months 4 Twelve months

Ans. (4)

➲ *Exp.* As per Article 249(2) of Constitution of India, 1949, a resolution passed under Clause (1) of Article 249 shall remain in force for such period not exceeding one year (twelve months) as may be specified therein.

Article 249(1) says that if the Council of States has declared by resolution supported by not less than two thirds of the members present and voting that it is necessary or expedient in national interest that Parliament should make laws with respect to any matter enumerated in the State List specified in the resolution, it shall be lawful for Parliament to make laws for the whole or any part of the territory of India with respect to that matter while the resolution remains in force.

The Article 249(2) further provides that if and so often as a resolution approving the continuance in force of any such resolution is passed in the manner provided in clause (1), such resolution shall continue in force for a further period of one year from the date on which under this clause it would otherwise have ceased to be in force.

6 The President's rule under Article 356 of the Constitution of India remains valid in the State for maximum period of

1 One month 2 Three months
3 Six months 4 One year

Ans. (3)

➲ *Exp.* The President's rule under Article 356 of the Constitution remains valid in the state for maximum period of six months.

According to Article 356, President's rule can be imposed on any state of India on the grounds of the failure of the constitutional machinery of that particular state.

7 The power of the Parliament to amend the Constitution of India is a constituent power laid down in Article 368 by

1 Twenty Fourth Amendment Act
2 Twenty Sixth Amendment Act
3 Forty Second Amendment Act
4 Forty Fourth Amendment Act

Ans. (1)

➲ *Exp.* The power of the Parliament to amend the Constitution of India is a constituent power laid down in Article 368 by Twenty Fourth Amendment Act, 1971.

The Twenty Fourth Amendment Act amended Article 368 on 5th November, 1971. The Twenty Fourth Amendment inserted Article 13(4) and 368(3) in the Constitution. Article 13 (4) says that an amendment under Article 368 is not subject to judicial review.

Article 368 of Constitution of India provides that Parliament may in exercise of its constituent power amend by way of addition, variation or repeal any provision of this Constitution in accordance with the procedure laid down in this Article.

8 'Jurisprudence is as big as law and bigger'. Who said this ?

1 Austin 2 Lloyds
3 Llewellyn 4 Holland

Ans. (3)

➲ *Exp.* Karl Llewellyn describes Jurisprudence as 'Jurisprudence is as big as law and bigger'.

The statement implies that the scope of Jurisprudence is much wider than law, because it encompasses various factors related to law as against a law which merely includes the bare text of law.

Austin defines 'Jurisprudence' as 'the philosophy of positive law.'

Holland defines 'Jurisprudence' as 'Jurisprudence is the formal science of positive law.'

9 "Rousseau is a Janus like figure in the history of national law" – who said this ?

1 Hobbes 2 J. S. Mill
3 Locke 4 Barker

Ans. (4)

➲ *Exp.* "Rousseau is a Janus like figure in the history of national law" is said by Robert Samuel Barker.

This statement was made in relation to the Social Contract approach to natural law reflected in the works of Rousseau. Barker observed that Rousseau turns to national law and belongs to it, he turns away from it and it belongs elsewhere.

10 Match List I (Jurist) with List II (Assumption) and select the correct answer using the codes given below the lists.

List I	List II
A. Aquinas	I. Jural postulates
B. Pound	II. Spirit of people
C. Kelson	III. Grund norm
D. Savigny	IV. Reason and will in law

Codes

	A	B	C	D		A	B	C	D
1	II	IV	III	I	2	IV	II	III	I
3	II	IV	I	III	4	IV	II	I	III

Ans. (1)

➲ *Exp.* The correct matching is A-II; B-IV; C-III; D-I.

Aquinas is related to spirit of people. Aquinas says that the law is made for the generality of men, the majority of whom are not perfect. This is certainly a practical and common sense observation.

Pound is related to reason and will in law. Pound defines law as a social institution to satisfy social wants. He says law is social engineering, which means that law is a instrument to balance between competing or conflicting interests.

Kelson is related to Grund norm. Kelson's legal system is one single unit and is a normative legal system or order.

Savigny is related to Jural postulates.According to Savigny, the origin of law lies in the Volksgeist. For the purpose of this, he made a whole new school known as the Historical school of Jurisprudence.

11 Match List I with List II and select the correct answer using the codes given below the lists.

	List I		List II
A.	Law in a Changing Society	I.	Fuller
B.	Human Law and Human Justice	II.	Friedmann
C.	The Morality of law	III.	Stone
D.	Ancient law	IV.	Maine

Codes

	A	B	C	D		A	B	C	D
1	I	III	II	IV	2	III	I	II	IV
3	II	I	IV	III	4	I	II	IV	III

Ans. *(*)*

Exp. The correct matching is A-II, B-III, C-I, D-IV.

Wolfgang Friedmann in Law in a Changing Society argues that law must adapt itself to social change if it is to remain the strength of creating social order in society.

Julius Stone is the author of the book 'Human Law and Human Justice'. Published in 1965, it is the first comprehensive study in the English language of the growth of human ideals of justice in their relevance for the law, and their relation to the legal, social, and economic conditions from which they spring.

Lon Fuller in 'the Morality of Law' published in 1964 has proposed a set of principles which he asserts should be used to decide the propriety of legal doctrines, popular will to the contrary notwithstanding.

Henry Sumner Maine is the author of the book 'Ancient Law'. His narrative spans the ancient world, in which individuals were tightly bound by status to traditional groups, and the modern one, in which individuals are viewed as autonomous beings, free to make contracts and form associations with whomever they choose.

12 Which one of the following schools of Jurisprudence considers that "a reasoned scale of values can be discovered as a basis for legal development" ?

1 Sociological 2 Historical
3 Analytical 4 Philosophical

Ans. *(4)*

Exp. Philosophical school of Jurisprudence considers that "a reasoned scale of values can be discovered as a basis for legal development."

Philosophical School is also called the Ethical School, Metaphysical School or the Law of Nature School.

The school concerns itself with the connection that law has with certain factors. Instead of studying law as it is, the school makes an attempt to explore the possible reasons that motivated the formulation of law. It is because of this enquiry, it is known as philosophical school.

The famous Jurists belonging to the school are : Hugo Grotius (1583-1645), Immanuel Kant (1724-1804), Hegel (1770-1831)

13 According to Salmond, the correlative of liberty is

1 Duty 2 No rights
3 Subjection 4 Disabilities

Ans. *(2)*

Exp. According to Salmond, the correlative of liberty is no rights.

Salmond also believed that no right can exist without a corresponding duty. Every right or duty involves a bond of legal obligation by which two or more persons are bound together.

Thus, there can be no duty unless there is someone to whom it is due; there can be no right unless is someone from who it is claimed and there can be no wrong unless their's someone who is wronged, that is to say someone whose right has been violated.

Liberty is merely an absence of a duty to abstain from the action. The correlativity of this jural relationship shows that the person against whom the liberty is held has a no-right concerning the activity to which the liberty relates.

14 Given below are two statements, one is labelled as Assertion (A) and the other is Reason (R).

Assertion (A) Customs to have the force of law must be immemorial.

Reason (R) Custom represents common consciousness of people.

Codes

1 Both (A) and (R) are true and (R) is the correct explanation of (A)
2 Both (A) and (R) are true and (R) is not a correct explanation of (A)
3 (A) is true, but (R) is false
4 (A) is false, but (R) is true

Ans. *(1)*

Exp. Both (A) and (R) are true, and (R) is the correct explanation of (A).

The Assertion is true because a custom must be immemorial to have force of law. If the custom has to be recognized as a source of law, and to receive an equal amount of force that any ordinary law of the land has, then it must have been followed for a long period of time. Antiquity or consistent usage of custom is an important element to confer the status of law.

The Reason is correct because custom needs to have sufficient longevity as it represents consciousness of people, which is equally essential for the determination whether the people desire to follow the said custom. It is worth noting that custom depends upon the will of people, and they must prove their constant desire to rely on it in order to convert the same into a law.

15 Given below are two statements, one is labelled as Assertion (A) and the other is Reason (R).

Assertion (A) International Court of Justice has power to decide cases on the basis of equity.

Reason (R) Equity is one of the general principles of law recognised by civilised nations.

Codes

1 Both (A) and (R) are true and (R) is correct explanation of (A)
2 Both (A) and (R) are true, but (R) is not a correct explanation of (A)
3 (A) is true, but (R) is false
4 (A) is false, but (R) is true

Ans. *(1)*

Exp. Both (A) and (R) are true, and (R) is the correct explanation of (A).

The Assertion is true as the International Court of justice has power to decide cases on the basis of equity. The term equity could be understood as balancing of interests, or proportionate rights and obligations resulting in fair decisions. It also includes principles of fairness and reasonability. For instance, good faith, res judicata, and impartiality of judges.

The Reason is true because Equity is one of the general principles of law recognised by civilised nations. The sources of international law under Article 38 of the International Court of Justice Statute are "general principles of law recognized by civilized nations" which includes, inter alia, principles of fairness and justice which apply in legal systems around the world.

16 Match List I with List II and select the correct answer using the codes given below the lists.

	List I (Subject Matter)		List II (Cases)
A.	International Custom	I.	SS Lotus (France Vs Turkey) PCIJ, Series A, No. 10
B.	Res Judicata	II.	UN Administrative Tribunal case, International Law Reports, 1954, P. 310
C.	Legal status of General Assembly Resolutions on decolonisation and self determination	III.	Western Sahara Case, Advisory Opinion, ICJ Rep., 1975, P. 12
D.	Human Rights	IV.	Lawless Case, American Journal of International Law, Vol. 56, 1962, P. 187

Codes

	A	B	C	D		A	B	C	D
1	I	II	III	IV	2	II	I	III	IV
3	III	II	I	IV	4	IV	II	III	I

Ans. *(1)*

Exp. The correct matching is A-I, B-II, C-III, D-IV.

SS Lotus (France Vs Turkey) PCIJ, Series A, No. 10 is related to International Customs. In this case, it was held that a rule of international law, which prohibits a state from exercising criminal jurisdiction over a foreign national who commits acts outside of the state's national jurisdiction, does not exist. Failing the existence of a permissive rule to the contrary is the first and foremost restriction imposed by international law on a state and it may not exercise its power in any form in the territory of another state.

In *UN Administrative Tribunal Case,* it was held that the principle of Res Judicata extends to bar proceedings on an issue that must necessarily have been determined in the earlier proceeding even if that precise issue was not then in dispute.

Western Sahara Case dealt with the legal status of General Assembly Resolutions on decolonisation and self determination. The International Court of Justice on 16th October, 1975, delivered an Advisory opinion on the Western Sahara case. The opinion dealt with legal issues which had arisen from the international controversy surrounding the proposed Spanish decolonization of the phosphate-rich territory. The Court first found that it was competent to comply with the General Assembly's request for an advisory opinion.

Lawless case is related to Human Rights. The European Court of Human Rights, a newly established international tribunal, recently decided its first case. This case, known as the Lawless case, concerns an alleged violation by the Government of Ireland of the Convention for the Protection of Human Rights and Fundamental Freedoms.

17 UN Commission on Human Rights has been discarded and replaced by

1 Economic, Social and Cultural Rights Committee
2 Amnesty International
3 Human Rights Committee
4 Human Rights Council

Ans. *(4)*

Exp. The United Nations Commission on Human Rights (UNCHR) was a functional commission within the overall framework of the United Nations from 1946 until it was replaced by the United Nations Human Rights Council on 15th March, 2006.

It was a subsidiary body of the UN Economic and Social Council (ECOSOC), and was also assisted in its work by the Office of the United Nations High Commissioner for Human Rights (UNHCHR). It was the UN's principal mechanism and international forum concerned with the promotion and protection of human rights.

18 Which of the following is not a primary source of International law ?

1 International Treaty
2 Decision of International Court of Justice
3 International Custom
4 General Principle of Law recognised by Civilized Nations

Ans. *(2)*

Exp. The decision of International Court of Justice (ICJ) is not a primary source of International law.

As per Article 38 of the Statute of ICJ, the Sources of International law include treaties, International customs, general principles of law as recognised by civilised nations, the decisions of national and lower courts and scholarly writings. They are the materials and processes out of which the rules and principles regulating the international community are developed. They have been influenced by a range of political and legal theories.

19 Which of the following cases relates to retroactive nature of the act of recognition of government ?

1 Aksionairnoye Obschestro AM Luthar Vs James Sagor & Co., (1921) 3 KB P 532
2 Trendtex Trading Corporation Vs. Central Bank of Nigeria, (1977) B P 529
3 Central Air Transport Inc. Vs. Central Air Transport Corporation, (1953) A C P 70
4 Nicaragua Vs USA, ICJ Rep., 1984, P. 169

Ans. (3)

Exp. The case titled as Central Air Transport Inc. Vs. Central Air Transport Corporation, (1953) BP 529 relates to retroactive nature of the act of recognition of government.

A retroactive or retrospective law is one that takes away or impairs vested rights acquired under existing laws, creates new obligations, imposes new duties, or attaches a new and different legal effect to transactions or considerations already past.

Common law principles do not favour the retroactive effect of laws in the majority of cases and canons of legislative construction presume that legislation is not intended as retroactive unless its language expressly makes it retroactive.

20 In a case concerning the legality of the threat or use of nuclear weapons, the International Court of Justice gave advisory opinion at the request of

1 UN Security Council
2 UN General Assembly
3 World Health Organisation
4 United Nations Educational and Cultural Organisation

Ans. (2)

Exp. In a case concerning the legality of the threat or use of nuclear weapons, the International Court of Justice gave advisory opinion at the request of UN General Assembly.

By a letter dated 19th December, 1994, filed in the Registry on 6th January, 1995, the Secretary-General of the United Nations officially communicated to the Registry a decision taken by the General Assembly, by its resolution 49/75 K adopted on 15th December, 1994, to submit to the Court, for advisory opinion, the following question : "Is the threat or use of nuclear weapons in any circumstance permitted under international law ?"

On 8th July, 1996, the Court rendered its Advisory Opinion, having concluded that it had jurisdiction to render an opinion on the question put to it and that there was no compelling reason to exercise its discretion not to render an opinion.

21 Which is not the modern source of Hindu Law ?

1 Equity, Justice and Good Conscience
2 Precedent
3 Sruti
4 Legislation

Ans. (3)

Exp. Sruti is a source of Ancient Law, not modern law. Sruti refers to the language of divine revelation through the sages. The Sruti comprise the four Vedas (Rig-Veda, Sum-Veda, Yajur-Veda and Atharva-Veda), the six Vedangas and eighteen Upanishads. The other Ancient sources are Smriti, Customs, Digests and Commentaries.

The modern sources of Hindu law are Equity, Justice and Good Conscience, Precedent and Legislation.

22 Consider the following propositions and select the correct answer.

I. A void marriage remains valid until a decree annulling it has been passed by a competent court.

II. A void marriage is never a valid marriage and there is no necessity of any decree annulling it.

III. A voidable marriage is regarded as a valid marriage until a decree annulling it has been passed by a competent court.

Codes

1 I, II and III are correct
2 I and II are correct
3 II and III are correct
4 I and III are correct

Ans. (3)

Exp. Among the given statements, only statements II and III are correct.

A void marriage is never a valid marriage and there is no necessity of any decree annulling it. It is void from the very beginning and is considered to have never existed. If it was never in existence, there is no need to get a declaration to that effect.

A voidable marriage, on the other hand, is regarded as a valid marriage until a decree annulling it has been passed by a competent court. Since, the status of a voidable marriage is dependent upon parties willingness whether they want to continue with the marriage or not, it operates as a valid marriage unless objected.

Statement I is incorrect because a void marriage remains void and unenforceable from the time it was made, and is not dependent upon an annulment by a court.

23 Given below are two statements, one is labelled as Assertion (A) and the other is Reason (R).

Assertion (A) Break down of marriage as such is not a ground for Divorce.

Reason (R) It may result into an easy way of dissolution of marriage and shall result into instability in the society.

Codes

1 Both (A) and (R) are correct
2 (A) is correct, but (R) is incorrect
3 Both (A) and (R) are incorrect
4 (R) is correct, but (A) is incorrect

***Ans.* (1)**

Exp. Both (A) and (R) are correct.

The breakdown of marriage as such is not a ground for Divorce in itself. This implies that no party can seek a divorce from the other party, merely on the ground that the marriage between them has failed to survive or that they have decided not to continue in the marriage any further.

The divorce may be granted only on the basis of grounds stated in the relevant laws. Section 13 of the Hindu Marriage Act 1955 and Section 27 of the Special Marriage Act 1954 provide the grounds and reasons for divorce which are as follows; Adultery, Cruelty, Desertion, Conversion, Mental Disorder, Venereal Disease, Renunciation, Not Heard Alive, No Resumption of Cohabitation, etc. Thus, Assertion (A) is correct.

The breakdown of marriage has not been incorporated as a ground in itself because it would be a very easy way out of marriage without any strong basis for dissolution of marriage. This way, the parties can approach the court for divorce on any trivial issue without any substance and that is certainly not the aim of legislation behind personal law as provided. Thus, Reason (R) is correct.

24 Dastane Vs. Dastane is a case decided by the Supreme Court relating to

1 Adultery 2 Dessertion
3 Cruelty 4 None of these

***Ans.* (3)**

Exp. Dastane Vs Dastane (1975) is a case decided by the Supreme Court relating to cruelty.

The Supreme Court examined scope and application of cruelty in relation to matrimonial remedy of divorce and found that cruelty could be a ground to end the marriage.

The court identified that the persistent threats by wife to end life amounts to cruelty. It is important to note that cruelty was not a ground of divorce under Hindu Marriage Act, 1955 before this case and an amendment of cruelty as a ground of divorce was incorporated only in the year 1976.

25 Marriages of all persons who are citizens of India belonging to various religions should be made compulsory registrable in their respective states where the marriage is solemnised. This was held by the Supreme Court in the case of

1 Githa Hariharn Vs. RBI
2 Seema Vs Ashwani Kumar
3 John Vallamathom Vs Union of India
4 None of the above

***Ans.* (2)**

Exp. In Seema Vs. Ashwani Kumar (2006), the Supreme Court held that the marriages of all persons who are citizens of India belonging to various religions should be made compulsory registrable in their respective states where the marriage is solemnised.

This was done since the Registration of Marriage, if made compulsory, can help in reducing the menace of Child Marriage which was prevalent at that time. The Court also directed the States and Union Territories to respective States to notify the procedure of marriages within three months.

26 Given below are two statements, one is labelled as Assertion (A) and the other is Reason (R).

Assertion (A) The Hindu Marriage Act, 1955 brought changes like prohibition of polygamy and bigamy and permission for inter-caste marriages.

Reason (R) The changes were brought under social pressure.

Codes

1 Both (A) and (R) are true and (R) is correct explanation of (A)
2 Both (A) and (R) are true, but (R) is not the correct explanation of (A)
3 (A) is true, but (R) is false
4 (A) is false, but (R) is true

***Ans.* (3)**

Exp. (A) is true, but (R) is false.

The Hindu Marriage Act, 1955 brought changes like prohibition of polygamy and bigamy and permission for inter-caste marriage. It is very well reflected in Section 5 of the Act, wherein essential conditions for a valid marriage have been provided.

The changes were made in order to make the law more advanced and progressive, in line with the modern requirements. It is wrong to say that such changes were made under social pressure. In fact, they were very well thought decisions arrived only after adequate deliberations.

27 An agreement made by mistake is

1 Void 2 Voidable
3 Illegal 4 Immoral

***Ans.* (1)**

Exp. An agreement made by mistake is void.

Section 20 of the Indian Contract Act, 1872 states that where both the parties to an agreement are under a mistake as to matter of fact essential to agreement, the agreement is void.

As an instance, 'A' agrees to sell to 'B' a specific cargo of goods supposed to be on its way from England to Bombay. It turns out that, before the day of the bargain the ship conveying the cargo had been cast away and the goods lost. Neither party was aware of these facts. The agreement is void.

28 Which of the following statements are true ?

I. Minor's contract can be ratified on attaining majority.

II. Minor's contract cannot be ratified on attaining majority.

III. Minor's contract can be ratified jointly by both the parties to the contract.

IV. Minor is not liable under minor's contract.

Codes

1 I and III
2 II and IV
3 I and II
4 II and III

Ans. *(2)*

Exp. Among the given statements, only statement II and IV are true.

No ratification of a minor's agreement is permitted and an agreement entered into by a minor is void ab initio. One of the reasons for the rule that a minor cannot ratify an agreement after attaining majority is that when the agreement was entered into during the minority, there was no 'proper consideration' and the 'bad consideration' is not enough for validating that agreement by its ratification. According to Privy Council stated that, a ratification in law is treated as equivalent to a previous authority, and it follows that as a general rule, a person or body of persons, not competent to authorise an act can't give validity after ratifying it.

Under Section 11 a minor is not competent to contract he is disqualified from contracting. He can, therefore, neither make valid proposal nor make a valid acceptance as defined in Section-2, Clause (a) and (b). He cannot, therefore, for the purposes of this Act be strictly called a promisor within the meaning of Clause (c). Nor can, therefore, anything done by the promise be strictly called a 'consideration' at the desire of a promisor as contemplated by Clause (d). It may, therefore, be urged that an argument by a minor cannot be strictly as being for 'consideration'.

The statements I and III are incorrect because it has already been observed that a minor's agreement cannot be ratified subsequently, either by himself alone or jointly by the other party to the agreement. In any case, it would not be valid and the agreement will remain void ab initio.

29 Given below are two statements, one is labelled as Assertion (A) and the other is Reason (R).

Assertion (A) Damages must be related to damage.

Reason (R) Damage is damaging and damages are compensating.

Codes

1 Both (A) and (R) are true, but (R) is not correct explanation of (A)
2 Both (A) and (R) are true and (R) is correct explanation of (A)
3 (A) is true, but (R) is false
4 (A) is false, but (R) is true

Ans. *(4)*

Exp. The Assertion is false, but the Reason is true.

The damages for a wrong are provided for violation of a legal right under civil laws including for a tortious wrong. It is not necessary to prove damage in order to claim damages, as a violation of legal right in itself is sufficient to claim damages in accordance with the principle of Injuria Sine Damnum.

The term 'damage' means suffering any harm or damage, such as loss of property, bodily harm, damage to reputation, etc., while the term 'damages' mean compensation in the form of money which is provided to restore the position of plaintiff to what it was before the wrong was committed.

30 Arrange the following concepts in sequence in which they appeared. Use the codes given below :

I. Offer by X to Y

II. Undue influence of X over Y

III. Demand of damages by Y from X

IV. Acceptance of the offer by Y.

Codes

1 I, II, III, IV
2 I, IV, III, II
3 II, I, IV, III
4 II, IV, I, III

Ans. *(3)*

Exp. The correct sequence of concepts in which they appeared is II, I, IV, III i.e., firstly Undue influence of X over Y, Offer by X to Y, then Acceptance of the offer by Y, and finally Demand of damages by Y from X.

In order to claim damages on the basis of a voidable agreement entered into by a person due to undue influence, he has to first establish undue influence over him by another which can be proven by showing dominance over his will either because of subsisting relations or some distressing position.

After establishing undue influence, the aggrieved can prove that defendant made an offer to him which was accepted by him under such undue influence. Eventually, he may ask for damages upon successful claim.

31 Which one of the following pairs is correctly matched ?

1 In India, consideration must follow.....from promisee only
2 In India, consideration must follow......from only promisor or only promisee
3 In India, consideration must follow.....from promisor or any other person
4 In India, consideration must follow.... from promisee or any other person

Ans. *(4)*

Exp. Consideration must follow either from the promisee himself or any other person.

According to Section 2(d) of the Indian Contract Act "when at the desire of the promisor, promisee or any other person has done or abstained from doing or does or abstains from doing or promises to do or to abstain from doing something, such act or abstinence, or promise is called a consideration for the promise. It is the benefit that each party receives, or expects to receive, when entering into a contract.

Consideration is often monetary, but it can be a promise to perform a specific act, or a promise to refrain from doing something. In order for a contract or agreement to be legally binding, every party to the contract must receive some type of consideration.

32 Given below are two statements, one is labelled as Assertion (A) and the other is Reason (R).

Assertion (A) Collateral transactions to wagering agreements are valid.

Reason (R) Only wagering agreements are declared void under Section 30 of the Indian Contract Act.

Codes

1 (A) is true, but (R) is false
2 (A) is false, but (R) is true
3 Both (A) and (R) are true, but (R) is not correct explanation of (A)
4 Both (A) and (R) are true and (R) is correct explanation of (A)

Ans. (4)

Exp. Both (A) and (R) are true and (R) is the correct explanation of (A).

Section 30 of the Indian Contract Act states that agreements by way of wager are void; and no suit shall be brought for recovering anything alleged to be won on any wager, or entrusted to any person to abide the result of any game or other uncertain event on which any wager is made.

A collateral transaction is related to wager and may be for the purpose of satisfaction of wager, but may not be wager in itself. For instance, 'X' and 'Y' enter into a bet (wager) in which 'X' loses money. If 'X' borrows the money from 'Z' to satisfy his debt owed under the wager, the agreement between 'X' and 'Z' is a collateral transaction to the wager and hence, is valid.

It may be observed that the collateral transactions to wagering agreements are valid because Section 30 declares only a wager agreement to be void.

33 Liability in torts depends on

1 quantum of damages suffered
2 involvement of intention
3 infringement of legal right
4 effect of public interest

Ans. (3)

Exp. Liability in torts depends on infringement of legal right.

Legal liability is the liability of a party imposed by a court for its actions or, in some cases, inactions, and for which the courts will award pecuniary damages as a form of redress. A legal wrong is either a violation of a person's rights or the failure to perform a legal duty for a party.

The legal maxim Injuria Sine Damnum guarantees actionable claim for a mere violation of legal right and there is no need to establish damage as such. However, according to Damnum Sine Injuria, if a person suffers only the damage, but no violation of legal right, then he is not entitled to a legal action on that basis.

34 Which of the following ingredients are essential to make master liable for the acts of the servant ?

I. Tort was committed by the servant.
II. Tort was committed in the course of employment.
III. Express authority was given by master.
IV. Master has knowledge of all constituent offers of tort.

Codes

1 I, II and III
2 I, II and IV
3 III and IV
4 I and II

Ans. (4)

Exp. Among the given statements, only statement I and II are true.

As per the principle of Vicarious Liability, a master is liable for the wrongs committed by a servant in the course of employment.

The test of liability is whether a person was acting as a servant of another, and if yes, if he committed wrong and whether such wrong was committed as a part of scope of his employment.

A person is said to be a servant of another, if he is under an obligation to obey the directions or instructions made by the master for the purpose of performance of his duties. A course of employment refers to an authorised act or even a wrongful mode of performing an authorised act.

It must be noted that there is no essential of express authority of master in order to impose liability upon him, since the master can be held liable as long as the servant acted within course of employment, either upon express or implied authority, or even when there is no authority at all in certain cases. It is also not relevant whether the master had knowledge of constituents of torts for the reasons explained above.

35 Which of the following is an essential constituent of negligence ?

I. Defendant was under or legal duty to exercise due care.
II. This duty was owed to plaintiff.
III. Defendant committed breach of such duty.
IV. That the breach of such duty was the direct and proximate cause of the damage alleged.

Codes

1 I, II and III
2 I, II, III and IV
3 II, III and IV
4 I, II and IV

Ans. (2)

Exp. All the statements I, II, III and IV are true.

Negligence is defined as a breach of duty by a person causing damage to another. It is found under civil or criminal law.

The essentials of negligence are required to be proven by the plaintiff, as generally the burden of proof is upon him.

The plaintiff must establish that defendant owed a duty of care towards him. Such duty can be established by the rule of neighbour, that is the plaintiff was most reasonably likely to be affected by the conduct of defendant.

The defendant must have caused breach of duty, that is non-observation of his duty.

The breach of duty must result in damage to the plaintiff. Damage may be of various kinds including harm against body, property, reputation or even a psychiatric injury in certain conditions.

Also, it must be established that the damage caused to the plaintiff was the direct and proximate result of defendant's conduct, that is it must be reasonably foreseeable on the part of defendant to anticipate the kind and extent of injury.

36 Which one of the following is not a good defence in suits for damages on negligence ?

1 Contributory Negligence
2 Express contract with plaintiff
3 Express contract where statute prohibits
4 Voluntary assumptions of risk

Ans. (3)

Exp. An express contract where statute prohibits does not serve as a valid defence to a claim against negligence.

When parties to a transaction or dispute had express contract that one party would not sue the other in any circumstance, such agreement is not valid if the circumstance described is prohibited by law. For instance, where a doctor has an agreement with a patient that the patient would not sue the doctor in case of medical negligence, even resulting into death.

This is not valid agreement as its object is unlawful and prohibited by law. Thus, the clause will not serve as a defence and the defendant would not be able to escape liability merely on the basis of such agreement.

Contributory negligence is a valid defence, wherein the plaintiff himself contributes to the damage caused himself, apart from the role played by defendant. Here, the amount of damages may be reduced to the extent plaintiff had contributed. The valid defences also includes assumption of risk, when a plaintiff assumes the risk involved in an obviously dangerous activity but proceeds to engage in the activity anyway, he or she may not be able recover damages for injuries.

An express contract with plaintiff may also be a valid defence provided the contract does not prevent plaintiff from taking an action against unlawful activity.

37 Match List I with List II and select the correct answer using the codes given below the lists.

List I	List II
A. Ryland Vs. Fletcher	I. Compensation for pain and suffering
B. Donoghue Vs. Stevenson	II. Loss caused by Competition in business
C. Gloucester Grammer School Case	III. Strict liability
D. Rose Vs. Ford	IV. Liability of minor for tests
	V. Liability for negligence

Codes

	A	B	C	D
1	I	II	III	IV
2	I	III	IV	V
3	III	V	II	I
4	III	IV	II	I

Ans. (3)

Exp. The correct matching is A-III, B-V, C-II, D-I, is correct.

In *Rylands Vs. Fletcher* (1868) the rule of strict liability was developed. It was held that a person who for his own purposes brings on his lands and keeps there anything likely to do mischief if it escapes, must keep it in at his peril and if he does not do so, is prima facie answerable for all the damage which is the natural consequence of its escape.

Donoghue Vs. Stevenson, (1932) is related to liability for negligence. The court held that manufacturers owe the final consumer of their product a duty of care. There need not be a contractual relationship in order for the final consumer to sue in negligence.

Gloucester Grammar School (1410) is related to loss caused by Competition in business. It was held that no legal action would succeed merely on the basis of monetary loss suffered in the absence of violation of legal right.

In *Rose Vs. Ford* (1937), it was held that compensation for pain and suffering and loss of expectation of life are just and equitable remedy and form a legitimate part of expectation of damages.

38 Given below are two statements, one is labelled as Assertion (A) and the other is Reason (R).

Assertion (A) Tort is a civil wrong redressible by an action for unliquidated damages only.

Reason (R) Law does not provide compensation in the nature of liquidated damages.

Codes

1 Both (A) and (R) are true and (R) is correct explanation of (A)
2 Both (A) and (R) are true but (R) is not the correct explanation of (A)
3 (A) is true but (R) is false
4 (A) is false but (R) is true

Ans. (3)

Exp. (A) is true, but (R) is false.

Tort is a civil wrong redressible by an action for unliquidated damages only. The tort law provides compensation which is not predetermined (unliquidated) as there is no contract between the parties necessarily and possible damage and compensation cannot be fixed beforehand. In that case, the court provides compensation based on the principles of justice, equity and conscience, or the precedents. Thus, Assertion is true.

However, it is wrong to say there is no provision for liquidated compensation in the entire law. The contract law contains provisions for such damages. As per Section 74 of the Indian Contract Act, 1872, enables an aggrieved to claim pre decided compensation (liquidated) in case of breach of contract. In such cases, the parties are at discretion to decide beforehand the amount of compensation to be provided by the party committing breach of contract to the other party. Thus, Reason is false.

39 'Z' while walking along a deserted road at night during winter saw a just born baby abandoned on a side. For a moment, he realised that he could save the baby without appreciable trouble, expense or loss of his time and also felt that if the baby is left over unprotected, it might die. But he did nothing and went away. 'P' another person also passed through that road and saw the baby and acted just like 'Z' and went away. Next morning the infant baby died of exposure. Decide who is responsible ?

1 Only 'Z' who saw first
2 'P' for omitting to be compassionate
3 Both 'Z' and 'P' for negligence
4 Neither 'Z' nor 'P' is responsible

Ans. *(4)*

Exp. In the given case neither 'Z' nor 'P' is responsible.

In order to be liable for negligence, the defendant must owe a duty of care towards plaintiff. Such duty must be the one imposed by law, and not merely motivated by morals or ethics.

In the present case, neither 'Z' nor 'P' had any such legal duty towards the just born baby. Therefore, the elements of negligence are not satisfied and hence, none of them could be held liable.

40 Decide on whom criminal liability can be fixed on the following.
The accused 'P' caught hold of the victim and exhorted on the main accused 'L' to strike the victim; upon which he inflicted a kirpan wound and consequently the victim died.

Assertions :

I. 'P' is liable for punishment
II. 'P' and 'L' are both liable for common intention
III. 'P' and 'L' are both responsible for victims death for having common object
IV. 'P' is not liable for any offence

Reasons :

1 I is quite possible
2 II is reasonable
3 III is as occasion demands
4 IV is most accurate

Ans. *(4)*

Exp. In this case, 'P' is not liable for any offence.

The situation is based on a case decided by Supreme Court of India, titled as Ajay Sharma Vs. State of Rajasthan (1998). The court held that the person escorting the victim to the main accused did not share common intention to cause death. He had merely agreed for a strike, but not for a strike resulting in death. The accused lacked requisite mens rea and hence, not held liable.

Criminal liability is generally made up of two elements: the guilty act or omission known as the 'actus reus' and the prohibited state of mind or guilty mind known as the 'mens rea'. The mental element generally requires the proof of an intention on the part of the person who commits the criminal act.

41 'M' a quack, an uneducated in matters of surgery, had performed an operation on a man for internal piles with the help of ordinary knife, unlike previous occasions, for which the man died due to haemorrhage. Decide on 'M''s liability.

I. 'M' is a recognised quack and hence not liable.
II. 'M''s profession is not legally acceptable hence liable.
III. 'M' is not liable because the man consented for such operation.
IV. 'M' is not liable because it was a post – operational syndrome

Codes

1 Statement I is correct
2 Statement II is correct
3 Statement III is correct
4 Statement III and IV are correct

Ans. *(2)*

Exp. Statement II is correct as 'M' was not professional medical personnel competent to perform the operation, so he is liable.

A quack is a 'fraudulent or ignorant pretender to medical skill'.

The facts disclose that 'M' was uneducated in matters of surgery and that he performed the operation with the help of an ordinary knife. This amounts to gross negligence on the part of 'M' for which he must have foreseen the irreparable damage as a consequence of his actions. He could control the damage here by not involving himself with the surgery and hence, he is liable.

42 Fill in the gap.
'P' in support of a just claim of 'Q' has stated against 'Z', for a sum of rupees one thousand and falsely sweared on a trial that he heard 'Z' admitted as to the just claim of 'Q'. The court decides that it was an affirmation of ________.

1 Statement of truth
2 False evidence
3 Making a declaration
4 None of the above

Ans. (2)

Exp. In the given case, the court decides that it was an affirmation of false evidence.

As per Section 191 of IPC, whoever, being legally bound by an oath or by an express provision of law to state the truth, or being bound by law to make a declaration upon any subject, makes any statement which is false, and which he either knows or believes to be false or does not believe to be true, is said to give false evidence.

The Section 193 of IPC provides that whoever intentionally gives false evidence in any stage of a judicial proceeding, or fabricates false evidence for the purpose of being used in any stage of a judicial proceeding, shall be punished accordingly.

Here, 'P' has falsely stated swearing on the trial that he heard 'Z' admitting to the just claim of 'Q'. This is clearly false evidence within the meanings of Sections 191 and 193 of IPC as provided above.

43 One of the essentials of holding a person responsible for dowry death is

1 subjected to harrassment by peer groups
2 subjected to harrassment for dowry
3 subjected to harrassment under suspicious circumstances
4 All of the above

Ans. (2)

Exp. One of the essentials for holding a person liable for dowry death is that he subjected a woman to harassment for dowry.

Section 304 B of IPC mentions Dowry death and states that where the death of a woman is caused by any burns or bodily injury or occurs otherwise than under normal circumstances within seven years of her marriage and it is shown that soon before her death she was subjected to cruelty or harassment by her husband or any relative of her husband for, or in connection with, any demand for dowry, such death shall be called "dowry death", and such husband or relative shall be deemed to have caused her death.

It is clear from the above definition that harassment by peer groups is not relevant. Also, to attract this provision, death should have been caused under suspicious circumstances.

It is important to note that the provision under Section 113B of IPC creates a presumption against husband or relatives for dowry death which is rebuttable upon sufficient evidence in their favour.

44 Fill in the gap.
An act of grievous hurt is always inferred through enormity to ________ and not merely a slight more than a frolic.

1 Murder
2 Bodily injury
3 Amputation
4 All of the above

Ans. (1)

Exp. An act of grievous hurt is always inferred through enormity to murder and not merely a slight more than a frolic.

The distinction between simple and grievous hurt is not always easy to determine.

This is intended by the framers of IPC that grievous hurt be understood to be proximate or similarly grave to the offence of murder. It implies that a hurt is classified as grievous when it could lead to death or in other words, could be life threatening.

However, a simple hurt is understood as injury which is quite trivial in nature and is slightly more than a mere frolic which is referred to as playful behaviour.

45 Given below are two statements, one is labelled as Assertion (A) and the other is Reason (R).

Assertion (A) Before Bangalore Water Supply case educational institutions were excluded from the definition of an industry.

Reason (R) Main purpose of such institutions is to impart education and not to run business or trade.

Codes

1 Both (A) and (R) are true and (R) is the correct explanation of (A)
2 Both (A) and (R) are true but (R) is not the correct explanation of (A)
3 (A) is true but (R) is false
4 (A) is false but (R) is true

Ans. (1)

Exp. Both (A) and (R) are true, and (R) is the correct explanation of (A).

The case titled Bangalore Water-Supply Vs. R. Rajappa and Others (1978) is a landmark decision on the interpretation of term 'industry' under Section 2(j) of the Industrial Disputes Act, 1947.

The judgement is known for giving wider application to the term and meaning of industry by extending its scope to include even hospitals, educational institutions and other related bodies. Before this decision, educational institutes were excluded from the definition of industry.

According to Section 2(j) of the Act, "Industry means any business, trade, undertaking, manufacture or calling of employees and includes any calling, service, employment, handicraft or industrial occupation or avocation of a workman."

The Supreme Court also laid down the triple test to determine status of an industry as an entity with systematic and organised activity, cooperation of employers and employees, for the production of goods and services. It can be observed that prior to this case, educational institutions were not included within the definition of industry and the underlying reason was education was understood to be a pure service, rather than a business or trade of any kind, similar to an ordinary trade involving production or supply of goods and services of commercial nature.

46 An individual dispute becomes industrial dispute when it is taken up by

1 Union only
2 Union or substantial number of workmen
3 Continuous support of union
4 Subsequent support of union

Ans. *(2)*

Exp. An individual dispute becomes industrial dispute when it is taken up by Union or substantial number of workmen.

It is worth noting that before insertion of Section 2-A of the Industrial Disputes Act, an individual dispute could not per se be an industrial dispute, but it could become one if taken up by the Trade Union or substantial number of workmen. The position is true based on the decisions of Bombay Union of Journalists Vs. The Hindu (1961), and Workmen of Indian Express Newspapers Ltd. Vs. Management Indian Express Newspapers (1970).

It is further pertinent to note that Section 2A does not declare all kinds of individual disputes to be industrial disputes, but only when a dispute is connected with discharge, dismissal, retrenchment or termination of workmen.

47 Which of the following statements are true ?

I. All employees are workmen.
II. All employees are not workmen.
III. All workmen are employees.
IV. All managerial staff are workmen.

Codes

1 I and II 2 II and III
3 III and IV 4 I and III

Ans. *(2)*

Exp. Among the given statements, only statements II and III are true.

Section 2(s) of Industrial Disputes Act, 1947 defines workmen as any person employed in any industry to do any manual, unskilled, skilled, technical, operational, clerical or supervisory work, for hire or reward, terms of employment be express or implied and includes any such person who has been dismissed, discharged or retrenched in connection with, or as a consequence of dispute.

It excludes persons employed in Army/Navy/Air Force/Police and those employed in mainly managerial or administrative, supervisory capacity and drawing wages of more than INR 6500.

An employee in ordinary meaning could be understood as someone serving another. It can be observed from the above definition that all employees are not workmen since workmen's definition is quite restrictive and narrow which includes only a certain kind of employee within itself. However, all workmen can be classified as employees because they are ultimately serving their employers.

48 In which of the following cases the Supreme Court held that medical representative is not workman ?

1 Standard Vacuum Oil Company Vs Commissioner of Labour
2 Anand Bazar Patrika Vs Its Workmen
3 Workmen Vs. Greaves Cotton & Co.
4 J and J Dechane Vs State of Kerala

Ans. *(4)*

Exp. In the case titled as J. and J. Dechane Distributors Vs. State Of Kerala and Ors (1974), the Supreme Court held that the medical representative in this case cannot be regarded as a workman.

The court relied on the decisions made earlier in a case D.S. Nagaraj Vs. The Labour Officer, Kurnool and Anr. (1972) where the Andhra Pradesh High Court ruled that a medical representative whose duty consisted of advertising and canvassing for sales of the products manufactured by Sandoz (India) Ltd. could not be regarded as a workman under the Industrial Disputes Act.

It also relied on the decision in Burmah Shell Oil Storage and Distributing Co. of India Ltd. and Anr. Vs. The Burmah Shell Management Staff Association and Ors., where the Supreme Court ruled that a district sales representative was not a "workman". It was true that in the course of his functions, he had to carry on some correspondence, but this was merely incidental to his main work of pushing up the sales. It was held, therefore, that his work was not either manual, clerical, technical or supervisory, and he was, therefore, not a "workman".

49 Which one of the following statements is true ?

1 The general funds of a registered trade union shall not be spent on the payment of salaries
2 A registered trade union may constitute a separate fund for the promotion of the civic and political interests
3 No appeal lies against the order of refusal of the Registrar to register a trade union
4 Every registered trade union shall not be a body corporate

Ans. *(2)*

Exp. A registered trade union may constitute a separate fund for the promotion of the civic and political interests is true.

Section 16 of Trade Unions Act, 1926 provides for constitution of a separate fund for political purposes. It states that a registered Trade Union may constitute a separate fund, from contributions separately levied for or made to that fund, from which payments may be made, for the promotion of the civic and political interests of its members, in furtherance of any of the objects specified.

The objects generally cover expenses incurred related to elections, maintenance or holding meetings necessary to give effect to the union.

50 Match List I with List II and select the correct answer using the codes given below.

List I (Subject)	List II (Provisions of Trade Union Act, 1926)
A. Appointment of Registrar	I. Section 24
B. Appeal	II. Section 10
C. Amalgamation of Trade Unions	III. Section 3
D. Cancellation of Registration	IV. Section 11

Codes

	A	B	C	D		A	B	C	D
1	II	IV	I	III	2	IV	I	III	II
3	III	IV	I	II	4	IV	III	II	I

Ans. (3)

Exp. The correct matching is A-III, B-IV, C-I, D-II.

Section 3 of the Trade Unions Act, 1926 mentions appointment of Registrars and states that the appropriate Government shall appoint a person to be the Registrar of Trade Unions for each State and may appoint as many Additional and Deputy Registrars of Trade Unions as it thinks fit.

Section 11 makes provision for Appeal and says that any person aggrieved by any refusal of the Registrar to register a Trade Union or by the withdrawal or cancellation of a certificate of registration may appeal at designated places.

Section 24 provides for amalgamation of Trade Unions, and says that any two or more registered Trade Unions may become amalgamated together as one Trade Union with or without dissolution or division of the funds of such Trade Unions or either or any of them under certain conditions.

Section 10 is related to Cancellation of Registration. As per Section 10, a certificate of registration of a Trade Union may be withdrawn or cancelled by the Registrar- (a) on the application of the Trade Union or (b) if the Registrar is satisfied that the certificate has been obtained by fraud or mistake or any other ground as specified therein.

PAPER III

1 "The new Constitution establishes, indeed a system of Government which is at the most quasi-federal, almost devolutionary in character, a unitary state with subsidiary federal features rather than the federal state with unitary features" said by

1 Dr KC Wheare
2 Dr Rajendra Prasad
3 Dr BR Ambedkar
4 Pandit Jawaharlal Nehru

Ans. (1)

Exp. "The new Constitution establishes, indeed a system of Government which is at the most quasi-federal, almost devolutionary in character, a unitary state with subsidiary federal features rather than the federal state with unitary features" said by Dr KC Wheare.

KC Wheare, described the Indian Constitution as 'quasi federal', that is "a unitary state with subsidiary federal features rather than a federal state with unitary features". He has observed that the federal principle is the method of dividing powers so that the general and regional governments are co-ordinate and independent.

2 In which of the following case it was held that 'Right to Life does not include Right to Die'?

1 Gian Kaur Vs. State of Punjab
2 Chenna Jagdeshwar Vs. State of A.P
3 State of UP Vs. Sanjay Kumar Bhatia
4 Deena Vs. Union Bank of India

Ans. (1)

Exp. In the case titled as Gian Kaur Vs. State of Punjab (1996), the court held that 'Right to Life does not include Right to Die'.

Whether suicide is in consonance with the Constitution is a matter widely debated. It first came to light in the case of P. Rathinam Vs Union of India wherein suicide was adjudged to be permissible and acceptable. This judgement was over ruled in the case of Gian Kaur Vs. State of Punjab.

The 5 judge bench in Gian Kaur Vs. State of Punjab held that the Right to Life cannot be considered the same as the Right to end life through unnatural means such as suicide.

These judgements are based on different interpretations of Article 21 of the Constitution of India (COI) which deals with 'Right to Life and Personal Liberty'. They also seek to determine the legality of Section 306 of the Indian Penal Code (IPC) which punishes abettors to suicide and Section 309 of the IPC which punishes the person who attempted suicide. Since the act of committing suicide is itself illegal, the act of abetting suicide is also automatically a punishable offence.

3 Given below are two statements, one is labelled as Assertion (A) and the other is Reason (R).

Assertion (A) An accused person cannot be compelled to give his signature or thumb impression.

Reason (R) An accused person cannot be compelled to be a witness against himself.

Codes

1 (A) is true, but (R) is false
2 (A) is false, but (R) is true
3 Both (A) and (R) are true
4 Both (A) and (R) are false

Ans. (2)

Exp. (A) is false, but (R) is true.

According to Article 20(3) of Indian Constitution, no person accused of an offence can be compelled to be a witness against himself. However, such compulsion is prohibited only in case of testimonial evidence; wherein interference with mind or memory is caused. In case where there is no testimonial evidence, such as a signature or thumb impression, the compulsion is permitted.

The testimonial evidence amounts to information obtained by narco analysis, lie detector tests, which cannot be forcibly employed without legal sanction.

4 After a Money Bill has been passed by the House of the People, within how many days it is transmitted to the Council of States for its recommendations ?

1 Thirty days
2 Twenty four days
3 Sixty days
4 Fourteen days

Ans. (4)

Exp. After a Money Bill has been passed by the House of the People, within fourteen days, it shall be sent to the Council of States for its recommendations.

A Money Bill after having been passed by the Lok Sabha, and sent to Rajya Sabha for its recommendations, has to be returned to Lok Sabha by the Rajya Sabha, with in a period of fourteen days from the date of its receipt, with or without recommendations.

It is open for the Lok Sabha, to either accept or reject all or any of the recommendations of the Rajya Sabha. In case a Money Bill is not returned by the Rajya Sabha to the Lok Sabha within a period of fourteen days from the date of its receipt, it is deemed to have been passed by both Houses in the form in which it was passed by the Lok Sabha after the expiry of said period.

5 Given below are two statements, one is labelled as Assertion (A) and the other is Reason (R).

Assertion (A) Directive Principles are not enforceable by any Court.

Reason (R) Directive Principles are more or less fundamental in the governance of the country.

Codes

1 Both (A) and (R) are true, but (R) is not the correct explanation of (A)
2 Both (A) and (A) are true and (R) is the correct explanation of (A)
3 (A) is false, but (R) is true
4 (A) is true, but (R) is false

Ans. (1)

Exp. Both (A) and (R) are true but (R) is not the correct explanation of (A).

The Directive Principles of State Policy (DPSPs) are not enforceable in a court of law, meaning thereby, that no legal action can be taken for or against implementation of any idea mentioned therein. It is because the principles contained therein are discretionary for the government and depends upon availability of necessary resources.

The fact that DPSPs are fundamental in governance of country is correct in itself but does not support the Assertion, as the fundamental nature must have rendered DPSP to be enforceable, but that is not the case clearly.

6 The Supreme Court does not have original jurisdiction regarding a dispute between

1 a citizen and a State
2 the Government of India and one State
3 two States
4 the Government of India and one State on one side and one State on the other side

Ans. (1)

Exp. The Supreme Court does not have original jurisdiction regarding a dispute between a citizen and a State.

Article 131 of Indian Constitution mentions Original jurisdiction of the Supreme Court, which will have original jurisdiction in any dispute between the Government of India and one or more States; or between the Government of India and one State or States on one side and one or more other States on the other; or between two or more States, if and in so far as the dispute involves any question (whether of law or fact) on which the existence or extent of a legal right depends.

7 In the Constitution of India, provision relating to the formation of new states can be amended by

1 A Parliamentary resolution which should be ratified by majority of State Legislatures
2 A simple majority in each House of Parliament
3 3/4th majority in the Parliament
4 2/3rd majority in the each House of Parliament provided they also constitute the majority of total members of each House

Ans. (2)

Exp. In the Constitution of India, provision relating to the formation of new states can be amended by a simple majority in each house of Parliament.

Article 3 of the Indian Constitution says that Parliament of India can form new states by separation of a territory from any state. e.g., State of Bombay was bifurcated in Gujarat and Maharashtra on 1st May, 1960.

The Parliament has power to increase or decrease the area of a state. It can diminish the area of the state and alter the boundaries. The name of the state can also be changed using powers given by Article 3.

8 Holding of periodic, free and fair elections by the Election Commission is part of the basic structure of the Constitution as per the following

1 Election Commission of India Vs. AIADMK
2 SS Dhanoa Vs. Union of India
3 In Gujarat Assembly Election matter
4 Sadiq Ali Vs. Election Commission of India

Ans. (3)

Exp. Holding of periodic, free and fair elections by the Election Commission is part of the basic structure of the Constitution as per in Gujarat Assembly Election matter.

The case was filed under Article 143(1) of the Constitution of India as Special Reference Case 1 of 2002. The Supreme Court held that it is no doubt true that democracy is a part of the basic structure of the Constitution and periodical, free and fair election is substratum of democracy. If there is no free and fair periodic election, it is end of democracy.

9 Writ of Mandamus cannot be issued, where a Fundamental Right is infringed by

1 A Statute
2 A Statutory Order
3 An Executive Order
4 Private Body

Ans. (4)

Exp. Writ of Mandamus cannot be issued, where a Fundamental Rights is infringed by Private Body.

'Mandamus' means 'we command'. It is issued by the Court to direct a public authority to perform a legal and public duty as a part of discharge of obligations.

It can be issued by the Court against a public official, public corporation, tribunal, inferior court or the government. It cannot be issued, inter alia, against a private individual or body, the President or Governors of States or against Parliament.

Further, it cannot be issued when the duty in question is discretionary and not mandatory, for the performance of a non-statutory function, performance of the duty involves rights of purely private nature, where such direction involves violation of any law, where there is any other remedy available under the law.

10 Given below are two statements, one is labelled as Assertion (A) and the other is Reason (R).

Assertion (A) The principles of natural justice ensures fair hearing.

Reason (R) It requires unbiased judge to decide after hearing all parties.

Codes

1 Both (A) and (R) are true and (R) is the correct explanation of (A)
2 Both (A) and (R) are true and (R) is not the correct explanation of (A)
3 (A) is true, but (R) is false
4 (A) is false, but (R) is true (R)

Ans. (1)

Exp. Both (A) and (R) are true and (R) is the correct explanation of (A).

Natural justice comprises of certain principles that need to be followed in order to have a fair and just procedure. One of the most important principles is 'NEMO JUDEX IN CAUSA SUA', which means no man shall be a judge in his own cause'. In other words, the deciding authority must be impartial and without bias.

The bias may arise in many situations, such as the judge being personally interested in the matter, or having a pre-existing relation with the parties to the case, or otherwise not competent to decide the matter on merit. A judge is expected to recuse himself from such matter in which he appears to have possibility of bias.

Therefore, it is clear that principle of natural justice ensures fair hearing because according to it, the judges must be impartial and unbiased in any given matter.

11 Prerogative writs to review an administrative action are

1 Two : Writ of Habeas Corpus and Writ of Mandamus
2 Three : Writ of Habeas Corpus, Writ of Mandamus and Writ of Prohibition
3 Four : Writ of Habeas Corpus, Writ of Mandamus, Writ of Prohibition, Writ of Certiorari and Writ of Quo Warranto
4 Five : Writ of Habeas Corpus, Writ of Mandamus, Writ of Quo Warranto, Writ of Certiorari and Writ of Prohibition

Ans. (4)

Exp. There are five Prerogative writs to review an administrative action which are Writ of Habeas Corpus, Writ of Mandamus, Writ of Quo Warranto, Writ of Certiorari and Writ of Prohibition.

A writ is a prerogative order by appropriate court issued for enforcement of a right; fundamental or legal. In India, the remedy of writ is available before Supreme Court under Article 32 only for enforcement of fundamental right, while before a high court, under Article 226 for either a fundamental or legal right.

A Writ of Habeas Corpus is issued to release a person under unlawful detention. Such writ may be issued against a state as well as a non state party.

The Writ of Mandamus is issued against a public official to perform a public and official duty. It cannot be issued against a private person.

A Writ of Quo Warranto is issued to question authority of a person holding a public office.

A Writ of Prohibition and Certiorari may be issued in order to prevent or rectify a jurisdictional error. While the former is issued after a legal proceeding has been initiated wherein there is a jurisdictional error but it has not concluded as of now to prevent the proceeding from continuing, the latter is issued when such proceeding has concluded in which the higher court will examine the records of lower court and may strike the decision if required.

12 A mandatory procedural requirement for an administrative tribunal must be

1. Legal representation
2. Cross examination
3. Reasoned decision
4. All of the above

Ans. (4)

Exp. A mandatory procedural requirement for an administrative tribunal must be Legal representation, Cross examination and Reasoned decision.

The Constitution of India empowers the government to establish tribunals for certain matters under Article 323A and for other matters under Article 323B.

Tribunal is a quasi-judicial institution that is set up to deal with problems such as resolving administrative or related disputes.

Administrative Tribunals are agencies created by specific enactments to adjudicate upon controversies that may arise in the course of the implementation of the substantive provisions of the relative enactments.

The tribunals are generally given the power of a civil Court enjoyable under the code of Civil Procedure in the matters of summoning witness, compulsory production and discovery and documents, receiving of evidence on oath and on affidavit, issuing commissions etc.

Apart from this, they are required to follow the principles of natural justice in deciding the cases. It is because of this that legal representation, cross examination and reasoned decisions are mandatory even for a tribunal.

13 Judicial review of an administrative action means

1. Review by the Parliament
2. Review by the Government
3. Review by the Legislative Assembly
4. Review by the Judiciary

Ans. (4)

Exp. Judicial review of an administrative action means review by the judiciary.

Judicial Review is the power exercised by courts to examine actions of legislatures and administrative functions of government.

It is important to note that it has been considered a basic structure of the constitution in the case Indira Gandhi Vs. Raj Narain (1975).

Some provisions in the constitution supporting the process of judicial review are; Article 372 (1) establishes the judicial review of the pre-constitution legislation. Article 13 declares that any law which contravenes any of the provisions of the part of Fundamental Rights shall be void.

Articles 32 and 226 confer status of the protector and guarantor of fundamental rights to the Supreme and High Courts. Article 137 gives a special power to the SC to review any judgment pronounced or order made by it. An order passed in a criminal case can be reviewed and set aside only if there are errors apparent on the record.

14 Match an item in List I with correct answer in List II.

List I		List II
Institution of Lokpal and Lokayukta	I.	Law should be able to control the numerous wide discretionary powers
	II.	Ensure fair hearing
	III.	Evaporate maladministration and corruption to bring good governance
	IV.	Check and control abuse of power and executive excesses

Ans. (3)

Exp. Institution of Lokpal and Lokayukta is to evaporate maladministration and corruption to bring good governance.

The lokpal and lokayuktas Act, 2013 act was enforced in 2014, to provide for the establishment of a body of Lokpal for the Union and Lokayukta for States to inquire into allegations of corruption against certain public functionaries and for matters connected therewith or incidental thereto.

These institution are statutory bodies without any constitutional status. They perform the function of 'ombudsman' and inquire into allegations of corruption against certain public functionaries and for related matters.

15 Which of the following statements is correct?

1. Administrative law is a branch of public law and is only a part of Constitutional law. It cannot control the Constitutional law
2. Administrative law is a branch of private law
3. Administrative law is independent to Constitutional law
4. Administrative law is neither the branch of public law nor of private law, but a part of Constitutional law

Ans. (1)

Exp. Statement 1 is correct regarding Administrative Law.

Administrative Law is a branch of public law and is only a part of constitutional law. It cannot control the constitutional law.

Administrative law has only very recently been developed as a separate branch of legal studies. Earlier it was considered to be a part of Constitutional Law.

There is no precise definition of administrative law, it could be understood as a law that has certain principles which help in the administration of the country.

The Constitution of India is the highest source of administration in the country. Terms such as rule of law, judicial review and separation of power are as such no where mentioned in the Constitution, but these are some of the very essential principles of the administrative law.

Since the Constitution is placed above all, nothing including administrative law can control or influence the Constitution. On the contrary, all laws need to be in compliance with Constitution.

16 Bentham's definition of law is imperative in nature because

1 law is an assembling of signs
2 law is a declaration of violation conceived or adopted by sovereign in a state
3 because it is adopted by non-sovereign State
4 Both 1 and 2

Ans. (4)

Exp. Bentham's definition of law is imperative in nature because law is an assembling of signs and law is a declaration of violation conceived or adopted by a sovereign in a state.

Bentham's definition of a law is that a law may be defined as an assemblage of signs declarative of a violation conceived or adopted by the sovereign in a state, concerning the conduct to be observed in a certain case by a certain person or class of persons, who in the case in question are or are supposed to be subject to his power.

17 The term 'Legal theory' has been first time used by

1 Llewlyn
2 Ihring
3 Salmond
4 W Friedmann

Ans. (4)

Exp. 'Legal theory' term has been used first time by W Friedmann.

Legal theory can be understood to be the study of philosophical notion of law. It reflects the struggle of law between tradition and progress, stability and change, certainty and flexibility.

The word 'legal theory' was coined by Dr.W. Friedmann in 1945. Philosophers of legal theory have been categorised into different schools of thoughts on the basis of their approach to law, such as natural law, analytical school, historical, sociological and realist schools.

18 Bracket Theory of corporate personality is also known as

1 Concession theory
2 Symbolist theory
3 Fiction theory
4 Will theory

Ans. (2)

Exp. The Bracket Theory of corporate personality is also known as the Symbolist Theory.

This theory was propounded by Rudolph Ritter von Jhering (also Ihering). According to Ihering, the conception of corporate personality is essential and is merely an economic device by which we can simplify the task of coordinating legal relations.

Hence, when necessary, it is emphasised that the law should look behind the entity to discover the real state of affairs. This is also similar to the concept of lifting of the corporate veil. This group believed that the juristic personality is only a symbol to facilitate the working of the corporate bodies. Only the members of the corporation are 'persons' in real sense of the term and a bracket is put around them to indicate that they are to be treated as one single unit when they form themselves into a corporation.

19 'A' says to 'B' that he will give a sum of rupees five thousand if 'B' marries his daughter, this is

1 Vested Right
2 Contingent Right
3 Primary Right
4 Secondary Right

Ans. (2)

Exp. 'A' says to 'B' that he will give a sum of rupees five thousand if 'B' marries his daughter, this is Contingent right.

The word 'contingent' denotes that there is no present interest or right but only a conditional one which will become effective upon the happening of the designated condition.

A contingent remainder is the right to possess property after the death of a person who holds a life estate in the land provided a specified condition is fulfilled.

An owner of land who grants a life estate to a son, with a remainder to a daughter if she marries, has created a contingent remainder, the contingency being the daughter's marriage.

20 Given below are two statements, one is labelled as Assertion (A) and the other is Reason (R).

Assertion (A) Kelson follows Kant in distinguishing between 'is' and 'ought'.

Reason (R) Kelson is a forerunner of Philosophical school.

Codes

1 Both (A) and (R) are true, and (R) is the correct explanation of (A)
2 Both (A) and (R) are true but (R) is not a correct explanation of (A)
3 (A) is true, but (R) is false
4 (A) is false, but (R) is true

Ans. (1)

Exp. Both (A) and (R) are true, and (R) is the correct explanation of (A).

Hans Kelson was great jurist of the analytical school, who gave a theory "the Pure Theory of Law". This theory is known as Pure Theory of Law because he separates law from politics, sociology, history, economic ,psychology ,ethics etc. Kelson said law must be "As it is" not "ought to be". Kelson follows Kant in distinguishing between 'is' and 'ought'.

Kelson was a forerunner of Philosophical school or Natural law and therefore did not enjoin law and morality. Natural law or the philosophical school is the moral theory of jurisprudence which states that laws should be on the basis of ethics and morals.

21 The possession is the

1 five point in ownership
2 seven point in ownership
3 nine point in ownership
4 ten point in ownership

Ans. (3)

Exp. The possession is the nine point in ownership.

It's an idiom reflects that once someone actually has physical custody of something, it's generally far more difficult to get it back from them than it might be to prevent them from taking it in the first place.

Legally, it reflects the difficulty of establishing ownership of a physical good without having actual possession of that good.

22 Which of the following duties have been included by Austin in the category of 'absolute duties' ?

I. Duties owed to persons indefinitely

II. Self regarding duties

III. Duties owed to the sovereign

IV. Duties owed to the parents

Select the correct answer using the codes given below

1 I, III and IV
2 II, III and IV
3 I, II and IV
4 I, II and III

Ans. *(4)*

Exp. According to Austin, absolute duties includes duties owed to persons indefinitely, self regarding duties, duties owed to the sovereign.

Austin said absolute duties are those duties which exist without any right as a natural corollary. These bind the people in entirety in any condition.

Austin suggested four kinds of absolute duties (i) Duties to those who are not human beings, such as duty towards god, (ii) Duties towards indeterminate persons or public at large, such as duty not to commit nuisance, (iii) Self-regarding Duties, such as duty not to commit suicide or duty not to become intoxicated, and (iv) Duty towards State or sovereign. He also classified Relative duties, on the otherhand, as those to which there is a corresponding right in some person or definite body of persons eg. duty to pay one's debt to the creditor.

23 Which one of the following get along correctly ?

1 Trust and co-ownership
2 Legal and contingent ownership
3 Sole and limited ownership
4 Legal and equitable ownership

Ans. *(4)*

Exp. Among the given choices, Legal and equitable ownership get along correctly.

Jurists have defined ownership in different ways. All of them accept the right of ownership as the complete or supreme right that can be exercised over anything. Thus, according to Hibbert ownership includes four kinds of rights within itself; Right to use a thing, Right to exclude others from using the thing, Disposing of the thing, Right to destroy it.

Ownership may be of various kinds. Broadly, it may be classified under the following heads; (1) Vested and Contingent ownership,(2) Sole and Co-ownership, (3) Corporeal and Incorporeal ownership,(4) Legal and Equitable ownership,(5) Trust and Beneficial ownership, (6) Absolute and Limited ownership.

24 A person who causes bodily injury to another who is labouring under a disorder, disease or bodily infirmity and thereby accelerates the death of the person. Under which it shall be deemed to have caused his death ?

1 Explanation I to Section 299
2 Explanation I to Section 300
3 Explanation II to Section 299
4 Explanation II to Section 300

Ans. *(1)*

Exp. In the given case study, Explanation I to Section 299 shall be deemed to have caused of his death.

Section 299 of IPC defines Culpable homicide and states that whoever causes death by doing an act with the intention of causing death, or with the intention of causing such bodily injury as is likely to cause death, or with the knowledge that he is likely by such act to cause death, commits the offence of culpable homicide.

Explanation I to Section 299 states that a person who causes bodily injury to another who is labouring under a disorder, disease or bodily infirmity, and thereby accelerates the death of that other, shall be deemed to have caused his death.

25 In which provision of Indian Penal Code the definition of 'valuable security' is explained ?

1 Section 29
2 Section 30
3 Section 31
4 Section 13

Ans. *(2)*

Exp. Section 30 of Indian Penal Code explains 'valuable security'.

According to this provision, the words 'valuable security' denote a document which is, or purports to be, a document whereby any legal right is created, extended, transferred, restricted, extinguished or released, or where by any person acknowledges that he lies under legal liability or has not a certain legal right.

As an instance, 'A' writes his name on the back of a Bill of exchange. As the effect of this endorsement he can transfer the right to the bill to any person who may become the lawful holder of it, then the endorsement is a 'valuable security'.

26 State the age limit prescribed under Section 82 of Indian Penal Code in which if a child commits an overt act is not considered as an offence ?

1 Under the age of 12 years
2 Under the age of 7 years
3 Under the age of 16 years
4 Under the age of 18 years

Ans. *(2)*

Exp. Section 82 in the Indian Penal Code states that an act of a child under 7 years of age is not an offence.

The provision is based on legal maxim Doli Incapax, which means incapability of committing a crime. Since, a child below seven years of age is mentally incompetent and lacks requisite mens rea under the criminal law, which is one of the essential ingredients for commission of a crime and imposing liability, he/she is exempted from punishment by the above provision.

27 When the injury is intentional and sufficient to cause death in the ordinary course of nature and death follows. The offence is of the category

1 Attempt to murder
2 Culpable homicide not amounting to murder
3 Murder
4 Attempt to suicide

Ans. *(3)*

➲ *Exp.* When the injury is intentional and sufficient to cause death in the ordinary course of nature and death follows, the offence is of the category of Murder.

Section 300 of Indian Penal Code, 1860 provides definition of Murder when the act by which the death is caused is done with the intention of causing death, it is done with the intention of causing such bodily injury as the offender knows to be likely to cause the death of the person to whom the harm is caused, it is done with the intention of causing bodily injury to any person and the bodily injury intended to be inflicted is sufficient in the ordinary course of nature to cause death, the person committing the act knows that it is so imminently dangerous that it must, in all probability, cause death or such bodily injury as is likely to cause death and commits such act without any excuse for incurring the risk of causing death or such injury as aforesaid.

28 Principle : Theft + Violence or Threat to violence = Robbery.
Facts 'M' meets 'B' and her child on a river bridge. M takes the child and threatens to fling it down to the river unless 'B' delivers her purse. 'B' in consequence delivers her purse. What offence 'M' has committed ?

1 'M' is liable for theft
2 'M' is liable for coercion
3 'M' is liable for robbery
4 'M' is liable for extortion

Ans. *(3)*

➲ *Exp.* In this case 'M' is liable for robbery.

Section 30 of IPC defines 'Robbery' and states that in all robbery there is either theft or extortion. Theft is "robbery" if, in order to the committing of the theft, or in committing the theft, or in carrying away or attempting to carry away property obtained by the theft, the offender, for that end, voluntarily causes or attempts to cause to any person death or hurt or wrongful restraint, or fear of instant death or of instant hurt, or of instant wrongful restraint.

Extortion is "robbery" if the offender, at the time of committing the extortion, is in the presence of the person put in fear, and commits the extortion by putting that person in fear of instant death, of instant hurt, or of instant wrongful restraint to that person or to some other person, and, by so putting in fear, induces the person so put in fear then and there to deliver up the thing extorted.

29 Fill in the gap.
A disability for _______ days constitutes grievous hurt.

1 A week
2 A fortnight
3 A month
4 A minimum of twenty days

Ans. *(4)*

➲ *Exp.* A disability for a minimum of twenty days constitutes grievous hurt.

In accordance with Section 320 of IPC, the following kinds of hurt only are designated as 'grievous'; Emasculation, Permanent privation of the sight of either eye, Permanent privation of the hearing of either ear, Privation of any member or joint, Destruction or permanent impairing of the powers of any member or joint, Permanent disfiguration of the head or face, Fracture or dislocation of a bone or tooth, any hurt which endangers life or which causes the sufferer to be during the space of twenty days in severe bodily pain, or unable to follow his ordinary pursuits.

30 Fill in the gap with appropriate word.
Wrongful restraint means keeping a person from out of his _______ of his residence.

1 House   2 Place   3 Hotel   4 Guest House

Ans. *(2)*

➲ *Exp.* Wrongful restraint means keeping a person from out of his place of his residence.

Section 339 in the Indian Penal Code defines wrongful restraint and states that whoever voluntarily obstructs any person so as to prevent that person from proceeding in any direction in which that person has a right to proceed, is said wrongfully to restrain that person.

The offence under the above provision can be committed as soon as a person is kept out of any place of his residence and not necessarily a house, hotel or guest house.

However, the obstruction of a private way over land or water which a person in good faith believes himself to have a lawful right to obstruct, is not an offence within the meaning of this Section.

31 Fill in the gap which is more appropriate.
Inducing a girl under 18 years of age to go away with him from _______ is an offence.

1 Normal home   2 Place of work
3 Domestic area   4 Any place

Ans. *(4)*

➲ *Exp.* Inducing a girl under 18 years of age to go away with him from any place is an offence.

The offence in this situation amounts to procuration of minor girl. The provision says that whoever, by any means whatsoever, induces any minor girl under the age of eighteen years to go from any place or to any act with intent that such girl may be, or knowing that it is likely that she will be, forced or seduced to illicit intercourse with another person shall be punishable with imprisonment which may extend to the years, and shall also be liable to fine.

32 Find the correct answer.
The principle of intergenerational equity envisages

1 Conservation of options
2 Conservation of quality
3 Conservation of access
4 All of the above

Ans. (4)

Exp. The principle of intergenerational equity envisages Conservation of options, Conservation of quality and Conservation of access.

The principle of intergenerational equity states that every generation holds the Earth in common with members of the present generation and with other generations, past and future. The principle articulates a concept of fairness among generations in the use and conservation of the environment and its natural resources (see also Conservation of Natural Resources; Environment, International Protection). The principle is the foundation of sustainable development.

The concept aims to preserve the alternative measures for environment protection, the quality of resources which are replaced with the older ones and assures their access for generations to come in future.

33 Find the correct answer.
The Supreme Court allowed compensation of ₹ 23.84 lakhs and later allowed additional compensation of ₹ 47 lakhs to the farmers whose crops got damaged, being irrigated by subsoil water drawn from a stream which was polluted from untreated effluents of industries. It was decided in the case of

1 Vellore Citizens Welfare Forum Vs. Union of India
2 Indian Council For Environment Action Vs. Union of India
3 S Jagannath Vs. Union of India
4 Narmada Bachao Andolan Vs. Union of India

Ans. (2)

Exp. The given situation was decided in the case of Indian Council for Environment Action Vs. Union of India (1996).

The Supreme Court in this case developed the concept of polluters pay, according to which enterprises engaging in activities leading to damage to environment or climate, are required to legally restore the cost suffered by victims.

The court also made it clear that the principle of polluters pay is applicable despite having taken reasonable care which will have no impact while imposition of the aforesaid liability.

34 The concept of sustainable development contains which of the following essentials ?

1 The precautionary principle
2 The polluter pays principle
3 The doctrine of public trust
4 All of the above

Ans. (4)

Exp. The concept of sustainable development contains the precautionary principle, the polluter pays principle, the doctrine of public trust.

Environmental Law is one of the fastest growing aspects of law. Various laws have been enacted domestically and internationally prohibiting certain practices that harm the environment or ways to conduct activities that might potentially harm the environment in an environmental friendly way.

Thus, to create a balance between development and environmental protection the concept of sustainable development was introduced.

The essentials of sustainable development include precautionary principle for which the Supreme Court in M. C. Mehta Vs. Union of India (2004) stated that the principle requires anticipatory action to be taken to prevent harm. The harm can be prevented even on a reasonable suspicion.

Further, the need and implementation of polluters pay principle has been highlighted in the case of Indian Council For Environment Action Vs. Union of India (1996) wherein the court has said that the person damaging environment must make good the loss suffered at the hands of activities undertaken.

The Supreme Court in the case of M.C. Mehta Vs. Kamal Nath (1997) applied the Public Trust Doctrine and stated that it rests on the principle that certain resources like air, sea, waters and forests have such great importance to the people as a whole that it would be unjustified to make them a subject of private ownership.

35 Given below are two statements, one is labelled as Assertion (A) and the other is Reason (R).

Assertion (A) The Supreme Court in Banwasi Seva Ashram Vs. State of Uttar Pradesh, permitted the government agency to acquire the forest land, ousting certain tribal dwellers to implement a power project only after they agreed to provide certain facilities approved by the Court.

Reason (R) Because the governmental action had an environmental impact that threatened to dislocate poor forest dwellers and disrupt their life-style infringing their Fundamental Right to Life, which include the right to livelihood.

Codes

1 (A) is true but (R) is false
2 (A) and (R) both are true, but (R) is not a correct explanation of (A)
3 (A) is false but (R) is true
4 Both (A) and (R) are true and (R) is correct explanation of (R)

Ans. *(4)*

Exp. Both (A) and (R) are true, and (R) is the correct explanation of (A).

The Supreme Court of India accepted a letter written to the Court as writ petition in the Seva Ashram Vs. State of Uttar Pradesh case. The court had to consider issues relating to the claim to land and related rights of the Adivasis living within Dudhi and Robertsganj Tehsils in the District of Mirzapur in Uttar Pradesh.

It came to light that Adivasis and other backward people living within the forest used the forest area as their habitat. They had raised several villages within these two Tehsils and for generations had been using the forests around for collecting the requirements for their livelihood.

It is for this reason to protect their livelihood and habitat, the court ordered provision of certain facilities of necessity before acquisition of their lands by government authorities.

36 The Supreme Court observed that noise pollution cannot be tolerated, even if such noise was a direct result of and was connected with religious activities in the case of

1 AP Pollution Control Board Vs. from MV Naidu
2 Church of God (Full Gospel) in India Vs. KKR Majestic Colony Welfare Association
3 KM Chinappa Vs. Union of India
4 Narmada Bachao Andolan Vs. Union of India

Ans. *(2)*

Exp. The Supreme Court observed that noise pollution cannot be tolerated even if such noise was a direct result of and was connected with religious activities in the case of Church of God (Full Gospel) in India Vs. KKR Majestic Colony Welfare Association, (2000).

The Supreme Court in this case said that the right to freedom of religion under Articles 25 and 26 of the Constitution is not absolute, and are subjected to the reasonable restrictions on the basis of health of other people as well.

Further, that the use of drums, amplifiers loudspeakers, etc. at a religious place is to be done in a manner so that the peace of others may not be disturbed.

37 Given below are two statements, one is labelled as Assertion (A) and the other is Reason (R).

Assertion (A) Nobody can claim a Fundamental Right to create noise pollution by amplifying the sound of his speech with the help of loudspeaker.

Reason (R) While one has a right to speech, others have a right to listen or decline to listen. Anyone who wishes to live in peace, comfort and quiet within his house has a Fundamental Right to prevent the noise as pollution reaching him.

Codes

1 (A) is true, but (R) is false
2 (A) is false, but (R) is true
3 Both (A) and (R) are true, but (R) is not a correct explanation of (A)
4 Both (A) and (R) are true and (R) is correct explanation of (A)

Ans. *(4)*

Exp. Both (A) and (R) are true, and (R) is the correct explanation of (A).

As per the observations made by the Supreme Court in the case titled as Church of God (Full Gospel) in India Vs. K.K.R. Majestic Colony Welfare Association., (2000) 7 SCC 282, nobody can claim a Fundamental Right to create noise pollution by amplifying the sound of his speech with the help of loudspeaker, is true because while one has a right to speech, others have a right to listen or decline to listen.

Anyone who wishes to live in peace, comfort and quiet within his house has a Fundamental Right to prevent the noise as pollution reaches him. This explains the concept of reasonable restriction on the fundamental rights in the interest of the larger public.

38 In which of the following cases it was held that there is no reason to compel non-smokers to be helpless victims of air pollution ?

1 Samantha Vs. State of AP
2 MC Mehta Vs. Union of India
3 Murli Deora Vs. Union of India
4 Sheela Barse Vs. Union of India

Ans. *(3)*

Exp. In Murli Deora Vs. Union of India (2001) it was held that there is no reason to compel non-smokers to be helpless victims of air pollution.

In an attempt to protect the health of non-smokers, the Court held that allowing smoking in public places would amount to an indirect violation of the right to life of non-smokers. It said that smoking in public was injurious to the health of passive smokers who were helpless victims of air pollution caused by smoking.

39 Protection and improvement of environment and safeguarding forests and wildlife is

1 A Fundamental Right
2 One of the Directive Principles of State Policy.
3 One of the Fundamental Duties
4 Both one of the Directive Principles of State Policy and one of the Fundamental Duties

Ans. *(4)*

Exp. Protection and improvement of environment and safeguarding forests and wildlife is both one of the Directive Principles of State Policy and one of the Fundamental Duties.

Article 48A in the Constitution Of India 1949 under the chapter IV as Directive Principles of State Policy provides that the State shall endeavour to protect and improve the environment and to safeguard the forests and wild life of the country.

Similarly, under Article 51A(g) in the Constitution, a fundamental duty to protect and improve the natural environment including forests, lakes, rivers and wild life, and to have compassion for living creatures is imposed.

It is worth noting that both the Directive Principles of State Policy and Fundamental Duties are not enforceable before a court of law and therefore, no legal action may be taken either against or for their enforcement.

40 Who stated that international law is not true law but 'positive international morality' only, analogous to the rules binding a club or society ?

1 Oscar Schachter
2 John Austin
3 Louis Henkin
4 Hans Kelson

***Ans.* (2)**

Exp. John Austin stated that, "International law is not true law but 'positive international morality' only analogous to the rules binding a club or socicty".

Austin said that international law cannot be called law proper in the true sense, because there is no competent legislature as such to formulate rules based on International Law, and also that there is no proper legal sanction behind the enforcement of such rules, which is otherwise seen in a domestic or municipal law.

He believed that international law is a code of conduct with moral force and nothing more. It consists of opinions or sentiments current among nations generally.

41 Opinio juris sive necessitatis means

1 Opinions of jurists is necessary evidence for determining rules of international custom
2 Opinions of jurists is not necessary for ascertaining the rules of international law
3 The feeling on the part of States that in acting as they do they are fulfilling a legal obligation
4 None of the above

***Ans.* (3)**

Exp. Opinio juris sive necessitatis means the feeling on the part of states that in acting as they do they are fulfilling a legal obligation.

Opinio juris refers to a subjective obligation, rather an impression on behalf of a state that it is bound to a certain law. The International Court of Justice provides this in ICJ Statute, Article 38 by expressing that the custom to be applied must be "accepted as law".

The concept of opinio juris still remains debatable notion in international law. Opinio juris sive necessitatis ("an opinion of law or necessity") or simply opinio juris ("an opinion of law") is the belief that an action was carried out as a legal obligation.

42 Which of the following cases supports constitutive theory of recognition, namely, the act of recognition alone confers international personality on an entity purporting to be a state or clothes new government with an authority to enter into international relations ?

1 The Arantzazu Mendi, (1939) AC P 256
2 AM Luther Vs. James Sagor and Co, (1921) 3 KB P.532
3 Tinoco Concessions, (1923) 1 United Nations Reports of International Arbitral Awards P 369
4 None of the above

***Ans.* (4)**

Exp. None of the cases supports the constitutive theory of recognition.

In the The Arantzazu Mendi case, it was held that when there is effective control over the territory of a government of de facto (recognition) a foreign court can not apply its jurisdiction over its matter.

In AM Luther Vs. James Sagor and Co it was held that the court cannot interfere in an internal matter of another state, if a state was given the De Facto Recognition. The court also in effect declared that there is no practical difference between de jure and de facto recognition.

In Tinoco Concessions case, a government need not conform to a previous constitution if the government had established itself and maintained a peaceful de facto administration and non-recognition of the government by other government does not destroy the de facto status of the government.

43 Which of the following statements is true ?

1 Nationality is the evidence of the link or relations of an individual with the State whereas domicile denotes de facto residence of an individual in a state with an intention to permanently settle there
2 Nationality is an evidence of residence of an individual with an intention to permanently settle there
3 Domicile denotes the link or relations of an individual with the state
4 None of the above

***Ans.* (1)**

Exp. Nationality is the evidence of the link or relations of the individual with the State whereas domicile denotes de facto residence of an individual in a state with an intention to permanently settle there is a true statement.

Nationality means the status of an individual belonging to a particular state. Fenwick defines it as a bond which unites a person to a given state which constitutes his membership in the particular state, which gives him a claim to the protection of that state and which subjects him to the obligation created by the laws of that state. The basis of nationality is the membership of a particular community.

Domicile, on the other hand, is an attribute of nationality and denotes a person's place of residence. It is the relationship between the individual and locality, where he has his permanent home.

44 The Charter of the United Nations came into force on

1 26th June, 1945
2 10th, December, 1945
3 24th October, 1945
4 1st November, 1945

Ans. (3)

Exp. The Charter of the United Nations came into force on 24th October, 1945.

The Charter of the United Nations is the founding document of the United Nations. It was signed on 26th June, 1945, in San Francisco, at the conclusion of the United Nations Conference on International Organisation, and came into force on 24th October, 1945.

The UN Charter is an instrument of international law, and UN Member States are bound by it. The UN Charter codifies the major principles of international relations, from sovereign equality of States to the prohibition of the use of force in international relations.

Since the UN's founding in 1945, the mission and work of the Organisation have been guided by the purposes and principles contained in its founding Charter, which has been amended three times in 1963, 1965, and 1973.

45 A member of the United Nations which has persistently violated the principles contained in the Charter may be expelled from the United Nations by the

1 Security Council
2 General Assembly
3 General Assembly upon the recommendation of the Security Council
4 Security Council upon the recommendation of the General Assembly

Ans. (3)

Exp. A member of the United Nations which has persistently violated the principles contained in the Charter may be expelled from the United Nations by the General Assembly upon the recommendation of the Security Council.

The above provision is found in Article 6 of the UN Charter. It is important to note that no member has been expelled as of now in accordance to the said provision.

46 The Judges of the International Court of Justice are elected by the

1 General Assembly
2 Security Council
3 General Assembly upon recommendation of the Security Council
4 General Assembly and the Security Council independently of one another

Ans. (4)

Exp. The judges of the International Court of Justice are elected by the General Assembly and the Security Council independently of one another.

The above position is found in Article 8 of UN Charter. The International Court of Justice is composed of 15 judges elected to nine-year terms office. In order to be elected, a candidate must receive an absolute majority of the votes in both bodies.

In order to ensure a degree of continuity, one third of the Court is elected every three years. Judges are eligible for re-election. Should a judge die or resign during his or her term of office, a special election is held as soon as possible to choose a judge to fill the unexpired part of the term.

47 Under Section 6 of the Hindu Minority and Guardianship Act, 1956 the natural guardian of a minor child is

1 Mother
2 Father
3 Both Mother and Father
4 Either Mother or Father

Ans. (2)

Exp. According to Section 6 of the Hindu Minority and Guardianship Act, 1956 the natural guardian of a minor child is father.

As per Section 6 of the Act, the natural guardian of a Hindu minor, in respect of the minor's person as well as in respect of the minor's property (excluding his or her undivided interest in joint family property), are in the case of a boy or an unmarried girl; the father, and after him, the mother.

48 A Muslim wife can relinquish her Mahr

1 When she is minor
2 When she has attained the age of puberty
3 When she is not less than 18 years of age
4 When she is not less than 21 years of age

Ans. (2)

Exp. A Muslim wife can relinquish her Mahr when she has attained the age of puberty.

Mahr or dower is a sum of money which becomes payable by the husband to his wife on marriage, either by agreement between the parties or by operation of law.

It is important to note that husband can increase the amount of dower at any time and also the wife can remit the dower wholly or partially but it should be done by her free consent. A Muslim girl who has attained the age of puberty can relinquish her dower, and it is not mandatory that she has attained majority (which is 18 years according to Indian Majority Act) or not.

The remission of Mahr by wife is called Hibe-e-Mahr. In any case after the death of husband, wife suffers mental distress, then remission of dower at that condition will be considered against her free consent and will not be binding on her.

49 In Islamic Law 'Faskh' means

1 Restitution of conjugal rights
2 Judicial separation
3 Dissolution or rescission of the contract of marriage by judicial decree at the instance of the husband
4 Dissolution or rescission of the contract of marriage by judicial decree at the instance of the wife

***Ans.* (4)**

Exp. In Islamic law 'Faskh' means dissolution or rescission of the contract of marriage by judicial decree at the instance of the wife.

The Judicial Divorce is by obtaining a decree from a Civil Court for dissolution of marriage under Section 2 of the Dissolution of Muslim Marriages Act 1939, which also amounts to divorce (under the law) obtained by the wife. It is also called as 'Faskh' and refers to the power of a Muslim Kazi to annul a marriage on the application of the wife.

The Quranic basis of the faskh is lying in Sura Nissa which begins with an appeal to the solidarity of the mankind, the rights of women and children and implications of the family relationship.

50 Muta marriage is recognised by

1 Hanafi School
2 Maliki School
3 Athna Ashari School
4 Hanbali School

***Ans.* (3)**

Exp. Muta marriage is recognised by Athna Ashari School.

The word "muta" literally means "enjoyment, use". It is a 'marriage for pleasure' for a fixed period of time, also known as temporary marriage.

The institution of muta, which was fairly common in Arabia before and at the time of the prophet, is now not recognized by any school of Muslim law in India, except the Athna Ashari Shiite or Shia school.

51 The term 'Hindu' denotes the person

I. Professing Hindu Religion.
II. Professing Buddh, Jain or Sikh Religion.
III. Who are not professing Muslim, Christian, Parsi or Jew Religion.

In respect of the aforesaid propositions which is correct ?

1 I and II are correct but III is incorrect
2 II and III are correct and I is incorrect
3 I and III are correct and II is incorrect
4 I, II and III are all correct

***Ans.* (4)**

Exp. All the statements I, II and III are true.

The term 'Hindu' denotes the person professing Hindu religion, professing Buddh, Jain or Sikh Religion, who are not professing Muslim, Christian, Parsi or Jew religion.

The term 'Hindu' is a general term, it denotes all those persons who profess Hindu religion either by birth or by conversion to the Hindu faith. Till this day there is no precise definition of the term 'Hindu' available either in the statute or in any judicial pronouncement.

Therefore, the meaning and scope of the term Hindu is derived by the application of Hindu Law on people belonging to different faiths or communities.

52 Match the List I with List II and select the correct answer by using the codes given below.

List I	List II
A. Void Marriages	I. Section 9
B. Voidable marriages	II. Section 11
C. Divorce	III. Section 13
D. Restitution of Conjugal Rights	IV. Section 12

Codes

	A	B	C	D		A	B	C	D
1	II	IV	III	I	2	IV	III	II	I
3	III	I	II	IV	4	I	II	III	IV

***Ans.* (1)**

Exp. The correct matching is A-II, B-IV, C-III, D-I.

Section 11 of Hindu Marriage Act, 1955 mentions Void marriages and states that any marriage solemnised after the commencement of this Act shall be null and void and may on a petition presented by either party thereto, be so declared by a decree of nullity if it contravenes any one of the conditions specified in clauses (i), (iv) and (v) of Section 5.

Section 5 (i) provides neither party has a spouse living at the time of the marriage; (iv) the parties are not within the degrees of prohibited relationship and (v) the parties are not sapindas of each other.

Section 12 mentions voidable marriages and states, inter alia, that any marriage shall be voidable if the respondent was impotent at the time of the marriage, the consent of the petitioner was obtained by force or fraud or the respondent was at the time of the marriage pregnant by some person other than the petitioner.

Section 13 of the Act deals with matrimonial remedy in the form of Divorce. It is provided that any marriage solemnized may be dissolved on a petition presented by either the husband or the wife on the ground that the other party has committed an act falling under certain conditions such as cruelty, desertion, conversion, etc.

Section 9 mentions about Restitution of Conjgual Rights and provides when either the husband or the wife has, without reasonable excuse, withdrawn from the society of the other, the aggrieved party may apply, by petition to the district court, for restitution of conjugal rights and the court may decree restitution of conjugal rights accordingly.

53 In which of the following case the Court held that Section 9 of the Hindu Marriage Act was Constitutionally violative of right to Human dignity and privacy ?

1 Bipin Chandra Vs. Prabhavati
2 T. Sareetha Vs. T Venkatasubah
3 Lachman Vs. Meena
4 None of the above

***Ans.* (2)**

Exp. In T Sareetha Vs. T Venkatasubah (1983) case, the Court held that Section 9 of the Hindu Marriage Act was, constitutionally violative of right to human dignity and privacy.

It was held that the right to privacy belongs to an individual, and is not lost by marital association. The court observed that the enforcement of section 9 against an individual compelled her to have sexual relations with her spouse, thus depriving her of control over her body.

This, according to the court, was a serious breach of the right to privacy as it transfers the choice of whether or not to have marital intercourse to the State from the concerned individual.

54 Match the List I with List II and indicate the correct answer using the codes given below.

List I	List II
A. Pre-Marriage Pregnancy	I. Divorce
B. Marriage within Prohibited Degree Relationship	II. Voidable Marriage
C. Cruelty	III. Void Marriage
D. When any spouse without reasonable excuse withdraws from the society of the other	IV. Restitution of Conjugal Rights

Codes

	A	B	C	D
1	II	IV	I	III
2	II	III	I	IV
3	IV	II	III	I
4	I	II	III	IV

Ans. *(2)*

Exp. The correct matching is A-II, B-III, C-I, D-IV.

A marriage can be categorised as *voidable* on the ground of Pre-marriage pregnancy. Section 12(1)(d) of Hindu Marriage Act, 1955 provides that the marriage will be voidable when the respondent was at the time of the marriage pregnant (Pre-marriage Pregnancy) by some person other than the petitioner.

Void marriage is related to marriage within Prohibited Degree Relationship. Section 11 declares marriage in contravention to Section 5 (iv) as void; when the parties are not within the degrees of Prohibited Relationship.

According to Section 13(1)(i)(a), any marriage solemnised be dissolved by a decree of *divorce* on the ground that the other party has, after the solemnisation of the marriage, treated the petitioner with cruelty.

Section 9 provides when either the husband or the wife has without reasonable excuse withdrawn from the society of the other, the aggrieved party may apply, by petition to the district court, for *Restitution of conjugal rights* and the court may decree restitution of conjugal rights accordingly.

55 International Women's Day is celebrated every year on

1 2nd March
2 4th March
3 6th March
4 8th March

Ans. *(4)*

Exp. International Women's Day is celebrated every year on 8th March.

International Women's Day (IWD) is a global holiday celebrated annually on 8th March to commemorate the cultural, political, and socio-economic achievements of women.

It is also important to note that the date brings attention to the idea of gender equality and women empowerment, among various issues.

56 Which one of the following is correct according to Article 1 of the Universal Declaration of Human Rights, 1948 ?

1 All human beings are born free and equal in rights
2 All human beings are born free, equal and dignity
3 All human beings are equal in dignity and rights
4 All human beings are born free and equal in rights and dignity

Ans. *(4)*

Exp. Article 1 of the Universal Declaration of Human Rights, 1948 states that all human beings are born free and equal in dignity and rights.

It is a milestone document in the history of human rights. According to this, human beings are endowed with reason conscience and should act towards one another in a spirit of brotherhood.

The Declaration was proclaimed by the United Nations General Assembly in Paris on 10th December 1948 (General Assembly resolution 217 A) as a common standard of achievements for all peoples and all nations. It sets out, for the first time, fundamental human rights to be universally protected.

57 Regional Human Rights Court does not exist in

1 Africa
2 Europe
3 America
4 Asia

Ans. *(4)*

Exp. Regional Human Rights Court does not exist in Asia.

The Regional Human Rights systems, consisting of regional instruments and mechanisms, are tremendously important for protection of human rights.

Regional human rights instruments such as treaties, conventions, declarations, etc. help to localise international human rights norms and standards, reflecting the particular human rights concerns of the region.

Regional human rights mechanisms further help to implement these instruments on the ground. Currently, the three most well-established regional human rights systems exist in Europe, the Americas and Africa.

58 Which protocol to the European Convention on Human Rights has abolished European Commission of Human Rights ?

1 Protocol 1
2 Protocol 2
3 Protocol 3
4 Protocol 11

Ans. *(4)*

Exp. The Protocol 11 to the European Convention on Human Rights has abolished European Commission of Human Rights.

The European Convention of Human Rights became obsolete in 1998 with the restructuring of the European Court of Human Rights

European Commission of Human Rights was a special body of the Council of Europe. From 1954 to the entry into force of Protocol 11 of the European Convention on Human Rights, individuals did not have direct access to the European Court of Human Rights; they had to apply to the commission, which if it found the case to be well-founded would launch a case in the Court on the individual's behalf.

Protocol 11 which came into force in 1998 abolished the commission, enlarged the Court, and allowed individuals to take cases directly to it.

59 Which one of the following convention has neither interstate communication procedure nor individual communication procedure ?

1 International Convention on Civil and Political Rights
2 International Convention on Economic, Social and Cultural Rights
3 Convention on the Rights of Child
4 Convention on the Rights of persons with Disabilities

Ans. *(3)*

Exp. Convention on the Rights of Child has neither interstate communication procedure nor individual communication procedure.

The communications procedure is a mechanism contained in several international conventions that gives the opportunity for an individual or group of individuals to bring a complaint, alleging violations of certain treaty rights to the body of experts set up by the treaty for quasi-judicial adjudication.

Some human rights instruments allow States parties to initiate a procedure against another State party, which is considered not to be fulfilling its obligations under this instrument.

60 The term of the office of the Chairperson and Members of the NHRC under Protection of Human Rights Act, 1993 is

1 5 years from the date on which he enters the office or until he attains the age of 70 years whichever is earlier
2 4 years from the date on which he enters the office or until he attains the age of 70 years whichever is earlier
3 3 years from the date on which he enters the office or until he attains the age of 68 years whichever is earlier
4 5 years from the date on which he enters the office or until he attains the age of 68 years whichever is earlier

Ans. *(1)*

Exp. The term of the office of the Chairperson and Members of the NHRC as per Section 6 under Protection of Human Right Act, 1993 is 5 years from the date on which he enters the office or until he attains the age of 70 years whichever is earlier.

It is also stated that a person appointed as a Member shall hold office for a term of five years from the date on which he enters upon his office and shall be eligible for re-appointment for another term of five years: provided that no Member shall hold office after he has attained the age of seventy years. On ceasing to hold office, a Chairperson or a Member shall be ineligible for further employment under the Government of India or under the Government of any State.

61 The Chairperson of National Commission on Minorities shall be deemed member of

1 Human Rights Council
2 Law Commission of India
3 National Human Rights Commission
4 International Law Commission

Ans. *(3)*

Exp. The Chairperson of National Commission on minorities shall be deemed member of National Human Rights Commission.

As per Section 3(3) of the Protection of Human Rights Act, 1993, the Chairpersons of the National Commission for Backward Classes, the National Commission for Minorities, the National Commission for Protection of Child Rights, the National Commission for the Scheduled Castes, the National Commission for the Scheduled Tribes and the the National Commission for Women and the Chief Commissioner for Persons with Disabilities shall be deemed to be Members of the Commission.

62 Which one of the following is an 'actionable' wrong?

1 Injuria Sine Damnum
2 Damnum Sine Injuria
3 Both of the above
4 None of the above

Ans. *(1)*

Exp. Injuria sine damnum is an 'actionable' wrong.

The legal maxim Injuria Sine Damnum guarantees actionable claim for a mere violation of legal right and there is no need to establish damage as such. However, according to Damnum Sine Injuria, if a person suffers only the damage, but no violation of legal right, then he is not entitled to a legal action on that basis.

63 Which of the following is the gist of tortious liability ?

1 Legal damages
2 Violation of legal right
3 Availability of legal duty
4 None of these

Ans. *(2)*

Exp. Violation of legal right is the gist of tortious liability.

The damages for a wrong are provided for violation of a legal right under tort law. It is not necessary to prove damage in order to claim damages, as a violation of legal right in itself is sufficient to claim damages in accordance with the principle of Injuria Sine Damnum.

64 The rule of Absolute Liability is subject to

1 All the exceptions mentioned in the rule of Rylands Vs. Fletcher
2 Half of the exceptions mentioned in the rule of Rylands Vs. Fletcher
3 None of the exceptions mentioned in the rule of Rylands Vs. Fletcher
4 All the exceptions mentioned in rule of MC Mehta Vs. Union of India

Ans. (3)

Exp. The rule of Absolute Liability is subject to none of the Exceptions mentioned in the rule of Rylands Vs Fletcher.

The Absolute liability applies to impose liability upon an enterprise engaged in inherently dangerous activity and resulting damage. The amount of damage in such cases is generally huge and the enterprise is usually established for profit motive.

There is no defence available for an absolute liability, unlike in case of a strict liability, wherein certain exceptions are provided such as Act of God, plaintiff's consent or fault, third party fault and statutory authority.

65 Given below are two statements, one is labelled as Assertion (A) and the other is Reason (R).

Assertion (A) If a person speaks ill of the business which X is doing, it amounts to defamation.

Reason (R) Slander is actionable per se.

Codes

1 Both (A) and (R) are true and (R) is the correct explanation of (A)
2 Both (A) and (R) are true but (R) is not the correct explanation of (A)
3 (A) is true but (R) is false
4 (A) is false but (R) is true

Ans. (3)

Exp. The Assertion is true but Reason is false.

The wrong of defamation is committed when a person makes imputation concerning another resulting in loss of reputation in the eyes of right thinking members of society. Defamation is generally of two types; Libel and Slander. While the former refers to publication of defamatory content in some permanent form such as in a newspaper, a painting, a photograph, etc., the latter refers to content in transient form. Libel is actionable per se, that is, an action against it can be taken without proving damage. However, slander is not actionable per se and a successful claim needs to establish damage.

66 In Res ipsa Loquitor

I. Presumption of negligence is there.
II. Plaintiff has to bring direct evidence.
III. Plaintiff is discharged from the duty of proving negligence on the part of the defendant.
IV. Court does not give chance to defendant to avoid his liability

Codes

1 I and II are correct 2 I, II and IV are correct
3 I, II and III are correct 4 I and III are correct

Ans. (4)

Exp. Among the given statements, only statement I and III are correct.

In Res ipsa Loquitor, presumption of negligence is there and plaintiff is discharged from the duty of proving negligence on the part of the defendant.

The rule of Res ipsa Loquitor says that in certain cases, negligence is apparent and the plaintiff need not establish clear negligence by evidence, which is the rule in ordinary cases of negligence. Here, the burden of proof is shifted on the defendant to show that he was not negligent.

However, such a presumption against defendant is subject to rebuttal and evidence led by defendant, and may turn out to be true or false.

The statements II and IV are incorrect as in such cases, the plaintiff need not bring direct evidence, as it otherwise is necessary in a general case of negligence and the liability of defendant is only tentative subject to final evidence.

67 Which one of the following statements is true ?

1 Both public as well as private nuisance are punishable under criminal law
2 Only private nuisance is punishable under criminal law, while there is no punishment for general nuisance
3 Public nuisance is punishable under criminal law, while private nuisance is a moral wrong only
4 Public nuisance is punishable under criminal law, while private nuisance under civil law

Ans. (4)

Exp. Public nuisance is punishable under criminal law while private nuisance under civil law is true.

As per Section 268 of IPC, a person is guilty of a public nuisance who does any act or is guilty of an illegal omission which causes any common injury, danger or annoyance to the public or to the people in general who dwell or occupy property in the vicinity, or which must necessarily cause injury, obstruction, danger or annoyance to persons who may have occasion to use any public right. A common nuisance is not excused on the ground that it causes some convenience or advantage.

The law of tort provides remedy for private nuisance wherein a person unlawfully or unreasonably interferes with the right to use or enjoy another's property causing damage.

68 For constituting tort of nuisance, there should be

1 Unreasonable interference
2 Interference should be with the use of enjoyment of land
3 Damage
4 All of the above

Ans. (4)

Exp. For consituting tort of nuisance, there should be unreasonable interference, interference should be with the use of enjoyment of land and damage.

The law of tort provides remedy for private nuisance wherein a person unlawfully or unreasonably interferes with the right to use or enjoy another's property causing damage.

Nuisance may be committed by using tangible or intangible objects. It can be committed through smoke, vibrations, smell, and even by blocking access to a rightful place, among other things.

69 Partnership is based on

1 Mutual trust
2 Mutual benefit
3 Mutual interest
4 Mutual agency

Ans. (4)

Exp. Partnership is based on Mutual agency.

The Mutual agency in partnership denotes to an arrangement among people to share obligations and powers to represent one another. As per Section 18 of the Partnership Act, 1932, a partner is the agent of the firm for the purposes of the business of the firm. Also, as per Section 19, the act of a partner which is done to carry on, in the usual way, business of the kind carried on by the firm, binds the firm.

In partnership, each partners has the authority to enter into contracts or perform obligations on behalf of the other partners. Their relations are similar to that of a relationship between a principal and agent.

70 Which statements are correct ?

I. An undisclosed principal can intervene against express terms
II. An undisclosed principal cannot intervene against express terms
III. An undisclosed principal cannot intervene when he knows that the other party would not have dealt with him
IV. An undisclosed principal can intervene when he knows that the other party would not have dealt with him.

Codes

1 I and II are correct
2 II and III are correct
3 III and IV are correct
4 IV and I are correct

Ans. (2)

Exp. Among the given statements, only statement II and III are correct.

As per Section 231 of Indian Contract Act, 1872, if an agent makes a contract with a person who neither knows nor has reason to suspect, that he is an agent, his principal may require the performance of the contract; but the other contracting party has, as against the principal, the same right as he would have had as against if the agent had been the principal. So, an undisclosed principal cannot intervene against express terms.

As per Section 232, where one man makes a contract with another, neither knowing nor having reasonable ground to suspect that the other is an agent, the principal, if he requires the performance of the contract, can only obtain such performance subject to the right and obligations subsisting between the agent and the other party of the contract. So, an undisclosed principal cannot intervene when he knows that the other party would not have dealt with him.

The statements I and IV are incorrect as they violate Sections 231 and 232 as provided above.

71 Read the following passage and match the column. A negotiable instrument contains a contract and therefore must be supported by consideration. In order to be a holder in due course, the holder must have obtained the instrument before its maturity. An instrument payable on demand is current at least as long as no demand for payment is made. To make a holder in due course, the instrument must be complete and regular. A post-dated cheque may not be complete and regular.

List I	List II
A. Negotiable instrument	I. Before maturity
B. Holder in due course	II. Demand for payment
C. Currency of instrument	III. Post dated cheque
D. Complete and regular	IV. Consideration

Codes

	A	B	C	D		A	B	C	D
1	I	IV	II	III	2	II	III	I	IV
3	IV	I	II	III	4	IV	III	I	II

Ans. (3)

Exp. The correct matching is A-IV, B-I, C-II, D-III.

According to the passage given, a negotiable instrument contains a contract and therefore must be supported by consideration. In order to be a holder in due course, the holder must have obtained the instrument before its maturity. An instrument payable on demand is current at least as long as no demand for payment is made. To make a holder in due course, the instrument must be complete and regular. A post-dated cheque may not be complete and regular.

72 Given below are two statements, one is labelled as Assertion (A) and the other is Reason (R).

Assertion (A) Every public company shall have at least three and every private company shall have at least two Directors.

Reason (R) Directors are trustees for the company and not for individual shareholders.

Codes

1 (A) and (R) are true, but (R) is not the correct explanation for (A)
2 (A) and (R) are true and (R) is the correct explanation for (A)
3 (A) is true, but (R) is false
4 (R)is true, but (A) is false

Ans. (1)

Exp. Both (A) and (R) are true, but (R) is not the correct explanation of (A).

The appointment of directors is permitted because Section 149(1) of the Companies Act, 2013 requires that every company shall have a minimum number of three directors in the case of a public company, two directors in the case of a private company, and one director in the case of a One Person Company.

A company can appoint maximum 15 directors. A company may appoint more than fifteen directors after passing a special resolution in general meeting and approval of Central Government is not required.

73 Arrange the following concepts in a sequence in which they appeared. Use the code given below :

I. Right of an unpaid seller to stop goods in transit.
II. Agreement to sell goods.
III. Damages for breach of contract of sale of goods.
IV. Conditions and warranties.

Codes

1 II, IV, III, I　　2 IV, II, I, III
3 II, I, IV, III　　4 I, II, IV, III

Ans. (*)

Exp. The correct sequence is II, IV, I, III.

Section 4 of Sale of Goods Act, 1930 is related to agreement to sell goods. It provides for Sale and agreement to sell and states that a contract of sale of goods is a contract whereby the seller transfers or agrees to transfer the property in goods to the buyer for a price. There may be a contract of sale between one part-owner and another.

Section 12 is related to condition and warranty. It provides that a stipulation in a contract of sale with reference to goods which are the subject thereof may be a condition or a warranty. A condition is a stipulation essential to the main purpose of the contract, the breach of which gives rise to a right to treat the contract as repudiated.

Section 45 and 46 provide for rights of unpaid seller to stop the goods in transit.

Section 56 and 57 is related to damages for breach of contract of sale of goods. It deal with damages for non-acceptance or non-delivery of goods.

74 Which statements are correct ?

I. Partner has a duty of good faith.
II. Partner has duty not to compete.
III. Partner has duty of due diligence.
IV. Partner has duty to indemnify for fraud.

Codes

1 Only I is correct
2 Only I and II are correct
3 Only I, II and III are correct
4 I, II, III and IV are correct

Ans. (4)

Exp. All the statements (I), (II), (III) and (IV) are true.

Section 9 and 10 of the Act lay down the basic duties of every partner and they said duties are not subject to any contract to the contrary. Therefore, partners are bound to carry on the business of the firm to the greatest common advantage, to be just and faithful to each other and to render accounts and full information of all things affecting the firm to any partner or his legal representative and every partner is bound to indemnify the firm for any loss caused to it by fraud in the conduct of the business of the firm.

Subject to any contract to the contrary such duties and rights of each partner are provided in Section 12 and Section 13 of the Partnership Act. They are, inter alia, every partner has a right to take part in the conduct of the business, every partner is bound to attend diligently to his duties in the conduct of business.

75 Match an item in List I with an item in List II.

List I	List II
A. Removal of Directors by Company Law Board	I. Section 318
B. Duty of Directors to disclose interest	II. Sections 299–300
C. Compensation for loss of office of Director	III. Section 402
D. Director with unlimited liability	IV. Sections 322–323

Codes

	A	B	C	D		A	B	C	D
1	III	II	I	IV	2	II	III	I	IV
3	II	III	IV	I	4	II	I	III	IV

Ans. (1)

Exp. The correct matching is A-III, B-II, C-I, D-IV.

Section 402 of the Companies Act, 1956 provided for power with company law board to remove the directors.

Section 299-300 deals with duty of directors to disclose interest. It stated that every director of a company who is in any way, whether directly, or indirectly, concerned or interested in a contract or arrangement, or proposed contract or arrangement, entered into or to be entered into, by or on behalf of the company, shall disclose the nature of his concern or interest at a meeting of the Board of directors.

Section 318 is related to compensation for loss of office of directors. It provided that payment may be made by a company, except in the cases specified in sub-section (3) and subject to the limit specified in sub-section (4), to managing director, or a director holding the office of manager or in the whole-time employment of the company, by way of compensation for loss of office, or as consideration for retirement from office, or in connection with such loss or retirement.

Section 322-323 is related to Directors with unlimited liability. It used to provide that in a limited company, the liability of the directors or of any director or manager may, if so provided by the memorandum, be unlimited.

PRACTICE SETS (1-5)

UGC-NET LAW

PRACTICE SET 1

PAPER II

1 Jurisprudence is
1 study and systematic arrangement of general principles of law
2 lawyer's extroversion
3 study of Government's behaviour
4 None of the above

2 Rights and duties exist
1 together
2 separately
3 opposite to each other
4 complementary to each other

3 Liberty is without independent jural significance was propounded by
1 Hans Kelsen 2 Duguit
3 Rosquo Pound 4 Mill

4 A legal system is only the sum total of laws and that one only needs to identify a law was propounded by :
1 Bentham 2 Austin 3 Salmond 4 Ihring

5 The difference between judicial and legislative creativity has been that "the creative power of the court is limited by existing legal material at their command. They find the material and shape it. The legislature may manufacture entirely new material." This statement was stated by :
1 Ehrlich 2 Rosquo Pound
3 Kelson 4 Savigny

6 Estrada doctrine is related to
1 Mexico 2 Spain 3 Portugal 4 Grenada

7 'Uniting for Peace Resolution' came into being in the year
1 1949 2 1950 3 1951 4 1952

8 Article 23 of the UDHR corresponds with which article of the Indian Constitution ?
1 Article 41 2 Article 39 (d)
3 Article 43 4 Article 38

9 Section 19 of the Protection of Human Rights Act, 1993 provides protection to
1 Police
2 Army
3 Navy
4 All of the above

10 A malignant act likely to spread infection or disease dangerous to life and making atmosphere noxious to health are punishable offences for environment protection. But the punishment are meagre to meet objectives. Under which of the following law such meagre punishment is given?
1 Environment Protection Act, 1986
2 Indian Penal Code
3 The Air (Prevention and Control of Pollution) Act, 1981
4 The Water (Prevention and Control of Pollution) Act, 1974

11 In the British Constitution there is no such thing as the absolute separation of Legislative - Executive and Judicial powers. In practice it is inevitable that they overlap. In the Constitution of France and USA, attempts to keep the organs of the government rigidly apart have been made but have proved unsuccessful. This position of doctrine of separation of powers has been summed-up by
1 Ullman
2 KT Shah
3 Wade and Phillips
4 Donoughmore Committee

12 In which of the following cases, the Supreme Court held that any Member of Parliament, Member of Legislative Assembly or Member of Legislative Council who is convicted of a crime and given a minimum of two years imprisonment loses membership of the House with immediate effect?
1 SM Sharma Vs. Sri Krishna Sinha
2 Ramakrishna Hegde Vs. State of Karnataka
3 Hardwari Lal Vs. Ch. Bhajhan Lal
4 Lily Thomas Vs. Union of India.

13 The law declared by the Supreme Court is binding on all the courts within the territory of India, but the Supreme Court is not bound by its own decisions, was decided by the Supreme Court itself in
1 Kesavananda Bharati Vs. State of Kerala
2 Indira Nehru Gandhi Vs. Raj Narain
3 Madhavrao Scindia Vs. Union of India
4 Bengal Immunity Co. Ltd. Vs. State of Bihar

14 In which of the following case, the High court held that 'the presence of Qazi is not necessary at the time of marriage ceremony under the Muslim law'?
1 Qazi Mohd. Najmuddin Hussain Vs. State of AP
2 Mohd. Yunus Vs. Malooki
3 Shamim Ara Vs State of U.P
4 Bai Tahira Vs. Ali Hussain

15 In the case of Mc Gregor Vs. Mc Gregor, (1888) 21 Q. B.D. 424, the wife withdrew her complaints as the husband entered into an agreement with her on the condition that if she withdrew her complaints and refrained from pledging his credit, he will pay her an allowance.
1 The agreement is a social agreement and is not binding
2 The agreement is a family agreement and is not a contract
3 The agreement is based on love and affection and is binding
4 Parties had the intention to have a binding contract between them

16 Principle of law in Hadley Vs. Baxendale is related to
1 Quasi-Contract
2 Fraud
3 Remoteness of damage
4 Unjust enrichment

17 In which of the following case, the Court held that "Dower is a sale price of women".
1 Humara Begum Case
2 Subrunnissan Case
3 Shah Bano Case
4 Abdul Kadir Case

18 If a Husband compare his wife with his real sister, this form of divorce is called
1 Zihar
2 Khula
3 Illa
4 Mubarrah

19 Muta marriage is recognised by
1 Hanafi School
2 Maliki School
3 Ithna Ashari School
4 Hanbali School

20 The Supreme Court has awarded twenty lakhs rupees as a compensation in the case of 'Bandh' calls given by political party/parties. Select the correct one from among the following
1 Communist Party of India
2 BJP
3 Both 1 and 2
4 Congress Party

21 Point out the correct statement
'A' and 'B' went to cause murder of 'C'. 'A' was with a spear and 'B' was with a stick. 'B' caught 'C' and beat 'C' with stick. 'A' did nothing while 'B' was beating. When 'C' fell down and became unconscious 'A' took him to a nearby hospital for care where he died.
1 'A' and 'B' both are liable under Sections 302 and 34 of Indian Penal Code.
2 'A' is liable under Section 302 of the Indian Penal Code but 'B' is liable for nothing.
3 'B' is liable for murder and 'A' is liable for abetment of murder.
4 None of the above

22 Retrenchment means
1 Voluntary retirement
2 Dismissal
3 Discharge of surplus labour
4 None of the above

23 Article 21-A and Article 51-A (k) are
1 interrelated and integrated as right and obligation
2 not interrelated and integrated as right and obligation
3 mutually exclusive
4 independent and not inter-dependent

24 With the deletion of Article 31 from the Fundamental Rights of the Constitution of India, Schedule IX seems to have outlived its
1 Utility
2 Importance
3 Both (1) and (2)
4 Neither (1) and (2)

25 The doctrine of prospective overruling established in the case of IC Golaknath Vs. State of Punjab 1967 can be applied
1 by any Court of the country
2 by any Administrative Tribunal of the country
3 only by the highest Court of the country
4 only by the revenue authorities under the Land Ceiling Acts

26 Who among the following is related to historical school of jurisprudence ?
1 Salmond
2 Bentham
3 Rawls
4 Henry Maine

27 In contributory negligence plaintiff is injured because of the wrong of
1 The plaintiff
2 Plaintiff as well as the defendant
3 Defendant
4 None of the above

28 The principle of Novus actus interveniens applies to determine
1 Vicarious liability
2 Remoteness of damage
3 Strict liability
4 Act of God

29 Which one of the following statement is correct?
1 Abetment of an offence is an incomplete offence.
2 Abetment of an offence is a continuing offence.
3 Abetment of an offence is a complete offence.
4 Abetment of an offence is an offence depending upon circumstances of the case.

30 A village Vaidya used to successfully operate wounds with shaving blade. Victim who was suffering from piles was operated with shaving blade by the Vaidya. Due to profound bleeding, the victim died and the Vaidya was prosecuted for causing death of the victim. If you are a defence counsel under which of the following sections of the Indian Penal Code you can defend the Vaidya.
1 Section 87 2 Section 88
3 Section 92 4 None of these

31 During the murder trial it was proved that the murder was committed by six persons. Out of the six accused persons, identity of two accused persons could not be verified. Hence the two accused persons were acquitted. Rest of the four accused persons claimed acquittal. Point out the correct answer in determining liability of the four accused persons.
1 Shall be liable u/s 302/149 of the Indian Penal Code
2 Shall be liable u/s 302/34 of the Indian Penal Code
3 Liable for negligence
4 Shall not be liable for murder

32 In which of the following case the Supreme Court recognised the theory of 'Hire and Fire' in labour law?
1 The Steel Authority Workers Corporation case
2 The Air India Authority Corporation case
3 Mohini Jain case
4 The Gujarat Electricity Workers case

33 Strike is a legitimate right in the hands of
1 The employer 2 Workman
3 Both (1) and (2) 4 None of these

34 Lock-out to is
1 anti-thesis of strike
2 anti-strike
3 equal to strike
4 None of the above

35 In the Islamic Academy of Education case guidelines were laid down for
1 Fixing fees by Private Educational Institutions
2 State Government Committee to conduct admission test
3 Admissions by Minority Professional Institutions to admit students of their own community
4 All of the above

36 Who of the following jurists said that "law is a Command of Sovereign"?
1 Salmond 2 Julius Stone
3 Hans Kelson 4 Austin

37 Who of the following jurists propounded Volksgeist theory?
1 Salmond 2 Savigny
3 Ihering 4 Ehrlich

38 Hypothesis of Grundnorm was propounded by
1 Austin 2 Duguit 3 Hart 4 Kelson

39 Monism and Dualism theories are
1 Complementary to each other
2 Different from each other
3 Similar to each other
4 None of the above

40 The Naulilaa Incident relates to
1 Obstruction of ships
2 Reprisals
3 Retorsion
4 Embargo

41 Some, all or none of the following statements are right. Answer using the code.
I. A minor's liability for necessaries depends on his consent to supply the necessaries to him.
II. An infant is capable of making a contract of purchase of necessaries.
III. A minor has to pay agreed price for necessaries.
IV. In Peter Vs. Fleming, (1840) 6 M and W 92, the court took judicial notice that it was Prima Facie unreasonable that an undergraduate at a college should have a watch and a watch chain.

Codes
1 I, II, III, IV 2 II and III
3 I, II, III 4 Only II

42 Arrange the following concepts in which they appeared. Use the code given below

I. Invitation to offer II. Damage
III. Offer IV. Damages

Codes
1 I, III, II, IV 2 I, III, IV, II
3 III, I, II, IV 4 I, IV, III, II

43 Arrange the following concepts in sequence in which they appeared.
Use the codes given below

I. Offer by 'X' to 'Y'
II. Undue influence of 'X' over 'Y'
III. Demand of damages by 'Y' from 'X'
IV. Acceptance of the offer by 'Y'.

Codes
1 I, II, III, IV
2 I, IV, III, II
3 II, I, IV, III
4 II, IV, I, III

44 Arrange the following concepts in sequence in which they occur, using codes given below

I. Offer is communicated
II. Counter offer is made
III. Offer is rejected
IV. Counter offer is accepted

Codes
1 I, III, II, IV
2 I, II, III, IV
3 I, IV, II, III
4 II, I, III, IV

45 Arrange the following Supreme Court decisions on the justification of torts in chronological order by using the codes given below:

I. Vinod Kumar Shantilal Gosalia Vs. Gangadhar Narsingdas
II. Sodan Singh Vs. New Delhi Municipal Committee
III. Anwar Hussain Vs. Ajay Kumar
IV. Nizam's Institute of Medical Sciences Vs. Prasanth S. Dhananka

Codes
1 I, III, IV, II 2 II, IV, I, III
3 III, I, II, IV 4 III, II, IV, I

46 Arrange the following leading cases in order, pronounced by the Supreme Court by using the code given below

I. Selvi Vs. State of Karnataka
II. Official Liquidator Vs. Dayananda
III. IR Coelho Vs. State of Tamil Nadu
IV. PA Inamdar Vs. State of Maharashtra

Codes
1 IV, I, III, II 2 IV, III, II, I
3 III, II, IV, I 4 II, III, IV, I

47 Preparation consists in devising or arranging means necessary for the commission of the offence. Such attempt is not punishable because

I. The motive was harmless
II. Impossibility to reach wrongful end
III. Does not affect the security of any person
IV. It remained without culmination

The reasoned answer is
1 Only I is correct.
2 The most probability is I and II.
3 There is quite likelihood of I and III.
4 All the reasons I, II, III and IV have to be examined.

48 No person employed in a public utility service shall go on strike

I. Without giving notice of strike to employer.
II. Within 14 days of giving such notice.
III. After expiry of date specified in notice for strike.
IV. Within 7 days of conclusion of conciliation proceeding.

Codes
1 I and IV 2 I and III
3 I and II 4 II and III

49 Which of the following statements are true?

I. Minor's contract can be ratified on attaining majority.
II. Minor's contract cannot be ratified on attaining majority.
III. Minor's contract can be ratified jointly by both the parties to the contract.
IV. Minor is not liable under minor's contract.

Codes
1 I and III 2 II and IV
3 I and II 4 II and III

50 Consider the following statements on Industrial dispute

I. Industrial dispute will subsist inspite of closure of industry.
II. An industrial dispute can arise when a demand is made by the workman and denied by the employer.
III. Once a dispute is referred for adjudication, the presumption is that it is an industrial dispute.
IV. Employer's failure to keep his verbal assurances is an industrial dispute.

Codes
1 I and II are correct 2 II and III are correct
3 III and IV are correct 4 I, II and III are correct

51 Match items in List-I with items in List-II using the codes given below.

List I	List II
A. Marriage during Iddat period is	I. Voidable
B. Marriage with an impotent person is	II. Valid
C. Marriage below the age of 18 years is	III. Voidable
D. Marriage with a person of unsound mind is	IV. Voidable

Codes

	A	B	C	D
1	I	II	III	IV
2	I	III	IV	II
3	I	III	II	IV
4	III	II	I	IV

52 Match List-I with List-II and indicate the correct answer using the codes given below.

List I	List II
A. Ashok Hurra Vs. Rupa Hurra case	I. Restitution of Conjugal-Rights
B. Bipin Chandra Vs. Prabhavati	II. Uniform Civil Code
C. Sarla Mudgal Vs. Union of India	III. Dessertion
D. T. Sareetha Vs. State of A.P.	IV. Divorce by Mutual Consent

Codes

	A	B	C	D
1	I	II	III	IV
2	IV	III	II	I
3	II	III	I	IV
4	IV	III	I	II

53 Match List-I and List-II and give the correct answer using the code given below

List I (Subject)	List II (Decided cases)
A. Defence of insanity	I. King Vs. Barendra Kumar Ghosh
B. Common intention	II. King Vs. McNaughton
C. Necessity	III. State of Maharashtra Vs. KM Nanawati
D. Causing death due to grave and sudden provocation	IV. King Vs. Dadle Stephens

Codes

	A	B	C	D
1	I	II	III	IV
2	II	I	IV	III
3	III	II	IV	I
4	IV	II	III	I

54 Match List I with List II using the code given below

List I (Theory)	List II (Subject)
A. Retributive theory	I. Legal Right
B. Sociological theory	II. Source of law
C. Theory of Precedent	III. Punishment
D. Theory of Property	IV. Roscoe pound

Codes

	A	B	C	D
1	I	IV	III	II
2	III	IV	II	I
3	III	II	I	IV
4	IV	III	II	

55 Match List I and List II with the help of code given below

List I	List II
A. Mohd. Ahmed Vs. Shah Bano	I. Oral gift
B. Mukku Rathod Vs. State of Kerala	II. Maintenance
C. Maina Bibi Vs. Chaudhry Vakil Ahmed	III. Life Interest
D. Nawazish Ali Khan Vs. Ali Raza Khan	IV. Dower

Codes

	A	B	C	D
1	II	I	IV	III
2	I	II	III	IV
3	II	III	IV	I
4	I	IV	III	II

56 Match List I with List II using the code given below

List I (Judicial decision)	List II (Item)
A. Coir Board Ernakulam	I. Employer
B. Pipraich Sugar Mills Ltd. Vs. Pipraich Sugar Mills Mazdoor Union	II. Industry
C. Sundarambal Vs. Govt. of Goa	III. Workman
D. Western India Automobile Association Vs. I.T.	IV. Retrenchment

Codes

	A	B	C	D
1	III	II	IV	I
2	II	IV	III	I
3	I	II	III	IV
4	IV	III	I	II

57 Match List I with List II using the code given below

List I	List II
A. National Emergency	I. Article 316
B. President's Rule	II. Article 360
C. Financial Emergency	III. Article 356
D. Public Service Commission for Union	IV. Article 352

Codes

	A	B	C	D		A	B	C	D
1	IV	III	II	I	2	II	III	I	IV
3	III	II	I	IV	4	I	II	IV	III

58 The reasons why International law does work are

I. The common good

II. The flexible nature of International law

III. Practitioners of International law are lawyers

IV. The effective Institutions

Codes

1 I and II are correct
2 III and IV are correct
3 I, II, III and IV are correct
4 I, II and III are correct

59 Match List I with List II using the code given below :

	List I (Subject Matter)		List II (Decisions)
A.	Territorial boundary treaty	I.	Rann of Kutch Arbitration
B.	Regional custom	II.	Temple of Preah Vihear case
C.	Principle of estoppel	III.	The Asylum case
D.	Principle of equity	IV.	Case concerning Kasikili/ Sedudu Island
		V.	The Danube Dam case

Codes

	A	B	C	D		A	B	C	D
1	III	V	I	IV	2	IV	V	III	II
3	IV	III	II	I	4	V	IV	II	III

60 Match List I with List II and select the correct answer using the codes given below

	List I (Concepts)		List II (Jurists)
A.	Minimum content of law	I.	Fuller
B.	Inner morality of law	II.	Hart
C.	Law with a variable content	III.	Kohler
D.	Law as a phenomenon of civilisation	IV.	Stammler

Codes

	A	B	C	D		A	B	C	D
1	III	I	II	IV	2	II	III	IV	I
3	II	I	IV	III	4	I	II	III	IV

61 Arrange the following decisions in order in which they appeared. Use the code given below

I. East Timor case

II. Western Sahara

III. Namibia case

IV. South West Africa case

Codes

1 II, III, I, IV
2 I, IV, II, III
3 III, I, II, IV
4 IV, III, II, I

62 Match List I with List II using the code given below

	List I (Principles)		List II (Decisions)
A.	Concept of limited liability	I.	The South West Africa case
B.	Principle of subrogation	II.	The Barcelona traction case
C.	Concept of trust	III.	The Danube case
D.	Duty to pay compensation for proven injury	IV.	The Mavrommatis Palestine concessions case
		V.	Frontier Dispute case

Codes

	A	B	C	D		A	B	C	D
1	II	I	V	III	2	II	IV	I	III
3	I	II	III	V	4	III	IV	II	I

63 Match the List I with List II using the code given below

	List I		List II
A.	Right to Strike	I.	University of Delhi Vs. Ramnath
B.	Industry	II.	Gujarat Steel Tubes Vs. Gujarat Steel Tubes Mazdoor Sabha
C.	Lay-off	III.	Pipraich Sugar Mills Vs. Mazdoor Union
D.	Retrenchment	IV.	Workman Vs. Firestone Tyre and Rubber Co.

Codes

	A	B	C	D		A	B	C	D
1	III	IV	I	II	2	IV	II	III	I
3	II	I	IV	III	4	IV	III	II	I

64 Consider the following statements :

I The Trade Unions Act prescribe time limit for the grant of registration of Trade Unions.

II The certificate of registraton issued by Registrar is a conclusive evidence.

III The Registrar of Trade Union is duty bound to hear existing unions before granting registration to a new Trade Union.

Which of the given statements is/are correct?

1 Only I
2 I and II
3 I, II and III
4 Only II

65 Under the Companies Act 2013, which of the following company is required to constitute a Corporate Social Responsible Committee?

I. company having net worth of ₹ 500 crore or more.

II. company having turnover of ₹ 1,000 crore or more.

III. company having net profit of ₹ 5 crore or more.
IV. company having net profit of ₹ 2 crore or more during any financial year.

Choose the most appropriate option:
1 I, II, III, and IV
2 I and IV
3 I, II and III
4 I, III and IV

66 Constitution of India assure "Dignity of the Individual" in the language of
1 Article 14 2 Article 21
3 Article 19 4 Preamble

67 Consider the following statements:
Under Article 36(2) of the Statute of International Court, the State party to the statute may confer 'compulsory jurisdiction' upon the International Court of Justice in respect of the following matter(s):
I. Interpretation of a Treaty.
II. Any question of National law.
III. The existence of any fact which, if established, would constitute a breach of international obligations
IV. The nature and the extent of the separation to be made for the breach of a domestic obligation

Choose the correct answer from the codes given below:

Codes
1 Only I and II are correct
2 I and III
3 I, II and IV
4 I, II, III and IV

68 Dower in Muslim law is
I. Dowry
II. An obligation imposed upon husband as a mark of respect for wife
III. Sale price of woman
IV. Consideration for Marriage

Select the correct answer by using the code given below :

Codes
1 I, III and IV 2 II and III
3 II and IV 4 I and III

69 Consider the following judicial decision on the meaning of industry :
I. Indian Red Cross Society Vs. Additional Labour Court, Chandigarh
II. Dhanrajgiri Hospital Vs. Workmen
III. State of Punjab Vs. Kuldeep Singh
IV. Prema Govinda Vs. Karnataka Small Scale Industries Association, Bangalore

The correct order in which these judicial decisions were rendered is
1 I, III, I and IV 2 III, II, IV and I
3 IV, III, I and II 4 II, I, III and IV

70 Give below are two statements, one is labelled as Assertion (A) and the other is labelled as Reason (R).
Assertion (A) Before Bangalore Water Supply case educational institutions were excluded from the definition of an industry.
Reason (R) Main purpose of such institutions is to impart education, and not to run business or trade.
In light of the above statement, choose the correct answer from the options given below.

Codes
1 Both (A) and (R) are true and (R) is the correct explanation of (A).
2 Both (A) and (R) are true but (R) is not the correct explanation of (A).
3 (A) is true but (R) is false.
4 (A) is false but (R) is true.

71 Give below are two statements, one is labelled as Assertion (A) and the other is labelled as Reason (R).
Assertion (A) The Hindu Marriage Act, 1955 brought changes like prohibition of polygamy and prigamy and permission for inter-caste marriages.
Reason (R) The changes were brought under social pressure.
In light of the above statement, choose the correct answer from the options given below.

Codes
1 Both (A) and (R) are true and (R) is correct explanation of (A).
2 Both (A) and (R) are true but (R) is not the correct explanation of (A).
3 (A) is true but (R) is false.
4 (A) is false but (R) is true.

72 Give below are two statements, one is labelled as Assertion (A) and the other is labelled as Reason (R).
Assertion (A) Human Rights occupy a significant place in the UN Charter.
Reason (R) Members of the UN have committed themselves to promote respect for and observance of Human Rights and Fundamental Rights.
In light of the above statement, choose the correct answer from the options given below.

Codes
1 Both (A) and (R) are individually true and (R) is the correct explanation of (A).
2 Both (A) and (R) are individually true, but (R) is not the correct explanation of (A).
3 (A) is true, but (R) is false.
4 (A) is false, but (R) is true.

73 Which of the following is an essential constituent of negligence?

I. Defendant was under legal duty to exercise due care.

II. This duty was owed to plantiff.

III. Defendant committed breach of such duty.

IV. That the breach of such duty was the direct and proximate cause of the damage alleged.

Codes

1 I, II and III 2 I, II, III and IV
3 II, III and IV 4 I, II and IV

74 When an injury is caused by the act of an enterprise engaged in a hazardous or inherently dangerous activity, the enterprise is absolutely liable for the injury because

I. it has not taken reasonable care.

II. the enterprise owes an absolute and non-delegable duty to the community to ensure that no harm results from the activity.

III. it is considered as a part of the social cost for carrying on the hazardous or inherently dangerous activity.

IV. it is difficult to prove lack of care on the part of enterprise.

Select the right code

1 I and II are correct 2 I and IV are correct
3 I and III are correct 4 II and III are correct

75 A valid contract can be entered into between parties under Indian Contract Act. Which of the following gives legal recognition to such contract?

I. Section 10-A of Information Technology Act

II. Section 65-B of Indian Evidence Act

III. Section 14 of Information Technology Act

IV. Section 63 of Indian Evidence Act

Choose the correct option:

1 I and IV 2 I and II
3 I and III 4 III and IV

76 Indicate the order in which the following words appear in the definition of 'workmen' as given in Section 2 (s) of the Industrial Disputes Act :

I. Operational II. Manual
III. Technical IV. Supervisory Work

Codes

1 III, II, I, IV 2 II, III, IV, I
3 I, II, III, IV 4 II, IV, III, I

77 Which of the following statements are true?

I. Past consideration is no consideration under Indian and English Law.

II. Past consideration is no consideration under Indian Law.

III. Past consideration is no consideration under English Law.

IV. Past consideration is made in past.

Codes

1 I and II 2 II and III
3 III and IV 4 IV and I

78 Consider the following set of legal propositions:

I. A person can claim damages for all wrongs he has suffered.

II. A person can claim damages for wrongs only if they are caused intentionally.

III. A person can claim damages for a wrong if it is caused by infringement of the legal right.

IV. A person can claim damages even if he has suffered no loss.

Of these above propositions which are correct?

1 I and II 2 III and IV
3 I and III 4 II and IV

79 The general principles as to protection of an accused is based on:

I. Autrefois acquit and Autrefois convict.

II. Reasonable doubt as to presumption of innocence.

III. Natural Justice.

IV. Conviction can not be based without proving the guilt even if it was admitted.

Which statement is correct?

1 I is correct.
2 I and II are correct.
3 I, II and III are correct.
4 I, II, III and IV are correct.

80 Consider the following statements :

An accused person can be compelled to

I. give his finger prints

II. give evidence against himself

III. participate in the identification parade

Which of the above statements are correct?

1 I, II and III
2 II and III
3 I and II
4 I and III

81 Identify the correct order in which the following bases of Jurisdiction appear in the statute of the International Criminal Justice :

I. Consent ad hoc

II. As provided in the UN Charter

III. Consent under the optional system

IV. Transferred Jurisdiction

Codes

1 IV, III, I and IV 2 III, I, II and IV
3 II, I, III and IV 4 I, II, IV and III

82 Which of the following is/are exception(s) to the rule of strict liability recognised by Rylands Vs. Fletcher?

I. Defendant's default
II. Act of God
III. Consent of the third party
IV. Statutory Authority

Choose the correct answer from the code given below:

Codes

1 I and II are correct
2 III and IV are correct
3 II and III are correct
4 II, III and IV are correct

83 Which of the following statements are correct in relation to 'administrative control' of forums and commission under Section 24-B of the Consumer Protection Act, 1986?

I. National Commission shall have administrative control over all State Commissions.
II. National Commission shall call for the periodical return of 'pendency of cases' before the State Commissions.
III. State Commission shall have administrative control over all district forums.
IV. State commission can issue instructions to district forums to furnish english translation of judgment written in any language.

Choose the correct answer from the code given below:

1 I and II are correct
2 II and IV are correct
3 I, II and III are correct
4 I, II, III and IV are correct

84 Which of the following statements are correct?

I. The Chairperson and Members of the State Human Rights Commission shall be appointed by the President under his hand and seal.
II. The Chairperson or a Member of a State Human Rights Commission may, by notice in writing under his hand addressed to the Governor, resign his office.
III. The President of India may, by order, remove from office the Chairperson or any Member as the case may be, if adjudged an insolvent.
IV. On ceasing to hold office, a Chairperson shall be eligible for further employment under the Government of India.

Choose the correct answer from the code given below

1 Only I and II are correct
2 Only I and III are correct
3 Only II and III are correct
4 All of these

85 Consider the following statements.

Statement I The Legislative Council of a state in India can be larger in size than half of the Legislative Assembly of that particular State.

Statement II The Governor of a State nominates the Chairman of Legislative Council of that particular State.

Choose the correct answer from the options given below.

1 Both Statement I and II are true
2 Both Statement I and II are false
3 Statement I is true but II is false
4 Statement I is false but II is true

86 Consider the following statements.

Statement I The Governor of Punjab is concurrently the administrator of Chandigarh.

Statement II The Governor of Kerala is concurrently the administrator of Lakshadweep.

Choose the correct answer from the options given below.

1 Both Statement I and II are true
2 Both Statement I and II are false
3 Statement I is true but II is false
4 Statement I is false but II is true

87 Which of the following are included among the duties of the Chief Minister in relation to the Governor?

I. Communication to the Governor of all the decisions of the Council of Ministers.
II. Advising the Governor to recommend to the President that the Government of the State cannot be carried on in accordance with the provisions of the Constitution.
III. Supplying to the Governor, information on such matters relating to the administration of the state as he call for.
IV. Assisting the Governor in making appointments in the State Government.

Select the correct answer using the codes given below :

1 I, II and III
2 I, III and IV
3 II, III and IV
4 All of these

88 Consider the following statements

I. Zonal Councils have been established under an Article of the Constitution.
II. The Constitution provides for setting up of an Inter-State Council by the Parliament.
III. Union Home Minister is the common Chairman of all the Zonal Councils.

Select the correct answer using the codes given below :

1 I and II 2 Only III
3 Only II 4 II and III

89 The function(s) of the finance commission is/are

I. to allow the withdrawal of the money out of the Consolidated Fund of India.
II. to allocate between the States the shares of proceeds of taxes.
III. to consider the application for Grant-in-aid from States.
IV. to supervise and report on whether the Union and State Governments are levying taxes in accordance with the budgetary provisions.

Which of the statement(s) given above is/are correct?

1 Only I 2 II and III
3 III and IV 4 I, II and IV

90 Which of the following are the discretionary powers given to the Governor of the State?

I. Sending a report to the President of India for imposing the President's Rule
II. Appointing the Ministers.
III. Reserving certain bills passed by the State Legislature for consideration of the President of India.
IV. Making the rules to conduct the business of the State Government.

Select the correct answer using the codes given below :

1 I and II
2 I and III
3 II, III and IV
4 All of the above

Directions (Q. Nos. 91-96) *Read the given passage and answer the following questions :*

Broadly speaking, legal theory involves a study of the characteristic features essential to law and common to legal systems and analysis of the basic elements of law which made it law and distinguish it from other forms of rules and standards, from systems which cannot be described as legal systems and from other social phenomena. In fact, it is not possible to reach our dogmatic answer to the question what is law or provide exclusive answers to many questions which are asked about its essential nature.

The nature of legal theory lies in a study of the right which other theories may shed on distinctive attributes of law by an examination of the relative merits and demerits of the principal expositions of the subject. In the same strain legal theory is linked at one end with philosophy and at the other end, with political theory.

Sometimes, the starting point is philosophy and political ideology plays a secondary part .... sometimes the theory of knowledge and political ideology are welded into one coherent system, of course, it is true that some legal philosophies have been philosophers first and foremost and juristic because they felt the need to express their political thought in legal form.... In short, before the nineteenth-century legal theory was essentially a by-product of philosophy, religion, ethics or politics.

The new era of legal philosophy arises mainly from the confrontation of professional lawyers in his legal work, with problems of social justice. The modern jurists legal theory, no less than scholastic philosopher is based on ultimate beliefs whose inspiration comes from outside the law itself.

91 As the science of law or philosophy of law emerged, which of the following approach came into existence

1 Analytical positivist approach
2 Socio-legal approach
3 Historical approach
4 Realist approach.

92 Law must remain free from social sciences, metaphysical, ethical and moral elements. This was propounded by

1 Austin 2 Pound 3 Kelsen 4 Salmond

93 Who defined jurisprudence as a formal science of positive law?

1 Austin 2 LA Hart 3 Salmond 4 Holland

94 Law is always in a state of continual change. This is the basic tenet of

1 Realist Jurisprudence
2 Sociological Jurisprudence
3 Philosophical Jurisprudence
4 Analytical Jurisprudence

95 Who, among the following jurists, says "legal theory is linked at one end with philosophy and, at other end, with political theory"?

1 John D. Finch 2 Friedmann
3 Wayne Morrison 4 Jeremy Bentham

Directions (Q. Nos. 96-100) *Read the given passage and answer the following questions:*

The thrust of Article 14 is that the citizen is entitled to equality before law and equal protection of laws. In the very nature of things the society being composed of unequals a welfare State will have to strive by both executive and legislative action to help the less fortunate in society to ameliorate their condition so that the social and economic inequality in the society may be bridged.

This would necessitate a legislative application to a group of citizens otherwise unequal and amelioration of whose lot is the object of state affirmative action. In the absence of the doctrine of classification such legislation is likely to flounder on the bed rock of equality enshrined in Article 14.

The Court realistically appraising the social and economic inequality and keeping in view the guidelines on which the State action must move as constitutionally laid down in Part IV of the Constitution evolved the doctrine of classification.

The doctrine was evolved to sustain a legislation or State action designed to help weaker sections of the society or some such segments of the society in need of succour. Legislative and executive action may accordingly be sustained if it satisfies the twin tests of reasonable classification and the rational principle correlated to the object sought to be achieved.

The concept of equality before the law does not involve the idea of absolute equality among human beings which is a physical impossibility. All that Article 14 guarantees is a similarity of treatment contra-distinguished from identical treatment. Equality before law means that among equals the law should be equal and should be equally administered and that the likes should be treated alike. Equality before the law does not mean that things which are different shall be as though they are the same. It of course means denial of any special privilege by reason of birth, creed or the like.

The legislation as well as the executive government, while dealing with diverse problems arising out of an infinite variety of human relations must of necessity have the power of making special laws, to attain any particular object and to achieve that object it must have the power of selection or classification of persons and things upon which such laws are to operate.

96 Right to equality, one of the fundamental rights, is enunciated in the Constitution under Part III, Article:

1 (A)12 2 13 3 14 4 15

97 The main thrust of Right to equality is that it permits

1 class legislation
2 equality before law and equal protection under the law
3 absolute equality
4 special privilege by reason of birth

98 The social and economic inequality in the society can be bridged by

1 executive and legislative action
2 universal suffrage
3 identical treatment
4 None of the above

99 The doctrine of classification evolved to:

1 help weaker sections of the society
2 provide absolute equality
3 provide identical treatment
4 None of the above

100 While dealing with diverse problems arising out of an infinite variety of human relations, the government

1 must have the power of making special laws
2 must not have any power to make special laws
3 must have power to withdraw equal rights
4 None of the above

ANSWERS

1 *(1)*	**2** *(4)*	**3** *(3)*	**4** *(2)*	**5** *(3)*	**6** *(1)*	**7** *(2)*	**8** *(1)*	**9** *(4)*	**10** *(2)*
11 *(4)*	**12** *(4)*	**13** *(4)*	**14** *(2)*	**15** *(4)*	**16** *(3)*	**17** *(2)*	**18** *(1)*	**19** *(3)*	**20** *(2)*
21 *(1)*	**22** *(3)*	**23** *(1)*	**24** *(1)*	**25** *(3)*	**26** *(4)*	**27** *(2)*	**28** *(2)*	**29** *(1)*	**30** *(2)*
31 *(2)*	**32** *(2)*	**33** *(2)*	**34** *(1)*	**35** *(4)*	**36** *(4)*	**37** *(2)*	**38** *(4)*	**39** *(2)*	**40** *(3)*
41 *(3)*	**42** *(1)*	**43** *(3)*	**44** *(2)*	**45** *(3)*	**46** *(2)*	**47** *(4)*	**48** *(3)*	**49** *(2)*	**50** *(4)*
51 *(1)*	**52** *(2)*	**53** *(2)*	**54** *(2)*	**55** *(1)*	**56** *(2)*	**57** *(1)*	**58** *(1)*	**59** *(3)*	**60** *(3)*
61 *(4)*	**62** *(1)*	**63** *(3)*	**64** *(3)*	**65** *(3)*	**66** *(2)*	**67** *(4)*	**68** *(3)*	**69** *(4)*	**70** *(1)*
71 *(3)*	**72** *(2)*	**73** *(2)*	**74** *(4)*	**75** *(2)*	**76** *(1)*	**77** *(3)*	**78** *(2)*	**79** *(4)*	**80** *(4)*
81 *(3)*	**82** *(4)*	**83** *(4)*	**84** *(3)*	**85** *(2)*	**86** *(3)*	**87** *(2)*	**88** *(4)*	**89** *(2)*	**90** *(2)*
91 *(2)*	**92** *(3)*	**93** *(4)*	**94** *(1)*	**95** *(2)*	**96** *(3)*	**97** *(2)*	**98** *(1)*	**99** *(1)*	**100** *(1)*

UGC-NET LAW

PRACTICE SET 2

PAPER II

1 Which of the following is principal organ of the United Nations ?
1 Human Rights Committee
2 Economic and Social Council
3 International Labour Organisation
4 International Law Association

2 India is not a party to
1 International Covenant on Economic, Social and Cultural Rights, 1966
2 International Covenant on Civil and Political Rights, 1966
3 Optional Protocol to International Covenant on Civil and Political Rights, 1966
4 Convention on Elimination of Discrimination Against Women (CEDAW), 1979

3 Which of the following can request the International Court of Justice to give an advisory opinion ?
1 State
2 General Assembly
3 International Law Commission
4 Individual

4 Which of the following is not a leading case on immunity of trade unions from criminal proceedings?
1 Jay Engineering Works Ltd. Vs. State of West Bengal
2 Standard Chartered Grindlays Bank Ltd. Vs. Grindlays Bank Employees
3 Onkarnath Tiwari Vs. Chief Engineer, Minor Irrigation Department
4 Piperaich Sugar Mills Ltd

5 The Supreme Court of India for the first time struck down the 'Carry Forward Rule' as unconstitutional in the following case :
1 Balaji Vs. State of Mysore
2 Rangachari Vs. General Manager, Southern Railway
3 Ashok Kumar Thakur Vs. State of Bihar
4 Devadasan Vs. Union of India

6 Which of the following is not a ground for divorce under the Dissolution of Muslim Marriage Act, 1939 ?
1 Treating the wife with cruelty.
2 The whereabouts of the Husband have not been known of a period of more than four years.
3 The Husband has been sentenced to imprisonment for a period of two years or upwards.
4 The Husband has been insane for a period of two years or more.

7 Which of the following do not relate to 'industrial dispute' ?
1 Dispute or difference connected with employment of workers.
2 Dispute or difference connected with non-employment of workers.
3 Dispute or difference connected with the terms of employment or with the conditions of labour.
4 Dispute or difference connected with the election of a trade union.

8 Requirement of 'reasonableness' runs like a golden thread through the entire fabric of Fundamental Rights is held in
1 Keshavananda Bharati Vs. State of Kerala
2 Indra Sawhney Vs. Union of India
3 Vishaka Vs. State of Rajasthan
4 Maneka Gandhi Vs. Union of India

9 An acceptance given by post
1 can be revoked at any time
2 cannot be revoked at all
3 can be revoked, if it does not reach to the proposer
4 can be revoked, even if it comes to the knowledge of proposer

10 A promise to pay time barred debt is
1 not enforceable
2 enforceable at the discretion of debtor
3 enforceable under Section 25 (3)
4 None of the above

11 Which of the following statements is correct ?
1 Third party can always sue for breach of contract.
2 Wagering agreements are illegal.
3 When consent is not free, agreement will always be voidable.
4 Catalogue is an invitation to offer.

12 An agreement with minor is void, but
1 Minor is never allowed to enforce such agreement.
2 Minor is allowed to enforce such agreement, if it was made for his benefit.
3 Minor is always allowed to enforce such agreement.
4 Minor is allowed to enforce such contract when other party makes no objection.

13 'A' s services were terminated without complying with retrenchment compensation provision :
1 'A' is entitled to reinstatement without back wages
2 'A' is entitled to back wages
3 'A' is entitled to retrenchment compensation
4 'A' is entitled to reinstatement and back wages as determined by the Court

14 Where a Hindu Male and a Hindu Female contract their Marriage under the Special Marriages Act 1954, Hindu Personal Law
1 applies to such marriage
2 does not apply
3 applies with some modifications
4 applies with the Indian Contract Act

15 A Muslim woman observing iddat period marries with another man. The marriage is
1 Sahih 2 Batil
3 Fasid 4 None of these

16 In which of the following case, the court held that 'Triple divorce' is not a valid Talaq?
1 Ziauddin Vs. Anwara Begum
2 Mohammad Ahmed Khan Vs. Shah Bano
3 Bai Tahira Vs. Ali Hussain
4 None of the above

17 A marriage under Muslim Law between persons with Fosterage relationship is
1 Sahih 2 Batil
3 Fasid 4 None of these

18 Promissory estoppel against Government agencies is decided in
1 Tweddle Vs. Atkinson
2 Dutton Vs. Poole
3 Delhi Cloth and General Mills Ltd. Vs. Union of India
4 Kedarnath Bhattacharji Vs. Gorie Mohammad

19 'Qui facit per alium facit per se' establishes the
1 Liability under the Indian Penal Code
2 Liability under the law of torts
3 Vicarious liability
4 Liability under the Indian Contract Act

20 The rule of Strict Liability was first laid down by
1 Lord Atkin in 1635
2 Justice Blackburn in 1868
3 Winfield in 1765
4 Chief Justice Holt in 1868

21 If 'A' gives lift in his car to 'B' upto a certain place and on the way due to negligence of 'A' an accident is caused. 'A' has
1 no responsibility towards 'B'.
2 no legal duty to take care of B's safety.
3 a legal duty to take care of 'B' also and is liable for compensation.
4 All of the above

22 A 2003 enactment provided for doing away with the requirement of a candidate to be resident of a particular state, to contest the election to the Rajya-Sabha. In 2006 the Supreme Court of India has held such enactment :
1 Unconstitutional
2 Constitutional
3 Partly valid and partly invalid
4 Subject to judicial review

23 A five judge Constitution bench of the Supreme Court in October 2006 has held that the exclusion of 'Creamy Layer' among the Scheduled Castes and Scheduled Tribes is :
1 Subject to Judicial review
2 Unconstitutional
3 Constitutional directive
4 A matter of policy decision of the government

24 In Gur Corporation's case the issue before an English court was whether the Government of Ciskei could sue as claimant in its own name. The court of Appeal answered this question in the affirmative by applying :
1 The Foreign Corporation Act
2 Foreign Relations Act
3 Doctrine of acts of a delegated sovereign
4 Estrada doctrine

25 In which of the constitutional Amendment it has been laid down that the total number of Ministers including Prime-Minister in the Union Council of Ministers, shall not exceed 15 percent of the total members of the House of people?
1 The Constitution [Eighty-Eighth Amendment] Act
2 The Constitution [Eighty-Nineth Amendment] Act
3 The Constitution [Ninety-First Amendment] Act
4 The Constitution [Ninety-Third Amendment] Act

26 In which of the following case, the Supreme Court held that "The three talaq would be treated as a single talaq and not a valid talaq" :
1 Shamim Ara Vs. State of U.P
2 Mohammad Ahmed Khan Vs. Shah Bano
3 Bai Tahira Vs. Ali Hussain
4 None of the above

27 A marriage under Hindu Marriage Act, 1955 between persons within Sapinda relationship is :
1 Valid 2 Voidable 3 Void 4 Irregular

28 Realist school is a branch of :
1 Sociological approach
2 Positive approach
3 Historical approach
4 Analytical approach

29 International law is :
1 Collection of legislations of various countries.
2 Body of rules and principles of action which are binding upon civilised states in their relation with each other.
3 Collection of customs of various countries
4 A legal instrument in service of domestic policy

30 International treaties are the most important source of :
1 Environmental Law
2 Cyber Law
3 International Law
4 None of the above

31 Which one of the following statements is correct ?
1 Directive Principles of State Policy are part and parcel of Fundamental Rights
2 Directive Principles of State Policy override Fundamental Rights
3 Fundamental Rights override Directive Principles of State Policy
4 Neither override each other

32 Point out the correct answer :
Right to education by the 86th Amendment of the Constitution has provided :
1 education upto any level
2 free and compulsory education upto 14 years
3 education subject to financial capacity of the state
4 education without considering the financial capacity of the state

33 A member of a House is disqualified if :
1 he resigns from his party
2 he becomes a Speaker of the House
3 he is expelled from his party
4 all the above grounds are correct

34 A constitutional amendment requires :
1 a majority of the total membership of the House
2 not less than two third majority of members present and voting
3 a simple majority of the total members present and voting
4 Both 1 and 2

35 The harmony between Fundamental Rights and Directive Principles was laid down by the Supreme Court in :
1 The AK Gopalan's case
2 The Golaknath case
3 The Minerva Mills case
4 The Champakam Dorairajan case

36 To strive towards excellence in all spheres of individual and collective activity is a part of
1 GATT
2 ICCPR
3 Directive Principles of State Policy
4 Fundamental Rights

37 Which one of the following Article is not suspended during enforcement of Article 356 of the Constitution ?
1 Article 20 2 Article 21
3 Article 20 and 21 4 Article 32

38 Which among the following is not a Fundamental Right ?
1 Right to Privacy
2 Right to Speedy Trial
3 Right to Clean Environment
4 Right to Property

39 The President shall revoke a proclamation of emergency if the house of people passes a resolution disapproving the proclamation of emergency by a :
1 Majority of total membership of the house
2 Majority of not less that two third of the house present and voting
3 Simple majority
4 Both 1 and 2

40 The Supreme Court is a court of record means :
1 It has the powers of a court to punish for contempt of itself
2 Its judgements are binding on all courts
3 It has got powers to pass orders for enforcement of its own judgements
4 Full faith and credit shall be given to all its judgements

41 Give below are two statements, one is labelled as Assertion (A) and the other is labelled as Reason (R).
Assertion (A) The Preamble to the Constitution of India clearly indicates the ideals set before the Nation.
Reason (R) The ideals set before the Nation are Justice, Equity, Fraternity of the individual and unity and integrity of the Nation.

In light of the above statement, choose the correct answer from the options given below.

Codes

1 Both (A) and (R) are true and (R) is the correct explanation of (A)

2 Both (A) and (R) are true but (R) is not the correct explanation of (A)

3 (A) is true but (R) is false

4 (A) is false but (R) is true.

42 Give below are two statements, one is labelled as Assertion (A) and the other is labelled as Reason (R).

Assertion (A) No person is eligible for appointment as Governor unless he is a citizen of India and has completed the age of Thirty Five Years.

Reason (R) He is debarred from holding any other office of profit during his term of office.

In light of the above statement, choose the correct answer from the options given below.

Codes

1 Both (A) and (R) are true and (R) is the correct explanation of (A)

2 Both (A) and (R) are true but (R) is not the correct explanation of (A)

3 (A) is true but (R) is false

4 (A) is false but (R) is true.

43 Give below are two statements, one is labelled as Assertion (A) and the other is labelled as Reason (R).

Assertion (A) A perfect duty is one which a person not merely ought to perform, but may be justly compelled to perform.

Reason (R) A perfect duty is one which is not merely recognised by law but enforceable.

In light of the above statement, choose the correct answer from the options given below.

Codes

1 (A) and (R) both are correct and (R) is the correct explanation of (A)

2 (A) and (R) both are correct but (R) is not the correct explanation of (A)

3 (A) is correct but (R) is wrong

4 (A) is wrong but (R) is correct.

44 Mention the following decisions in a chronological order on Extradition:

I. Mobarik Ali Ahmed Vs. State of Bombay

II. Hans Muller of Nuremberg Vs. Suptt. Presidency Jail Calcutta and Others

III. Ram Babu Saxena Vs. State

IV. State of Madras Vs. C.G. Menon

Choose the correct option :

1 IV, III, I, II   2 III, IV, II, I
3 II, I, IV, III   4 IV, III, II, I

45 Arrange the provisions of Trade Marks Act, 1999 in chronological order (section wise):

I. classification of goods and services

II. regulation in case of honest concurrent use etc.

III. limitation as to colour

IV. absolute grounds for refusal of registration

Choose the correct option:

1 I, II, III, IV   2 I, III, IV, II
3 I, IV, III, II   4 II, III, IV, I

46 Mention the following cases in a chronological order on Election Commission:

I. Kuldip Nayar Vs. Union of India

II. TN Seshan Vs. Union of India

III. People's union for Civil Liberties Vs. Union of India

IV. S.S. Dhanoa Vs. Union of India

Choose the correct option:

1 II, III, IV, I   2 III, IV, II, I
3 I, IV, II, III   4 IV, II, I, III

47 Arrange the following decisions in the order in which they appeared. Use the code given below:

I. Baroda Borough Municipality Vs. Its workmen

II. D.N. Banerji Vs. PR Mukherjee

III. Samishta Dubey Vs. City Board, Etawah

IV. Lalit Hari Ayurvedic College Pharmacy case

Codes

1 I, II, III, IV   2 II, I, IV, III
3 III, IV, II, I   4 IV, II, III, I

48 Arrange the grounds of divorce in the order in which they appear in the Hindu Marriage Act 1955. Use the code given below :

I. Mutual Consent   II. Breakdown
III. Fault   IV. Customary

Codes

1 III, II, I, IV   2 II, III, IV, I
3 I, II, III, IV   4 IV, I, III, II

49 Select correct code combination relating to 'Closure'.

I. Suspension of Employment relationship

II. End of bargaining

III. Permanent closing down of employer's business

IV. Deliberate temporary closing of a place of employment

Codes

1 I, II, III, IV   2 IV, II, III, I
3 II, I, III, IV   4 III, I, IV, II

50 Consider the following statements.

Statement I If the Legislative Assembly of a State in India is dissolved in mid-term, the speaker continues in office till the process of formation of next Legislative Assembly.

Statement II When the speaker of a Legislative Assembly resigns, he addresses his letter to the Deputy Chairman of the Assembly.

Select the correct answer from the options given below.

1 Both Statement I and II are true
2 Both Statement I and II are false
3 Statement I but II are false
4 Statement I is false but II is true

51 Consider the following statements.

The Constitution of India provides that

Statement I The Legislative Assembly of each State shall consist not more than 500 members chosen by direct election from territorial constituencies in the State.

Statement II A person shall not be qualified to be chosen to fill seat in the Legislative Assembly of a State if he/she is less than 25 years of age.

Select the correct answer from the options given below.

1 Both Statement I and II are true
2 Both Statement I and II are false
3 Statement I is true but II is false
4 Statement I is false but II is true

52 A company can convert into Limited Liability Partnership:

I. By complying with requirements of the third schedule of Limited Liability Partnership Act, 2008.
II. It can convert if there is no security interest in its assets subsisting at the time of application.
III. Partners of Limited Liability Partnership are the erstwhile shareholders of the company and no one else.
IV. All the assets, interests, rights and privileges of the company are transferred to the firm.

Choose the correct answer from the options given below :

1 I only 2 II only
3 III only 4 I, II, III, IV

53 Which of the following statements are correct. Answer using the codes given below:

I. Ascertainment of goods for sale is done by buyer.
II. Appropriation of goods for sale is done by seller.
III. Distinction between ascertainment of and appropriation of goods that former involves 'the element of common intention between buyer and seller', whereas later can be a unilateral act by buyer.
IV. Property in goods does not pass to buyer till appropriation.

Codes

1 I, III and IV are correct
2 II is correct
3 IV is correct
4 III is correct.

54 Which of the following are presumptions as to a negotiable instrument under Section 118 of the Negotiable Instruments Act? Answer using codes given below:

I. Presumption of contractual capacity
II. Presumption of consideration
III. Presumption of maturity of instrument
IV. Presumption of date

Codes

1 I and III 2 II and IV
3 I and IV 4 All of these

55 Which of the following statement/statements is/are incorrect?

I. Long duration is an essential element for International Custom.
II. The custom should be completely uniform and consistent to be an International custom.
III. In an International custom, Universality of practice is not necessary, the practice should have been generally observed or repeated by numerous states.
IV. Opinio juris is present, that is to say, customary practice to be a International Custom, must be recognised as being required by International law.

Codes

1 Only I 2 I and II
3 II, III and IV 4 All of these

56 Which of the following statements are correct as per Article III of agreements establishing WTO? The main functions of the WTO are:

I. To administer and promote agreements on individual and multi-national agreements.
II. To administer the rules and procedures governing the settlement of disputes.
III. To administer the Trade Policy Review Mechanism (TPRM).
IV. To coordinate IMF, TBRD and World Bank on regional economic policies.

Choose the correct option:

1 I and II 2 I and III
3 II and III 4 All of these

57 Which of the following could be considered to be advantages of Legislation over Precedent?

I. Abrogative capability
II. Fore knowledge

III. Prospective application
IV. Systematic arrangement
Choose the correction option:
1 I, II, IV only 2 I, II, III only
3 I, II, III and IV 4 I and III only

58 Which of the following factors are responsible for judicial activism in India?
I. Denial of court access to the poor, downtrodden and underprivileged sections of the society who do not have sufficient means to approach the court.
II. Maladministration, misuse of public and rampant corruption.
III. Increasing social problems as environmental pollution, child labour, smoking in public places, pitiable conditions of prisoners and exploitation of women etc.
IV. Gross violation of Human Rights.
Choose the correct option:
1 I, II and III 2 II, III and IV
3 I, III and IV 4 All I, II, III and IV

59 Which of the following statement are correct?
I. Convention of Nationality was adopted in 1928.
II. Convention of Nationality of married women was adopted in 1957.
III. Convention on the reduction of statelessness was adopted in 1961.
IV. Convention on the Nationality of newborn child was adopted in 1938.
Select the correct answer using the codes given below :
1 I and II 2 II and III 3 I, II, III 4 II and IV

60 To constitute the offence of kidnapping from lawful guardianship under Section 361 of Indian Penal Code the age of the minor should be:
I. Under eighteen years if male.
II. Under sixteen years if male.
III. Under eighteen years if female.
IV. Under sixteen years if female.
Choose the correct option:
1 I and II 2 I and III 3 II and III 4 I and IV

61 Consider the following statements and point out which statements are related to Positivism?
I. Laws are command.
II. Analysis of legal concept is distinct from Sociological and Historical analysis.
III. Decisions can be deducted logically with recourse to morality.
IV. The 'Law as it is' has to be kept separate from 'Law ought to be'.
Choose the correct option :
1 I, II and III only 2 I, II and IV only
3 II, III and IV only 4 I and IV only

62 The provisions given under Article 13 of the Indian Constitution are as follows :
I. All laws in force in the territory of India immediately before the commencement of this Constitution will be void to the extent of the inconsistency.
II. 'Laws in force' includes all laws passed or made by the legislature or other competent authority in the territory of India before the commencement of this constitution and not previously repealed.
III. The state shall not make any law which takes or abridges right conferred by Part III and any law made in the contravention shall be void.
IV. Law does not include any ordinance, order, bye-law, rule, regulation, notification, custom or usage etc.
Choose the correct answer from the options given below:
1 II and IV only 2 IV and V only
3 I and V only 4 I, II, and III only

63 The provision relating to 'Solid Waste Management' is contained under which Schedule of the Constitution of India?
I. Schedule VII II. Schedule IX
III. Schedule XI IV. Schedule XII
Choose the correct answer from the options given below :
1 I only 2 II only 3 III only 4 IV only

64 Under Section 5 of the Sale of Goods Act, 1930, a contract for the sale of goods can be made:
I. By writing and must be registered.
II. By word of mouth.
III. By partly in writing and partly word of mouth.
IV. By writing or partly in writing and partly by word of mouth.
Choose the correct answer from the options given below :
1 I and III only 2 I and IV only
3 I and II only 4 II and IV only.

65 In which of following cases originator of defamatory statement will be liable for the damage resulting from repetitive publication by third persons?
Answer by using codes below:
I. He himself authorised repetition.
II. Repetition was the natural and probable consequence of his act.

III. There was immoral obligation on the person in whose presence the slander was made to repeat it.

IV. There was moral obligation on the person in whose absence the slander was made to repeat it.

Codes

1 I and II 2 I and III 3 I and IV 4 II and IV

66 Give the chronological order of the following in which they came into existence

I. Charter of United Nations.

II. Universal Declaration of Human Rights.

III. International Covenant on Civil and Political Rights.

IV. International Covenant on Economic, Social and Cultural Rights.

Codes

1 I, II, III, IV 2 IV, II, I, III

3 I, II, IV, III 4 IV, III, II, I

67 Which of the following statements are wrong?

I. Human rights are created by legislation.

II. Legal duty to protect human rights is not duty to respect them.

III. International concern with Human Rights as enshrined in the United Nations Charter is a modern innovation.

IV. A human right violation is now conceived as violation of those personally and directly aggrieved, but not of everyone.

Codes

1 I and II 2 II and III

3 III and IV 4 All of these

68 Which of the following statements are correct? In order that a person can be called a holder in due course, he must show

I. that he is the drawer of the negotiable instrument.

II. that he has obtained it without consideration.

III. that he has obtained it before the maturity of the negotiable instrument.

IV. that he has obtained the negotiable instrument in good faith.

Select the correct statement from codes given below :

1 I and II are correct 2 II and III are correct

3 III and IV are correct 4 I and IV are correct

69 Which of the following are not available to a Hindu husband as grounds of Judicial Separation?

Answer with the help of codes given below:

I. Extra marital sex by wife

II. Conversion of wife to a non-Hindu religion

III. Wife's pre-marriage pregnancy

IV. Non consummation of marriage owing to impotence of wife

Codes

1 I and II only 2 II and III only

3 IV and I only 4 III and IV only

70 To which of the following International Conventions on Human Rights, India has become party to such conventions? Give correct answer with the help of codes given below:

I. Convention on the Political Rights of Women.

II. Convention on the Right of the Child.

III. Convention for the Suppression of the Traffic in Person and of exploitation of the prostitution of others.

IV. Convention on International Recovery of Child Support and Other Forms of Family Maintenance.

Codes

1 Only I 2 I and IV only

3 I, II and III 4 I, II, III and IV

71 In which among the following cases malice becomes relevant to determine a person's liability in law of torts. Answer by using codes below

I. Malice may result in aggravation of damages.

II. In torts of deceit and conspiracy one of the essential is malice.

III. When act is lawful, intention can be gathered from past circumstances.

IV. Causing of personal comfort by lawful means may turn lawful act into a tort.

Codes

1 I and II 2 I and III

3 I, II and III 4 None of these

72 Which are essentials of sale of goods?

I. Contractual capacity

II. Bilateral contract

III. Profit for seller

IV. Mutual and free consent of parties to the contract of sale of goods

1 I, II, III 2 I, II, IV

3 II, III, IV 4 I, III, IV

73 Which are essentials of a contract of sale of goods?

I. Offer

II. Acceptance of offer

III. Exchange of goods for money

IV. Transfer or property in goods from seller to buyer

Select the correct answers from codes given below :

1 I and II

2 III and IV

3 II and III

4 I, II, III and IV

74 Which of the following statements is/are correct regarding Constitutional Amendment Bill? Give correct answer by using the codes given below :

I. Prior permission of President is required before introducing the Constitutional Amendment Bill in Parliament.

II. Constitutional Amendment Bill can be introduced in either House of Parliament.

III. President is bound to give his assent to the Bill if duly passed by both Houses of Parliament and ratified, if required, by the Legislature of not less than one-half of the States.

IV. President may return the Bill to the Houses for reconsideration.

Codes

1 I, II and III   2 II and III
3 I, III, III and IV   4 All of these

75 The guilt theory of divorce, on the one hand implies a guilty party and on the other, it implies that the other party is innocent. In view of this which of the following is/are correct?

I. If cruelty is provoked, divorce will be refused.

II. In innocent party condones the act of the guilty party, no divorce can be granted.

III. If both parties were guilty, divorce would not be granted to either.

IV. Unreasonable delay in filing petition is no bar for the relief of divorce.

Codes

1 I and III are correct   2 II and III are correct
3 I, II and III are correct   4 III and IV are correct

76 Which of the following are included in the list of Fundamental Duties in the Constitution of India? Answer using codes given below

I. To uphold and protect the sovereignty, unity and integrity of India and the states.

II. To defend the country and render national service when called upon to do so.

III. To value and preserve the rich heritage of our composite culture.

IV. To develop the Scientific temper, humanism and the spirit of inquiry and reform.

Which of the statement(s) given above are correct?

1 I, II and III   2 I, II and IV
3 I, II, III and IV   4 I, III and IV

77 Which of the following statement/statements is/are correct?

I. Fundamental Rights are not absolute. They are subject to reasonable restrictions.

II. Freedom of Press is implict in Article 19 of the Constitution.

III. Socially and economically backward classes of persons are entitled to get benefit under Clause 4 of Article 15 of the Constitution.

IV. Equal protection of laws under Article 14 of the Constitution is based upon English law.

Select the correct answer using the codes given below :

1 I and II are correct   2 I, II and III are correct
3 III and IV are correct   4 All of the above

78 As per the Constitution of India, which of the following statement(s) is/are correct?

I. The State may make provision for securing just and humane conditions of work.

II. The state shall endeavour to provide early childhood care and education for all the children until they complete the age of six years.

III. The state shall not endeavour to secure for the citizens a Uniform Civil Code in the territory of India.

IV. The state shall endeavour to protect and improve the environment and to safeguard the forests and wildlife of the country.

Which of the statement(s) given above are correct

1 I, II and II   2 II, III and IV
3 II and IV   4 III and IV

79 In which of these cases, Fundamental Duties are judicially invoked?

Answer using codes given below.

I. Prem Parkash Vs. Punjab University

II. Suresh Koshy George Vs. University of Kerala

III. Rural Litigation and Entitlement Kendra Vs. State of Uttar Pradesh

IV. Shri Sachidanand Pandey Vs. State of West Bengal

Select the correct answer using the codes given below:

1 I and II are correct   2 II and III are correct
3 III and IV are correct   4 All of the above

80 Match List I with List II and give the correct answer by using the codes given below.

List I (Sources of Public International Law)	List II (Case related)
A. General principles of law recognised by the civilised countries	I. North Sea Continental Shelf case
B. Juristic Work	II. Burkina Faso Vs. Mali
C. International Customs	III. Portugal Vs. India
D. Justice and Equity	IV. Paquete Habana case

Codes

	A	B	C	D		A	B	C	D
1	I	II	III	IV	2	II	III	IV	I
3	III	IV	I	II	4	IV	I	III	II

81 Match List I with List II and give the correct answer by using the codes given below the lists.

List I	List II
A. The Principles of constructive res judicata are also applicable to writ petition	I. Woman's Education Trust Vs. State of Haryana
B. Writ petition dismissed for want of prosecution can be restored	II. M Nagabhushana Vs. State of Karnataka
C. Direction given by the High Court under Article 226 cannot be altered by the State Government	III. Ratan Singh Vs. State of Rajasthan
D. The disposal of several writ petitions in a batch by a single order would be permissible if facts of all cases are similar or almost similar	IV. V Parukutty Mannadissiar Vs. State of Kerala

Codes

	A	B	C	D		A	B	C	D
1	II	III	IV	I	2	III	IV	I	II
3	II	I	IV	III	4	IV	III	II	I

82 Match List I with List II and give the correct answer by using the codes given below the list

List I	List II
A. Mr Jose Ayala Lasso	I. President of International Court of Justice
B. Justice Nagendra Singh	II. Secretary General of UN
C. Kofi Annan	III. Chairperson of Commission on Human Rights
D. Mrs FD Roosevelt	IV. UN High Commissioner for Human Rights

Codes

	A	B	C	D
1	IV	I	II	III
2	II	IV	III	I
3	III	II	I	IV
4	III	II	IV	I

83 Match List I with List II and give the correct answer by using the codes given below the list

List I	List II
A. Article 136	I. Appellate jurisdiction of Supreme Court with regard to criminal matters
B. Article 134	II. Seat of Supreme Court
C. Article 131	III. Special leave to appeal jurisdiction of the Supreme Court over any court of administrative tribunal
D. Article 130	IV. Original jurisdiction of the Supreme Court

Codes

	A	B	C	D		A	B	C	D
1	IV	I	III	II	2	I	III	IV	II
3	II	IV	I	III	4	III	I	IV	II

84 Match List I with List II and give the correct answer by using the codes given below the list

List I	List II
A. Article 221	I. Transfer of a judge from one High Court to another
B. Article 222	II. Appointment of acting Chief Justice of a High Court
C. Article 223	III. Appointment of additional and action judges of High Court
D. Article 224	IV. Salaries of High Court Judges

Codes

	A	B	C	D		A	B	C	D
1	IV	I	II	III	2	II	IV	I	III
3	III	IV	II	I	4	III	I	IV	II

85 Match List I with List II and give the correct answer by using the codes given below.

List I	List II
A. Section 54 of the Sale of Goods Act	I. Risk where goods are delivered at distant place
B. Section 40 of the Sale of Goods Act	II. Delivery of wrong quantity
C. Section 37 of the Sale of Goods Act	III. Sale by description
D. Section 15 of the Sale of Goods Act	IV. Rights of unpaid seller against the goods

Codes

	A	B	C	D		A	B	C	D
1	I	IV	II	III	2	IV	I	II	III
3	IV	I	III	II	4	II	III	I	IV

86 Match List I with List II and give the correct answer by using the codes given below the list.

List I (Provisions)	List II (Articles of statue of International court)
A. Law applied by the International Court of Justice	I. Article 62
B. Transferred Jurisdiction	II. Article 59
C. Court power to allow a state to intervene in case to which it is not a party	III. Article 38
D. Binding force of the decisions of the International Court of Justice	IV. Article 36(5)

Codes

	A	B	C	D		A	B	C	D
1	I	II	III	IV	2	IV	III	II	I
3	III	IV	II	I	4	II	I	IV	III

87 Match List I with List II and give the correct answer by using the codes given below.

List I (Provisions)	List II (Articles of UN Charter)
A. Voting procedure of the General Assembly	I. Article 23
B. Composition of Security Council	II. Article 96
C. Composition of Trusteeship Council	III. Article 4
D. Provisions regarding Membership in the Untied Nations	IV. Article 18

Codes

	A	B	C	D		A	B	C	D
1	II	III	IV	I	2	I	II	III	IV
3	III	I	II	IV	4	IV	II	I	III

88 Match List I with List II and give the correct answer by using the codes given below.
Answer in context of the Negotiable Instruments Act.

List I	List II
A. Time and place for presentment	I. Section 19
B. Cheques are payable in demand	II. Section 8
C. Holder of a negotiable instrument	III. Section 61
D. Fictitious drawer of payee	IV. Section 42

Codes

	A	B	C	D		A	B	C	D
1	I	IV	II	III	2	III	II	IV	I
3	II	III	IV	I	4	II	III	I	IV

89 Match List I with List II and give the correct answer by using the codes given below

List I	List II
A. Inchoate stamped instrument	I. Union Bank of India Vs. Ankur Corporation
B. Liability of acceptor of negotiable instrument	II. Section 31 of the Negotiable Instrument Act
C. Liability of an endorser	III. Section 35 of the Negotiable Instrument Act
D. Liability of the drawee of a cheque	IV. Section 20 of the Negotiable Instrument Act

Codes

	A	B	C	D
1	I	IV	III	II
2	IV	I	III	II
3	IV	I	II	III
4	III	II	I	IV

90 Match List I with List II in the light of Geneva Convention relating to the treatment of prisoners of War.

List I	List II
A. Categories of prisoners to be treated as prisoners of war	I. Article 13
B. Prisoners of war to be humanly treated	II. Article 91
C. No physical or mental torture	III. Article 4
D. Escape of prisoners of war	IV. Article 17

Codes

	A	B	C	D		A	B	C	D
1	I	III	II	IV	2	I	III	IV	II
3	III	I	II	IV	4	III	I	IV	II

Directions (Q. No. 91-95) *Read the passage carefully and answer the questions that follow:*

The right to live with dignity has been recognised as a human right on the international front and by the number of precedents of this Court and therefore, the Constitutional courts must strive to protect the dignity of every individual, for, without the right to dignity, every other right would be rendered meaningless.

Dignity is an inseparable facet of every individual that invites reciprocative respect from others to every aspect of an individual which he/she perceives as an essential attribute of his/her individuality, be it an orientation or an optional expression of choice. The Constitution has ladened the judiciary with the very important duty to protect and ensure the right of every individual including the right to express and choose without any impediments so as to enable an individual to fully realise his/her fundamental right to live with dignity.

Sexual orientation is one of the many biological phenomena which is natural and inherent in an individual and is controlled by neurological and biological factors. The science of sexuality has theorised that an individual exerts little or no control over who he/she gets attracted to. Any discrimination on the basis of one's sexual orientation would entail a violation of the fundamental right of freedom of expression.

91 The consensual sexual act of an adult is criminalised under which of the following legislations?

1 Indian Penal Code
2 POCSO
3 Criminal Law (Amendment) Act 2013
4 None of the above

92 The Fundamental right of the freedom of expression is contained in the following articles of the Indian Constitution:

1 Article 19(1)(a)
2 Article 19(1)(f)
3 Article 181
4 Article 21

93 Discrimination on the basis of sexual orientation is violative of which of the following fundamental rights?
1 Article 21 only
2 Article 14, 15 only
3 Article 15, 19 only
4 Articles 14,15,19,27

94 The above paragraph reflects the judgement in case of
1 Navtej Singh Johar Vs. Union of India
2 Machhi Singh Vs. State of Punjab
3 State of UP Vs. Ram Swaroop
4 Chairman Railway Board Vs. Chandrima Das

95 Which one of the following judges were part of the judgement referred to in the paragraph?
1 Deepak Mishra 2 R.F. Nariman
3 D.Y. Chandrachud 4 Indu Malhotra

Directions (Q. No. 96-100) *Read the following passage carefully and answer the questions that follow.*

The Constitution guarantess every citizen the Fundamental Right to equality. Yet after 50 years of independence, just one perusal of the female infant mortality figures, the literacy rates and the employment opportunities for women is sufficient evidence that discrimination exists. Almost predictably, this gender, bias is evident in our political system as well. In the 13th Lok Sabha, there were only 43 women MPs out of total of 543; it is not a surprising figure, for never has women's representation in Parliament been more than 10 per cent. Historically, the manifestos of major political parties have always encouraged womens participation. It has been merely a charade. So, women's organisations, denied a place on merit, opted for the last resort; a reservation of seats for women in Parliament and State Assemblies. Parties, which look at everything with a vote bank in mind, seemed to endorse this. Alas, this too was a mirage.

But there is another aspect also. At a time when caste is the trump card, some politicians want the bill to include further quotas for women from among minorities and backward castes. There is more to it. A survey shows that there is a general antipathy towards the bill.

It is actually a classic case of doublespeak: in public, politicians were endorsing women's reservation but in the backrooms of Parliament, they were busy sabotaging it. The reasons are clear: Men just don't want to vacate their seats of power.

96 The problem raised in the passage reflects badly on our:
1 Political system
2 Social behaviour
3 Individual behaviour
4 Behaviour of a group of people

97 According to the passage, political parties have mostly in mind
1 Economic prosperity 2 Vote bank
3 People welfare 4 Patriotism

98 'Trump card' means
1 Trying to move a dead horse
2 Playing the card cautiously
3 Sabotaging all the moves by others
4 Making the final jolt for success

99 The sentence "Men just don't want to vacate their seats of power" implies :
1 Lust for power
2 Desire to serve the nation
3 Conviction in one's own political abilities
4 Political corruption

100 What is the percentage of women in the Lok Sabha :
1 10 2 7.91
3 43 4 9.1

ANSWERS

1 (2)	**2** (3)	**3** (2)	**4** (3)	**5** (4)	**6** (3)	**7** (4)	**8** (4)	**9** (3)	**10** (3)
11 (4)	**12** (2)	**13** (3)	**14** (1)	**15** (2)	**16** (2)	**17** (2)	**18** (3)	**19** (3)	**20** (2)
21 (3)	**22** (2)	**23** (3)	**24** (1)	**25** (3)	**26** (2)	**27** (3)	**28** (1)	**29** (2)	**30** (3)
31 (3)	**32** (2)	**33** (4)	**34** (4)	**35** (3)	**36** (3)	**37** (3)	**38** (4)	**39** (4)	**40** (4)
41 (3)	**42** (2)	**43** (1)	**44** (2)	**45** (3)	**46** (4)	**47** (2)	**48** (1)	**49** (1)	**50** (1)
51 (1)	**52** (4)	**53** (3)	**54** (4)	**55** (2)	**56** (4)	**57** (4)	**58** (4)	**59** (3)	**60** (3)
61 (2)	**62** (1)	**63** (4)	**64** (4)	**65** (2)	**66** (3)	**67** (4)	**68** (3)	**69** (4)	**70** (3)
71 (1)	**72** (2)	**73** (4)	**74** (1)	**75** (2)	**76** (3)	**77** (1)	**78** (3)	**79** (3)	**80** (4)
81 (2)	**82** (1)	**83** (4)	**84** (1)	**85** (4)	**86** (3)	**87** (1)	**88** (1)	**89** (2)	**90** (4)
91 (1)	**92** (1)	**93** (4)	**94** (1)	**95** (1)	**96** (2)	**97** (2)	**98** (4)	**99** (1)	**100** (2)

UGC-NET LAW

PRACTICE SET 3

PAPER II

1 The Charter of the United Nations requires that the organisation and its members shall act in accordance with the principles enumerated in the Charter. Which of the following is not one of such principles ?
1 Sovereign equality
2 Settlement of international disputes by peaceful means
3 Promotion of human rights
4 Prohibition of threat or use of force

2 Non-amendability of the Basic Structure of the Constitution was declared firstly in :
1 Sajjan Singh Vs. State of Rajasthan, 1965
2 Minerva Mills Vs. Union of India, 1980
3 Shankari Prasad Vs. Union of India, 1951
4 Kesavananda Bharati Vs. State of Kerala, 1973

3 The Supreme Court of India gave direction to the fact that the marriages of all persons, citizen of India, belonging to various religions should be made compulsorily registerable in those respective States where marriage is solemnised. These directions were issued in which of the following cases ?
1 R.D. Upadhyay Vs. State of A.P.
2 Sastri Yagnapurushadji Vs. Muldas
3 Seema Vs. Ashwanikumar
4 Kailash Sarkar Vs. Maya Devi

4 The decision given in M.C. Mehta Vs. Union of India is on :
1 Vicarious liability
2 Absolute liability
3 Strict liability
4 Simple liability

5 'A', a police constable tortured a person under the order of his senior police officer. The person lost one eye because of the torture. Which of the following will be the basis of defence which can be invoked by the accused police constable
1 torture was under the order of senior police officer.
2 torture was given because he was under the threat of losing service.
3 torture was given because he was under the threat of suspension from service.
4 torture was given because there was imminent threat to death.

6 Propositions are :
I. Consent theory makes the divorce very easy.
II. Consent theory makes the divorce very difficult.
Which of the following is correct in respect of the aforesaid propositions :
1 I is correct but II is incorrect
2 I and II both are correct
3 II is correct but I is incorrect
4 I and II both are incorrect

7 The Hindu Marriage Act, 1955, provides for .... theory/theories of divorce.
1 Breakdown
2 Fault
3 Consent
4 All of the above

8 In which of the following cases Supreme Court held 'Talaq-e-Biddat' is not a valid divorce?
1 Bai Tahira Vs. Ali Hussain Fissalli
2 Shamim Ara Vs. State of UP
3 Shayara Bano Vs. Union of India
4 Yusuf Vs. Sowramma

9 Under which of the following Section of the Indian Contract Act, 1872, remedies for breach of contract are available?
1 Section 72
2 Section 73
3 Section 74
4 Section 32

10 The maxim 'injuria sine damno' has been explained in the following case :
1 Donough Vs. Stevenson
2 Rylands Vs. Fletcher
3 Ashby Vs. White
4 Bradford Vs. Pickles

11 Under the doctrine of 'vicarious liability', a master is liable for the acts of his servant :
1 only if the servant is under the control of the master as regards the manner in which work is to be done.
2 only if the servant is not under the control of the master as regards the manner of doing work.
3 irrespective of whether the servant is under the control of the master or not as regards the manner of doing the work.
4 None of the above

12 The verdict of the 'Donough Vs. Stevenson' was delivered by the following Judge
1 Justice Black Stone
2 J. Douglas
3 Lord Denning
4 Lord Atkin

13 Lay-off means
1 removing a workman
2 retirement of a workman
3 dismissing a workman
4 inability of employer to provide work to a workman

14 Constitution of India assures the 'Dignity of the Individual' in the language of
1 Article 14
2 Article 19
3 Article 21
4 Preamble

15 Secularism is one of the five constituents of the Constitution of India and has been held to be the only permissible religion in a pluralistic Indian Society in the case of
1 I.C. Golaknath Vs. State of Punjab
2 Kesavananda Bharati Vs. State of Kerala
3 S.R. Bommai Vs. Union of India
4 S.L. Kapoor Vs. Union of India

16 Schedule IX was inserted in the Constitution of India by
1 1st Amendment, 1951
2 42nd Amendment, 1976
3 44th Amendment, 1978
4 52nd Amendment, 1985

17 The difference between possession and ownership is as follows
1 Full enjoyment of the property is restricted in possession and there is no restriction in ownership
2 The right of ownership consists of excluding others from using it and there is no such right in possession
3 Both 1 and 2
4 None of the above

18 Precedent is a source of Law in
1 Common law system
2 Civil law system
3 International law
4 All of the above

19 An incorporated service of successive person is called
1 Corporate person
2 Corporate aggregate
3 Corporate animation
4 Incorporeal possession

20 UN Human Rights Council has taken the place of
1 Human Rights Committee
2 Human Rights Commission
3 UN Commission for Human Rights
4 Economic, Social and Cultural Rights Committee

21 Mark the correct statement.
1 Under the Hindu Marriage Act, 1955, the husband can claim maintenance.
2 Unchaste wife can live separate and claim maintenance under Hindu Adoptions and Maintenance Act, 1956.
3 Under the Hindu Adoptions and Maintenance Act, 1956, Father-in-law is personally liable to pay maintenance to the widowed daughter-in-law.
4 The term 'maintenance' under the Hindu Adoptions and Maintenance Act, 1956 does not include marriage expenses of unmarried daughter.

22 To give constitutional sanction to democracy at the grassroot level through Panchayat and Municipalities, 73rd and 74th Amendments were made in 1992. Which one of the following subjects related to environment is not found in the Twelfth Schedule?
1 Urban planning including town planning
2 Regulation of land use and construction of buildings
3 Animal husbandry, Dairying and Poultry
4 Public health, sanitation, conservancy and solid waste

23 Which of the following Articles define the term 'State'?
1 Article 12
2 Article 13
3 Article 14
4 Article 15

24 In which one of the following cases, the Supreme Court made it explicit that 'even when the authority has statutory power to take action without hearing, it would be arbitrary to take action without hearing and, thus, violative of Article 14 of the Constitution'?
1 AK Kraipak Vs. Union of India
2 Satish Chandra Vs. Union of India
3 AK Roy Vs. State of Punjab
4 HL Trehan Vs. Union of India.

25 Law is a social engineering to remove the existing imbalance and to further the progress, serving the needs of the Socialist Democratic Bharat under the rule of Law. This was the observation of Justice K. Ramaswamy in

1 Delhi Transport Corp. Vs. DTC Mazdoor Congress
2 Indra Sawhney Vs. Union of India
3 State of Karnataka Vs. Appa Balu Ingale
4 Parmanand Katara Vs. Union of India

26 "Secularism as the basic structure of the constitution has been held to be so on the basis of more than 50 years experience of the working of the constitution. The complete apathy for all kinds of religious teachings in institutions of the State have not helped in removing mutual misunderstanding and intolerance inter se between sections of the people of different religious faith and beliefs". This was stated by the Supreme Court of India in

1 Aruna Roy Vs. Union of India
2 Arundhati Roy Vs. Union of India
3 PA Inamdar Vs. State of Maharashtra
4 Unni Krishnan Vs. State of AP

27 Sexual harassment of women at working place was recognised as violation of human right to human dignity in

1 Sarla Mudgal Vs. State of TN
2 Vishakha Vs. State of Rajasthan
3 Nargesh Meerza Vs. Air India
4 Maneka Gandhi Vs. Union of India

28 The Fundamental Right to move to the Supreme Court has been described as the cornerstone of the democratic edifice raised by the Constitution and as such the Supreme Court must always regard it as its solemn duty to protect the said Fundamental Rights zealously and vigilantly. This has been stated by the Supreme Court in

1 Daryao Vs. State of UP 1962
2 Bandhua Mukti Morcha Vs. Union of India 1984
3 Sheela Barse Vs. Union of India 1988
4 MC Mehta Vs. Union of India 1989

29 Which of the following Articles do not contain the power of the highest Court of the country to punish for the contempts of the Court?

1 Article 141 2 Article 142
3 Article 129 4 Both 1 and 2

30 In a Wrestling match 'A' tells 'B' that Wrestler no.1 will win. 'B' challenges the statement of 'A'. They bet with each other over the result of the match. This is

1 Unlawful agreement
2 Wagering agreement
3 Contingent contract
4 Voidable contract

31 Contract becomes impossible of performance if

1 goods are not available in the market
2 workers are on strike
3 subject matter of the contract was destroyed at the time of contract
4 money is not available

32 In Donoghue Vs. Stevenson, the duty of a manufacturer was fixed towards

1 Retailer only 2 Buyer from retailer
3 Ultimate consumer 4 None of these

33 The term 'Workman' under IDA includes

1 a person employed for doing any manual unskilled, skilled, technical, clerical or supervisory work for hire or reward
2 a person employed mainly for managerial or administrative capacity
3 Both 1 and 2 are correct
4 Only 1 is correct

34 Under which of the following sections, a Registered Trade Union is immuned from its criminal liability where an act done by the members in furtherance of their Trade Disputes?

1 Section 15 of the Trade Union Act, 1926
2 Section 16 of the Trade Union Act, 1926
3 Section 18 of the Trade Union Act, 1926
4 Section 20 of the Trade Union Act, 1926

35 In which of the following cases it is well established that, any settlement between the employer and with one or more concerned union in a conciliation proceeding would bind all other workman unions who were not made parties to the settlement ?

1 Ramnagar Cane and Sugar Co. Ltd. Vs. Jatin Chakravorty
2 Shambhu Nath Goel Vs. Bank of Baroda
3 Workers of Dimakuchi Tea Estate Vs. Management of Dimakuchi
4 None of the above

36 University of Petroleum, Energy, Gas and Oil has been created by a statute of a State on self-financing scheme. It

1 Shall not be 'the State' under Article 12.
2 Shall be 'the State' having the trappings of the State under Article 12.
3 Shall not be 'the State' with no liability and obligations to the public under Article 12.
4 Shall not be 'the State' because of its governing relationship with other people under Article 12.

37 Hugo Grotius is regarded as the father of

1 Realist School
2 Analytical School
3 Historical School
4 Philosophical School

38 The task of Social engineering is to build as efficient structure of the society as possible with minimum friction and waste, was said by

1 Kelsen
2 Karl Marx
3 Roscoe Pound
4 Savigny

39 The meaning of per incuriam is as follows

1 A decision which ignores a statute on the subject.
2 A decision which ignores the case law on the subject.
3 A decision which ignores the constitution on the subject.
4 All of the above

40 In which case has the Supreme Court of India held that there is no reason to compel non-smokers to be helpless victims of air pollution ?

1 Salem Advocate Bar Association Vs. Union of India
2 Onkar Lal Bajaj Vs. Union of India
3 Ramakrishnan Vs. State of Kerala
4 Murli S. Deora Vs. Union of India

41 Give below are two statements, one is labelled as Assertion (A) and the other is labelled as Reason (R).

Assertion (A) Culpable homicide becomes murder when the act causes death and is done with the intention of causing death.

Reason (R) One of the conditions to be satisfied for treating it murder provide the injury intended to be inflicted is sufficient in the ordinary course of nature to cause death.

In light of the above statement, choose the correct answer from the options given below.

Codes

1 (A) is true, but (R) is false
2 Both (A) and (R) are true, but (R) is not the correct explanation of (A).
3 (A) is false and (R) is true.
4 Both (A) and (R) are true and (R) is the reasonable explanation of (A).

42 Give below are two statements, one is labelled as Assertion (A) and the other is labelled as Reason (R).

Assertion (A) Common intention implies a pre-arranged plan, prior meeting of minds and prior consultation between all the persons committing the crime.

Reason (R) The law makes no distinction between the persons or the part played by them in doing the criminal act.

In light of the above statement, choose the correct answer from the options given below.

Codes

1 (A) is true and (R) is false.
2 Both (A) and (R) are true, but (R) is not the correct explanation of (A).
3 (A) is false and (R) is true.
4 Both (A) and (R) are true and (R) is most nearest explanation of (A).

43 Give below are two statements, one is labelled as Assertion (A) and the other is labelled as Reason (R).

Assertion (A) Ownership is not only a juridical concept, but also a social concept and an instrument of social policy.

Reason (R) The right of alienation is not a necessary incident of ownership.

Codes

1 Both (A) and (R) are true and (R) is correct explanation of (A).
2 Both (A) and (R) are true, but (R) is not the correct explanation of (A).
3 (A) is true, but (R) is false.
4 (A) is false, but (R) is true.

44 Arrange the following enactments in chronological order enacted to provide social justice:

I. Equal Remuneration Act
II. Immoral Traffic (Prevention) Act
III. Medical Termination of Pregnancy Act
IV. Maternity Benefit Act

Choose the correct option:

1 I, II, III, IV
2 II, III, I, IV
3 II, IV, III, I
4 IV, III, II, I

45 Arrange the provisions of Hindu Succession Act 1956 in chronological order (Section wise).

I. Presumption in case of simultaneous death
II. Failure of heirs
III. Act not to apply to certain properties
IV. Full blood preferred to half blood

Choose the correct option :

1 I, II, III, IV
2 IV, III, II, I
3 III, IV, I, II
4 IV, I, III, II

46 Arrange the following judgements on Torts in chronological order:

I. Ashby Vs. White
II. MC Mehta Vs. Union of India
III. Ryland Vs. Fletcher
IV. Donoghue Vs. Stevenson

Choose the correct option:

1 II, IV, III,
2 I, III, IV, II
3 I, III, II, IV
4 IV, II, I, III

47 Arrange the following judgements of the Supreme Court on the issue of constitutionality of death penalty in chronological order:

I. Rajendra Prasad Vs. State of UP
II. Machhi Singh Vs. State of Punjab
III. Jagmohan Singh Vs. State of UP

IV. Bachan Singh Vs. State of Punjab

Choose the correct option:

1 I, II, III, IV
2 III, II, I, IV
3 IV, III, II, I
4 III, I, IV, II

48 Starting from the earliest, arrange the following countries in chronological order where the Office of Ombudsman was created:

I. Sweden
II. United Kingdom
III. New Zealand
IV. Finland

Choose the correct option:

1 I, II, III, IV
2 I, IV, III, II
3 I, III, II, IV
4 I, II, IV, III

49 Arrange the grounds of divorce in the order in which they appear in the Hindu Marriage Act, 1955. Use the codes given below:

I. Mutual consent
II. Break down
III. Fault
IV. Customary

Codes

1 III, II, I, IV
2 II, III, IV, I
3 I, II, III, IV
4 IV, III, I, II

50 Read the following propositions and give correct answer with the help of codes given below. Propositions are

I. A voidable Hindu marriage is regarded as a valid marriage until a decree annulling it has been passed by a competent court.

II. A void Hindu marriage is never a valid marriage and there is no necessity of any decree annulling it.

III. A void Hindu marriage remains valid until a decree annulling it has been passed by a competent court.

IV. Children of void and voidable Hindu marriages are legitimate.

Codes

1 Only I and II are correct, but IV is incorrect
2 I, II and IV are correct, but III is incorrect
3 I, II, III and IV are correct
4 I and IV are correct, but II and III are incorrect

51 Consiider the following statements. The Fundamental Rights under the Indian Constitution are fundamental because

I. They are protected and enforced by the Constitution.

II. They can be suspended only in the manner prescribed by the Constitution.

III. They are enforceable against the State.

IV. They cannot be amended.

Which of the statement(s) given above are correct.

1 I and III
2 I, II and III
3 I, III and IV
4 All of these

52 Using the codes given below indicate the chronological sequence in which the following judgements were delivered by the International Court of Justice?

I. Right of passage over Indian Territory case
II. South-West Africa case
III. Frontier Dispute
IV. Temple of Preah Vihear

Codes

1 I, II, III, IV
2 II, IV, I, III
3 I, IV, II, III
4 III, II, IV, I

53 Which of the following statement(s) is/are not correct?

I. United Nations Declaration of Territorial Asylum was unanimously adopted in 1977 by the General Assembly.

II. Article 14 of the 1948 Universal Declaration of Human Rights make obligatory by states to grant Asylum.

III. The International Court of Justice explained the distinction between 'Territorial Asylum' and 'Diplomatic Asylum' in the Colombia. Vs. Peru.

IV. The Convention on the Status of Refugees, 1951 entered into force on 22nd April, 1954

Codes

1 Only I
2 I and IV
3 I, II and III
4 All of these

54 Which of the following statement(s) is/are correct? Answer by using the codes given below.

I. In tort duty is imposed by law and is owed to the community at large.

II. A tort is founded upon consent of parties.

III. A tort is civil wrong for which the remedy is a common law action for liquidated damages.

IV. In tort 'motive' for the violation of right is immaterial.

Codes

1 Only I
2 I and II
3 I, II and III
4 I, II, III and IV

55 Which of the following statement(s) is/are correct?

I. In Nottebohm's case the International Court of Justice held that in respect of grant of nationality there is no obligation of the states if that man has no relationship with the State of Naturalisation.

II. In famous Re Lynch case, it was held that if a person is not a citizen of any State he will be called stateless.

III. Nationality is the principal link between an individual and international law.

IV. The Convention on the Reduction of Statelessness was adopted in 1959 by the General Assembly.

Codes

1 Only I 2 I, II and III
3 II, III and IV 4 I and III

56 Which of the following statement(s) is/are incorrect? Give correct answer by using the codes given below.

I. 'Subjugation' is a mode of 'acquisition' of nationality under the international law.

II. Stoeck Vs. The Public Trustee is a case related to double nationality.

III. Article 3 to 6 of the Hague Convention of 1930 provide the provisions for solving the problem of Double nationality of married women.

IV. 'Cession' is a mode of 'Loss' of Nationality under the international law.

Codes

1 Only II 2 I, II and III
3 II, III and IV 4 I, II, III and IV

57 Which of the following statement(s) is/are not correct?

I. There are four main theories of Recognition.

II. Anzilotti is a exponent of Declaratory Theory of Recognition.

III. Civil Air Transport Incorporated Co. Vs. Central Air Transport Corporation is a case on Retrospective Effects of Recognition.

IV. Pitt Corbett is one of Chief Exponent of Constitutive Theory of Recognition.

Codes

1 I, II and III 2 II, III and IV
3 I, II and IV 4 I, II, III and IV

58 Which of the following statement/statements is/are correct?

I. Custom is the oldest and the original source of International as well as of law in general.

II. In Barcelona Traction case, the International Court applied the general rule of subrogation.

III. In Chorzow factory (Indemnity) case, the Permanent Court of Justice ruled that the International law is based on justice, equity and good conscience.

IV. In Nicaragua Vs. USA, the World Court has taken the view that the sources of International law are not hierarchical but are necessarily complimentary and inter related.

Codes

1 Only I 2 I, II and III
3 I and IV 4 All of these

59 Which of the following statement/statements is/are incorrect?

I. There are five prominent theories of relationship between International law and Municipal law.

II. According to Dualism Theory law is a unified branch of knowledge.

III. 'Monism' and 'Dualism' are diametrically opposed to each other.

IV. Wright, Kelson and Duguit are prominent exponents of Dualism Theory.

Codes

1 II and IV 3 I, II and IV
3 Only IV 4 All of these

60 An individual dispute becomes an industrial dispute when it is espoused by

I. a trade union

II. the appreciable number of workman

III. falls under Section 2A of the Industrial Disputes Act.

IV. One fifth of the total work force in the concerned establishment.

Codes

1 I, III and IV are correct 2 II and III are correct
3 I, II and III are correct 4 Only IV is correct

61 Indicate the correct order in which the following decisions appeared :

I. Namibia case

II. Naulilaa case

III. Nauru Vs. Australia

IV. Nicaragua Vs. Honduras

Codes

1 I, III, IV, II 2 II, I, III, IV
3 III, IV, II, I 4 IV, III, II, I

62 Consider the following Judgements of the Supreme Court, which dealt with the appointment and transfer of Judges of the Supreme Court and High Courts :

I. SP Gupta Vs. Union of India

II. Sankal Chand Vs. Union of India

III. In re special Reference No. 1 of 1998

IV. Supreme Court Advocate on Record Association Vs. Union of India

Which one of the following is correct chronological order in which the above judgements were delivered ?

Codes

1 I, II, III, IV
2 II, I, III, IV
3 II, I, IV, III
4 I, II, IV, III

63 The purpose of the United Nations are

I. To maintain International Peace and Security

II. To establish World Government

III. To develop friendly relations among Member's States

IV. To secure International cooperation in solving problems of social, economic and humanitarian character.

Select the correct choice from the options given below

1 I, II and III
2 II, III and IV
3 II and III
4 I, III and IV

64 Which of the following is a ground for judicially attacking the exercise of administrative discretion?

I. Ultra vires the law
II. Malafide intent
III. Arbitrariness
IV. Irrelevant considerations

Codes

1 I and II
2 II and III
3 I, II and III
4 All of these

65 The provisions of the Paris Convention may be sub-divided into following categories.

I. A first category contains rules of substantive law.
II. A second category establishes right of priority.
III. A third category defines a certain number of common rules in the field of substantive law.
IV. A fourth category deals with the administrative framework.

Which of the statements given above is/are correct?

1 I and II
2 III and IV
3 II and III
4 All of these

66 Consider the following statements.

I. The UCC was developed by UNESCO as an alternative to the Berne Convention.
II. WIPO Convention was signed at Stockholm, Sweden.
III. WIPO's main objective is to promote the protection of IP worldwide.
IV. India became a member of WIPO in 1998.

Which of the statement(s) given above is/are correct?

1 I, II and III
2 II, III and IV
3 All of these
4 None of these

67 Consider the following statemets.

Statement I In case of any conflict between Part III and Part IV of the Constitution, the former should prevail in the Court.

Statement II Part IV (containing the Directive Principles of the State Policy) is not a part of the Constitution.

Choose the correct answer by using the options given below:

1 Both Statement I and II are true
2 Both Statement I and II are false
3 Statement I is true but II is false
4 Statement I is false but II is true

68 Consider the following statemets.

Statement I The chapter named registration of firms in Parnership Act is applicable to Hindu Trading Familes.

Statement II Registration of firms is designed primarly to protect third parties and the absence of registration need not prevent disappearance of an unregistered or imperfectly registered firm.

Choose the correct answer by using the options given below:

1 Both Statements I and II are true
2 Both Statements I and II are false
3 Statement I is true but II is false
4 Statement I is false but II is true

69 Match List I with List II and select the correct answer using the codes given below :

List I (Principle)	List II (Associated Case)
A. Absolute Liability	I. Gloucester Grammar School
B. Damnum sine injuria	II. Ashby Vs. White
C. Injuria sine damnum	III. Stanley Vs. Powell
D. Inevitable accident	IV. Rylands Vs. Fletcher

Codes

	A	B	C	D		A	B	C	D
1	I	II	III	IV	2	II	III	IV	I
3	IV	II	I	III	4	III	I	II	IV

70 Match List I with List II and give the correct answer by using the codes given below :

List (Provisions)	List (Articles of UN Charter)
A. Suspension of Members	I. Article 5
B. Veto Power	II. Article 97
C. Appointment of Secretary General	III. Article 27
D. Composition of Trusteeship Council	IV. Article 86

Codes

	A	B	C	D		A	B	C	D
1	I	III	II	IV	2	IV	III	II	I
3	III	II	IV	I	4	II	I	III	IV

71 Match List I with List II and select the correct answer by using the codes given below the lists.

List I	List II
A. Directive Principles of State Policy	I. American Constitution
B. Emergency Provisions	II. United Kingdom
C. Fundamental Rights	III. German Reich
D. Parliamentary form of Government	IV. Ireland

Codes

	A	B	C	D		A	B	C	D
1	IV	III	I	II	2	IV	I	III	II
3	I	II	III	IV	4	III	II	I	IV

72 Match List I (Name of principle) with List II (Related Case) and answer by using the codes given below.

List I	List II
A. Res judicata	I. SP Gupta Vs. Union of India
B. Legitimate expectation	II. Motilal Padampat Sugar Mills Vs. State of Uttar Pradesh
C. Promissory estoppel	III. Daryao Vs. State of Uttar Pradesh
D. Locus standi	IV. Monnet Ispat and Energy Ltd. Vs. Union of India

Codes

	A	B	C	D		A	B	C	D
1	II	IV	III	I	2	III	IV	II	I
3	I	III	IV	II	4	IV	III	II	I

73 Match List I with List II and select the correct answer by using the codes given below the lists.

List I	List II
A. Right to speak includes right not to speak	I. R Rajagopal Vs. State of TN
B. Government has no monopoly on electronic media	II. Tata Press Ltd. Vs. Mahanagar Telephone Nigam limited
C. Commercial Advertisement is part of Freedom of Speech and Expression	III. Secretary Ministry of Information and Broadcasting Vs. Cricket Association of Bengal (WB)
D. Government cannot impose prior restraint on publication of defamatory material against its officials	IV. Bijoe Emmanuel Vs. State of Kerala

Codes

	A	B	C	D		A	B	C	D
1	IV	III	II	I	2	III	II	I	IV
3	I	IV	III	II	4	II	I	IV	III

74 Match List I with List II and select the correct answer by using the codes given below the lists.

List I	List II
A. Justice is realised only through good law	I. Jerome Hall
B. Moral value needs to be included in a definition of positive law	II. John Finnis
C. Natural law with a variable content	III. Morris
D. A sophisticated version of Natural Law has been put forward in the tradition of Aristotle and Aquinas	IV. Stammler

Codes

	A	B	C	D		A	B	C	D
1	II	IV	I	III	2	I	II	III	IV
3	III	I	IV	II	4	IV	III	II	I

75 Match List I with List II and select the correct answer using the codes given below the lists.

List I	List II
A. Equal justice and free legal aid	I. Article 44
B. Uniform Civil Code for citizens	II. Article 48A
C. Protection and improvement of environment and safeguarding of forests and wildlife.	III. Article 39A
D. Promotion of international peace and security	IV. Article 51

Codes

	A	B	C	D		A	B	C	D
1	III	II	IV	I	2	III	I	II	IV
3	I	II	III	IV	4	IV	I	II	III

76 Match List I with List II and select the correct answer using the codes given below.

List I (Constitutional Provisions)	List II (Subjects)
A. Article 249	I. Power of Parliament to legislate for two or more States by consent and adoption of such legislation by an other state
B. Article 250	II. Power of Parliament to legislate with respect to any matter in the State List if a Proclamation of Emergency is in operation
C. Article 252	III. Legislation for giving effect to international agreements
D. Article 253	IV. Power of Parliament to legislate with respect to a matter in the State List in the national interest

Codes

	A	B	C	D
1	I	II	III	IV
2	IV	II	I	III
3	III	II	IV	I
4	II	III	I	IV

77 Match List I with List II and select the correct answer using the codes given below.

List I (Veda)	List II (Deals with)
A. Yajurveda	I. Praise of forces of nature
B. Samaveda	II. Magic, spell and incantation
C. Atharvaveda	III. Rituals
D. Rigveda	IV. Dance

Codes

	A	B	C	D
1	I	II	IV	III
2	II	IV	I	III
3	IV	II	III	
4	III	IV	II	I

78 Match List I with List II and select the correct answer using the codes given below.

List I	List II (Jural Correlatives)
A. Right	I. Liability
B. Privilege	II. Disability
C. Power	III. Duty
D. Immunity	IV. No-right

Codes

	A	B	C	D		A	B	C	D
1	I	II	III	IV	2	I	III	IV	II
3	II	III	IV	I	4	II	I	III	IV

79 Match List I with List II and select the answer using the codes given below :

List I (Book)	List II (Author)
A. The Concept of Law	I. Gray
B. The Nature and Sources of the Law	II. Julius Stone
C. Some Reflections on Jurisprudence	III. Buckland
D. The Province and Function of Law	IV. HLA Hart

Codes

	A	B	C	D		A	B	C	D
1	IV	I	III	II	2	IV	II	I	III
3	IV	I	II	III	4	I	III	IV	II

80 Which are essentials of a partnership?
I. Contract of two or more competent persons
II. Agreement to share profits
III. Mutual agency
IV. Lawful business
Select the correct statement from codes given below :
1 I, II and III 2 I, II and IV
3 II, III and IV 4 All of these

81 Which of the following partnerships are legal?
I. Twelve members forming a banking firm.
II. A partnership to create a monopoly.
III. Twenty members forming a firm for tea trade on a railway platform.
IV. Trustees carry on business of a firm in their own name.
Select the correct statement from codes given below
1 I, II, III and IV 2 II, III and IV
3 II and III 4 III and IV

82 Who can be a partner in a firm?
I. A trustee
II. Another firm
III. A Hindu Undivided Family
IV. Wakfs
Select the correct statement from codes given below :
1 I, II, III and IV
2 I, III and IV
3 Only I
4 Only III

83 Which of the following statements are true?
I. Past consideration is no consideration under Indian and English Law.
II. Past consideration is no consideration under Indian Law.
III. Past consideration is no consideration under English Law.
IV. Past consideration is made in past.
Codes
1 I and II 2 II and III
3 III and IV 4 IV and I

84 Consider the following set of legal propositions:
I. A person can claim damages for all wrongs he has suffered.
II. A person can claim damages for wrongs only if they are caused intentionally.
III. A person can claim damages for a wrong if it is caused by infringement of the legal right.
IV. A person can claim damages even if he has suffered no loss.
Of these above propositions which are correct?
1 I and II 2 III and IV
3 I and III 4 II and IV

85 The general principles as to protection of an accused is based on:
I. Autrefois acquit and Autrefois convict.
II. Reasonable doubt as to presumption of innoconce.
III. Natural Justice.

IV. Conviction can not be based without proving the guilt even if it was admitted.

Which of the statements is/are correct?

1 I is correct
2 I and II are correct
3 I, II and III are correct
4 I, II, III and IV are correct

86 Which section of IPC mandates that every offence is to be understood subject to Chapter IV (General Exceptions)?

1 Section 4 2 Section 6
3 Section 76 4 Section 75

87 Which Constitutional amendment estabilished National Commission for SCs and STs?

1 61st 2 71st 3 65th 4 74th

88 Which of the following ingredients are essential to make master liable for the acts of the servant?

I. Tort was committed by the servant.
II. Tort was committed in the course of employment.
III. Express authority was given by master.
IV. Master has knowledge of all constituent offers of tort.

Codes

1 I, II, III 2 I, II, IV 3 III, IV 4 I, II

89 Which of the following is an essential constituent of negligence?

I. Defendant was under or legal duty to exercise due care
II. This duty was owed to plantiff
III. Defendant committed breach of such duty
IV. That the breach of such duty was the direct and proximate cause of the damage alleged.

Codes

1 I, II and III 2 I, II, III and IV
3 II, III and IV 4 I, II and IV

90 Which of the following statements are true?

I. All employees are workmen.
II. All employees are not workmen.
III. All workmen are employees.
IV. All managerial staff is workmen.

Codes

1 I and II 2 II and III
3 III and IV 4 I and III

Directions (Q. No. (91-95) *Read the passage carefully and answer the following questions:*

The Preamble of the Constitution is an integral part of the Constitution. Democratic form of government, federal structure, unity and integrity of the nation, secularism, socialism, social justice and judicial review are basic features of the Constitution. The Union of India shall protect the State Government and as corollary under Article 356 it is enjoined that the government of every state should be carried on in accordance with the provisions of the Constitution. On receipt of a report from the Governor or otherwise the President (Council of Ministers) on being satisfied that a situation has arisen in which the Government of a State cannot be carried on in accordance with the provisions of the Constitution is empowered to issue Proclamation under Article 356 (1) and impose President's rule in the state in a manner laid down in sub-clause (a) to (c) of Article 356 (1) of the Constitution.

The exercise of the power under Article 356 is an extraordinary one and needs to be used sparingly when the situation contemplated by Article 356 warrants to maintain democratic form of government and to prevent paralysing of the political process. The exercise of power under Article 356 should under no circumstances be for a political gain to the party in power in the Union government. It should be used sparingly and with circumspection that the government of the State functions with responsibility in accordance with the provisions of the Constitution.

Rule of law has been chosen as an instrument of social adjustment and resolution of conflicting social problems to integrate diverse sections of the society professing multi-religious faiths, creed, caste or region fostering among them fraternity, transcending social, religious, linguistic or regional barriers. Citizen is either by birth or by domicile and not as a member of religion, caste, sect, region or language. Secularism has both positive and negative constants.

91 Which one of the following provisions of the Constitution imposes an obligation on the Union to ensure that the Government of the State is carried on in accordance with the provisions of the Constitution?

1 Article 352 2 Article 355
3 Article 356 4 Article 360

92 In which of the following cases, the Supreme Court held that the Preamble is the part of the Constitution:

1 Buckingham and Carnatic Co. Ltd Vs. Venkatiah
2 Keshavananda Bharati Case
3 Golaknath Vs. State of Punjab
4 In Re Berubari case

93 On which grounds of the following a restriction can be imposed on freedom of religion under Article 25 of the Constitution?

1 Public order, decency and morality
2 In the interest of general public
3 Public order, morality and health
4 In the interest of general public

94 'Rule of law' has been recognised by the Constitution of India under

1 Article 14 2 Article 19
3 Article 21 4 Article 22

95 Article 356(I)(b) provides that

1 Any proclamation under Article 356 (1) may be revoked by a subsequent proclamation.
2 Every proclamation under Article 356 (1) shall be laid before each House of Parliament.
3 A Proclamation under Article 356 (1) shall cease to operate on the expiration of six months from the date of issue of proclamation.
4 The President may by proclamation under-Article 356 (1) declare that the powers of the legislature of the state shall be exercisable by or under the authority of Parliament.

Directions (Q. No. (96-100) *Read the passage below carefully and answer the questions that follow :*

The state of Uttar Pradesh and Uttarakhand have not cooperated with the Central government to constitute a Ganga Management Board. The Uttarakhand High Court in the exercise of its 'parens patriae' jurisdiction, ordered conversation of Ganga and Yamuna rivers as juristic/legal persons/living entities, having the status of a legal person. The rivers Ganga and Yamuna are thus legal persons with corresponding rights of a living person. The director NAMAMI Ganga, the Chief Secretary and Advocate General of Uttarakhand states were declared as persons in 'loco parentis'.

The division bench of Uttarakhand High Court sharply berated the state terming their non-cooperation as the 'sign of non-governance. The deterioration of Ganga and Yamuna is a classic case of 'desperate times, desperate measures, the court granted the juristic entity at par with Hindu idol. The Uttarakhand High Court in another case reiterated the constitution of the Ganga Management Board has become all the more necessary for the purpose of irrigation, water supply, hydropower generation, and navigation.

96 'The division bench of Uttarakhand High Court sharply berated...non-governance' was observed in which of the following cases?

1 Indian Council for Enviro-Legal Action Vs. Union of India
2 Rural Litigation and Entitlement Kendra Vs. State of Uttarakhand
3 Divya Pharmacy Vs. Union of India
4 Lalit Miglani Vs. State of Uttarakhand

97 The term 'Parens Patriae' refers to

1 Common Suit
2 Descent from parent
3 Parent of his/her own country/state
4 Barred by Res judicata

98 The term 'loco parentis' refers to

1 In equal fault
2 In place of parent
3 Hizanat period
4 Indigent suit

99 Hindu Idol is a juristic entity capable of holding property, was laid down in

1 Bengal Immunity Co. Ltd Vs. State of Bihar
2 Yogendra Nath Naskar Vs. Commissioner of Income Tax
3 M. Basheer Vs. Lona Chackola
4 Nanak Chand Vs. State of UP

100 Why 'the Ganga Management Board' is important?

1 To care the holy river
2 To better management for multipurpose project
3 They are forced by public at care of the river
4 Both 1 and 2

ANSWERS

1 (3)	**2** (4)	**3** (3)	**4** (2)	**5** (3)	**6** (2)	**7** (4)	**8** (3)	**9** (2)	**10** (3)
11 (1)	**12** (4)	**13** (1)	**14** (4)	**15** (3)	**16** (1)	**17** (3)	**18** (4)	**19** (2)	**20** (3)
21 (1)	**22** (3)	**23** (1)	**24** (4)	**25** (1)	**26** (1)	**27** (2)	**28** (1)	**29** (4)	**30** (2)
31 (3)	**32** (3)	**33** (1)	**34** (3)	**35** (4)	**36** (4)	**37** (4)	**38** (3)	**39** (2)	**40** (4)
41 (4)	**42** (4)	**43** (2)	**44** (3)	**45** (3)	**46** (2)	**47** (4)	**48** (2)	**49** (4)	**50** (2)
51 (2)	**52** (3)	**53** (3)	**54** (1)	**55** (4)	**56** (3)	**57** (1)	**58** (3)	**59** (1)	**60** (3)
61 (2)	**62** (1)	**63** (4)	**64** (4)	**65** (4)	**66** (1)	**67** (3)	**68** (4)	**69** (4)	**70** (1)
71 (1)	**72** (3)	**73** (1)	**74** (1)	**75** (2)	**76** (2)	**77** (4)	**78** (1)	**79** (1)	**80** (4)
81 (4)	**82** (3)	**83** (3)	**84** (2)	**85** (4)	**86** (2)	**87** (3)	**88** (4)	**89** (2)	**90** (2)
91 (2)	**92** (2)	**93** (3)	**94** (1)	**95** (4)	**96** (4)	**97** (3)	**98** (2)	**99** (2)	**100** (4)

UGC-NET LAW

PRACTICE SET 4

PAPER II

1 For an adjudicating officer, which of the following factors need to be taken into account according to the IT Act, 2000?

1 The amount of gain of unfair advantage
2 The amount of loss caused to any person
3 The repetitive nature of the default
4 All of the above

2 In which of the following cases, the Supreme Court held that 'death penalty is constitutionally valid'?

1 Balraj Singh Vs. State of UP
2 Saheli Vs. Commissioner of Police
3 Bachan Singh Vs. State of Punjab
4 Hari Kishan and State of Haryana Vs. Sukhbir Singh

3 The Section 299 of the IPC provides for which of the following offences?

1 Theft
2 Culpable homicide
3 Kidnapping
4 Sexual offences

4 Which section of the Indian Penal Code, 1860 lays down the rule of 'doli incapax'?

1 Section 81
2 Section 82
3 Section 83
4 Section 84

5 The Section 121 of IPC provides for which of the following?

1 Waging or attempting to wage war or abetting waging of war, against the Government of India.
2 Collecting arms, etc with intention of waging war against the Government of India.
3 Concealing with intent to facilitate design to wage war.
4 Assaulting President, Governor etc.

6 Which of the following statement(s) is/are true?

I. Use of someone else property constitute strict liability.

II. In Rylands Vs. Fletcher case, the huge water body was dangerous thing.

III. Gas, electricity, sewage, explosives consists dangerous things.

Select the correct answer using the codes given below :

1 I and III
2 II and III
3 I and II
4 Only I

7 Consider the following statements regarding offences

I. Offences are anti-social in nature.

II. Offences are part and parcel of the society.

III. The socio-economic condition of society does not play significant role in occurrence of offences.

Choose the correct statement(s) using the given codes :

1 I and II
2 II and III
3 I and III
4 All of these

8 Which of the following statements is true?

I. Power of state government to constitute claim tribunal is compulsory.

II. This was displayed in Minu B. Mehta Vs. Bal Krishna case.

Select the correct answer using the codes given below :

1 Only I
2 Only II
3 Both I and II
4 None of these

9 Consider the following statements.

I. The Constitution in a unitary government is relatively flexible.

II. It is very much suitable during emergency.

Choose the correct answer using the codes given below :

1 I is correct
2 II is correct
3 Both I and II are correct
4 None of the above

10 Which of the following statement(s) is/are incorrect?

I. Section 41 of the Parsi Marriage and Divorce Act, stipulates for payments of alimony.

II. Section 37 of Special Marriage Act, 1954 deals with Permanent Alimony.

III. Section 7 of Divorce Act, deals with 'Permanent Alimony'.

Select the correct answer using the codes given below :

1 II and III   2 Only II
3 I and II   4 All of these

11 Consider the following statements.

I. Commercial law is significant in economic growth.

II. Commercial law protect the intellectual property right.

III. Sale of Goods Act was enacted in 1930.

Select the correct statement from the codes given below :

1 I and II   2 II and III
3 I and III   4 All of these

12 With reference to the Indian Contract Act, 1872, consider the following statements.

I. After independence, this act has been replaced by the Indian Evidence Act.

II. This has provision, which explicitly talks about frustration of contract.

III. Indian Contract Act was inspired from the American legislation.

Choose the correct statement from the given codes

1 I and II
2 II and III
3 I and III
4 None of the above

13 Arrange the following in correct chronological order.

I. The Partnership Act

II. The Sale of Goods Act

III. The Limited Liability Partnership Act

IV. The Negotiable Instruments Act

Select the correct statement from the codes given below.

1 III, I, II, IV   2 IV, II, I, III
3 II, IV, I, III   4 IV, III, II, I

14 Consider the following statements regarding the Sale of the Goods Act, 1930.

I. It is based on the English Sale of Goods Act, 1893.

II. Section 24 deals with the agreement to sell of valuation.

III. The Act has 8 chapters.

IV. It provide certain rights to buyer to examine goods.

Select the incorrect statement by using the given codes.

1 I and II   2 1, II and III
3 II and III   4 None of these

15 To avail qualified privilege defence, which of the following points are required?

I. The statement was made on a privileged occasion.

II. The matter comment upon must be of public interest.

III. The statement was made without any malice.

Select the correct statement(s) using the codes given below :

1 Only II   2 I and II
3 Both I and III   4 Only I

16 Consider the following statements.

I. Transfer of CBI officers investigating cases referred by Lokpal can be done with the approval of the watchdog.

II. The Lokayukta is generally a retired judge of the High Court or the Supreme Court .

Which of the above statement(s) is/are true?

1 Only I   2 Only II
3 Both I and II   4 None of these

17 Consider the following statements.

I. YK Alagh Committee was of the view that poverty line must be derived from the expenditure that was enough to provide 2250 calories per day in both urban and rural areas.

II. The Planning Commission constituted a task force under the chairmanship of YK Alagh in 1979.

III. Lakdawala Committee submitted its report in the year 1993.

Which of the following statement(s) given above is/are correct?

1 II and III   2 I and III
3 Only III   4 Only I

18 Match List I with List II using the codes given below.

List I (Jurists)	List II (Theories of Property)
A. Spencer	I. Labour Theory
B. Henry Maine	II. Historical Theory
C. Blackstone	III. Functional Theory
D. Roscoe Pound	IV. Natural Law Theory

Codes

	A	B	C	D		A	B	C	D
1	I	II	IV	III	2	III	I	IV	II
3	II	IV	I	III	4	IV	II	III	I

19 When the Security Council is exercising, in respect of any dispute or situation, the functions assigned to it in present Charter, the General Assembly

1 shall not make any recommendation with regard to that dispute or situation unless the Security Council so requests.
2 cannot make any recommendation with regard to that dispute.
3 can make any recommendation with regard to that dispute or situation.
4 None of the above

20 Match List I with List II using the codes given below.

List I (Jurists)	List II (Theories of Property)
A. Kant	I. Metaphysical Theory
B. Bentham	II. Psychological Theory
C. Roscoe Pound	III. Functional Theory
D. Grotius	IV. Natural Law Theory

Codes

	A	B	C	D
1	III	I	II	IV
2	IV	I	III	II
3	I	II	III	IV
4	II	I	III	IV

21 Match List I with List II using the codes given below.

List I (Jurists)	List II (Definitions of International Law)
A. Starke	I. Defends international law as 'law' and says "a weak law nevertheless is still law."
B. Oppenheim	II. International law as "rules of conduct which states feel themselves bound to observe and therefore do commonly observe in their relations with each other."
C. Russel	III. International law, "as the aggregate of the rules to which the nations have agreed to their conduct towards one another."
D. Holland	IV. The rules of international law are voluntary,though habitually observed by every State in its dealings with the rest, can be called 'law' only by courtesy.

Codes

	A	B	C	D		A	B	C	D
1	II	I	IV	III	2	II	I	III	IV
3	I	IV	III	II	4	IV	II	I	III

22 The modernist approach and experiments in the field of arts were visible across Europe in between the year ____ and ____ .

1 1820, 1910
2 1890, 1930
3 1890, 1910
4 1845, 1920

23 The term 'civil law' is derived from the _____ 'jus civile'.

1 Latin
2 Roman
3 Greek
4 French

24 Consider the following statements.

I. Tendulkar Committee was constituted by the Planning Commission in the year 2007 under the chairmanship of Suresh Tendulkar.
II. Tendulkar Committee recommended the incorporation of private expenditure on health and education in poverty estimation.
III. Rangarajan Committee was constituted in the backdrop of national outrage over the Planning Commission's suggested poverty line of ` 22 a day for rural areas.

Which of the following statement(s) given above is/are correct?

1 I and II
2 II and III
3 I and III
4 All are correct

25 Section 147 of 1988 Act deals with

1 Amount of liability incurred
2 Maximum limit to which, statutory liability of insurer is there
3 Both 1 and 2
4 Nonc of thc above

26 Consider the following statements;

I. Duties imposed by law of torts are not towards the world at large, but they are towards any specific individual.
II. Damages is the main remedy both in an action for the breach of contract as well as in an action for tort.
III. Damages are said to be unliquidated when the sum payable by way of damages is predetermined.

Which of the statement(s) given above is/are correct?

1 Only I
2 Only II
3 Only III
4 I and III

27 Match List I with List II using the codes given below.

List I (Theory of Punishment)	List II (Content or Meaning)
A. Deterrent	I. Change in character
B. Reformative	II. Moral satisfaction
C. Retributive	III. Prevent further crime
D. Preventive	IV. Capital punishment

Codes

	A	B	C	D		A	B	C	D
1	IV	I	II	III	2	III	II	I	IV
3	I	II	IV	III	4	II	III	I	IV

28 Match List I with List II using the codes given below.

List I (Sections)	List II (Provisions)
A. Section 83	I. Act of a child above seven and under twelve of immature understanding
B. Section 89	II. Act done in good faith for benefit of child or insane person or by consent of guardian
C. Section 90	III. Consent known to be given under fear or misconception
D. Section 92	IV. Act done in good faith for benefit of a person without consent

Codes

	A	B	C	D		A	B	C	D
1	IV	I	III	II	2	II	IV	I	III
3	III	I	IV	II	4	I	II	III	IV

29 Which of the following statement(s) is/are true?

I. Maintenance of the army is a non-sovereign function.

II. State will not be liable for any act by army personnel.

III. In Smt Meinam Ongbi Bina Devi Vs. State of Manipur, the defendent was found liable.

Select the correct answer using the codes given below

1 Only I
2 Only II
3 Only III
4 I, II and III

30 Consider the following statements.

I. The rules applicable in case of tort are generally different from those in the case of crime.

II. As tort is considered to be a private wrong, the injured party himself has to file a suit as a plaintiff.

III. The criminal proceedings against the wrongdoer are brought by the State.

Which of the statement(s) given above is/are correct?

1 Only III
2 II and III
3 Only I
4 All are correct

31 Consider the following statements.

I. Fiscal federalism is the type of federalism in which the money bag controls everything.

II. The federalist party of US was opposed by Democratic-Republican.

III. On 17th September, 1787, the delegates approved and signed an entirely new Constitution for the United States of America.

Which of the following statement(s) given above is/are correct?

1 Only I
2 I and II
3 II and III
4 All of these

32 When a law obliges a person to do an act, the obligation is called ______ .

1 mandatory
2 compulsory
3 negative
4 positive

33 Match List I with List II using the codes given below.

List I (Jurists)	List II (Definitions)
A. Zitelmana	I. Personality is the legal capacity of will, the bodily-ness of men for their personality a wholly irrelevant attribute.
B. GW Paton	II. Legal personality is a medium through which some units are created in whom rights can be vested.
C. Salmond	III. Defines 'person' as 'any being to whom the law regards as capable of rights or duties'.
D. Gray	IV. Defines a 'person' as 'entity to which right and duties may be attributed'.

Codes

	A	B	C	D		A	B	C	D
1	IV	I	III	II	2	I	II	III	IV
3	III	I	IV	II	4	II	III	I	IV

34 Consider the following definitions of law and choose the incorrect definition.

1 According to Duguit, "Law emanates and is enforced by the State. He firmly believed that there is a confluence of command, sanction and sovereignty in law."

2 Hegel defines law, "as the abstract expression of the general will existing in and for itself."

3 According to Ihering, "Law is the form of guarantee of, the conditions of life in society, assured by State's power of constraint."
4 According to Salmond, "Law is the body of principles, recognised and applied by the State, in the administration of justice."

35 Which of the following is not an example of Critical legal theory?
1 Feminism
2 Legal realism
3 Race theory
4 Postmodernism

36 Which of the following factors leads the emergence of administrative law and enhance its importance?
1 Change in the nature of the state
2 Limitations of the judicial system
3 Declining population
4 Both 1 and 2

37 Match List I with List II using the codes given below.

List I (Schools of Jurisprudence)	**List II** (Jurists)
A. Historical School	I. Savigny
B. Analytical School	II. Bentham
C. Philosophical School	III. Kant
D. Sociological School	IV. Roscoe Pound

Codes

	A	B	C	D
1	IV	II	I	III
2	I	III	II	IV
3	III	I	IV	II
4	I	II	III	IV

38 Given below are two statements, one is labelled as Assertion (A) and the other is labelled as Reasons (R).

Assertion (A) One of the principles of natural justice is, 'No man shall be judge in his own case.'

Reason (R) Principles of natural justice require fair play in action.

In the light of the above statements, choose the correct answer from the options given below.

Codes
1 Both (A) and (R) are true and (R) is the correct explanation of (A)
2 Both (A) and (R) are true, but (R) is not the correct explanation of (A)
3 (A) is true, but (R) is false
4 (A) is false, but (R) is true

39 The purpose of which law is to provide remedy to the person who has suffered?
1 Civil Law
2 Criminal Law
3 Constitutional Law
4 None of these

40 Where is the headquarters of the WTO?
1 New York
2 Washington DC
3 Geneva
4 Austria

41 In which case, the idea of post decisional hearing has been developed by Supreme Court?
1 Murlidhar Vs. Kadam Singh
2 Syed Yakoob Vs. Union of India
3 Shankari Prasad Vs. Union of India
4 Maneka Gandhi Vs. Union of India

42 Match List I with List II using the codes given below.

List I	List II
A. There is no rigid formula for principles of natural justice	I. RS Dass Vs. Union of India
B. Choice of application of rules of natural justice	II. R Vs. Sussex Justices
C. Justice should not only be done, but manifestly and undoubtedly be seen to be done	III. Union of India Vs. PK Roy
D. Meaning of bias	IV. Secretary to Government Transport Department Vs. Munuswamy

Codes

	A	B	C	D
1	I	II	III	IV
2	III	I	IV	II
3	I	III	II	IV
4	III	I	II	IV

43 Which of the following will be the consequences of declaration of National Emergency by the President?
I. The President can issue directives to the State Executives.
II. The President can extend the normal tenure of the Lok Sabha.
III. The President can suspend all the Fundamental Rights of citizens.
IV. The President can modify the distribution pattern of financial resources between Centre and States.

Select the correct answer using the codes given below :

1 I, III and IV
2 I, II and IV
3 1, II and III
4 All of the above

44 Which of the following is not an anti-federal character of Indian Constitution?

List I	List II
A. Writ of Habeas Corpus	I. Available against private individuals as well
B. Writ of Quo Warranto	II. Available against the legality of claim of a person to a public office
C. Writ of Certiorari	III. Available against state only
D. Writ of Prohibition	IV. Available against judicial and quasi-judicial authorities

Codes

1 Only III
2 I, II and III
3 I, II and IV
4 I, III and IV

45 The power of the Supreme Court of India to decide disputes between the Centre and the States falls under its

1 Advisory Jurisdiction
2 Appellate Jurisdiction
3 Original Jurisdiction
4 Writ Jurisdiction

46 When a writ is issued to an inferior court or tribunal on grounds of exceeding its jurisdiction or acting contrary to the rules of natural justice, it is called a writ of

1 Certiorari
2 Mandamus
3 Quo Warranto
4 Habeas Corpus

47 Article 168 states that Supreme Court shall be a court of record and shall have all the powers such as including the power to punish for contempt of itself.

1 'Contempt of itself' means the contempt of Supreme Court only
2 It includes Supreme Court and all subordinate courts
3 It includes Supreme Court and High Court
4 None of the above

48 Which of the following types of authorities attributed to the President of India?

1 Real and Popular
2 Titular and De-jure
3 Political and Nominal
4 Constitutional and Real

49 Match List I with List II using the codes given below.

List I (Jurists)	List II (Views)
A. Pound	I. Since law exists to harmonise the purpose of individuals, law itself strives towards justice.
B. Paton	II. Law and morals have a common origin, but they diverge in their development.
C. Bentham	III. Law has just the same centre as morals but it has by no means the same circumference.
D. Pollock	IV. Though much ground is common to both, the subject-matter of law and ethics is not the same.

Codes

	A	B	C	D		A	B	C	D
1	II	I	III	IV	2	II	I	IV	III
3	I	II	III	IV	4	IV	I	III	II

50 In which of the following cases, Parliament can make laws in any matter enumerated in the State List?

I. During National Emergency
II. During Presidents Rule
III. To implement international agreements

Select the correct answer using the codes given below

1 Only I
2 I and IV
3 II and III
4 All of these

51 The practice of most of the States including Great Britain is to consider de facto and de jure recognition at par in relation to the property within the jurisdiction of recognising state. The English courts took this view in

1 Republic of Spain Vs. Arantzazu Mendi
2 Madhavrao Scindia Vs. Union of India
3 Republic of Spain Vs. Felipe Campuzano
4 None of the above

52 Which of the following statements is/are true about Centre-State relations?

I. During the proclamation of emergency (Article 352), the Centre can give direction to a State on any matter.
II. During the proclamation of emergency (Article 352), President can modify the Constitutional distribution of revenues between the Centre and the States.

III. Word 'cabinet' is mentioned only once in the Constitution under Article 352.

Select the correct answer using the codes given below

1 Only I 2 II and III
3 Only III 4 All of these

53 Consider the following explanations regarding interrelation of Articles 14, 19 and 21.

I. In Maneka Gandhi Vs. Union of India case, the SC held that Article 19 has no application to laws depriving a person of his life and personal liberty enacted under Article 21 of the Constitution.

II. In Gopalan's case, the SC held that Article 21 does not exclude Article 19.

Which of the statement(s) given above is/are correct?

1 Only I 2 Only II
3 Both I and II 4 None of these

54 What is the minimum age required to become a member of Parliament?

1 Not less than 25 years
2 Not more than 25 years
3 35 years
4 21 years

55 Which of the following qualification(s)/are laid down by the constitution for a person to be appointed as the Governor of a State?

I. He should be a citizen of India.
II. Must have completed the age of 35 years.
III. He shall not belong to the state where he is appointed.

Select the correct answer using the codes given below

1 Only I 2 I and II
3 Only II 4 All of these

56 Which jurist defined ownership as, "ownership is the entirety of the powers of use and disposal allowed by law"?

1 WN Hohfeld 2 Buckland
3 Keeton 4 Pollock

57 Match List I with List II using the codes given below.

List I	List II
A. Directive Principles of State Policy	I. American Constitution
B. Emergency Provisions	II. United Kingdom
C. Fundamental rights	III. German Reich
D. Parliamentary form of Government	IV. Ireland

Codes

	A	B	C	D		A	B	C	D
1	IV	III	I	II	2	IV	I	III	II
3	I	II	III	IV	4	III	II	I	IV

58 The following are enshrined in the Preamble to the Constitution of India.

I. Equality of status and opportunity.
II. Liberty of thought, expression, belief, faith, and worship.
III. Justice social, economic and political.
IV. Fraternity assuring the dignity of the individual.
V. Unity and integrity of the nation.

Which one of the following is the correct order in which they appear in the Preamble?

1 V, I, II, IV, III 2 III, II, I, IV, V
3 III, I, II, V, I 4 I, II, IV, III, V

59 An accused person has been provided with the following protections by Constitution of India.

I. Ex-post facto law
II. Safeguard against arrest and detention
III. Double jeopardy

Arrange the protections in the order in which they appear in the Indian Constitution with the help of codes given below

1 I, III, II 2 I, II, III
3 III, I, II 4 II, I, III

60 The UN Charter provides that the voting right of a member may be suspended by the General Assembly. What is the basis of the suspension of this right?

1 Violation of the direction of the General Assembly or the Security Council
2 Failure to assist the Security Council in its enforcement measures
3 Failure to pay its UN subscription for two years
4 Failure to assists the General Assembly in its peace-keeping efforts

61 The word 'secular' denotes

1 keeping away from all religions
2 freedom of religion and worship to all religions
3 belief in one god
4 practicing different religions

62 International Court of Justice was set

1 as a principal judicial organ of the UN
2 independent organ of the UN
3 as an organ of the Five Big Powers
4 as a part of North-South dialogue

63 Among the following doctrine, which was based on the principle of 'ex injuria jus non oritur'?

1 Estrada doctrine 2 Hallstein doctrine
3 Stimson doctrine 4 None of these

64 Imperative theory of law was propounded by

1 Pound 2 Kelsen
3 Austin 4 Salmon

65 Membership of the UN is open to all those states which are peace loving and accept the obligations under the UN Charter. How is a new member admitted?

1 By the Security Council
2 By the General Assembly
3 By the General Assembly on the recommendation of the Secretary General
4 On the recommendation of the Security Council made in a resolution passed with nine affirmative votes including those of Big Powers by the General Assembly with two-third majority

66 Match List I with List II using the codes given below.

List I (UN Initiatives)	List II (Years)
A. UN Charter	I. 1946
B. Commission on the Status of Women	II. 1945
C. UDHR	III. 2006
D. UNHCR	IV. 1948

Codes

	A	B	C	D		A	B	C	D
1	III	IV	I	II	2	IV	III	I	II
3	II	I	IV	III	4	I	IV	III	II

67 Consider the following statements.

I. As per Patent Act, 1970, literary work includes computer programmes, table and compilations.
II. Patent Act, 1970 was adopted and came into force on 20th April, 1982.

Which of the statement(s) given above is/are correct?

1 Only I 2 Only II
3 Both I and II 4 Neither I nor II

68 Which of the following statement(s) is/are true?

I. In Section 94, the act for which someone has been forced by death threats.
II. Section 95 has been done in the act of committing frivolous kidnapping.
III. Section 96 to 106 deals with acts done in private defence.

Which of the statement(s) given above is/are correct?

1 Only I 2 Only II
3 I and II 4 All of these

69 Arrange the following in correct order, on the basis of their establishment.

I. International Committee of the Red Cross
II. International Fact-Finding Commission
III. United Nations Declaration on Human Rights
IV. International Criminal Court

Select the correct answer using the codes given below

1 III, II, IV, I 2 IV, III, II, I
3 II, IV, III, I 4 I, III, II, IV

70 Which of the following Convention or Declaration is considered as a first step towards the enaction of International Humanitarian Law?

1 Declaration of Paris
2 Geneva Convention of 1864
3 Hague Convention
4 Treaty of Versailles

71 Whish of the following statement(s) is not true?

1 GI has been defined in TRIPS.
2 Members countries of GI shall provide the legal means for the protection of GI.
3 It came into effect on 1st January, 1995.
4 All of the above

72 Where is the Headquarter of the WHO?

1 New York 2 Washington DC
3 Geneva 4 Austria

73 Consider the following statements.

I. Arbitration and Embargo are peaceful method of dispute settlement.
II. In Mediation, decision are binding on disputing parties.
III. Retorsion and reprisal have same meaning.
IV. Conciliation is type of coersive mechanism of dispute settlement.

Which of the statements given above are correct?

1 I and II 2 I, II and III
3 III and IV 4 None of these

74 The highest cess charged under Water (Prevention and Control of Pollution) Cess Act, 1978 is for which category of purpose?

1 Domestic use of water being supplied by municipality.
2 Water getting contaminated with biodegradable pollutants.
3 Water getting contaminated with non-biodegradable and toxic pollutants.
4 Industrial cooling, spraying in mine pills or boiler feed.

75 With reference of NCSC and NCST, consider the following statements.

I. Both of them were formed together.

II. They play significant role in protection and enforcement of human rights for SC and ST communities.

III. They submit annual report to the President.

Select the incorrect statement(s) from the codes given below

1 Only I 2 II and III
3 I and III 4 All of these

76 Consider the following statements.

I. The Bill of Right was enacted by the Parliament of England.

II. It has a provision, which prohibited levying taxes without grant of Parliament is illegal.

III. It was signed in the year 1689.

Which of the given statements are correct?

1 I and II 2 II and III
3 II and IV 4 All of these

77 Which of the following acts are exempted from criminal liability under the section of IPC?

I. The act done by a person who is believed to be bound by law in Section 76 or due to mistake of fact.

II. The work of a judge acting judicially in Section 77.

III. Work in Section 81, which is likely to cause hijacking, but which is done without criminal intent and for the prevention of other abductions.

Which of the statement(s) given above is are correct.

1 Only I 2 I and II
3 II and III 4 All of these

78 Clearance for projects is required by Ministry of Enviornment in which of the following CRZs?

1 CRZ I, II 2 CRZ II, III
3 CRZ I, IV 4 CRZ III (A)

79 In which case Supreme Court held that, "Right to live includes the right to enjoyment of pollution free water and air for full enjoyment of life"?

1 State of Bihar Vs. Murad Ali Khan
2 Narmada Bachao Vs. Union of India
3 Subash Kumar Vs. State of Bihar
4 A.P Pollution Control Board Vs. MV Nayudu

80 Consider the following statements.

I. National Commission was set up by an Executive Resolution in 1978.

II. Later in the year 1995, it became statutory body.

III. It is not entitled with power of civil court.

IV. It evaluates the progress of the development of minority section.

Which of the statement(s) given above is/are correct?

1 I and II 2 II and III
3 III and IV 4 I and IV

81 Which of the following institutions recognises the hiba?

I. Aariat

II. Sadaqah

III. Wakf

IV. Hiba-ba-shart-ul-iwaz

Select the correct answer using the codes given below :

1 I and II 2 III and IV
3 II, III and IV 4 All of these

82 Consider the following statements.

I. The first statutory law related to trademark in India was the Trademarks Act, 1940.

II. ® (the registered trademark) may only be used by the owner of mark following registration with the relevant national security.

III. A duration of registration of a trademark is 20 years.

Choose the correct statement(s) from the codes given below

1 I and II 2 II and III
3 I and III 4 All of these

83 Match List I with List II using the codes given below.

List I (Types of Covernment)		List II (Features)
A. Unitary	I.	All powers in the single central government.
B. Parliamentary	II.	Executive is selected from among the members of the legislature.
C. Presidential	III.	Executive is constitutionally independent of the legislature.
D. Federal	IV.	Divide powers between strong Central government and local regional government.

Codes

	A	B	C	D		A	B	C	D
1	I	II	III	IV	2	III	II	IV	I
3	IV	III	I	II	4	I	IV	II	III

84 How many sections are there in the Indian Contract Act 1872, (including repealed)?

1 265 2 266
3 267 4 268

85 Which section of the Indian Contract Act deals with 'Agreement in Restrain of Trade'?
1 26 2 27
3 28 4 29

86 Consider the following statements.
I. Government in which the constitution concentrates all powers in the single central government is called Unitary government.
II. It exists in the UK, France and Italy.
Choose the correct answer using the codes given below
1 I is correct
2 II is correct
3 Both I and II are correct
4 None of the above

87 Punishment prescribed under Section 18 of Hindu Marriage Act, 1955 for procurement of marriage between two sapindas is
1 imprisonment only
2 Fine only
3 imprisonment or fine or both
4 imprisonment and fine or both

88 Which of the following statement(s) is/are incorrect regarding prospectus?
I. The Companies Act, 2013 does not define prospectus.
II. Prospectus intends to issue a public appeal for subscription of its shares and debenture.
III. A company has to issue red herring prospectus prior to the issue of a prospectus.
Choose the correct answer using the given codes given below
1 Only I 2 Only II
3 I and II 4 All of these

89 Which Section of the Companies Act, 2013 deals with the provisions related to the Removal of Directors?
1 Section 169 2 Section 170
3 Section 171 4 Section 172

90 Which of the following statement(s) is/are true?
I. In Section 88, an act done in good faith by consent for the benefit of a person, which does not have the intention of causing death.
II. Act done in good faith by the guardian or with his consent in Section 89 for the benefit of the infant or insane person.
III. Consent in Section 90, in relation to which it is known that it is given under fear or misconception.
Select the correct answer using the codes given below
1 Only I 2 I and III
3 II and III 4 All of these

91 Issues related to Uniform Civil Code got heat especially after which of the following case?
1 Bommoi Case
2 Maneka Gandhi Case
3 Keshavananda Bharati Case
4 Shah Bano Case

92 The guardian has been given a power to give his ward in adoption in what circumstances?
I. If both the parents are dead.
II. If parents have finally and completely renounced the world.
III. If parents have abandoned the child.
IV. Parents have been judicially declared to be of unsound mind.
Select the correct answer from the given codes below
1 I, II and III
2 II and III
3 II, III and IV
4 I, II, III and IV

93 Who may be taken in adoption under the Hindu Adoptions and Maintenance Act, 1956?
1 The child whose mother could not have been married by adopter
2 Child must be Hindu
3 Legitimate child
4 All of the above

94 In which condition, the quantum of maintenance of wife, children and aged or infirm parents lays down under sub-section 92?
I. Reasonable wants of claimant.
II. If the claimant is living separately.
III. The number of persons are entitled to be maintained.
Select the correct answer using the codes given below:
1 I and II
2 II and III
3 All of these
4 None of the above

95 Which of the following cases are related to the live-in relationship?
I. S Khushboo Vs. Kannaiammal and Anr
II. Badri Prasad Vs. Union of India
III. Tulsa Vs. Durghatiya
IV. Indra Sarma Vs. VKV Sarma
Select the correct answer using the codes given below
1 I, II and III
2 I, III and IV
3 I, II and IV
4 All of the above

96 Which of the following are the ways to distribute the property under Muslim law?
1 Per capita distribution
2 Per strip distribution
3 Both 1 and 2
4 None of the above

97 Which of the following statement(s) is/are true?
I. The act of a person who is unable to reach a decision due to intoxication against his will as given under Section 85.
II. In Section 86, an offence committed by a person who is under the influence of liquor, is required to have special intent or knowledge.
III. Act done with consent in Section 87, which does not meant to cause death or grievous hurt.
Which of the statement(s) given above is/are correct?
1 Only I
2 II and III
3 I and II
4 All of these

98 The Fundamental Duties were added by
1 42nd Amendment
2 44th Amendment
3 52nd Amendment
4 31st Amendment

99 It was on 1st November, 1943, that the foundation of the UN Charter was laid when Foreign Ministers of the Big Four Powers met. This is known as
1 Moscow Declaration
2 Foreign Ministers Declaration
3 London Conference
4 Paris Declaration

100 Which statement is not correct about Parliamentary privileges?
1 The courts are prohibited to inquire into the proceedings of a House.
2 Members cannot be arrested during the session of Parliament for any case.
3 No member is liable to any proceedings in any court for anything said or any note given by him in Parliament.
4 It can punish members as well as outsiders for breach, of the privileges.

ANSWERS

1 (4)	2 (3)	3 (2)	4 (3)	5 (1)	6 (2)	7 (1)	8 (4)	9 (3)	10 (4)
11 (3)	12 (4)	13 (2)	14 (3)	15 (3)	16 (3)	17 (1)	18 (1)	19 (1)	20 (3)
21 (4)	22 (1)	23 (2)	24 (2)	25 (2)	26 (2)	27 (1)	28 (4)	29 (3)	30 (4)
31 (4)	32 (2)	33 (2)	34 (1)	35 (2)	36 (4)	37 (4)	38 (1)	39 (1)	40 (3)
41 (4)	42 (4)	43 (2)	44 (3)	45 (3)	46 (1)	47 (2)	48 (2)	49 (4)	50 (4)
51 (1)	52 (4)	53 (2)	54 (1)	55 (2)	56 (1)	57 (1)	58 (2)	59 (1)	60 (3)
61 (2)	62 (1)	63 (3)	64 (3)	65 (4)	66 (3)	67 (4)	68 (4)	69 (4)	70 (2)
71 (1)	72 (3)	73 (4)	74 (3)	75 (1)	76 (4)	77 (4)	78 (3)	79 (3)	80 (4)
81 (4)	82 (1)	83 (1)	84 (2)	85 (2)	86 (3)	87 (3)	88 (1)	89 (1)	90 (4)
91 (4)	92 (4)	93 (4)	94 (3)	95 (4)	96 (3)	97 (3)	98 (1)	99 (1)	100 (2)

UGC-NET LAW

PRACTICE SET 5

PAPER II

1 "Law emanates and is enforced by the state. He believed that there is a confluence of command, sanction and sovereignty in law." Who gave this definition?

1 Austin 2 Parker 3 Blackstone 4 Savigny

2 The emission of air pollutants from automobiles was first regulated under which law?

1 The Environment (Protection) Act, 1986
2 The Air (Prevention and Control of Pollution) Act, 1981
3 The Air (Prevention and Control of Pollution) Rules, 1982
4 The Air (Prevention and Control of Pollution) Amendment Act, 1987

3 Under which law, the manufacturing processes, materials and substances that are likely to cause environmental pollution should be examined?

1 The Factories Act, 1948
2 The Water Act, 1974
3 The Environment Act, 1986
4 The Air Act, 1981

4 Consider the following statements.

I. The Estrada doctrine was followed by Britain.
II. The Stimson doctrine is the policy of non-recognition of States created as a result of aggression.

Which of the following statement(s) given above is/are correct?

1 Only I 2 Only II
3 Both I and II 4 None of these

5 Which theory views punishment from the prism of bringing reform in the criminal?

1 Retributive Theory
2 Preventive Theory
3 Reformative Theory
4 Compensation Theory

6 Give below are two statements, one is labelled as Assertion (A) and the other is labelled as Reason (R).

Assertion (A) A lease is that form of encumbrance of property vested in one person by a right to possession and use of it is vested in another.

Reason (R) A lease may be either for a certain specified period or in perpetuity?

1 Both (A) and (R) are true and (R) is the correct explanation of (A)
2 Both (A) and (R) are true, but (R) is not the correct explanation of (A)
3 (A) is true, but (R) is false
4 (A) is false, but (R) is true

7 The Central and State Boards for Prevention and Control of Pollution were first constituted under which law?

1 The Environment (Protection) Act, 1986
2 The Air (Prevention and Control of Pollution) Act, 1981
3 The Water (Prevention and Control of Pollution) Act, 1974
4 The Water (Prevention and Control of Pollution) Cess Act, 1978

8 In India, the offences are described in which of the following codes?

1 Indian Criminal Code, 1870
2 Indian Penal Code, 1860
3 Indian Offence Code, 1860
4 Indian Punishment Code, 1870

9 Articles 132(2), 133(1) and 134(1)(c) provides that High Court may grant certificate, to 'fit cases' for appeal to Supreme Court, High Court may do so

1 on its own motion
2 on an oral application made on behalf or by the aggrieved party
3 Both (1) and (2) are true
4 (1) is false, but (2) is true

10 Give below are two statements, one is labelled as Assertion (A) and the other is labelled as Reason (R).

Assertion (A) The law in its concrete sense means a statute, enactment, ordinance or other exercise of legislative authority.

Reason (R) Savigny said that law grows with the growth of people, strengthens with the strength of people and finally dies away as the nation loses its nationality.

Codes

1 Both (A) and (R) are true and (R) is the correct explanation of (A)
2 Both (A) and (R) are true, but (R) is not the correct explanation of (A)
3 (A) is true, but (R) is false
4 (A) is false, but (R) is true

11 A minister who is not a member of either house (Note: A person can remain a minister for six months, without being a member of either house of Parliament)

1 can participate in the proceedings of Lok Sabha only.
2 can participate in the proceedings of Rajya Sabha only.
3 can participate in the proceedings of either house of Parliament.
4 cannot participate till he becomes a member of either house of Parliament.

12 Article 356 empowers President to issue a proclamation in State where the Government of a State cannot be carried on in accordance with Constitution

1 on receipt of report from the Governor of the State only
2 on receipt of a report from the Government or otherwise
3 on receipt of a report from the Council of Ministers
4 on receipt of a report from Chief Justice of India

13 The provisions related to elections to Panchayat are given under which Article of the Indian Constitution?

1 Article 243 D
2 Article 243 F
3 Article 243 G
4 Article 243 K

14 "Agreement is an expression by two or more persons communicated to each other, of a common intention to affect the legal relations between them." Which of the following jurists gave this statement?

1 Paton
2 Austin
3 Bentham
4 None of these

15 If a person is not the member of either house of Parliament, he cannot be appointed as a minister at the centre for a period more than

1 1 month
2 6 months
3 3 months
4 it is not essential to be a member of either house to remain a minister

16 Consider the following statements regarding the State Legislature

I. Articles 168 to 212 deal with the organisation, composition, duration etc. of the State Legislature.
II. The State Legislative Assembly consists of 500 fixed members and 60 minimum members.
III. The State Legislative Council has the maximum strength fixed at one-third of the total strength of the assembly and the minimum strength is fixed at 40.

Which of the statement(s) given above is/are correct?

1 I and II
2 Only I
3 I and III
4 All of these

17 Give below are two statements, one is labelled as Assertion (A) and the other is labelled as Reason (R).

Assertion (A) It is true that in any intensive form of government, the government cannot function without the exercise of some discretion by its official.

Reason (R) Giving discretion to government officials is necessary for the welfare of people.

Codes

1 (A) and (R) are correct and (R) is the correct explanation of (A)
2 (A) and (R) are correct, but (R) is not the correct explanation of (A)
3 (A) is correct, but (R) is incorrect
4 (A) is incorrect, but (R) is correct

18 Doctrine of forum prorogatum means

1 Jurisdiction cannot be conferred upon an existing tribunal not otherwise competent by the litigants during the proceedings
2 Jurisdiction can be conferred upon an existing tribunal not otherwise competent by the litigants during the proceedings
3 Jurisdiction can be conferred upon an existing tribunal not otherwise competent by the litigants after the proceedings
4 None of the above

19 Who among the following jurists is the supporter of psychological theory of property?

1 Bentham
2 Blackstone
3 JC Gray
4 Dicey

20 Which of the following statements are correct?

I. Indian territory can be ceded to a foreign state without amending the constitution as mentioned in Article 368.

II. Resolution of boundary dispute between India and another country does not require constitutional amendment.

III. Constitution amendment procedure is provided under Article 368 of the Constitution.

Select the correct answer using the codes given below

1 I, II and III 2 II and III 3 I and III 4 I and II

21 Match the following.

List I (Years)	List II (Schemes)
A. 2001	I. Sampoorna Grameen Rozgar Yojana
B. 2000	II. Sarva Shiksha Abhiyan
C. 2014	III. Sansad Adarsh Gram Yojana
D. 2016	IV. Pradhan Mantri Gramin Awas Yojana

Codes

	A	B	C	D		A	B	C	D
1	IV	I	II	III	2	II	IV	I	III
3	I	II	III	IV	4	III	IV	I	II

22 "Administrative law is the law concerning the powers and procedures of administrative agencies, including especially the law governing judicial review of administrative action." This definition of administrative law is given by

1 Ivor Jenning 2 Garner
3 KC Davis 4 Wade

23 In which of the following cases, the Supreme Court held that the principles of natural justice are applicable to administrative proceedings?

1 MC Mehta Vs. Union of India
2 Maneka Gandhi Vs. Union of India
3 AK Kraipak Vs. Union of India
4 Smt. Indira Nehru Gandhi Vs. Raj Narain

24 Which of the following are the essentials of a valid custom?

I. The custom must have existed since time immemorial.

II. The custom must have been in operation with small interruptions only.

III. The custom must have been exercised peaceably, openly and as of right.

IV. The custom must not be unreasonable in the eyes of law.

Codes

1 I, III and IV 2 II, III and IV
3 II and III 4 All are correct

25 Match the following

List I (Jurists)	List II (Definitions)
A. Salmond	I. A security is an encumbrance the purpose of which is to ensure or facilitate the fulfilment or enjoyment of some other right vested in the same person.
B. Paton	II. Agreement is an expression by two or more persons communicated to each other, of a common intention to affect the legal relations between them.
C. Hibbert	III. Ownership includes within it four kinds of rights.
D. Black's Law Dictionary	IV. Defined ownership as "collection of rights to use and enjoy property including right to transmit it to other's.

Codes

	A	B	C	D		A	B	C	D
1	IV	II	I	III	2	III	I	II	IV
3	II	IV	I	III	4	I	II	III	IV

26 Consider the following statements.

I. A lease is that form of encumbrance of property vested in one person by a right to the possession and use of it is vested in another.

II. A lease may be terminated on the happening of the events referred to in Section 112 of Transfer of Property Act, 1882.

III. Encumbrances prevent the owner from exercising some definite rights with regard to his property.

Which of the statement(s) given above is/are correct.

1 I and II 2 I and III
3 II and III 4 All are correct

27 A President's rule can be imposed under the provisions of

1 Article 356 2 Article 360
3 Article 352 4 Article 366

28 Match the following.

List I (Jurists)	List II (Views)
A. Puchta	I. Considers that psychology of asserting claim is the basis of legal right.
B. Vinogradoff	II. A legal right is a power over an object which by means of his right can be subjected to the will of the person enjoying the right.
C. Austin	III. Will is not an essential element of a legal right or law. The real basis of law is solidarity.
D. Duguit	IV. Concept of right is based on sovereign power of the state.

Codes

	A	B	C	D		A	B	C	D
1	I	II	III	IV	2	IV	II	I	III
3	II	I	IV	III	4	III	I	II	IV

29 The Preamble to the Constitution of India
1 was adopted by the Constituent Assembly after the Constitution had been approved
2 was adopted by the Constituent Assembly before the draft Constitution had been approved.
3 was adopted by the Constituent Assembly simultaneously with draft Constitution.
4 was adopted along with National Security Act.

30 Who among the following said that "legislation includes formal utterances of the Legislative organs of the Society"?
1 TE Holland 2 Gray
3 Austin 4 Blackstone

31 Who among the following defined International law as "rules of conduct which States feel themselves bound to observe and therefore do commonly observe in their relations with each other"?
1 Salmond 2 Austin
3 Starke 4 Holland

32 Which one of the following is a leading case on Article 14?
1 Anwar Ali Sarkar Vs. State of WB
2 Kesavananda Bharti Vs. UOI
3 Golaknath Vs. State of Punjab
4 Hakam Singh Vs. M/S Gammon (India) Limited

33 Consider the following statements.
I. In case of any conflict between Part III and Part IV of the Constitution, the former should prevail in the Court.
II. Part IV (containing the Directive Principles of the State Policy) is not a part of the Constitution.
Which of the statement(s) given above is/are correct?
1 Only I
2 Only II
3 Both I and II
4 Neither I nor II

34 Consider the following statements with regard to Calling Attention Motion and Zero Hour
I. Both are Indian innovation in the parliamentary procedure.
II. Both are not mentioned in the rules of procedure.
III. Only Zero hour is Indian innovation.
IV. Only Zero hour is not mentioned in the rules of procedure.
Which of the statements given above are correct?
1 I and II 2 III and IV
3 II and III 4 I and IV

35 Consider the following statements regarding nationality.
I. Nationality is a legal status.
II. The status is acquired by different means such as birth, inheritance or naturalisation.
III. On the basis of constitutional provision every State sets the criteria which determine who can be national of that country.
Which of the following statement(s) given above is/are correct?
1 Only I
2 Only II
3 Both 1 and 2
4 All of these

36 Match List I with List II and select the correct answer using the codes given below

List I (Theories)	List II (Concepts)
A. Dualist	I. Every State has a right to decide itself when provision to be implemented
B. Monistic	II. International and municipal laws are distinct
C. Transformation	III. There is only one system of law
D. Delegation	IV. Transformation of treaty into national law

Codes

	A	B	C	D		A	B	C	D
1	I	II	III	IV	2	I	IV	III	II
3	II	III	IV	I	4	IV	II	III	I

37 Which of the following theories relate to subjects of International law?
1 Only States are the subjects of International Law.
2 Only individuals are the subjects of International Law.
3 States, individuals and certain non-State entities are subjects of International Law.
4 All of the above.

38 Consider the following statements regarding the United Nations
I. The UN Charter was adopted on 24th October, 1945.
II. The UN is a inter-governmental body.
III. Locarno treaty was signed under the aegis of UN.
Which of the following statement(s) given above is/are correct?
1 I and III 2 II and III
3 I and II 4 All of these

39 The Hague Conferences of 1897 and 1907 tried to limit the right of resorting to war and the Paris Pact of 1928 did succeed in outlawing it to some extent, but the first successful attempt to organise nations in this direction was made

1 by League of Nations
2 at Triple Alliance
3 by Council of Europe
4 by Amphictyonic Council

40 Which of the following cases propounds the view that recognition is not necessary for becoming an international person?

1 Tinto Arbitration
2 Albama Arbitration
3 Re-conditions of Membership of the UN (1948) ICJ
4 Luther Vs. Sagor

41 The decisions in Trusteeship Council are taken

1 by the majority of the members present and voting
2 by the majority of the members present and voting with the five concurring votes of the Great Powers
3 by the two-third majority of the members present and Voting
4 by the majority of votes of the total membership of the Council

42 Which article of the UN Charter says that it is purpose of the UN to achieve international co-operation in promoting and encouraging respect for Human Rights?

1 Article 1 2 Article 3
3 Article 4 4 Article 55

43 "Human rights are right inherent to all human beings regardless of race, sex, nationality, ethnicity, language, religion or any other status."
This definition of human rights was given by

1 Hague Convention
2 European Commission
3 United Nations
4 Geneva Convention

44 The general exception, which was made under the Indian Penal Code to avoid the need to repeat multiple boundaries with the penal clause repeatedly is cited in which section?

1 Sections 76 to 106 2 Sections 75 to 105
3 Sections 80 to 106 4 Sections 85 to 90

45 Which authority will prescribe the procedure for the purpose of authenticating electronic signature, according to section 3A of the IT Act?

1 The State Government
2 NITI Aayog
3 Central Government
4 None of the above

46 Which of the following cases explains the relation of adopted child with the family of the adopter?

1 Arumugam Vs. Valliammai Case
2 Vijayalak shmamma Vs BT Shankar
3 Both 1 and 2
4 None of the above

47 Section 32 of the Competition Act deals with

1 international cartel
2 power to impose lesser penalty
3 establishment of commission
4 composition of commission

48 Under which act, maintenance is provided under Hindu law?

1 Hindu Adoptions and Maintenance Act, 1956
2 Hindu Marriage Act, 1955
3 Special Marriage Act, 1954
4 Criminal Procedure Code, 1973

49 Consider the following statements.

I. Federal government is the most suitable one for vast states with hetrogenous populations.
II. The federal system prevents despotism.
III. Power divides between central and local government.

Choose the correct answer using the codes given below

1 I is correct
2 I and II are correct
3 I, II and III are correct
4 None of the above

50 Under which act or order, a guardian may bc appointed for the management of an estate is vested?

1 Section 11 of Hindu Minority and Guardianship Act
2 Order 32 of Criminal Procedure Code
3 Order 32 of Indian Penal code
4 None of the above

51 With Regard to Constitutional Amendment Bill

1 the President can reject the Bill but cannot return the Bill.
2 the President cannot reject the Bill but can return the Bill.
3 the President can neither reject the Bill nor return the Bill.
4 the President can either reject the Bill or return the Bill.

52 Among the following theories, which one of them is considered as oldest?

1 Retributive Theory
2 Preventive Theory
3 Deterrent Theory
4 Compensation Theory

53 Who is appointed as a chairperson of the NGT?
1 Retired Chief Justice of India
2 Retired Chief Justice of respective High Court
3 Judges of High Court
4 Retired Judges of Supreme Court

54 Consider the following statements.
I. A positive right aims at some positive benefit while negative right aims at not to be harmed.
II. A positive right has a mediate and indirect relation to the object while a negative right is immediately related to the object.
III. A positive right requires only passive acquiescence of other persons.
Which of the statements given above are correct?
1 Only III 2 I and II
3 II and III 4 All of these

55 The Section 354 of IPC contain provision regarding
1 intercourse by public servant with woman in custody
2 rape
3 assault or criminal force to woman with intent to outrage her modesty
4 sexual harassment

56 Under Section 83 of the Indian Penal Code, an offence is punishable if it is done by a child
1 of below seven years of age
2 of above seven years of age but below 12 years, if he has not attained sufficient maturity and understanding
3 of above seven years of age but below 12 years having attained sufficient maturity and understanding
4 All of the above

57 The motive under Section 81 of the Indian Penal Code should be the
1 prevention of harm to property
2 prevention of harm to person
3 Both 1 and 2
4 Either 1 or 2

58 Under Section 98, right to private defence is available against a
1 person who does not have maturity of understanding
2 person of unsound mind
3 Neither 1 nor 2
4 Both 1 and 2

59 According to which theory, property was first acquired by occupation of an ownerless object as a result of individual labour?
1 Labour theory
2 Historical theory
3 Functional theory
4 Natural law theory

60 Who among the following gave this definition, "law has its basis in social conduct. Morals go on intrinsic value of conduct. Hence, it is vain to talk about law and morals. The legal criterion is not an ethical criterion"?
1 Capitant 2 Vinogradoff
3 Pollock 4 Duguit

61 In which case in Great Britain, it was held that international law is not ipso facto regarded as a part of the UK law?
1 Pinchon's case
2 Duke of Norfolk's case
3 Rylands Vs. Fletcher
4 Franconia case

62 "Interests of personality like security of one's physical being, privacy, honour, reputation, etc. can be realised only through some access to property." Who made this observation?
1 Roscoe Pound 2 Jenks
3 Laski 4 Locke

63 The Constitutive Theory of Recognition of a new State is advanced and supported by
1 Holland 2 Oppenheim
3 Hall 4 Both 1 and 2

64 Who said that, "sources of law includes material from which the judge obtains rules for deciding cases"?
1 Fuller 2 Professor Dias
3 Dr CK Allen 4 Harold Laski

65 Which of the following statements is/are regarding the Preamble of Indian Constitution?
I. Preamble is non-justiciable, i.e. its provisions are not enforceable in courts of law.
II. The Preamble to the Indian Constitution is based on the 'Objective Resolution' drafted and moved by BR Ambedkar.
III. It secures political justice to all its citizens.
IV. The idea of Preamble is borrowed from the Constitution of USA.
Select the correct answer using the codes given below
1 I and II 2 II and III
3 III and IV 4 I, III and IV

66 The Section 6(2) (b) of Environment (Protection) Act, 1986 deals with making rules relating to
1 disposal of hazardous wastes
2 handling of hazardous wastes
3 maximum allowable limits of environmental pollutants
4 penalties for violating the Environment Act

67 Under Article 371B, the President is empowered to provide for the creation of a committee of the .... legislative Assembly.

1 Nagaland
2 Assam
3 Manipur
4 Sikkim

68 Under which sections of Indian Criminal Procedure Code, the maintenance rights are provided in India?

1 Section 125 to 128
2 Section 124 to 128
3 Section 123 to 129
4 None of the above

69 To avail qualified privilege defence, which of the following points is/are required?

I. The statement was made on a privileged occasion.
II. The matter comment upon must be of public interest.
III. The statement was made without any malice.

Select the correct statement(s) using the codes given below

1 Only II
2 I and II
3 Both I and III
4 Only I

70 Which of the following statement(s) is/are true?

I. Act of God is an exemption from rule of strict liability.
II. If the escape is due to action of defendant, it is considered an act of God.
III. Nichols Vs. Marsland was not considered an act of God.

Select the correct answer using the codes given below

1 Only I
2 I and II
3 II and III
4 I and III

71 Consider the following statements.

I. The Negotiable Instruments Act was enacted in 1881.
II. The above act does not have provisions regarding compensation and rules of evidence.
III. The Chapter XIV deals with the crossed cheque.

Select the correct statement by using the given codes

1 I and II
2 II and III
3 I and III
4 All of these

72 Which of the following statement(s) is/are correct?

I. Every listed company shall have at least one-half of the total number of directors as independent director.
II. An independent director shall have term of 5 years.
III. Section 164 contain provision for the disqualification for appointment of director.

Choose the correct statement using the given codes

1 Only I
2 Only II
3 II and III
4 All of the above

73 Consider the following statements.

I. ECOSOC consists of 54 members.
II. Security Council has five permanent and ten non-permanent members.
III. Germany and Japan are permanent members of Security Council.
IV. There can be more than one judges from the same country.

Select the correct answer from the codes given below

1 I and II
2 II and III
3 II, III and IV
4 All of these

74 Which of the following is true about Section 79?

I. There is a difference in Section 79 that a person is treated as bound in the preceding section and in the latter, there has been a distinction in actual or permitted legal justification in performing a specific act, in other words justified by law.
II. Under both these clauses, the intention should be to forward the law in good faith, which is reflected in the circumstances related to the work which is the subject of the charge.
III. The accused party cannot say that it was generally good for him, but would have to specifically specify that in doing whatever he did, he was confident that he had acted with good judgement in good faith.

Which of the statement(s) given above is/ are correct?

1 Only I
2 I and II
3 II and III
4 All of these

75 According to the provisions of the Companies Act, 2013, what do you understand by the Government Companies?

1 It refers to those companies in which 51% or more of the paid-up share capital is held by the Central Government or by one or more State Government or partly by Central Government or partly by one or more State Government.
2 It refers to those companies in which 75% or more of the paid-up share capital is held by the Cental Government only.
3 It refers to those companies in which 69% or more of the paid-up share capital is held by the State Governments only.
4 All of the above

76 According to Section 339 IPC, what is an offence?
1 Wrongful restraint 2 Wrongful confinement
3 Wrongful attachment 4 Wrongful force usage

77 What is the minimum number of members to be appointed by Central Government in CCI, as per the Competition Act, 2002?
1 1 2 2
3 3 4 4

78 Consider the following statements in the context of shares and debentures?
I. Section 43 contains provision regarding kinds of share capital.
II. Preference share would carry preferential right with respect to payment of dividend, repayment, etc.
III. Equity share gives voting right to the people.
Choose the correct statement using the given codes
1 I and II 2 II and III
3 I and III 4 All of these

79 Which of the following statements are correct?
I. Indian Constitution is mix of flexible and rigid feature.
II. While US Constitution is rigid in nature.
III. The Constitution of South Africa is flexible in nature.
Which of the above statement(s) is/are correct?
1 I and II 2 II and III
3 I and III 4 All of these

80 Which of the following statements are correct regarding judicial activism?
I. It is enshrined in the Indian Constitution.
II. It aims at helping people of lower strata.
III. When judicial activism croses its limit, it is referred to as judicial overreach.
Choose the correct statement using the given codes
1 I and II 2 II and III
3 I and III 4 All of these

81 Choose the correct statement with reference to the Information Technology law in India.
I. IT Act was enacted in 2004.
II. It contains provision regarding cyber crime and electronic governance.
III. IT Act, 2000 was amended in 2008.
Choose the correct statement(s) using the codes given below
1 I and II 2 II and III
3 I and III 4 All of these

82 Which of the following statements is/are correct?
I. Parties of UNFCCC are required to create National Biodiversity Strategies and Action Plan (NBSAP).
II. Nagoya and Cartagena Protocols are part of Agenda 21.
Select the correct statement using the codes given below
1 Only I 2 Only II
3 Both I and II 4 None of these

83 Consider the statement(s) in the context of the International Covenant on Human Rights.
I. They were adopted in 1966.
II. International covenant on Civil and Political Rights contain 53 Articles.
III. International Covenant on Economic, Social and Cultural rights was also adopted in the same year.
Select the correct answer using the codes given below
1 I and II 2 II and III
3 I and III 4 All of these

84 Which of the following statements regarding Green Climate Fund is/are correct?
I. It is intended to assist the developing countries in adaptation and mitigation practices to counter climate change.
II. It is founded under the agencies of UNEP, OECD, Asian Development Bank and World Bank.
Select the correct statement using the codes given below
1 Only I
2 Only II
3 Both I and II
4 Neither I nor II

85 Consider the following statements in the context of Human Rights in Indian Constitution.
I. Article 21A was inserted to provide right to compulsory education to all children in the age group 6-14.
II. Article 23 prohibits the employment of children below the age of 14 years in hazardous employment.
III. Articles 25-28 of the Constitution deal with the freedom of conscience and religion.
Which of the statement(s) given above is/are correct?
1 I and II 2 I and III
3 II and III 4 All of these

86 Which of the following judgements is/are related to the live-in relationship?
1 Badri Prasad Vs. Dy. Director of Consolidation
2 Tulsa Vs. Durghatiya
3 Both 1 and 2
4 None of the above

87 Hindu Marriage Act, 1955
1 does not prescribe the ceremonies requisite for solemnisation of marriage but leaves it to the parties to choose a form of ceremonial marriage which is in accordance with any custom or usage applicable to either party.
2 does not prescribe the ceremonies requisite nor leaves it to the parties to choose.
3 does prescribe the ceremonies and does not leave it to the parties to choose.
4 does prescribe the ceremonies and at the same time leaves it to the parties to choose.

88 The main objectives of the Wildlife Protection Act, 1972 are
I. Restricting hunting, killing or overexploitation of species
II. Protection of wildlife, preservation of natural habitats and environment
III. Recognising the right of people to a healthy environment

Which of the statements given above are correct?
1 I and II
2 II and III
3 I and III
4 I, II and III

89 Which of the following statements is correct with reference to quasi-contractual obligations?
1 There is no real contract in existence
2 There is no offer and acceptance
3 There is no intention to make a contract
4 All of the above

90 Consider the following statements about National Biodiversity Authority?
I. Its main mission is to oversee the effective implementation of Environmental Protection Act.
II. The Chairman of NBA is appointed by the Central Government.
III. Biodiversity Management Committee is a sub committee under the NBA.

Which of the statements given above are correct?
1 I and II
2 II and III
3 I and III
4 I, II and III

91 In the context of geographical indications, select incorrect statement?
I. GI is not considered as IPR.
II. It is valid for 10 years.
III. Initiative of both national and international level have been taken to curb its infringement.
IV. Geographical Indication (Registration and Protection) Act was amended in 2002.

Choose the correct statement(s) using the codes given below :
1 I and II
2 II and III
3 III and IV
4 I and IV

92 Consider the following statements.
I. Protection of Inventions Acts were consolidated in 1888 as the Inventions and Designed Act.
II. AGI is a sign used on products that have a specific geographical origin and reputation that are due to that origin.

Which of the statement(s) given above is/are correct?
1 Only I
2 Only II
3 Both I and II
4 Neither I nor II

93 Which of the given statements are incorrect?
I. Patentability refers to the substantive condition that must be met for a patent to be held valid.
II. Any invention that is detrimental for plant and animal life can get patent.
III. The request for examination of patent has to be filed within 12 months of the application date or date of priority.

Choose the incorrect statements from the given codes
1 I and II
2 II and III
3 I and III
4 All of the above

94 How many sections and schedules are there in the Partnership Act, 1932?
1 Sixty-nine sections and four schedules
2 Seventy-four sections and two schedules
3 Seventy-six sections and three schedules
4 Seventy-eight sections and five schedules

95 As per Section 20, the authority of a partner to bind the firm conferred by this section is called
1 Hidden authority
2 Sovereign authority
3 Dominating authority
4 Implied authority

96 Adultery is matrimonial offence punishable under
1 Section 494 of Indian Penal Code
2 Section 497 of Indian Penal Code
3 Section 498 of Indian Penal Code
4 Section 498-A of Indian Penal Code

97 Which of the following are criticisms of the amendment procedure of the Indian Constitution?
I. The process is flexible as well as rigid.
II. The process of amendment is similar to that of a legislative process except for the special majority.
III. Parliament has almost the entire power to initiate amendments.
IV. There is no provision for holding a joint sitting to solve deadlock in case of constitutional amendment bill.
Which of the above statements are correct?
1 I and II 2 III and IV
3 II, III and IV 4 All of these

98 With reference to punishment, which of the following statements are correct?
I. Punishment plays definite role in reducing crime.
II. Punishment vary according to the offence.
III. The only purpose of punishment is to take revenge.
Choose the correct statements using the given codes
1 I and II
2 II and III
3 I and III
4 All of the above

99 With reference to the trademark, consider the following statements.
I. Product trademarks are used to identify the services of an entity.
II. Service trademarks are those that identify goods.
III. Collective trademarks are registered in the name of groups, associations or other organisations.
Choose the correct statement(s) using the given codes
1 Only I 2 Only II
3 Only III 4 None of these

100 Which of the following is not dependent under Section 21 of Hindu Adoption and Maintenance Act, 1956?
1 Son's of widow
2 Minor illegitimate son
3 Widowed daughter
4 Son's son's major son

ANSWERS

1 (1)	2 (2)	3 (3)	4 (2)	5 (3)	6 (1)	7 (3)	8 (2)	9 (3)	10 (2)
11 (3)	12 (2)	13 (4)	14 (1)	15 (2)	16 (4)	17 (1)	18 (2)	19 (1)	20 (2)
21 (3)	22 (3)	23 (3)	24 (1)	25 (3)	26 (2)	27 (1)	28 (2)	29 (1)	30 (2)
31 (3)	32 (1)	33 (1)	34 (4)	35 (4)	36 (3)	37 (4)	38 (3)	39 (1)	40 (1)
41 (1)	42 (4)	43 (3)	44 (1)	45 (3)	46 (1)	47 (1)	48 (1)	49 (3)	50 (2)
51 (3)	52 (1)	53 (4)	54 (3)	55 (3)	56 (3)	57 (4)	58 (4)	59 (1)	60 (4)
61 (4)	62 (2)	63 (4)	64 (1)	65 (4)	66 (3)	67 (2)	68 (1)	69 (3)	70 (1)
71 (3)	72 (3)	73 (1)	74 (4)	75 (1)	76 (1)	77 (2)	78 (4)	79 (1)	80 (4)
81 (2)	82 (4)	83 (4)	84 (1)	85 (2)	86 (3)	87 (1)	88 (4)	89 (4)	90 (3)
91 (4)	92 (3)	93 (2)	94 (2)	95 (4)	96 (2)	97 (3)	98 (1)	99 (3)	100 (4)